A CULTURAL THEORY
INTERNATIONAL RELATIONS

In this exciting new volume, Richard Ned Lebow introduces his own constructivist theory of political order and international relations based on theories of motives and identity formation drawn from the ancient Greeks. His theory stresses the human need for self-esteem, and shows how it influences political behavior at every level of social aggregation. Lebow develops ideal-type worlds associated with four motives: appetite, spirit, reason and fear, and demonstrates how each generates a different logic concerning cooperation, conflict and risk-taking. Expanding and documenting the utility of his theory in a series of historical case studies, ranging from classical Greece to the war in Iraq, he presents a novel explanation for the rise of the state and the causes of war, and offers a reformulation of prospect theory. This is a novel theory of politics by one of the world's leading scholars of international relations.

RICHARD NED LEBOW is James O. Freedman Presidential Professor of Government at Dartmouth College and Centennial Professor of International Relations at the London School of Economics and Political Science. He is the author of *The Tragic Vision of Politics* (Cambridge, 2003) which was the winner of the Alexander L. George Book Award of the International Society of Political Psychology, 2005.

A CULTURAL THEORY OF INTERNATIONAL RELATIONS

RICHARD NED LEBOW

CAMBRIDGE
UNIVERSITY PRESS

CAMBRIDGE UNIVERSITY PRESS
Cambridge, New York, Melbourne, Madrid, Cape Town, Singapore, São Paulo, Delhi

Cambridge University Press
The Edinburgh Building, Cambridge CB2 8RU, UK

Published in the United States of America by Cambridge University Press, New York

www.cambridge.org
Information on this title: www.cambridge.org/9780521691888

First published 2008

Printed in the United Kingdom at the University Press, Cambridge

A catalogue record for this publication is available from the British Library

Library of Congress Cataloguing in Publication data
Lebow, Richard Ned.
A cultural theory of international relations / Richard Ned Lebow.
p.   cm.
Includes bibliographical references and index.
ISBN 978-0-521-87136-5 (hardback)
1. International relations – Philosophy.   2. Constructivism (Philosophy)   I. Title.
JZ1305.L43   2008
327.101 – dc22   2008027833

ISBN 978-0-521-87136-5 hardback
ISBN 978-0-521-69188-8 paperback

To Carol, Kate, Andrew, Eli and David

CONTENTS

List of figures and tables   *page* viii

Acknowledgments   ix

1   Introduction   1

2   Fear, interest and honor   43

3   The spirit and its expression   122

4   The ancient world   165

5   Medieval Europe   222

6   From Sun King to Revolution   262

7   Imperialism and World War I   305

8   World War II   371

9   Hitler to Bush and beyond   439

10   General findings and conclusions   505

Bibliography   571

Index   741

FIGURES AND TABLES

Figures

9.1	System transformation	*page* 498
10.1	Motives	510
10.2	Fear	511
10.3	Identity	564

Tables

2.1	Foundational assumptions	59
2.2	The spirit	64
2.3	Motives, emotions, goals and means	90
7.1	Prospect theory	367
10.1	Prospect theory	537

ACKNOWLEDGMENTS

In *The Tragic Vision of Politics* I attempt to develop a new ontology for social science that assumes change as the norm, and attempts to study and track it in terms of the series of compromises that actors make with respect to key and often conflicting values. I argue that these compromises are inherently unstable and that changes in any one of them can be dampened or amplified as they interact with other accommodations and work their way through the system. In this volume I build on this ontology to develop a theory of international relations embedded in a proto-theory or political order. In a follow-on volume I hope to develop a full-blown theory of political order drawing on the findings of this study and additional research.

If orders are unstable and constantly evolving, so are theories. My theory of international relations has been and remains a work in progress, although it has progressed far enough to warrant publication. I expect that feedback will push me to think further about my theory and to introduce changes in the course of writing the follow-on volume. My theory builds on works of social science, history, philosophy and literature and has compelled me to turn to colleagues for help in understanding relevant works and controversies in these several fields. Once again I have been struck by the interest and generosity of so many colleagues in different fields. Wthout their initial guidance and subsequent willingness to read and comment on drafts I could not have attempted, let alone completed, this project.

My greatest debt goes to Dartmouth College and colleagues and staff in its Department of Government and John Sloan Dickey Center for International Understanding. The College and Department have provided a comfortable and supportive home base and my colleagues have been helpful for discussing relevant literature and draft chapters. The Dickey Center provided the venue for these reviews and I am grateful to its Director, Ambassor Kenneth Yalowitz, and Associate Director, Christianne Hardy Wohlforth, for sponsoring two seminars at which draft chapters were discussed and critiqued. Among my Dartmouth colleagues, special thanks go to Stephen Brooks, Michael Mastanduno, James Murphy, Jennifer Lind, Roger Masters, Daryl Press, Lucas Swaine, Benjamin Valentino and William Wohlforth.

I spent the spring of 2003 as a visiting research professor in the Department of Political Science at the University of California at Irvine, where I was able to read and think and share my thoughts with welcoming colleagues. They subsequently invited me back to give a talk about the book. For these opportunities l am particularly grateful to David Easton, Cecelia Lynch, Kristin Monroe, Mark Petracca, Sean Rosemberg, Wayne Sandholz, Kamal Siddiq, Etel Solingen and Katherine Tate. My former Cornell friend, colleague and role model, the late Robin Williams, was also in residence in Irvine during this period, and supportive of my project as he had been of earlier ones.

For two terms during the five years I worked on this book I was a fellow of the Centre for International Studies at the University of Cambridge and a fellow of first Wolfson and then St. John's College. For their support and intellectual compansionship I am indebted to Centre Director Christopher Hill, and to collegues Duncan Bell, John Forsyth, Charles Jones, Amrita Narilkar, Shogo Suzuki and Philip Towle. Other Cambridge colleagues, including Paul Cartledge, Andrew Preston and Ricardo M. S. Soares de Oliveira, also became valued friends and intellectual companions. At St. John's I owe thanks to Master Richard Perham and President John Leake. Pembroke College was also welcoming and for this I thank Lorraine Gelthorpe and Mark Wormald.

Various institutions invited me to give seminars where I had the opportunity to lay out arguments from the book and receive criticism and suggestions. Over the course of the last few years I have given presentations at the University of Brisbane, the University of Bristol, the University of California, Berkeley and Irvine, the Centre for International Studies at the University of Cambridge, the Institute of War and Peace Studies at Columbia University, the University of Hobart, the Institute of Defense and Strategic Studies at the National Technical University of Singapore, the Mershon Center at the Ohio State University, the PIPES seminar at the University of Chicago, McGill University, the Olin Institute at Harvard University, the Psychology Department of the New School, Rutgers University, the Institut d'Études Politiques de Paris (Sciences Po), the School of Pacific and International Studies of the Australian National University, St. Andrew's University, the University of Toronto and the Victoria University of Wellington. For making these presentations possible and for hosting my visits, I offer thanks to Bertrand Badie, Alex Bellamy, Roland Bleiker, Emanuele Castano, Dan Drezner, Greg Fry, Avery Goldstein, Ray Goldstein, Rick Herrmann, Chris Hill, Bob Jervis, Jia Quingguo and Yu Tiejun, Sebastian Kaempf, Jack Levy, Charles Lipson, Richard Little, Catherine Lu, Ed Mansfield, Kate McMillan, Jan Pakulski, T. V. Paul, Chris Reus-Smit, Nick Rengger, Matthew Sussex, Shiping Tang, Bill Tow, Steve Weber and David Welch.

In the course of research and writing, various colleagues agreed to read draft chapters, and Martin Heisler, David Lebow, Nick Onuf and Chris Reus-Smit read the entire manuscript. I am deeply indebted to them for their criticism and suggestions. For thoughtful comments on chapters I thank Tomoko Akami, Duncan Bell, Jens Bartelson, Chris Brown, Paul Cartledge, Holger Herwig, Jacques Hymans, Chris Hill, Fritz Kratochwil, Andrew Lawrence, Ian Lustick, Dorothy Noyes, Paul Schroeder, Simon Reich, Nick Rengger, Dick Samuels, Janice Gross Stein, Shogo Suzuki and Dan Tompkins. All of these readers, and an anonymous one from Cambridge University Press, helped to make the book better than it would otherwise have been.

This is the second book I have written with the guidance and support of editor John Haslam of the Cambridge University Press. During the course of research and writing he was substantively as helpful as any academic colleague, and did a superlative job of overseeing the production of the book. At Dartmouth, I had the assistance of departmental administrators Lisa Wallace and Christine Gex and departmental assistant Katherine Donald. All three provided assistance above and beyond the call of duty, and I am deeply grateful.

Finally, a special thanks to Carol Bohmer, who provided feedback and emotional support, and did so, moreover, while writing her book on political asylum.

1

Introduction

Poetry can give some satisfaction to the mind, wherein the nature of things doth seem to deny it.

Francis Bacon

There are few general theories of international relations. One reason for this may be its relatively late emergence as a field of study. The first department and chair of international relations – both at the University of Wales in Aberystwyth – were established only in 1919.[1] More fundamentally, the nature of the subject inhibits theoretical development. International relations is at the apex of multiple levels of social aggregation, and is significantly influenced, if not shaped, by what happens at other levels. A good theory of international relations presupposes a good understanding of politics at all these other levels. It would be something akin to a unified field theory in physics. Einstein devoted his mature decades to this goal, and failed, as anyone would in the absence of more knowledge about the individual forces that have to be subsumed by a general theory. Our knowledge of politics at all levels of interaction is even more fragmentary, as is our understanding of how other disciplines can augment this knowledge.

There is more than one way to skin a cat, and clever political scientists have devised alternative strategies for theorizing about international relations. The most obvious move is to ignore the need to understand politics holistically and to assume that patterns of international behavior can be studied independently of what transpires at other levels of interaction. If system-level relations could somehow be studied in splendid isolation, without any reference to the character and politics of its units, its dynamics might be described by a parsimonious, deductive theory. This

---

[1] International law and diplomacy were studied before 1919, and the Chichele Chair of International Law and Diplomacy had been created at Oxford in 1859. Schmidt, *The Political Discourse of Anarchy*, on the evolution of the field of IR in the United States.

is a variant of the claim advanced to justify international relations as an independent discipline. Theorists and academic empire-builders alike had strong incentives to argue that anarchy and its consequences differentiated international relations from politics at all other levels of social aggregation.[2] This claim was facilitated by the widely accepted Weberian definition of the state as representing a social community and territory, and with a monopoly of legitimate violence within that territory.[3] It allowed theorists to distinguish rule (*Herrschaft*) at the domestic level from anarchy at the international level, thereby creating the necessary binary.[4]

Attempts to build theories at the system level have been prominent but notoriously unsuccessful. Almost from the beginning of the enterprise scholars were drawn to other levels of analysis, to the structure and character of states and societies, domestic politics, bureaucracies and the role of leaders. They offer additional analytical purchase, especially when it comes to explaining foreign policies. To theorize about international relations is to say something systematic about the character of relations among the actors that comprise the system, and also about who those actors are and how they become recognized as such by other actors. To develop meaningful insights into these questions we must go outside of international relations because the patterns of interactions among actors is determined not by their number and relative power but by the nature of the society in which they interact.[5] Society also determines who counts as an actor. Any theory of international relations must build on or be rooted in a theory of society and must address the constitution of actors, not only their behavior.

Existing paradigms are inadequate in this regard. Realism all but denies the existence of society at the international level and treats the character of international relations as universal, timeless and unchanging. Liberalism posits a strong two-way connection between the domestic structure of state actors and the nature of their relationships. It says little to nothing about what shapes the structure of these actors, and is restricted to one

---

[2] Ashley, "The Poverty of Neorealism"; Little, "Historiography and International Relations," note the success of this strategy.

[3] Weber, *The Profession and Vocation of Politics*, p. 78, and *Economy and Society*, I, p. 54; Wendt, *Social Theory of International Politics*, pp. 199–201, for different views of the state.

[4] Guzzini, unpublished comments on the roundtable on " 'Power' in International Relations: Concept Formation between Conceptual Analysis and Conceptual History," American Political Science Association, Philadelphia, PA, 2006. Derrida, *Of Grammatology*, pp. 24–33, and *Positions*, p. 41, on the central role binary oppositions play in the creation of a scientific or philosophical language.

[5] Onuf, "Alternative Visions," also makes this point.

historical epoch: the modern, industrial world. It is also wed to a parochial Anglo-American telos that assumes that only one kind of state structure (liberal democracy) is a rational response to this world. The English School recognizes society at the international level, but understands it to be thin, limited and a conscious artifact. It generally rejects the idea of progress, although Hedley Bull and Adam Watson welcome it in their discussion of outlawing the slave trade and the legal regulation of war.[6] Marxism links society and international relations in a more comprehensive manner, because it is fundamentally a theory of society. It nevertheless fails in its accounts of history and of international relations in the nineteenth and twentieth centuries. Constructivism also emphasizes the decisive role of society in constituting actors and their identities, but constructivist scholars have not as yet produced a full-blown theory of international relations.[7]

A theory of society, or of aspects of it most relevant to the character and evolution of politics at the state, regional and international levels, is a daunting task. It involves something of a Catch-22 because understandings of society and politics at least in part presuppose each other. Their co-dependency troubled Greek philosophers of the fifth and fourth centuries BCE and led to Plato's paradox: if true knowledge is holistic, we need to know everything before we can know anything.[8] Plato developed his theory of a priori knowledge to circumvent this dilemma. He posited a soul that had experienced multiple lives in the course of which it learned all the forms. Knowledge could be recovered with the help of a dialectical "midwife" who asked appropriate questions.[9] Thucydides pursued a more practical strategy; he nested his analysis of the Peloponnesian War in a broader political framework, which in turn was embedded in an account of the rise and fall of civilization. By this means, the particular could be understood, as it had to be, by reference to the general. Knowledge, once retrieved and transcribed, could become "a possession for all time."[10] I hope to emulate Thucydides, not in writing a possession for all time,

[6] Bull and Watson, *The Expansion of International Society*. Vincent, *Human Rights and International Relations*. More recently, Buzan, *From International to World Society*; Wheeler, *Saving Strangers*; Linklater and Suganami, *The English School of International Relations*.
[7] Alexander Wendt, who describes his theory as constructivist, is better categorized as a structural liberal.
[8] Dumont, "The Modern Concept of the Individual," for the conception of holism.
[9] Plato, *Meno*, 86b1–2, and *Cratylus*, 400c, for his theory of rebirth and its connection to knowledge.
[10] Thucydides, *History of the Peloponnesian War*, 1.22.4. Lebow, *Tragic Vision of Politics*, chs. 3, 4 and 7 for an account of this framework.

but in attempting to explain the particular with reference to the general. I offer my theory of international relations as a special case of political order.

Society is a catch-all term that encompasses all aspects of a group of people who live together. Order describes any kind of pattern or structure. It enables societies to function because it provides guidelines for behavior, making much of it routine and predictable. Vehicular traffic is a simple case in point. It could not flow if drivers did not drive on the same side of the road when moving in the same direction, stop at red lights and adhere to other important "rules of the road" (e.g., signaling for turns, passing in the outside lane, not blocking intersections).[11] Drivers enact most of these rules out of habit, and if they reflect upon them, generally recognize that they are in everyone's interest. There are, of course, violations, and the more often they occur the more difficult it is to maintain or enforce order. When enough people violate a rule – as in the case of speeding – it becomes increasingly difficult to enforce. At every level of human interaction, from interpersonal to international, order requires a high degree of voluntary compliance.

Order also refers to some kind of arrangement or rank, among people, groups or institutions.[12] On the road equality is the rule, but ambulances, police cars and fire engines have the right of way. Off the road, social hierarchies embed inequalities. Some actors are consistently treated better than others because of their social standing, wealth, connections or willingness to push themselves to the head of the line. Inequalities are usually self-reinforcing. Wealth allows better educational opportunities, which lead to better connections, better jobs and higher status. Inequalities are also self-sustaining when those who benefit from them can pass on advantages to their progeny. Given the inequalities of all social orders, and the exclusions, restrictions and compulsions they entail, it is nothing short of remarkable that most people in most societies adhere to stipulated practices and rules.

Philosophers and social scientists have come up with four generic explanations for compliance: fear, interest, honor and habit. The power of fear has been self-evident from the beginning of civilization, if not before, and is probably a component of most social orders. Tyrannies are the regimes most dependent on fear; Thucydides, Plato and Aristotle thought they

---

[11] Lewis, *Convention*, for this now famous example.
[12] Weber, *Political Writings*, p. 311. For a reminder that not all systems are hierarchical, Luhmann, *Social Systems*, pp. 298–9.

would survive only as long as they had the power and will to cow their subjects, or the wisdom and commitment to transform themselves into more consensual kinds of regimes.[13] The interest explanation is associated with Hobbes and is central to modern social science. It assumes that people are willing to accept relatively inferior positions and benefits in return for the greater absolute rewards they receive by belonging to a society in which their physical security and material possessions are protected.[14] Honor refers to the seemingly universal desire to stand out among one's peers, which is often achieved by selfless, sometimes even sacrificial, adherence to social norms. Homer might be considered the first theorist of honor, and his account in the *Iliad* is unrivaled in its understanding of this motive and its consequences, beneficial and destructive, for societies that make it a central value. In modern times, the need for status and esteem is described as "vanity" by Hobbes and Smith, and for Rousseau it is at the core of *amour propre*.[15] The importance of habits was understood at least as far back as Aristotle, who observed that children mimic adult behavior and are taught how to act and toward what ends by their mentors. They are socialized into behaving in certain ways and may ultimately do so unreflexively.[16] Habit can ultimately be traced back to one or more of the other three explanations. Children emulate adults because they fear the consequences of not doing so or in expectation of affection, approval or material rewards.

These explanations for compliance draw on universal drives (appetite and spirit), a powerful emotion (fear) and routine practices (habit). Their relative importance varies within and across societies and epochs. Fear, interest and honor operate at every level of social aggregation. Reflecting the conventional wisdom of his day, Thucydides has the Athenians explain their drive to empire and their subsequent commitment not to relinquish it to all three motives.[17] I contend that each of these motives gives rise to

---

[13] Plato, *Republic*, 571c8–9 and 579d9–10; Aristotle, *Politics*, 1315b11; Thucydides, *passim*, but especially the Melian Dialogue.

[14] Hobbes, *Leviathan*, I.11.9. Although fear is central to Hobbes, it is a secondary means of control. He recognizes that sovereigns must govern by legitimacy if coercion is to be effective against any minority that resists. His sovereign encourages citizens to concentrate on their material interests, as appetite combined with reason is likely to make them more compliant. Williams, "The Hobbesian Theory of International Relations," on this point.

[15] Chapter 7 offers a fuller account.

[16] Aristotle, *Politics*, 1252a1–7, 1155a22–613, 162b5–21, 1328b7–9, 1335b38–1336a2, 1336b8–12.

[17] Thucydides, 1.75.2–5. All English quotations from Thucydides are from the Richard Crawley translation in *The Landmark Thucydides*.

a particular kind of hierarchy, two of which – interest and honor – rest on distinct and different principles of justice. All three motives also generate different logics concerning cooperation, conflict and risk-taking. These logics are intended to sustain the orders in question, although, depending on the circumstances, they can also work to undermine them. This dynamic holds true at every level of social order, and the nature of hierarchies and their degree of robustness at any level has important implications for adjacent levels.

Of necessity, then, my project has a double theoretical focus: order and international relations. As each theory is implicated in the other, a simple linear approach will not work. I can neither formulate a theory of political orders and extend it to international relations, nor develop a theory of international relations and derive a theory of political order from it. Instead, I adopt a layered strategy. I begin with the problem of order, and propose a framework for its study, but not a theory. This framework provides the scaffolding for a theory of international relations, the major part of which I construct in this volume. In a planned follow-on volume, I intend to use this theory and additional evidence to transform my framework of order into a theory of order, and use that to further develop my theory of international relations. Like the calculus or the hermeneutic circle, such a series of approximations can bring us closer to our goal, if never actually there.

Why international relations?

International relations is the hardest, if in many ways the most interesting, case for any theory of political orders. Given the thinness of order at the international level, does it make sense to start here? Why not approach the problem of order at the levels of the individual or the group? Plato opts for this strategy; he develops a theory of individual order in the *Republic*, which he then extends to society. Thucydides uses a roughly similar formulation to bridge individual, polis and regional levels of order. Modern psychology also starts with the individual and builds on this understanding to study group and mass behavior. I do something similar, starting with the individual and working my way up to international society and systems. Following the Greeks, I develop a model of the psyche and argue that order at the individual or any social level of aggregation is a function of the balance among its several components. At the macro level, balance sustains practices that instantiate the principles of justice on which all successful orders are based.

The most important analytical divide is between individuals and social units. In the literature it is generally assumed that different levels of order are sustained by different kinds of norms. Groups are thought to be governed by social norms, societies by legal and social norms, and regional and international systems primarily by legal norms.[18] In developing his concept of organic solidarity, Durkheim theorizes, and subsequent research tends to confirm, that legal and social norms are more reinforcing, and informal mechanisms of social control more effective, in small social units (e.g. villages and towns) where the division of labor is relatively simple.[19] Moral disapproval of deviance is more outspoken in these settings and serves as a powerful force for behavioral conformity.[20] Paradoxically, deviance is also more likely to be tolerated when it is understood as closing ranks against outside interference.[21] On the whole, however, tolerance of deviance varies with the division of labor; it is more pronounced in larger and more complex social systems.[22] Order is accordingly more difficult to achieve and sustain at higher levels of social aggregation for reasons that have nothing to do with the presence or absence of a Leviathan.

Regional and international orders are particularly challenging because they inevitably have competing as well as reinforcing norms, and glaring contradictions between norms and behavior. The lack of normative consensus, the paucity of face-to-face social interaction and the greater difficulty of mutual surveillance, make effective social control more difficult, but by no means impossible, at the regional and international levels. It is most effective among states and societies that subscribe to a common core of values. In eighteenth- and nineteenth-century Europe, where there was a reasonable degree of mechanical solidarity at the regional level, group

---

[18] Regional orders come in between and display considerable variance. Regional order in Europe more closely resembles a domestic society, whereas regional orders in the Middle East or South Asia – to the extent that we can even use the term order – more closely resemble international relations. Thucydides and Plato distinguished Greece from the rest of the ancient world on the basis of its cultural unity, which led to a different structure of relations among its political units. For the same reason, Buzan and Waever, *Regions and Powers*, wisely argue that since the end of the Cold War, regional clusters have become the most appropriate level at which to study international politics.

[19] Durkheim, *The Division of Labor in Society*, pp. 400–1.

[20] Erikson, *Wayward Puritans*; Shilling and Melor, "Durkheim, Morality and Modernity."

[21] Brian Lavery, "Scandal? For an Irish Parish, It's Just a Priest with a Child," *New York Times*, January 22, 2005, p. A6, describes local support for a 73-year-old Roman Catholic priest who fathered the child of a local schoolteacher and unwillingness to talk about it to representatives of outside media. The local bishop was also supportive and did not remove the priest from his pastoral duties.

[22] Glaser, "Criminology and Public Policy," pp. 24–42.

pressures to adhere to accepted norms and practices were more effective than the balance of power in restraining actors.[23] The Montreal Protocol and subsequent agreements to ban chlorofluorocarbons (CFCs) and restore the ozone layer indicate that this kind of suasion serves not only as a source of social control but as a catalyst for change.[24] Although generally framed in terms of great power pressure on recalcitrant actors, social pressures arising from moral outrage can be effectively utilized by the weak, and even by agents who are not even recognized as legitimate actors. A striking example is the boycott of South Africa to end apartheid, which arose from successful appeals to Britain and the United States by non-state actors to pursue foreign policies in accord with their professed values.[25] As informal social mechanisms of control are at least as important as threats, bribes and institutions in bringing about self-restraint and compliance, the robustness of society – and not the absence of central authority, as modern-day realists insist – should be considered *the* determining characteristic of regional and international systems.[26] Both sources of control have their limitations, which we will explore in due course.

Regional and international orders are set apart by another phenomenon: the consequences of the seeming human need to generate social cohesion through distinctions between "us" and "others." The research of Tajfel and others on "entitativity" suggests this binary may be endemic to all human societies and certainly operates at the group level.[27] It was first conceptualized in the eighteenth century in response to efforts by Western European governments to promote domestic cohesion and development by means of foreign conflict. Immanuel Kant theorized that the "unsocial sociability" of people draws them together into societies, but leads them to act in ways that break them up. He considered this antagonism innate to our species and an underlying cause of the development

---

[23] Wight, *Systems of States*, pp. 23, 149; Schroeder, "International Politics, Peace and War, 1815–1914"; Kissinger, *A World Restored*, p. 1.

[24] Parson, *Protecting the Ozone Layer*, on the role of moral outrage.

[25] Klotz, *Norms in International Relations*.

[26] Finnemore and Toope, "Alternatives to 'Legalization,'" make a variant of this argument in the context of compliance with international law. The international society and international system are distinct but overlapping, and given the complexity of contemporary political, economic and social relations, it is probably impossible to distinguish the two categorically. We should nevertheless be aware of the problem, which I will return to later in this volume. For some of the relevant literature, see Bull, "The Grotian Conception of International Society"; Buzan, *From International to World Society?*, pp. 133–4; Dunn, "System, State and Society."

[27] Tajfel, *Human Groups and Social Categories*; Brewer, "The Psychology of Prejudice"; Brown, "Social Identity Theory," for a literature review.

of the state. Warfare drove people apart, but their need to defend themselves against others compelled them to band together and submit to the rule of law. Each political unit has unrestricted freedom in the same way individuals did before the creation of societies, and hence is in a constant state of war. The price of order at home is conflict among societies. The "us" is maintained at the expense of "others."[28]

Hegel built on this formulation, and brought to it his understanding that modern states differed from their predecessors in that their cohesion does not rest so much on preexisting cultural, religious or linguistic identities as it does on the allegiance of their citizens to central authorities who provide for the common defense. Citizens develop a collective identity through the external conflicts of their state and the sacrifices it demands of them. "States," he writes in the *German Constitution*, "stand to one another in a relation of might," a relationship that "has been universally revealed and made to prevail." In contrast to Kant, who considers this situation tragic, Hegel rhapsodizes about states as active and creative agents which play a critical role in the unfolding development of the spirit and humankind. Conflict among states, he contends, helps each to become aware of itself by encouraging self-knowledge among citizens. It can serve an ethical end by uniting subjectivity and objectivity and resolving the tension between particularity and universality. After Hegel, peace came to be seen as a negotiated agreement between and among states, and not the result of some civilizing process.[29]

International relations as a zone of conflict and war was further legitimized by the gradual development of international law and its conceptualization of international relations as intercourse among sovereign states. In the seventeenth century, Grotius, Hobbes and Pufendorf endowed states with moral personalities and sought to constrain them through a reciprocal set of rights and duties.[30] In the eighteenth century, the state was further embedded in a law of nations by Vattel.[31] The concept of sovereignty created the legal basis for the state and the nearly unrestricted

---

[28] Kant, "Idea for a Universal History," pp. 44–7; "Perpetual Peace," p. 112.

[29] Hegel, "The German Constitution," pp. 15–20, *Elements of the Philosophy of the Right* and "The Philosophical History of the World," for the development of his thought on the state. See also Pelcynski, "The Hegelian Conception of the State"; Taylor, *Hegel*, ch. 16; Avineri, *Hegel's Theory of the Modern State*.

[30] Grotius, *De jure belli ac pacis libri tres* (1625); Hobbes, *De Cive* and *Leviathan*; Pufendorf, *De jure naturae et gentium libri octo*; Onuf and Onuf, *Nations, Markets and War*, ch. 4; Keene, "Images of Grotius," for a critical review of contrasting interpretations and the application of his ideas to international relations theory.

[31] Vattel, *Le droit de gens*; Koskenniemi, *The Gentle Civilizer of Nations*, ch. 1.

right of its leaders to act as they wish within its borders. It also justified the pursuit of national interests by force beyond those borders so
long as it was in accord with the laws of war. Sovereignty is a concept with
diverse and even murky origins, that was first popularized in the sixteenth
century. At that time, more importance was placed on its domestic than
its international implications. Nineteenth- and twentieth-century jurists
and historians, many of them Germans influenced by Kant and Hegel
(e.g. Heeren, Clausewitz, Ranke, Treitschke), developed a narrative about
sovereignty that legitimized the accumulation of power of central governments and portrayed the state as the sole focus of a people's economic,
political and social life. The ideology of sovereignty neatly divided actors
from one another, and made the binary of "us" and "others" appear a natural, if not progressive, development, as did rule-based warfare among
states.[32]

This binary was reflected at the regional level in the concept of European or Christian society, which initially excluded Russia and the Ottoman
Empire as political and cultural "others." There was no concept of the
"international" until the late eighteenth century, and its development
reflected and hastened the transformation of European society into an
international system in the course of the next century.[33] New standards
of legitimacy enlarged the boundaries of the community of nations following the Napoleonic Wars.[34] By 1900, non-Western states were being
admitted to the community, and the number of such units burgeoned
with decolonization in the late 1950s and 1960s. In recent decades, non-
governmental organizations (NGOs) and diverse social movements have
pushed a more cosmopolitan notion of democracy that extends to units
beyond states and challenges the legitimacy of many recognized international organizations.[35]

Equally sharp distinctions were made at the outset between the European "us" and Asian and African "others," facilitated by the fact that

---

[32] Kant, "Idea for a Universal History," pp. 44–7; "Perpetual Peace," p. 112; Bartelson, *A Genealogy of Sovereignty*, pp. 220–9; Osiander, "Sovereignty, International Relations, and the Westphalian Myth"; Schmidt, *Political Discourse of Anarchy*, on these developments more generally.

[33] Bartelson, *A Genealogy of Sovereignty*, ch. 5; Ziegler, "The Influence of Medieval Roman Law on Peace Treaties"; Lesaffer, "Peace Treaties from Lodi to Westphalia." According to Halliday, *Rethinking International Relations*, p. 6, Jeremy Bentham coined the term international relations in the early nineteenth century.

[34] Clark, *The Hierarchy of States*, ch. 6.

[35] Held, *Democracy and the Global Order*; Bernstein, "The Challenged Legitimacy of Inter-national Organisations."

most of these societies were not yet organized along the lines of the European state. In 1859, John Stuart Mill held that it was a "grave error" to "suppose that the same international customs, and the same rules of international morality, can obtain between one civilized nation and another, and between civilized nations and barbarians."[36] Samuel Huntington has recently attracted a lot of attention – and criticism – for his concept of the clash of civilizations, which makes invidious distinctions somewhat along the lines of Mill.[37] Basing their claims on Kant, but really acting in the tradition of Mill, liberal advocates of the Democratic Peace update his dichotomy to divide the world into liberal states and authoritarian "others." In sharp contradiction of Kant's categorical imperative, some liberals justify economic penetration or military intervention as necessary to bring the benefits of democracy to these states and their peoples.[38] American domestic and foreign policy since 9.11 indicate how easy it remains for political leaders to exploit fear of "others" à la Carl Schmitt to create solidarity at home.[39]

Research on social movements and work in psychology give us grounds for questioning the need for binaries that generate hostile feelings toward outgroups. "Oppositional consciousness," as Jane Mansbridge call it, may be far less common in practice than generally supposed.[40] Psychologists find negative affect toward other groups least likely to develop when oppositional identities are formed within a larger social context in which the actors are embedded. Muzafer Sherif, who first noted this effect, hypothesizes that "transcendent" identity groupings mute feelings of hostility because they provide some base for common identity and empathy.[41] In

---

[36] Mill, "A Few Words on Non-Intervention"; Onuf, *Republican Legacy in International Thought*, p. 250; Jahn, "Classical Smoke, Classical Mirror."

[37] Huntington, *Clash of Civilizations*, pp. 21, 129.

[38] Doyle, "Kant, Liberal Legacies, and International Affairs," parts 1 and 2, for the most influential statement linking Kant to the Democratic Peace, although not to intervention. Tesón, *A Philosophy of International Law*, p. 25; Burley (now Slaughter), "Law Among Liberal States"; Feinstein and Slaughter, "A Duty to Prevent," for so-called Kantian justifications of differential treatment of non-liberal governments. For critiques of how Democratic Peace advocates misread Kant, Lawrence, "Imperial Peace or Imperial Method"; MacMillan, "Immanuel Kant and the Democratic Peace," Franceschet, "'One Powerful and Enlightened Nation'"; Jahn, "Classical Smoke, Classical Mirror."

[39] Schmitt, *Concept of the Political*.

[40] Mansbridge, "Complicating Oppositional Consciousness"; Hopf, *Social Construction of International Politics*, p. 263.

[41] Sherif, "Subordinate Goals in the Reduction of Intergroup Conflict," Kelman, "The Interdependence of Israeli and Palestinian Identities," and Hymans, *Psychology of Nuclear Proliferation*, for a more recent applications of the concept.

international relations the "us" and "others" binary has not infrequently been mobilized for beneficial ends. Ole Waever contends that the European Union has been constructed against the negative temporal "other" of pre-1945 Europe.[42] Recent work on Kant and Hegel suggests that their "othering" was a response by intellectuals from relatively backward parts of Europe to the challenge posed by the French Revolution.[43] Robert Shilliam suggests that Kant and Hegel constructed the German "self" by incorporating important elements of the French "other."[44] Virgil makes a similar argument about Rome. His *Aeneid* foregrounds the foreignness that helped to constitute Rome from its very beginning and leads readers to the conclusion that *Romanità* is a multiple, open and evolving identity, constructed *with* more than in opposition to others.[45] The creation of "others" should properly be seen as only one means of identity construction, and one, moreoever, that has the potential to transcend hostile binaries.

Twentieth-century international relations theory took shape against the background of the Westphalia myth, which became foundational for realists.[46] The writings of realist scholars made interstate war appear the norm, and enduring cooperation an anomaly that required an extraordinary explanation. They cherry-picked quotes from Thucydides, Rousseau and Hobbes, seriously misreading all three, to lend authority to their claim that the international arena was fundamentally distinct from the domestic one and that anarchy and warfare were its norm.[47] Watered-down versions of the realist world view dominate policy communities on a nearly worldwide basis. Sovereignty and untrammeled pursuit of the national interest reveal themselves to be mutually constitutive. They are also in part self-fulfilling, as foreign policies based on narrow constructions of self-interest, made possible by the legal edifice of sovereignty, appear to confirm realist depictions of international relations. Writing in the mid-1960s, before the emergence of constructivism, Martin Wight lamented

---

[42] Waever, "European Security Identities."

[43] Shilliam, "The 'Other' in Classical Political Theory"; Pinkard, *Hegel*, pp. 61–8; Dickey, *Hegel*, pp. 278–81; Habermas, *Theory and Practice*.

[44] Shilliam, "The 'Other' in Classical Political Theory." Keene, "Images of Grotius," for a similar argument.

[45] Virgil, *Aeneid*; Reed, *Virgil's Gaze*, for a thoughtful analysis of his views of nation and of Rome in particular.

[46] Morgenthau, *Politics among Nations*, 3rd edn, p. 312; Krasner, *Sovereignty*, pp. 73–82. Osiander, "Sovereignty, International Relations, and the Westphalia Myth," on the myth itself.

[47] Lebow, *Tragic Vision of Politics*, chs. 3 and 4; Aiko, "Rousseau and Saint-Pierre's Peace Project"; Williams, "The Hobbesian Theory of International Relations," for critiques of realist readings.

that the realist project precluded any serious theorizing about international society. The "theory of the good life," he observed, is only applicable to orderly societies, and realists framed the international arena as a "precontractual state of nature," where no real theory is possible.[48] Within this framework, the most theorists could do was to describe patterns of interaction among units.[49]

If the challenge of studying order at the international level is intriguing, the prospect of doing so has become a little less daunting. There has been mounting dissatisfaction with the normative implications of the foundational binary of international relations theory.[50] It is apparent that the degree of order varies at least as much among domestic societies as it does between them and regional and international systems. So too does the degree of dissensus about fundamental political, religious and social values. These empirical realities compel us to look beyond the domestic–international dichotomy to study how relatively thin societies at all levels of aggregation can sometimes maintain a reasonable degree of order, but also how they are vulnerable to serious disruption. Greek understandings of politics and Durkheim's insights into the nature of social control provide conceptual tools for tackling these questions and developing an alternative understanding of order and disorder based on a society's thickness and the behavior of its elites.[51] Important differences between domestic and international politics at these levels would still remain, and between both of them and individual behavior. One of the key insights of the Enlightenment, since elaborated by social science, is the extent to which systems produce outcomes that cannot be predicted or explained by knowledge about the actors that constitute the system or their behavior. Emergent properties are important and unpredictable, and greatly complicate the task of theory-building. However, investigation may reveal that the kinds of dynamics that lead to emergent properties in domestic societies are not all that dissimilar from those at the regional and international levels.

---

[48] Wight, "Why There Is No International Theory." Linklater, "The Problem of Harm in World Politics," for a thoughtful assessment of Wight's writings.

[49] Bull, "The Grotian Conception of International Society," and *The Anarchical Society*, ch. 1; Watson, "Hedley Bull, States, Systems and International Society."

[50] Walker, *Inside/Outside*; Brown, *Sovereignty, Rights and Justice*; Agamben, *Homo Sacer*; Campbell, *Writing Security*; Connolly, *Identity/Difference*; Edkins and Pin-Fat, "Through the Wire."

[51] Lebow, *Tragic Vision of Politics*, pp. 258–64, makes a preliminary case for this approach based on the understandings of order shared by Thucydides, Clausewitz and Morgenthau.

A wise scholar might still stop here. There are nevertheless compelling normative reasons to forge ahead with the effort to develop a better theory of international relations. The most powerful one is to prevent pessimism from turning into fatalism by keeping alternative visions alive.[52] Justice is best served by an ordered world, but one that must be pliable and open enough to allow, if not encourage, the freedom, choice and overall development of actors. Many domestic societies come closer to meeting these conditions than regional orders or the international system. Failed states (e.g. Somalia, Afghanistan, Haiti) and the international system as a whole are undeniably the least ordered kinds of political systems, and the most in need of our attention, practical and theoretical.[53] Understanding "order" and disorder comparatively can generate insights that cannot be gained by studying them in isolation. Given the connection between theory and practice, it is important to create an alternative narrative that lends additional support to those scholars and practitioners who are attempting to move beyond narrow concepts of sovereignty and understandings of international relations that take war as an unavoidable fact of life. For intellectual, ethical and practical reasons, we need to pursue our investigations even if our answers are partial, tentative and certain to be superseded. Like political philosophy, international relations theory should reflect on how to create and maintain order and the principles on which it rests.[54]

The spirit

Modernity affirmed the value of ordinary life, and with it the quest for material well-being. The classical concern with virtue and the Christian emphasis on salvation were both downgraded.[55] Enlightenment thinkers developed a novel understanding of the psyche that reflected and possibly accelerated this shift in values. For Plato and Aristotle the psyche consisted of three drives: appetite, spirit and reason, each seeking its own ends.[56] They considered appetite dangerous and corrupting, valued the spirit

---

[52] Morgenthau, *Politics among Nations*, and Wight, *International Theory*, both make this point.

[53] Rotberg, *When States Fail*, is a good starting point.

[54] Wolin, *Politics and Vision*, p. 9, for this characterization of political philosophy. For similar views about the role of international relations theory, see also Kratochwil, *Rules, Norms and Decisions*; Onuf, *A World of our Making*; Alker, *Rediscoveries and Reformulations*.

[55] This is a central theme of Charles Taylor, *Sources of the Self*.

[56] "Spirit" is the widely used translation for *thumos* or *to thumoeides*, a word derived from the *megathumos*, the organ that supposedly roused Homeric heroes to action. Since the

because it motivated people to participate in civic life, but had the highest regard for reason. Reason sought to understand what made for a happy life and had the potential to constrain and educate appetite and spirit to collaborate with it toward that end. Moderns rejected the spirit altogether, largely because of its association with the aristocracy.[57] They upgraded appetite, reconceiving it as the source of economic growth and political order. Reason was reduced to a mere instrumentality, "the slave of the passions," in the words of David Hume.[58]

The spirit may have dropped out of the philosophical and political lexicon, but it has not ceased to be a fundamental human drive. As Plato and Aristotle understood, it gives rise to the universally felt need for what we call self-esteem. It makes us admire and emulate the skills, character and achievements of people considered praiseworthy by our society. By equaling or surpassing them, we gain the respect or esteem of people who matter, and feel good about ourselves. The spirit craves autonomy because it is so essential to this goal, and responds with anger to any impediment to self-assertion in private or public life. The spirit desires to avenge all slights and challenges to our autonomy and that of our friends. As we will see, modern psychology has also made self-esteem a key research focus, although it is conceptualized quite differently than it is by Plato and Aristotle.[59] Plato and Aristotle also have their differences, which become relevant when we examine the role of the spirit for politics in detail. This I do in chapter 2, where I also discuss some of the ways in which they differ.

Conventional paradigms of politics and international relations are rooted in appetite. Liberalism and Marxism describe politics as driven by material interests, and realism acknowledges their primacy after security. Scholars who work in these paradigms attempt to penetrate what they believe to be the smokescreen of culture and ideology to get at the

advent of Christianity, spirit has taken on quite a different set of meanings in English. Readers are urged to lay them aside and conceive of spirit in the sense it was intended by Greeks of the fifth and fourth centuries BCE. The alternative, the use of one of the Greek terms throughout my text, I have rejected for two reasons: it would be awkward, especially as I use the English words for appetite and reason for their Greek equivalents; and different Greek authors use different terms for *thumos*, and the choice of any one of them would privilege one or more of these thinkers over others.

[57] Hume, *Political Essays*, p. 294, describes honor as the concern of aristocratic "debauchees" and "spendthrifts."

[58] Hume, *A Treatise of Human Nature*, 2.3.3.4, and *An Inquiry Concerning the Principles of Morals*, appendix I, p. 163.

[59] Rubin and Hewstone, "Social Identity Theory's Self-Esteem Hypothesis," for a useful review of the relevant psychological research.

political, economic and military realities they are understood to obfuscate. Constructivism recognizes that culture and ideology do more than offer rationalizations for behavior that actors engage in for other reasons. They provide people with identities that offer meaning, order and predictability to their lives.[60] Identity can also be regarded as a vehicle for attaining self-esteem. People want to belong to high-status groups and institutions for this reason, and act in ways that secure them admission and standing within these groups and institutions. Driven by the needs of their members and leadership, these groups and institutions in turn act to maintain or enhance the respect they receive from other actors in the environment in which they function. Individuals, groups and institutions who are denied the respect to which they believe they are entitled often engage in deviant and disruptive behavior. Alternatively they can pursue the more creative and difficult strategy of trying to change the reward structure of their societies. Behavior of both kinds is manifested by states, responding to the psychological needs of their leaders, elites, and, not infrequently, their populations as well. States are certainly not people, but we see nothing implausible about describing their behavior in terms of the security and material needs of their populations. Just as the drive for wealth and security inform international relations theory, so too must the drive for self-esteem.

Following Thucydides, Plato and Aristotle, I maintain that the spirit animates all human beings and that the need for self-esteem is universal, although manifested differently across societies. In the chapters that follow, I develop a paradigm of politics based on the spirit, and incorporate it in a general theory of international relations based on a more comprehensive understanding of human motives and their implications for political behavior. In the process, I confront the concept of identity, one of the foundational concepts of constructivism. Perhaps because of its roots in historical sociology, constructivism is a curious beast: an interactionist paradigm in a psychological vacuum. To make identity a more meaningful concept, we need to be more precise about its purposes and components, learn more about how they evolve at individual and social levels, and what their implications are for behavior. I take some hesitant steps in this direction, laying the foundations for a psychology of identity appropriate to a constructivist theory of international relations.

---

[60] There is a vast literature on this subject. For two very different but reinforcing arguments about the importance of identity, see Taylor, *Sources of the Self*; March and Olsen, "The Logic of Appropriateness."

International relations is undoubtedly the hardest domain in which to make the case for the spirit as an important, if not a dominant motive. Honor, as opposed to standing – more about this difference in due course – can only be achieved in a society, and theories of international relations either deny the existence of international society or consider it relatively thin. The last 150 years of international relations are also the most difficult period in which to document the importance of the spirit. Monarchies and their dynastic rivalries gave way to modern states, an increasing number of them democratic in their governance. They are no longer led by aristocrats and warriors but by elected officials, bureaucrats and lawyers who must respond to important constituencies, many of them motivated by economic concerns. From Tocqueville to Nietzsche, philosophers have lamented the degree to which modern society has become plebian, focused on the most immediate of appetites and unsympathetic to grand projects that fire the imagination and require sacrifice. Has the spirit disappeared from public and international life as it has from political philosophy and social science?

Historically we associate the goals of honor and standing with dynastic political units, but nationalism indicates the they are at least as important for modern democratic, industrial and postindustrial states. Drawing on psychological research, recent work on nationalism contends that people manifest strong desires for group membership and identification because they provide a "heightened level of self worth."[61] My argument goes a step further to contend that people who identify with nationalities or nations to some degree seek vicarious fulfillment and enhanced self-esteem through their victories, and suffer a corresponding loss of esteem, even humiliation, when they suffer setbacks. We witness a similar phenomenon with sports teams, where the sense of affiliation can be just as strong. In today's Germany one rarely sees anybody carrying or flying the national flag. On weekends in the season, however, the S-Bahns are filled with fans, many in team shirts, proudly carrying the pennants of their team and singing its songs. The two domains sometimes come together, as in the World Cup. When their team plays Germany, English fans routinely shout "two to one" to remind Germans that they won two world wars to Germany's one World Cup victory against England. They goose-step, yell *Sieg Heil* to referees and hold their fingers under their noses in imitation of the Führer's

---

[61] Greenfield, *Nationalism*; Migdal, *Boundaries and Belonging*; Hall, *National Collective Identity*, p. 37, for the quote.

moustache.[62] "Project X," one of the most popular television series in Japan, dramatizes the conception, design and manufacture of world-class Japanese products such as hand-held calculators, ink-jet printers and digital cameras. The show appeals to and attempts to build national esteem, and is strikingly at odds with the recent rash of recalls of defective products that has triggered national hand-wringing in the press, talk shows and hallways of government ministries. In neighborhood noodle shops, concern is voiced that Japan is losing its competitive edge at the very moment Korea and China are demonstrating theirs. The soul-searching is less about economics than about standing and the national honor. "Craftsmanship was the best face that Japan had to show the world," said a lathe operator in an auto parts factory in Kawasaki. "Aren't the Koreans making fun of us now?"[63]

We should not be surprised by this phenomenon. The modern world led to the emergence of the individual, which is often considered one of its defining features.[64] Cut loose, at least in part, from socially determined roles and clientalist relationships, people suffered from psychological isolation, or anomie. Thinkers as diverse as Kierkegaard, Nietzsche, Simmel, Tönnies, Durkheim, Heidegger, Sartre and Arendt describe it, or its equivalent, as an expression of modernity. People forced to look somewhere else for identities, self-esteem and purpose in life often turned to states. Others turned to class, race or professional affiliations, or combinations of them.[65] I will show how the search for self-esteem via class and national affiliations was an important underlying cause of imperialism and both world wars, and continues to influence not only contemporary conflicts but efforts to put international relations on a more orderly footing.

One of the more radical claims I make concerns the relationship of the spirit to other motives, notably appetite (interest) and fear. Realists from Morgenthau to Waltz consider survival the most fundamental national interest, as do prominent liberals and constructivists.[66] Hobbes and Rousseau consider self-preservation the highest directive of human nature, and Waltz takes serious liberties with their texts to draw an analogy

---

[62] *The Independent* (London), June 2, 2006, p. 4.
[63] Martin Fackler, "Japanese Fret that Quality Is in Decline," *New York Times*, September 21, 2006.
[64] Seigel, *The Idea of the Self*, pp. 4–5.
[65] Lasswell, *World Politics and Personal Insecurity*, pp. 40–56.
[66] Morgenthau, *Politics among Nations*, 3rd edn, p. 10; Waltz, *Theory of International Politics*, pp. 92, 204; Berenskoetter, "Friends, There Are No Friends?," for a discussion of the role of survival in international relations theory.

between states and individuals.[67] Martin Wight, I noted earlier, believes that students of domestic politics can allow themselves to think about "the theory of the good life" in contrast to those who study international relations and must develop a "theory of survival."[68] When the spirit is dominant, when actors seek self-esteem through honor, standing or autonomy, they are often willing to risk, even sacrifice, themselves or their political units in pursuit of these goals. From the ancient Greeks to Iraq, my cases offer strong evidence to support this contention.

The literature

Homer began a tradition of thinking about the spirit and its behavioral consequences that endured down to the Enlightenment and still finds the occasional echo in our own day. At military academies future warriors read the *Iliad* with interest, and some are reported to have even taken copies with them to Iraq. Significantly, a survey of West Point cadets reveals that Achilles – the most skilled but least disciplined of warriors – is no longer the most admired figure in the epic. Students offer a victorious Hector as their role model, explaining that he is acting in defense of his family and city. Even in the military world, the quest for glory, love of battle and the appeal of sacrifice is no longer acceptable unless it is for the higher good of the nation. Glory and honor are less comprehensible to civilians. To make the Trojan War credible to contemporary audiences, the screenwriters for Wolfgang Petersen's 2003 film, *Troy*, dropped honor as a motive for war in favor of an invented trade rivalry between Greeks and Trojans.[69]

International relations theory beat Hollywood to the punch. Post-World War II theorists all but expunged the spirit from the political lexicon. Like Petersen's screenwriters, they invoked power and material interests to account for foreign policies that were intended to maximize honor, prestige or standing. Earlier generations of scholars were more attuned to the spirit. It features prominently in Max Weber, who distinguishes

---

[67] Waltz, *Theory of International Politics*, pp. 92, 204. Hobbes is more complex than Waltz allows. Hobbes recognizes two universal drives – vanity and self-preservation – and mobilizes the latter to control the former. See Strauss, *Political Philosophy of Hobbes*, pp. 23–9; Stauffer, "Reopening the Quarrel between the Ancients and the Moderns." Williams, "The Hobbesian Theory of International Relations," for an alternative, non-realist reading of Hobbes. Aiko, "Rousseau and Saint-Pierre's Peace Project," on Waltz's misreading of Rousseau.

[68] Wight, "Why There Is No International Theory."

[69] Coker, *The Warrior Ethos*, pp. 23, 25. Personal communication with Christopher Coker, June 23, 2007.

honor from interest and considers leaders more sensitive to challenges to the former. "A nation," he maintains, "will forgive damage to its interests, but not injury to its honour, and certainly not when this is done in a spirit of priggish self-righteousness."[70] International politics for Weber is driven by the desire of states to have their superior worth recognized. They acquire power over other states to gain power-prestige (*Machtprestige*), defined as "the glory of power over other communities." Competition for standing among states, but especially among the major powers, introduces an irrational element into international relations that exacerbates tensions, military preparations and conflict. Weber offered Franco-German relations as an example. Domestic politics is an additional source of international conflict because territorial expansion is an important means by which those in power can enhance their standing vis-à-vis domestic opponents.[71]

Dutch cultural historian Johan Huizinga makes even more sweeping claims than Weber. In a classic study on the play element in culture, first published in 1938, he describes the inherent ludic qualities of agon (contest or competition). War is a violent variant that takes on the appearance of a game so long as "it is waged within a circle whose members acknowledge each other as equals, or, at least, as equals before the law." Huizinga identifies glory (what I call honor and standing) as a motive distinct, and in competition with, material gain.

> Even in highly developed cultural relations, and even if statesmen who are preparing the conflict interpret it as a question of power, the desire for material gain remains, in general, subordinate to motives of pride, glory, prestige and the appearance of superiority or supremacy. The general term *glory* furnishes a much more realistic explanation of all the great wars of conquest from antiquity to the present day, than any theory of economic forces and political calculations.

Ludic wars are easy to recognize because the place and time of combat are usually agreed upon in advance, and both sides consider themselves bound by the rules, because victory achieved in any other way would not confer honor. They stress single combats, which are tests of wills, but also considered "judgments of god" that determine which side possesses right or justice.[72] This definition, it will be seen, draws on Homer and subsequent descriptions of warfare in classical Greece.

[70] Weber, "The Profession and Vocation of Politics," p. 356.
[71] Weber, *Economy and Society*, p. 911.
[72] Huizinga, *Homo Ludens*, especially pp. 110–26. Caillois, *Man, Play, and Games*.

Not all wars are ludic according to Huizinga. Some cannot be described as games because they are neither limited in their goals nor fought in accordance with rules. Non-ludic wars are usually waged against peoples or political units outside of one's society. "If it is a question of combat against groups which are not, actually, acknowledged as men, or at least as being possessed of human rights – whether they are called 'barbarians,' 'devils,' 'pagans,' or 'heretics' – this combat will remain within the 'limits' of culture only as long as a group which imposes limits on itself for the satisfaction of its own honor."[73]

There are serious limitations to Huizinga's analysis. He describes ludic warfare as a mark of civilization and an improvement on "the violence of savage peoples." He fails to recognize that tribal warfare is often rule-governed and fought for standing within and between tribal groups, and that so-called civilized states can fight wars *à outrance* among themselves. He unreasonably imparts a telos to warfare, describing a progression from simple violence to ludic warfare, and from wars fought for glory to those centered on justice. He also describes the "rivalry for first rank" as an inherently civilizing drive that leads to "young" honor cultures, and ultimately to more complex civilizations.[74] Such optimism – or naïveté – may once have been possible, but not after the experience of two world wars. Huizinga displays no awareness that the competitive phenomenon he describes in the modern world – notably, the rise of organized sports – was closely linked with imperialism. Native Americans were taught football to "civilize" them, and the playground movement arose to control and assimilate new immigrants to American cities. Writing after these practices had become "naturalized," Huizinga unselfconsciously reflects the values of his culture.

Once we move beyond Weber, twentieth-century international relations theory downgrades honor and standing as independent motives. Prominent postwar theorists either ignore the spirit or treat its manifestations as instrumentalities for demonstrating and maximizing power.[75] Hans Morgenthau is typical. States, like individuals, he writes, seek to

---

[73] Huizinga, *Homo Ludens*.

[74] Ibid. Caillois, *Man, Play, and Games*, offers a more sophisticated take on play, but from quite a different perspective. He considers the reconstruction of agon in modernity as having to do with notions of individual responsibility versus alea, the subjection to outside forces.

[75] This point is also made by Markey, "Prestige and the Origins of War." Among major theorists, Raymond Aron perhaps comes the closest to acknowledging the independent importance of prestige. He includes three long quotes from Huizinga in his *Homo Ludens*. They come in a final note at the end of this massive volume, along with the immediate disclaimer that "reality seems more complex."

increase, maintain or demonstrate their power. A state that aims at acquiring more power, pursues a policy of "imperialism." A state whose foreign policy has the goal of maintaining its power pursues "a policy of the status quo." A state that wants to demonstrate power pursues "a policy of prestige." It attempts to "impress other nations with the power one's own nation actually possesses, or with the power it believes, or wants the other nations to believe, it possesses."[76] A policy of prestige is not an end in itself, but a strategy for supporting or challenging the status quo. It can be based on actual power, or bluff. Morgenthau confesses that its underlying purpose is often difficult to fathom.[77]

Morgenthau's relegation of prestige-seeking from an end to a means is all the more surprising given his interest in Aristotle, who considered striving for recognition a fundamental human drive.[78] He attended Weber's lectures at the University of Munich and made his conception of power the foundation of his own theory of international relations. Weber's understanding of the drive for power, which Morgenthau calls the *animus dominandi*, is best understood as an expression of the spirit. The lust for power "concerns itself not with the individual's survival but with his position among his fellows once his survival has been secured."[79] Committed to constructing a parsimonious theory, Morgenthau reversed the relationship between power and prestige, making the former subordinate to the latter, and theorized about how the power was achieved and maintained. He ignored Weber's admonition that power was a means to an end, not an end in itself, and that any theory about politics must be rooted in some understanding of those ends.

Following Morgenthau, Robert Gilpin distinguishes prestige from power, and at first appears to give it singular prominence in international relations. In *War and Change in International Relations* he describes it as the most important component of the international system after power and the "everyday currency of international relations." Prestige for Gilpin has a moral as well as a functional basis, with the former deriving from the leading state's ability to provide public goods and advance or protect common ideological, religious or other values. Lesser states follow the lead of more powerful ones in part because they accept the legitimacy of the

---

[76] Morgenthau, *Politics among Nations*, 4th edn, pp. 69–82.
[77] Ibid., chs. 4–6 devoted to the three foreign policies. Morgenthau had first introduced the three-fold distinction among states in *La notion du "politique" et la théorie des différends internationaux*, pp. 42 ff and 61.
[78] Morgenthau, *Political Theory and International Affairs*.
[79] Morgenthau, *Scientific Man vs. Power Politics*, p. 165.

existing order. Every dominant state accordingly promotes a religion or ideology to justify its domination over other states.[80] Gilpin all but repudiates this sensible formulation a few pages later when he redefines prestige as a mere manifestation of power. It is "largely a function of economic and military capabilities, and achieved primarily through the successful use of power, and especially through victory in war."[81] He acknowledges the liberal claim that a shift is underway from military to economic power as the basis of international prestige, but insists that Japan and Germany have only increased their prestige "because they could translate their economic capabilities into military power."[82]

Prestige and conflict are closely linked for Gilpin. Peace is most likely when the prestige hierarchy is clearly understood and unchallenged. A weakening of this hierarchy, or ambiguity concerning it, generally precedes eras of conflict and war. Prestige is distinct from power because perceptions of power can lag behind the actual capabilities of states. The greater the asymmetry between perceptions and the distribution of power in the system, the more likely war becomes, especially when it is the power of rising states that is undervalued. "The rising state or states in the system increasingly demand changes in that system that will reflect their newly gained power and their unmet interests." Governance in the system breaks down until "perceptions catch up with the realities of power." This often requires war, and the principal function of war among leading powers is to reestablish the prestige hierarchy.[83]

There is a tension in Gilpin between his understanding of the importance of legitimacy and his desire to produce a parsimonious deductive theory of international relations. He frequently cites Thucydides and appears at first to agree with him that prestige has a moral as well as a material basis, and that power derived from material capabilities is only one source of influence, and by no means the most effective.[84] He quickly jettisons this more nuanced understanding of influence, and the way in which prestige contributes to it, because it is culturally dependent and incompatible with a theory that purports to be universal.

Leading scholars of the English School are uninterested in honor and prestige. They are modernist in their orientation and concerned with the emergence of the international society in law and practice.[85] Recognition

---

[80] Gilpin, *War and Change in International Relations*, pp. 30–4. Quote on p. 31.

[81] Ibid., p. 35. [82] Ibid., pp. 33–4. [83] Ibid., pp. 34–5.

[84] On this point, see Lebow, *Tragic Vision of Politics*, ch. 4.

[85] Bull, *The Anarchical Society*, p. 36, describes as a positive development the concept of the "great power," as developed by Ranke, because it replaced the ranking of states in terms of

interests them only in so far as it determines who is admitted to international society, because they maintain that the character of its membership
largely determines its structure.[86] Kenneth Waltz makes no reference to
prestige, standing or honor in his *Theory of International Politics*.[87] More
recently, he asserts that states compete only for wealth and security.[88]
Alexander Wendt acknowledges that self-esteem is important because
human beings need to feel good about themselves. It is a throwaway line,
as the concept is not developed any further.[89] Nicholas Onuf is the only
constructivist to take the spirit seriously. In *World of our Making*, he contends that "standing, security and wealth are the controlling interests of
humanity. We recognize them everywhere."

The spirit is staging a comeback, albeit in an indirect and undertheo-
rized way. In *Honor, Symbols, and War*, Barry O'Neil argues that appeals
to honor are less common today than in the past, but that patterns of
international conflict share much in common with past disputes over
honor. He cites statements by officials of both superpowers to show that
honor was at the core of their arms race, and especially the deployment
of theater-range nuclear systems in Europe in the 1980s. In a subsequent
paper, he argues that states have historically sought prestige by acquiring certain kinds of weapons systems, most recently nuclear weapons.
Weapons and other admired possessions or attributes confer influence,
and are emulated by others.[90] David Sylvan, Corinne Graff and Elisabetta
Pugliese draw on Weber's formulation of *Machtprestige* to argue that states
are concerned about their relative status in the system and willing to go
to war to preserve it. They offer short case studies of the origins of the
Crimean War and the outbreak of the First World War to document their
claims and also discuss the foreign policy of de Gaulle's France.[91] Inspired
by Thucydides, Hobbes and Rousseau, Daniel Markey investigates the role
of prestige in international relations, but never effectively distinguishes it
from power.[92]

the inherited status of their rulers. Once ranking was based on relative power, as assessed
by the major actors themselves, it could be formally expressed in the "Concert of Europe."

[86] Ibid., pp. 33, 208. Also Dunne, "Society and Hierarchy in International Relations."
[87] Onuf, *World of our Making*, p. 278.   [88] Waltz, "Structural Realism after the Cold War."
[89] Wendt, *Social Theory of International Politics*, p. 132.
[90] O'Neill, "Nuclear Weapons and the Pursuit of Peace," unpublished but available on-line
at http://cowles.econ.yale.edu.
[91] David Sylvan, Corinne Graff and Elisabetta Pugliese, "Status and Prestige in International
Relations," unpublished paper presented at the Pan-European International Relations
Conference, Vienna, 1998.
[92] Markey, "Prestige and the Origins of War."

The links between honor and identity are stressed in constructivist writings on "ontological security." The concept was developed by R. D. Laing, but given a wider audience by Anthony Giddens, who reformulated it in his theory of structuration.[93] Drawing more on the work of Goffman and Erikson than on Laing, Giddens contends that people need to reduce anxiety by developing confidence in their understandings of the physical and social world and the patterns of responses they sustain. The largely routinized nature of social intercourse helps people structure their identities and enhance their capacity for agency, and accordingly becomes a powerful component of their security system. People suffer acute anxiety when these routines are disrupted by novel or critical situations.[94] The concept of ontological security has been applied to international relations on the assumption that states, like people, seek ontological security.[95] They are said to require consistent concepts of self that are generated and sustained through foreign policy routines. These routines are embedded in biographical narratives that government officials, media and intellectuals develop and invoke to explain and justify foreign policies. Policies at odds with these narratives and the values they encode can bring shame on officials if public opinion judges their behavior incongruent with their states' identity.[96]

Thucydides' account of the origins of the Peloponnesian War is in every way consistent with the ontological security hypothesis. The narrative of Book 1 indicates that Sparta's decision for war in 431 BCE had more to do with threats to its identity than to its security. The rise of Athenian power was sufficiently steep to threaten Sparta's standing as the leading hegemon, and with it the identities and self-esteem of its citizens.[97] Erik Ringmar suggests that wars are not only fought to protect well-established identities but to forge new ones. In its effort to develop a national identity, Sweden declared itself to be the leading Lutheran power and the heir to

---

[93] Laing, *The Divided Self*, ch. 3.

[94] Giddens, *The Constitution of Society*, pp. 50–1, 86, 375, *The Consequences of Modernity*, pp. 92–100, and *Modernity and Self-Identity*, pp. 36, 39–40. Rotter, "Generalized Expectancies for Internal vs. External Control of Reinforcement," for a similar argument to the effect that belief systems provide a sense of predictability and control, reducing stress to a level that permits coping behavior.

[95] Bull, *Anarchical Society*, pp. 7–8, suggests that people value order because it allows predictability.

[96] Huysmans, "Security! What Do You Mean?"; McSweeny, *Security, Identity and Interests*; Mitzen, "Ontological Security in World Politics"; Manners, "European [Security] Union"; Steele, "Self-Identity and the IR State," draft book manuscript, introduction, p. 3; Berenskoeter, "Creating (In) Security from Within."

[97] Lebow, *Tragic Vision of Politics*, ch. 3.

the Goths and their heroic myths. This biographical narrative, not just strategic considerations, required it to intervene in the Thirty Years War to protect Lutherans from the Catholic armies of the Holy Roman Empire.[98] Jennifer Mitzen contends that states can become dependent on security dilemmas because the routines they provide, while dangerous, help to stabilize their identities. Leaders can adhere to these routines rigidly or reflexively, which has important consequences for conflict management and resolution.[99]

There is an obvious overlap between my project and the ontological security research program. Ontological security recognizes that identities are structured around diverse narratives and values, which once established give leaders strong incentives to act consistently with them, or at least to defend their policies with reference to them. Self-esteem, I will argue, is a critical component of identity, and is maintained through the quest for honor or standing. Understanding this relationship, how it functions at both the individual and state levels, and how they are linked, can provide insights into a largely neglected but important set of motives for state behavior.

Overview of the argument

My theory of international relations is based on a simple set of assumptions about human motives. Following the Greeks, I posit spirit, appetite and reason as fundamental drives with distinct objects or ends. They give rise to distinctive forms of behavior that have different implications for cooperation, conflict and risk-taking. They also require, and help generate, distinct forms of hierarchy based on different principles of justice. Order at the individual, state, regional and international levels is sustained by these hierarchies, and weakens or breaks down when the discrepancy between behavior and the principles of justice on which they rest becomes great and obvious. Order and disorder at any level have implications for order at adjacent levels.

I begin with a description of spirit, appetite and reason, and go on to describe the characteristics of ideal-type worlds based on each of these motives, the kinds of behavior to which they give rise and the nature of the hierarchies and principles of justice associated with them. In real worlds, I contend, all three motives are to varying degrees present, and often fear as

[98] Ringmar, *Identity, Interest and Action.*
[99] Mitzen, "Ontological Security in World Politics."

well. Real worlds are lumpy, in that their mix of motives differs from actor to actor and among the groupings they form. Multiple motives generally mix rather than blend, giving rise to a range of behaviors that can often appear contradictory.

Reason-based worlds are those in which reason is able to constrain and educate spirit and appetite to work with it to achieve a happy life. Such a state of balance is rare among individuals, hardly ever approached by societies and has never been seen in regional or international systems. Imbalance occurs when reason fails to gain control of the spirit or appetite, or subsequently loses it to either. Imbalance is a matter of degree, as is the disorder it brings to individuals, societies and the systems in which they function. Imbalance, when it occurs, is almost always one-sided in the direction of either spirit or appetite. I offer two reinforcing explanations for imbalance: the failure of elites to adhere to the restraints or "rule packages" associated with their status or office, and changing conceptions of justice that deprive the existing hierarchy of its legitimacy. The two processes are often related in that the former encourages the latter.

I describe the mechanisms that translate imbalance into social disorder and breakdown. Spirit- and appetite-based societies are delicately balanced even when well-functioning. Both motives are advanced through competition, and spirit-driven competition for standing is particularly intense because of its relational nature. When not held in check by reason, competition for either honor and standing (spirit) or wealth (appetite) can transgress the accepted constraints and lead to a rapid unraveling of order. Imbalance in the direction of spirit can intensify intra-elite competition to the point where a critical mass of elite actors come to fear that they will be denied standing or even forfeit their lives. This fear becomes paramount when one actor or faction (or state or alliance) appears on the verge of capturing the mechanisms of state (or abusing its power to establish unwanted authority over others) in pursuit of its parochial goals. In these circumstances, violence or warfare may break out, brought about through a bid for domination by one side or preemption by the other. Imbalance in the direction of appetite on the part of an elite is likely to lead to both emulation and resentment by other actors. It risks unraveling the social order through widespread violation of *nomos* and increasing class tensions that ultimately lead to the same kind of fear and responses to it associated with an excess of spirit.

Social orders at every level undergo cycles of consolidation and decline. As it is always easier to enter fear-based worlds than to escape from them, realism is the default social condition. Human history at this level is cyclical, as realists contend. There are also historical trends. Over the span of human existence, societies, which are originally appetite-based, have evolved into spirit-based worlds, and then back into worlds of appetite, but ones that emphasize material well-being at the expense of other appetites. I raise the prospect of further evolution in the form of a return to a spirit-based world that would not be a warrior society, but one with diverse, if still competitive, forms of recognition and standing. This evolution is discontinuous, far from uniform, and driven by neither a single nor necessarily dialectical process. Breakdowns of existing orders are an essential component, as they make way for change, but also stimulate learning (in the form of a renewed commitment to constrain and educate spirit and appetite). Although spirit, appetite and fear-based worlds have existed in pre- and postindustrial societies, with strikingly similar characteristics, technological, intellectual and social changes have contributed to transitions between them. Future advances in bio- and nano-technology, and the ways in which they shape our thinking, might be expected to do the same.

Chapter outline

Developing a new paradigm of politics and theories nested within it is a daunting task, not only conceptually, but also in terms of presentation. This chapter is a kind of teaser that opens with a short description of the concept of the spirit and advances the claim that it is germane to a wide domain of social interactions. I develop both the concept and its application in greater detail in the chapters that follow. It makes sense to lay out the theory before proceeding to the cases, and to elaborate, extend and refine the theory on the basis of evidence from historical cases. With respect to cases, there are tradeoffs to consider between a small number that allows in-depth examination of the role of the spirit in politics, and a larger sample that demonstrates the range of conditions in which the spirit is relevant and the diverse ways in which it finds expression. I have chosen the latter strategy, and use cases from the ancient, medieval, early modern and modern worlds. Artists often start paintings with broad brush strokes with the goal of capturing the essence of what they want to represent. I do the same, with the understanding that my cases will be more illustrative than demonstrative.

Chapter 2 lays out the ontological and epistemological premises of my theory. My starting point is the three-fold ancient Greek characterization of the human psyche. I assume that appetite and spirit are universal drives whose expression varies across cultures and epochs. Reason is also universal, and the degree to which it constrains and educates appetite and spirit varies enormously within as well as across cultures. I briefly describe the characteristics of ideal-type worlds based on each of these and their different implications for cooperation, conflict and risk-taking. I do the same for fear-based worlds, another ideal type in which appetite and spirit are entirely unconstrained by reason. Each ideal-type world generates a different kind of hierarchy, and all but that of fear are based on some principle of justice. Ideal-type worlds, by definition, do not map on to historical worlds, all of which are mixed in motives, behavior and the hierarchies. These ideal types nevertheless help us make sense of real worlds and the mixtures these reveal. The chapter concludes with an extended discussion of what I believe to be the most problematic aspects of my theory and how I have attempted to address them.

Chapter 3 further elaborates the character, behavior and tensions of spirit-based worlds. Plato and Aristotle provide the philosophical foundation for my ideal type, as they were the first to theorize about the spirit and its implications for human behavior and political orders. They were deeply influenced by Homer. His *Iliad* describes a traditional warrior society and identifies its core values and inner tensions that threaten its survival. It became the prototype for later European conceptions of honor, and for this reason too it is the most useful text for my analysis. Comparing real honor worlds to this ideal-type one will help us better understand these societies and how many of them gradually evolve into something more diverse and complex.

Chapter 4 turns to the real world and the first three of my historical cases. It begins with an analysis of classical Greece (480–325 BCE). It is an "easy" case because contemporaries and modern-day scholars alike describe it as a society in which honor was an important, if not the dominant, value for the elite. It is also a productive case because of the many differences between it and the Homeric ideal-type honor society. These differences, and the complexities to which they give rise, provide additional insights into the nature of honor societies and their tensions. I extend my analysis into the Hellenistic and Roman periods. Both epochs offer interesting variants on honor cultures, and I describe some of their salient features and compare them to classical Greece. The late Republic and Roman Empire are no longer warrior societies. Nor are they honor societies, as the rules governing the competition for standing were violated so regularly that they broke down. The spirit was manifested in the drive for standing, increasingly unconstrained by rules and more profligate in its expression. There were nevertheless some survivals of honor-based behavior, especially in the military sphere, where they tended to be counterproductive in their consequences.

Chapter 5 extends my analysis to Europe, from the early Middle Ages to the Hundred Years War. I begin with the Merovingian and Carolingian dynasties, which are theoretically interesting because, in contrast to classical Greece and the early and middle Roman Republics, they are warrior societies not based on honor. Standing was all-important, and in the absence of honor the struggle for standing, as in the Roman Empire, was unconstrained by norms. My next topic is Anglo-French relations from the Norman invasion through the Hundred Years War. This is another violent era in which honor nevertheless became an increasingly important goal for rulers and aristocratic warriors with the rise of chivalry. The creation of intellectuals and churchmen, chivalry was a self-conscious and largely unsuccessful attempt to create an honor society by drawing on understandings of past Roman practices. Chivalry nevertheless created an ideal, which, along with its Homeric predecessor, significantly influenced later European thinking and practice.

In chapter 6 I examine Europe from Westphalia (1648) to the French Revolution (1789). During this period, the quest for *gloire* was the dominant dynastic motive, and found expression in expansion and war, although economic considerations and security were of course present as well. Striving for standing and honor provides the basis for an alternative explanation for the rise of the state. Leaders extracted resources to fight wars, but for their initiators most of these wars had little to do with security; they were waged to gain territory to increase dynastic standing and served as a vehicle for individual combatants to obtain honor and wealth. Leaders also extracted resources and developed bureaucracies for purposes of display, another means by which they gained honor and standing. In the eighteenth century, there was an enormous increase in resources European states devoted to palaces and other kinds of display, and in some cases a corresponding decline in funds allocated for war. On the basis of these cases, I revisit and expand my model of an honor society and its implications for politics and international relations.

Chapter 7 confronts modernity, a world in which the spirit has been relegated to ghost-like status and appetite is assumed to dominate. I describe this transition and the writings of Rousseau and Smith, who recognize that the spirit remains a powerful human motive, but one that has become increasingly entwined with appetite. My account of international relations in the nineteenth and early twentieth centuries are the "hard cases" for my theory. International relations nevertheless reveals a striking continuity with past practices. One reason for this is that down to 1914 the majority of political leaders, diplomats and generals were aristocrats imbued with many of the values that had motivated their predecessors. The quest for honor and standing, initially a preserve of the aristocracy, penetrated deeply into the middle classes, many of whose members took their cues from the aristocracy and sought to assimilate its values and practices. My case studies of imperialism and the origins of World War I focus on the social structure of European society, especially Germany, to show how the need for self-esteem was deflected outward in the form of international competition and willingness to use force in defense of the national "honor." Schumpeter attributed World War I to the malign influence of aristocrats more concerned with honor than wealth. I critique and refine his argument and offer an explanation for this conflict based on different aristocratic responses to modernity, the relative political power within countries of aristocrats with largely premodern values, and the relative size and economic power of the middle and commercial classes of these countries. I contend that the spirit offers a better account for the origins of World War I than explanations based on fear and interest.

I use my case studies of imperialism and World War I to reformulate and extend prospect theory. Prospect theory tells us that people are willing to take greater risks to prevent losses than they are to make gains.[100] It was developed and tested with respect to material gains and losses, so it is above all a theory about appetite. My cases indicate different patterns of risk acceptance for actors motivated by fear or honor. When actors are motivated by the spirit, and are attempting to gain or preserve honor or standing, they are risk-accepting with respect to both perceived losses and gains. When seeking gain, they may welcome threats to their survival because they gain honor by surmounting them or dying in the attempt. When motivated by fear, they cannot distinguish between gain and loss, as security is relational. They are equally risk-accepting or averse, depending on the intensity and context of the threat.

Chapter 8 analyzes the origins of World War II. Given the seeming dominance of appetite and fear, the 1920s and 1930s should be the hardest case in which to demonstrate the importance of the spirit as a foreign policy motive. I contend that spirit-based explanations are absolutely essential to account for the aggressive foreign policies and wars of conquest of

---

[100] Kahneman and Tversky, "Prospect Theory", and *Choices, Values, and Frames*.

Italy, Germany and Japan because these policies were so sharply at odds with their security and economic interests. The spirit, which generates the need for self-esteem, also helps to explain the public appeal of Hitler and Mussolini, without which they could never have come to power. My treatment of Germany, Italy and Japan emphasizes the survival of prefeudal values, which found expression in an aggressive search for standing. This dynamic rewarded ambitious politicians or leaders who promised, or successfully pursued, aggressive policies, but not war against other great powers. The late acceptance of all three countries as great powers, and perceived prior humiliation at the hands of other great powers, made leaders and politically relevant publics more willing to use force to achieve recognition, revenge and standing. These several phenomena were related and reinforcing, and together with agency, in the form of psychologically imbalanced leaders, led to World War II.

In the conclusion to this chapter I return to two themes I introduced earlier: the restraining role of reason and the character of warfare. In chapter 2 I identify three kinds, or levels, of reason: instrumental, *phronēsis* and wisdom. I find that spirit- and appetite-dominated worlds function well when *phronēsis*, or second-level reason, restrains actors because they recognize the extent to which the advancement of their goals depends on the preservation of the system and its norms. When it loses its hold over either spirit or appetite, systems are likely to undergo a phase transition into fear-dominated worlds. Such worlds involve wars that are often fought *à outrance* to destroy, or at least seriously weaken, opposing states and regimes. World War II conformed to this pattern, and on the eastern front revealed many of the characteristics of an ideal-type fear-based world.

Chapter 9 takes up another hard case for my theory: the Cold War. I argue that all three motives were present in the origins and early years of that conflict, but that standing increasingly became the principal goal of both Moscow and Washington as the conflict became more stable in the years after the Cuban missile crisis. The competition between the superpowers came to resemble that between the colonial powers in the latter part of the nineteenth century. The Cold War ended primarily because Soviet president Mikhail Gorbachev and his principal advisors considered the superpower competition for standing too costly, risky and inimical to their goals of domestic reform. I go on to examine the American intervention in Iraq and show how it cannot be explained with reference to material well-being or security. We must look to spirit-based explanations that stress anger and the desire to exploit America's comparative advantage in military power to prevent or deter future challenges to its hegemony.

In the second part of this chapter, I address the question of system transformation. In the West, international standing has almost always been claimed on the basis of military and economic power. Periodic challenges from revolutionary regimes to claim standing on an alternative basis have consistently failed. Multiple challenges to traditional conceptions of standing are now underway, and constitute an important, and largely neglected, dimension of international politics. I examine these challenges, and consider the possibility that we are in the early stages of a reformulation of the nature and criteria for standing that reintroduces the concept of honor. I explain why any such change would have profound consequences for the identities of actors, the goals and means of their foreign policies and the nature of power and influence. I suggest criteria for tracking such evolution and assessing its likely consequences.

In chapter 10, the conclusion, I evaluate my theory on the basis of my principal empirical findings. In the process, I briefly recapitulate my arguments concerning the rise of the state, prospect theory and parvenu powers. I situate my discussion of the latter in a broader analysis of the strategies open to states seeking recognition, honor or standing. I go on to elaborate some of the radical implications of my theory and empirical findings for our understandings of political order and the relationship between power and influence. I conclude by offering a dynamic model of the relationship of identity to interest and behavior and how this process shapes and can transform the character of the political systems.

Do we need another grand theory?

Social scientists have been working away at the problem of order for a long time: not that any of them, to my knowledge, have analyzed it in terms of Plato's and Aristotle's categories. Scholars have worked from the bottom up – tackling small and more manageable pieces of the puzzle – and from the top down – in the form of grand theories in the tradition of Hegel and Marx. Both approaches are valuable, although, as I noted earlier in my discussion of Plato's paradox, either is difficult to do in the absence of the knowledge generated by the other. Grand theories are nevertheless valuable because they provide frameworks for conducting research and suggest propositions that are amenable to empirical research. As Thomas Kuhn so persuasively argued, most research takes places within paradigms or grand theories – and the two are often closely related – and it would be difficult, perhaps impossible, to establish and follow research programs in their absence.[101]

Most people use theories to approach the world, although they may be no more aware of using them than Molière's Monsieur Jourdain is of speaking prose. Most politicians and journalists are like Monsieur Jourdain; they have half-formed and unarticulated theories of how the world works that they use to confront and make sense of new situations. Social scientists are distinguished by their efforts to make their theories explicit, to articulate their assumptions, justify their propositions in terms of them and to test, or at least evaluate, them against appropriate evidence. Not all social scientists work within the positivist framework; many are more interested in understanding the background conditions and cultures that constitute the social reality and make actors and action meaningful. Scholars in both the *Verstehen* and *Erklärung* traditions resort to theory, albeit of different kinds, that direct our attention to certain problems, relationships and evidence, and often to the tests or methods of evaluation considered relevant to them.[102] Theories, of course, have a downside. They ignore or dismiss certain problems, discourage certain kinds of inquiry and encourage the kind of cognitive consistency that leads us to assimilate discrepant information to our expectations. Hans Morgenthau was bemused by how events such as the rapid defeat of France in 1940 were considered impossible beforehand, because they were at odds with reigning theories, but were interpreted in terms of those same theories in retrospect. By such sleights of hand the social scientists indulge their "inveterate tendency to stick to their assumptions and to suffer constant defeat from experience rather than to change their assumptions in the light of contradicting facts."[103]

Competing paradigms and grand theories are a partial palliative to some of these problems. They open our eyes to new or different problems, give us reasons for thinking them important as well as ways to approach them. They also make it more difficult for us to ignore evidence that is inconsistent or anomalous with particular grand theories. And when we do, proponents of other theories and paradigms are almost certain to point to our failings. International relations already has several competing paradigms: realism, liberalism, Marxism, constructivism. The

[101] Kuhn, *Structure of Scientific Revolutions*.
[102] Lebow and Lichbach, *Theory and Evidence in Comparative Politics and International Relations*, for essays that explore how the concern for theory, evidence and evaluation cuts across research traditions.
[103] Morgenthau, *Decline of Democratic Politics*, p. 282.

English School, feminism, pragmatism, cognitive psychology, sociological institutionalism and philosophical realism further enrich our menu of choice. They provide intellectual diversity and encourage intellectual honesty, although they have also brought about considerable fragmentation of the field.

Why then do we need another paradigm and associated grand theory? I believe there are compelling reasons. The first and most important of these concerns the limited representation of human motives by existing paradigms and the theories nested in them. As I noted earlier, liberalism and Marxism are rooted in appetite, and so is realism at one remove. It is a paradigm based on fear, and the theories within it contend that in anarchical environments actors must make security their first concern, and only then can they indulge their desires for material well-being. There is no paradigm or theory that builds on the motive of the spirit and the human need for self-esteem and describes the ways in which strivings for honor and standing influence, if not often shape, political behavior. My theory of international relations is necessary to explain behavior other theories cannot, identify new problems, reframe existing ones in helpful ways and, more generally, to establish a new and fruitful research program.

The heyday of grand theories in the social sciences was the late eighteenth to the early twentieth century.[104] For scientific and normative reasons they became an increasingly disreputable enterprise. Theories of the period were generally blind to the extent to which their concepts and premises were the products of specific historical and cultural circumstances. They devalued agency and were hostile to individual expression and development by actors. Wittgenstein and Feyerabend in philosophy, Benedict and Geertz in anthropology, and Mills in sociology were committed to developing local, contingent understandings.[105] Postmodernism is even more hostile to grand theory. Jean-François Lyotard defines postmodernity "as incredulity toward metanarratives" and the idea of progress they encode. He calls upon scholars to replace them with open-ended, multicultural, relativistic, non-judgmental accounts.[106] Some of the opponents of grand theories (e.g. Feyerabend, Kuhn and Foucault)

---

[104] They are a prominent feature of the Scottish Enlightenment and marked in the writings of Smith and Hume.

[105] Wittgenstein, *Philosophical Investigations*; Feyerabend, *Against Method*; Benedict, *Patterns of Culture*; Geertz, *Local Knowledge*.

[106] Lyotard, *The Postmodern Condition*, "Introduction," p. xxiv.

have been accused of favoring a relativism that borders on incoherence.[107] Quentin Skinner notes with irony that some of the authorities most opposed to theory (e.g. Wittgenstein, Foucault, Derrida) are themselves authors of such theories.[108] Other prominent critics, such as Althusser, Habermas and Rawls, returned quite self-consciously to the project of grand theory in the 1960s and 1970s.[109]

Many early modern and Enlightenment figures, and all nineteenth-century grand theories assume epistemological and historical progress.[110] Reason, or a dialectical process that encodes reason, is expected to bring a better world into being. Marxism is the quintessential example of such a theory, but many modern thinkers – Locke, Kant and Hegel among them – were optimistic about the future. Like Rousseau, Nietzsche broke with this tradition; to the extent he envisaged an "end to history" it took the form of cultural desolation. Two world wars and the Holocaust did away with philosophical optimism and appeared to many to confirm Nietzsche's pessimistic view of history. Poststructuralists such as Foucault and Derrida not only reject the Enlightenment "project" but condemn progressive narratives of history as particularly dangerous falsehoods.[111]

Epistemological optimism, which may have reached its high water mark in prewar Popperian neopositivism, is also on the wane. Hermeneutic approaches have made great inroads. They stress the importance of understanding and self-reflection – a kind of knowledge that cannot be captured or described by science. Thoughtful social scientists have come to understand that theory is limited in a double sense: it cannot possibly encompass all there is to know, and it is undermined by self-reflection, which leads people to remake their worlds, and in the course of doing so invalidate any social "laws" that may have described their practices.[112] Hermeneutics reduces epistemology to a subset of knowledge, but, Richard Rorty

---

[107] Davidson, *Inquiries into Truth and Interpretation*; Putnam, *Meaning and the Moral Sciences*.

[108] Skinner, "Introduction: The Return of Grand Theory," pp. 12–16.

[109] Althusser, *For Marx*; Habermas, *The Theory of Communicative Action*; Rawls, *A Theory of Justice*.

[110] Koselleck, *The Practice of Conceptual History*, pp. 218–35, on the development of the concept of progress.

[111] Foucault, *Language, Counter-Memory, Practice*, pp. 153–4.

[112] Habermas, *Knowledge and Human Interests*; Gadamer, *Truth and Method* and *Philosophical Hermeneutics*, pp. 18–82. Weber, "'Objectivity' in Social Science and Social Policy," made this latter point during the *Methodenstreit*.

points out, it is not inalterably opposed to epistemology.[113] It rejects all privileged standpoints, but is not relativistic.

I appreciate these objections to grand theory and the need, as hermeneutic approaches insist, to put all understandings in historical perspective. The post-World War II disillusionment with the Enlightenment represents a predictable response to the horrors of that conflict, recurrent episodes of ethnic cleansing and genocide, the threat of nuclear annihilation, most recently associated with the Cold War, and the ever more real possibility of environmental catastrophe. Like all historical moments, it is unique, and not a privileged position from which to make objective judgments. There was probably more pessimism at the end of Thirty Years War, yet within a century it gave way to the extraordinary, if short-lived, elite optimism of the Enlightenment. Even with the looming threat of environmental disaster, we cannot categorically rule out a similar reversal in the future, as the moods and practices of philosophy and social science alike are so sensitive to broader developments of society. There are nevertheless sound epistemological reasons for questioning metanarratives of progress. Even those that rely on a dialectic to move history forward do so through a series of progressive stages and toward a predetermined telos that represents an end to history. Immanuel Kant, for one, assumed the inevitability of progress. He was willing to accept human servitude and exploitation as part of nature's "*hidden plan*" toward this end.[114] Adam Smith embeds a conception of moral progress in his theory of history; the middle class is the vanguard of a superior economic and moral order.[115] Marx's views are well known. Why should history be progressive, and why should it come to an end? And where do we derive the warrants to make these assessments when any reasons for judging one epoch or social-economic order superior to another are culturally specific, ideologically motivated and epistemologically arbitrary?

Grand theories can be purged of normative assumptions and telos. We can describe changes in human societies and their organizing principles without making judgments about which societies are superior, more just or better able to meet human needs. We can incorporate a concept of "development" (although not of "progress") in our analysis without smuggling in normative assumptions, if by development we mean

[113] Rorty, *Philosophy and the Mirror of Nature*, part III.
[114] Kant, "Idea for a Universal History with a Cosmopolitan Purpose," pp. 41–53.
[115] Smith, *Theory of Moral Sentiments*, III.vi.9–10, pp. 174–5.

nothing more than increasing complexity.[116] The theory of evolution understands development in this way. In the course of the last few decades, biologists, and other serious students of the subject, have moved away from the long-standing portrayal of evolution as the upward ascent of life to the pinnacle of *Homo sapiens* to recognition of it as a process not driven by any purpose and not leading to any particular end.[117] We can also be alert to the possibility that some trajectories are more likely than others. To cite one example, agricultural societies replaced hunter-gatherer societies almost everywhere because they provided more food and could support larger populations.[118]

Postmodernists also oppose grand theory on the grounds that it is inimical to freedom, self-definition and choice because it imposes analytical categories on societies and their members and creates strong pressures on them to conform to these archetypes. Sophisticated social scientists recognize that typologies and propositions cannot possibly capture the diversity of behavior and beliefs. Such formulations do not, of necessity, deny agency, although most theories that rely on so-called structures to do their heavy lifting have strong incentives to downplay the role of actors.[119] I am sensitive to the need for organizing principles and the ability of actors to transcend them. This is one of the reasons why my foundational concepts are based on the Greek understanding of the psyche. It generates a useful set of ideal types that do not describe real individuals or societies, who almost always display a mix of motives expressed in a variety of different ways. My theory celebrates diversity and explores its consequences for order *and* agency.

The hermeneutic challenge

A more serious challenge for a grand theory is the relativistic one posed by hermeneutics. Grand theory is distinguished by the generalizations it makes across cultures and epochs. It must, of necessity, deploy conceptions that arose in one cultural context to describe behavior in others. This was not a problem for post-Kantian empiricists who were drawn

---

[116] For evidence of the increasing complexity of human societies, see Smith and Szathmáry, *Origins of Life*; Christian, *Maps of Time*; Marx and Mazlish, *Progress: Fact or Illusion?*; Chaisson, *Cosmic Evolution*, on larger trends towards complexity.

[117] Gould, *Dinosaur in a Haystack*, pp. 252–5, and *Wonderful Life*, pp. 23–52.

[118] Diamond, "The Diffusion of Language Groups in Africa"; Inglehart, *Modernization and Postmodernization*, p. 17.

[119] Mazlish, "Progress in History," on how theories of progress and agency can be reconciled.

to semantic understandings of language, and conceived of concepts and their objects as ontologically separate.[120] Frege described concepts as distinct from objects, although even he recognized that they are essentially predicates, and cannot exist without the objects they describe.[121] Russell thought it was possible to infer the universality of concepts from their logical properties.[122] Much of social science still operates on this outmoded assumption.

The linguistic turn effectively undermined the proposition that language could serve as a neutral and transparent medium of analysis and communication. Deleuze and Guattari rightly observe that "Every concept relates back to other concepts, not only in its history but in its becoming or its present connections." As concepts are built from components imported from other concepts, they have no independent or intrinsic meaning, and can only be understood in terms of other concepts. They are best described as "centers of vibration" that resonate rather than cohere or correspond with one other.[123] Concepts do not have fixed meanings. Wittgenstein demonstrated that meanings derive from concrete usages that vary across subjects, but also vary with the same subject who may mobilize contrasting meanings in differing contexts.[124] To the extent that concepts possess any autonomy, it is because they are constitutive of social reality. That reality, as well as the concepts deployed to describe it, are products of historical context and local, fluid circumstances.[125]

Historians of political thought have documented how concepts have connotations that evolve in response to their use by actors.[126] They spurn reductionist discourses, and with them the allegedly perennial questions and problems around which they were structured.[127] Quentin Skinner insists that the great philosophical texts of the past "cannot be concerned

[120] Frege, "On Sense and Meaning"; Ogden and Richards, *The Meaning of Meaning*.
[121] Frege, "On Concept and Object."   [122] Russell, *Problems of Philosophy*, pp. 56–7.
[123] Deleuze and Guattari, *What is Philosophy?*, pp. 17–21, 25.
[124] Wittgenstein, *Philosophical Grammar*, pp. 64, 202–7.
[125] Farr, "Understanding Conceptual Change Politically"; Gunnell, *The Orders of Discourse*; Toews, "Intellectual History after the Linguistic Turn."
[126] Richter, *History of Political and Social Concepts*, for the intellectual background of the transformation. Toews, "Intellectual History after the Linguistic Turn," for an overview. Exemplars of linguistic, contextualist and discourse analysis approaches include Dunn, "The Identity of the History of Ideas"; Skinner, "Meaning and Understanding in the History of Ideas"; Koselleck and Gadamer, *Hermaneutik and Historik*; Pocock, *Virtue, Commerce and History*; Pagden, *The Languages of Political Theory in Early Modern Europe*; Shöttler, "Historians and Discourse Analysis."
[127] Strauss, *Natural Right and History*, is a case in point.

with our questions, but only their own."[128] There is an evolving dialogue within and between political theory and philosophy about the ways in which conceptual meanings should be understood and the implications of these understandings for their respective projects and mutual relationship.[129]

The protocols of the hermeneutic approach would all but cripple social science. They would restrict comparison to cultures and eras bounded by shared concepts. Even that condition would be hard to meet as concepts are continually evolving and are usually not understood or used the same way by actors within the same discourse.[130] Applied with rigor, the principle of comparability of fundamental concepts would restrict research to individual texts – as it tends to in the history of political philosophy – or to tracking the evolution of discourses they sustain. Such an analysis requires hermeneutic reconstruction of texts, a feasible if difficult enterprise. Comparative analysis of concepts is an altogether different matter. Nietzsche observed that only concepts that have no history can be defined.[131] His insight is particularly applicable to foundational concepts in political science. Liah Greenfeld has documented the irresolvable ambiguity of the concept of democracy, John Dunn has done the same for civil society and Jens Bartelson for the state. They show how the very centrality of these concepts renders them ambiguous. Their meanings cannot fully be determined by examining their semantic components or their inferential connections to other concepts because they are partially constitutive of these components by virtue of the theoretical significance and metaphorical possibilities they impart to them. No amount of rigorous, analytical work will come up with common, widely useful definitions, and attempts to do will only reduce the utility of the concept. It makes more sense to try to understand the role such foundational concepts serve for a discourse.[132]

Fortunately, there is a fundamental difference between the goals of political theory and social science. The former approaches concepts as objects of investigation, while the latter uses them as analytical resources.[133] If we were to limit ourselves to concepts embedded in a

---

[128] Skinner, "Meaning and Understanding in the History of Ideas," p. 65.

[129] Bartelson, "Political Thought and the Linguistic Turn" (unpublished) for a thoughtful overview.

[130] On this point, see Benhabib, *Claims of Culture*.

[131] Nietzsche, "'Guilt,' 'Bad Conscience' and the Like," in *On the Genealogy of Morals*, pp. 493–532.

[132] Greenfeld, *Nationalism*; Bartelson, *The Critique of the State*; Dunn, "The Contemporary Significance of John Locke's Conception of Civil Society."

[133] This point is also made by Bartelson, "Political Thought and the Linguistic Turn."

local discourse, we could only compare societies that share this discourse and its associated concepts. This is unsatisfactory on the face of it. Concepts as diverse as class, stratification, civil society, anomie, evolution and projection were developed in the eighteenth and nineteenth centuries, and our analysis of earlier and later economics, history, politics and social life would be severely impoverished without them. Such concepts must nevertheless be applied with caution. Those who use them must avoid "ontological gerrymandering," which involves the manipulation of boundaries to make the phenomena we study problematic, but leaves the categories we use to study them unquestioned.[134] We must also resist the temptation to shoehorn social reality into the conceptions we use to describe it. Classic examples of the latter include Marxist efforts to describe societies as diverse as sixteenth-century Russia and eighteenth-century China and India as "feudal," and the characterization by international relations scholars of fifth-century Greece and the second half of the twentieth century as "bipolar."[135]

In *The Tragic Vision of Politics*, I employed the hermeneutic approach to reconstruct concepts used explicitly by Carl von Clausewitz and Hans J. Morgenthau and, implicitly, by Thucydides. In this volume I do the reverse: I transport concepts developed or used by Thucydides, Plato and Aristotle to other cultures and epochs. Anthropologists call this an "etic" framework.[136] I justify this practice on the grounds that these concepts capture universal attributes of human nature that find expression in all cultures at all times, with the very important caveat that they are manifested and described in a wide variety of ways. I am interested in their manifestations *and* their conceptualization (or lack of them) as both reveal important features about the societies in question. Changes in discourses concerning these motives, or their absence, have profound consequences for the behavior associated with them and can tells us something important about the nature of social evolution.

Aristotle thought it unlikely that human investigations could ever produce *epistēmē*, which he defined as knowledge of essential natures reached through deduction from first principles. Like some critics of neopositivism, he was more inclined to accept the possibility of generalizations that held true for the most part (*epi to polu*) under carefully specified

---

[134] Woolgar and Pawluch, "Ontological Gerrymandering."

[135] Copeland, *The Origins of Major War*, for a misreading of international relations in classical Greece; Barshay, "Double Cruelty," on Marxism's conceptual injustices to the development of capitalism in Japan.

[136] Bernstein, *Beyond Objectivism and Relativism*.

conditions.[137] My model for such a theory is derived from the writings of Thucydides, Clausewitz and Morgenthau. All three aspired to provide a universally valid understanding by describing the underlying dynamics that govern particular social processes, in full recognition that their real-world manifestations would vary in unpredictable ways due to idiosyncratic features of context.[138] The proper goal of social theory is to structure reality and make it more comprehensible by describing the relationship between the parts and the whole. By doing so, I hope to offer scholar and practitioner alike a good first cut into the problem of political order at the regional and international levels, and the patterns of politics associated with different distributions of motives.

[137] Aristotle, *Nicomachean Ethics*, 1141a–b, on Aristotle's contrast between theoretical and practical wisdom.
[138] See my *Tragic Vision of Politics* for a comparative analysis of their respective approaches to war and politics.

2

Fear, interest and honor

And the nature of the case first compelled us to advance our empire to its present height; fear being our principal motive, though honor and interest afterwards came in.

Athenian speakers to the Spartan assembly[1]

Political scientists have rightly been accused of "physics envy." I do not want to open myself up to the charge of "polis envy." I do, however, want to go back to the Greeks and their thoughts about politics for the conceptual foundations of my theory. I recognize that the Greeks of the classical period lived in a very different world, where the city state (polis) was the principal unit and source of identity, and where politics, and all important relationships, were conducted face to face among people long acquainted with one another. Democracy, where it existed, was direct, with most or all important issues being debated and voted on in public assemblies. Politics was entirely the preserve of adult male citizens, and the criteria for citizenship, even in Athens, were extremely restrictive. Women, children, slaves and resident aliens performed, at most, ceremonial roles.

Despite these striking differences, the great playwrights and political thinkers of classical Greece still speak to us and their writings remain the starting point of our reflections on a wide range of ethical and political issues. Thucydides (460–c. 390 BCE), Plato (427–347 BCE) and Aristotle (384–322 BCE) provide the foundations for theories of politics and international relations. Their insights are timeless, but only in part due to their indisputable genius. Their writings reflect a collective Greek wisdom about human motives and behavior and the purpose of life. Greek playwrights, historians and philosophers wrote before symmetry was broken. In physics, this refers to that period after the Big Bang when the universe began to cool, but before it had cooled enough for the four forces that

---

[1] Thucydides, *Peloponnesian War*, 1.75.2–5.

govern all interactions to emerge. In fifth-century Greece, inquiry into the social and physical world was well developed but separate disciplines had not yet developed. What we know today as physics, philosophy, poetry and history were all intertwined, and influenced one another in form and substance. The philosopher Democritus of Abdera (early fifth century BCE) wrote numerous texts, including one on farming. Hippias of Elis, a contemporary of Socrates, specialized in astronomy and mathematics, but also made contributions to language, poetry, music, archeology and history. Antiphon, another contemporary, worked primarily in the physical sciences but also composed poetry and speeches. The Hippocratic physicians described Scythian customs, Herodotus wrote about medicine, and Aristotle wrote about almost everything.[2]

The Greeks were not only polymaths, but sought to integrate knowledge across what for us are separate disciplines. The tragic poets addressed politics and its relationship to order and justice. Thucydides borrowed concepts from medicine and his plot line from tragedy, and used both to impart a deeper meaning to the events he described. He applied tragedy's spare plot line to history to craft an abstract, stylized narrative that directs our attention to the deeper meanings of events. Plato trashed Homer and the tragic poets in his *Republic*, but devised dialogue as an art form and used it to convey wisdom that could not be captured by concepts. These Greeks are the last thinkers to approach knowledge holistically, as must any general theory involving human behavior.

In the pages that follow, I elaborate some of the epistemological and substantive conceptions that shape the tragedies of Aeschylus, Sophocles and Euripides, the histories of Herodotus and Thucydides and the philosophy of Plato and Aristotle. As my purpose is to build the *Grundbegriffe* for my own theory, I do not go into detail about the many differences among these figures, highlighting only those relevant to my arguments. The principal themes I treat are human motives and their implications for order and justice. I will contrast the Greek approach to these questions with their modern counterparts to demonstrate the utility of the former. The body of the chapter builds on this introduction to elaborate a framework for the study of politics. I conclude with a discussion of what I consider to be some of its principal conceptual problems and how they can be addressed.

---

[2] Aristotle, *On Airs, Waters, Places*, ch. 22; Herodotus, *Histories*, 1.105.

Foundational assumptions

Motives

The Enlightenment constituted a sharp break with past thinking and practice. Its rejection of Aristotelian telos (the end something is intended to achieve, and how that end drives its development) helped pave the way for modernity.[3] Rejection of telos required a corresponding reconceptualization of reason. It was reduced from an end in itself to a mere instrumentality – "the slave of the passions," in the words of David Hume.[4] Max Weber would later coin the term "instrumental reason" to describe this transformation, which he recognized had come to dominate the modern world and our approach to it. Freud incorporated it in his model of the mind; the ego embodies reason and mediates between the impulses of the id and the external environment. Rational choice employs a similar understanding of reason; it assumes that actors rank-order their preferences and engage in the kind of strategic behavior best calculated to obtain them.

The modern conceptualization of reason as instrumentality was part and parcel of the shift in focus away from the ends we should seek to the means of best satisfying our appetites. Strategic action models take preferences as given, or assume they will be revealed in the course of interaction with other actors and the environment. They acknowledge the critical importance of preferences, but cannot tell us how they form or when and why they change. Their epistemology is unsuitable to this task. Rational choice and other theories of strategic action often derive preferences from substantive assumptions, as neorealists do when they stipulate that relative power must be the principal goal of states in an anarchic international environment. Deduction of this kind, whether in economics or politics, almost invariably leads to a single motive like wealth or power, or at least to its prioritization. By making human, institutional or state preferences unidimensional, theorists homogenize and oversimplify human motivation while divorcing it from contexts that give it meaning. To introduce additional motives, any hierarchy among them would require additional theories to stipulate which motive, or combination of them, will

---

[3] For Aristotle, this is one of four kinds of causality: efficient, material (by virtue of an object's composition), formal (the way the structure of an object gives it form) and final causality (telos).

[4] Hume, *A Treatise of Human Nature*, 2.3.3.4, *An Inquiry Concerning the Principles of Morals*, appendix I, p. 163.

dominate under what set of conditions. Such theories would have to be rooted in relatively sophisticated understandings of human psychology and culture.[5]

Freud, to his credit, grappled with this problem and valiantly attempted to formulate a theory of human desire. In the Freudian model, people are driven by impulses associated with the libido. They seek to satisfy these impulses, or channel them into other expressions, when their primary outlets are unavailable or prohibited. In contrast to Freud, social science privileges structure over agency, and most of its theories and models assume that people and other actors respond primarily to external stimuli.[6] The most casual observation of the social world indicates that people and states are moved by a combination of internal and external stimuli. It is often difficult to distinguish between them, let alone assess their relative weight, or how they interact, without detailed knowledge of the actors and their setting. Economists assume that people seek wealth, but have devoted surprisingly little thought to the origins and nature of this most fundamental proposition of economic theory. At least as far back as King Midas, wealth has been sought as an end in itself. It is also a means to such ends as security, material possessions, leisure and good health care, to mention that just some of the things that money can buy. To the extent that people want wealth for what it can provide, their desire is to a large degree socially determined. Rousseau and Adam Smith both grasped this truth when they observed that one of the distinguishing features of the modern world is the extent to which material goods and luxuries are sought for the standing and prestige they confer.[7] John Kenneth Galbraith wryly observes that this is why advertising campaigns regularly succeed in generating demand for useless and cost-ineffective products.[8]

Assume for the moment that people have a preference for wealth when making economic choices. To have a workable theory, we would need to know the range of choices people frame as economic (as opposed to political, social, religious, etc.). We also need to know something about why they seek wealth, because only then could we begin to estimate (for individuals and other actors) how they frame and make tradeoffs between

---

[5] Brennan and Pettit, *Economy of Esteem*, to their credit, recognize that people are often motivated by esteem as opposed to wealth. They do not theorize about the circumstances in which this might occur or the tradeoffs that are involved.

[6] Lebow, "Reason, Emotion and Cooperation," for a fuller critique.

[7] Rousseau, *Discourse on the Origin and Foundation of Inequality*; Smith, *The Theory of Moral Sentiments*, I.iii.2.1 and 3.1.

[8] Galbraith, *The Affluent Society*.

wealth and other values (e.g. security, status, leisure, job satisfaction), and how much risk they will assume in its pursuit. We cannot analyze means without knowing something about the ends they are intended to achieve.[9]

This truth was obvious to the ancient Greeks, who framed the problem of choice differently. Their principal concern was human goals, and from an early date they distinguished between two kinds of human motives: appetite and spirit. The former pertained to bodily needs, like food, shelter and sex, and the latter to the competitive quest for recognition as a means of building self-esteem. Plato and Aristotle maintained that reason also generates desires of its own, and was a third, independent motive. Reason had the potential to lead people to understand the nature of happiness and to constrain and educate appetite and spirit to collaborate with it toward this end.

The ancients differ from the moderns in apportioning desires among three separate motives, each distinct in its character and consequences for human behavior and happiness. This three-fold characterization of motives provides the foundation for an analytical framework for a theory of preferences. It also generates a typology of political orders applicable to individuals, societies and regional and international systems. Plato and Aristotle use variants of this typology to probe the causes of order and disorder within individuals and societies. I will do the same for political orders, and use it as the starting point for a theory of history.

Balance and imbalance

Modern conceptions of balance and imbalance are rooted in our physical understanding of the world. They derive from the scale, which, along with the clock – initially based on the pendulum – is central to the Newtonian conception of the universe.[10] Enlightenment philosophers extended this conception to the social world, where it became an organizing principle for programs of reform. The separation of powers built into the American constitution represents one of the most successful political applications of this concept; it is intended to preserve a balance among the three branches of government, and between the federal and state governments. Critical analyses of American institutions and politics often assume that

---

[9] Lasswell, *Politics: Who Gets What, When, How*, postscript, pp. 202–3, is one of the few social scientists who address this problem. He posits a plurality of motives, each of which can be an end in itself or a means toward achieving other ends.

[10] Butterfield, *The Origins of Modern Science*, pp. 19, 105, 130–2.

problems are the result of imbalance among these branches or levels of government.[11]

There is a concept of justice implicit in the scale analogy. The scale was intended to provide a fair measure of the product being offered for sale. Balance became associated with fairness more generally, a connection graphically represented by the many statues of a goddess holding a balanced scale that grace entrances to American courthouses. This association may date back to the ancient Egyptians, who thought the gods employed a scale to weigh the souls of the dead to see if they were worthy of an afterlife.

Social science modeled itself on nineteenth-century physics and adopted many of its key metaphors, including that of balance. Equilibrium has been a foundational concept for many theories or approaches to psychology, economics, political science and sociology, game theory among them. The balance of power has been central to the theory and practice of international relations since the eighteenth century, and is central to most realist theories. Imbalance, in the form of a dialectic, is foundational to Marxism, where it drives history until order and equilibrium are reached under communism. More recently, sociologist Niklas Luhmann, influenced by work in chaos and complexity, has developed conceptions of dynamic interactions between balance and imbalance.[12]

Greek philosophers were fascinated with mathematics, especially geometry. They used mathematical concepts as metaphors in epistemology (Plato's forms) and metaphysics (*meden agan*, or the golden mean). Like post-Enlightenment philosophy and literature, Greek writings are also rich in organic analogies, and conceive of balance in a biological sense. The life cycle of birth, growth, decline and death is routinely applied not only to people but to social entities, including the polis and its constitutions. It also provides the basis for telos, which for Aristotle is the kind of growth and maturation that enables living things to express their respective natures. *Phuein*, the verb "to grow," may have given rise to the noun *phusis*, meaning "nature." For Greeks, the two concepts were inseparable almost from the beginning. Proportion (*to analogon*) comes into play because growth is an expression of one's nature, and healthy growth is by definition proportional.[13]

---

[11] A prominent example is Schlesinger, *The Imperial Presidency*.

[12] According to Luhmann, *Social Systems*, p. 282, "Unstructured complexity is entropic complexity, which can at any time disintegrate into incoherence. The formation of structure *uses this disintegration* and constructs order out of it."

[13] Although Aristotle is careful not to confuse conceptual considerations with those of a natural scientist, his interest in the physiology of emotional response is very important.

For Greeks, power could not easily be understood apart from its purpose, and this was usually considered to be expansion and growth. Such an understanding couples power to proportionality and, indirectly, to fairness and justice, because proportionality is a measure and expression of fairness and justice. It follows that the several parts of the individual psyche, and the constituent parts of the city, should also be in balance. Each must perform its particular function and cooperate with the others in a harmonious manner. Fairness, justice and balance are so closely related that it is not too much of a stretch to understand them as different expressions of the same thing. Aristotle associates nobility and the good life with order, symmetry and decisiveness in action. These are all expressions of the doctrine of the mean. For every virtue, he describes two associated vices: an excess and a deficiency of that virtue. This holds true for cities as well as for people.[14]

The relationship among balance, the psyche and human fulfillment is an underlying theme of Plato's *Republic*. His Socrates acknowledges that appetites and spirit are frequently in conflict not only with each other, but also with reason. He calls these conflicts "afflictions and diseases," and associates them with different pathologies. Timocratic man is ruled by his spirit, and has a correspondingly exaggerated concern for his honor. Honor is a limited good because it is relational, and timocratic man is often disappointed. Repeated setbacks provide the incentive for him to accede to the incessant demands of appetite.[15] Oligarchic man is ruled by his appetite. His spirit finds narrow expression in a desire for wealth and the esteem it brings. Lacking judgmental criteria based on reason, he finds it

Having *pathē* is never merely having certain thoughts – although those provide the efficient causes of the emotion – but also feeling certain sensations of pain or pleasure, which provide the material causes of the emotion. According to Aristotle, those causes have to do primarily with changes in body temperature. Fear, for example, involves a drop in temperature. Cowards, who are deficient in courage, are constantly "chilled"; they suffer from a bodily disturbance (*tarache*) as well as a moral failing. There is every reason to think that Aristotle considers the moral mean of action and reaction to have a psycho-physiological corollary in bodily homeostasis. In his teleological system, the parts of the soul are arranged such that it may adjust successfully to the various social situations in which individuals will find themselves (inter alia, by adopting medial states of character); similarly, the body is arranged such that it may achieve success in adjusting to its environment. The task of modifying emotions, to bring them into harmony with the mean in each case and for each individual, is thus at the same time a task of altering individual physiology. It follows that each specific emotional trait is part of a general emotional trait that admits of a physiological medial state: a homeostasis. Specific anomalous emotional traits are not simply to be gotten rid of – any more than your hand is to be considered expendable and cut off if it feels too cold – but rather brought into line by adjusting the "body temperature".

[14] Aristotle, *Politics*, 1273a3–b17.
[15] Plato, *Republic*, 403c9–404e1, 537c9–540c2, 548c1–2, 549a9–550b7.

impossible to discriminate among his competing appetites and will adopt
the democratic decision rule of trying to satisfy whatever desire makes the
most insistent demand at the moment.[16] The democratic person can find
no way of resisting his appetites – unlawful ones aside – and is vulnerable
to the appeal of tyranny.[17] Oligarchic, democratic and tyrannical people
are ruled by different aspects of their desires, and all are unhappy.[18] Aristotle offers a different evolution and logic of transformation, but based
on a similar understanding of the psyche.[19] Socrates' accounts are the
starting point for his arguments on both subjects, and when discussing
constitutions Plato is present as a kind of silent interlocutor.[20]

Plato's Socrates makes an explicit analogy between the psyche and the
polis, and insists that both individuals and cities require a consensus
about who is to rule. In a just city, every person performs his assigned
role, making civic justice a collective representation of individual justice.
Socrates also draws parallels between individual and political pathologies.
He describes four deviant constitutions – timocracy, oligarchy, democracy and tyranny – each of which comes about in the same way as its
individual counterparts. This happens to be the progression that Athens
went through in Socrates' lifetime, and the *Republic* can be read as a
commentary on that city's constitutional history. For people to live good
and just lives, Socrates concludes, their appetites and spirit must be well-
trained by reason and willing to do the right thing. At the level of the
polis, this requires the active collaboration of all citizens, making justice

---

[16] Ibid., 553a1–555b1, 554d2–3, d10–e5 and 559d4–561a5.

[17] Ibid., 560e5, 561a6–562a2, 561c6–d5 and 572b10–573b4.

[18] The tyrannical person (ibid., 571a1–576e2) is the most pathological because he is ruled
by lawless appetites. He is overcome by *pleonexia*, or unlimited desires (343e7–344c8,
348b8–350c11, 542a2–b1, 571a1–592b6). The democratic person (558c8–562a2) is ruled
part of the time by unnecessary appetites, but never by illegal ones. The oligarchical
person (554a5–8, 553a6–555b1) is ruled by his necessary appetites. In addition to external
constraints, he imposes internal ones. The timocratic person (548d6–550d4) is ruled by
his spirit, to which he has surrendered completely. He has moderated his necessary and
unnecessary appetites, and is less likely to succumb to *pelonexia*. Only the philosopher
(473c11–541b5) is ruled by reason and has moderated his appetite and spirit.

[19] According to Aristotle, *Politics*, 1286b19–21, the early polis had few citizens and was ruled
as an extension of the household (*oikos*) by kings. When many persons equal in merit
arose, they all felt themselves worthy of kingship, and set up a commonwealth with a
constitution. The ruling class sooner or later succumbed to its appetites and enriched
themselves at public expense. Riches also became paths to honor, so oligarchies developed. They degenerated into tyrannies, and then into democracies, because love of gain
among rulers diminished their numbers while strengthening the people (*dēmos*). Aristotle,
Rhetoric, 1365b33–1366a16, also describes regime types.

[20] Rowe, "Aristotelian Constitutions."

on the individual level the prerequisite of civic harmony. For individual and city alike, the three parts of the psyche must be in balance and work together harmoniously.[21]

Aristotle's analysis of constitutions also parallels his understanding of the individual; lack of discipline (*akrasia*) in individuals and cities leads to instability. The institutional arrangements he thinks most likely to maintain discipline in cities are an extrapolation from his preferred regimen for the individual. It is self-evident, he writes in the *Politics*, that "the same life is best for each individual, and for states and for mankind collectively."[22] Thucydides extends this understanding to foreign policy. Social relations among fifth-century Greeks were embedded in a dense web of relationships, governed by an elaborate set of conventions that encouraged expectations of support while imposing constraints and obligations. Relations with fellow citizens were conceptualized as an extension of domestic household relations, as were, to a significant extent, relations between Greek cities. The fifth-century Greek lexicon did not have a word for international relations. Like Herodotus, Greeks most often used *xenia* – a Homeric term best translated as guest friendship – to describe relations among cities.[23]

Levels of analysis

Social science has become specialized in a double sense. It is divided into disciplines and divided within disciplines. Much of the latter division is on the basis of level of social aggregation. The traditional subfields of economics are micro and macro, the former pertaining to the firm, and the latter to the larger economic environment in which firms and other economic actors operate. Principal specializations within psychology include neuro and cognitive (about the individual), group and social (about smaller and larger collectivities). Political science is different in that its subfields are defined by subject, but most of them are then further divided by level of aggregation. International relations, for example, has long been organized in terms of the system, state, substate and individual levels of analysis.[24] For the most part, different problems are assigned to different levels of analysis, and different approaches and theories are generally used to address them.

---

[21] Plato, *Republic*, 430e6–431a2, 441d12–e2.   [22] Aristotle, *Politics*, 1325b30–2.
[23] Herodotus, *Histories*, 1.69.
[24] Singer, "The Level-of-Analysis Problem in International Relations," is the classic statement of this framework.

Thucydides, Plato and Aristotle distinguish between individuals and cities, and describe politics at what we call the individual and state level. Thucydides extends this analogy to the regional level, to Hellas as whole. None of these thinkers frames problems in terms of levels of analysis, and efforts to map their writings on to this formulation do an injustice to their understandings of the social world. They do not conceptualize political behavior in horizontal, if permeable, layers, each with its own appropriate mode of explanation. They conceive of social interactions of all kinds as taking place in a discrete number of nested domains, each characterized by similar dynamics and amenable therefore to the same kind of analysis. If we need a modern analogy, fractals come closest to capturing the Greek understanding of human behavior. They replicate the same patterns at different orders of magnification.

As we have seen, Plato and Aristotle begin with a description of the individual psyche, whose categories and pathologies they then extend to the polis. People and *poleis* alike are motivated by appetites, spirit and reason. Order or disorder in either is attributable to balance or imbalance among these three motives. Plato's *Republic* describes a city, but it is offered as a collective representation of a well-ordered human psyche, with its philosophers embodying the drive of reason. The constitution Plato lays out for Kallipolis is similar in all important respects to what he believes is best for the individual. It is derived from first principles by philosophers whose wisdom comes from their holistic understanding of the good. They know how to order the life of the polis to the benefit of all citizens regardless of their particular skills and intellectual potential. They rely on guardians to impose correct opinion on the polis and enforce the constitution, including its provision of denying its citizens contact with outsiders, as far as possible.[25] The physical isolation of Kallipolis is necessary because of the absence of other virtuous cities.

Greek understandings of psyche and balance are the basis of a parsimonious theory of order that nicely bridges levels of analysis. They also reveal – as Thucydides documents – how balance or imbalance at any level of aggregation (i.e. individual, city, region) has important implications for balance and order at other levels. Plato talks about the direction of change (with tyranny his default condition), and Aristotle describes some of the mechanisms of change, but neither offers a theory of change. Such a theory is implicit in Thucydides, and is based on the interplay of material and intellectual forces and how they affect individual and

---

[25] Plato, *Republic*, 506c, *Statesman*, 309c6–10.

collective balance. I will explicate, draw out and expand upon these insights, and extend them to modern foreign policy and international relations. I use both terms because a theory of international relations embedded in a theory of society is also a theory of foreign policy. There can be no meaningful theory of international relations just at the system level. For this reason, as we shall see, it becomes more difficult to differentiate a theory of international relations from one of foreign policy.

Ontology and epistemology

The dominant ontology treats actors as autonomous, egoistic and often without history. It assumes that politics is best studied through the choices made by these actors. Rationalist theories nevertheless assume that these choices are shaped, if not determined outright, by environmental pressures and constraints. Constructivists start from the premise that people and their societies are mutually constitutive, but in practice many constructivist scholars treat identities and interests as social constructions. Each paradigm emphasizes one side of a complex social reality, and confronts difficulties in determining the respective roles of agents and structures. The tension between individual and social identities, and individual and collective interests, are only two of the tensions that characterize the relationship of human beings to each other and their societies. Other key polarities pit honor against interest, socially assigned roles against personal preferences, religious beliefs and practices against family loyalties and both of these against civic obligations.[26] Societies face similar tensions. In a recent book, Diana Mutz explores the tensions between deliberative and participatory democracy, which, she contends, requires a tradeoff between maximizing the participation of citizens and respect and tolerance for their differences.[27]

Greek tragedy explores many of these dualisms.[28] It reveals the generally destructive consequences of rejecting a middle ground in favor of unwavering commitments to any extreme. In Sophocles' *Antigone*, Antigone's loyalty to her brother and the gods brings her into conflict with Creon, who is just as committed to upholding civic order and his authority as head of the family. There are lesser collisions between Antigone and her sisters, Creon and his son and Creon and Teresias, each of them equally

[26] Lebow, *Tragic Vision of Politics*, pp. 323–54, and "Reason, Emotion and Cooperation," develop this argument at greater length.
[27] Mutz, *Hearing the Other Side*.   [28] Lebow, *Tragic Vision of Politics*, chs. 8 and 9.

emblematic. These conflicts arise not only as a result of the choices these characters make, but also from their inability to empathize with one another. They understand the other's position as a reality without justification. Tragic conversations, like their real-world counterparts, are self-defeating when protagonists talk past each other, fail to develop empathy and learn nothing new about themselves. Antigone and Creon interact in this way with catastrophic consequences for themselves, their family and their polis.

By dramatizing extreme commitments and their consequences, tragedy makes us sensitive to the way in which even ordinary human beings in their quotidian lives are pulled in opposite directions by conflicting needs, multiple identities and the different loyalties to which they give rise. As a general rule, these conflicts become more acute in periods of transition when discourses, and the values, conventions and practices they sustain, are questioned or breaking down. At most times and in most societies, human behavior is arrayed somewhere along the continuum between the polar extremes that tragedy describes. Very rarely does it mirror any of these poles, and invariably with destructive consequences. Like tragedy, we must start from the premise that these polarities define the extremes of the human condition and are not themselves good starting points for understanding behavior. We must represent, not suppress, the diversity and inherent instability of individual and collective identities, interests and motives, and their complex interactions with the discourses, social practices and institutions they generate and sustain.

I argued in *Tragic Vision of Politics* that multiple discourses encourage multiple identities, which are inherently unstable and accelerate the pace of social and political change. In contrast to most theories that take stable structures, societies and identities as the norm, tragedy encourages us to emphasize the complexity and dynamism of social life. The accommodations individuals and societies make with key polarities are temporary and fragile. They are uneasy compromises that can never be adequately justified by logic, may be difficult to legitimize politically and are likely to encounter a succession of moral and political dilemmas. Like the moon's tug and pull on the oceans, they give rise to inner tides that find outward expression in breaking waves of conflicting obligations and loyalties. Our search for ontological stability must give way to acceptance of the truth that social life, and our understandings of it, are, and must always be, in a state of flux.[29] We must accordingly privilege process over structure as

---

[29] Lapid, "Introduction" to *Identities, Borders, Orders.*

our principal category of metaphysical understanding, a subject to which I will return in the next section.

A focus on change dictates a radical break with the dominant epistemology in political science. Individuals and societies, I contend, adapt to changing circumstances by ever-shifting understandings of and accommodations to key polarities. As there are only so many quasi-stable sites along any of these continua, a new accommodation may be quite different from the one its replaces. Polarities are interconnected in complex ways. Changes in one can affect other accommodations, as their consequences ripple through the system. The system can return to something close to its prior state, but even minor changes can sometimes produce major systemic change by setting off something akin to a chain reaction.

For these reasons, equilibrium is not a useful concept in studying political order even in the short term. It assumes a state or states of equilibrium to which the system returns. In practice, changing accommodations, even when they are minor, generate new pressures and new accommodations, bringing about significant change over time. Evolution of this kind renders the concept of stability something of an oxymoron. Some of the most "stable" political systems – measured in terms of their longevity – are those that have evolved significantly over the course of time, so much so in some cases that comparisons between these systems at time T and T plus 100 years suggests that we are really looking at two very different systems. Georgian England in comparison to late Victorian Britain, or Victorian Britain in comparison to late twentieth-century Britain offer nice illustrations. The institutions governing the country were more or less unchanged, but the nature of the political culture, the distribution of power across classes, the demography of the country and many of its key social and political values underwent significant change, transforming the way in which these institutions functioned and the roles they performed for society.

Shifts in the nature of accommodations along any fault line can be dampened or amplified as they work their way through the society. Order is an open system. None of its key components can be studied in isolation from the rest of the social world, because important sources of instability and change for the components in question can emanate from any of them. Physical scientists study non-linear processes by modeling them. They often start with linear processes that are reasonably well understood, to which they add additional variables, and arbitrarily vary their value, or rate of change, in the hope of discovering the outer boundaries of linearity, and beyond them possible patterns or domains of order that may develop in non-linear domains. Turbulence is the paradigmatic example. At a certain point, flow becomes turbulent and unpredictable. Within this turbulence, areas of stability can form, where flow can be described by linear models or equations. The Great Red Spot of Jupiter is a case in point, and is an island of relative and temporary stability in the storm raging throughout Jupiter's atmosphere. Durable political orders may be best understood as islands of this kind; they are in a state of flux, just less so than the sea of political turbulence that surrounds them. By identifying such islands, the ways in which they evolve, maintain their apparent stability, and where they come up against the edge of chaos, we can learn a lot about the processes that build, maintain and destroy orders.

Process philosophy

From the time of the ancient Greeks there has been a deep divide between philosophers who believe nature should be understood in terms of its units and those who think it is best described as a process. The atomistic conception began with Leucippas and Democritus, two fifth-century thinkers, who, according to Aristotle, sought to reconcile the plurality, motion and change with the Eleatic denial of the processes of coming and ceasing to be. They assumed the existence of primary, unchanging particles whose combination and separation accounted for the observable phenomena of generation, corruption and death.[30] Heraclitus of Ephesus, who wrote around 500 BCE, is difficult to interpret by virtue of the limited fragments we possess and the oracular style of many of them. He has nevertheless been read as a philosopher who emphasizes the primacy of process, as suggested by his often-quoted line to the effect that you cannot step twice into the same river. Everything is in motion and a matter of activity which brings about continual change (*panta rhei*).[31] Since Aristotle, the atomistic formulation has dominated philosophy and, until quite recently, the physical sciences. Quantum mechanics has compelled us to reject the notion of stable particles and to question the distinction between substance and process. At the macro level, there are a host of phenomena, among them storms, that cannot effectively be analyzed

---

[30] Aristotle, *On Coming to Be and Passing Away*, 324a35–325a31; Taylor, "The Atomists."
[31] Heraclitus, B4 9a, in Diels and Kranz, *Die Fragmente*; Hussey, "*Heraclitus*"; Barnes, *The Presocratic Philosophers*, I, pp. 57–81.

in terms of objects or statics. Dynamic processes are more the work of "forces" than of "agents."

In modern times, Leibniz was among the first scientists and philosophers to adopt a dynamic of view of nature. He invented the concept of "appetition" to distinguish human from animal souls and describe the striving and conscious, logical process through which humans recognize, order and reorder reality.[32] The early twentieth-century French philosopher Henri Bergson also rebelled against the fixity and rigidity that the logicians and materialists ascribed to reality. He popularized the idea of process, and its implication for human autonomy. If change was real, he insisted, so was novelty, and with novelty came freedom. The physical and social worlds were fluid by nature, and atomistic approaches at best convey the illusion of change the way the cinema does by displaying still pictures at rapid intervals.[33]

Process philosophy in its modern form developed with the writings of Alfred North Whitehead and his disciples Paul Hartshorne and Paul Weiss. Building on Bergson's idea of "nature as a process," Whitehead emphasizes the centrality of temporality, change and passage to our world.[34] In his world view, "Becoming is as important as being, change as stability."[35] Nicholas Rescher, the most prominent contemporary advocate of process philosophy, defines a process "as an actual or possible occurrence that consists of an integrated series of connected developments unfolding in programmatic coordination: an orchestrated series of occurrences that are systematically linked to one another either causally or functionally."[36] Process philosophy is committed to five fundamental propositions:

1. Time and change are among the principal categories of metaphysical understanding.
2. Process is a principal category of ontological description.
3. Processes are more fundamental, or at least not less fundamental, than things for purposes of ontological theory.
4. Several, if not all, major elements of ontological repertoire (nature, persons, substances) are best understood in process terms.
5. Contingency, emergence, novelty, creativity are among the fundamental categories of metaphysical understanding.[37]

---

[32] McCrae, *Leibniz*, pp. 30–6, 131–45, and "The Theory of Knowledge"; Wilson, *Leibniz' Metaphysics*, pp. 131–7; Rescher, *Leibniz's Metaphysics of Nature*.
[33] Bergson, *The Creative Mind*, p. 332.   [34] Whitehead, *The Concept of Nature*, ch. 3.
[35] Rescher, *Process Philosophy*.   [36] Ibid., p. 22.   [37] Ibid., pp. 5–6, 22.

Existing theories of international relations are atomistic in that their base units are states and other actors that are said to comprise a system. They also rely on so-called structures for their independent variables. For realist theories, the putative anarchy of the international system rewards and punishes certain kinds of behavior. For neorealism, the number of actors and their relative power determines the polarity of the system which in turn determined frequency of war and the stability of the system. Liberals emphasize the character of the units that make up the system and the way a system shaped by liberal, trading states provides incentives for other units to become liberal, trading states. Hedley Bull and Alexander Wendt posit three kinds of international systems (Hobbesian, Lockean and Kantian) which arise from the "identities" of actors and their interactions. Marxists direct their attention to the mode of production, which determines not only the character of economic and political relations, but legal and social relations as well. Realism, liberalism and Wendtian constructivism hold their actors and structures constant because they would lose their analytical purchase if they were allowed to vary.[38] These theories acknowledge the possibility of change but its causes, of necessity, lie outside the theories. Only Marxism, to its credit, allows its structures to evolve, and understands change as an interactive process between the economic-political consequences of structures (feudalism, capitalism and socialism) and the way in which that behavior in turn reshapes those structures.[39]

In contrast to these theories, I privilege process over structure and change over stability, and attempt to describe the dynamics that bring about change. I build my theory around ideal types, which can be described as non-existent structures. Spirit-based worlds have distinctive characters that give rise to a range of related behaviors, but real worlds only resemble such an ideal-type world in part and so do their behaviors. Realism describes another ideal type: a fear-based world. Liberalism is one variant of a third ideal type: an interest-based world. Real worlds generally contain some elements of all three, are unstable and are constantly in flux. Over time, they move toward or away from one or more of these ideal-type worlds. Reality is further complicated by the fact that these societies and the systems in which they interact almost invariably contain considerable local variation, making them "lumpy," more difficult to describe and correspondingly more volatile.

---

[38] Lawrence, "Imperial Peace or Imperial Method," criticizes the "democratic peace" paradigm and its static definition of democracy for this reason.

[39] Marx, *Capital*, I.25, pp. 612–21, for one of many examples.

Table 2.1. *Foundational assumptions*

Assumptions	Ancients	Moderns
Human motives	Three-fold	Appetite
Balance	Mechanical	Organic
Source of balance	Internal	External
Levels of analysis	Similar	Distinct
System state	Change/cycle	Equilibrium
Ontology (actors)	Embedded	Autonomous

For these reasons, a general theory of international relations must be more a theory of process than of structure. It must establish templates for determining the character of particular worlds and their subsystems, but also identify the dynamics that move them to and away from these states, and how they are related to or even arise from the character of these worlds. We must recognize, in the language of Bergson, that our understanding of the international system is a "snapshot" that freezes the moment and gives it an artificial appearance of stability.[40] To comprehend that order, we need to examine the previous frames through which it has progressed, and the dynamics that drove that progression. They may also give us an inkling of where it is heading, and just possibly when it is likely to undergo a rapid phase transition or more gradual evolution into some other kind of world. I say an inkling, because we are describing a non-linear process in which simple projections of the past into the future are almost certain to be misleading.

The preceding discussion of the foundational assumptions of my theory is intended to provide a roadmap for readers and distinguish my theory from other ones. For the most part my assumptions derive from the Greeks, although they are by no means all shared by even Plato and Aristotle. Table 2.1 summarizes these assumptions and compares them to their modern counterparts.

In the sections that follow, I elaborate the outlines of a combined theory of politics and order that builds on these foundational assumptions. I start with motives and their associated hierarchies and principles of justice. I contend that each motive generates a distinctive logic concerning cooperation, conflict and risk-taking. I then turn to order and its breakdown and

---

[40] Bergson, *The Creative Mind*, p. 232.

examine the dynamics associated with the latter. The dynamics of break-down are more or less universal, although the sources of tensions within societies vary according to which motive is dominant. I recognize that single-motive worlds are, by definition, ideal types, and that real worlds always reveal multiple motives. I argue that for the most part motives mix, not blend, which has important implications for behavior. Lastly, I address the question of change and transformation.

Motives

Plato and Aristotle posit three fundamental drives – appetite, spirit and reason – each seeking its own ends. Three paradigms of international relations – realism, liberalism and Marxism – are rooted in appetite. Liberalism assumes that people and states seek wealth, and use reason instrumentally to design strategies and institutions conducive to this goal. Realism differs from liberalism in arguing that concern for security must come first in an anarchical world. As I noted in the introduction, real-ists root their paradigm in Hobbes's observation – generally taken out of context – that people are motivated to find ways out of the state of nature, not only to preserve their lives, but to protect their property and create an environment in which they can satisfy other appetites.[41] Marxism is also anchored in appetite, although the young Marx was equally con-cerned with the spirit. He wrote about man's alienation from his labor, and how socialism would restore workers' self-esteem by reordering their relationship to what they produced. Marx was a close reader of the Greeks, and appreciated their richer understanding of human motives and related understanding that human happiness required more than the satisfaction of appetites.

The spirit has not been made the basis for any paradigm of politics or international relations, although, as Machiavelli and Rousseau recog-nized, it has the potential to serve as the foundation for one, and Hobbes described "vanity" – his term for the spirit – as a powerful, fundamental drive and principal cause of war.[42] I attempt to remedy this conceptual oversight. With Homer's *Iliad* as my guide, I construct an ideal-type honor society in chapter 3, and use it as a template to understand the role of the spirit in real worlds, ancient and modern. In this chapter, I provide a

---

[41] Hobbes, *Leviathan*, p. 126.
[42] The quest for prestige, and its political consequences, are discussed at some length by Machiavelli in the *Prince* and the *Discourses*, Hobbes in the *Leviathan* and Rousseau in his "Fragments on War" and *Discourse on the Origins of Inequality*.

brief overview of the characteristics and tensions of spirit-based worlds and their implications for foreign policy. I do the same for interest- and fear-based worlds, showing how these ideal-type worlds differ from each other in their organizing principles and behavior.

Spirit

A spirit-based paradigm starts from the premise that people, individually and collectively, seek self-esteem. Simply put, self-esteem is a sense of self-worth that makes people feel good about themselves, happier about life and more confident about their ability to confront its challenges. It is achieved by excelling in activities valued by one's peer group or society and gaining the respect of actors whose opinions matter. By winning their approbation we feel good about ourselves. Self-esteem requires some sense of self, but also recognition that self requires society, because self-esteem is impossible in its absence. There is a large literature in psychology about self-esteem and its beneficial consequences, although efforts to build self-esteem in the absence of substantive accomplishments have come in for serious criticism.[43]

The spirit is fiercely protective of one's autonomy and honor, and for the Greeks the two are closely related. According to Plato, the spirit responds with anger to any restraint on its self-assertion in private or civic life. It wants to avenge all affronts to its honor, and those against its friends, and seeks immediate satisfaction when aroused.[44] Mature people are restrained by reason, and recognize the wisdom of the ancient maxim, as did Odysseus, that revenge is a dish best served cold.

Self-esteem is a universal drive, although it is conceived of differently by different societies. For the Greeks, identity was defined by the sum of the social roles people performed, so esteem (how we are regarded by others) and self-esteem (how we regard ourselves) were understood to be more or less synonymous because the latter depended on the former. For modern Westerners, esteem and self-esteem are distinct words and categories and are no longer synonymous. We also distinguish external honor – the only kind the Greeks recognized – from internal honor, a modern Western concept associated with behavior in accord with our values. We can behave in ways that provoke the disapproval of others but still feel good about ourselves if that behavior reflects our values and

---

[43] Dechesne *et al.*, "Terror Management and Sports Fan Affiliation."
[44] Plato, *Republic*, 440c–441c.

beliefs and confers internal honor. We must nevertheless be careful about making hard and fast distinctions between Greeks and moderns, because there is some evidence that internal honor was not entirely foreign to Athenians. Socrates accepts his death sentence, when it may have been intended to make him go into exile, which is what his friends plead with him to do, because he insists on behaving in a manner consistent with his beliefs.[45]

Even more than appetite, the spirit is mediated by society. People can satisfy some appetites by instinct, but must be taught how to express and satisfy the spirit through activities deemed appropriate by the society. They need appropriate role models to emulate. For Aristotle, emulation, like many behaviors, is motivated by pain and pleasure. We feel pain when we observe people, who are much like us, and who have good qualities and positions we do not have but might. To escape this pain we act in ways that make it possible for us to possess these goods and feel good when we obtain them.[46]

Societies have strong incentives to nurture and channel the spirit. It engenders self-control and sacrifice from which the community as a whole prospers. In warrior societies, the spirit is channeled into bravery and selflessness from which the society also profits. All societies must restrain, or deflect outwards, the anger aroused when the spirit is challenged or frustrated. The spirit is a purely human drive; organizations and states do not have psyches and cannot be treated as persons. They can nevertheless respond to the needs of the spirit in the same way as they do to the appetites of their citizens. It is readily apparent, as I noted in the introduction, that people join or support collective enterprises in the expectation of material and emotional rewards. They can build self-esteem in the same way, through the accomplishments of nations with which they affiliate. Arguably the most important function of nationalism in the modern world is to provide vicarious satisfaction for the spirit.

There are a bundle of concepts associated with the spirit that must be defined with some care. Thee first of these is self-esteem, which I have described as a universal human need on a par with appetite. For Plato and Aristotle, and classical Greek literature more generally, self-esteem or self-worth is an affect, and like all emotions for the Greeks, is mediated by the intellect. We only feel good about ourselves when we recognize that we are esteemed for the right reasons by other actors whom we respect and admire.

---

[45] Plato, *Crito.*   [46] Aristotle, *Rhetoric*, 1388a29–1388b30.

Esteem and self-esteem – for me the more relevant concept – map on to different conceptions of identity. In the ancient world, I noted above, identity is conceived of as social in nature.[47] People did not lack a concept of self, but that self was relationally defined and has been described as the sum of their socially assigned roles.[48] Our word for person derives from *persona*, the Latin for mask, and describes the outer face that one presents to the community.[49] In the modern world, individual identity is thought to have become increasingly important, and with it, the concept of self-esteem has emerged. Durkheim observed that the replacement of the collectivity by the individual as the object of ritual attention is one of the hallmarks of transitions from traditional to modern societies. From Rousseau on, Enlightenment and Romantic ideologies emphasized the uniqueness and autonomy of the inner self.[50] Modernity created a vocabulary that recognizes tensions between inner selves and social roles but encourages us to cultivate and express our "inner selves" and original ways of being.[51]

Self-esteem is a subjective sense of one's honor and standing and can reflect or differ from the esteem accorded by others. Tension and conflict can arise, internally and socially, when actors' self-esteem is considerably lower or higher than their external esteem. Esteem and self-esteem can also be described as respect and self-respect. The opposite of esteem is shame, an emotion that arises in response to the judgments, or expected judgments, of others. Both forms of esteem are stipulatively social. Aristotle describes shame as a "pain or disturbance in regard to bad things, whether present, past or future, which seem likely to involve us in discredit." Examples he provides include throwing away one's shield in battle, withholding

[47] Yack, *The Fetishism of Modernities*; Fitzgerald, *Metaphors of Identity*, p. 190; Lapid, "Culture's Ship."
[48] Durkheim, *Division of Labor in Society*, preface and pp. 219–22; Finley, *The World of Odysseus*, p. 134.
[49] Hobbes, *Leviathan*, part I, xvi, p. 112; Andrew, *Worlds Apart*, pp. 98–103.
[50] Hegel, *Phenomenology of Spirit*, Bb, Cc, described the "authentic" Romantic as a "beautiful soul," pure in its inwardness and uncorrupted by modernity's divisiveness. Norton, *The Beautiful Soul*; Berman, *The Politics of Individualism*. On Durkheim, see his *Elementary Forms of the Religious Life* and *The Division of Labor in Society*; Parsons, *The Structure of Social Action*, pp. 378–90; Lukes, *Emile Durkheim*; Collins, "Categories, Concepts or Predicaments?"
[51] Many concepts of self rely on the idea of interpellation developed by Althusser in "Ideology and Ideological State Apparatuses." For the development of the concept of the relational self, see Shotter, "Social Accountability and the Social Construction of 'You'"; Butler, *Excitable Speech*; Eakin, *How our Lives Become Stories*; Gergen, *An Invitation to Social Construction*.

Table 2.2. *The spirit*

Motive	Goal	Instrument
Spirit	Self-esteem	Honor/standing

payment from someone deserving of it, making a profit in a disgraceful way and having sexual relations with forbidden persons or at the wrong times or places.[52] Aristotle is clear that we shrink from knowledge of our behavior, not the acts themselves, as we are primarily concerned with how we appear in the eyes of those who matter most to us.[53] We must exercise due caution with the binaries of social and individual identities, and esteem and self-esteem, because Greek tragedy (e.g. Sophocles' Ajax and Euripides' Medea) reveals that self-esteem to some degree existed in fifth-century Athens. Even in the ancient world, these binaries may describe differences of degree than of kind.

Self-esteem is closely connected to honor (*timē*), a status for the Greeks that describes the outward recognition we gain from others in response to our excellence. Honor is a gift, and bestowed upon actors by other actors. It carries with it a set of responsibilities, which must be fulfilled properly if honor is to be retained. By the fifth century, honor came to be associated with political rights and offices. It was a means of selecting people for office and of restraining them in their exercise of power. Table 2.2 summarizes the relationships among the several concepts I have introduced in this section. It suggests that the spirit is best conceived of as an innate human drive, with self-esteem as its goal, and honor and standing the means by which it is achieved.

Honor is inseparable from hierarchy. Hierarchy is a rank ordering of status, and in honor societies honor determines the nature of the statuses and who fills them. Each status has privileges, but also an associated rule package. The higher the status, the greater the honor and privileges, but also the more demanding the role and its rules. Almost wherever they have appeared, kings, at the apex of the social hierarchy, have been understood to mediate between the human and divine worlds and derive their authority and status from their latter connection. This is true of societies as diverse as ancient Assyria, Song China and early modern Europe.[54] Status can be ascribed, as in the case of kings, or achieved, and in

---

[52] Aristotle, *Rhetoric*, 1383b15–1884a21.   [53] Ibid., 1384a22–8.
[54] Machinist, "Kingship and Divinity in Imperial Assyria"; Yates, "Song Empire." In Europe, the divine right of kings is reflected in key texts from Augustine to Bossuet.

traditional honor societies the two are expected to coincide. The king or chief is expected to be the bravest warrior and lead his forces into battle. Other high-ranking individuals must assume high-risk, if subordinate roles. Service and sacrifice – the means by which honor is won and maintained – have the potential to legitimize hierarchy. In return for honoring and serving those higher up the social ladder, those beneath them expect to be looked after in various ways. Protecting and providing for others is invariably one of the key responsibilities of those with high status and office. The Song dynasty carried this system to its logical extreme, integrating all males in the kingdom into a system of social status signified by seventeen, and then twenty, ranks. Obligations, including labor and military service, came with rank, as did various economic incentives. As in aristocratic Europe, the severity of punishments for the same crime varied by rank, but in reverse order.[55]

Great powers have had similar responsibilities in the modern era, which have been described by practitioners and theorists alike.[56] The Security Council is an outgrowth of this tradition. Its purpose, at least in the intent of those who drafted the United Nations Charter, was to coordinate the collective efforts of the community to maintain the peace. Hierarchies justify themselves with reference to the principle of fairness; each actor contributes to the society and the maintenance of its order to the best of its abilities and receives support depending on its needs.[57]

Honor is also a mechanism for restraining the powerful and preventing the kind of crass, even brutal exploitation common to hierarchies in modern, interest-based worlds. Honor can maintain hierarchy because challenges to an actor's status, or failure to respect the privileges it confers, arouse anger that can only be appeased by punishing the offender and thereby "putting him in his place." Honor worlds have the potential to degenerate into hierarchies based on power and become vehicles for exploitation when actors at the apex fail to carry out their responsibilities or exercise self-restraint in pursuit of their own interests.

I define hierarchy as a rank order of statuses and use the term in this way throughout the book. Max Weber offers a different understanding of hierarchy: an arrangement of offices and the chain of command linking them together. Weber's formulation reminds us that status and office

---

[55] Yates, "Song Empire."
[56] Onuf, *The Republican Legacy*, on Pufendorf, Grotius, Vattel and Wolff; Kratochwil, *Rules, Norms, and Decisions*; Neumann, "Russia as a Great Power"; Bukovansky, *Legitimacy and Power Politics*, p. 70; Reus-Smit, *The Moral Purpose of the State*, p. 137; Clark, *Legitimacy in International Society*, p. 100.
[57] For a thoughtful modern take on fairness, see Rawls, *Justice as Fairness*.

are not always coterminous, even in ideal-type worlds. In the *Iliad*, as we shall see, the conflict between Agamemnon and Achilles arises from the fact that Agamemnon holds the highest office, making Achilles his subordinate, and Achilles, the bravest and most admired warrior, deeply resents Agamemnon's abuse of his authority. In international relations, great powerdom is both a rank ordering of status and an office. As in the *Iliad*, conflict can become acute when the two diverge, and states – more accurately, their leaders and populations – believe they are denied an office commensurate with the status they claim.

Standing and honor are another pair of related concepts. Standing refers to the position an actor occupies in a hierarchy. In an ideal-type spirit world, an actor's standing in a hierarchy is equivalent to its degree of honor. Those toward the apex of the status hierarchy earn the requisite degree of honor by living up to the responsibilities associated with their rank or office, while those who attain honor by virtue of their accomplishments come to occupy appropriate offices. Even in ideal spirit worlds there is almost always some discrepancy between honor and standing because those who gain honor do not necessarily win the competitions that usually confer honor. In the *Iliad*, Priam and Hector gain great honor because of their behavior on and off the battlefield but lose their lives and city. In fifth-century Greece, Leonidas and his band of Spartan warriors won honor and immortality by dying at Thermopylae. Resigning office for the right reasons can also confer honor. Lucius Quinctius Cincinnatus was made dictator of Rome in 458 and again in 439 BCE. He resigned his absolute authority and returned to his humble life as a hardscrabble farmer as soon as he saved his city from the threat of the Volscians and Aequi. His humility and lack of ambition made him a legendary figure after whom a city in the wilderness of Ohio was named.[58] George Washington emulated Cincinnatus and retired to his plantation at the end of the Revolutionary War. Later, as first president of the new republic, he refused a third term on principle and once again returned to Mt. Vernon. His self-restraint and commitment to republican principles earned him numerous memorials and a perennial ranking as one of the three top presidents in history.

Honor and standing can diverge for less admirable reasons. Honor worlds are extremely competitive because standing, even more than wealth, is a relational concept. Hobbes compares it to glory and observes that "if all men have it, no man hath it."[59] The value placed on honor in spirit-based worlds, and the intensity of the competition for it, tempt actors to take short cuts to attain it. Once actors violate the rules and get

---

[58] Livy, *The Early History of Rome*, III, 26–9.   [59] Hobbes, *De Cive*, 1.1.

away with it, others do the same to avoid being disadvantaged. If the rules governing honor are consistently violated, honor becomes a meaningless concept. Competition for honor is transformed into competition for standing, which is more unconstrained and possibly more violent. As we shall see, this is a repetitive pattern, especially in international relations.

The quest for honor generates a proliferation of statuses or ranks. These orderings can keep conflict in check when they are known and respected and effectively define the relative status of actors. They intensify conflict when they are ambiguous or incapable of establishing precedence. This is most likely to happen when there are multiple ways (ascribed and achieved) of gaining honor and office. Even when this is not a problem, actors not infrequently disagree about who among them deserves a particular status or office. This kind of dispute has particularly threatening consequences in international relations because there are no authorities capable of adjudicating among competing claims.

External honor must be conferred by others and can only be gained through deeds they regard as honorable. It has no meaning until it is acknowledged, and is more valuable still when there is a respectful audience. The Greek word for fame (*kleos*) derives from the verb "to hear" (*kluein*). As Homer knew, fame not only requires heroic deeds but bards to sing about those deeds and people willing to listen and be impressed by them. For honor to be won and celebrated there must be a consensus, and preferably one that transcends class or other distinctions, about the nature of honor, how it is won and lost and the distinctions and obligations it confers. This presupposes common values and traditions, even institutions. When society is robust – when its rules are relatively unambiguous and largely followed – the competition for honor and standing instantiates and strengthens the values of the society. As society becomes thinner, as it generally is at the regional and international levels, honor worlds become more difficult to create and sustain. In the absence of common values, there can be no consensus, no rules and no procedures for awarding and celebrating honor. Even in thin societies, honor can often be won within robust subcultures. Hamas and other groups that have sponsored suicide bombing, have publicized the names of successful bombers, paid stipends to their families and encouraged young people to lionize them.[60] Such activity strengthens the subculture and may even give it wider appeal or support.

---

[60] Levitt and Ross, *Hamas*, pp. 59–60, report monthly stipends of $5–5,500 to prisoners of Israel and $2–3,000 to widows or families of those who have given their lives.

Honor societies tend to be highly stratified and can be likened to step pyramids. Many, but by no means all, honor societies are divided into two groups: those who are allowed to compete for honor and those who are not. In many traditional honor societies, the principal distinction is between aristocrats, who are expected to seek honor, and commoners, or the low-born, who cannot. This divide is often reinforced by distinctions in wealth, which allow many of the high-born to buy the military equipment, afford the leisure, sponsor the ceremonies or obtain the education and social skills necessary to compete. As in ancient Greece, birth and wealth are never fully synonymous, creating another source of social tension. Wealth is generally a necessary, but insufficient, condition for gaining honor. Among the egalitarian Sioux, honor and status were achieved by holding various ceremonies, all of which involved providing feasts and gifts to those who attended. Horses and robes, the principal gifts, could only be attained through successful military expeditions against enemy tribes, or as gifts from others because of the high regard in which brave warriors were held.[61]

Recognition in the elite circle where one can compete for honor is the first, and often most difficult, step in honor worlds. The exclusiveness of many honor societies can become a major source of tension, when individuals, classes or political units demand and are refused entry into the circle in which it becomes possible to gain honor. What is honorable, the rules governing its attainment, and the indices used to measure it are all subject to challenge. Historically, challenges of this kind have been resisted, at least initially. Societies that have responded to them positively have matured, and in some cases gradually moved away from, completely or in part, their warrior base.

A final caveat is in order. Throughout the book I use the term recognition to mean acceptance into the circle where it is possible to compete for honor. Recognition carries with it the possibility of fulfillment of the spirit, and it is not to be confused with the use the term has come to assume in moral philosophy. Hegel made the struggle for recognition (*Kampf um Anerkennung*) a central concept of his *Philosophy of Right*, which is now understood to offer an affirmative account of a just social order that can transcend the inequalities of master–slave relationships.[62] In a seminal essay published in 1992, Charles Taylor applied Hegel's

---

[61] Hassrick, *Sioux*, pp. 296–309.

[62] Hegel, *Phenomenology of Spirit*, III.A.178–96. For interpretations, see Williams, *Hegel's Ethics of Recognition*; Markell, *Bound by Recognition*, esp. ch. 4; Onuf, "Late Modern Civil Society."

concept to the demands for recognition of minorities and other marginalized groups. He argues that human recognition is a distinctive but largely
neglected human good, and that we are profoundly affected by how we
are recognized and *mis*recognized by others.[63] The political psychology
of recognition has since been extended to international relations, where
subordinate states are assumed have low self-images and low self-esteem.
Axel Honneth stresses the importance of avoiding master–slave relationships among states.[64] Fernando Cornil argues that subaltern states enjoy
the trappings of sovereignty but often internalize the negative images of
them held by the major powers.[65]

I acknowledge the relationship between status and esteem, but make
a different argument. In terms of at least foreign policy, it is powerful
states, not weak ones, who feel the most humiliation. My explanation for
this phenomenon draws on Aristotle's understanding of anger, which is
narrower than our modern Western conception. It is a response to an
oligōria, which can be translated as a slight, lessening or belittlement.
Such a slight can issue from an equal, but provokes even more anger
when it comes from an actor who lacks the standing to challenge or insult
us. Anger is a luxury that can only be felt by those in a position to seek
revenge. Slaves and subordinates cannot allow themselves to feel anger. It
is also senseless to feel anger towards those who cannot become aware of
our anger.[66] In the realm of international relations, leaders – and often
peoples – of powerful states are likely to feel anger of the Aristotelian kind
when they are denied entry into the system, recognition as a great power
or treated in a manner demeaning to their understanding of their status.
They will look for some way of asserting their claims and seeking revenge.
Subordinate states lack this power and their leaders and populations learn
to live with their lower status and more limited autonomy. Great powers
will feel enraged if challenged by such states.[67] I believe we can profit from
reintroducing the Greek dichotomy between those who were included in
and excluded from the circle in which it was possible to achieve honor and
Aristotle's definition of anger. Both conceptualizations help to illuminate
important social and political phenomena that would otherwise not be
noticed or flagged as important.

[63] Taylor, "Politics of Recognition."
[64] Honneth, *The Struggle for Recognition*; Honneth and Fraser, *Recognition or Redistribution?*
[65] Cornil, "Listening to the Subaltern."
[66] Aristotle, *Rhetoric*, 1378b10–11, 138024–9. Konstan, *Emotions of the Ancient Greeks*, pp. 41–76, for an analysis.
[67] Aristotle, *Rhetoric*, 1379b10–12, on the anger provoked by slights from our inferiors.

Let us turn to the wider implications of honor as a motive for foreign policy. First and foremost is its effect on the preferences of states and their leaders. Realists and other international relations scholars insist that survival is the overriding goal of all states, just as domestic politics explanations assert that it is for leaders.[68] This is not true of honor societies. As we shall see in the next chapter, Achilles spurns a long life in favor of an honorable death that brings fame. For Homer and the Greeks fame allows people to transcend their mortality. Great deeds carry one's name and reputation across the generations where they continue to receive respect and influence other actors. In the real world, not just in Greek and medieval fiction, warriors, leaders, and sometimes entire peoples, have opted for honor over survival. We encounter this phenomenon not only in my case studies of ancient and medieval societies but also in nineteenth- and twentieth-century Europe and Japan. Morgenthau and Waltz draw on Hobbes, and Waltz also on Rousseau, to argue that survival is the prime directive of individuals and political units alike. Leo Strauss sees Hobbes as an important caesura with the classical tradition and among the first "bourgeois" thinkers because he makes fear of death and the desire for self-preservation the fundamental human end in lieu of aristocratic virtues.[69] A more defensible reading of Hobbes is that he aspired to replace vanity with material interests as a primary human motive because he recognized that it was more effectively controlled by a combination of reason and fear. For Hobbes the spirit and its drive for standing and honor remained universal, potent and largely disruptive forces.

As Thucydides and Hobbes understand, the quest for honor and the willingness to face death to gain or uphold it make honor-based societies extremely war-prone. Several aspects of honor contribute to this phenomenon. Honor has been associated with warrior societies, although as we will see not all warrior societies are honor societies, and not all warrior societies are aristocratic. In warrior societies that are aristocratic, the principal means of achieving honor is bravery in combat. War is not only

---

[68] Morgenthau, *Politics among Nations*, 3rd edn., p. 10, holds that "successful political action [is] inspired by the moral principle of national survival." Waltz, *Theory of International Politics*, p. 92, draws on Hobbes and Rousseau to stress the individual's will for self-preservation as the primary human goal in the hierarchy of human motivations. The assumption that survival is the core objective of states is undisputed in the field. See also Wight, "Why There Is no International Theory"; Mearsheimer, *The Tragedy of Great Power Politics*, p. 46; Wendt, *Social Theory of International Politics*.

[69] Strauss, *The Political Philosophy of Hobbes*. See also Macpherson, *The Political Theory of Possessive Individualism* and "Introduction" to Hobbes, *Leviathan*; Hayes. "Hobbes' Bourgeois Moderation."

considered a normal activity in such societies but a necessary one, because without it young men could not demonstrate their mettle or distinguish themselves. More fundamentally, war affirms the identity of warriors and their societies. I have argued elsewhere that Thucydides considered the threat Athenian power posed to Spartan identity, not their security, the fundamental reason why the Spartan assembly voted for war.[70] Erik Ringmar makes a persuasive case that it was the principal motive behind Sweden's intervention in the Thirty Years War, where standing was sought as a means of achieving a national identity.[71] In chapters 6 through 9 I will show that such considerations were important for leaders and peoples from post-Westphalian Europe to the post-Cold War world.

In honor societies, status is an actor's most precious possession, and challenges to status or to the privileges it confers are unacceptable when they come from equals or inferiors. In regional and international societies, statuses are uncertain, there may be multiple contenders for them and there are usually no peaceful ways of adjudicating rival claims. Warfare often serves this end in honor societies. It often finds expression in substantive issues such as control over disputed territory, but can also arise from symbolic disputes (e.g. who is to have primacy at certain festivals or processions, or whose ships must honor or be honored by others at sea).

For all three reasons, warfare in honor worlds tends to be frequent, but the ends of warfare and the means by which it is waged tend to be limited. Wars between political units in honor societies often resemble duels.[72] Combat is highly stylized, if still vicious, and governed by a series of rules that are generally followed by participants. As we will see, warfare among the Greeks, Aztecs, Plains Indians, and eighteenth-century European states offer variants on this theme. By making a place for violence in community-governed situations it is partially contained and may be less damaging than it otherwise would be.[73] These limitations, however, apply only to warfare between recognized members of the same society. War against outsiders, or against non-elite members of one's own society, often has a no-holds-barred quality. Greek warfare against tribesmen

---

[70] Thucydides, book 1; Lebow, *Tragic Vision of Politics*, ch. 4.

[71] Ringmar, *Identity, Interest and Action*.

[72] In book 1, ch. 1, pp. 75–6, of *On War*, Clausewitz equates war to a duel in which each combatant tries through physical force to compel the other to do his will. "His *immediate* aim is to *throw* his opponent in order to make him incapable of further resistance." Countless duels make a war, but their purpose is the same. "*War is thus an act of force to compel our enemy to do our will.*"

[73] Hobsbawm, "Rules of Violence" makes this point.

or against the Persians at Marathon, Salamis and Plataea, and American warfare against native Americans in the nineteenth century, illustrate this nasty truth.

Despite the endemic nature of warfare in warrior-based honor societies cooperation is not only possible but routine. Cooperation is based on appeals to friendship, common descent and mutual obligation more than it is on mutual interest. The norms of the hierarchy dictate that actors of high status assist those of lower status who are dependent on them, while those of lower status are obliged to serve as their clients. Friendship usually involves the exchange of gifts and favors, and provides additional grounds for asking for and receiving aid. Cooperation in honor societies is most difficult among equals because no actor wants to accept the leadership of another, and thereby acknowledge its higher standing. This situation makes cooperation difficult even in situations where there are compelling mutual security concerns.

As honor is more important than survival, the very notion of risk is framed differently. Warrior societies are risk-accepting with respect to both gain and loss. Honor cannot be attained without risk, so leaders and followers alike welcome the opportunity to risk limbs and lives to gain or defend it. Actors will also defend their autonomy at almost any cost because it is so closely linked to their honor, unless they can find some justification for disassociating it from honor that is convincing to their peers. Risk-taking will be extended to the defense of material possessions and territory to the extent that they have become entwined with honor.

To summarize, honor-based societies experience conflict about who is "recognized" and allowed to compete for standing; the rules governing agon or competition, the nature of the deeds that confer standing and the actors who assign honor, determine status and adjudicate competing claims. Tracking the relative intensity of conflict over these issues, and the nature of the changes or accommodations to which they lead, provides insight into the extent to which honor remains a primary value in a society and its ability to respond to internal and external challenges. It also permits informed speculation about its evolution.

Appetite

Appetite is the drive with which we are all familiar. Plato considered wealth to have become the dominant appetite in Athens, a development that has found an echo in all societies where some degree of affluence becomes possible. There are, of course, other appetites, including sex, food, drink, clothing and drugs, but contemporary economists and liberals either ignore them or assume their satisfaction depends on, or is at least facilitated by, wealth.

Appetites can be satisfied outside of society, but more easily within it. Many appetites are innate, but their expression is socially constructed. Sex, undeniably a universal drive, finds expression in diverse ways depending on the culture. In some societies women are not expected to derive pleasure from the sex act, and in Victorian Europe there is evidence that many did not.[74] In some societies, post-pubescent boys are considered appropriate sexual partners for men, while in others, this is considered unnatural and taboo. For Athenians, playing the role of penetrator versus the penetrated distinguished manly sex from its effeminate counterpart. For many modern Americans sexual preference is determined by the gender of one's partner. In the modern era, Smith and Hegel comment on the extent to which our desires, especially for luxuries, which we feel as needs, are products of our imagination and induced by the society in which we live.[75]

Material well-being is generally abetted by the well-being, even prosperity, of other actors. This is a hard-won insight.[76] Early efforts at wealth accumulation often involved violence, as it appeared easier and cheaper to take other people's possessions than to produce them oneself or generate the capital necessary for their purchase. Until recent times piracy was an honored profession, and slavery, often the result of raiding expeditions, was considered an acceptable means of acquiring wealth. Riches gained through conquest became an important goal of empires, and the norm against territorial conquest only developed in the twentieth century. Even trading economies (e.g. the Carthaginians, Portuguese and British) historically viewed wealth as a zero sum game and sought to exclude competitors from access to raw materials and markets they controlled. Recognition dawned only slowly that generating surplus through production and trade made societies and their rulers richer than obtaining it through conquest, that production and trade benefited from peace, and that affluence was as much the result of cooperation as it was of conflict. It was not until the late eighteenth century that even economists began

---

[74] Gay, *Schnitzler's Century*, pp. 81–6, 267, 282. Marie Stopes, *Married Love or Love in Marriage*, first published in 1918, was offered as a corrective and made the radical – at the time – case for female sexual satisfaction in marriage.

[75] Hegel, *Philosophy of Right*, 197.

[76] Hont, *Jealousy of Trade*, for the development of arguments in the eighteenth century that stressed the importance of reciprocity in trade over traditional approaches emphasizing the autonomy of the state and its economic competition with other units.

to understand that the free exchange of capital, goods, people and ideas is in the long-term common interest of all trading states.[77]

Modern appetite-based worlds are based on the principle of equality, of which Rousseau is the outstanding theorist.[78] By the third decade of the nineteenth century, Tocqueville noted, equality was well on its way toward becoming the only principle on which legitimate government could be based.[79] In such an order everyone is supposed to be recognized as an ontological equal and have the same opportunities for advancement. The hierarchies that result – based on wealth – are no less steep than their spirit-based counterparts, but are entirely informal. They come with no defined statuses or privileges and without attached rule packages. Status is not as evident as in traditional hierarchies, so actors must actively seek to display their wealth in support of their claims for standing.[80] Not everyone seeks to be identified and ranked this way. In the absence of rule packages there is also no requirement to share resources with others who are less well-off. Redistribution of wealth, to the extent this occurs, must be imposed by governments through progressive income and estate taxes and deductions for charitable donations. Proponents of egalitarian orders assert that they benefit everyone with skills and commitment because status is based on personal qualities. Adam Smith maintains that one of the great benefits was the ending of personal dependency, allowing people to sell their skills and labor on the open market. Personal freedom and unrestricted markets are alleged to make more efficient use of human potential and encourage people to develop their potential. They are also defended on the grounds that they generate greater wealth, making those who end up at the bottom of the hierarchy substantially better off than they would be in traditional, clientalist orders.[81]

Plato describes appetite and spirit as two distinct drives or motives. He provides examples to show how they can come into conflict, as when

---

[77] Smith, *Wealth of Nations*, ch. 1, was among the first to observe that the division of labor permitted more efficient production and wealthier societies. Ferguson, *An Essay on the History of Civil Society*, for a contemporaneous and somewhat more jaundiced account of the social consequences of the division of labor.

[78] Rousseau, *Du contrat social*, which explicitly rejects contracts of submission and the clientalist hierarchies they instantiate. Every citizen, he insists, must be bound by the same laws and obligations.

[79] Tocqueville, *Democracy in America*, I, introduction, pp. 3–6.   [80] Ibid., II.3.2, p. 540.

[81] Smith, *Theory of Moral Sentiments*, I.iii.3.6. For extreme formulations of this position, see Hayek, *Road to Serfdom* and *Constitution of Liberty*; Kristol, *Two Cheers for Capitalism*; Berger, *The Capitalism Revolution*.

someone is thirsty but drinking in the circumstances would be socially inappropriate. In this example behavior allows a culturally informed observer to determine which motive is dominant. In other instances this might not be apparent, as wealth and honor have been implicated with each other from the beginning of human history and are sometimes difficult to disentangle. In ancient Greece, as in many societies, wealth was a prerequisite for honor.[82] In Europe, titles were not infrequently sold or awarded on the basis of wealth, and in seventeenth-century France conferred privileges that were a vehicle for increasing one's wealth. In much of Western Europe by the mid-nineteenth century, and earlier in some countries, aristocrats were primarily distinguished from the rich bourgeoisie by the age of their wealth. More confusing still is the seeming fusion of wealth and standing in our epoch. Rousseau describes *amour propre*, the passion to be regarded favorably by others, as the dominant passion of modernity. In contrast to savage man, who sought esteem directly, his "civilized" counterpart seeks it indirectly, though the attainment and display of material possessions.[83] According to Adam Smith, we better our condition "to be observed, to be attended to, to be taken notice of with sympathy, complacency, and approbation."[84] Modernity, at least in the West, has arguably transformed wealth into an ever more instrumental good because it has become the chief source of standing. According to Schumpeter, entrepreneurs are motivated by "the dream to found a private kingdom" in the form of an eponymous company that carries one's name and fame across the generations. Like Greek and Trojan heroes on the battlefield, financial success for entrepreneurs is "mainly valued as an index of success and as a symptom of victory."[85]

Ideal-type actors in an appetite world would behave differently than they would in a spirit-based world. Cooperation would be routine, indeed the norm, and built around common interests. It would endure as long as actors shared interests and end when they diverged. As interests change, or others became more salient, alliances (formal and informal) would shift, and yesterday's partners might become today's opponents. Relations among units would resemble the kind of shifting coalitions the authors of *Federalist* no. 10 expected to developed in the Congress.[86] Conflict would be as common as cooperation, as actors would have opposing interests

---

[82] Aristotle, *Politics*, 1286b15, recognizes that riches have become a path to honor.
[83] Rousseau, *Discourse on the Origin and Foundation of Inequality*, pp. 147–60, 174–5.
[84] Smith, *The Theory of Moral Sentiments*, I.iii.2.1.
[85] Schumpeter, *The Theory of Economic Development*, p. 82.
[86] Hamilton *et al.*, *Federalist Papers*, no. 10 by James Madison.

on numerous matters of importance. Their conflicts, however, would be non-violent and rule-governed because all actors would recognize their overriding interest in maintaining peaceful relations and the institutions, procedures and general level of trust that enabled peaceful relations. The outcome of disputes would depend very much on the relative power of actors, the structure and rules of the institutions in which their conflicts were adjudicated and their skill in framing arguments, bargaining with opponents and building coalitions. Actors might even be expected to develop a set of rules about changing the rules of the game.

Because interests – primarily economic interests – dictate policy preferences, conflicts within political units would mirror those between them. Domestic and transnational coalitions would form to advance common interests and provide mutual assistance. Risk-taking in interest-based worlds is described by prospect theory: actors are willing to assume more risk to avert loss than they are to make gains.

Liberalism is the quintessential paradigm of politics and international relations based on the motive of interest. Theories and propositions rooted in this paradigm, including those associated with the democratic peace research program, do a comprehensive job of laying out the assumptions of an interest-based world and the behavior to which it gives rise. Many liberals nevertheless make the mistake of confusing their ideal-type descriptions of an interest-based world with the real world, in which interest is only one important motive. Liberals further err in thinking that the world they describe – one composed of capitalist democracies – is the only efficient response to the modern industrial world. A compelling argument can be made that it is only one of several possible interest-based responses, and that its emergence was a highly contingent outcome.

Reason

We also lack a paradigm for reason, but with more reason, so to speak. Just and ordered worlds do not exist at any level of aggregation. Greek and modern philosophers have had to imagine them. For Plato, it is Kallipolis of the *Republic* or Magnesia of the *Laws*. For Aristotle, it is *homonoia*, a community whose members agreed about the nature of the good life and how it could be achieved. For Augustine, it is a culture in which human beings use their reason to control, even overcome, their passions, and act in accord with God's design.[87] For Marx, it is a society in which

---

[87] Augustine, *City of God*.

people contribute to the best of their abilities and receive what they need in return. For Rawls, it is a utopia that conforms to the principles of distributive justice. As most of these thinkers acknowledge, disagreements would still exist in reason-informed worlds, but would not threaten the peace because they would not be about fundamental issues of justice and would be adjudicated in an environment characterized by mutual respect and trust. Plato, Aristotle and Rawls understand their fictional worlds as ideals toward which we must aspire, individually and collectively, but which we are unlikely ever to achieve. Their worlds are intended to serve as templates that we can use to measure how existing worlds live up to our principles. As Plato might put it, even imperfect knowledge of any form can motivate citizens and cities to work toward its actualization. Partial progress can generate enough virtue to sustain reasonable order in individuals and societies. Thucydides offers Periclean Athens as an example – one that Plato unambiguously rejects – while Aristotle makes the case for polity, a mixture of oligarchy and democracy.

Order in reason-informed worlds arises from the willingness of actors to cooperate even when it may be contrary to their immediate self-interest. All actors recognize that cooperation sustains that *nomos* that allows all of them to advance their interests more effectively than they could in its absence. Conflict exists in reason-informed worlds, but it is tempered not only by recognition of the importance of order, but, as Aristotle notes in his description of an *homonoia*, by a fundamental agreement about underlying values that minimizes the nature of conflict and the cost of being on the losing end. To maintain this consensus, actors often favor compromise over outright victory in conflicts. Compromise that allows common projects is also a vehicle for building and sustaining the common identities that maintain the underlying value consensus. Rawls's difference principle incorporates a risk-averse propensity on the part of actors which he assumes is a universal human trait that will still operate behind the veil of ignorance, even though all other social orientations have been shorn away.[88] He has rightly been criticized for this move and it is more reasonable to assume that even in a reason-informed world risk propensity will depend on the characteristics of the society and actors in question.

Reason-informed worlds may or may not have hierarchies. Plato's Republic has a hierarchy based on the principle of fairness. Everyone, including women, occupies a position commensurate with their abilities and character. Aristotle's aristocracy, for him the ideal form of

---

[88] Rawls, *Theory of Justice*, pp. 8, 53, 57, 65, and "Some Reasons for the Maximum Criterion."

government, is also hierarchical and combines principles of fairness and justice. It is hierarchical in that aristocrats are in a superior position to the demos because of their superior qualities, but egalitarian in the ways aristocrats relate to one another and their understanding that honor and office should be assigned on the basis of merit.[89] Rawls recognizes a hierarchy based on wealth and attempts to offset the principle of equality with that of fairness. The veil of ignorance allegedly leads actors to conclude that everyone should have the same opportunities to better themselves. The principle of difference dictates that the only inequalities (hierarchies of wealth) that are allowed are those that demonstrably permit the poorest members of society to become better off.[90] Plato and Aristotle recognize that their reason-informed worlds would be short-lived. Plato expects his republic to become corrupt after a few generations, while Aristotle expects aristocracies to degenerate, even to the point of revolution, when a few actors monopolize the honors of state.[91]

Theories of cooperation in international relations – realist, liberal institutionalist, social capital and "thin" constructivist alike – tell us next to nothing about how the commitment to restore order comes about or how it is translated into political action. These theories address the narrower problem of issue-based cooperation. For analytical purchase they rely on the same explanatory mechanisms imported from microeconomics: external stimuli in the form of environmental constraints and incentives and the choices of other actors. They frame the problem of cooperation on a case-by-case basis, with actors cooperating or defecting in each instance on the basis of instrumental calculations of self-interest. The more interesting and fundamental question is the underlying propensity and willingness to cooperate with a given set of actors. In its absence, order is impossible, and cooperation, if possible at all, is unlikely to extend beyond the most obvious, important and self-enforcing issues.[92]

Plato and Aristotle address this question. For their answers, they turn to reason – not instrumental reason, but reason the drive – because of its potential to construct ordered and just worlds by constraining and educating appetites and spirit. These are separate but related processes. The initial stage consists of limiting expressions of appetite (e.g. overindulgence in food or alcohol) and spirit (ill-chosen methods of competition or ill-timed expressions of anger) that are self-defeating or self-destructive.

---

[89] Aristotle, *Politics*, 1307a27–8.   [90] Rawls, *Theory of Justice*, p. 65.
[91] Aristotle, *Politics*, 1306b23–7.
[92] Finnemore and Toope, "Alternatives to 'Legalization'"; Lebow, "Reason, Emotion and Cooperation."

Reason must go on to teach appetite and spirit alike to become more discriminating, develop more refined tastes and seek higher goals. Plato distinguishes between *epithumia*, which are unreasoning or animal desires, and *eros*, which can be educated by reason and directed toward the good and the beautiful and even the kind of wisdom concerned with the ordering of states and families.[93] For Aristotle, reason can constrain and educate appetite and spirit alike. Together with education it can lead people to more sophisticated appetites and ways of satisfying the spirit, which in turn require greater self-constraint and longer postponement of gratification. For both Plato and Aristotle, reason the drive must also deflect people and their societies from seeking wealth as an end in itself, as opposed to acquiring it as a means of satisfying the requisites of a good life. They condemn the appetite for wealth on the grounds that it can never be satisfied; when people become consumed by its pursuit, they have no time for leisure and reflection. Both activities are important components of the educational process because from time to time we need to take ourselves out of our daily routines and reflect upon them and the lessons they can teach us about life and happiness. For intellectually gifted people, leisure also allows the pursuit of wisdom through philosophy.[94]

Education is a life-long project whose object Plato describes as the attainment of mental health in the form of psychological balance.[95] Aristotle characterizes it as a process that teaches people to follow the mean between excess and deficit in almost everything.[96] Justice is not an overarching virtue for Aristotle as it is for Plato, but for both philosophers it is a mental state that we might not unreasonably equate with truly enlightened self-interest.[97] Justice has several key components, the first of which – the exercise of appropriate self-restraint – I have already noted. Education not only teaches reasons for self-restraint, it seeks to make its exercise habitual. With maturity, education increasingly becomes a self-guided process:

[93] Plato, *Symposium*, 209a–b; Hall, *Trouble with Passion*, p. 65.

[94] These arguments are developed by Plato, in the *Republic*, and by Aristotle, in the *Nicomachean Ethics*, the *Eudaimonian Ethics* and *Politics*.

[95] Plato, *Republic*, 430e6–431a2, 441d12–e2, 444e7–445a4.

[96] Aristotle, *Nicomachean Ethics*, 1106b35–1107a4.

[97] Their conceptions of justice differ. For Plato, it was balance and harmony among the components of the psyche or city, with each performing its proper function. For Aristotle, *Nicomachean Ethics*, 1106a15–24, 1129b17–19, 1129b25–6, justice is not an attribute a person can possess in isolation, but a quality that can only develop and find expression in social relations. Justice is an active virtue that requires people to make, implement and adjudicate laws, not just follow them. It is the "complete" or "perfect" virtue because it requires possession and exercise of all other virtues. Aristotle accordingly distinguishes virtue, which applies to individuals, from justice, which operates at the communal level.

reason, experience and reflection combine to provide more sophisticated grounds for self-restraint. Reason widens citizens' horizons and circle of concerns by convincing them of their dependence on their community, not only for physical protection, but for creating and maintaining the conditions and fostering the relationships that enable appetite and spirit to be satisfied in the most fulfilling ways.[98]

For reason to constrain spirit and appetite, it must educate them, just as it must constrain them to educate them. This seeming tautology is resolved by the active involvement of parents and guardians who impose on young people the kind of restraints they are incapable of imposing on themselves, and educate them by means of the examples of their own lives.[99] Role models are critical components of individual and civic education necessary to bring about reason-informed worlds.[100] Unfortunately, as Socrates discovered, people are at least as likely to resent, even punish, others who lead just lives. Plato and Aristotle sought unsuccessfully, I would argue, to find some way out of this bind, and the difficulty of doing so was an important reason for their general pessimism. Plato resorted to the "noble lie" to create his fictional city of Kallipolis; its founders agree among themselves to tell their descendants that their *nomos* was established by the gods. He does not tell us how the founders themselves gained enough wisdom and insight to devise these laws and willingly submit themselves to their constraints.

The understanding of reason shared by Thucydides, Plato and Aristotle differs in important ways from modern conceptions of reason. For the ancients, as we have seen, reason is an instrumental facility and a drive with goals of its own. A second important difference is its relation to affect. Plato and Aristotle believe that reason can only have beneficial effects in concert with the proper emotions.[101] Dialogue is valuable for Plato because of its ability to establish friendships. When we feel warmly

---

[98] Tocqueville, *Democracy in America*, II. 2.8, pp. 501–3 for the doctrine of self-interest well understood.

[99] Aristotle, *Nicomachean Ethics*, 1101b14–1103b26.

[100] Plato, *Republic*, book II, 377b to III, 399e, spends a lot of time talking about the poets as inappropriate role models. The Guardians and the literature they approve are intended as their replacement. Aristotle (see below) had a more favorable view of literature, and especially of tragedy, which he believed could have powerful beneficial consequences.

[101] Aristotle makes the most explicit case for the beneficial interaction of reason and emotion in his discussions of mimesis and tragedy in *Poetics*. In *Poetics*, 1448b7, he contends that we have impulse toward mimesis (*kata physin*), and in 1448b5–6, that the pleasure we derive from looking at representations of reality made by artists is connected to our ability to learn from them, and also functions as an incentive to learn from them. We learn from tragedy (1450) because of the pity and fear it inspires in us through our ability to imagine

toward others, we empathize with them and can learn to see ourselves through their eyes. This encourages us to see them as our ontological equals. Affect and reason combine to make us willing to listen to their arguments with an open ear, and, more importantly, to recognize that our understandings of justice, which we think of as universal, are in fact parochial. We come to understand a more fundamental reason for self-restraint: it makes it possible for others to satisfy their appetites and spirits. Self-restraint is instrumentally rational because it makes friendships, wins the loyalty of others and sustains the social order that makes it possible for everyone to satisfy their appetites and spirit. Self-restraint also brings important emotional rewards because spirit and appetite are best gratified in the context of close relations with other people.

For Thucydides, Plato and Aristotle, what holds true for individuals holds true for their cities. The most ordered and just cities are those with properly educated citizens. Guided by reason and love for their polis, they willingly perform tasks to which they are best suited and take appropriate satisfaction from their successful completion. The foundation of the city is the friendship (*philia*) that citizens develop with one another, and regional peace is built on friendship among cities (*poleis*).[102] At both levels, relationships are created and sustained through a dense network of social interaction and reciprocal obligations that build common identities along with mutual respect and affection.[103]

Despite the modern emphasis on reason as an instrumentality, we find echoes of Plato and Aristotle in the writings of some influential eighteenth- and nineteenth-century figures. Adam Smith maintains that reason can teach prudence, discipline and honesty to self-interested people – a set of qualities he calls "propriety" – that lead them, among other things, to defer short-term gratification to make longer-term gains.[104] This is very similar to Aristotle's concept of *phronēsis*, often translated as practical reason or prudence. It arises from reflection upon the

---

ourselves in the role of the tragic hero. This association in turn produces catharsis, a purging of our soul.

[102] Aristotle, *Nicomachean Ethics*, 1155a21, 25–7, 1159b25, 1161a26–8, 1161b12. In 1155a32, he writes "when men are friends they have no need of justice, but when they are just, they need friendship as well." Plato's vision of an ideal community was not dissimilar. In the *Republic*, 419a–421a, Socrates describes such a community as one in which benefits are distributed fairly, according to some general principle of justice.

[103] Thucydides, 1.37–43, has the Corinthians express the same sentiments in a speech to the Athenian assembly. Their invocation of justice is unintentionally ironic, as they have just subverted this very traditional notion of justice in their off-hand dealings with Corcyra.

[104] Smith, *Theory of Moral Sentiments*, I.i.5, VI.i.

consequences of our behavior and that of others. It is concerned with particulars, but can help us make better lives for ourselves, by influencing how we go about attempting to achieve goals that are important to us.[105] Hegel is even closer to Aristotle in arguing that reason must combine with affect, and together they can teach people to act ethically and affirm their civic obligations. Insight grounded in reason (*eine Einsucht durch Gründel*) has the potential to liberate us, at least in part, from our appetites, give direction to our lives and help us realize our full potential as individuals.[106]

Order and its breakdown

Real worlds at best approximate this ideal, and most do not even come close. Those that function reasonably well must, of necessity, contain enough reason to constrain appetite and spirit and direct them into productive channels. They must restrain actors, especially powerful ones, by some combination of reason, interest, fear and habit. Self-restraint is always difficult because it involves deprivation, something that is noticeably out of fashion in the modern world where instant gratification and self-indulgence have increasingly become the norm. Experimental evidence indicates that about one-third of Americans put their personal material interests above shared norms when there are no constraints on them other than conscience. This behavior can only effectively be constrained by high levels of normative consensus, resource dependence on other actors and dense links to these actors and a broader community.[107]

Spirit and appetite-based worlds are inherently unstable. They are intensely competitive, which encourages actors to violate the rules by which honor or wealth is attained. When enough actors do this, those who continue to obey the rules are likely to be seriously handicapped. This provides a strong incentive for all but the most committed actors to defect from the rules. This dilemma is most acute in spirit-based worlds because of the relational nature of honor and standing, which makes it a zero sum game unless there are multiple hierarchies of honor and standing. Appetite-based worlds need not be this way, but actors often frame

---

[105] Aristotle, *Nichomachean Ethics*, 1139a29–1141b20.
[106] Hegel, *Philosophy of Right*, 132, 144, 147, 149–52. On Hegel's grounding in Aristotle, see Lear, *Aristotle*, pp. 160–74; Wood, *Hegel's Ethical Thought*, pp. 33–4.
[107] Zelditch, "Process of Legitimation"; Zelditch and Walker, "Normative Regulation of Power"; Johnson *et al.*, "Legitimacy as a Social Process"; Tyler, "Psychological Perspectives on Legitimacy and Legitimation."

the acquisition of wealth as a winner-take-all competition and behave competitively even when cooperation would be mutually beneficial. Here too, lack of self-restraint encourages others to emulate their behavior. Disregard for rules accordingly takes two forms: non-performance of duties (including self-restraint) by high-status actors, and disregard of these status and associated privileges by actors of lesser standing. The two forms of non-compliance are likely to be self-reinforcing and have the effect of weakening hierarchies and the orders they instantiate.

Thucydides and Plato lived through the Peloponnesian War, the succession of demagogues it brought to power, the short-lived but brutal tyranny of the Four Hundred and the subsequent restoration of democracy. Thucydides was exiled from Athens for twenty years, possibly as a result of efforts by Cleon to deflect attention from his defeat at Delium.[108] In 399 BCE, Plato's mentor Socrates was condemned to death on the trumped-up charges of atheism and corrupting youth. Aristotle had an easier life; the Athens of his day was a relatively stable democracy. He nevertheless had to leave the city on two occasions, and give up the Lyceum he had founded, when relations between Athens and his native Macedonia became strained. Each of these thinkers accordingly drew upon a store of personal as well as historical experiences to reflect upon the causes of disorder.

All three attributed civil disorder to lack of self-restraint, especially on the part of high-status actors, and considered it a consequence of psychological imbalance.[109] For Plato, oligarchic people and regimes are ruled by their spirit, and democratic people and regimes by their appetite. The difficulty of appeasing the spirit or appetite, or of effectively discriminating among competing appetites, sooner or later propels both kinds of people and regimes down the road to tyranny.[110] Tyranny is initially attractive because a tyrant is unconstrained by laws. In reality, the tyrant is a true slave (*tōi onti doulos*) because he is ruled by his passions and is not in any way his own master.[111] Thucydides tells a similar story about the two leading protagonists of the Peloponnesian War. In Sparta, reason loses control to the spirit, and in Athens, to both spirit and appetite.

Building on their understandings, we can formulate propositions about why and how psychological balance and imbalance and their dynamics lead to order and disorder. My starting point is the different principles of

---

[108] Thucydides, 5.26.5.

[109] Aristotle also observes, *Politics*, 1302b34–1303a21, that changes in the demographic balance among classes can also lead to civil disorder.

[110] Plato, *Republic*, 439d1–2, 553d4–7.   [111] Ibid., 571c8–9, 579d9–10.

justice and hierarchies associated with spirit- and interest-based worlds. Traditional spirit-based worlds, I noted earlier, are based on the principle of fairness, and their hierarchies are clientalistic. Every status in their hierarchies, the bottom rungs aside, has responsibilities for those who occupy lower statuses and has the right to look to those above them for support. In return for the benefits they receive from those of higher rank, people honor and serve them. The rule packages associated with different statuses require different kinds of self-restraint, and the closer one moves toward the apex of the hierarchy, the more extensive these constraints become. Honor is not only a function of rank, but of how well actors of high status and office perform their respective roles. Clientalist hierarchies are designed to restrain selfishness and its consequences by embedding actors with resources in a social order that requires them to protect and support those who are less advantaged and feel shame if they do not meet their responsibilities. When clientalist orders are robust, they satisfy the spirit of those with high status and the security and appetites of those with low status. In appetite-based worlds, hierarchies arise from the different degree of success actors have in accumulating wealth. When society in appetite worlds is robust, rewards are roughly proportional to merit because each actor has a relatively equal opportunity to compete.

In both kinds of orders the most common and destructive kind of imbalance is at the elite level. When high-status actors, whether individuals or political units, no longer restrain their spirit or appetite, they subvert the principles of justice associated with their respective hierarchies. Unconstrained spirit, which intensifies the competition for honor, is likely to generate acute and disruptive conflict *within* the dominant elite. It has wider consequences for the society because it intensifies conflict, not infrequently leads to violence, and reduces, if not altogether negates, the material and security benefits clientalist hierarchies are expected to provide for non-elite members of society. Unconstrained appetite also undermines an elite's legitimacy and arouses resentment and envy on part of other actors. It can encourage a more diffuse imbalance in the overall society when other actors emulate elite self-indulgence and disregard the norms restraining the pursuit of wealth at the expense of others. Loss of control to the spirit was a persistent threat to order in the ancient world and early modern Europe, where it was a major cause of civil and interstate wars. Loss of control to the appetite was not unknown in Greece, where it was initially associated with tyrants and oligarchies. In our world, it is endemic to all kinds of regimes and their elites, and has made rapacity a principal source of conflict at every level of order.

Spirit-based societies are vulnerable to other kinds of imbalance. For much of history, spirit-based societies have also been warrior societies where competition, and the aggression associated with it, is deflected outwards in warfare against communal adversaries. Skill in battle and defense of the homeland in turn provide a justification for a warrior elite's claim to honor, standing and political authority.[112] The elite's standing and authority can be threatened when changes in the conduct of warfare require the participation and skills of lower-status groups. In Athens, the development and growing importance of the navy, staffed largely by less-wealthy citizens, paved the way for wider democratization of society.[113] If external threats recede, warrior classes have an interest in generating new conflicts to sustain their authority and to avoid destructive, inward deflection of competition and aggression. The combination of external peace and internal lack of elite restraint will generate strong pressures to limit its authority. Warrior societies accordingly have incentives to have frequent wars, but to limit and regulate such conflicts so they do not disrupt society or demand extraordinary resources. They can also devise alternative forms of competition. The original Olympic Games were intended to serve this end, and their modern counterpart was envisaged, at least in part, as a substitute for war. It was no accident that competition in the modern Olympics was initially limited to so-called "gentlemen" athletes.

For Thucydides, Plato and Aristotle, elite imbalance results in the same behavioral pathology: high-status actors violate the principles on which their elite status is based. They fail to exercise the prudence and self-restraint (*sophrosunē*) of their predecessors. Thucydides and Plato believe that intellectuals accelerate this process of decay by undermining the values that encourage public service, sacrifice and self-restraint by the elite. They problematize social orders that were previously accepted and reproduced as natural practice. Politicians skilled in the art of rhetoric are another source of corruption. In Athens, Thucydides laments, they used "fair phrases to arrive at guilty ends."[114] They twisted and deconstructed the language, giving words meanings that were often the opposite of their traditional ones, and used them to justify behavior at odds with

---

[112] Schumpeter, *Imperialism and Social Classes*, is the classic work on the subject.

[113] Aristotle, *Politics*, 1297b16ff, 1305a18; Raaflaub, "Equalities and Inequalities in Athenian Democracy"; Hanson, "Hoplites into Democrats"; Strauss, "The Athenian Trireme, School of Democracy," who makes the case from the perspective of the *thetes*, arguing that trireme service created a sense of class solidarity and entitlement which translated into political influence.

[114] Thucydides, 3.82.

conventional practices and values. By the late fifth century the code of "ancient simplicity" (*eūthēs*), so admired by Thucydides and Plato, had not merely declined, Thucydides reports, it had been "laughed down and disappeared."[115] Aristotle notes that elite corruption stimulates the appetites of poorer people, making them want a greater share of the wealth and more supportive politicians who promise it to them. Such a process appears to be underway in the United States where elite greed is increasingly open and extreme and marked by ever increasing gaps between the compensation of employees and CEOs, and increases in all forms of tax evasion by the wealthy.[116] This dynamic is not limited to affluent societies; Mao Zedong made a parallel argument about revolutionary bureaucracies and how quickly they become corrupted.[117]

Thucydides' account of Athenian politics during the Peloponnesian War indicates that intra-elite competition stimulates wider imbalance in societies. Members of the elite, intent on advancing their political standing, mobilize support among non-elite actors. Cleon appealed to the masses in language that encouraged them to put their self-interests above those of the community. E. E. Schattschneider describes a similar process in American politics: individuals or groups who lose a political struggle in one arena seek to expand the struggle into new arenas of contestation if they expect it to improve their chances of success.[118]

For Thucydides and Aristotle, the defining moment of civic breakdown is when actors or factions capture the institutions of state for partisan purposes. The assembly and courts no longer serve to regulate and constrain competition for wealth and honor, but intensify it by enabling one faction to advance its standing or enrich itself at the expense of others. Those in power may use these institutions to expel, punish or kill opponents. At the international level this kind of behavior often takes the form of attempting to so improve one's strategic position as to make challenge all but impossible. Aristotle observes that when conflict becomes sufficiently acute, a leader, faction or state can feel the need to act preemptively; they prepare to strike out before they are victimized. Once a cycle of violence and retribution begins, it becomes difficult to stop. Thucydides provides a chilling description of how runaway civic tensions escalated into an utterly destructive civil war (*stasis*) in Corcyra.[119] Aristotle offers Rhodes, Thebes, Megara and Syracuse as his examples of breakdown (*stasis*) and revolution (*metabolē*).[120]

---

[115] Ibid., 3.83.   [116] Lebow and Lebow, *Running Red Lights and Ruling the World*.
[117] Young, "Mao Zedong and the Class Struggle in Socialist Society."
[118] Schattschneider, *The Semisovereign People*.   [119] Thucydides, 3.69–85.
[120] Aristotle, *Politics*, 1302b22–34.

Thucydides describes an important cognitive-linguistic component of this process. One of the most famous passages of his history describes a feedback loop between words (*logoi*) and deeds (*erga*). As language is stretched, words not only lost their meaning, but took on new ones that justify, even encourage, behavior at odds with traditional *nomos*. In my follow-on volume I will return to this passage and its thoughtful analysis of the relationship between words and deeds because it suggests a useful empirical way of tracking the transition to and from fear-based worlds.

For Lenin and some academic students of revolution, civic unrest and revolution is most likely to occur when a sharp economic downturn follows a period of sustained economic growth.[121] The Greeks are also sensitive to class conflict, but believe it will be most acute when the discourses that reconcile diverse classes through a widely shared and overarching commitment to the community as a whole lose their authority. In this situation, the wealthy and high-born become more rapacious and the *dēmos* less accepting of their subordinate economic and political status. Thucydides and Plato understood that learning to live with affluence can be just as difficult as accommodating poverty. Plato described both extremes as destabilizing because wealth makes for luxury and idleness, and poverty for mean-mindedness and bad work.[122] Their observations suggest the proposition that neither wealth nor poverty per se produce instability and revolution, but lack of empathy and self-restraint. Hegel makes a similar argument.[123]

To summarize, breakdown is the result of imbalance. Reason loses control of spirit or appetite. The most damaging kind of imbalance is that of an elite. When reason loses control of the spirit among an elite it provokes destructive conflicts within the elite. When reason loses control to appetite, elite overindulgence arouses envy, resentment and emulation by the rest of the population. Elite imbalance in the direction of the spirit encourages the subversion of institutions for parochial ends and encourages counter-responses, or even preemption, by those who are threatened. Elite imbalance in the direction of the appetite also leads to violation of *nomos*, which is aggravated by a process of elite appeals for support to other actors on the basis of mutual self-aggrandizement. In extreme circumstance, the competition in

---

[121] Lenin, *State and Revolution.*   [122] Plato, *Republic*, 421e4–422a3.
[123] Hegel, *Philosophy of Right*, 195, 239, 244, 253, 266, 271–2, argues that the polarization of wealth between the rich and poor, brought about by the love of luxury and extravagance of the business (*gewerbetriebenden*) classes, encouraged a sense of inward resentment and rebellion against the rich, the society and the government.

"outbidding" not only threatens other members of the elite, it exacerbates relations between the elite and the demos and encourages preemption by threatened actors. External forces enter into the picture when they create or contribute to imbalance by exposure to different societies with different practices and levels of affluence, or by removing the basis, or changing the character, of outwardly directed elite competition for honor and standing.

These forms of imbalance can occur at the individual, domestic, regional and international levels. Their consequences are more or less the same, as are the dynamics that undermine order once we move beyond the individual level. As we shall see, there is also a considerable contamination effect in which imbalance at any level threatens balance at neighboring levels. Balance can also encourage balance at other levels, but has a weaker effect. This is another reason why orders are more likely to unravel than be sustained and strengthened. The Greek understanding of order offers a critical perspective on current practices and the discourse of maximization so central to them. Western theories of economics sanction the pursuit of maximal objectives, and not only in economics. These theories rest on a broader, modern valuation of appetite more generally that looks favorably, even encourages, actors to pursue their satisfaction to the limit. The only self-restraint that is considered worthwhile is tactical. Greek conceptions of balance, by contrast, emphasize deeper reasons for self-restraint as this often makes it possible for others to achieve their goals. Doing so helps sustain the community that is essential to the satisfaction of appetite and spirit alike.

A final, complicating caveat must be entered. If order depends on robust hierarchies, the maintenance of those hierarchies by elites can contribute to disorder when entry into the elite is restrictive and increasingly challenged. It will also have this effect when the distribution of motives in a society has changed, undermining the legitimacy of the principle on which the hierarchy is based. So depending on the circumstances, efforts to defend a hierarchy and its associated values can have differential consequences for order.

Fear

Aristotle defines fear "as a pain or disturbance due to imagining some destructive or painful evil in the future." It is caused "by whatever we feel has great power of destroying us, or of harming us in ways that tend to cause us great pain." It is the opposite of confidence and is associated with danger, which is the approach of something terrible. It is aroused by the expectation, rather than the reality, of such an event and encourages a deliberative response. It is often provoked by another actor's abuse of its power and is threatening to the social order, not just to individuals.[124]

Following Aristotle, I argue that the principal cause of the breakdown of orders is the unrestricted pursuit by actors – individuals, factions or political units – of their parochial goals. Their behavior leads other actors to fear for their ability to satisfy their spirit and/or appetites, and perhaps for their survival. Fearful actors are likely to consider and implement a range of precautions which can run the gamut from bolting their doors at night to acquiring allies and more and better arms. Escalation of this kind is invariably paralleled by shifts in threat assessment. Actors are initially regarded as friends, colleagues or allies and evoke images rich in nuance and detail, which give way to simpler and more superficial stereotypes of adversaries or, worse still, of enemies.[125] This shift, and the corresponding decline in cognitive complexity, undermines any residual trust and encourages worst-case analyses of their motives, behavior and future initiatives. Mutually reinforcing changes in behavior and framing can start gradually but at some point can accelerate and bring about a phase transition. When they do, actors enter into fear-based worlds.

Fear is an emotion, not a fundamental human drive. In this sense it differs from appetite, spirit and reason. It arises from imbalance and the application of human imagination to its likely, or even possible, consequences. Fear triggers a desire for security which can be satisfied in many ways. In interstate relations, it is usually through the direct acquisition of military power (and the economic well-being that makes this power) or its indirect acquisition through alliances. It is also a catalyst, as it is at the domestic level, for institutional arrangements that provide security by limiting the capabilities and independence of actors who might do one harm. Table 2.3 compares fear to appetite, spirit and reason.

My take on fear-based worlds differs from that of most realists in two important respects. I do not attribute fear-dominated worlds to anarchy, but to a breakdown in *nomos* caused by the lack of constraint by elite actors. The logic of anarchy assumes that those who are weak are the most threatened in a fear-based world, and the most likely to balance or

---

[124] Aristotle, *Rhetoric*, 1382a21–33, 1382b28–35. Konstan, *Emotions of the Ancient Greeks*, pp. 129–55, for a discussion.

[125] Herrmann, *Perceptions and Behavior in Soviet Foreign Policy*; Tetlock, "Accountability and Complexity of Thought"; Levi and Tetlock, "A Cognitive Analysis of Japan's 1941 Decision for War,"; Levy, "Learning and Foreign Policy."

Table 2.3. *Motives, emotions, goals and means*

Motive or emotion	Goal	Instrument
Appetite	Satiation	Wealth
Spirit	Esteem	Honor/standing
Fear	Security	Power

bandwagon. The breakdown of *nomos* thesis suggests that it is elite actors who set the escalatory process in motion, and are often the ones who feel most threatened. The history of the last two centuries provides numerous examples of this phenomenon at the domestic and international levels. The same kinds of breakdowns occur within states and the systems in which they interact and are the result of the same dynamics. I believe Thucydides intends his account of the slide to civil war and barbarism in Corcyra to be read as a parallel in almost every respect to the process that spread war throughout Hellas. Both outcomes are described by the Greek word *stasis*, translated as civil war, acute conflict or the breakdown of order.

Fear-based worlds differ from their appetite and spirit-based counterparts in important ways. They are highly conflictual, and neither the ends nor the means of conflict are constrained by norms. Actors make security their first concern and attempt to become strong enough to deter or defeat any possible combination of likely adversaries. Arms races, reciprocal escalation, alliances and forward deployments intensify everyone's insecurity, as the security dilemma predicts. Precautions are interpreted as indicative of intentions, which provoke further defensive measures and can lead to acute conflict, and perhaps outright warfare brought about by preemption, loss of control or a decision to support a threatened third party. Thucydides suggests that the Spartan declaration of war on Athens was the result of this process.[126] Such patterns of escalation are well described in the international relations literature.[127]

In traditional spirit-based worlds (those dominated by warrior elites) wars tend to be frequent but limited in their ends and means. In fear-based worlds wars may be less frequent because they tend to be more unrestrained in their ends and means, and hence are often – although not

---

[126] Thucydides, 1.81–9.
[127] Herz, "Idealist Internationalism and the Security Dilemma," *Political Realism and Political Idealism*, p. 24, and "The Security Dilemma in International Relations"; Waltz, *Theory of International Politics*; Jervis, "Cooperation under the Security Dilemma."

always – recognized as riskier and more costly. They are also more difficult to prevent by deterrence and alliances, the stock-in-trade realist tools of conflict management. One of the most revealing aspects of Thucydides' account of the Peloponnesian War is the absolute failure of all alliances and all forms of deterrence intended to prevent war. They almost invariably provoked the behavior they were intended to prevent.[128] General and immediate deterrence failed in fifth-century Greece for the same reasons they often do in modern times: they appeared to confirm worst-case fears of their targets, convincing them of the need to demonstrate more, not less, resolve, in the equally false expectation that it would deter their adversaries from further aggressive initiatives.[129] When target actors are focused on their own problems and needs, and are committed to their own strategic plans as the only means they see of addressing those problems, deterrence is likely to fail. Challengers are highly motivated to deny, distort, explain away or discredit obvious signs of adversarial resolve.[130] Both sets of conditions are less likely in appetite- and spirit-dominated worlds, and for this reason deterrence is least likely to succeed in precisely those circumstances where realists consider it most needed and appropriate.

Fear of a common adversary creates strong incentives for cooperation, but cooperation will only last as long as the threat. Under some conditions, fear encourages bandwagoning – that is, cooperation with the threatening actor, not with those allying against it.[131] Risk-taking is prevalent because security is such an important goal, and loss of security is understood to have catastrophic consequences. As I will discuss in chapter 7, actors find it difficult, if not impossible, to distinguish between loss and gain because security, as Waltz properly reminds us, is relational in nature.

Hierarchies can exist in fear-based worlds, but do not always do so. In Hobbes's war of all against all there are no hierarchies, only anarchy, although he leaves open the possibility of people going into league with

---

[128] Lebow, "Thucydides and Deterrence."

[129] Lebow, *Between Peace and War*, chs. 4–6; Lebow and Stein, "Deterrence: The Elusive Dependent Variable," "Rational Deterrence Theory," and *We All Lost the Cold War*, chs. 3, 12; Hopf, *Peripheral Visions*; Chang, *Friends and Enemies*; Chen, *Mao's China and the Cold War*.

[130] Lebow, *Between Peace and War*, chs. 4–6; Jervis *et al.*, *Psychology and Deterrence*, chs. 3 and 5; Lebow and Stein, *We All Lost the Cold War*, ch. 3.

[131] On balancing and bandwagoning, see Walt, "Alliance Formation and the Balance of World Power," and "Testing Theories of Alliance Formation"; Christiansen and Snyder, "Chain Gangs and Passed Bucks"; Kaufman, "To Balance or Bandwagon?"; Schweller, "Bandwagoning for Profit."

others to protect themselves or take what they want from third parties.[132] Modern-day realists describe anarchy as the opposite of order, but nevertheless recognize the possibility of hierarchies. Under bipolarity, for example, many lesser powers attach themselves to one or the other of the hegemonic alliance systems in the expectation of protection or other benefits. Such a hierarchy can function along the lines of a traditional spirit-based hierarchy, as did the Spartan alliance or, arguably, NATO. Alternatively, it can be another fear-based order, as was the Athenian alliance or the Warsaw Pact.

Fear-driven worlds are the opposite of honor and interest worlds in the sense that they are like lobster traps: easy to enter and difficult to leave. Once fear is aroused it is hard to assuage. Worst-case analysis, endemic to fear-based worlds, encourages actors to see threat in even the most benign and well-meaning gestures. It creates a snowball effect, making fears of such worlds self-fulfilling. Actors who contemplate steps toward trust and accommodation rightfully worry that others will misunderstand their intent or exploit their concessions. Pure fear-based worlds are few and far between, but most political units for most of their history have had to worry to some degree about their security. For this reason, realists see fear-driven worlds as the default, and the state to which human societies inevitably return. History gives ample cause for pessimism, but also for optimism. If Thucydides' account of the Peloponnesian War reveals how lack of self-restraint and the fear it arouses can quickly lead actors into destructive realist worlds, his "Archeology" shows that escape is possible, as civilization arose from barbarism.[133] Recent history provides no shortage of examples of both processes. Competition for colonies in the late nineteenth century, sought primarily for reasons of standing, got out of hand, led to increasingly unrestrained competition in the Balkans, and helped to push the European powers into World War I.[134] Beggar-thy-neighbor policies during the Great Depression reveal how quickly a partially liberal trading world can be destroyed.[135] Europe's phenomenal economic and political recovery after World War II, based in large part on the consolidation of democracy in Germany, Italy, Spain, Portugal and Greece, has transformed that continent in ways that would have been dismissed

---

[132] Hobbes, *Leviathan*, ch. 13, para 8, and ch. 17, para. 13.
[133] Thucydides, 1.2–13. Lebow, *Tragic Vision of Politics*, ch. 3.
[134] The most forceful exponent of this thesis is Schroeder, "World War I as Galloping Gertie," and "Necessary Conditions and World War I as an Unavoidable War." For a rejoinder, Lebow, "Contingency, Catalysts and International System Change."
[135] Kindleberger, *The World in Depression*.

out of hand as idle dreams if offered as a prediction as late as the early 1950s.

Mixed worlds

Greek descriptions of constitutions could be abstract and idealized, or more specific when describing a particular city. Thucydides, Plato and Aristotle understood that real polities were more complex and often combined elements of more than one type of regime. Aristotle offers his typology of constitutions as ideal types, and the constitution he favors is a mixed world. He regards a polity as the second-best constitution, but the best among attainable worlds.

The concept of an ideal type is implicit in Plato's forms as well as Aristotle's constitutions, but was only developed by Max Weber at the beginning of the twentieth century. Weber had two somewhat different understandings of ideal types. He devised the concept initially to replace intuition as a means of understanding the behavior of societies with different values and world views. Ideal types of this kind have no external validity because they do not correspond to any historical reality. He offered his typology of authority as an example.[136] He later reconceptualized ideal types to give them a more empirical connection to the societies he studied. He described them as an analytical accentuation of aspects of one or more attributes of a phenomenon to create a mental construct that will never be encountered in practice, but against which real-world approximations can be measured. Such ideal types were not intended as a basis for comparison, but a schema for understanding a specific culture or situation.[137]

All four of our worlds qualify as ideal types according to Weber's first definition. Worlds of spirit, appetite, reason and fear are analytical constructs, useful to understand the behavior of societies, but without direct correspondence in reality. This is most evident in the case of reason-informed worlds, which have remained a remote ideal ever since they were conceived by Socrates or Plato. In such a world, appetite and spirit

---

[136] Turner, "Introduction" to *The Cambridge Companion to Weber*. Underlying the concept of ideal types is the assumption, made explicit by Weber, that people in different cultures and historical epochs have different world views (*Weltanschauungen*). These world views are based on value choices that require no additional justification. In Turner's informed reading of Weber, world views determine what it is we seek to explain, and what "facts" we consider relevant.

[137] Weber, " 'Objectivity' in Social Science and Social Policy," pp. 90–5.

have been constrained and shaped to desire only what produces true happiness and behavior that accords with justice.

Worlds of spirit, appetite and fear, but probably not reason, also fit Weber's later understanding of ideal types. They are abstractions of societies that exist, or have existed. All these worlds require some degree of reason, but it is instrumental reason. If actors constrain their appetite or spirit, it is for the same reason that Odysseus did when he discovered his house full of suitors importuning his wife Penelope: he understood that by suppressing his rage now he would increase his chances of subsequent revenge. Reason as an end in itself operates at another level of abstraction. It constrains spirit and appetite, but in order to reshape and redirect them to enable a happier, ordered and more just life. All relatively stable systems depend on this process, but in practice, reason's control over appetite and spirit never progresses to the point of bringing about anything close to a reason-driven world. I will accordingly limit myself to three ideal-type worlds, and keep a reason-informed world in the background as a kind of ideal or Platonic form.

Realists do not think of their paradigm as an ideal type, but as a description of the real world of international relations. The validity of this claim depends very much on the formulation in question. Strong claims, like Waltz's assertion that "In international politics force serves, not only as the *ultimo ratio*, but indeed as the first and constant one," describe few, if any, actual worlds, and can only be considered ideal types.[138] Weaker claims bear a closer relationship to reality. Robert Gilpin contends that anarchy and the primacy of the state do not imply a world of constant warfare, only the recognition that "there is no higher authority to which a state can appeal for succor in times of trouble."[139] By relaxing their assumptions, realist, liberal or Marxist theories can make a better fit between their claims and real worlds. In doing so, they must give up making determinant claims and acknowledge that there is more going on in the world than can be described by their respective theories.

Some theorists avoid this tradeoff and insist on the primacy of their paradigm. Through selective attention or interpretation, they stretch their theory's reach into domains where competing theories have staked out claims. A well-known article by Stephen Krasner purports to demonstrate the relevance of realism to international political economy by showing that trade negotiations are characterized by intense struggles over the shape and terms of agreements in which relative power is the most important

---

[138] Waltz, *Theory of International Politics*, p. 113.   [139] Ibid., p. 17.

predictor of outcome.[140] His findings are not incorrect but only take on meaning in context, and that context indicates just how constrained the exercise of power was in the negotiations he studied. Force, or threats of force, were not considered – and would have shocked participants if they had been made – nor were threats of economic boycotts mooted. Power was exercised in more subtle ways, in accord with the norms that developed to govern trade negotiations among actors who recognize the mutual benefits of cooperation. What Krasner's findings demonstrate is that so-called realist and liberal worlds are both mixed. Power struggles are everyday occurrences among states who are members of what Karl Deutsch called "pluralistic security communities," just as certain kinds of restraint are common in warfare in all but the most hostile realist environments.[141]

Weber was adamant about the need to distinguish ideal types from real worlds. The former give us a clear picture of what a "pure" world of its kind would be like, and a benchmark for measuring how closely it is approached by real worlds. By determining which features of real worlds conform most closely to one or more ideal-type worlds we get a better sense of what kind of worlds they are. By tracking changes over time we can get an inkling of where such worlds are heading. If we could chart the courses of multiple worlds over time, we could search for patterns that might tell us more about the paths – past and future – of worlds that interest us. Such a project would lay the groundwork for a common research agenda for scholars working within different paradigms. It would focus attention on the ways in which elements of their respective paradigms combine to shape the character and politics of a unit or system. Examining the tensions generated by mixed states, and mixed states within mixed systems, would also be helpful in understanding short-term change by identifying the fault lines along which it is most likely to occur.

In this volume, I take only an initial step toward this ambitious goal. I examine the ways in which all three motives found expression in the societies I analyze from ancient to modern times. All three motives are present in every society, although the relative stress put on them by societies and actors within those societies varies considerably. As noted earlier, motives are sometimes very difficult to separate out analytically, and all the more so in the modern world where material possessions have become a marker of standing. Another complicating factor – again most apparent in the

---

[140] Krasner, "Global Communications and National Power".
[141] Deutsch *et al.*, *Political Community and the North Atlantic Area*, pp. 6–7.

modern period – is the tendency of actors to respond to one motive but explain and justify their behavior with respect to another. Governmental officials routinely invoke security to justify policies motivated by spirit or interest because they believe it is easier to sell them to the public. As the spirit all but dropped out of the political and philosophical lexicon during the Enlightenment, although honor and "national honor" did not, behavior motivated by the spirit is the least likely to be acknowledged by contemporary actors. Despite these problems it is often possible to make judgments about the actors' motives and how they are reflected in their foreign policies, and in due course I will discuss the methods appropriate to such an enterprise. My supposition, validated by my case studies, is that multiple motives interact as mixtures, not solutions. They do not blend, but coexist, and often in ways that makes the behavior of actors appear contradictory. As no simple explanation will reconcile such behavior, it offers prima facie support for the inference that mixed motives are at work.

Change and transformation

Marxism aside, most theories of international relations attempt to explain stability, and do so by invoking allegedly enduring structures. They do not address change, or if they do, they frame it such a way that its causes lie outside the theory. Plato and Aristotle explicitly, and Thucydides implicitly, use the traditional Greek three-fold division of the psyche to develop proto-theories of change that bridge levels of analysis. Their core insight is that balance or imbalance at any level of analysis – but especially imbalance – are likely to produce similar changes at adjacent levels of analysis. Greater balance across individual, domestic and regional levels will produce or sustain order at these levels of interaction, and imbalance will do the reverse. A theory of change should also say something about its direction. It can be aimless and unpredictable (like Brownian motion), cyclical (as most Greeks and realists contend) or toward some end (as liberals and Marxists maintain). It is useful here to review these several positions, before presenting my own.

Thucydides, Plato and Aristotle understand the rise and fall of social orders as a cyclical process. They are deeply pessimistic about the ability of human beings to construct orders that incorporate principles of justice and doubtful about the longevity of such orders. Thucydides, like Protagoras, nevertheless recognizes that there has been progress from subsistence-level barbarism to the wealth and civilization of the polis.[142] In his *Symposium*, Plato acknowledges that law-givers and philosophers aspire to create something enduring but insists that only philosophers have any chance of success. All constitutions, even the best ones, are destined to decay.[143] In the *Republic*, he acknowledges that this would also happen to his Kallipolis.[144] Aristotle considers the life cycle of a constitution no different in principle from that of living things. He laments that "time is by its nature the cause . . . of decay, since it is the number of change, and change removes what is."[145]

Modern realists have drawn on these understandings, especially that of Thucydides, to construct their own theories, all of which see order as precarious and fear-based worlds as the default. They conceive of the history of international relations in cyclical terms, as Thucydides certainly did – a series of accommodations to fear-based worlds or doomed attempts to escape from them. Liberals and Marxists posit an end to history; for liberals it is a world of democratic, trading states, and for Marxists, a world of communism, in which classes seek to exist and the state withers away. "End" should be understood in a double sense here: as telos, it is the expression of something's latent potential, and the goal toward which history propels societies. Neither Marxism nor the many variants of liberalism acknowledge the possibility of further evolution. Wendtian liberalism, which posits the inevitable triumph of a Kantian world in the context of a world state, is another representative of this genre.[146]

In contrast to these telos-driven theories, I conceptualize the problem of change at multiple, but interrelated levels. Each level involves different time scales and kinds of change. The overall scheme incorporates concepts of both cycle and evolution. As with biological evolution, there is no linear path, as evolutionary principles of adaptation have the potential to produce considerable diversity even after natural selection has had its effect.[147] Nor is there any preordained goal toward which evolution strives.

Level 1

The most superficial level of change is the one described by realists: a pattern of repeated attempts, temporary successes but ultimate failures to escape permanently from fear-based worlds. They are the default state

---

[142] Hegel and Weber also conceive of history as cyclical and repetitive, but composed of non-repetitive acts, and incorporating the idea of progress.

[143] Plato, *Symposium*, 206c–207c.   [144] Plato, *Republic*, 546d5–547a5.

[145] Aristotle, *Physics*, 222b.   [146] Wendt, "Why a World State Is Inevitable."

[147] Kehoe, *Humans*, p. 107, on the non-linearity of human development.

because, for reasons already noted, they are easy to enter and difficult to leave.[148]

Political units and the systems in which they interact experience periods of relative order, followed by a decline, even a breakdown or collapse, which prompts efforts at reconstruction.[149] These orders can be unitary or pluralist, hierarchical or coalition-based, limited to a narrow elite or encompassing a broader circle of actors, and based on any one or a combination of the hierarchies I have described. They must nevertheless incorporate some widely accepted principle of justice if they have any hope of longevity. Plato, Aristotle, Machiavelli and Max Weber all observe that tyranny is the shortest-lived of all political regimes because it is the only order not founded on some principle of justice.[150]

There are important causal links between order at the individual and system levels; both are sustained by balance and undermined by imbalance, defined in terms of reason's success in constraining – and, at least in part, in educating – the spirit and appetite. Changes in the internal balance of actors – especially powerful actors – are likely to have profound effects on balance and imbalance at the system level. Powerful actors are not immune to changes in balance at the system level. It is possible, although difficult, for well-ordered units to survive, at least for a while, in a system that has become increasingly disorderly. The reverse is more difficult. System order depends on the internal order of key units. If those actors are powerful enough, they can impose order, or create strong incentives for certain kinds of order, as did the concert of powers after the Congress of Vienna, and the United States in Western Europe after World War II. If powerful units succumb to imbalance – Periclean Athens, the France of Louis XIV, Wilhelmine and Nazi Germany, and the United States under George W. Bush are cases in point – it is very difficult for less powerful units to sustain order at the international level.

The responsible mechanisms at this most superficial level of change are not the ones posited by contemporary realists. To the extent that realist theories address change and order, it is through the balance of

[148] Wendt, *Social Theory of International Politics*, p. 255, makes the mistake of thinking they are the easiest worlds to escape from because their culture matters so little. This is, of course, what makes them so hard to leave.

[149] Lebow, *Tragic Vision of Politics*, defines classical realism in reference to its efforts to reconstruct order after catastrophic wars by attempting to combine the best of the old with the most promising of the new.

[150] Plato, *Republic*, 571c8–9 and 579d9–10; Aristotle, *Politics*, 1315b11, who considers oligarchy a short-lived constitution for the same reason. Weber, *The Profession and Vocation of Politics*, p. 311.

power. Power transition theories differ in their specific predictions, but they all assume that changes, or impending changes, in the balance of power between hegemons and challengers have the potential, if not the near certainty, of triggering war. Hegemonic war, whether initiated by a declining hegemon or rising challenger, can change the character of the system by altering its polarity. For some power transition theorists and neorealists, miscalculations of the balance are important catalysts of war, because if both sides could calculate the balance properly they would adjust their relationship accordingly.[151]

I invoke miscalculation, but in the deeper, almost structural sense it is understood by Greek tragedy. Tragedy treats miscalculation of the military balance as merely one example of the more general inability of human beings to understand and control their environment. The tragic poets and Thucydides understood that we live in an open-ended and reflexive world whose interconnections are beyond the ken of any actor, and especially those whose judgments are influenced by their political and psychological needs.[152] Human behavior not infrequently leads to outcomes that are tragic in the sense of producing consequences that are the reverse of those intended.[153] This is most likely to happen to actors who are powerful and have been successful in past ventures. Tragic heroes are self-centered, hubristic figures who revel in their own importance and come to believe they are no longer bound by the laws and conventions of man. Reason has lost control over their spirit or appetites. Tragic poets explore this pathology through a standard plot line: success intoxicates heroes and leads them to inflated opinions of themselves and their ability to control man and nature alike. They trust in hope and become susceptible to adventures where reason would dictate caution and restraint. The Greeks used the word *atē* to describe the aporia this kind of seduction induces, and the *hamartia* (miscalculation) it encourages.[154] *Hamartia* ultimately leads to catastrophe by provoking the wrath of the gods (*nemesis*). The

---

[151] Organski, *World Politics*; Organski and Kugler, *The War Ledger*; Gilpin, *War and Change in World Politics*; Doran and Parsons, "War and the Cycle of Relative Power," on power transition. Waltz, *Theory of International Politics*, pp. 168–70; Jervis, "War and Misperception," and Mesquita, *The War Trap*, on miscalculation and war.

[152] Thucydides, book 1, offers several examples of miscalculation of actors' intentions or of the military balance of Corinth, Corcyra, Athens and Sparta for these reasons.

[153] Frost, "Tragedy, Ethics and International Relations"; Mayall, "Tragedy, Progress and the International Order"; Rengger, "Tragedy or Skepticism?"; Lebow, "Tragedy, Politics and Political Science."

[154] English translators of Aeschylus often render *atē* as delusion, but it also suggests a more onerous connotation suggestive of the potential for self-destruction. Dawe, "Some

Persians of Aeschylus, produced in the spring of 472 BCE, at the height of Themistocles' power, is an early example of this genre and is seemingly intended as a cautionary tale about the consequences of hubris. Herodotus and Thucydides apply the pattern to Persia and Athens to explain their imperial overstretch and the *nemesis* to which it leads at Salamis and Sicily respectively.[155]

The phenomenon of hubris is universal and common to individuals, organizations and political units. It brings us back to motives and their importance. Hubris and miscalculations of the balance of power are not innocent cognitive errors as most realist theories assume but more often the result of motivated bias. As Diodotus argues in the Mytilenian Debate, people greedy for honor (which requires autonomy) or wealth are attracted to risky ventures and convince themselves that they will succeed even in the face of contradictory evidence.[156] Janice Stein and I have shown how motivated bias lay behind many of the most important twentieth-century deterrence failures. In most of our cases the challenger was motivated by need arising from a combination of strategic and domestic political problems or pressures. However, the results were the same as Diodotus' description of people driven by seeming opportunity: hubris that led actors to embrace complex, risky and unrealistic schemes and to deny, distort, explain away or ignore information indicating that they were unlikely to succeed.[157]

Level 2

At this level, change is directional and long-term, and consists of movement to and away from different ideal-type worlds. Making allowance for considerable variation, human history begins with societies that are appetite-driven and subsequently transition to worlds of the spirit, and later back to appetite. The first iteration of appetite revolves around hunger, as hunter-gatherers and early agricultural settlements are consumed with the problem of subsistence. The second iteration of appetite dominance takes place in more affluent societies, where it is possible, at

---

Reflections on *ate* and *hamartia*"; Doyle, "The Objective Character of *Atē* in Aeschylean Tragedy."

[155] Lebow, *Tragic Vision of Politics*, ch. 4 for an analysis and comparison.

[156] Thucydides, 3.41–8; Lebow, "Thucydides and Deterrence."

[157] Lebow, *Between Peace and War*, chs. 4–6; Lebow and Stein, "Deterrence: The Elusive Dependent Variable," "Rational Deterrence Theory," and *We All Lost the Cold War*, chs. 2–7.

least for the elite, to indulge more varied appetites, and more sophisticated variants of basic appetites. This transformation, and the in-between
transition to a spirit-based world, reflects increasing complexity in the
division of labor. Smith, Marx and Durkheim offer theories of historical
development to which this increasing complexity is central and responsible for the progression of society from subsistence, through agricultural
to commercial or industrial societies.[158]

Early social orders are egalitarian, as Smith noted, because everyone
is poor.[159] Anthropologists have observed that many subsistence societies are organized around their food needs and this is reflected in their
relatively simple division of labor and assignation of status.[160] Some of
these units prosper and accumulate enough surplus to sustain a more
complex social order, and with it statuses emerge that are unrelated to
an actor's role in acquiring, producing, processing or distributing the
means of sustenance. Often higher status requires distance from such
primary activities, as it did for aristocracies in Europe, Meso-America,
China and Japan. The spirit is given more leeway for expression, and is
not infrequently directed by society into the display of bravery and military skill in combat with external foes. Such a need was pronounced
in many pre-literate societies, as warfare was endemic and the cost of
defeat often catastrophic.[161] The increasing frequency of warfare is itself a
function of the success of small societies in rising above subsistence levels.
Surplus allows population growth, greater propinquity of settlements and
greater competition for territory and other scarce resources. As external
competition becomes more acute, or its material benefits more obvious,
warriors increase their standing and authority in the society. Some of
these societies become warrior societies and expand at the expense of
their neighbors.[162]

---

[158] Smith, *An Inquiry into the Nature and Causes of the Wealth of Nations*, I.i, on the division of labor, and *Wealth of Nations*, I.iv and *Lectures on Jurisprudence*, "Report of
1762–63," on the ages of man. According to the student who took notes on Smith's
lectures, he divided history into hunting-gathering, shepherding, agricultural, and commercial societies; Kant, "Conjectures on the Beginning of Human History," pp. 221–34;
Durkheim, *The Division of Labor in Society*, pp. 400–1 for his distinction between traditional and modern societies. On Smith, see Meek, *Social Science and the Ignoble Savage*.

[159] Smith, *Wealth of Nations*, I.iv; Ross, "An Overview of Trends in Dietary Variation from
Hunter-Gatherer to Modern Capitalist Societies"; Cohen, "The Significance of Long-Term
Changes in Human Diets and Food Economy."

[160] Fried, *The Evolution of Political Society*; Flannery, *The Early Mesoamerican Village*.

[161] Keeley, *War before Civilization*, for compelling evidence from Europe and North America.

[162] Schumpeter, *Imperialism and Social Classes*, pp. 23–2, argues that the imperialism of early
empires is an irrational policy judged from the interests of the political unit, but not for

Not every successful social order is a warrior society, but those that are have definitive advantages at this stage of historical development. The Mongols offer a particularly striking example. A nomadic, illiterate people, they nevertheless conquered highly developed, wealthy societies with much larger populations. Societies that use high levels of agricultural surplus to support warriors, equip them with the best weapons the technology of the day has to offer and display a gift for organization, expand their domains, which provide the resources for futher expansion. This is how great empires like those of Egypt, Assyria, Persia, Athens and Rome came into being.[163] The swords of empires are nevertheless double-edged. Territorial overextension and overexpenditure on military forces can make empires vulnerable and hasten their demise.

Successful empires do more than expand their territorial reach. They foster internal peace and the conditions for economic development. Development gives rise to new classes, including wealthy farmers, who control large tracts of land; producers or finishers of goods, like potters and tanners; and merchants who sell produce and manufactures at home and abroad. When permitted, members of the new classes adopt the language, dress and values of the dominant elite, and seek acceptance by it, and entry into higher political and social circles. Failure to incorporate at least some members of the commercial or professional classes impedes unity and ultimately weakens the political unit vis-à-vis more progressive competitors. It also makes it difficult to sustain the elite. Sparta's aristocracy underwent a demographic decline that drastically reduced the size of the army it could field. The political and social exclusion of groups, whose position is based on wealth, but increasingly also on public service, encourages them to assert themselves and their class values. Their affluence and visibility, even when they are not integrated into the dominant elite, is usually enough to set in motion the transition from spirit to interest-based worlds. Such a process takes place in roughly the same way in preindustrial and industrial worlds. It is not surprising, therefore, that

the warrior classes, whose vocation and claim to power rested on conquest. This is a one-sided account because empires only arise and prosper because of their warrior classes. At a certain point in their history, warrior classes may push them to expand beyond what their capabilities for conquest or administration permit, leading to disaster. More recently, Tin-bor Hui, *War and State Formation*, argues that empires expand when they improve their ability to extract resources and mobilize armies at reasonable cost, both of which depend on effective centralized bureaucracies. Cooley, *Logics of Hierarchy*, maintains that empires give evidence of both centralized and decentralized bureaucracies, which have different implications for expansion and integration.

[163]   Pagden, *Lords of All the World*; Armitage, *The Ideological Origins of the British Empire*.

political, social and intellectual developments in fifth-century Greece and eighteenth-century Europe reveal striking parallels.[164]

Transformations from appetite to spirit to interest-based worlds are progressive but not linear. They are not infrequently interrupted by breakdowns in order, and the decay, even disappearance, of key political units, as well as retrogression toward fear-based worlds. These breakdowns can and do occur at any stage of historical development. They may be repeated more than once in a unit or system before it transitions to the next stage of development. All of these transitions occur first in units, and can transform the system when enough units change and pressure mounts on other units to do so as well. For reasons I will also make clear in the course of my case studies, environmental pressures of this kind generally have opposing effects: they encourage change in some units but also strenuous opposition on the part of some others to the new order. These latter units may attempt to halt or slow change through aggressive foreign policies, as Germany arguably did in 1914. Not all units make all of the transformations I have described at the same time, as some are almost certain to lag far behind. Such a delay is more likely to work against than for transformation, because such units or regions will become increasingly disadvantaged and socially and politically threatened by the ongoing transformation. Their orders will become less stable, their leaders more insecure and their intellectuals more hostile to other cultures by virtue of their own low self-esteem. Much of the contemporary Middle East gives evidence of this phenomenon.

Ancient Greece had multiple breakdowns of order at the unit and system level. The Peloponnesian War, as portrayed by Thucydides, was the result of imbalance in small powers like Corcyra, middle powers like Corinth, and between the two most powerful units in the regional Greek political system, Athens and Sparta. Their imbalance became more acute as the war progressed, which spread the conflict to previously uninvolved third parties, and destroyed order throughout most of the Greek world. At a deeper level, breakdown of order at the unit and regional level was due to social, intellectual and economic changes in Greece. In *Tragic Vision of Politics*, I argue that fifth-century Greece underwent a process of modernization that began to transform Athens from a spirit-based to an interest-based society. This transformation was a fundamental cause of imbalance within Athens, and between the Athenian and Spartan alliance systems.

---

[164] Smith, *Wealth of Nations*, I.iv, and *Lectures on Jurisprudence* offer a similar four-stage model of historical development.

Similar changes took place in early modern and modern Europe and in Japan, where they also helped to bring about imbalance, breakdown of order and destructive wars. It is not accidental, I will argue, that the Peloponnesian War and World Wars I and II occurred when those transitions were only partially completed. Transitions are danger periods because they led to reason's loss of control over the spirit without offsetting this by more effective control over the appetite. Modern transition from spirit- to appetite-based societies in Europe were accompanied by three devastating wars (the Napoleonic Wars and World Wars I and II). A seemingly stable regional order has emerged, but a stable global order is nowhere in sight.

Level 3

A still deeper level of change involves both a transformation in the ordering principles of the system (e.g. from appetite to spirit), and an evolution in the ways these drives find expression. The present age may herald the tentative beginnings of such a transformation, a theme I develop in chapter 9. The kind of double transformation I envisage at level 3 does not preclude further transformations in the character of the system or in its ordering principles. There is no visible end to human history, unless we destroy ourselves as a species.

Appetites are unchanging but not their expression. As Aristotle understands, appetites are often learned; we come to enjoy things that at first appeared unpleasant to us.[165] Food provides the most obvious example. Many hunter-gather societies have monotonous diets and their meals are simply prepared and without much in the way of garnishes. With the emergence of a division of labor a more varied and sophisticated diet becomes possible, at least for the elite. It includes high price-tag items in short supply – eels and imported wines for classical Athenians – which are consumed and served to others as both a matter of taste and a demonstration of or claim to status.[166] Imperial cuisines may subsequently develop, which are even more complex and labor-intensive. Then comes a shift from gourmand to gourmet, from stuffing one's belly to filling it well, and with food presented in a way that pleases. There is also a shift (college students excepted) from consuming as much alcohol as possible to

---

[165] Aristotle, *Rhetoric*, 1369b16–19.
[166] Appalled by this display, Plato, *Republic*, 373a–b distinguishes between necessary and unnecessary appetites.

drinking high-quality spirits, wine or micro-brews in moderation. Staple foods of earlier times that provided sustenance and protein to the masses (e.g. polenta, herring) are shunned, but may reenter the diet later in sophisticated variants or as complements to what are understood to be elegant and refined dishes (as polenta is now served with *funghi porcini*, or seaweed as a wrapper for sushi). Paralleling this development may come a change in body image: large and fat – an indicator of successful childbirth – is replaced by svelte as desirable and sexually attractive, along with a taste for clothes that show off such figures. These developments indicate how change in one appetite can serve as a catalyst for changes in others, and vice versa.

The spirit undergoes an even more dramatic transformation. Most spirit-based worlds are warrior societies in their earliest iterations. Status is achieved through military prowess or related activities like winning athletic competitions. High status is often restricted to an aristocratic elite, making ascribed status a precondition of achieved status. As spirit-based societies evolve, or return in subsequent iterations, more pathways for winning honor open up, and more members of societies are allowed to compete for honor. In classical Athens, skill in rhetoric and poetry became additional routes to honor. In the course of the last two centuries, numerous other routes to honor have emerged at the national and local levels. Hierarchies have proliferated, allowing individuals to win honor in increasingly diverse and multiple ways. I hypothesize that advanced honor societies are no longer warrior societies, as other means of competition replace war and are seen as less disruptive to order and other social goals. Efforts to substitute sports competitions for wars and surrogate competition through scientific and cultural accomplishments are all steps in this direction.

As equality became the dominant principle of justice in the modern world, all of these hierarchies became increasingly open to entry from people from any class of the society. In theory, it should be possible, at least in the Western world, for any individual with commitment and some skills to find a route to winning honor. As the Special Olympics and Paralympics indicate, we have even designed areas for competition for the handicapped to win honor and enhance their self-esteem. We are witnessing a similar development in international relations where recognition as a great power was once closed to non-Caucasian political units and where non-whites and professionals were frequently excluded from international sports competitions. It would have been unthinkable a century ago for any kind of international congress or organization to be chaired by anyone not representing a great power. Recent secretaries-general of the United Nations have come from less powerful, non-Caucasian countries (e.g. Ban Ki-moon, Kofi Annan).

Change at all three levels has profound implications for the principles of order and their associated hierarchies. Hierarchies emerge with the division of labor that transforms subsistence-level, appetite-based societies into spirit-based worlds. These hierarchies are generally hereditary, allow little mobility and divide actors into a small elite who are able to compete for honor and standing and a large majority who are not. Those at the top feel superior and have their status confirmed by high office and the deference and subordination of those at the bottom. They in turn are expected to assume responsibilities toward those who honor them. They justify themselves with reference to the principle of fairness. In such societies there is usually a single hierarchy, although tensions within it emerge when high status and high performance do not coincide, or when the elite fail to exercise the self-restraint and responsibilities associated with office. Appetite-driven worlds often inherit hierarchies of this kind, and its actors struggle to free themselves from the vertical pattern of relations and to replace it with a horizontal pattern based on the principle of ontological equality. Such a process was evident in early modern Europe and accelerated during the Enlightenment where the concepts of the state of nature and contracts were mobilized to justify orders based on the original equality of actors.

Mature appetite-based worlds – those with a more advanced division of labor and fewer restraints on individual actors – reflect more fully the principle of equality. For Adam Smith, the truly liberating feature of commercial society was its ability to end hierarchies based on personal dependency that justified the domination of one man by another. To the extent that everyone became a merchant or free laborer, rather than a lord, retainer, serf or peasant, horizontal ties would proliferate, freeing people of direct, personal, even inherited, forms of dependency.[167] Hierarchies also develop in such worlds and they are based on wealth and its display. Display is central because, as Smith observes, people generally seek wealth not for the material advantages it confers but for the status it brings.[168] The hierarchies that result are informal in the sense that they are not institutionally defined, are not associated with office and do not entitle actors to particular privileges. Nor do they carry associated rule packages, allowing, if unconstrained by law and custom, the practice of

---

[167] Smith, *The Theory of Moral Sentiments*, I.iii.3.5–6.   [168] Ibid., I.iii.2.1 and 3.1.

an undiluted selfishness which is far more difficult to indulge in traditional hierarchies.[169] Tensions arise when practice betrays principle, as it does when some actors, or group of actors, are excluded from using their physical and mental resources to better themselves, or unfair obstacles are put in their way, or when actors who are rich and powerful use their influence in public institutions to lock in their advantages and pass them on to their descendants.

Levels 2 and 3 of historical change involve a multiplication and blurring of hierarchies. New and more sophisticated appetites develop, new domains open up or are recognized as arenas where actors can compete for honor and standing, hierarchies become less exclusive, and the expressions of appetite and spirit become increasingly intertwined and difficult to distinguish from one another. This diversity, as Simmel suggests, allows us to gravitate towards realms of activity in which we can excel.[170] Societies may ultimately develop in which the best (or worst) principles of fairness and equality combine to produce new forms of hierarchy that support more freedom, opportunity, affluence and self-esteem (or tyranny, poverty, oppression and constraint). The contemporary world is not short of examples of societies that have moved, however imperfectly, in both directions.

When we examine the international system in light of the historical development of domestic societies the difference is striking. Its evolution has been minimal, and only partially reflects changes evident in so many of its units. Honor has largely diverged from standing and the latter is still achieved primarily on the basis of military might, although economic power has become increasingly important in its own right. The international system remains a single hierarchy, with the great powers, or a single superpower, at the apex. Regional systems, some of them based on different principles, have nevertheless developed. The international system underwent its last transformation in the seventeenth and eighteenth centuries with the emergence of the post-Westphalian order.[171] This international hierarchy and its associated principle of order constitute something of an atavism in today's world, and one, for this reason, that is unlikely to endure. The state became the principal actor and

---

[169] Tocqueville, *Democracy in America*, II.4.6, p. 662, on "individualism" and its consequences.

[170] Simmel, *Philosophy of Money*, 468–70.

[171] This evolution and its causes are a highly contentious issue. For some of the relevant literature, see Ruggie, *Constructing the World Polity*; Spruyt, *The Sovereign State and its Competitors*; Ertman, *Birth of the Leviathan*; Teschke, *The Myth of 1648*.

the concept of political friendship was mobilized to free units from hierarchies and their dependent relationships – at least in theory – and create equality among them.[172] Today, practices based on equality (e.g. one state, one vote in many international fora) are widespread and often in sharp conflict with the hierarchy that places great powers at its apex. In effect, two principles of order are in conflict, and many different outcomes are possible. I return to this question in chapters 9 and 10 where I use evidence from my historical cases to asses the prospects for a transformation of the international system.

The future

In units and systems in which wealth has become paramount, the spirit can give the appearance of being in sharp decline. The spirit is everpresent as a motive, and, as Rousseau and Smith suggest, can find expression in material acquisition and its display. Affluence can become a new means of achieving standing, replacing, or at least supplanting, other criteria like high birth, military prowess, education and public service. To some degree this has happened in the West, and most markedly in the United States, which, as Tocqueville observed, was at the cutting edge of modernity because it possessed ample land for settlement and lacked an aristocracy and traditions to forestall, slow down or mask the pace of change.[173] More traditional expressions of the spirit nevertheless endure. Adam Smith lamented that the most obvious manifestation of "public spirit" in eighteenth-century Europe was reveling in the "glory" of victories in foreign wars.[174] In today's United States, this remains the case; yellow ribbons adorn numerous cars and so do bumper stickers that proudly proclaim "These Colors Don't Run."

To the extent that wealth, and the material possessions and leisure it permits, become increasingly widespread, they can no longer serve as effectively as a source of standing. High-status items and pursuits are increasingly purchased or imitated by "lesser folk." In Europe, this process was facilitated by urbanization, which produced concentrated markets and more fluid conceptions of self. The middle classes and the poor spent an increasingly large percentage of their disposable income on

---

[172] Roshchin, "The Concept of Friendship."
[173] Tocqueville, *Democracy in America*, I, pp. 3–19.
[174] Smith, *Theory of Moral Sentiments*, VI.ii.2, pp. 340–1.

luxury items.[175] They were particularly interested in what Sidney Mintz calls "drug foods," which include sugar, tobacco, coffee, tea and cocoa. These were exotic luxuries in the sixteenth century but household items by the end of the nineteenth.[176] Romans, Europeans, Chinese and Japanese introduced sumptuary laws to prevent the spread of distinguishing markers of clothing and consumer goods to the lower orders. Ming China attempted to regulate dress and tableware but their laws seem to have had little effect. As we shall see in chapter 6, Louis XIV was also frustrated in his attempt to regulate clothing, and similar efforts in seventeenth-century Italy, Spain, England, and even in increasingly bourgeois Holland, were no more successful.[177] New ways had to be found to distinguish between old and new wealth, or wealth and mega-wealth, a problem Veblen described nicely in the early years of the twentieth century.[178] The barriers erected between old and new wealth in nineteenth-century Europe and America ultimately fell under the assault of democracy. Even clothing, once the most visible class marker in China and Europe, became increasingly uniform and even misleading.[179] In Latin America and the developing world, jeans have become a leveler, not only of classes, but of nationality. In Costa Rica, wide access to jeans, and foreign clothing more generally, helps to sustain the fiction of a classless society.[180]

There is still a sharp pyramid in material well-being in almost all developed societies, and between them and the lesser-developed world. For some decades, the gap between rich and poor nations has been increasing; roughly 85 percent of the world's income now goes to the richest 20 percent of the population, while only 6 percent goes to the poorest 60 percent. For the time being, wealth remains a sharp delineator of status in much of the world. Barring environmental catastrophe – at which point, all bets are off – the current trend conceals a broader historical one towards a significant across-the-board regional, if not global, improvement in material well-being. Absolute wealth is increasing, even if relative differences have become more pronounced and might ultimately lead, as Smith predicted, to "universal opulence."[181]

---

[175] Sombart, *Luxury and Capitalism*, p. 95; Medick, "Plebian Culture in the Transition to Capitalism"; Pomeranz, *The Great Divergence*, pp. 114–15, 135.

[176] Mintz, *Sweetness and Power*, p. 108; Pomeranz, *The Great Divergence*, pp. 114–15.

[177] Clunas, *Superfluous Things*, pp. 8–39, 151; Yamamura, *A Study of Samurai Income and Entrepreneurship*, pp. 41–7; Pomeranz, *The Great Divergence*, p. 131.

[178] Veblen, *Theory of the Leisure Class*.

[179] Benn, *China's Golden Age*, pp. 100–13; Pomeranz, *Great Divergence*, p. 131.

[180] Biesanz *et al.*, *The Ticos*, p. 101.   [181] Smith, *Wealth of Nations*, I.i.

If absolute wealth continues to increase, I expect two related developments. The first, I have already noted, is the increasing difficulty of using wealth and lavish display as sources of standing. Producers, advertisers and some rich people will still be motivated to find new means of differentiation, and to some extent will succeed. As I write, a signal sign of status in Manhattan is the ability to book a table and suffer a *prix fixe* dinner at Masa, a Japanese restaurant with only twenty-six tables, whose chef decides what you will eat, how much of it you will eat, in what order and at what pace. Diners pay $350 – not including drinks, tip or taxes – for this dubious privilege. The high, if not exorbitant, price of the meal only adds to its draw. Body work is another increasingly popular vehicle for displaying wealth. Tummy tucks, breast enhancement, face lifts and eye makeovers are increasingly widespread, and new, even costlier procedures are likely to come on line that will prove attractive to the wealthy.

The second development is increasing boredom with possessions and grooming (the other great source of display) and a corresponding search for meaning elsewhere. We witnessed glimmers of this in the ideology of the "flower power" children of the 1960s and in the lifestyle of an increasing number of people who come from old wealth and live lives of comfort, but not of extravagance. Ronald Inglehart's studies of values in forty-three societies offer some empirical support for my prediction. He finds a strong positive correlation between economic development and cultural change. In the wealthiest countries, a gradual shift is underway, most marked among the young, from "materialist" values (emphasizing economic and physical security) toward "postmaterialist values" (emphasizing self-expression and the quality of life).[182] While this is not quite what I am talking about, Inglehart's data indicates the extent to which people attempt to satisfy other needs once they attain a certain level of well-being. The most important need beyond appetite is the spirit.

The search for meaning beyond affluence can only go in the direction of the spirit, to honor and recognition, and with it self-esteem, achieved on the basis of one's accomplishments or public service. In traditional societies, honor was the preserve of warriors, and achieved in combat, or at least maintained by the promise to serve in the front line in future conflicts. Warrior societies are *passé*, and if liberals are correct in their assumption that a peaceful democratic trading world is on the way, interstate war itself may become increasingly uncommon, and ultimately an atavism. In these circumstances, the nature of honor and standing will have to be reformulated.

---

[182] Inglehart, *Culture Shift in Advanced Society* and *Modernization and Postmodernization*.

I contend, and will try to demonstrate, that this is already taking place within advanced societies and is beginning to have important consequences for the international system. State standing has traditionally been based on military power, which is usually, but not always, backed by economic power. The United States currently claims standing on these grounds, but it can be demonstrated that this claim to standing – as opposed to cautious respect for American military power – is increasingly falling on deaf ears. We may be in the early stages of a shift of the very definition, not just the indices, of standing, that has profound and long-term implications for state identity and the practice of foreign policy and international relations.

Problems

All theories have problems, and I want to flag some challenges and difficulties to my theory. I address in order problems of scope, drivers, actors, levels of analysis and evaluation.

Scope

All systems have boundaries. They divide the system from the environment in which it operates. Boundaries cannot be imposed by fiat, and various strategies to identify them, including Luhmann's contention that systems define their own boundaries in the course of reproducing themselves, encounter difficulties. By insisting on the ontological priority of the state most international relations theories, and certainly those of Waltz and Wendt, all but rule out the possibility of shifting boundaries. Boundary issues are nevertheless receiving increasing attention in both security and political economy, where they have been shown to be unstable and porous.[183] Stefano Guzzini wryly observes that we do not really know what international relations is but nevertheless claim to have theories that describe it.[184]

Like all social domains, international relations is fuzzy. There is general agreement that it encompasses anything and everything that has to do with relations among states and other important actors (e.g. non-state political groups, non-governmental and international organizations,

---

[183] Stubbs and Underhill, *Political Economy and the Changing Global Order*; Cerny; "Globalization and Collective Action"; Jacobson and Lapid, *Identities, Borders, Orders*; Kratochwil, "Constructing a New Orthodoxy?"

[184] Guzzini, *Realism in International Relations and International Political Economy*; Behnke, "Grand Theory in the Age of its Impossibility."

multinational corporations) whose activities and influence extend beyond the confines of a single political unit. Attempts to define international relations more precisely only elicit controversy; a line drawn anywhere will almost certainly provoke a response from scholars or practitioners that it is too limiting or too encompassing. The practical solution to this problem was suggested long ago by Samuel Johnson, who observed that there was great uncertainty about when dawn and dusk began and ended, but that everybody could agree about the existence of night and day.

As my theory addresses what are generally considered to be core problems of international relations (e.g. the nature and goals of political units, the character and stability of regional and international political systems, the likelihood and character of international cooperation, the probability of war and peace, the causes of system change), I intend to finesse boundary questions. I claim, with some justification, I believe, to be addressing problems that are unambiguously night or day. This answer is not meant to be flippant but to highlight the truth that boundary problems arise from our desire to divide the physical and social worlds into manageable categories. Despite the holistic nature of knowledge we require artificial categories of knowledge, and with them artificial divisions that isolate some phenomena for study while excluding others. As none of these categories and boundaries we impose are natural, the only appropriate criteria for their assessment is their utility. Do they tell us something interesting and useful, and perhaps in an elegant manner? Boundaries, like order, are products of theories and not things that can be determined in the abstract. This is not a novel argument but harks back to Francis Bacon, one of the fathers of modern science, who recognized the extent to which his project was, like literature, involved in the imposition of clever artifice on reality to give it the appearance of order. "Poetry," he reminds us, "can give some satisfaction to the mind, wherein the nature of things doth seem to deny it."[185]

Drivers

Powerful theories explain a lot on the basis of a few assumptions. This is very difficult in the social sciences because of the complexity, openness and reflexivity of social systems. Parsimonious grand theories do not take us very far and require secondary drivers and additional typologies to

---

[185] Bacon, *The Advancement of Learning*, book 2, p. 34.

extend their reach.[186] In keeping with my Greek foundations I try to strike a middle ground between a parsimonious theory of limited empirical value and a richer one that would be unwieldy in its complexity. I try to demonstrate that my starting assumptions of the three-fold nature of the psyche, the different kinds of orders to which they give rise, and the related concept of balance and imbalance, go a long way in accounting for the goals of actors, their approaches to cooperation, conflict and risk, and the causes of order and disorder in individuals, societies, and regional and international systems. To explain the causes of balance and imbalance, I invoke balance and imbalance at adjacent levels, which is simply an extension of one of my core assumptions. I offer additional reasons for changes within levels. The causes for these changes are in turn amenable to explanation and I attempt to provide a partial answer by developing the outlines of a theory of history. It puts changes in balance into a broader context, and offers underlying explanations for them (e.g. imbalance is most likely in times of transition between spirit-based and appetite-based worlds). My theory of history requires additional drivers and typologies, but it retains considerable parsimony by drawing on attributes of appetite and spirit to help explain the historical progression between appetite- and spirit-based worlds and the changing character of these worlds. By developing two parallel theories – one of order, the other of the historical progression of orders – and building them around the same units (my ideal-type worlds), I attempt to maximize the explanatory power of my analytical categories while keeping them relatively parsimonious.

Some readers may be troubled or confused by the use of several different but related typologies: the three-fold nature of the psyche, and the four kinds of ideal-type worlds, and, in my follow-on volume, four principles of justice. I struggled without success for ways of dispensing with the first or second of these typologies, or of merging them in some elegant manner. The typologies are related but different, and both, I am convinced, are necessary. All three psychic drives give rise to ideal-type worlds, but so does fear, which is not a drive of the psyche, but an emotion that comes to the fore in proportion to reason's loss of control over spirit and appetite. Dispensing with the psyche would eliminate reason, essential to explain balance and imbalance, and equally critical to account for learning. Doing away with my four-fold typology of ideal-type worlds would

---

[186] In the introduction I discussed this problem in the context of neorealism, and its need to introduce distinctions among types of actors to make it relevant to the world of foreign policy.

eliminate fear, which is the basis of the realist paradigm. By retaining both typologies, I can account for all existing paradigms of international relations, demonstrate the need for an additional paradigm of politics, and lay its foundation. I can also say something about how these several paradigms are related in theory and practice. In the conclusion, I expand upon this theme, and believe this is the appropriate place to do it because by then the reader will be quite familiar with all of my categories and many of the ways in which they relate to one another.

Ontology

Theories must define their units. Most theories of international relations make states their units, an understandable if controversial choice given their political importance and legal standing in the modern age. Limiting units to states nevertheless provokes the reasonable objection that they are not the only important international actors. In this chapter I have talked about individuals, societies, states and regional and international systems. This is admittedly confusing, but defensible, I believe, if we think of these categories in terms of units and systems. My irreducible starting point, as it was for the Greeks, is the individual psyche, whose several components interact in ways that help us understand the individual as a system. Individuals are the units for societies and states, which I treat in turn as units of higher levels of systems.

This still leaves me with the problem of distinguishing between societies and states. Do we need both categories? This was not a question that would have occurred to the Greeks, as the polis and the society were more or less coterminous. This is not true in the modern world, where state and society have become conceptually as well as empirically and legally distinct.[187] Unlike the polis, Durkheim observed, "the state is too remote from individuals, its connections with them too superficial and irregular, to be able to penetrate the depths of their consciousness and socialise them from within."[188] I cannot dispense with either category. Society is important because it is the system in which individuals interact, and the one most directly affected by their collective balance and imbalance. Modern

---

[187] Luhmann, "The 'State' of the Political System," for a strong statement of the distinction between state and society, and the dominance of the state over society. On the blurring of the distinction between state and society, see Koselleck, *Critique and Crisis*; Keane, "Despotism and Democracy," pp. 35–71.

[188] Durkheim, *The Division of Labor in Society*, preface to the second edition, p. liv.

states are certainly affected by balance and imbalance in the society, but they are partially insulated from it by institutional and other mechanisms. I need states because, for better or worse, they are the principal units in regional and international systems. Balance and imbalance in states does not always reflect, and at times may be quite different from, balance and imbalance in societies. This creates a double complication for my theory: the need to address both society and state and the need to distinguish effectively between them.

My use of Greek conceptions of the psyche and the notion of nested layers of social aggregation creates a framework that might appear to exclude non-state actors like international organizations and multinational corporations. They are not direct expressions of individuals or societies, so are not part of the chain of units and systems I use to trace the consequences of balance and imbalance. Although they are not presently included in my theory, they are by no means precluded from incorporation. Non-state actors can be analyzed in terms of the same typology of goals (spirit, appetite and reason) as other actors, as can the key actors, individuals or organizations that constitute their membership or leadership. Non-governmental organizations are particularly interesting theoretically, because some of them may come the closest of all actors at the international level to being motivated by reason. They are substantively important as examples because actors learn in part through a combination of mimesis and reflection.

Levels of analysis

I offer and attempt to justify the Greek understanding of nested units as an alternative to the levels of analysis framework so common to social science and international relations theory. This allows me to explain order and disorder at different levels of social aggregation in a parsimonious manner. My theory assumes extensive homology in the rules that govern balance and imbalance in individuals, societies, states and regional and international systems, thus permitting the claim that changes at one level can affect (or alternatively, mirror) changes at adjacent levels. In a follow-on study I intend to make a strong empirical case for the existence of these similarities. I recognize but downplay the differences within and across these levels. For purposes of exposition this is an appropriate strategy because it allows for greater clarity. Stressing uniformities can hinder analysis if it ignores critical differences that would confound a theory, or prevent it from recognizing and addressing important anomalies. I will accordingly relax my insistence on the full comparability of systems, and the rules governing balance and imbalance within them, in the course of my treatment of this phenomenon and that of change.

Cities are treated as reifications of individuals by Plato, Aristotle and Thucydides on the grounds that their constitutions are analogous to different expressions of the human psyche. Plato describes a progression of constitutional pathologies that he believes to mirror exactly the progression within individuals. Even if we acknowledge these parallels, individuals and cities differ in important respects and we need to be very careful not to treat them as equivalent. Parallels in structure or process enable a theory to bridge levels of aggregation, but to do this effectively we must acknowledge differences that might influence, hinder or distort these comparisons. Affect is one of the most important differences. The small size of most Greek cities and the personal basis of their politics made it more likely that the emotions of citizens and their city ran along parallel tracks. In modern states, size, the social divide and many layers of institutions between the political elite and voters confound the comparison. The problem is more acute when we move from the level of political units to regional and international systems. We cannot convincingly attribute affect to states and the systems in which they operate, only to those individuals who occupy important positions within them.

The larger problem here is reification: treating the state as if it were a person. This fiction is recognized by international law, and prominent theorists like Waltz, Jervis and Wendt routinely refer to the "motives," "beliefs," "feelings," even the "personalities" of states.[189] To some extent this is a linguistic convention; Jervis is absolutely explicit about the problems of psychologizing states.[190] Wendt goes the furthest in treating states as persons; his "alter" and "ego" blur the distinction between the two and in a subsequent article he makes the case for treating states as persons.[191] My comparison between persons and states (and by extension, regional and international systems) falls somewhere between these two theorists. I argue that order and disorder have the same effects for all, and that it comes about in the same way: reason gains or loses control over spirit and appetite. At the same time, I recognize important differences in the

---

[189] Vincent, *Theories of the State*, ch. 6, on the state as a legal person and its critics. Waltz, *Theory of International Politics*, pp. 91–2, on the survival motives of states; Jervis, *Perception and Misperception in International Politics*, p. 71, on state beliefs; Wendt, *Social Theory of International Politics*, pp. 291–4, on states as psychological persons.

[190] Jervis, *Perception and Misperception in International Politics*, pp. 18–19.

[191] Wendt, "The State as Person in International Theory," and "Social Theory as Cartesian Science."

ways in which this occurs at different levels of analysis. What goes on in the head of the individual is not what happens in the councils of state, and states usually differ from regional or international systems by virtue of the density of their institutions and enforcement capabilities. My comparison is only an analogy, but one I believe offers considerable analytical purchase.

Comparisons across levels of analysis run into a second problem: systems differ in the extent to which their characteristic patterns of behavior are emergent properties, determined, but not predicted, by unit behavior. Such an outcome underlies Adam Smith's understanding of capitalism in the *Wealth of Nations*, and is nicely characterized by Hegel as "the cunning of reason." It assumes that beneficial outcomes can emerge at the system level from entirely self-interested behavior at the agent level.[192] Following the pioneering work of Friedrich Hayek, emergent properties has become an increasingly important field in economics and political science.[193] In sharp contrast to much research in the social sciences that is *within* levels of analysis, this research stresses the connections *between* levels. Outcomes at the system level are the result of the ways in which the consequences of behavior are mediated by rules at the system level. These rules can remain hidden, making it difficult to compare systems in the absence of numerous iterations of interactions based on real or simulated data.

I posit fairly direct and traceable links between motives and behavior, and system-emergent properties enter the picture when we progress from behavior to social structure. The hierarchies I describe are the result of unintentional behavior by actors, although efforts to maintain or transform them are often quite conscious and deliberate. The transformations between spirit and appetite worlds, and the kinds of developments within each that I associate with the third level of change, can also be characterized as emergent properties. To the extent they are successful, these worlds encourage behavior that undermines the *nomos* that sustains them. In this dialectical process, actors produce unintended changes of the kind that have the effect of making the goals they seek more difficult, if not impossible, to achieve.

[192] Smith, *Wealth of Nations*, IV.ii.4 and 9; Hegel, *Lectures on the Philosophy of World History*, II.(2).§37; Burbidge, "The Cunning of Reason."
[193] See Deutsch *et al.*, *Problems of World Modeling*; Bremer, *Simulated Worlds*; Cusack, and Stoll, *Exploring Realpolitik*; Axelrod, *The Evolution of Cooperation*; Cederman, *Emergent Actors in World Politics*, and "Modeling the Size of Wars"; Epstein and Axtell, *Growing Artificial Societies*.

Evaluation

Scientific theories must avoid tautology in the statement of the theory and elaboration of measures appropriate to their evaluation. They must have independent variables whose presence can be detected independently of their supposed effects. This is an endemic problem of even the best scientific theories; Newtonian mechanics and Darwinian evolution have both been accused of tautology.

Within social science, the problem of tautology is endemic to theories that rely on cultural or psychological variables. Both to some degree require us to look inside the heads of people for drives, inclinations, understandings or commitments to practices of which they may be unaware or unable to conceptualize or articulate. According to David Elkins and Richard Simeon:

> Several characteristics of political culture pose special problems for measuring and describing it. First, it is often hard to disentangle from structural or psychological variables. Second, it is an abstract concept, not a concrete thing. It cannot be directly seen, heard, or touched; therefore it must be inferred from other clues. Third, for most of the members of a society, culture is unconscious, inexplicit, taken for granted; hence we cannot easily ask people about it directly. Fourth, while individuals participate in a culture, as a collective attribute of society, we do not describe a culture by simply aggregating all the individuals. How then do we find it?[194]

These problems are encountered by most categories and variables in social science; markets, polarity and the balance of power are as unobservable as anxiety or fear- or interest-driven worlds. Cultural explanations may be held in especially low esteem in political science because of the unsophisticated way in which they have been used by the authors of such prominent works as *The Civic Culture* and *Clash of Civilizations*.[195] Culture is badly defined, treated as static and monolithic, and not distinguished from other aspects of society or the environment that would establish its autonomy.[196] To the extent that the concept of culture is operationalized in these studies, it is in terms of the very behavioral attributes it is intended to explain.

---

[194] Elkins and Simeon, "A Cause in Search of its Effect, or What Does Political Culture Explain?"

[195] Huntington, *Clash of Civilizations and the Remaking of World Order*; Almond and Verba, *The Civic Culture*.

[196] Jackman and Miller, *Before Norms*, pp. 188–96.

My theory relies heavily on cultural and psychological explanations. I employ culture in a double sense. Like Weber, I use it to explain human goals and their variation across societies and epochs. Like Durkheim, I use it to account for the means by which people and their societies pursue these goals. Psychology enters the picture because I use variation in the hierarchy and expression of the drives of appetite, spirit and reason as my criteria for distinguishing one culture from another. To use both sets of explanations properly, I need to define them carefully – and independently of their putative effects. I must also explicate the causal chain linking them and the behavior I want to explain. To avoid tautology my characterization of culture must have manifestations other than the behavior I expect them to produce. A similar problem arises from my constructivist emphasis on actors understanding their environment. I posit fear as the cause of transitions from appetite and spirit-based worlds to fear-based ones. Fear is an affect, and a highly subjective one. It is based on idiosyncratic, and at times irrational, assessments of others' motives. There can be no objective measures of fear or of the amount of fear necessary to prompt a phase transition. Its presence and effect will vary across actors, and our measures of fear must somehow tap their understandings. Ideally, we require measures independent of the behavior we attribute to fear, and they are very difficult to devise. Realism attempts, unsuccessfully, to finesse this problem by holding fear a constant in anarchical systems. The level of fear demonstrably varies from epoch to epoch, regardless of the polarity of the system, as a function of the judgments actors make of others' intentions.

Appropriate measures and indices are doubly important because my independent and dependent variables are not discrete but continuous. Even discrete variables, like shifts from bi- to multi-polarity, pose serious measurement challenges. Neorealism's failure to develop explicit protocols for determining the polarity of the international system makes it tautological and unfalsifiable. Continuous variables require us to track shifts along a continuum. Even if there are only a certain number of stable states along this continuum, measurement still demands reasonable precision. Most of my variables are continuous. Worlds are more or less spirit-, appetite- or fear-based, and all three motives can be observed to varying degrees in a unit or system. Reason too is a matter of degree, as are balance and imbalance, which reflect the degree of reason present. With relatively precise cardinal measures (i.e. dollar values for wealth), we could look for the intervals at which phase transitions were most likely to take place between different kinds of worlds. My measures are less precise and, at best, allow me to say something about the range in which transitions occur. Fuzzy measures create the temptation, which I do my best to avoid, of measuring critical variables in terms of their theorized consequences. The task of understanding ultimately requires what Weber calls *sympathetisches Nacherleben*, an empathetic reliving of the motives, feelings and actions of others, established through careful attention to culture, texts and behavior.

One way to establish the role of culture is to track its evolution over time; in the case of my theory, transitions to and away from one or more of the ideal-type worlds I describe. If the indices for this evolution are different from the behavior I seek to explain I can determine the presence, or degree of presence, of these worlds independently of the kinds of foreign policy behavior they manifest, and thus avoid tautology. I attempt to do this in all but my most modern cases. For the classical Greeks and Romans I begin with an analysis of the society to determine the extent to which it meets the criteria of an honor society on the basis of internal criteria. My evidence is drawn largely from contemporary literature, philosophy and social practices. I then turn to foreign policy and warfare to see the extent to which they mirror the character of the society I have described. This becomes more difficult to do in the modern period where motives are mixed and interact in complex ways. So I adopt a different strategy in addressing nineteenth-century imperialism and subsequent cases. I show the ways in which the spirit found expression in these societies and attempt to document links between it and aggressive foreign policies. As further evidence of my explanation I attempt to demonstrate that these policies cannot adequately be explained with reference to appetite or fear.

A general theory of international relations is a grand theory. It is commonly assumed, Kal Holsti writes, that such theories can "bring together the essential, if not all, the animals of world politics into one theoretical ark."[197] Stephen Brooks makes the case for a more "minimalist" role for grand theory. It should make few predictions itself, but offer a framework that orders a phenomenon, creates novel links and associations and inspires development of "middle range" theories.[198] According to Robert Merton, who coined the term, middle range theory is "intermediate to the minor working hypotheses evolved in abundance during the day-by-day

---

[197] Holsti, "Retreat from Utopia."
[198] Brooks, *The Globalization of Production and International Security*, ch. 2.

routines of research, and the all-inclusive speculations comprising a master conceptual scheme."[199]

My own view of grand theory mirrors that of Brooks. It should have something to say about all aspects of international relations, but not necessarily in the form of testable propositions. It should establish a research program, or at least lay the foundation for one, generate fresh perspectives, raise novel questions, and stimulate research that is relevant to theory and practice. I believe I meet these criteria. I propose a general framework for studying politics in terms of dynamic status hierarchies. I derive several theories from this framework, having to do with the rise of the state, the kinds of states that are most likely to be aggressive, the causes, character and frequency of cooperation and warfare, and the propensity of actors to seek or eschew risk. My framework also identifies a series of important questions that are not being asked, and provides some of the conceptual tools necessary for seeking answers to them.

Kant understood science as internally self-perpetuating; answers generated new questions and answers.[200] Positivists harbor the goal of cumulative theory that builds on previous research and knowledge. For Kant, however, science advances by finding new questions, not only answers to them; it is a dialectical process. Progress in our questions is every bit as important as progress in the answers we find to them. In this connection we can discover new answers to old questions, new questions or the inappropriateness of existing questions. Epistemic change, as Nicholas Rescher points out, "relates not only to what is *known* but what can be asked."[201] It is on this basis that my framework and related theories ought to be judged.

---

[199] Merton, *Social Theory and Social Structure*, pp. 5–6.
[200] *Kant, Prolegomena to any Future Metaphysic*, sec. 57.
[201] Rescher, *Process Philosophy*, pp. 60–1.

3

The spirit and its expression

> Rage – sing, goddess, the rage of Achilles, the son of Peleus, the destructive
> rage that brought countless griefs upon the Achaeans.
>
> Homer[1]

This chapter develops a paradigm of politics based on the spirit and the
need for self-esteem to which it gives rise. Following Plato and Aristotle,
I contend this need is universal and distinct from appetite. The spirit is
an individual drive but has great importance for politics because people
seek self-esteem not only through their personal activities, but vicariously
through the achievements of social units to which they feel attached, such
as sports teams and nations.[2] In classical Greece, citizens achieved standing and self-esteem individually and collectively through the triumphs of
their city states. In the modern era, often called the age of nationalism,
people achieve self-esteem in a variety of ways and many bask in the glory
of their nations. Harold Lasswell and Hans Morgenthau, among others,
argue that nationalism involves a degree of transference by individuals of
their aspirations on to states.[3] More recent research suggests that this relationship works in both directions. To build identities and mobilize public
support, states construct and project characters and narratives of themselves to which many of their citizens become deeply attached. Policymakers find it in their interests to act – or give the appearance of acting –
in terms of these characters and narratives, which can restrain their

---

[1] Homer, *Iliad*, 1.1–2.

[2] Heider, *The Psychology of Interpersonal Relations*; Cialdini, *et al.*, "Basking in Reflected
Glory: Three (Football) Field Studies," demonstrate that identification with a sports
team enhances self-esteem when the team is successful. Dechesne, Greenberg, Arndt and
Schimel, "Terror Management and Sports Fan Affiliation," demonstrated the links among
mortality, self-esteem and identification with sports teams. Those subjects primed beforehand to think about mortality showed a higher rate of identification with their favorite
team.

[3] Lasswell, *World Politics and Personal Insecurity*, pp. 23–39; Morgenthau, *Scientific Man vs.
Power Politics*, p. 169; Kelman, "Patterns of Personal Involvement in the National System."

freedom of action and at times compel them to pursue policies at odds with their preferences.[4] For citizens and leaders alike, questions of standing and honor can be very important and interrelated.

The concept of the spirit all but disappeared from the philosophical and political lexicon as a result of the Enlightenment and French Revolution. The spirit found expression in honor, a value and way of life associated with the *ancien régime*, that was considered politically retrograde. Adam Smith is a notable exception. He hoped to transform the potentially destructive "jealousy of trade" into a peaceful competition for national glory and honor.[5] Tocqueville, who insists that "every time men are gathered in a particular place, honor is immediately established among them," is the last major theorist to speak of honor and the positive role it can perform for democracy, although not the last to write about its consequences for international affairs.[6] I hope to bring the discourse of the spirit back to life – although not in the context of aristocratic values – by describing the key characteristics of the spirit, its principal behavioral manifestations and how they have been conceptualized in the past. I intend to show how the spirit remains not only relevant, but essential, to understanding contemporary individual and collective political behavior.

Plato and Aristotle provide the philosophical foundation for my paradigm, as they were the first to theorize about the spirit and its relationship to political order. I accordingly discuss their conceptions of the spirit and its relationship to political order. They were deeply influenced by Homer. The *Iliad* illustrates the values, characteristic modes of behavior and sources of stability of spirit-based worlds, as well as their tensions and pathways to their destabilization. I use the *Iliad* to construct a Weberian ideal-type honor society and template to study several real societies in which honor or standing were key state goals.

Many historical honor societies were warrior societies. Such societies value bravery on the battlefield most highly, and through its display – ideally in one-on-one combat – warriors achieve status and the possibility of political office. Warrior societies are governed by complex codes, although, as we shall see in the case of Homeric Greece, these codes are

---

[4] This is a central contention of those who emphasize "ontological security" as a prime motive of state behavior. The argument and relevant literature are discussed later in this chapter.

[5] Smith, *Wealth of Nations*, I, chs. 1, 5; Rothschild, *Economic Sentiments*, p. 656; Hont, *Jealousy of Trade*, pp. 6, 354–88.

[6] Tocqueville, *Democracy in America*, II.3.17–18, 587–9, 593 (for quote); Krause, *Liberalism without Honor*, pp. 67–96.

neither unproblematic nor accepted by everyone in the society.[7] Warrior societies are highly competitive, but seek to constrain internal competition and violence through friendship, marriage and gift-giving and
the selflessness, self-restraint and reciprocity they entail. Warrior societies are another ideal type, because most societies in which warriors and
honor play important, if not dominant, roles are more complex and varied
than any abstract description would suggest. Fifth-century Greece, Macedon under Philip and Alexander, early and middle Republican Rome, the
Frankish kingdoms, the Vikings, Shang China (*c.* 1600–1050 BCE), India
at various stage of its history, the Maori of New Zealand, the Inca and
Aztec Empires and the American Plains Indians are cases in point. Many,
but not all, of these societies were aristocratic, as of course were the Greeks
and Romans. The Vikings and Plains Indians were not.[8]

Outside of the most isolated regions of the Amazon Basin and New
Guinea, warrior societies no longer exist, although some of their characteristics are found in the kinds of gangs that thrive in various inner-city
and subaltern settings.[9] Even fifth-century Greece, where warfare was
frequent and the principal means of obtaining honor, had moved considerably beyond the world described by Homer. As we shall see, individual
pursuit of honor was partly incorporated and sublimated into the city
state's striving for honor and standing. Within the polis, especially in
Athens, other forms of standing and honor emerged, among them public
speaking and private expenditure for the benefit of the city. Appetite was
also a powerful motive, and one that gradually gained more acceptance.
Europe from the Middle Ages to the French Revolution deviates further
from the Homeric model. Europe of the nineteenth and twentieth centuries is even further removed, although the spirit was still influential, if
generally unacknowledged.

The *Iliad* is the prototype for other European honor worlds, and an
essential starting point for analysis. Comparing real honor worlds to this
ideal-type warrior society will help us better understand these societies
and how some of them developed into something more diverse and complex. All societies retain some traditional practices, even when the values
that initially sustained them have disappeared. In modern societies, it is
not difficult to identify practices, or variants of them, that originated in
warrior societies and still influence status hierarchies and the conduct

---

[7] Finley, *World of Odysseus*, p. 113; Taplin, *Homeric Soundings*, pp. 7, 50.
[8] Byock, *Medieval Iceland*, pp. 103–36, and *Viking Age Iceland*, pp. 134–7.
[9] White, *Street Corner Society*; Cohen, *Delinquent Boys*, for the honor aspects of gang culture.

of politics, diplomacy and war. Understanding how the spirit is encouraged and channeled in warrior societies makes it easier for us to identify its manifestations in other kinds of honor societies and in more mixed societies, and in those like ours that are assumed to be dominated by appetite.

Outline of a paradigm

The most useful starting point for any discussion of recognition, standing and honor is Plato's *Republic* because it offers the first explicit account of the spirit. Plato has Socrates describe the appetite (*to epithumētikon*) as encompassing all primitive biological urges (e.g. hunger, thirst, sex and aversion to pain) and their more sophisticated expressions. Socrates divides appetites into those that are necessary (e.g. food and water) and unnecessary (e.g. relishes and fancy garments). We are unable to deny the former and benefit from their satisfaction. The latter we can avoid with proper training and discipline. Socrates uses the example of thirst, which he describes as a desire for a drink qua drink, to argue that appetites are a distinct set of desires and not a means to other ends.[10]

Socrates infers that there are desires beyond the appetites because someone can be thirsty but abstain from drink. The principal alternative source of desire is the spirit (*to thumoeides*), a word derived from the *thumos*, the organ that supposedly roused Homeric heroes to action.[11] Socrates attributes all kinds of vigorous and competitive behavior to the spirit. It makes us admire and emulate the skills, character and positions of people considered praiseworthy by society. By equaling or surpassing their accomplishments, we gain the respect of others and buttress our self-esteem. The spirit is honor-loving and victory-loving. It responds with anger to any impediment to self-assertion in private or civic life. It desires to avenge all sleights of honor or standing to ourselves and our friends. It demands immediate action, which can result in ill-considered behavior, but can be advantageous in circumstances where rapid responses are necessary.[12]

The spirit requires conceptions of justice, esteem and shame. Indeed, our very sense of self depends on them. Justice and shame are acquired through imitation and education – what we today, call socialization – and

---

[10] Plato, *Republic*, 439b3–5, c2–3, 553c4–7, 558d11–e3, 559a3–6 and 580d11–581a7.
[11] Homer, *Iliad*, 9.561, 18.109.
[12] Plato's conceptions of the spirit are developed in books V, VIII and IX of the *Republic*.

tend to be common to a family, peer group, and sometimes the wider society. Plato has Socrates distinguish the spirit from appetite and reason. His defining example is Leontius, who experiences pleasure from looking at corpses, but is angry at himself for indulging this shameful appetite. The spirit can also come into conflict with reason. When Odysseus returns home in disguise, he is enraged to discover that some of Penelope's maids have become willing bedmates of her suitors. He suppresses his anger because it would reveal his identity and interfere with his plans to address the more serious threat posed by the numerous and well-armed suitors.[13]

Reason (*to logistikon*) is the third drive of the psyche. It has the capability to distinguish good from bad, in contrast to appetite and spirit which can only engage in instrumental reasoning. For Socrates, reason has desires of its own, the most important being discovery of the purposes of life and the means of fulfilling them. It possesses a corresponding drive to rule. Reason wants to discipline and train the appetite and the spirit to do what will promote individual happiness (*eudaimonia*) and well-being.[14]

Plato conceives of the psyche's components as quasi-independent agents. He has Socrates compare the appetitive part to a many-headed beast, the spirited part to a lion and the rational part to a human being. Reason knows what is best for the psyche as a whole but must persuade the appetite and spirit that it is in their interests to accept its leadership. In healthy individuals, the appetite and spirit come to accept the rule of reason. Socrates acknowledges that few people attain this state of mastery, but insists that the closer they come, the happier they are.[15] Justice is analogous to mental health because it trains and constrains the appetite and spirit in a manner best suited to human nature. It leads people into close relationships with others and teaches them respect for their fellow citizens and other Greeks. There is no conflict between justice and *enlightened* self-interest because the former is essential for the latter. It follows that justice ought to take precedence over other goals.[16] One of the principal purposes of the *Republic* is to demonstrate that the happy life is also the just life and that self-restraint and respect for others, rather than depriving one of pleasures, make those we have more enjoyable and satisfying.

[13] Homer, *Iliad*, 20.1–37; Plato, *Republic*, 439e1–440b.
[14] Plato, *Republic*, 441c1–2, 441e4, 442c5–6, 580d7–8, 8505d11–e1.
[15] Ibid., 441d12–442b4, c6–8, 443c9–444a3, 472b7–d2, 580c1–4, 588c7–d5.
[16] Ibid., 430e6–431a2, 441d12–e2, 444e7–445a4.

For Aristotle, the principal division in the human psyche is between the desires (*epithumiai*) and reason, or "the calculating part" (*to logistikon*). Aristotle describes two kinds of desires. The first, which arises from "necessary" sources of pleasure (*epithumia*) – eating, drinking, sex and, more generally, touch and taste – is equivalent to Plato's appetite. The second is passion (*pathē*), which encompasses Plato's spirit because it generates desires for wealth, honor or victory. People whose appetites are unrestrained by reason succumb to passions and act against their better judgment, often in ways that are destructive to themselves and those around them. A product of an honor culture, Aristotle contends that giving in to the spirit (*thumos*) is less reprehensible and less damaging than overindulging appetites.[17]

Aristotle's understanding of the spirit is somewhat more elaborate than Plato's. He describes it as an impulsive desire, and a source of both courage and anger.[18] The spirit strives for honor through victory in competition, which is pleasing because it produces an image of superiority which all human beings desire. It also makes people see themselves as good characters, especially when they are honored as such by others whom they respect.[19] For the same reason, people are sensitive to anything that threatens their sense of individual worth, and grow angry in response to what they perceive as attempts to disparage them publicly, especially from people whom they regard as their inferiors.[20] Honor is "the token of a man's being famous for doing good." It is recognized through sacrifices, commemoration in verse, prose or statues, privileges, grants of land, front seats at civic celebrations, state burial, public grants and precedence at home and abroad.[21]

Aristotle follows Plato in his belief that "all men by nature desire to know." He distinguishes theoretical from practical reasoning. The former is conceptual knowledge (*epistēmē*) about the fundamental nature of things.[22] Practical wisdom (*phronēsis*) is deliberative but directed toward action. It leads to knowledge about what is worthwhile in life, and seeks to educate the desires to act in accord with these goals. *Phronēsis* is the product of an arduous educational process that must begin in childhood and gradually allows reason to shape the psyche by weeding out

---

[17] Aristotle, *Nicomachean Ethics*, 1098a4, 1102b13–31, 1147b25–8 and b31–5, 1148a8–9, 1247b18–19, 1378a20–2, and *Rhetoric*, 1369b16–19, 1370a18–1370b4.

[18] Aristotle, *Nicomachean Ethics*, 5.10, 1135b25–9, 1149a21–b23.

[19] Aristotle, *Rhetoric*, 1370b32, 1371a8–18.   [20] Ibid., 1379a30–b37.

[21] Ibid., 1361a28–b1.   [22] Aristotle, *Posterior Analytics*, I.2, *Physics*, 2.3,194b23–35.

some pleasures, and reshaping others, all the while encouraging a taste for more complex ones. If successful, reason promotes a life of "moral virtue" (*ēthikē aretē*).[23]

The good life consists of enjoying pleasures in a refined way. It also requires public service, which allows pursuit of the noble. Successful public service demands character traits that have been shaped by training, experience and reason. They enable us to make good judgments, build stable, trust-based relationships and gain the admiration of other virtuous people. Public service requires a high degree of maturity and self-discipline. We need to overcome the temptation to seek self-esteem and respect on improper grounds – notably, military prowess or wealth – because they come to us through good fortune, not through the exercise of our moral qualities.[24]

Plato and Aristotle understand self-esteem as a powerful and universal drive, although its expression is culturally determined because esteem depends on conceptions of shame and justice, which vary across cultures and epochs. I follow Plato and Aristotle in assuming that people everywhere crave recognition for some kind quality or achievement, and feel better about themselves when they receive it. And all the more so when they gain the approbation of those whom they admire or who occupy positions of high status within their society. As Plato's example of Leontius indicates, people are usually willing to make sacrifices to maintain or achieve honor and standing. This usually requires tradeoffs between honor and appetite, but in warrior societies it can entail one between honor and life.

Two caveats are in order. The first pertains to the cultural framework in which the spirit finds expression, a particularly relevant consideration for a study whose cases span several continents and 2,500 years. We must identify the diverse ways in which the spirit is encouraged, the varied expressions in which it is challenged and the different ways it can be stymied and arouse anger and desires for revenge. We must be sensitive to the links between individual self-esteem and the honor or standing of the collectivities with which people identify. This too varies across cultures. Finally, we must recognize that the language that we use to describe the spirit and its behavioral manifestations is culturally embedded. The societies in question sometimes embed the spirit in a different discourse, or

---

[23] Aristotle, *Nicomachean Ethics*, 1099a4–5, 1103a2, 1139a29–30, 1139a29–30, 1140a25–8.
[24] Aristotle, *Eudaimonian Ethics*, 1215a25–16a10, *Politics*, books 5 and 8.

do not describe or theorize about it at all. These discourses – or lack of them – in turn have important behavioral ramifications.

Since Darwin, modern conceptions of neurophysiology have attempted to explain emotions as states triggered by biochemical reactions in response to external stimuli and thus universal in nature.[25] David Konstan ably demonstrates that emotions, like understandings of colors, are mediated by culture. The Greek lexicon of the emotions is not the same as ours, and Greek terms for seemingly shared emotions do not necessarily coincide with ours. This is most evident with respect to love, friendship and anger.[26] For our purposes it is important to recognize that Greek conceptions of honor and shame differ in many ways from their nineteenth-century Southern United States and contemporary Mediterranean and Middle Eastern counterparts.[27] For both, however, shame is a pain or disturbance concerning bad things that appear to lead to loss of reputation.[28] Greeks and moderns differ in the greater diversity among moderns in their naming and describing of emotions.[29] There are even greater differences between contemporary Western and non-Western understandings of emotions. The Japanese word for self-esteem – *serufu esutimu* – comes from English as there is no indigenous term that captures the concept of feeling good about oneself.[30]

Unlike modern Europeans, the Greeks did not conceive of emotions as internal states of agitation. They understood them to be mediated, actually aroused, by the interpretations we place on the words, deeds and intentions of others. Thucydides and the playwrights recognized that emotions can be made self-validating when action based on them provokes the expected behavior.[31] Aristotle considers emotions to be the result of reasoning and malleable because they can be altered by changing

---

[25] Konstan, *Emotions of the Ancient Greeks*, ch. 1, for a critical discussion of this approach.

[26] Konstan, "*Philia* in Euripides' *Electra*," *Friendship in the Classical World*, *Pity Transformed*, and *Emotions of the Ancient Greeks*; Konstan and Rutter, *Envy, Spite and Jealousy*.

[27] Cicero, *On Duties*, I, §15, 7 and 153, 9. Southern honor has been extensively studied. See, for example, Greenberg, *Honor and Slavery*, chs. 1–2; Franklin, *The Militant South, 1800–1861*, chs. 3–4; Wyatt-Brown, *Southern Honor*, ch. 4; Ayers, *Vengeance and Justice*.

[28] Aristotle, *Rhetoric*, 1383b12–15; Konstan, *Emotions of the Ancient Greeks*, pp. 91–110.

[29] See, for example, Smith, *Theory of Moral Sentiments*, II.ii–iii, on hatred, indignation and contempt. Unlike Cicero, Smith recognizes that the conceptions of justice, which ultimately determine the meaning of honor, are culturally bound.

[30] Nisbett, *The Geography of Thought*, p. 54.

[31] Konstan, *Emotions of the Ancient Greeks*, pp. xii–xiii, 28, 37.

the attributions we make about others' motives.[32] In *Philoctetes*, Sophocles shows how successful persuasion can turn on the ability to reshape another actor's attributions and emotions.[33]

Emotion (*pathos*) and its plural (*pathē*) are closely related to the verb *paskhō*, meaning to suffer or experience. This verb is also the source of the words passive and passion in English. *Paskhō* in turn derives from the Indo-European stem *pa-*, to suffer.[34] Perhaps reflecting a common Greek understanding, Aristotle describes every *pathos* as evoking pain or pleasure. For Aristotle, pain and pleasure are not emotions, but sensations (*aisthēseis*) mediated by the intellect. Anger is accompanied by both pain and pleasure; the former because a slight that arouses the anger diminishes one's dignity, and the latter from the anticipation of revenge. Aristotle defines anger as something that is "properly felt when anyone gets what is not appropriate for him, though he may be a good man enough. It may also be felt when anyone sets himself up against his superior."[35] As for revenge, he quotes Homer to the effect that "Sweeter it is by far than the honeycomb dripping with sweetness."[36] People suffer pain when they fail to get revenge.[37] Anger is not aroused by affronts from people who are more powerful than we are, because it is unlikely that we can gain revenge. We can, however, experience this pleasure vicariously when offenders receive their comeuppance.[38] This response is nicely captured by the German concept of *Schadenfreude*.

Anger is a key emotion for Aristotle because so much of Greek life revolves around public competition and confrontation. Citizens are constantly judging one another and making their opinions known.[39] Anger is equally important for my paradigm because it is aroused by slights to honor or impediments that stand in the way of the spirit achieving honor or standing, and is a powerful incentive for action. The Greeks have a narrower and more precise understanding of anger than contemporary Westerners, for whom anger can be provoked in many ways. Harm is a case in point. For the Greeks, it does not trigger anger, even when it is intentionally inflicted. Harm provokes hostility (*misein*), unless it also entails

---

[32] Aristotle, *De Anima*, 1.1403a16–b2, *Rhetoric*, book II. The latter describes various emotions and how they are a function of our understanding of others' motives, worthiness and comparative status.

[33] Lebow, "Power and Ethics."   [34] Konstan, *Emotions of the Ancient Greeks*, p. 1.

[35] Aristotle, *Rhetoric*, 1387a31–1380a4, *Nicomachean Ethics*, 1117a6–15; Konstan, *The Emotions of the Ancient Greeks*, pp. 41–76.

[36] Aristotle *Rhetoric*, 1370b11–12; Homer, *Iliad*, 18.109.

[37] Aristotle, *Rhetoric*, 1370b30–2.   [38] Ibid., 1379b17–19.

[39] Konstan, *The Emotions of the Ancient Greeks*, p. 45.

a slight. Anger is a luxury for Greeks because only people who have the power to seek revenge can allow themselves to experience this emotion. This generally excluded slaves, women, the poor, and weak city states. For Aristotle, it can only be directed at individuals – unlike hatred, which can be felt towards entire peoples – and only toward individuals who can feel your anger.[40] Reflecting a widely shared understanding, Aristotle considers someone who is in a position to avenge a slight and fails to do so servile and contemptible, and unworthy of being Greek.[41] Classical Greeks nevertheless recognized that anger not infrequently provokes ill-considered actions that have serious adverse practical consequences. Thucydides tells us how Athenians voted out of anger (*hupo orgēs*) to kill all Mytilenean males as punishment for their unsuccessful rebellion.[42] Diodotus convinces the assembly to reverse its decision, and in Thucydides' account does so on the grounds that it is not in the Athenian interest.[43]

Where does this leave us? Although our understandings of fear, envy, shame, anger and hatred are different from the Greeks', we see ample evidence of the kind of emotions Aristotle describes and that motivate Greek tragedies. In children, denial of sweets, toys and the like often leads to rage, and one sign of maturity is the suppression of such anger and general mastery over the appetites. The spirit and the sense of self-esteem it can build are also innate but require a social context to find full expression. The spirit is shaped in the course of socialization and responds the same way the appetite does when frustrated. Road rage offers a nice example. It is triggered by the belief that someone who has just cut you off has intentionally insulted you or shown you disrespect. Mature people learn not to treat all behavior of this kind as challenges, nor to respond to challenges they cannot win or involve more risk or cost than victory is worth, and to think carefully before acting in instances where they feel compelled to respond. Challenges to our self-esteem threaten our identities and sense of self-worth, and the fury they arouse is generally more difficult to suppress than that arising from denials of appetite. Thucydides makes it apparent that challenges to self-esteem and collective identities, not to security, were the underlying cause of the Peloponnesian War.[44] Following Thucydides, I try to demonstrate that affronts to honor, and thus to self-esteem, have been at least as great a source of war as threats to material well-being or security.

---

[40] Aristotle, *Rhetoric*, 387a31–3, 138024–9, 1382a2–14.
[41] Ibid., 1370b13–14; Konstan, *The Emotions of the Ancient Greeks*, pp. 46, 58.
[42] Thucydides, 3.36.2.   [43] Ibid., 3.42.1.
[44] Lebow, *Tragic Vision of Politics*, ch. 3, for this argument.

A second caveat concerns the Greek understanding of the psyche with its three fundamental and different impulses. Modern authorities have offered different descriptions of the psyche and human needs. I noted Freud's conception of the psyche in the introduction and how it reduces all fundamental drives to appetite (primarily sexual) and reason to an instrumentality. Another prominent formulation is Abraham Maslow's hierarchy of needs, developed from his study of great people and what accounted for their accomplishments.[45] On several occasions when I gave talks about the psychological foundations of my theory, colleagues from psychology and political science asked why I did not base it on Maslow instead of the Greeks. Maslow, to his credit, captures some of the qualities of the spirit under his category of "ego needs," which describes the need for self-respect and respect from others. Unlike Plato and Aristotle, he does not analyze any of its behavioral attributes or the consequences of ego frustration, which are essential for any analysis of political behavior. More troubling from my perspective is the hierarchical nature of Maslow's scheme, with self-actualization at the apex.

Self-actualization is a Western concept associated with the Romantic movement of the late eighteenth and early nineteenth centuries. It would have provoked a quizzical response from earlier Europeans, as it does today from many non-Westerners. Some Western psychologists, moreover, believe the emphasis on self-actualization in American education and health care to be overblown and counterproductive.[46] Maslow has taken a purely local understanding of human excellence and transformed it without justification into a universal one. His description of the so-called "B-values" associated with self-actualization – truth, goodness, beauty, unity, transcendence, aliveness, uniqueness, perfection, justice, order and simplicity – are more virtues than values, making the concept of self-actualization fuzzy and all but impossible to operationalize even within the confines of a single culture.[47] Empirically, Maslow is also on shaky ground as more recent biographers of at least some of the figures

---

[45] Maslow, *Motivation and Personality*, and *Toward a Psychology of Being*.

[46] Baumeister, Campbell, Krueger and Vohs, "Does High Self-Esteem Cause Better Performance, Interpersonal Success, Happiness, or Healthier Lifestyles?," and "Exploding the Self-Esteem Myth"; Lerner, "Self-Esteem and Excellence." Mruk, *Self-Esteem Research, Theory, and Practice*; Mecca et al., *The Social Importance of Self-Esteem*, for a more positive view.

[47] Mruk, *Self-Esteem Research, Theory, and Practice*, p. 34, noting that, like all other key concepts, it is "always connected to many other self-related phenomena and processes, from consciousness to identity."

whom Maslow associates with these values or virtues (e.g. Jefferson, Schweitzer, Huxley) draw very different and far less idealized portraits of them.[48]

Although the spirit all but dropped out of the political and philosophical discourse during the Enlightenment, self-esteem has been rediscovered by modern social science, especially psychology.[49] Inspired by the pioneering work of Fritz Heider, psychologists have framed the concept very differently than did Plato and Aristotle.[50] Another important line of research that relates to the spirit is the work of Henri Tajfel and his successors on collective identity. Tajfel emphasizes the social construction of identity and defines collective identity as "that part of an individual's self-concept which derives from his knowledge of his membership in a social group."[51] Tajfel and his co-researchers contend that social identities buffer anxiety and build self-esteem by allowing individuals to bask in the reflected glory of a group's achievements. In-group identification leads to a bias in favor of those who are part of the in-group and can lead to prejudice against those who are not, providing a psychological explanation for the tendency, noted in the introduction, of people to invoke binaries of "us" and "others." There is evidence that people will allocate resources differentially across groups in response to this bias even when it is disadvantageous to themselves.[52]

Social identity theory suggests that people join and maintain groups for varied and multiple reasons.[53] The evidence for self-esteem as a motive nevertheless remains strong. Research indicates that members of low-status groups usually define their choices as collective action to improve

---

[48] For example, Randall, *Thomas Jefferson*; Hitchens, *Thomas Jefferson*.

[49] Turner, *Status*; Berger and Zelditch, *Status, Power, and Legitimacy*; Rosen, *War and Human Nature*; Frank, *Choosing the Right Pond*; Thaler, *The Winner's Curse*, all suggest that status hierarchies are a universal aspect of social life.

[50] Rubin and Hewstone, "Social Identity Theory's Self-Esteem Hypothesis," for a critical review.

[51] Tajfel, *Differentiation between Social Groups*, p. 63.

[52] Tajfel, *Human Groups and Social Categories*; Tajfel *et al.*, "Social Categorization and Intergroup Behavior"; Tajfel and Turner, "The Social Identity Theory of Intergroup Behavior"; Turner, Brown and Tajfel, "Social Comparison and Group Interest in Intergroup Favoritism"; Turner, Oakes, Reicher and Wetherell, *Rediscovering the Social Group*; Turner, Oakes, Haslam and McGarty, "Self and Collective."

[53] Tajfel, *Human Groups and Social Categories*; Tajfel and Turner, "The Social Identity Theory of Intergroup Behavior"; Rubin and Hewstone, "Social Identity Theory's Self-Esteem Hypothesis"; Abrams and Hogg, "Comments on the Motivational Status of Self-Esteem in Social Identity and Intergroup Discrimination," and *Social Identity Theory*; Brown, "Social Identity Theory"; Huddie, "From Social to Political Identity."

the standing of their group or defection to a group with higher standing.[54] Studies using sports teams as the foci find that people tend to identify with highly ranked teams and disassociate themselves from teams that decline in the rankings.[55] Cross-cultural research supports the finding that people prefer to identify with high-status groups, and that the pattern of group identification (social versus political) varies across countries.[56] Group and contextual variables, of course, complicate the relationship between self-esteem and group identification, making the choice of identity maintenance strategies very sensitive to context.[57] There is evidence that these preferences are also displayed by state actors.[58]

Collective identities allow individuals to overcome some of the limitations of self-hood and its finitude. They require groups with a real existence, and D. T. Campbell coined the term "entitativity" to describe this quality.[59] In the 1990s, social psychologists were drawn to entitativity as a means of studying prejudice.[60] Recent research shows that entitativity leads to heightened perceptions of agency, security and standing, all of which encourage group affiliation and maintenance of group boundaries.[61] This research has important implications for international relations. Castano, Yzerbyt and Bourguignon found that identification with the European Union increased among EU citizens when perception of its

---

[54] Elmers, "Individual Upward Mobility and the Perceived Legitimacy of Intergroup Relations"; Abrams and Hogg, "Social Identification, Social Categorization and Social Influence."

[55] Dechesne, Greenberg, Arndt and Schimel, "Terror Management and Sports Fan Affiliation."

[56] Taylor, "Multiple Group Membership and Self-Identity"; Freeman, *Liking Self and Social Structure*; Oldmeadow and Fiske, "System-Justifying Ideologies Moderate Status = Competence Stereotypes."

[57] Tajfel, "Social Categorisation, Social Identity and Social Comparison"; Kruglanski, *Lay Epistemics and Human Knowledge*; Kruglanski, "Motivated Social Cognition: Principles of the Interface"; Shah *et al.*, "Membership Has its (Epistemic) Rewards"; Dechesne, Janssen and van Knippenberg, "Derogation and Distancing as Terror Management Strategies"; Brown, "Social Identity Theory"; Huddie, "From Social to Political Identity."

[58] For example, Johnston, "Treating International Institutions as Social Environments"; Flockhart, "Complex Socialization"; Zhiumin, "Nationalism, Internationalism and Chinese Foreign Policy"; Narilkar, "Peculiar Chauvinism or Strategic Calculation?"; Suzuki, "China's Quest for Great Power Status."

[59] Campbell, "Common Fate, Similarity, and Other Indices of the Status of Aggregates of Person as Social Entities."

[60] Yzerbyt *et al.*, *The Psychology of Group Perception,* for a recent review of the relevant literature.

[61] Sacchi and Castano, "Entitative is Beautiful"; Castano, Yzerbyt and Bourguignon, "We Are One and I Like It."

entitativity was heightened and declined when it was lessened.[62] Castano and Dechesne argue that individuals have a strong incentive to see their in-groups as more entitative when they perceive their sense of continuity as human being as being at risk.[63]

The self-esteem and the social identity explanations of group existence and solidarity might be subsumed within a larger research program known as Terror Management Theory (TMT). Pioneered by Greenberg, Pyszczynski and Solomon, it seeks to develop and test a general theory of human behavior based on the existential dilemma posed by mortality. It assumes that the inevitability of death would give rise to paralyzing terror in the absence of psychological mechanisms to cope with it. The most prominent of these mechanisms is a cultural system of meaning, or world view, that imposes meaning, order, stability and continuity on life. It confers symbolic immortality on those who perform well the social roles derived from this world view, or live up to its behavioral standards. The second mechanism is self-esteem, also derived from performing roles well and acting consistently with the expectations of a shared world view. It has been described as a stimulus for our species to develop and sustain complex social orders and to improve the quality of life through a range of social and scientific innovations.[64]

Terror Management Theory has stimulated considerable research, much of it lending support to the claim that culture is an important buffer for anxiety associated with death.[65] Taubman, Ben-Ari, Florian and Mikulincer carried out two interesting experiments in which they examined the relationship between self-esteem and risky driving. Participants whose self-esteem was not enhanced by reckless driving expressed lower intention to drive recklessly after being reminded about death than participants for whom self-esteem and reckless driving were linked. Participants who admitted that reckless driving buttressed their self-esteem also drove

[62] Castano, Yzerbyt and Bourguignon, "We Are One and I Like It."
[63] Castano, Yzerbyt, Paladino and Sacchi, "Transcending Oneself through Social Identification"; Castano and Dechesne, "On Defeating Death."
[64] This last point is made by Castano and Dechesne, "On Defeating Death." For a general review, Solomon, Greenberg and Pyszczynski, "The Cultural Animal."
[65] Rosenblatt, Greenberg, Solomon, Pyszczynski and Lyon, "Evidence for Terror Management Theory I"; Greenberg, Pyszczynski, Solomom et al., "Evidence for Terror Management II"; Greenberg, Pyszcynski, Solomon, Simon and Breus, "Role of Consciousness and Accessibility of Death-Related Thoughts in Mortality Salience Effects"; Greenberg, Simon, Pyszcynski, Solomon and Chatel, "Terror Management and Tolerance"; Greenberg, Porteus, Simon, Pyszcynski and Solomon, "Evidence of a Terror Management Function of Cultural Icons."

more recklessly in a simulator.[66] A related experiment showed that people who derive self-esteem from sex rated it more appealing still after being primed about death.[67] Mortality salience is also known to increase in-group bias, another finding with obvious political implications.[68] Castano, Yzerbyt, Paladino and Sacchi found that Italians primed by thoughts of mortality identified more strongly with their nation than did fellow citizens in the control condition. Their judgments of Germans was unaffected.[69] When subjects are primed with thoughts about mortality, they are likely to predict that their favored team will score a higher number of goals in its next match.[70]

The spirit also draws empirical support from research on self- and other-reactive emotions. Fritz Heider's "balance theory" implies that the success of others is a psychological resource that we can exploit to buttress our self-esteem. The Self-Evaluation Maintenance (SEM) model builds on the insight that someone else's performance relative to one's own can be consequential for self-evaluation. It hypothesizes that reflected glory in another's outstanding performance can enhance self-esteem, but only when the domain in which they perform is of low relevance to the actor. Comparison to someone else's superior performance in an area of high relevance is likely to generate negative affect and lower self-esteem.[71] In modern societies there are many routes to standing, and the SEM model reasonably suggests that we are most likely to resent those who do better than us in those competitive realms in which we try to excel because they are important to our sense of self-worth.[72]

The psychological research of the last three decades has not in any way been influenced by the writings of Plato and Aristotle. There are nevertheless striking parallels between the ancient Greek understanding of the psyche and research associated with the TMT and SEM research programs. The core assumption of TMT is that people fear death because

---

[66] Taubman *et al.*, "The Impact of Mortality Salience on Reckless Driving."

[67] Goldenberg *et al.*, "The Body as a Source of Self-Esteem."

[68] Harmon-Jones, Greenberg, Solomon and Simon, "The Effects of Mortality Salience on Intergroup Bias Between Minimal Groups"; Gaertner and Schopler, "Perceived Ingroup Entitativity and Intergroup Bias."

[69] Castano, Yzerbyt, Paladino and Sacchi, "Transcending Oneself through Social Identification."

[70] Dechesne, Greenberg, Arndt and Schimel, "Terror Management and Sports Fan Affiliation."

[71] Tesser and Collins, "Emotion in Social Reflection and Comparison Situations"; Smith, "Assimilative and Contrastive Emotional Reactions to Upward and Downward Social Comparison."

[72] Kristjánsson, "Justice and Desert-Based Emotions," for a critique.

it disrupts continuity. They seek to overcome the acute anxiety mortality would otherwise arouse through comprehensive world views and self-esteem. The former provides order, continuity and meaning to their lives, and with them a sense or feeling of permanence. The latter provides figurative immortality, and is achieved by living up to the behavioral standards associated with the world view. Individuals attempt to transcend mortality by membership and contribution to groups that endure beyond their lifetimes.

Plato and Aristotle also posit the drive for self-esteem as innate and universal. Unlike TMT, they offer no explanation for why human beings so desperately seek self-esteem. They nevertheless make an implicit connection between self-esteem and death, as they recognize that for Greeks the most satisfying traditional means of achieving self-esteem is through deeds that bring enduring, if not immortal, fame. They offer a richer and more nuanced formulation of self-esteem, which stresses its competitive and social aspects, and emphasizes the extent to which honor and standing are relational qualities. This makes them difficult to achieve and maintain, and this is why threats to self-esteem or one's ability to achieve it provoke anger, if not rage. Plato and Aristotle are interested in the social and political consequences of the spirit, which are only hinted at by psychologists working in the TMT program. In contrast to TMT, which frames the problem of mortality and the mechanisms for coping with it as entirely cognitive, Plato and Aristotle envisage self-esteem as cognitive and affective. It has an important cognitive component because it is more socially dependent than appetite. It requires conceptualization, observation, imitation and reflection. However, self-esteem is a psychological state; we feel good or bad about ourselves, and these feelings generate other emotions such as pleasure, anger and envy.

Plato and Aristotle also have a different understanding of the social. The TMT program, and social psychologists more generally, take the individual as their unit and retain the essentialist character of the individual regardless of the extent to which people interact with or associate with collectivities. Group membership benefits individuals but does not change them ontologically. For the Greeks, involvement in families, friendships, fraternal associations and cities is transformative. Positive relationships with other human beings stretch our identities, together with our conceptions of ourselves and our self-interest. More significantly, relationships provide rewards not available to autonomous individuals, allowing people to realize their full potential as human beings. This is why Aristotle insists that the good life is only possible in the polis. For Plato and Aristotle, relationships allow individuals to overcome their inherent limitations by extending themselves in space as well as in time.

The Greek understanding that competition evokes elation, satisfaction and anger, and builds or weakens self-esteem, provides a link with the SEM research program. Plato and Aristotle provide a conceptual framework that accounts for divergent responses to competition, something currently lacking in the SEM program. TMT and SEM researchers could profit from a careful reading of the relevant Greek philosophers and playwrights.

There are also unexplored connections between the TMT and ontological security research programs. Giddens's variant of ontological security assumes that people require confidence in their understandings of the physical and social world and the patterns of responses they sustain. The largely routinized nature of social intercourse helps us to structure our identities and enhances our capacity for agency and accordingly becomes a major component of our security system. As we have seen, the concept of ontological security has been applied to states. Researchers attribute concepts of self to states which are embedded in biographical narratives and sustained through foreign policy routines. Leaders can feel pressure to act in accord with these narratives and can feel compelled to risk war to build or defend state identities. Terror Management Theory provides a more profound explanation for the importance of biographical narratives and behavior consistent with them. Such narratives not only prevent disorder, but build self-esteem and encourage the illusion of immortality by enhancing continuity, provided the groups, organizations or states in question and the ideals they represent are perceived as enduring.

I neither assess the relative merits of these research programs nor use them to build my theory. It is derived largely from the ancient Greeks and supplemented with insights from modern philosophers and social scientists. I have discussed these research programs to show that some of the most important insights of Greek philosophy and literature find resonance, even empirical support, in contemporary research. My theory and cases are relevant to these programs in a double sense. They can enrich our understanding of self-esteem and the strategies by which it is achieved, embed them in a more comprehensive understanding of human needs, and root that conception in a larger and ever-changing cultural and historical setting. By revealing the important links among partially parallel research programs in sociology, international relations and psychology, they highlight the need for greater exchange across disciplines. They also demonstrate the need to go outside of social science to literature, philosophy and the arts for ideas, insights and defining examples.

In this sense too, this book continues the project I began in *The Tragic Vision of Politics*.

The world of Achilles

Troy was a Bronze Age city for over two thousand years, from about 3000 to 950 BCE. It is in the Troad, that part of western Anatolia bounded by the Dardanelles in the north and the Gulf of Edremit in the south. The ruins of what we think of as Troy consist of dozens of layers of settlement, sometimes sharply divided, covering about 75 acres. The city is built around a natural rock citadel that overlooks a fertile plain and the sea, and its Bronze Age economy depended on local agriculture, horse-breeding and trade. Its location made it a convenient stopping point for ships transiting the Dardanelles, plying between Europe and Asia, as part of a long-distance trading network. Trojans spoke a language akin to Hittite and were culturally distinct from the Greeks.[73] The Trojan War – if it actually occurred – took place before the so-called Greek dark age (ca. 1150–750 BCE), sometime between 1230 and 1180. In about 1180, Troy was consumed by fire, and discoveries of arrowheads, spear points, sling stones and unburied human bones all point to a sack.[74]

There is a general consensus that the *Iliad* was composed, or at least put into its final form, sometime between 800 and 650 BCE. The epic offers us an ideal-type description of a warrior-based honor society. It illustrates the dominant values, behavior and inner tensions of such a world. The Greeks, whom Homer refers to as Achaeans, Danaans or Argives, have been fighting on the plain before the walls of Troy (*Ilios*) for ten years. They will ultimately triumph and destroy the city and its inhabitants. Homer tells us nothing about the outcome of the war in the *Iliad*, and confines his tale to a mere fourteen days, with most of the action taking place over the course of three days.[75]

According to Greek myth, the Trojan War is the direct result of Paris' seduction of Helen, wife of the Greek King Menelaus, and their elopement to Troy. It is a violation of her husband Menelaus' honor and of guest friendship (*xenia*), a convention common to most traditional societies.[76] In Greece, the obligation to receive guests was considered so important that hospitality was made one of the epithets of the father of the gods:

---

[73] Latacz, *Troy and Homer.*   [74] Strauss, *Trojan War*, p. 10.
[75] Taplin, *Homeric Soundings*, pp. 14–22.
[76] Kant, *Perpetual Peace*, pp. 105–8, thought that *xenia* was probably the one universal form of conduct.

Zeus Xenios.[77] In return, the guest must not abuse his host's hospitality or overstay his welcome. Menelaus defends his honor by attempting to punish Paris and regain Helen. He is also defending his position, as he would be regarded as weak by rivals and neighbors if he failed to act. He asks Zeus to grant him revenge "so that any man born hereafter may shrink from wronging a host who has shown him friendship."[78] Honor requires Greeks connected to him by ties of obligation, family or guest friendship to come to his aid.[79] On the Trojan side, honor and guest friendship compel King Priam to offer refuge to his son Paris and the woman he has abducted even though he and most Trojans thoroughly disapprove of the pair.

Much of the *Iliad* focuses on the conflict between Achilles and Agamemnon, which is also driven by honor. In an act of moral blindness (*atē*), Agamemnon takes a slave girl from Achilles to replace the one he must return to her father. Achilles is furious, withdraws from the struggle, refuses gifts subsequently offered him by Agamemnon, and only returns to the fighting to avenge the death of his beloved Patroclus. Homer ends his tale while the war is still raging, but his listeners know that Troy will be captured and its inhabitants slaughtered or enslaved, though not before Achilles and many other Greek heroes die. Menelaus will bring Helen home but his brother Agamemnon will be murdered by his unfaithful wife Clytemnestra, who has never forgiven him the sacrifice of their daughter.

In honor-driven societies, honor is so highly valued that one's survival and that of one's family become secondary considerations. In Aeschylus' *Oresteia*, Agamemnon sacrifices his daughter Iphigenia at Aulus to gain a fair wind to carry the Greek fleet to Troy. In the *Iliad*, Achilles opts for immortal fame over a homecoming and long life, knowing full well that participation in the war will bring his own death.[80] King Priam provides sanctuary for his son Paris (Alexandros) and Helen, although he recognizes that it could lead to the destruction of Troy.[81] His son Hector, makes a similar choice when he seeks battle with Achilles, knowing that his death will hasten the fall of Troy, the enslavement of his wife and the death of their young son.[82]

---

[77] Finley, *The World of Odysseus*, pp. 99–101 on guest friendship in the Homeric world.
[78] Homer, *Iliad*, 3.351–4. All quotes from the Fagles translation.
[79] Seaford, *Reciprocity and Ritual*, pp. 13–25, on gift exchange in the *Iliad*; Taplin, *Homeric Soundings*, pp. 56–8, on the problematic nature of these obligations.
[80] Homer, *Iliad*, 9.413, 497–505.   [81] Ibid., 2.189.
[82] Taplin, *Homeric Soundings*, p. 125, argues that Hector must win *kleos* while he can because he knows his city will be destroyed.

Emphasis of the spirit leads to a corresponding depreciation
of the appetite

Wealth is not valued for what it can buy, but for the standing it can confer. Tripods, cauldrons, bars of iron, shields, livestock, female slaves and other booty taken in raids are the mark of heroes. These possessions enable warriors to claim status and to make friends and gain influence when they give them to others as gifts. Glaucus and Diomedes exchange gold and bronze armor, Hector and Ajax end their duel by exchanging gifts, Achilles awards prizes ranging from unworked iron to talents of gold at Patroclus' funeral games, and Menelaus presents Telemachus with a silver mixing bowl.[83] Many of these items had been previously received as gifts, and their histories add value to them and create links of friendship along the chain of givers and receivers.[84] Gift-exchange represents and sustains the long-term social order, in contrast to trade which maintains it in the short term. When short-term, individual-oriented exchange supports the longer-term communal exchange, it has beneficial effects.[85] In this connection it is interesting to note that the Indo-European root for gift is *ghab(h)*, which also means to take hold or have. Habit has the same root, implying that at least for peoples who speak Indo-European languages gifts were once the basis for social relations and the *nomos* that sustained it.

In honor societies markets are considered a necessary evil, as are the people who make their livelihood in trade. In the *Iliad*, the presence of markets is acknowledged because the two armies are continually resupplied with animals and other needs, but never apparently by Greeks. No details are provided, and there is no mention of money.[86] Homer's banishment of trade to the periphery presages Marx's observation that commerce first develops on the margins of communities, where they come into contact with foreigners.[87]

There is feasting in the *Iliad*, but the diet is monotonous. Appetites are sated, not indulged. Sheep and goats are slaughtered and roasted, but

---

[83] Homer, *Iliad*, 4.589–619; 6.230–6; 7.302; 15.99–120; 23.257–897.

[84] Ibid., 4.125–9, 23.807–8, for illustrations.

[85] Parry and Bloch, *Money and the Morality of Exchange*, pp. 23–30. Seaford, *Money and the Early Greek Mind*, develops this theme, and its implications for Greek philosophy and politics.

[86] There are three instances of exchange of goods in Homer: *Iliad*, 8.506, 546; 18.291–2; *Odyssey*, 15.416, 445, 452.

[87] Marx, *Contribution to the Critique of Political Economy*, p. 50; Seaford, *Reciprocity and Ritual*, pp. 18–19, for a discussion of trade in Homer.

the finest cuts are burned as offerings to the gods. The meat is consumed with bread and simple relishes and washed down with wine mixed with water. Food and drink are distributed equitably among those present, and Homer tells us at the end of each meal or feast that every man ate until he was satisfied.[88] Homer never uses the word *nomos*, which first occurs in Hesiod, where it refers to sacrifice or the eating habits of animals. Sacrifice is, of course, a kind of gift, but not one necessarily to be returned because the giver does not have the receiver's standing.[89] By the fifth century *nomos* had become a term that encompassed laws, rules, procedures and customs, but still retained a connotation of equality in the word *isonomia* (equality of political rights). Homer uses *nemein*, and the compound *epinemein*, whenever he refers to food and drink in the active voice. As *nomos* derives from *nemein*, this usage suggests the degree to which early Greeks and Homer envisaged the system of food distribution as a core constituent of the political order.[90]

Despite the symbolic importance of food, honor societies on the whole consider appetite an addictive distraction that can weaken, if not dissolve altogether, men's commitment to risk their lives in the pursuit of honor and the safety of their community. Appetite is blamed for making men flabby, effeminate and unfit for battle. The most corrupting appetite is considered lust for women. Honor societies tend to propagate stereotypes of women as sensuous, weak-willed, seductive and addicted to luxury.[91] The beautiful, sexy and exquisitely dressed and perfumed Helen personifies these qualities and holds lovesick Paris in thrall. Her elopement causes war between two distant cities and peoples who have had no previous quarrel. Paris lets Hector and his other brothers and half-brothers bear the brunt of the fighting. He is finally goaded into a combat with Menelaus, and saved from death by Aphrodite, who wraps him in a deep mist and snatches him away from the battlefield. While Menelaus is stalking the battlefield in search of him, Paris is making love to Helen on a fancy bed in a secluded chamber inside the walls of Troy.[92]

---

[88] Homer, *Iliad*, 1.602, 4.48, 7.318–20, 9.225, 15.95, 23.24–35, 23.56, 24.69 for formulaic sentences to this effect.

[89] Gifts may be returned indirectly by the gods. Chryses prays to Apollo for help when Agamemnon will not return his daughter, and the god sends a plague on the Greek camp. He is responsive because of the many sacrifices Chryses has made to him.

[90] Seaford, *Money and the Early Greek Mind*, pp. 49–50.

[91] They are not alone in doing this; misogyny is common to Hebrew, Greek, Christian and Islamic culture.

[92] Homer, *Iliad*, 3.245–447.

The need for self-esteem is transformed into a quest for fame
and even immortality

In ancient Greece, life was short and often filled with pain and suffering. The ancient Greek religion held out no hope of an afterlife. In the *Odyssey*, Achilles confirms to Odysseus on his visit to the underworld that Hades is a place of darkness and decay.[93] Immortality can only be achieved figuratively, through heroic deeds that will carry one's name and reputation across the generations. Achilles' famous choice of a short glorious life over a long dreary one must be understood in this context.[94] By opting for glory, he assures himself eternal recognition. A Google search for Achilles gets 17,700,000 hits, and another 238,000 under his Greek name of Achilleus. Napoleon surpasses him with 26,000,000 hits, but is a much more recent figure.[95] Achilles became a role model for generations of young Greeks raised on the *Iliad* and taught to equate manhood with courage, as he was more than two millennia later for Europeans with a classical education. In the nineteenth and twentieth centuries Britain and New Zealand named warships after him. In 1939, the New Zealand *Achilles*, and its sister ship *Ajax*, played a vital and courageous role in disabling the German pocket battleship *Graf Spee* off the coast of South America.[96]

Honor worlds are extremely competitive

This is because honor is highly valued and in limited supply. Competition is accordingly intense and can readily become disruptive of the social order. It does not take long for Achilles and Agamemnon to develop strong mutual hostility. Achilles resents Agamemnon appropriating an inordinate share of the booty the Greeks took on raids when he has done the most difficult fighting. Agamemnon resents Achilles' insolence and lack of respect for his person and authority. Upon learning that he is about to be deprived of the slave girl Briseis, Achilles contemplates drawing his sword against Agamemnon, but depending on one's reading of Homer, decides against it or is restrained by Athena.[97] Briseis is not just booty; she is a *geras*,

---

[93] Homer, *Odyssey*, 11.475.
[94] Edwards, "Achilles in the Odyssey"; Nagy, *The Best of the Acheans*, p. 184; Loraux, *The Experiences of Tiresias*, pp. 63–100.
[95] Accessed on 2 May 2006. Multiple searches reveal frequent changes in the numbers, but not in the overall ranking.
[96] Waters, *"Achilles" at the River Plate*; Weinberg, *A World at Arms*, pp. 70–1.
[97] Homer, *Iliad*, 1.88–214; Williams, *Shame and Necessity*, pp. 29–30.

a gift bestowed by the community, and thus a special prize of honor.[98] The conflict is political as much as personal, because to give Briseis up is to renounce his standing in the community. Agamemnon should understand this because his loss of Helen had similar consequences for his standing, which is why the Greeks have gone to war. Agamemnon's selfishness, just like Paris' lust, threatens the system of centralized reciprocity that binds together the community of warriors. Achilles also removes himself from this system and its conflict-healing potential when he refuses the compensation and apology that Agamemnon is persuaded by other Greeks to offer him. "Hateful to me are his gifts," he sputters.[99]

In preindustrial societies, there are limited ways of gaining honor; it is most often won through prowess in hunting or battle or skill in medicine or necromancy. Women generally have to achieve status through their relationships with powerful men (fathers, brothers, husbands or lovers). Because of her faithfulness and guile, Odysseus' wife Penelope would become a role model for later Greek women. "Hero" nevertheless has no feminine gender in Homeric Greek.[100] Modern societies offer a wider range of possible routes to standing, but status can still be subject to caste or class restrictions. If so, competition for standing within particular castes or classes can be more intense than it is between them. This is arguably true in the *Iliad*, where the feuds between Achilles and Agamemnon and Achilles and Odysseus are constructed by Homer as conflicts between social equals, and accordingly have an emotional intensity absent in the wider dispute between the Greeks and Troy.[101]

Competition for honor is restricted to an elite

In Homeric Greece, as in many traditional societies, competition was open only to warriors of aristocratic background. Feelings among equals are highly ambivalent as they are characterized by in-group solidarity but also by rivalry and jealousy. Members of the elite are likely to express disdain,

---

[98] Homer, *Iliad*, 1.118–20; 9.328–36, 367–8; Taplin, *Homeric Soundings*, pp. 60–3.

[99] Homer, *Iliad*, 9.378. Seaford, *Money and the Early Greek Mind*, pp. 37, 39, notes that Achilles' rejection of Lycaon's offer of ransom, and of gifts from Hector, is a continuation of this crisis.

[100] Finley, *The World of Odysseus*, pp. 32–3. Foley, *Female Acts in Greek Tragedy*. Penelope was contrasted to powerful women in Greek tragedy such as Clytemnestra and Medea who violate norms of female behavior: they speak and act decisively, often violently, in their own interests and represent puzzling deviations from the cultural norm.

[101] Marks, "The Ongoing *Neikos*: Thersites, Odysseus and Achilleus."

contempt, hostility or pity toward others, depending on the circumstances in which they interact. In the several assemblies Greeks convene, only the high-born are invited or allowed to speak.[102] Homer does his best to make the distinction between elite warriors (*aristoi*) and the ordinary people (*dēmos*) appear a natural one. The only rank-and-file soldier he names and describes is Thersites, son of Agrius (the name implies a savage). He is lame and hollow-chested, with a pointed head shaped like a sugar loaf. He is also vulgar, with a mouth "full of obscenities [and] teeming with rant," and wants to return home, having had enough of the bloody business of war fought for the glory of kings. Thersites incurs Odysseus' wrath when he calls Agamemnon greedy and Achilles a coward. Odysseus strikes Thersites on the head with Agamemnon's royal scepter for mocking his sorrow over the death of Penthesilea. The weapon is symbolic because the scepter was a symbol of royal authority and of rightful procedure (*themis*), and was held in turn by each speaker in an assembly. Homer tells us that no one grieved when Thersites spat out teeth and fell to the ground.[103] Many honor worlds are divided into two groups: an aristocratic elite that is allowed to compete for honor, and everyone else. These others do not count, even though they perform essential roles for the society. Entry into the elite – what I term recognition – is the first and essential step into the world of standing and honor.

Honor societies generally have limited possibilities for upward mobility

The exclusiveness of honor creates two hierarchies: one separating the elite from the rest of society, and another ranking members of the elite. The initial division, especially if its two categories are impermeable, can become a major source of tension when individuals, classes or political units demand, but are denied, entry into the circle in which the pursuit of honor becomes possible. The elite is usually hereditary, and not a club to which one can apply for admission. Demands for entry into the elite usually meet strong resistance, at least initially. So do challenges to the kind of behavior that is considered honorable and the rules governing its attainment. The *Iliad* indicates that these criteria are by their nature

---

[102] Homer, *Iliad*, 2.84–94; 9.9–79; 14.109–27.
[103] Ibid., 2.212–77. In *Troilus and Cressida*, I, iii, Shakespeare refers to Thersites as "a slave whose gall coins slanders like a mint."

somewhat ambiguous and therefore open to challenge. In the *Iliad*, there are no challenges from below except from Thersites, who openly expresses resentment. The mass of ordinary soldiers and servants remain nameless and voiceless. Homer is writing for the well-off elite.

Standing is signaled and sustained by mutually understood markers

Standing may be informal and affirmed by outward signs of deference. It can be associated with titles, ranks, privileges and membership in elite bodies. In the *Iliad*, there is a formal (ascribed) hierarchy with kings at the top, followed by their sons, other aristocrats and their followers (*hetairoi*). Agamemnon is at the apex of this hierarchy on the Greek side, and Homer gives him the title *anax* – a variant of *wanax* – a Bronze Age term for a king. On several occasions Agamemnon refers to himself as "the best of the Achaeans" (*āristos Achaiōn*) or its equivalent, and is described once by Homer as the "best" (*āristos*).[104] There is also an informal (achieved) hierarchy, where standing is primarily a function of valor, but secondarily of wisdom. Old Nestor, in his day a brave warrior and champion wrestler, is now admired for his sage advice.[105] Odysseus is respected for his fighting skills and cool head. Achilles unquestionably has the highest achieved status, a position conferred on him by his peers, who show him many signs of respect, and Homer, who repeatedly refers to him as "the best of the Achaeans."[106] Achilles' conflict with Agamemnon accordingly takes on an additional and symbolic dimension because Agamemnon is attempting to usurp an honor that is rightfully Achilles'. Homer encourages us to conclude that strife is inevitable whenever there are multiple hierarchies headed by different people with at least one of them unreconciled to the status of the other. Upward (or downward) mobility within the achieved status hierarchy is possible, but only among warrior aristocrats who are allowed to compete.

The conflict between Agamemnon and Achilles indicates that *standing and honor are not always equivalent*. Agamemnon has standing – high status and office – because of his kingship, but his anger, imperiousness and selfishness imperil the Greek cause and arouse grumbling among his followers. He loses honor while Achilles gains it through valorous displays,

---

[104] Homer, *Iliad*, 1.191; 2.82, 580, 760; 5.14; 11.288. Nagy, *Best of the Achaeans*, pp. 30–1 for a discussion.
[105] Homer, *Iliad*, 2.16–18.
[106] Ibid., 1.244, 412; 16.271, 274; Nagy, *Best of the Achaeans*, pp. 26–7.

the games he holds in Patroclus' honor and his killing of the much feared Hector in one-on-one combat. Honor does not always require success. In many ways, Priam is the most honorable and sympathetic figure in the *Iliad*. He is also the biggest loser in the Trojan War; he, his sons and grandsons are killed, his city is destroyed and his wife Hecuba is carried off to Greece as a slave. He is sympathetic because he is the victim of a dilemma not of his own making, in which the choice open to him – expelling Paris and Helen, or sheltering them at the cost of war with the Greeks – forces him to choose between the good of his city and the code by which he is expected to live. He honors the same *xenia* that Paris, his son, violated, with equally tragic consequences for himself, his family and his city.

People with standing are expected to feel a strong sense of obligation toward their society and those who honor them

The elite must uphold the values and *nomoi* of the society through their everyday behavior and serve as a role model to others. Like Priam, they may have to do so at enormous personal cost, a sacrifice which only enhances their honor. Homer provides numerous examples of how this code operates in everyday practice. At the end of the Cyclops episode in the *Odyssey*, Odysseus and his followers break up into groups to hunt. They share the spoils, with each man getting ten goats, except for Odysseus, who gets eleven, including the ram that was Cyclops' favorite. He promptly gives the ram as a gift to his companions, and they roast it and feast together.[107] The leader (*basileus*) has accepted a gift and bestowed one in return, acknowledging his primacy and his charity. By contrast, the conflict between Agamemnon and Achilles is the result of Agamemnon's double violation of the norm of reciprocity. In the most insulting manner, he rejects the generous ransom that Chryses, a priest of Apollo, offers for the return of his daughter Chryseis, who had been taken by the Greeks on an earlier raid. Chryses prays to Apollo for revenge and, as noted, Apollo, in acknowledgment of his priest's service over the years, sends a plague to decimate the Greek army. The Greek seer Calchas tells Agamemnon that he must return Chryseis to end the plague, and Agamemnon agrees to do this if he is compensated with somebody else's prize. He insists on taking

---

[107] Homer, *Odyssey*, 9.549–52. For exchange in the *Iliad*, see Donlon, "Reciprocities in Homer," and "Political Reciprocity in Dark Age Greece"; Zanker, "Beyond Reciprocity"; Postlethwaite, "Akhilleus and Agamemnon"; Seaford, *Reciprocity and Ritual*, pp. 13–25.

Briseis from Achilles, even though she had been awarded to him for valor during the raid.[108] The two principal conflicts of the *Iliad* are both driven by a "crisis of reciprocity."[109]

Honor worlds require a robust society

The Greek word for fame (*kleos*) derives from the verb to hear (*kluein*). As Homer knew, fame not only requires heroic deeds, but bards to sing about them and people willing to listen and be impressed. There must be a consensus, and preferably one that transcends class distinctions, about the nature of honor, how it is won and lost and the distinctions and obligations it confers. There must be rules and procedures for awarding honor and recording and commemorating the names and deeds of those who achieve it are also essential. This requires a society with shared values, traditions and institutions. Competition for honor and standing can sustain these values and institutions and socialize others into assimilating and acting in terms of them. It nevertheless has the potential to destabilize society when it becomes so intense that actors ignore or violate the norms and procedures that govern and constrain competition.

The *Iliad* provides stunning examples of destructive and constructive behavior by Achilles in response to the death of Patroclus, who is first wounded and then run through by Hector's spear. Achilles seeks out Hector and rejects his appeal that each of them promise, if victorious, to return the other's body for a proper burial.[110] After a prolonged chase, he kills Hector, then pierces his "Achilles tendons," passes rawhide straps through them, ties him to the back of his chariot and drags him back across the battlefield to the Greek camp and twelve times around Patroclus' funeral pyre. Achilles flings Hector's body face down into the dust, subjecting him, in Homer's words, to "shameful treatment."[111] He announces to his Myrmidons and the dead Patroclus that he has fulfilled his promise to drag Hector's body before him, give it to the dogs to eat raw and slit the throats of twelve splendid Trojan children before his funeral pyre. Apollo now compares him to a lion "going his own barbaric way, giving in to his power, his brute force and wild pride, as down he swoops on the flocks of men to seize his savage feast."[112] Achilles feels no pity and has no sense of shame, and has become more animal than human.

---

[108] Homer, *Iliad*, book 1.   [109] Seaford, *Reciprocity and Ritual*, ch. 1.
[110] Homer, *Iliad*, 22.247–70.   [111] Ibid., 22.23.1–28.
[112] Ibid., 24.39–45. While he is still alive, Achilles, 22.407–9, taunts Hector with the threat that he will "hack your flesh away and eat you raw [*ōmos*]." Eating cooked meat is one

The funeral and feast that follow, both arranged by Achilles, offer a sharp contrast to his treatment of Hector. So do the games, where the Greeks compete in chariot-racing, running, boxing and dueling. Achilles wisely and calmly adjudicates disputes, awards an array of prizes and fully acts the part of a leader. In the final book of the saga, Zeus intervenes and has Hermes smuggle Priam into the Greek camp, where he pleads with Achilles for the return of his son's body. Achilles has previously been informed by his mother, the sea nymph Thetis, that his treatment of Hector has angered the gods. He honor's Priam's pleas, has Hector's body washed and wrapped in linen and treats Priam as his guest. The two men share a meal, which symbolizes an end to mourning, but also a token of their common humanity. *Nomos* is restored.

Cooperation is both more difficult and easier in honor worlds

Cooperation among individuals or political units invariably involves some degree of coordination and leadership. Actors are continually measuring themselves against others and are loath to accept subordinate status, making it difficult, at times impossible, to cooperate when it involves recognizing the authority of another and accepting the loss of autonomy this may entail. This is another reason why Achilles is so resentful of Agamemnon. Honor societies nevertheless inculcate a strong sense of obligation to leaders, kinsmen, guest friends and others to whom actors are linked through gifts or favors. In the *Iliad*, this makes it possible for Agamemnon and Priam to mobilize a wide range of relatives, friends, clients and their retainers to fight for them in a conflict in which many have no direct stake, and to remain committed to the struggle for ten years.

Warfare is frequent in honor societies, but generally limited in its ends and means, and governed by rules

Warfare between political units that are members of the same society frequently resemble duels.[113] They are arranged beforehand, fought in

---

of the things that distinguished human beings from animals for the Greeks, so here too Achilles is showing his animal nature.

[113] Clausewitz, *On War*, book 1, ch. 1, pp. 75–6, equates war to a duel in which each combatant tries through physical force to compel the other to do his will. "His *immediate* aim is to *throw* his opponent in order to make him incapable of further resistance." Countless duels make a war, but their purpose is the same. "*War is thus an act of force to compel our enemy to do our will.*"

an agreed-upon location and with the goal of establishing precedence or reestablishing honor. Honor in warrior cultures produces a class of fighters ready to serve at a moment's notice and face death unflinchingly for their homeland. Honor societies, in effect, encourage aggression and deflect it outwards. We must nevertheless avoid the inference that such societies are a rational response to anarchical international environments and the security threats they generate. In the *Iliad* and historical honor worlds, warriors frequently seek honor at the expense of their community's security and other fundamental interests.

Warfare ideally takes the form of highly stylized combat or contest (agon) between two warriors, closely governed by a series of rules, well-understood and respected by all participants, that encourage a fair fight. Single combats are widely attested to in honor societies. The Torah gives a vivid description of the contest between David and Goliath, and David's victory becomes the basis for his subsequent kingship.[114] We find numerous examples of single combats in other warrior cultures, including Republican Rome, the Aztec Empire, among the Plains Indians and in Papua New Guinea. Homer's battles are set pieces to provide descriptions of such encounters. Combatants are generally – although not always – keen to win honor by fair means. At one point, Ajax invites Hector to strike first, and Hector in turn warns Ajax that he should be on his guard because he does not want to kill him "with a sneaking shot, with an eye for my chance, but in open fight."[115] The purpose of war is as much to provide a stage for individual aristocratic participants to gain honor as it is to advance any broader goals of their political units. *Iliad* battlefield scenes depict champions dismounting from chariots or stepping forward from the ranks to challenge warriors in the opposing army. Chariots are taxis, that transport heroes to and from the battlefield, not weapons of war. Combat is always brief and nearly always fatal, with compatriots on both sides observing, but generally not interfering once the contest begins. Wounded warriors die quickly, unless they are just nicked, but sometimes survive just long enough to utter final words.

As the old adage has it, exceptions prove the rule, and Homer offers several with telling effect. The Trojan Lycaon, stunned with terror, dodges Achilles' blow, grabs his knees and pleads for his life. Achilles rejects his promise of ransom, telling him that better men have died in the war. Lycaon's spirit collapses and he sits down with both hands outstretched. Achilles thrusts downwards with his sword, sinking it into his body up to

---

[114] 1 Samuel.   [115] Homer, *Iliad*, 7.42–3.

the hilt.[116] If no mercy is shown on the battlefield, there are restrictions on who can fight. In book 4, Glaucus and Diomedes, both eager for battle, advance to confront each other. In the course of announcing their lineages and exploits, they discover that their families are linked and they are accordingly "guest friends." They grasp hands and exchange armor, even though it requires Glaucus to give away his gold armor in return for bronze. Homer tells us that Zeus must have taken away Glaucus' wits, offering evidence that the system of gift exchange was breaking down at this stage in the war.[117]

More fundamentally, the desire to gain honor determines the strategy of war. The Greeks have no choice but to take war to the Trojans, but they never try to besiege and starve the city into submission. Instead, they offer fair combat on the plain below Troy. For their part, the Trojans do not seriously oppose the Greek amphibious landing on their shores, and play their game by coming out from behind their walls to fight. They would have been much better advised to have worn the Greeks down with indirect resistance in the form of ambush, harassment, raids and efforts to cut off the long supply line on which the Greeks depended for their food. We know from Homer that the Greek army was tired of fighting and only kept from sailing away by Odysseus acting on instructions from Athena.[118] Hector's strategy of frontal assault played up to the Greek strengths, and only makes sense, as does his decision to remain outside the walls to do combat with Achilles, as a reflection of his commitment to gain glory through decisive battle.[119]

Tensions

The *Iliad* is a saga, not a rule book, and Homer shows us how norms and human nature interact and give rise to serious tensions even in this ideal-type representation of an honor society. The structure and beauty of the poetry suggest an ordered and stable world in which gods, people and words have a proper place. The narrative tells us how the defense of *nomos* nearly destroys it, and transforms handsome, accomplished and noble young men into ugly, rotting corpses that become carrion for wild dogs and vultures. The jarring juxtapositions of beauty and tragedy, life and death and order and disorder heighten our awareness of the fragility of

---

[116] Ibid., 21.64–134. A similar incident between Tros, son of Alastor, and Achilles is reported in 20.462–9.
[117] Ibid., 6.230–6.   [118] Ibid., 2.248–51.
[119] Strauss, *Trojan War*, pp. 140–3, 158, makes a similar argument.

honor-based warrior societies. This fragility derives in the first instance
from the intense competition such societies encourage. It is channeled
into violence, where it can readily escalate out of control, as it does for
Greeks and Trojans, and almost does for Achilles and Agamemnon. Violence arouses intense emotions, among them fear, anger and the desire
for revenge – what anthropologists call negative reciprocity. Greeks and
Trojans come close to a settlement in book 3 when they agree to a contest
among champions, with Helen and all her possessions going to the winner.
Athena persuades an angry Trojan archer to violate the truce and wound
Menelaus. Agamemnon, his brother, is enraged, and swears to destroy
Ilium. The fighting resumes and from that point on moves inexorably
toward its tragic finale.[120]

Achilles embodies within himself the central tension of warrior societies. His uncompromising sense of self-worth is the source of extraordinary vitality, and his god-like wrath (*mēnis*) energizes him on the battlefield.[121] It also gives rise to implacable anger that makes him a threat
to the social order. Unlike Odysseus, he finds it difficult to exercise self-
restraint. In the opening book of the *Iliad*, he refrains from drawing
his sword against Agamemnon, but insults him publicly and withdraws
from the fighting on the grounds that the Trojans have never done him
any harm.[122] He returns to the battle for the wrong reasons – personal
revenge as opposed to social obligation – and kills without restraint. His
defilement of Hector's body is a violation of *nomos* that ranks with Paris'
violation of *xenia*. In the closing book of the epic, Achilles facilitates a
restoration of *nomos*. He returns Hector's body to Priam, suitably oiled
and wrapped, and lifts it on to the wagon that Priam has brought with
him from Troy. He becomes a participant in Hector's funeral, symbolically
bridging the gaps between Greece and Troy, peace and war and life and
death.

In battle Achilles is like an animal, and his murderous wrath makes his
adversaries become animal-like in expressing their hostility to him. They
want to tear his flesh apart and eat his liver raw, actions Greeks associate
with animals.[123] His human qualities resurface only when he empathizes
with Priam over the loss of his son. He softens when he pictures his father
mourning him. This scene concretizes a traditional Greek understanding
of the nature of community embedded in many tragedies and, we will see

[120] Homer, *Iliad*, 4.100–274.
[121] Ibid., 1.1; Clarke, "Manhood and Heroism," pp. 82–3; Nagy, *Best of the Achaeans*,
pp. 142–4; Muellner, *The Anger of Achilles*.
[122] Homer, *Iliad*, 1.148–71.   [123] Ibid., 24.253.

in chapter 4, made explicit by Pericles in his funeral oration and Plato in his *Protagoras*. Community is based on expanding circles of friendship. War narrows those circles, destroys empathy, makes human beings animal-like and has the potential to destroy community.

There is a striking contradiction between the goals and means of war. The Greeks have come to Troy to retrieve Helen or destroy the city for harboring her and Paris. They have no strategic plan to achieve this goal beyond engaging Trojan forces in a war of attrition on the plain in front of their city. The combats that ensue are not really battles, with the possible exception of the melee that erupts when Hector and the Trojans breach the Greeks' defensive wall and threaten to burn their ships. Armies are only occasionally organized by either side to make maximum use of the forces on hand, and almost always in exceptional circumstances[124] Most of the fighters on both sides do not appear to engage and merely observe individual combats between heroes. Some of the most intense and bloodiest fighting is over trophies, as one hero and his supporters attempt to strip the armor from a dead opponent, while the other side struggles to regain the body and its armor.[125] None of this violence contributes to the broader objectives of war.

Homer does not recount a single strategy session in which Greek leaders make reasoned arguments for or against different courses of action. Their councils are dominated by quarrels about disputed claims for precedence in which participants attempt to intimidate one another with harsh words and threats.[126] The only significant strategic advice on the Greek side is given by Nestor, who suggests they build a protective wooden wall in front of their beached ships. The Greeks heed his advice, and the wall saves their ships from being burned by Hector and the forces under his command. On the Trojan side, Polydamas urges the Trojans, and Hector in particular, to withdraw behind the walls of the city and wage a defensive war. His sound advice is angrily rejected by Hector, who spurns omens and good counsel as cowardice. "One omen is best," he insists, "to fight back for one's fatherland." Hector goes outside the walls to do

---

[124] Important examples are Nestor's careful arrangement of his infantry and cavalry, along with his orders that "Let no man in the pride of his horsemanship and his manhood dare to fight alone with the Trojans in front of the rest of us," 4.293–308; Ajax, mustering his troops in defense of Patroclus's body, 17.354–9; and Polydamas arranging the dismounted Trojans into five companies to attack the Greek ships, 12.61–107. Lendon, *Soldiers and Ghosts*, pp. 29–30.

[125] Homer, *Iliad*, 17.352–65, for the fight over Patroclus' body and armor.

[126] Finley, *World of Odysseus*, p. 114.

combat with Achilles, only to lose his life and his city.[127] Personal honor routinely triumphs over strategic considerations, and is often pursued at their expense. In Homer's fictional Greece, social obligation requires heroism. Nestor and Odysseus are nevertheless admired for their strategic wisdom and good counsel, which sometimes favors restraint. They can voice reason-based arguments because they have reputations as great warriors.

There is an equally prominent and unresolved tension in combat itself, Killing other warriors in close engagements, generally in one-on-one encounters, constitutes a claim for glory (*euxos*). The *Iliad* is nevertheless filled with examples of heroes killing unheroically. Hector slaughters Periphetes while he lies on the ground, and delivers a *coup de grâce* to the wounded and dazed Patroclus. Deiphobos kills Hypsenor by mistake. Achilles throws spears through the backs of fleeing warriors and kills others who are cowering along the banks of a raging river.[128] Such unheroic violence can be attributed to the aroused state of the warriors, but it also reflects the standing of the fighters who are killed. The fame won from victory is very much proportional to the status of the dead hero, which is why Homer often provides us with long genealogies of these warriors and their accomplishments. When Hector is killed, the Greeks tell themselves: "We have won ourselves enormous fame. We have killed the great Hector whom the Trojans glorified as if he were a god in their city."[129] At the other end of the spectrum, less distinguished warriors and unnamed soldiers can be killed by any available means because their defeat does not constitute a claim for *euxos*.

Homer's take on archery points to another contradiction. When Paris hits Diomedes from a distance with an arrow, the wounded Diomedes calls him a "foul fighter," and dismisses his arrow as "the blank weapon of a useless man, no fighter."[130] "Arrow fighter" is on the whole synonymous with cowardice because courage involves risk, and this demands fighting at close quarters.[131] In the funeral games, archery is nevertheless one of the competitions. Teucer, brother of Ajax, wins fame for bringing down so many Trojans with his bow, as does Odysseus in the *Odyssey*, for killing

---

[127] Homer, *Iliad*, 22.105–22, 243.
[128] Ibid., 15.638–52; 13.402–17; Wees, "Heroes, Knights and Nutters," for elaboration of further instances.
[129] Homer, *Iliad*, 22.443–59; Lendon, *Soldiers and Ghosts*, pp. 26–7.
[130] Homer, *Iliad*, 8.146–55.
[131] Ibid., 4.242; 11.385–90; Lendon, *Soldiers and Ghosts*, p. 34.

the suitors with a bow that only he can string.[132] The codes governing combat in the *Iliad* are at least in part at odds with themselves.[133]

The *Iliad* can be read as the first great work of literature with an anti-war theme. It glorifies warfare and the heroes it creates, but depicts combat as a thoroughly bloody and gruesome affair. Homer provides graphic descriptions of the various ways in which warriors die. Spears pierce their skulls, teeth, tongues, necks and torsos, and swords slash their necks, abdomens and limbs. Eyes and teeth pop out, blood gushes from wounds and orifices, heads and joints are severed or remain attached by folds of skin or all-but-severed ligaments. The wounded scream, double up in agony, reach out for their intestines, claw the earth or silently collapse as black night covers their eyes.[134] Greek and Trojan heroes willingly enter into combat and are killed in large numbers. Countless others succumb to disease. Self-aggrandizing generals such as Agamemnon, tricksters such as Odysseus, and cowards such as Paris are the most likely to survive.[135]

Myth has it that when Troy fell the hatred and rage of the Greek army found release in the slaughter of a defenseless civilian population. If it had been described in the *Iliad*, the sharp contrast between this dénouement and the bloody but honorable combat between warriors would have pushed this unheroic aspect of the conflict into the background. Greek legend attributes victory to a desperate, clever ploy: the famous Trojan Horse of Odysseus. Calm, rational and courageous, Odysseus was also calculating and indirect. Helen describes him to Priam as "the master of all kinds of trickery and clever plans."[136] Homer emphasizes the sly nature of his tactics early in the *Iliad*, where he recounts a nighttime ambush that Odysseus and Diomedes carried out to capture Trojans from whom useful intelligence might be gleaned.[137] Odysseus' balance and judgment are a nice counterpoint to the anger and questionable leadership of Agamemnon and Achilles, but his behavior on and off the battlefield clashes with the heroic code that emphasizes direct and open engagements between

---

[132] Homer, *Iliad*, 23.850–83; 13.313–14; *Odyssey*, 8.215–28, 22.1–118. Lendon, *Soldiers and Ghosts*, pp. 34–5.

[133] Lendon, *Soldiers and Ghosts*, p. 28.   [134] *Iliad*, book 5 for particularly graphic examples.

[135] According to myth, Paris is killed in the fighting by Philoctetes, and Agamemnon by his wife shortly after he returns home at the end of the war. Neither event is described by Homer.

[136] Homer, *Iliad*, 3.199–202. In *Philoctetes*, lines 407–8, Sophocles has Philoctetes proclaim that Odysseus "would attempt with his tongue every evil word and villainy."

[137] Homer, *Iliad*, book 10. This theme is further developed in the *Odyssey*, where Odysseus relies on bravery and a knack for stealth to preserve himself and many of his men through a series of arduous ordeals and challenges.

opposing champions and denigrates the use of tricks to overcome an enemy, or indeed any tactic that minimizes the risk of warfare. Odysseus' trickery is all the more threatening because of its success.[138]

The final book of the *Iliad* describes the dramatic encounter between Priam and Achilles. There are striking parallels in language and detail between this scene and the opening scene of the saga where another old father, Chryses, appeals unsuccessfully to Agamemnon for the return of his daughter. On this occasion, the supplication succeeds and forges a momentary bond between the two men. Both know their reconciliation is temporary, that war will resume and that Priam is at great risk within the Greek camp, as is Achilles for receiving him. By focusing our attention on the story of two families of honorable men from opposing sides, Homer leaves us with a tragic understanding of war and its consequences. For political as well as artistic reasons, he had every reason to end his story with the walls of Troy intact.

Historical worlds

The *Iliad* is a fictional work that describes a fictional world. Ruins and artifacts aside, much of what we know about the age of heroes – Bronze Age Greece in the Late Minoan period – comes from myths, later writers such as Homer and Hesiod, and the poems of the "Epic Cycle." Six of these poems narrate events from the Trojan War that are not described in either the *Iliad* or the *Odyssey*.[139] Homer, if he actually existed, lived sometime in the ninth or eighth centuries BCE, some three or four hundred years after the Trojan War is supposed to have occurred. It is possible that the *Iliad* portrays a real war on the basis of stories passed down by word of mouth through the Greek Dark Ages. At some stage, bards combined these stories into larger narratives – the *Iliad* is 15,000 lines – and improvised many of these lines in retelling them according to a sophisticated set of rules.[140] Improvisation inevitably, perhaps purposefully, introduced

---

[138] Vidal-Nacquet, *The Black Hunter*, constructs an elaborate theory around the contrast between straightforward combat and hunting and subterfuge. Drawing on anthropology, he argues that initiation rites often involve a logic of inversion, in which young men are encouraged to act out proscribed roles, including those inimical to hoplite warfare.

[139] The *Cypria* describes the outbreak and first nine years of the Trojan War; the *Aethiopis* is about Troy's Ethiopian and Amazon allies; the *Little Iliad* provides detail on the Trojan Horse; the *Nostoi* describes the return of those Greek heroes, especially Agamemnon, who made it back safely from the wars; and the *Telegony* picks up where the *Odyssey* leaves off.

[140] Auerbach, *Mimesis*; Kirk, *Homer and the Oral Tradition*; de Jong, *Narrators and Focalizers*; Parry, *The Making of Homeric Verse*; Nagy, *The Best of the Achaeans*; Bakker, *Poetry in*

some of their society's values, ideals and practices. The bards constructed what Max Weber would call an ideal type: a mental construct that will never be encountered in practice but nevertheless offers insights into real worlds.[141]

With this ideal type at hand, let us turn to the analysis of historical societies, beginning with fifth-century Greece, in which honor seems to have been of paramount importance. I start with classical Greece because Athens and Sparta took Homer as their model, just as Rome and Europe from the Renaissance on were influenced by Homer and classical Greece. There were over 1,000 city states in fifth-century Greece, and we have little or no information about most of them. We know something about Sparta, and a lot about Athens, so must be careful about generalizing to Greece as a whole. From Greece I move to the Hellenistic period and then to the early, middle and late Roman Republics and the Roman Empire. In later chapters I analyze feudal and early modern Europe, and Europe and the United States in the nineteenth and twentieth centuries. Ancient Greece and Europe illustrate not only the characteristics of honor-oriented societies but their principal tensions. The ways in which these societies coped with these tensions, and their different degrees of success, sheds further light on the character of honor worlds.

All my cases are European, but honor-based worlds and warrior societies are by no means exclusively Western phenomena. In the absence of Homer, they developed on roughly parallel tracks in the Middle East, Southeast Asia, China and Japan, Scandinavia, Oceania and Meso- and North America at different stages of their history. Honor has been extensively studied in some of these societies, revealing practices in many ways similar to those of Homeric Greece and historical European honor societies. I include one non-European case: Japan in the late nineteenth and early twentieth centuries.

Classical Greece and Europe differ in important ways from the world described by Homer. They are larger and more developed, especially with regard to their political institutions. In the Greece of Homer and fifth-century playwrights, the state was more or less synonymous with the leader, and the army with his followers and their dependants. There is no levels-of-analysis problem because the goals of kingdoms generally reflect those of their leaders. It is straightforward and credible to describe

---

Speech; Lord, *The Singer of Tales*; Fowler, "The Homeric Question"; Foley, *Homer's Traditional Art* and "Epic as Genre"; Dowden, "The Epic Tradition in Greece."

[141] Weber, "'Objectivity' in Social Science and Social Policy," pp. 90–5.

politics as driven by desires for honor and the related emotions of anger and revenge. This becomes more difficult when political institutions (e.g. assemblies, armies, courts, bureaucracies) take form and achieve some degree of independence from rulers, and when rulers become increasingly dependent on other groups in the society. Pericles wielded enormous influence in Athens, but unlike Agamemnon, he had to consider other groups and their interests and govern more by persuasion than by fiat.[142]

When a political unit develops an identity of its own, it is usually reflected in the contemporary discourse. Leaders and non-leaders begin to speak of the existence of the city or state independently of that of its rulers, and may even distinguish, as does Pericles, the loyalty citizens owe their community as distinct from its rulers. Fifth-century playwrights read the idea of the polis back into Bronze Age Greece; Oedipus and Creon speak of their responsibilities to the city. One of the important themes of *Oedipus Turannus* and *Antigone* is the conflict between the civic responsibilities of leaders and their personal and family interests.

The separation of state and ruler, even if only partial, requires us to conceptualize the former as an abstract entity. We cannot attribute personhood to it in any sense but the juridical, and that only in recent times. Nor can we project on to political units the kinds of drives and emotions natural to people.[143] This problem exists for all paradigms, not just one based on recognition, honor and standing. Fear is absolutely central to realist paradigm, just as greed is to its liberal counterpart. Realists attempt to get around the level-of-analysis problem by referring to reasons of state, a concept developed by Machiavelli to counter princely waste of resources in pursuit of their passions. Realists assume that leaders are motivated by some conception of national interest as distinct from their personal or political interests. This move from fear to reason involves a remarkable sleight of hand because at least since Thucydides – the putative father of realism – fear has been recognized as the emotion least amenable to mastery by reason. It is also a questionable move empirically because there is ample evidence that leaders across cultures and epochs often put their personal interests above those of the state, or convince themselves that they are one and the same. Moreover, when leaders consciously try to act in terms of the national interest, as Machiavelli recognized, there is rarely

---

[142] Thucydides, 2.56.9–10 tells us that behind the facade of democracy, lay the rule of one man (*ergōi de hupo tou prōtou andros archē*), Pericles. However, Thucydides' account also indicates that Pericles had to work hard to win the support of the assembly for his key foreign policy decisions. See also, Plato, *Menexenus*, 238c–d; Plutarch, *Cimon*, 15.2.

[143] This question is discussed in chapter 2.

any consensus about its substance.[144] Critics of realism have long contended that the national interest is a fuzzy concept at best, and one that
is more useful as a normative goal or rhetorical ploy than an empirical
description of policymaking.[145]

Liberals make a similar and equally problematic move with respect to
interest. They assume the majority of people in the modern world have
material well-being as their primary goal, and that governments, to the
extent they are democratic, must satisfy their desires to stay in power.
States accordingly act as if they were motivated by appetite. Public opinion polls and elections reveal that electorates have wider goals, and that
material interests are not always paramount. In the 2004 American election, a significant percentage of the working class and middle class voted
against their economic interests. They cast their ballots for Republican
candidates for the White House and Congress on the basis of their social
agenda and security concerns. In a poll conducted by the Pew Foundation, 44 percent of Bush voters said moral values were the single most
important issue for them in the campaign.[146] When governments privilege economic concerns, they are not always those of the electorate. They
can act to the benefit of powerful special interests which can be at odds
with those of the community as a whole.

To assert that political units are motivated by fear, interest, honor,
or any other motive, is not the same as demonstrating it. To do this,
we must show that important decisions over time reflect these motives.
Alternatively, we can engage in process-tracing and show that leaders acted
on the basis of these motives. We can also search for revealing cases where
different motives, say interest and honor, pulled leaders, or appeared to
pull them, in opposite directions. None of these tests is particularly easy,
let alone definitive. In the conclusion to chapter 2, I noted how difficult
it is to devise good indices for motives, and how much more difficult still
it is to identify the motives behind actions that appear to be consistent
with multiple motives. On the eve of the Peloponnesian War, Thucydides
has Athenians tell the Spartan assembly that "the nature of the case first

---

[144] Machiavelli, *Discourses*, writes that "without an unambiguous brief, reason of state was
liable to become a general doctrine of prudence and a technique of secretive statecraft."
Translation from Hont, *Jealousy of Trade*, p. 12.

[145] In 1950, Morgenthau, *In Defense of the National Interest*, felt compelled to write a book
identifying the national interest because there were such differences of opinion about it
and a general tendency to describe American policies in other terms with reference to
other goals.

[146] Pew Research Center, "Voters Liked Campaign 2004, But Too Much 'Mud-Slinging',"
released November 11, 2004.

compelled us to advance our empire to its present height; fear being our principal motive, though honor and interest afterwards came in."[147] The actions in question – the Corcyraean alliance, the siege of Potidaea and the Megarian Decree – are consistent with all three motives, and it is apparent that Spartans assign them a reverse order from the Athenians.[148] Thucydides' account of this and other episodes makes us aware that actors are not necessarily in touch with their own motives, let alone those of their adversaries. It is hardly surprising that the key decisions leading up to the Peloponnesian War remain a subject of intense debate among scholars.

These problems should not deter us from making careful efforts to determine the hierarchy of motives behind foreign policy decisions. They nevertheless make it essential that we supplement these efforts with other approaches. One promising line of inquiry focuses on the dominant discourses of the society. What motives do they recognize as legitimate? What hierarchy, if any, do they establish among them? Do actors justify their behavior in terms of these motives and their associated ends? Do they do this even when it appears likely or obvious that they are acting in response to other motives? Does admission of illegitimate motives, or those that are considered inappropriate in the circumstances, provoke shock, protest or other negative consequences? Even partial answers to these questions ought to provide valuable clues about the value structure of the society, the degree to which these values represent a distant ideal or are expected to govern everyday practice, the extent to which they do, and the ability and the willingness of actors to police practice.

We must also be sensitive to changes in discourse as they can be powerful indicators of changes in the hierarchy of motives. Shifts in the relative emphasis and evaluation of motives can presage, accompany or follow shifts in practice, so we must exercise care in making inferences directly from a discourse without also examining behavior. The problem is further complicated by the presence of multiple discourses in many, if not most, societies. Shifts in the appeal and primacy of these discourses are likely to tell us something about changes in values or behavior, which are, of course, related. It is useful, indeed essential, to supplement our analysis of a society's discourses with the observations of its members, especially when they are recognized by contemporaries as astute observers of their culture. What I am describing here is a variant of the hermeneutical approach to texts.[149]

---

[147] Thucydides, 1.76.11–13.   [148] Ibid., 1.24–66.
[149] On hermeneutics, see Berger and Luckmann, *The Social Construction of Reality*; Gadamer, *Truth and Method*, and "Text and Interpretation"; Habermas, *On the Logic of the Social*

I make use of all these strategies in my analysis of Greece, Rome and Europe. I quote extensively from contemporary sources, relying on what they have to say about the value hierarchies of their societies, the tensions they embody and the nature of challenges to them. I also offer my own analysis of texts and practices. With respect to the latter, I look for patterns indicative of value hierarchies in the practice of foreign policy and for illustrative cases where different values appear to be pitted against each other in the choices policymakers confront. As I am treating multiple societies over a span of more than two millennia, I use these several strategies in a selective rather than a systematic manner. My case studies are intended to be illustrative and provocative, not definitive, and to highlight key features of value hierarchies and their political consequences.

Real political units differ from ideal types in another important respect. One motive may be dominant, but others are also important, giving rise to mixed societies with complex interactions that are correspondingly more difficult to analyze. Classical Greece, Macedonia, the early and middle Roman Republics and eighteenth-century Europe put sufficient emphasis on the honor and standing that it is appropriate to describe them as honor societies. Appetite was also an important motive for individuals and political units, as was fear, which in some circumstances was dominant. We cannot ignore these other motives when analyzing the spirit and its consequences because they constrain it and shape its expression in important ways. Each motive, like the spirit, embodies its own tensions. I have described those associated with Greece of the *Iliad*. In the next chapter I do this for classical Greece. In fifth-century Greece, Macedonia, the early and middle Roman Republics and pre-French revolutionary Europe, I treat these drives as relatively distinct and describe these societies as mixtures. In the modern world, we shall see, appetite and spirit increasingly blend, leading to worlds that are more solutions than mixtures, and accordingly with a somewhat different set of characteristics and tensions.

Theoretical summary

Before turning to my cases, I think it useful to recapitulate for the reader in abbreviated form the principal characteristics of honor-based societies

Sciences; Ricoeur, *Freud and Philosophy*, and "The Model of the Text"; Searle, *Construction of Social Reality*; Shapiro and Sica, *Hermeneutics*; Lebow, *Tragic Vision of Politics*, pp. 50–8. For an overview and the controversies surrounding hermeneutics, see Diesing, *How Does Social Science Work?*, pp. 104–48.

and the tensions associated with them. I revisit and expand upon these propositions at the end of chapter 4, drawing on my ancient world case studies and, in the theoretical conclusion to the book, drawing on all my case studies.

The starting point of the paradigm of recognition, standing and honor is the universal need for self-esteem, which the ancient Greeks associated with the spirit. It finds expression in a competitive quest for honor and standing, which are defined and pursued differently depending on the society and epoch. Plato's and Aristotle's model of the psyche includes two other drives: appetite and reason. They also generate ideal worlds. Classical liberal theory portrays an ideal world of interest, although does not acknowledge it as such. Plato's *Republic* constructs an ideal world based on reason.

Real worlds are mixes of all three motives, and in those I refer to as honor-based societies honor is more important for the elite than appetite. The reverse is true in interest-based worlds. For either kind of society to exist in practice, reason must to some degree restrain and educate spirit and appetite alike. When reason loses its hold over either, other actors become increasingly concerned about the prospects of achieving honor, satisfying their appetites or preserving their lives. This can prompt a rapid phase transition into a fear-based world.

My analysis of the *Iliad* suggests that honor-based worlds have the following generic characteristics:

1. Honor takes the form of external honor, defined as acceptable, or, better yet, outstanding performance of socially determined roles. Failure to act honorably induces shame.
2. Death is preferable to dishonor for individuals and political units. Survival is an important but secondary goal. It will be put at risk, or even knowingly sacrificed for the prospect of honor and immortal fame or of avoiding dishonor.
3. Honor and standing are intended to be synonymous. Societies aspire to have as perfect an overlap as possible between achieved and ascribed statuses.
4. In their earliest iterations, honor-based societies are warrior societies. Bravery in battle is the most highly regarded social activity, and the principal claim to honor and standing. It may be an essential prerequisite for political office.
5. To the extent that honor is valued, appetite is correspondingly devalued. Excessive appetite for wealth or women is considered corrupting.

Luxuries and women are thought to make men less capable warriors and less willing to risk their lives for honor. Homosexual love is often encouraged and channeled by warrior societies to stimulate bravery in battle.

6. Honor societies are relatively closed societies. They do not easily admit or assimilate outsiders. Some honor societies are rigidly stratified, as was Bronze Age Greece of the *Iliad*. Others are not, cases in point being the Vikings, Plains Indians or many tribes of Papua New Guinea. Entry into the elite in these societies is most often achieved through bravery in battle.

7. Honor societies are commonly divided into a relatively undifferentiated mass and an elite. The elite usually consider themselves to be ontological equals, but are organized hierarchically on the basis of ascribed and achieved status. Hierarchy often involves multiple gradations in rank.

8. Honor and standing are conveyed by generally understood markers. These can include special titles, costumes and privileges. Failure to acknowledge or respect them arouses anger because it is considered a slight to one's honor.

9. Honor worlds require a robust society based on a core of widely shared values. Honor can only be achieved in societies where there is a consensus about what it is, how it is won and lost, and who awards or takes it away.

10. The hierarchies that constitute honor worlds come with rule packages for each status that must be followed for the hierarchy to remain legitimate and effective. Statuses and their associated privileges must also be enforced and defended when challenged by those who benefit from them.[150]

11. Honor requires public recognition, and actors are willing to make sacrifices to achieve it only if they believe they will be honored in their lifetimes or afterwards.

12. Warfare between honor societies is frequent and rule-governed. The ends and means of war are limited, and its principal goal is to establish precedence through competitive displays of bravery. A secondary goal of war is to seek revenge for sleights to one's honor or standing.

13. Warfare between honor- and non-honor-based societies is usually about security (defense) or conquest (offense) and is neither

---

[150] Pitt-Rivers, "Honour and Social Status," on how honor depends on the ability to silence anyone who disputes one's standing or the system that confers honor and standing.

rule-governed nor limited in its objectives. Prisoners are rarely taken unless they are held for ransom or used or sold as slaves.

Honor societies incorporate key tensions:

1. There is tension between competition for honor and the *nomos* that makes that competition possible and meaningful. Honor hierarchies are steep and competition for them is correspondingly intense. Actors are sorely tempted to take short-cuts to attain honor. If the rules are consistently violated, honor becomes meaningless.
2. The quest for honor requires a proliferation of ranks or statuses. These gradations intensify conflict when they are ambiguous, and create difficulty in establishing precedence across rankings of achieved and ascribed status or among multiple forms of achieved status.
3. In practice, ascribed and achieved status hierarchies are often distinct and diverge. The relative standing of these hierarchies and those within them can constitute a powerful source of conflict.
4. Warfare conducted by the rules of honor societies privileges the honor of individual warriors over the honor and security of the society as a whole. Adherence to these rules can make defeat more likely by adversaries who are not similarly constrained. Strategies and tactics intended to maximize the chances of victory are equally threatening to the survival of honor societies.

The survival and stability of real-world honor societies depend on their ability to moderate and control these four tensions. As they interact synergistically, failure to do so can lead to a rapid transformation of an honor-based world into a fear-based one. However, success and the orders it brings make the accumulation of wealth more likely and threaten to transform honor-based societies into worlds dominated by appetite. Honor-based societies are inherently fragile and subject to decay and transformation by two distinct dialectical processes.

4

The ancient world

This is *aretē* (excellence), the best possession that man can have,
The noblest thing that a young man can endeavor to win.

Tyrtaeus[1]

Honor is a great thing for the sake of which people will make
every conceivable effort and face every conceivable danger.

Xenophon[2]

Honor is clearly the greatest of external goods.

Aristotle[3]

What else is an enemy but a perpetual opportunity for you to
show your mettle and win glory?

Camillus[4]

Classical Greece (480–325 BCE) is the first of my historical cases in which
to demonstrate the power of the spirit and the central role it played in
politics, foreign policy and international relations. It is an "easy" case
because Greeks and modern-day scholars alike consider it a society in
which honor was an important, if not the most important, value for
the elite. The quote from Aristotle above expresses a belief that would
have met little dissent from fifth- and fourth-century aristocrats, and
a nod of agreement from citizens of other Greek city states. Although
it is an "easy" case, it is a theoretically productive one because of the
many differences between it and the Homeric ideal-type honor society.
These differences, and the complexities to which they give rise, provide
additional insights into the nature of honor societies, their tensions and
the interaction between the spirit and other motives.

[1] Tyrtaeus, 12.13–14 in the Lattimore translation. Tyrtaeus was a seventh-century poet who
lived in Sparta.
[2] Xenophon, *Hiero*, 7.1–3.   [3] Aristotle, *Nicomachean Ethics*, 1123b20.
[4] Livy, *The History of Rome from its Foundation*, 6.18.7.

The polis emerged in the archaic age (750–480 BCE), by which time Greeks already had a sense of common identity. By the fifth century, democracy had emerged as a powerful political movement, and defeat of the two Persian invasions of 490 and 480–479 BCE ushered in a golden age of Greek creativity and accomplishments in politics, art, literature, history and philosophy. As Greek culture was so heavily dependent on the polis and its independence, the classical period came to an end when these city states become subordinate, first to Macedon and then to Rome. If we need a defining moment, it was the autumn of 338, when the armies of Philip of Macedon decisively defeated a Greek coalition at the Battle of Chaeronea.

The polis encouraged citizens to regard one another as members of an extended family, to project their strivings for greatness on to the city and to compete for honor in its service. The citizen to some degree merged with the city, a development reflected in hoplite warfare where the individual fought in close order as part of a larger unit, and where excellence (*aretē*) on the battlefield was won by the unit and the city. The phalanx, devised in Argos about 670 BCE, only achieved its centrality at the beginning of the fifth century, when paintings no longer depict archers alongside hoplite infantry, and hoplites no long carry throwing spears. At around the same time, grave-markers in many Greek cities became more uniform, another sign of the individual being submerged into the community. Gravestones become differentiated again in Athens in the 420s, after the city has lost its independence.[5] Classical Greece represents a high point of civic association not witnessed again until the Roman Republic.

Classical Greece was followed by the Hellenistic age (323–30 BCE), a period beginning with the conquests of Alexander (338–323) and the spread of Greek culture and political influence throughout the eastern Mediterranean basin and the former Persian Empire. After Alexander's death, there were three major kingdoms in Greece and the Middle East. A fourth, based in Pergamum, arose in the third century. In the First and Second Macedonian Wars (215–213, and 200–197 BCE), Rome became an increasingly powerful player in Macedonia and Greece. After the Battle of Actium in 31 BCE, Greece and the Greek east were incorporated into the Roman Empire where they would remain for the next four hundred years.

Most of this chapter focuses on a narrow if key slice of Greek history. The justification for doing so lies in part with the availability of sources.

---

[5] Lendon, *Soldiers and Ghosts*, p. 65.

They become much richer in the fifth century, both in historical records and contemporary texts. The fifth century is also a period of incredible cultural and political vitality, and encompasses the emergence of democracy, the growth of the Athenian Empire, rapid economic development and the spread of trade, devastating wars with the Persians and within the Greek community, the "proto-Enlightenment" and reflection on these developments by some of the most creative playwrights, historians and philosophers in the Western canon. Greek culture underwent a notable evolution, and appetite emerged as an increasingly powerful motive. Fear also became pronounced, especially during the Persian invasions and the Peloponnesian War (431–404). The classical period gives us the opportunity to examine a society based on honor, but also one in which its primacy was challenged.

I extend my analysis into the Hellenistic and Roman periods. Both societies offer interesting variants on honor cultures, and I describe some of their salient features and compare them to classical Greece. There are also interesting comparisons to be made between the early and middle Roman Republics and the late Republic and Empire.

Classical Greece

Greeks everywhere considered themselves the cultural, if not the biological, descendants of the Bronze Age heroes portrayed by Homer and the playwrights. The sign of an educated man was his ability to recite sections of the *Iliad* and the *Odyssey*, and there were people who knew both epics by heart.[6] Greeks assimilated Homeric values to such a degree, according to Socrates, that there were Greeks who thought they should mould their lives around the characters and values of his epics.[7] This was especially true in military affairs where a rhapsode – one who sang Homer professionally – could assert his right to a generalship on the basis of his knowledge of the bard.[8] The relationship between Homer and classical Greece was reciprocal and reinforcing. The *Iliad* occupied a central place in the education and culture of classical Greece because it showcased the values and deeds admired by Greeks wherever they lived, and by the fifth century BCE their city states stretched from the Black Sea coast to colonies in Sicily, and what today constitutes mainland Italy, France and Spain.

[6] Plato, *Symposium*, 3.5, 4.6–7; Xenophon, *Symposium*, 3.5.
[7] Plato, *Republic*, 606e; Hunter, "Homer and Greek Literature"; Robb, *Literacy and Paideia in Ancient Greece.*
[8] Plato, *Ion*, 541B.

Striving for honor

Greeks were fed Homer with their mother's milk, and nowhere was the diet so rich as in Sparta, where respect for the past and its values was actively fostered by the state. Spartan customs, as Thucydides has the Corinthians hastening to point out, were positively antediluvian and unchanging. Spartiates rejected a money economy and material goods, and the citizens of Sparta were prohibited from engaging in commerce or becoming artisans. They were full-time soldiers and judged on the basis of their bravery, courage, honor and other personal attributes such as wisdom and self-control.[9] As they departed for war, Spartan mothers were alleged to tell their sons: "Come home with your shield – or on it." Sparta encouraged internal rivalry to an unusual extreme. Beginning as young boys, Spartiates competed with one another in their education, for membership in the mess and the cavalry (*hippeis*) that surrounded the king in battle. As old men, they competed for membership in the Gerousia, the council of elders.

In Athens, the most commercial and democratic polis, honor was also a core value. Thucydides' Athenians offer it as one of their motives for winning and maintaining empire.[10] According to Xenophon, "Athenians excel all others not so much in singing or in stature or in strength, as in love of honor, which is the strongest incentive to deeds of honor and renown."[11] In contrast to Homer's Bronze Age, honor was extensively theorized, not only by philosophers such as Plato and Aristotle, but by the playwrights. The *Oresteia*, *Philoctetes*, *Electra* and *Antigone* explore different understandings of honor and the clashes that arise from unyielding commitments to them. *Ajax*, *Seven against Thebes* and, arguably, *Oedipus Turannus* examine the destructive consequences of unrestrained competition. Honor was unquestionably the dominant value of classical Greek society. Aristotle describes it as "the greatest of external goods."[12] For Xenophon it was a defining characteristic of human beings, and made people willing to "make every conceivable risk and face every conceivable danger."[13]

---

[9] Thucydides, *Peloponnesian War*, 1.119–25; Crane, *Thucydides and the Ancient Simplicity*, ch. 8; Cartledge, *Spartans*. All English quotations from Thucydides are from the Richard Crawley translation in *The Landmark Thucydides*.
[10] Thucydides, 1.76.11–13.   [11] Xenophon, *Memorabilia*, 3.3.13.
[12] Aristotle, *Nicomachean Ethics*, 2.39–42, 1123b20.   [13] Xenophon, *Hiero*, 7.1.3.

Appetite

As we would expect in an honor-oriented society, appetite was frowned on in classical Greece. Pindar (circa 518–438 BCE) warned that monetary exchange threatened to turn the Muse into a whore because it placed her outside of personal relationships.[14] Scorn of trade and of the low-born who profited from it was a sign of the increasing insecurity of the aristocracy. By mid-fifth century, *agōraios* (merchants and traders who set up shop every day in the agora) had become a general term of contempt.[15] Xenophon, Plato and Aristotle, all of whom wrote in the fourth century, opposed the money economy on philosophical grounds.[16] Wealth provided the leisure for a man to engage in politics, gain honor, seek wisdom and lead a virtuous life, none of which would happen if the desire for wealth became unlimited and self-reinforcing. In his *Republic*, Plato has Socrates defend a simple, largely vegetarian diet based on bread, salt, olives, cheese, onions and wine on the grounds that more elaborate meals inevitably encourage the desire for conquest.[17] Plato's *Laws* represents the intellectual highpoint of the conservative reaction to proto-modernity. It envisages a rural community on Crete – the most traditional part of Greece – modeled, at least in part, on old Sparta. Private property is regulated and restricted, and no money, industry, commerce or foreign contacts were to be permitted.[18]

Where there is smoke, there is often fire, and the pronounced criticism of appetite in late fifth- and fourth-century Greece is indicative of how important it had become.[19] As in Homeric Greece, sexual appetites were allowed open, if highly regulated, expression. Unmarried women were expected to remain chaste, and monogamous once married. Men were allowed relations with their wives and prostitutes of both sexes. Sex with younger male protégés, while not officially sanctioned, seems to have been a common practice. In keeping with the overall emphasis on honor and manliness, Greeks categorized sexual relationships in terms of roles, not

---

[14] Pindar, *Isthmian Odes*, 2.1–11; Kurke, *The Traffic in Praise*, pp. 240–56.

[15] Herodotus, *Histories*, 2.167; Connor, *New Politicians of Fifth Century Athens*, pp. 153–4.

[16] Xenophon, *Oeconomicus*, 7.29; Aristotle, *Politics*, 1256a1–1259a36 on the dangers of unlimited acquisition, and 1337b23–1338b8 on the importance of leisure.

[17] Plato, *Republic*, 372c. Also *Gorgias*, 494f, about the Charadris, a bird that must eat continuously, used metaphorically by Socrates.

[18] Plato, *Laws*, 4.704d–705b, 5.739c–745b, 9.855a–856e, 11.923a–924a, 929b–e.

[19] On this point, see Balot, *Greed and Injustice in Classical Athens*.

gender preferences. *Erastes* referred to the dominant, active penetrating partner. Those who were submissive, passive and penetrated – male or female – were described, pejoratively, as *erōmenoi*. For Greeks, masculinity was something to be achieved and defended through a combination of active and energetic but self-controlled behavior.[20]

The other Greek passions were food and drink. Athenians went into rapture over seafood, especially eels. Seafood was expensive, and eels and tuna were luxury items.[21] Wine, mixed with water and occasionally other ingredients, was the most common beverage, and by the fifth century there was an extensive seaborne wine trade. Wine from some locations was much admired, and priced accordingly. Wealthier citizens participated in symposia where they drank, conversed and were entertained by flute girls. The yearning for good wine and food was one of many incentives citizens had to earn money.

Competition

Classical Greece was an intensely agonistic society. Individuals and cities alike competed for fame and honor. Valor and success on the battlefield was the principal means of gaining it, although victory in sporting contests, as in the *Iliad*, emerged as an alternative at an early date. The Olympic Games, founded in 776 BCE, were not restricted to the sons of aristocrats, but in practice competitors needed enough free time and resources to pay their way to and from the games unless they had sponsors. After the middle of the fifth century, athletes from the lower classes began to participate in larger numbers. Through their control of victory memorials, aristocrats sought to impose interpretations of athletic contests conducive to their values and efforts to defend their power. They excluded any reference to training or participants, like jockeys, who came from the lower orders.[22] There were no team competitions, and as in the ideal of warfare, competitions were often one-on-one and always "winner take all." No second or third prizes were awarded.[23]

---

[20] Wohl, *Love Among the Ruins*; Keuls, *The Reign of the Phallus*; Nussbaum, *The Fragility of Goodness*, chs. 6 and 7; Dover, *Greek Homosexuality*; Cohen, "Sexuality, Violence and the Athenian Law of *Hubris*"; Winkler, *The Constraints of Desire*.
[21] Davidson, *Courtesans and Fishcakes*, pp. 11–20.
[22] Finley and Pleket, *The Olympic Games*, pp. 45, 72; Nicholson, *Aristocracy and Athletics in Archaic and Classical Greece*, esp. pp. 16–17.
[23] Miller, *Ancient Greek Athletics*, p. 19.

Traditional Greek ideology justified political authority on the basis of the contribution citizens made to the defense of the polis. Infantry warfare was largely the preserve of the wealthy, especially after the advent of the hoplite phalanx.[24] Other forms of warfare existed – cavalry, light infantry, archers and slingers – and, cavalry aside, used the skills (*technai*) that were the preserve of the less wealthy, non-citizens and mercenaries. Non-hoplite forms of warfare nevertheless often played an important, and sometimes decisive, role on the battlefield, but Greeks tended not to acknowledge or write about them because they were at odds with their cultural definition of warfare as face-to-face encounters between heavily armed elites.[25] Hoplite warfare was justified with reference to the *Iliad*, although it is sharply at odds with the kind of combat Homer describes. Hoplite warfare was read back into an imaginary past on fifth-century vases that reveal Homeric heroes dressed in hoplite panoply.[26] In all probability, Homer's depiction of Bronze Age war bore little relationship to how wars were fought during the so-called Dark Ages. What matters is how later generations *thought* they were fought, and how they assimilated Homeric values and modeled themselves on Homeric heroes even when it required taking considerable liberties with his texts. Ancient heroes were revered and considered to possess great powers, especially the ability to heal and defend. Heracles had numerous shrines, and before Marathon Athenian hoplites encamped in two of these sanctuaries. In the years after the victory, Heracles' festival at Marathon was given greater prominence, no doubt in the hope that it would help maintain his assistance in defending Athens.[27]

A full classical hoplite panoply – which included shield, helmet, breastplate, greaves (plate armor worn around the lower leg), sword, spear, and tunic – cost around 75–100 drachmas, roughly three months' wages for a skilled worker. The armor consisted of very fine sheets of hammered bronze, and offered little more protection than cheaper and more comfortable leather. It was primarily a status symbol and a relatively effective means of restricting the field of honor to the wealthier classes.[28] In Athens, poorer citizens, some of them landless (*thetes*), and many residents, or metics, found employment in the fleet, dockyards or chandleries, and were essential to the security of the city and the expansion of its empire. After the Battle of Salamis in 480 BCE, where the Athenian navy and its

[24] Wees, *Greek Warfare*, pp. 184–97 on the classical phalanx.
[25] Ibid., p. 85.   [26] Lendon, *Ghosts and Soldiers*, p. 45.
[27] Boedeker, "Athenian Religion in the Age of Pericles."   [28] Ibid., pp. 52–3.

allies decisively defeated the Persian fleet, service in the fleet provided a strong claim for participation in the affairs of state by the large class of citizens who could not afford a hoplite panoply.[29]

In the course of the fifth century, especially in Athens, other forms of excellence (*aretē*) were recognized. Skill in public speaking conferred honor and standing, as did winning play-writing prizes at festivals. Wealth could buy honor only when it was used voluntarily for the benefit of the polis by underwriting triremes or the production of plays performed at the Dionysia. By the end of the fifth century, *aretē* had progressed through three stages of meaning: from its original Homeric sense of fighting skill, to skill at any activity to moral goodness.[30] Thucydides uses all three meanings, and has Pericles introduce a fourth in his funeral oration, where *aretē* describes the reputation a state can develop by generous behavior toward its allies.[31] The aristocratic conception of *aretē* was extended in a double sense: to activities other than military combat, and to cities as well as individuals. One of the striking features of fifth-century Greek culture, especially Athenian, is how *aretē* was adopted as a value by members of the non-aristocratic classes. In part, this was due to its extension to domains where non-aristocrats could hope to achieve it.

Immortality

Like Achilles, Greek warriors aspired to everlasting renown by extraordinary exploits on the battlefield. King Leonidas of Sparta (4,500,000 hits on Google) achieved immortality at Thermopylae. The 7,000 Greeks he commanded successfully withstood a Persian army some sixty times their number. When the Persians, helped by a traitor, found an alternative route through the mountains, Leonidas understood that his position was no longer tenable. He dismissed all but the remaining Spartans and the Thespians who elected to stay with him. He "considered it unseemly to leave the post which they had come to defend."[32] Herodotus portrays the fighting as brutal, even for hoplite combat. As their numbers diminished, the Greeks retreated to a small hill in the narrowest part of the pass. With their spears gone or broken, the Spartiates and Thespians kept fighting with their short swords (*xiphos*) and, after these broke, with their bare hands and teeth.[33] The Athenians similarly displayed *aretē* at Marathon

[29] Ober, *Mass and Elite in Democratic Athens*, pp. 83–4; Wees, "Politics and the Battlefield."
[30] Thucydides, 2.42.2.   [31] Ibid., 2.39; Hooker, "Χαρις and αρειη in Thucydides."
[32] Herodotus, *Histories*, 7.210–20.   [33] Ibid., 8.223–4.

and Salamis where they risked their lives for the freedom of Greece.[34] Aeschylus, the great Athenian playwright, fought in both battles, and it is revealing that he chose to be remembered for his military service rather than his poetry. For his gravestone, he prepared the following inscription: "Under this monument lies Aeschylus the Athenian, Euphorion's son, who died in the wheatlands of Gela. The grove of Marathon with its glories can speak of his valor in battle. The long-haired Persian remembers and can speak of it, too."[35]

Cities evolved elaborate rituals to honor those who had died in their defense. In Athens it was an annual event in time of war. According to Thucydides:

> Three days before the ceremony, the bones of the dead are laid out in a tent which has been erected; and their friends bring to their relatives such offerings as they please. In the funeral procession cypress coffins are borne in cars, one for each tribe; the bones of the deceased being placed in the coffin of their tribe. Among these is carried one empty bier decked for the missing, that is, for those whose bodies could not be recovered. Any citizen or stranger who pleases, joins in the procession: and the female relatives are there to wail at the burial. The dead are laid in the public sepulcher in the beautiful suburb of the city, in which those who fall in war are always buried; with the exception of those slain at Marathon, who for their singular and extraordinary valor were interred on the spot where they fell. After the bodies have been laid in the earth, a man chosen by the state, of approved wisdom and eminent reputation, pronounces over them an appropriate eulogy.[36]

In the winter of 431, Athens laid to rest the first victims of the Peloponnesian War. Pericles, chosen to deliver the eulogy, spoke of the power and greatness of Athens that made it "the school of Hellas." He describes the accomplishments of its citizens as everlasting monuments that do not require the skill of poets to make others respectful:

> The admiration of the present and succeeding ages will be ours, since we have not left our power without witness, but have shown it by mighty proofs; and far from needing a Homer for our panegyrist, or other of his craft whose verses might charm for the moment only for the impression which they gave to melt at the touch of fact, we have forced every sea and

[34] Ibid., book 7, and Strauss, *Battle of Salamis,* for accounts of these battles.
[35] Aeschylus, Grene and Lattimore translation. Gela refers to the city in Sicily whose tyrant was Aeschylus' patron. He visited frequently and died there.
[36] Thucydides, 2.34.2–7.

land to be the highway of our daring, and everywhere, whether for evil or for good, have left imperishable monuments behind us. Such is the Athens for which these men, in the assertion of their resolve not to lose her, nobly fought and died; and well may every one of their survivors be ready to suffer in her cause.[37]

Pericles encouraged citizens to regard their city as an extended family to which they owed their primary loyalty. By sacrificing their lives to preserve or extend its glory, they could share in its immortality:

> For this offering of their lives made in common by them all they each of them individually received that renown which never grows old, and for a sepulcher, not so much that in which their bones have been deposited, but that noblest of shrines wherein their glory is laid up to be eternally remembered upon every occasion on which deed or story shall call for its commemoration. For heroes have the whole earth for their tomb; and in lands far from their own, where the column with its epitaph declares it, there is enshrined in every breast a record, unwritten with no tablet to preserve it, except that of the heart.[38]

Markers of standing

Unlike armor, clothing was not a particularly important signifier of status in the *Iliad* or in classical Greece. Fancy dress was frowned on in fifth-century Athens, where it was associated with Asian luxury and tyrants. Spartans were famous for their disdain of luxury. They dressed simply, in rough wool cloaks, and ate a frugal diet dominated by beans. Classical Greeks associated fine clothes with evil deeds. In *Agamemnon*, Clytemnestra rolls out an elegant, red velvet cloak for her husband, ostensibly to honor and welcome him home from Troy. Agamemnon initially refuses to step on it, insisting that he is only a man and should not be honored like a god. Clytemnestra appeals to his hubris, and he finally assents to her request. He walks across the cloak barefoot, and they enter the house, where she repeatedly stabs him in the bath she has prepared. Agamemnon's willingness to be treated like a god makes him something of an accomplice in his destruction.

Warfare and sports – the two dominant arenas for earning honor – came together at Delphi, which housed the Temple of Zeus and hosted

[37] Ibid., 2.41.4–5.
[38] Ibid., 2.43.2–3; Loraux, "Mourir devant Troie, tomber pour Athènes."

the Pythian Games. City states erected treasuries at Delphi to house and display booty won in wars, especially against non-Greeks. The treasuries were offerings to the gods and visible signs of the standing cities claimed. The Pythian and Olympic Games were open to all Greek athletes who swore before Zeus to abide by the rules. Those who were caught committing fouls were fined or flogged. Victors were rewarded with an olive wreath. The wreath itself was intentionally worthless, and meant to signify that athletes competed only for honor, not for financial gain.[39] The Persians found this inexplicable.[40] In the *Iliad*, and in other contests, athletes did compete for cash prizes or their equivalents.

Cities built monuments and shrines on their own territories that were also intended to convey their wealth and power. Monumental architecture was by no means a Greek invention; the Egypt and Mesopotamian Empires had built massive palaces, temples and tombs for political as well as religious purposes. Athens followed suit and outdid its rivals. In the aftermath of the Persian Wars, Pericles used funds from the Delian League and white marble from Pentelicon to rebuild the Acropolis, a twenty-year project that resulted in the Propylaea, with its monumental gates and columns, the Temple of Nike and the Parthenon. The new buildings on the Acropolis celebrated Athens' victory over Persia, and its north bastion incorporated stones and other elements from the earlier structures destroyed by the Persians. Construction was not finished until 421, during a truce in the Peloponnesian War.[41] With sculpture by Phidias, including a large Athena inside, the splendid Parthenon was regarded as one of the marvels of the ancient world. Athenian reconstruction on the Acropolis encouraged other cites to follow suit, and monumental architecture became another site of agon in the Greek world.

Threats to honor and standing

How people and cities respond to threats and slights to their standing and honor is indicative of the importance of honor in their society. In classical Greece, disrespect from other cities could lead to war. Sparta's war against Elis (*c.* 402) was the result of symbolic mistreatment at Olympic Games

---

[39] Finley and Pleket, *The Olympic Games*, pp. 15–16; Miller, *Ancient Greek Athletics*, pp. 17–19.
[40] Herodotus, *Histories*, 8.26.
[41] Beard, *The Parthenon*, pp. 141–4; Rhodes, *Architecture and Meaning on the Athenian Acropolis*, pp. 2–34.

and the altar of Zeus.[42] Insults led to war with Thebes.[43] Individuals and cities alike sometimes made decisions to fight for their honor at the expense of their security. Athens could easily have remained uninvolved when the Ionians revolted against Persian rule in 499, but its assembly rashly succumbed to the appeal of Aristagoras, the local tyrant of Meletus, to come to the aid of people of common descent. Athens intervened on a symbolic scale – the assembly sent a mere twenty ships – to show support for people felt to be their kinsmen. Herodotus tells us that this was enough to infuriate the Persians and was the catalyst for Darius' invasion of Greece.[44]

The two Persian invasions of Greece aroused enormous fear and encouraged many cities to privilege security over honor. Most Greek cities directly on the path of advancing Persian armies "Medized": they offered water and earth to the Persian king or his representatives, and threw themselves on their mercy. Some thirty cities resisted, some of them, such as Plataea, were even astride the invasion route. Greek negotiations with Gelon, the tyrant of Syracuse, provide powerful evidence of the importance of honor, even in the face of great danger. Syracuse was one of the wealthiest and most powerful cities in Greece, and Gelon offered to send 300 ships to augment the Greek navy. This force was almost equal to the 380 ships the Athenians were able to muster at Salamis. Gelon insisted that he be made the commander-in-chief. The Spartans suggested that he content himself with command of the joint Greek fleet, but the Athenians, citing Homer as their authority, asserted their right to this position. Denied the standing he desired, Gelon sat out the war. Sparta rejected aid from two other powerful Greek states in preference to sharing the military leadership. Argos withdrew from the coalition when it was offered only one-third of the command.[45]

Leonidas and the Spartiates under his command chose to fight and die at Thermopylae to gain honor, when they could have withdrawn along with the other Greeks without any loss of honor. They had repulsed repeated attacks by superior forces, demonstrating their superior motivation and skill. The Greek army had already retreated to the south, and the Greek

---

[42] Xenophon, *Hellenica*, 3.8.4.

[43] Ibid., *Hellenica*, 6.5.33–48.

[44] Herodotus, *Histories*, 5.98–104; Meiggs, *The Athenian Empire*, p. 32.

[45] Herodotus, *Histories*, 7.145, 148–9, 157–63. Gelon then sent ships to Delphi with treasure to offer to Xerxes if he emerged the victor. It is possible that Gelon insisted on command knowing that his offer would be spurned, thus leaving him free to concentrate on the threat posed closer to home by Carthage.

navy had abandoned its position at Artemisium for Salamis, and the Spartans served no useful strategic purpose by staying behind.[46] Sparta did not always behave honorably. The Greeks retreated as the Persian army advanced, and the Athenians abandoned their city for the island of Salamis in the Saronic Gulf. Themistocles, the Athenian leader, was convinced of the necessity of enticing the Persians to fight in the narrow straits between Salamis and Attica, where the smaller, less seaworthy, but more maneuverable Greek ships would have an advantage. A victory here was also the only hope the Athenians had of regaining their homeland. Eurybiades, the Spartan in command of the Greek navy, wanted to retreat to the mainland, behind the defensive walls that the Greeks were building across the narrow Isthmus of Corinth.[47] If defeated here – a likely outcome because the Persians could outflank the Greek forces and attack them from behind – the Spartan army could withdraw to its homeland and hope the Persians would not follow. Themistocles insisted on a council of war that brought together the leaders of the allied forces. The Corinthian admiral taunted Themistocles over the loss of his city. Eurybiades became so enraged by what he perceived as Themistocles' challenge of his authority, that he raised his staff of office and threatened to bring it down on the Athenian's head, reminiscent of Odysseus' treatment of Thersites. Themistocles remained calm and finally cajoled the allies into fighting at Salamis by threatening to sail off to Sicily with his ships and all the Athenians they could transport to found a new colony out of reach of the Persians.[48]

In the *Iliad*, honor almost always trumps fear. The Greek response to the Persian invasions indicates that in fifth-century Greece honor was an important but not exclusive motive that was sometimes sacrificed in the name of security. Interest entered into the picture in proportion to the Greek success in expelling Persia and reducing the threat it posed to Hellas as a whole. If Thucydides is to be believed, the Athenians were quite conscious of the mix. He has them invoke all three motives on the eve of the Peloponnesian War to justify their city's policies. They explain to the Spartan assembly that Athens acquired its empire

---

[46] Ibid., 8.8–23, 8.40, on the sea battle and abandonment of Artemisium.

[47] According to Herodotus, ibid., 8.2, Eurybiades was given leadership of the Greek naval forces because the other Greeks, while acknowledging Athenian naval prowess, did not want to serve under a city many considered their equal. In this instance, Athenians put their security above their honor, and agreed to Spartan leadership.

[48] Ibid., 8.62.

because you were unwilling to prosecute to its conclusion the war against the barbarian, and because the allies attached themselves to us and spontaneously asked us to assume the command. And the nature of the case first compelled us to advance our empire to its present height; fear being our principal motive, though honor and interest afterwards came in. And at last, when almost all hated us, when some had already revolted and had been subdued, when you had ceased to be the friends that you once were, and had become objects of suspicion and dislike, it appeared no longer safe to give up our empire; especially as all who left us would fall to you. And none can quarrel with a people for making, in matters of tremendous risk, the best provision that it can for its interest.[49]

The Athenian speech reveals the degree to which motives can be reinforcing or cross-cutting. Fear and honor were conjoined at the outset; resistance to Persia, understood as the only way to save their lives and independence, required Athenians to cobble together a coalition of Greek states to resist the Persian invader, evacuate their city and risk everything on a naval battle in the Straits of Salamis. Individual Athenians were also motivated by fear and honor; they fought to gain honors as they struggled to save their families and homeland.[50] Athenian courage and risk-taking, so critical to success against the Persians, are the hallmarks of honor-based societies.

By the time of the Peloponnesian War, it is fair to say that honor and interest had become coequal motives for most of the cities directly involved in the events leading up to its outbreak. The precipitating cause of that war was a conflict between Corcyra and Corinth that drew in Athens and Sparta on opposing sides. Corinth's hostility to Corcyra derived, at least initially, from that colony's failure to pay the expected homage towards its Corinthian founders at festivals. For some time, Corinth had been consolidating its hold over the coast of northwest Greece, an important way-station for seaborne trade to Magna Grecia.[51] When Corcyra turned a deaf ear to the appeals of envoys from Epidamnus for help in defending their city against local tribesmen in league with exiled nobles, the city turned to Corinth for assistance. The Corinthians responded with alacrity, according to Thucydides, because of their hatred of Corcyra. The Corcyraeans, outraged by Corinthian intervention, promptly laid siege to

---

[49] Thucydides, 1.75.2–5.

[50] Strauss, *Battle of Salamis*, pp. 157–74, gives a nice sense of how these motives combined for Athenian and other captains of triremes.

[51] Herodotus, *Histories*, 3.49.1; Thucydides, 1.23.3; Graham, *Colony and Mother City in Ancient Greece*, pp. 4–8, 118–51; Crane, *Thucydides and the Ancient Simplicity*, pp. 95–100.

Epidamnus. Corinth readied a fleet to come to the aid of the city. Fearful of war with Corinth and its allies, Corcyra proposed negotiations and then arbitration. Corinth refused, and sent its fleet toward Epidamnus, where it was defeated by Corcyra at Leucimme. Corinth now prepared for war in earnest, and Corcyra appealed to Athens for support.[52]

The Athenian assembly at first rejected the Corcyraean appeal for a defensive alliance, but then reversed the decision at the urging of Pericles. With Athenian assistance, the Corcyraeans repulsed a second Corinth naval expedition, this time directed against them. The Corinthians and other allies with grievances against Athens appealed to the Spartan assembly, who voted for war in 431 on the grounds that Athens had broken the Thirty Years Peace.[53] The Athenians concluded that the alliance was attractive because the Corcyraean fleet would significantly enhance Athenian naval capabilities in a war with Corinth and its allies.[54] Fear nevertheless seems a remote motive because war with Corinth was unlikely in the absence of a Corcyraean alliance. Nor was the Corcyraean fleet an important enough asset to risk war as Athens already possessed a fleet much larger than Corinth and other Spartan allies combined. In the same sentence in which he describes Athenian strategic concerns, Thucydides tells us that Corcyra lay conveniently on the coasting passage to Italy and Sicily, suggesting that interest was an important motive.[55]

Pericles probably welcomed the Corcyraean alliance, not because he really thought war was inevitable, but because he regarded it as an opportunity to extend and consolidate Athenian power. He may have reasoned that the alliance would deter Corinth from attacking, but that if deterrence failed, Sparta would remain neutral and Corinth would be humbled. If Sparta entered the war, he made clear his intention not to oppose their expected invasion of Attica, but conduct a campaign of naval harassment around the Peloponnese, raising the prospect of a helot rebellion. The Spartans would become increasingly frustrated by their inability to engage Athens, tire of war and reach a new agreement with Athens.[56] Such a policy was clearly motivated by reinforcing considerations of interest and honor.

In his often-cited authorial statement in book 1, Thucydides writes that "the growth of the power of Athens, and the alarm which this inspired

---

[52] Thucydides, 1.32–6.
[53] Ibid., 1.88, and book 1 more generally for the origins of the war; Plutarch, *Pericles*, 29.1, on the first Athenian assembly.
[54] Thucydides, 1.44.1–2.   [55] Ibid.
[56] Lebow, *Tragic Vision of Politics*, ch. 2, and pp. 264–5.

in Sparta, made war inevitable."[57] I have argued elsewhere that in the narrative of book 1 Thucydides leads thoughtful readers to the conclusion that Sparta's decision for war had less to do with fear than it did with honor. The Spartan "war party" did not fear Athenian military power, which it grossly underestimated. "War party" and "peace party" – to the extent that we can use these terms to distinguish between the supporters of Sthenelaïdas and those of Archidamus – were concerned about honor and the Spartan way of life.[58] *Timē*, and sometimes *axioma*, define honor with respect to standing or status. They also encompass dignity and self-respect, which require people to act in the right way, quite independently of its implications for their security. Most Spartiates saw both forms of honor on the line in 431. If they stood aside, Athens would increase its absolute power and relative standing at their expense. Failure to come to the aid of their allies would be dishonorable. For centuries, Spartans had been driven by a fierce ambition to achieve and then maintain hegemony in Hellas. Spartiates lived to serve their polis and internalized its goals. Their self-esteem was inextricably connected with Sparta's honor and international standing, and respect for the bravery and accomplishments of its hoplites. Spartiates were deeply offended by the power and confidence of Athens, and charges by their allies that they had left them to fend for themselves. They sought honor and glory, aims that had little to do with more tangible interests. The Spartan decision for war was not motivated by concern for physical security but by ontological security: the need to defend Spartan values and identity.

Obligation

Competition among individuals and cities was softened by family ties and friendships that created and sustained dense networks of responsibilities and mutual obligation. These ties existed at the personal and political levels, as they did in the *Iliad* and the *Odyssey*, but also at the city level as the polis replaced the household (*oikos*) as the unit of political and economic life in the late eighth century.[59] At both levels, they were sustained by gift-exchange and the ritual that surrounded it. Not surprisingly, the political structure of the early polis copied the *oikos*; it was hierarchical and

---

[57] Thucydides, 1.23.6.   [58] Lebow, *Tragic Vision of Politics*, pp. 101–3, 155–9.
[59] Nagy, *Best of the Achaeans*, p. 7, suggests that this was the period in which the *Iliad* and the *Odyssey* achieved their final form, and that this reflected the need for pan-Hellenic heroes.

centered on the king, his retainers, servants and slaves.[60] By 700 BCE, most kingdoms had given way to aristocratic rule. This was a major transformation because the ruling class, although small, had always been conceived of as a group of equals despite its hierarchy. Henceforth, expanding political rights to more, or even all citizens, as in the case in Athens, became a change in degree, not of kind.

Friendship and gratitude encouraged loyalty, self-restraint and generosity based on the principle of reciprocity. In the *Republic*, Plato has the simple but honest Polemarchus define justice in terms of reciprocity: it consists of doing good to one's friends and harm to one's enemies.[61] Reciprocity is also emphasized by Xenophon in his *Hellenica*.[62] For the ancient Greeks, as understood by Émile Durkheim and Marcel Mauss, participation in a network of ritual exchange and mutual obligation built community by creating affective ties among individuals, providing important shared experiences, and stretching their identities into what Durkheim called *la conscience collective*.[63] Modern scholars consider reciprocity the foundation of traditional interpersonal and inter-*oikos* relations.[64] They disagree about whether reciprocity and kinship ties survived the transition from *oikos* to polis, and the extent to which it was supplanted by the new ideal of communal solidarity.[65] One incentive for this transition was the high political cost of reciprocity. While hospitality and gifts elicited friendship and return gifts, transgression against oneself or family required vengeance, which led to escalating family and political feuds of the kind responsible for the tragedy of the *Iliad*. Aeschylus reworked

[60] Aeschylus' *Seven against Thebes* and *Oresteia*, and Sophocles, *Oedipus Turannis*, portray such cities where there is no distinction between the politics of the household and the city.

[61] Plato, *Republic*, 1.332a.

[62] Xenophon, *Hellenica*, 4.v.41. The Phliasian Procles argues in the aftermath of the Battle of Leuctra that if Athens comes to the aid of Sparta, it will feel duty bound to offer help in return when Athens needs support.

[63] Durkheim, *The Division of Labor in Society*, pp. 229–30; Mauss, *The Gift*.

[64] Vidal-Naquet, *The Black Hunter*; Booth, *Households*; Sahlins, *Stone Age Economics*; Seaford, *Reciprocity and Ritual*; Reden, *Exchange in Ancient Greece*; Donlon, "Reciprocities in Homer," and "Political Reciprocity in Dark Age Greece"; Zanker, "Beyond Reciprocity"; Postlethwaite, "Akhilleus and Agamemnon"; Low, *Interstate Relations in Classical Greece*, pp. 43–53.

[65] Connor, "Civil Society, Dionysiac Festival, and the Athenian Democracy," makes this argument in the case of fifth-century Athens. Seaford, *Reciprocity and Ritual*, suggests that solidarity largely replaced reciprocity. The case for continuing reciprocity in social, economic and political relationships is made by Millett, "The Rhetoric of Reciprocity in Classical Athens," and *Lending and Borrowing in Ancient Athens*, esp. pp. 24–52, 109–26 and 148–59; Allen, *The World of Prometheus*; Schofield, "Political Friendship and the Ideology of Reciprocity."

this theme in his *Oresteia* to demonstrate the need for and possibility of substituting courts and public justice for private revenge.[66] Reciprocity also encouraged expectations of private gifts and rewards, and was thus a source of corruption in the polis.[67] Pericles solved the corruption problem by living a simple and relatively isolated life. He was famous for his refusal to socialize with his peers, presumably to avoid becoming enmeshed in any personal relationships and their concomitant obligations.[68] He had his house burned when Athenians took refuge behind their walls for fear that Archidamus would spare it is an act of friendship.[69]

For much of recorded history, there was no conceptual, organizational or juridical divide separating international from domestic politics. In fifth-century Greece there was no word or set of concepts to signify this difference. This may seem strange to contemporary readers, but was perfectly natural to Greeks. Athens aside, there were no police forces to maintain domestic order, which meant that the polis technically existed in a state of anarchy. People depended for the most part on the good will and support of their neighbors.[70] If someone raised a cry of alarm in the night, it was customary for neighbors to come running. Cities like Athens ultimately developed courts for citizens to bring complaints, and they were very active in the fifth century. Good will and trust nevertheless remained the foundation of order. They allowed Greeks to go about unarmed, of which they were proud because they believed it distinguished them from barbarians.[71] As Durkheim observed, such a system of informal enforcement works best in small, tight-knit communities where everybody knows everybody else.[72]

---

[66] Seaford, *Reciprocity and Ritual*, on the role of tragedy in general in serving this end.
[67] On bribery and reciprocity, see Adkins, *Merit and Responsibility*; Dover, *Greek Popular Morality in the Time of Plato and Aristotle*; Blundell, *Helping Friends and Harming Enemies*, ch. 2. Vlastos, *Socrates*, pp. 194–9, argues that there was an explicit rejection of reciprocity in the democratic polis, especially of its retaliatory aspects, because of the destructive consequences. Xenophon, *Memorabilia*, 2.4.6, notes the damaging aspect of reciprocity as used by politicians to buy votes for undemocratic ends.
[68] Plutarch, *Pericles*, 7.4–5, reports that Pericles only traveled on one street in the city: the road leading to the agora and the assembly. The only social event he is known to have attended was the wedding feast of his kinsman Euryptolemos, and he left immediately after the libations were made. Thucydides, 2.60.5, 2.65.8.
[69] Thucydides, 2.13.
[70] Fifth-century Athens had a rudimentary police force of about 300 Scythian slaves who helped the magistrates maintain order at public meetings, control crowds, arrest criminals and guard prisoners. There were no public prosecutors, and the Athenian police force may have been unique.
[71] Thucydides, 1.5–6; Lintott, *Violence, Civil Strife and Revolution in the Classical City*, pp. 13–33; Rahe, *Republics Ancient and Modern*, I, p. 55.
[72] Durkheim, *The Division of Labor in Society*, pp. 400–1.

Relations among city states – Greek city states – were in theory, and often in practice, governed by the norms of guest friendship (*xenia*), and considered an extension of domestic relations. Cities would routinely invoke their common heritage, prior good will or past assistance as justification for their demands on others to come to their aid. These requests would sometimes be honored in circumstances involving high risks or costs, as in the case of Athenian support for the Ionian rebels. On the eve of the Peloponnesian War, Corinth appealed unsuccessfully to Athens to refrain from allying with its adversary Corcyra on the grounds that Corinth had opposed those in the Spartan alliance who pushed for war with Athens in 441–40 while it was struggling to suppress rebellion in Samos.[73]

Pericles' funeral oration indicates that he considered gift-giving (*charis*), and the reciprocity it entailed, an appropriate model for foreign as well as domestic policy. Athens is different from other empires, he tells his listeners, because of the generosity it shows its allies, offering them more than it takes from them.[74] By 431, as Pericles knew better than anyone else, the Athenian Empire was held together as much by force as by loyalty, and the flow of resources was largely unidirectional. Athens suppressed piracy, instituted common weights and coinage, opened its markets and law courts to allies, provided employment, especially as rowers, for poorer allied citizens, but also moved the treasury from Delos to Athens and increased the tribute it levied on allies to pay for the war, which caused grumbling and occasional rebellion.[75] In the last speech Pericles makes before succumbing to the plague, he acknowledges that the Athenian Empire has many attributes of a tyranny.[76] He nevertheless presents a model of empire that shares a striking similarity with Homer's depiction of the ideal Bronze Age king (*basileus*), whose authority rests not only on his power, but on how it is used to benefit his followers. Fifth- and fourth-century Greeks, had their own term for this relationship: *hēgemōnia*. It was a form of legitimate authority and was associated with *timē*, the gift of honor. *Timē* meant "esteem" in the abstract, but also the "office" to which one was therefore entitled.[77] It symbolized the linkage between honor and office that I associated in chapter 2 with clientalist hierarchies in

---

[73] Thucydides, 1.37–43.

[74] Thucydides, 1.40. Pericles is using erotically charged imagery. He is urging his countrymen to assume the masculine role with respect to their city (*erōmenos*), and by extension to the rest of Greece. See Monoson, *Plato's Democratic Entanglements*, pp. 64–87; Wohl, *Love among the Ruins*, pp. 30–73; Lebow, *Tragic Vision of Politics*, pp. 278–81.

[75] Meiggs, *The Athenian Empire*, pp. 538–61.   [76] Thucydides, 2.63.

[77] Perlman, "Hegemony and *Archē* in Greece".

traditional honor worlds. Sparta and Athens earned *timē* and the honorific status of "hegemons" by virtue of their contributions to Greece during the Persian Wars. *Timē* was also conferred on Athens in recognition of her literary, artistic and intellectual, political and commercial accomplishments that had made her, as Pericles noted in his funeral oration, the "school of Hellas."[78]

Society

Community was originally organized around the household (*oikos*), but during the eighth century it was replaced by the polis. In both forms of community, security and sustenance were principal ends, and the interest of the individual was advanced through the group's attainment of common goals.[79] All communities were organized around the principles of hierarchy and *philia*. The latter embraced affection, friendship and belonging, and at its core signified some form of freely chosen association.[80] *Philia* was routinely used to describe the bonds of marriage and the political "friendship" of citizens who chose to associate with one another in a political community.[81] In the last third of the fifth century, as Pericles' speech indicates, the term was also used to characterize a citizen's relationship to his polis, and responsibility for its well-being.[82] Without intended irony, Athenian playwrights describe as "demos-lovers" people who have the same degree of affection for their polis as for their family and friends.[83]

As society becomes thinner, honor worlds become more difficult to sustain. Sports offers a nice illustration. Olympic victors, who sometimes

---

[78] Thucydides, 2.4.

[79] Aristotle, *Politics*, 1252a1, notes that "Every state is a community of some kind, and every community is established with a view to some good." See also Finley, *The Ancient Economy* and *The World of Odysseus*; Vidal-Naquet, *The Black Hunter*; Booth, *Households*.

[80] Aristotle, *Nicomachean Ethics*, 1155a14, 1159b25, 1161a23, 1161b12, and *Politics*, 1280b39, observes that, for Greeks, political community is a common project that requires affection and a common commitment among citizens, and that friendship is often considered more important than justice.

[81] On *philia*, see Aristotle, *Nicomachean Ethics*, 1155a1–1172a16, and *Eudemonian Ethics*, 1234b19–1249a24; Connor, *The New Politicians of Fifth-Century Athens*, ch. 2; Hunter, *Politics as Friendship*; Konstan, "*Philia* in Euripides' *Electra*"; Lacey, *The Family in Classical Greece*; Vernant, *Mythe et pensée chez les grecs*, pp. 208–9; Cooper, *Reason and Emotion*, chs. 14 and 15.

[82] Aristotle, *Politics*, 1320b7–11, 1329b39–1330a2.

[83] In *Antigone*, Sophocles uses *philia* in a double sense: as kinship and as affection toward the polis. See Winnington-Ingram, *Sophocles*, p. 129; Connor, *The New Politicians of Fifth-Century Athens*, pp. 99–100.

had odes written in their honor, not infrequently exploited their fame for material gain. The Olympic Games were always preceded by a truce so that athletes from all over Hellas could participate and spectators travel to and from Olympia in safety. At times, this truce broke down. In 364 BCE, the organizers lost control of the games because of their improper involvement in politics. To get revenge, they attacked the new organizers in the midst of a wrestling match. This led to a pitched battle inside the sanctuary, with archers participating from some of the temples. The fans stopped watching the wrestling match and directed their attention to the battle, applauding the two sides as if they were opposing teams at a sports match.[84]

A similar development occurred in relations among cities, and is one the principal themes of Thucydides' history. Pericles appears to be the model of the wise statesman because of his ability to get citizens to rise above their parochial concerns to support policies that are in the best interest of their polis. Thucydides attributes Pericles' success to self-mastery; he suppresses his appetites in pursuit of honor for himself and his city. He succeeds as long as his appetite and spirit are constrained and guided by reason. In 431 BCE, he nevertheless succumbs to hubris, and convinces himself, and an initially reluctant Athenian assembly, that a defensive alliance with Corcyra is a low-cost means of increasing Athenian power and humbling its Corinthian rival. Pericles is irrationally confident about his ability to manage events to prevent the outbreak of war, or, failing that, to limit its scope and duration.[85] His hubris is emblematic of his city. In their speech to the Spartan assembly on the event of war, Thucydides has the Corinthians portray the Athenians as driven by *polypragmosunē*, literally "trespass," but widely used in the late fifth century by critics of modernity to signify a kind of metaphysical restlessness, intellectual discontent and meddlesomeness that found expression in *pleonexia* (envy, ambition, search for glory, monetary greed, lust for power and conquest).[86] Athens cannot resist the prospect of gain held out by the Corcyraean proposal of alliance. These characteristics become increasingly more pronounced as the war progresses, and find their most extreme and destructive expression in the assembly's irrational enthusiasm for the Sicilian expedition.

Thucydides leads thoughtful readers to a parallel conclusion about Sparta. Reason loses control of the spirit. King Archidamus offers the Spartan assembly an accurate account of Athenian power, and urges his

---

[84] Finley, and Pleket, *The Olympic Games*, pp. 74–8, on compensation.
[85] Lebow, *Tragic Vision of Politics*, ch. 7.   [86] Thucydides, 1.68–71.

compatriots to reflect carefully before embarking on a war that they are likely to pass on to their sons. His argument carries less weight than the emotional plea of the ephor Sthenelaïdas, who insists that the Athenians have wronged long-standing allies and deserve to be punished. In Athens, Pericles appeals to the Athenian appetite for wealth and power, while in Sparta, Sthenelaïdas speaks to his countrymen's spirit and yearning for honor. In showing the disastrous consequences of the unrestrained pursuit of either set of desires, Thucydides reaffirms the importance of the traditional Greek value of the middle way (*meden agan*), something that can only be attained in practice when reason constrains both appetite and spirit.[87]

Up to the death of Pericles in 429, the ideal of empire nevertheless remained *hēgemōnia*. Six years later, in the Mytilenean debate, Cleon tells the Athenian assembly that their empire is an *archē* and despotism (*turannis*) based on military power and the fear it inspires.[88] In the interim, the Athenians had suffered grievous losses in the plague, tightened their control over dependent states and increased their demands for tribute. By the time of the Melian Dialogue in 416, Athens has given up all pretense of acting in terms of accepted values, and its spokesmen make no attempt to justify their self-interested behavior with reference to them.

The breakdown of society and the unrestrained pursuit of self-interest come together in the Melian Dialogue.[89] The Athenian generals, Cleomedes and Tisias, dispense with all pretense about their motive. They deny the relevance of justice, which they assert only comes into play between equals. "The strong do what they can and the weak suffer what they must," and the Melians should put their survival first and submit.[90] The Melian aristocrats rule out submission even though they recognize that resistance is almost certain to be futile and lead to their destruction. They put their honor – conceived as freedom and independence – above their security. Contemporary Greeks would have been shocked by Athens' failure to offer any justification (*prophasis*) for their invasion, and even more by their rejection of the Melian offer of neutrality on the grounds that "your hostility cannot so hurt us as your friendship [*philia*]."[91]

---

[87] Ibid., 1.80–5, 86–8, for the two speeches. The war developed as Archidamus predicted, and Sparta was forced to sue for peace after a sizeable number of its hoplites were taken prisoner on the island of Sphacteria in 426. Athens subsequently broke the truce and was defeated in 404, but Sparta's victory left it weak and unable to maintain its primacy in Greece.

[88] Thucydides, 3.37.2.   [89] Ibid., 5.84–116.   [90] Ibid., 5.89.   [91] Ibid., 5.95.

Fifteen years into the war the Athenians have repudiated, indeed inverted, core Greek values.

The rhetorical style of the Athenian generals reinforces the impression conveyed by their words. Dionysius of Halicarnassus judged their language "appropriate to oriental monarchs addressing Greeks, but unfit to be spoken by Athenians to Greeks whom they liberated from the Medes."[92] Thucydides appears to have modeled his dialogue on a passage in Herodotus where the Persian king Xerxes discusses the wisdom of attacking Greece with his council of advisors.[93] The language is similar and so are the arguments; Xerxes also alludes to the law of the stronger and the self-interest of empires. Later in his account, Herodotus describes an offer of peace and friendship that Xerxes makes to Athens and Sparta on the eve of his invasion. The Athenians spurn his olive branch and accept the danger of confronting a seemingly invincible force in the name of Greek freedom, just as the Melians reject Athens' offer of alliance because of the value they place on their freedom.[94] These parallels would not have been lost on contemporary readers. For Thucydides, as for many Greeks, the Athenians of 416 have become the Persians of 480 and the symbol of rank despotism.[95]

War

According to Hans van Wees, the most respected authority on Greek warfare, city states fought one another "to demonstrate their 'excellence' [aretē] that entitled them to a place at the top of the tree, and at the same time they fought to stop inferiors from acting like equals, equals from acting like superiors, and superiors from demanding more deference than they deserved."[96] Material gain was "a secondary issue at best," as attested to by the demands victors made on the defeated. They frequently included acknowledgments of superiority, which often took the form of entering into an alliance as a subordinate partner, and only rarely required payments or other kinds of material compensation such as cattle or slaves.[97] Hatreds nevertheless arose in the course of time; the feud

---

[92] Dionysius of Halicarnassus, *On Thucydides*, ch. 38, p. 31.
[93] Herodotus, *Histories*, 7.8. Cornford, *Thucydides Mythistoricus*, pp. 176–82; Connor, *Thucydides*, pp. 155–7; Crane, *Thucydides and the Ancient Simplicity*, pp. 241–6; Rood, "Thucydides' Persian Wars," on the parallels between Herodotus and Thucydides.
[94] Herodotus, *Histories*, 8.140, 144; Thucydides, 5.112; Connor, *Thucydides*, pp. 156–7.
[95] This point is also made by Crane, *Thucydides and the Ancient Simplicity*, pp. 246 ff.
[96] Wees, *Greek Warfare*, p. 22.   [97] Ibid., pp. 24–5.

between Corinth and Corcyra helped to trigger the first phase of the Peloponnesian War, and the one between Thebes and Argos to renew it after the Spartan–Athenian truce. It influenced city behavior as much as it did individual behavior. Modern scholars attribute the internecine warfare of the period to an endemic and competitive desire on the part of cities for honor and prestige.

In honor worlds, warfare is frequent, but its ends and means are limited. This was true on the whole of classical Greece. War was a normal part of city life, and hoplite service was nearly universal for those who could afford a panoply.[98] Until the Peloponnesian War, conflicts among Greeks had generally been about disputed territory, relative standing or insults to civic honor. Campaigns were designed to seek out and engage the other side's army. A single battle often sufficed to achieve the goals of war if it gave one or the other a victory. Peter Krentz estimates that in the hoplite battle, losses were 5 percent for the victors and 14 percent for the losers.[99] Warfare rarely threatened the existence of combatant cities or the lives of their inhabitants, because its goal generally was to establish precedence among cities. Their destruction would have led to dishonor and destroyed the community that made precedence meaningful.[100] Greek practice nevertheless frequently departed from this Homeric ideal. On sixty-five occasions Herodotus uses the verb "to conquer" (*katastrephein*) to describe one city imposing its will on another.[101]

Battles were intense and bloody affairs, but governed by extensive rules. The emphasis was on a fair encounter, because standing was based on courage, and relative courage only became apparent in a fight between equals. Opposing armies would sometimes camp out opposite each other for several days until they could agree on a time and place to engage. The agonal spirit requires acceptance of combat, but not under unfavorable conditions. Heralds and sacred places were inviolable, as was the Olympic truce. If the engagement involved allies, the opposing phalanxes were arrayed on the basis of standing, with the far-right wing of each being the principal place of honor. There was often as much, if not more, debate about the order of precedence as there was about the strategy for fighting the battle.[102] Generals were also expected to lead their troops into battle,

---

[98] Finley, *Politics in the Ancient World*, p. 67; Ma, "Fighting Poleis in the Ancient World," p. 338.

[99] Krentz, "Casualties in Hoplite Battles."

[100] Raaflaub, "Expansion und Machtbildung in frühren Polis-Systemen."

[101] Eckstein, *Mediterranean Anarchy*, p. 42.

[102] Pritchett, *The Greek State at War*, I, pp. 147–55; Wees, *Greek Warfare*, pp. 134–5.

and we have the names of at least thirty military leaders from classical Greece who died in the front lines.[103]

Before battle both armies would make a sacrifice and sing a paean to the gods, which also had the effect of preventing a surprise attack. The opposing phalanxes would then advance and push against each other and thrust with their spears until one or the other gave way, and possibly shed its armor and fled the field of battle. The restrictions on pursuit were more tactical than normative; soldiers in a phalanx feared loss of cohesion and facing a sudden rally of the enemy. However, armies that could not escape were sometimes massacred. Mutilation of the dead was prohibited, but victors were allowed to strip their armor, clothing and possessions. They could show special consideration to opponents who had fought well by leaving their bodies in their tunics. There were also procedures for determining the victor. By the middle fifth century, the decisive consideration was control of the battlefield and the bodies on it. Asking the other army to retrieve one's dead was an admission of defeat. The winner was required to grant a truce so that these bodies could be recovered. The victor was allowed to erect a trophy on the battlefield, and the loser was required to leave it intact until it collapsed or was destroyed by the elements. The Greek word *tropē*, from which our word "trophy" derives, signified the turning point in the battle at which one side turned and fled. Trophies were also erected at temples, especially at Delphi, and were claims for prestige and honor.[104]

The test of courage, for cities and hoplites alike, was not giving ground. In the words of Euripides, it consists of "standing fast staring at the rushing line of spears, and holding one's place in the ranks."[105] In the fifth century, some cities ranked their citizens on the basis of their bravery in battle. Sparta awarded a prize to the bravest man in major battles. A product of this culture, Herodotus usually tells us who, in his opinion, were the bravest combatants in the engagements he describes. Conflicts with barbarians, whether tribesmen or empires, were about security, sometimes about survival, and generally fought with no holds barred. At Marathon, Salamis and Plataea, Greeks took few if any prisoners, excepting those that

---

[103] Hanson, *Western Way of War*, pp. 113–14.
[104] Euripides, *Heracles*, 191–4; Xenophon, *Hellenica*, 4.2.18, 6.5.16; Pritchett, *The Greek State at War*, I, pp. 105–9, II, pp. 147–55, 246–70; Wees, *Greek Warfare*, pp. 134–8; Hanson, *Hoplites*, pp. 197–227; Lendon, *Soldiers and Ghosts*, pp. 40–3; Eckstein, *Mediterranean Anarchy*, pp. 211–14.
[105] Euripides, *Heracles*, 163–4. Translation from Lendon, *Soldiers and Ghosts*, p. 50.

might be ransomed for significant sums.[106] It is nevertheless also true that in the Peloponnesian War Sparta killed sailors and merchants alike that they captured at sea, and killed the 3,000 Athenians they took at prisoners in the final naval battle of that conflict. Worse still, they are alleged to have left their bodies to rot.[107]

Warfare between cities was largely the preserve of the aristocracy, or the wealthy, the only classes who could gain honor, and who could afford a hoplite panoply. Hoplites were arrayed in a tightly knit phalanx, eight or more ranks deep, with their length varying as a function of terrain and the size of the opposing force. Kings and generals often fought in the front ranks – the place of honor – where they sustained unusually high casualties.[108] Like their Homeric predecessors, fifth-century Greeks on the whole disparaged cavalry, archery and slinging because they were safer forms of warfare and provided less opportunity to display bravery. In Sparta, the cavalry was transformed into an elite corps of three hundred hoplites who fought in a phalanx. In Athens, a citizen who elected to serve in the infantry when he could have been in the cavalry could claim this as a badge of courage.[109] The influence of Homer is further apparent in the occasional agreement of cities to settle their disputes by a battle of champions.[110] The purely ritual aspect of warfare had nevertheless on the whole been superseded by a more centralized, hierarchical military structure and the prominence of strategic considerations that reduced the opportunities for "free-form" warfare between heroes.[111]

In practice, there was a nastier side to warfare, conducted by cavalry and infantry alike. It consisted of ambushes, sieges of cities and devastation of crops, especially olive trees, which took thirty years to mature. Slashing and burning (*kaptein kai kaiein*) conferred no honor, but was not uncommon before the Peloponnesian War, and much more so during it.[112] At the outset of that conflict, the Spartans invaded Attica and ravaged its countryside when Athenians sought refuge behind the walls of their city. Later, they established a permanent fort for this purpose on the border of Attica

---

[106] Herodotus, *Histories*, 7.226–7; Aeschylus, *Persians*, 418–28; Strauss, *Battle of Salamis*, pp. 149–50, 194–5; Lendon, *Soldiers and Ghosts*, pp. 45–6.

[107] Thucydides, 2.67.4; Xenophon, *Hellenica*, 2.1.31–2; Plutarch, *Lysander*, 13.1; Wees, *Greek Warfare*, p. 215.

[108] Wees, *Greek Warfare*, pp. 52–3.   [109] Ibid., p. 67, citing Lysias.

[110] The most famous of these, between Sparta and Argos, involved a fight to the death between 300 champions from each city. Herodotus, *Histories*, 1.82.

[111] Wees, *Greek Warfare*, p. 165.

[112] Thucydides, 1.96, 2.14.1, 2.19.2, 2,23.2, 2.80.8 and *passim*; Xenophon, *Hellenica*, 4.1–7.1, 4.6.2–6; Pritchett, *The Greek State at War*, II, pp. 177–89; Wees, *Greek Warfare*, pp. 116–17, 121–3.

and Boeotia.[113] The Athenian triumph at Pylos in 425 BCE that resulted in the death or capture of 440 Spartan hoplites, and encouraged Sparta to sue for peace, was the result of clever generalship, the use of archers and peltasts to pick off Spartan soldiers from a distance and a blockade to starve survivors into submission.[114] In words reminiscent of Homer's Diomedes, a Spartan prisoner, when asked if those killed on the island had been more worthy than those who surrendered, scornfully responded that "the arrow would be worth a great deal if it could pick out the noble and good men from the rest."[115] From the eighth century down to the conquest of Greece by Alexander, and then by Rome, total warfare of the kind described above rivaled agonal warfare, and attacks on settlements, sieges of cities, ambushes and standoff warfare were as common as agonal warfare conducted in accord with its well-specified rituals.

Like their Homeric counterparts, fifth-century Greeks had great respect for clever ruses that contributed to victory. At Salamis, Themistocles behaved like a latter-day Odysseus. His bravery and eloquence were matched by his cunning. Afraid that he would be overruled by the Spartan admiral Eurybiades, he sent one of his slaves to pose as an informer to the Persian king Xerxes to make him believe that the Greeks would withdraw during the night. Xerxes believed him and sent his Egyptian squadron around Salamis to blockade the western outlet of the straits and unwittingly removed it from the main battle.[116]

Throughout the night the Persian ships were on the lookout for the Greek retreat, but the Greeks slept alongside their moored ships. When Themistocles learned that his ruse had worked, he ordered his fleet into battle the next morning. The Greeks rowed toward the Persians until it became evident that the fleets would meet in the middle of the channel, where the Persians would have room for maneuver and their numerical advantage could be put to telling use. The Greeks retreated, hoping to gain time until the early morning wind rose, which it did, churning up waves that began to break up the Persian formation. The Greeks attacked, ramming the leading Phoenician ships, and throwing javelins and shooting arrows at the soldiers on their decks. The Phoenician triremes were taller and rode higher in the water, making them that much more difficult to maneuver in the wind and an unsteady platform for their soldiers. The battle turned into a rout, with the Persians losing more than 200 ships, and many more sailors, as most of them could not swim. The Greeks

---

[113] Thucydides, 2.21, 2.47, 2.55–8.   [114] Ibid., 4.34.   [115] Ibid., 4.40.2.
[116] Aeschylus, *Persians*, 353–74; Herodotus, *Histories*, book 8, for Themistocles' ploys and the battle; Strauss, *Battle of Salamis*, pp. 151–4.

192 A CULTURAL THEORY OF INTERNATIONAL RELATIONS

killed all the Persians they could find on land and in the water. Xerxes was forced to retreat, leaving Mardonius behind with a land army that the Greeks would defeat at Plataea the following year.[117] Sparta subsequently awarded Themistocles a prize for his cleverness.[118]

Herodotus provides us with a striking example of cunning on the Persian side, significantly by another Greek. Artemisia, the queen of Halicarnassus in Asia Minor and an ally of Xerxes, commanded a trireme, the only woman to do so on either side. Dangerously pursued at one point in the melee by a Greek ship, she deliberately turned and rammed a Persian vessel, and the Greek captain abandoned the chase, convinced that her ship must be an ally. On a hillside, sitting on his golden throne, Xerxes watched the destruction of his fleet. He subsequently commended Artemesia for her bravery in ramming and destroying nine Athenian triremes, announcing that "My female general has become a man, and my male generals have all become women."[119]

As Homer recognizes bravery, courage and skill on both sides of the Trojan War, so does Herodotus in the Battle of Salamis, and more generally in his account of the Persian Wars. Thucydides' follows suit in his account of the Peloponnesian War. Although an Athenian, his model military leader is the Spartan general Brasidas, and his model political leader is Hermocrates of Syracuse. Thucydides' praise of Brasidas is all the more remarkable as his lightning move against Amphipolis and its surrender, before Thucydides and reinforcements could arrive, were a great embarrassment to him and led to his banishment from Athens for twenty years.[120] The even-handed treatment of combatants on both sides by Herodotus, Thucydides and Xenophon indicates conformity to another important characteristic of war in honor societies: it is as much about the opportunity for warriors to gain honor and fame as it is about achieving any political goals sought by opposing political units.

Tensions

The tension concerning military strategy is only one of many apparent in classical Greece. If we group them by categories, there are those internal to the spirit, and those involving the spirit and other motives. Both sets

---

[117] Herodotus, *Histories*, book 9.   [118] Ibid. 8.124.

[119] Ibid., 8.88. Artemisia had wisely argued against giving battle in the Straits of Salamis as it would put the larger Persian ships at a disadvantage. Xerxes rejected her advice in favor of his chief advisor Mardonius, who pressed for an attack.

[120] Ibid., 4.105–9.

of tensions were reinforcing and ultimately responsible for the transformation of an honor society into a largely fear-based world during the Peloponnesian War.

The most important internal tension was between the striving for honor and the nomos *that sustains and gives it meaning*

In the *Iliad*, violations of *nomos* cause the Trojan War and the hostility between Achilles and Agamemnon. Both conflicts have the potential to destroy the society, an outcome that is prevented only by the intervention of the gods.[121] In classical Greece, the gods remained on the sidelines, and the tensions between agon and *nomos* set in motion a negative feedback cycle. Competition for standing within city states and among them broke through the constraints imposed by convention and a dense web of mutual obligations in which individuals and city states alike were embedded. As standing is relative, the success of some cities in achieving it led to the loss, or threat of loss, of standing for others. Denial of honor aroused anger and intense desires for revenge that were even more destructive of the social–political order, as we observed in case of Corinth.

The Corcyraean alliance is another telling example. In a strictly technical sense, it was consistent with the terms of the Thirty Years Peace because no allies changed sides. It was nevertheless unacceptable to Sparta because it threatened a further, perhaps irreversible, erosion of its status as a hegemon, and with it its self-esteem. The Spartan declaration of war is best understood as an act of preemption of the kind Aristotle describes to forestall this possibility. Both hegemons made their fear of war self-fulfilling. Thucydides provides a parallel account of how the same fears drove democratic and aristocratic factions in Corcyra to civil war.[122]

Once violence begins, stronger emotions come into play. Driven by hatred of opponents who have killed one's comrades, friends or families, desires for revenge become acute among individuals, factions and cities. In the Corcyraean civil war the spiral of escalation these emotions produce lead to *stasis*, defined as a complete breakdown of order. The same thing happened in Greece as a result of the Peloponnesian War. Reason and

---

[121] Homer, *Iliad*, 1.155–65, tells us that the siege of Troy was proving so difficult that the frustrated Greeks went down to their ships to sail for home. Gray-eyed Athena sped down the peak of Olympus and instructed Odysseus to prevent the departure of the Argives, which he did. Withdrawing from the battle and going home would have involved sufficient shame to threaten the very survival of an honor culture.

[122] Thucydides, 3.70–81.

emotion can combine in the most pernicious way to destroy honor-based worlds. Thucydides constructs his accounts of the Corcyraean and Greek civil wars to make us aware of the parallels.

The tension between honor and *nomos* was particularly acute because war was the principal, although not exclusive, means for cities to gain honor and relative standing. Writing in the aftermath of the Peloponnesian War, Plato rather describes peace as a state of undeclared war among all city states.[123] This was probably intended as a theoretical statement, and should not be read as an expression of his conversion to realism, because elsewhere Plato describes the "natural relationship" between Greeks as a form of kinship and described *stasis* and slavery among Greeks as unacceptable.[124] Fifth-century Greeks distinguished themselves from barbarians (*barbaroi*, literally meaning anybody other than a Greek), and had higher expectations for intra-Greek relations.[125] There was a strong sense of "pan-Hellenic" community going back at least as far as the eighth century, reflected in the final form taken by Homer's epics, the poetry of Archilocus, colonization, the spread of the Greek alphabet, the establishment of the Pythian and Olympic Games and Apollo's sanctuary and oracle at Delphi. Herodotus tells us that the Athenians resisted the Persians in the name of "our common brotherhood with the Greeks: our common language, the altars and sacrifices of which we all partake, the common character which we bear."[126] In the classical period we have records of more than 250 treaties of friendship and peace among Greek cities, which is certainly indicative of an effort to put their relations on an orderly footing.[127] In the aftermath of the Peloponnesian War, this sentiment was still very much alive. There were widespread calls for an all-Greek effort to conquer the Persian Empire, distribute its wealth and give its richest land to poor Greeks to colonize.[128] Aristophanes' *Lysistrata*, produced in 411, pleads for Greeks to unite against barbarians instead of killing one another and destroying each other's cities. In Euripides' *Iphigenia at Aulis*, written in about 407, Iphigenia declares that it is noble to die for Greece, and that Greeks are superior to barbarians because they are free, not enslaved.[129]

---

[123] Plato, *Laws*, 626a.   [124] Plato, *Republic*, 469b–471c.
[125] Harrison, *Greeks and Barbarians*; Perlman, "Panhellenism, the Polis and Imperialism"; Cartledge; *The Greeks*, ch. 3; Low, *Interstate Relations in Classical Greece*, pp. 54–67.
[126] Herodotus, *Histories*, 8.144.
[127] Eckstein, *Mediterranean Anarchy*, p. 38.
[128] Isocrates, Frg. 4.3, 15–17, 199–23, 126, 130.
[129] Euripides, *Iphigenia at Aulis*, lines 1377–98.

These ideals remained unrealized for many reasons, chief among them perhaps the importance of honor and its continuing relationship to war. Ironically, the only serious attempts to create a common peace (*koinē eirēnē*) were by outside powers like Persia and Macedonia.

The tension between warfare as agon and warfare to achieve political goals

In the *Iliad*, neither Achilles, Agamemnon nor Hector hesitates to put his personal goals above those of the common cause. Strategic need finally compels Agamemnon to offer rewards and an apology to Achilles. Achilles returns to the fighting to avenge Patroclus, not out of any commitment to the Greek cause. Within the polis, private quarrels that threatened civic interests were frowned upon, although not infrequent. John Finley observes, "the community could only grow and prosper by taming the hero and blunting the free exercise of his prowess, and a domesticated hero was a contradiction in terms."[130]

   In fifth-century Greece the struggle for honor was internal as well as external, and factions were as much a reflection of personal rivalries as they were of class interests. In Athens, at the time of the second Persian invasion, Cimon and Themistocles, representing the aristocrats and democrats respectively, overcame their differences in the interest of the city. Athenian history in the decades after the Battle of Salamis was once again intensely factional, with the leaders of the losing side ostracized and expelled from the city for ten years. Thucydides tells us that domestic conflict became more divisive during the Peloponnesian War, with demagogues using their rhetorical skills to advance their political standing at the expense of the city. The most talented of these demagogues was Alcibiades, a character of almost Homeric proportion. He was handsome, rich, skilled at horse-racing, a brilliant strategist, brave in battle, and utterly unscrupulous and self-serving. He rose to political prominence by agitating for a renewal of the war against Sparta after the Peace of Nicias, and convinced the assembly to embark upon the disastrous Sicilian expedition. Alcibiades was then accused of sacrilegious speech, and fled Athens for Sparta after conveying useful military information to Syracuse. He gave excellent strategic advice to Sparta, but had to abscond again when his affair with the wife of the Spartan king Agis II was discovered. He went

---

[130] Finley, *The World of Odysseus*, p. 117.

to Persia, where he gained the support of a powerful satrap, and hatched further complicated schemes. He ultimately returned to Athens where he was elected a general, fought a naval campaign, and subsequently fled to Lydia, where he was murdered.[131] In today's world, Alcibiades would be regarded as a traitor by virtue of his first defection. The accounts of Thucydides and Plutarch (*c.* 46–27) reveal considerable ambiguity. They decry his duplicity but admire his skill and cleverness.

The tension between warfare as ritual and a means to political ends was most evident in its conduct. As I noted earlier, the rules of agonal warfare were frequently violated by participants who, throughout the course of Greek history, not infrequently resorted to all kinds of ruses, standoff warfare and sieges to defeat adversaries, and on occasion massacred Greek prisoners and left their bodies unburied. Greeks sometimes regarded the discrepancy between their values and their practice as an aberration and imagined a past in which they had behaved properly. Demosthenes and Polybius indulged in such fictional nostalgia.[132] One of the remarkable features of the culture of the Greeks was their ability to recognize, accept and even profit from contradictions they recognized in their behavior. They drive the plots of many Greek tragedies, and are used by playwrights to highlight the benefits and dangers of Athenian values and practices. Elsewhere I argue that Thucydides exploits contradictions to lead readers to deeper levels of understanding of the relationship between words and deeds, nature and convention, and the necessity but fragility of the foundations of political order.[133] Tensions in warfare could be treated in similar fashion. Excellence was achieved by standing firm, regardless of the consequences, but also won by clever stratagems that violated all the conventions of hoplite warfare. To recognize these seemingly contradictory ways of gaining victory, Sparta sacrificed a bull to Ares for a victory gained by stealth, and a rooster for a triumph achieved by holding one's ground.[134] One reason perhaps that both traditions flourished – and could be acknowledged – was the ability of their practitioners to find precedents for them in Homer.[135]

---

[131] Thucydides, 5.42–7, 52–6, 61, 76, 84; 6.8, 15–19, 28–30, 48–54, 60–1, 74, 88–93; 7.18, 8.11–18, 26, 45–57, 63–6, 76, 81–90, 97, 108; Plutarch, *Alcibiades, passim.*

[132] Plutarch, *Demosthenes*, 9.47–8; Polybius, *Histories*, 13.3.1–8; Wees, *Greek Warfare*, pp. 115–16.

[133] Lebow, *Tragic Vision of Politics*, ch. 4.   [134] Herodotus, *Histories*, 9.71.

[135] Lendon, *Soldiers and Ghosts*, pp. 83–90, 105–6, on the contradictions inherent in fifth- and fourth-century Greek warfare and the appeals to Homer.

*Honor societies are characterized by tension between equality
and hierarchy*

The aristocratic warrior elite consider themselves ontological equals. In the *Iliad*, this is symbolized by their equal opportunity to gain honor on the battlefield and in athletic competitions and their equal shares at feasts.[136] There is nevertheless a pronounced hierarchy within the elite that reflects their ascribed and achieved status. The tension between equality and hierarchy can become acute when those at the apex of a hierarchy flaunt their social superiority or exploit their position for personal gain in violation of conventions and practices. Tension can be muted when they respect those conventions and collaborate with the less powerful or less honored in practices that affirm their ontological equality. As a general rule, hierarchy among equals is only tolerable when it is seen to benefit all concerned and is masked by rituals that allow the powerful and powerless to pretend they are equals. Pericles is fully aware of these social truths, and appears to have modeled his approach to the Athenian *dēmos* on Odysseus' relationship with his shipmates.

As individual strivings for honor were increasingly transferred to the polis, the city state became the main actor in the competition for standing and honor. City states came to be regarded as ontological equals, just as aristocrats were in an earlier age. Many of the same practices and conventions governed their interactions, although they too were not infrequently violated. Claims for honors and precedence were fiercely resisted by city states who felt themselves as deserving as the cities making them. Resentment of this kind was responsible for Athens being denied leadership of the Greek fleet at the outset of the second Persian invasion. The victory at Salamis and willingness to pursue the war against Persia after Sparta recalled its general Pausanias, earned Athens *hēgemōnia*, and with it the willingness of others to accept its leadership. Thucydides describes how Athens subsequently lost that *hēgemōnia* by exploiting its position to enrich itself at the expense of its allies. It became a tyranny when it used force to extract tribute and suppress allied rebellions. Thucydides comes to describe Athens' allies as subjects (*hypekooi*) and has his speakers do so as well.[137] By the time of the Melian Dialogue, the Athenians understand that their empire is largely held together by fear, which is why they feel compelled to make an example of the Melians. They must keep expanding to demonstrate their power to others, and inevitably overextend themselves and lose their empire when they are defeated.

[136] Homer, *Iliad*, 7.318–20, 23.24–35, for example.   [137] Thucydides, 1.139.3, 140.3.

Thucydides encourages us to draw a general principle from the Athenian experience. In honor societies, power is most effectively transformed into influence when hegemons exercise self-restraint and use their power to advance their interests by serving those of the community as a whole. In this circumstance, they can usually persuade others to support common initiatives. As their basis of authority shifts from *hēgemōnia* to *archē*, they must increasingly make use of threats and bribes to enlist support. This is costly and inefficient. Sophocles makes much the same argument in his *Philoctetes*, probably written in 409, late in the Peloponnesian War, but set during the Trojan War. Friendship and persuasion triumph over threats, tricks and force.[138] Put another way, fifth-century cities confronted the same choices as individuals in Homeric Greece. They could seek to demonstrate *aretē*, and by doing so achieve standing and influence through their excellence. Or they could exploit their power for selfish ends, as did Agamemnon in the *Iliad*, tyrants and the Athenian Empire.

The case of Thersites aside, there is no overt tension in the *Iliad* between the aristocratic elite and the mass of ordinary solders, servants and slaves. In fifth-century Greece there was profound tension in many societies between the wealthy and well-born and the powerless masses. These conflicts led to revolutions and civil wars, as in Epidamnus and Corcyra. Athens was Greece's greatest democracy, and tensions between aristocrats and low-born, and between wealthy and poor, were relatively muted as the result of a series of democratic reforms dating back to the end of the sixth century. Traditional Greek ideology justified political authority on the basis of the contribution citizens made to defense of the polis, and service in the fleet provided a strong claim for participation in the affairs of state by the large class of citizens who could not afford a hoplite panoply.[139] The importance of the fleet, and service in it for some hoplite infantry, may also have made the upper classes more receptive to these demands.[140]

The second category of tensions is between honor and other motives.

---

[138] Knox, *The Heroic Temper*, ch. 5; White, *Heracles' Bow*, pp. 3–27; Lebow, "Power and Ethics," for analyses of *Philoctetes*.

[139] Thucydides, 1.142; Sinclair, *Democracy and Participation in Athens*, pp. 218–19; Ober, *Mass and Elite in Democratic Athens*, pp. 83–4.

[140] Aristotle, *Politics*, 1297b16ff; Raaflaub, "Equalities and Inequalities in Athenian Democracy," sees a strong connection between naval service by *thetes* and attainment of political rights. Hanson, "Hoplites into Democrats," suggests that service of "middling" hoplites on Athenian warships created solidarity with rowers and support for their incorporation into the body politic. Strauss, "The Athenian Trireme, School of Democracy," makes the case from the perspective of the *thetes*, arguing that trireme service created a sense of class solidarity and entitlement which translated into political influence. Wees, *Greek Warfare*, pp. 52–3, is not so convinced.

In honor societies, desire for honor generally succeeds in triumphing over fear

In the *Iliad*, fear is omnipresent. It waxes and wanes with the fortunes of war, but with rare exceptions warriors keep it under control. In real worlds, as Socrates recognizes in the *Republic*, fear is more difficult to suppress.[141] It is evident in decisions to emphasize security over honor. Even Sparta, the quintessential warrior society, struggled with this problem, not on the battlefield, where Spartiates were notoriously courageous, but in the war rooms, so to speak. On key occasions, they privileged security above honor; they stayed away from the fighting, presumably waiting to see the outcome before committing themselves. During the first Persian invasion Spartan forces arrived too late to take part in the Battle of Marathon, ostensibly because they could not leave home until their religious festival ended. At Salamis, the Spartans and their allies were quite open about their preference for security over honor. They wanted to retreat to the narrow Corinthian Isthmus and make their stand there against the Persians, abandoning the Athenians to their fate. After Salamis, the Spartans were reluctant to go on the offensive, and it took enormous efforts by Athens to move the Spartan army out behind its fortifications on the Isthmus to join them in the joint offensive that led to the decisive victory against the Persians at Plataea in 479.

The most serious tension in fifth-century Greece was between the spirit and appetite on the one hand and reason on the other

For Plato, oligarchic people and regimes are ruled by their spirit, and democratic people and regimes by their appetite. The difficulty of appeasing the spirit or appetite, or of effectively discriminating among competing appetites, sooner or later propels both kinds of people and regimes down the road to tyranny.[142] Tyranny is initially attractive because a tyrant is unconstrained by laws. In reality, the tyrant is a true slave because he is ruled by his passions and is not in any way his own master.[143] Thucydides tells a similar story about Athens and Sparta. Reason loses control over the spirit in Sparta, and over both spirit and appetite in Athens. The truest cause of war for Thucydides was psychological imbalance in individuals, which replicates itself in their cities, and then in Hellas more generally.[144]

---

[141] Plato, *Republic*, 3.336a.   [142] Ibid., 439d1–2, 553d4–7.
[143] Ibid., 571c8–9, 579d9–10.
[144] Lebow, *Tragic Vision of Politics*, chs. 3–4 for an elaboration of this argument.

Our analysis of honor societies permits further refinement of our understanding of reason. It takes three forms, each of which plays an important role in bringing about and sustaining societies. The first, and simplest kind, is instrumental reason. For Plato, the appetite and spirit require reason for coordination, even reflection, if they are to attain their goals. Instrumental reason of this kind serves the same end for Freud; it is associated with the ego, which mediates between libido and the external world. Social science has made instrumental reason the central mechanism of rational choice and other strategic interaction models. Instrumental reason can explain cooperation on a case-by-case basis, but not an underlying propensity to cooperate with another group of actors, especially in situations where their immediate self-interest repeatedly suffers. Nor can it explain self-restraint in the face of opportunity to make immediate short-term gains. To account for this kind of behavior, which sustains all communities and their hierarchies, we need to invoke second-level, or reflective, reason.

Honor societies are fiercely competitive because honor is relational. Competition can undermine an honor society when it gets out of hand, as it threatened to do in the *Iliad*, and did in fifth-century Greece. The principal check against destructive behavior of this kind is *nomos*, to which people are socialized and which they learn to respect. Conventions, rules, procedures and laws are never self-enforcing. Reflexive reason of the second kind is required, above all the understanding it brings that neither honor nor appetite can be satisfied effectively, if at all, in the absence of a robust society. This is especially true of honor, because it depends on rules. It requires a consensus about what honor is, how it is won and lost, and the presence of actors willing to show respect and honor to the memory of those who have achieved it. Actors who grasp these truths have a more holistic understanding of honor and the context in which it is earned and takes on meaning. They understand why self-restraint and respect for *nomos* is in their interest.

The third level of reason is motive. Plato and Aristotle further stretch the lexical field of *aretē* to encompass excellence of the human soul. For Plato, it is a form of true happiness and justice, achieved through wisdom about the purpose of life and the appropriate means of obtaining it. Reason alone cannot produce holistic wisdom of this kind. It must work in tandem with the emotions and open itself to their insights. The most important emotion in this regard is affection. Affection develops through dialogue with others. This builds empathy, as Protagoras and Plato both argue, which allows us to perceive ourselves through the eyes of others.[145] Empathy not only encourages us to see others as our onto-logical equals, but to recognize and feel the self-actualizing benefits of close relationships with others. Affection and reason together make us seek cooperation, not only as a means of achieving specific ends, but of becoming ourselves. They bring individuals and social actors of all kinds to expand their identities and to think of others as an extension of them-selves. Their well-being and interests become important to us, and in the case of family members, can become more important than our own. Collective identities reshape our understanding of self-interest, provide additional incentives to constrain our spirit and appetites, and transform meaningful cooperation with others into something that is valuable in its own right. Honor worlds – indeed, all well-functioning societies – are brought into being and sustained by the positive reinforcement of affect and reason.

Thumos to *gloria*

In fourth-century Greece honor continued as a powerful motive for cities and individuals. Sparta, Athens and Thebes jockeyed for primacy, and all three cities used honor to mobilize the kind of sacrifice on the battlefield toward that end. In the prospectus it sent around to other cities in 378 in an attempt to enlist them in a Second Athenian League, Athens promised that the alliance would be purely defensive, based on mutual freedom and autonomy, and that it would not display the impe-rial pretensions it had in the Delian League.[146] Thebes was famous for its Sacred Band, composed of 150 pairs of male lovers, each of which feared being shamed in his partner's eyes. Spartan lovers were stationed alongside each other in the hoplite phalanx for the same reason.[147] The era of Greek city states all but came to an end with the conquest of central Greece by Philip II of Macedon at the Battle of Chaeronea in 338 BCE.

Macedon

Philip's son Alexander, known to posterity as "the Great," extended his reign over all of Greece, Persia, Egypt and lands beyond the Hindu Kush

---

[145] This insight also goes back to Homer, whose reference to *dialegesthai*, the ancestor of dialectic, implies detaching oneself from oneself to debate a moral decision.

[146] Rhodes, "Democracy and Empire."

[147] Plutarch, *Pelopidas*, 18–19; Plato, *Symposium*, 178e–79a; Xenophon, *Symposium*, 8.35; Ogden, "Homosexuality and Warfare in Ancient Greece."

and the Indus, all in the course of thirteen years. There can be no doubt that posterity thinks he deserves this title. He features in the national literatures of some eighty countries, and in the opinion of at least one prominent historian, "is probably one of the most famous of the few individuals in human history whose bright light has shone across the firmament to mark the end of one era and the beginning of another."[148] He receives 76,200,000 hits on Google, ten times more than Achilles.[149]

The accepted rite of passage to manhood in Macedon was hunting and killing a wild boar without a net. This entitled a young man to recline rather than sit at the daily symposium. Killing an enemy in battle earned a warrior the right to wear a special belt. It was "a visual signal and reminder of his attainment and prestige," and a spur to others to equal or surpass his accomplishments.[150] Macedon had about 500,000, inhabitants, making it twice the size of Athens.[151] Philip and his generals had welded its army into an unrivaled instrument in its training, *esprit de corps* and effective use of combined arms. At the age of twenty, Alexander inherited the Macedonian throne, and may have killed his father to guarantee his succession.[152] He used his father's army as an instrument of conquest. He succeeded in part because of his clever generalship, but also as a result of the extraordinary aggressiveness of his officers and soldiers, something he effectively inspired and encouraged.

Greeks did not regard Macedonians as particularly Greek because their language was incomprehensible and their Greek was laced with many Macedonian words and expressions. Demosthenes called Alexander a "lone wolf" and rather condescendingly dismissed Macedonia as a country that could not even provide good slaves.[153] Macedonians considered themselves Greek because they shared the same Greek myths and claimed lineal descent from Temenus of Argos.[154] Mount Olympus, home of many Greek gods and goddesses, was in Macedonia. As part of their effort to assert "Greekness," Macedonians built the sacred city of Dium on its northeastern flank, making it the site of the Olympic Games. Alexander claimed descent from Heracles, and declared himself the defender of the shrine at Delphi for similar reasons.[155]

---

[148] Cartledge, *Alexander the Great*, p. 4.   [149] Search carried out on June 14, 2006.
[150] Cartledge, *Alexander the Great*, p. x.   [151] Ibid., p. 30.
[152] Plutarch, *Alexander*, 11; Cartledge, *Alexander the Great*, pp. 56, 63–5.
[153] Plutarch, *Demosthenes*, 23.   [154] Lendon, *Soldiers and Ghosts*, p. 28.
[155] Buckler, *Theban Hegemony*, pp. 78–9, 145–7 on Philip and Greece; Plutarch, *Alexander*, 1.1.

Plutarch tells us that Alexander "cared nothing for pleasure or wealth but only for deeds of valor and glory." Every conquest made by his father left him with the dread that there would be nothing left to conquer by the time he ascended to the throne.[156] We can speculate that one reason why Alexander sought recognition with a vengeance was his origin in a peripheral society. Several powerful Roman emperors, Napoleon, Hitler and Stalin came from similar backgrounds. According to some of their biographers, the trio of modern conquerors compensated for their backgrounds by attempting to make themselves and their adopted cultures as powerful as possible.[157] Alexander's drive to conquer the known world was also related to his passionate attachment to Homer. He had been introduced to the *Iliad* by his tutor, who dubbed him Achilles, his friend Hephaestion Patroclus, and his father Peleus, after Achilles' father.[158] He envied Achilles because he had Homer to preserve the memory of his great deeds.[159] Alexander's identification with Achilles continued throughout his life, as did his propaganda to demonstrate how Greek he was. He let it be known that he traveled with a copy of Homer at his side, with his friend Hephaestion laid wreaths on what he supposed were the tombs of Achilles and Patroclus, surrounded himself with Greek courtiers and proclaimed his campaign against Persia a pan-Hellenic one.[160] He attempted to universalize Greek culture, giving rise to Hellenism. The Greek language became the vehicle for this cultural dispersion and retained its primacy in the eastern Mediterranean for a long time after the decline of Greek and Byzantine power. Alexander also encouraged Greeks, with somewhat less success, to define themselves and their status less in terms of their cities and more as members of the dominant Greek culture.

Alexander sought to mimic Achilles by displaying extraordinary *aretē* in battle. He took ancient armor from the temple of Athena at Troy and wore it at the Battle of Granicus, 334 BCE, the first of the three major battles against Persia. His emblazoned shield and the high crest on his helmet made him very visible, and was charged by the two Persian commanders. He killed one and was struck on the helmet by the other's battleaxe.[161] At Gaugamela, the last of the three great battles, Alexander led his cavalry in a decisive charge in the direction of the Persian king Darius. He was

---

[156] Plutarch, *Alexander*, 5.

[157] Lefebvre, *Napoleon*, p. 64; Bullock, *Hitler*, pp. 42–3; Tucker, *Stalin as Revolutionary*, pp. 137–43.

[158] Plutarch, *Alexander*, 8.   [159] Arrian, *Campaigns of Alexander*, 1.12.

[160] Plutarch, *Alexander*, 15.   [161] Ibid., 16; Arrian, *Campaigns of Alexander*, 1.14–16.

wounded, but Darius was intimidated and fled the battlefield.[162] Alexander later bragged about the various wounds he had received in these battles. He continued to describe himself as the new Achilles, and his companion, and lover, Hephaestion, as his Patroclus.[163] Like Achilles, he tirelessly encouraged competition among his officers, and held games in which they could compete for prizes. He would also die young because of his pursuit of glory. He complained that Achilles had Homer to sing about his deeds, but that he had to do it for himself.[164]

The Romans

Rome had an indigenous honor culture which took on Homeric trappings when they began to have extensive cultural interchanges with the Greeks. Roman culture, not merely its literature, became deeply infused by Homer.[165] His epics, but especially the *Iliad*, occupied a special place in the curriculum. Horace remembered that his schoolmaster made his pupils memorize whole sections of it in Greek and Latin.[166] Scipio Aemilianus is supposed to have wept at the destruction of Carthage and quoted Hector's prescient warning to Andromache: "There will be a day when holy Troy will perish, and Priam, and the people of the good ash-spear."[167]

In the early and middle Roman Republics (509–123 BCE), the primary value was *virtus* (military valor). According to Plutarch, "prowess was honored and prized at Rome above all other virtues."[168] It was a prerequisite for political office and the defining criteria of nobility. It found expression in the almost unquenchable desire of young aristocratic warriors to compete with one another for glory achieved in single combats with foreign foes.[169] Romans convinced themselves that one-on-one engagements of the kind described in the *Iliad* had been common in their early history. They celebrated ancient champions like Titus Manlius, who allegedly killed a gigantic Celtic chief in single combat, and the Horatii and Curatii triplets who fought a duel to the death over a matter of honor.[170] As one authority puts it: "Romans imagined a heroic culture not too far distant from the military culture depicted in the *Iliad* but even

---

[162] Plutarch, *Alexander*, 31–4; Arrian, *Campaigns of Alexander*, 2.11.15.
[163] Cartledge, *Alexander the Great*, pp. 11–15.   [164] Plutarch, *Alexander*, 15.4–5.
[165] Farrell, "Roman Homer"; Fantham, "Literature in the Roman Republic"; Putnam, "Troy in Latin Literature."
[166] Horace, *Epistles*, 2.2.41–2.   [167] Horace, *Epistles*, 2.2.41–2.
[168] Plutarch, *Life of Coriolanus*, 1.1.   [169] Polybius, *Rise of the Roman Empire*, 3.19.4.
[170] Livy, *The History of Rome from its Foundation*, 6.42.8, 7.9–10.2 on Titus Manlius.

more ceremonious and ritualized."[171] Like Homer's Greeks, they aspired to reputations for themselves and their families that would give them immortality.[172]

Rome was a highly stratified society from the early days of the Republic. Old aristocratic families, many of Etruscan origin, sought to preserve their monopoly on power. The ruling class, known as patricians, were descendants of the "fathers" (*patres*) who had been members of the Senate under the kings. Their right to rule was upheld by custom (*mos maiorum*) and religion. Religion was entwined with politics, as every leading political figure was a member of one of the colleges of priests and was expected to preside at various sacrifices and ceremonies. In the fifth century BCE new wealthy families arose, but were denied entry into the political–religious elite by the shrinking circle of older patrician families. The demands of war created the first opening in the form of the chief magistracy – tribunes of soldiers with consular authority – a position which could be filled by non-patricians. Disturbances in the 370s led to a law, adopted in 367, that decreed that every year one of the consuls might be a plebian. Bravery in battle and service to the state provided the justification, as they did in Athens, for a widening of the elite.[173]

The Roman Republic was increasingly ruled by an alliance of patrician and plebian aristocrats who excluded others, especially the lower classes, from positions of honor and leadership. War ultimately forced further changes. The Samnite Wars, waged on and off from 343–290, greatly enriched successful generals. Many of them invested in land, and to make their estates profitable, replaced peasant smallholdings with large-scale operations worked by slaves. The Samnite Wars required the extensive conscription of ordinary citizens and long service away from home. Returning veterans gravitated towards Rome, as their farms could not compete with the produce of large estates, and they became urban proletariat. By the end of the fourth century, this class became a powerful force in Roman politics, especially when mobilized by politicians like Ap. Claudius. As a censor in 312, he introduced public works to provide employment for plebians; redistributed the poor among all the tribes, thus securing for them a majority in the tribal assembly; made sons of freedmen eligible for election to the Senate; and changed manipular tactics to give ordinary soldiers more responsibility. Aristocratic families

---

[171] Ibid., 1.10.4–7; Wallace-Hadrill, "*Mutatas Formas*"; Goldsworthy, *The Roman Army at War*, pp. 264–71; Lendon, *Ghosts and Soldiers*, pp. 175, 182, for the quote.

[172] Cicero, *Brutus*, 62, on the role of family honor and history.

[173] Livy, *The History of Rome from its Foundation*, 6.39.6–42.8; Oakley, "The Early Republic."

nevertheless continued to monopolize power and honor well into the imperial period.[174]

Athens and Rome differed in their response to foreigners. Foreign residents (*metics*) could not by law become citizens in Athens, and Pericles made it more difficult for their progeny to do so by having the assembly pass legislation in 451 making citizenship dependent on the citizenship (*astoi*) of both one's parents.[175] Rome was a more open society, extending citizenship from the beginning, although sometimes without voting rights, to conquered peoples and allies. Athens and Rome indicate the tradeoff warrior-based honor societies must make between expansion and preservation of the old elite and its values. Athens could to some degree do both because it was among the largest of Greek cities and was able to enlist *metics* and allies in military service. Rome could not have conquered Italy, let alone the Mediterranean basin, without extending citizenship to foreign elites.

Plautus, Ennius and Pliny the Elder describe martial courage as the most admired quality in their society.[176] Pursuit of *virtus* may help explain why Rome was constantly at war. From 327 to the end of the Republic in 27 BCE, there were at most five years of peace.[177] *Virtus* and the promise of posthumous fame may also account for why Romans of the middle Republic were willing to sustain a level of casualties and hardships that far exceeded those of Athens, Macedon, the Etruscans, Carthage or Egypt.[178]

Despite the strong cultural emphasis on loyalty, mutual obligation and obedience to superiors, Roman commanders repeatedly encountered difficulty in restraining soldiers; they were prone to rush ahead in search of combat. The phalanx, which the Romans copied from the Etruscans or Carthaginians, was incompatible with the ethos of *virtus*. Like the hoplite phalanx in classical Greece, it exposed the tension between communal needs and identity on the one hand and individual striving for honor on the other. The manipular legion, which became the dominant military formation of the early and middle Roman Republic, may have been designed in part in recognition of the difficulty of restraining troops. At the very least, it represented a nice compromise between bravery and discipline.[179] The legion was composed of 4,000 infantry and 300 cavalry. Skirmishers (*velites*) were positioned out in front, composed of the youngest soldiers, who had an opportunity to seek out individual

---

[174] Oakley, "The Early Republic."   [175] Patterson, "Other Sorts".
[176] Plautus, *Amphitruo*, 648–53, quoted in Lendon, *Soldiers and Ghosts*, p. 176.
[177] Harris, *War and Imperialism in Republican Rome*, p. 10.   [178] Ibid., p. 2.
[179] Lendon, *Ghosts and Warriors*, pp. 185–90.

combats prior to the engagement of the main forces. It was later replaced by the cohort legion, favored by commanders because it gave them more versatility in the deployment and use of their forces.[180] The legion did not fully succeed in restraining individual initiative, a problem that continued to plague commanders in the late Republic (121–49 BCE). Writing about his campaign in Gaul in 52 BCE, Caesar describes the foolhardy bravery of his centurions, whose death rate was many times that of the soldiers. During the siege of Gergovia, centurions ignored the efforts of tribunes and legates to restrain them and forced Caesar into a costly engagement he had wanted to avoid.[181]

For Polybius, the First Punic War was evidence that Rome "aimed boldly at universal domination" and that this was an end in itself.[182] Roman historian Sallust and Church Father Augustine attribute Roman expansion to the passion for glory that animated almost every level of Roman society.[183] So do many modern historians. William Harris, author of a highly regarded study of Roman conquests, attributes expansion to the warrior culture of Rome, and only secondarily to ways in which plunder could enrich tribunes, generals and their armies. *Luxuria* and *avaritia*, pronounced in the late Republic were unfairly read back into Roman history by Sallust, Livy and later historians to explain empire. In a case-by-case examination of Republican wars, Harris reviews alternative explanations for empire, including the desire for plunder, defensive imperialism and efforts by the aristocracy to protect or expand their wealth and power, and finds them wanting.[184] For whatever reason, Rome underwent a transformation in the mid-fourth century which led to an increase in warfare, lengthier, longer and more successful confrontations with its enemies, and conflicts fought further away from home.[185]

The role of honor becomes even more evident when we look at strategies and tactics. They were generally dictated by cultural norms, not considerations of security. Romans frequently relied on their past and Greek history for tactical guidance even when they were anachronistic and

---

[180] Polybius, *Rise of the Roman Empire*, 1.16; Goldsworthy, *The Roman Army at War*, pp. 12–36; Potter, "The Roman Army and Navy."

[181] Caesar, *Conquest of Gaul*, 7.46–51.   [182] Polybius, *Rise of the Roman Empire*, 2.63.9

[183] Sallust, *Bellum Catilinae*, vii, quoted by Augustine, *The City of God*, V.12 in support of his contention that, for Romans, the desire for glory was the primary passion.

[184] Harris, *War and Imperialism in Republican Rome*. Eckstein, *Mediterranean Anarchy*, esp. pp. 1–6, for a realist interpretation that attributes Roman expansion to anarchy, which put pressure on Rome and other states to become warlike.

[185] On this point, see Eckstein, *Mediterranean Anarchy*, p. 231.

inappropriate to the situation. They emulated ways of fighting described in the *Iliad*. Following Homer, the aristocratic cavalry of the early Republic dismounted to fight.[186] In the Second Punic War, Republican legions, which repeatedly attacked their adversary's center, suffered grievously from Hannibal's superior tactics. One army after another was mauled, and at Lake Trasimeno, Flaminius and all of his legions were destroyed. Fabius Maximus subsequently sought to avoid a direct battle with Hannibal, convinced that he could overcome him by a policy of harassment that would deny him recruits and supplies. This strategy was anathema to Roman soldiers, imbued with *virtus*, and he was accused of cowardice in the Senate. His successors were instructed to engage Hannibal, which they did in a head-on assault at Cannae in 216 BCE, Hannibal's cavalry encircling the legions sent against them led to the destruction of 50,000 Roman soldiers. Subsequent Roman armies still sought to engage Hannibal and were consistently defeated.[187]

Roman generals learned strategy from the Greeks, from fighting in their phalanxes and reading their books. Cato the Elder produced the only widely circulated Roman military textbook. Plutarch published a lost treatise, *Tactics*, and claims to have given military advice to Scipio at the time of the siege of Carthage.[188] By the late Republic, some Roman generals, Scipio Africanus and Caesar among them, were masterful in their strategies and tactical use of stratagems. Rome was nevertheless conservative and resisted innovation, even in military affairs where its value was demonstrable. The evolution from phalanx to manipular to cohort legion was very gradual due to the resistance it encountered in the army and Senate. The authority of generals over their soldiers only became effective in the late Republic, by which time the nature of the army had changed.

The old Republican army had been composed of independent citizens with property. By the first century BCE, legionaries and officers were increasingly drawn from the poorer classes and joined the army in search of advancement and plunder. They owed their primary allegiance to their generals, which in turn strengthened the power of the generals vis-à-vis the Senate. Only at this point did economic consideration loom large as a motive for war for both officers and men. For this reason, many of

---

[186] Lendon, *Soldiers and Ghosts*, p. 188.
[187] Polybius, *Rise of the Roman Empire*, 3.107–18, 264–75; Livy, *The History of Rome from its Foundation*, books 22–30; Potter, "The Roman Army and Navy"; Lendon, *Soldiers and Ghosts*, pp. 201–2.
[188] Walbank, "Introduction," p. 14.

the ensuing campaigns were waged on pretexts against richer provinces of the empire where more plunder could be extracted. Generals were often supported by magistrates, who were elected for a year, and sought to gain as much booty and fame as they could in their limited window of opportunity. The Senate was generally reluctant to assume overseas obligations, and this created additional tension within the political system. The Senate gradually lost power to generals, and expansion, or at least war, became the norm.[189]

The generals' independent political base encouraged them to defy the state in pursuit of personal gain and political power. The tribunate of Tiberius Gracchus (133–32 BCE) marks the beginning of the spiral of violence that ultimately led to the collapse of the Republic. The "optimates" (Senate and aristocrats) felt threatened by Tiberius, who had a large following among his former soldiers and the poor of Rome, and they killed him in a scuffle that broke out on the Senate floor. Sullus was the first general (91 BCE) to take advantage of his troops' loyalty to control the political process in Rome. He was followed by the great warlords of the first century: Caesar, Pompey, Antony and Octavian.[190] In imperial times – from the death of Alexander Severus, in 234 CE, to the accession of Diocletian in 284 – there was almost constant civil and foreign war. All third-century Roman emperors save one after Severus met violent ends, most at the hands of their soldiers or competitors for the throne.

Typical of all honor cultures, appetite was regarded with suspicion. Cato, who held the censorship in 184, campaigned for office with the promise to stamp out luxury and effeminacy.[191] Echoing Cato and his Greek predecessors, Cicero describes all bodily pleasures as corrupting. Along with Bacchic cults, they made men effeminate and destroyed *virtus*. When wealth and riches became valued, the ideal of public service declined, and the public interest was replaced by the private one (*communis utilitatis*).[192] Sallust warns that avarice (*avaritia*) emasculates men and makes the frugal life repugnant.[193] Livy maintains that the early Republic was great because it was poor. Contact with the Greeks and Asia corrupted Rome, encouraged an inappropriate lifestyle of *luxuria* and led to

---

[189] Appian, *Civil War*; Polybius, *Rise of the Roman Republic*, 6.9; Potter, "The Roman Army and Navy."
[190] Plutarch, *Life of Tiberius Gracchus*; Ungern-Sternberg, "The Crisis of the Republic."
[191] Plutarch, *Life of Cato*, 16; Culham, "Women in the Roman Republic."
[192] Cicero, *Tusculan Disputations*, 3.17, *Pro Flacco*, 28, *De Finibus*, 3.64, *Offices*, 2.12.
[193] Sallust, *Bellum Catalinae*, 11, 12, *Histories*, 1.13.

the city's moral decline.[194] Juvenal echoes this theme.[195] The late Republic – the second half of the second century – witnessed the emergence of appetite as an increasingly powerful motive, and not just among the generals and their legions.[196] The aristocracy increasingly gave up military pursuits for commercial ones, and reveled in luxury and its display. Aristocrats who enlisted no longer had to serve five years in the ranks before offering themselves for election to the tribunate. The lower reaches of the aristocracy supplied large numbers of officers who gave orders but rarely fought. Individual combat declined as a marker of honor as military service became another means of accumulating wealth.

Glory-seeking was still evident in the late empire, and sometimes led to military policies that were directly at odds with security needs. The most dramatic example may be the Persian campaign of Julian in 363 CE. Despite the pleas of advisors to campaign against the Goths in the north, Julian wanted a "worthier enemy," and chose to invade quiescent Persia. The Persians were the traditional enemy of Greeks and Romans, and Julian wanted to follow in the footsteps of Themistocles, Alexander and Trajan and go down in history for having conquered Persia. He conducted his campaign without regard to military requirements, but brought a large library which he studied in the hope of emulating the deeds of his predecessors. At Prisabora on the Euphrates, Julian led a small detachment in a risky and unsuccessful charge against the gate of the city because he had read that Scipio Aemilianus entered Carthage by this means. Despite a series of victories, his campaign ended in disaster, and Julian was one of its casualties.[197]

Fifteen years later, another Roman army was destroyed for much the same reason, this time by the Goths at the Battle of Adrianople (378 CE). Emperor Valens had allowed the Visigoths to settle south of the Danube, where they were joined by the Ostrogoths. Both groups were treated badly by local governors, and nearly starved in resettlement campus. They rebelled, defeated a Roman army and held off a second. Sebastianus, the general Valens sent to deal with the situation, wisely sought to put down their rebellion by using his cavalry to channel the Goths into mountain defiles were they could be contained and starved into

---

[194] Livy, *The History of Rome from its Foundation*, preface, 34.4.3, 36.17.4–5, 37.54.18–23, 39.6.7.

[195] Juvenal, *Satire*, 6.

[196] Polybius, *Rise of the Roman Empire*, 18.35.1 on the rise of bribery as an institution.

[197] Ammianus Marcellinus, *The Later Roman Empire*, books 22–5; Lendon, *Soldiers and Ghosts*, pp. 290–305.

submission. Valens sought to engage the Visigoths in battle, and to do so before additional forces under Gratian arrived so he would not have to share the glory of victory with him. He unwisely confronted the Goths in open terrain that left his army vulnerable to the Gothic cavalry, and lost his life along with 40,000 of his legionaries. Adrianople was the beginning of the end for the empire in the west. The military initiative everywhere passed to the barbarians and was never regained by Rome.[198]

Individual actions and state policies that consciously put security and survival at risk are contrary to the most fundamental tenet of realism, and probably strike many people as irrational. There is no reason to suppose that Greeks and Romans were any less rational or intelligent than their modern counterparts. Their behavior appears irrational because we have a different hierarchy of values. Or do we? Psychological studies indicate that individuals adhere to groups for many reasons, among them the apparently strong and universal need to overcome the inherent limitations of individual identities.[199] Belonging to and supporting groups can transform them into real entities, allowing their members to share in their existence and transcend their own limitations and mortality. If death's greatest horror is the denial of continuity, group membership can guarantee continuity beyond the grave.[200] If the individual contributes significantly to the group, his name may also endure. This was the

[198] Ammianus Marcellinus, *The Later Roman Empire*, book 31; Nicasie, *Twilight of Empire*, pp. 233–56.

[199] Greenberg, Pyszcynski and Solomon, "The Causes and Consequences of a Need for Self-Esteem"; Rosenblatt *et al.*, "Evidence for Terror Management Theory I"; Solomon *et al.*, "A Terror Management Theory of Social Behaviour"; Solomon *et al.*, "Terror Management Theory of Self Esteem"; Solomon *et al.*, "The Cultural Animal"; Greenberg, Pyszczynski, Solomon, Rosenblatt, Veeder, Kirkland *et al.*, "Evidence for Terror Management II"; Greenberg, Pyszczynski, Solomon, Simon and Breus, "Role of Consciousness and Accessibility of Death-Related Thoughts in Mortality Salience Effects"; Greenberg, Porteus, Simon, Pyszczynski and Solomon, "Evidence of a Terror Management Function of Cultural Icons"; Greenberg, Simon, Pyszczynski, Solomon and Chatel, "Terror Management and Tolerance"; Halloran and Kashima, "Social Identity and Worldview Validation"; Hamilton and Sherman, "Perceiving Persons and Groups"; Harmon-Jones, Greenberg Solomon, and Simon, "The Effects of Mortality Salience on Intergroup Bias Between Minimal Groups"; Goldenberg, McCoy, Pyszczynksi, Greenberg and Solomon, "The Body as a Source of Self-Esteem"; Harmon-Jones, Simon, Greenberg, Pyszczynski, Solomon and McGregor, "Terror Management Theory and Self-Esteem"; Heine *et al.*, "Terror Management in Japan"; Castano, Yzerbyt and Bourguignon, "We Are One and I Like It"; Castano, "On the Advantages of Reifying the Ingroup."

[200] In addition to the above, see Becker, *The Birth and Death of Meaning, The Denial of Death*, and *Escape from Evil*. On Terror Management Theory, see Castano, Yzerbyt and Bourguignon, "We Are One and I Like It"; Greenberg, Arndt, Schimel, Pyszczynski and Solomon, "Clarifying the Function of Mortality Salience-Induced Worldview Defense";

strategy adopted by Achilles, when he opted for a short and glorious life over a long and uneventful one. Many other ancient warriors and military leaders followed suit.

The striving for immortality at the risk – even the certainty – of extinction is a strategy that is also open to groups and political communities. Leonidas and his Spartan colleagues at Thermopylae, the Melians versus Athens, and Celtic cities who fought the Romans knowing they would lose are examples. Plataea, Athens and some other Greek cities in the path of the Persian invasions chose to resist with only the slimmest odds of success. Even if the community is destroyed, many of its members may reason that its name and deeds, and theirs by association, will become synonymous with courage and commitment to autonomy and achieve immortality. Jewish resistance to subjugation by Greeks and Romans offers another example. The Jews fought costly, even suicidal, wars against both, culminating in the destruction of Jerusalem and its temple and the expulsion of the Jews from their homeland. Such resistance makes sense if those who fight, suffer and die achieve recognition and remembrance in the eyes, not only of surviving and future Jews, but of the Lord. For believers, the latter is far more significant than fame among fellow mortals.[201]

Concluding observations

My paradigm of recognition, standing and honor offers a compelling explanation for the domestic politics and international relations of the ancient world. It accounts for the frequency of war in classical Greece, the ends it was intended to serve and the means by which it was fought. It explains Alexander's unremitting drive for conquest that put an end to the independence of Greek city states and ushered in the Hellenistic era. It offers important insights into the Roman Republic and the Roman Empire. Appetite and fear are increasingly evident in these periods as motives, making domestic politics and foreign policies more complex. I do not address the Hellenistic era, but here too honor was an important motive. Even though mercenary armies became the norm in this period, the leader was still expected to fight in the van of his forces. Individual combats between leaders were not infrequent, and commanders

---

Castano, "In Case of Death, Cling to the Ingroup"; Castano, Yzerbyt, Paladino and Sacchi, "I Belong, Therefore, I Exist"; Castano, Yzerbyt and Paladino, "Transcending Oneself Through Social Identification"; Castano and Dechesne, "On Defeating Death."

[201] Josephus, *Jewish War*, Harkabi, *The Bar Kokhba Syndrome*, pp. 1–84.

who killed enemies in person were greatly honored.[202] Greek cities that lost their independence found new ways to compete with one another for standing. Antioch, Alexandria and Pergamum gained recognition for their commerce, wealth and public buildings and monuments. Rome was drab by comparison until Augustus' great building program transformed it from a city of bricks to one of marble.[203]

In chapters 2 and 3 I speak repeatedly of recognition, standing and honor. I distinguish recognition from standing and honor. It represents admission into the circle of ontological equals in which it is possible to compete for standing and honor. In the *Iliad*, this circle was coterminous with the aristocracy, and was largely restricted to it in classical Greece and the early and middle Roman Republics. The aristocracies of the late Republic and Empire were more porous and those of Macedonia and the Hellenic world more open still.[204] In all these epochs, non-aristocrats usually entered the inner circle by virtue of their military accomplishments and service to rulers and the power and influence they conferred. In Rome, as in fifth-century Greece, law and public speaking were also ways of winning honor.[205]

While not synonymous, standing and honor are very closely related in the *Iliad*. This is because the ascribed and achieved hierarchies overlap so nicely and *nomos* is generally maintained; the greatest warriors (e.g. Achilles, Ajax, Hector, Menelaus) are also among the highest-ranking aristocrats. Agamemnon is the principal exception, and his conflict with Achilles seriously threatened the Greek cause. In historical worlds, status across hierarchies is rarely reinforcing the way it is in the *Iliad*. Honor and standing frequently diverge. People and states can gain honor without achieving standing, as did the soldiers and cities in classical Greece who fought bravely but were defeated. On the eve of the Battle of Salamis, the Corinthians claimed that the undefeated Athenians no longer had standing because they had lost their city.[206]

Standing is often easier to gain than honor because it does not require winning in accordance with elaborate rules, one goal of which is to put competition on as even a footing as possible so that victory is more likely to be the result of bravery and virtue. The transformation of the Delian

---

[202] Chaniotis, *War in the Hellenistic World*, pp. 31, 80–2.
[203] Favro, "Making Rome a World City"; Beacham, "The Emperor as Impresario."
[204] Syme, *The Augustan Aristocracy*, on the rapid promotion of new men by Augustus; Oakley, "The Early Republic."
[205] Harris, *War and Imperialism in Imperial Rome*, p. 257, citing Cicero.
[206] Herodotus, *Histories*, 8.57–62.

League into the Athenian Empire is a striking example. Under Pericles and his successors, Athens increasingly violated the norms of reciprocity and self-restraint in its efforts to assert effective control over its allies and extract greater tribute from them. Its empire underwent a transition in the eyes of other Greeks from a *hēgemōnia* into an *archē*, symbolizing the separation of honor from standing. Athens was recognized as the dominant power of Greece, if not in the eastern Mediterranean, but achieved this standing at the expense of its honor. Most subsequent ancient empires – including those of Alexander and his successors, but not that of the Romans – were really closer to an *archē*. Ernst Badian's influential account of Roman imperialism emphasizes the one-sided nature of political authority, which took the form of clientalist (*clientelae*) relationships with allies and conquered political units.[207] Eric Gruen has successfully challenged this interpretation. He demonstrates that Rome made at most nine, and perhaps as few as four, alliances in the Hellenic East between 229 and 146 BCE, but entered into dozens, if not hundreds, of more informal "friendship" pacts or *amicitia*.[208] Gruen equates the *clientela* model with ineffectiveness, describing it as "toothless," and thus indicative of Roman lack of interest in imperial expansion. Burton offers persuasive evidence to the effect that *amicitia* was understood by Romans and Greeks alike as a direct extension of personal friendship, which created close ties and involved both parties in a set of reciprocal obligations. Like many friendships, *amicitia* recognized unequal power and the hierarchy to which it gave rise. This required generosity on the part of the Romans, the dominant party, and loyalty by the Greek friends. Rather than being an alternative to expansion, it was the most efficient way to extend and maintain Roman influence.[209]

Amicitia was possible between Greeks and Romans because they shared a common understanding of friendship and honor, creating the basis for a society that transcended political boundaries. This was not the case with respect to most of the other peoples who became subordinate to Rome. There was no broader community in the ancient world, as there had been in classical Greece, toward which political units and their actors could look for approbation. For much of the Republic, honor was accordingly a domestic question. Individuals and military units competed with one another, often intensely as in Alexander's army or the Roman army, to

---

[207] Badian, *Foreign Clientelae*, and *Roman Imperialism in the Late Republic*.
[208] Gruen, *The Hellenistic World and the Coming of Rome*, who also engages Harris. Bleicken, Review of E. Badian, "Foreign Clientelae," for another thoughtful critique.
[209] Burton, "*Clientela* or *Amicitia*?"

achieve honor, invariably at the expense of foreigners who were the objects of their hostility and conquests.

The divergence of standing and honor has everything to do with the framing and value of power. In the *Iliad*, power generally reinforces standing and honor. The one exception is Achilles. Driven by godlike wrath, and a descendant of a goddess, he is disproportionately powerful on the battlefield and accordingly a challenge to Agamemnon's authority. In fifth-century Greece, the pursuit of power gradually became divorced from the pursuit of honor, as interest became an increasingly powerful motive for domestic actors and the cities. To dramatize this point, Thucydides puts words associated with money and economics in the mouths of speakers considering critical foreign policy decisions.[210] His narrative makes it apparent that this transformation was underway in domestic and foreign policy, and that changes in the character of one accelerated changes in the other. Plato has Socrates make a similar argument in the *Republic*. Pursuit of unlimited wealth (*epi chrēmatōn apeiron*) is the source of war, if not of all evils, private and public.[211] In Hellenic Greece and the late Roman Republic, as we have seen, interest also became increasingly important.

Fear is not an innate motive like the spirit and appetite, but enters into the picture when actors believe that others threaten their ability to gain honor or appetite, and possibly their lives. It surfaces most visibly on the Greek side in the *Iliad* when the Trojans break through the wooden wall protecting the Greek ships. This is one of the few occasions when the Greeks marshal their forces according to a tactical plan and engage their adversary en masse. In classical Greece, fear was considered one of the three motives driving individuals and their cities. On the eve of the war, the Athenians invoke it as their principal motive for gaining an empire, and one of the three motives for retaining it. By the time of the Melian Dialogue it has become their dominant motive. During the Persian invasion, fear inspired rational strategies, risk-taking by cities and bravery by individuals, much like the Greek response to the Trojan threat to burn their ships. During the Peloponnesian War, it led to irrational strategies and risk-taking, as Thucydides documents at Melos and in the Sicilian debate.

These different responses are explained by the condition of society. When it is robust, fear is likely to encourage cohesion and rational

---

[210] Thucydides, 1.32–6 for the Corcyraean speech where it is most evident; Crane, *Thucydides and the Ancient Simplicity*, p. 106; Lebow; *Tragic Vision of Politics*, pp. 155–9.

[211] Plato, *Republic*, 2.373a–e.

discussion, stimulate the quest for honor and inspire the kind of sacrifice that led to victory at Marathon, Salamis and Plataea. When society begins to break down, fear encourages a *sauve qui peut* response, intensifies division and bickering within leadership groups, and provides opportunities for actors to advance their parochial interests at the expense of the community. In Rome, this difference helps to account for the divergent responses to the threats posed by the Celts and the Goths.

As a general rule, the more robust the society, the more honor and standing are synonymous. This is evident in Greece during the first half of the fifth century and in the early Roman Republic. When honor and standing diverge, as they did in Greece in the second half of the fifth century, and more dramatically in the late Roman Republic, the society and its values come under stress. In Athens, the career of Alcibiades was made possible by the growing separation between honor and standing. It is equally evident in Athenian foreign policy, in which Alcibiades played a leading role. In Rome, appetite gradually replaced spirit as the leading value of the aristocracy. Wealthy aristocrats became more interested in their estates and investments than in winning honor, and wealth became a means to acquire power and standing. For Sallust and the Stoic philosopher Posidonius, this "corruption" was the underlying cause of the collapse of the Republic.[212]

As honor and standing diverge, the ends and means of warfare undergo a transformation. In Greece, this led to more wars in which the objective was no longer a symbolic victory to establish precedence but decisive defeat of adversaries. The rules of warfare became correspondingly more relaxed. There was greater reliance on ambushes, sieges, peltasts, non-Greek allies, slaves and mercenaries. This in turn eroded the traditional meaning and purpose of battle. It further undermined the honor culture, by making fear an increasingly paramount motive given the consequences of defeat. The late Roman Republic underwent a similar transformation, but with respect to the internal competition. The struggle for power became so acute that office was increasingly achieved through violence rather than election. Assassinations and riots encouraged ambitious generals to make their own bids for power, leading to Caesar's march on Rome and the end of the Republic. Caesar's assassination in turn, triggered off a struggle for power that pitted Roman generals and their armies against each other. Fear and interest became mutually supporting

---

[212] Sallust, *Histories*, 1.10–14; Moatti, *La raison de Rome*, pp. 44–6.

in such a situation, because failure to gain power usually meant one's demise.[213]

As honor and standing diverge, hypocrisy becomes more pronounced. Individuals and their political units are intent on achieving standing, now increasingly equated with power, but feel the need to justify their standing on traditional grounds. They speak the language of the honor culture, although their deeds are motivated by interest or fear. At a certain point, hypocrisy becomes stretched and self-defeating, and the culture may become more accepting of motives other than honor. The Melian Dialogue is a watershed in this regard as the Athenians dispense with any pretense (*prophasis*), and justify their invasion of Melos on purely utilitarian grounds.[214] In Rome, generals coerced the Senate into granting them triumphs, whether they were deserved or not. The practice became sufficiently widespread that one way Augustus sought to establish his bona fides was to refuse triumphs voted him by the Senate.[215] He is nevertheless the quintessential example of a ruler who gained standing by illegitimate means and sought legitimacy by making himself appear honorable in the eyes of others.[216] By the end of the Republic, this was not enough, and rulers had to provide bread and circuses for the masses as well. There was a similar but more muted version of the same kind of appeal in Athens during the Peloponnesian War. Cleon sought to buy votes by throwing feasts, and Alcibiades appealed to the assembly to support invasion of Sicily on the ground that its conquest would make citizens rich.[217]

Standing and honor have important implications for influence. When standing is a function of honor, leadership is more likely to be regarded as legitimate by other members of the community. Initiatives that sustain common identities and values are likely to gain support and coopera-tion. When standing is based entirely on power, it is more difficult to institutionalize and less readily transformed into influence. Bribes and threats become the principal levers of influence, and they can be costly

---

[213] There are exceptions to this rule, as the success of Tiberius indicates. He absented himself from Rome and public office to avoid giving the appearance of threatening the succession to power of Agrippa's sons, Gius and Lucius. Only when they died of natural causes did he reemerge and eventually succeed Octavian.

[214] Lebow, *Tragic Vision of Politics*, pp. 124–6, 148 for an analysis. Greek culture still demanded a *prophasis* – an explanation for behavior that made it appear legitimate – so the Melian Dialogue was shocking to contemporary readers.

[215] Eder, "Augustus and the Power of Tradition."

[216] Ibid.; Gruen, "Augustus and the Making of the Principate," for details.

[217] Thucydides, 6.16–19.

in terms of resources.[218] The Greek understanding of the psyche suggests that capability-based influence always has the potential to provoke internal conflict and external resistance because of how it degrades the spirit – and all the more so when no effort is made to give it any aura of legitimacy through consultation, institutionalization, soft words or self-restraint.

Greece and Rome indicate that a kind of dialectic is at work in honor societies. The more a society values honor, the more intense the competition for it becomes. In the *Iliad*, Greece and Rome, this intensity made actors even more sensitive about slights to their honor, and gave rise to conflicts that threaten to tear apart the society. Honor societies are also threatened by the rise of other motives, notably interest. The pursuit of women or wealth – the *Iliad* illustrates the dangers of the former, and the Athenian Empire of the latter – leads to violations of honor codes which provoke acute conflict with others. Either process can prompt fear and lead to the kind of behavior that makes it self-fulfilling and destroys the *nomos* on which honor society is based. These dangers highlight the value of the ancient Greek conception of *meden agan* (the middle way).

The honor societies of the ancient world were warrior societies. Honor was achieved primarily through the display of bravery in battle – what the Romans called *virtus*. Additional ways to gain honor opened up in fifth-century Greece, such as public speaking, playwriting and expenditure of wealth for civic purposes. These alternative routes to honor were all internal to the society, and for the most part secondary to honor won on the battlefield. This is probably why Aeschylus chose to be remembered for his valor at Marathon and Salamis. Honor among states was also a function of military victories, albeit achieved according to the rules governing warfare. Athens also gained some recognition for its cultural accomplishments, but this was secondary. In Macedon, bravery in hunting and battle was the only means of gaining standing in the eyes of Alexander. In the Hellenistic era, cities had less independence, as they were usually part of larger political units. Competition among them was undiminished, but claims for standing were now based on literary, artistic and architectural achievements and the fame of their favorite sons. In the Roman Republic, public speaking and service augmented honor won in war.[219] When we turn to Europe and the modern world, we will see an increasing diversity in the ways in which honor and standing can be achieved domestically,

---

[218] Polybius, *Rise of the Roman Empire*, 6.9; Lebow, "Power, Persuasion and Justice," for an elaboration of this argument.

[219] Cicero, *On Duties*, 1.74, 76–8.

and thus a greater divergence in the conceptions of honor that operate in domestic versus international society.

Honor for Greeks, Macedonians and Romans was an important constituent of identity. For Plato and Aristotle alike honor is a two-edged sword. It makes communities central to individuals and encourages the kind of self-restraint and sacrifice necessary to sustain them. The desire for honor can also prompt actors to violate key *nomoi* in pursuit of this goal. For Aristotle, lack of discipline (*akrasia*) in individuals and cities leads to instability.[220] Thucydides extends this understanding to foreign policy. Social relations among fifth-century Greeks were embedded in a dense web of relationships, governed by an elaborate set of conventions that encouraged expectations of support while imposing constraints and obligations. Relations with fellow citizens were conceptualized as an extension of domestic household relations, as were, to a significant extent, relations between Greek cities.

There is no indication that Thucydides or any of his contemporaries thought the kind of order they deemed possible among the Greeks could ever be extended to non-Greek political units. The most benign explanation for this limited vision was the understanding that ordered relations could only take place within a society, and a particular kind of society. As the Peloponnesian War demonstrated, it was extremely difficult to maintain order in Hellas, let alone among political units representing different cultures and practices. There is also a darker interpretation. Moderns, from Kant and Hegel on, have conceived of identity as constituted through the creation and even celebration of difference. Following their lead, some students of the ancient world have suggested that the concept of a Hellenic "us" required barbarian "others," and that civic solidarity in Athens was equally dependent on the interlocking binaries of citizen–foreigner, master–slave, male–female and dominant–submissive (*erastai–eremonos*) sexual partners.[221] In modern times, "others" are frequently differently religious or ethnic groups, and nation-building in Spain, England and France – three among many historical examples – was accompanied, if not based, on religious zeal and exclusion.[222] So too was the concept of "the West" based on Christianity and defined in opposition and hostility

---

[220] Aristotle, *Politics*, 1325b30–2.

[221] For example, Monoson, *Plato's Democratic Entanglements*; Wohl, *Love among the Ruins*; Keuls, *The Reign of the Phallus*; Cartledge, Miller and von Reden, *Kosmos*; Strauss, "The Melting Pot, the Mosaic and the Agora"; Hedrick, "The Zero Degree of Society"; Honig, *Democracy and the Foreigner*.

[222] Anthony W. Marx, *Faith in Nation*.

to Islam. Scholarship that stresses binaries of this kind appears to affirm the Kantian notion that order is constructed in a similar way at every order of magnification.

I believe this is far too facile an explanation for identity. I argued in the introduction that identities are more often constructed in conjunction with others, as Virgil thought Roman identity was from the city's founding.[223] Alternatively, they are constructed against one's prior self, as Ole Waever maintains the European Union was in opposition to the negative temporal "other" of pre-1945 Europe.[224] The evolution of Athenian identity gives evidence of both these processes, especially the use of the past as a vehicle for negotiating new identities. This project is central to Greek tragedy, where Bronze Age Greece and myths surrounding other *poleis*, most notably Thebes, were used as points of reference to problematize contemporary practices and identities.[225] Sophocles' *Oedipus* is a prominent example.[226] Tragedies could also facilitate the transition to new identities and practices, as Aeschylus's *Oresteia* attempts to by emphasizing civic over family identities and civil justice as a replacement for private revenge.[227] For Macedonians, and Alexander in particular, Homer's depiction of Achilles was a critical reference point, and one that drew on a semi-foreign tradition. Macedonian identity, I suggested, was also built with reference to a past, in this case a fictional past that Alexander attempted to make a reality.

Herodotus uses Asians in general, and Persians in particular, as a foil for Greeks to construct common identities. In book I, Thucydides' casts Athenians and Spartans as polar opposites for much the same purpose. As both narratives progress, this simple formulation is undermined. For Herodotus, Greek identity cannot be understood in isolation from other cultures. Even though he finds Greek culture the most admirable, it is because it represents a balance among human capabilities, a conception that cannot be understood in isolation or by framing other cultures as polar opposites or foreign "others." Thucydides' account of the Peloponnesian War reveals that Sparta and Athens become more alike in how they fight the war and treat other cities. The Melian Dialogue and Sparta's trial of the Plataean are clearly intended as analogs, and reveal how war has not only reshaped Athenian and Spartan identities but made them . His

---

[223] Virgil, *Aeneid*; Reed, *Virgil's Gaze*, for a thoughtful analysis of his views of nation and of Rome in particular.

[224] Waever, "European Security Identities."   [225] Zeitlin, "Thebes."

[226] Knox, *Oedipus at Thebes*, pp. 61–106; Segal, *Oedipus Tyrannus*, pp. 11–13.

[227] Lebow, *Tragic Vision of Politics*, ch. 3 for a discussion.

Melian Dialogue also builds on Herodotus' account of Persia's stern warn-ings to Athens that resistance would be futile and suicidal to collapse the binary of Persia-Greece. He has the Athenians make the same arguments to the Melians that the Persians made to them, suggesting that they have become the Persians, or their Greek equivalents in word as well as deed.[228]

The Greek and Macedonian cases, and the Roman case too, if we credit Virgil's account, indicate that there are a variety of strategies for building identities and that the creation of oppositional binaries is only one of them. I will return to this question in the conclusion, integrating evidence from other cases.

---

[228] Lebow, *Tragic Vision*, ch. 4, for an elaboration of this argument.

5

Medieval Europe

Men do not seek each other's company for its own sake, but for honour or profit.

Hobbes[1]

Drawing on Homer's *Iliad*, chapter 3 developed an ideal-type description of an honor-based warrior society. Chapter 4 applied it to classical Greece, Macedonia and Rome. I now extend my analysis to Europe, from the early Middle Ages to the French Revolution. I use these cases to refine and extend my argument and to show how the spirit was still important in eras when society was weak and honor all but non-existent.

The *Iliad* offers a fictionalized account of Bronze Age Greece. My analysis of classical Greece relies on contemporary texts, notably those of Thucydides, Plato and Aristotle, all of whom were influenced by Homer. To a surprising degree, Homeric values and conceptual categories shaped Greek practice, and thinking about their practices. The influence of Homer on the Greeks, and of Homer and the Greeks on the Romans, raises fascinating questions. Chief among these is the extent to which the texts we possess are good guides to the societies they purport to describe. In medieval Europe, as we will see, they present a greatly idealized portrait of Charlemagne and his kingdom. Later texts, notably the poetry of the troubadours, and court literature more generally, depict a fictional world, some of it based on a equally mythical portrait of Rome.

Unlike Bronze Age Greece, we have considerable evidence about the medieval world. We can compare and contrast historical and fictional worlds, and ask why the latter was created. I argue that it was because the real world was so unacceptable. It was disorderly, violent and ruled by the passions. The literature of chivalry seeks to create an honor society and related norms that encourage the self-restraint and selflessness it depicted.

---

[1] Hobbes, *De Cive*, 1.2.

To do so, it created a fictional past that it could draw upon as a model and justification for the values and practices it sought to instantiate. Its heroes are reminiscent of Achilles and are sometimes described with Homeric metaphors and similes.

I begin my examination of Europe with the Merovingian and Carolingian dynasties. Charlemagne's imperial coronation on Christmas Day 800 has long been considered a defining if controversial moment in European identity. Since the end of World War II, it has also become a symbol for European integration. The Frankish Empire resembles Bronze Age Greece in that its influence on later generations had less to do with any reality than with its mythical representation by later bards. The Merovingian and Carolingian dynasties are nevertheless interesting because, in contrast to classical Greece and the early and middle Roman Republic, they are warrior societies that are not based on honor. Standing was all-important, and in the absence of honor, the struggle for standing was unconstrained by norms. Political orders were highly unstable, and the Frankish Empire and many other European political units of the era were relatively short-lived. Charlemagne is an interesting figure because of his partially successful effort to draw on German and Roman traditions to achieve legitimacy by reintroducing the concept of honor.

My next topic is Anglo-French relations from the Norman invasion through the Hundred Years War. This is another particularly violent era of European history in which honor nevertheless became an important motive for rulers and aristocratic warriors. Toward the end of the thirteenth century, the scale of war increased substantially, as evidenced by the large-scale English invasions of Wales and Scotland and the French invasion of Flanders. In 1294 England and France went to war in what turned out to be a prelude to the Hundred Years War, the name given to a series of wars between these protagonists that began in 1337 and ended in 1453. Chivalry developed in the twelfth and thirteenth centuries and reached its peak in the fourteenth and fifteenth centuries during the Hundred Years War. It propagated values and military practices that, while not directly modeled on Homer, claimed Rome and Greece as their antecedents. Chivalry was a project by writers and warriors of an intellectual and religious bent to create an honor culture and a class of knights to police society and protect women, orphans and the poor. In practice, knights were more often a cause of disorder, and the wars they and their kings fought bore only a passing resemblance to the world of troubadours and romances. In the words of Johan Huizinga: "This illusion of society based on chivalry curiously clashed with the reality of things."[2]

Chivalry nevertheless laid the post-Roman foundations for a European honor culture. Some of its values endured down to the First World War and even afterwards. Recruiting posters and war memorials from all the major European participants in World War I feature knights as icons of bravery and service, and volunteers as their lineal descendants.[3] Postwar memorials, especially in Germany and Britain, also drew on chivalry and knighthood to make sense of a generation's sacrifice.[4]

Chivalry inspired various conceptions of conflict management in later centuries that might be described as the "aristocratic peace." None of these peace plans came to fruition, but they offer an interesting contrast with later bourgeois conceptions of the "democratic peace."

This chapter and the next span more than 1,200 years of European history. My cases are not so much case studies, as mini-cases used primarily for purposes of illustration. Where appropriate, they are organized around the categories I used to analyze Greece and Rome. They serve to demonstrate the importance of the spirit for foreign policy and international relations in a series of differing contexts. They lend further support to the central argument of this book: that the conduct of what we call interstate relations is fundamentally different in honor-, appetite- and fear-driven worlds. In mixed worlds, like those of Britain and France during the Hundred Years War and post-Westphalian Europe (the subject of the next chapter), all three motives are well represented and often influence foreign and military policy in seemingly contradictory ways. Understanding the multiplicity of motives at work helps us make sense of these patterns.

Charlemagne

For the great Belgian historian Henri Pirenne, the coronation of Charlemagne as Roman emperor signaled the transition from late antiquity to the medieval world.[5] Subsequent research indicates that this change was more prolonged than sudden, more subtle than dramatic and driven more by internal developments than by Islamic closure of the Mediterranean to

---

[2] Huizinga, *Waning of the Middle Ages*, p. 56.
[3] Frantzen, *Bloody Good*, for a detailed exposition.
[4] Goebel, *Great War and Medieval Memory*.
[5] Pirenne, *Mohammed and Charlemagne*, p. 26. Hodges and Whitehouse, *Mohammed, Charlemagne and the Origins of Europe*, for a modern reconstruction.

Christian traffic. By the ninth century, the former empire of the West was divided into a number of squabbling political jurisdictions whose political structure and economic base bore little relationship to antiquity. The political units of this period have been described as "a rather loose collection of persons and institutions exercising power perceived to be derived from royal authority, an arrangement in which (at least in our eyes) the boundary between 'public' and 'private' uses of power was blurred."[6] Contemporary writers used the Latin term *res publica* to describe the Frankish kingdom, implying the existence of a state independent of its rulers.[7] In practice, the Merovingian and Carolingian kingdoms came close to what Weber calls a patrimonial regime as they rested on the personal authority of rulers, and were to a large degree an extension of their households.[8]

Rulers were not always kings. On his deathbed in 712, Charles Martel felt free to divide his domains between his two sons, Pepin the Short and Carloman. The actual king, the Merovingian Childeric III, was a puppet who was replaced by Pepin the Short in 751 with the tacit compliance of Pope Zacharias. Three years later, Pope Stephen travelled to Gaul to anoint Pepin. The two leaders swore a pact of friendship. The Vatican was anxious to solidify its alliance with the Franks to counter the Lombard threat in northern Italy – the Lombards had recently captured Ravenna – and to use them as a replacement for Byzantium, which was no longer able to protect Rome. The Church was also increasingly at odds with the Eastern Empire, then consumed by a raging controversy over icons.[9]

Pepin died in 768, and Carloman succumbed to an illness a few years later. Pepin's son Charles, born in about 742, assumed the throne.[10] Living up to his name, which means virile in Frankish, he acted decisively to preserve the integrity of kingdom, threatened along its peripheries by Vikings in the north, Saxons in the east, Lombards in the southeast and Arabs in Spain. He fought successful wars against most of these

---

[6] Fouracre, "Frankish Gaul to 814."   [7] Nelson, "Kingship and Empire."

[8] Weber, *Economy and Society*, I, pp. 231–41, II, pp. 1006–10; Nelson, "Kingship and Empire in the Carolingian World"; Barbero, *Charlemagne*, pp. 147–51.

[9] McKitterick, *The Frankish Kingdoms under the Carolingians*, pp. 41–66; Favier, *Charlemagne*, pp. 59–63; Barbero, *Charlemagne*, pp. 75–80; Werner, *Histoire de France*, I, pp. 335–9, 342–9, 363–88; Collins, *Early Medieval Europe*, pp. 157–61, 245–71; Noble, "The Papacy in the Eighth and Ninth Centuries"; Fouracre, "Frankish Gaul to 814."

[10] The three principal sources on Charlemagne are the *Continuations of the Chronicle of Fredegar*, the *Prior Metz Annals* and Einhard's *Life of Charlemagne*. They are all highly partisan and imaginative, and I have been guided in my use of them by respected secondary sources. On the Royal Annals and the difficulty of determining dates from them, see Favier, *Charlemagne*, pp. 139–42; Barbero, *Charlemagne*, p. 22.

neighbors, and incorporated Bavaria and northern Italy into his king-dom. He then confronted a new enemy, the Avars, who had launched raids into northern Italy from their base in Pannonia. His conquests and punitive campaigns were carried out with papal support. By the time he was crowned emperor in Rome in 800, he had unified most of Christian Europe, aside from England, Spain and Italy south of Lombardia. By 806, Charlemagne's multiethnic empire stretched from the Baltic to the Adriatic and the Atlantic to the Hungarian plain. It was a European rather than a Roman society, as its commerce was oriented toward the Atlantic, not the Mediterranean. Because Pope Leo III was weak, corrupt and increasingly reliant on Frankish support, Charlemagne gradually extended his authority over the Church, approving, if not dictating, its key policies and appointments.[11]

The kingdom that Charlemagne inherited and expanded was built on a very weak society. Its predecessor, imperial Rome, had a long-standing symbiotic relationship with landowners, who collected taxes and served as intermediaries between the central government and local populations. This system was in terminal decline, and a new system of patronage was emerging in its place. Carolingian rulers encouraged nobles to serve them in the expectation of gaining land and other material rewards they extracted through taxes, tolls, gifts and booty. This system harked back to the old German tribal practice of the warrior retinue described by Tacitus. It was based on the personal bond between a leader and his followers; they swore fealty and in return were rewarded with food and booty.[12] German tradition endowed victorious kings or chieftains with *Mund*, a kind of magical charisma. Defeat was a sign that they no longer possessed this quality, depriving them of their *bannum* (the right to punish) and often led to their removal by assassination.[13] Even when it did not lead to their overthrow, military failure by the king could provoke considerable internal discord.

In Charlemagne's time, the nobility was not restricted by birth, but drawn from a class of educated freemen, which was larger than it would be later in the Middle Ages because many of the traditions of Roman education continued through the Merovingian and Carolingian periods.

---

[11] Einhard, *Vita Karoli*; Fouracre, "Frankish Gaul to 814." Barbero, *Charlemagne*, pp. 97–9, 224–6; Noble, "The Papacy in the Eighth and Ninth Centuries."
[12] Tacitus, *Germania*, 13.1–15.1; Rives, "Commentary," in Tacitus, *Germania*, pp. 183–8; Goetz, "Social and Military Institutions."
[13] Rouche, "Break-Up and Metamorphosis of the West."

Members of this class looked favorably upon war and conquest as a means of enriching themselves and improving their status.[14]

To govern his expanding empire Charlemagne expanded his household, doubling the number of administrators, and relied on the parallel hierarchy of the Church to oversee the activities of the 700 or so counts (as Soviet leaders would later use the parallel hierarchy of the KGB as a check on the Soviet military) spread out over his increasingly vast domain. He rewarded those who supported him with land and other forms of wealth, which required fairly frequent raiding expeditions and territorial expansion. Lombardia and the Avar "ring" provided particularly rich lodes of booty, which is undoubtedly one reason why Charlemagne sought to conquer them. The nobility were the king's partner in these ventures, but their relationship was an uneasy one.[15] The Carolingians had come to power by deposing the Merovingians, and rebellion was a constant threat.[16] In 792, Charlemagne's own son, Pippin (the Hunchback), rose against him. After suppressing the revolt and punishing those responsible, he felt compelled to reward those members of his entourage who had remained loyal with gold, silver and silks.[17] Charlemagne's followers swore an oath of fealty to him, and he could punish recalcitrant or rebellious nobles by humiliating them publicly, removing their offices, exiling them or confiscating their property. In extreme cases, he could have rebels blinded or executed.[18] In the aftermath of Duke Tassilo of Bavaria's unsuccessful revolt in the spring of 788, Charlemagne imposed a loyalty oath on all freemen in his kingdom. Not surprisingly, the *chanson de geste*, which emerged about two centuries later, and celebrates events in Charlemagne's reign, has

---

[14] Innes, "Charlemagne's Government"; McKitterick, *The Frankish Kingdoms under the Carolingians, 715–987*, p. 87; Ganshof, "Charlemagne et les institutions de la monarchie franque"; Airlie, "Charlemagne and the Aristocracy"; Barbero, *Charlemagne*, pp. 314–21; Nelson, "Kingship and Empire"; Airlie, "The Aristocracy"; Collins, *Early Medieval Europe*, pp. 75–93, on the effects of grants of land to German tribesmen and their leaders on the late Roman tax base.

[15] Reuter, "Plunder and Tribute in the Carolingian Empire"; McKitterick, *The Frankish Kingdoms under the Carolingians*, p. 78; Randsborg, *The First Millennium A.D. in Europe and the Mediterranean*, p. 167; Fouracre, "Frankish Gaul to 814."

[16] Harouel *et al.*, *Histoire des institutions de l'époque franque à la Révolution*, p. 64; Contamine, *Histoire militaire de la France*, I, p. 28; McKitterick, *The Frankish Kingdoms under the Carolingians*, pp. 87–8, 93–7; Ganshof, "Charlemagne et les institutions de la monarchie franque," and *Qu'est-ce que la féodalité?*

[17] McKitterick, *The Frankish Kingdoms under the Carolingians*, pp. 41–66; Airlie, "Charlemagne and the Aristocracy."

[18] Nelson, "Kingship and Empire in the Carolingian World."

betrayal (*trahison*) as a dominant motif.[19] This problem became more pronounced after Charlemagne's death, when aristocratic factionalism provoked a long and costly civil war (829–43) and division of his empire into two kingdoms.[20]

Like most clever rulers, Charlemagne sought to enhance his authority as best he could. His height – he was reputed to be seven feet tall – his skill at hunting boar and his military successes were helpful in this regard. Being crowned emperor by Pope Leo III provided an additional prop of legitimacy, although Charlemagne later had second thoughts about his symbolic subordination to the pope. When his son succeeded him, Charlemagne, and not the pope, placed the crown on his head.[21] He had his imperial seal inscribed with the words *renovatio romani imperii*. *Renovatio*, meaning "renewal," had gained currency in the seventh century through its application to the kingdom of the Franks in the phrase *renovatio regni Francorum*.

The clerics who advised Charlemagne now sought to mobilize this biblical image, associated with rebirth through baptism, to imply a new Christianization of the barbarian world.[22] Charlemagne was widely hailed as "a new Constantine," although as his chief advisor Alcuin recognized that he was only one of many kings (*regna*), and exercised a limited form of *imperium* that consisted of lordship over other peoples (*gentes*) divided by language and customs. Charlemagne claimed equal status with the Byzantine emperor, who recognized his title in 812. Einhard, a member of Charlemagne's court, was encouraged to write his biography, which he based on Suetonius' life of Augustus. Charlemagne overtly exploited the Roman imperial model to support his claim of ruling an *imperium christianum*. One of his Frankish chroniclers made this claim explicit: Charlemagne, he wrote, "assumed the title of Emperor in accordance with the will of God and at the request of all his Christian people." As God's elected representative, rebellion against him was rebellion against God.[23]

---

[19] Barbero, *Charlemagne*, pp. 58–9; Nelson, "Kingship and Empire."
[20] McKitterick, *The Frankish Kingdoms under the Carolingians*, pp. 169–73; Collins, *Early Medieval Europe*, pp. 296–300; Nelson, "The Frankish Kingdoms, 814–898: the West"; Fried, "The Frankish Kingdoms, 817–911: the East."
[21] Dutton, *Charlemagne's Mustache*, pp. 4–36.
[22] Rouche, "The Carolingian 'Renewal'"; Noble, "The Papacy in the Eighth and Ninth Centuries."
[23] Herrin, *The Formation of Christendom*, pp. 451–62; Saintfaller, *Zur Geschichte der Ottonisch-Salischen Reichskirchensystems*, pp. 20–6; Nelson, "Kingship and Empire in the Carolingian World"; Innes, "Charlemagne's Government"; Brown, "Introduction to the Carolingian Renaissance" for the quote.

Charlemagne sought to balance and integrate Christian and German traditions and profit politically from identification with both, as well as the Roman past. His efforts gave rise to discourses and practices that provide insight into the problems of his age, and, suitably reworked and mythologized, became an important model for later Europeans. Charlemagne played up his Frankish connection. He spoke Frankish and wore the national dress. He had ancestral songs about great Frankish warriors of the past transcribed, and upheld the myth, which had great currency among the clergy, that the Franks were descended from the Trojans. Here too, the Romans were a model as they claimed descent from Priam through Aeneas, who was alleged to have fled to Latium after the fall of Troy. Hair was another important cultural marker. The Romans were clean-shaven, while Franks had long hair and traditionally did not shave until they had killed their first enemy. Charlemagne had the head of the last Merovingian tonsured to indicate his loss of authority among the Franks, and, copying earlier Theodosian German emperors, shaved his beard but cultivated a large moustache. He had coins minted identifying him as emperor with his face in profile sporting a drooping moustache that curled down around his lips.[24] Most importantly, he continued the Frankish custom of annual meetings in which royal authority was ritually affirmed by his aristocratic followers.[25]

A small circle of intellectuals aside, most of Charlemagne's followers appear to have been driven by appetite. They sought wealth, and few gave evidence of having any qualms about how it was acquired or displayed. Nobles regularly flaunted their possessions despite priestly exhortations for self-restraint. The Christian ethos was nevertheless very prominent, in conflict with avarice, and did affect some prominent figures in Charlemagne's circle. William of Gellone retired to a monastery, and Wido sought out Alcuin for spiritual advice.[26] Alcuin was an English cleric and principal advisor to Charlemagne, who was handsomely rewarded for his biblical translation and political advice. He was never required to take monastic vows and received five abbeys, including the richest in the kingdom, St. Martin at Tours. His writings extol the virtues of poverty, but he lived a life of luxury made possible by the labor of 20,000 slaves. Toward the end of his life he felt remorse and gave large donations to churches back in England.[27] Many of the clergy were equally self-indulgent and

---

[24] Barbero, *Charlemagne*, pp. 13, 104–5, 117–19, 213–15; Dutton, *Charlemagne's Mustache*.
[25] Fouracre, "Frankish Gaul to 814."
[26] Innes, "Charlemagne's Government"; Nees, *A Tainted Mantle*, p. 47.
[27] Barbero, *Charlemagne*, pp. 216–17.

had a reputation for keeping multiple concubines, drinking, feasting and hunting. Their principal loyalty was to the king, whom they served as local agents with a primary responsibility for raising soldiers for his wars.[28]

There is little evidence of glory-seeking by nobles to impress their peers or to gain a reputation that might last beyond the grave. Valor was a means of gaining wealth. In the summer of 782, Charlemagne sent Count Theoderic, one of his relatives, with a powerful force to attack the Slavs. Nobles already in the field worried that Theoderic would get the credit and the material rewards for victory and charged into battle without him, only to be cut to pieces.[29] Nobility and clergy alike collected books, not because they had an interest in learning, but because libraries were a visible sign of wealth and status. They gave books to their friends, and to churches and monasteries to enhance their standing and save their souls.[30]

Charlemagne comes across as a more complex character. He was pious, intellectually curious and driven by spirit as well as appetite. He was interested in good food and female companionship, but honored fasts and dressed simply. In his old age, he spurned advice from doctors and priests to give up roast meat and concubines. He sought glory through territorial expansion and, following his coronation as emperor, issued proclamations and minted coins to establish himself as the successor to the emperors of Rome. He positively relished, and probably encouraged, references to himself as the new David, Augustus or Constantine. He enjoyed his wealth, although he shared with Rome some of the treasure he captured from the Avars. He demonstrated his superiority over his followers and other rulers by supporting learning and an elaborate building campaign. He constructed multiple palaces, the most impressive of which was in Aachen, in scale and style modeled on older Roman palaces. More than one hundred people could fit into its pool at the same time. Charlemagne was consciously following the precedents of Augustus and the later Theodosian emperors of the fourth century, who had sponsored poetry and the rebuilding of Rome and Ravenna.[31]

In school, Charlemagne was exposed to the standard *trivium* and *quadrivium*. He developed an interest in astronomy as the heavenly bodies were thought to encode messages from the deity. Although he never learned to read or write, he personally initiated efforts to reinvigorate

[28] Ibid., pp. 220–1.   [29] Airlie, "Charlemagne and the Aristocracy."
[30] McKitterick, *Carolingians and the Written Word*, pp. 148–64.
[31] Barbero, *Charlemagne*, pp. 122–4, 137–9; Innes, "Charlemagne's Government." Nees, *A Tainted Mantle*, ch. 5, argues that Charlemagne's imperial ambitions developed only gradually, and were not a motive for his territorial acquisitions.

learning, and encouraged those with the requisite skills to live and teach in his kingdom. His court became a recognized center of culture and scholarship. He had a circle of friends with an interest in producing and distributing correct texts from the compilation of different manuscripts. We have 1,800 manuscripts and fragments from the first 800 years of Christian culture, and 7,000 alone from the ninth century. Most of these texts concern grammar and religion. Charlemagne had little interest in secular texts, but was committed to producing a grammar in Frankish in the hope of keeping his native tongue alive.[32] He also wanted to produce and distribute accurate bibles and provide better Latin instruction and training for priests.[33]

If society was weak within the Frankish kingdom, it was much weaker still in the wider world in which that kingdom functioned. Christians thought of themselves as members of a community but the ties that bound them were minimal. The Vatican and the Byzantine Empire were religious and political adversaries, and neither had the moral or political authority to impose order in their respective domains.[34] Most of the groups against whom Charlemagne made war (Saxons, Vikings, Spanish Muslims, Avars) were not Christian, the principal exception being the Lombards. As we would expect, there were no rules governing combat against these foes. The war against the Saxons was one of "unparalleled ruthlessness" and dragged on for twenty years. No restraint was shown by either side; Saxons sacrificed captives and Franks killed Saxons who would not convert. In one afternoon in 782, Charlemagne had 4,500 Saxons decapitated after they had peacefully surrendered. He authorized pogroms against unbelievers, and issued draconian legislation that imposed the death penalty for not fasting on Fridays. His war against the Avars was even more savage. Thousands of them, women and children included, were murdered or enslaved, with joyous poems written to celebrate these "accomplishments."[35] Charlemagne established a precedent for dealing with

[32] Barbero, *Charlemagne*, pp. 213–15; Brown, "Introduction to the Carolingian Renaissance"; McKitterick, "The Carolingian Renaissance of Culture and Learning," and "Eighth-Century Foundations"; Contreni, "The Carolingian Renaissance."

[33] Barbero, *Charlemagne*, pp. 213–48, 234–7; Brown, "Introduction to the Carolingian Renaissance"; McKitterick, "The Carolingian Renaissance of Culture and Learning," and "Eighth-Century Foundations"; De Jong, "Charlemagne's Church"; Contreni, "The Carolingian Renaissance"; Ganz, "Book Production in the Carolingian Empire and the Spread of Caroline Miniscule."

[34] Noble, "The Papacy in the Eighth and Ninth Centuries."

[35] Favier, *Charlemagne*, pp. 239–51; Barbero, *Charlemagne*, pp. 46–7, 72–3.

non-Christian peoples that Europeans would follow with a vengeance for the next 1,000 years.[36]

Charlemagne's chroniclers did their best to excuse or explain away his violence. Even before his death, he became a figure of veneration and was offered as a role model for other leaders. Beginning in 788, the Carolingians produced Royal Annals that came to link Charlemagne to Christ.[37] Einhard's *Vita Karoli*, written sometime between 817 and 830, presents a highly idealized picture of Charlemagne and his court as part of a plea for the patronage of liberal arts. Notker Balbulus, a monk in St. Gallen, composed *Gesta Karli Magni* in about 886–7. It is a collection of real and fictional stories that glorify Charlemagne.[38] These texts began a tradition of hagiography that found its widest circulation in the twelfth-century *Chanson de Roland*, where Charlemagne is portrayed as a brave and civilized warrior and the very embodiment of virtue and wisdom. These representations propagate a Christian concept of empire that influenced kings in the Middle Ages. They also posit a link between god and earthly rulers that laid the basis for the divine right of kings.

The Frankish kingdoms demonstrate the extent to which honor requires a robust society. In its absence, there may be rules governing competition for standing, but they are unlikely to be followed. More probable is "a race to the bottom" where contenders for wealth and standing use whatever means are available to achieve their goals, encouraging others by their example to follow suit. This was evident in the struggle for power in the Frankish kingdom, where coups were the principal means of changing dynasties or simply hastening the retirement of one's father from power. Violent struggles for succession were averted on more than one occasion by fortuitous natural deaths of uncles and brothers. Charlemagne found it necessary to forbid his sons "to kill, blind, mutilate their nephews, or force them to be tonsured [i.e. sent into monasteries] gainst their will."[39] Warfare was also relatively unrestrained, although Charlemagne behaved differently toward his Christian and non-Christian adversaries,

---

[36] In fairness, we should acknowledge that Charlemagne and his successor, Louis the Pious, were protective of the Jews who lived in their realms. Market day was changed from Saturday, to allow Jews to rest on the Sabbath, and they were even permitted to practice their religion within the imperial palace. Barbero, *Charlemagne*, p. 290.

[37] Innes and McKitterick, "The Writing of History."

[38] Barbero, *Charlemagne*, pp. 38–42.

[39] *Monumenta Germania Historia*, cap. 1, no. 45, c. 18, pp. 129–30, quoted in Nelson, "Kingship and Royal Government."

indicating the presence of some conventions governing warfare among those considered part of the community.[40]

In the Frankish kingdom honor, in the sense that it was understood by Homer or fifth-century Greeks or Aristotle, simply did not exist. Nor, interestingly, did the traditional Germanic conception of honor, which so struck Tacitus. The Germanic *comitatus*, or retinue, that he describes applied to a group of men who voluntarily attached themselves to chieftains in search of honor more than booty. They were committed to fight to the death, if necessary, for their leader, and their relative status depended on how well they served him.[41] We can speculate that German occupation of Roman lands, and the enormous increase in wealth this brought, overwhelmed many traditional values. Carolingian texts use the word honor to describe high office. It also came to include lands that came with offices or were granted by the ruler. Individuals are deprived of their *honores* for losing battles or otherwise disgracing themselves.[42] *Honores* were actively sought as a means of security by men who did not have a large inheritance. The wealth it conferred also enabled counts to strengthen their local authority.[43] Honor in this sense was no different from standing, and standing desired in large part as a means of satisfying appetites. It was associated with ascribed and achieved status. Being born into a royal line conferred standing, as did the accumulation of wealth and power, regardless of the means by which it was acquired. For princely scions to adhere to the unwritten, and generally disregarded, rules of comportment could evoke respect or scorn in others depending on the circumstances. Bravery and ruthlessness in gaining wealth and power invariably generated respect. Respect was distinct from honor, and referred to others' recognition of your skill, bravery, cunning or other characteristics deemed responsible for success. Then as now, respect can be coupled with loathing or admiration, depending on the values and interests of those making the evaluation.

Honor can only be gained by competing according to an accepted set of rules. Charlemagne undeniably sought honor in addition to standing, which is one reason he attempted to legitimate his primacy through his coronation as emperor, and used that position as emperor to advance Christian values. He achieved honor in a very thin international society, which was an extraordinary accomplishment. He was unable to use it to

---

[40] Fouracre, "Frankish Gaul to 814"; Nelson, "The Frankish Kingdoms, 814–98."
[41] Tacitus, *Germania*, 13.1–15.1; Lindow, *Comitatus, Individuals and Honor*, pp. 10–11.
[42] Nelson, "Kingship and Royal Government."   [43] Airlie, "The Aristocracy."

legitimize his own rule, let alone his dynasty. His grandson, Louis the German, faced constant threats from his brothers, and later from his own sons, leading to destructive, internecine wars.[44] Not surprisingly, those in the later Middle Ages who sought to foster a thicker society found Charlemagne a useful role model. They gave him an extraordinary posthumous reputation. In doing so, they explained away or simply ignored his more ruthless policies, greatly exaggerated his piety and accomplishments and invented stories to make them appear more impressive still.

The high Middle Ages

The high Middle Ages in Europe are generally described as spanning a period from roughly 1050 to 1400. During these centuries, a brief Mongol interlude aside, barbarian invasions all but ceased, new lands were cleared or reclaimed, and the population increased dramatically until the great famine, the Black Death and the disruption caused by wars and associated economic stagnation. The dominant political development was the collapse and re-formation of the state, a phenomenon most evident in Latin Europe. Beginning in the last decades of the tenth century, French, Italian and Spanish nobles built castles with the surplus funds generated by their estates. Castles enabled nobles to impose their will on local inhabitants and resist the encroachments of competitors, with the result that in much of Western Europe political power became dispersed in large numbers of relatively small, largely independent castellanies. Kings or would-be kings had to exercise authority in alliance with hundreds, if not thousands, of local, despotic rulers.[45]

The thirteenth century witnessed the collapse of the imperial *dominium mundi*. The Holy Roman Empire, although it survived to the age of Napoleon, never recovered from the death of Frederick II in 1250 and the ensuing interregnum. Civil and canon lawyers throughout Europe advanced arguments to justify the de facto independence of their respective domains, invoking the formula, *rex in regno suo imperator est* (the king is emperor in his kingdom).[46] State formation was a long uphill struggle,

---

[44] Goldberg, *Struggle for Empire*, on this period.

[45] Hodges, *Dark Age Economics*, pp. 153–60, 188–97; Randsborg, *The First Millennium A.D. in Europe and the Mediterranean*, pp. 167–8, 181; Bois, *La mutation de l'an mil*, pp. 205–6, 246–58; Duby, *La société aux XIe et XIIIe siècles dans la région mâconnaise*, pp. 137–90; Poly and Bournazel, *La mutation féodale*, pp. 59–103; Wickham, *Early Medieval Italy*, pp. 97–8, 172–5.

[46] Rigaudière, "The Theory and Practice of Government in Western Europe."

which benefited from a revival in Church learning and the concomitant revival of Roman, canon and administrative law, primogeniture and the advantages location gave to certain regions and their rulers. The feudal estates in the Seine valley, which became the core of the French state, were ideally situated to meet the food needs of Flanders, which was rapidly urbanizing in the eleventh century by virtue of its cloth industry and commerce. The influx of wealth from Flanders enabled Henri I (1031–60) to field large enough forces to win his first victories over castellans. His son and grandson would continue to extend their domains, increasing their resources in the process relative to those of competitors.[47] Similar developments occurred elsewhere in Europe, as small advantages, successfully exploited by clever and ambitious leaders, led to ever greater advantages over their neighbors. By the end of the twelfth century, Western Europe had become a patchwork quilt of polities, many of them sizeable, which engaged in frequent internecine warfare and whose leaders struggled to raise the funds necessary to sustain competition and expansion. There was as yet no word for "state." *Status republicae, status regni, status coronae* were all commonly used, but the state – defined à la Weber as a unit whose rulers exercise a monopoly of force over the territory they govern – was becoming ever more a reality.

The rivalry between England and France began in earnest with the Norman invasion of 1066. It reached its medieval apex in the Hundred Years War, fought off and on from 1337 to 1453. The Norman invasion occurred at the early stages of state formation, when confrontation for standing among leaders was acute, and unconstrained by any of the norms associated with honor societies. It was fought at the beginning of the so-called age of chivalry, but its conduct was largely, although not entirely, at odds with chivalry's values and practices. The period offers us insight into the incentives for setting up honor societies and the difficulties these efforts encounter. It reveals how nascent honor societies attempt to cope with practices distinctly at odds with their values.[48]

The Norman Conquest

The Norman invasion is most often examined from the perspective of England, where it was an undeniable watershed. It changed the regime,

[47] Dunabin, *France in the Making*, pp. 105–6, 162–4.
[48] Pounds, *An Historical Geography of Europe*, p. 116; Duby, *Guerriers et paysans*; Lopez, *The Commercial Revolution of the Middle Ages*; Fossier, *Enfance de l'Europe*.

language and culture of England and created close ties with France and also acute antagonism that endured down to the twentieth century. It brought about a regrouping of powers in northern Europe, strengthened the power of the Roman Church and stimulated a reformist movement within it. It linked England more closely to the Latin peoples, and helped to jump-start the so-called twelfth-century Renaissance. It also imposed high feudalism. Within a generation or two, there were few independent smallholders left in England.

The underlying cause of the conflict between William, duke of Normandy, and Harold, king of England had nothing directly to do with security. It arose, as did most conflicts of the time, from the ambitions of powerful men in an era when competition for standing was almost entirely unconstrained by norms. Standing was achieved through birth and on the battlefield, where victory could enhance a warrior's status and add to his domains and titles. Conquest required no particular justification; the Danes and Normans, like the Angles and Saxons before them, carved out kingdoms by the sword in lands that now constitute England and France. Invaders killed, displaced or intermarried with local inhabitants. Of eight English kings who reigned between 939 and 1016, only three – Edmund, Eadreed and Eadwig – came to the throne uncontested.

By the eleventh century, life in parts of Western Europe had become more ordered, although violence and threats against rival kings remained commonplace.[49] In Normandy, still very much a state in the making, poison was commonly used to remove rivals and adversaries.[50] William, born in 1027, was the illegitimate son of Robert, duke of Normandy, known as *Le Diable*. His father went on a pilgrimage to the Holy Land and his uncles and mentors were murdered in his absence. Only a young boy at the time, William barely escaped with his life, and took refuge with Henri I of France. Quarrels among his would-be successors to the dukedom kept any of them from consolidating their power. In 1047, at age twenty, William won an important victory at Val de Dunes over Guido of Mâcon, a powerful competitor, and in 1054 he defeated another rival, Guillaume, count of Arques. In both struggles he was assisted by the French.[51] In the course of the next decade he consolidated his hold over Normandy in alliance with the French crown and reformist clerics.

---

[49] Strickland, "Against the Lord's Anointed."
[50] Douglas, *William the Conqueror*, appendix F, pp. 408–15; Gillingham, "1066 and the Introduction of Chivalry into England," for a counter-argument that defeated rivals for power were better treated in Normandy than in England.
[51] Douglas, *William the Conqueror*, pp. 48–51.

In England, Godwine, the earl of Essex, twice mobilized armies against Edward the Confessor.[52] Inheritance had become the generally accepted but by no means the only method of acquiring thrones. There was a complicated succession procedure that required the approval of the Witan (literally, "the wise men"), an assembly composed of nobility and churchmen. Harold was voted the kingship in January 1066, following the death of the heirless Edward, largely to forestall Norman influence. His election violated the expectations of William of Normandy, who had told everyone that he was Edward's chosen successor. William claimed – truthfully or not – that Harold had come to Normandy two years earlier at Edward's bidding to anoint him as his successor.[53]

William was not the only contender for the throne. Tostig, son of Godwine, who was the exiled earl of Northumbria, had been waiting in Ireland for an opportunity to act. In May 1066, he began harrying the Sussex coast, but was decisively defeated by a local English naval force.[54] Harald Hardraada, the powerful king of Norway, believed that the treaty between Magnus of Norway and King Harthacnut of England put him in line for the succession. In September 1066, he invaded northern England with an armada of more than 300 ships. He moved his fleet upriver and disembarked to capture York. King Harold rushed two hundred miles north with his army and defeated the Vikings – killing Harald Hardraada and Tostig – at the Battle of Stamford Bridge on September 25.[55] He then marched south to deal with William, who in the interim had landed his army at Hastings. Harold moved his forces within close proximity of the Normans, where he intended to await reinforcements. This was a fatal tactical error because it allowed William to attack and overwhelm Harold's exhausted troops in a long, hard-fought but decisive battle.[56]

William was successful for many reasons. His forces included heavy cavalry that had prior experience fighting as units and were able to retreat and double back on vulnerable groups of English who had broken formation to pursue them. He had worked hard to neutralize or win the support of neighbors who might otherwise have rebelled or attacked Normandy

---

[52] Stenton, *Anglo-Saxon England*, pp. 424–6, 561–8; Douglas, *William the Conqueror*, pp. 163–9.

[53] Stenton, *Anglo-Saxon England*, pp. 560–2; Douglas, *William the Conqueror*, pp. 175–8, 184.

[54] Stenton, *Anglo-Saxon England*, pp. 579, 586–90; Douglas, *William the Conqueror*, pp. 172, 179–81, 191–4.

[55] Stenton, *Anglo-Saxon England*, pp. 560, 569, 575, 587–8; Douglas, *William the Conqueror*, pp. 173, 180–3, 190–4.

[56] Stenton, *Anglo-Saxon England*, pp. 593–6; Douglas, *William the Conqueror*, pp. 194–209.

in his absence. He managed to convince important third parties, most notably the Vatican, of the legitimacy of his cause. Rome's support was something of a quid pro quo for his prior support of ecclesiastical reform in Normandy and rebuilding of the Church in Rouen. Hildebrand, the archdeacon, later Pope Gregory VII, interceded on William's behalf. Pope Alexander II issued a judgment calling upon others to support William and provided a banner for him to carry into battle. Gregory may have expected William, if successful, to remove London Archbishop Stigand, an opponent of his reforms. Holy Roman Emperor Henry IV also publicly declared his support of William. His backing made it possible for William to recruit forces and mercenaries from outside his realm.[57]

The struggle to succeed Edward the Confessor reveals important similarities and differences with Carolingian Gaul. Like Gaul, Normandy was a warrior society in which the competition for standing was fierce and more or less unconstrained. England was a more developed society with institutions and traditions and something approaching national sentiment, which, as Edward the Confessor discovered, could only be ignored at considerable political risk. Like Charlemagne, William sought to mobilize local sentiment and legitimate his claims through the support of respected third parties. These were astute political moves having nothing to do with honor, which was not yet a meaningful political concept in either Normandy or England. The spirit was nevertheless omnipresent. It was behind the drive for standing, and the anger and violent responses its frustration provoked. Tostig, Harald Hardraada and William's assaults on England are all cases in point.

The biggest difference between the two epochs may be the causes of war. At the outset, Charlemagne's campaigns were motivated as much by security concerns as they were by the desire to enhance his standing through territorial expansion. The Frankish kingdom was vulnerable to Saxon and Muslim marauders. After the conquest of Lombardia, Avar incursions became a serious problem, as did Viking raids along the Channel coast. Harold's hold on England was threatened by rival Danish, Norwegian and Saxon claimants to the throne, and above all by William. None of these conflicts had security concerns at their core; they were triggered by a quest for standing on the part of the principals, and expectations of increased status and wealth by their followers. The same was true, we shall see, of the more prolonged and destructive conflict known as the Hundred Years War.

---

[57] Stenton, *Anglo-Saxon England*, p. 586; Douglas, *William the Conqueror*, p. 187.

Chivalry

The concept of chivalry developed between the late eleventh and the fifteenth century. Together with the rise of courtliness, it can be understood
as, at best, a partly successful attempt to transform the elite culture of Western Europe into a more sophisticated honor-based society.[58] Chivalry is
rooted in legends about Arthur and Charlemagne, the *chansons de geste*
and romantic poems. It looked back to Rome, Alexander of Macedon and
Greece for historical examples. Chrétien de Troyes, the greatest writer of
courtly romances and inventor of Camelot, portrayed medieval France as
the successor to Greece and Rome.

Ce nos ont nostre livre apris,	[Our books have taught us
Que Grèce ot de chevalrie	That chivalry and learning
Le premier los et de clergie.	First flourished in Greece;
Puis vint chevalerie à Rome	Then to Rome came chivalry,
Et de la clergie la some,	And the sum of knowledge,
Qui ore est en France venue.	Which now has come to France.
Deus doint qu'ele i soit retenue.[59]	God grant they be retained here.]

In the fourteenth century, the Valois kings paid translators to produce
readable texts of Latin and Greek classics. Centered in France, chivalry
became an international discourse constructed around the mounted, aristocratic warrior, or *chevalier* (knight). It quickly spread to Flanders, England, Spain, Germany and Italy, where it took slightly different forms.
There were numerous attempts to distil a set of behavioral norms from
the literature espousing chivalry. Two of the most widely read were
fourteenth-century books by the Majorcan mystic Ramon Llull and the
French knight Geoffroi de Charny.[60] Llull's *Book of the Order of Chivalry*,
written in Catalan in about 1280, was translated into French and English,
and purports to convey the wisdom of an old hermit who was once a
knight. Charny was one of the most renowned warriors of his age. His
Livre de Chivalry, written around 1350, offers sketches of famous knights,
and equates martial accomplishments with self-worth. It was part of a

---

[58] Elias, *The Civilising Process*, claims that behavior was increasingly censured socially, producing feelings of shame, that became feelings of guilt when these social constraints were
internalized. Vale, *Princely Court*; Jaeger, *The Origins of Courtliness*; Goody, *The Theft of
History*, pp. 154–79, for thoughtful and persuasive critiques.

[59] De Troyes, *Cligès*, lines 27–34, in *Arthurian Romances*, p. 123.

[60] Llull, *Book of the Order of Chivalry*; Charny, *Book of Chivalry*; Keen, *Chivalry*, pp. 18–43,
110–13.

general effort to create behavioral norms for chivalry and became the most popular medieval manual for knights.[61]

Chivalry emphasizes prowess (*prouesse*), which more or less encompasses courage, competitive assertiveness, loyalty, self-restraint, discipline and service. It is modeled on Roman *virtu*, and the texts of chivalry rely heavily on Sallust, Livy and other Roman writers. In *Lancelot*, Pharian announces that it is "the honour of this world towards which all prowess struggles."[62] Like Homeric heroes, fictional knights seek out tests of their prowess. They challenge rivals to one-on-one combats, and generally display courtesy by dismounting to engage opponents they have unhorsed. Like Odysseus, the only man strong enough to string his bow, they perform superhuman feats: they pull swords from rocks and defeat magic chessboards.[63] Lancelot kills five knights and five men-at-arms with five blows. With one stroke, Galahad slices through his opponent, his saddle and his horse so that "half the horse fell one way and half the other in the middle of the road." King Arthur cleaves the Roman emperor from head to waist with his great sword.[64] In the *Iliad*, Apollo compare Achilles to a lion "who gives in to his great force and overmanly heart and goes against the flocks of mortals, to seize his feast."[65] English poet John Gower (1330–1408) describes the Black Prince as a lion breaking through the ranks of the enemy and a ravenous wolf among the sheep.[66]

Depreciation of the appetite goes hand-in-hand with emphasis on the spirit. The Lady of the Lake teaches Lancelot to value honor above survival and put his life on the line to dispel the merest hint of shame or cowardice.[67] In *The Quest for the Holy Grail*, Owein tells Gawain that he is content to die "at the hand of so fine a knight as you."[68] In some romances, knights seek out warriors of legendary prowess like Galahad, expecting to be killed but to win great honor in the process.[69] In the

---

[61] Kaeuper, "Charny's Career," pp. 25, 52–3.

[62] Lacey, *Lancelot*, part I, p. 39, quoted in Kaeuper, *Chivalry and Violence*, p. 130.

[63] Vale, *War and Chivalry*, pp. 18–19, and Keen, *Chivalry*, pp. 122–3 on Greek and Roman influences and texts.

[64] Lacey, *Lancelot*, part 5, pp. 161–2; and *Quest for the Holy Grail*, quoted in Kaeuper, *Chivalry and Violence in Medieval Europe*, pp. 137, 48.

[65] Homer, *Iliad*, 24.39–45.   [66] Gower, *Vox Clamantis*.

[67] Kennedy, *Lancelot do Lac*, I, pp. 142–5, Kaeuper, *Chivalry and Violence in Medieval Europe*, pp. 155–6.

[68] *Quest for the Holy Grail*, p. 168.

[69] Lacey, *Lancelot*, part 3, p. 272, quoted in Kaeuper, *Chivalry and Violence in Medieval Europe*, p. 153.

Chanson de Roland, the eponymous hero refuses to sound his horn and bring help from Charlemagne so he and his rearguard can gain more honor by fighting the Saracens alone and outnumbered even though it means certain death. When Roland's companion Oliver urges him to call for reinforcements, Roland tells him: "That would be the act of a fool! I would forfeit the fame I have in Sweet France."[70] Honor occasionally gives rise to wealth. Lancelot's grandfather acquires land because of his valor on the battlefield. This was more likely to occur in practice than in fiction where, religious orders aside, knights did not have to forsake wealth to gain honor. Prowess also provided access to sex, as women were socialized into seeking bed partners among successful knights. In some tournaments, women offered themselves as prizes to the victors.[71]

Most of the great texts of chivalry treat women as property and propagate stereotypes similar to those found in Homer and the Roman literature emphasizing *virtu*. These stereotypes are most pronounced in works by authors with monastic associations, such as *The History of the Holy Grail* and *The Quest for the Holy Grail*, but they also pervade more secular *chansons de geste*. Women are depicted as unstable, wily and corrupting creatures dominated by appetites and emotions. Knights come to blows over women because their unfaithfulness or abduction is an offense to manly honor. In the "Tale of Balin," the hero decapitates a lady who has sought a favor from Arthur. The king feels no sympathy for the woman, only shame because her murder violates guest friendship and the expectation of protection offered by his court.[72] The few women who are praised in these fictional accounts generally sacrifice themselves, as does Alde, Roland's betrothed, when Charlemagne informs her of Roland's death. He offers her his son Louis as a replacement. She declines, preferring not to live if Roland is dead, and successfully calls upon God, his saints and angels to end her life on the spot. With tears in his eyes, Charlemagne has countesses escort her body to a convent for burial.[73] Like its ancient Greek counterpart, chivalry created strong bonds among fellow fighters. Male fellowship, which gives meaning to life, was as important as prowess. The

---

[70] Merwin *Chanson de Roland*, line 83.
[71] Kaeuper, *Chivalry and Violence in Medieval Europe*, pp. 219–25.
[72] Lacey, *The Merlin Continuation*, cited in Kaeuper, *Chivalry and Violence in Medieval Europe*, p. 213.
[73] Merwin *Chanson de Roland*, line 258.

ultimate violations of chivalry according to Llull were slaying one's lord, surrendering his castle or sleeping with his wife.[74]

As in the *Iliad*, the literature of chivalry tries to suppress any tension between ascribed status (lineage) and achieved status (prowess). The assumption, often made explicit, is that noble birth brings with it qualities that encourage and allow young men to accomplish great deeds.[75] In *The Crowning of Louis*, Charlemagne warns his son not to take any "lowborn man" as a counselor because he "would betray his trust in a minute for money."[76] In the *Song of Aspremont*, the duke of Burgundy insists that all lay officials must come from a "good family."[77] In the early Middle Ages, the reverse was closer to the truth in practice. Fighting men, described as *milites*, were often landless men of low status.[78] The decline of royal power ultimately led to the rise in the status of knighthood, envisaged by the Church and intellectuals as an alternate source of order. In twelfth-century France, the terms knight and noble began to be used synonymously, a practice that soon followed in Germany. A distinct nobility was never defined by law in England, but here too a class emerged that claimed the right to engage in violence in defense of its honor. In much of Europe, this development was increasingly symbolized by entry into knighthood through simple inheritance in lieu of ceremonies like dubbing.[79]

Like Homer and the early Romans, chivalry put great store in civilized manners, courtesy and generosity. It was part and parcel of an increasingly sophisticated court-based culture that sought to recapture or recreate some of the imagined values and practices of the past. Unlike the ancients, it was infused with a romantic ethos that created idealized visions of women while seeking to make them available as sex objects. Round Table knights swore to uphold the honor of damsels. In Chrétien de Troyes' *Lancelot*, the Lovesome Damsel coyly advises Lancelot that a knight who takes advantage of a woman will be dishonored in all lands, but if he wins her in battle by defeating another knight, "he can without shame do with

---

[74] Llull, *Book of the Order of Chivalry*, cited in Keen, *Chivalry*, p. 10.
[75] Kennedy, "Quest for Identity"; Kaeuper, *Chivalry and Violence*, pp. 130–1.
[76] *The Crowning of Louis*, quoted in Kaeuper, *Chivalry and Violence in Medieval Europe*, p. 105.
[77] *The Song of Aspremont*, quoted in Kaeuper, *Chivalry and Violence*, p. 105.
[78] Strayer, *Medieval Statecraft and the Perspectives of History*, pp. 655–69.
[79] Barber, *The Knight and Chivalry*, p. 41; Keen, *Chivalry*, p. 143; Kaeuper, *Chivalry and Violence in Medieval Europe*, pp. 189–90.

her as he will."[80] Significantly, the verb *esforcer* in Old French is used to describe great military efforts and rape.[81]

Chivalry also differed from its ancient counterparts in its close connection with Christianity. In ancient times, immortality could only be achieved figuratively through everlasting fame as a hero. In the Middle Ages, knights, and the population more generally, believed in the possibility of eternal life through salvation.[82] In the *Chanson de Roland*, Archbishop Turpin, himself a knight, tells Roland's warriors, who are about to face an overwhelming Saracen force: "If you die, you will be holy martyrs and will sit in the topmost parts of paradise."[83] In various versions of *Lancelot*, Pharian assures his fellow knights that if we die for our liege lords "we die as sure of salvation as if we were slain fighting the Saracens."[84] In *The Quest for the Holy Grail*, Galahad was uncomfortable if a day went by without his attending mass. In the *Mort Artu*, Lancelot regularly says his prayers and makes confession. Other knights pray before combat or listen to mini-sermons on the battlefield. In the *Marvels of Rigomer*, Gawain wields a sword on which the Father, Son and Holy Ghost have been incised. Divine support of chivalry is signaled by the Angel Gabriel's cameo appearance in the eleventh-century *Chanson de Roland* to escort Roland's soul to heaven and buck up Charlemagne, who is wearying from battle fatigue.[85] Geoffroi de Charny repeatedly tells his readers that prowess is a gift of God, who opens the doors of paradise for brave knights.[86]

Romances and guidebooks to chivalry emphasize the responsibility of knights to protect the Church, widows, orphans and the poor. The *Chanson de Roland* depicts Charlemagne as the great defender of Christendom and contrasts his valor, loyalty and wisdom with the cowardice, betrayal and foolishness of the traitor Ganelon. In Thomas Malory's *Morte Darthur*, written in the mid-fifteenth century, Arthur compels his knights

---

[80] De Troyes, *The Knight of the Cart*, in *Arthurian Romances*, p. 223. Gravdal, "Chretien de Troyes, Gratian, and the Medieval Romance of Sexual Violence," contends that Troyes helped to legitimize rape and make it an accepted, even preferred form, of heterosexual relations in the West.
[81] Kaeuper, *Chivalry and Violence in Medieval Europe*, pp. 225–30 on sexual violence.
[82] Kantorowicz, *The King's Two Bodies*, on military sacrifice and salvation in the Middle Ages.
[83] Merwin, *Chanson de Roland*, line 89.
[84] Lacey *Lancelot*, part 1; Kennedy, *Lancelot do Lac*, I, p. 73, quoted in Kaeuper, *Chivalry and Violence in Medieval Europe*, p. 72.
[85] Merwin, *Chanson de Roland*, lines 175, 179, 261.
[86] Kaeuper and Kennedy, *Book of Chivalry*, pp. 132–3.

to swear upon pain of death to succor "ladies, damsels, and gentlemen."[87] Ramon Llull traces knighthood back to the creation, and God's choice of one of a thousand men as brave, loyal and strong enough to sustain the difficult trials necessary to serve humankind.[88] Chivalry has been described "as the male aristocratic form of lay piety."[89] However, knights rarely considered themselves bound by the Church, which condemned tournaments and private wars, albeit with little effect.[90]

Knights read these immensely popular romances and accepted the historicity of their key figures.[91] Many sought to emulate their heroes, and presumably internalized their putative values. William Marshall, who died in 1219, made a pilgrimage to Cologne, fought in a crusade, founded a religious house and became a Templar. Geoffroi de Charny, who died in 1356, was a crusader and founded a religious house.[92] Kings and prominent aristocrats instituted tournaments and honorific orders to recreate the lifestyle of Arthur, Lancelot, Gawain and the Knights of the Round Table. The first order of knighthood, the Society of St. George, may have been founded by King Charles-Robert of Hungary in about 1325. It was an elite band, limited to fifty knights who wore their own habit, met on a regular basis and swore to uphold religious and knightly obligations. Other orders followed quickly, among them the Band (Castile, 1330), the Garter (England, 1349), the Star (France, 1351), the Collar (Savoy, 1364) and the Ermine (Brittany, 1381). Their membership was restricted to warriors of noble birth and high character. Edward III founded the Order of the Garter after the Battle of Crécy to commemorate his victory and the valor of those who had served under him. Secular orders of knighthood soon proved an effective means of binding high-born nobles to the service of their monarchs.[93] It benefited knights to the extent that displays of honor on the battlefield, in the tournament stalls and in court led to royal support and amorous liaisons.

Chivalry found its most characteristic expression in the tournament, a form of staged warfare that became popular in mid-eleventh-century France. In its initial form, the *mêlée* or *haslitude*, opposing teams of knights had a go at one another on a level field. They sometimes paid an entrance

---

[87] Malory (d. 1471), *Le Morte Darthur* quoted in Lynn, *Battle*, p. 82.
[88] Llull, *Book of Knighthood and Chivalry*, book II, p. 15.
[89] Kaeuper, *Chivalry and Violence*, p. 47; Keen, *Chivalry*, pp. 21, 102–4, 197–9.
[90] Barker, *The Tournament in England*, pp. 70–83; Keen, *Chivalry*, pp. 44–63, 94–8; Kaeuper, *Chivalry and Violence in Medieval Europe*, pp. 45–62, 85.
[91] Keen, *Chivalry*, p. 113; Kaeuper, *Chivalry and Violence in Medieval Europe*, p. 31.
[92] Kaeuper, *Chivalry and Violence in Medieval Europe*, p. 47.
[93] Boulton, *Knights of the Crown*, pp. 30–6, 194–5, 229–30; Keen, "Chivalry and the Aristocracy."

fee, were accompanied by foot soldiers and had roped-off areas where they could catch their breath and recuperate. Captured knights lost their armor and could be held for ransom. By the thirteenth century, English tournaments excluded armed foot soldiers and required all weapons to be blunted to reduce fatalities. Such contests were still bloody: in 1241, eighty knights are reported to have died at a tournament in Neuss, a city on the west bank of the Rhine, most of them from suffocation. Casualties were also heavy at the so-called "little battle of Chalons" at Hertford in 1241, where the count of Chalons put a headlock on King Edward I in an attempt to unhorse him. Footmen and spectators immediately joined the fray. In some cases, tournaments were bloody because they were used to settle private disputes and grudges. From the thirteenth century on, these combats increasingly became one-on-one contests.[94]

The more valued tournaments became, the more they were limited to an elite drawn from the nobility. Like the hoplite panoply in ancient Greece, the necessary equipment was expensive. In addition to weapons, a warhorse and armor for oneself and the horse, knights needed a palfrey to ride to the tournament and squires to assist them. They were expected to live in style befitting their status, which often involved a sizeable house, hawks and hounds. Tournaments became a means of preserving the barriers between the nobility and rich bourgeoisie, which is why wealthy merchants in Flanders began to stage their own tournaments. In some locales, notably in the Low Countries, members of the merchant class were allowed to participate and could even be ennobled for displaying prowess. Elsewhere, class barriers were strengthened, and often made more visible, through the adoption of coats of arms and other regalia. The principle of *dérogeance*, which declared a variety of occupations including retail trading as incompatible with nobility, first arose at this time. This principle, and class barriers more generally, were justified on the grounds that generosity (*largesse*) was an inbred, or at least acquired, characteristic of the nobility, in contrast to the avarice of merchants. Presaging relations between aristocrats and merchants in the modern era, impecunious knights not infrequently crossed the class barrier and married the daughters of wealthy merchants.[95]

[94] Keen, *Chivalry*, pp. 83–102; Vale, *War and Chivalry*, pp. 63–9, and *Princely Court*, pp. 184–200; Barker, *The Tournament in England*, pp. 19–20, 23, 48–9, 57–9, 142–3; Kaeuper, *War, Justice, and Public Order*, pp. 199–211; Vale, "Violence and Tournament"; Gillingham, "War and Chivalry in the *History of William the Marshal*."
[95] Keen, *Chivalry*, pp. 90, 144, 153–5, and "Chivalry and the Aristocracy"; Kaeuper, *Chivalry and Violence in Medieval Europe*, pp. 194–9.

The thirteenth century witnessed the development of jousting, an event facilitated by the spread and adoption of the stirrup, which provided more stability in the saddle and greatly enhanced the value of cavalry. Champions armed with lances charged each other on horseback, often in lists, with the goal of unseating their opponent or at least breaking their lance against his armor. In the course of the next two hundred years, *pas d'armes*, as these contests became known, spread through much of Western Europe and became increasingly elaborate. They were often accompanied by lavish feasts, dancing and desirable damsels as spectators or rewards. Edward III, like Edward I, was a great warrior and a fan of jousting. He used these contests to emphasize his association with King Arthur, and at his "round table" of 1344 established the Order of the Garter in imitation of Arthur.[96] On the continent, pavilions were erected next to artificial lakes and hills dominated by images of the Virgin Mary or of damsels and unicorns looking down on the combat. Challengers routinely appeared in color-coordinated armor, and winners might receive golden swords and lances. Pomp and show became the order of the day and fatalities declined. Huizinga rightly describes the tournaments of this era as an elaborate form of sport.[97] The centrality of tournaments to aristocratic culture of the time allowed kings to draw nobles into their ambit, making them more dependent on them, while at the same time it enmeshed to some degree the king and his court in the values and practices of chivalry.[98]

Some knights, like William Marshall, were famous for their simple lives and service to their lords and the Church. Others indulged in gratuitous violence against those they were supposed to protect, or extorted or robbed them, leading clerics to describe them as a scourge.[99] Real warfare, as the Hundred Years War indicates, deviated considerably from the one-on-one combats or fair fights characteristic of the literature.

---

[96] Barnie, *War in Medieval English Society*, p. 66; Barker, *The Tournament in England*; pp. 145–8; Keen, *Chivalry*, pp. 22–3.

[97] Keen, *Chivalry*, pp. 23–4, 87–8, 200–12; Barker, *The Tournament in England*; pp. 84–111; Huizinga, *Waning of the Middle Ages*, p. 72.

[98] Keen, "Aristocracy and Chivalry," portrays these as alternative developments. I consider them coexisting and in some ways reinforcing.

[99] *The Chronicle of Jean de Venette*, p. 34, quoted in Kaeuper, "Charny's Career," p. 50; Newton, *Fashion in the Age of the Black Prince*. For the debate on knights and their role in spreading or limiting violence, see Elias, *Civilizing Process*, II, p. 72, and the discussion in Kaeuper, "Chivalry and the 'Civilizing Process'."

The Hundred Years War

In the centuries after William's invasion, the Norman elite dispossessed its English counterpart and established its hold on the country. England and France drew closer together, linked by language, the culture of chivalry and an increasingly intermarried aristocracy. This propinquity was also a fundamental source of conflict.

Edward III's mother and her lover Roger Mortimer forced his father, the inept loser of Bannockburn, to abdicate in 1326. The following year they disposed of him for good by having him buggered with a red hot poker. Fourteen-year-old Edward III became a puppet monarch until 1330, when he broke into his mother's bed chamber with a band of friends and took her and her lover prisoner. They had him tried, and he was hanged, drawn and quartered at the gallows at Tyburn. Queen Isabella was confined to a country estate for the rest of her life. Isabella was first cousin to Philip VI of France and sister of King Charles IV, the last member of the Capetian dynasty, who died in February 1328. On his deathbed, Charles declared that if his pregnant wife produced a son he would become king, but if she bore a daughter, the crown would pass to Philip of Valois. At an assembly convened by Philip to anoint him king, two English envoys demanded that the crown go to Queen Isabella, but the notables ruled, in the words of a contemporary chronicler, that "the realm of France was of so great noblesse that it ought not by succession to fall into a woman's hand."[100] This was a convenient means of excluding Isabella, whom the French knew all too well from reputation and her earlier visit to Paris in 1326.

Edward III had a reasonable claim on the throne of France, but was not powerful enough to challenge Philip. His more immediate concern was retention of the duchy of Aquitaine, also known as Guyenne, which ran along the French coast from La Rochelle to the Pyrenees with its capital in Bordeaux. It was the last remnant of Henry II's Angevin Empire, which Edward inherited and held as a feudatory to the king of France, although he regarded the territory as an integral part of England. The duchy generated more income for the king from tolls, taxes and wine than all of England. It was well fortified, being defended by a series of strong points, or *bastides*, situated in strategic towns and along the border with Gascony. In 1329, Edward traveled to Amiens to swear fealty to Philip as his representative in Guyenne.[101]

---

[100] Ormrod, "England: Edward II and Edward III"; Jones, "The Last Capetians and Early Valois Kings, 1314–1364"; Froissart, *Chronicles*, book 21 for the quote.

[101] Ormrod, "England: Edward II and Edward III"; Vale, *English Gascony*, pp. 1–55.

Philip VI was the most powerful monarch in Europe at the time. France's population was a multiple of England's – about 17 to 7 million people before the Black Death arrived in 1348 – and Philip's predecessors had subjugated unruly nobles and effectively established their authority over the kingdom. Philip controlled the papacy, then in exile in Avignon, and ruled in theory, although not in practice, over Flanders, Brittany and Guyenne. For several years, Edward attempted to negotiate a border settlement with Philip, but discontinued these efforts when Philip gave refuge to his enemy the Scottish king. French privateers began to attack English shipping in the Channel, and an aroused parliament voted Edward money to fight France. Both sides prepared for war, which was triggered in 1337 by a proclamation issued by Philip to the effect that Edward had forfeited Guyenne through disobedience. Edward sent a formal letter to Philip claiming the French throne. Philip responded with an attack on Guyenne.[102]

There are two equally compelling and compatible explanations for the war: the medieval and the modern. The medieval directs our attention to ambiguous or contradictory status hierarchies, one of the tensions I have described as inherent in honor societies. In the *Iliad*, the clash between achieved and ascribed status drove the conflict between Achilles and Agamemnon. In Anglo-French relations, a similar problem arose because of Edward III's dual status as a king and a vassal. The former made him an equal of Philip, but the latter made him his subordinate.[103] This situation was irritating to both leaders, and perhaps intolerable, because Edward's claim to the throne of France was as least as good as Philip's. The fact that both men were active, ambitious and risk-accepting, and driven by concerns for their respective honor and standing, made compromise impossible. As is so often the case when the spirit is aroused, slights to one's honor (e.g. offering refuge to Edward's adversary, the Scottish king) aroused anger and countermoves that quickly transformed a personal conflict into a violent, national one.

The modern explanation has to do with the emergence of states. Successive monarchs of France and England gradually consolidated what would become two powerful national states. English kings still had to contend with considerable opposition in Wales and Scotland and many English barons remained unwilling to accept the authority of the crown.

[102] Ormrod, "England: Edward II and Edward III"; Jones, "The Last Capetians and Early Valois Kings, 1314–1364."
[103] Le Patourel, "Origins of the War."

In the first half of the fourteenth century France had largely suppressed regional and baronial autonomy, and this may explain why it ended up a more highly centralized political unit. Slowly but inexorably, the kings of France were reducing the lordship of dukes to mere ownership of land and thus transforming their de jure suzerainty into de facto sovereignty. Edward was being asked to renounce England's control of Guyenne in both theory and practice at a time when the English were attempting to strengthen their position in the duchy. The medieval and modern explanations see England and France on a collision course and their monarchs moved by personal anger as well as more rational calculations.

The Hundred Years War consisted of a series of raiding expeditions, sieges of cities and towns, a few pitched battles and naval encounters and long truces or periods of inactivity. The English were surprisingly successful at first, capturing considerable French territory and raiding almost at will. In 1346, Edward won an impressive victory at Crécy, where the French heavy cavalry was all but eliminated. The Black Prince (the Prince of Wales) invaded Gascony, and won a stunning victory at Poitiers in 1356. The French, under Charles V (1360–1400), avoided battle with the main English army, but recaptured much of their lost territory, including the city of Poitiers. Under Henry V (1400–22), the English regained the upper hand, extending their operations deep into the Pas-de-Calais and winning a major victory at Agincourt in 1415. In 1429, Jeanne d'Arc lifted the siege of Orléans, and helped to clear the English from the Loire valley. The war ended in July 1453 when the French finally expelled the English from the continent, their stronghold in Calais aside.

The Hundred Years War was a form of state-sponsored brutality. *Chevauchée*, which literally means "ride," came to describe the English strategy of terrorizing the population through pillage, burning, rape and murder. The English carried out eleven *chevauchées* between 1339 and 1380, devastating large swaths of western, central and southern France. They killed every person, regardless of age, who fell into their hands.[104] In 1360, Petrarch lamented that English armies had so "reduced the entire kingdom of France by fire and sword" that I "had to force myself to believe that it was the same country I had seen before."[105] As the French largely avoided pitched battles, the *chevauchée* served as a substitute for actual combat, and in some circumstances as a vehicle to compel the French to stand and fight. It deprived the French government of resources,

---

[104] Seward. *Hundred Years War*, pp. 84–5; Lynn, *Battle*, p. 85.
[105] Petrarch, *Letters of Old Age*, book II, pp. 366–7.

conscripts and taxes. By exposing Philip's inability to protect the French peasantry, *chevauchées* sought to undermine the legitimacy of his contested claim to the French crown. They generated booty and hostages for ransom, and provided ordinary soldiers with the opportunity for rapine and pillage. One common practice that combined the two was to lock a husband in a chest and gang-rape his wife on the lid until he agreed to reveal where he had buried his treasure.[106]

Pillage, rape, murder and efforts to pick off stragglers coexisted uneasily with the practice of chivalry. Some contemporary writers like Froissart struggled vainly to reconcile theory and practice. He describes plunder and ransom as consistent with the code of chivalry. Those who fought at Poitiers, he writes, were "*riche d'onneur et d'avoir*" (rich in honor and possessions). Following Huizinga, some modern authors suggest that chivalry had become decadent by virtue of its failure to sustain crusading zeal against the Turks and was on the decline in the fourteenth and fifteenth centuries.[107] More recent works distinguish between social decline and moral decadence, and recognize that striking differences between the theory and practice of war do not necessarily indicate a decline in the ideal and culture of chivalry.[108]

On the macro level, war was undeniably waged by both sides for political goals, and strategies chosen or developed to attain those ends regardless of their consequences for non-combatants or the social hierarchy. At the micro level, both armies were brutal and rapacious, but chivalrous practices were also apparent. Discipline was weak, and knights behaved the way their namesakes, the *milites*, did in the early Roman Republic. They charged ahead in search of glory and captives, heedless of the risk and the tactical disadvantage of acting in an uncoordinated manner. Engagements threatened to dissolve into a series of Homeric style one-on-one combats, with the killing of adversaries or the taking of prisoners regarded by participants as more important than routing the enemy.[109] On other occasions, honor was regarded as more important than life. Sir William

---

[106] *The Chronicle of Jean de Venette*, pp. 99–100, cited in Lynn, *Battle*, p. 89; Wright, *Knights and Peasants*, p. 73.

[107] Huizinga, *Waning of the Middle Ages*; Kilgour, *The Decline of Chivalry as Shown in the French Literature of the Late Middle Ages*, who contends that chivalry became a code of display increasingly divorced from real life. Hewitt, *The Organization of War under Edward III*, pp. 131–3. Ferguson, *The Indian Summer of English Chivalry*, on the fifteenth century.

[108] Vale, *War and Chivalry*, pp. 1–12, contra Huizinga, and his *The Princely Court*; Allmand, *The Hundred Years War*; Keen, *Chivalry*; Ainsworth, *Jean Froissant and the Fabric of History*, pp. 80–2.

[109] Vale, *War and Chivalry*, p. 104; Kaeuper, *Chivalry and Violence in Medieval Europe*, p. 145.

Felton was killed in Castile when he chose to charge a Spanish force sin-glehandedly.[110] At the Battle of Mauron in Brittany in 1352, eighty French knights, all members of the Company of the Star, died rather than with-draw because of an oath they had sworn never to retreat.[111]

Caste solidarity united English and French knights. Edward III held tournaments during the Hundred Years War and invited knights from everywhere in Europe, including France, although only knights allied with him participated.[112] When English knights fell at Longeuil, their compatriots mourned them on the grounds that "it was too much that so many of their good fighters had been killed by mere peasants."[113] Gascon captain Jean de Grailly is said to have asked his captor if he was a man of noble birth, "For I would sooner die than surrender to one who was not."[114] After King John's capture at Poitiers he was enter-tained royally by the Black Prince, who held a feast in his honor, and served him in person, as there was nobody else of appropriate rank to do so.[115] In the tradition of Homer, Herodotus and Thucydides, contem-porary chroniclers and leaders celebrated feats of bravery by adversaries. Chandos Herald speaks well of French generals at Poitiers, especially the Marshal d'Audrehem, whom he call "a very goodly knight." Charles V praised his nemesis, the Black Prince, for having ruled "mightily and bravely."[116]

Some of the barbarities of the Hundred Years War were attributable to the hyper-acute sense of honor fostered by chivalry. Limoges was held for the English by Jean de Cros, a trusted advisor of the Black Prince. In 1370, he betrayed Edward and let the French into the city. The Black Prince and his brother, John of Gaunt, laid siege to Limoges when its inhabitants would not surrender. When they captured it, the Black Prince ordered its inhabitants slaughtered as compensation for their governor's treason. "More than three thousand persons, men, women and children, were dragged out to have their throats cut."[117] Like the Greeks at Troy, treachery was considered collective, and revenge was required to satisfy honor.

---

[110] Chandos Herald, II, line 2725, quoted in Barnie, *War in Medieval English Society*, pp. 90–1.
[111] Boulton, *Knights of the Crown*, p. 36.
[112] Barnie, *War in Medieval English Society*, p. 84.
[113] *The Chronicle of Jean de Venette*, pp. 99–100, quoted ibid., p. 72.
[114] *Quatre premiers Valois*, p. 241, quoted, ibid.
[115] Chandos Herald, II, lines 141–4, cited ibid., pp. 80–1.
[116] Chandos Herald, II, lines 938ff, cited ibid., p. 85.   [117] Froissart, *Chronicles*, book 8.

Chivalry not infrequently trumped strategic considerations. Bertrand du Guesclin, constable of France, and one of his country's foremost military commanders, was captured by the English in Spain in 1367 at the Battle of Nájera. Within a year, the Black Prince released him for a sizeable ransom against the advice of his principal advisors, who rightly worried that he would stiffen French resistance. Du Guesclin succeeded in renewing the war by helping to install a new king of Castile, and was then recalled by Charles V to manage his country's defense. Recognizing what a dangerous adversary du Guesclin was, the Black Prince asked for an extraordinary ransom of 100,000 francs. When the king of France offered to pay this sum, Edward's honor required him to release his prisoner.[118]

In some key encounters, chivalry dictated the tactics of armies. At Crécy in 1346, Edward, outnumbered three to one, counted on the French commitment to the chivalrous code. He arrayed his men accordingly, with dismounted knights and squires in the center and longbow archers on the flanks extending forward to provide enfilading fire against the expected cavalry charge of the English center. His forces dug ditches in front of their lines to trip the horses of any French cavalry that reached them. Philip failed to rest his tired men, who had endured a long march to reach the English. When he saw the English, "his blood boiled." His knights were so eager for battle that they pressed forward, preceded by Genoese crossbow archers sent to soften up English resistance. The longbow outranged the crossbow and had a more rapid rate of fire, allowing the English to pick off the Genoese at will. An infuriated Philip, convinced that his Italian archers were cowards, called upon his cavalry to run them down and charge the English line. The English longbowmen now let loose barrage after barrage against the cavalry, bringing down horses and riders. Cavalry that reached the English line were repelled and subsequently cut down by pursuing English knights and infantry. The English used spears to penetrate the armor, or knives to slit the throats of fallen French knights, rousing protest from some of Edward's knights, who thought the action not chivalrous and denying them the opportunity of taking prisoners for ransom. The French made fifteen consecutive sorties, losing considerable forces on every attempt to arrows and spears. Between assaults, longbowmen went out on to the field of battle to retrieve arrows, often pulling them out of wounded and dead Frenchmen. By nightfall, it was obvious that the French had lost, and Philip was finally persuaded to break off

---

[118] Barnie, *War in Medieval English Society*, pp. 78–9.

the battle and retreat. The English, who had sustained only minor losses, identified the bodies of more than 1,500 dead French knights.[119]

There was nothing novel about Edward's strategy. Longbows devastated cavalry formations because they could penetrate helmets and chain mail. Cavalry could also be stopped by massed infantry wielding pikes, a tactic used successfully by the Flemish, Swiss and English at Courtain, Morgarten, Laupen and Bannockburn.[120] The French stressed the psychological "shock" function of heavy cavalry, and charging horsemen inspired fear and could deal handily with troops that broke formation and ran.[121] Contemporary observers attributed French tactics and defeat to pride. The eagerness of individual French knights to win reputations for glory worked to their collective disadvantage.[122]

Tensions

Chivalric literature highlights the central tension I attribute to honor societies: the extent to which competition and violence threaten the political–social order that makes honor possible. In *Lancelot do Lac*, an insignificant but astute man-at-arms observes that "Everyone would be disinherited and ruined if King Arthur were overthrown because the stability of all of us is his concern."[123] As he fears, the fellowship of the Round Table is destroyed by internecine conflict. There is an obvious parallel to the *Iliad*. The Trojan War is set in motion by Paris's liaison with and abduction of Helen, while civil war among Arthur's knights is triggered by Lancelot's adulterous liaison with and abduction of Guinevere. In both conflicts, violation of norms abases the honor of husbands and arouses anger that is only satisfied by vengeance. Loyalty, another key principle of chivalry, was supposed to restrain intra-elite competition and direct aggression against external adversaries. It failed to do so in many medieval romances and in real life.

The Hundred Years War provides ample empirical evidence of this phenomenon. It arose from an internecine quarrel at the highest levels of the Anglo-Norman-French nobility, and quickly led to the kind of violent

---

[119] Froissart, *Chronicles*, books 129, 161–2; Le Baker, *Chronicle*, p. 43; Ayton and Preston, *The Battle of Crécy*, Lynn, *Battle*, pp. 74–7; on Philip and the English. Sumption, *The Hundred Years War*, I, pp. 525–32 for Crécy.

[120] Vale, *War and Chivalry*, pp. 100–5.   [121] Fuller, *Armament and History*, p. 23.

[122] Barker, *The Tournament in England*, pp. 21–2; Beeler, *Warfare in England*, pp. 88–92; Gaier, "Le cavalerie lourde en Europe occidentale du XXIIe au XVIe siècle."

[123] Kennedy, *Lancelot do Lac*, I, p. 35, quoted in Kaeuper, *Chivalry and Violence in Medieval Europe*, pp. 93–4.

unraveling described in the romances. The English and French sought
to overcome this tension by making a sharp distinction between men of
gentle birth, most of them knights, and ordinary soldiers and civilians,
drawn from the lower classes. The former, who made up less than half of
the forces on either side, were treated relatively well, and often in accord
with the principles of chivalry. But not always when military necessity
dictated otherwise. At Agincourt, while the English were awaiting a third
French attack, King Henry V ordered the execution of all prisoners except
the wealthiest because he could not afford to release soldiers to guard
them. Archers let loose with arrows, infantry flailed about with poleaxes
and daggers and other knights were burned alive in a hut where they were
confined.[124]

Like the Peloponnesian War, the Hundred Years War escalated out of
control with devastating consequences for participants. The English kings
nearly went bankrupt in paying for the expeditions to France, and were
compelled to accept the growing powers of parliament.[125] The French
expected an easy victory, but lost three major battles to the English –
Crécy, Poitiers and Agincourt – and two generations of the upper ranks
of French nobility. The war divided the country, provoked a succession
struggle and civil war, and a nasty peasant uprising, the bloody *jacquerie*
of 1358. Peasants in the Beauvaisis rose up and slaughtered lords who
had been unable to protect them against the English and who had con-
fiscated their crops to help make up their losses or pay ransoms. The
insurrection moved up the Seine until the king of Navarre massed enough
troops to massacre the ill-armed army of peasants at Meaux.[126] Because
public opinion became engaged on both sides, extremists – defined here
as those wanting to continue the war – always found an audience and
degree of popular support, especially in England. Successive generations
of nobles also had an interest in war to prove their prowess and gain
honor.

In contrast to classical Greece, but similar to the late Roman Republic
and Empire, appetite entered the picture in a major and complex way. It
encouraged fighting, given the extraordinary ransoms that nobles could
earn and the plunder and percentages on ransomed prisoners captured
that could make common soldiers rich. If the historians of the conflict are
to be believed, war functioned something like today's lotteries. Ordinary

---

[124] Seward, *Hundred Years War*, pp. 168–9; Keen, *Chivalry*, p. 221.
[125] Ormrod, "England: Edward II and Edward III"; Barron, "The Reign of Richard II."
[126] Wright, *Knights and Peasants*, pp. 2–22, 80–116.

soldiers ignored the odds against them and focused instead on the gain they might achieve through plunder and hostage-taking – in sharp contradiction to the predictions of prospect theory. For the elite, appetite should have functioned as a restraint, given the staggering cost of the war. If the Peloponnesian War was sustained by the combination of spirit and fear, the Hundred Years War was kept going by spirit and appetite.

As I noted earlier, the other big contrast with the ancient world was Christianity. The pacific tradition was strong in the early Church; in its early history Christ was routinely represented as the Prince of Peace who urged Peter to sheathe his sword. Under Constantine, the Church became more militant in defense of an increasingly Christian realm. Augustine, writing a century later, laid the foundations for just war theory. By the time of the crusades, the Church relied on military forces to uphold the Peace of God and extend the territory in which Christianity was the dominant religion. Soldiers of Christ (*milites Christi*) came to refer equally to monks who used the weapon of prayer against evil, and knights who wielded their swords allegedly for the same end.[127] Military orders like the Templars, the Hospitalers and the Teutonic and Spanish knights, swore vows of obedience and chastity, and were freed from secular obligations in return for accepting ecclesiastical authority. Such groups became isolated from the emerging courts by virtue of their piety and international orientations.

Maurice Keen contends that we must look elsewhere for the origins and appeal of the more secular, romantic form of chivalry. In the *chansons de geste*, chivalry's key virtues of *largesse* (charity), *prouesse* (prowess) and *loyauté* (loyalty) are offered as models for noble behavior. These are the core values of traditional warrior societies and can be traced back to the pre-Christian German past. They animate *Beowulf*, which may have been written in the eighth century, and the German Latin epics of *Ruodlieb* and *Waltharius*, which date from the tenth and eleventh centuries. In Christian German poetry, the secular and religious traditions are brought together in the depiction of Christ as a noble leader and his disciples as devoted warriors. The Germanic Church was staffed with monks and priests who were themselves products of this tradition and kept alive the oral tradition – and preserved manuscripts like *Beowulf* that told of the great deeds of their ancestors. Leading church authorities came from noble families and were closely related to those who became feudal knights. By the eleventh century, the twin goals of an active, heroic life and salvation had become

---

[127] Kaeuper, *Chivalry and Violence in Medieval Europe*, pp. 67–8.

intertwined in the ideal of knighthood. Geoffroi de Charny explicitly urges young men to pursue "noble skill and exercise of arms, through which one can certainly acquire one's salvation."[128]

One of the most important catalysts of chivalry was the decline of kingly authority following the breakup of the Frankish kingdom in the late ninth century. Post-Carolingian Europe was afflicted with near-constant violence and civil disorder, and knighthood was created to fill the void. *chansons de geste* were explicitly concerned with institutions of governance. Thomas Malory's *Morte Darthur* calls upon knights to become a force for stability and the rule of law. The *chansons* created role models like Charlemagne, whose values and behavior bore little relationship to the historical figure. He was nevertheless a good choice because the character and preoccupations of the Carolingian world were not so far removed from those of the Middle Ages, and readers could more readily put themselves into the lives of knights featured in these tales.[129] Clerics gave the enterprise their blessing, and continued to uphold the ideal of knighthood even when its practice bore little relationship to their expectations. Offending practices, like "accursed tournaments," as St. Bernard described them, they consistently condemned.[130]

Quests are central to chivalric romances. They take the format of warriors in search of adventure who refashion their inner selves in the process. The quest becomes a vehicle for interrogating contemporary society and for socializing knights into playing a more positive role by supporting law and order.[131] Along with medieval romances more generally, the quest drives home the lesson that unrestricted competition in tournaments or in battle, and unbridled lust for women, can have tragic consequences for the social order and the survival of honor as a meaningful value.

By the time of the Hundred Years War, chivalry had largely outlived its usefulness. In England, war had long been acknowledged to be the business of the king, although there had been periodic violent disputes about who should be king. English rulers nevertheless faced a serious deterioration in law and order that began in the late thirteenth century

---

[128] Nelson, "Kingship and Empire," and Frantzen, *Bloody Good*, pp. 33–9, on Christ as a warlord. Keen, *Chivalry*, pp. 44–63; Charny, *Le Jouvencel*, I, p. 5, quoted in Vale, *War and Chivalry*, p. 31.

[129] Keen, *Chivalry*, p. 107.

[130] *Bernard of Clairvaux*, letter 405, quoted in Lacey, *Lancelot*, part 1, p. 32, Kennedy, *Lancelot do Lac*, I, p. 73, quoted in Kaeuper, *Chivalry and Violence in Medieval Europe*, p. 85.

[131] Kaeuper, *Chivalry and Violence in Medieval Europe*, pp. 253–72.

and continued for the next two hundred years.[132] In France, Capetian authority was gradually extended over the nobility, transforming the Truce of God into the King's Peace (*pax regis*).[133] Louis IX restricted trial by battle and private wars, and used whatever legal excuse came his way to destroy the castles of nobles.[134] Later Capetians, notably Philip IV and his sons, had *ordonnances* passed stipulating that the king's wars took precedence over all other kinds of violence, and outlawing tournaments, private wars and duels during wartime. The rapid growth of royal courts aided the peaceful, or at least state-run, implementation of justice.[135] Rather than constituting a force for order, knights and their traditions were increasingly a source of disorder, and central authorities searched for ways of reining them in and refocusing their loyalties on the state.

Johan Huizinga observes that restraints in war are only effective when protagonists recognize each other as equals.[136] Chivalry encouraged this perception, although, as we have seen, it limited its domain of equality to aristocratic combatants. To some degree it softened war, making fighting less barbaric for the "officer class" of knights. There was also a sharp decline in the torture and slaughter of prisoners, and a growing awareness that clerics and civilians should not be treated the same way as combatants.[137] Chivalry created a precedent, ultimately based on Homer, that helped to shape interstate European warfare down to the First World War. The spirit was both a source of war and of the development of international law and rules governing the conduct of war, especially of sieges and the treatment and exchange of prisoners.[138]

Motives and honor revisited

In chapter 2 I constructed ideal-type worlds of spirit, appetite and reason. Real worlds, of course, contain elements of all three, and are found within the triangle in which each ideal type is a vertex. When reason declines,

---

[132] Kaeuper, *War, Justice and Public Order*, pp. 136–7; Phillips, "Simon de Montfort (1250), the Earl of Manchester (1644), and Other Stories."

[133] Baldwin, *The Government of Philip Augustus*, pp. 373–5.

[134] Jordan, *Louis IX and the Challenge of the Crusade*; Kaeuper, *War, Justice, and Public Order*, pp. 211–35.

[135] Kaeuper, *Chivalry and Violence in Medieval Europe*, pp. 100–2.

[136] Huizinga, *Homo Ludens*, pp. 110–11.

[137] Gillingham, "1066 and the Introduction of Chivalry into England"; Contamine, "Introduction," in *War and Competition between States*.

[138] Vale, *War and Chivalry*, p. 8.

and systems move closer to pure appetite- or spirit-driven worlds, there is a possibility that they can undergo a phase transition into a fear-based world, where security concerns are paramount. The balance of motives underwent significant evolution in the period of European history under discussion. Different configurations led to different kinds of political orders, with different imperatives for political order and warfare.

In the Frankish kingdoms of the eighth and ninth centuries, appetite and spirit were coequal and largely unconstrained by reason. Domestic society was accordingly weak, and nearly non-existent at the regional and international levels. As a result, leaders established their authority with difficulty, and used their tax- and war-making powers to build up and sustain networks of support. They became vulnerable when they could no longer reward supporters with wealth and status, or when supporters, including their own sons, grew greedy and impatient. These sentiments were by no means uncommon in a weak society, and were also more likely to be acted upon in the absence of effectively internalized restraining norms. To survive, leaders required territorial conquests or other sources of wealth. Only unusual leaders like Charlemagne were able to build up loyal followings and use their power to make alliances, in his case with the Church, that provided him with extraordinary status. Even so, he faced rebellions, one of them organized by his son.

Warfare was frequent and brutal in such worlds. It generated wealth in the form of booty, tribute and land, conferred status to leaders and warriors alike and thus sustained leaders in power. Charlemagne was constantly at war and, as my theory predicts, behaved differently towards fellow Christians and so-called barbarians and infidels. Regional society was just strong enough to allow a distinction between "us" and "them." Fellow Christians were treated with a certain degree of restraint in both warfare and the subsequent occupation of their territories. Non-Christian "barbarians" were treated brutally, and conflicts against them more closely resembled wars of extermination. This difference was reinforced by the different motives for warfare. Most of the wars against "barbarians" (i.e. Saxons, Avars, Vikings) were fought largely for reasons of security, the principal exception being Charlemagne's unsuccessful and costly incursion into Spain, where his principal adversaries were Christian princes allied to Muslim overlords. The wars in Spain, and those against other Christians, were wars of conquest, and restraint was exercised for political and economic reasons. As Charlemagne was seeking to establish his position as emperor and protector of Christians, he had to show some respect for local populations.

Similar conditions prevailed in the early Middle Ages. Normandy was much like the Frankish kingdom; the struggle for power was fierce and unconstrained by norms. Once in power, leaders had to reward their supporters with land, titles and sinecures, which generally required territorial expansion. Spirit and appetite alike compelled William to invade England. Government in England was more rule-based, and William hastened to do what he could to legitimize his kingship in keeping with his need to reward his own supporters. His policies in England were not dissimilar in this respect from Charlemagne's in Lombardia.

The Hundred Years War took place in the aftermath of efforts to create an honor society through the efforts of chivalry. Society had become robust enough in many Western European kingdoms and city states to sustain the quest for honor. The spirit thus vied with the appetite, and both often competed with fear. Neither appetite nor spirit were effectively constrained or educated by reason. The Hundred Years War was caused by competing claims of authority to Guyenne and the French throne. Both sets of claims – and the absolute unwillingness of either king to consider compromise – were manifestations of their respective drives for honor and standing, for themselves and their respective countries. As Guyenne was an extraordinarily rich province, appetite also entered into the picture, for kings and their supporters alike. As we have seen, the spirit and its associated code of honor also influenced the conduct of the war, but only in relations among warriors of noble status. Sometimes it trumped strategic necessity, as in the Black Prince's decision to release Bertrand du Guesclin, while on other occasions it was not allowed to interfere with actions considered essential for victory, as when Henry V ordered the execution of all prisoners except the wealthiest on the eve of Agincourt. This action is also a nice example of the kinds of tradeoff that were routinely made between spirit and appetite.

The Hundred Years War was sustained by a combination of spirit and appetite, as large sections of the nobility expected to gain both wealth and honor from the conflict. So did many ordinary English combatants, although they had little say in decision-making. The human and economic costs of war were extraordinary, and in France the political costs were also high, as the war provoked a civil war and the *jacquerie*. Greed and anger were pronounced and truces did not hold. War could only be ended by outright victory, which took the form of the expulsion of the English from all their holdings in France save Calais. France won the war, the house of Valois enhanced its authority and prestige and expanded its territory, but at tremendous cost to the country.

Honor can only exist in a relatively robust society, and there was no such society regionally or internationally during the entire period in question. In the Frankish kingdom and Normandy, the struggle for standing was unconstrained, and violence and assassination were the norm. There was no meaningful difference between domestic and international relations, and little, if any, distinction between personal and political wars. In the absence of an honor society, there were also fewer barriers to mobility, and educated non-nobles who successfully served leaders could readily improve their standing and wealth, and become ennobled in the process. Standing, wealth, and power were not really conceptually distinct, as each was very much an expression of the others. In Old French, which evolved out of Romance dialects and Frankish in the tenth century, honor (*honneur*) was not a personal quality, but described a noble man's worldly goods (*biens*), including fiefs and benefices. Possessions served as markers of status well into the fourteenth century and the emergence of Middle French.[139]

In Carolingian times, the Roman concept of *virtu* still lurked somewhere in the background. There were proportionately more educated people than later in the Middle Ages as a result of the lingering survival of Roman educational practices. Educated people read Latin and had more than a passing familiarity with the great literature and historical works of Rome, and through them the historical and mythical Greek past. They were aware of the important differences between their society and those of antiquity. They were also steeped in Christianity and the writings of the Church fathers, and knew Augustine's view of the creation and survival of the Roman *imperium* as evidence of the ability of divine providence to harness the spirit to produce something beneficial to humanity.[140] The pope and lesser church authorities, including intellectuals like Alcuin, could not ignore the problem of security and order. Charlemagne capitalized on this yearning to offer a synthesis of Christianity and honor, and in the process created a more secure society and a new political niche for himself.

Charlemagne's empire was transient; the Treaty of Verdun in 843 divided it into three successor states, and in 911 the German branch of the Frankish successor family died out. The Holy Roman Empire was brought into being by a later Saxon dynasty, whose most prominent ruler

---

[139] Godefroy, *Dictionnaire de l'ancienne langue française*, IV, pp. 224–5; Duby, "Lineage, Nobility and Chivalry in the Region of Mâcon during the Twelfth Century"; Nye, *Masculinity and Male Codes of Honor in Modern France*, pp. 34–6.

[140] Augustine, *Confessions*, 8.9.21; *City of God*, V.12–13.

Otto I (the Great) was crowned emperor in 962. The Middle Ages was nevertheless a period of political fragmentation and disorder in which neither political competition nor the striving for wealth was restrained by effective norms. It is hardly surprising that thoughtful clerics and poets would look to an honor society as a possible solution of the security problem, and to a greatly idealized Charlemagne as the role model for such a society. The *chansons de geste* and medieval romances were vehicles for teaching literate laymen, and those to whom they would read aloud, the values and practices of an honor society, and for inspiring them to emulate their mythical depictions of Charlemagne, Roland, Arthurian knights and more recent exemplars of knighthood. The project succeeded in an unexpected way. It inspired many aristocrats to style themselves as knights and to seek the kind of glory achieved by heroes of the past through legendary military exploits. It also taught a code of behavior toward fellow knights and others in the society in need of their protection. This code was only appropriate to an honor society, and the world of medieval Europe was far from that. Tournaments and jousts, and the rituals and gatherings that accompanied them, were invented as an alternative artificial world in which the spirit could be satisfied through competition for honor.

To a limited degree the values and practices of chivalry carried over to the real world of medieval competition where they helped to inspire military valor, loyalty to one's liege and the generous treatment and ransom of aristocratic warriors taken prisoner. They acted as an additional spur to conflict and war because they intensified competition and made compromise of all kinds appear dishonorable. Honor societies are threatened not only by the competition they encourage, but by the inevitable ambiguities, even contradictions, within and across their multiple hierarchies. The Hundred Years War was the direct result of such a non-negotiable tension: the subordinate status of the English king versus his French counterpart by virtue of their respective authority over Guyenne. The absence of any established practices or institutions for settling such disputes led to wars when they involved powerful lords or heads of state. Those wars were unconstrained when it came to the treatment of local populations, and difficult to terminate short of outright victory by one side. The partial blending of honor and standing was arguably more of a curse than a blessing for medieval society.

6

From Sun King to Revolution

Glory is like a circle in the water.
Which never ceaseth to enlarge itself,
Til by broad spreading it disperse to naught.
Shakespeare[1]

From the late Middle Ages I move to seventeenth and eighteenth-century Europe. After the Peace of Westphalia in 1648, honor became an increasingly powerful motive, if not a way of life for much the European elite. The quest for *gloire* was the dominant dynastic goal, and found expression in expansion and war, although economic and security considerations were not insignificant. The period between Westphalia and the French Revolution offers insights into how concern for honor can shape foreign policy and the conduct of war, and also how it interacts with other motives to produce complex, and at times contradictory, patterns of behavior. The quest for *gloire* was limited to the great powers whose monarchs waged war for largely personal ends. War also served to find a new basis for legitimizing dynastic rule in an era when the commercial classes were becoming more important and were increasingly the arbiters of taste.[2] Europe included Protestant and Catholic states and their dependencies stretching from Ireland to Russia, and non-Christian powers, most notably the Ottoman Empire, played an important if unofficial role in the political system they constituted. I will discuss developments within and from the perspective of a number of these units but will devote most of my attention to France because, under Louis XIV and his successor, it was far and away the dominant political, military and cultural force in Europe.

In the conclusion to this chapter, I compare and contrast the tensions associated with honor societies in Greece, Rome and the late Middle Ages with those of post-Westphalian Europe, and analyze their implications

[1] Shakespeare, *Henry VI*, I.2, lines 133–7.
[2] Blanning, *The Culture of Power and the Power of Culture*, on this latter point.

for cooperation, conflict and political order. One of my more important findings concerns the role of states who are late developers and intent on gaining admission into the community where competition for honor and standing is possible. Governments of such states (e.g. Sweden, Russia and Prussia) mobilize a greater percentage of their available resources to support policies of expansion than their contemporaries, in pursuit of their goal of recognition as a great power. I also offer a novel spirit-based explanation for the rise of the state.

The modern era of European history is often dated from 1648 and the Peace of Westphalia. It was the product of the treaties of Münster and Osnabrück, the first ever pan-European congresses that brought together 145 representatives from 55 political units. Westphalia ended the Thirty Years War (1618–48), the last and most violent eruption of the religious wars that divided post-Reformation Europe. The Treaty of Osnabrück attempted to defuse religious wars by accepting the right of private worship and the principle of *curius regio, eius religio*, which left the regulation of religious practice to the state. The Treaty of Münster recognized the Dutch Republic and the Swiss Confederation. The 1659 Treaty of the Pyrenees ended the war between France and Spain. In the 141 years between Westphalia and the French Revolution of 1789 the state become the dominant political unit, and a European society emerged that facilitated the development of rules and procedures to regulate interstate relations. Aristocrats governed almost everywhere and maintained family and political loyalties that took little notice of state boundaries. Many aristocrats were multilingual, and most educated aristocrats could converse in French. Edward Gibbon described eighteenth-century Europe as "one great republic" with common standards of "politeness and cultivation" and a common "system of arts, and laws, and manners." "Fear and shame," he maintained, and "some common sense of honor and justice" induced leaders to moderate their ambitions. "In peace, the progress of knowledge and industry is accelerated by the emulation of so many active rivals: in war, the European forces are exercised by temperate and undecisive contests."[3] Hans Morgenthau invoked Gibbon's description to differentiate international relations in this epoch from that of the late nineteenth and twentieth centuries, when society broke down and actors

---

[3] Gibbon, *The Decline and Fall of the Roman Empire*, II, pp. 93–5. Voltaire, *Dictionnaire philosophique*, "Des Loix," section 1, makes a similar prediction: that Europe is becoming "a kind of great Republic" that will be governed in accord with universally accepted principles.

no longer followed the rules intended to govern competition and make it meaningful.[4]

Gibbon's characterization of Europe of the *ancien régime* involves considerable rhetorical flourish but contains an important element of truth. Actors who seek recognition, standing and honor in the eyes of others are intensely competitive but tend to play by the rules of the game when they understand that this makes their goals attainable. The other important incentive to exercise self-restraint was the recent experience of the consequences of failure to do so. The religious wars of the seventeenth century had left much of Europe in ruins. Burgundy, the Netherlands and much of Germany were seriously depopulated. Some scholars estimate that Germany's overall population declined from thirteen to four million, although a consensus has emerged around the figures produced by Günther Franz that indicate a decline in urban dwellers of about one-quarter and of the rural population by one-third. Of some 35,000 villages in Bohemia, no more than 600 were left intact.[5]

Self-restraint and rule-oriented behavior were also facilitated by the number of rulers related by blood or marriage. Consolidation had reduced Europe to no more than about twenty major political units, of which no more than about six at any one time qualified as great powers, a category that did not become fully conceptualized until the early nineteenth century.[6] The leading powers were France, Spain, England (after 1688), Austria (beginning in the eighteenth century), the United Provinces (Holland), Sweden (until 1711), Prussia (after 1742) and Russia (after 1712). Medium-sized states such as Sardinia, Bavaria and Saxony played an important role in the system. The smaller German states, the Swiss Federation, Denmark and Poland, prior to its three partitions, served as buffer states. The Ottoman Empire was also a great power, but it was outside the Christian community and network of reciprocal diplomacy.[7]

Spirit

Kings and other rulers were aristocrats, and some aspired to be autocrats. In the seventeenth century, Louis XIV (1643–1715), Leopold I of Austria (1657–1705), Frederick I, elector of Brandenburg, then king of Prussia

---

[4] Morgenthau, *Politics among Nations*, pp. 159–66, 270–84; Morgenthau, *In Defense of the National Interest*, p. 60.

[5] Perré, *Les mutations de la guerre moderne*, p. 409; Burckhardt, *Richelieu and his Age*, III, ch. 11; Holsti, *Peace and War*, pp. 28–9; Blanning, *Pursuit of Glory*, p. 54.

[6] Kratochwil, *Rules, Norms, and Decisions*; Neumann, "Russia as a Great Power."

[7] Scott, *Birth of a Great Power System*, pp. 2–7, for a ranking of the great powers in this period.

(1688–1701) and Peter the Great of Russia (1682–1725) invoked the divine right of kings and attempted to rule their states with an iron hand. In the eighteenth century, Frederick II (the Great) (1740–86), Empress Catherine of Russia (1762–6), Joseph II of Austria (co-regent from 1765 and sole ruler from 1780 to 1790), Gustav III of Sweden (1771–92), Charles III of Spain (1759–88) and Leopold (1765–90), Grand Duke of Tuscany were to varying degrees patrons of the Enlightenment, but most were intent on monopolizing power as far as was possible. So too were the rulers of the smaller Italian principalities, the Marques of Pombal in Portugal and the kings of Denmark. The most important exceptions were Leopold I, who as Grand Duke and later Emperor of Austria, aspired to introduce constitutional monarchy, and the United Provinces and Great Britain, where the *Stadhouter* and monarch respectively were constrained by constitutions and electoral political processes.

In the 1930s, the concept of enlightened absolutism was developed to characterize the continental autocrat of the period. By the 1960s it was regarded as an outdated stereotype. The independence of most rulers is now seen as sharply circumscribed by the impossibility of governing without the support of local elites, established systems of law, rights and customs, or even public opinion. Rulers also required increasingly large armies for expansion or defense, and the finances and the administration necessary to support them. This too required negotiation with local elites, and often some degree of dependence on burgeoning bureaucracies. Chief ministers assumed considerable power: Mazarin and Colbert in France, Walpole and Pitt in Britain, de Witt and Heinsius in the Netherlands and Haugwitz and Kaunitz in Austria.[8]

No monarch, not even Louis XIV, was an absolute ruler, although Louis did his best to encourage an absolutist culture. He ascended the throne as a child in 1643, and lived through the Fronde (1648–53), a series of revolts by peasants and Paris mobs against high taxes, and by nobles who sought to halt the centralizing of power by Richelieu, the king's first minister, and his successor, Cardinal Mazarin. Louis established a system of patronage that bypassed nobles of questionable loyalty and employed officials (*intendants*) to collect taxes and gather information.

---

[8] Anderson, *Europe in the Eighteenth Century*, pp. 121–9, and Goodwin, *The American and French Revolutions*, pp. 16, 19, 296–7, 331–61. Beik, *Absolutism and Society in Seventeenth Century France*, for critiques of absolutism. Some of the contributors to the Goodwin volume deny the concept of absolutism altogether. Blanning, *Joseph II and Enlightened Despotism*, for a nuanced account of Maria Theresa and Joseph II. Scott, *Enlightened Absolutism*, pp. 1–4, for the evolution of the debate.

As finance minister, Jean-Baptiste Colbert extracted revenue at the price of rampant nepotism and the development of clientalist networks that retarded the development of a modern bureaucracy.[9] Louis compelled many aristocrats to reside at Versailles, but never succeeded in taming them, and their resentment over loss of many of their privileges endured long after his reign. He failed fully to establish his authority over the army, as traditional attitudes were too strong.[10] Other contemporary rulers, and their successors in the eighteenth century, faced similar constraints.

Nicholas Henshall contends that these men brought their monarchs to a new conception of foreign policy, one that made the interests of state, not of the royal house, paramount.[11] The distinction between private and state interest was only just developing in France and readings of the period like Henshall's incorrectly impose modern understandings of *Realpolitik* on Louis XIV and other monarchs of the period. Louis thought of the state as his estate, and *la gloire*, which meant his prestige (*considération*) and standing relative to other leaders, as its appropriate end. "The love of *gloire*," he wrote, "surpasses all the others in my soul."[12] His advisor Mazarin spoke of *gloire* and *raison d'état* in the same breath, telling Louis that "I am interested in your *gloire* and the conservation of your state more than anything else in the world."[13] Louis XIV's idea of the state as a personal patrimony was widely shared by other rulers and prevailed up to and even past the French Revolution, although the conception of the ruler as the servant of the state made some headway.[14] It nevertheless made little difference in practice as rulers and most of their advisors saw "the glory of the state and its monarch" as roughly equivalent, and their primary goal.[15]

---

[9] Dessert, *Fouquet*, pp. 206–25, and *Argent, pouvoir et société au Grand Siècle*, pp. 354–65; Bonney, *The King's Debts*, p. 326; Durand, *Les fermiers généraux au XVIIIe siècle*, p. 51; Matthews, *The Royal General Farms in Eighteenth Century France*, pp. 47–50; Mettam, *Power and Faction in Louis XIV's France*, p. 279. Yates, "Song Empire," for a more effective attempt by the First Emperor of Qin to create an alternative bureaucratic structure that bypassed the inherited status of powerful families.

[10] Beik, *Absolutism and Society in Seventeenth Century France*, for an insightful and balanced treatment.

[11] Henshall, *The Myth of Absolutism*, pp. 62–3.

[12] Quoted in Lavisse, *Louis XIV*, pp. 134–5, and Elias, *Court Society*, p. 147.

[13] Mazarin to Louis XIV, June 29, 1658. Quoted in Luard, *War in International Society*, p. 155; Blanning, *Pursuit of Glory*, pp. 286–7, contends that Frederick the Great is the only ruler who came close to the conception of a state with interests independent of the ruler.

[14] Swann, "Politics and the State in Eighteenth Century Europe"; Lynn, *Giant of the Grand Siècle*, pp. 251–4.

[15] Schroeder, *The Transformation of European Politics*, p. 8.

Regardless of the internal constraints rulers everywhere faced, they sought to preserve foreign policy as a *domaine réservé*. Louis's vast expenditure on armies and war was a choice, not a necessity, as it was for all the so-called absolutist rulers of the seventeenth and eighteenth centuries. Up to 1672 and the Dutch War, Louis could perhaps have enjoyed a peaceful hegemony in Western Europe, but this was because of the extraordinarily favorable situation he enjoyed by virtue of the accomplishments of Richelieu and Mazarin and concurrent developments, including Habsburg weakness in Spain and Austria, the Ottoman menace to Austria and Spain, the Dutch War with England, the restoration of an English monarch whose instinct for survival led him to become a French client, divisions in the Holy Roman Empire and client rulers with whom to ally. The fact that Louis nevertheless sought to extend his hegemony by force is indicative of how little war had to do with security and how much with *gloire*.

According to Guy Rowlands, "The king of France's standing army in the seventeenth and early eighteenth centuries developed on the rock of private – and essentially dynastic – interest."[16] Standing among rulers was determined primarily by their success in war. For this reason, so-called enlightened despots tended to be *more* aggressive than other rulers. Like Louis XIV, many of them also faced pressures from below to make war a preferred route to reputation, office and wealth for noblemen in France, Sweden, Austria, Prussia and Russia. By 1691, at least 3,000 nobles were serving in Louis's elite corps, and more than 10 percent of all nobles did military service.[17] In his memoirs, Louis confesses that there were so many "fine men . . . enthusiastic for my service who seemed to be constantly urging me to furnish some scope for their valour."[18] He was not really pushed into war by nobles seeking glory through military service, but those nobles were supportive. His army was the most top-heavy in Europe; it contained 60,000 officers, far too many to offer more than one in five a command. At one point the king wryly observed that "I have officers whom I do not need. But I am sure they need me."[19]

Although Louis XIV went to war for *gloire*, he developed a strategic conception of war aims. He sought to acquire key territories that he called the "gates" to France, and expanded France's borders, especially in the northeast. Other countries followed suit, but strategic conceptions only gradually came to dominate their foreign and military policies. Britain

---

[16] Rowlands, *The Dynastic State and the Army under Louis XIV*, p. 336.
[17] Blanning, *Pursuit of Glory*, p. 215.
[18] Louis XIV, *Memoirs for the Instruction of the Dauphin*, pp. 258–60.
[19] Treasure, *Making of Modern Europe*, p. 207.

fought for Gibraltar and other strategic locations, but did not systematically set out to control the sea lanes globally until the French Revolutionary
and Napoleonic Wars.[20] Its empire in India and elsewhere was acquired as
much by accident as by design, and only after 1763 was its defense considered a strategic necessity.[21] Austria and Prussia struggled to consolidate
and extend their territories. Frederick the Great's smash-and-grab attack
on Austrian Silesia in 1760 was part of his quest for personal glory, but
also aimed at securing the rich resources of Silesia. Empress Maria Theresa
was subsequently consumed by the desire for revenge against Frederick the
Great.[22] Kaunitz, the real architect of Austrian foreign policy after 1749
thought in rational-strategic terms. Russia sought access to a warm-water
port, but mostly its rulers sought recognition for it as a great power, and
Catherine waged war to consolidate her hold on the throne. Monarchs
had family and dynastic interests, which were sometimes at odds with
state interests, especially when they concerned the pursuit or defense of
thrones. Thrones conferred standing and were a major source of conflict, although somewhat less so than had been the case in early modern
Europe.[23] Marriages, like alliances, were considered a form of statecraft,
and intended to enhance a ruler's claims to a throne or a territory while
undercutting those of rivals. Many of the important wars between 1688
and 1748 were wars of succession, and succession questions in Poland and
Bavaria triggered later wars.

Through the second half of the seventeenth century, Spain continued
to decline as a power and Louis XIV's France was at the apex of the
European status hierarchy. Voltaire compared its level of civilization to
classical Greece and Augustan Rome, and French became the language of
diplomacy and culture.[24] Other leaders emulated Louis's pursuit of *gloire*
through building as well as waging war. Palaces sprang up all over Europe –
including the Amalienborg in Copenhagen, the Drottningholm outside
of Stockholm, the Royal Palace and Charlottenburg in Berlin, Sans Souci,
the New Palace and the Town Palace in Potsdam, the Winter Palace in St.
Petersburg, the Great Palace at Tsarkoe Selo, the Royal Palace in Warsaw,
the Schönbrunn in Vienna, the Royal Palace in Naples, and the Royal
Palace in Madrid. While not copies of Versailles, their sponsors sought
to emulate its grandeur and become the focus of equally elaborate court

[20] Frost, *The Global Reach of Empire.*
[21] Marshall, *The Making and Unmaking of Empires,* for the best statement of this thesis.
[22] Blanning, *Joseph II and Enlightened Despotism,* p. 39.
[23] Black, *European International Relations,* p. 10.
[24] Voltaire, *The Age of Louis XIV,* pp. 1–5.

rituals. Rulers like Peter I of Russia and Frederick I and II of Prussia also built up their armies for conquest.[25]

Peter was the classic outsider – a misfit in traditional Russia, a country considered barbarian by the rest of Europe – whose visit to the West – the so-called "Grand Embassy" of 1697 – reinforced his desires to modernize his military and win fame for himself. He had previously transformed his two "play regiments," presented to him as a child, into real ones, and during the course of his reign added forty other regiments and a navy. They were initially led by foreigners, who were also imported to establish munitions and shipbuilding industries. The Russian nobility was transformed into a service nobility, and commoners reaching a specified rank were given a hereditary title. As the old boyar class died out, they were replaced by a new hierarchy with Western titles awarded on the basis of service to the state. Peter also approached the state as its servant. He started service in the army as a bombardier, and began to use language that depersonalized the state, formerly described as the private property of the tsar. His efforts at modernization led him ape the West in matters of appearance as well, and he outlawed beards and traditional dress for all but church officials and peasants.[26]

Peter incurred the wrath of the traditional military and palace guard (Strel'tsy), nobles who resented their increasingly subordinate position, and the Church, whose power and wealth he sharply reduced. Peter faced revolts from the Strel'tsy in 1698, nobles and assorted discontents in Astrakhan (1704–5) and Don Cossacks (1704–8). Despite his frustration with the pace of change, his army, after initial setbacks, bested the Swedes in the Great Northern War. The Treaty of Nystad (1721), signed at its conclusion, awarded Russia Ingria, Estonia, Livonia and part of Karelia. Peter made Russia into a great power, and the kings of Poland, Prussia and Sweden recognized his claim to be an emperor. This status did not come cheaply. Louis XIV devoted up to 75 percent of his income to war, and Peter, who had fewer revenues to draw on, spent an astounding 85 percent of Russia's income on the military and the financing of Poland and other allies. By the end of the Great Northern War, Russia was on the verge of bankruptcy.[27]

---

[25] Blanning, *Pursuit of Glory*, pp. 423–5.

[26] Massie, *Peter the Great*, pp. 65–79; Blanning, *Pursuit of Glory*, pp. 235–47; Cracraft, *The Revolution of Peter the Great*; Hughes, *Peter the Great*.

[27] Massie, *Peter the Great*, pp. 289–515; Frost, *State and Society*; Parker, *The Military Revolution*, p. 62; Blanning, *Pursuit of Glory*, pp. 557–61.

Prussia had patiently been constructed and expanded over the course of several generations of Hohenzollern rule, which had transformed it from a scattered collection of war-torn holdings into a kingdom that could field 83,000 men and was regarded an important regional power. Frederick I (1657–1713) unilaterally proclaimed himself king of Prussia in January 1701, and to buttress his claim he hosted elaborate festivities, highpoints of which were a cavalcade of carriages drawn by 30,000 horses and a coronation robe with diamond buttons each costing 3,000 ducats. During the course of his reign, he more than doubled the size of Prussia's army and bequeathed his son an enormous war chest.[28] Frederick II (1712–86), commonly described as brutal, bluff and tyrannical, spoke five languages, displayed a serious interest in French literature and philosophy and performed and composed music for the flute. By dint of his organizational skill and tactical genius, he made Prussia a great European power through victories in the First Silesian War (1740–2) and the War of Austrian Succession (1740–8). He conquered Silesia in these wars – part of his "rendez-vous with fame," as he put it – but nearly lost the province in the Seven Years War (1756–63). He participated in the first partition of Poland (1772), which gained him additional territory in the east. In the last years of his life he was recognized as the most heroic figure in Europe. For the Hohenzollerns, states existed to support armies. By 1740 Frederick was able to extract one-third of the yield of the land with a collection system of ruthless efficiency based on noble district councilors (*Landräte*) established by his father. Following French practice, he introduced a number of state monopolies to raise further income. The civil service, which required entrance exams, also served as his vehicle for checking the power of the nobility, although he only appointed nobles to senior positions in the civil service and army. The *Junker* class of landowners upon whom he depended was having difficulty in holding on to its estates; by 1800, 10 percent of them would be owned by commoners. *Junker* families and their estates were also decimated by war. Frederick's officer corps sustained an extraordinary rate of casualties, and his wars provoked temporary occupations of Prussian territory by the armies of France, Sweden, Austria and Russia. Late in his life, Frederick came to understand and acknowledge that the balance of power and the internal limitations of his state made it increasingly difficult to make additional territorial gains by dint of war.[29]

---

[28] Blanning, *Pursuit of Glory*, p. 229.
[29] Scott, "Prussia's Emergence as a European Great Power"; Schieder, *Frederick the Great*, pp. 90–100, 115–48; Anderson, *The War of the Austrian Succession*, p. 61 for the Frederick

All three rulers succeeded in enhancing their prestige and that of their states. Louis (12.7 million hits on Google) became known as "the Sun King." Peter (27.3 million hits) and Frederick (46 million) both have "the Great" attached to their names. In Frederick's case, the honorific came into use within five years of his ascending the throne. Peter wound up the most celebrated and commemorated tsar in Russian history, with a reputation equally vaunted in the Soviet and post-communist eras.[30] "Old Fritz" was lionized by subsequent generations of Prussians, but was spurned by liberals and Romantics in the aftermath of Prussia's defeat by Napoleon in 1806–7. His reputation was revived by nationalists, he took on the trappings of an all-German hero in the 1830s and this remained the case until 1945. In the 1960s, revisionist historians began to ask if his glorification of the military had created a lineage that ran through later Hohenzollerns to Hitler.

Appetite

If the spirit dominated the age of absolutism, appetites were hardly suppressed. The courts of Louis XIV and XV were famous for their lavishness and indulgence of all kinds. Louis XIV had numerous mistresses, as did many members of his court. They welcomed social events and performances, in which they sometimes performed, as opportunities to display their charm and virility.[31] High officials were rewarded handsomely, and had no compunction about flaunting their wealth. Mazarin sent an enormous sum of money to his father in Rome, along with a casket of jewels as dowry for his three sisters. The well-born shunned visible bribes because of the honor code, but many seemed willing to accept money if it could be kept out of sight. Corruption and fraud were a constant problem, made that much easier by the absence of any effective accounting and auditing systems.[32] Gambling was another pervasive vice among the nobility, and occasionally led to exile or suicide when debts could not be repaid.[33] Illegitimacy was so widespread that it became acceptable, with all kinds of indulgences and honors given to bastards. Saint-Simon, who did his best

quote; Showalter, *The Wars of Frederick the Great*; Gooch, *Frederick the Great*, p. 318; Gagliardo, *Germany under the Old Regime*, pp. 67–93, 293–311; Blanning, *Pursuit of Glory*, pp. 230–5.

[30] Duffy, *The Military Life of Frederick the Great*; Hughes, *Peter the Great*, pp. 226–50.

[31] Treasure, *Louis XIV*, pp. 180–99.

[32] Rowlands, *The Dynastic State and the Army under Louis XIV*, pp. 135–49; Kimmel, *Absolutism and its Discontents*, pp. 67–74.

[33] Ladurie, *Saint-Simon and the Court of Louis XI*, pp. 51–2.

to ingratiate himself with Louis, privately railed against the "foul muck" and "sewer of sensuality" of the French court.[34]

Appetites were equally unconstrained at the Russian court. As a child, Peter was presented with the most elaborate and costly confections, and traveled in a gilded carriage pulled by dwarfs. As an adult, he preferred to live in small wooden houses with low ceilings. He nevertheless had a voracious appetite for food, alcohol, sex and violence. He was said to eat enough for seven men, and amazed Parisians and Viennese alike with his ability to consume and hold his drink. His formal attire was richly decorated with gold and silver threads and encrusted with jewels. He had embossed saddles, carved and velvet-lined carriages, and icons with jeweled casings. He supported workshops to manufacture these items with materials imported from all over the world. He also enjoyed traveling incognito, assuming a humble demeanor and posing as a lowly official or bombardier in one of his regiments.[35] The Hohenzollern court of this period was modest by comparison. Frederick the Great engaged in display for political purposes. He lived in Sans Souci, a palace he had built for himself, where he received visitors without pomp. He was often shabbily dressed, and could be seen sporting an old coat, reeking of snuff and patched where it had been shot through by bullet.[36]

Restrictions on competition

In honor worlds, competition for honor and standing is an elite activity. In seventeenth- and eighteenth-century Europe this was true at the domestic and international levels. One way to differentiate elite from mass is by means of rituals and codes of deportment. Louis XIV introduced an elaborate set of manners at his court to transform aristocratic warriors into courtiers, where it had quite an unintended effect. Court civility emphasized courtesy and sociability, and honor (*honnêteté*) became increasingly associated with politeness, charm, taste and social grace. This code was adopted more widely by nobles and gradually spread throughout society, bringing greater peace and civility to the country.[37] The rise of civility

---

[34] Ibid., pp. 97, 100.
[35] Massie, *Peter the Great*, pp. 65–75, 155–275; Hughes, *Peter the Great*, pp. 9–10, 35, 43, 116–17.
[36] Schieder, *Frederick the Great*, pp. 33–53.
[37] Elias, *The Civilizing Process*, and *The Court Society*; Magendie, *La politesse mondiane*; Kettering, *French Society*, pp. 70–1; Krailsheimer, *Studies in Self-Interest from Descartes to La Bruyère*, pp. 81–4; Keohane, *Philosophy and the State in France*, pp. 283–9; For critiques,

exacerbated noble fears of debasement, and voices of protest were raised throughout Louis XIV's reign.[38]

Elite and mass were nevertheless porous categories, and an actor's station within the elite was often a matter of contestation. As a general rule, the finer the distinctions that were invoked, the sharper the conflict about these signifiers and related privileges. In Louis XIV's court such conflicts were often resolved by inclusion, and led to a "trickle-down" of privileges, in the words of Emmanuel Le Roy Ladurie.[39] Clothing initially restricted to the upper nobility came to be worn by the lesser nobility, and ultimately by the bourgeoisie, undermining any role it might have had as a marker of social standing. Louis XIV struggled to maintain hierarchies of birth but, like Peter, sought a more professional corps of advisors, loyal to him not to family interests. Both monarchs increasingly filled important positions with non-aristocrats. Jules Cardinal Mazarin (Giulio Mazzarino) was the grandson of an Italian artisan. Both grandfathers of finance minister Jean-Baptiste Colbert were merchants. In eighteenth-century France, few bishops were commoners, but it was not unheard of, and some commoners became cardinals.[40] Under Louis XV, the majority of *intendants* came from recently ennobled families.[41] Upward mobility was more common in the military, although not in France, where Louis XIV and his successor supported the exclusive right of the nobility to become officers in an effort to produce an officer corps imbued with the ethos of honor and service to the monarch. Edicts of 1718 and 1729 reaffirmed the nobility's military monopoly, but one of 1750 made it possible to ennoble families and individuals on the basis of their service to the state.[42] The purchase of commissions was common practice in Austria and France until the second half of the eighteenth century. Austria and Bavaria had a much higher percentage of middle-class officers than France or Prussia.[43] In France, but elsewhere in Europe as well, the seventeenth and eighteenth centuries witnessed the rise of a new nobility, distinct from the old feudal one, which partially bridged social orders, but the

Meyer, *La noblesse bretonne*; Schalk, "The Court as Civilizer"; Jouanna, "Recherches sur la notion d'honneur."

[38] Kettering, *French Society*, p. 76.
[39] Ladurie, *Saint-Simon and the Court of Louis XI*, pp. 28–30.
[40] Péronnet, *Les évêques de l'ancienne France*, I, pp. 524, 1483; Ladurie, *Saint-Simon and the Court of Louis XI*, pp. 30–1.
[41] Gruder, *The Royal Provincial Intendants*, pp. 168–73, 180–6.
[42] Furet, *Interpreting the French Revolution*, p. 106.
[43] Kroener, "The Modern State and Military Society in the Eighteenth Century"; Kimmel, *Absolutism and its Discontents*, pp. 52–67.

new nobility often sought to close the door to others attempting to use the same means to enhance their social standing.

The circle of states and rulers that could compete for honor was limited to Christians. Royalty and high birth overcame religious differences after 1648, and the European system included Catholic (France, Spain, Austria, Savoy) and Protestant (Britain, Holland, Sweden, Prussia) monarchies. The Muslim Ottomans were excluded, even though they had been a de facto part of the European system since the fifteenth century. Developing states on the periphery of the continent were gradually included in the system, and some, like Sweden and Prussia, became leading powers. Heavy Swedish, Prussian and Russian investments in their armed forces reflected their monarchs' desire to gain recognition, and their understanding that it could only be achieved through conquest. Peter's attempts to Westernize his elite, construct a new, architecturally impressive capital on the Baltic, and found an academy of sciences indicate his understanding that status required more than a big stick. His efforts, while monumental, were only partly successful as Russia continued to be regarded as a quasi-oriental, backward country. In the aftermath of Russia's defeat of the Swedes, Leibniz wrote to the Russian envoy in Vienna to describe the European amazement at Peter's success and the belief that he was becoming "a sort of Turk of the north."[44]

Markers of standing

Johann Christian Ludwig contended that rulers had a divine commission to differentiate themselves from other mortals by external signs (*euerliche Marquen*).[45] With Louis XIV in mind, Montesquieu wrote that "the magnificence and splendor that surrounds kings form part of their power."[46] The Sun King set the standard when it came to display, starting with his *grands bâtiments*. His pride and joy was Versailles, a collection of palaces, pavilions, gardens and lakes built during the last three decades of the seventeenth century.[47] According to Jacques-Bénigne Bossuet, bishop, court preacher and theologian, Versailles was intended "to make people respect

---

[44] Quoted in Hughes, *Peter the Great*, p. 86.
[45] Quoted in Blanning, *Pursuit of Glory*, p. 445.
[46] Montesquieu, *Spirit of the Laws*, book V, 8, lines 11–13.
[47] Elias, *The Court Society*, pp. 42–65 on the political and social implications of architectural design; Berger, *A Royal Passion*, on Louis's personal role in the design and construction of Versailles and other buildings; Dunlop, *Louis XIV*, pp. 109–20; Treasure, *Louis XIV*, pp. 180–99; Olwig, *Landscape, Nature, and the Body Politic*, on the broader political role of gardens and landscaping; Blanning, *Pursuit of Glory*, pp. 428–36, 440–2, 534–5.

him."[48] It contained numerous theatrical spaces for the performance of ballet, theater, concerts and opera, spectacular *fêtes* of all kinds, more intimate scenes of romance and seduction, and royal religious and civil ceremonies. Most of these productions encouraged audiences to regard the king as the embodiment of France and its *gloire* – and especially those in which he danced dressed as Apollo.[49] This impression was reinforced by the architecture and decoration. A stunning example was Charles Le Brun's 1681–4 paintings in the Hall of Mirrors, arrayed around a large central painting that Racine entitled "The King governs for himself." Louis is grasping a rudder while being crowned by the Graces. Below, under dark storm clouds, a France-figure quells discontent, while above, Hymen offers Louis a horn of plenty and Minerva leads the way to wisdom and glory. The Gobelin tapestries told a similar story. "In every piece," John Locke observed, "Lewis le Grand was the hero."[50]

The carefully crafted orderliness of Versailles was mirrored in the hierarchy of the French court. The king came first, followed by his family: "le Grand Dauphin" and other "children of France"; Louis's brother and his children, the "princes of blood," which included the Condé and Conti cousins; and finally, various bastards and illegitimate daughters. Then came dukes and peers, who had an elaborate and far from static ranking system of their own.[51] Everyone had a position and place, made visible by their residence, dress, privileges and proximity to the king at ceremonies. Louis's household troops, the envy of all who saw them, according to Voltaire, had uniforms covered with gold and silver.[52] At mass, people were accustomed to sitting, kneeling or standing, according to the stage of the ceremony. This practice was copied at civil events, where, Saint-Simon reports, some people had to stand while others sat on chairs with or without backs or on stools, all according to their rank.[53] Rank also determined the number of valets or ladies-in-waiting one was entitled to, the presence and amount of velvet in cloaks and jerkins, who could wear

---

[48] Bossuet, quoted in Treasure, *Louis XIV*, p. 180; Keohane, *Philosophy and the State in France*, pp. 251–8.

[49] Burke, *The Fabrication of Louis XIV*, pp. 45–6. Elias, *Court Society*, pp. 121–2. More broadly on the assertion of power through performance in this era and later, see Baecque, *The Body Politic*; Orgel, *The Illusion of Power*; Yates, *Theatre of the World*.

[50] Lough, *Locke's Travels in France*, p. 150. The tapestries were also designed by Le Brun.

[51] Elias, *The Court Society*, pp. 29, 82–90; Ladurie, *Saint-Simon and the Court of Louis XIV*, pp. 24–5.

[52] Voltaire, *The Age of Louis XIV*, p. 93.

[53] Saint-Simon, *Mémoires*, described and quoted in Ladurie, *Saint-Simon and the Court of Louis XIV*, pp. 24–7.

hats in the presence of the king and how one kissed and was kissed (or not) when greeting.[54] According to Norbert Elias, these gradations intensified the struggle for prestige because they made it possible to define, as with money, the value of every increment with respect to another. It allowed the king to emphasize his standing above all his courtiers, but also gave them an interest in his *gloire* because it improved their standing relative to those in other courts and ordinary Frenchmen.[55] Emmanuel Le Roy Ladurie notes that such a hierarchy, while it emphasized social differences, also created a holistic conception of society in which individuals and social groups could feel integrated. From this sentiment too the king benefitted.[56]

Tim Blanning observes that "Versailles was only the most spectacular manifestation of a much wider cultural project which aimed at nothing less than hegemony of French culture in Europe."[57] With patronage at his disposal, Louis attracted the finest architects, gardeners, artists, writers and composers of the age (e.g. Le Vau, Mansart, Le Nôtre, Le Brun, Rigaud, Girardon, Corneille, Racine, Molière, Lully, Couperin), and used their creations in very direct and calculated ways to augment his *gloire*. French increasingly became the accepted language of European courts and of diplomacy. Frederick the Great insisted that the Berlin Academy publish its proceedings in French so they would reach the widest audience. The Treaty of Utrecht, signed in 1713, was the first international agreement written in French instead of Latin. By the last quarter of the century even treaties not involving France were often drafted in French. In 1686, Pierre Bayle predicted that "in the future it will be the French language which will serve as the means of communication for all the peoples of Europe."[58]

Other European courts copied the French. Existing palaces were renovated along the lines of Versailles. In 1701, King Max Emanuel of Bavaria added pavilions and gardens to the Nymphenburg Palace in Munich. Leopold I (1640–1705) built the Schönbrunn, a Viennese Versailles, later extended and remodeled by Maria Theresa. Peter the Great built an entirely new city as his capital and graced it with Summer and Winter Palaces (1710–14) with Versailles as his inspiration.[59] The Habsburgs built numerous churches in addition to palaces, and Frederick II established the tradition of supporting music and opera. Other aristocrats followed suit, and in the fifty years after 1683 almost 300 palaces were constructed

[54] Ladurie, *Saint-Simon and the Court of Louis XIV*, pp. 28–32, 54–5.
[55] Elias, *Court Society*, pp. 120–1, 127, 146.   [56] Ibid., p. 29.
[57] Blanning, *Pursuit of Glory*, pp. 434–5.   [58] Ibid.
[59] Jones, "Why St. Petersburg?"

in Vienna and its environs. Peter and Frederick the Great each created an academy of sciences, and Peter established a tapestry factory modeled on the Gobelins. German princes also sought standing through the creation of universities, fourteen of which were established between 1648 and 1789. Following general European practice, Peter I created an elaborate table of ranks for his military, civil and court officials.[60] Rank was everywhere accompanied by uniforms, especially in the military. Weapons commonly had names, another sign of the extent to which war is fought for honor and standing. Fancy uniforms reached their peak between 1790 and 1830. Their decline was hastened by rapid-fire weapons, but also changes in the character of war. Dress uniforms became increasingly differentiated from combat uniforms and remained elaborate.

Courts generally spared no expense for ceremonies appropriate to the status their ruler claimed. Ambassadors were received with pomp; in France, this involved a procession in coaches in which the ambassador was escorted by footmen, servants, pages, soldiers and musicians, and accompanied by the pealing of church bells. The size of the procession and the mansion to which a new ambassador was escorted and how he was presented to the monarch depended on his country's status. Louis XIV dressed in his most luxurious costume to met his Spanish bride at a crossroads where a triumphal arch was erected solely for the purpose of the encounter.[61] On his 1670 trip to the newly conquered territories of Dunkirk and Lille, Louis travelled with 30,000 men, his queen and ladies from the court, and offered gold and jewels and other bounty to prominent residents. Voltaire offered his judgment that "The pomp and splendour of the ancient kings of Asia were eclipsed by the magnificence attending this journey."[62]

Slights to standing – real or imagined – could provoke violence, if not wars. France claimed to be the "Court of King," and Louis XIV insisted that Spain acknowledge the primacy of his ambassadors over theirs at every European court. In 1677 Colbert demanded that all states acknowledge French primacy at sea. The English refused and sought to avoid French ships on the high seas. When the Genoese spurned a French squadron's request for a first salute, the French bombarded their city. In 1685, Admiral Tourville attacked the Spanish fleet after its commander refused to salute

---

[60] Blanning, *Pursuit of Glory*, pp. 449–50, 502; Hughes, *Peter the Great*, pp. 165–6.
[61] Voltaire, *The Age of Louis XIV*, pp. 259–60; Burke, *The Fabrication of Louis XIV*, pp. 19, 43–4.
[62] Burke, *The Fabrication of Louis XIV*, p. 90.

the French colors.[63] Personal pique also entered the picture. Peter the Great had strategic reasons for challenging Sweden, but also personal ones arising from how badly he felt he was treated on his first visit to Swedish territory. He explained to other Europeans that "We were avenging the insult dealt to us and our ambassadors in Riga."[64]

Warfare

Between Westphalia and the French Revolution, warfare displays most of the characteristics I associate with honor societies. Wars were less frequent, although often on a far grander scale than in the past. Between 700 and 1000, extant chronicles rarely describe a peaceful year. Data sets indicate that early modern Europe was proportionately the most warlike in terms of the number of years in which there was war, with one new war on average every three years. In the sixteenth and seventeenth centuries the great powers were at war 95 percent of the time. The frequency of war drops to 71 percent in the eighteenth century, and to 29 percent in a long nineteenth century. The years between 1815 and 1914 formed the first century-like span in which there were more years of peace than of war.[65]

Although the trend is clear, we must exercise caution about any statistical measures of warfare from the sixteenth through the eighteenth centuries because there was no clear-cut distinction between war and peace. Frontiers were poorly defined, and generally consisted of zones of contact rather than demarcated lines, and central governments often had little control over commanders and other officials in these zones, who not infrequently engaged in violence against their opposites without provoking war. Central authorities sometimes sponsored raids and other forms of violence against neighboring political units while technically at peace with them. In the seventeenth and eighteenth centuries, the frontier between the Habsburgs and the Ottomans was a site of non-stop small-scale warfare even when the two empires were at peace. This was also true of the lands dividing France and Spain in the seventeenth century. The situation at sea was even more ambiguous, as navies only belatedly developed into organized and centrally controlled forces.

---

[63] Treasure, *Making of Modern Europe*, p. 194.
[64] Quoted in Hughes, *Peter the Great*, p. 58.
[65] Wright, *A Study of War*, pp. 121, 237, 242, 248, 638; Levy, *War in the Modern Great Power System*, pp. 139–41. Hamilton, "The European Wars: 1815–1914," for an overview.

Privateering was commonplace, and governments at loggerheads might engage in open warfare at sea while technically at peace.[66]

The ends and means of war were limited in comparison to the recent European past. Rulers on the whole no longer attempted to assassinate or poison their adversaries and they addressed each other in the most respectful terms, even when their countries were at war.[67] They treated ambassadors and other representatives with civility. The Italian and German wars in the first half of the sixteenth century fostered the development of diplomatic missions and chanceries to assist rulers in the conduct of foreign policy. The religious wars froze, even set back, these developments because ambassadors were not infrequently considered sources of contamination likely to spread heretical doctrines. After 1648, Catholic and Protestant Europe were again in contact, and diplomatic representatives worked together at successive peace conferences, including Rastadt (1714), Carlowitz (1718) and Nystad (1721). International law underwent a correspondingly rapid development and was part of the effort to regulate and civilize the practice of war. Rules developed concerning the exchange of honors, the billeting of troops on foreign territory, extraction of contributions from the population of war zones and the treatment of prisoners. The concept of neutral countries emerged, although such countries still had to allow armies to pass through their territories (*trasitus innoxius*) provided they made good any damage they caused in the process. Officer prisoners were routinely exchanged on the basis of rank, but ordinary soldiers could still be sent to the gallows. That practice changed in the course of the eighteenth century, when conscripts came to be regarded as people doing national service, not criminals.[68]

In the seventeenth century, Louis XIV's France was the only state large and rich enough to follow in the footsteps of Philip II of Spain (1527–98) and aspire to continental hegemony. According to a prominent French biographer, France's war against the Dutch (1672–8), "had no other cause than Louis XIV's thirst for glory."[69] There was also an important element of Aristotelian anger. Traditionally allies of France, the Dutch chose to ally with England and Sweden. Slighted by a political inferior, Louis was enraged, declared war against the Dutch Republic in 1672, and on the

---

[66] Anderson, *War and Society in Europe of the Old Regime*, pp. 16–17.

[67] An important exception was Catherine the Great, who gained the throne by colluding in the murder of her husband, Peter III.

[68] Luard, *War in International Society*, pp. 160–1; Best, *Humanity in Warfare*, pp. 53–60; Anderson, *War and Society in Europe of the Old Regime*, p. 15.

[69] Bluche, *Louis XIV*, p. 246.

verge of total victory – which he did not attain because an uprising of the common people brought the more intransigent William of Orange to power – he decreed that a Dutch delegation should abase themselves before him once a year and present him with a medallion that graphically represented their subservient status.[70]

The War of Spanish Succession (1702–14) removed the threat by averting the union of Spain and France and expelling France from the Netherlands, Germany and Italy. The war developed gradually, and ultimately embroiled France, Spain, Portugal, England, the Dutch Republic, some German states and Austria. It was fought in the Spanish Peninsula, the Spanish Netherlands, Italy, Germany and North America. The Treaty of Utrecht (1714), which ended the war, officially enshrined the balance of power as a principle of continental order. The more or less contemporary Great Northern War (1700–21) pitted the coalition of Russia, Denmark–Norway, the north German states, and later Russia, against Sweden and the Ottoman Empire. It ended in 1721, with the Treaty of Nystad and the Stockholm treaties. Russia supplanted Sweden as the dominant northern power and became a major player in wider European politics.

Other conflicts remained, in northern Europe, India and North America, and new ones were created by the Polish, Bavarian and Austrian successions. They led to the Seven Years War (1756–63), described by Winston Churchill as the first world war because it involved most European states and their colonies in North America and Asia. The continental struggle ended in a draw: Prussia survived, but barely, and Russia retired into profitable neutrality. Overseas, Britain was the biggest winner, and France the biggest loser. France had to cede its remaining holdings in Canada to Britain, and retained only minor territories in the New World. The British also consolidated their hold on India through the British East India Company, and became the world's dominant colonial power. It was also a more secure empire because the French navy lost key battles and would never again be in a position to challenge the Royal Navy.[71]

The Peace of Paris in 1763 is often described as ushering in an era of relative stability. One reason for the years of relative peace that followed is that the Seven Years War left the major powers exhausted and many of them deeply in debt. Great Britain, the victor, had almost doubled its debt, which now amounted to £147,000,000, something made possible by the creation of the Bank of England. Subsequent attempts to make the

[70] Blanning, *Pursuit of Glory*, pp. 538–40; Schama, *Embarrassment of Riches*, pp. 273–4.
[71] Scott, *Birth of a Great Power System*, pp. 72–116 on the Seven Years War.

Americans contribute to servicing this debt through the Sugar Act of 1764 and the Stamp Act of 1765 helped to trigger their revolt against Britain.[72] The Peace of Paris nevertheless failed to establish an effective balance of power. In Paul Schroeder's judgment, it weakened France and stalemated the German powers, leaving Russia free to pursue an aggressive policy toward Poland and the Ottomans. The Peace of Paris also undermined several smaller powers and ushered in a cold war between Austria and Prussia for domination of Germany. The postwar European system tended toward escalation, not diminution of conflict, and can more properly be regarded as a twenty-four-year interlude before the next, and far more destructive world war, triggered by the French Revolution.[73]

As many authorities have noted, warfare was limited for reinforcing technical and economic reasons. The introduction of the bayonet and more mobile and robust artillery made combat far more deadly. It was also difficult to finance, supply and control large armies in the field, especially as their size increased dramatically. In 1552, Charles V's advisors calculated that they were supporting 148,000 men in Germany, the Low Countries, Lombardy, Naples, North Africa and Spain. In 1625, Philip IV of Spain could muster 300,000 regular troops and 500,000 militiamen. Louis XIV's army rose from 273,000 in 1693 to 395,000 in 1696. Even a small state like the emerging Dutch Republic had 60,000 men at arms by 1606. In 1756, the total number of Europeans in arms is estimated at 1.3 million. These forces engaged more in maneuvers and small-scale engagements and sieges than they did pitched battles. The Duke of Marlborough, famous for his aggressiveness, fought only four major engagements in the course of ten continental campaigns. One of them, the Battle of Malplaquet in 1709, was brought about by Marlborough's political need for a decisive victory. It was the largest engagement in Europe prior to Borodino, involving 200,000 British, Dutch, French and Imperial forces. When the smoke cleared, 30,000 of them were casualties.[74] We should nevertheless be careful about attributing the limits of warfare to either its destructiveness or cost. Sieges were often as bloody and costly as battles. The great growth in standing armies was paralleled by a growth in population and the ability of some states to raise money for war. And by

[72] Blanning, *Pursuit of Glory*, pp. 301, 595–9.
[73] Schroeder, *The Transformation of European Politics*, pp. 1–4.
[74] Chandler, *The Art of Warfare in the Age of Marlborough*; Weigley, *The Age of Battles*; Anderson, *War and Society in Europe of the Old Regime*, p. 17; Duffy, *The Military Experience in the Age of Reason*, p. 17; Black, *European Warfare, 1660–1815*, pp. 58–9, and *A Military Revolution?*, p. 7; Demel, *Europäische Geschichte des 19. Jahrhunderts*, pp. 230–2.

the end of the eighteenth century the pattern of warfare would change dramatically. Between 1792 and 1815 – the years of French revolutionary and Napoleonic warfare – there were 713 pitched battles.[75]

The more fundamental reason for the limits on warfare was the nature of the goals sought by combatants. After 1648 they were for the most part struggles over precedence, and only occasionally involved the destruction of other major political units or recognized buffer states. Louis XIV's bid for the throne of Spain on behalf of his grandson, which provoked a major European war, had little to do with *raison d'état* and everything to do with dynastic standing.[76] In his memoirs, Louis XIV is absolutely explicit about his motives for the Dutch War (1672–8): "I shall not attempt to justify myself. Ambition and [the pursuit of] *gloire* are always pardonable in a prince, and especially in a young prince so well treated by fortune as I was."[77] William of Orange and Frederick the Great also spoke of *gloire*. Protagonists, including Louis XIV, only accepted limits on their territorial expansion and political influence through control of their thrones for the sake of the system as a whole. French delegates to the Rijswick peace conference of 1697 were instructed by Louis to make significant concessions "for the general peace of Christendom."[78] Relative standing could sometimes be decided by one victory, as in the case of fifth-century Greece, or by campaigns of maneuver that secured a province or recognition of a ruler's right to that province. The general aim of campaigns was to dislodge opposing forces and occupy territory at minimum cost. Sieges were considered preferable to open battle.

War nevertheless remained a brutal affair, and strategic considerations, or sometimes mere pique, not infrequently overrode courtesy in the treatment of civilians. French armies committed all kinds of atrocities during the Dutch campaigns of the 1670s. Under Marshal Tessé, they ravaged the Palatinate in 1688–9, and were authorized by Louis XIV to destroy Heidelberg, Mannheim, Worms and Speyer. The Duke of Marlborough cut a swathe of destruction across Bavaria in 1704. Charles XII devastated Poland in 1706–7, and Peter the Great did the same in the Baltic, leaving many of its inhabitants without enough food to survive. Peter had few compunctions about using civilians and prisoners of war in his quest for grandeur. St. Petersburg was built by Swedish prisoners, many of whom

---

[75] Blanning, *Pursuit of Glory*, p. 643.   [76] Ibid., p. 213.
[77] Zeller, "French Diplomacy and Foreign Policy in the European Setting."
[78] *Commission des Archives Diplomatiques*, XX, p. 510, quoted in Holsti, *Peace and War*, p. 45.

perished in the process.[79] In 1677, Louis XIV nevertheless ordered that no more taxes could be extracted from occupied territories than they had paid to their former sovereign. The duke of Marlborough gained honor in the Netherlands by virtue of his respectful treatment of civilians and fair adjudication of disputes between them and his forces.[80]

The quest for *gloire* also contributed to the brutality of war, and was responsible, as it was in Roman times, for consistently higher casualty rates among officers.[81] The French in particular sought to achieve fame through their audacity. Marshal Charles Villars, the most successful commander on the French side in the War of the Spanish Succession (1701–14) praised "the air of audacity so natural to the French," whose preferred method of battle "is to charge with the bayonet."[82] For much of the seventeenth century, the French army put less emphasis on victory than on their ability to maintain order while suffering casualties inflicted by the other side.[83] This was increasingly suicidal in an age when artillery and musket fire could destroy formations at a considerable distance, and a further indication of the overriding importance of *gloire*. For Louis XIV, it was all about bravery: "Good order makes us look assured, and it seems enough to look brave, because most often our enemies do not wait for us to approach near enough for us to have to show if we are in fact brave." The king personally led regiments into battle as late as 1692 making sure to give orders within musket range of the enemy.[84]

Another common misconception among students of the eighteenth century, which seems to have arisen with Gibbon, is that warfare was largely ineffective and inconclusive.[85] Jeremy Black reminds us that there were numerous decisive battles including Poltava (1709), which ended Swedish supremacy in northern Europe, Blenheim (1704), which drove the French from Germany, and Ramillies (1706) and Oudenaarde (1708) which expelled them from the Low Countries. Other decisive conflicts included suppression of the Rakoczi uprising in Hungary (1703–11), of the Jacobites in Britain (1745–6), of Pugachev in Russia (1773–5), and the Irish rebellion of 1798. All of these successes involved pitched and often

---

[79] Blanning, *Pursuit of Glory*, pp. 54–5, 307–8; Massie, *Peter the Great*, pp. 522–6.
[80] Anderson, *War and Society in Europe of the Old Regime*, pp. 137–8.
[81] Lynn, *Battle*, p. 140.
[82] Ibid., quote on p. 127; Lynn, *Giant of the Grand Siècle*, pp. 453–512, on French army tactics.
[83] Lynn, *Battle*, pp. 128–9.
[84] Louis XIV, *Mémoires de Louis XIV pour l'instruction du dauphin*, II, pp. 112–13.
[85] Weigley, *The Age of Battles*; Kroener, "The Modern State and Military Society in the Eighteenth Century."

costly battles.[86] Blenheim reduced 30,000 of its combatants to casualties. Five years later, at Malplaquet, one-quarter of the forces of the anti-French coalition were killed or wounded.[87] Civil wars were also bloody, but in contrast to foreign wars, few prisoners were taken, and those that were were often executed as they were deemed rebels or traitors. The different treatment accorded prisoners of interstate war, whether ordinary people or nobles, is indicative of the extent to which the conceptual category of the international had emerged, and how warfare in this domain, among Christians at least, became associated with honor.

Motives

Wars almost invariably have multiple motives, and it is not easy to identity and evaluate them. Paul Schroeder, arguably the most distinguished diplomatic historian of eighteenth- and nineteenth-century Europe, concludes that "The motive and rule of all action was to advance the interest of the state – meaning first of all its power, security and wealth, but also, almost equally, its monarch's honour and prestige (*considération*) and rank among other princes."[88] For the period in question, I contend that honor and prestige were even more important than security and wealth if we distinguish states who initiated wars from those who were forced to fight them. For the former, interstate war was most often an expression of competition for standing. This goal was frequently pursued at the expense of state interests.[89] Louis XIV rejected the Dutch Republic's desperate peace offers following his initial campaign, although he had achieved his strategic goals. Out of hubris and his insatiable search for *gloire*, he insisted on complete conquest, which turned the war into a long struggle and led to the creation of a powerful anti-French coalition. Against the advice of more sensible advisors (e.g. Vauban, Colbert, Hugue de Lionnes), he repeatedly began military ventures he could not bring to a successful conclusion and had to settle at Rijswijk and Utrecht for more modest gains, a draw or even defeat. Charles XII of Sweden rejected a reasonable peace in 1714 after fourteen years of war on the grounds that "better times would not come till we get more respect in Europe than we

---

[86] Black, *European Warfare, 1660–1815*, pp. 67–86.
[87] Anderson, *War and Society in Europe of the Old Regime*, p. 136; Blanning, *Pursuit of Glory*, p. 553.
[88] Black, *European Warfare*, p. 8.
[89] Swann, "Politics and the State in Eighteenth Century Europe."

now have."[90] In the Great Northern War (1699–1721), which ended in the total defeat of Sweden, Charles foolishly invaded Russia and led his army into an exposed position deep in what is now Ukraine, where it was crushed at Poltava. Charles could not restrain his spirit. He was apparently driven by a burning desire to avenge the Danish-Russian-Saxon attacks in 1700 on the Swedish empire and its German ally.[91]

Security entered into the picture because the expansionist policies of those countries vying for primacy or recognition as great powers threatened the interests, or sometimes the survival, of other states, as they did in the case of Holland, Spain, Poland and some of the German principalities.[92] Austria was also threatened by the Ottoman Empire, and with Polish assistance decisively defeated a Turkish army outside the gates of Vienna in 1683. The Ottoman assault on Europe reveals a lot about the motives of key European actors. The Turks, then at the height of their military power, were widely regarded as the Muslim enemy. To the extent that security was a dominant concern, the European powers had a strong incentive to put aside their parochial differences and balance against any power attempting to impose hegemony, as many religious authorities called upon them to do. However, this rarely happened. After the fall of Constantinople in 1453 and of Negroponte in 1470, Turkish expansion in the west threatened Italy, especially Venice, whose wealth derived from its commerce with the eastern Mediterranean. Italian city states never unified or coordinated their strategies against the Turks. Instead, they took advantage of them to weaken rival states. When Otranto fell to the Turks in 1480, Florence and Venice were delighted by the difficulties this posed for the southern kingdom controlled by Aragon.[93] Europeans did coalesce a century later at the Battle of Lepanto, fought off the coast of western Greece in October 1571. In the last major sea battle involving rowed vessels, the Ottomans were defeated by the Holy League, a ramshackle coalition of the papacy, Spain, Venice, Genoa, Savoy and Malta. Louis XIV broke with this united front to ally with the Ottomans, and urged Turkish grand vizier Kara Mustafava to press his assault against Austria. For quite different reasons, the leader of the Hungarian Calvinists, Imre Thököly, also appealed to the vizier to attack Vienna. On the whole, therefore, the quest for

[90] Quoted in Hatton, *Charles XII of Sweden*, p. 375.
[91] Holsti, *Peace and War*, pp. 68–9.
[92] Black, *European Warfare*, p. 8; Holsti, *Peace and War*, pp. 93–4, for a list of eight planned European partitions and three executed partitions (all of Poland) from 1713 to 1814.
[93] Covini, "Political and Military Bonds in the Italian State System, Thirteenth to Sixteenth Centuries."

standing – and of religious autonomy – trumped the security of Europe as a whole against outside threats.

Economic motives also came into play, but were only occasionally decisive. The English were sometimes opposed to war because it interrupted trade, but were willing to make war against Holland in the mid-seventeenth century to secure trade benefits. Samuel Pepys noted in his diary that the merchants and court were "mad for a Dutch war."[94] The English again rallied for war in 1739 when it promised to enhance commercial prospects. For most continental countries, economics was framed in terms of its contribution to honor and standing. One reason Louis XIV went to war against Holland in 1672 was to reduce its commercial preeminence and secure it for France. For Colbert, commerce was tied to prestige. He feared that the Dutch would use the profits of trade to augment the army and navy and supplant France as arbiter of Europe.[95] In 1740 Frederick the Great invaded Silesia to attain *gloire*, but also because it was a rich province and its 40,000 square miles could be expected to generate additional resources for his army.[96]

K. J. Holsti has made the most serious comparative effort to evaluate the causes of the wars of the period. Between 1648 (Westphalia) and 1713 (the Treaty of Utrecht), he identified twenty-two wars, associated with fifty-one sources of conflict. Contests over territory, which caused twelve of the wars and accounted for 44 percent of all issues, were the most significant source of war. Disputed claims concerning commerce, dynastic succession and control of territories having strategic significance came next. National or dynastic survival was at stake in only 23 percent of the wars. Holsti suspects that territory featured so prominently because it was the foundation for new revenues.[97] Between 1715 and 1814, Holsti counts thirty-six wars, almost all of them involving the great powers. Territory is once again the principal source of conflict, being responsible for twenty-four wars or 67 percent of the total. Commerce and navigation and dynastic succession come next, followed by state or regime survival, the latter dropping to 17 percent of the total. In this period too, Holsti attributes the striving for territory to diverse motives, including

---

[94] Pepys, *Diary*, February 9, 22, 1664, I, pp. 485, 490.

[95] Luard, *War in International Society*, p. 168; Jean-Baptiste Colbert to Louis XIV, 1664. Quoted ibid., p. 158.

[96] Ritter, *Frederick the Great*, pp. 73–92; Showalter, *The Wars of Frederick the Great*, pp. 38–89; Schieder, *Frederick the Great*, pp. 90–100.

[97] Holsti, *Peace and War*, pp. 46–63.

the desire of leaders to increase their resource base, to consolidate their holdings and enhance their strategic situation. He describes a progression from concern for *gloire* in the 1648–1713 period, which made certain territories much more valuable than others because of dynastic connections or claims to them, to a more strategic approach to territory in the 1715–1814 period. Territories were routinely swapped in the eighteenth century, usually as a result of war, and dynastic claims declined as causes of war but continued to be voiced as ex post facto justifications for territorial aggrandizement.[98]

Holsti exaggerates the ease and benefit of territorial aggrandizement in both epochs. The pursuit of territory for *gloire* or any other reason was extremely costly. Evan Luard calculates that few wars of territorial aggrandizement succeeded, and even fewer of them were economically profitable. They entailed a considerable outlay of forces, mercenaries, allies and third parties, and often involved fighting and occupying distant territories in the face of opposition from the local populations.[99] The scale of the forces involved, on land and at sea, also increased enormously in the seventeenth and eighteenth centuries.[100] Toward the end of his reign, Louis XIV spent three-quarters of his income on his wars, an expenditure that included not only his armed forces but subsidies to allies and third parties, among them Hanover, Hesse, Brunswick and Prussia. When the War of Spanish Succession ended in 1714, the French government was saddled with a debt thirty times its annual income. Louis XIV was forced to sell his silver plate and cherished collection of 5,000 silver toy soldiers.[101] In his memoirs, he admitted that the French people "deprived of my relief by the expenses of such a great war, could suspect me of preferring my personal glory to their welfare and tranquillity."[102] Louis XV (1715–54) put France even deeper in debt to fight the War of Austrian Succession. It cost his government the phenomenal sum for its day of 757 million livres, of which only half was covered by taxes.[103] The Seven Years War was even more expensive for France, with an estimated cost of between

---

[98] Ibid., pp. 83–102.   [99] Luard, *War in International Society*, pp. 237–43.

[100] Anderson, *War and Society in Europe of the Old Regime*, pp. 82–99.

[101] Parker, *The Military Revolution*, pp. 62–5; Luard, *War in International Society*, pp. 346–7; Bonney, *The King's Debts*; Rowlands, *The Dynastic State and the Army under Louis XIV*; Blanning, *Pursuit of Glory*, pp. 599–603.

[102] Louis XIV, *Memoirs for the Instruction of the Dauphin*, p. 260.

[103] Morineau, "Budget de l'État et gestion des finances royales en France au dux-huitième siècle"; Ertman, *Birth of the Leviathan*, p. 141; Scott, *Birth of a Great Power System*, pp. 38–95 on the war.

1 and 1.3 billion livres, with only 29 percent coming from tax revenues. The country stood at the edge of bankruptcy.[104]

The Habsburgs also had to sell private assets to keep their armies in the field.[105] After the Great Northern War, France and Prussia were on the verge of financial collapse. The high costs and low success rate of war undercuts the claim that they were motivated by material gain. Neither condition would, however, deter leaders intent on achieving *gloire*. The high cost of war might even make it more attractive, just as rich people seeking status today often flock to vastly overpriced hotels and restaurants in the hope of being seen by those they want to impress.

Society and warfare

In warrior-based honor societies, competition for honor and standing threatens the order that sustains competition and makes it meaningful. In post-Westphalian Europe, war as the sport of kings required political units in which their authority was secure enough for them to mobilize resources to wage war in pursuit of dynastic as opposed to national interests. Louis XIV, Charles XII, Peter I and Frederick II were all beneficiaries of such a system, but dissatisfied with the standing they achieved. They created more effective bureaucracies to establish greater authority over their respective countries and extract more resources for war. They developed more ambitious war aims and three of the four overreached themselves. France and Prussia were on the losing side of the Seven Years War, and Sweden lost its Baltic empire as a result of Charles's unnecessary and impetuous invasion of Russia. As Paul Schroeder observes, there was a near-perfect correlation between so-called enlightened absolutist states and foreign policy aggressiveness. France, the least aggressive of the lot in the second half of the eighteenth century, also had the least successful attempt at absolutism.[106]

Greater resources and more effective bureaucracies facilitated advances in training, discipline, equipment, logistics, strategy, tactics, weaponry and organization of staff and support services, all of which made war more "rational," efficient and deadly. It did not change the goals for which wars were fought, which offers compelling evidence that motives, not resources,

---

[104] Égret, *Louis XV et l'opposition parlementaire*, pp. 103–10, 142; Ertman, *Birth of the Leviathan*, pp. 141–2.
[105] Dickson, *Finance and Government under Maria Theresa*, II, pp. 272–99.
[106] Schroeder, *The Transformation of European Politics*, p. 50.

administration or technology were the most important determinant of the character of warfare.

Better administration did extend the scope of European war to the New World and Asia.[107] Each of the major wars of the eighteenth century was costlier in men and money and wider in its geographical scope. Paul Schroeder offers structural explanations for these wars having to do with the size, structure, power and geographical distribution of the great powers. The flanks became dominant, the center vulnerable, threatening intermediaries and bringing about a general crisis of security. He further contends that the balance of power failed to contain conflict because once it became accepted as a governing principle it justified the pursuit of narrow self-interest.[108] Both arguments are in the European tradition of *der Primat der Aussenpolitik* (literally, the primacy of foreign policy), which, like realism, gives precedence to foreign policy over domestic goals.

Schroeder's argument has damning implications for any claims about the utility of the balance of power as a mechanism of conflict management. Historians and international scholars alike commonly regard the eighteenth century as the golden age of the balance of power. Europe was multipolar, with up to six great powers – seven if we include the Ottoman Empire. No one state, not even France, was unambiguously more powerful than any combination of two other great powers. Sea power offset land power, and wealth tended to offset numbers; in contrast to later centuries, there were no sharp ideological divisions among states; offense was not perceived to have great advantage over defense, giving ample time for diplomacy to resolve crises; and after 1714, none of the great powers had hegemonic goals, but rather sought to best particular rivals (England vs. France, Russia vs. Sweden, Prussia vs. Austria). All the structural conditions realists envisage for a balance to restrain conflict were present. Most realists understand that balancing is not driven by an invisible hand, but requires conscious efforts on the part of powers to join together to oppose others who threaten the status quo.[109] This condition was also met. The principal actors understood the concept of the balance of power and agreed that a balance was in their common interest. They actively sought to maintain a balance through compensations, indemnities and alliances. They recognized that alliances could be offensive or defensive and were generally short-lived because they functioned according to the

---

[107] Black, *European Warfare, 1660–1815*, pp. 234–7; Schroeder, *The Transformation of European Politics*, pp. 50–1.

[108] Schroeder, *The Transformation of European Politics*, pp. 9, 46–7.

[109] On this point, Morgenthau, *Politics among Nations*, pp. 43–5.

principle of *pacta sunt servanda rebus sic stantibus* (to be observed until circumstances change).[110]

Under these optimal conditions the balance failed to prevent major wars or to resolve them rapidly when they broke out. According to Schroeder, it made matters worse because it was "the basis for many arguments, filled with strange mixtures of sincere conviction, sophistry, cynicism, and hypocrisy, which served to justify open breaches of faith, naked aggression, and obvious imbalances of power."[111] If the balance of power did not prevent war in the eighteenth century, or account for the decline in war from the previous century, it certainly could not be expected to do so in the nineteenth century, when the structural conditions were less than ideal. Yet there was an even sharper drop in the number and destructiveness of wars from 1815 to 1914. We must accordingly look elsewhere for our explanations of peace and war, and the obvious focus is on the nature of the society and the motives it reflects and shapes.

In between came the irruption of the French revolutionary and Napoleonic Wars, Within France, the struggle for power became increasingly violent; parliamentary government gave way to the reign of terror, restrained by the Directory and replaced by Napoleon's dictatorship. Spirit and appetite, increasingly unchecked by reason, prompted wars of conquest, culminating in a classic policy of overextension with Napoleon's invasion of Russia. Napoleon returned from exile to challenge Europe a second time. He was narrowly defeated at Waterloo in 1815, but given the enormous superiority of the allied coalition, a French victory would likely only have postponed an inevitable French defeat.

France's adversaries initially failed to understand the revolutionary force and potential of "the nation in arms," but were subsequently driven to emulate in part French methods to defeat Napoleon. Post-Napoleonic Europe was organized to repress nationalism, maintain the territorial status quo and allow the great powers once again to compete for primacy without war, or by means of limited wars. It was an attempt to apply reason to escape from a fear-driven world, and was partially successful. Like Westphalia, it ultimately failed because the system it sought to instantiate or preserve was both inherently unstable and the victim of underlying changes in society that could be neither prevented nor effectively controlled by a balance or concert of powers. The next chapter, which

---

[110] Anderson, "Eighteenth-Century Theories of the Balance of Power"; Schroeder, *The Transformation of European Politics*, pp. 5–11.

[111] Schroeder, *The Transformation of European Politics*, p. 9.

contains mini-case studies of imperialism and the origins of World War I, documents this contention. There are interesting lessons to be drawn from these efforts at order-building, and from the third, post-World War II order-building project, a subject I will take up in the follow-on volume. For our purposes here, it is enough to note that these several cases indicate that reason is a necessary but insufficient cause of order. The structure and goals of order-building must not only reflect the mix of motives in society, but through practices, institutions and leadership help constrain and shape those motives so actors behave in more productive and constructive ways.

Balance and imbalance among motives are arguably more helpful in helping us understand war and political order. The last two chapters have tried to demonstrate that the distribution of motives also explains the frequency and character of war, even the different character of wars fought by the same states and leaders. In making these claims, I have sought to establish the boundaries and character – the mix of motives – of the societies in question independently through references to domestic discourses and practices. Theories of foreign policy and international relations all too easily become tautological. By not establishing the presence of my independent variables with reference to the dependent variables I hope to explain, I have tried to avoid this problem.

Standing and honor

Europe between 1648 and 1789 offers an informative contrast to the era of the Hundred Years War. Domestic and international society were more robust, especially in Western Europe, making honor a feasible ordering principle. By the sixteenth century, honor had come to be regarded as more a personal quality, closely associated with physical appearance, military prowess and reputation, qualities which were considered the natural inheritance of the nobility. Honor was thought to elude those who sought it too actively, but to attach itself to those who achieved or displayed it with a cultivated nonchalance.[112] Honor, standing and wealth were now conceptually distinct categories, although not fully differentiated in practice.

Nobles claimed status on the basis of military service and old wealth, meaning they did not have to work for their living. There was some

---

[112] Huguet, *Dictionnaire de la langue française*, pp. 497–8; Nye, *Masculinity and Male Codes of Honor in Modern France*, p. 16.

substance to their claim, especially in France where many nobles died in the service of the French kings, although by the eighteenth century it tended to be the less well-off members of the nobility who sought glory through military service.[113] Two marshals of France under Louis XIV – Catinat and Vauban – came from minor noble families.[114] Nobles looked down on the bourgeoisie, who made or inherited its wealth from commercial activities. By differentiating honor from wealth, and defining the character manifestations of honor as largely inherited qualities, the nobility could justify its higher standing and exclusionary practices. This stratagem dated back to the Middle Ages, where there had been a long-standing debate over the respective merits of "birth" and "worth."[115] Nobles competed with one another for honor within their respective societies, and a smaller number of royal dynasties (e.g. Bourbons, Habsburgs, Wittelsbachs, Czartoryskis) competed internationally, often through the vehicle of the political units they controlled. As we have seen, this competition took the forms of display and warfare, and the latter was constrained and rule-bound in ways that it was not during the religious wars, the Renaissance or the Middle Ages.

Competition for honor and standing in the seventeenth and eighteenth centuries was far from unproblematic. In France, the *noblesse d'épée* (nobility of the sword) was under pressure from several directions. From above, its status and freedom was being reduced by monarchs who were outlawing or restraining private wars and duels. Louis XIV did this early in his reign in an effort to establish his sole authority over the use of force. In France, as elsewhere, the concept of honor, which bound a liegeman to his lord, was redefined to bind noblemen to their country. From within, the *noblesse d'épée* was being challenged by the *noblesse de robe* (nobility of the gown), individuals and families who had been ennobled through administrative and legislative service. As the French state grew, administrators became more important, and the balance of power between them and warriors began to shift. Louis XIV also violated with impunity the hierarchy among nobles that he had previously sought to maintain by increasingly appointing *intendants* from lesser families and lower ranks because they were more dependent on him and correspondingly more loyal.[116] As noted, he also sold patents of nobility to raise money for his wars. The sale of offices declined sharply between Louis's death and the

---

[113] Best, *War and Society in Revolutionary Europe*, p. 25.
[114] Anderson, *War and Society in Europe of the Old Regime*, p. 133.
[115] Keen, *Chivalry*, p. 177; Best, *War and Society in Revolutionary Europe*, pp. 24–6.
[116] Elias, *Court Society*, p. 172; Gruder, *The Royal Provincial Intendants*, pp. 168–73, 180–6.

1750s, but rose to new levels in the latter part of the eighteenth century given the expanding financial requirements of the state.[117] Frederick the Great instituted a civil service with entrance exams, which proved to be another way of checking the nobility.[118] He nevertheless purged the army of commoners, and by 1739 every colonel was a noble. In Prussia, it was easier for an aristocrat from another country to gain a commission than it was for a Prussian commoner.[119]

From below, the nobility had to confront an increasingly powerful bourgeoisie. The character of warfare was gradually changing, putting an increasing premium on professionalism and training, and, outside of Prussia, weakening aristocratic claims that leadership and ability were purely characteristics of birth.[120] As monarchs became more strapped for income, they had strong incentives to encourage commerce and tap the wealth of merchants and manufacturers. Rich commoners had always managed to find a way to become ennobled, but this process accelerated and became more open in the second half of the seventeenth century. Louis XIV, Maria Theresa and her son Joseph II established public fee schedules for buying titles.[121] Under Joseph, it cost 20,000 gulden to become a count, but only 386 gulden to be ennobled.[122] Surviving older families, relatively few in number, resented these intrusions, but their need for money drove many of them into the arms of the bourgeoisie. Matches between impoverished noble sons and daughters of rich merchants became increasingly common. The difference between nobles and the bourgeoisie also diminished because of the entry of commoners into the military profession and noble investment in commerce. Perceptions count for everything, and the *anobli* family of the eighteenth century had less prestige than it did in the seventeenth century, and considerably less than in the fifteenth century.[123]

The conflict between the nobility and the bourgeoisie was muted because the latter developed no class-consciousness or distinctive set of values. The middle class on the whole adopted aristocratic values and practices and sought to gain social acceptance.[124] Increasingly, the real social difference in France was between those who invested their capital in land and annuities (*rentes*) and venal office, which brought returns on

[117] Furet, *Interpreting the French Revolution*, p. 105.
[118] Johnson, *Frederick the Great and his Officials*, p. 132. Rosenberg, *Bureaucracy, Aristocracy, and Autocracy*, for the rise of Prussian bureaucracy in historical perspective.
[119] Anderson, *War and Society in Europe of the Old Regime*, p. 132.   [120] Ibid., p. 23.
[121] Dipper, "Orders and Classes."   [122] Buford, *Germany in the Eighteenth Century*, p. 61.
[123] Lucas, "Nobles, Bourgeois and the French Revolution."
[124] Elias, *Court Society*, pp. 292–300, 319; Dumard, *Les bourgeois de Paris au XIXe siècle*, pp. 165–6.

average of between 2 and 4 percent, and those who sought greater returns from capitalist investments. The first group, composed of nobles and commoners alike, adhered to more traditional social values and continued to regard trade and business as ignoble and dishonorable.[125]

Variants of the French pattern were common throughout western, northern and central Europe. In Britain, Scandinavia and the Habsburg domains, the middle class emulated aristocratic values and practices, and the gap between the rich bourgeoisie and the nobility narrowed, forcing nobles who wished to maintain the status hierarchy to find new and increasingly artificial ways of distinguishing themselves. In Prussia, where the landed gentry (*Junkers*) occupied an unusual niche and sustained distinct values and a related code of honor, and in Russia, even more backward and possessed of a smaller bourgeoisie, there was less mobility across class barriers. This did not prevent the emerging middle class from adopting aristocratic values, and they helped to keep the concept of honor alive. This was to have profound consequences for foreign policy in the nineteenth and twentieth centuries, as we shall see in the next chapter.

Interestingly, the bourgeoisie, even when challenging the old order, had doubts about itself and its ability to sustain the kind of commitment to public service and sacrifice that many of its representatives considered essential to maintaining national power. This was most pronounced in Britain, the country in which the bourgeoisie and commercialism had made the greatest inroads. Writers of bourgeois origin attributed the initial successes of Bonnie Prince Charlie's invasion of England in 1745 and British defeats in the early stages of the Seven Years War to a decline in "the public spirit" due the changing values of a rapidly industrializing society. Admiral John Byng's failure to intercept the French fleet in 1756, which led to the loss of Minorca and his subsequent execution, was attributed to his supposed effeminacy and corruption. Sir James Lowther, an independent Whig, warned that Britain would be "undone as a nation" by gambling and other entertainments. John Brown complained that commerce and the wealth it generated led to effeminacy, secularism and decadence.[126] Other critics attributed British military setbacks to alcohol, Italian opera, debasement of British womanhood by virtue of the Marriage Act of 1753 and talk of easing restrictions on Jews. There were also complaints about

---

[125] Lucas, "Nobles, Bourgeois and the Origins of the French Revolution."
[126] John Brown, *An Estimate of the Manners and Principles of the Times* (1757), cited in Blanning, *Pursuit of Glory*, p. 111.

the fancy dress of military commanders and calls for a national militia to revive martial ardor among the people.[127]

Late developers and late competitors

Alexander Gerschenkron focused our attention on the relationship between development and state intervention in the economy. The greater the degree of economic backwardness, he reasoned, the more state intervention is required to channel capital and entrepreneurial talent to nascent industries. More comprehensive and coercive measures are also required to reduce domestic consumption and compel national saving. England, the first country to industrialize, was under no pressure from competitors, and could develop in accord with the principles of the free market as described by Adam Smith. Germany, which began to industrialize later, required greater state intervention and large banks to provide needed capital. Russian backwardness led to an even later start, and much greater state intervention, reflected in Stalin's forced collectivization of agriculture, five-year plans and the command economy of the Soviet Union.[128] China under Mao followed the same strategy.

The Gerschenkron thesis has rightly been criticized for its economic determinism, and it is not my purpose here to enter into this controversy. Rather, I want to use Gerschenkron as the inspiration to make a parallel but quite different argument concerning late entry into the game of competition for honor and standing and the intensity and goals with which that competition is pursued. My proposition, developed more extensively in chapter 8, is that states that are late entrants into the arena where they can compete for international standing do so with greater intensity. They devote a higher percentage of their national incomes to military forces and pursue more aggressive foreign policies. Their leaders and populations, to the extent they are mobilized, will also be relatively more concerned with standing than with honor. These responses will be more pronounced if the leaders or relevant publics of the states in question believe they have been unfairly denied recognition, honor and status in the past. Latecomers to the game of international standing also tend to be late developers, and Germany, Italy, Japan and the Soviet Union, all of whom qualify as late developers, were among the more aggressive states of the twentieth

---

[127] Harris, *Politics and the Nation*, pp. 4–6, 283, 333; Sims, "The Connections between Foreign Policy and Domestic Politics in Eighteenth-Century Britain."

[128] Gerschenkron, *Economic Backwardness in Historical Perspective*, and "Agrarian Policies and Industrialization: Russia 1861–1917."

century. The phenomenon is likely to be more pronounced if the political elites and relevant public opinion of late developers feel an acute sense of humiliation by reason of their past treatment by the great powers.

In the seventeenth and eighteenth centuries, three states gained recognition into the limited circle of European major powers: Sweden under Gustavus Adolphus, Russia under Peter the Great and Prussia under Frederick the Great. Their rulers spent a higher percentage of their available income on the military than did other European states. European rulers in the eighteenth century typically spent between 20 and 40 percent of their income on their military establishments, and more during wars. Peter the Great added forty new regiments to his army during the course of his reign, and throughout the Northern War used up to 80 percent of revenues for war or war-related industries.[129] In 1786, the last year of his reign, Frederick the Great spent 75 percent of his state's income on the army, and directed another 5 percent to his war treasury.[130]

All three leaders were the most aggressive of their day. This was neither coincidence nor idiosyncrasy. Frederick's father, Frederick William I, had begun Prussia's transformation into a garrison state, and Gustavus Adolphus and Peter were followed by aggressive monarchs. Peter and Catherine also spent vast sums on display in the form of a new capital city, palaces and art and other valuable objects to fill their corridors. In Peter's later years, military spending declined relative to display.[131] Under Catherine, state expenditure rose 500 percent, and far exceeded income. On average, 37 percent went to the army and navy, 13.5 percent to the court and less than 1.5 percent to education and welfare. There were peaks of greater spending on the court: Catherine's infamous journey to the Crimea in 1787 consumed 12.5 percent of that year's budget.[132]

Humiliation entered into the picture to varying degrees. Sweden was seeking recognition in the early seventeenth century, at a time when Protestant rulers were still considered outsiders by the great Catholic powers. Erik Ringmar makes it apparent that Sweden's outside status rankled Gustavus Adolphus and the Swedish elite, and that its recognition as a major power would build not only self-esteem but identity as a nation.[133] Russia was ignored and disregarded until the end of the seventeenth century, and not even considered by many to be part of Europe. In the 1680s and 1690s, Russia, together with Poland, the Habsburgs and Venice, waged

---

[129] Hughes, *Peter the Great*, pp. 61–2.   [130] Schulze, "The Prussian Military State."
[131] Anderson, *War and Society in Europe of the Old Regime*, p. 142.
[132] Dukes, *Catherine the Great and the Russian Nobility*, p. 110.
[133] Ringmar, *Identity, Interest and Action.*

war against the Ottoman Empire. At the peace settlement in 1700, Russia's allies entirely ignored its interests.[134] Memory of this and other insults made Peter acutely aware of Russia's image in the West as a largely uncivilized and quasi-Asian kingdom, and clearly felt a strong sense of cultural inferiority. Even after his military successes against Sweden, Russia, we have seen, was considered the "Turk of the north." His construction of St. Petersburg, like his earlier policy concerning beards and attire, appears to have been motivated in large part by the desire not only to make Russia a Western nation but to have it accepted as one. Russia never fully lived up to Western standards in its internal politics or economic development, and, although a member of the club, was never fully trusted despite its large army and impressive territorial expansion. Peter, it was known, had his son arrested and tortured to death, and Catherine the Great was thought to have murdered her husband. Prussia was more accepted, but still regarded as something of an odd fellow by virtue of its single-minded focus on its military. Frederick William I was another known despot, who imprisoned his son and executed his son's lover. Great power status required more than success on the battlefield and the construction site. The bar to membership would be consistently raised in the nineteenth and twentieth centuries to include adherence to a set of domestic and international norms and practices.[135] As with academic tenure, newcomers to the club were often held accountable to higher standards than existing members.

My thesis is difficult to operationalize because of problems of definition and measurement. Backwardness and late development can be readily defined and measured, but what is important here is a state of mind that, I suspect, does not always track nicely with economic indicators of wealth and development. This is even more true of humiliation, which is an entirely subjective emotion. In the countries I identify – Sweden, Prussia and Russia in the seventeenth and eighteenth centuries, and Germany, Italy and Japan in the late nineteenth and first half of the twentieth century – the sense of humiliation was pronounced. Rather than external indicators, we must turn to the telltale discourses in which these feelings find expression. I will return to this problem later in the book.

---

[134] Anderson, *War and Society in Europe of the Old Regime*, p. 79.
[135] Bukovansky, *Legitimacy and Power Politics*, p. 70; Reus-Smit, *The Moral Purpose of the State*, p. 137; Clark, *Legitimacy in International Society*, p. 100; Neumann, "Russia as a Great Power"; Suzuki, "Seeking 'Legitimate' Great Power Status in Post-Cold War International Society."

The rise of the state

In Western Europe, the nation state developed slowly and in stages, and only later, but at a more accelerated pace, in central and eastern Europe. For purposes of analysis, it is useful to break down state development into stages. The first stage, which I call the Weberian transformation, is arguably the most critical. It is characterized by the increasing monopolization of force by kings or central governments, which in Western Europe was a long, slow process, beginning in the eleventh century, and continuing off and on over the next 700 years. It was accompanied by conceptualization of the state as being something beyond the ruler of the moment. These two developments are related but not always coterminous; power became increasingly centralized in the Frankish kingdom, which nevertheless remained a patrimonial political order. Later in the Middle Ages and in early modern Europe both processes took place in tandem in Spain, France, England and the United Provinces. In much of southern and eastern Europe, the Weberian transformation did not begin until the modern era.

The drive to monopolize armies and violence was part and parcel of a struggle for power between kings and nobles. So-called "private wars" were common practice throughout the Middle Ages, as were rebellions against royal authority. As standing among aristocrats was generally determined by proximity to the throne (ascribed status) and the size, wealth and autonomy of one's domain (achieved status), kings had a strong incentive to centralize power while provincial nobles had equal incentives to resist them. Lesser figures, who hoped to obtain status and property through military service to kings or their noble opponents, had a decided interest in such conflicts and their outcomes. As mercenaries – whom Hobbes called "worms in the intestines of state" – became important from the fourteenth century onwards, the side with the most resources had a definite military advantage.[136] In Spain, France and England, this was generally the king, and helped to consolidate monarchical authority. This process accelerated by virtue of a tipping phenomenon. Kings exploited their relative advantage to hire more mercenaries, which increased their chances of cowing or defeating rebellious nobles. Success in turn brought them more resources and power, making allegiance to them more attractive

---

[136] Keen, *Chivalry*, pp. 229–32; Waley, "The Army of the Florentine Republic from the Twelfth to the Fourteenth Century"; Garcia, "Types of Armies." Grundmann, "Rotten and Brabanzonen"; Prestwich, "War and Finance in the Anglo-Norman State," on the earlier use of mercenaries. Hobbes, *Leviathan*, p. 375.

to mercenaries and ambitious individuals. Those opposed to centralization often waged unsuccessful rebellions, which further strengthened the
power of monarchs.

The process of establishing royal control over the use of force was
still underway in the seventeenth and eighteenth centuries. In France,
the country most advanced in this regard, kings confronted the most
warlike nobility in Europe and had difficulty in making them serve in
organized regiments of the regular army. In 1676, central authority was
further extended by compelling aristocrats to recognize that the officers
commanded on the basis of military rank, not according to their inherited
social status. Regiments were still largely local forces beholden to their
aristocratic colonels and not to the central government. It was only in the
1680s that French regiments began to be referred to by provincial titles
instead of the names of the colonels who recruited them. In 1712, the
British substituted numerical designators for the names of commanders
in their regiments.[137] Central control of military forces came more slowly
further east.

Social scientists and historians rightly consider warfare to have played
a critical role in the development of the state. In the words of Charles Tilly,
"the state made war and war made the state."[138] Wars required extraordinary resources, which drove leaders to centralize authority to extract
those resources and develop the bureaucracies that could transform them
into ever larger standing armies and navies.[139] This strategy did not work
everywhere, as attempts to centralize authority in some countries, most
notably Spain, the Holy Roman Empire and Poland, wrecked the political
unit or undermined its regime.

Thomas Ertman makes a persuasive case for the timing of state-building
having a determining effect on the state structures that developed. Political units that responded to geopolitical pressures and differentiated their
infrastructures before about 1450 (early state-builders) did so with methods and institutional arrangements that became increasingly outmoded
but which proved difficult to replace because of the power of vested interests and their material and ideological stakes in existing structures. States

[137] Anderson, *War and Society in Europe of the Old Regime*, pp. 132, 105.
[138] Tilly, "Reflections on the History of European State-Making," p. 42.
[139] Hintze, *The Historical Essays of Otto Hintze*; Anderson, *Lineages of the Absolutist State*;
Tilly, *Coercion, Capital, and European States, The Formation of National States in Western
Europe*, and "War Making and State Making as Organized Crime"; Mann, *The Sources
of Social Power*; Parker, *The Military Revolution*; Downing, "Constitutionalism, Warfare,
and Political Change in Early Modern Europe"; Ertman, *Birth of the Leviathan*; Anderson,
War and Society in Europe of the Old Regime, pp. 82–99.

that were affected by these pressures after 1450 (late state-builders) were able to adopt the latest techniques in administration and finance. As there was a great expansion of qualified administrative personnel in the early modern period, this enhanced the bargaining position of these rulers. Early state-builders – England and Scotland in 1100s and 1200s, and Spain and the Italian city states before 1450 – had to use available feudal and ecclesiastical models. It gave them an early lead, but at the cost of substantial loss of control to proprietary officeholders, tax farmers and officeholder-financiers who did not view the state as an instrument of princely power but a source of income and social standing. Later state developers, including German states, the northern Netherlands, Scandinavia and Poland, were able to create dependent bureaucracies and were better able to resist or overcome local elites.[140]

According to Ertman, timing alone is insufficient to explain state structure. We must also take into account the organization of local and larger governments. In England, the strength of parliament permitted the country to move off a path of development that would have otherwise led to patrimonial constitutionalism, and instead to develop a form of bureaucratic constitutionalism. In Poland, where the parliament had a *liberum veto*, and was blocked by factional division, this was not possible. The onset of state-building and the strength of parliamentary institutions generate a two-by-two matrix, and with it four kinds of state structure: patrimonial absolutism, patrimonial constitutionalism, bureaucratic absolutism and bureaucratic constitutionalism. These structures nicely describe the historical reality of countries in western, southern and eastern Europe. Ertman insists that the catalyst in all cases was geopolitical competition and the wars it generated.[141]

Ertman's last claim is highly questionable, or at least in need of reformulation, because, as we have seen, most of the wars fought in early modern Europe, and indeed up to the French Revolutionary wars, were less a response to insecurity than they were part of the quest for honor and standing by kings and aristocrats. Moreover, many of the resources extracted by new state organizations were not directed to warfare, but to display in the form of palaces, churches, cultural events and festivals.

In Charlemagne's time, in the age of William the Conqueror and during the Hundred Years War, it is difficult to distinguish internal from foreign wars. States were not fully formed, political jurisdictions were overlapping and, depending on precedent and the nature of conflicting claims,

---

[140] Ertman, *Birth of the Leviathan.*   [141] Ibid.

a war might be framed as a domestic matter by one protagonist and a foreign invasion by another. After 1648, the distinction between domestic and foreign became more distinct, which allows me to offer generalizations about the different character of civil and international wars in the seventeenth and eighteenth centuries. In the course of this chapter, I have demonstrated that the principal motive for war was standing. Monarchs gained and maintained standing and *gloire* through military victories and the territorial expansion it allowed. Appetite was a secondary consideration as wars often cost far more than any economic benefits new territories might be expected to confer. Even when conquered territories generated wealth, it was most often sought – as in the case of Frederick II's conquest of Silesia – to augment a ruler's military might. As wars became larger in scale and costlier after 1500, monarchs were increasingly strapped for cash and driven to organize "bureaucracies" – a neologism coined in 1765 by the French *philosophe* Vincent de Gournaym – to extract more resources from their societies. The spirit, not appetite or fear, was the root cause of state-building.

The conceptualization of the state or kingdom as a *res publica* went hand-in-hand with royal consolidation of power because it helped to legitimize it. To the extent that the kingdom was conceived of as an entity in its own right, the monarch's position, as representative of the state, put him or her on a qualitatively different plane than other nobles. This involved a tradeoff because monarchs could no longer claim the state as personal property, but their more impersonal states could make more farreaching claims on the loyalty and resources of citizens, from which monarchs benefited. In France, this transition is visible during the course of the long reign of Louis XIV (1643–1715). Early depictions of Louis in literature and the plastic arts portray him as Jupiter, Apollo, the sun and famous heroes. He was compared to Solomon, Augustus, Constantine, Justinian, Clovis and Charlemagne.[142] By the late 1680s, classical and mythical imagery and associations were on the wane, reflecting the general decline of antiquity as a cultural model in literature. Louis was increasingly represented in modern dress, in contemporary settings and surrounded by symbols of commerce, military might, science and the productive arts. "French order" columns were designed for the Louvre in lieu of classical Ionic, Doric or Corinthian ones.[143]

---

[142] Burke, *The Fabrication of Louis XIV*, pp. 12, 35.
[143] Ibid., pp. 126–7; Blanning, *Pursuit of Glory*, pp. 428–40.

There was a corresponding change in the rhetoric of legitimacy. Mystical associations were on the wane as part of what Max Weber would later call the "disenchantment of the world" (*Entzauberung der Welt*).[144] The intellectual revolution of the seventeenth century, prompted by the works of Descartes, Galileo and Newton, among others, reconceived the world in mechanical rather than organic terms.[145] The commitment by scientists to understand the universe as a rational, if enormously elaborate, machine, in which each part had its place, was reflected in the effort by political theorists to understand, if not construct, the state along similar lines. As kings became demystified they lost some of what Bourdieu calls their symbolic capital.[146] Not surprisingly, the symbolism invoked by Louis XIV and his advisors became more self-consciously rational, with the king portrayed as the indispensable cog in the machine or the source of its energy and direction.[147]

Michael Walzer rightly observes that the state is invisible and must be personified before it can be seen and symbolized to be imagined. Symbolization does not create unity, but units of discourse "around which emotions of loyalty and assurance can cluster."[148] Encouraging citizens to identify with and take pride in their nation, and to regard the monarch as its embodiment, requires courts, palaces, public squares and new or renovated capital cities. As with Louis XIV, art, architecture, literature and ritual were often manifestations of a coordinated and carefully supervised strategy to shape perceptions of monarchs at home and aboard.[149] These projects can also be understood in less personal terms as efforts to create the roles and symbols critical to a centralizing state. Clifford Geertz argues, in the context of nineteenth-century Bali, that royalty can be considered an end in itself. "Power served pomp, not pomp power."[150] As monarch and state were so inextricably entwined, either reading emphasizes the importance of the spirit as an end in itself and a means of state-building.

Additional evidence for my thesis is provided by the extraordinary sums European rulers during this period spent on their courts, palaces,

---

[144] Weber, "Science as a Vocation," p. 30.

[145] On the older organic metaphors and their political uses, see Archambault, "The Analogy of the Body in Renaissance Political Literature"; Kantorowicz, *The King's Two Bodies.*

[146] Bourdieu, *Language and Symbolic Power*, pp. 75–6, 163–70.

[147] Burke, *The Fabrication of Louis XIV*, *passim*, for examples.

[148] Walzer, "On the Role of Symbolism in Political Thought."

[149] Shils, *Center and Periphery*; Eisenstadt, "Communication Patterns in Centralized Empires"; Burke, *The Fabrication of Louis XIV*, pp. 39–45, and 158–65 on influencing foreign audiences; Blanning, *Pursuit of Glory*, pp. 207–17.

[150] Geertz, *Negara*, p. 13; Burke, *The Fabrication of Louis XIV*, pp. 11–12.

churches, theaters, other public buildings – entire cities in some cases – processions, festivals and other grand events. Louis XIV not only built Versailles but Vaux-le Vicomte, and he extensively renovated the Louvre. He employed a stellar array of writers and artists, among them the playwrights Corneille, Molière and Quinalt, the poet La Fontaine, the painter Le Brun, the sculptors Augurier and Girardon, the architect Le Vau and the landscape designer Le Nôtre. Louis was a patron of the sciences and founded the Académie des Sciences on the model of the English Royal Society. To demonstrate the king's interest in erudition, his minister Colbert spent freely to collect books, manuscripts, art and scientific curiosities and commissioned leading artists to design and issue medals of Louis.[151] The rays of the Sun King illuminated other courts, as Versailles inspired a spate of new construction. Louis's grandson, Philip V of Spain, had his portrait painted by the same artist, Hyacinthe Rigaud, for whom Louis had sat, and had his palace redecorated and re-modeled in the style of the court at Versailles. Max Emmanuel of Bavaria spent 75 percent of his state's income on his court, while Ernst August of Hanover and Friedrich Karl von Schöborn, prince-bishop of Würzburg, both spent over 50 percent on their courts. The latter instructed his architect to visit Versailles and to re-create its grand staircase in his own palace. Charles II of England followed Louis's example in founding the Royal Observatory (1675) and the Chelsea Hospital (1681). In Vienna, display determined status, and a very high percentage of the Viennese economy was based on supplying servants, goods, comestibles and buildings to the Residenz and the lesser establishments in its orbit. In Hungary and Poland, the Esterházys, Radziwills and Czartoryskis built enormous palaces on their estates, and spent small fortunes on servants, orchestras, dependent gentry and private armies, all in pursuit of standing and political goals. Peter the Great, I noted previously, wanted his Peterhof in Saint Petersburg to be recognized as a new Versailles.[152]

There was considerable variation in relative expenditure on courts and armies within and across states. In a number of major powers, expenditure on display regularly exceeded that of armies. In France, high-profile expenditure on display continued regardless of military requirements. On average, almost 50 percent of the state budget in 1770 went to the court, while only 20 percent went to the army. However, at peak periods of war,

[151] Burke, *The Fabrication of Louis XIV*, pp. 66–9, 53–4.
[152] Swann, "Politics and the State in Eighteenth Century Europe"; Blanning, *Pursuit of Glory*, pp. 113–14; Burke, *The Fabrication of Louis XIV*, pp. 169–78.

military spending could rise as high as 75 percent. In 1768, Vienna spent 23 percent on the court and 48 percent on the army, but this percentage dropped sharply afterwards when the army reforms were completed. In Bavaria in 1770, the court received 42 percent and the army 30 percent. In Russia, Peter the Great devoted 80 percent of his income to his war machine, but his priorities underwent a considerable shift in favor of display after the Great Northern War.[153] The two great outliers were Saxony and Prussia. Toward the end of Frederick the Great's reign, Prussia directed 80 percent of its revenues to war-making. The Saxon kings of Poland, Augustus II (1697–1733) and Augustus III (1733–63) went to the other extreme. They devoted almost all of their resources to display, transforming Dresden into one of the most culturally exciting and beautiful courts of Europe. Augustus II, known as the Strong, was also famous for fathering 354 illegitimate children with the legion of mistresses he supported. Their neglect of its military made Saxony an inviting target for Prussian conquest. Such conquest in the eighteenth century was hardly the norm, and did not deter other rulers from continuing to spend vast sums on display.

In both war and peace, the spirit played a large, if not dominant, role. The quest for standing and honor cannot by itself explain the rise of the modern state, but its development cannot be understood without taking them into account. In the next chapter, we will see that they remained significant motives for leaders and national elites long after their states were well established and help to explain imperialism and the First World War.

[153] Schulze, "The Prussian Military State"; Parker, *The Military Revolution*, pp. 62–5.

7

Imperialism and World War I

> Oft of one wide expanse had I been told
> That deep-brow'd ruled as his demesne;
> Yet did I never breathe its pure serene
> Till I heard Chapman speak out loud and bold:
> Then I felt like some watcher of the skies
> When a new planet swims into his ken;
> Or like stout Cortez when with eagle eyes
> He star'd at the Pacific – and his men
> Look'd at each other with a wild surmise –
> Silent, upon a peak in Darien.
>
> John Keats[1]

Traditional Europe is often considered to end with the French Revolution. Many historians treat it as a transformative event that separates the old regime from republicanism and traditionalism from modernity.[2] The Revolution is undeniably an important historical marker, although many of the historians who use it as such wisely hedge their claims with various

---

[1] Keats, "On First Looking into Chapman's Homer." Of course, it was Balboa, not Cortez, who was the first European to "discover" the Pacific Ocean.

[2] I follow Bernard Yack's understanding of modernity. In *The Fetishism of Modernities*, pp. 32–5, he identifies four distinct conceptions of modernity: philosophic, sociological, political and aesthetic. Philosophic modernity represents a self-conscious break with authority, initiated by Bacon, Descartes and later Enlightenment philosophers. It is a project whose roots can be traced back to the Renaissance. The sociological conception describes changing social relationships and conditions, and is generally thought to have been ushered in by the development of capitalism in the late eighteenth century, and the break it initiated with traditional forms of authority. The political conception of modernity focuses on the emergence of egalitarian and democratic forms of political legitimacy, and the corresponding decline of aristocratic political hierarchies. The watershed here is the French Revolution. The aesthetic conception of modernity is associated with styles of art and literature that understand beauty and meaning as ephemeral, and are opposed to the orthodoxy of the moment regardless of its content. Modernism in this sense did not appear until the late nineteenth century. See also Eley, "German History and the Contradictions of Modernity," for a discussion of modernization and its specific application to Germany.

caveats.[3] They recognize that important developments we associate with modernity often had their origins in pre-revolutionary Europe, and that many characteristic practices of the old regime survived the Revolution, some of them down to our day, albeit in muted or altered form.[4] The politics and international relations of the nineteenth and twentieth centuries is best understood in terms of the uneasy coexistence and tensions between values and practices of pre-revolutionary Europe with those that emerged with modernity. These centuries represent a period of transition, and one that is not yet complete despite claims by some that we have already entered a postindustrial, postmodernist age.

Modernity, of which the French Revolution has become the principal symbol, affirms the value of ordinary life and the quest for material well-being. As I noted in the introduction, the classical concern with virtue and the Christian fixation on salvation were correspondingly downgraded.[5] Enlightenment thinkers streamlined our understanding of the psyche and legitimized appetite as drive, reconceiving it as the source of economic growth and political order. With some notable exceptions, they ignored or consciously rejected the spirit and downgraded reason to a mere instrumentality. This reformulation provided a justification for larger political and economic projects, including the French Revolution.

In the last three chapters, I concentrated on the spirit to demonstrate its relevance to international relations. In this chapter, I extend my analysis to other motives as well, because from the Enlightenment on they become that much more important in discourse and practice. I do not claim that the spirit can explain all politics and international relations, only that they cannot be understood without taking it into account. For this reason, it is essential not only to examine other motives but show how they interact with the spirit. Are these combinations best described as mixtures, or do they combine to form something else as solutions do? In medieval and post-Westphalian Europe, they generally manifested themselves as

---

[3] Furet, *Interpreting the French Revolution*, pp. 1–17, for an enlightening discussion of the historiography of the French Revolution, the extent it has been interpreted as a new beginning or a culmination of the old, and how these choices reflect the political or sociological projects of the politicians and historians in question. Blanning, *Pursuit of Glory*, pp. 349–50, for substantive continuity and change.

[4] Tocqueville, *Democracy in America*, and *The Old Regime and the French Revolution*, is an interesting case in point. He understands the Revolution as the culmination of the centralization process begun during the reign of Louis XIV, but novel in the sense that it enshrined and legitimized the idea of equality. By destroying the aristocratic principle, the Revolution hastened the development of an absolutist state.

[5] This is a central theme of Taylor, *Sources of the Self*.

mixtures; each motive prompted the kind of behavior associated with it, making the aggregate behavior of actors appear inconsistent, even irrational. Rousseau, Smith and Veblen suggest that appetite and spirit can also blend, and consider this phenomenon a defining feature of modernity. Solutions of the kind they describe make their first dramatic appearance in the age of Louis XIV, when, as we observed, status was achieved through display as well as war. The practice became widespread and routine by the nineteenth century. It complicates analysis by making it more difficult to differentiate among motives. I attempt to do so in the case of imperialism and World War I by examining the dominant discourses of policymaking elites in Britain, France, Germany and Russia and the extent to which their policies appear consistent with the motives of fear, interest and honor.

Intellectual discourses do not necessarily mirror behavior, especially when they describe human motives. In classical Greece, the philosophical discourse in Athens emphasized the spirit at the very moment when appetites had become increasingly uncontrolled among the elite. Throughout the Middle Ages appetite was also a powerful motive, but disparaged by discourses rooted in the spirit. The Enlightenment and the French Revolution reversed this emphasis, at least in some countries. In Britain, the Low Countries and the United States, appetite increasingly came to dominate the philosophical and political discourses and was considered beneficial for society.[6] In Germany and Austria, the dominant discourses still centered on the spirit and continued to disparage the appetite. In Britain and the United States, the spirit nevertheless remained a powerful motive for individuals, groups and their governments, but the behavior to which it gave rise was ignored, disparaged or reinterpreted as an expression of appetite. This approach continues to the present day. As we observed, Anglo-American international relations try unsuccessfully to explain the strivings of states and their leaders for prestige as a tactic intended to maximize power, and thus motivated by fear or appetite.

In central Europe, traditional elite discourses survived and even prospered in the nineteenth century. In Germany, the Greeks provided an inspiration for humanists and an alternative cultural space for artists and intellectuals alienated by Prussian authoritarianism.[7] German idealism drew heavily on the Greeks, especially Greek tragedy. Beginning with Kant and continuing through Fichte, Hegel and Schelling, it led to a renewed

---

[6] See Hirschman, *The Passions and the Interests*; Hont, *Jealousy of Trade*; Force, *Self-Interest before Adam Smith*.

[7] Butler, *The Tyranny of Greece over Germany*; Marchand, *Down from Olympus*; Schmidt, *On Germans and Other Greeks*; Taylor, *Hegel*, pp. 25–9.

emphasis on the spirit among the educated classes and a corresponding depreciation of more pedestrian pursuits such as making money and the low politics associated with governance. In Britain, renewed interest in the Greeks came earlier, and centered on Homer. Chapman's famous translation appeared in 1598. A nineteenth-century reissue inspired a famous poem by John Keats, which I have reproduced as the epigraph to this chapter. Shelley and other young radicals took heart in what they saw as the heroic defiance of the Greeks.[8] The Victorian fascination with the Greeks was such that Matthew Arnold came to believe that "Marathon and Salamis were more actual to the governing culture of nineteenth century England than was the Battle of Hastings."[9] In Britain and the United States, Latin and Greek were mandatory school subjects. Harvard required all entering students to write and speak Latin, a requirement which they eased for science students only in 1912. Through their education, the elite assimilated more traditional aristocratic values, values that were reflected to varying degrees in their behavior, especially in foreign policy and warfare. Homer's appeal may well reflect the increasing disappearance of the spirit from other discourses in Britain and the United States, and hence explain the attraction of a text in which heroism, great deeds and sacrifice feature so prominently.

My account of international relations in the nineteenth and early twentieth centuries stresses a continuity in values. The most important actors in international relations continue to be states. The majority of their rulers, diplomats and generals were aristocrats imbued with many of the same values that had motivated their predecessors.[10] One of the most important of these was honor. Max Weber described honor as determining the relative status of groups (*Ständische Lage*). It dictated a "specific conduct of life" for the nobility that emphasized "distance and exclusiveness." Honor made the conduct of personal relations a primary consideration of life, and aristocrats were socialized into believing that their code of behavior was shared throughout Europe and was a central pillar to their identity and prestige. Ever since chivalry, Weber noted, honor was closely connected to the "ideal of manliness." This way of life, reinforced through education, intermarriage and social exclusiveness, stood in direct

---

[8] Jenkyns, *Victorians and Ancient Greece*; Turner, *The Greek Heritage in Victorian Britain*.
[9] Quoted in Steiner, *Antigones*, p. 285.
[10] I use the terms aristocracy and nobility interchangeably, although T. C. W. Blanning, among others, has suggested that aristocracy is a political term and nobility is more neutral. For a discussion see Urbach, *European Aristocracies and the Radical Right*, pp. 4–5.

contrast and opposition to "the pretensions of sheer property" and the idea of classes defined in terms of their respective wealth.[11]

The quest for honor and standing, initially a preserve of the aristocracy, penetrated deeply into the middle classes, many of whose members took their cues from the aristocracy and sought to assimilate at least some of its values and practices. In central Europe, the rise of the middle classes and their semi-feudalization was more threatening than reassuring to large segments of the nobility, and a major source of domestic tension and more aggressive foreign policies. The military in particular regarded honor as its "inviolable possession," and took offense at the pretenses of the wealthier bourgeoisie. Officers and diplomats alike, both drawn from the nobility, intensified their commitment to honor, which was increasingly personified in the name of the nation. They identified honor with strength, courage and decisiveness and shame with weakness, hesitation and compromise. Their letters, pronouncements and cables are redolent with allusions to national "insults," "challenges" and "humiliation," and the need to seek "satisfaction" to avoid "shame."[12] We should be clear, however, that agency remains important because there is considerable individual variation within policymaking elites, the intelligentsia and the middle classes in both the nineteenth and the twentieth centuries.

There were important changes in the arenas in which great powers competed for standing. In the seventeenth and eighteenth centuries, great power wars were frequent; victory and territorial conquest were the principal means by which states became great powers and ranking was established among them. In the nineteenth century, there were few such wars: the Crimean War (1853–6), and the wars of Italian and German unification being the exceptions. These five intra-European wars had important results, but were relatively limited in their duration, scope and casualties. The great powers of 1815 were still great powers in 1914, although their ranking had altered, and they had been joined by Japan and the United States. All the lesser European powers survived the century, except for those absorbed, mostly willingly, in mid-century unifications. Considerable amounts of money were spent on armies and fleets, but the great powers on the whole acted with restraint toward one another. Paul Schroeder is struck by how much self-restraint the great powers exercised, and how their ambitions were otherwise checked, not so much by a balance of power as by the efforts of other states to use "group pressures to

---

[11] Weber, *Economy and Society*, II, pp. 932–7, 1068–9.
[12] Frevert, *Men of Honor*, p. 47; "Honor, Gender, and Power."

enforce norms and treaties."[13] Durkheimian social pressures, as noted in the introduction, were once again more effective than formal means of control at the regional level.

With the decline in great power warfare, secondary arenas of competition became more important. Most of the great powers used their armed forces to make extra-European conquests. Imperialism became the "great game" in which major and minor powers competed to plant their respective flags in the furthest reaches of the globe. The British, the premier colonial power, could proudly proclaim that the sun never set on their empire. In sharp contrast to the eighteenth century, there were no European wars over colonial possessions, although competition was intense and led to the occasional acute crisis like Fashoda in 1898 that almost brought France and Britain to blows over control of the Sudan.

Display was a prominent means of claiming standing in the seventeenth and eighteenth centuries, and became even more evident in the second half of the nineteenth century. The major powers extensively renovated, expanded and beautified their capitals. They built museums, concert halls and opera houses in their cities, and railroads and canals throughout their countries and the world. France and the United States built canals in Egypt and Panama, at least as much to gain prestige as to advance any security or economic interest.[14] The major powers also competed to achieve primacy in the creative and performing arts and in science and engineering. By the end of the century, sports competitions and races involving athletes (the modern Olympics began in 1896), sailing ships, and horses grabbed public attention and became international in scope; competition among nations abetted claims to status and helped to sell newspapers.[15] In the first decades of the twentieth century, horseless carriages and air races were added to the list. It was hoped by many that sporting events would become surrogates for more violent forms of competition.[16] Many of these activities, like canal-building, involved prodigious expenditures and represented national manifestations of what Veblen called conspicuous consumption. Time for practice and money for uniforms and equipment, while not limiting sports to the wealthy, gave them an advantage, and it was primarily their sports and competitions (e.g. shooting, yachting, rowing,

---

[13] Schroeder, "International Politics, Peace and War, 1815–1914."
[14] Collin, *Theodore Roosevelt's Caribbean*, pp. 127–340; McCulloch, *The Path between the Seas*, pp. 101–51, 243–69.
[15] Guttmann, *The Olympics*; Huggins, *Victorians and Sport*, pp. 111–41, on the commercialization of sport.
[16] Sombart, *Händler und Helden*, p. 121; Veitch, "Play up! Play up! and Win the War!"; Newbolt, *The Book of the Happy Warrior*.

coursing, cricket) that were covered by the elite press.[17] International competitions also mirrored international relations in that indigenous races and non-Causcasian countries were at first excluded from participation. In Britain, press coverage of sporting events helped to propagate the imperial idea, and victories over other European teams were interpreted as more evidence of British superiority. As the United States rose in its power and influence, the British press began to denigrate baseball as a sport.[18]

European competition for standing offers evidence of a striking continuity with the past, but its manifestations were increasingly novel. From the ancient empires to pre-revolutionary Europe, wealth was a means to the end of standing. It allowed its owners to purchase hoplite panoplies, armor or the armies they needed to enter the lists. It also bought splendor, a generally accepted marker of standing, although not in pre-classical Greece. Under Pericles, this changed in Athens, and throughout the ancient Mediterranean world palaces and public buildings became accepted symbols of power. Modernity brought subtle but significant changes. As the appetite gained acceptance, and was even regarded as beneficial to society, wealth became an acknowledged source of standing, not just one of its markers. Major public expenditures of all kinds accorded standing, from beneficial projects like the Paris sewers to more outrageous forms of conspicuous consumption such as France's Eiffel Tower and America's "Great White Fleet."

Between 1815 and 1914, Europe's transnational society sustained and constrained competition among the great powers. It generated rules and procedures that helped to mute the consequences of major changes in both standing and the balance of power associated with the unification of Germany and Italy, the rise of Japan and the United States. It was somewhat less successful in addressing the decline of the Ottoman Empire. Traditional narratives of the origins of World War I explain it with reference to the breakdown of this order and the increasing lack of restraint of the great powers. Realists attribute this behavior to the ways in which opposing alliance systems and offensive dominance exacerbated fears of strategic disadvantage and general insecurity. They also emphasize the rising power of Germany and its challenge of the existing order. Marxist and Marxist-inspired analyses emphasize class divisions that encouraged aristocratic regimes to pursue increasingly aggressive foreign policies. Intellectual historians draw our attention to the *Zeitgeist* and the ways in which Social Darwinism, acute nationalism and

---

[17] Huggins, *Victorians and Sport*, pp. 21, 237–8, 100.   [18] Ibid., pp. 236–44.

adulation of military heroes made conflict and war appear attractive and inevitable.[19]

My account of imperialism and World War I begins with a critique of these several explanations. I argue that the policies that are understood to be responsible for this war (e.g. imperial competition, offensive military strategies, support for allies, preference for preemption, willingness to go to war) cannot successfully be accounted for by appetite or fear. Most of these policies were a drain on the national economy and strategically questionable, if not downright disadvantageous. Some leaders even understood how ill-advised the policies they pursued were when evaluated in material or strategic terms. I accordingly turn to the spirit to explain imperialism and the First World War. I argue that competition for colonies, like earlier forms of interstate competition, was driven by a desire to achieve national recognition and standing, and through them individual self-esteem. In the nineteenth century, this competition was a core concern of some leaders, most notably the German Kaiser, but increasingly of politically relevant middle-class voters who sought to buttress their self-esteem vicariously through the successes of their nation.

Interstate competition became more acute because of the problems aristocratic regimes had in coping with modernity. Some of this difficulty involved challenges to the authority and privileges of the nobility by other classes, but ironically it also reflected the efforts of the upper middle class to emulate at least some of their values and practices. This phenomenon was most pronounced in societies where the spirit remained the dominant discourse. It threatened to blur the distinction between new and old wealth, and with it the exclusive status of the latter. It led powerful members of the nobility to emphasize the importance of "high politics," the domain where they still exercised unquestioned authority through their control of the armed forces and foreign ministries. The most threatened aristocratic regimes – Germany and Austria-Hungary – exercised less self-restraint in their foreign policies and increasingly violated the norms that governed interstate competition.

My account differs in significant ways from standard "social imperialist" explanations for European expansion overseas and World War I. Standard accounts stress the insecurity of aristocratic–authoritarian regimes confronted with the rising power of the middle and working classes, and the extent to which aggressive foreign policies were calculated to divide

---

[19] For a review of the literature on the origins of World War I, see Lebow, "Contingency, Catalysts and International System Change"; Williamson and May, "An Identity of Opinion."

theses classes and reconcile significant parts of them to the domestic political status quo. There is strong evidence for this interpretation in the case of Britain in the 1870s, and concern for the rising power of the middle and working classes was one of several reasons behind Bismarck's brief flirtation with imperialism in the 1880s and Bülow's a decade later. It does not provide a persuasive explanation for German willingness to risk war in 1914. Even where it is relevant, the social imperialist thesis fails to identify the most important pressures for expansionist policies. They emanated more from the middle classes than from the aristocracy, and weak aristocratic governments, especially in early twentieth-century Germany, felt an increasing political need to respond to this constituency.

My account of World War I also stresses the role of honor in the immediate causes of that conflict. The war hawks responsible for the Austrian ultimatum to Serbia – Berchtold and Conrad von Hötzendorf – acted less from fear for their country's security and rather more from a desire to uphold its honor and their own. Kaiser's Wilhelm's "blank check" was similarly motivated. French support for Russia reflected strategic calculations, but also concern for honor. In Britain, the cabinet was divided, and prime minister Herbert Asquith was only able to muster a majority for war by appealing to the need to "honor" Britain's commitment to defend the neutrality of Belgium. His foreign secretary, Edward Grey, also regarded the treaty to uphold Belgium's neutrality as a moral commitment.[20]

In previous chapters I began my mini-case studies with an assessment of the extent to which the societies in question can be described as honor societies. In this chapter I follow a different procedure. As I noted earlier, Europe of the nineteenth and twentieth centuries is composed of mixed societies in the sense that appetite and spirit are both present and influential. In some states, and certainly in the regional system these countries constitute, fear is present as well. Rather than attempting to assess the relative importance of these motives, and then predict the mix of foreign policy behavior that should result, I select behavior I want to explain – imperialism and World War I – and attempt to ascertain the degree to which the spirit is implicated. Toward this end, I focus on the political–social structure of European society, especially that of Germany, to show how the need for self-esteem was deflected outwards in the form of international competition and willingness to use force in defense of the national "honor." This dynamic, I contend, was the most important underlying cause of imperialism and World War I.

[20] Joll, *1914*, pp. 11–12.

Superficially, my arguments resemble those of Joseph Schumpeter, who attributes war to the power of the aristocracy and its premodern values. He dismisses aristocratic values as "atavistic," in contrast to those of appetite, which he contends are more "rational" and peace-oriented. I maintain that there was considerable diversity in the responses of European aristocrats to modernity, just as there was among the middle classes in their response to the aristocracy and its values. The most aggressive policies were pursued by countries where (1) there was a sizeable middle class; (2) a significant portion of that class became semi-feudalized; and (3) aristocrats with premodern values dominated the government. These conditions were most evident in Germany and Austria, less so in France and Russia (for different reasons) and least evident in Great Britain.

I have a more fundamental objection to Schumpeter. I reject any formulation that evaluates one motive (appetite in his case) as by definition preferable to another, and defines reason solely in reference to that motive and its expected behavioral manifestations. As we have seen, appetite, spirit and fear each has its own logic and associated behavioral expressions, and human action and rationalism must be assessed with reference to all three motives. Behavior intended to build or enhance self-esteem cannot be evaluated in terms of the implications for material well-being, and vice versa. Appetite and spirit also have different implications for risk-taking, as does fear. In the last section of the chapter I describe these differences and show how they offer a nice account for the variation in risk-taking evident among the European great powers in 1914. This pattern suggests a reformulation, or at least an extension, of prospect theory, which until now has been entirely based on appetite-driven choices.

The modern mind

One of the defining features of modernity is the salience of personality and the psyche. The heroes of Greek tragedies and the major figures in the histories of Herodotus and Thucydides are archetypes who embody different combinations of strengths and weaknesses. Little, if anything, is ever said about their personalities or idiosyncrasies because the central convention of fifth-century Greek epic poetry, tragedy and prose is to show the typicality, not the uniqueness, of characters and the situations they confront. The tragic heroes of Shakespeare and Goethe also act out moral philosophies, and reveal the nature of evil and virtue in the course of confronting dangers and challenges. They differ from their classical predecessors in having distinctive personalities and inner lives, which are thoroughly explored and exploited to drive the narrative forward. The modern novel goes a step further and often reverses the traditional relationship between plot and characters by using situations and plot line to expose the inner lives, tensions and contradictions of their characters. This tendency is particularly evident in post-Freudian literature.

Despite its abiding fascination with the human mind, modernity has impoverished our understanding of the psyche. The process began with Descartes, who not only disembodied the mind, but purged it of the higher goals posited by Plato and Aristotle.[21] Rejection of Aristotelian *telos* (the end something is intended to achieve, and how that end accounts for its development) paved the way for modern social science by focusing attention on immediate instead of final causation. Reason was accordingly reduced from an end in itself to a means, to "the slave of the passions" in the words of David Hume.[22] Max Weber coined the term "instrumental reason" to capture this transformation.

Many Enlightenment philosophers and writers rejected the spirit as an independent drive. They were moved by political as well as philosophical concerns. The classical understanding of the spirit associated it with the quest for honor and glory, generally achieved through prowess on the battlefield. A long line of prominent writers, among them Thomas Aquinas and Dante, condemned glory-seeking as sinful, but the tradition remained alive, in practice and literature, and reached its apotheosis in the writings of Machiavelli, Hobbes and Corneille. "Demolition of the hero" was a major seventeenth-century project; writers like La Rochefoucauld, Racine and Pascal sought to discredit glory-seeking as crass self-interest, self-love and an escape from the real world.[23] Pursuit of honor and glory was associated with the aristocracy, and provided a justification for its authority based on administrative and military service to the state. In the eighteenth century, devaluation of the spirit – indeed its eradication as a category of the psyche – became part and parcel of the strategy of the rising bourgeoisie to undercut the authority of the aristocracy. The only remaining drive was appetite, to which the bourgeoisie catered.

These conceptual changes were accompanied and made possible by a fundamental philosophical and psychological transformation. Traditional conceptions of morality were based on obedience to external authorities: church, state and paterfamilias. During the seventeenth and

---

[21] Lakoff and Johnson, *Philosophy in the Flesh*, pp. 337–40, 400–14.

[22] Hume, *A Treatise of Human Nature*, 2.3.3.4, and *An Inquiry Concerning the Principles of Morals*, appendix I, p. 163.

[23] Lafond, *La Rochefoucauld, Augustinisme et littérature*.

eighteenth centuries, there was a general assault on these authorities and their self-serving claims that they were essential to maintaining order.[24] Enlightenment philosophers conceived of morality as self-governance, which in turn provided the justification for people to assume control of their lives in a wide range of domains. Reid, Bentham and Kant are all major figures in this development. The strongest formulation of the argument may once again be that of Rousseau, who exclaimed in *Émile* that "the heart receives laws only from itself."[25] He was also the most optimistic, believing, in contrast to the ancient philosophers and their modern disciples, that entire peoples could be made virtuous through education. Virtue for Rousseau was no longer defined in terms of compliance with external norms, but their internalization as part of a transformative project.

The reformulation of the psyche brought about by modernity is nicely captured by the Freudian model of the mind, which integrates appetite, instrumental reason and internalized restraint. At the core is the libido, which is the repository of all psychic energy. It generates sexual urges and other appetites, as well as perception, imagination and thought processes. The ego embodies reason and mediates between the impulses of the libido and the external environment. The superego is the site of self-governance and constrains and channels the outward flow of libidinal energy. It performs a useful function for the individual and the society by constraining certain impulses, channeling others into socially acceptable outlets and generally maintaining order. Freud reasoned that too strong or too weak a superego are both dangerous. The former prevents libidinal energy from finding release, leading to a situation where, like water behind a dam, it will find some way to break through, often in dramatic fashion. He offered the euphoria that greeted the outbreak of war in 1914 as an example, and interpreted it as a response to the overly repressive Victorian superego.[26] The latter fails to restrain or properly channel the libido, leading to the kind of behavior that threatens the social order.

Not all moderns went along with the parsimonious reformulation of the psyche. Rousseau sought to refute Hobbes's claim that all human behavior is driven by self-interest. He describes sympathy as an important motive, as does Adam Smith. Rousseau embeds his theory of human motives in a historical account of the emotional and cognitive development of humankind. He posits three stages: savage, primitive (both part

---

[24] Schneewind, *The Invention of Autonomy*, p. 4; Taylor, *Sources of the Self*, p. 83.
[25] Rousseau, *Émile*, p. 234.   [26] Freud, *Beyond the Pleasure Principle*, pp. 49–50.

of the state of nature) and civilized. Man is driven by *amour de soi* (love of self) and *identification* (pity and sympathy) in his original, savage state. *Amour de soi*, which man shares with animals, is a prerational instinct for survival, tempered by pity for the suffering of others. For want of reason, primitive man is "always yielding to the first feeling of humanity."[27] Primitive man is distinguished by his ability to think and reflect. Comparative modifiers creep into his vocabulary as he compares himself to other people and recognizes that others make comparisons to him. Those who excel in the various comparative categories gain standing and self-esteem. Standing now becomes the dominant goal, and *amour propre* (the passion to be regarded favorably by others) becomes the principal motive for human actions. Material goods are valued in so far as they contribute to this end.[28] Slights and insults are intolerable because they are interpreted as contempt for one's person and "more unbearable than the harm itself." Vengeance becomes terrible, and men turn "bloodthirsty and cruel." Civilized man is also moved by *amour propre*, but a subtle yet important transformation occurs. His cognitive faculties increase, and his calculations and goals become correspondingly more complex. He is driven to postpone gratification for long periods of time, if not endlessly, in the pursuit of affluence. Whereas savage man sought esteem directly, civilized man seeks it indirectly, through the attainment and display of material possessions.[29]

Rousseau's concept of *amour propre* and its manifestation in the competitive search for standing bears more than a passing resemblance to the ancient Greek conception of the spirit. His primitive man would be at home in a traditional honor culture. Like many moderns, Rousseau collapses the motives of appetite and spirit into one category, but unlike most of his contemporaries, he makes the spirit dominant. He differs from the ancients in his understanding of reason. Thucydides, Plato and Aristotle admired reason (the motive) because they thought it had the potential to restrain and educate the spirit and appetite. Rousseau holds reason responsible for *amour propre* and the resulting quest for respect and esteem. It is not a faculty to be admired, but one that increasingly distances man from his real nature. For the Greeks, the spirit was an original and natural part of the psyche. For Rousseau, it is an artificial passion inspired by reflection.[30]

[27] Rousseau, *Discourse on the Origin and Foundation of Inequality among Men*, pp. 115–16.
[28] Ibid., pp. 147–60.   [29] Ibid., pp. 174–5.   [30] Rousseau, *Émile*, p. 213.

Rousseau's *Social Contract* can be read as a normative response to the sorry state of modern man depicted in his *Discourse on the Origin of Inequality*. It is impossible to return to a primitive, let alone savage, state of nature. However, politics and reason – which here has a positive role – can restore our freedom, reconcile us to who we really are and teach us to live together in peace. This can only happen when free and equal persons come together and organize themselves into a community aimed at advancing the collective welfare, and make policy with reference to the "general will," not merely the "will of all." Individual wills reflect individual interests, but the general will, once formed, is directed towards the common good, as it is collectively understood. It has the potential to create and sustain a community similar to Aristotle's conception of a *homonoia*.[31]

Adam Smith advances a strikingly similar argument in *The Theory of Moral Sentiments*.[32] In modern commercial society, people work very hard to obtain material possessions out of all proportion to any physical need. They do so because they are driven by vanity to gain the esteem and admiration of others. We better our condition "to be observed, to be attended to, to be taken notice of with sympathy, complacency, and approbation."[33] Material goods are a means of acquiring "attention," "approbation," "respect," and "rank."[34] Smith is describing the same kind of vanity that Rousseau attributes to *amour propre*, and like Rousseau he considers such behavior corrupting because it compels people to debase themselves in the process of seeking favors from others. It also inspires envy, which Smith considers the most serious threat to the social–political order. Most disturbing of all, the attainment of wealth does not make human beings any happier.[35]

Rousseau and Smith differ from most moderns, not in their reduction of the psyche, but in subsuming appetite to spirit rather than the other way around. Thorstein Veblen makes a similar argument. By the end of the nineteenth century, he observed, wealth had not only become "the definitive basis of esteem," but "a conventional basis for reputability." It was now regarded as "intrinsically honourable and confers honour on its

---

[31] Rousseau, *Du contrat social*, ch. 3, pp. 252–3.
[32] Force, *Self-Interest before Adam Smith*, pp. 157–64, lays out the parallels. For thoughtful commentaries on Smith, see Winch, *Riches and Poverty*; Hont and Ignatieff, *Wealth and Virtue*; Griswold, *Adam Smith and the Virtues of Enlightenment*; Rothschild, *Economic Sentiments*; Wood, *Adam Smith*; Hont, *Jealousy of Trade*.
[33] Smith, *The Theory of Moral Sentiments*, I.iii.2, p. 71.   [34] Ibid., VI.i, pp. 310–12.
[35] Ibid., IV.i, pp. 257–68.

possessor."[36] The automobile, as Sinclair Lewis understood, became the perfect status symbol because of its visibility and the many graduations of cost and style in which it was produced. A passage from his 1922 novel, *Babbitt*, describes a conversation between his children about cars and indicates the extent to which advertising had imparted a romantic aura to them that evoked images of chivalry and a world in which honor was imagined to have been a central value.

> They went, with ardor and some thoroughness, into the matters of stream-line bodies, hill-climbing power, wire wheels, chrome steel, ignition systems, and body colors. It was much more than a study of transportation. It was an aspiration for knightly rank. In the city of Zenith, in the barbarous twentieth century, a family's motor indicated its social rank as precisely as the grades of the peerage determined the rank of an English family – indeed, more precisely, considering the opinion of old country families upon newly created brewery barons and woolen-mill viscounts. The details of precedence were never officially determined. There was no court to decide whether the second son of a Pierce Arrow limousine should go in to dinner before the first son of a Buick roadster, but of their respective social importance there was no doubt; and where Babbitt as a boy aspired to the presidency, his son Ted aspired to a Packard twin-six and an established position in the motored gentry.[37]

Veblen is best known for his concept of conspicuous consumption, which describes expenditures and activities that are costly in money or time and have little practical payoff. The more wasteful the expenditure of money or time the more prestige it confers. Two of the author's passionate interests – classics and amateur athletics – are offered by Veblen as prime examples of activities that confer status because they are "a prodigious waste of time."[38] Veblen understands that his views represent a complete repudiation of the Aristotelian understanding of the value of leisure. "From the Greek philosophers to the present," he writes, "a degree of leisure and of exemption from contact with such industrial processes as serve the immediate everyday purposes of human life has ever been recognised by thoughtful men as a prerequisite to a worthy or beautiful, or even a blameless, human life."[39] Now the life of idleness is an end in itself and a means of gaining stature in the eyes of others. As society develops, however, purposeless leisure is increasingly held in ill-repute,

---

[36] Veblen, *Theory of the Leisure Class*, p. 29.   [37] Lewis, *Babbitt*, pp. 74–5.
[38] Veblen, *Theory of the Leisure Class*, pp. 75, 92, 112, 396–7.
[39] Ibid., pp. 37–8 for the quote, and 43.

making it necessary to engage in all kinds of activities, like charities, that are non-productive but socially worthwhile ways of passing one's time.[40]

Veblen knew that modern man confronts a problem Greeks did not. In the ancient world, and until very recent times, only a small percentage of people were wealthy in even the richest societies. When affluence and leisure become commonplace, they can no longer serve effectively as markers of standing. New ways must be found to distinguish old from new wealth. By the end of the twentieth century, even this distinction had all but disappeared, but wealth and its display remain the primary source of standing. This social reality is nicely captured by the bumper sticker, occasionally found on yachts or other expensive conveyances: "He who dies with the most toys wins."

The social transformation described by Rousseau, Smith and Veblen met with considerable resistance, especially in Europe, where the aristocracy remained a powerful, or at least influential, class. Elements of the aristocracy, in alliance with the Roman Catholic Church and conservative intellectuals, fought a rearguard action to uphold the spirit and the values of service and sacrifice associated with it, and to denigrate the appetite and the "crass" pursuit of Mammon. To some degree, this discourse was self-serving because it justified the special privileges, political, legal and social, from which the aristocracy still benefited.

This discourse can be put in a broader perspective that relates it back to the theory of history I outlined toward the end of chapter 2. To do this it needs to be conjoined with changing Western conceptions of wealth. But let us start with the development that parallels the depreciation of the spirit: the upgrading of appetite as beneficial for human beings and their society. The key conceptual innovation associated with this transformation was the insight that collective consequences of individual behavior might be different from what any individual envisaged or intended. It is central to the writings of thinkers as diverse as Pascal, Vico, Mandeville and Smith. "Out of ferocity, avarice, and ambition," Vico writes, "society makes national defense, commerce, and politics, and thereby causes the strength, the wealth, and the wisdom of the republics."[41] Mandeville argues that greed and pride stimulate the passion for material goods and luxury and have the potential to transform them from a "private vice" into "publick benefits."[42] Pascal wonders at the ability of human beings

---

[40] Ibid., pp. 96–7.   [41] Vico, *New Science*, para. 132, p. 20.
[42] Mandeville, *The Fable of the Bees*, I, p. 51; II, p. 78.

"to tease out of concupiscence an admirable arrangement."[43] Adam Smith uses the term "Invisible Hand," previously associated with divine intervention, to describe the ways in which the interests of society are served by individual behavior motivated by self-interest.[44]

The strongest support for the beneficial effects of capitalism came from Montesquieu and his Scottish Jacobite protégé and mercantilist economist Sir James Steuart.[45] The "Montesquieu–Steuart doctrine," as Hirschman dubs it, rested on the premise that passion can be checked by opposing another passion to it. Montesquieu provides a paradigmatic example of countervailing passions in his *Spirit of the Laws*, where he describes how greedy kings robbed Jewish merchants and sent them into exile. The merchants invented the bill of exchange to protect their property, and effectively made it impossible for rapacious leaders to expropriate their property. By facilitating the movement of goods and money, the bill of exchange provided an enormous boon to commerce and the development of capitalism.[46] This conception of self-interest, Hirschman contends, was originally applied to rulers, but was gradually expanded, as the Montesquieu example illustrates, to explain group and individual behavior.[47]

The interests of individuals, and of states, became increasingly focused on appetite, which, like honor, was initially understood to be relational. From Roman times until the eighteenth century, the conventional wisdom assumed that the world's total wealth was a finite quantity. Adam Smith's *Wealth of Nations* ultimately convinced people that it was expandable thanks to increases in the division of labor. As we observed in the last chapter, Louis XIV was convinced that any increase in Holland's wealth due to its success in the carrying trade would, of necessity, be at France's expense. One of his incentives for going to war against the United Provinces was that a relative increase in its standing with respect to wealth was an insult to a great power like France. Mercantilism, developed by his minister Colbert, was as least as much an expression of the politics of standing as it was of economics.[48]

---

[43] Pascal, *Pensées*, nos. 502, 503.

[44] Smith, *Theory of Moral Sentiments*, IV.i.10, pp. 265–8; *Wealth of Nations*, II.iv.2, p. 427.

[45] Force, *Self-Interest before Adam Smith*, pp. 135–68.

[46] Montesquieu, *The Spirit of the Laws*, book XXI, p. 389; Hirschman, *Passions and Interests*, pp. 72–4.

[47] Hirschman, *Passions and Interests*, pp. 113, 117–20, 123–4, 128.

[48] Ames, *Colbert, Mercantilism, and the French Quest for Asian Trade*; Hont, *Jealousy of Trade*, pp. 21–3, 78–9, 115–23.

Even after intellectuals and political leaders came to understand that the division of labor and access to new sources of raw materials and energy could expand the sum total of wealth, the link between wealth and standing remained for the reasons that Rousseau and Smith identified. In effect, the legitimation of appetite, and especially of material possessions, made it an increasingly acceptable arena for competition, by states as well as individuals. The renewed interest in colonial expansion in the second half of the nineteenth century is an expression of this development. It was not driven by the search for wealth, as Lenin and his followers contend. Political authorities in all the major powers recognized that colonial expansion was a drain, not a gain; it benefited some investors and businesses at the expense of the national economy as a whole. Competition for colonies, and efforts to paint the globe red (Britain), green (French), brown (Holland), yellow (Spain), orange (Portugal) and blue (Germany), were struggles for standing. The more money colonies cost, the more attractive they became for some because of their greater significance as status symbols. Many Germans were desperate to get colonies for this reason, even out-of-the-way chunks of land of little economic value.

The story, of course, does not end here. Colonies were to lose their appeal after World War II, in large part because local opposition and uprisings made it them too costly to maintain. Other markers developed to take their place, among them national airlines, hosting the Olympics, nuclear weapons and space programs. They too had the virtue of being expensive and the nuclear weapons and space programs were dependent on the kind of technology and organization that only large rich states possessed. As the century progressed, first national airlines, then nuclear weapons became more widely accessible. The non-proliferation regime, usually treated as a means of reducing the likelihood of nuclear war, can also be understood as an effort by the "club" of nuclear powers to limit membership, making their possession of these weapons more valuable in terms of the status they confer.

Growing wealth among the developed countries, the increase in the number of developed countries and the greater wealth within countries is gradually bringing us to the stage of history where wealth is beginning to lose its value as a marker of standing, almost regardless of the means of its expression. I noted in chapter 2, that these means become increasingly arcane – jeans with diamond studs being my favorite example. There are strong incentives to abandon wealth as a marker, that is to disaggregate appetite and spirit, and find new forms of competition for honor and standing.

Imperialism

The merging of spirit and appetite Rousseau and Smith were describing was a social transformation that had already begun in Western Europe. In politics, it was evident in the ways leaders and their states sought legitimacy at home and standing abroad. In the previous chapter we observed how display became increasingly prominent in European courts, especially that of Louis XIV. He set a trend that was imitated elsewhere in Europe. Although the term "conspicuous consumption" would not be invented for another 150 years, the practice was well established in the first half of the eighteenth century. Kings and princes not only competed with one another in building lavish palaces, churches and extensive gardens, but went deeply into serious debt to do so. This practice continued into the nineteenth century, but the focus of spending shifted to public buildings, and from conquest in Europe to empire overseas. As we will see, the imperial project sometimes brought together opponents and proponents of modernity. For the former, it was a grand project that sought *gloire* and gave meaning to life in addition to serving parochial political ends. For many of the latter, it was a vicarious means of buttressing their self-esteem through close identification with a powerful nation.

Imperialism is generally understood to be the expansion of a state beyond its borders with the goal of establishing a formal or informal empire.[49] European imperialism has a long history, dating back to the Middle Ages when crusaders established colonies in what they called the Holy Land. Overseas expansion began again in earnest in the fifteenth century when Portuguese and Spanish caravels ventured out into the Atlantic and worked their way down the coast of Africa. In the next two centuries, European powers occupied or established their control over vast tracts of the Americas and Asia. Imperialism is considered to have entered a new phase between 1870 and 1914, as European powers, joined by the United States and Japan, sought to divide up much of the rest of the available world among themselves. They penetrated into the hinterlands of many areas, particularly in Africa, in which they had previously been content to control coastal strips. Britain, France, Germany, Portugal and Belgium made inroads in Africa, Russia in the Caucasus and Far East, France, Britain and Japan on the Asian coastal rim, and Britain, Germany, Japan and the United States in the Pacific.

---

[49] Porter, *European Imperialism*, p. 2.

The "new imperialism" had multiple reinforcing causes. The industrial revolution and related advances in science, technology, medicine and administration removed many of the constraints on European expansion or penetration of African and Asian hinterlands. Among the positive incentives, Paul Schroeder includes "great power competition, the pull of the periphery, the breakdown of traditional regimes and societies, the push of local imperialisms, men on the spot, turbulent frontiers, the white man's burden and manifest destiny, racism, the struggle for markets, the patterns of European economic development and competition, imperialism as a lightning rod for European energies."[50] We must be wary of monocausal explanations because, as Robinson and Gallagher warn: "The gaudy empires spatch-cocked together in Asia and Africa . . . were linked only obliquely to the expansive impulses of Europe."[51] I want to unravel one important thread of this complex skein: social imperialism. It consists of efforts by politicians to mobilize middle- and working-class support for colonial expansion as a means of maintaining the power and privileges of the landed aristocracy. Analyses of social imperialism routinely frame it as a question of elite politics and direct our attention to the variety of domestic incentives that led politicians like Disraeli, Bismarck and Bülow to embrace colonial projects. They tend to ignore the other side of the equation: the conditions that made middle- and working-class opinion so receptive to appeals that were so obviously at odds with their economic and political interests. Most studies also overlook the fact that in some countries, most notably Germany, the colonial project was pushed strongly and independently by lobby groups with largely middle-class memberships.[52] Imperialism was at least as much a "bottom-up" as it was a "top-down" project.

Middle- and working-class enthusiasm for colonialism is best understood as an expression of the spirit. It was an important means by which

---

[50] Schroeder, "International Politics, Peace and War."

[51] Robinson and Gallagher, *Africa and the Victorians*, p. 5; Fieldhouse, *Economics and Empire*, for a similar view. Louis, *Imperialism*, for a critical review of the Robinson and Gallagher thesis.

[52] We must be careful about our understanding of the term "middle class," which in Germany is used to describe strands of society generally on the basis of their putative socioeconomic interests. *Der Mittelstand, die Mittelschicht, das Bürgertum* encompass what we refer to in English as the middle class. The lower middle class, or *Kleinbürgertum*, includes artisans, shopkeepers and salaried employees on the lower rungs of the ladder. Fundamentally, all of these groups, like their English middle-class equivalents, exist somewhere between the working and upper classes. Support for imperialism came more from the professional and intellectual representatives of the middle class.

members of new classes, largely excluded from the arenas in which honor and standing could be achieved, sought to build or enhance self-esteem. The starting point of my argument is the continuing dominance of the nobility in European politics, especially in foreign and military affairs, where it helped to transform honor and standing from class into national goals. The European bourgeoisie did not behave as Marx expected; its members often placed social over class interests, assimilated many aristocratic ambitions and accepted their leadership of foreign policy. This novel and largely unexpected alignment, as Weber noted, allowed the aristocracy to maintain its privileges, and in some countries its power, in the face of the twin political and economic challenges of working-class democracy and finance capital allied to export-oriented industry.[53] Imperialism was an expression of the partial "feudalization" of the European middle classes that encouraged them to buttress their self-esteem through the competitive achievements of their respective nations. As in more traditional honor societies, it made them angry in the Aristotelian sense of the term when their nation was checked or challenged, and correspondingly willing to resort to force in its defense.

In 1835, Tocqueville recognized that the increasingly positive emphasis on self-interest by philosophers was indicative of the extent to which equality had become the hallmark of modernity, in theory as well as practice. Modern people, he writes in *Democracy in America*, have an "ardent, insatiable, eternal and invincible passion for equality; they want equality in liberty and, if they cannot obtain it they still want it in slavery. They will suffer poverty, enslavement, barbarity, but will not suffer the aristocracy." Only republican governments, he maintains, can gain legitimacy in the modern age.[54] In 1815, all of the great powers were aristocracies or kingdoms, and the Holy Alliance was committed to maintaining the constitutional status quo. By the end of the century, three of the European powers (France, Britain and Italy) were republics or constitutional monarchies. Germany was a mixed regime, and under growing pressure to democratize further. Russia, Austria-Hungary and the Porte were autocratic empires ruled by monarchs, but in five years Russia would be shaken by revolution, and none of the three empires survived past 1918. Outside Europe, the United States, the world's largest democracy, and had just become a great power. Fulfilling Tocqueville's prediction, the United

---

[53] Weber, *Economy and Society*, II, pp. 920–1.
[54] Tocqueville, *Democracy in America*, II.2.1, p. 482.

States and the Soviet Union were destined to become the world's first superpowers.[55]

As Tocqueville expected, aristocracies were everywhere on the defensive in the second half of the nineteenth century. They developed a range of strategies to preserve their authority and privileges. One of the most successful was "social imperialism." Austrian socialist Karl Renner may have been the first to use this term, but it quickly became commonplace among socialists and left-liberals. Building on John Hobson, Hilferding and Lenin, Renner wrote about the efforts of *Finanzkapital* to provide a mass base for imperialism, from which it profited.[56] Franz Neumann later applied the argument to the Nazi regime.[57] All these treatises account for imperialism in terms of the economic interests of leading classes, although some of them also note its utility in mobilizing working-class support for the existing order.[58]

There is little evidence that the more developed sectors of European capitalism supported imperialism. Industrialists, like diplomats, on the whole considered colonialism wasteful of resources and risking unnecessary conflict with other powers. Numerous studies indicate that trade, and even more, investment, were largely between major colonial powers, or between them and developing countries like the United States and Argentina, not between metropoles and their colonies.[59] Imperialism was much more the policy of traditional conservative elites, army and navy officers in search of adventure and promotion, and nationalist intellectuals and businesses with specific colonial interests.

There is more evidence for the political utility of imperialism to the governing elite. In Britain, imperialism was combined with efforts to reconcile the working class to the factory system by mitigating some of its worst evils. Benjamin Disraeli, who initially denounced colonies as "a millstone around our neck," later embraced imperialism as a means of binding the middle and working classes to the landed aristocracy and the

[55] Ibid., I, 2.10, pp. 395–6.

[56] Hobson, *Imperialism*; Hilferding, *Finanzkapital*; Renner, *Marxismus, Krieg und Internationale*; Lenin, *Imperialism*; Neumann, *Behemoth*, pp. 153–5.

[57] Hilferding, *Finanzkapital*.

[58] Hobson, *Imperialism*, stressed the role of England's anachronistic political structure that permitted the upper classes to use the institutions of state to advance their parochial economic interests. See also Luxemburg, *The Accumulation of Capital*.

[59] Feis, *Europe: The World's Banker*; Fieldhouse, *Economics and Empire*; David and Hutenback, *Mammon and the Pursuit of Empire*; Edelstein, *Overseas Investments in the Age of High Imperialism*; Offner, "Costs and Benefits, Prosperity and Security, 1870–1914"; Platt, *Britain's Investment Overseas on the Eve of the First World War*.

political status quo.[60] He sought to expand the arena in which competition for standing took place. It was now the nation, he reasoned, that competed against other nations and peoples. As Britain ruled over a larger empire and more diverse lot of peoples and "races" than any other power, Englishmen in the middle or even at the bottom of the social hierarchy at home could enhance their self-esteem by imagining themselves at the top of a global hierarchy. In his famous Crystal Palace speech of 1872, Disraeli committed himself to an ambitious program of colonial expansion. His carefully staged incorporation of India into the British Empire in 1877 and the crowning of Queen Victoria as Empress of India aroused enormous enthusiasm. Combined with a far-reaching extension of suffrage, welfare legislation and recognition of trade unions, imperialism led to large Tory electoral gains.

Disraeli's opponent, William Gladstone, leader of the free-trade Liberals, had also opposed imperialism at first but subsequently had little choice but to embrace it. Responding to public pressure and circumstances, Gladstone asserted British authority over Egypt in 1882.[61] By the 1890s, liberal imperialism was a powerful force, and its leader, Joseph Chamberlain, justified it as necessary to maintain Britain as a great power. In 1897, he argued that "the tendency of the time is to throw all power into the hands of the greater empires, and the minor kingdoms . . . seem destined to fall into a secondary and subordinate place."[62]

Charles Morazé calls the period between 1848 and 1870 in France the age of *les bourgeois conquérants* (the triumphant bourgeoisie).[63] While there is much truth to this claim, the nobility kept their lands and continued to staff key positions in the church, army and civil service throughout the Restoration and the Empire, as it would under the Third Republic (1871–1940) and the Vichy regime (1940–4). Noble families would not have survived as a class without constant replenishment from the bourgeoisie. Many *grande bourgeoisie* families simply added the particle "de" to their names and maintained the fiction of being aristocratic long enough and with sufficient panache to be accepted. Others were coopted through intermarriage. The traditional nobility eschewed investments in industry as opposed to land, and sent their sons into the church, the army and

---

[60] Malmesbury, *Memoirs of an Ex-Minister*, p. 343, for the quote. McKenzie and Silver, *Angels in Marble*; Feuchtwanger, *Disraeli, Democracy and the Tory Party*; Smith, *Disraelian Conservatism and Social Reform*; Semmel, *Imperialism and Social Reform*.

[61] Cain and Hopkins, *British Imperialism*, pp. 312–17.

[62] *Mr. Chamberlain's Speeches*, II, p. 5, quoted in Mommsen, *Theories of Imperialism*, p. 6.

[63] Morazé, *Les bourgeois conquérants*.

high-status ministries. A sizeable percentage of the nobility nevertheless invested in commercial enterprises, either openly or through individuals and groups that fronted for them.[64] The majority of the middle class remained untitled and more connected to the capitalist economy, but largely accepted aristocratic social values even if they were staunchly republican in their political outlook. There was little sign of emerging class consciousness among the French bourgeoisie.[65]

The foreign policy of Napoleon III (emperor from 1852 to 1870) reflected the deep tensions between the republican left and the monarchist right, which would dominate French politics down to the end of World War II. He embraced imperialism in an effort to placate both groupings, appealing to their mutual desires for national glory. France expanded its presence in Algeria and established protectorates over Indochina and Senegal. Imperialism was supported by special economic sectors, the military, expansionist bureaucrats in the ministry of colonies and many members of the middle class who were desperate for successes for the *grande nation* in the aftermath of its humiliating defeat at Sedan in 1870.[66] In the late 1870s, the Opportunists came to power, a conservative, bourgeois faction of the republican movement committed to economic development and overseas expansion. They were able to exploit the weak state to advance their colonial project.[67]

In contrast to Britain, preindustrial values continued to thrive in France. Many members of the landed aristocracy felt threatened by capitalism, republicanism and the spirit of equality, all of which resulted in declining deference and the erosion of class barriers between themselves and the rich bourgeoisie. Like their British counterparts, they attempted to outflank their bourgeois republican opposition, but their strategy had a much harder edge. They allied with conservative members of the upper bourgeoisie, the army and the church, and made appeals to the artisan

[64] Blanning, *Pursuit of Glory*, p. 108, notes that such investment began in earnest after French nobles were allowed to own ships and engage in overseas trade in 1629. After 1701, they were allowed to engage in any form of wholesale trade without losing their noble status.

[65] Cobban, *The Social Interpretation of the French Revolution*; Forster, "The Survival of the Nobility during the French Revolution"; Moore, *Social Origins of Dictatorship and Democracy*, p. 51; Lucas, "Nobles, Bourgeois and the Origins of the French Revolution"; Nye, *Masculinity and Male Codes of Honor in Modern France*.

[66] Brunschwig, *French Colonialism, 1871–1914*, pp. 182–3.

[67] Andrew, Grupp and Kanya-Forstner, "Le mouvement colonial française et ses principales personnalités," "French Business and French Colonialists," and "The *groupe coloniale* in the French Chamber of Deputies"; Brunschwig, "Le parti coloniale français," and *French Colonialism, 1871–1914*; Marseille, *Empire colonial et capitalisme français*; Wesseling, *Divide and Rule*, pp. 13–14.

class and rural population on the basis of race, nationalism and the glory of empire. Their proclaimed enemies were the Jews and the socialists, often lumped together and hated for their cosmopolitanism and embrace of the Enlightenment and its political and social values. They were at least as hostile to Britain, the historical enemy and source of liberal, capitalist values, as they were to Germany, the occupier of Alsace and Lorraine.[68] The establishment of a protectorate over Tunisia in 1881 has been rightly described as a form of social imperialism intended to appease the middle classes and consolidate class rule.[69]

From 1871 on, two rival perspectives, one continentalist and the other colonialist, both with important aristocratic representation, vied for control of the foreign policy of the French Republic. The continentalists, centered in the foreign ministry, were wary of colonial expansion, convinced that it diverted resources from the nation's important objective, the containment of Germany. It also courted conflict with Britain, with whom they favored rapprochement, and considered, along with Russia, a counterweight to German power. The colonialists, dominant in the colonial ministry and the navy, considered colonial empire the sine qua non of national greatness. They looked to Germany to strengthen France's hand in its struggle with Britain, its long-standing competitor overseas. The struggle between these ministries came to a head in the Fashoda crisis of 1898. With the backing of the *groupe coloniale*, the colonial ministry had persuaded the Chamber of Deputies to allocate funds for a mission to travel overland from West Africa to the Sudan. The ministry and Comité de l'Afrique insisted that control of the Sudan would fulfill their dream of a French empire stretching from the Atlantic coast to Somalia. On 10 July 1898, Captain Jean-Baptiste Marchand, in command of a French expeditionary force, hoisted the tricolor on the banks of the White Nile at Fashoda in defiance of British warnings that French penetration of the Sudan would constitute a "hostile act." Before the crisis was resolved by Marchand's withdrawal, France and Britain came within a hair's breadth of war.[70]

---

[68] Brunschwig, *French Colonialism, 1871–1914*, pp. 182–3.
[69] Elwitt, *The Making of the Third Republic*, pp. 290–2. Lebovics, *The Alliance of Iron and Wheat in the Third Republic*.
[70] Persell, *The French Colonial Lobby*, pp. 7–24, 54–74; Brown, *Fashoda Reconsidered*; Newbury, "The Development of French Policy in the Lower and Upper Niger"; Leaman, "The Influence of Domestic Policy upon Foreign Affairs in France"; Sanderson, *England, Europe, and the Upper Nile*; Lebow, *Between Peace and War*, pp. 73–4.

In September 1898, as the Fashoda crisis neared its dénouement, the Dreyfus Affair also entered its most acute phase following the revelations of the *faux Henri* on 31 August. The two crises reinforced each other and brought the country to the brink of civil war. The colonialists were monarchist, pro-clerical and anti-Dreyfusard. The continentalists were pro-Republic, anti-clerical and overwhelmingly Dreyfusard. At issue were competing visions of the destiny of France: one authoritarian, anti-British and expansionist; the other democratic, anti-German and more conscious of the limits of French power. For both sides, the glory of France was important, but the continentalists were not willing to allow this objective to tale precedence over French security. The humiliation of Fashoda and the exposure of the conspiracy against Dreyfus led to the victory of La Défense Republicaine coalition in the 1900 parliamentary election. The new government reduced the term of military service, excluded the church from public education and sought a rapprochement with Britain.[71] The election was only a temporary triumph, as conservative, pro-colonial, anti-British and anti-Semitic forces, linking aristocrats with premodern values with dissatisfied members of the middle and lower agricultural classes, resurfaced in the 1930s. This coalition dominated the Vichy regime and collaborated with Germany in the rounding-up of Jews for transportation to death camps. The National Front of Jean Marie Le Pen has a similar political base.

In Germany it is more difficult to analyze the response of the nobility to modernity in national terms. In Silesia, nobles were generally willing to put money into commercial ventures, and found it easier to accommodate rich bourgeoisie. Elsewhere this was often not the case, and German heavy industry was built almost entirely on a base of foreign investment. In Prussia, the East Elbian nobility – the *Junkers* – expressed nothing but disdain for "money grubbing capitalists," and into the twentieth century their estates were for the most part still run in a precapitalist manner. In his *Wanderungen durch die Mark Brandenburg* ("Travels in the Mark of Brandenburg"), Theodor Fontane portrays the nobility as a class without higher standards or purpose, leading a life of narrow self-interest that revolves around archaic rituals and social customs.[72] Aristocratic greed nevertheless led to an amalgamation through marriage of the young capitalist nobility (*Goldadel*) with the older, landowning nobility

[71] Brown, *Fashoda Reconsidered*, pp. 1–58; Lebow, *Between Peace and War*, pp. 71–4.
[72] Fontane, *Wanderungen durch die Mark Brandenburg*; Mommsen, *Imperial Germany*, pp. 119–20.

(*Grundadel*).[73] Hans Rosenberg argues that this led to a kind of "pseudo-democratization" of the *Junkers*, in which they felt compelled to justify their robust materialism in the rhetoric of idealism and nationalism.[74] It also promoted rapid "feudalization" of rich bankers, merchants and industrialists who sought to compensate for their lack of noble blood by emulating the lifestyle of the nobility.[75] They bought East Elbian estates, rode about in expensive carriages with baronial liveries and hosted elegant dinner parties for ministers and diplomats. In 1873, Gerson Bleichröder, Bismarck's banker, became the first German Jew to be ennobled without first converting to Christianity, and purchased the estate near Potsdam of Field Marshal von Roon, Moltke's chief-of-staff during the wars of unification.[76]

In Germany too, the bourgeoisie failed to achieve the kind of class consciousness Marx expected. Writing about the 1848 Revolution, a much disappointed Marx compared the Prussian bourgeoisie to "an accursed old man, who found himself condemned to lead and mislead the first youthful impulse of a robust people in his own senile interests – sans teeth, sans eyes, sans taste, sans everything."[77] Max Weber offered an equally jaundiced view of the German middle class at the end of the century. He lamented its failure to follow the liberalism of its British counterpart and develop a modern "capitalist" culture to offset the largely feudal culture of the aristocracy.[78] Left critiques of Germany in the twentieth century continued this stress on their country's arrested liberalism and preindustrial traditions.[79]

In the *Iliad*, feelings among equals are characterized by in-group solidarity but also by rivalry and jealousy. Elites regard their social inferiors with contempt, disdain, hostility, or, alternatively, with a sense of

[73] Weber, "Suffrage and Democracy in Germany."
[74] Rosenberg, "Die Pseudodemokratisierung der Rittergutsbesitzerklasse"; Pflanze, *Bismarck and the Development of Germany*, III, pp. 15–16.
[75] See Loen, *Der Adel*, pp. 61–5; Bramsted, *Aristocracy and the Middle Classes in Germany*, II, p. 17.
[76] Pflanze, *Bismarck and the Development of Germany*, II, p. 16; Cecil, "The Creation of Nobles in Prussia"; Stern, *Gold and Iron*, pp. 167–70.
[77] Marx, "The Bourgeoisie and the Counter-Revolution."
[78] Weber, "Die Handelshochschulen," *Berliner Tageblatt*, no. 548, October 27, 1911, quoted in Mommsen, *Max Weber and German Politics*, p. 95.
[79] Rosenberg, *Imperial Germany*; Veblen, *Imperial Germany and the Industrial Revolution*; Gerschenkron, *Economic Backwardness in Historical Perspective*, and *Bread and Democracy in Germany*; Dahrendorf, *Society and Democracy in Germany*; Moore, *Social Origins of Dictatorship and Democracy*. Eley, "The British Model and the German Road," for a critical review.

responsibility or pity. In Germany, the rural nobility was largely une-ducated, coarse and uncultured, while the court nobility tended to be foppish and imitative of everything French. Negative feelings toward the middle class predominated in both groups, and kept alive practices that established social distance and signaled aristocratic superiority. Nobles insisted on precedence at all social occasions where classes mixed, and on the right to wear elegant costumes, including hats with feathers. A noble's word remained equivalent to a statutory declaration.[80]

In post-Napoleonic Germany, aristocratic hatred of the middle class intensified, and was fanned by romanticists like Adam Müller and Friedrich Schlegel who saw the nobility as defenders of traditional Ger-man values against the materialism and destructive equality of the West. Even Goethe's romantic poetry, avidly devoured by the emerging mid-dle class, portrays the nobility in relatively rosy terms while gener-ally being disparaging of the bourgeoisie.[81] Anti-bourgeois sentiment was a European-wide phenomenon, but was especially pronounced in Germany. It reflected the long-standing aristocratic abhorrence of trade and of social inferiors who made money this way. This attitude, as we have seen, can be traced back to the Greeks and Aristotle, and resurfaced in the Middle Ages when a class of wealthy merchants first emerged. In Germany, it was given an additional boost by Luther's depiction of money and profit as evil, an attitude that was still being encouraged by sermons in nineteenth-century Lutheran churches. It was also a byproduct of German idealism and its rejection of Western values, and especially capitalism and its emphasis on profit. In this cultural setting, the middle-class response to the nobility vacillated between feelings of superiority, which found expression in hostility, and inferiority, that prompted emulation and a desire for acceptance.

The German middle class did not begin to organize politically until the 1830s, and did not become a powerful economic force until after 1848. Middle-class political assertiveness reached its peak in the 1860s, when the National Liberals challenged the Prussian monarchy by refus-ing to vote credits for the army. Bismarck successfully divided the Lib-erals by offering them national unification and a laissez-faire economy of scale at the expense of constitutional government. The three wars of German unification against Denmark (1864), Austria (1866) and France

---

[80] Loen, *Der Adel*, p. 232; Goethe, *Wilhelm Meisters Lehrjahre* for a colorful description; Bramsted, *Aristocracy and the Middle Classes in Germany*, pp. 27, 154.
[81] Bramsted, *Aristocracy and the Middle Classes in Germany*, pp. 38–9.

(1870–1) resolved the Prussian constitutional crisis by creating the infamous alliance of "iron and grain" between conservative industrialists and East Elbian landowners. The middle and working classes were effectively excluded from any responsible role in government.[82]

The German Empire, brought into being at Versailles in 1871, was a mixed political system in which parliamentary democracy coexisted uneasily with political privileges reserved for the nobility. The chancellor was appointed by the emperor and responsible to him. Foreign and military policy was also the prerogative of the emperor and not subject to parliamentary review. Even more than in France, the foreign ministry and army remained the preserve of the nobility. The army's stunning victories in the wars of unification, and especially its triumph over France, made it the darling of the middle classes and halted the previously powerful momentum of the liberals. The National Liberal Party lost power in 1874, and made only brief comebacks in 1880 and 1885. The Conservative Party remained dominant for the rest of the century.[83]

Writing in the first decade of the twentieth century, Weber noted that "feudal pretensions" had become widespread among the middle class. Students at universities assimilated the *Junker* sense of honor and "capacity for giving satisfaction" through membership of dueling fraternities. A reserve commission became a highly vaunted status symbol, and the middle-class reserve officer did not so much bring civilian values to the army as help to militarize society.[84] Professors declined in status. They enjoyed high standing among the middle class, but were not acceptable at court. Nor were middle-class wives of nobles, including Bismarck's mother, a professor's daughter. Business and professional activities were still looked down upon by the aristocracy, a feudal attitude that had wider resonance in the society and, judging from memoirs and novels,

[82] Rosenberg, *Imperial Germany*, pp. 5–7; Pflanze, *Bismarck and the Development of Germany*, I, pp. 111–16; III, p. 27.
[83] The German *Sonderweg* – the thesis that Germany's development was different from other European countries – rests on the assumption that modern industrial societies should have liberal, constitutional government, and that Germany's failure to develop one rested in large part with the failure of the liberals in 1848 and the 1860s. This left Germany with sharp contradictions between its social and political structures, which were an underlying cause of aggressive foreign policies in both the Wilhelmine and fascist periods. In addition to the works of Veblen, Dahrendorf and Moore, already cited, see Bracher, *The German Dilemma*; Wehler, *Das deutsche Kaiserreich*.
[84] Weber, "Die Handelschochschulen," *Berliner Tageblatt*, no. 548, October 27, 1911, quoted in Mommsen, *Max Weber and German Politics*, p. 95; Ritter, *Sword and Scepter*, II, pp. 93–104; Mommsen, *Imperial Germany*, p. 120; Pflanze, *Bismarck and the Development of Germany*, III, pp. 17–18.

influenced the self-assessment of many otherwise successful members of the bourgeoisie.[85] Professional and business men increasingly expected to be addressed by their full titles. Commenting on this practice among the Viennese, German novelist Karl Gutzkow reasoned: "It is not politeness that causes people in Austria to address the whole world as 'Herr von So-and-so,' but self defense. It is too oppressing, too humiliating, to appear as a burgher in the midst of this general nobility of birth."[86] By such means, large sections of the German middle class came to terms in effect with the empire and their restricted place within it. In 1917, Walther Rathenau astutely observed that the German aristocracy had controlled the middle class the same way Louis XIV had his nobility, by encouraging admiration and imitation.[87]

In the 1880s, Bismarck sought to repeat his success of the 1860s with a policy of social imperialism. Previously a critic of imperialism, the Iron Chancellor appears to have embraced imperialism as a short-term strategy for creating greater political stability, overcoming an economic downturn and securing markets for export-oriented industry.[88] Social democracy had by now replaced the liberals as the principal threat to authoritarian rule, and taking a page out of Disraeli's play book, he sought to divide the working class through a policy of imperialism and social legislation, as he had the liberals with national unification. Bismarck engineered the passage of the Sickness Insurance Law in 1883, Accident Insurance Laws in 1884–5, and the Old Age Insurance Law in 1889. He was nevertheless a cautious imperialist. Between 1884 and 1886, he acquired Southwest Africa, Togoland, the Cameroons, East Africa and some Pacific islands. Samoa and Kiao-Chow, Germany's economic zone in China, were added later. Bismarck insisted that colonial rule be indirect, through chartered companies that would assume primary financial responsibility for administration and infrastructure. He turned against imperialism when the German government was compelled to assume these costs.[89] General Leo von Caprivi, his successor, also embraced imperialism as a means of "diverting

[85] Bramsted, *Aristocracy and the Middle Classes in Germany*, pp. 150–99, 228–70.

[86] Karl Gutzkow, *Gesammelte Werke*, III, p. 329, quoted in Bramsted, *Aristocracy and the Middle Classes in Germany*, p. 191.

[87] Walther Rathenau, *Von kommenden Dingen*, p. 273, quote in Bramsted, *Aristocracy and the Middle Classes in Germany*, p. 192.

[88] Wehler, *The German Empire*, pp. 170–80; Pflanze, *Bismarck and the Development of Germany*, II, pp. 119–27; Mommsen, *Imperial Germany*, pp. 80–1; Loew, *The Great Powers, Imperialism, and the German Problem*, pp. 95–6.

[89] Wehler, *The German Empire*; Pflanze, *Bismarck and the Development of Germany*; Mommsen, *Imperial Germany*; Loew, *The Great Powers, Imperialism and the German Problem*.

revolutionary elements." He nevertheless antagonized the colonial lobby by arranging with Britain to swap Zanzibar for the North Sea islands of Helgoland (Heligoland).[90]

Wolfgang Mommsen identifies three strands of German imperialism: governmental, radical nationalist and informal economic.[91] Governmental imperialism was associated with Bismarck's short-lived social imperialism, and with Holstein and Bülow's *Weltpolitik*. Bülow proclaimed his *Weltpolitik* in the Reichstag on December 6, 1897 when he demanded equal entitlement (*Gleichberechtigung*) and "a place in the sun" for Germany. Privately, he made it abundantly clear that he envisaged his initiative as a response to domestic political problems; it was intended "to reconcile, pacify, rally, unite."[92] He hoped to rally the support of the bourgeois parties, including the Catholic Zentrum, to slow the growth of social democracy and strengthen governmental authority. Bülow was aware of the risks of too aggressive a foreign policy and his *Weltpolitik* consisted more of flamboyant rhetoric than actual deeds.[93] Otto Pflanze, one of the most astute students of imperial Germany, concludes that colonies "were retained not for economic gain, but as symbols of national pride and power, proof that Germany was a world power (*Weltmacht*) with far-flung possessions and a rival, if not the equal, of Britain, whose achievements had so often in so many ways incited Germans to envy and emulation."[94]

Radical nationalist imperialism was also motivated by a concern for prestige, and found expression in a simple syllogism: Germany is a great power, great powers have empires, Germany deserves an empire. Historian and publicist Heinrich von Treitschke complained that "Up to the present Germany has always had too small a share of the spoils in the partition of non-European territories ... yet our existence as a state of the first rank is vitally affected by the question whether we can become a power beyond the seas."[95] Radical nationalist imperialism in the 1880s was spearheaded by colonial lobby groups like the Pan-German League (Alldeutscher Verband) and the Navy League (Flottenverein). These groups had some backing from traditional elites, including former civil servants and aristocrats, but their leading figures were intellectuals and other upwardly mobile

[90] Nichols, *Germany after Bismarck*, pp. 59, 102–4; Mommsen, *Imperial Germany*, p. 80.
[91] Mommsen, *Theories of Imperialism*, pp. 73–5.
[92] Quoted in Röhl, *Germany without Bismarck*, p. 252.
[93] Mommsen, *Imperial Germany*, p. 81; Kaiser, "Germany and the Origins of the First World War."
[94] Pflanze, *Bismarck and the Development of Germany*, III, p. 141; Herwig, *Germany's Vision of Empire in Venezuela*, p. 242, for a similar assessment.
[95] Treitschke, *Politik*, I, p. 42, quoted in Mommsen, *Theories of Imperialism*, p. 5.

members of the middle class. Between 1897 and 1906, 270 so-called "fleet professors" lobbied on behalf of the navy and its shipbuilding goals.[96] Popularist nationalism, with its lack of restraint or consideration of any other state's interests, had little appeal for the political elite.

Liberal imperialism, which received a better hearing, helped to legitimize imperialism in the eyes of the political elite. It was the project of more temperate nationalists like sociologist Max Weber, political scientist Ernst Francke, and Friedrich Naumann, founder of the weekly magazine *Die Hilfe* (Help). At his inaugural address in Freiburg in 1895, Weber proclaimed: "We must realize that the unification of Germany was a youthful exploit performed by the nation in its old age, at so high a price that it should not have been undertaken if it was to be the end and not the beginning of a policy of turning Germany into a world power."[97] Weber believed that the fate of German culture depended on the success of the nation, and that success required Germany to become a world economic and military power. He favored construction of a large navy, joined the Pan-German League in 1893 and came grudgingly to respect the *Junker* class and Bismarck as agents of Germany's "will to power."[98] After 1895, the *Preussische Jahrbücher*, under the editorship of Max Delbrück, became the principal organ of middle-class intellectuals and an exponent of imperial expansion. Successive chancellors felt an increasing political need to reach some accommodation with both radical and liberal imperialists, and reached out to them through the funding of a blue water navy, despite the tension this caused with Britain. Admiral Tirpitz and the Navy Office, in alliance with the Navy League, effectively channeled nationalist sentiment to their advantage.[99]

Informal imperialism was the result of German trade and investment. In comparison to Britain and France, German investment in their colonies was meager. The great majority of businessmen and bankers had little interest in imperialism. The prevailing view in the business community in the 1890s was that Germany's growing trade, largely with other colonial powers, would be damaged by a policy of imperialism. In contrast to Britain, Germany suffered a chronic capital shortage. The problem was

---

[96] Kehr, "Soziale und finanzielle Grundlagen der Tirpitzschen Flottenpropaganda"; Eley, *Reshaping the German Right*, for the most comprehensive analysis of these pressure groups, their ideologies and influence; Herwig, *"Luxury" Fleet*, p. 2.

[97] Weber, *Gesammelte politische Schriften*, p. 23, quoted in Mommsen, *Theories of Imperialism*, p. 7; Mommsen, *Max Weber and German Politics*, pp. 40–8 for background.

[98] Mommsen, *Max Weber*, pp. 40–84, 139.

[99] Kehr, *Primat der Innenpolitik*, pp. 130–48; Wehler, *The German Empire*, pp. 126; 165–6; Mommsen, *Imperial Germany*, p. 77.

not finding markets for excess capital but attracting foreign investment. The Baghdad Railway, begun in 1888, was an important exception, but the Deutsche Bank actively sought foreign partners for the venture for economic and political reasons.[100]

Eckhart Kehr depicts German *Weltpolitik* as straightforward social imperialism. Hans-Ulrich Wehler and Volker Berghahn maintain that imperialist sentiment and naval construction were encouraged by the conservative ruling elite as a means of preserving the country's class structure by winning support from the middle classes while isolating social democracy. Geoff Eley emphasizes the extent to which radical nationalism after 1900 succeeded in neutralizing popular democratic antagonism to the political system. These authors ignore the extent to which the drive for colonies was a middle-class project, a means by which middle-class intellectuals especially sought to gain the esteem and honor denied to them within Germany. Imperialism may be best understood as a result of unintended consequences. In the early 1880s, Bismarck embraced a policy of social imperialism, and by doing so aroused or fanned enthusiasm among the middle classes for Germany as a world power. Bülow's *Weltpolitik* was as much a response to middle-class demands for German colonial assertiveness as it was an attempt to harness them for his domestic political goals.[101] Conservatives did less well in the polls in the twentieth century, making conservative governments more dependent on the radical right and the middle classes. As we shall see, their weakness would make Chancellor Bethmann Hollweg even more dependent on these groups in 1914.

Rousseau and Smith noted the extent to which appetite and standing increasingly converged in the modern world. Within countries, this was apparent in the upgrading of the social utility of wealth and the recognition and honors accorded to rich bourgeois in Western Europe. Between countries, wealth had always been to some degree linked to standing. Ancient empires engaged in extensive building programs to claim status vis-à-vis other dynasties and empires. In the seventeenth century, conspicuous consumption of this kind reached new levels at the court of Louis XIV, and was emulated elsewhere in Europe. Status symbols

---

[100] Mommsen, *Imperial Germany*, pp. 84–8.
[101] Kehr, *Primat der Innenpolitik*, 149–75; Wehler, *The German Empire*, pp. 165–6, 176–9; Berghahn, *Imperial Germany*, pp. 272–6; Mommsen, *Imperial Germany*, pp. 77, 95; Mayer, "Internal Causes and Purposes of War in Europe," for an earlier statement of the link between domestic politics and aggressive foreign policies. Eley, *Reshaping the German Right*, pp. 356–7.

remained equally important in the eighteenth and nineteenth centuries, but their character had changed dramatically by the last third of the nineteenth century. Palaces, balls and support for the arts remained *de rigueur* for ruling houses, but the standing of the state was increasingly separate from that of its rulers. Museums, theaters, opera houses, monuments commemorating victories and great cultural figures, as well as advances in science, engineering, transportation and public health measures became the accepted currency of national standing. Great powers were also expected to have colonies and fleets. French colonial policy was motivated in addition by efforts to recover status and prestige lost in 1870. The United States laid claim to an entire hemisphere for reasons that had as much to do with prestige as with economics and security.[102] Colonies became the sine qua non of great powership, so Britain and France were emulated by Russia, Japan, Italy, Spain, Portugal, the Netherlands and even Belgium. Among the great powers, Austria-Hungary was the only exception. It did attempt to expand in the Balkans, but for different reasons.

Empire was widely recognized as expensive; it was only a money-making proposition for those businesses with a direct interest in the colonies, and they frequently made their profit at the expense of metropolitan society as a whole. Even more costly than empire were the fleets that made them possible. In Germany's case, naval construction became another important symbol of *Weltpolitik*, and was pursued beyond any reasonable commercial need and at considerable strategic risk, as it provoked an otherwise avoidable conflict with Britain. In 1907 Germany spent about 291 million marks on its fleet, and between 1897 and 1914 naval shipbuilding added 1,040,700,000 marks to the national debt.[103] Imperialism was the ultimate nineteenth-century expression of conspicuous consumption, a kind of mega-potlatch, from which, we will see, none of the players felt capable of retiring.

World War I

It is traditional to analyze wars in terms of their underlying and immediate causes, and World War I is no exception. There is an extensive literature at both levels of analysis, and much of it is characterized by efforts to

[102] LaFeber, *Inevitable Revolutions*, on how these motives are entangled.
[103] Herwig, *"Luxury" Fleet*, p. 61.

find "rational" explanations for war, or the behavior that led to war.[104] Rational is rarely defined by the authors of these arguments, but is generally used to signify behavior calculated to advance strategic, political or economic goals. These goals reflect fear and interest, but are all reducible to appetite. This is self-evident in the case of economic explanations for war, and underlies strategic and domestic political explanations. Scholars who attribute the war to domestic politics or structures generally interpret aggressive foreign policies as a strategy to preserve the class structure, and by extension the material benefits that accrue to the elite. Those who emphasize security invariably conceive of it as a precondition for material well-being.

Very little attention has been paid to the role of honor and standing in bringing about World War I. A long-standing exception is Joseph Schumpeter's famous essay on imperialism. In sharp contrast to the socialists, Schumpeter argues that true bourgeois regimes operating in a free market system would spurn war and imperialism as economically wasteful. He attributes the First World War to irrational and precapitalist desires "for self-glorification and violent self-assertion" that were prevalent among the aristocracy. He describes imperialism as an "atavism" and a consequence of the power wielded by "high military circles" committed to feudal values. It was most pronounced in countries where "the officer corps is linked to a definite social class" and can assimilate middle-class entrants to its practices and values. Military leaders allied with those elements of the bourgeoisie who stood to profit from war and expansion. "This alliance kept alive war instincts and ideas of overlordship, male supremacy, and triumphant glory – ideas that would have otherwise long since died."[105]

A more recent article by Avner Offer explains German decisions for war in terms of the military honor code. He draws the parallel between a personal insult and a national one, and the extent to which the Kaiser interpreted the assassination of Archduke Franz Ferdinand as an intolerable insult to Austria for which Emperor Franz Josef had to "demand satisfaction." The Kaiser conceived of his role in the crisis as Franz Josef's "second" in the forthcoming duel.[106] Offer understands an honor code as "a cultural script," but also explains the Kaiser's behavior in terms of

---

[104] For reviews, see Lebow, "Contingency, Catalysts and International System Change"; Mombauer, *The Origins of the First World War*; Hamilton and Herwig, *The Origins of World War I*.

[105] Schumpeter, *Imperialism and Social Classes*, pp. 12, 95–8.

[106] Offer, "Going to War in 1914."

his depressive personality, repressed internal conflicts and propensity to throw temper tantrums. Cultural and personal traits were reinforcing, at least in the case of Wilhelm, and Offer does not consider the counter-factual of whether Germany would have supported Austria to the hilt, so to speak, if someone else had been Kaiser. While noting the pervasive embeddedness of the honor code in Germany in contrast to Britain, he does not attempt to explain this difference or its relationship to broader developments in German and European society. This question is central to understanding the underlying causes of war.

My account of World War I, an extension of my analysis of imperialism, once again foregrounds the spirit. It builds on a familiar narrative: how competition among actors becomes more intense when reason loses control of the spirit, and how these actors increasingly violate the unwritten rules that govern and restrain their competition. In chapter 3, drawing on Homer and Greek philosophers, I hypothesized that honor-based worlds incorporate important tensions. First and foremost is that between competition for honor and preservation of the *nomos* that makes that competition possible and meaningful. Status hierarchies are steep, and competition for them is correspondingly intense. Actors are sorely tempted to take short-cuts to improve their position. If the rules are consistently violated, society loses its cohesion and honor becomes meaningless. In the course of such a transition, honor and standing diverge and actors generally opt for standing over honor. This dynamic captures the progression of European international relations in the late nineteenth and early twentieth centuries. It explains why Germans considered Britain, the country that threatened them the least, their most serious adversary, a phenomenon that constitutes a serious anomaly for any security-based or realist account of German foreign policy. A preference for standing over honor also explains German willingness to invade Belgium in spite of its treaty obligation to uphold Belgian neutrality dating back to 1839. German chancellor Theobald Bethmann Hollweg publicly acknowledged that the invasion was an "injustice," which he nevertheless justified on the grounds of necessity.[107] A similar willingness to gain standing at the expense of honor explains Austria's annexation of Bosnia-Herzegovina in 1908, viewed as a "disgrace" by the other powers, and leading to its temporary isolation, and Austria's ultimatum to Serbia in 1914. The latter was widely regarded as an even more egregious violation of accepted

---

[107] Thompson, *In the Eye of the Storm*, quoting from the diary of Kurt Riezler, p. 92.

diplomatic practice, and triggered off the chain of events leading to a continental war.[108]

Honor and standing are likely to diverge when ascribed and achieved status hierarchies become distinct. The relative standing of these hierarchies and status within them constitutes a powerful source of conflict. In the *Iliad*, Agamemnon was at the top of the ascribed status hierarchy, and Achilles at the apex of the achieved status one. The jealousy and hostility between these two men threatened Greek unity. In prewar Europe, achieved and ascribed hierarchies were once again very much in evidence, with the novelty that this tension was not within the elite but between a traditional and newer elite. The conflict between these hierarchies was not significantly muted, and may well have been exacerbated by middle-class emulation of aristocratic values. Powerful elements of the traditional, aristocratic hierarchy also sought the more aggressive pursuit of international standing as both an end in itself and as a means of preserving their values, way of life and identities.

The starting point of my argument is the continuing power of the aristocracy everywhere in continental Europe and the uneasy relations between it and the middle class. Like Schumpeter, I stress the importance of honor as a value in its own right for the nobility, and not just a strategic vehicle for preserving the class structure.[109] I differ from Schumpeter in key respects. He treats the nobility as relatively uniform in their values, but not all aristocrats had premodern values or were imperialists. In Germany and Austria-Hungary, arguably the countries most responsible for the war in 1914, the nobility was divided on the question of imperialism and the pursuit of aggressive foreign policies. Schumpeter ignores the middle class, as he simply assumes that most people who make their livelihood from industry and commerce are inclined to peace. As we have seen, the middle class in some countries was more committed to imperialism than the aristocracy. Schumpeter not only reduces all goals to material appetite, but further assumes that all behavior is strategic, and is calculated to advance an actor's material well-being. This is a remarkably myopic understanding of human motivation and behavior. It also stands in sharp contradiction to the claim that the aristocracy is committed to what he calls "pre-modern" and "atavistic" values that run counter to

---

[108] Bridge, *The Habsburg Monarchy among the Great Powers*, pp. 288, 293, 298–9 on Austria, Bosnia and the European reaction.

[109] Schumpeter, *Sociology of Imperialism.*

their material interests. Given Schumpeter's assumptions, middle-class preference for standing over wealth represents an even greater anomaly.

Werner Sombart observes that the aristocracy gained wealth in the premodern world by virtue of its political authority, while the modern bourgeoisie uses its wealth to gain political power.[110] For more traditional members of the aristocracy, wealth and power were not fungible. As Weber reminds us, money-making through commercial enterprise had been taboo among the aristocracy since ancient times. The income generated by landed property was intended for consumption, not for profit or investment.[111] In premodern times, nobility and commoners alike considered themselves to exist within a single hierarchy. The Enlightenment challenged the legitimacy of that hierarchy, and sought to expose the superstition and repression on which these social distinctions were based. Spokesmen for the rising middle classes justified their commercial activities as beneficial to society as a whole, reversing the long-standing deprecation of money-making as corrosive of social values and communal well-being.[112] Following the French Revolution, the social structure of Western and then central Europe threatened to develop into two parallel hierarchies, each claiming legitimacy with reference to different values and principles of justice. The prospect of this double hierarchy generated tensions, and all the more so since the more class-conscious members of the bourgeoisie held themselves out as the future of the human race and demanded equality in status (*Gleichberechtigung*). Many nobles also believed that the bourgeoisie represented the future and saw their own way of life as very much threatened and on the decline.

Sharper conflict was voided by two moderating developments: many nobles, especially in Western Europe, became more commercial and "modern" in their values, and many wealthy members of the commercial classes embraced the values and lifestyle of the aristocracy. The latter sought to overcome their inferior social status by fusing with the nobility. In Germany, the accommodation of the bourgeoisie with the landowning nobility sustained *Honoratiorenpolitik*: the leading role of the prefeudal nobility in the politics and social life of the country. This accommodation might have reassured anxious aristocrats and convinced them that their values, way of life and class could survive into the industrial age. Instead, it seems to have made many more concerned and threatened, not only in

---

[110] Sombart, *Der Moderne Kapitalismus*, I, pp. 586–90.
[111] Weber, *Economy and Society*, II, p. 1106.
[112] See Hirschman, *Passion and Interests*; Force, *Self-Interest before Adam Smith*; Hont, *Jealousy of Trade*.

Germany, but elsewhere in central Europe as well. German army chief-of-staff Helmuth von Moltke voiced a fear, widespread among his military colleagues, that assimilation would lead the nobility to adopt bourgeois values and become more interested in money than honor.[113]

Aristocratic support for imperialism and the kinds of aggressive policies that provoked war in 1914 was very much a function of the extent to which nobles accommodated to modernity. Their choices were not random. A gradient ran across Europe from west to east, with the nobility more reconciled to modernity in the west and less so the further east one went. Nobles more accepting of modernity had the highest rates of intermarriage with the bourgeoisie and were most likely to invest in commerce and industry. In Britain, aristocratic investment in capitalist enterprises was quite common and had begun before the English Civil War when landed aristocrats became the chief supporters of capitalist agriculture.[114] In the eighteenth and nineteenth centuries, these aristocrats acted as "the political advance guard for commercial and industrial capitalism."[115] In 1727, a Swiss traveler noted that "In England commerce is not looked down upon as being derogatory, as it is in France and Germany. Here men of good family and even of rank may become merchants without losing caste."[116] Voltaire was struck by the tendency of younger sons of aristocrats to seek their fame and fortune in commerce.[117]

In France, there were important regional exceptions. In the vicinity of Toulouse, aristocrats were deeply involved in commercial enterprises. Fearful of social ostracism, they frequently resorted to bourgeois fronts for their investments.[118] Further east, in Prussia, Poland, Hungary and southern Italy, nobility tended to scorn money-making through commercial enterprises and were most strongly opposed to the ennoblement of successful commoners.[119]

A second gradient ran across Europe from west to east marking the emergence and size of the bourgeoisie. England, Scotland and the Low Countries had the largest middle classes and urban populations. France's middle class developed later, and was considerably smaller. Those of eastern and southern Europe and Russia developed later still and were an

---

[113] Helmuth von Moltke to Eliza von Moltke, in Moltke, *Erinnerungen*, p. 362.
[114] Moore, *Social Origins of Dictatorship and Democracy*, pp. 11, 15, 19.
[115] Ibid., pp. 30–1.
[116] César de Saussure quoted in Blanning, *Pursuit of Glory*, p. 110.
[117] Muller, *Mind and Market*, p. 36.
[118] Ibid., p. 51; Forster, *Nobility of Toulouse*, pp. 26–7.
[119] On Hungary, see Blanning, *Joseph II and Enlightened Despotism*, p. 57.

even smaller percentage of the overall population. Industry appeared in Germany and Austria-Hungary after it did in France, but developed more rapidly, with the result that both empires had larger middle classes. In Germany, the middle class was most concentrated in the Rhineland, the former Hanseatic cities, Silesia and Berlin. Nevertheless, in 1910, only slightly over 20 percent of the population lived in cities with a population greater than 100,000, while more than half lived in communities of less than 5,000 people.[120]

Germany was unique in the degree to which it had both a large middle class and a high percentage of nobility unreconciled to modernity. Not unexpectedly, class tensions were pronounced and quite evident during the constitutional crisis of the 1860s. On the eve of the war, tensions were rising again as indicated by the Zabern Affair.[121] Germany and Austria were nevertheless the countries in which the middle class was most feudalized, a development due less to any conscious efforts on the part of the nobility than to the insecurity of the bourgeoisie in a political and social environment in which they were marginalized and denied entry into the elite circle where it was possible to compete for honor. These middle classes were correspondingly more nationalistic because they sought honor and standing vicariously through the attainments of their respective empires.

Another marked feature of Germany and Austria was the tyranny of small differences. As equality in wealth or status became more widespread, visible distinctions among classes, groups and individuals receded, and those intent on maintaining separation had to find new status markers. As Rousseau, Smith and Veblen observed, old ever finer distinctions in privileges, dress, manners, speech or rank are likely to emerge in these conditions. We encountered this phenomenon in the court of Louis XIV, where numerous gradations of rank, dress and privilege were introduced into an already elaborate social hierarchy.[122] The value of these markers was quickly undermined as courtiers successfully pleaded for special dispensations and the *grande bourgeoisie* began to copy court manners and dress, often in violation of sumptuary laws.

In the nineteenth century, class barriers everywhere became more porous in response to the rising numbers and wealth of the bourgeoisie and the relative decline in wealth, even impoverishment, of many noble families. Aristocrats opposed to modernity and to mixing with other classes sought new barriers to erect between themselves and

[120] *The Statesman's Year Book, 1914*, p. 889.
[121] Kitchen, *The German Officer Corps*, ch. 8; Cecil, *Wilhelm II*, II, pp. 189–92.
[122] Saint-Simon, *Mémoires*, described and quoted in Ladurie, *Saint-Simon and the Court of Louis XIV*, pp. 24–7, 28–32, 54–5.

others. Nowhere was this more evident than in Germany. The complexity of the Kaiser's court was so great that it was necessary to publish a yearly handbook to describe the proliferation in ranks and their order of precedence.[123] The Court Precedence Regulations established sixty-two grades. The Austrian and Saxon courts had only five, and the Bavarians merely three grades. State expenditure on the court increased accordingly. Between 1881 and 1907, the Prussian civil list (the Kaiser's expenditures on his court) rose from 12.2 to 19.2 million marks, an increase of more than 50 percent. The court cost more than the Reich chancellor and chancellery, the foreign office, the colonial office and the justice administration combined. There were twenty other courts within Germany. The Bavarians spent 5.4 million marks on their court in 1910, making it the eighth most costly in the world. The money lavished on courts and the constant publicity they received throughout the Reich in commercial and official publications reinforced the status and sense of entitlement of the nobility and had an enormous effect on the mentality of the middle and working classes.[124]

A third significant gradient running from west to east had to do with the nature of government. After 1871 Britain and France had governments responsible to national legislatures and electorates. Germany, Austria-Hungary and Russia had written constitutions, but they reserved the powers of monarchs to appoint and dismiss ministers and decide questions of war and peace.[125] Article 11 of the German Constitution gave the emperor the exclusive right to "to declare war and conclude peace." With respect to other questions, the lower house (Reichstag) of the parliament could only suggest legislation to the chancellor and upper house (Bundesrath). The Kaiser had full authority of military command (*Kommandogewalt*). Wilhelm imposed his *Immediatsystem*, to further facilitate his personal rule: Prussian state secretaries reported privately to him without the responsible minister being present. The circle of German officials who made policy in the July crisis consisted of the Kaiser, Chancellor Bethmann Hollweg, war minister Erich von Falkenhayn and chief-of-staff Moltke.[126]

---

[123] *Handbuch über den koeniglich-preussischen Hof und Staat.*
[124] Röhl, *The Kaiser and his Court*, pp. 72–91; Sösemann, "Hollow-Sounding Jubilees."
[125] Williamson, "Influence, Power, and the Policy Process," on the extent to which foreign policy decision-making in Austria-Hungary was formulated by a narrow circle of officials, and all the more so after the assassination of Franz Ferdinand.
[126] State secretary of foreign affairs Gottlieb von Jagow and Admiral Tirpitz were not in Berlin during the crisis. Hull, *The Entourage of Kaiser Wilhelm II*; Kennedy, "The Kaiser and German *Weltpolitik*"; Deist, "Kaiser Wilhelm II in the Context of his Military and Naval Entourage."

The major powers, with the exception of Britain and France, were dominated by the nobility. Foreign ministries and armies were all but aristocratic preserves. In 1914, the German foreign service consisted of eight princes, twenty-nine counts, twenty barons, fifty-four untitled nobles and eleven commoners.[127] Of the 548 diplomats who served between 1870 and 1914, 377, or 69 percent, were from the nobility. This percentage was considerably higher if we include only diplomats stationed abroad, and not officials employed at home by the foreign office.[128] The domestic civilian administration had many more high-ranking officials of bourgeois origin, but the overwhelming majority of officials were Prussian and from noble families.[129]

The political power of the nobility and the nearly closed circle in which foreign policy decisions were made makes a mockery of the economic explanation for war and raises serious problems for realist accounts that attribute aggressive policies in the July crisis and the decade leading up to it to security concerns. Developed by radical liberal and socialist critics of imperialism, it stresses capitalist competition and understands the war as the outgrowth of an escalating struggle for markets and raw materials. It has repeatedly been demonstrated that there was little correlation between empire on the one hand and trade and investment on the other.[130] Germany, as noted, was a net importer of capital – one reason why leading industrialists and bankers were not keen on the imperial project, or foreign policies that antagonized foreign lenders or risked a continental war they did not believe their country could afford. Nor did leading capitalists have any perceived need for territorial expansion, as political barriers were not a significant impediment to the export of German goods. Equally important, they were not powerful enough to impose their preferences on the German government, and nor were they involved in the decisions that led to war in 1914.[131]

Between 1890 and 1913, the population of the Reich burgeoned, from 49 to 65 million, making it the most populous country in Europe aside from Russia. By 1914, its coal output equaled Britain's, and its steel

---

[127] Morsey, *Reischsverwaltung*, p. 246, cited in Röhl, *The Kaiser and his Court*, p. 136.
[128] Cecil, *The German Diplomatic Service, 1871–1914*, pp. 66–8, 84, 110–12.
[129] Lerman, "The Kaiser's Elite?"
[130] Feis, *Europe: The World's Banker*; Fieldhouse, *Economics and Empire*; Davis and Huttenback, *Mammon and the Pursuit of Empire*; Edelstein, *Overseas Investments in the Age of High Imperialism*; Offner, "Costs and Benefits, Prosperity and Security, 1870–1914"; Platt, *Britain's Investment Overseas on the Eve of the First World War*.
[131] Hamilton, "On the Origins of the Catastrophe," for a good discussion of the pro-peace attitudes of German and other business communities.

production was equal to the combined output of Britain, France and Russia. Between 1890 and 1914, its exports rose from £166 to £505 million. After Britain, it was the world's largest trading nation, and the number 1 industrial power after the United States.[132] The great industrialist Hugo Stinnes was optimistic about Germany's economic future and a leading spokesman for peace. On the eve of war he voiced a sentiment common to many of his peers:

> Give us three or four more years of peaceful progress and Germany will be the undisputed economic master of Europe. The French are lagging behind us; they are a nation of small *rentiers*. And the English dislike hard work and lack the mettle for new ventures. Apart from them, there is no one in Europe to compete with us. Three or four years of peace, then, and I assure you that Germany will secretly come to dominate Europe.[133]

Walter Rathenau, chairman of General Electric (AEG), also preferred trade to war.[134] Albert Ballin, founder and head of the Hamburg-Amerika Shipping Line, derided war as a response "grounded in fear, vanity and megalomania."[135] A week before Sarajevo, Hamburg banker Max Warburg advised the Kaiser against war. "Germany," he insisted, "becomes stronger with every year of peace."[136] The only important industrialist who favored imperial expansion was Gustav Krupp von Bohlen und Halbach, whose firm received many important naval contracts. There is no evidence that he advocated an aggressive policy in 1914.[137]

Against such testimony Fritz Fischer offers the "September Program" as evidence of the bellicose intentions of German industrialists.[138] It called for far-reaching territorial annexations and economic concessions that would have greatly benefited German industry. It was prepared in the first flush of seeming victory in France. The September Program undeniably reflects greed, but greed encouraged by a German government intent on maximizing its strategic advantage by strengthening other heavy

---

[132] Figures from Kennedy, "The Kaiser and German *Weltpolitik*."

[133] Heinrich Class, *Wider den Strom*, pp. 217–18, quoted in Mommsen, *Imperial Germany*, pp. 84–8, quote on p. 91.

[134] Quoted in Herwig, "Germany."   [135] Cecil, *Albert Ballin*, pp. 165–6.

[136] Max Warburg, *Aus meinen Aufzeichnungen*, p. 29, quoted in Fischer, *War of Illusions*, pp. 657–8 and Hamilton, "On the Origins of the Catastrophe."

[137] Fischer, *Germany's Aims in the First World War*, p. 55. Once the war broke out, pp. 169–70, Krupp came to favor a dictated peace that would weaken France and Britain.

[138] Ibid., pp. 98–118, and Fischer's follow-on *War of Illusions*; Mayer, "Domestic Causes of the First World War"; Wehler, *Das deutsche Kaiserreich*; Geiss, *German Foreign Policy*. Ritter, "Eine neue Kriegsschuldthese?"; Geiss, "The Outbreak of the First World War and German War Aims," for early pro and con reactions.

military industry and weakening France "to make her revival as a great power impossible for all time."[139] Bethmann Hollweg himself observed that "*l'appétit vient en mangeant*" (appetite comes from eating).[140] Germany's leaders did not go to war for the benefit of the industrialists, whose pursuit of profit they regarded as crass, but rather sought to enlist them for purposes of their own once war was underway. Fischer has his arrow of causation reversed.[141]

The strategic explanation for war has long been a staple of historians and realist international relations scholars. In its broadest formulation, it attributes the war to the growing insecurity of all the major powers, reflected in their arms buildups and greater perceived need to support allies in crisis.[142] In the case of Austria, strategic explanations emphasize the growing power of Serbia, backed by Russia, and the alienation of Romania.[143] Perceptions of acute strategic vulnerability are alleged to have persuaded Austrian policymakers to exploit the assassination of the archduke and his wife at Sarajevo on June 28, 1914 as a pretext for humbling, if not eliminating, Serbia. As many scholars recognize, strategic calculations cannot be considered independently of domestic political concerns, and Austrian leaders worried that a powerful Serbia encouraged south Slav nationalism within the empire. They convinced themselves that Serbia's destruction would deflate that nationalism and strengthen the empire.[144]

This account has merit to it, but encounters some striking anomalies. Austrian officials and historians agree that the central figure in determining Austria's response to the assassination was chief-of-staff Conrad von

---

[139] Theobald Bethmann Hollweg, "Provisional Notes on the Direction of our Policy on the Conclusion of Peace," September 9, 1914. Quoted in Fischer, *Germany's Aims in the First World War*, p. 103.

[140] Riezler, Diary, August 20, 1914. Quoted in Stern, "Bethmann Hollweg and the War."

[141] For critiques of the Fischer thesis and the broader argument that German foreign policy was intended to serve domestic political and economic goals, see Eley, *Reshaping the German Right*; Kaiser, "Germany and the Origins of the First World War"; Mommsen, "Domestic Factors in German Foreign Policy before 1914"; Gordon, "Domestic Conflict and the Origins of the First World War"; Lebow, *Between Peace and War*, pp. 101–47.

[142] Stevenson, *Armaments and the Coming of War*, for a strong claim about the relationship between arms races and war.

[143] Williamson, "The Origins of World War I," "Influence, Power, and the Policy Process," and *Austria-Hungary and the Coming of the First World War*, pp. 170–80; Bridge, *The Habsburg Monarchy among the Great Powers*, pp. 329–30. Jelavich, *Russia's Balkan Entanglements*, pp. 210–34, on Russian penetration of the Balkans.

[144] This thesis originated with former Austro-Hungarian socialist Otto Bauer and is reflected in the more recent writings of Ritter, *Sword and Scepter*, II, p. 228; Bridge, *The Habsburg Monarchy among the Great Powers*; Williamson, *Austria-Hungary and the Coming of the First World War*; Herwig, *The First World War*, pp. 8–18; Tunstall, "Austria-Hungary."

Hötzendorf. A depressive personality, who developed a nervous tic when under stress, and sixty-two years old in 1914, he was a man of action, always urging his emperor to draw the sword.[145] Since 1907, he had repeatedly demanded war against Serbia, and sometimes against Montenegro, Italy and Russia as well. In each instance he maintained that a victorious war that led to the incorporation of Serbia would slow down the centrifugal forces of nationalism within the empire.[146] "War, war, war," was how foreign minister Count Leopold von Berchtold described Conrad's response to the assassination.[147] Upon closer inspection, Conrad's desire for war appears to have had less to do with security – international or domestic – than with honor – national and personal. He repeatedly lamented the "foul peace which drags on and on" and branded foreign minister Count Alois Lexa von Aehrenthal and prime minister Count Leopold Berchtold "idiots" for failing to have developed a "firm, positive, expansive goal."[148] He told defense ministry colleagues and Aehrenthal that peace denied Austria the opportunity to overcome its humiliation at the hands of Prussia in 1866 through a military victory against one or more of its hated foes. The assassinations were another pretext for action, but in addition required immediate military response to avenge Austria's honor.[149] Conrad also wanted war to legitimize his relationship with his beloved mistress, Virginie. She was married to a brewery magnate who exploited the affair to justify his philandering and make important social contacts through his wife's lover. Conrad wrote "Gina" that their affair aroused in him the desire "to achieve great things."[150] He desperately desired a "war from which I could return crowned with success that would allow me to break through all the barriers between us . . . and claim you as my

---

[145] Sondhaus, *Franz Conrad von Hötzendorf*, pp. 75, 94–5, 117.

[146] Conrad, *Aus meiner Dienstzeit*, IV, p. 31; Ritter, *Sword and Scepter*, II, pp. 227–30; Herwig, *First World War*, pp. 8–10; Williamson, *Austria-Hungary and the Coming of the First World War*, pp. 190–216; Kronenbitter, *Krieg im Frieden*, pp. 317–68.

[147] Hantsch, *Leopold Graf Berchtold*, II, pp. 558–9, quoted in Herwig, *First World War*, p. 9; Kronenbitter, *Krieg im Frieden*, pp. 461–86; Sondhaus, *Franz Conrad von Hötzendorf*, pp. 95, 135–49.

[148] Conrad to Gina, Vienna, September 30, 1912, and October 3, 1912. Cited in Sondhaus, *Franz Conrad von Hötzendorf*, p. 117.

[149] Virginia Conrad von Hötzendorf, *Mein Leben mit Conrad von Hötzendorf*, letter of December 26, 1908, pp. 30–1; Conrad's talk with Aehrenthal, February 18, 1909. Both cited in Herwig, *First World War*, p. 10; Tunstall, *Planning for War against Russia and Serbia*, pp. 167–88; Kronenbitter, *Krieg im Frieden*, pp. 455–86, on the role of revenge more generally for the Austro-Hungarian leadership.

[150] Conrad to Gina, Vienna, May 25, 1907 (never mailed), cited in Sondhaus, *Franz Conrad von Hötzendorf*, p. 111.

own dearest wife." A war, he confided, "would bring the satisfaction in my career and private life which fate has so far denied me."[151]

There is reason to believe that Conrad's strategic arguments were more rationalizations than motives. In his memoranda there are numerous assertions that preventive war would cut the head off the "snake" Italy and the "dog" Serbia, but no reasoned arguments that offer a logic, as opposed to a claim, of why war with either country would deal a serious setback to nationalism within the empire as opposed to stimulating it. Conrad never doubted that war against Serbia would involve war against Russia as well, although he hoped that Austria might conquer Serbia quickly enough – another pipedream – which would allow it to send its army north in time to take the offensive against Russia.[152] In reality, the Austrian offensive against Serbia stalled in 1914, and the empire had inadequate troops to prevent Russia in its initial offensive from occupying Galicia up to the heights of the Carpathian range. If security was Conrad's principal concern, we would expect him to be reluctant to start a war he did not believe Austria could win. He knew that in a European war Germany would go on the offensive in the west, covering the east with only eight Prussian divisions, composed largely of elderly reservists.[153] Austria would be left exposed to a Russian offensive. Conrad tried to resolve his two-front predicament by creating a reserve force that could be sent against Serbia or Russia, as the need arose. He was nevertheless determined to destroy Serbia and had no intention of diverting any forces northeast to face the Russian threat until that goal had been accomplished. Strategic logic would have dictated just the opposite disposition of forces, as Serbia constituted no offensive threat. Austrian war plan "R" had been prepared with this contingency in mind, in contrast to war plan "B," which sent the empire's forces south against Serbia. Conrad drew from both plans and met the goals of neither. He may have reasoned that an

---

[151] Conrad to Gina, Vienna, December 26, 1908 (never mailed). Text in Virginia Conrad von Hötzendorf, *Mein Leben mit Conrad von Hötzendorf*, pp. 30–1. For Conrad's relationship with Gina, see Williamson, "Vienna and July 1914"; Kronenbitter, *Krieg im Frieden*, pp. 108–35; Harmat, "Divorce and Remarriage in Austria Hungary"; Sondhaus, *Franz Conrad von Hötzendorf, passim*, for the most complete account of their relationship.

[152] Sondhaus, *Franz Conrad von Hötzendorf*, p. 145. Kageneck, the German military attaché in Vienna, informed Conrad as early as July 25 that Russia would support Serbia in any war; *Tagebuch Kageneck*, cited in Herwig, *The First World War*, p. 54. Franz Josef took it for granted that Russia would intervene because Russia could not possibly tolerate (*sich . . . gefallen lassen*) the Austrian ultimatum. Kann, *Kaiser Franz Josef und der Ausbruch des ersten Weltkrieges*, p. 12.

[153] Showalter, "The Eastern Front and German Military Planning, 1871–1914"; Herwig, *First World War*, pp. 51–2 on communications between the Austrian and German staffs.

immediate offensive against Serbia – made possible by his tampering with plan "B" – began hostilities almost immediately, making the decision for war all but irrevocable. His strategy was based at best on "wishful thinking," as there was no possible way that Austria could fight a two-front war. Conrad's plan ignored improvements in Russia's mobilization capability, about which he had been fully informed by Moltke, and wrongly assumed that there was ample time to defeat Serbia before Russia posed a threat.[154]

Conrad's military dispositions – Serbia first, and Russia second – make his preferences transparent. Serbia posed no military threat, but Russia most certainly did, and he was willing to put the empire's security at risk to "show Serbia who was boss."[155] Three days into the war, Conrad's colleagues prevailed upon him to send the Second Army, earmarked for the Serbian offensive, northeast to the Russian threat.[156] Conrad's insatiable desire to crush Serbia was dictated by anger. Anger in the Aristotelian sense is aroused by challenges from one's inferiors, and this is how Serbia was viewed by Conrad and other top Austrian officials.[157] There is evidence that Conrad recognized the nature of his tradeoff between anger and security and its possible consequences, because in late June he admitted to his beloved Gina that "It will be a hopeless struggle." He was undeterred by the prospect of defeat because he expected that he personally and Austria more generally would at least gain satisfaction and "such an ancient monarchy and such an ancient army cannot perish ingloriously."[158]

Emperor Franz Josef shared Conrad's outlook. He felt humiliated by Austria's defeats at Solferino in 1859 and Sadowa in 1866, and deeply resented his empire's decline in prestige. According to Gerhard Ritter, his "resentment and injured pride simply boiled over," making him receptive to the idea of war.[159] Unlike Conrad, he was plagued by doubts, worried

[154] Ritter, *Sword and Scepter*, II, p. 237; Williamson, "Introduction" and "Origins of World War I"; Rothenberg, *The Army of Francis Joseph*, p. 178; Herwig, *The First World War*, pp. 52–6; Tunstall, *Planning for War against Russia and Serbia*, pp. 159–88; Kronenbitter, *Krieg im Frieden*, pp. 487–520.

[155] Ritter, *Sword and Scepter*, II, p. 234, quoting from minutes in the General Staff section of the Austrian War Archives; Tunstall, *Planning for War against Russia and Serbia*, p. 163.

[156] Regele, *Conrad*, p. 266; Kronenbitter, *Krieg im Frieden*, pp. 487–518, on Austrian mobilization and changes in the strategic plans.

[157] See the discussion in chapter 3.

[158] Hötzendorf, *Mein Leben mit Conrad von Hötzendorf*, letter of June 28, 1914, p. 114, quoted in Ritter, *Sword and Scepter*, II, p. 236.

[159] Ritter, *Sword and Scepter*, II, p. 235; Beller, *Francis Joseph*, pp. 213–30, for a more moderate account.

about the military threat posed by Russia and refused his chief-of-staff's request for mobilization until he was assured of German support.[160] In the end, Franz Josef stoically accepted the need to war to preserve the honor of the empire. "If we must go under," he told Conrad, "we better go under decently."[161] Berchtold, who held the balance between the committed Conrad and the wavering emperor, came down decisively on the side of war after Sarajevo. Influenced by the so-called "Young Rebels" in the foreign office, he spoke of a *"final and fundamental reckoning"* with Serbia.[162] Led by Count János Forgách and Franz Baron von Matscheko, these officials hoped that a successful war against Serbia would compel respect from the other great powers.[163] Prestige and honor were the underlying causes of war against Serbia, and anger its immediate precipitant. "Failure to act decisively," as Berchtold put it, would be "renunciation of our Great Power position."[164] The emperor aside, leading Austrian civilian and military officials pretended that Russia, and the threat it posed, did not exist.

Historians and political scientists put equal stress Germany's putative strategic dilemma. Chief-of-staff Helmuth von Moltke repeatedly warned the Kaiser, Chancellor Bethmann Hollweg and foreign secretary Gottlieb von Jagow that an offensive war plan would be unworkable by 1917. This plan, long assumed to be the conception of Moltke's predecessor, Count Alfred von Schlieffen, was a response to the prospect of war on two fronts. France, the stronger of Germany's adversaries, was to be invaded by almost all available forces, allowing the more slowly mobilizing Russians to advance in the east against only thin covering forces. When France was defeated, German military might would be turned rapidly against Russia. The plan, really devised by Moltke and his staff, counted on Germany's ability to knock France out of the war quickly enough to redeploy German armies in the east in time to stop the Russians from advancing too deeply

---

[160] Conrad's memorandum to Franz Josef, July 1, 1914, in *Österreichs-Ungarns Aussenpolitik von der bosnischen Krise 1908 bis zum Kriegsausbruch 1914*, VIII, no. 9978; Williamson, *Austria-Hungary and the Origins of the First World War*, pp. 192–3; Herwig, *First World War*, pp. 11–12; Beller, *Francis Joseph*, pp. 213–30.

[161] Hötzendorf, *Mein Leben mit Conrad von Hötzendorf*, August 18, 1914, p. 118, quoted in Herwig, *First World War*, p. 11.

[162] Tschirschky to Bethmann Hollweg, June 30, 1914, quoted in Geiss, *July 1914*, pp. 64–5, italics in the original; Bridge, *The Habsburg Monarchy among the Great Powers*, pp. 335–6; Williamson, *Austria-Hungary and the Origins of the First World War*, pp. 190–212; Kronenbitter, *Krieg im Frieden*, p. 483.

[163] Tunstall, "Austria-Hungary."   [164] Bridge, *Habsburg Monarchy*, p. 335.

into Prussia. Time pressure dictated an invasion of Belgium as the terrain along the Franco-German border was unsuitable for the rapid advance of large armies. The German army was to overrun Belgium – attacking Liège within hours of the mobilization order – and then wheel south to outflank and encircle the French army behind Paris.[165]

From the moment he became chief-of-staff in 1906, Moltke urged the Kaiser and successive chancellors to find some pretext for preventive war against France and Russia. With foreign minister Bernhard von Bülow, he worked to transform the Austro-German defensive alliance into an offensive one.[166] In the so-called "war council" of December 1912 – a meeting between the Kaiser and his military chiefs – Moltke "wanted to launch an immediate attack."[167] During the July crisis, he was an unrelenting advocate of war, a goal widely shared within the general staff and ministry of war.[168] The Kaiser, Bethmann Hollweg and Jagow were influenced by Moltke's aggressive outbursts, which grew more intense in 1913 and 1914, as did his demands for a larger army.[169] The Kaiser largely cut himself off from civilian advisors, and relied primarily on his military entourage for military and civilian advice, and all the more so in times of crisis. As a favored member of this entourage, Moltke had the emperor's ear.[170] On June 21, 1914, on the eve of Sarajevo, the Kaiser, reflecting Moltke's concerns about the pace of Russian railway construction, wondered "whether it might not be better to attack than to wait."[171]

---

[165] Ritter, *The Schlieffen Plan*; Snyder, *The Ideology of the Offensive*, pp. 107–56; Mombauer, *Helmuth von Moltke and the Origins of the First World War*, pp. 72–105; Rothenberg, "Moltke, Schlieffen and the Doctrine of Envelopment"; Showalter, "German Grand Strategy." Zuber, *Inventing the Schlieffen Plan*, and *German War Planning*, critiques earlier works on the so-called Schlieffen Plan and demonstrates that Schlieffen actually intended to wage a defensive war on both fronts. The war plan Germany executed in 1914 was of more recent origin, and reflected the commitment of Moltke and his colleagues to the offensive.

[166] Mombauer, *Helmuth von Moltke and the Origins of the First World War*, pp. 1–2, 108, 110–11, 114; Mommsen, *Grossmachtstellung und Weltpolitik 1870–1914*, p. 203.

[167] Theobald von Bethmann Hollweg's account of the meeting in Fischer, *War of Illusions*, pp. 161–4.

[168] Ibid., pp. 142–3, 180, 188–226.

[169] Mombauer, *Helmuth von Moltke and the Origins of the First World War*, pp. 5–6, 114, 122, 133, 140, 179–80.

[170] Hull, *The Entourage of Kaiser Wilhelm II*, p. 205; Röhl, *Germany without Bismarck*, p. 161; Mombauer, *Helmuth von Moltke and the Origins of the First World War*, p. 24.

[171] Fischer, *War of Illusions*, p. 471, quoting Max Warburg, *Aus meinen Aufzeichnungen*, printed privately.

The Kaiser's biographers portray him as full of bravado, but lacking the temperament or courage of a wartime leader.[172] He found it difficult to cope with ambiguity or complexity, and this may be another reason why he sought a simple frame of reference for the problem posed by the assassination of Archduke Franz Ferdinand.[173] Instead of approaching the issue strategically, the Kaiser framed it as a challenge to Austria's honor that demanded satisfaction.[174] Two days after the assassination, he penned a note on a foreign office telegram: "The Serbs must be disposed of, *and* that right *soon*."[175] When he pledged German support to Count Hoyos at their luncheon meeting on July 5 – undoubtedly the most crucial German decision of the crisis – he acknowledged Austria's need to preserve its national dignity in the face of an intolerable affront by Serbia. More than two weeks later, he was still furious with Serbia, writing on the margin of a cable that "Serbia is nothing but a band of robbers that must be seized for its crimes! I will meddle in nothing of which the Emperor [Franz Josef] is alone competent to judge!"[176] The next day he penned yet another revealing comment: "in *vital* questions and those of honor, one does not consult with others."[177] On July 6 in Kiel, the Kaiser made an interesting confession to his friend, Krupp von Bohlen und Halbach. He told the steel magnate: "This time I shall not cave in" – and repeated himself three times.[178] Perhaps Sarajevo had also become a matter of internal honor for Wilhelm, anxious to convince himself and others that he was a man of courage.

Moltke also influenced Bethmann Hollweg, who displayed what was for him an unusually aggressive self-confidence in the early stages of the July crisis. He subsequently confessed that his support for Austria in 1914 had been the result of Moltke's pleading to go to war before 1917:

> Yes, by God, in a way it was a preventive war [*Präventivkrieg*]. But if war was in any case hovering above us; it would have come in two years' time, but even more dangerously and even more unavoidably, and if the military

---

[172] Cecil, *Wilhelm II*, pp. 194–5; Hull, *The Entourage of Kaiser Wilhelm II*, p. 265, and Röhl, *Wilhelm II*, pp. 541–5.

[173] Cecil, *Wilhelm II*, pp. 194–5.

[174] Offer, "Going to War in 1914," is persuasive on this point.

[175] Marginalia on report from Tschirschky to Bethmann Hollweg, June 30, 1914. Quoted in Geiss, *July 1914*, p. 65, italics in original.

[176] Marginalia on telegram from Lichnowsky to Jagow, July 23, 1914. Quoted in Geiss, *July 1914*, p. 171.

[177] Marginalia on telegram from Lichnowsky to Jagow, July 24, 1914. Quoted ibid., p. 184, italics in original.

[178] Quoted in Fischer, *War of Illusions*, p. 478.

leaders declared that then it was still possible without being defeated, in two year's time no longer! Yes, the military.[179]

Such a counterfactual is patently self-serving because it portrays the chancellor as a victim rather than an accomplice, but it does drive home the extent to which Bethmann Hollweg at least was influenced by strategic calculations.

The difficulty with the strategic explanation for war is that Germany's war plan was less a response to Germany's strategic dilemma than it was the principal cause of that dilemma. French investment allowed the Russians to extend and improve their railway network, significantly reducing the time Germany had to defeat France, in turn putting pressure on the generals to go to war sooner rather than later. The obvious solution was a defensive strategy, which would have been very much in Germany's national interest, and was apparently Schlieffen's conception of how to fight a two-front war.[180] Had the German army of Moltke's day adopted a defensive strategy, the First World War might never have occurred because a Russian mobilization would not, of necessity, have triggered a German invasion of France. Nor would German leaders have been as concerned as they were with closing their "window of vulnerability." If war had broken out, Germany would have been unassailable. In the west, Britain would almost certainly have remained neutral in the absence of a German invasion of Belgium.[181] The French army would have exhausted itself in unsuccessful offensives in the Ardennes. To the embarrassment of the offensively oriented general staff, war games indicated that even modest German forces could blunt a French attack, and the French still failed to advance when the game was rigged in their favor.[182] Reality recapitulated simulations: France launched costly and unsuccessful

---

[179] Bethmann Hollweg's conversation with Conrad Haussmann, quoted in Fischer, *War of Illusions*, p. 671. On Bethmann Hollweg and the outbreak of war see Stern, "Bethmann Hollweg and the War"; Zechlin, "Deutschland zwischen Kabinettskrieg und Wirtschaftskrieg"; Jarausch, *The Enigmatic Chancellor*, pp. 148–84.

[180] Lebow, "The Soviet Offensive in Europe: The Schlieffen Plan Revisited?"; Snyder, *Ideology of the Offensive*, pp. 121–2; Zuber, *Inventing the Schlieffen Plan* and *German War Planning* on Schlieffen's intentions to wage a defensive war on both fronts.

[181] Kennedy, *The Rise of Anglo-German Antagonism*, pp. 425–65; Steiner, *Britain and the Origins of the First World War*, pp. 211, 228–37; Wilson, *The Policy of the Entente*, pp. 135–47.

[182] Zoellner, "Schlieffens *Vermachtnis*," *Militärwissenschaftliche Rundschau*, supplementary issue, 1938, pp. 46–8 on the war games. Cited in Snyder, *Ideology of the Offensive*, p. 142; pp. 46–8 on the war games.

assaults in 1914 against the strong, natural German defensive position in Alsace.[183]

In the east, where Germany initially took the defensive, the Russian offensive into Prussia was repulsed in disorder with grave losses. If, after a series of defensive victories of this kind, German leaders had declared their commitment to a peace on the basis of the *status quo ante bellum*, they almost certainly would have prevailed. It seems unlikely that there would have been much support in either France or Russia for continuing the war after a series of disheartening defeats. Nor could these two powers have resisted British, even American, pressures to lay down their arms and accept a peace on the basis of the *status quo ante bellum*. The Austro-Hungarian Empire would have been preserved, although the Russian Empire might have succumbed to revolution. German preeminence on the continent would not only have been maintained but greatly strengthened.[184]

A defensive strategy was anathema to Moltke and other generals, who constantly reproached the navy for its defensive orientation and lack of "offensive spirit."[185] Karl von Bülow, who would command the Second Army in the invasion of France, even considered Clausewitz's and Moltke's strategy of encirclement not quite cricket. Epitomizing what Bismarck called the *Schneidigkeit* (brainless virility) of German generals, he advocated a full frontal attack instead.[186] Moltke recognized that by 1917 the offensive would no longer be a feasible strategy for the army, but was unprepared to plan any defensive alternative.

The German "cult of the offensive" was not unique; military organizations all over Europe were drawn to the offensive, even small countries like Belgium with purely defensive goals. The literature on this phenomenon for the most part stresses the organizational roots of offensive strategies.[187] European generals ignored – perhaps deliberately – the writings of Clausewitz about the Napoleonic Wars and the lessons of the American Civil and

---

[183] Strachan, *First World War*, pp. 213–15; Gilbert, *First World War*, p. 52.

[184] Lebow, "The Soviet Offensive in Europe" for an elaboration of this argument.

[185] Karl von Einem, *Errinerungen eines Soldaten 1853–1933*, pp. 51ff, cited in Mombauer, *Helmuth von Moltke and the Origins of the First World War*, p. 21.

[186] Bavarian military plenipotentiary Gebsattel to Minister of War, November 2, 1905, reporting on a conversation with then Lt.-Col. Wilhelm Groener. Cited ibid., p. 68.

[187] Snyder, "Civil Military Relations and the Cult of the Offensive, 1914 and 1984," and *Ideology of the Offensive*. Evera, *Causes of War*, in search of a rational explanation for this most irrational of commitments, argues that offensive dominance reflected the widespread belief that territorial conquest was easy.

Russo-Japanese Wars, to which all the major powers had sent observers.[188] The latter two wars demonstrated that offensives against well-defended positions were costly, if not suicidal, especially against entrenched forces equipped with machine guns and protected by barbed wire. European armies were dominated by the cavalry, whose principal mission was spearheading offensives, and a defensive strategy would have relegated them to a subordinate role. Class considerations reinforced organizational imperatives. The cavalry was everywhere the preserve of the aristocratic elite, as it had been since the days of chivalry. It was the darling of the Kaiser, who enjoyed leading decisive cavalry charges in maneuvers, even though there he appears to have understood that they would be of no practical value in a real war.[189] A defensive strategy would have relegated the cavalry to the sidelines and foregrounded the role of infantry, artillery and specialized units, many of them commanded by non-aristocratic reserve officers.

These explanations offer an "efficient cause," but say nothing about why it was so important for the nobility to lead offensives, especially when they were likely to lead to its destruction. Seventy-seven percent of Prussia's highest-ranking officers belonged to the ancient nobility of the sword. Not unexpectedly, the sons of the most distinguished German military families were killed in large numbers during the First Battle of the Marne, just as the flower of French knighthood had been destroyed at Crécy and Agincourt. During the course of World War I, thirty-three Bülows, twenty-six Arnims, twenty-four Wedels, twenty-one Puttkamers, nineteen Schwerins and eighteen Prittwitzs were killed.[190] In the tradition of their forebears, who had fought for the electors and kings of Prussia against Napoleon, Denmark, Austria and France, these officers adhered to an aristocratic honor code that put courage above survival. For French knights and their German successors, their identities and way of life were at stake, not merely questions of strategy, tactics and class preferences. As in the *Iliad*, the highest born were expected to perform the bravest feats on the battlefield and aggressively to challenge their opponents. Aviators aside, they no longer did so in single combats, but the rules of honor remained unchanged. Moltke's war plan relied on rapid mobilization, a good railway network, careful organization, but above all, as Schlieffen himself never tired of saying, success required the will to victory

---

[188] Clausewitz, *On War*, book 6; Luvaas, *The Military Legacy of the Civil War*; Travers, "Technology, Tactics, and Morale."

[189] Afflerbach, *Falkenhayn*, p. 61.

[190] Görlitz, *Die Junker*, p. 319, cited in Herwig, "Germany"; Trumpener, "Junkers and Others," for figures on the rise of non-noble officers before 1914.

(*Siegeswille*), reckless daring (*Kühnheit*), self-sacrifice and utter disdain of death (*Todesverachtung*).[191] It was a senseless strategic plan for many reasons, but the very embodiment of the offensive spirit of the German officer corps.

Germany's top generals gave ample evidence that they sought war as an end in itself.[192] In 1900, Colmar von der Goltz proclaimed that "I could do with a war, a truly hard, invigorating, joyful war."[193] By 1914, he was convinced that any campaign against France would be "tenacious and protracted," but still favored war.[194] For Prussian war minister Erich von Falkenhayn, the advent of war was more important than its outcome. On August 4, 1914, he confided to his diary: "Even if we go under as a result of this, still it was beautiful."[195] Moltke wanted war because he was a soldier, and soldiers fought wars. His political motives for war were correspondingly vague. He hated France, yearned to see it humbled, and hoped that a war would give extended shelf life to an honor culture within Germany.[196] He aroused strategic anxiety in the Kaiser and civilian leadership to make them more receptive to his pleas for war. He withheld critical evidence that would have made them risk-averse, most notably his deep-seated doubts, shared by Falkenhayn, about the feasibility of victory.[197] He and Falkenhayn were both convinced that a short war was impossible, but encouraged hopes that an offensive would quickly bring France to its knees.[198] Moltke made sure that the army had no alternative plans for fighting just against Russia in the east, to put more pressure on Germany's leaders to go to war before 1917.[199]

---

[191] Hull, "The End of the Monarchy."

[192] On the militarism of the army's officers and leadership, see Haeussler, *General William Groener and the German Army*, p. 72; Jarausch, *The Enigmatic Chancellor*, pp. 181–6; Ritter, *The Sword and Scepter*, II, pp. 227–75; Kitchen, *The German Officer Corps*, pp. 96–114.

[193] Colmar von der Goltz to Colonel von Morgen, February 10, 1900, quoted in Herwig, "Germany."

[194] Reichsarchiv, *Der Weltkrieg 1914 bis 1918*, I, p. 327, quoted in Herwig, "Germany"; Mombauer, *Helmuth von Moltke and the Origins of the First World War*, p. 69.

[195] Falkenhayn diary, August 1, 1914, quoted in Herwig, "Germany."

[196] Helmuth von Moltke to Eliza von Moltke, in Moltke, *Erinnerungen*, p. 362.

[197] Herrmann, *The Arming of Europe and the Making of the First World War*, p. 208, on Moltke's certainty that Germany would, of necessity, fight a two-front war. Mombauer, *Helmuth von Moltke and the Origins of the First World War*, pp. 101, 145 on Moltke's pessimism. Afflerbach, *Falkenhayn*, pp. 259–60, 294–5, 300–7, on Falkenhayn's doubts.

[198] Mombauer, *Helmuth von Moltke and the Origins of the First World War*, pp. 210–13, citing relevant correspondence.

[199] Gasser, *Preussischer Militärgeist und Kriegsentfesselung 1914*, p. 5; Mombauer, *Helmuth von Moltke and the Origins of the First World War*, pp. 103–4.

Moltke and his staff also dealt dishonestly with their Austrian ally. They kept Austrian chief-of-staff Conrad in the dark about their strategic plans, and he reciprocated their mistrust. They encouraged the Austrians to believe that Germany might attack Russia, when in fact the bulk of the German army would be deployed in the west against Belgium and France.[200] The Austrians, who knew they were being lied to, encouraged the Germans to believe that they would also attack Russia, when they were planning an offensive in the south, against Serbia.[201] German generals looked down their noses at Austria as a poorly governed, multiethic empire with a slowly mobilizing and ineffective army that Schlieffen had all but written off. The Austrians had exaggerated regard for German military prowess, which provided the psychological cover that Conrad needed to concentrate his forces against Serbia.[202] Military leaders who placed security above other considerations would certainly not have mobilized the lion's share of their forces against their least threatening adversaries. For his part, Moltke half-counted on what he called *Nibelungentreue* (loyalty to the German spirit) to bind Austria to Germany.[203] Such behavior is typical of honor cultures where elite actors regard each other with suspicion and envy, put their own goals first and find it difficult to cooperate even when it is very much in their mutual interest. At the same time, they expect unquestioning loyalty from their "followers," and there is no doubt that Moltke and the Germans considered Austria their junior if not subordinate partner.

The German naval challenge to Great Britain rivaled the army's plan in its political and strategic lunacy. If France was a sworn enemy and Russia a dangerous neighbor, Britain was a natural ally, or at the very least a neutral party in defensive continental war. Social Democrats admired Britain and lobbied for a pro-British foreign policy.[204] By the turn of the century, however, Germany was in the grip of Anglophobia, especially pronounced among conservative nationalists and liberal bourgeois

---

[200] Ritter, *Sword and Scepter*, II, pp. 239–47; Mombauer, *Helmuth von Moltke and the Origins of the First World War*, pp. 119–20; Tunstall, *Planning for War against Russia and Serbia*, pp. 138–40, 149–58, 161–88, and "Bundesgenossen?"

[201] Conrad, *Aus meiner Dienstzeit*, III, p. 670; Williamson, *Austria-Hungary and the Origins of the First World War*, pp. 180–4; Tunstall, "Bundesgenossen?"; Kronenbitter, *Krieg im Frieden*, pp. 448–54.

[202] Fellner, "Die Mission Hoyos," reporting the recollection of the Austrian ambassador to Germany, Count Hoyos. Mombauer, *Helmuth von Moltke and the Origins of the First World War*, pp. 213–15.

[203] Mombauer, *Helmuth von Moltke and the Origins of the First World War*, p. 119.

[204] Kehr, *Economic Interest, Militarism and Foreign Policy*, pp. 30–4.

imperialists. Hostility to Britain by the middle classes can only be understood as envy for its acknowledged imperial primacy. The German navy, the vehicle intended to challenge that supremacy, was enormously expensive, and largely responsible for the big increase in defense spending in the first two decades of the twentieth century. In 1901–3, the navy consumed one-fifth of defense expenditure, and the percentage rose to a quarter in 1907–9. By 1911, the navy budget was 54.8 percent of the army budget.[205] Germany had to cut back on its naval building program in 1912. It could not keep pace with Britain, which was now committed to outbuild Germany, because it also had a large army to support.[206]

Admiral Tirpitz claimed that a powerful navy would make Germany a more attractive ally (*Bündnisfahig*) and strengthen Germany's hand in its struggle to become a world power. His "risk theory" was directed against Great Britain, whom he hoped to deter by building a fleet large enough to make the Royal Navy shy of attacking Germany.[207] None of this made any sense, because, as World War I would prove, it was the German navy that was deterred by a superior British battle fleet. Moreover, the British navy in no way interfered with German trade and colonization – until the war – as German businessmen freely acknowledged. Tirpitz's plan for sixty capital ships triggered a naval arms race with Britain and nudged the country out of its "splendid isolation" into increasingly close arrangements with France and Russia. The failure of Anglo-German naval discussions in January 1902 led to a British arrangement with Japan. The Entente with France followed in April 1904. The German naval slowdown in 1912 opened the way for a reduction of tensions with Britain, but in subsequent talks with Lord Lansdowne Germany insisted on terms that were unacceptable to the British and only further convinced Lansdowne and other powerful figures in London of German hostility.[208]

The strategic and economic absurdity of the High Seas Fleet has encouraged historians to look for domestic political motives.[209] While these were

---

[205] Witt, *Finanzpolitik des deutschen Reiches von 1903 bis 1913*, pp. 380–1; Stevenson, *Armaments and the Coming of War*, p. 18; Herwig, *"Luxury" Fleet*, p. 75.

[206] Herrmann, *The Arming of Europe and the Making of the First World War*, pp. 1–5, on the relative expenditures of Britain and Germany on their armies and navies.

[207] Tirpitz, *Erinnerungen*, p. 51.

[208] On the British reactions and responses to Germany's naval buildup, see Kennedy, *The Rise of Anglo-German Antagonism*, parts 3–5; Steinberg, "The German Background to Anglo-German Relations, 1905–1914"; Sweet, "Great Britain and Germany, 1905–1911"; Steiner, *Britain and the Origins of the First World War*, pp. 42–78; Röhl, *Wilhelm II*, pp. 999–1039.

[209] This literature is discussed in the previous section of this chapter.

not insignificant, they were secondary. The navy was so important to Tirpitz, the Kaiser and liberal imperialists because their dream was to replace Britain as Europe's leading power, and *pax Britannica* with a *pax Germanica*.[210] In December 1889, Tirpitz confided to the Saxon military representative in Berlin that "the naval expansion is aimed primarily against England."[211] The Kaiser considered the High Seas Fleet "his navy," and greatly valued his honorary appointment to the British navy. He never tired of wearing his Royal Naval uniform whenever he met the British ambassador.[212] At the same time, he was notoriously hostile to England, so much so that the use of English, in which he was fluent, was all but banned at the Potsdam court.[213] He came to regard Britain as Germany's arch-rival, and admitted that he was motivated in large part by envy. He reacted with undisguised anger at any suggestion that Germany should accept British naval primacy.[214] On a visit to London in 1908, and asked by Sir Charles Hardinge of the foreign office if the Germans could make fewer ships or build more slowly, Wilhelm blurted out: "Then we shall fight, for it is a question of national honour and dignity."[215]

More compelling evidence about the extent to which concern for honor drove German strategy is provided by the response of the army and navy chiefs to war and defeat. In August 1916, Field Marshal Hindenburg acknowledged that strategic logic required a withdrawal from Verdun and termination of the unsuccessful campaign of attrition against the French. He nevertheless wanted to persevere because too many Germans had died to withdraw voluntarily. The "honor of Germany was at stake."[216] In late October and early November of 1918, Prince Max of Baden's cabinet considered an armistice in the hope of protecting important national interests. Tirpitz and Ludendorff were violently opposed, and argued for a "last battle," which they had no expectation of winning, to be fought on German soil to uphold military honor. Without such a costly engagement,

---

[210] On Tirpitz and the navy, see Epkenhans, *Die Wilhelminische Flottenrüstung 1908–1914*; Berghahn, *Tirpitz Plan*; Herwig, *Das Elitekorps des Kaisers, passim*; Herwig, *"Luxury" Fleet*, pp. 20–1.

[211] Quoted in Herwig, *"Luxury" Fleet*, p. 37.

[212] Herwig, *Das Elitekorps des Kaisers*, p. 34.

[213] Cecil, "History as Family Chronicle"; Röhl, *Wilhelm II*, pp. 966–98.

[214] Cecil, "History as Family Chronicle"; Röhl, *Wilhelm II*.

[215] Wilhelm to Bülow, August 13, 1908, in *Die Grosse Politik der Europäischen Kabinette*, XIX, pp. 126–9, quoted in Epkenhans, "Wilhelm II and 'His' Navy, 1888–1918."

[216] Neiberg, *Fighting the Great War*, p. 169.

the nation would be "ruined."[217] The allies required Germany to hand over its High Seas Fleet, and Admiral von Reuter scuttled it at the British naval base of Scapa Flow in June 1919. He was following the ex-Kaiser's orders "that in case of bad luck, an honorable sinking of my ships will preserve them from striking the flag."[218] This action came at the same time as the Germans were presented with the draft peace treaty at Versailles, and angered the allies, making them less willing to compromise.

Paul Schroeder offers a variant of the strategic thesis that links it to imperialism and economics. He argues that imperialism served as a "safety valve" until the mid-1890s. It was a hunt for prizes,

> like an Easter egg hunt, carried on in fierce competition on the ground between individuals in and out of governments (entrepreneurs, firms, explorers and adventurers, settlers, careerists in politics and the military, and so on), but pursued more cautiously by most governments, usually aware of the dubious value and high costs of acquisitions. Even when imperialist ambitions and programmes clashed, deals and compromises were the normal outcome; there seemed enough for everyone, and losers could be compensated elsewhere.

Schroeder contends that preemptive actions to seize prizes eroded the rules of the game. Governments increasingly sought sole possession of territories or at least spheres of influence, creating conflicts between Britain and France in Egypt, Britain and Russia in Persia and Afghanistan, Germany and France in Morocco, and, most threatening of all, Russia and Austria in the Balkans. Purely commercial ventures also began to be regarded as threatening by other colonial powers. *Weltpolitik* became so important because it was widely believed that survival depended upon securing a dominant, or at least satisfactory, economic and territorial position in the world.[219]

Schroeder's argument maps nicely on to a spirit-based explanation. Aristotle contends that honor societies decline when competition gets out of hand. When actors no longer exercise self-restraint and break the rules in pursuit of standing, they threaten the self-esteem of others by limiting their chances of gaining honor and standing. Everyone then has a strong incentive to play hard and fast with the rules, which negates

---

[217] Ludendorff note of October 31, 1918; Tirpitz to Max of Baden, October 17, 1918 and Tirpitz, *Deutsche Ohnmachtspolitik im Weltkriege*, pp. 617–18, both cited in Hull, "The End of the Monarchy."

[218] Krause, *Scapa Flow*, p. 270.   [219] Schroeder, "International Politics, Peace and War."

the possibility of achieving honor and hastens the transformation of an honor world into a fear-based one. Aristotle bases his analysis in part on both Homer's *Iliad* and the experience of fifth-century Greece, and these dynamics were analyzed in chapters 3 and 4. Late nineteenth-century imperialism qualifies as a "game" conducted to achieve standing, and was often described as such by contemporaries. According to Schroeder, it was a game that got out of hand, especially in the Balkans, where it made Austro-Hungarian leaders particularly insecure. I am not persuaded by his claim that colonial empire was perceived as essential to "survival." I offer evidence to the contrary in this chapter, and explain the quest for empire largely in terms of the quest for standing. There can be little doubt, however, that the intensity of this conflict exacerbated tensions among the great powers and encouraged the widely shared view that war was likely, if not inevitable.[220]

Finally, we come to theories that root war in domestic politics. They are anchored in the efforts of groups and classes to advance or preserve their political prerogatives and associated material benefits. Critics rightly point out that these arguments encounter a problem that physicists describe as action at a distance. They assume the importance of underlying causes (i.e. class tensions and other social factors) without demonstrating how they were responsible for the decisions that led to war.[221] In the case of Germany, internal conflict was made more acute by the rising power of social democracy, concentrated in well-organized trade unions and a political party. In the 1912 election, the Social Democrats mobilized enough working-class support to gain 110 seats, making it the largest single party in the Reichstag.[222] Historians of the period differ about the degree to which German leaders feared social democracy or exaggerated its putative threat to mobilize support for aggressive foreign policies. Eckhart Kehr, Hans-Ulrich Wehler and Volker Berghahn place their emphasis on the willful role of leaders. I have argued that Bülow's *Weltpolitik* was as much a response to middle-class demands for empire as it was an effort to mobilize support for domestic political goals. By the time of Bethmann Hollweg's chancellorship, the governing elite was in thrall to both middle-class opinion and the more conservative elements of the aristocracy. Wolfgang Mommsen rightly observes that Germany's aggressive nationalism was the result of "the relative

[220] On perceptions of inevitability, see Lebow, *Between Peace and War*, pp. 254–63.
[221] Kaiser, "Germany and the Origins of the First World War"; Groh, "'Je eher, desto besser!'"
[222] Schorske, *German Social Democracy*, parts 1–4, on the rise of social democracy.

powerlessness of the traditional elites, and not any masterful manipulation of public opinion."[223]

Mommsen's interpretation brings us back to the world of the spirit. Nationalism in Germany was primarily a means of achieving self-esteem. Liberals and intellectuals of diverse persuasions were infatuated with war, and without much if any political rationale. Thomas Mann was "tired, sick and tired" of peace and embraced war as "a purification, a liberation, an enormous hope."[224] Herman Hesse believed it was very much in the interests of Germans "to be torn out of a dull capitalistic peace."[225] Philosopher Max Scheler predicted that war would arouse the "noble beast" in young Germans.[226]

Further evidence of the extent to which personal striving for self-esteem was transferred to the Reich was provided by the extraordinary reaction of intellectuals, and the middle class more generally, to the Agadir crisis of 1911, in which Germany overplayed its hand and had to back down in the face of Anglo-French opposition.[227] The crisis unleashed a torrent of national outrage that the navy and army successfully exploited for their own ends. It inspired Friedrich von Bernhardi's *Germany and the Next War*, which called for the total annihilation of France. Bernhardi offered as his justification the widely shared belief among educated Germans that *deutsche Kultur* (German civilization) was superior to Anglo-French materialism with its crass emphasis on "material prosperity, commerce and money making." His book became an influential bestseller, going through six editions by 1913.[228] The generally sensible Max Weber voiced similar sentiments. He thought Morocco worth a war to defend German prestige, and called for more armaments in the aftermath of the crisis.[229] The rhetoric of conservative nationalists, liberal imperialists and the government was redolent with the language of honor, as it would be for Germany and Austria in 1914. Political leaders were not immune from

---

[223] Mommsen, "Domestic Factors in German Foreign Policy before 1914"; Kehr, *Der Primat der Innenpolitik*, 149–75; Wehler, *The German Empire*, pp. 165–6, 176–9; Berghahn, *Imperial Germany*, pp. 272–6; Mommsen, *Imperial Germany*, pp. 77, 95; Mayer, "Internal Causes and Purposes of War in Europe," for an earlier statement of the link between domestic politics and aggressive foreign policies.

[224] *Tagebuch Wenninger*, quoted in Herwig, *The First World War*, p. 35.

[225] Morton, *Thunder at Twilight*, p. 333.

[226] Quoted in Herwig, *The First World War*, p. 35.

[227] On Agadir, Albertini, *Origins of the War*, I, pp. 318–34; Barlow, *The Agadir Crisis*; Fischer, *War of Illusions*, pp. 71–94.

[228] Bernhardi, *Deutschland und der nächste Krieg*; Mombauer, *Helmuth von Moltke and the Origins of the First World War*, p. 130; Herwig, "Germany."

[229] Mommsen, *Max Weber and German Politics*, pp. 79, 154.

this sentiment. In July 1911, following the Anglo-French naval agreement, foreign secretary Kiderlen-Wächter told Bethmann Hollweg: "Our reputation abroad has deteriorated, we must fight."[230]

Prospect theory and foreign policy

Prospect theory tells us that people are willing to take greater risks to prevent losses than they are to make gains. Loss and gain are determined with reference to subjective benchmarks established by actors.[231] Prospect theory was developed and tested with respect to material gains and losses, so it is above all a theory about appetite. It has nevertheless been applied to international relations with some degree of success.[232] If we analyze the July crisis in terms of prospect theory, it is apparent that Britain's foreign policy in 1914 and during the prior decade conforms nicely with its expectations. British leaders were notably risk-averse when it came to making gains, and more willing to accept risk (e.g. the two Moroccan crises, the July crisis) when they framed the issue as loss avoidance.[233]

Germany should have behaved similarly if its leaders were motivated primarily by wealth or security. A few more years of peace, leading business figures pointed out, were likely to consolidate Germany's economic dominance in Europe. A defensive military policy would have made Germany all but impregnable and allowed a risk-averse foreign policy. The Kaiser and his military spurned a defensive strategy, and the Kaiser pursued an increasingly risk-acceptant policy, culminating in his "blank check" to Austria in July 1914. Such policies only become explicable with reference to the hierarchy of motives shared by the Kaiser and his principal advisors. In contrast to British officials, most of whom appear to have ranked appetite above spirit, and security over both, the Germans, I have shown, emphasized the spirit over appetite and security. They were accordingly much more willing to risk for several reinforcing reasons. Standing, and

[230] Kiderlen-Wächter to Bethmann Hollweg, July 30, 1911. Quoted in Fischer, *War of Illusions*, p. 129.
[231] Kahneman and Tversky, "Prospect Theory," *Choices, Values, and Frames*, and "Loss Aversion in Riskless Choice."
[232] Levy in special issue of *Political Psychology* and "Loss Aversion, Framing, and Bargaining"; Farnham, *Avoiding Losses/Taking Risks*; McDermott, *Risk-Taking in International Politics*; Boettcher, *Presidential Risk Behavior in Foreign Policy*; Welch, *Painful Choices*.
[233] On British policy in the Moroccan crises, see Albertini, *Origins of the War*, I, pp. 145–90, 318–33; Steiner, *Britain and the Origins of the First World War*, pp. 33–6, 71–8, 140–3; Dockrill, "British Policy during the Agadir Crisis of 1911"; Grey, *Twenty-Five Years*, pp. 67–98, 210–39.

the esteem it was expected to confer, was a central goal for German leaders and public opinion alike. They accordingly downgraded security and wealth as primary concerns of foreign policy, and so did not value as highly what they were putting at risk. Honor also entered the picture, as we have seen in the Kaiser's responses to the assassinations at Sarajevo and Moltke's desire for war and the offensive regardless of the circumstances or consequences. Honor for the military can only be achieved or maintained by accepting risk. This is why Moltke was willing to risk everything on a single throw of the "iron dice," which was not only acceptable, but attractive to German leaders.

Similar values prevailed in Vienna, as we have seen, and in St. Petersburg. Foreign minister S. D. Sazonov looked hard to find some evidence of Serbian complicity in the files that Vienna circulated to the other powers in defense of its ultimatum to Serbia so he could distance St. Petersburg from Belgrade.[234] When Austria failed to provide any evidence substantiating the link alleged to exist between Serbia and the assassins, Sazonov reframed the problem as one of upholding Russian prestige and honor. At a decisive meeting of the Russian Council of Ministers on the afternoon of July 24, he insisted that Russia fulfill its historic mission of defending Slavic peoples. Failure to do so would reduce Russia to a "decadent state" and "second-place" power.[235] Another influential voice, the diplomat M. N. Giers, a moderate Slavophil, insisted that any capitulation to Austria would "result in the total destruction of our prestige and of our position in the Near East [the Balkans]."[236] Risk was acceptable to the Russians because the alternative, loss of standing and honor, was not.

My analysis suggests that prospect theory needs to be reformulated to take into account the motives of actors. Judging from the World War I case, propensity for risk-taking varies not only in response to whether gains or losses are perceived to be at stake, but, more importantly, the nature of those gains and losses. Table 7.1 lays out this relationship.

When appetite is dominant, that is when actors are concerned with material gains and losses, prospect theory, as presently formulated,

---

[234] *Pièces diplomatiques relative aux antecedents de la Guerre de 1914*, III, no. 6, Szapary to Berchtold, July 29, 1914, pp. 17–19. Cited in Lieven, *Russia and the Origins of the First World War*, p. 140.

[235] Bakhmetev Archive, Columbia University. Quoted in Lieven, *Russia and the Origins of the First World War*, pp. 141–2; Jelavich, *Russia's Balkan Entanglements*, pp. 248–65, on the role of Serbia in Russian calculations before and during the July crisis.

[236] *Mezhdunarodnye otnosheniiya v epokhu imperializma*, no. 154, Giers to Sazonov, July 27, 1914, pp. 168–70, quoted in Lieven, *Russia and the Origins of the First World War*, pp. 141–2.

Table 7.1. *Prospect theory*

	Gains	Loss avoidance
Appetite	Risk-averse	Risk-accepting
Fear	Risk-averse	More risk-accepting
Spirit	Risk-accepting	Very risk-accepting

describes the risk propensity of actors. However, capitalism is, by definition, a risk-prone activity; this characteristic helps to distinguish it from other forms of economic activity. Early capitalists were buccaneers, although they looked for ways of reducing risk and increasing profits.[237] Mature capitalism becomes increasingly less risk-prone, although capitalism in the first two decades of post-communism in Russia especially bears a striking resemblance to early capitalism in its level of risk – and not just to one's pocketbook – and willingness of at least some actors to assume those risks in search of profits. Prospect theory does not capture this pattern of development.

When actors frame the issue as one of security, they will also be risk-averse when it comes to making gains, and risk-accepting when it comes to avoiding loss. Complications can nevertheless arise. Unlike appetite, security is relational, linking gains and losses in a way that is not generally true in appetite where another actor's gain or loss of wealth does not necessarily affect your wealth. When another's gain is understood as your loss, and vice versa, it becomes correspondingly difficult to separate gains from losses, a conceptual distinction that lies at the core of prospect theory. When fear becomes pronounced, as it does when the losses in question are understood to be great, likely, and imminent, as in the prospect of conquest by another state, I hypothesize that actors find it increasingly difficult to distinguish loss from gain and become either much more or much less willing to assume risk. The former will lead to balancing, or possibly preemption, and the latter to bandwagoning. My cases in this chapter and the next offer evidence in support of this proposition.

Although I distinguish security from appetite on the grounds that loss and gain are relational in the former, this is not always the case. Failure to clinch a big deal does not necessarily result in loss – unless you are

---

[237] Greif, *Institutions and the Modern Economy*, on risk-taking by Medieval Jewish merchants and how they sought to reduce their risks.

expected to make the deal, in which case failure may entail a serious loss of reputation. In some circumstances, another's material success may also adversely affect your own. If a competitor's gain of more market share will allow it to sell its product more cheaply and possibly drive you out of the market, gain and loss will become mirror images of each other, as they do in all adversarial contests where fear becomes the dominant motive. So even when appetite is the dominant motive, conditions may make fear paramount, bringing about a shift in how gains and losses are framed. Context can be as important as motive.

When actors are motivated by the spirit – that is, when they are concerned with winning or preserving honor or standing – they should be risk-accepting with respect to either losses or gains. Loss of honor is intolerable to such actors, and even certain death is unlikely to deter them from action intended to avoid it. They will also be willing to accept high risk when it comes to gain because acceptance of risk is an essential precondition of standing and honor. For the warriors of the *Iliad*, knights in the Middle Ages, and Prussian officers in the nineteenth and early twentieth centuries, honor was proportional to the nature of the risk that actors ran. To behave well, especially in circumstances where survival was doubtful, earned respect in the eyes of others, which is why Leonidas and the Spartans at Thermopylae remain to this day the ultimate symbol of honor and role models for military officers around the world.

Agency

My focus in this chapter has been more on the underlying than the immediate causes of war. This emphasis could convey the impression that I privilege structure over agency. I argue that there were structural conditions – chief among them the continuing political domination of a nobility with premodern values, and its social and psychological consequences for the German middle class – that made it likely that Germany would pursue aggressive and high-risk foreign policies. Somewhat similar conditions prevailed in Austria-Hungary, where the middle class was weaker, but where nationality problems provided an additional impetus for an aggressive foreign policy. However, none of these orientations made war inevitable.

Elsewhere I have argued that Austrian, German and Russian leaders became more risk-accepting in 1914 than they were in 1913 or 1912 as the result of a confluence of three largely independent chains of causation. In the absence of this confluence, not only would leaders have been less risk-prone, those in favor of war under any circumstances (e.g. Moltke and Conrad) would have found other officials less receptive to their pleas.[238] The problem of causation is further complicated by recognition that the precipitants of war (immediate causes) can be important causes in their own right, with origins quite independent of any underlying causes. In 1914, Sarajevo was such a precipitant. It met a number of conditions without which a continental war would have been unthinkable. It removed the principal Austrian opponent to war, Franz Ferdinand; angered Emperor Franz Josef and Kaiser Wilhelm in ways that made them more receptive to strong action against Serbia; made it possible for German chancellor Bethmann Hollweg to win over the Social Democrats by making Russia appear responsible for any war; and allowed the Kaiser and the chancellor, men unwilling to accept responsibility for war, to convince themselves that support for Austria would not escalate into a continental war, and that if it did, responsibility would lie elsewhere. Sarajevo was not a match that set the dry kindling of Europe alight, the metaphor routinely invoked by historians and international relations scholars. It was more like a permissive action link on a nuclear weapon: a trigger at least as complicated as the weapon itself.

It is improbable that some other provocation would have met these conditions, or that another combination of great powers would have started a war for different reasons. Without the twin assassinations at Sarajevo, Europe might have remained at peace for another several years. Even in that short a time, some of the pressures making Austrian, German and Russian leaders risk-prone would have eased, and other developments might have further altered their risk calculus. Take the case of Austria. The death of Franz Josef in 1916 – and there is no reason to think that he would have lived any longer in time of peace – would have brought Franz Ferdinand to the throne. Motivated by hatred of Hungarians and the *Ausgleich* of 1867 that had created the dual monarchy, the anointed successor (*Thronfolger*) had considered several strategies toward this end, including a triple rather than a dual monarchy that would include southern Slavs as the third "pole" and a looser form of federalism. The documents he had prepared for his succession indicate that he probably would have introduced universal suffrage in Hungary at the outset of his reign in the hope of increasing the power of minorities at the expense of the Magyars. This would have provoked a strong reaction from Budapest, and further

---

[238] Lebow, "Contingency, Catalysts and International System Change"; Thompson's rejoinder, "A Streetcar Named Sarajevo," and Lebow "A Data Set Named Desire."

attempts by Franz Ferdinand to undercut the *Ausgleich* would have raised the prospect of civil war. Vienna would not have been in any position to start a war with Serbia.[239] If Vienna was consumed by a constitutional crisis and Germany compelled after 1917 to adopt a defensive strategy, it is conceivable that Europe might have evolved in ways in which the Great War and many of the horrors of the twentieth century could have been avoided.[240]

War and peace ultimately depended entirely on the policies and decisions of leaders, and Germans and Austrians had the misfortune to be governed by men of poor character, lacking good political instincts or insights and devoid of moral courage. The Kaiser was unprepared to face up to the consequences of his warmongering early in the crisis, suffered a dissociative reaction and remained incommunicado in Potsdam during the most critical phase of the crisis. Bethmann Hollweg possessed neither the courage nor the independence to oppose Moltke's push for war, even when it became apparent that it would not be a limited war in the east, but a continental war with Britain intervening on the side of Germany's enemies.[241] The Austrian emperor was old and on the whole peacefully inclined; he was goaded into war by Conrad and Berchtold once they were assured of German support. Neither man was professionally or emotionally equipped for their position, and Conrad appears to have acted at least in part on the basis of inappropriate personal motives. Different men could well have made different decisions. Learning that he is to be deprived of the slave girl Briseis, Achilles is about to draw his sword against Agamemnon, but suppresses his fury and restrains himself for compelling practical and political reasons.[242] None of the principal actors in Vienna and Berlin had the courage or presence of mind to act as responsibly.

---

[239] Zeman, "The Balkans and the Coming of War"; Dedijer, *Road to Sarajevo*, ch. 7.

[240] Lebow, "Contingency, Catalysts and International System Change."

[241] Lebow, *Between Peace and War*, ch. 4, for a psychological analysis of German decision-making in the July crisis.

[242] Homer, *Iliad*, 1.88–214.

8

World War II

"One cannot obtain a tiger's claw unless he braves the tiger's den."

Yōsuke Matsuoka[1]

The twentieth century is generally considered the age of appetite. Politics in the developed countries is thought to have revolved around the distribution of resources – about who gets what, when and how, in the well-known phrase of Harold Lasswell.[2] International relations, by contrast, is portrayed as a realm dominated by security concerns for much of the century. Two world wars, the Cold War and the breakup of colonial empires and the disputes they spawned – in short, the tragic history of the twentieth century – encouraged realist claims that states must always make security their primary concern and strive to maintain, if not extend, their power. Realists transformed the striking contrast between the domestic and foreign politics of many developed states into another law-like statement: these domains are fundamentally different because of the anarchy of the international system and the fear it engenders. Liberals, by contrast, emphasize the importance of appetite in both international and domestic politics, and the preference of democratic trading states for peaceful relations among themselves. They regard the two world wars and the Cold War, if not as an aberration, as growing pains of a democratic, postindustrial order that has the potential, even likelihood, to usher in a "Kantian world" in which the frequency of war will sharply recede.

The cleavage between realists and liberals reflects their relative emphasis on fear and appetite as the primary motive of state actors. As we have seen, the international relations literature almost entirely ignores the spirit, and those few theorists who speak of standing or prestige as state goals reduce them to instrumental concerns intended to advance a state's influence, and

---

[1] Quoted in Hosoya, "Retrogression in Japan's Foreign Policy Decision-Making Process."
[2] Lasswell, *Politics: Who Gets What, When and How?*

thus its security or material well-being.[3] In this chapter, I demonstrate once again that they are important ends in themselves and often pursued at the expense of security or wealth. Given the seeming dominance of appetite and fear, the twentieth century should be the hardest case for which to demonstrate the importance of the spirit, and World War II the most difficult set of international events in the century in which to make this case. I attempt to show that neither appetite nor fear arising from insecurity is capable of explaining the decisions of Germany, Italy and Japan to go to war. Explanations based on spirit offer more compelling accounts, and can also help explain why leaders like Hitler and Mussolini came to power.

I begin my analysis with post-World War I Germany, and the consequences of defeat for the German people. There was deep resentment toward the allies and the terms of the Treaty of Versailles. Revealingly, its most hated feature was not the loss of territory, reparations or restrictions on the German military that this treaty imposed, but the articles that required Germany to accept responsibility for the war and hand over the Kaiser and other individuals for trial as war criminals. Compelled to sign the treaty by the allies, the Weimar Republic never achieved legitimacy. Economic shocks further weakened the Republic. Right-wing opponents, Hitler among them, gained popular support by promising to restore Germany's position in Europe, and with it the self-esteem of the German people. Hitler's own motives for going to war were pathological because they went far beyond restoration of *status quo ante bellum* to the conquest of Europe, if not the world.[4] Many of his foreign policy and defense initiatives – withdrawal from the League of Nations, rearmament of Germany, the *Anschluss* and the dismemberment of Czechoslovakia – were welcomed enthusiastically by most Germans and Austrians. His wars against Poland, Western Europe, Yugoslavia, Greece and the Soviet Union were decidedly less popular, but what support they did have derived in large part from the same motives.[5] The importance of honor to the officer corps secured Hitler the quiescence, if not the active support, of the German army, and its willingness to keep fighting long after officers of every rank realized the hopelessness, if not the evil character, of their cause.

[3] See chapter 2.
[4] Weinberg, *The Foreign Policy of Hitler's Germany*, I, p. 358; Rich, *Hitler's War Aims*, I, pp. 3–10; Bullock, *Hitler*, pp. 10–11, 622; Fest, *Hitler*, pp. 213–18.
[5] Kershaw, *The "Hitler Myth,"* pp. 151–68, reports that Hitler's high point in support came after the fall of France and before his failure to conquer Britain or force it to sue for peace.

The spirit was an equally important motive for Italy and Japan. Neither was attempting to live down the consequences of defeat and partial territorial dismemberment, but their aggressive, expansionist policies can be described in large part as efforts to gain standing in the international system. Both countries achieved great power status only belatedly. Italy emerged as a nation state in the latter half of the nineteenth century, and was considered the weakest of the great powers. It was the last European country to obtain a colonial empire, suffered a grievous defeat in Ethiopia in 1896 and arguably put in the worst military performance of any major combatant in World War I. Although on the winning side, Italy satisfied only some of its far-ranging territorial ambitions, and right-wing anti-republican forces convinced many Italians that Britain and France had robbed them of their due. Their success in transforming Italy into a revisionist power was not merely the result of tactical skill, but of the predisposition of middle-class Italians to see themselves and their country as weak, lacking respect and vulnerable to the machinations of other powers. Territorial aspirations, disillusionment with a stagnant parliamentary system and a severe economic crisis made it possible for Mussolini to achieve power by a combination of legal and extra-legal means and gradually impose a dictatorship. His foreign policy, increasingly at odds with Italy's strategic and economic interests, was intended to consolidate and strengthen his regime by creating a modern-day Roman *imperium* that would enhance the self-esteem of Italians. Germany posed the principal threat to Italy, but Mussolini chose to ally with it against Britain and France because these latter two countries were the principal barriers to colonial expansion in the Mediterranean. Mussolini entered World War II erroneously believing that a German victory was all but inevitable, and that Italy could only satisfy its territorial ambitions by being on the winning side. While his decision for war was idiosyncratic and based on bad judgment, his invasion of France was supported by wide segments of the Italian elite.

The Japanese had even more compelling reasons for hostility to the status quo powers, as they had been the object of European economic exploitation and racism and only grudgingly accepted as a great power. In an earlier stage of their history, they had struggled to assert their equality with China, from whom, via Korea, Japan had received much of its culture. Japanese colonialism in China and Korea was in large part motivated by the desire for recognition and standing, from Asian as well as European audiences. This goal lay behind Japan's aggression against China in the 1930s, although it was also motivated by the desire for economic autarchy and cannot be fully understood without also taking into account the struggle for power between the army and the civilian leadership. That conflict in turn had much to do, as it did in Wilhelmine Germany, with problems of modernity and the extent to which many threatened aristocrats clung to premodern values, and the middle class failed to develop the kind of world view Marx associated with the bourgeoisie. Japanese failure to bring the war in China to a successful conclusion led to a wider war with the European powers. The attack on Pearl Harbor made no strategic sense, given the military commitment Japan already had in China and the far greater military potential of the United States. Both the Japanese calculations about the American response, and their willingness to take extraordinary risks with their own security must be understood in terms of the spirit-driven values of a warrior class.

Security should have been the primary concern of states who were the intended targets of Japanese, German, Italian or Soviet aggression. Even in the face of unambiguous threats of invasion, the leaders of some of these states put other goals first and bandwagoned unsuccessfully with the aggressor (e.g. the Soviet Union with Nazi Germany until June 1941), or refused to cooperate with one another (e.g. Britain, France and the Soviet Union) in spite of strong security incentives to do so. The motives and calculations behind such behavior were complex, and cannot be understood adequately with reference to just security or appetite.

Esteem is a difficult concept to operationalize. As it is a subjective emotion I have not attempted to devise some standard measure of esteem, either in an actor's own eyes (self-esteem) or those of others. Rather, I attempt to construct estimates of esteem through the eyes of actors themselves. I also look at the efforts of intellectuals and politicians to play on those feelings, as they did so successfully in Italy and Germany. Discourses are largely inseparable from practices.

In my case studies of Germany, Italy and Japan, I appear to offer four different explanations for World War II: the survival of prefeudal values; leaders' needs to pursue aggressive foreign policies to sustain themselves in power; pathological leaders driven to commit acts of aggression at home and abroad for personal rather than political reasons; and the late recognition of these three countries as great powers. These explanations, I contend, are related and reinforcing, and highlight the importance of the spirit as a motive for key actors in all three countries. They also suggest that we must look at the spirit as a motive for leaders and peoples alike, and also as a resource to which leaders can appeal to gain power and mobilize support for their own goals. Bismarck was not a nationalist, but aroused and exploited German national feeling to make Prussia the dominant unit in a unified Germany from which Austria was excluded. Mussolini and Hitler shared nationalist sentiments and quite consciously sought to strengthen particular discourses and held themselves out as their personification. Their skill at bricolage propelled them into power and strengthened the appeal of these discourses. In the case of Mussolini, it may have made him their prisoner. Once again, agency proved important and helps us to understand why some leaders' appeals to the spirit are more successful than others.

In the conclusion I return to two themes I broached in earlier chapters: the character of warfare and the foreign policies of parvenu great powers. I describe the progression that is evident from the Napoleonic Wars through World War I to World War II with respect to the goals and character of warfare. In each war, more extensive goals were pursued with fewer constraints on the use of force. This progression reflects, and also helped to bring about, the gradual breakdown of the European regional order. These cases suggest some propositions about conditions in which war sustains or undermines order. With respect to parvenu powers, I treat postwar Germany as an extension of its Wilhelmine predecessor and extend my analysis to Japan, Italy and the Soviet Union. I demonstrate that parvenu powers share a common discourse – one of their markers – that portrays each of them as culturally distinct from and superior to the dominant powers in the system by virtue of their allegedly more spiritual and collectivist cultures.

Germany

My account of Nazi Germany builds on my earlier analysis of German imperialism and the origins of World War I. In chapter 6, I emphasized the survival of premodern values among a powerful aristocracy, the partial feudalization of the German middle class and the deflection outward of its strivings for self-esteem.[6] The commitment of the *Junker* aristocracy to preserve its power and way of life, and the vicarious association of the middle class with the state, provided reinforcing incentives for an aggressive foreign policy as well as political backing for it. The German Empire came to an abrupt end in 1918, and was replaced by a republic that drew support from socialists, Catholics and some members of the middle class. It was opposed by nationalists on the right and communists on the left, and ultimately lost support to both, paving the way for extra-parliamentary government and Hitler's dictatorship. Historians

---

[6] See my discussion of the meaning of middle class in Germany in chapter 7.

have offered many reasons for the Weimar Republic's failure. They include the success of the right in hanging the hated Treaty of Versailles around its neck; the growth of independent, anti-republican paramilitary forces; the economic crises of the early 1920s and 1930s and their consequences for the middle and working classes; middle-class fears of socialism; alienation of the intellectuals; a flawed constitution; and bad leadership.[7] Historians also point to deeper causes, among them the schism between German and Western political thought and the sense of a special German mission to which it gave rise in opposition to the more commercial and democratic values of France and Britain.[8] German idealism encouraged deep respect, if not reverence, for the state and the subordination of the individual to it. The German middle class and intellectuals were predisposed to look to the state for unity, purpose and guidance, a role a querulous, controversial, weak and threatened republic could not possibly fulfill.[9]

I do not pretend to offer a comprehensive explanation for Hitler's rise to power and Germany's role in bringing about World War II. Rather, I offer an account that highlights the role of the spirit in understanding these events, and advance the claim that concern for self-esteem was not only an underlying cause of this conflagration, but a necessary condition. As we saw in chapter 6, self-esteem was a key, if frustrated, ambition for the semi-feudalized German bourgeoisie. This need became more acute after the humiliation of defeat in World War I and the imposition of what Germans widely regarded as the punitive Treaty of Versailles. In this circumstance, it was difficult for the Weimar Republic to build legitimacy, and comparatively easier for its right-wing opponents to win support in the name of nationalism. Hitler was particularly adept at playing on the desires of the middle class for self-esteem. The Nazi emphasis on the *Volksgemeinschaft* held out the promise of a higher purpose to be achieved through unity, sacrifice and struggle in a showdown with the nation's internal and external enemies.[10] Hitler's defiance of the Western powers and the Treaty of Versailles was widely popular with the middle classes, who were his largest supporters at the polls.

---

[7] Eyck, *History of the Weimar Republic*; Mommsen, *The Rise and Fall of Weimar Democracy, passim*; Bracher, *The German Dictatorship*, pp. 168–78, 191–8; Aycoberry, *The Nazi Question*; Stachura, "Introduction."

[8] On the revolt against modernity, see Lukács, *The Destruction of Reason*; Plessner, *Die Verspätete Nation*; Mosse, *The Crisis of German Ideology*; Stern, *The Politics of Cultural Despair*; Herf, *Reactionary Modernism*.

[9] Krieger, *The German Idea of Freedom*; Ringer, *The Decline of the German Mandarins*.

[10] Kershaw, *Popular Opinion and Political Dissent in the Third Reich*, pp. 1–2; Dahrendorf, *Society and Democracy in Germany*, p. 404.

In November 1918, allied advances on the Western front and German war-weariness led to mutinies and worker uprisings. On November 9, socialist leader Philip Scheidemann proclaimed a republic on the steps of the Reichstag and Kaiser Wilhelm fled to Holland the next day. Prince Max of Baden, the last imperial chancellor, had opened negotiations with the allies in October for an armistice, which came into effect on November 11. The victorious allied leaders, meeting in Paris, summoned a German delegation to Versailles in May 1919 to receive a draft treaty. The allies gave the Germans fifteen days to submit objections and questions in French or English, a deadline that was later extended by a week.[11]

The treaty required Germany to return Alsace-Lorraine to France, hand over Eupen and Malmédy to Belgium, northern Schleswig to Denmark, Hultschin to Czechoslovakia, and parts of West Prussia, Posen and Upper Silesia to Poland. East Prussia was separated from West Prussia by a corridor of territory given to Poland to guarantee it access to the Baltic Sea. The Saar, Danzig and Memel were put under the control of the League of Nations, and Germany was required to give up all of its colonies and the land it had taken from Russia under the Treaty of Brest-Litovsk. The German army was reduced to 100,000 men, and severe restrictions were placed on its navy and air force. The Rhineland was to be demilitarized permanently. Germany was forbidden from incorporating Austria, despite strong sentiments for unification in both countries. It had to accept responsibility for starting the war, and assume the burden of reparations, in an amount to be determined, the bulk of which was to go to Belgium and France to compensate them for damages caused by the war and four years of German occupation.[12]

The German reaction to the draft treaty is revealing in two respects. The first is the state of shock and denial that it provoked. By all accounts, Germans of all classes were stunned by the peace terms, having convinced themselves that Woodrow Wilson would compel a reluctant Britain and France to offer a generous peace based on the American president's Fourteen Points. The draft treaty was in fact mild in comparison to either the September Program of 1914, prepared by the German government in the expectation of victory over Belgium and France, or the Treaty of Brest-Litovsk, imposed on Bolshevik Russia by Germany in March 1918. The latter forced Russia to cede or give independence to all of its western

[11] French, "Had We Known How Bad Things Were in Germany"; Stevenson, "French War Aims and Peace Planning"; MacMillan, *Paris 1919*, pp. 460–3.

[12] See http://history.sandiego.edu/gen/text/versaillestreaty/vercontents.html for the text of the Treaty of Versailles (accessed December 2006).

territories (Finland, the Baltic provinces, Poland, Belarus and Ukraine). It
offers evidence of the kind of harsh terms Germany would have imposed
on the Western powers if its 1918 offensive had succeeded in breaking
allied resistance. Germans on the whole failed to make this comparison
and saw themselves as undeserving victims. The German military deluded
itself into believing that it would receive allied backing for a *Drang nach
Osten* (march to the east) to St. Petersburg to overthrow the Bolshevik
regime.[13]

It is equally revealing that Germans gave evidence of being more upset
by those articles of the treaty they considered offensive to their honor than
by those inimical to their security or well-being.[14] Article 228 allowed the
allies to indict and try people "for acts against the laws and customs of war."
Almost across the political spectrum, Germans opposed this demand as a
matter of national pride, without any concern for the possible substance
of the allegations. It was a largely symbolic issue as the Kaiser had taken
refuge in Holland. Article 231, the so-called "war guilt clause," demanded
reparations for allied and associated governments "as a consequence of
the war *imposed* upon them *by the aggression of Germany* and her allies."
The German delegation summoned four experts with international reputations to draft a response. The document they submitted insisted that
the question of war guilt could only be determined by a careful comparative analysis of the archives of all the warring powers. The allied
reply, written by Lloyd George's private secretary Philip Kerr (later Lord
Lothian), played to allied public opinion and excoriated the Germans for
their wartime actions. In the judgment of Wolfgang Mommsen, it "paved
the way for the passionate, often demagogic, discussion of the 'war-guilt
lie' which helped kindle German nationalism once again."[15]

With respect to territory, public opinion accommodated itself readily
to the loss of Alsace-Lorraine, but was least reconciled to ceding territory

---

[13] See www.lib.byu.edu/rdh/wwi/1918/brestlitovsk.html for the Treaty of Brest-Litovsk
(accessed December 2006).
[14] Mommsen, *The Rise and Fall of Weimar Democracy*, pp. 89–128, and "Max Weber and
the Peace Treaty of Versailles"; Krüger, *Deutschland und die Reparationen*; Wengst, *Graf
Brockdorff-Rantzau und die aussenpolitischen Anfänge der Weimarer Republik*; Heinemann,
Die verdränge Niederlage.
[15] Eyck, *A History of the Weimar Republic*, I, pp. 90–128; Mommsen, *The Rise and Fall of
Weimar Democracy*, pp. 89–128, and "Max Weber and the Peace Treaty of Versailles";
Krüger, *Deutschland und die Reparationen*; Wengst, *Graf Brockdorff-Rantzau und die
aussenpolitischen Anfänge der Weimarer Republik*; Heinemann, *Die verdränge Niederlage*;
Schwabe, "Germany's Peace Aims and the Domestic and International Constraints," on
the German response to the Treaty of Versailles. MacMillan, *Paris 1919*, pp. 463–74.

to Poland. Harald von Riekhoff reasons that Germans respected France as an equal or superior power and thus more readily acquiesced in the loss of Alsace-Lorraine. They looked down on the Poles as their inferiors, and had no respect for anything associated with them, which made it more difficult to relinquish territory to them.[16] This phenomenon offers more evidence for Aristotle's understanding of anger as an emotion primarily aroused by slights from those we consider beneath us.[17] With respect to both reparations and territory, the spirit, not appetite or fear, appears to have dictated the German response.

Prime minister Scheidemann told the Reichstag that the Treaty was unacceptable. Even moderates rejected its terms and spoke about revenge.[18] Hans Delbrück wrote in the *Preussische Jahrbücher* that "The day and hour will come when we will demand everything back."[19] Only one deputy, an Independent Social Democrat, was willing to affirm the treaty on the sensible grounds that Germany had no choice but to make peace. In France, Marshal Ferdinand Foch drew up very public plans for an invasion of Germany, while British prime minister David Lloyd George pleaded with the French to accept some revision of the treaty in the hope of reaching an accommodation. French prime minister Georges Clemenceau agreed to some changes, the most important of which was a plebiscite to decide the political future of Upper Silesia. The draft treaty had awarded the territory outright to Poland. The German government sent representatives back to hold out the prospect of signing the treaty without its two most objectionable provisions concerning war guilt and war criminals. The same day word reached Paris that the German navy had scuttled its battle fleet in Scapa Flow. The French, Americans and British were furious, and refused to consider any further revisions. The German government had no choice but to accept the treaty, making the Republic vulnerable to charges by the right-wing nationalists that its socialist leaders were responsible for Germany's humiliation.[20]

[16] Riekhoff, *German–Polish Relations*, p. 383.
[17] Aristotle, *Rhetoric*, 1379b10–12, 1387a31–3.
[18] Mommsen, "Max Weber and the Peace Treaty of Versailles"; Schwabe, "Germany's Peace Aims and the Domestic and International Constraints."
[19] Mommsen, *The Rise and Fall of Weimar Democracy*, p. 91.
[20] Schwabe, "Germany's Peace Aims and the Domestic and International Constraints"; Lentin, *Lloyd George, Woodrow Wilson, and the Guilt of Germany*, pp. 93–4, and "A Comment," pp. 221–43; French, "Had We Known How Bad Things Were in Germany"; Stevenson, "French War Aims and Peace Planning"; Goldstein, "Great Britain"; MacMillan, *Paris 1919*, pp. 463–83.

The treaty became a central issue of Weimar politics, and all parties save the independent socialists (USPD) condemned it. The *Burgfrieden* – the truce among parties at the outset of the First World War – had made criticism of prewar diplomacy all but impossible during the war. The treaty controversy effectively foreclosed exposure and criticism of the ills of the former monarchical political system under the Republic.[21] It deprived pro-Republican forces of what in other circumstances would have been a powerful political tool, while shackling them with treaty terms arising from a war for which they were not responsible.

The army and right-wing forces successfully propagated the fiction that the German army had not been defeated, but had been stabbed in the back by socialists on the home front.[22] *Freikorps*, composed of former veterans, coalesced into extra-legal armies, and fought to suppress socialism in Berlin and further east, and intimidate voters in plebiscites, especially in Silesia in 1920–1. *Freikorps* also participated in the Kapp putsch of March 1920, an unsuccessful attempt to overthrow the Republic.[23] The foreign ministry conspired with conservatives to propagate the fiction that Germany bore no responsibility for the war. In a coverup that would continue into the 1960s, an entire department within the Wilhelmstrasse cleansed, edited, forged, hid and destroyed incriminating memoranda, letters and cables, and paid scholars and journalists at home and abroad to refute what it called "the war-guilt lie."[24] With a few exceptions, the German historical profession was a willing participant in this "patriotic" self-censorship and self-delusion. In 1930, Hermann Hesse lamented to Thomas Mann that "of 1,000 Germans, even today, 999 still know nothing of [our] war guilt."[25]

Pro-Republican parties – Social Democrats (SPD), Democrats and the Zentrum – won over 70 percent of the vote in first postwar national election in January 1919.[26] The inauspicious beginning of the Weimar Republic did not bode well for its survival, and some scholars see its demise as inevitable. Theodore Hamerow attributes not only the collapse of Weimar, but World War I, the rise to power of the Nazis and World War II to the failure of the German liberals in 1848 to develop constitutional

[21] Broszat, *Hitler and the Collapse of Weimar Germany*, p. 47.
[22] Mommsen, *The Rise and Fall of Weimar Democracy*, pp. 105–6.
[23] Eyck, *History of the Weimar Republic*, I, pp. 150–4.
[24] Röhl, *1914: Delusion or Design?*, pp. 21–36; Geiss, "The Outbreak of the First World War and German War Aims," on the foreign office in the 1960s; Herwig, "Introduction" and "Clio Deceived."
[25] Quoted in Herwig, "Clio Deceived."
[26] Broszat, *Hitler and the Collapse of Weimar Germany*, p. 45.

democracy as an effective alternative to the conservative authoritarianism of Prussia. "The penalty for the mistakes of 1848 was paid not in 1849, but in 1918, in 1933, and in 1945."[27] Hamerow's argument is a quintessential expression of the *Sonderweg* (special path) thesis, which attempts to explain the Nazi period as the inevitable, or at least the most likely, outcome of earlier developments in German history which mark it off from that of its Western neighbors. Ironically, the *Sonderweg* thesis originated with conservatives in the imperial era to justify Germany's constitution as a reasonable compromise between the inefficient authoritarianism of Russia and the decadence of Western democracy.[28] It was given new meaning by left-leaning historians in the post-World War II period. Historians Fritz Fischer and Hans-Ulrich Wehler mobilized it to combat the claims of their conservative–nationalist counterparts that the Hitler period was an extraordinary development, unrelated to past German history.[29] Critics of the *Sonderweg* thesis rightly note that it assumes a questionable "normal" course of history to which Britain and France conformed and from which Germany deviated.[30]

Other historians emphasize the contingency of Nazi Germany. In an early and still highly regarded history of the Weimar Republic, Erich Eyck makes a credible case that the synergism between the economic downturn and bad leadership brought Hitler to power.[31] In a variant of the *Sonderweg* thesis, Wolfgang Mommsen maintains that the collapse of Weimar was inevitable, but the rise of Hitler to power was not.[32] Henry Turner uses counterfactuals to make the case that Hitler's survival during the First World War and a later automobile accident were both remarkable, and that without Hitler Weimar's failure would likely have led to a conservative, authoritarian regime with revanchist goals in the east but no stomach for another continental war. It would have been anti-Semitic, but unlikely to have carried out draconian measures against Jews.[33]

---

[27] Krieger, *The German Idea of Freedom*; Hamerow, *Restoration, Revolution, Reaction*, p. viii; Puhle, *Von der Agrarkrise zum Präfaschismus*; Dahrendorf, *Society and Democracy*, p. 398.

[28] Kocka, "German History before Hitler."

[29] Fischer, *Germany's Aims in the First World War*; Wehler, *Der deutsche Kaiserreich*. The *Sonderweg* thesis has been revived recently by Winkler, *The Long Shadow of the Reich*, and *Der lange Weg nach Westen*, who attributes Germany's special character to developments in the Middle Ages.

[30] Eley and Blackbourn, *The Peculiarities of German History*; Evans, *Rethinking German History*.

[31] Eyck, *A History of the Weimar Republic*.

[32] Mommsen, *The Rise and Fall of Weimar Democracy*.

[33] Turner, *Geissel des Jahrhunderts*.

The determinists sensitize us to all the serious impediments that stood in the way of the success of the Republic, and those who emphasize contingency alert us to the need to separate the fate of the Republic from the question of what kind of regime might have succeeded it. The forces arrayed against the Republic were on both ends of the political continuum. The communists on the left opposed a constitutional bourgeois order. Led by intellectuals, their base consisted of workers, whose support waxed and waned as a function of the economic situation.[34] By 1928, there was very little inclination on the part of the conservatives to cooperate with the socialists, and the pro-Republican parties did not have enough seats to cobble together a center–left coalition. The grand coalition that attempted to govern lasted less than six months, the victim of Gustav Stresemann's death and the stock market crash.[35] The nationalist–conservative opposition was divided among several parties, and in the last years of the Republic the National Socialists (Nazis) became by far the strongest of these parties. In July 1932, the Nazis won 38.2 percent of the overall national vote, making anti-Republican forces a majority in the Reichstag. Government had to be conducted by emergency decree, which shifted power to President Paul von Hindenburg, and paved the way for the appointment of Hitler after the failure of the short-lived von Papen and Schleicher regimes.[36] Hindenburg could have used his emergency power to support a pro-Republican government, but preferred to rule through a conservative *fronde* that excluded the socialists from power. He set in motion a chain of events that had an outcome very different from what he imagined.[37] So did the communists. On instructions from Moscow, they made a fatal error in refusing to support the grand coalition, composed of the socialists, Zentrum and moderate parties on the right. They welcomed the Nazi regime in the expectation that it would quickly fail and pave the way for a workers' revolution.[38]

According to Karl Dietrich Bracher, the nationalist, anti-Republican front was composed of people and groups representing four orientations:

[34] Mommsen, *Rise and Fall of Weimar Democracy*, pp. 456, 494–5, 535–7.
[35] Eyck, *A History of the Weimar Republic*, II, pp. 203–52; Broszat, *Hitler and the Collapse of Weimar Germany*, pp. 94–115.
[36] Eyck, *A History of the Weimar Republic*, II, pp. 350–488; Dorpalen, *Hindenburg and the Weimar Republic*, pp. 301–446. Broszat, *Hitler and the Collapse of Weimar Germany*, pp. 115–49; Mommsen, *The Rise and Fall of Weimar Democracy*, pp. 357–432.
[37] Dorpalen, *Hindenburg and the Weimar Republic*, pp. 302–3, 316–17, 472; Mommsen, *The Rise and Fall of Weimar Democracy*, pp. 357–432; Broszat, *Hitler and the Collapse of Weimar Germany*, pp. 80–1.
[38] Mommsen, *Rise and Fall of Weimar Democracy*, pp. 456, 494–5, 535–7.

imperialistic nationalism; conservative authoritarianism; a nationalist and romantic variant of socialism; and supporters of a *völkisch*, race-based ideology.[39] Imperialistic nationalism focused on territorial revisionism, and Weimar's foreign policy, which "vacillated between East and West, resistance and compliance, cooperation and revision, was incapable of putting a brake on this dynamic."[40] Revisionist demands were intense between 1918 and 1923, and again after the depression began in 1929.[41] Conservative authoritarianism was well established in Prussia under the Hohenzollerns, and in Germany more generally since the creation of the Reich in 1871. It continued under the Republic, and sustained a predisposition, formerly directed toward the person of the Kaiser, to support a strong leader.[42] Nationalism had been actively encouraged under the empire, but its combination with a romantic variant of socialism was relatively novel. *Völkisch* sentiment was also strong within the middle class, and initially found expression as straightforward xenophobia, but increasingly morphed into racial anti-Semitism under the influence of the Nazi Party.

Hitler cleverly sold himself as the personification of all four orientations. He rallied the middle-class on the basis of his nationalism, opposition to socialists and Jews and promises of full employment. Analyses of party rolls and election data indicate that Hitler appealed not only to the lower middle class (*Kleinbürgertum*), but other middle-class groups as well. He won over conservative business and political elites by conveying the impression that he would serve as their pliant tool once in power.[43] The success of National Socialism, at home and abroad, was very much a history of the fatal underestimation of Hitler by the army, industrialists, bankers, conservative politicians and President Hindenburg. Hitler pandered to their shared illusion that they could "box him in" and exploit him for their own ends. He did the same in his foreign policy, where he communicated willingness to negotiate while making threats, preparing for war and engaging in faits accomplis. Above all else, he displayed great flexibility; he made extreme demands, but was willing to pull back

---

[39] Bracher, *The German Dictatorship*, p. 10.   [40] Ibid., p. 21.

[41] Broszat, *Hitler and the Collapse of Weimar Germany*, pp. 11–17, on the political consequences of the Great Depression.

[42] Mosse, *The Nationalization of the Masses*, chs. 1–4; Nipperdey, "Nationalidee und Nationaldenkmal in 19. Jahrhundert"; Kershaw, *The "Hitler Myth"*, p. 14.

[43] Schoenbaum, *Hitler's Social Revolution*, pp. 119–58; Kershaw, *Popular Opinion and Political Dissent in the Third Reich*, pp. 113–14; Childers, *The Nazi Voter*, pp. 1–51.

when opposed, and to push ahead when his opponents appeared weak or vacillated.[44]

Once in power, Hitler and Goebbels propagated the "Führer myth," which encouraged his idolization among the middle classes.[45] It stressed Hitler's ability to transcend class divisions, revitalize the economy, restore growth and stability, and restore German rights, territory and dignity. He was portrayed as personally unattached, selfless, incorruptible and above party politics. The Hitler cult made some inroads among workers, although the groups least receptive to his propaganda were the organized sections of the working class, Catholics and the educated elite.[46] In 1928, the Nazis garnered a mere 2.6 percent of the vote. Once the depression set in, this figure rose to 18.1. In the March 1933 elections, held two months after Hitler took office, the Nazis still received considerably less than half of the vote, but more votes than any party had in the Weimar era.[47] The Nazis received enough working-class support to shock and surprise the Marxists associated with the Institute for Social Research (the Frankfurt School), some of whom – Marcuse, Horkheimer and Fromm – turned to Freud to look for non-rational, non-economic explanations for this baffling behavior.[48]

Hitler's foreign policy successes greatly increased his support. Fully 95.1 percent of Germans supported his withdrawal of Germany from the League of Nations.[49] His popularity soared because he "liberated" the Saar and the Rhineland, brought Austria into the Reich, together with Memel and the Sudetenland, and established protectorates over Bohemia and Moravia, and all without war.[50] The twin humiliations of defeat and Versailles had been largely overcome. As Hitler put it in a well-publicized

---

[44] Bracher, *Nazi Dictatorship*, pp. 48, 287–303; Eyck, *Weimar Republic*, II, pp. 449–87; Mommsen, *Rise and Fall of Weimar Democracy*, pp. 433–89; Bracher, *German Dictatorship*, pp. 169–214; Bullock, *Hitler*, pp. 369–70; Weinberg, *Foreign Policy of Hitler's Germany*, I, pp. 358, 363.

[45] Kershaw, *"Hitler Myth"*; Schoenbaum, *Hitler's Social Revolution*; Mommsen, *Rise and Fall of Weimar Democracy*, p. 47.

[46] Kershaw, *"Hitler Myth,"* pp. 34, 53, and *Opinion and Political Dissent in the Third Reich*, pp. 71–110; Allen, *The Nazi Seizure of Power*, pp. 69–90; Broszat, *Hitler and the Collapse of Weimar Germany*, pp. 15–16; Mommsen, *Rise and Fall of Weimar Democracy*, pp. 318–56; Childers, *The Nazi Voter*, pp. 1–51.

[47] Berend Stöver, *Berichte über die Lage in Deutschland. Die Meldungen der Gruppe Neu Beginnen as dem Dritten Reich 1933–36*, cited in Frei, "People's Community and War"; Mommsen, *Rise and Fall of Weimar Democracy*, pp. 314–17.

[48] Jay, *Dialectical Imagination*, chs. 3 and 4; Wiggershaus, *Frankfurt School*, ch. 3.

[49] Kershaw, *"Hitler Myth,"* pp. 120–39.

[50] Weinberg, *Foreign Policy of Hitler's Germany*, I, pp. 159–79, 239–63, on Hitler's successes.

speech of April 28, 1939: "I have further attempted to tear up page for page that Treaty, which contained in its 448 articles the most base violations ever accorded to nations and human beings. I have given back to the Reich the provinces stolen from us in 1919."[51] Hitler's appeal extended well beyond those who thought of themselves as Nazis, and included people who were critical of his domestic policies and ideology.[52] Despite support for Hitler, there was very little support for war. Most Germans desperately wanted to believe that peace could be maintained. When Germany invaded Poland in September 1939, there was none of the enthusiasm for war that had been so visible in 1914.[53]

Hitler's rhetorical strategy and the basis of his support indicate the extent to which the spirit was central to his rise to power and subsequent popularity. Ian Kershaw, author of the most comprehensive study of Hitler's speeches, concludes that he "always enjoyed a particular talent, approaching demagogic genius, for appealing to the populist national emotions, hopes, and aggression of increasing numbers of ordinary Germans, in particular by exploiting the deep-rooted resentments which the name 'Versailles' conjured up." He wisely refrained from talking about his wider imperialist aims, as they could not be achieved without a second world war.[54] Hitler's racism, which vaunted the superiority of the Aryans over other races, was also intended to enhance his listeners' self-image and self-esteem. Economic improvements and stability, valued in their own right, were also portrayed as a means of restoring German dignity and self-esteem. *Triumph of the Will*, the most carefully crafted and justly famous of all Nazi propaganda films, is a direct appeal to the spirit. The movie encourages Germans to find self-esteem and personal fulfillment through subordination of their bodies and minds to the Führer and the national mission he is bringing to fruition. The Christian symbolism is blatant from the opening scene of Hitler's plane descending over the stadium and casting a shadow in the shape of a cross over the bodies of the massed stormtroopers. Hitler and his uniformed soldiers arrayed in columns evoke knights preparing for a quest and sworn to uphold their honor and that of their liege. Both images are reinforcing, as they were in medieval imagery and in many World War I recruiting posters.[55] For

[51] Quoted in Kershaw, *"Hitler Myth,"* p. 256.

[52] Ibid. p. 5; Schoenbaum, *Hitler's Social Revolution*, pp. 77–118, on Hitler and labor.

[53] Kershaw, *"Hitler Myth,"* pp. 139–47; Frei, "People's Community and War."

[54] Kershaw, *"Hitler Myth,"* p. 122.

[55] Diephouse, "Triumph of Hitler's Will"; Welch, *Propaganda and the German Cinema, 1933–1945*; Kershaw, *"Hitler Myth,"* p. 69.

quite different reasons, knights and chivalry featured very prominently in postwar memorials in Britain and Germany.[56]

The spirit is easily angered by real or imagined slights, and readily responds to opposition with hostility. This process drives the action in Sophocles' *Ajax*, when the armor of the dead Achilles is awarded to Odysseus. Convinced that he deserves it, but that it was denied him by virtue of the hostility of others, Ajax seeks revenge against Odysseus, the Atridae clan and the Greek army. Paranoia of this kind is often associated with heroic actors, and, I have argued, is particularly prevalent in societies with low self-esteem. Such paranoia was evident in the German Empire, where Fritz Stern notes that visions of politics were "blurred by clouds of evil fantasy."[57] Publicists and anti-Semites charged England and France with plotting Germany's encirclement, and Jews and socialists of boring away from within. These conspiracies also flourished in the Weimar period, augmented by the new charge of a *Dolchstoss* (stab in the back) made by Hindenburg to a parliamentary committee in 1919.[58] The socialists and Jews – "November criminals" – were made responsible for defeat and the hated Treaty of Versailles.[59] The widespread success of conspirational theories under the empire and in Weimar is further evidence of the degree to which German politics was driven by the spirit.

Many historians contend that the most fundamental cause of the Third Reich was the deep schism between German and Western political thought that opened up in the late eighteenth century and its consequences for German political and national development.[60] It resulted in a special German sense of destiny with strong anti-Western overtones. This latter outlook found expression in Kant's effort to discipline French individualism with German enlightened corporatism and Fichte's *Address to the German Nation*. In the latter, written in 1807–8 in response to the French occupation, Fichte praised the "German spirit," whose ideals transcended the selfish goals of Western culture, and described Germans as the only Europeans capable of profound and original thought. Anti-Western diatribes became a constant theme of German literature and intellectuals

[56] Goebel, *Great War and Medieval Memory*, contends that the crusades, chivalry and medieval spirituality provided tropes and narratives to personalize loss and provide meaning to the war and its legacy.
[57] Stern, *Failure of Illiberalism*, p. xxxviii.
[58] Dorpalen, *Hindenburg and the Weimar Republic*, pp. 51–2.
[59] Krumeich, "Die Dolchstoss-Legende"; Seiler, "'Dolchstoss' und 'Dolchstosslegende.'"
[60] Lukács, *Destruction of Reason*; Plessner, *Verspätete Nation*; Mosse, *The Crisis of German Ideology*; Stern, *Politics of Cultural Despair*; Holborn, "Origins and Political Character of Nazi Ideology"; Bracher, *Nazi Dictatorship*, pp. 23, 494–5; Herf, *Reactionary Modernism*.

in the nineteenth and early twentieth centuries. Thomas Mann's *Reflections of a Non-Political Man*, written toward the end of World War I, praises Germany's musical and metaphysical culture, which he contrasts with the more skeptical, analytic and political culture of the West. He rejects democracy as "foreign and poisonous to the German character" and endorses the *Obrigkeitstaat* (authoritarian state) as most suitable to the German character.[61] In the 1920s, writing in the aftermath of another defeat and partial French occupation, Oswald Spengler advanced a variant of this argument in his bestselling *Decline of the West*. Western thought, he wrote, was "merely rational," and the Germans, who were capable of great accomplishments, had to be protected from it.[62] The German middle class was particularly susceptible to *völkisch* ideas, as events of 1848, 1866, 1870, 1918 and 1933 revealed.[63] Nazi ideology was admittedly a more extreme variant, but one that played to a largely receptive audience, and for reasons having largely to do with the need for self-esteem.

Italy

The other two powers most responsible for World War II were Italy and Japan. They pursued foreign policies that were grossly irrational from the perspective of national security. Italy was a great power in name only. It had a sizeable population – some 35 million on the eve of the First World War – but its rate of literacy was the lowest of any major country, and malaria and pellagra were endemic in its countryside. The peninsula was almost entirely lacking in coal, compelling Italy to import most of its fuel from Britain. Its steel output was a mere fraction of Britain's or Germany's, and its rail network was far less dense, largely single-track and almost entirely dependent on foreign financing.[64] In the 1930s, Italy suffered a severe balance of payments deficit, and remittances from its large numbers of emigrants had largely dried up due to the world depression. Its bureaucracy and government were inefficient and corrupt, and its military was poorly trained and led by aristocrats who were more interested in status than leadership. The incompetence of the Italian army had

---

[61] Mann, *Reflections of a Nonpolitical Man*, p. 16 for quote. Mann wrote this work during the war, although it was published in 1918, and in the years afterwards he gradually underwent a shift in his politics, ending up a supporter of the Republic.
[62] Spengler, *Decline of the West*.   [63] Bracher, *Nazi Dictatorship*, pp. 27–8.
[64] Cafagna, *Industrial Revolution in Italy*, pp. 11–13; Fenoaltea, "Italy"; Bosworth, *Italy, the Least of the Great Powers*, pp. 2–5.

been revealed at Adowa in 1896, where it suffered a humiliating defeat at the hands of Ethiopia, and in World War I, where it was no match for even Austria-Hungary. Italy was a great power as a matter of courtesy and encouragement, a diplomatic fiction that went to the head of liberal Italy in 1915, as it did again in fascist Italy in 1940. In private, Bismarck sneered: "As to Italy, she does not count."[65] At the turn of the century, Lord Salisbury dismissed Italy as "the *quantité négligeable*."[66] In 1914, Edward Grey derided Italians as "the blue bottle flies of international politics: always buzzing when one wants to be quiet."[67] At Versailles, Charles Hardinge referred to the Italians as "the beggars of Europe."[68]

In Italy, World War I strengthened right-wing nationalist forces. The country entered the war in May 1915, paid an enormous human price for Trieste and Trentino, the territory it gained from Austria at the end of the war, and faced an antagonistic Yugoslavia in the east. The Italian middle class was nearly ruined by the postwar inflation, dramatic increases in the price of coal, high unemployment and a growing trade imbalance.[69] The peasant struggle for land became increasingly acute as did industrial unrest, which took the form of strikes and violence by and against workers. Mazzini's vision of a modernizing left-oriented republic lost ground to a cruder form of nationalism, personified by Gabriele D'Annunzio and Benito Mussolini.[70] In September 1919 D'Annunzio and 2,000 *arditi* – mostly demobilized soldiers – attempted to redeem Fiume (now Rijeka in Croatia) for the motherland, but were forced to withdraw in the face of an Italian naval blockade.[71] Mussolini, a socialist turned nationalist, distanced himself from D'Annunzio to made his own bid for power. He played on Italian anger at *la vittoria mutilata* (hijacked victory), blaming it on "the evil brood" of *caporettisti* (generals and politicians) who had "stabbed the nation in the back."[72] By helping to foster the myth that Italy was somehow robbed of its rightful due, he and other politicians on the right laid the foundations for revisionism and Italian cooperation with Nazi Germany in the 1930s.[73]

---

[65] Quoted in Taylor, *Struggle for the Mastery of Europe*, p. 283.   [66] Ibid.
[67] Quoted in Bridge, *Great Britain and Austria-Hungary*, p. 146.
[68] Lowe and Marzari, *Italian Foreign Policy*, pp. 160–72; quote from Bosworth, *Italy, the Least of the Great Powers*, p. 5.
[69] Lowe and Marzari, *Italian Foreign Policy*, p. 173.
[70] Chabod, *History of Italian Fascism*, pp. 22–8; Lyttelton, *Seizure of Power*, p. 3; Samuels, *Machiavelli's Children*, pp. 35–7.
[71] Mack Smith, *Italy*, p. 335; Samuels, *Machiavelli's Children*, p. 113.
[72] Chabod, *History of Italian Fascism*, pp. 19–20, 48–9; Samuels, *Machiavelli's Children*, p. 36.
[73] Lowe and Marzari, *Italian Foreign Policy*, pp. 179–80.

Fascism arose from the split between interventionists and neutralists, which generated an acute political division in the country. By the war's end, democracy was considered obsolete by many intellectuals and members of the middle class, raising the prospect of a fascist or socialist takeover. The Italian government was hobbled by the limited power of the executive and an increasingly immobilized legislature. There were frequent changes in party alignments and governments, but very little, if any, effort at governing. At its core, this *immobilisme* was attributable to the deep division between the increasingly industrial north and a rural south, whose poverty and illiteracy allowed clientalism to flourish.[74]

Fascism was a largely urban, middle-class movement that had little success in attracting workers or ex-combatants. In 1921, the party had 310,000 party members, of whom only 22,418 were workers and only 36,847 peasants. It appealed to journalists, artists, writers and unemployed intellectuals anxious to secure a livelihood and some degree of recognition, to marginal groups from the petty bourgeoisie like shopkeepers and low-salaried employees, and to anyone attracted to the emotional excitement and turmoil associated with a radical and violent political movement. Mussolini actively sought the support of conservative landowners and businessmen, holding out the prospect that a fascist government would serve their economic interests and serve as a bulwark against socialism. Like the Nazis, the fascists never received an electoral majority in contested elections. In May 1921 they won a mere 36 out of 535 seats in the national assembly. In 1924, after two years in power, Mussolini's fascists captured only 65 percent of the vote in an election in which they used every means of intimidation against their opponents.[75]

The key to Mussolini's success was his paramilitary organization, the *squadristi* (Black Shirts) which he used to cow or silence opponents and sweep the opposition from streets.[76] In October 1922, Mussolini marched on Rome with 30,000 supporters after his *squadristi* had already taken power in most of the cities of the Po Valley. Supported by the military, the business community and a wide segment of the middle classes, and badly advised by Giolitti, King Vittorio Emanuele rejected the government's demand that he call out the army to suppress the fascists and

---

[74] Lyttelton, *Seizure of Power*, pp. 3, 8–9; Samuels, *Machiavelli's Children*, pp. 121–4.

[75] Salvemini, *Origins of Fascism in Italy*, p. 419; Chabod, *History of Italian Fascism*, pp. 49–51; Lyttelton, *Seizure of Power*, pp. 48–76; Mack Smith, *Mussolini*, pp. 35–51; Samuels, *Machiavelli's Children*, p. 49.

[76] Chabod, *History of Italian Fascism*, pp. 55–61.

instead handed power over to Mussolini.[77] In June 1924, Mussolini used the assassination of Giacomo Matteotti, an anti-fascist writer, probably carried out by his own henchmen, as a pretext to establish a dictatorship.[78]

More than most leaders, Mussolini was a man of ideas, and had been a leading socialist intellectual in the prewar years. Fascist ideology was nevertheless "remarkably nebulous" because Mussolini above all wanted to convey an impression of action.[79] Not surprisingly, the fascist program of 1919 proved a poor guide to the party's subsequent behavior. To the extent the regime developed an ideology, it emerged in response to Mussolini's efforts to create a hierarchical, corporatist state based on anti-hedonist and virile myths that belligerently advocated "a policy of grandeur, power and conquest aimed at creating a new order and a new supranational civilization."[80] In 1910, Enrico Corradini, a co-founder of the Nationalist Association, had compared nations to classes, arguing that "Italy is, materially and morally, a proletarian nation." "Just as socialism taught the proletariat the value of the class struggle," he wrote, "we must teach Italy the value of the international struggle."[81] Mussolini appropriated and elaborated this idea, and increasingly used national assertion as a substitute for economic reform and development.

Mussolini was no more able to address Italy's economic problems than his predecessors because any serious attempt to do so would have involved confrontations with key backers of his regime. He did, however, try to satisfy Italian cravings for greater standing in the world. Early nationalists had invoked Rome as an idea and Italy as a culture in their efforts to build a common identity.[82] Mussolini built on this base, invoking past Roman glories and modern Italy's achievements as a nation "of poets, of artists, of heroes, of saints, of scientists, of explorers, and of emigrants."[83] He promised to make Italy another Rome and the Mediterranean into *mare nostrum*, introduced the Roman salute, dress and symbols, and quietly encouraged the practice of the ancient polytheistic religion.[84] Denis Mack Smith, author of a respected biography of Mussolini, argues that "By

[77] Chabod, *History of Italian Fascism*, p. 41; Samuels, *Machiavelli's Children*, pp. 112–14.
[78] Mack Smith, *Mussolini*, pp. 56–61; Lyttelton, *Seizure of Power*, pp. 237–68.
[79] Chabod, *History of Italian Fascism*, pp. 19–20, 48–9; Samuels, *Machiavelli's Children*, p. 36.
[80] Gentile, *Fascist Ideology*, p. xiii.
[81] Corradini, "Report to the First Nationalist Congress."
[82] Tullio-Altan, *La conscienza civile degli Italiani*; Romano, "La cultura della politica esterna italiana"; Procacci, *History of the Italian People*, p. 327.
[83] Chabod, *History of Italian Fascism*, pp. 19–20, 48–9; Samuels, *Machiavelli's Children*, p. 36.
[84] Zunino, *L'ideologia del fascismo*, p. 85; Chabod, *Italian Foreign Policy*, p. 170; Mack Smith, *Mussolini's Roman Empire*, pp. 82–4.

convincing Italians that he and he alone could lead them to greatness and riches at negligible cost to themselves, he won the plenitude of power for himself without much opposition."[85] No less of an authority than Hitler was impressed by the passions that Il Duce aroused among his countrymen.[86]

Mussolini is an enigmatic and complex figure, an intellectual fond of quoting Plato, Machiavelli, Kant and Nietzsche, and part *animale poco socievole* (barely socialized ruffian), whose thinking underwent a considerable evolution, and whose behavior often appears at odds with his apparent goals. These contradictions have allowed remarkably diverse interpretations of Il Duce to flourish. Italian liberals have been dismissive of Mussolini and his regime, condemning it in the words of Benedetto Croce as "antihistorical" and a mere "parenthesis" in Italian history.[87] The more conservative Renzo de Felice offers an apologetic assessment in his multi-volume biography, depicting Mussolini as humane, widely supported by the Italian people in the early and mid-1930s and later victimized by Hitler who left him little choice in foreign policy.[88] Gaetano Salvemini, a prominent anti-Fascist exile, portrays Mussolini as a man driven by ego, possessed of great demogogic skills, but operating "from hand to mouth" without any strategic goals.[89] Marxist historians have taken Mussolini more seriously, and have documented the extent to which he was, like Hitler, a *sanguinario* (blood-stained murderer). Predictably, but unconvincingly, they invoke Lenin and his theory of imperialism to explain Italy's entry into the Second World War.[90] Prominent diplomatic historians and Mussolini biographers consider Mussolini's foreign policy to have been motivated by a desire to consolidate and maintain his domestic authority by creating the appearance of Italy as a power of primary importance. They acknowledge the tension between this goal and Mussolini's day-to-day conduct, which was often dictated by his desire to cut a figure for himself, defer to the interests of others when successfully flattered, and overreact to what he considered slights to his or Italy's

---

[85] Mack Smith, *Mussolini's Roman Empire*, p. viii.
[86] Trevor-Roper, *Hitler's Secret Conversations*, nos. 132, 268.
[87] Croce, "Chi è fascista?"; Mack Smith, "Benedetto Croce: History and Politics."
[88] De Felice, *Mussolini*, and *Interpretations of Fascism*.
[89] Salvemini, *Prelude to World War II*.
[90] Togliatti, *Lectures on Fascism*. For more subtle Marxist accounts, Ragionieri, *Dall'unità a oggi*, and Santarelli, *Storia di movimento e de regime fascista*. Webster, *Industrial Imperialism in Italy*, and Bosworth, *Italy*, for arguments that Mussolini, not industrialists, dictated colonial expansion, and that the latter had more to gain from an economy open to trade with Western Europe.

prestige.[91] Torn between realism and desire, he ultimately succumbed to the latter.

The publication of Fritz Fischer's *Griff nach der Weltmacht* (literally, "Grasping for World Power") in 1962 made apparent the extent to which Hitler's goals did not differ fundamentally from those of Imperial Germany.[92] Since then, historians have generally come to accept the Nazi era more as a continuation of the German past than a sharp break with it. The same is true of fascist Italy and its liberal predecessor. Both were powers on the make, "looking for a bargain package deal which would offer the least of the Great Powers a place in the sun."[93] Before the First World War, Italians were aware of the low esteem in which they were held by the other powers. Former foreign minister Francesco Guicciardini recognized that foreigners were impressed by "our sky, our countryside, our cities," and to overcome this humiliation, Italy must be "more respected" as a power.[94] In 1911, British ambassador Rennell Rodd was struck by Italy's "adolescent inferiority complex."[95]

Mussolini's foreign policy was motivated by the pursuit of *grandezza*, which he initially pursued with some degree of caution. He promised to drive Britain out of the Mediterranean and turn it into an "Italian lake," which played well with the public.[96] He made demands on Britain and France in Africa, and did not hide his ambition to conquer Abyssinia (Ethiopia), but waited to do so until he was convinced he could get away with it. His incentive to act grew in proportion to the stagnation of the economy. As a result of the depression, the stock market lost a third of its value between 1929 and 1932, gold flowed out of the country, production and exports declined, emigrant remittances more than halved, real wages fell, unemployment grew. Mussolini's feeble efforts to make the country economically self-reliant only made matters worse.[97] The invasion of Abyssinia on October 3, 1935 was greeted with "unimaginable

---

[91] Lowe and Marzari, *Italian Foreign Policy*; Weinberg, *The Foreign Policy of Hitler's Germany*; Coverdale, *Italian Intervention in the Spanish Civil War*; Mack Smith, *Mussolini*, *Roman* and *Mussolini's Roman Empire*; Bosworth, *Mussolini*.

[92] An English version appeared in 1966 with the insipid title, *Germany's Aims in the First World War*.

[93] Bosworth, *Italy, the Least of the Great Powers*, p. viii.

[94] *Atti parlamentari, Camera dei Deputati*, XXIII, xiii, June 7, 1911, p. 15348. Quoted in Bosworth, *Italy, the Least of the Great Powers*, p. 7.

[95] Rennell Rodd to Edward Grey, November 27, 1911, in Rodd Papers, Bodleian Library, Oxford. Quoted in Bosworth, *Italy, the Least of the Great Powers*, p. 8.

[96] Salvemini, *Origins of Fascism in Italy*, p. 33; Lowe and Marzari, *Italian Foreign Policy*, p. 291; Mack Smith, *Mussolini*, pp. 170–87.

[97] Bosworth, *Mussolini*, pp. 288–92; De Felice, *Mussolini*, I, pp. 63–74.

excitement" by the Italian people.[98] Its timing was serendipitous because Hitler had repudiated the disarmament provision of Versailles the day before, making Britain and France more willing to accommodate Italy in light of the greater threat posed by Hitler.[99] The conventional explanation that the conquest of Abyssinia was an expression of "exasperated nationalism seeking to divert internal discontent into foreign adventures" is fundamentally sound.[100]

Between 1933 and 1936, Mussolini supported the status quo in Europe and appeared alert to the dangers of Hitler and a revisionist Germany. He had every reason to maintain forces on the Brenner Pass to prevent an *Anschluss*, as it would give Germany entry into eastern Europe and the Balkans and put direct pressure on the Tyrol, where Mussolini was using coercive measures to Italianize its German-speaking population.[101] His invasion of Ethiopia in October 1935 alienated Britain and France, provoking mild sanctions from the League of Nations. Italy lost any leverage it had over Hitler, who now felt free to occupy Austria.[102]

In June 1934, Mussolini met Hitler in Venice and came away convinced that he was a "dangerous fool."[103] In May 1939, he nevertheless signed the Pact of Steel with Hitler, helping to shift the European balance of power in Germany's favor.[104] Hitler's alliance with the Soviet Union in August – euphemistically advertised as a "non-aggression pact" – permitted him to invade Poland and then the west with his eastern and southern flanks secured. Mussolini now made the further, and fatal, error of entering the war on the side of Germany in the spring of 1940, when he sent Italian troops into France following Germany's invasion of that country.

Mussolini's volte-face was due in part to his invasion of Ethiopia, which alienated France and Britain, led to mild sanctions, and pushed him in the direction of Germany. So did his intervention in the Spanish Civil War. Nor could he not resist the temptation to weaken France by flirting with Hitler because the French government gave succor to anti-fascist émigrés. Along with Britain, France was regarded by Italian nationalists

---

[98] De Felice, *Mussolini*, I, p. 758. Mack Smith, *Mussolini*, pp. 196–202; Bosworth, *Mussolini*, pp. 308–9, concur on the popularity of the invasion.

[99] Lowe and Marzari, *Italian Foreign Policy*, p. 262.

[100] Ibid., p. 240; De Felice, Mussolini, I, pp. 610–14, for the claim that it was externally motivated.

[101] Lowe and Marzari, *Italian Foreign Policy*, pp. 174–5, 202–4.

[102] Weinberg, *Foreign Policy of Hitler's Germany*, II, pp. 261–312.

[103] Salvemini, *Origins of Fascism in Italy*, p. 151 for the quote. Weinberg, *Foreign Policy of Hitler's Germany*, I, p. 332; II, p. 263.

[104] Weinberg, *Foreign Policy of Hitler's Germany*, II, pp. 304–12.

as their principal Mediterranean and colonial antagonist.[105] Mussolini accordingly refused to oppose German reoccupation of the Rhineland in 1935 and subsequently eased his vigilance on the Brenner, making it possible for Hitler to march unopposed into Austria.[106]

Mussolini routinely used the police to report on the public mood, and was disturbed to discover that a decade into fascism his attempts to transform Italian youth were not succeeding.[107] His intervention in the Spanish Civil War in 1936 was unpopular and costly. Italy lost 3,000 soldiers and untold military equipment, some of which Franco's government sold to his enemy Yugoslavia. Mussolini admitted privately that this conflict "bled his country white."[108] He visited Germany in September 1937, where the Nazis dazzled him with military parades, visits to arms factories and an audience, estimated at a million people, that wildly cheered his speech, which was in less than perfect German. Hitler persuaded him that Germany could not be defeated and that Italy could be its equal partner in victory. Mussolini returned home believing that territorial gains in Europe could only be made with Hitler as an ally. To demonstrate his bona fides as an ally, he began to impose restrictions on Italian Jews, only to meet opposition from within the fascist hierarchy.[109] Mussolini convinced himself that he could restrain Hitler and use his association with him to gain concessions from Britain and France and expand Italian territory control in the Balkans. On May 22, 1939, he signed the Pact of Steel and committed Italy to follow Germany to war.[110]

By August 1939, Mussolini was having second thoughts. He understood that Hitler was planning war sooner rather than later, would not supply him with the materials Italy needed to become more combat ready, and whose unexpected pact with Stalin transformed him and Italy into very junior partners. Ciano was "disgusted" with the way German leaders "have tricked us and lied to us," and began a campaign to keep Mussolini from going to war.[111] The military, aware of their lack of preparedness, feared

[105] Weinberg, *Foreign Policy of Hitler's Germany*, II, p. 263.
[106] Lowe and Marzari, *Italian Foreign Policy*, pp. 291–314; Weinberg, *Foreign Policy of Hitler's Germany*, I, pp. 256, 332–4; II, pp. 261–312.
[107] De Felice, *Mussolini*, III, pp. 359–61.
[108] Mack Smith, *Mussolini's Roman Empire*, p. 105.
[109] Ciano, *Diary, 1937–38*, February 6, September 4, October 6, November 12, 1938, pp. 71, 150–1, 172, 193; Mack Smith, *Mussolini's Roman Empire*, p. 97; Lowe and Marzari, *Italian Foreign Policy*, p. 301.
[110] Lowe and Marzari, *Italian Foreign Policy*, pp. 331–6.
[111] Ciano, *Diary, 1939–43*, August 13, 1939, p. 125; Lowe and Marzari, *Italian Foreign Policy*, pp. 340–62; Bosworth, *Mussolini*, pp. 354–6.

the prospect of a prolonged war.[112] Mussolini's alliance with Hitler was not at all popular, and the Italian people were generally horrified by the prospect of a European war.[113] Ciano did not succeed in turning Mussolini away from Hitler, and confided to his diary that "The Duce is really out of his wits. His military instinct and his sense of honour were leading him to war. Reason has not stopped him."[114]

German successes in the spring of 1940 against Poland in the east and Denmark, Norway, Holland, Belgium and France in the west convinced Mussolini that time was running out. He told Ciano on May 13 that "Any delay is unthinkable."[115] Ciano wrote in his diary that Mussolini "believes the Germans will succeed and will succeed quickly" and that Italy had to join them if they were to make territorial gains.[116] On May 29 Mussolini communicated the same message to Marshal Badoglio and other military leaders: Italy needed "a few thousand dead to be able to attend the peace conference as a belligerent."[117] Mussolini now also worried about his standing in the country. He told Ciano that "The Italians will laugh at me. Every time Hitler takes a country he sends me a message."[118] Il Duce now became victim of his own motto: *Chi si ferma è perduto* (he who stops is lost). He succumbed to "the delusions of invincibility to which successful dictators are prone."[119]

On one level, Italy's foreign policy was the creation of one man: Mussolini. He decided to invade Abyssinia, seek territory at the expense of France, Yugoslavia, Albania and Greece, and was responsible for Italy's accommodation of and fatal dependence on Germany. His decision to invade France and join the war on the side of Hitler was actively opposed by his foreign minister and led to disaster. Mussolini's authority and seemingly idiosyncratic foreign policy has led apologists like De Felice, and Italian historians more generally, to hold him, not their country, responsible for the horrors the Italian army inflicted on Balkan populations and that Italy suffered at the hands of the allies and the Germans.[120] There are,

[112] Ciano, *Diary, 1939–43*, August 21, 1939, pp. 130–1.
[113] Ibid., September 2, 1939, p. 143; Coverdale, *Italian Intervention in the Spanish Civil War*, pp. 266–71; Aquarone, "Public Opinion in Italy before the Outbreak of World War II"; Mack Smith, *Mussolini*, pp. 213–50.
[114] Ciano, *Diary, 1929–43*, August 26, 1939, pp. 285–6.
[115] Ibid., May 13, 1940, pp. 249–50.   [116] Ibid.
[117] Badoglio, *Italy in the Second World War*, p. 15.
[118] Ciano, *Diary, 1939–43*, March 15, 1939, pp. 44–6.
[119] Lowe and Marzari, *Italian Foreign Policy*, p. 276.
[120] De Felice, *Interpretations of Fascism*, and *Rosso e nero*; Bosworth, *Mussolini*; Dondi, "The Fascist Mentality after Fascism"; Fogu, "*Italiani brava gente*."

however, reasons to question Mussolini's absolute power with respect to these decisions and the extent to which he pursued a policy at odds with significant segments of elite and middle-class opinion.

Mussolini's territorial ambitions in the Adriatic, North Africa and Abyssinia had a long genealogy, and were widely supported by elite and broader public opinion. The conquest of Abyssinia, despite its senselessness and brutality, aroused euphoria at home. As for entry into World War II, fascist Italy behaved in a manner reminiscent of its liberal predecessor. In 1914–15, the Italian government waited to see which side was likely to emerge victorious, and joined them after long bargaining to extract the maximum in territorial concessions.[121] Mussolini did the same, and was quietly supported by all who wanted Italy to turn its myth of being a great power into a reality. Students of Italian public opinion suggest that there was a notable shift toward a pro-war policy in May 1940, and this even affected the Catholic Church, whose leaders were prepared to support a brief, victorious war.[122] Bosworth concludes that "There is every reason . . . to think that, in the special circumstances of mid-June 1940, Mussolini made a 'decision' from which few demurred."[123] It is important to remember in this connection that Mussolini was not removed from power for starting a war, but for losing it. As Max Weber noted, charismatic leadership thrives on the promise of success but rarely survives failure.[124]

Like its German counterpart, the Italian case illustrates the extent to which the middle classes and intellectuals can seek self-esteem through the political–military success of their nation and the standing it confers. In both countries, nationalist, anti-republican forces appealed to these groupings, evoking strikingly similar anxieties that included betrayal and a "stab in the back" by socialists and republicans. In Italy, the nationalist right had to convince Italians that they should resent the peace settlement, a sentiment that needed no advertising campaign in Germany. Italian fascists and other nationalists made no efforts to scapegoat a minority, and Mussolini's later racial laws and roundups of Italian Jews, intended to placate Hitler, aroused little sympathy among fascists.[125] Even in Germany,

---

[121] Lowe and Marzari, *Italian Foreign Policy*, pp. 133–60.
[122] Colarizi, *L'opinione degli italiani sotto il regime 1929–1943*, pp. 336–8; Padrone, "Le reazioni dell'opinione pubblica italiana all'intervento nella seconda guerra mondiale."
[123] Bosworth, *Mussolini*, p. 370.
[124] Weber, *Economy and Society*, pp. 114–15.
[125] Michaelis, *Mussolini and the Jews*; Zuccotti, *Italians and the Holocaust*; Steinberg, *All or Nothing*; Carpi, *Between Mussolini and Hitler*; Bosworth, *Mussolini*, pp. 342–4, 391–4, 407.

where anti-Semitism was rife, there is little evidence that Hitler's anti-Semitism won him popular support in his bid for power, as opposed to being accepted or tolerated by those who backed him largely for other reasons.[126] The fascist and Nazi movements profited from sharp economic downturns, which brought them support from members of the middle classes attracted to their ideology and fearful of socialism. Mussolini and Hitler promised to improve the economy and reduce unemployment, but only Hitler succeeded: extraordinary expenditure on defense led to nearly full employment by the end of 1936.[127] Mussolini was compelled to seek foreign successes to maintain support for his regime. In his rise to power, Hitler copied Mussolini with great success. In his bid for supremacy in the Mediterranean, Mussolini tried to mimic Hitler and failed miserably. His failure not only revealed his incompetence as a leader, but more fundamentally exposed the unreality of the Italian desire to pursue political–military greatness in the near total absence of its organizational, economic and social prerequisites.

Japan

Japan was the dominant power in northeast Asia, ruling over Korea, Manchuria, Taiwan and other Pacific islands. If reason is defined in terms of a state's security and economic interests, Japanese foreign policy became increasingly irrational in the 1930s with the army's occupation Manchuria, withdrawal from the League of Nations in March 1933, the signing of the Anti-Comintern Pact with Germany and Italy in November 1936, and the July 1937 invasion of China. The Japanese attack against the US fleet in Hawaii, on December 7, 1941, followed by assaults against the Philippines and British and Dutch colonies, rested on a best-case scenario, and a very unrealistic one at that. To understand these foreign policy and military initiatives, we must turn to the history of Japan, the tensions associated with its modernization and the ways in which its leaders and the Japanese people sought recognition and standing.

---

[126] Merkl, *Political Violence under the Swastika*, pp. 33, 453; Noakes, *Nazi Party*, pp. 209–10; Kershaw, *"Hitler Myth,"* pp. 229–54, and "Ideology, Propaganda, and the Rise of the Nazi Party" suggest that anti-Semitism was a motivating force for the early activist core of the Nazi Party, but quite secondary to subsequent electoral successes, with the possible exceptions of Middle Franconia and parts of Hesse, Westphalia and the Rhineland where Jews traditionally dominated local trade and rural credit.

[127] Weinberg, *Foreign Policy of Hitler's Germany*, II, pp. 348–51.

Like Italy, Japan was economically underdeveloped in comparison to the other great powers.[128] The two countries shared other formative experiences.[129] Both were unified by means of civil wars. The Italian Risorgimento was a conflict between the old and new ruling classes, and the Japanese Restoration one with the old ruling class. Neither ruling class had to face a serious challenge from a well-organized bourgeoisie. Both successfully blocked agrarian reform.[130] The political systems that emerged had parliamentary facades, but effectively concentrated power in the hands of a small elite who ruled through backroom deals. In both countries, there was widespread dissatisfaction with this kind of regime, which intensified after World War I. In Italy, Mussolini was able to exploit this sentiment to establish an extra-parliamentary system of personal rule. In Japan, the military, and especially the army, usurped parliamentary authority and by the mid-1930s had a relatively free hand in determining foreign policy.

In the late nineteenth and early twentieth centuries the elites of Italy and Japan were conscious of their backwardness and fearful of foreign domination. Both countries were "catch-up imperialists." Italy fought colonial wars in North Africa in the late nineteenth and early twentieth century, while Japan built an empire in northeast Asia as a result of successful wars against China and Russia. These wars were enormously popular in both countries, and leaders and public opinion alike felt cheated when their battlefield gains were to varying degrees annulled at the conference table. Japanese negotiators were greeted with mass protests when they returned home in 1905 from the Portsmouth Peace Conference. Like Italy, Japan fought on the allied side in World War I, but at the Paris Peace Conference in 1919 was denied the territorial rewards promised earlier by Britain and France because they were glaringly at odds with the principles embodied in Woodrow Wilson's Fourteen Points.[131]

The starting point for any analysis of Japanese self-esteem is the country's relationship with China, historically its most important neighbor. Japan was never in the Chinese political orbit, but received from it its

---

[128] Howe, *The Origins of Modern Japanese Trade Supremacy*; Lockwood, *The Economic Development of Japan*; Tolliday, *Economic Development of Modern Japan*, I, on prewar Japanese trade and development.

[129] Samuels, *Machiavelli's Children*, for an elaboration of this theme. Knox, *Common Destiny*, for comparisons of Italy and Germany.

[130] Samuels, *Machiavelli's Children*, p. 21; Waswo, "The Origins of Tenant Unrest."

[131] Okamoto, *Japanese Oligarchy and the Russo-Japanese War*, pp. 167, 184, 218–21; Nish, *Japanese Foreign Policy*, pp. 93–125; LaFeber, *The Clash*, pp. 120–7.

religion, general culture and writing system.[132] During the Ming dynasty, Asia was dominated by a Sinocentric order that assumed division of the world between the Chinese and uncivilized barbarians. It found expression in a tribute or "investiture" system, that defined the ethical norms of Confucianism as the foundation of civilization. As these norms were allegedly embodied in the Chinese state and personified by the emperor, other peoples could become civilized and contribute to order by proclaiming themselves "subjects" of the Son of Heaven. This entailed signing a document, known as *piao*, by which vassals accepted the Chinese calendar, which was seen as the equivalent of accepting the emperor's role as mediator between cosmos and man.[133] Augustus had similarly demanded acceptance of his calendar as a sign of submission.[134]

The Chinese world order had willing participants, among them Korea and Siam, but not Japan. The Japanese were unwilling to enter into a subordinate relationship with China because of their own sense of centrality and their core myth of imperial divinity. Acceptance of any superior authority would have violated this self-image. The Japanese acknowledged Chinese suzerainty only briefly in the Muromachi period to allow advantageous trade. The act of submission was made by a shogun seeking to liberate himself from Japanese imperial sanction.[135] By the eighteenth century, some thinkers urged rejection of China as a model. In the Tokugawa period, the Chinese literary heritage became even more important for the Japanese, but China as a country was seen to have declined under Manchu rule.[136] In the first decades of the twentieth century, Japanese attitudes toward China were complex: contempt for China's present coexisted with respect for its past, and yearnings for solidarity competed with feelings of superiority and disdain.[137]

In premodern times the Japanese set about creating an alternative international order centered on themselves, but still acceptable to other Asians and allowing trade and cultural contact.[138] They engaged in trade and other relations only with those countries that accepted the protocols associated with a Japan-centered (*ka'i*) order. Brief submission in the Muromachi period aside, the Japanese avoided any relationship with China that

---

[132] Jansen, *Japan and its World*, pp. 9–14.
[133] Nelson, *Korea and the Old Orders in East Asia*; pp. 11–20; Fairbank, *Chinese World Order*, pp. 8–9, 20–2, 63–89, 190, 211.
[134] Beacham, "The Emperor as Impresario."
[135] Toby, *State and Diplomacy in Early Modern Japan*, pp. 170–2.
[136] Jansen, *Japan and its World*, pp. 24–5, 18–19.
[137] Duus, "Japan's Informal Empire in China, 1895–1937."   [138] Ibid., p. 173.

sacrificed the appearance of Japanese primacy.[139] This orientation would also govern Japan's approach to the West: they would freely borrow while trying to avoid dependence.[140] The first Europeans to reach Japan, Portuguese sailors blown off course in 1542, were regarded as curiosities. Seven years later, Jesuit missionaries arrived and quickly made converts. In 1587 they were expelled, and Christians, homegrown and foreigners alike, were crucified. In 1640, the Tokugawa terminated contact with the West, although a small community of Dutch merchants was allowed to reside on an island near Nagasaki. Henceforth, the Japanese would define themselves in opposition to both Chinese and Europeans.

In 1853, Commodore Perry and his four black ships arrived in Tokyo Bay and forced Japan to open its doors to the West. Europeans and Americans subsequently compelled the Shogunate to lift the taxes it had imposed on foreign and Japanese traders and to reduce tariffs. The treaties of 1859 committed Japan in perpetuity to an across-the-board tariff of only 5 percent. For nearly half a century, the Japanese chafed at the terms imposed by the Western powers. Desire to escape from degrading, "unequal treaties" was a key incentive for Japanese development, the study missions sent abroad and the import of foreign teachers, all of which was intended to make Japan self-sufficient. By becoming a developed and rich trading nation – the Meiji-era slogan was "rich country, strong army" (*fukoku kyōhei*) – Japan sought to end humiliation at the hands of the West.[141]

The Meiji Restoration of 1868, generally described as the principal watershed in modern Japanese history, developed institutions to unify and rule over what were formerly 260 quasi-independent feudal domains.[142] Japanese bureaucrats used Shinto, the indigenous religion, to mobilize the population and arouse nationalism.[143] The emperor, a secluded figure, was recast as a symbol of national unity and focus of authority. Japan was depicted as a "family nation" (*kazoku sei kokka*) with the emperor as the father-figure. He was referred to as *Tenno*, meaning "heavenly ruler" or "son of heaven." The imperial institution served as an effective agent

---

[139] Ibid., pp. 229–30.   [140] See Westney, *Imitation and Innovation*.

[141] Marshall, *Capitalism and Nationalism in Prewar Japan*; Duus, "Introduction"; Iriye, *Japan and the Wider World*, p. 3; Howe, *Origins of Modern Japanese Trade Supremacy*; Barshay, "'Doubly Cruel'."

[142] Beasley, *The Meiji Restoration*; Jansen, *Japan in Transition from Tokugawa to Meiji*, are standard accounts of the Restoration and its consequences. Westney, *Imitation and Innovation*, on the development of national institutions based on foreign models.

[143] Kimio, "The Invention of *Wa* and the Transformation of the Image of Prince Shōtoku in Modern Japan."

of change, modernization and unity, but once feudal divisions were overcome, it was used as a bulwark against future political evolution.[144] In
1889 a constitution was promulgated, and the following year a national
assembly was created. Both institutions created a facade of popular rule.
Hirobumi Ito, author of the constitution, made certain that it reserved
real power for bureaucrats acting in the name of the emperor.[145] Aritomo
Yamagata, war minister and creator of Japan's modern army, ensured
that the military was independent and reported to the emperor through
the general staff office. The minister of the army was responsible to the
prime minister on administrative matters, but only to the commander of
the general staff, and indirectly to the emperor, on military matters. These
arrangements made military and bureaucratic intervention in politics
"not only possible but virtually certain of success."[146]

Confucian tradition demanded that the ruling class display virtue, generally defined as selfless devotion to duty. It looked down on profit and
other forms of personal gain or indulgence.[147] Under the Shogunate, the
merchant class (*chōnin*) had been relegated to a status below that of the
peasantry, given its goal of profit-making.[148] It nevertheless existed in a
symbiotic relationship with the warrior aristocracy. It processed and sold
rice and other agricultural products, providing great lords (*daimyō*) and
warriors (samurai) with cash and consumer goods. Merchants looked
to the aristocracy for political tolerance and protection. This relationship became increasingly imbalanced after the Restoration as the samurai
lost their authority and *raison d'être* in an era of peace, while the merchant class became wealthier and more powerful. This situation provoked
unsuccessful samurai rebellions.[149]

The social position of the merchants did not change under the Meiji
(1868–1912) because their glorification of the emperor reinforced traditional scorn of private gain.[150] Far-sighted aristocratic leaders of the

[144] Jansen, *Japan and its World*, p. 75; Fujitani, *Splendid Monarchy*, p. 11; Gluck, *Japan's Modern Myths*.
[145] Storry, *Double Patriots*, pp. 1–2; Gluck, *Japan's Modern Myths*, pp. 17–41, 102–35.
[146] Samuels, *Machiavelli's Children*, pp. 39, 59–60; Gluck, *Japan's Modern Myths*, p. 44.
[147] Bellah, *Tokugawa Religion*, for a good discussion of traditional values.
[148] Shively, "Popular Culture."
[149] Vlastos, "Opposition Movements in Early Meiji, 1868–1885." Marshall, *Capitalism and Nationalism in Prewar Japan*, pp. 2–10; Moore, *Social Origins of Dictatorship and Democracy*, pp. 234–41. Moore's fundamental thesis is that industrialization without any funda-mental transformation of the property and labor system of agriculture was the underlying cause of the tensions of the 1930s. Dore and Ōuchi, "Rural Origins of Japanese Fascism," offer a sympathetic but compelling critique.
[150] Marshall, *Capitalism and Nationalism in Prewar Japan*, pp. 5–7.

Restoration nevertheless encouraged industrialization as necessary to make Japan a powerful state capable of regaining its economic independence and becoming a major player on the world stage. The Meiji government offered a generous settlement to the formerly independent *daimyō*, and to the rebellious samurai class, which enabled many of them to invest in industry and became part of the new financial–industrial elite. Over time, the generally non-productive class of aristocrats was transformed from tax collectors to tax payers, a process made more palatable by buying many of them off with peerages. Japanese industry made great strides during World War I and in the decade afterwards. It nevertheless remained a small factory system dominated by a few great firms (*zaibatsu*) which extended their reach to almost every corner of the economy through financing, technical assistance and purchase. The *zaibatsu* system reached its peak in 1929, but remained powerful through the war, as it would in the postwar period.[151]

In Japan, as in Germany, the landed aristocracy not only survived into the modern period but remained powerful.[152] It supported the invention of a Japanese past by dissatisfied intellectuals that idealized the spirit of *wa* (harmony) and the community (*kyōdōtai*), and denigrated individualism and profit-making.[153] The emphasis on social and national harmony worked against capitalism and liberal democracy, as open differences, competition and conflict – the core dynamics of business and parliamentary government – were frowned upon.[154] Businessmen had to act deferentially toward politicians and at least publicly disassociate themselves from Western-style capitalism and personal gain. Leading industrialists advocated a more communal approach based on patriotism and willingness to sacrifice for the common good. One of the most powerful Meiji businessmen, Shibusawa Eichi, felt compelled to deny profit as a legitimate motive.[155] To some degree these genuflections were a matter of show as traditional values had lost much of their purchase, but industrialists like Mutō Sanji understood that there were economic rewards in supporting

---

[151] Yamamura, "The Founding of Mitsubishi"; Masaki, "The Financial Characteristics of the Zaibatsu in Japan."

[152] Bendix, "Preconditions of Development."

[153] Gluck, *Japan's Modern Myths*; Vlastos, "Tradition," and "Agrarianism without Tradition"; Kimio, "The Invention of *Wa* and the Transformation of the Image of Prince Shōtoku in Modern Japan"; Scheiner, "The Japanese Village."

[154] Dore and Ōuchi, "Rural Origins of Japanese Fascism"; Tiedemann, "Big Business and Politics in Prewar Japan."

[155] Scalapino, *Democracy and the Party Movement in Prewar Japan*, p. 272; Marshall, *Capitalism and Nationalism in Prewar Japan*, pp. 2–5.

corporate paternalism and the invented tradition of "warm heartedness" (*onjôshug*). Production costs could be kept down by avoiding British-style trade unionism.[156] Lip service to the collectivist ideology made it that much more difficult for alternative discourses to emerge and gain legitimacy, which in turn had important implications for the balance of political power in Japan.

In these circumstances it is hardly surprising that Itagaki's Liberal Party (Jiyūtō), which attempted to challenge the financial–industrial oligarchy in the interests of small landlords, gained little traction and was defeated in the 1870s and 1880s. The Jiyūtō split and dissolved in 1884, when the landlords who had founded it, threatened by the peasant revolts of 1884–5, feared that the party would be pushed further left.[157] At the same time the government became increasingly authoritarian, and the Peace Preservation Law of December 1887 allowed the police, but in practice General Yamagata, to remove anyone living within a seven-mile radius of the Imperial Palace whom they judged to be a threat to public tranquility. Nearly 500 people, including nearly all opposition leaders, were exiled from Tokyo. The struggle for power became more acute and further removed from electoral politics. The politicians competed among themselves for office, the interior ministry and the army vied with each other for control of the police, and the army contested the navy for control of the military. Led by scions of the landed aristocracy, the army effectively assumed the role of king-maker: governments survived only as long as they kept its confidence. The fall of the Itō government in 1901 signaled the end of any kind of independent civilian rule. After Itō's assassination in 1909, General Yamagata became the dominant figure in Japanese politics.[158]

Japanese imperialism was motivated by a combination of fear and standing. There was concern, as foreign minister Komura Jutarō put it in 1904, that Japan had to expand to protect its interests against Europeans who were staking out territorial claims in Asia. Japan should "not fall behind" the imperialists but use the opportunity "to expand our interests in Manchuria, Korea, and the Maritime Province."[159] Fear of the European presence in Asia was also a convenient rationalization for

---

[156] Dore, *British Factory: Japanese Factory*; Samuels, *Machiavelli's Children*, pp. 128–31.

[157] Scalapino, *Democracy and the Party Movement in Prewar Japan*, pp. 68–71, 101–10; Dore, *Land Reform in Japan*, pp. 56–107; Havens, *Farm and Nation in Modern Japan*, chs. 3 and 4; Gluck, *Japan's Modern Myths*, pp. 178–86.

[158] Titus, *Palace and Politics in Prewar Japan*, p. 324; Akira, "The Role of the Japanese Army."

[159] Iriye, *Japan and the Wider World*, p. 8.

imperialists like Taguchi Ukichi, Shiga Shigetaka and Tokutomi Shohō who sought colonies to put Japan on an equal footing with the West.[160] There was a widely shared belief that empire was the sine qua non of great power status, and that Japan should accordingly acquire colonies. In addition, imperialism helped consolidate the modern Japanese state, and was supported for this reason by a range of intellectuals and bureaucrats.[161] Material reward played a surprisingly insignificant role in Japanese expansion, but was used as a carrot to sell imperialism to public opinion. In 1894, when 8,000 Japanese troops were sent to Korea, foreign minister Mutsu Munemitsu admitted that he pressured the Korean government to make railway, mining, telegraph and other concessions to justify the risk of war with China raised by Japanese intervention.[162] In 1910, Japan's trade with China was about five times that with its de facto colonies of Korea and Taiwan combined. Private investment also went to China, rather than to these colonies.[163]

In 1894–5, Japan sent its army to Korea, defeated the Chinese and advanced into Manchuria. Under the Treaty of Shimonoseki, China ceded Formosa, the Pescadores and the Liaotung Peninsula, and agreed to pay a large indemnity.[164] In 1902 Japan entered into its first foreign alliance, with Britain to block Russian expansion in Asia, but also to gain acceptance as an equal member of the great power club.[165] *Mainichi Shimbun* hailed the victory as "the beginning of a new era of Japanese greatness."[166] In 1904–5, Japan defeated Russia on land and at sea, and public opinion was enraged when the "Triple Intervention" of Russia, France and Germany forced Japan to give up its claims to the Liaotung Peninsula.[167]

The stunning success against Russia led to demands for further expansion and engagement with the wider world. Patriotic societies attributed victory to unique national qualities, and emphasized the importance of maintaining racial purity in a growing colonial empire. The favorable

[160] Quoted in Iriye, *Pacific Estrangement*, p. 45.
[161] Iriye, "Japan's Drive to Great Power Status."
[162] Yanabe Kentarō, *Nik-Kan gappei shōshi*, cited in Iriye, *Pacific Estrangement*, p. 44; Munemitsu, *Kenkenroku*, for records of Japanese decision-making.
[163] Duus, "Japan's Informal Empire in China, 1895–1937."
[164] Conroy, *The Japanese Seizure of Korea*; Duus, *The Abacus and the Sword*; Beasley, *Japanese Imperialism*. Lone, *Japan's First Modern War*, on the military aspects of the conflict. Myers and Peattie, *The Japanese Colonial Empire*, for essays on the management of this empire.
[165] Nish, *The Anglo-Japanese Alliance*; Iriye, *Japan and the Wider World*, p. 17 for the quote.
[166] Quoted in Samuels, *Machiavelli's Children*, p. 103.
[167] Nish, *Japanese Foreign Policy*, pp. 39–41; White; *The Diplomacy of the Russo-Japanese War*, on the international dimension of this conflict. Okamoto, *The Japanese Oligarchy and the Russo-Japanese War*, on decision-making and domestic politics.

impression that Japanese development and military successes made on the Western powers played into the hands of right-wing nationalists who cited it as evidence of the success of their policies. Nationalists defined Japan as a nation of divine warriors and promoted a heroic image of the samurai that stressed their loyalty, self-sacrifice and stoicism. Samurai dramas dominated the stage and were a popular subject of prints. *Bushidō* – the code of the warrior – was invented to describe a past that was increasingly romanticized, if not downright fictional. Eiko Ikegami contends that the symbolic idiom of the samurai was also important between the wars as a means of mediating a new compromise between the individual and the collectivity responsive to the conditions of modernity.[168] Despite nationalist propaganda – and perhaps in part because of it – the "rich nation, strong army" consensus of the Meiji, which found expression in rapid industrialization and efforts to end unequal tariffs, began to break down after the Sino-Japanese War. Liberal internationalists, who constituted a sizeable faction among intellectuals, divided between those like Kijūrō Shidehara who supported imperialism, and those like Tanzan Ishibashi, who opposed it. A debate ensued over whether Japan should be a great military power or a trading state, which was not resolved for some time in favor of the former.

Yamagata and Tanaka, his deputy, welcomed World War I and entered the conflict on the allied side in the expectation of making territorial gains in Asia and the Pacific.[169] Japan also took part in the allied intervention in the Russian civil war, sending forces into Siberia.[170] The First World War strengthened Japanese industry, and the death of General Yamagata in 1922 increased its political influence. For the first time, newspapers controlled by *zaibatsu* called for the army to remain aloof from politics. Politics at the national level was nevertheless characterized by the same kind of stasis that paralyzed Italy prior to Mussolini's march on Rome. Politicians continued to compete for office, largely because of the monetary rewards it brought from businesses. Violence and assassination became increasingly common. Hired thugs broke up labor union meetings and smashed the presses of liberal papers. The Tokyo earthquake of 1923 provided the police with the pretext to round up thousands of

---

[168] Pyle, *The New Generation in Meiji Japan*, p. 188; Iriye, *Pacific Estrangement*, pp. 126–50; Varley, *Samurai*, p. 12; Ikegami, *The Taming of the Samurai*; Vlastos, "Tradition"; Kimio, "The Invention of *Wa* and the Transformation of the Image of Prince Shōtoku in Modern Japan"; Shun, "The Invention of Martial Arts."

[169] Dickinson, *World War I and Japan*; Nish, *Japanese Foreign Policy*, pp. 93–104.

[170] Morley, *The Japanese Thrust into Siberia*.

socialists. Until 1928, rural landlords controlled a majority of the seats in both houses of the Diet, and the conservative majority was unwilling to accommodate major social forces. Parliament expanded the franchise, but increased the power of the police to silence dissenters. Right-wing groups proliferated – by 1936 there were 750 of them – many with close ties to the police or army. Nationalists portrayed politicians as "intruders who sundered a sacred and mystical bond between the emperor and his subjects."[171] The middle classes were responsive to the appeals of fascism; this was especially evident among small factory owners, building contractors, shopkeepers, skilled craftsmen, small landowners and independent farmers, school teachers, clerical workers, low-grade officials and Buddhist and Shinto priests.[172]

The desertion by intellectuals of democratic politics in the 1920s offers an important parallel with Germany. Prince Konoe Fumimaro, arguably the most important political figure in the late 1930s, invited prominent academics and journalists associated with the Shōwa Research Association, among them Rōyama Masamici, Ryū Shintarō and Miki Kiyoshi, to collaborate with him in developing the vision of what would become the "Greater East Asian Co-Prosperity Sphere." These intellectuals were drawn to European fascist ideas because of their repugnance for contemporary party politics and the free market economy. They imagined that fascism would be more efficient, avoid debilitating clashes between unions and companies and strengthen Japan internationally.[173] Other disillusioned intellectuals, following Ōyama Ikuo, joined the communists.[174]

By the 1920s, Japan was no longer a collectivist society – if it ever had been one. Tenant militancy, industrial strikes, parliamentary conflict and violent protests of various kinds and a growing disparity between the rich and poor were among the many signs of the uneven growth of capitalism. There was little understanding of this phenomenon, but a strong reaction to its outward manifestations that took the form of imagining a collectivist past with the alleged harmony of the family and village as its ideal.[175] The collectivist ideology, steadily reinforced by forces on the right, made it more difficult for the Diet and the cabinet to accommodate open

[171] Scalapino, *Democracy and the Party Movement in Prewar Japan*, pp. 282, 352–62; Storry, *Double Patriots*, pp. 26–31; Berger, *Parties out of Power in Japan*, p. 28; Dore and Ōuchi, "Rural Origins of Japanese Fascism"; Seiichi, "Cabinet, Emperor, and Senior Statesmen"; Large, *Emperor Hirohito and Shōwa Japan*, pp. 56–75 on the limited role of the emperor.
[172] Maruyama, *Thought and Behaviour in Modern Japanese Politics*, pp. 57–8.
[173] Fletcher, *Search for a New Order*, pp. 1–5.
[174] Duus, "Ōyama Ikuo and the Search for Democracy."
[175] Reischauer, "What Went Wrong?"; Vlastos, "Tradition."

conflicts of ideas and interests and achieve the kinds of compromises that democratic governance requires. The Japanese public and many intellectuals "turned away, either in disappointment or disgust," from a political system based on open acceptance and balancing among competing private interests. Their attention and interest were focused instead on the utopian project of recreating unity and harmony through some alternative system. Robert Reischauer observes that Japanese thinking had not kept pace with the reality of industrial development, "causing a dangerous imbalance between what actually existed and what people felt should exist."[176]

The Great Depression accelerated political decline while increasing the forces of right-wing nationalism. There was no single event to mark the transition from a parliamentary regime to a fascist dictatorship as there was in Italy and Germany, but a gradual slide that included assassinations, the occupation of Manchuria in 1931, and the radical right's unsuccessful coup attempt in May 1932. Unlike in Italy and Germany, fascism did not come to power by means of a revolution carried out by a mass movement, but from within the state where it was imposed by existing political forces, military organizations and the bureaucracy.[177]

Paralleling this developments was a shift in discourse in and out of government in which "political values such as expansionism, national prestige, and 'national mission,' increasingly took precedence over economic values in the process of foreign policy decision-making."[178] Anti-Western nationalism also reflected generational change. The world view of the so-called Meiji generation, who had made their country a great power, in part by virtue of their close relations with Britain and the United States, was now seen as out of date. The world had changed, and attractive opportunities had opened for Japanese expansion in Asia with the collapse of China and the demise of the German and Russian empires.[179] New cleavages emerged. Yamagata's control over policy had been achieved at the expense of Asianists who embraced modernization but rejected Westernization. They were supported by nativists, like Kita Ikki and Ōkawa Shūmei, who were intensely nationalist and committed to rectifying Japan's national

---

[176] Reischauer, "What Went Wrong?"; Fletcher, *Search for a New Order*, esp. pp. 28–50.

[177] Reischauer, *Japan*, p. 157; Scalapino, *Democracy and the Party Movement in Prewar Japan*, p. 243; Moore, *Social Origins of Dictatorship and Democracy*, pp. 299, 304; Maruyama, *Thought and Behaviour in Modern Japanese Politics*, p. 65; Pelz, *Race to Pearl Harbor*, pp. 125–66.

[178] Hosoya, "Retrogression in Japan's Foreign Policy Decision-Making Process."

[179] Jansen, *Japan and its World*, p. 80.

spirit (*yamato damashii*). Yamagata and these groups were opposed by "Big Japan liberals," such as Shidehara Kijūrō who favored expansion by economic rather than military means. They came to dominate both major conservative parties. "Small Japan liberals," such as Ishibashi Tanzan, opposed expansion and sought closer economic cooperation with the Western powers, whom they regarded as the source of technology and Japan's principal trading partners.[180] The post-World War I Japanese military was increasingly dominated by nationalists and Asianists, and the goal of regional hegemony established by the sword and organized according to racial principles bridged the otherwise sharp differences in preferences dividing the army and navy.

The sense of racial identity and national mission was intensified by continuing references in Western discourses to the so-called "yellow peril." In the United States, this found expression in a movement to ban Japanese immigration, culminating in the 1924 Exclusion Act. Western racial prejudice came as a shock to the Japanese, but the government did not feel strong enough to oppose it too openly. Foreign minister Hayashi Tadasu, convinced that Japanese–American relations should focus on economic and political issues, negotiated a "gentlemen's agreement" to restrict Japanese immigration to the United States. Weakness and fear combined to stimulate an "inferiority complex," and with it a desire to enhance national self-esteem through a policy of strength and assertiveness.[181] The perception was widespread that Japan was being treated unfairly by the West, and that this justified – even demanded – expansion onto the Asian mainland.[182]

The Japanese Diet debated and criticized foreign policy. The Siberian intervention from 1918 to 1920 was severely criticized, as was the 1927–8 Shantung expedition, the latter for giving a big boost to anti-Japanese movements in China and being prejudicial to Sino-Japanese relations.[183] Legislators became more cautious in their criticism in the years following the Mukden Incident – the seizure in September 1931 of this Manchurian city followed by the occupation of the entire province – and even more fearful of the army once the war against China began in

---

[180] Samuels, *Securing Japan*, ch. 3, characterizes the different ideological and political approaches to modernization and Westernization and their implications for foreign policy.

[181] Jansen, *Japan and its World*, pp. 19, 29; Iriye, *Pacific Estrangement*, pp. 126–7; LaFeber, *The Clash*, pp. 55, 65, 73, 88–91, 104–7, 144–6.

[182] Iriye, *Japan and the Wider World*, p. 45 for quotes from intellectuals and military spokesmen to this effect.

[183] Nish, *Japanese Foreign Policy in the Interwar Period*, pp. 53–61.

earnest. Some continued to be outspoken in their opposition to imperialism. Saitō Takao, highly critical of the army's role in China, was forced to retire from the Diet. Many legislators, infected by nationalism and influenced by the numerous and powerful right-wing political organizations in Japan, supported imperialism in China and withdrawal from the League of Nations.[184] The Wakatsuki cabinet, which fell in December 1931, was fairly craven in its efforts to have the army's independent actions in China accepted by the international community as a new status quo, and tried to avoid intervention by the League of Nations in Manchuria. It was consistently undercut by the army, which accelerated its efforts to conquer Manchuria and to resettle poor tenant farmers in the new puppet state of Manchukup.[185]

In 1936, Japan had a relatively free election in which the nationalist right fared poorly, winning only six seats in the Diet. The Labor Party (Shakai Taishūtō) doubled its vote, winning 18 seats, and the big and unexpected winner was Minseitō, which won 205 seats with its campaign slogan: "What will it be, parliamentary democracy or fascism?"[186] Power was nevertheless shifting from the Diet to the bureaucracy and the military. The bureaucracy benefited from the creation of cabinet super-agencies in the 1930s, and power within them was increasingly wielded by so-called "new bureaucrats," many of them men in their forties. They were less inhibited in pursuing tactics of acting across ministerial boundaries to promote their ideas and protégés. Many of these officials were opponents of the existing order and advocated ideological purification and state control of the economy in order to enhance the nation's spiritual and military strength. They tended to support the army, although they looked askance at its use of violence against domestic opponents.[187] While the bureaucracy was becoming more powerful, higher positions in the civil service were increasingly occupied by active-duty military officers.

Japanese rule in Manchuria was extended to incorporate the south as a result of the Mukden Incident of September 1931. Young officers acting

[184] Hosoya, "Retrogression in Japan's Foreign Policy Decision-Making Process"; Oka, *Konoe Fumimaro*, pp. 34, 97, 104; Shigeo and Saburō, "The Role of the Diet and Political Parties"; Takashi, "The Role of Right-Wing Organizations in Japan"; Akira, "The Role of the Japanese Army"; Iriye, *After Imperialism*, for Japan's foreign policy in the 1920s.

[185] Seiichi, "Cabinet, Emperor, and Senior Statesmen"; Shigeo and Saburō, "The Role of the Diet and Political Parties"; Nish, *Japan's Struggle with Internationalism*; Young, "Colonizing Manchuria."

[186] Moore, *Social Origins of Dictatorship and Democracy*, p. 300.

[187] Shigeo and Saburō, "The Role of the Diet and Political Parties"; Spaulding, "The Bureaucracy as a Political Force, 1920–45."

410 A CULTURAL THEORY OF INTERNATIONAL RELATIONS

on their own initiative blew up a section of the railway line in Mukden, held the Chinese nationalists responsible, and compelled the army to act. The general staff and war minister gave ex post facto approval.[188] In Manchuria especially, the army and navy joined forces to purge uncooperative bureaucrats and to replace them with officers. Bureaucrats from the ministry of commerce and industry and other ministries were nevertheless in Manchuria in large numbers, ran most of the machinery of government and honed their skills in industrial policymaking.[189] In 1932, the Saitō government in effect handed over Manchuria to the army by combining the posts of Japanese ambassador to the puppet government, governor-general of the railway zone and commander of the Kwantung Army.[190] By the end of 1936, the Kwantung Army had extended its control over Manchuria, and was in the process of doing the same elsewhere in Japanese-controlled China and in Japan itself. Generals frequently invoked "the right of supreme command" and the right of the chief-of-staff to communicate directly and privately with the emperor – shades of Kaiser Wilhelm's *Kommandogewalt* – to combat any kind of cabinet oversight.[191] Politicians who stood in the way were assassinated and premiers were unable to assert their authority in the face of military opposition, as indicated by the downfall of the second Konoe cabinet in October 1941.[192] Even at the zenith of their power, generals and admirals governed the way civilian cabinets had, through informal coalitions of high-ranking officers and career bureaucrats. The army and navy were nevertheless often at loggerheads, and their senior officers, who did not want to be derided as "weaklings," were vulnerable to pressures from subordinates to pursue more aggressive policies.[193]

The failure of intimidation to silence the opposition at home led army officers with radical, anti-capitalist beliefs to engage in assassinations

---

[188] Maxon, *Control of Japanese Foreign Policy*, p. 89.
[189] Johnson, *MITI and the Japanese Miracle*, pp. 116–33.
[190] Spaulding, "The Bureaucracy as a Political Force, 1920–45"; Storry, *Double Patriots*, pp. 126–8.
[191] Storry, *Double Patriots*, pp. 53, 82–6. The *Kommandogewalt* nevertheless worked in reverse fashion in Japan. Large, *Emperor Hirohito and Shōwa Japan*, demonstrates that the emperor was opposed to the war in China and many of the domestic moves of the Japanese military but did not express his opposition. The military exploited him for their ends, rather than the emperor using them to bypass civilian authority.
[192] Oka, *Konoe Fumimaro*, pp. 87–118; Storry, *Double Patriots*, pp. 271–95; Maxon, *Control of Japanese Foreign Policy*, p. 247.
[193] Spaulding, "The Bureaucracy as a Political Force, 1920–45"; Hosoya, "Retrogression in Japan's Foreign Policy Decision-Making Process"; Reischauer, "What Went Wrong?"; Akira, "The Role of the Japanese Army."

and coup attempts to discredit parliamentary government and strengthen their hold on power.[194] The attempted coups were an embarrassment to military leaders, although they did not hesitate to exploit them to advance their own goal of military hegemony. In the process, Japanese generals and admirals increasingly lost power to radical junior officers, whose coup attempts and assassinations largely went unpunished. In part, this situation reflected a long-standing practice that dated back to the adoption in the 1880s of the German army as a model. The Germans emphasized the importance of staff officers, which in the Japanese army led to the development of the phenomenon known as *gekokujō*, in which decision-making was dominated by field-grade officers. Senior Japanese commanders rarely issued orders on the basis of their own judgment, but were judged by the plans and performance of their subordinates. Many senior officers were also sympathetic to younger extremists, especially in Manchuria, where the Kwantung Army tried unsuccessfully to make itself economically self-sufficient and in a stronger position *vis-à-vis* the *zaibatsu*.[195] By 1939–40, army officials controlled the political system, and used their authority to impose national mobilization, dissolve trade unions, remove or silence opposing politicians, ban political parties and replace them with the Imperial Rule Assistance Association, modeled on Western totalitarian movements. The army encouraged patriotism, worship of the emperor and obedience to the needs of industry, all essential to its program of imperial expansion.[196]

Kita Ikki (1883–1937), the most influential nationalist ideologue of the 1920s, has been described as the father of Japanese fascism. He demanded Japanese domination of the Pacific rim from Siberia to Australia to strengthen Japan in its struggle against the West. His *Outline Plan for the Reconstruction of Japan*, published in 1906, proved the blueprint for Japan's wartime "Greater East Asia Co-Prosperity Sphere."[197] The Kwantung Army staff, committed to a policy of expansion, believed that it was only possible through the use of force against China. In a striking recognition of the primacy of standing as a foreign policy motive, a 1931 Kwantung Army memorandum proclaimed that "If we win the war

[194] Ogata, *Defiance in Manchuria*, pp. 90–106; Storry, *Double Patriots*, pp. 96–203.
[195] Crowley, *Japan's Quest for Autonomy*, pp. 187–243; Ogata, *Defiance in Manchuria*, pp. 27–33; Storry, *Double Patriots*, pp. 77–82, 144–5, 159–62; Cohen, *Japan's Economy*, p. 29; Akira, "The Role of the Japanese Army."
[196] Ogata, *Defiance in Manchuria*, pp. 137–94.
[197] Crowley, "Intellectuals as Visionaries of the New Asian Order"; Jansen, *Japan and its World*, pp. 75–7.

it should not matter what the world thinks of us."[198] By July 1937, the army had become strong enough to start a war with China and commit the country without prior governmental backing.

Japanese strategists talked about conquest in stages, envisaging first the conquest of Manchuria and northern China, followed by a victorious war against the Soviet Union, expulsion of Britain and France from the Pacific rim, the occupation of Australia and New Zealand, and finally war against the United States. A general staff memo of May 1939 declared the defeat of the Soviet Union and Britain "the basic strategic goal in the next world war," and went on to urge avoidance of such a conflict until 1942 or 1943 when the country would be better prepared.[199] In September 1940, Japan joined the anti-Comintern, officially allying itself with Germany and Italy in the expectation that it would deter the United States. The army also became a much stronger advocate of war with the United States and Britain than either navy or civilian officials.[200]

The Japanese military had expected the Chinese to accept their leadership, much as the Koreans had, on the grounds of racial solidarity.[201] Victory in China proved elusive, and Japanese forces were drawn deeper into the country on the assumption that occupation of more territory would compel the Nationalists to come to terms.[202] Chiang Kai-shek, his army, officials and assorted hangers-on retreated deeper into the hinterland. Japanese armies met increasing resistance from guerrilla fighters organized by the communists, making it more difficult to establish control over the countryside. The Japanese navy and the army hoped that economic cooperation with the United States would dishearten the Chinese Nationalists and convince them of the futility of resisting Japan. They convinced themselves that Washington would put pressure on Chiang to come to terms, a scenario the distinguished Japanese historian Akira Iriye describes as the height of "wishful thinking"[203]

---

[198] Quoted in Iriye, "The Failure of Military Expansionism."   [199] Ibid.

[200] Hosoya, "The Tripartite Pact, 1939–1940," who stresses the deterrent aspects of the pact; Akira, "The Role of the Japanese Army." Weinberg, *Foreign Policy of Hitler's Germany*, I, pp. 342–7; Fox, *Germany and the Far Eastern Crisis*, on German–Japanese relations; Nish, *Japanese Foreign Policy in the Interwar Period*, pp. 109–12.

[201] Iriye, *Pacific Estrangement*, pp. 125, 137.

[202] Crowley, "Intellectuals as Visionaries of the New Asian Order," on the advice of China "experts" that a "smashing victory" and occupation of more territory would compel capitulation. Crowley, *Japan's Quest for Autonomy*, pp. 301–78 on the China war; Iriye, *The Second World War in Asia and the Pacific*, pp. 41–9, 89–94; Nish, *Japanese Foreign Policy in the Interwar Period*, pp. 120–36.

[203] Iriye, "The Failure of Military Expansionism"; Nish, *Japanese Foreign Policy in the Interwar Period*, pp. 138–50.

Within Japanese military circles it became "an article of faith" that "only a German alliance could bring about the new order." Foreign minister Yōsuke Matsuoka urged that Japan exploit Germany's expected triumph "to construct a new order in East Asia." Japanese generals also thought that German and Italian victories in Europe would reduce Western interference in China, and might even pressure China to come to terms with Japan.[204] Like Mussolini, army leaders believed that Germany was on the verge of victory and that they had to act quickly to get in on the spoils. They also reasoned that occupation of Southeast Asia would cut the supply lines to Chungking, so vital to the nationalist regime. Army planners counted on American neutrality so long as Japanese military action was only directed against European colonies. The navy general staff was more realistic, warning in August 1940 that access to scrap and oil was "a matter of life and death," and that the occupation of Indochina could provoke an American economic embargo. Naval extremists nevertheless wanted to exploit Hitler's conquests in Europe to move south to grab Indochina and the Indonesian oil fields. Many of them had believed since the mid-1930s that war with the United States was all but inevitable. The foreign ministry and some industrial leaders were also concerned because they recognized Japan's dependence on Western raw materials and trade. Army leaders remained confident of American neutrality.[205]

Washington provided some material assistance to the Chinese nationalist army, and allowed American fliers to create a volunteer air force to assist the Nationalists. In July 1941, the Roosevelt administration froze Japanese assets, and on August 1 cancelled all licenses for the export of petroleum to Japan. The Dutch quickly followed suit, depriving Japan of its other major source of petroleum. Washington beefed up its air forces in the Pacific, began lend-lease aid to China and the training of Chinese pilots, and opened discussions on common defense with the British, Dutch and Chinese.[206] As the Roosevelt administration knew, Japan produced only enough oil of its own every year to meet the navy's needs for

---

[204] Iriye, *Power and Culture*, p. 11.

[205] Iriye, "The Failure of Military Expansionism," *Power and Culture*, pp. 7–13, and *Second World War in Asia and the Pacific*, pp. 100–67; Sadao, "The Japanese Navy and the United States"; Katsumi, "The Role of the Foreign Ministry."

[206] Butow, *John Doe Associates*, on Japanese-American negotiations; Heinrichs, *Threshold of War*, on Roosevelt's Far Eastern policy; Marshall, *To Have and Have Not* on the American decision to defend Southeast Asia and its resources; Sun, *China and the Origins of the Pacific War*, p. 150; Coble, *Facing Japan*, on the Chinese perspective.

several weeks, and its reserves, estimated at 9,4000,000 kiloliters, would last no more than two years.[207]

The embargo was intended to make it more costly and difficult for the Japanese to prosecute their war against China, but proved to be the catalyst for Japanese attacks against Hawaii, the Philippines, Hong Kong, Singapore, Indonesia and Burma. In the words of General Tōjō: "To yield [to the United States] on this question is like piercing the heart and tantamount to surrender."[208] As Admiral Yamamoto predicted, Japan won victory after victory during the first six months of the war, and its forces came within striking distance of India and Australia.[209] Ultimately, the superior American economy outproduced the Japanese in aircraft, aircraft carriers and every other category of weapon and war-related item. American submarines effectively blockaded Japan, while US long-range B-29 bombers destroyed its cities and war-making potential.[210]

The scenario behind the attack on the United States and other Western powers envisaged a more favorable outcome. Japanese military authorities reasoned that if they attacked Pearl Harbor and destroyed the American battleships and carriers, and captured Indonesia and its oil supply, they could go on to conduct operations anywhere in the western Pacific and Indian Oceans. The United States and China, they expected, would lose their will to resist.[211] Admirals Isoroku Yamamoto and Shigemi Inoue hastened to point out that this scenario rested on a number of unrealistic assumptions, the principal one being the likely response of the Roosevelt administration to an air attack against Pearl Harbor. As we know, the administration sought a declaration of war the next day from Congress, which passed with only one negative vote. The American people were so enraged by Pearl Harbor that it proved difficult for Roosevelt and the joint

---

[207] Iriye, *Power and Culture*, p. 28; Graebner, "Hoover, Roosevelt, and the Chinese," on how the administration erroneously concluded that this dependence would compel Japan to moderate its foreign policy. See also, Pelz, *Race to Pearl Harbor*, pp. 67–96; Marshall, *To Have and Have Not*, and the importance of raw material and the Roosevelt administration's understanding of the problem.

[208] Hattori Takushirō, *Dai-tōa sensō zenshi* [Complete History of the Great East Asia War], quoted in Iriye, "The Failure of Military Expansionism"; Iriye, *Second World War in Asia and the Pacific*, pp. 146–80; Pelz, *Race to Pearl Harbor*, pp. 212, 219–26. Ike, *Japan's Decision for War*, for the records of Japanese decision-making.

[209] Spector, *Eagle against the Sun*, pp. 73–165.

[210] On the Japanese-American war in the Pacific, see Costello, *The Pacific War*; Dower, *War without Mercy*; Butow, *Japan's Decision to Surrender*. For overviews, see relevant sections of Murray and Millett, *A War To Be Won*; Weinberg, *A World at Arms*.

[211] Iriye, "The Failure of Military Expansionism"; Sadao, "The Japanese Navy and the United States."

chiefs of staff to implement their strategy of defeating Germany first while conducting a holding operation in the Pacific.[212]

In an earlier book, I attributed unrealistic Japanese expectations about the United States to motivated bias.[213] Japanese leaders faced equally unpalatable choices – acquiescence to the demands of the Western powers, and with it presumed loss of autonomy and great power status, or war against a coalition they could not defeat. As Janis and Mann's conflict theory of decision-making predicts, actors in this situation seek to avoid the unpalatable alternative they can most readily imagine, in this case capitulation. The Japanese went to war with a strategy that they convinced themselves, in the face of all the available evidence, had a reasonable chance of success.[214] Once committed to this course of action, they distorted, reinterpreted, explained away or simply denied evidence that America would fight to the finish. Japanese generals were also attracted to war for cultural reasons. They saw themselves as representatives of a long military tradition that valued valor, sacrifice, loyalty and standing up to challenges rather than giving in or running away from them.

Pre-Tokugawa Japan contained many elements of a warrior-based honor society. It was dominated by war lords who competed for standing and commanded armies composed of relatives, allies and their retainers. Combat was governed by well-understood codes which shared much in common with their European counterparts. One-on-one combats were highly valued, and warriors distinguished themselves in pursuit of honor. As in Europe, this military tradition became romanticized in the literature and art of the premodern and modern eras. European chivalry, as we have seen, was more fiction than fact, and a social construction based on an idealized understanding of the Roman past. Subsequent epochs, but notably late nineteenth-century Europe, celebrated an idealized version of chivalry. Something similar happened in Japan, where fictional or heavily romanticized events from the country's mythical and samurai past were enacted on stage, and were the subject of popular woodcuts in the nineteenth-century. The code of *Bushidō* was invented to impose an honor code stressing valor and sacrifice in the past so it could be used

---

[212] Sadao, "The Japanese Navy and the United States"; Morley, *The Final Confrontation*, on Japan's decision and negotiations with the United States; Heinrichs, *Threshold of War*; Butow, *John Doe Associates*, on American decision-making and Japanese–American diplomacy. Costello, *The Pacific War*, pp. 74–6, 175–81, on US strategy.

[213] Lebow, "Conclusions," in Jervis *et al.*, *Psychology and Deterrence*.

[214] Janis and Mann, *Decision Making*, pp. 46–81, for an outline of their theory.

as a symbol and model for the present.[215] Like many nineteenth-century Europeans, Japanese aristocrats, as well as officers from non-aristocratic backgrounds, modeled themselves on a world that never was.

The Japanese version of a warrior society differed from its European counterpart in one very important respect. From Homer on, Europeans were at best ambivalent about clever ploys and subterfuges. In the *Iliad*, honor is won through single combats arising out of challenges, and fought on open ground with no protection beyond a shield. Odysseus represents an alternative approach to war – one that relies on intelligence, stratagems, stealthiness and ambush. The tension between the two approaches to war is left unresolved in Homer. Romantic accounts of the Japanese past are more forthright in their praise of cleverness. The idealized Japanese warrior is not only lightning fast in handling himself and his sword, he uses his equally nimble mind as a force multiplier and means of confusing and disorienting his foes.

Modern Japanese military strategy drew on this fictionalized past. Admiral Tōjō opened hostilities against Russia in 1904 with a devastating surprise attack on the Russian fleet at Port Arthur. Foreign minister Matsuoka, who concluded Japan's military alliance with Germany and Italy, was also drawn to risk-taking. He frequently reminded those who favored caution that "One cannot obtain a tiger's claw unless he braves the tiger's den."[216] At least some Japanese military officials were by no means confident of their ability to prevail against the United States. Admiral Isoroku Yamamoto and other naval moderates warned against going to war with Britain and the United States, whose industrial superiority would allow them to construct naval vessels rapidly to more than make up any losses.[217] Foreign minister Matsuoka countered that the Axis alliance, of which he was the major architect, would deter the United States.[218] War minister Tōjō Hideki brushed aside the concerns of his naval colleagues with the observation that "sometimes a man has to jump, with his eyes closed, from the veranda of Kiyomizu Temple."[219]

When viewed in this light, Japan's decision and strategy in December 1914 becomes more explicable. Withdrawal from China and pursuit of a more peaceful policy were unacceptable to Japanese generals, as retreat

---

[215] Pyle, *The New Generation in Meiji Japan*, p. 188; Gluck, *Japan's Modern Myths*; Fujitani, *Splendid Monarchy*; Shun, "The Invention of the Martial Arts"; Vlastos, "Tradition"; Samuels, *Machiavelli's Children*, p. 56, citing Hiroshi Minami, *Nihijinron*.

[216] Quoted in Hosoya, "Retrogression in Japan's Foreign Policy Decision-Making Process."

[217] Agawa, *Reluctant Admiral*, pp. 37–8.   [218] Ibid., pp. 100, 129–31, 144, 160–3.

[219] Hosoya, "Twenty-Five Years after Pearl Harbor."

and surrender would have undercut their hold on power. Of equal importance, it offended their sense of honor, violated their values and threatened
their identities. War was the only choice open to them, and even if they lost,
they would preserve their honor. They sought to maximize their chance
of victory through clever stratagems, and Pearl Harbor, like Port Arthur
before it, was carefully planned and executed and fully consistent with
the warrior's code. The "all or nothing" orientation shaped other critical
wartime strategies, most notably the decision in 1944 to risk everything
on a single naval battle with American forces in and around the Philippines. German admirals had considered a similar suicide battle toward
the end of World War I, intended to preserve the navy's "honor," but were
prevented from carrying it out by naval mutinies. Japanese admirals faced
no such resistance, and went to a glorious death with their battle wagons.

Warfare

Ancient Greeks explained policy decisions with reference to three distinct
motives: fear, interest and honor. Thucydides analyzes foreign policy in
terms of these motives, and has the Athenians invoke all three in explaining to the Spartans how they acquired their empire and why they are
committed to keeping it.[220] Beginning with classical Greece, I have analyzed the origins of wars in terms of these motives to show how all three
are often germane, and how honor often plays a central role. In chapter
6, I demonstrated how honor and standing drove European imperialism
and were principal underlying causes of World War I. This chapter makes
the case for the spirit as the key underlying cause of World War II in a
double sense. In Italy, Germany and Japan needs for self-esteem helped to
bring particularly nationalistic leaders to power, and generated support
for their aggressive foreign policies and high-risk military ventures.

Conventional interpretations of World War I stress fear and the willingness of leaders to take risks to preserve and enhance their security. I
found little evidence of fear or security as primary motives. In Austria
and Germany, fear was aroused by Conrad and Moltke and the German
military as a justification for a war they wanted for other reasons. Of all the
principal leaders, only Bethmann Hollweg arguably acted out of fear for
his country's security, and only because he was successfully manipulated
by Moltke. To the extent that fear played a role for other major actors it
was fear associated with the possible loss of honor or standing. Personal

---

[220] Thucydides 1.75.3 and 76.2 for fear, interest and honor.

and national honor was a central value to military officers, who generally placed it above material interest and survival. National standing was also a powerful motive for middle classes in central Europe, where it was an important component of personal self-esteem.

There is little evidence to support Marxist-Leninist interpretations that material interests were the principal motive for war. They came into the picture afterwards, as industrialists hoped to capitalize on seeming military successes, and political leaders sought to improve their economic situation, while weakening that of their enemies. Even demands for territory, the price of entry into the war by Italy and lesser powers, was motivated less by visions of profit than of national glory and relative standing.

The origins of World War II show important similarities and differences compared to World War I. Among the initiators of that conflict, honor was less important for key actors in Germany and Italy. Neither Hitler nor Mussolini was concerned with honor, nor could their behavior in any way be considered honorable. Both took a decided pride in duplicitous stratagems and violence to gain the upper hand against adversaries. Honor and standing were important goals for the middle classes and intellectuals in both countries, and both dictators played upon their populations' deep resentments over the outcomes of World War I to gain and consolidate power. Mussolini reached the highpoint of his popularity after the conquest of Abyssinia, and Hitler followed his success in escaping from or overturning the most offensive clauses of the Treaty of Versailles without provoking a war.

Fear played a complex role in the origins of World War II. For Hitler, fear came into the picture at the personal level. He was a hypochondriac who feared for his survival, and wanted war sooner rather than later.[221] Mussolini feared that Italian neutrality or late entry into a short European war from which Germany emerged victorious would deny him the territory gains he was so desperate to make. This provided a strong incentive for him to ally with Germany and to invade France in 1940. Fear of not making gains, sought for purposes of standing, domestically and internationally, is different from fear for security. Among the initiators of World War II, this latter kind of fear was pronounced in Japan, but only after the war in China had bogged down and provoked an embargo on oil and other strategic goods by the United States. The Soviet Union, another perpetrator of World War II by reason of Stalin's August 1939 non-aggression

[221] Weinberg, *Foreign Policy of Hitler's Germany*, II, pp. 306–7, 389–90.

pact with Hitler, had legitimate security concerns. Hitler's anti-Soviet rhetoric, Germany's growing military power and the reluctance of France and Britain to oppose his territorial ambitions in the east put Stalin in a difficult position. His alliance with Hitler can be interpreted as a means of protecting the Soviet Union by turning Hitler west against France and Britain and gaining additional territory in Poland and the Baltic states as a buffer against Germany. No doubt Stalin also regarded territorial expansion as an end in itself.[222]

Material interests were even less determining than fear. For Italy, colonial expansion was costly with little or no prospect of economic returns. Neither Mussolini nor his major backers expected to profit from invading France, Croatia, Albania or Greece. Hitler was not motivated by material gains, although he did consider the economic resources of the territories he conquered as necessary to strengthen his war machine. The Romanian oil fields, and those of Baku, were desirable for this reason, as was the black earth region of the Soviet Union, which Hitler planned to clear of most of its inhabitants and repopulate with Germans.[223] There is no evidence that Hitler went to war for these territories, although it is apparent that he expected the conquest of Europe to be a first step toward world empire for which the resources of Europe were critical. The territories were sought for strategic reasons, not to make Germans richer.[224]

In chapter 3 I hypothesized that the frequency, goals and conduct of war are significantly influenced by the distribution of motives. There is an interesting progression in this connection from the Napoleonic Wars to World Wars I and II. On the eve of the French Revolution, European society was more robust than it had ever been. The principal actors were kingdoms whose leaders sought honor and standing. As we would expect, competition among rulers was acute and warfare was frequent, but the goals of war were generally limited and it was conducted in accord with a well-understood set of rules. This was not true of warfare conducted against political units and peoples outside European society or rebels at home.

Honor-based warrior societies usually have fairly rigid class or caste structures. Not surprisingly, in seventeenth- and eighteenth-century Europe, the divide between officers and men was at least as great, if not

---

[222] Weinberg, "The Nazi Soviet Pact of 1939," in *Germany, Hitler and World War II*, pp. 168–81; Hochman, *Soviet Union and the Failure of Collective Security*.

[223] Rich, *Hitler's War Aims*, I, pp. 3–10, 206–7.

[224] Ibid., I, pp. 3–10; Bullock, *Hitler*, pp. 10–11, 622; Fest, *Hitler*, pp. 213–18; Weinberg, *Foreign Policy of Hitler's Germany*, I, p. 358; Thies, *Architekt der Weltherrschaft*, pp. 149–53.

greater, than that between officers of opposing countries. Officers kept themselves apart from mercenaries and conscripts, a social division that was maintained in the face of mortal threats. British officers considered command their responsibility and fighting the task of their troops. At Waterloo, they carried weapons of little value and on the whole no longer sought out one-on-one combats.[225] Officers and diplomats frequently fought for or represented states that were not their homelands, and had a class-based sense of mutual respect and camaraderie that transcended the political differences of the states they served. They corresponded and married across national lines, even when their respective political units were at war. If taken prisoner, officers were usually treated well, often being paroled or exchanged for someone of equivalent rank. In October 1806, the young Carl von Clausewitz was captured after repelling six French cavalry charges in the course of covering the retreat of the Prussian army. He was interned in Nancy, then in Soissons for six months, where he learned French, studied mathematics and familiarized himself with the institutions of local government. He was allowed a three-week furlough in Paris, where he took in all the usual sights. He was released after the Treaty of Tilsit in 1808.[226]

Revolutionary France rejected the old order and its constraining norms. The goals of war escalated. Representatives of the old regime – the First Coalition comprised Prussia, Austria, Spain, Portugal, Britain, Kingdom of Naples and Sicily, Sardinia and various smaller states – went to war to suppress the revolution and restore the Bourbons to the throne. The French fought at first to defend their revolution, and, when victorious, to expand their territory and replace monarchical governments with republican ones. The anti-French coalition, which now included Russia and Britain, triumphed because Napoleon overreached himself. In their desire to restore a balance of power, create favorable domestic conditions for the Bourbon restoration and avoid a new irruption of continental war, the allies did not impose punitive peace terms on France. At the Congress of Vienna, diplomats and soldiers from opposing sides negotiated with one another during the day and socialized together in the evening.[227]

Warfare in the imperial age also involved violence against non-European peoples, and here Europeans followed no rule other than convenience. They had no compunctions about using violence on a large scale, targeting civilians, using weapons that had not been used in

---

[225] Keegan, *Face of Battle*, p. 188.   [226] Paret, *Clausewitz and the State*, pp. 123–36.
[227] Nicholson, *Congress of Vienna*, pp. 160–3; Webster, *Congress of Vienna*, pp. 110–13.

intra-European warfare (e.g. dum-dum bullets, gas) and carrying out large-scale reprisals against local populations. Between 1904 and 1908 the Germans waged wars of genocide against the Herero people in South West Africa.[228] Lack of restraint was also apparent in dealing with more developed and respected cultures. After repressing the Boxer Rebellion, the combined European forces that occupied Peking committed widescale acts of looting, rape and murder. The Boer War, a colonial war fought against fellow Europeans, offers a striking counter-example. British losses were large and attributable to their commitment to the "proper" way of fighting. In the belief that training, camouflage and taking cover were just not cricket, green troops were exposed to hit-and-run tactics and murderous standoff fire from skilled Boer riflemen.[229]

World War I took place in an international society whose *nomos* had been rapidly breaking down. War aims became increasingly extreme on all sides as the war dragged on. The Treaty of Brest-Litovsk, which Germany briefly imposed on the Soviet Union in 1918, deprived it of its most valuable and populous territory and all but transformed the remaining rump state into an economic satellite. At Versailles, in sharp contrast to Vienna, the losers were excluded from the proceedings, and when German delegates were summoned to the palace to receive peace terms they were kept locked up and incommunicado in a local hotel.[230] The war involved violations of accepted rules from the outset. Germany invaded Belgium, although it was sworn to uphold and protect its neutrality, because it needed to march troops through its southeastern corner to invade France. The Austrian army committed atrocities against Serbians, and not infrequently hanged captured Serbian soldiers as if they were common criminals.[231] The Germans experimented with aerial bombing of cities from dirigibles; the first such attack was carried out against Liège on August 6, 1914 and killed nine civilians.[232] Warfare at sea provides a telling example of how initial intentions to honor the rules of war gave way to military exigencies. German submarines surfaced at first to allow the crews of tankers and merchantmen to take refuge in lifeboats before they sunk their vessels with torpedoes. The British began arming merchantmen, and disguising destroyers as merchantmen, so they could blow submarines out of the water when they surfaced. The Germans responded by torpedoing ships

---

[228] Bridgman, *Revolt of the Hereros*.

[229] Dixon, *On the Psychology of Military Incompetence*, pp. 54–5.

[230] Mommsen, *Rise and Fall of Weimar Democracy*, p. 95; Eyck, *History of the Weimar Republic*, I, p. 90.

[231] Gilbert, *First World War*, pp. 41–2.   [232] Strachan, *First World War*, p. 211.

without advance warning. The British then flew American flags on their ships, leading the Germans to declare a "war zone" in which any shipping, neutral or allied, would be sunk. Britain countered by imposing an economic blockade on Germany. Hoping to provoke Germany into a conflict with the United States, Britain authorized passenger ships to carry contraband goods. Germany rose to the bait and announced its intention of sinking such ships, which it termed "auxiliary cruisers." The sinking of the *Lusitania*, which was carrying contraband goods, provoked a war-threatening crisis between Germany and the United States.[233]

Some earlier practices survived or were adapted to new circumstances. World War I saw revival of the *aristeia* by aviators, who dropped challenges over enemy airfields. Airmen in general conceived of themselves as part of a fellowship of noble warriors, and they eschewed parachutes, initially favored one-on-one combats and provided downed enemy fliers with burials accompanied by full military honors. Despite claims by German fliers that "Every fight is a tournament for us, a chivalrous or . . . sporting duel," romantic warfare quickly gave way to more methodical kinds of killing, with airmen taking advantage of the sun, overhead positions and larger numbers to carry out ambushes and make kills at less risk to themselves.[234] Jean Renoir's *La grande illusion*, filmed in 1937, portrays the strong aristocratic sense of honor between infantry officers on opposing sides during World War I, and how it functioned as a psychological defense against the reality of undiscriminating industrial warfare. Football matches and Christmas truces between British and German troops served the same function for ordinary soldiers but higher-ups soon put an end to them.[235] For a least a year into the war, vestiges of an earlier, romantic approach survived in the press and public discourse. At the outbreak of war, the German light cruiser *Emden* successfully attacked commercial shipping in the Pacific and Indian oceans, and became something of a legend before being run down and destroyed by a British warship in June 1915. A *Daily Telegraph* leader proclaimed: "It is almost in our heart to

---

[233] Spindler, *Guerre sous-marine*, I; Birnbaum, *Peace Moves and U-Boat Warfare*; Lebow, *Between Peace and War*, pp. 45–53; Wilson, *Myriad Faces of War*, pp. 87–94; Chickering, *Imperial Germany and the Great War*, pp. 88–9; Hull, *Absolute Destruction*, on how the lack of civilian control over the military in imperial Germany allowed the military command to pursue the use of force unrestrained by ethical, legal, political or purely pragmatic constraints.

[234] Richthofen, *Der rote Kampfflieger*, p. 109 for the quote. Fritzsche, *A Nation of Fliers*; Wohl, *Passion for Wings*, for the romanticization of aerial combat. Wilson, *Myriad Faces of War*, pp. 362–76, 608–17, 694–704, on the reality of aerial warfare.

[235] Gilbert, *First World War*, pp. 69–71.

regret that the *Emden* has been destroyed . . . The war at sea will lose something of its piquancy, its humour and its interest now that *Emden* is gone."[236] No such sympathy for the other side remained by the end of the war. The British public demanded a punitive peace in the so-called "khaki election" of 1918, and fully supported the extension of the blockade of Germany and Austria after the war even though it was devastating to the civilian population.[237]

World War II made its predecessor appear positively chivalrous. War aims were more extreme on the Axis side, where they entailed the physical destruction of nations and peoples. Hitler intended to exterminate most of the Slavs after finishing off Europe's Jews and Roma, and had enough Zyklon-B poisonous gas on hand and on order in 1945 to more than begin the task.[238] The Soviet Union attempted to liquidate all non-communist intelligentsia in the Baltic countries and the part of Poland it occupied. At the end of the war it took territory from Germany, Poland and Czechoslovakia, and gave Poland German land that moved it 150 miles to the west. Italy was slightly more benign, but hardly lived up to the claim of its apologists that Italians, in comparison to Germans, were *brava gente* (good people).[239] Mussolini annexed part of French Provence, encouraged Italian forces to commit barbarities in the Balkans and imposed racial legislation at home, although he had no enthusiasm for killing Jews.[240] Allied war aims were more lenient. The Soviets, whose troops were turned free to rape and pillage in occupied territories, and whose occupying authorities arranged to send back home everything from furniture and art to dismantled industries under the guise of reparations, subsequently sought to rebuild eastern Europe, albeit on their own inefficient, authoritarian model.[241] The United States, Britain and France unified the sections of Germany they controlled, and rebuilt Germany economically and politically, making it within a generation one of the world's most prosperous countries. The United States did the same to Japan. Only a small number of Germans and Japanese were tried and convicted of war crimes.[242]

---

[236] Herwig, *"Luxury" Fleet*, p. 157.

[237] Taylor, *English History*; Wilson, *The Myriad Faces of War*, pp. 665–70.

[238] Marrus, *Holocaust in History*; Friedlander and Miltons, *Holocaust*; Rohwer and Jäckel, *Der Mord an dem Juden im Zweiten Weltkrieg*; Breitman, *Architect of Genocide*.

[239] Fogu, *"Italiani brava gente"*; Knox, *Mussolini Unleashed 1939–1941*, for a good description of Italian occupation policies.

[240] Steinberg, *All or Nothing*, on Mussolini and the Holocaust.

[241] Naimark, *Russians in Germany*.

[242] Taylor, *Anatomy of the Nuremberg Trials*; Marrus, *Nuremberg War Crimes Trial*; Dower, *Embracing Defeat*, pp. 444–84; Röling, *Tokyo Trial and Beyond*.

The conduct of the war was brutal even measured by the standards of World War I. In the east, Germans starved, shot or worked to death enemy soldiers who surrendered. They shot commissars and Jews on sight, and denuded the countries they occupied of food and other essential goods without any consideration of local needs.[243] The German air force conducted bombing campaigns against European cities, beginning with the destruction of Guernica during the Spanish Civil War, and followed by Warsaw and Rotterdam in 1939 and 1940. The Luftwaffe attempted to do the same to London, first with bombing attacks, then with V-1 and V-2 rockets.[244] Guernica offers a striking contrast with aerial warfare in World War I. The von Richtofen family had produced the Red Baron in the Great War, an airman feared but respected by his allied adversaries. The planner of the Guernica operation, a scion of the next generation of the Richtofen family, wrote in his diary "ganz toll" (what fun) when apprised that almost all of the town had been destroyed.[245] Some fighter pilots on both sides considered themselves, like their predecessors in World War I, knights of the air, but the idea of the warrior-hero was decisively repudiated by the Royal Air Force which refused, despite enormous pressure from the press, to recognize "aces" or release their names.[246]

The German army killed or starved somewhere between 700,000 and 1.5 million residents of Leningrad during 900 days of siege and air and artillery bombardment.[247] The Soviets in turn did not always allow German soldiers to surrender, and sent those who did off to labor camps from which most never returned.[248] They cleared minefields by marching their own soldiers, usually punishment battalions, through them.[249] All told, the Soviets lost over twenty-six million people during four years of war.[250]

The war in the Balkans resembled the war in the east but on a smaller scale. No quarter was given or asked for by rival partisan forces or the Germans and communist partisans who opposed them. The fighting was accompanied by widescale murders of Serbs and Jews.[251] The allies

---

[243] Dallin, *German Rule in Russia 1941–1945*; Schulte, *German Army and Nazi Policies in Occupied Russia*; Bartov, *Eastern Front, 1941–45*, pp. 106–41; Krausnick, *Truppe des Weltanschauungskrieges*, part I, chs. 1–3; Hillgruber, *Deutsche Grossmacht- und Weltpolitik im 19. und 20. Jahrhundert*, pp. 252–75; Bartov, *Eastern Front*, pp. 106–42.

[244] Weinberg, *World at Arms*, pp. 574–6.

[245] Quoted in Knox, "Everybody but Shakespeare."

[246] Coker, *Warrior Ethos*, pp. 107–8.   [247] Salisbury, *900 Days*, pp. 513–17.

[248] Merridale, *Ivan's War*, pp. 161, 241.

[249] Glantz, *Colossus Reborn*, p. 577; interview with Gregory Massell, December 8, 2006.

[250] Volkogonov, *Triumph and Tragedy*, p. 418.

[251] Weinberg, *World at Arms*, pp. 523–7.

committed their own atrocities, most of them in the form of aerial bombing, by day and night, of German cities; a single fire bomb attack on Dresden late in the war killed tens of thousands of people, almost all of them civilians.[252] Bomber crews were deliberately misled about their real targets in the strategic bombing campaign – German cities, workers and civilized life – by a British government that recognized the violations of international law this entailed.[253] Perhaps the most unrestrained warfare was in the Far East, where the Japanese often committed gratuitous violence against Asian civilians.[254] In Nanjing, Japanese soldiers went on a rampage and murdered hundreds of thousands of the residents of the city.[255] American bombing raids against Japanese cities were equally destructive; the fire bombing of Tokyo in June 1945 burned out 15.8 square miles of the city and killed an estimated 87,793 people.[256] The atom bombing of Hiroshima killed 145,000 people and signaled, as did the follow-on attack against Nagasaki, willingness to use weapons of unparalleled destructive potential.[257] Both Japanese and Americans frequently refused to accept the peaceful surrender of combatants from the other side.[258]

World War II combatants exercised some self-restraint. Germany's non-use of poison gas has drawn considerable attention, although no one has argued that Hitler and his generals were constrained by the laws of war. All of the major participants prepared nerve gases, but may have been deterred or simply found their use unnecessary.[259] Michael Bess contends that nations do not "check their values at the door" when they go to war. Neither governments nor their armed forces, he insists, can

---

[252] De Bruhl, *Firestorm*; Hastings, *Bomber Command*, pp. 411–12; Bundy, *Danger and Survival*, pp. 63–8; Weinberg, *World at Arms*, p. 616.

[253] Boog *et al.*, *Germany and the Second World War*, pp. 30–6.

[254] Dower, *Embracing Defeat*, pp. 41–9.

[255] Weinberg, *World at Arms*, p. 322; Fogel, *The Nanjing Massacre in History and Historiography*. The Japanese allow that 20,000 people may have died, while the Chinese insist it was 300,000. Wakabayashi, *What Really Happened In Nanking*, estimates 70,000 dead.

[256] Spector, *American War with Japan*, pp. 478–510; Selden and Seldon, *Atomic Bomb*, p. xvi, quoting the Strategic Bombing Survey.

[257] Rhodes, *Making of the Atomic Bomb*, p. 734; Craven and Cate, *Army Air Forces in World War Two*, V, pp. 616–17; Committee for the Compilation of Materials on Damage Caused by the Atomic Bombs in Hiroshima and Nagasaki, *Hiroshima and Nagasaki*, pp. 113, 115, 367–9. Hiroshima is estimated to have lost 130–150,000 people at the outset and upwards of 200,000 by the end of five years. Nagasaki lost somewhere between 60,000 and 80,000 in the first week.

[258] Dower, *War without Mercy*, pp. 11–12, 63–71.

[259] Price, *Chemical Weapons Taboo*, pp. 100–34; Legro, *Cooperation under Fire*; Harris and Paxman, *Higher Form of Killing*, ch. 3; Weinberg, *World at Arms*, pp. 108, 146, 181, 558–61, 784, 832.

operate in defiance of their states' values because they need to justify war and the sacrifice it entails in terms of those values.[260] This is a sensible argument, and well documented in the case of democracies such as the United States. It is more difficult to sustain in the case of Nazi Germany where Hitler's behavior was often blatantly at odds with his proclaimed goals and where German soldiers continued fighting after the cynicism of the Nazi leadership was apparent to many of them and when they knew defeat was inevitable.[261] Even Hitler at times sought to minimize the discrepancy between values and practice. Presumably because of his concern about the popular reaction, he never spoke publicly about the "Final Solution" or the euthanasia of the mentally ill, and gave strict orders that these killings, the death camps and the extermination campaigns of the Waffen SS and the Wehrmacht in the east be kept under wraps.[262] Hitler did, however, describe his extermination campaign to generally approving Wehrmacht officers.[263]

Concern for dissonance and its consequences is likely to be more pronounced in democracies, but here too the experience of World War II indicates that soldiers and civilians who feel threatened are willing to act in ways that are subsequently recognized to have been at odds with their values. The internment of Americans of Japanese descent is a case in point, being declared unconstitutional only after the war was over, and widely recognized as morally reprehensible only some decades after that.[264] The controversy and cancellation in April 1995 of the planned *Enola Gay* exhibit at the National Air and Space Museum indicates that service organizations, the military and conservative congressmen remain unwilling to reconsider the ethics of Hiroshima and Nagasaki.[265] The Indochina War experience nevertheless suggests that dissonance has limits; it spawned a large anti-war movement that kept Lyndon Johnson from seeking reelection, helped to defeat Hubert Humphrey in 1968 and ultimately compelled Nixon and Kissinger to end the war on decidedly unfavorable terms.[266] Of course, these two wars occurred under very different domestic political and social circumstances, making any generalizations difficult to sustain.

---

[260] Bess, *Choices under Fire.*
[261] Steinert, *Hitler's War and the Germans*; Herzstein, *War that Hitler Won*, chs. 11–12; Bartov, *Eastern Front*, pp. 26–39; Weinberg, *World at Arms*, pp. 479–83, 769.
[262] Kershaw, "Hitler Myth," p. 242.   [263] Wilhelm, "Wie geheim war die 'Endlösung'?"
[264] Ng, *Japanese-American Internment in World War II.*
[265] Harwit, *Exhibit Denied*; Kohn, "History at Risk."
[266] Schulzinger, *Time for War*, pp. 215–46, 274–304; Karnow, *Vietnam*, pp. 500–5, 558–65, 571–627.

Ironically, the part of society most affected by values may be the military. Honor, valor and patriotism are core concerns for almost all armies, navies and air forces, although they may be defined somewhat differently. In World War II, the American air force opted for the more costly daylight bombing of Germany on the grounds that it was less likely to cause collateral damage. This concern soon went by the board, and many civilian and military officials came to view civilian casualties as a positive benefit. By this time the British and the Americans already had a well-established division of labor, with the former bombing at night and the latter during the day.[267] Bombing by day was more costly, and the American air force developed external and disposable fuel tanks to extend the range of its fighters to provide constant coverage on long-range missions.[268]

Another military value that endures is the belief, going back at least as far as Homer, that combat should be an opportunity to display bravery, and that bravery requires putting oneself at risk. This concern was in part responsible for the German choice of an offensive strategy in World War I, and there are numerous accounts of how it shaped the behavior of individual officers in many armies.[269] The image of brave soldiers going over the top, regularly featured in novels and films, apparently encourages such risky behavior in combat. Correspondent Michael Herr describes young Marines charging the enemy in Vietnam in imitation of John Wayne in the film *The Sands of Iwo Jima*.[270] The commitment to protect one's own forces, but the belief that combat is valuable in part because it entails risks, clearly conflict. During the NATO intervention in Yugoslavia, French General Philippe Morillon was unhappy with long-range air strikes. "How can you have soldiers who are ready to kill," he complained, "who are not ready to die?"[271] Based on interviews with high-ranking officers in NATO, Christopher Coker contends there is now a growing distinction between American and European military organizations. The latter abhor war because they no longer associate it with status and self-esteem, in contrast to their American counterparts.[272]

Returning to our primary argument, the Napoleonic and two world wars indicate the extent to which the goals and conduct of war are

---

[267] Hastings, *Bomber Command*, pp. 201–5, 306–12; Murray and Millett, *War To Be Won*, pp. 304–35; Weinberg, *World at Arms*, pp. 574–81.
[268] Weinberg, *World at Arms*, pp. 540, 578; Murray and Millett, *War To Be Won*, p. 312.
[269] Keegan, *Face of Battle*; Holmes, *Acts of War*, for examples from Waterloo to Vietnam.
[270] Herr, *Dispatches*, p. 44.   [271] Pfaff, *Bullet's Song*, p. 132.
[272] Coker, *Waging War without Warriors*, "The Unhappy Warrior" and *Warrior Ethos*, pp. 16–43, 105–31.

influenced by society. When society is robust, honor and standing are closely linked, and actors correspondingly more restrained in their goals and the means they use to achieve them. When society is thinner, honor and standing more readily diverge, actors are less restrained and an escalation in goals and means is more likely to occur. Such escalation further undermines society, as it did in both world wars. Warfare is not always destructive of *nomos*; in some circumstances, it can sustain the values of society. Homer's *Iliad* and Thucydides' account of the Peloponnesian War indicate the conditions under which both outcomes occur. In societies where honor is paramount, warfare can strengthen communal bonds, and even those between adversaries, when both sides respect all the relevant conventions. Warfare is most likely to weaken or destroy society when reason loses control of the spirit or appetite and actors no longer feel constrained by the limitations governing warfare in their societies. Fear quickly becomes the dominant motive, and provides further incentives for violating *nomos*.

The world wars had unrelievedly negative consequences, not only because of the goals and strategies of the actors, but because of the ways in which they influenced each other. After the Napoleonic Wars, Clausewitz observed that force tends toward the extreme because if one side holds back the other will gain an advantage. Violence sets in motion a process of reciprocal escalation (*Wechselwirkung*). The use of poison gas and the course of submarine and anti-submarine warfare in World War I, and the bombing of cities in World War II, provide apt if disturbing illustrations. Clausewitz also recognized limiting factors to escalation. Like Homer and Thucydides, he argued that they derive from the social conditions of states and the nature of their relationships. They exist *prior* to war, and are not a function of fighting itself.[273] Conventional explanations for military escalation or restraint generally rely on rational or organizational explanations. These explanations ignore cultural determinants of military behavior, which, I have tried to show with cases from ancient times to the present, are at least as significant. Culture and not institutions establish the necessary preconditions for institutions to facilitate self-restraint and cooperation.[274]

Destructive wars can provide strong incentives for reconstituting society, and with it rules, norms and procedures that channel aggression into socially acceptable channels and minimize or regulate its expression in

---

[273] Clausewitz, *On War*, book 1, ch. 1, pp. 75–6.
[274] Lebow, "Reason, Emotion and Cooperation."

violence and warfare. This happened in Greece after the Peloponnesian War, in Europe after the Napoleonic Wars, and World War I, and again, and more successfully, in the aftermath of World War II.[275] The European project is based on such learning, and demonstrates the extent to which it can move societies away from fear-based worlds.

Parvenu powers

In chapter 6 I suggested that powers seeking acceptance as great powers are likely be more aggressive than existing great powers, and all the more so if their leaders or peoples have previously been ostracized, snubbed or otherwise humiliated by the dominant powers of the system.[276] As examples, I offered Sweden in the seventeenth century and Russia and Prussia in the eighteenth. In chapter 7, I extended this claim to imperial Germany, arguing that its aggressiveness was due in part to the same perceived need of parvenu great powers to push their weight around, and their greater sensitivity to real or imagined slights to their standing or honor. This sensitivity was strikingly apparent in the Kaiser and the military officers and civilian officials he gathered around him. German aggressiveness was also attributable to the semi-feudalization of the middle class, which had independent causes. German defeat in World War I intensified the need of the middle classes to externalize their need for self-esteem and, I have argued in this chapter, provided the political foundation for Hitler's rise to power.

Germany's sense of special mission and glorification of the state was neither arbitrary nor unique. This ideological framework served the spirit in a direct and instrumental manner. Measured against Western values and accomplishments in the eighteenth century, Germany was an under-achiever. It had failed to unify, and its leading states (Prussia and Austria) performed poorly on the battlefield, being defeated decisively by Napoleon at Jena, Auerstädt and Austerlitz. Subsequent victories against Napoleon (e.g. Leipzig and Waterloo) did not eradicate the sense of humiliation felt by many German aristocrats, military officers, intellectuals and members of the emerging middle class. A world view that offered a different set of criteria for excellence, that stressed German intellectual and artistic creativity and the solidarity and the world mission of the *Volk*, and down-graded the value of commerce and constitutional government, seemed

---

[275] Lebow, *Tragic Vision of Politics.*
[276] Suzuki, "China's Quest for Great Power Status," develops a similar argument.

to buttress the self-esteem of Germans of all classes. By emphasizing the role of the state as both the instrument and expression of this mission – a theme developed by Fichte that received its fullest expression in the philosophy of Hegel – power could be concentrated in ways that facilitated unification and the emergence of imperial Germany as the dominant military power on the continent. This power would ultimately enable it to compete for standing in more traditional ways.

Victory in the Franco-Prussian War (1870–1), national unification (1871) and recognition as the leading power on the continent should have boosted German self-esteem and reduced the need of its leaders and people to define themselves in opposition to France and Britain and the values they were thought to epitomize. Bismarck certainly behaved as a mature and satisfied leader. He was never drawn to nationalism as anything other than a means of advancing Prussian power, and under his leadership Germany acted as a satisfied nation and defender of the territorial status quo. He had a jaundiced view of colonies, although he briefly flirted with social imperialism, and consistently opposed a blue water navy as a provocation and a waste of money. Bismarck was considered old-fashioned by many Germans in the 1880s, and especially by those who considered empire the sine qua non of great power status. As we have seen, the pursuit of empire and a navy to challenge that of Britain's were widely supported, especially by the middle classes. Germans now felt strong enough, psychologically as well as physically, to compete on the playing fields valued by their competitors and adversaries, Britain and France. At the same time, they continued to enhance their self-esteem by defining themselves and their political culture in contrast to Britain and France. The *Sonderweg* thesis was mobilized to justify and extend the shelf life of quasi-authoritarian government. German music under Wagner sought to fuse *völkish* traditions with modernity in the form of a *Gesamtkuntswerk* (total art), and the composer and his followers vaunted its artistic superiority to the "decadent" operas of Italy and France. German literature continued to praise premodern values and heap scorn on the petty, commercial concerns of the middle class. Friedrich Meinecke, Germany's preeminent historian in the decade prior to World War I, praised German *Kultur*, which combined language, ethnicity, national identity and spiritual renewal, as superior to the French principles of liberty, fraternity and equality.[277] During World War I, Werner Sombart praised "the ancient German hero's spirit," which was rescuing Germany from becoming another corrupt capitalist nation

---

[277] Meinecke, *Weltbürgertum und Nationalstaat.*

and would make the German *Volk* the "chosen people" of the twentieth century.[278]

National neuroses – if we can use this term – are no more readily overcome by success than their individual counterparts. They are, however, greatly exacerbated by failure, which is what happened in Germany after its defeat in World War I. Defeat prompted denial, a search for scapegoats and an intense desire for revenge, emotions that made it difficult, if not impossible, for the Weimar Republic to gain legitimacy. To create a different political–psychological outlook, it took another round of war that left Germany defeated, in ruins and occupied and divided by powers intent on imposing their own political and economic systems and reshaping the country's culture.

Students of Germany attribute the country's *völkish*, anti-Western and pro-state orientation to the peculiar circumstances of its political and intellectual development. This explanation is not persuasive because roughly similar ideologies are found in other countries. If we look further east, to Poland and Russia, we see variations on the same theme. Poland developed a national culture in the nineteenth century but was not reunified until 1918. Poles chose to look back to their "golden age," spanning the sixteenth to the eighteenth centuries, when their country had been a great power, increasingly democratic and parliamentary, tolerant towards its numerous and multifarious minorities, a contributor to the civilization of Europe and champion of the Roman Catholic faith. Polish nationalism in the nineteenth and twentieth centuries, which developed in opposition to its German, Austrian and Russian overlords, not surprisingly stressed the country's special mission and unique position in Europe. Poles saw themselves as the easternmost outpost of Latin Christian Europe, and the "Christ among nations," forever a martyr, although not one accustomed to turning the other cheek. Poland was partitioned three times by its more powerful neighbors, and rose up against them in a series of unsuccessful rebellions. The Polish self-image also stressed military success and the country's role as the rescuer of Europe in 1683, when Polish forces routed the Turks in front of Vienna, and again in 1920, at the "Miracle on the Vistula," when they turned back the Red Army before the gates of Warsaw. Both victories were understood as triumphs of Latin Christian European civilization over non-European "infidels."[279]

---

[278] Sombart, *Händler und Helden*, pp. 125, 143.
[279] Davies, *God's Playground*; Orla-Bukovska, "New Threads on an Old Loom."

Marshal Józef Piłsudski, the first head of state and virtual dictator from 1926 to 1935, sought to make Poland entirely independent of Germany and the Soviet Union, refusing to accept a subordinate role to either. Under Colonel Józef Beck, foreign minister from 1932 through 1939, the goal of foreign policy was to regain great power status. Beck aspired to eliminate Czechoslovakia, establish a common border with Hungary and create a "Third Europe," composed of states from the Baltic to the Black Sea, that would be independent of Britain, France, Germany and Russia. Such dreams were foolhardy and dangerous for a country sandwiched between a revisionist Germany and the Soviet Union, intent on eliminating Poland as a country. Delusions of the spirit led Beck and his supporters to place so-called national considerations above security. Such a policy nevertheless received support from the nobility and that section of the middle class that, like its German counterpart before 1914, had become quasi-feudalized.[280]

Russian nationalism stressed moral over material forces, and contrasted the holy mission of the Russian people to Western rationalism and materialism. Slavophile ideology was *völkish*, emphasized the communal life of the Rus in contrast to the individualism of the West, and hailed the Russian Empire as the successor to Rome and Byzantium. Aleksei S. Khomiakov, Konstantin S. Aksakov and Fyodor Doestoevsky were among those who propagated the belief that Russia had inherited the Christian ideal of universal spiritual unification from Byzantium, while the decadent West, formed in the crucible of Roman Catholicism, preserved the old Roman imperial tradition.[281] Russia was the self-described "big brother" to Slavs elsewhere in Europe, an ideology that prompted provocative policy in the Balkans where Russia increasingly came into conflict with Austria by virtue of its nearly unqualified support of Bulgaria and Serbia.[282]

In Germany, romantic nationalism was always at odds with traditional conservatism, but had less difficulty in blending with more modern approaches to politics, including socialism. The Nazi Party appealed to romantic nationalist and *völkish* strands of opinion, but made only limited inroads with workers, and at best gained their tacit support of the traditional conservative elite by virtue of its successful economic and foreign

---

[280] Cienciala, *Poland and the Western Powers*, pp. 4–9; Polonsky, *Politics in Independent Poland*, pp. 470–83. Korbel, *Poland between East and West*, on Soviet and German policy toward Poland.

[281] Walicki, *The Slavophile Controversy*; Riasanovsky, *Russia and the West in the Teaching of the Slavophiles*; Pipes, *The Russian Intelligentsia*; Gleason, *European and Muscovite*.

[282] Lieven, *Russia and the Origins of the First World War*, pp. 141–2; Jelavich, *Russia's Balkan Entanglements*, pp. 248–65; Schroeder, "International Politics, Peace and War."

policies. In Russia, these different strands of opinion found expression in different political movements, although there was some degree of overlap. In prewar Russia, Slavophil sentiment was most prevalent within the aristocracy, but found some support among intellectuals, Dostoevsky being a case in point.[283] Liberal constitutionalism was represented by the Kadet Party, the largest party in the National Assembly (Duma). Socialism blended with nationalism, found expression in a series of movements, including Zemlya i Volya (land and liberty), which, in the 1880s, sent students, without notable success, to live with peasants and mobilize their support.[284] More Marxist socialists envisaged the workers as the vanguard of the revolution. The avowedly internationalist Bolshevik faction emerged as the dominant force in postwar Russia, now renamed the Soviet Union.[285] Despite its strong anti-nationalist ideology, part of the appeal of revolutionary socialism to Russian intellectuals had to do with their expectation that it would accelerate Russian development and gain new respect for their country as both a great power and a model for the rest of the world.[286]

Russia had been recognized as a major power since Peter's defeat of Sweden in the Great Northern War. It was nevertheless regarded with suspicion by other Europeans. The Russian army was considered "barbaric and Tatar-like," and Peter, as we observed, was described as "a sort of Turk of the north."[287] Russian arms prevailed against Napoleon, but only after a series of humiliating setbacks culminating in the evacuation and burning of Moscow. In the mid-nineteenth century, the Russians held their own in the Crimea against the French and the British, prevailed over the Turks, and extended their empire in the Caucasus and Turkic lands to the south and to the shores of the Pacific in the east. Their royal family and nobility intermarried with their Western counterparts – Nicholas II and Wilhelm II were first cousins – and Russian contributions to Western culture, especially in literature, music and ballet, were widely acknowledged. Russia nevertheless remained a semi-pariah because of its autocratic government, economic backwardness and pogroms against Jews. As Erik Ringmar observes, to become a great power, an aspiring state must convince existing great powers that it meets the normative requirements

[283] Pipes, *The Russian Intelligentsia*, Gleason, *European and Muscovite*.
[284] Venturi, *Roots of Revolution*, esp. pp. 253–84, 469–506.
[285] Ulam, *Expansion and Coexistence*, pp. 12–31.
[286] Pipes, "Historical Evolution of the Russian Intelligentsia."
[287] Quoted in Hughes, *Peter the Great*, p. 86.

of this exalted status.[288] Wight, Bull and Kratochwil all describe the most important of these normative requirements as the ability and willingness to protect the rules and core values of the society.[289] In the eyes of liberals, the Russian regime constituted a threat to these values. Russia was more acceptable, but still regarded with suspicion, by the ruling elites of the German and Austro-Hungarian Empires because of its commitment to uphold the principle of monarchy.

Defeat in the Russo-Japanese War (1904–5) and humiliation at the hands of Austria and Germany in the 1909 Bosnian Annexation crisis, made Russia's leaders fearful of losing their great power status. Their concern cannot be explained with reference to security because, as we have seen, the July crisis confronted them with a direct tradeoff between prestige and security, and they unanimously opted for the former. They were committed to supporting Serbia in 1914 even though they recognized that it was likely, if not certain, to lead to war with Austria-Hungary and Germany, adversaries they were militarily unprepared to fight.[290] The decision for war was widely supported by the nobility and middle class alike.[291]

The socialists, like their nationalist counterparts, shared a sense of inferiority vis-à-vis the West, which did not diminish when they achieved power. If anything, it was intensified by Russia's poor performance against Germany in World War I, the short but humiliating Treaty of Brest-Litovsk and the occupation of part of its territory by Western and Japanese forces during the Civil War.[292] In a famous 1931 speech urging rapid economic development, Stalin offered a vivid depiction of the past consequences of Russia's backwardness:

> To slacken the tempo would mean falling behind. And those who fall behind get beaten. But we do not want to be beaten. No, we refuse to be beaten! One feature of the history of old Russia was the continual beatings she suffered because of her backwardness. She was beaten by the Mongol khans. She was beaten by the Turkish beys. She was beaten by the Swedish feudal lords. She was beaten by the Polish and Lithuanian gentry. She was

---

[288] Russell, *Identity Diplomacy*. Suzuki, "Seeking 'Legitimate' Great Power Status in Post-Cold War International Society," for elaboration.

[289] Wight, *System of States*; Bull, *Anarchical Society*, p. 171; Kratochwil, *Rules, Norms, and Decisions*, p. 52.

[290] Lieven, *Russia and the Origins of the First World War*, pp. 141–2; Jelavich, *Russia's Balkan Entanglements*, pp. 248–65.

[291] Seton-Watson, *The Russian Empire*, pp. 6–8, 19.

[292] On Brest-Litovsk through the civil war, see Fischer, *Russia's Road from Peace to War*, pp. 9–39; Ulam, *Expansion and Coexistence*, pp. 51–110.

beaten by the British and French capitalists. She was beaten by the Japanese barons. All beat her because of her backwardness, military backwardness, cultural backwardness, political backwardness, industrial backwardness, agricultural backwardness. They beat her because to do so was profitable and could be done with impunity.[293]

Backwardness did not prevent Soviet leaders from attempting to export revolution by force into the heart of Europe. The Red Army was defeated in Poland in 1920, and in 1924 the Soviet Union adopt a foreign policy based on Stalin's concept of "socialism in one country."[294] During the 1920s, the Soviet Union was shunned by the victorious allies, who erected the so-called cordon sanitaire to isolate the Bolshevik regime from political and economic intercourse with the rest of Europe. The Soviet Union was gradually incorporated into the European regional system and came to play an increasingly important role in the 1930s. Security dominated the Soviet foreign policy agenda in the 1930s, although it is equally apparent that domestic politics – dominated by Stalin's paranoia – took precedence over security.[295] It is only in the postwar period, following Stalin's death and Khrushchev's consolidation of power, that the spirit reasserted itself in foreign policy, once again to compete with security as a motive. I address the role of the spirit in the Cold War in the next chapter.

Finally, we come to Japan. The nationalist creed taught the Japanese that they had been born in possession of important virtues as gifts of the gods. Their core character was described as *kokutai*, which translates as "the substance, or body, of the nation," or "the national entity." *Kokutai* was frequently used by politicians in the interwar period to refer to the nation or the "national honor."[296] Many Japanese intellectuals also stressed the superiority of their way of life in contrast to the objectionable values of the West. Nakano Seigō, an important early twentieth-century journalist, was typical in looking back on the Meiji Restoration as a source of inspiration that would perpetuate, but in modern form, the spirituality that unified Japan and made it unique. Nationalists of this period, among them Kuga Katsunan (1857–1907) and Miyake Setsurei (1860–1945), were Germanophiles and directly influenced by the Romantic belief that a

---

[293] Stalin, speech to industrial managers, February 1931, in *Problems of Leninism*, pp. 454–8.

[294] Fischer, *Russia's Road from Peace to War*, pp. 40–9, 118–43; Ulam, *Expansion and Coexistence*, pp. 105–11, 181–5.

[295] Hochman, *Soviet Union and the Failure of Collective Security*, p. 172; Volkogonov, *Stalin*, pp. 3–13, 70–1, 225–36; Tucker, *Stalin*, II, pp. 278–80, 317–19, 620, 625.

[296] Storry, *Double Patriots*, p. 5.

nation cohered around its *Geist*. Nakano Seigō insisted that Japan must struggle to preserve its distinctiveness, which he associated in large part with the strength and commitment of samurai like Saigō Takamori (1827–77) to the national cause, even when it required rebellion.[297] To a certain degree these nationalists drew on an older tradition of late Tokugawa thought that developed in the domain of Mito. Mito learning, as it was called, was nationalist and nativist and sought to enhance the standing of the emperor and expel the "barbarians."[298]

If Germany was reacting against France and Britain, and Russia against Western Europe more generally, the Japanese contrasted themselves to all the Western powers. Pan-Asian doctrines gained a favorable audience toward the end of the nineteenth century because their publicists justified them as a means of resisting Western imperialism and values. Japanese were urged to stop copying the West and return to their allegedly traditional values of cooperation, harmony, mutual respect, social integration and communal equality.[299] The Sino-Japanese War (1894–5) was welcomed as part of "an inner war to cleanse the Japanese mind of Western influences and modes of thought, not just as an action to bring the recalcitrant Chinese to their senses."[300] Subsequent Japanese imperialism was justified on a similar basis and widely appealing for this reason. A typical example from the 1930s was the effort of legal scholar Takigawa Seijirō to defend expansion in Asia as necessary to negate Western influence and cultural dominance. As the repository of Asian virtues, Japan had the responsibility to take the lead in liberating the region.[301]

The army propagated Japan's "Imperial Way" in other Asian countries.[302] Known as the *Kōdō* policy, it was defended as a selfless form of imperialism. Shiratori Toshio, a prominent foreign policy official, claimed that "Japan's continental policy is essentially based on its efforts to realize a cultural mission. No other cases are comparable in world history to Japan's present venture, which is designed to reconstruct human society

---

[297] Najita, "Nakano Seigō and the Spirit of the Meiji Restoration in Twentieth Century Japan."
[298] Harootunian, *Toward Restoration* and *Things Seen and Unseen*, on these developments; Wakabayashi, *Anti-Foreignism and Western Learning in Early-Modern Japan*, on Mito learning.
[299] Jansen, *Japan and its World*, pp. 78–9.   [300] Iriye, *Power and Culture*, p. 5.
[301] Ibid., pp. 5–6.
[302] Ogata, *Defiance in Manchuria*, pp. 3–4, 41–7; Nish, *Japan's Struggle with Internationalism*, pp. 169–74.

and to regenerate modern civilization."[303] During the Pacific War, the
Ministry of Education provided soldiers with an ideological manifesto,
The Way of the Subject (*Shinmin no Michi*) that explained the Japanese
mission in racial and political terms and justified the war as a struggle
against Western imperialism and acquisitiveness.[304]

These anti-Western, anti-materialist and anti-individualist orientations were largely invented by intellectuals and elites in these several
countries in response to the problems of modernization. Their common
emphasis on the special mission of their respective countries suggests
that national self-images are more a function of the relationship between
a political unit and the dominant powers of the system in which it operates
than they are an expression of unique national cultures and histories. And
this despite the emphasis of all these self-images on an allegedly unique
past and its determining influence on "national character." The vaunt-
ing of values directly opposed to a shared stereotypical understanding of
those thought to prevail within leading political units is neither a purely
Western phenomenon nor unique to modernity. The Swedes, Russians
and Prussians embraced such self-images prior to the French Revolution.
These self-images and related ideologies reflect the position of a state that
considers itself an outsider but wants recognition as an equal to the leading powers of the system. These discourses can also be taken as evidence
that the actors in question perceived themselves as underprivileged, if not
humiliated powers, as well as late arrivals to great powerhood.

Parvenu powers are also risk-accepting powers, as we saw in the case of
Germany in 1914. Indeed, whenever honor and standing become central
concerns, leaders are willing to accept considerable risks to avoid losses
or make gains. Italy and Japan offer more evidence in support of this
proposition. Hitler, Mussolini and the Japanese military were willing to
take the most extraordinary gambles. Hitler may have been idiosyncratic;
he had the authority to impose his preferences on a military elite that
wanted to act more cautiously. Mussolini lacked Hitler's authority, and
his policies were more reflective of elite preferences. In the Japanese case,
Tōjō was at best *primus inter pares*, and Japan's decision to attack Pearl
Harbor was widely supported by top military officials. Tōjō brushed aside

[303] Toshio Shiratori, *Kokusai Nihon no chii* [The Status of Japan in the World], quoted in
Hosoya, "Retrogression in Japan's Foreign Policy Decision-Making Process"; Crowley,
"Intellectuals as Visionaries of the New Asian Order," on conceptions of Japanese–Asian
relations under the new order.
[304] Dower, *War without Mercy*, p. 24.

minority objections with the insouciant but revealing remark that "Some-times people have to shut their eyes and take the plunge."[305]

Tōjō's remark might readily have sprung from the lips of President George Bush or one of his principal advisors in the context of the American decision to invade Iraq. In the next chapter, I will not only analyze this decision and the support it received among the American public but the extent to which at least in part this was attributable to America's self-image as a parvenu power.

---

[305] Konoe Fumumaro, *Ushinawareshi Seiji*, p. 131, quoted in Maruyama, *Thought and Behaviour in Modern Japanese Politics*, p. 85.

9

Hitler to Bush and beyond

We're an empire now, and when we act, we create our own reality. And while you're studying that reality – judiciously as you will, – we'll act again, creating other new realities, which you can study too, and that's how things will sort out. We're history's actors . . . and you, all of you, will be left to just study what we do.

Karl Rove[1]

Any system intended to bring liberty by open force to neighboring nations can only make liberty hated and prevent its triumph.

Talleyrand

The Cold War was the dominant international conflict of the post-World War II era. Other important developments, many of them related, include decolonization and the regional conflicts it spawned, the spread of democracy, the rising economic power of Pacific rim countries, the emergence of China as a great power and the collapse of the Soviet Union. The Cold War has been analyzed in terms of fear and appetite; realists and traditional historians emphasize the former and revisionists the latter. The study of foreign policy and international relations has once again ignored the spirit and the ways in which striving for recognition and standing helped to shape the Cold War and contributed to its demise. Two of the most serious crises of the Cold War – the Cuban missile crisis and the superpower confrontation arising out of the 1973 Middle East War – were provoked by anger; in each instance one superpower leader felt betrayed by the other and felt compelled to respond to what they considered an intolerable affront to themselves and their country.

The Cold War became less volatile after the missile crisis in response to expectations in Washington and Moscow that the risk of war could be reduced through understandings about how their rivalry should be

---

[1] Quoted in Ron Suskind, "Faith, Certainty and the Presidency of George Bush," *New York Times Magazine*, October 17, 2004.

managed. "Rules of the road" were developed during the short-lived era of détente of the late 1960s and early 1970s.[2] The superpowers remained committed to their rivalry and their pursuit of unilateral advantage undermined the promise of détente. The striking aspect of superpower goals in the 1970s and 1980s is how little they had to do with security and how much they reflected desires to gain the upper hand in a contest for standing. This orientation did not change until the era of Mikhail Gorbachev. He and his advisors had concluded that such competition was costly, dangerous and inimical to their domestic reform agenda. Their shift in goals made possible the agreements that ended the Cold War.

The American world view changed dramatically as a result of the events of September 11, 2001. Once again, security appeared to move to the top of the agenda. The invasions of Afghanistan and Iraq were justified in its name by the Bush administration, which did everything in its power to link Iraq's ruler to the terrorists responsible for the attack of 9.11. These invasions generated a large literature, much of which focuses on the intelligence failures preceding the Iraq invasion or the faulty execution of that invasion and the subsequent occupation. Critics point to the arrogance and ideological fervor of leading members of the Bush administration as underlying causes of these failures, and are certainly correct in doing so.[3] Elsewhere I argue that the hubris of the Bush administration was not only attributable to the influence of neoconservatives, but to a wider shift in American narratives of self-interest that was already apparent in the foreign policy of the Clinton administration.[4] In this chapter I explore the intensity of the Bush administration's hostility to Iraq and its concomitant desire to overthrow Saddam Hussein, both of which were evident from the moment it assumed office. The events of 9.11 provided the political cover for a long-planned invasion desired for reasons that had nothing to do with terrorism, but much to do with anger and standing. Equally significant was the enormous popular support for the invasions of Afghanistan and Iraq and the extent to which that support continued for a considerable time after it became evident that the occupation was a costly failure. Sustained support for these ventures sharply differentiates the American public from its closest allies, notably Great Britain, whose prime minister

[2] George, *Managing US–Soviet Rivalry* and George et al., *U.S.–Soviet Security Cooperation*.
[3] Hersh, *Chain of Command*; Daalder and Lindsay, *America Unbound*; Woodward, *Plan of Attack*; Fallows, "Blind into Baghdad"; Phillips, *Losing Iraq*; Suskind, *The One Percent Doctrine*; Ricks, *Fiasco*; Isikoff and Corn, *Hubris*; Woodward, *State of Denial*; Gordon, and Trainor, *Cobra II*; Galbraith, *End of Iraq*.
[4] Lebow and Lebow, *Running Red Lights and Ruling the World*.

committed forces to both operations and became enormously unpopular as a result. The difference was due to more than mere "spin control."

I turn to the spirit for help in explaining both phenomena. My starting point is once again Homer's understanding of anger, implicit in his treatment of the conflict between Greece and Troy and Achilles and Agamemnon, and made explicit by Aristotle in his *Rhetoric*. Americans would have been angry at any group who attacked the World Trade Center and the Pentagon and killed thousands of people, but there was an additional sense of outrage because of the relative insignificance of Al-Qaeda. Its hijackings were not just a travesty but an act of *lèse majesté*, given the quasi-imperial stature of the United States. The insult and resulting anger were made all the more acute by the failure of the Bush administration to kill Osama bin Laden or bring him to justice. Given public sentiment in the immediate aftermath of the attacks – sentiment shared within the administration – the president had little choice but to strike out at someone, and Afghanistan was the obvious target. Treating Al-Qaeda as a criminal group, best pursued by standard police measures, in collaboration with allies and other third parties, may have made more sense strategically, but was simply not perceived as a political option. The administration also appears to have desired a "war against terror" for a combination of domestic and foreign policy reasons.

The war against Iraq was another matter. There was no significant public pressure to invade Iraq, and what support became manifest was largely manufactured by the administration. The Iraq invasion was intended to showcase US military might and political will and send a message of power and resolve to diverse Middle East audiences. As a warning to hostile states such as Iran and Syria, the invasion was meant to demonstrate the ease with which Washington could topple regimes and establish friendly governments. For the same reason, it was expected to make Saudi Arabia, Jordan and the Palestinians more pliant. In a more fundamental sense, the Iraq invasion was part and parcel of the strategy, vocally espoused by neocons and widely supported within the administration, to act decisively in a world in which no serious opposition was in sight, and by so doing lock in the United States as the world's sole hegemon.

The Iraq War and the world's reaction to it indicate that world opinion has an increasingly restrictive view of the circumstances in which one state can legitimately use force against another. There is some evidence that this is part of a more fundamental shift in the views about the nature and basis of influence in the post-Cold War world among America's closest allies and trading partners, and other states as well. Intersubjective understandings about the nature of legitimate foreign policy goals and the means appropriate to achieving them shape the character of regional and international political systems. Culture, not the number of actors and their relative capabilities, determines who counts as an actor and how those actors define and pursue their interests. Changes in what is considered legitimate and appropriate have the potential to reshape not only the behavior of actors, but their identities as well, because we often revise our understandings of ourselves to bring them in line with our behavior.[5] Changes in the identities of enough important actors can transform the character of the international system. If such a transformation occurs, we may look back on the Iraq War, not so much as a turning point, but as an event that made us aware that such a process was underway. Indictors are often misleading, and many expected developments never occur, so it is also possible that international relations will remain a social domain in which standing continues to be associated with military power. I accordingly offer two scenarios, one leading to a transformation of the international system, and the other to its prolongation. I offer them not as predictions, but as useful means of exploring the interaction of ideas and behavior in regional and international systems.

The title of this chapter, "Hitler to Bush and beyond," will undoubtedly offend some readers. So a few explanatory words are in order. The title makes chronological sense as I begin my analysis with the collapse of Nazi Germany and the onset of the Cold War and conclude with the Bush administration's invasion of Iraq. There are, of course, telling differences between the two leaders. George Bush is not a pathological murderer who came to power intent on using the institutions of state to act out his most perverse fantasies and compulsions. Nor did he bring about the physical destruction and territorial division of his country. There are nevertheless disturbing parallels between the two nations and the tactics of their leaders. Both lashed out against what they regarded as national humiliations that had to be avenged by force and resorted to bald-faced lies to mobilize support for unsuccessful military adventures that most of the rest of the world condemned as unwarranted aggression. Both leaders continued to pursue their goals after it became evident that they were doomed to failure. Hitler's defeat led to the division of Europe, but also to the rise of a peaceful, economically integrated European community based on the reconciliation of former enemies. Since the end of the Cold War and the collapse of the Soviet Union, the European Union has been

---

[5] Bem, "Self-Perception," and "Self-Perception Theory."

extended further east to encompass much of the continent. America's failure in Iraq also has the potential to serve as a catalyst for learning – if it reshapes Washington's approach to the world.

The Cold War

The Cold War arose from the power vacuum created in central Europe by the defeat of Nazi Germany. Converging on Germany from opposite directions, allied forces and the Red Army sought to avoid any confrontation but also to impose their political and economic preferences on the countries they occupied. In these circumstances, some degree of conflict between the two superpowers and their allies was inevitable. It became acute by virtue of the antagonistic nature of their social systems and mutual resentment arising from past and present policies. Appetite (markets for the West, reparations for the Soviets), spirit (competition for standing in Europe) and fear (concern for the consequences of the other side gaining control of Europe's industrial base and resources) were all implicated and probably mutually reinforcing at the onset of the Cold War, and it would be fruitless to attempt to assess their relative weight. In the West, different concerns were paramount for different actors at different times. In the Soviet Union, Stalin's voice was dominant, and all we can do is speculate about his hierarchy of motives and the ways in which cunning and paranoia combined to shape his policies.[6]

As the Cold War progressed, it is sometimes possible to determine the motives of the superpowers and other actors. In some instances, appetite, spirit and fear were cross-cutting and required actors to make visible tradeoffs. In other cases, documents allow us to establish their presence, if not their relative weight. The written record is both revealing and obfuscating. Documents sometimes provide insight into the minds of policymakers and their advisors, and on other occasions are misleading. The Cold War was framed as a security issue by both superpowers, and arguments for and against courses of action generally had to be phrased in the language of security. The security discourse became so dominant that it was successfully used as a cover for a host of policies and programs in the United States that had little or nothing to do with security (e.g. foreign aid, the interstate highway system, secret classification of politically

---

[6] Volkogonov, *Stalin as Revolutionary*, pp. 3–13, 70–1, 225–36; Tucker, *Stalin in Power*, pp. 278–80, 317–19, 620, 625; Holloway, *Stalin and the Bomb*, pp. 153–60, 171, 283–8, 368–70.

embarrassing documents). Other motives and their associated discourses were correspondingly downgraded and even delegitimized. In the Soviet Union, there was the additional twist: all policies had to be justified with reference to Marxist-Leninist ideology.

Presidents could not defend any decisions, especially those concerning foreign policy, with reference to their political interests. In the Cuban missile crisis, neither Kennedy nor his closest advisors spoke about the domestic political consequences of the various options open to them in ExComm meetings even though they were very much on their minds. We have only hints in the form of the president's private asides to his brother.[7] The spirit was almost as *verboten*; government officials and prominent talking heads never openly spoke of the Cold War as a competition for standing. It nevertheless increasingly assumed this character in the decades after Stalin's death. If interrogated, policymakers undoubtedly would have described competition for its own sake as costly and irresponsible, and all the more so if it risked provoking war-threatening crises. American presidents were willing to talk about prestige, but only as a means of enhancing security. This approach is reflected in the international relations literature of the period, which, as we have seen, treats prestige as a useful resource, not an end in itself.[8] As policymakers may not have been willing to admit, even to themselves, that the Cold War was at least as much about standing as it was about security, its repression as a motive – and I think this psychological concept is justified – makes its documentation all the more elusive. The motive of appetite was more acceptable; policies intended to help American manufacturers and farmers sell their products abroad were welcomed by relevant constituencies and generally acceptable to the wider public. Even when paramount, however, appetite also had to appear to take a back seat to security in the realm of foreign policy.

American reactions to the communist takeover of China in 1949, the Soviet explosion of an atomic device in the same year and the launching of Sputnik in 1957 offer some insight into how deeply the spirit was implicated in the Cold War during its first decade. Chiang Kai-shek's defeat and the nationalist retreat to the island redoubt of Taiwan came as a shock to the American public. Politicians and opinion-makers spoke of the "loss of China," and right-wing Republicans associated with the China lobby blamed the Truman administration and communists within

---

[7] Lebow and Stein, We *All Lost the Cold War*, ch. 3, for the role of American domestic politics in the missile crisis.
[8] See the discussion of Morgenthau, Gilpin and other theorists in the introduction.

it for what they considered an otherwise inexplicable loss.[9] These charges were entirely unfounded, but were surprisingly credible to the American public, many of whom gave credence to the "Red" conspiracy and returned a Republican majority to the Congress. Since the early years of the twentieth century, China had been portrayed as a "younger brother" whom America was mentoring and Christianizing. Its "defection" to the "Reds" – as common parlance had it – was not considered the choice of the Chinese people, but of communist leaders beholden to Moscow who had, in the words of Dean Acheson, "brainwashed" other Chinese to follow their lead.[10] This kind of tortured logic, present in the administration, not just among its right-wing opponents, was indicative of the unwillingness of many Americans and their elected representatives to face political reality. American self-esteem had become increasingly tied to the country's standing in the world, and China's apparent rejection of America was not just a political loss, but a blow to that self-esteem. Thus the need, as in Weimar, to attribute an unacceptable outcome to a conspiracy and exculpate oneself by punishing a scapegoat. It is revealing that there was less discussion in the media about the security consequences of "losing" China than of the blow it constituted to American prestige in Asia.[11]

The Soviet explosion of a nuclear device in August 1949 was another shock to the government and the American public. Nuclear experts had predicted that it would take Russia at least ten years to join the nuclear club.[12] Their atomic test, which the administration at first considered keeping quiet, had obvious security implications because it put an end to America's nuclear monopoly and threatened in the not too distant future to make the United States vulnerable to a devastating attack. When the Soviet Union developed this capability, the American nuclear arsenal would be unusable for anything other than deterrence.[13] While security concerns were undoubtedly paramount in the minds of at least some policymakers, the Soviet Union's detonation of a nuclear device was widely

[9] Westerfield, *Foreign Policy and Party Politics*, pp. 296–382; Purifoy, *Harry Truman's China Policy*, pp. 125–232; Kahn, *The China Hands*.

[10] Shewmaker, *Americans and Chinese Communists*, on early assessments. On the 1949–50 period, Whiting, *China Crosses the Yalu*, pp. 169–70; McClellan, *Dean Acheson*, pp. 196–7, 211–14.

[11] Lebow, *Between Peace and War*, pp. 192–216 for an elaboration of this argument in the context of the Korean War.

[12] R. H. Hillenkoeter, Memorandum for the President, "Estimate of the Status of the Russian Atomic Energy Project," July 6, 1948, cited in Holloway, *Stalin and the Bomb*, p. 220; Bundy, *Danger and Survival*, pp. 199–214.

[13] Ibid., pp. 209–14.

considered a blow to American prestige that required a vigorous response. Part of that response was a crash program to develop a thermonuclear weapon, which the Truman administration desired on strategic grounds, but also to ensure that the Soviet Union was not the first country to acquire such a weapon.[14] The Soviet Union exploded a thermonuclear device in August 1953, less than a year after the United States. The Soviet device, although less powerful, was, unlike its American counterpart, a deliverable weapon.[15]

Concern for prestige was even more evident in the American reaction to Sputnik. Launched in October 1957, *Sputnik 1* carried a payload the size of a basketball and broadcast a beeping signal back to Earth that could be picked up by ordinary shortwave radios. It caught the attention of the world, was applauded as a major scientific achievement and appeared to support Soviet premier Nikita S. Khrushchev's claims that the Soviet system could compete with, if not surpass, the capitalist West economically and scientifically. *Sputnik 2*, launched in November 1957, carried the first life into orbit, a dog named Laika. These space coups were all the more mortifying to Americans and their government in light of two successive and highly publicized failures of the US Vanguard launches intended to loft the country's own satellite into space. The Eisenhower administration stepped up its efforts to put a satellite into orbit, established the National Aeronautic and Space Administration (NASA), and poured funds into science education.[16] Khrushchev exacerbated American insecurities by boasting that Soviet factories "were turning out missiles like sausages" and that Soviet rockets could "hit a fly in space."[17] Senator John F. Kennedy, out to win the Democratic nomination and the 1960 presidential election, exploited these developments by repeatedly asserting that there was "a missile gap" for which the Eisenhower administration was responsible. When Kennedy assumed office he learned that there was no missile gap, but still dramatically accelerated the US strategic buildup, and later promised to land a man on the moon.[18] The Soviet Union stepped up

[14] Holloway, *Stalin and the Bomb*, pp. 267, 294–303, 309–10, 318.
[15] Ibid., pp. 303–9, 317–18.
[16] Aliano, *American Defense Policy from Eisenhower to Kennedy*, pp. 204–22 on Eisenhower. On Kennedy, see Paul H. Nitze to McGeorge Bundy, June 17, 1963, enclosing "Memorandum for the Record: The Missile Gap, 1858–1960," John F. Kennedy Library, Boston, MA; Ball, *Politics and Force Levels*, pp. 15–25; Lebow and Stein, *We All Lost the Cold War*, pp. 34–6.
[17] Khrushchev interview with *Le Figaro*, excerpted in *Pravda*, March 27, 1958; *Pravda*, May 9, 1959 and January 15, 1961, Lebow and Stein, *We All Lost the Cold War*, p. 33.
[18] McNamara, Robert, "Memorandum for the President, The Missile Gap Controversy," March 4, 1963, John F. Kennedy Library; Sorensen, *Kennedy*, pp. 608–10; Schlesinger, *A*

its strategic program in response.[19] Pursuit of prestige, and the political capital to be made from it, triggered off a dangerous and costly arms race.

The Cuban missile crisis illustrates how the spirit can be a contributing cause of conflict. When President Kennedy was informed that Soviet missile sites had been discovered in Cuba, he exclaimed: "He [Khrushchev] can't do this to me!"[20] Most analysts of the crisis have interpreted Kennedy's anger as a response to the strategic and political dilemmas he suddenly confronted. The national interest and political survival alike demanded that Soviet missiles be kept out of Cuba, but the ongoing missile deployment could only be stopped by military action, or the threat of military action, and either involved enormous risk. There was an Aristotelian dimension to his anger. The Soviet premier had promised the American president through official and informal channels that he would not send missiles to Cuba nor do anything to embarrass him before the congressional elections. Kennedy felt betrayed and slighted. His first inclination was to seek revenge by attacking the missile sites, humiliating Khrushchev. He gradually overcame his anger, and conspired with Khrushchev to allow him to save face by means of a negotiated withdrawal of the missiles. Kennedy in turn agreed to withdraw the Jupiter missiles from Turkey after a decent interval.[21]

Standing and reputation dominated American calculations during the crisis. Kennedy and his secretary of defense Robert McNamara considered Soviet missiles in Cuba more a political than a military threat. From McNamara's perspective, it did not much matter if you were killed by an ICBM launched from the Soviet Union or an IRBM from Cuba. "A missile is a missile," he told his colleagues.[22] Kennedy and McNamara reasoned that a successful Soviet deployment would confer tremendous prestige on Moscow and its leader and damage the standing of the United States and its president. The repercussions of a successful challenge would be felt throughout the world, give heart and courage to pro-communist guerrilla movements in Latin America and Southeast Asia, and undermine

---

Thousand Days, pp. 288, 498–500; Bottome, *The Missile Gap*, pp. 229–31; Prados, *The Soviet Estimate*, pp. 111–26; Ball, *Politics and Force Levels*, pp. 88–95, 107–26; Lebow and Stein, *We All Lost the Cold War*, pp. 34–8.

[19] Lebow and Stein, *We All Lost the Cold War*, pp. 32–42.

[20] Quoted in Neustadt, *Presidential Power*, "Afterword," p. 187.

[21] Lebow and Stein, *We All Lost the Cold War*, ch. 5; Garthoff, *Reflections on the Missile Crisis*, pp. 43–55; Bundy, *Danger and Survival*, pp. 391–462.

[22] Transcript of "Off-the-Record Meeting, October 16, 6:30–7:55 p.m.," pp. 12–13, John F. Kennedy Library; Lebow and Stein, *We All Lost the Cold War*, pp. 98–102 for a discussion of this meeting.

the resolve of America's allies.[23] Kennedy and his advisors were considering prestige in its instrumental sense, but there is also reason to believe that Kennedy in particular framed it as an absolute goal. More than most politicians, Kennedy was committed to winning, whether in touch football, politics or foreign policy. His self-esteem, and that of his brother Robert, suffered a severe blow in the aftermath of the Bay of Pigs failure. By all accounts, the Kennedy brothers took the defeat of Cuban émigré forces personally, and former members of the CIA have hinted that Robert Kennedy, then attorney-general, was behind subsequent American efforts to assassinate Cuban leader Fidel Castro.[24] Victory, as Aristotle observes, is often more important than honor.[25]

Concern for standing was equally evident on the Soviet side. Khrushchev was desperate to have the Soviet Union recognized as a great power. When invited to visit the United States, he was troubled by President Eisenhower's decision to receive him at Camp David, a place unknown to the Soviet embassy. Khrushchev later confessed,

> One reason I was suspicious was that I remembered in the early years after the Revolution when contacts were first being established with the bourgeois world, a Soviet delegation was invited to a meeting held someplace called the Prince's Islands. It came out in the newspaper that it was to these islands that stray dogs were sent to die. . . . I was afraid maybe this Camp David was the same sort of place, where people who were mistrusted could be kept in quarantine.

Upon his arrival in Washington, he was greatly relieved to be received with full honors and delighted to discover that it was a sign of special favor to be invited to Camp David.[26]

This passage is one of many in Khrushchev's memoirs that reveals his desire for personal and national recognition and a corresponding sensitivity to the possibility of humiliation. As a peasant leader of a quasi-pariah socialist country, he was insecure in his dealings with the West and its more worldly and seemingly self-confident leaders. On more than one occasion, his insecurity led him to infer insults when none were intended.[27] Although reassured by the American ambassador that he would be treated

---

[23] Transcript of "Off-the-Record Meeting"; Lebow and Stein. *We All Lost the Cold War.*

[24] Schlesinger, *Robert Kennedy and his Times*, pp. 44–6, 485–94; Lebow and Stein, *We All Lost the Cold War*, pp. 24–7 on the Kennedy brothers' responses to the failure of the Bay of Pigs operation.

[25] Aristotle, *Rhetoric*, 1389a12–14.   [26] Khrushchev, *Khrushchev Remembers*, p. 420.

[27] Haykal, *The Sphinx and the Commissar*, p. 137, tells of a revealing encounter with Khrushchev. Alexei Adzhubei, Khrushchev's son-in-law, who accompanied him to Egypt,

as a head of state (although in point of fact, he was only the premier), Khrushchev still fretted about the discrimination he might encounter. He admitted to being "very sensitive" on this score and unwilling to tolerate "even a hint of anti-Sovietism."[28] The other side of Khrushchev's insecurity was his delight in acceptance. Khrushchev was so overwhelmed by his regal welcome to Cairo that "there were tears in his eyes."[29] He was equally thrilled by his red carpet treatment in Washington, and the many courtesies extended to him in the United States. "It made me immensely proud; it even shook me up a bit." Standing on the podium at Andrews Air Force Base, the Soviet visitors "felt pride in our country, our Party, our people, and the victories they had achieved. We had transformed Russia into a highly developed country."[30]

Some of Khrushchev's sensitivity was idiosyncratic, but it also reflected his understanding of the Soviet Union as a great country arising, like himself, from an inauspicious, if not underprivileged, background. He regarded his visit as a "colossal moral victory" for socialism.[31] "Who would have guessed," he told his Kremlin colleagues, "that the most powerful capitalist country would invite a Communist to visit? This is incredible. Today they *have* to take us into account. It's our strength that led to this – they have to recognize our existence and our power. Who would have thought the capitalists would invite me, a worker? Look what we've achieved in these years."[32] He was deeply moved when "Ike" called him "my friend" – which he interpreted as a sign of his respect for the USSR – and concluded that he was sincerely interested in ending the Cold War.[33]

Relations between the superpowers deteriorated quickly. Khrushchev was subjected to stinging criticism from hardliners at home for his search for détente with the United States, and Eisenhower, under pressure from Adenauer and his own hardliners, gradually backed away from his policy

---

reported that his father-in-law was angry with Heykal for his newspaper account of the visit. Haykal confronted Khrushchev, who told him that "It's something you wrote – about me being a peasant." Haykal protested: "But Mr. Chairman, you've always spoken with such pride of being a peasant." To which Khrushchev responded: "But you wrote I was like a peasant from a story by Dostoevsky – why didn't you say a peasant from Tolstoy?"

[28] Khrushchev, *Khrushchev Remembers: The Last Testament*, p. 483. Haykal, *The Sphinx and the Commissar*, p. 135, reports that Khrushchev expressed the same concerns prior to his Egyptian visit.

[29] Haykal, *The Sphinx and the Commissar*, p. 135.

[30] Khrushchev, *Khrushchev Remembers: The Last Testament*, p. 423.   [31] Ibid., p. 471.

[32] Sergei Khrushchev, *Khrushchev on Khrushchev*, p. 356.

[33] Khrushchev, *Khrushchev Remembers: The Last Testament*, p. 471; *New York Times*, September 30, 1959.

of accommodation.[34] Khrushchev understood he was vulnerable, and was "completely beside himself in rage," when Eisenhower undercut him further by sending a U-2 reconnaissance flight over the Soviet Union on April 9, 1960. Khrushchev had previously asked him not to do anything "to worsen the atmosphere" before their impending summit in Paris.[35] The Soviets had been quietly fuming about these overflights since they had begun in July 1956, which they regarded as an insult to the Soviet Union and its sovereignty. They developed the SA-2 missile specifically to deal with the threat, and used it for the first time on May 1 to bring down a U-2 along with its pilot over Sverdlovsk (now Ekaterinburg) in central Russia.[36] Given the timing of the flight – on May Day – Khrushchev was convinced that it was "an affront orchestrated by the president himself."[37] Soviet hardliners stepped up their attack on Khrushchev, and Mao Zedong publicly ridiculed him. Khrushchev told journalists that "the American militarists have placed me . . . in a very difficult position."[38] He used the U-2 incident to retract his invitation to Eisenhower to visit the Soviet Union and justification for his confrontational stance in Paris, which effectively torpedoed the summit.[39]

Khrushchev was pleased when Kennedy defeated that "son-of-a bitch" Nixon, but the April 1961 Bay of Pigs invasion convinced him that the new president had no interest in détente. So did his deployment of Jupiter missiles in Turkey and performance at the Vienna summit, where he brushed aside Khrushchev's complaints about these missiles and how they could only aggravate US–Soviet relations.[40] Khrushchev made many subsequent references to the Jupiters. On October 27, at the height of

[34] Lebow and Stein, *We All Lost the Cold War*, p. 55, reporting on interviews with Soviet political officials from the period.

[35] Interview, Oleg Grinevsky, Stockholm, October 24, 1992; Lebow and Stein, *We All Lost the Cold War*, p. 56.

[36] Wise and Ross, *The U-2 Affair*; Beschloss, *Mayday*; Khrushchev, *Khrushchev Remembers: The Last Testament*, pp. 504–7; Oleg Grinevsky to author, December 16, 1992. Lebow and Stein, *We All Lost the Cold War*, pp. 56–7.

[37] Interview, Alexei Adzhubei, Moscow, May 15, 1989; Lebow and Stein, *We All Lost the Cold War*, p. 57.

[38] News Conference, May 11, 1960, quoted in Tatu, *Power in the Kremlin*, p. 63; Lebow and Stein, *We All Lost the Cold War*, pp. 57–8.

[39] Interviews, Leonid M. Zamyatin, Moscow, December 16, 1991; Oleg Grinevsky, Vienna, October 11, 1991, and Stockholm, October 23, 1992; Tatu, *Power in the Kremlin*, pp. 41–68; Arbatov, *The System*, p. 96; Lebow and Stein, *We All Lost the Cold War*, p. 58.

[40] Khrushchev, *Khrushchev Remembers*, p. 458, and *Khrushchev Remembers: The Last Testament*, pp. 555–8, 567; "Record of Vienna Summit Meeting, 3 June 1961, 3 p.m., at residence of U.S. ambassador," John F. Kennedy Library; Lebow and Stein, *We All Lost the Cold War*, pp. 45–6.

the missile crisis, he wrote a long private letter to Kennedy, defending his deployment of missiles in Cuba as a justifiable response to the American deployment in Turkey.

> You are worried over Cuba. You say that it worries you because it lies at a distance of ninety miles across the sea from the shores of the United States. However, Turkey lies next to us. Our sentinels are pacing up and down and watching each other. Do you believe you have the right to demand security for your country and the removal of such weapons that you qualify as offensive, while not recognizing this right for us?
>
> You have stationed devastating rocket weapons, which you call offensive, in Turkey, literally right next to us. How then does recognition of our equal military possibilities tally with such unequal relations between our great states? This does not tally at all.[41]

Khrushchev did not regard the weapons as a military threat "because the Soviet Union had been surrounded by US Air Force bases since 1945." It was the *uselessness* of the weapons that offended him.[42] He told Richard Nixon that the missiles could only be used as first-strike weapons: "If you intend to make war on us, I understand; if not, why do you keep them there?"[43] Khrushchev interpreted the missiles as yet another American attempt, like the earlier U-2 overflights, to humiliate the Soviet Union and deny it the respect its military and economic accomplishments warranted.

From Khrushchev's perspective, American behavior defied Lenin's concept of the "correlation of forces," which was central to his understanding of superpower relations. Eisenhower had sought improved relations because of "our economic might, the might of our armed forces, and that of the whole socialist camp." "By the time Kennedy came to the White House and we had our first meeting in Vienna," he wrote, "there had already been a shift in the balance of power. It was harder for Kennedy to pressure us than it had been in the days of Dulles and Truman."[44] Blinded by American arrogance, Khrushchev reasoned, the American president behaved as if there had been no change in the correlation of forces. By

[41] Letter from Chairman Khrushchev to President Kennedy, October 27, 1962, in Lebow and Stein, *We All Lost the Cold War*, p. 46.

[42] Interview with Sergei Khrushchev, Moscow, May 17, 1989; Lebow and Stein, *We All Lost the Cold War*, p. 46.

[43] This conversation took place on July 26, 1959 in Moscow. "Compendium of Soviet Remarks on Missiles, 2 March 1961," quoted in Lebow and Stein, *We All Lost the Cold War*, p. 46.

[44] Khrushchev, *Khrushchev Remembers*, pp. 423, 568.

sending Soviet missiles to Cuba, Khrushchev hoped to shake Kennedy free from his illusions and pave the way for a more equal relationship.[45]

For Aristotle, harm provokes hostility (*misein*), and slights arouse anger, but only when the offended party has the power to get even.[46] Khrushchev and other Soviet officials had been compelled to suppress their anger at the U-2 overflights until their air defense forces had a missile capable of shooting one down. With Castro as a pliable ally, Khrushchev was now in a position to avenge the threatening forward deployments of American bombers and missiles by sending Soviet missiles to Cuba. Other considerations also came into play. Khrushchev expected the missiles to deter an expected American attack on Cuba and partially offset American strategic superiority.[47] Soviet officials of the era agree that the Jupiter missiles were the principal catalyst for the deployment, although it is not clear whether Khrushchev hit upon the idea before or during a state visit to Bulgaria in May 1961.[48] By one account, Khrushchev had a big lunch at the Bulgarian seashore resort of Varna and fell asleep in a deck chair with the book he was reading spread on top of his ample belly. He awoke late in the afternoon and extolled the tranquility of the scene to defense minister Rodion Ya. Malinovsky, seated in a nearby deck chair. Malinovsky reminded Khrushchev of something both men knew: beyond that "tranquil" horizon the Americans were deploying missiles tipped with nuclear missiles and aimed at the Soviet Union. Khrushchev grew angry and expressed his intention to send missiles to Cuba to "get even" with the Americans for their "intolerable provocation."[49] He later told his ambassador to Cuba that "Inasmuch as the Americans already have surrounded the Soviet Union with a circle of their military bases and missile installations of various designations, we should repay them in kind, let them try their own medicine, so they can feel what it's like to live in the nuclear gun sights."[50]

---

[45] General Dimitri Volkogonov, "Moscow Conference," pp. 28–9, in Allyn *et al.*, *Back to the Brink*; Khrushchev, *Khrushchev Remembers: The Last Testament*, p. 568, on the first Soviet atomic test and Sputnik as models for the Cuban missile deployment because of how they gained American attention and respect.

[46] Aristotle, *Nichomachean Ethics*, 1117a5–15, and *Rhetoric*, 2.2, 1387a31–3.

[47] Lebow and Stein, *We All Lost the Cold War*, chs. 2 and 3; Garthoff, *Reflections on the Missile Crisis*, pp. 6–42.

[48] Lebow and Stein, *We All Lost the Cold War*, pp. 72–3 for discussion and evaluation of conflicting accounts.

[49] Interview with Fedor Burlatsky, Cambridge, October 12, 1987.

[50] Alekseev, "Karibskii krisis," p. 29; interview with Anatoliy Dobrynin, Moscow, December 17, 1991.

Resolution of the missile crisis paved the way for détente. In May 1972, Soviet premier Leonid Brezhnev and President Richard Nixon met in Moscow, where they signed the first important strategic arms-limitation agreement and discussed ways of preventing war-threatening crises. In the spirit of détente, the two leaders attempted to develop some general principles and informal rules to govern their relationship. They negotiated the Basic Principles Agreement in 1972, and at the urging of the Soviet Union, the Agreement on Prevention of Nuclear War in June 1973.[51] The latter accord was aimed at reducing crises as it required both sides "to immediately enter into urgent consultation with each other and make every effort to avert this risk" if their direct relationship or relations with other countries "appear to involve the risk of a nuclear conflict."[52]

Preventing war was obviously an overriding goal of both superpowers, and Soviet leaders rightly hailed détente as a significant achievement in this regard.[53] They also emphasized the coequal superpower status they had gained by virtue of these agreements. Especially important to Moscow was the second article of the Basic Principles Agreement that referred to the "recognition of the security interests of the parties based on the principle of equality and the renunciation of the use or threat of force," and the recognition "that efforts to obtain unilateral advantages at the expense of others, directly or indirectly, are inconsistent with these objectives."[54] To Politburo members these agreements symbolized their long-standing goal of American acceptance of their country as a coequal global power. Speaking for Brezhnev, Leonid Zamyatin explained that as America's recognized equal, the Soviet Union now expected to participate fully in the resolution of major international conflicts.[55] The clear implication was that the Soviet Union would act more like a satisfied power once its status claims were recognized and honored.

From the late 1960s, the Cold War increasingly came to resemble European imperial competition in the latter part of the nineteenth century. It

[51] Kissinger, *Years of Upheaval*, pp. 274–86; Garthoff, *Détente and Confrontation*, 69–105, 289–359; George, *Towards a Soviet–American Crisis Prevention Regime*, and *Managing U.S.–Soviet Rivalry*.

[52] US Department of State, *The Washington Summit*, pp. 30–1.

[53] Georgi Arbatov, "Soviet-American Relations at a New Stage," *Pravda*, July 22, 1973. Quoted in Garthoff, *Détente and Confrontation*, p. 333.

[54] "Basic Principles of Relations."

[55] Quoted by Murrey Marder, "Brezhnev Extols A-Pact," *Washington Post*, June 24, 1973; TASS, Radio Moscow, June 25, 1973, in Foreign Broadcast Information Service, Daily Report: Soviet Union, June 25, 1973. Garthoff, *Détente and Confrontation*, pp. 344–5; Lebow and Stein, *We All Lost the Cold War*, pp. 153–5.

morphed from a conflict about postwar spheres of influence in Europe into a struggle for primacy in the so-called Third World, and all the more so after the 1978 Helsinki Accords ratified the European territorial status quo.[56] The biggest difference was in the number of players: Soviet–American competition in the Middle East, Africa, Asia and Latin America was dominated by the two superpowers, although, depending on the decade and region in question, Britain, France and China played lesser roles. Imperial competition in the late nineteenth century provoked crises (e.g. Fashoda, the First and Second Morocco crises, the Bosnian Annexation) when one power attempted to make gains at the expense of another by unilateral political or military action. The last serious crisis between the superpowers arose in a similar manner. American secretary of state Henry Kissinger sought to exploit the October 1973 Middle East War to wean Egypt away from its dependence on the Soviet Union and make it an American dependency.

In October 1973, Syria and Egypt launched a coordinated surprise attack against Israel and overwhelmed Israeli forces on the Golan Heights and in the Sinai Peninsula. With full mobilization, and additional weapons and ammunition supplied by an American airlift, Israel halted the Arab advances and went over to the offensive on both fronts. Within a week, Israel had recaptured the Golan, putting Damascus at risk, trapped the Egyptian Third Army on the west bank of the Suez Canal, and was conducting an increasingly powerful offensive on the east bank that threatened to cut off another Egyptian army, leaving the road open to Cairo. The United States was now in a position to broker a peace, and Egyptian president Anwar El Sadat understood that the only way he could regain the Canal and the Sinai was with American assistance. Egypt and Syria, with Soviet support, called for a ceasefire after their initial successes. In keeping with his desire to maximize leverage over both sides, Kissinger agreed to support a ceasefire once Israel had gone over to the offensive but before it had decisively defeated its Arab adversaries. He flew to Moscow where, on October 21, he worked with Brezhnev, Gromyko and Dobrynin to draft a joint ceasefire resolution. Kissinger flew on to Jerusalem the next morning to persuade the Israelis to stop fighting.[57]

[56] Garthoff, *Détente and Confrontation*, pp. 473–9 on Helsinki, and pp. 622–89, and Westad, *Global Cold War*, on the spread of the Cold War to other parts of the world. Westad, p. 5, offers his take on the similarities and differences between the Cold War and nineteenth-century colonialism.

[57] Kissinger, *Years of Upheaval*, pp. 539–54; Israelian, *Inside the Kremlin*; Garthoff, *Détente and Confrontation*, pp. 360–404; Lebow and Stein, *We All Lost the Cold War*, pp. 207–19, for

The catalyst for the 1973 superpower crisis, like the missile crisis a decade earlier, was personal anger, in this instance Brezhnev's. Soviet battlefield intelligence was seventy-two hours behind time because of satellite problems, and the Politburo thought that Israel was still pressing its offensive. Now back in Washington, Kissinger was doing his best to make sure that Israel honored the ceasefire. Brezhnev convinced himself that Kissinger had come to Moscow to lull him into believing that he supported a ceasefire and subsequently urged Israel to keep fighting. After some serious drinking, and behind the back of his colleagues, he added a sentence to the message the Politburo had authorized him to send to President Nixon urging joint action to enforce the ceasefire. Brezhnev raised the prospect of unilateral intervention if the United States did not agree to cooperate, and Kissinger and his colleagues, anxious to signal that they would not be blackmailed, responded with a strategic nuclear alert. The crisis ended as quickly as it began once Soviet intelligence learned that fighting in the Middle East had in fact stopped.[58]

Kennedy had been furious with Khrushchev because he conspired behind his back after assuring him that the Soviet Union would do nothing in Cuba to embarrass him.[59] Brezhnev mistakenly concluded that Kissinger had done something similar to him. Ironically, détente had increased the likelihood of misunderstanding by virtue of the unrealistic expectations it aroused. Each superpower expected the other to exercise more restraint and to treat it with greater respect. Each also recognized that it could provoke the other with greater impunity as both were so committed to avoiding any serious risk of war.

Kissinger hoped to use détente to enmesh the Soviets in a web of beneficial economic ties that would increase their incentives for exercising strategic and political restraint.[60] The Soviets rejected Kissinger's strategy of linkage, and sought to make mutual gains within well-defined policy domains. They wanted to negotiate beneficial economic agreements and isolate strategic arms control from outside political interference. They stepped up military aid to Egypt and Syria after 1969, but showed restraint in Latin America where they provided very little support for the Allende government for fear of antagonizing Washington. They allowed the 1972 summit to proceed despite American bombing and mining of Haiphong Harbor, and encouraged North Vietnam to make concessions at the Paris

Kissinger's trips to Moscow and Israel, and chs. 7–11 for the origins, history and resolution of the crisis.
[58] Lebow and Stein, *We All Lost the Cold War*, chs. 2–4 and 10, for these incidents.
[59] Ibid., pp. 68–9.   [60] Kissinger, *White House Years*, pp. 129–30.

Peace Talks, which began in January 1973.[61] Kissinger sought unilateral advantages in the Middle East, and used the Israeli–Egyptian disengagement agreement of January 1974, engineering Sadat's defection from the Soviet camp.[62]

Brezhnev was mightily displeased by this development but was positively enraged when Kissinger attempted to do the same thing with Syria in May 1974. The Soviet Union had invested billions of rubles in development and military aid and in training the Egyptian army and air force, and even more in Syria, where they had effectively consolidated their influence.[63] Kissinger's success with Sadat and his unsuccessful effort to undercut the Soviet position in Syria were followed by the Jackson–Vanik and Stevenson amendments to the US–Soviet Trade Agreement. These actions spelled the death knell of détente as Brezhnev and his colleagues understood these latter initiatives as attempts at coercion and strikingly at odds with their understanding of accommodation.[64] Beginning in 1975, the Soviets escalated their efforts to gain influence in the Third World at the expense of the United States. They increased their aid to North Vietnam, and arranged for the introduction of Soviet, East German and Cuban military advisors or combat forces into Angola (1975–6), Ethiopia (1978) and South Yemen (1978). They invaded Afghanistan in 1978 to protect their protégé and influence in the country, and Americans almost universally interpreted it as yet another offensive move.[65] The Soviet invasion helped to elect Ronald Reagan, who stepped up American support for anti-communist forces in Afghanistan and sought to confront the Soviet Union in other domains. Like a Greek tragedy, real or imagined injustices created incentives for revenge, and revenge brought further escalation in its wake.[66]

Moscow and Washington were locked into a global competition for standing, at great financial and material cost that was increasingly at odds with any legitimate security needs. Their leaders were nevertheless judged at home and abroad – and often by themselves as well – by how they fared in this competition. This situation bred anxiety, mistrust and extreme sensitivity to the possibility of being exploited by the other

---

[61] Breslauer, "Why Détente Failed"; Garthoff, *Détente and Confrontation*, pp. 248–61.

[62] Garthoff, *Détente and Confrontation*, pp. 381–5, 398–9.

[63] Lebow and Stein, *We All Lost the Cold War*, pp. 152–3; Garthoff, *Détente and Confrontation*, p. 362.

[64] Garthoff, *Détente and Confrontation*, pp. 966–1008.

[65] Westad, *Global Cold War*, chs. 5, 7–8; Garthoff, *Détente and Confrontation*, pp. 828–48, 887–965.

[66] Garthoff, *Détente and Confrontation*, pp. 966–1089 on this escalatory spiral.

side. It encouraged the kind of worst-case analysis that Soviets used to explain Kissinger's behavior during the October War, the later Carter–Reagan strategic buildup and Reagan's Strategic Defense Initiative (Star Wars). The Americans in turn drew the worst possible inferences about Soviet motives from their military aid to North Vietnam and invasion of Afghanistan.[67]

The Cold War came to an end as a result of the initiatives of Mikhail Gorbachev, elected general secretary in March 1985. The realist literature invokes Gorbachev's understanding of the Soviet Union's economic decline to explain his willingness to withdraw from Afghanistan, make the concessions necessary to reach an arms control agreement, allow the peoples of Eastern Europe to remove their pro-Soviet communist governments, and accept German unification on terms that effectively allowed the Federal Republic to annex the territory of the Democratic German Republic and thereby extend the borders of the NATO alliance eastwards.[68] Realists reason that Gorbachev sought to make the best arrangements he could before the Soviet Union's relative power declined more precipitously. There is no evidence for such an inference; there is no Politburo document or oral testimony by former Soviet officials that they or Gorbachev acted on this basis. Soviet documents, memoirs of former officials and their comments at scholarly conferences indicate that Gorbachev and his top advisors concluded that the Cold War was costly, dangerous and a serious impediment to their domestic reform program. They understood it as a self-sustaining competition that was inimical to the security of both superpowers and could only be stopped by dramatic, unilateral gestures on their part.

"New thinking" was the fundamental cause of the Cold War's demise because it led Gorbachev to prioritize domestic over foreign policy and encouraged him to make concessions to the West to jump-start the process of accommodation. Of equal importance, it provided a frame of reference that made feasible the kinds of concessions (e.g. a theater forces agreement in which the Soviet Union had to withdraw and destroy more weapons than the United States, unification of Germany within NATO) that previous Soviet governments would have considered utterly anathema. While Gorbachev was distancing himself from Lenin and his heritage, his strategy bore an uncanny resemblance to Lenin's approach to

---

[67] On Afghanistan, see Lebow and Stein, "Afghanistan, Carter and Foreign Policy Change."
[68] Zubok, "Why Did the Cold War End in 1989?"; Davis and Wohlforth, "German Unification"; Herrmann, "Learning from the End of the Cold War," for the argument and relevant literature.

imperial Germany. Lenin had been willing to sign the grossly one-sided and exploitative Treaty of Brest-Litovsk because he gambled that subsequent events – he was hoping for a socialist revolution in Germany – would negate the treaty and advance Soviet interests in a more fundamental way. Gorbachev's strategy rested on a similar premise: strategic and political concessions would be meaningless if they helped to end the Cold War and radically restructure the Soviet Union's relations with the West. Neither gamble worked out as planned. There was no successful revolution in Germany in 1918–19, and Gorbachev's unwillingness to use force to keep communist governments in power in Eastern Europe led to the unanticipated breakup of the Warsaw Pact and the subsequent dissolution of the Soviet Union. Gorbachev's gamble was still the better one if evaluated on the basis of the longer-term prospects for the people of the former Soviet Union.

After the fall of the Berlin Wall and the collapse of the Soviet Union, journalists and academics in Europe hailed the end of the division of their continent and the threat of war associated with it. Europeans debated how money no longer necessary for defense could be redirected and the best way of integrating former Eastern bloc countries into the economic and political life of the West. The American response was quite different. There was only momentary celebration of the fact that for the first time since the 1960s there were no nuclear weapons targeted against the United States. As the dominant American discourse had framed the Cold War as a competition between Washington and Moscow, its termination on terms highly favorable to the West was celebrated as an American "triumph." There was – and continues to be – enormous resistance to evidence that the Soviet Union's search for accommodation had little to do with American pressure, and was largely a response to "new thinking" by the Soviet elite.[69] American intellectuals, and the public more generally, have been remarkably receptive to what can only be called the myth that Washington "won" the Cold War by spending the Soviets into submission through the Reagan arms buildup and "Star Wars." Even liberal journalists such as Tom Wicker, who had no political incentive to build up Reagan's reputation, ended up propagating the myth that the Soviets "threw in the towel" because they could no longer compete.[70] Such a reading of the Cold war portrays it as a potlatch, a form of conspicuous consumption

---

[69] Lebow and Stein, "Reagan and the Russians," and *We All Lost the Cold War*, postscript; Herrmann, "Learning from the End of the Cold War."
[70] Tom Wicker, "Plenty of Credit," *New York Times*, December 5, 1989, p. A35.

and quintessential expression of a competition for standing. This interpretation, which has no basis in fact, can be taken as more evidence for how so many Americans framed the Cold War.

Iraq

The Anglo-American invasion of Iraq may prove the dominant military event of the first decade of the twenty-first century. Intended as a lightning strike to remove Saddam Hussein from power and to "shock and awe" friend and foe alike, it turned into a multi-year, increasingly costly and unsuccessful occupation whose consequences for the Middle East will be felt for years to come. It transformed the United States from a country for which there was enormous sympathy in the aftermath of the terrorist attack of 9.11 into an overextended, intensely disliked, quasi-pariah, whose military power was still enormous but unusable for anything but the most obvious defensive missions.[71]

When George Walker Bush assumed office in January 2001, his secretary of state Colin Powell cheerfully admitted to reporters that his predecessor's Iraq policy was successful: "We have kept Saddam contained, kept him in a box."[72] The president and his closest advisors were not satisfied with mere containment, nor with the international constraints under which they operated. Vice-president Cheney, secretary of defense Donald Rumsfeld, deputy secretary of defense Paul Wolfowitz and undersecretary of defense Douglas Feith wanted to remove Saddam from power, and made no attempt to hide their goals. Their neoconservative allies in the media and think-tanks had long been pushing for war against Iraq, and stepped up their campaign after the terrorists attacks on September 11.[73]

---

[71] "What the World Thinks in 2002," available at http://people-press.prg/reports/display.php3?ReportID = 165. There was overwhelming support in Europe for the war against the Taliban: 73 percent in the United Kingdom, 64 percent in France and 61 percent in Germany.

[72] Colin Powell, "Press Briefing en Route to Cairo Egypt," February 23, 2001, available at www.state.gov/secretary/former/powell/remarks/2001/931.htm.

[73] William Kristol and Zalmay Khalilzad, "We Must Lead the Way in Deposing Saddam," *Washington Post*, November 9, 1997; PNAC Statement of Principles available at the Project for a New American Century website, www.newamericancentury.org/statementof principles.htm; Woodward, *Bush at War*, pp. 349–50; Gordon and Trainor, *Cobra II*, p. 15, quoting from an interview with Lt.-Gen. Gregory S. Newbold in which he quotes Douglas Feith. Halper and Clarke, *America Alone*, pp. 201–31. Isikoff and Corn, *Hubris*, pp. 33–191, Alfonsi, *Circle in the Sand*, pp. 362–71, on the public relations campaign by neoconservatives and administration officials to win public support for war against Iraq. Ricks, *Fiasco*, pp. 13–28, on containment.

An open letter to the president, signed by William Bennett, Gary Bauer and the editors of *The New Republic* and *The Weekly Standard*, promised to brand the president a wimp, guilty of "surrender in the war on international terrorism" if he refused to make a concerted effort to get rid of Saddam Hussein – regardless of whether or not he was implicated in the attacks.[74]

The events of September 11 provided the much desired pretext for the American invasion, first of Afghanistan and then of Iraq. In the week following the attacks, Rumsfeld and his deputy Paul Wolfowitz, former CIA director James Woolsey and Cheney's chief of staff Scooter Libby made the case for the invasion of Iraq in addition to Afghanistan. Rumsfeld told General Richard Myers, vice chairman of the joint chiefs of staff, that "My instinct is to hit Saddam at the same time, not just bin Laden." He and Wolfowitz also made the case to the president.[75] George Bush would ultimately be persuaded by their appeals, and not advice to proceed cautiously offered by secretary of state Colin Powell, James Baker and Lawrence Eagleburger – his father's two secretaries of state – Republican majority leader Dick Armey, former national security advisor Brent Scowcroft and retired Marine Corps general Anthony Zinni.[76] "Fuck Saddam," Bush told Condi Rice. "We're taking him out."[77]

---

[74] William Kristol *et al.*, "An Open Letter to the President," *Weekly Standard*, October 1, 2001.

[75] Patrick Tyler and Elaine Sciolino, "Bush Advisors Split on Scope of Retaliation," *New York Times*, September 20, 2001, p. A5; Bob Woodward and Dan Balz, "At Camp David, Advise and Dissent," *Washington Post*, January 31, 2002, p. A1; Richard Cheney on *Meet the Press*, September 16, 2001; Fallows, "Blind into Baghdad"; Purdham, *A Time of our Choosing*, p. 10; Woodward, *Bush at War*, pp. 48–50, 83; Mann, *Rise of the Vulcans*, p. 302, citing a June 18, 2003 interview with Paul Wolfowitz; Gordon and Trainor, *Cobra II*, pp. 14–15, and Rumsfeld interview by Francis Brooke, p. 19.

[76] National Commission on Terrorist Attacks, *The 9/11 Commission Report* (henceforth *9/11 Commission Report*), pp. 334–5; Woodward, *State of Denial*, pp. 332–4 on the Powell–Bush meeting of August 5, 2002; transcript of interview with Brent Scowcroft, *Face the Nation*, August 4, 2002; Brent Scowcroft, "Don't Attack Saddam," *Wall Street Journal*, August 15, 2002, p. A12; Todd Purdum and Patrick E. Tyler, "Top Republicans Break with Bush on Iraq Strategy," *New York Times*, August 16, 2002, p. A1; James A. Baker II, "The Right Way to Change a Regime," *New York Times*, August 25, 2002, section 4, p. 9; transcript of Lawrence Eagleburger, *Crossfire*, August 19, 2002; interview with Lawrence Eagleburger, *Fox News Sunday*, Washington, DC, August 18, 2002; Walter Gibbs, "Scowcroft Urges Wide Role for the U.N. in Postwar Iraq," *New York Times*, April 9, 2003; Eric Schmitt, "Iraq is Defiant as G.O.P. Leaders Opposes Attack," *New York Times*, August 9, 2002, p. A6; Ricks, *Fiasco*, pp. 30–2, 50–2: Isikoff and Corn, *Hubris*, pp. 27–8.

[77] Quoted in Michael Elliot and James Carney, "First Stop Iraq," *Time*, March 31, 2003, p. 173; Gordon and Trainor, *Cobra II*, p. 17, quoting from an interview with Hugh Shelton.

In June 2002, Bush told West Point cadets that from now on the administration was prepared to preempt any adversary. "We must take the battle to the enemy, disrupt his plans, and confront the worst threats before they emerge."[78] In the fall of 2002, Powell began a diplomatic offensive in New York to secure Security Council approval for a tough resolution on Iraq.[79] Washington sought wording that would authorize it to take "all necessary means" to compel Saddam's regime to relinquish all weapons of mass destruction (WMDs). France and Russia, supported by other governments, thought military action premature and favored more aggressive weapons inspections, reserving any decision on the use of force to a later date. Under pressure, Powell settled for a compromise resolution to the effect that if Saddam did not yield his WMDs he would be in "material breach" of prior UN resolutions, which would in effect give the United States leeway to use force. On November 8, the Security Council approved the compromise resolution by a 15–0 vote.[80]

Powell's victory at the UN was a pyrrhic one. On the eve of the resolution Bush demanded publicly that Saddam disarm, and threatened to forcibly disarm him if he resisted.[81] Administration officials began talking in public about the liberation of Iraq and the spread of democracy through the Middle East. In February, the president gave an address at the American Enterprise Institute in Washington in which he insisted that "A new regime in Iraq would serve as a dramatic and inspiring example of freedom for other nations in the region."[82] The administration also began a media blitz with the goal of connecting Saddam to Al-Qaeda, the group responsible for the attacks on 9.11. On November 1, 2002, President Bush told the country: "We know [Iraq has] got ties with al

Bush is reported to have said: "We will get this guy but at a time and place of our choosing." Lott, *Herding Cats*, pp. 235–6, also reports that Bush indicated his intention to go to war in private conversations with him.

[78] "The President Delivers Graduation Speech at West Point," June 1, 2002, White House website, www.whitehouse.gov/news/releases/2002/06/20020601-3.html.

[79] President Bush, address to the United Nations General Assembly, September 12, 2002; Woodward, *Bush at War*, pp. 336, 344–9.

[80] Tyler Marshall, "A War of Words Led to Unanimous U.N. Vote," *Los Angeles Times*, November 10, 2002; Karen DeYoung, "For Powell, a Long Path to Victory," *Washington Post*, November 10, 2002, p. A1; Michael O'Hanlon, "How the Hard-Liners Lost," *Washington Post*, November 10, 2002, p. B7; Mann, *Rise of the Vulcans*, pp. 324–5; Daalder and Lindsay, *America Unbound*, pp. 127–42.

[81] White House transcript of remarks by President Bush, Cincinnati Museum Center, October 7, 2002.

[82] President George Bush speech to American Enterprise Institute, February 26, 2003.

Qaeda."[83] In his State of the Union Address on January 28, 2003, he described the kinds of WMDs Saddam possessed, spoke of his efforts to buy uranium in Africa and accused him of harboring Al-Qaeda terrorists.[84] All of these claims would later be discredited. British intelligence leaked a comprehensive report that no substantial links between Iraq and Al-Qaeda had been found, and experts in Britain, and US Middle East experts, ridiculed any connection on the grounds of mistrust and incompatible ideologies. Powell and Rice stood firm, and in a later speech Bush gave on the eve of war, he justified the invasion by citing the by now discredited link between Iraq and Al-Qaeda.[85] Bush and Cheney continued to voice these allegations publicly even after the National Commission on Terrorist Attacks Upon the United States – commonly known as the "9.11 Commission" – found absolutely no evidence connecting Saddam to Al-Qaeda and its attack on the United States. It reported that Mohammed Atta, leader of the attacks, considered Saddam an enemy and "a stooge" of the Bush administration.[86] As late as June 2004, Bush kept insisting that there were links between Saddam and Al-Qaeda, and Cheney criticized the press as "irresponsible," and the New York Times as "outrageous," for questioning the president.[87] Cheney maintained that such a connection existed even after the publication of a declassified Pentagon study in April 2007 that dismissed the allegation and decried earlier efforts by the Pentagon's own intelligence unit to give credence to such reports.[88]

The administration was determined to have its war, and George Tenet, director of the CIA, was not about to let lack of evidence stand in its way. Tenet was a skillful bureaucratic player who had developed a close relationship with the president, and according to former CIA executive

[83] George Bush, "President Bush Outlines Iraqi Threat", October 7, 2002, available at www.whitehouse.gov/news/releases/2002/10/20021007-8.html.
[84] State of the Union Address, January 28, 2003, available at www.whitehouse.gov/news/releases/2003/01/20030128-19.html.
[85] Speech to the Nation, March 17, 2003, available at www.whitehouse.gov/news/releases/2003/03/20030317-7 html.
[86] 9/11 Commission Report, pp. 61, 161, 334–5; Iraq Survey Group Final Report, Global Scan, available at www.globalsecurity.org/wmd/library/report/2004/isg-final-report/isg-final-report_vol3_cw_key-findings.htm (accessed March 4, 2007).
[87] David Milbank, "Bush Defends Assertions of Iraq-Al Qaeda Relationship," Washington Post, June 18, 2004, p. A9; Walter Pincus and Dana Milbank, "Al Qaeda Link Is Dismissed," Washington Post, June 17, 2004, p. A1. Hersh, Chain of Command, pp. 203–47; Rich, Greatest Story Ever Sold, pp. 64–70; Isikoff and Corn, Hubris, pp. 106–14.
[88] Rupert Cornwell, "Cheney still Insists al-Qaïda had Links with Iraq, despite Evidence," Independent (London), April 7, 2007, p. 31.

director "Buzzy" Krongard, supported Bush in a way that "was beyond professional loyalty."[89] He made no effort to alert the president of the fallacious, or at least questionable, nature of the claims he and Cheney were making in public. The Pentagon was equally successful in managing the media. Despite Cheney's outrage at the *New York Times*, press and television outlets generally served as docile conveyors of the administration's position on Saddam, WMD and terrorism. After White House attacks, ABC canceled the television show *Politically Incorrect*.[90]

In his study of post-Vietnam military intervention, Jonathan Mermin finds that the media rarely offer critical analysis of presidential policies unless they are first attacked in Congress or by high-ranking officials.[91] True to form, the Congress scurried for cover, not wanting to appear unpatriotic. Democratic leader of the House Dick Gephardt backed Bush's war resolution, rather than supporting Senator Joe Biden's alternative formulation. Commenting on his action, Dem. Rep. Jim McGovern explained: "He did not want the Democrats to be blamed for the next attack."[92] Many reporters were one-sidedly pro-war. A week after 9.11, CBS anchor Dan Rather told viewers on the David Letterman show: "George Bush is my president, he makes the decisions, and, you know, as just one American, if he wants me to line up, just tell me where." Rather said that he would willingly don a uniform if asked to serve.[93] Judith Miller of the *New York Times* allowed herself to become the mouthpiece of Cheney, and consistently reported as fact the unsubstantiated rumors and downright false information fed to her by administration hawks.[94] The *Times* would subsequently apologize for its handling of the war and events leading up to it.[95]

Secretary of state Powell was instructed to try once more to win UN support for military action against Saddam. On 5 February 2003 he made his now infamous speech, replete with American reconnaissance photographs of alleged Iraqi weapons facilities, asserting that Saddam

[89] Cited in Isikoff and Corn, *Hubris*, pp. 30–1.
[90] Bill Carter and Felicity Barringer, "In Patriotic Time, Dissent Is Muted," *New York Times*, September 28, 2001; Rich, *Greatest Story Ever Sold*, pp. 29–30.
[91] Mermin, *Debating War and Peace*, p. 143; Schechter, "Selling the Iraq War."
[92] Isikoff and Corn, *Hubris*, pp. 127–8, citing interviews.
[93] Dan Rather interview, *Late Show with David Letterman*, September 18, 2001, quoted in Entman, *Projections of Power*, p. 1.
[94] Judith Miller, "SECRET SITES: Iraqi Tells of Renovations at Sites for Chemical and Nuclear Arms," *New York Times*, December 20, 2001 for an example.
[95] Isikoff and Corn, *Hubris*, pp. 57–62, 215–21, for an account of her activities before and during the war.

was on the verge of developing WMDs.[96] France, Germany and Russian declared their opposition to an invasion of Iraq. A month earlier, secretary of defense Donald Rumsfeld, with his usual tact, dismissed France and Germany as the "old Europe" on a continent where power was shifting eastwards.[97] At Britain's insistence, the White House tried again to gain UN backing. The dénouement came on March 10 when French president Jacques Chirac announced that his country would not support the Anglo-American proposal for the use of force against Iraq. A week later, Bush and Blair gave up their efforts to win UN support.[98] On March 20, 2003, Anglo-American forces opened their campaign against Iraq with massive air strikes directed against military and political targets throughout the country. The following day, ground forces went on the offensive, and three weeks later US forces entered Baghdad. On May 1, aboard the aircraft carrier *Abraham Lincoln*, President Bush proudly proclaimed victory.[99] Little did he suspect that the real war was about to begin.

To make sense of the Iraq fiasco, we need to understand why the Bush administration was so committed to overthrowing Saddam that it was prepared to act unilaterally, manipulate and "cherry-pick" intelligence to support its claims that he possessed WMD, and ride roughshod over the advice and objections of high-ranking military officers concerning its on-the-cheap invasion plans. It made no preparations for an occupation beyond protection of the oil ministry and well heads, was dilatory in responding to the post-occupation insurgency, did so with tactics that only made the situation worse, installed a corrupt, "puppet" émigré leader with no local support and was subsequently slow and ineffective in building a coalition representative of Iraqi opinion. A large literature has developed to address intelligence, military planning and execution, the occupation and efforts to quell the insurgency, and attributes these failures largely to hubris.[100] The most fundamental question remains unanswered: what were the administration's reasons for invading Iraq rather than continuing its predecessor's policy of political, economic and military containment?

---

[96] Speech of secretary of state Colin Powell to the United Nations Security Council, February 5, 2003.

[97] Department of defense transcript of secretary of defense Donald Rumsfeld's remarks at the Foreign Press Center, January 22, 2003.

[98] Gerard Baker *et al.*, "Blair's Mission Impossible," *Financial Times*, May 29, 2003, p. 17; Mann, *Rise of the Vulcans*, pp. 352–6.

[99] Karen DeYoung, "Bush Proclaims Victory," *Washington Post*, May 2, 2003, p. A1.

[100] Daalder and Lindsay, *America Unbound*, pp. 143–83; Fallows, "Blind into Baghdad"; Phillips, *Losing Iraq*; Isikoff and Corn, *Hubris*, pp. 191–210; Ricks, *Fiasco*, pp. 149–202; Galbraith, *End of Iraq*, pp. 114–224.

Despite frequently voiced claims by Noam Chomsky and others that the invasion was driven by the desire to control Middle Eastern oil, such an explanation is unpersuasive.[101] The United States had traditionally allowed oil companies, interested only in the flow of reasonably priced oil, to make deals with all kinds of authoritarian regimes in the Middle East.[102] If the administration wanted access to Iraqi oil, all it had to do was end sanctions, as many people were urging on humanitarian grounds. Saddam would have been happy to sell oil to all comers as he was desperate for income, and the price of oil would have dropped as Iraq's production reentered the international market. The Republican radical right would not consider ending sanctions and buying Iraqi oil. Invasion and occupation were their preferred strategy. The war cost the United States an estimated $100 billion dollars a year in 2004–5 and the total cost was estimated at over a trillion dollars, far exceeding any conceivable economic benefit.[103] At the outset, the administration maintained that the invasion would pay for itself from Iraqi oil revenues, which can be taken as additional evidence that they were not motivated by material gain.[104] Any serious investor would have made a comprehensive estimate of the likely costs and gains and not have invested solely on the expectation of the best-case scenario. The administration's unrealistic but well-publicized claims about cost were almost certainly politically motivated and intended to undercut opposition to its planned invasion. The other charge made at the time – and even more far-fetched – is that Cheney convinced the president to eat the huge costs of an invasion for the benefit of his associates in

---

[101] Chomsky and Barsamian, *Imperial Ambitions*; "Imperial Ambition," interview with Noam Chomsky by David Barsamian, *Monthly Review*, May 2003, available at www.monthlyreview.org/0503chomsky.htm; "Iraq: Yesterday, Today, and Tomorrow," Michael Albert interviews Noam Chomsky, December 27, 2006, available at www.chomsky.info/articles/20050704.htm; Callinicos, *New Mandarins of American Power*, pp. 93–8; Phillips, *American Dynasty*, pp. 248–59, 313–14; Harvey, *The New Imperialism*, pp. 1–25.

[102] Ingram, "Pairing off Empires," makes this point.

[103] Reus-Smit, "Unipolarity and Legitimacy," on the relative cost of the Iraq and Persian Gulf Wars; MSNBC, "Cost of War Could Surpass One Trillion," March 17, 2006, available at www.msnbc.msn.com/id/11880954/.

[104] On September 15, 2002, White House economic advisor Lawrence Lindsay estimated the high limit on the cost to be 1–2 percent of GNP, or about $100–$200 billion. Mitch Daniels, director of the office of management and budget subsequently discounted this estimate as "very, very high" and stated that the costs would be between $50 and $60 billion. "Bush Economic Aide Says Cost of Iraq War May Top $100 Billion," *Wall Street Journal*, September 16, 2002; Elizabeth Bumiller, "Estimated Cost of Iraq War Reduced," *New York Times*, December 31, 2002; "Daniels Sees U.S. Iraq War Cost below $200 Billion," *Reuters News Service*, September 18, 2002.

the oil and construction industries. There are easier ways of aiding the oil industry, and the administration, with congressional backing, engaged in them. It is difficult to believe that the president, national security advisor and secretary of defense, none of whom had the same ties to the oil industry, could be persuaded to go to war on its behalf. American oil companies reaped windfall profits in the years following the invasion, but this had little to do with the Iraq War, and was certainly not foreseen by the administration, who expected the price of crude oil to drop when Iraqi production came back on-line.[105]

Security is an equally dubious motive. Saddam had been defeated in the Gulf War, although he was able to reassert his authority within Iraq. Iraq's air force and air defense network were in a shambles and "no-fly" zones had been imposed over the Shi'a and Kurdish regions of Iraq and enforced by NATO with frequent sorties. The UN maintained economic sanctions and interdicted any strategic materials that could assist in the development of WMDs. Saddam repeatedly limited inspections and expelled United Nations weapons inspectors, but there was never credible evidence indicating that he had recommenced his prewar efforts to acquire a nuclear arsenal. A band of uncertainty nevertheless remained, and it was reasonable, even prudent, to compel Saddam to readmit UN inspection teams and give them unrestricted access. The US military buildup accomplished this goal, and the UN inspectors found no evidence to support American claims that Iraq was attempting to acquire WMD. Saddam could have reneged on his agreement once American forces stepped down, but he would have played into the Bush administration's hand by so doing. Such a double cross would have lent some credence to their claims that he was up to no good and would have made it easier for Washington to secure Security Council authorization to remove him from power.[106] In the absence of WMD and a useable air force, and with a poorly equipped and trained army, Saddam was more a nuisance than a threat to his immediate neighbors. At conferences sponsored by the American Enterprise Institute and in op-ed pieces and in *The Weekly Standard*, neoconservatives nevertheless charged Saddam with supporting terrorism around the world. After

---

[105] *Debate*, March 5, 2007, "Is Oil or Big Business an Undisclosed Motive for the War on Iraq?" available at www.thedebate.org/thedebate/iraq.asp; MSNBC, November 11, 2002, "Oil: The Other Iraq War," available at www.msnbc.msn.com/id/3071526/, for a more moderate version of the argument.

[106] *9/11 Commission Report*, pp. 61, 161, 334–5; *Iraq Survey Group Final Report*, Global Scan, available at www.globalsecurity.org/wmd/library/report/2004/isg-final-report/isg-final-report_vol3_cw_key-findings.htm (accessed March 4, 2007); Cirincione *et al.*, *WMD in Iraq*, for the pre- and post-invasion non-discovery of WMD.

9.11, they accused him of being the guiding hand behind Al-Qaeda, an allegation that Cheney repeatedly referred to as established fact. There was never any evidence for this connection, as Cheney himself must have realized. So terrorism was even more transparent a rationalization than WMD for an invasion that high-ranking policymakers and their neocon supporters wanted to carry out for other reasons.

What about broader security motives? Iraq was not the only US concern in the Middle East. Policymakers worried about Saudi Arabia, along with Israel, the twin pillars of America's position in the region. Saudi Arabia was at best an ambiguous ally whose leadership confronted growing opposition from Islamic fundamentalists and sought to cope with them through a largely ineffective policy of repression and orthodoxy. Saudi fundamentalists were xenophobic and deeply resented the American military presence in their country and the region; Osama bin-Laden cited it as one of his motive for attacking the United States.[107] A much larger American presence in Iraq, even on a short-term basis, and a puppet government in Baghdad could only be expected to strengthen fundamentalist forces in Saudi Arabia and throughout the Muslim world, as opponents of the war predicted and as quickly came to pass.[108] The invasion of Afghanistan and Iraq – overwhelmingly opposed by the world's Muslims – compelled Middle East governments to distance themselves from Washington and seriously eroded American influence in the region.[109] It also reduced American influence in Europe and among allies elsewhere in the world.

On the eve of the Iraq invasion, a European poll found that in Italy, only 34 percent viewed the United States positively, compared to 70 percent in 2002. In Spain, only 14 percent had a favorable image of the US. In a worldwide poll of its readers, *Time* magazine asked "which country poses the greatest threat to world peace in 2003?" North Korea was identified as the great threat by 6.7 percent of the 700,000 respondents,

---

[107] *9/11 Commission Report*, pp. 88–91. Woodward, *State of Denial*, pp. 332–4, quoting Powell–Bush meeting of August 5, 2002; CNN.com, "Bin Laden on Tape: 'Attacks Benefitted Islam Greatly'," available at http://archives.cnn.com/2001/US/12/13/ret.bin.laden.videotape/.

[108] Johnson, *Blowback*, for the original statement of this position. Daniel L. Byman and Kenneth Pollack, "What Next?," *Washington Post*, August 20, 2006, p. BO1, for a more recent take.

[109] "Islamic Nations Totally Reject Iraq War," *Al-Jazeera News*, March 2003; Shibley Telhami, "Arab Public Opinion: A Survey in Six Countries," *San Jose Mercury*, March 16, 2003; Susan Page, "Poll: Muslim Countries, Europe Question U.S. Motives," *USA Today*, June 21, 2004; Saikal, "Reactions in the Muslim World to the Iraqi Conflict."

Iraq by 6.3, and the US by a whopping 86.9 percent.[110] The invasion of Iraq, the mistreatment and seeming murder of Iraqi prisoners and civilians, the holding of foreign nationals for years without charges at Guantanamo and the "extraordinary rendition" of prisoners to countries where they were tortured for information led to an even more precipitous drop in standing. Public opinion in Europe, extremely sympathetic to the United States after 9.11, reversed itself and came to consider it a greater threat to world peace than North Korea.[111] In Britain, those with favorable opinions of the United States dropped from 83 percent in 2000 to 56 percent in 2006. In other countries, the US underwent an even steeper decline.[112] This evaluation had not changed much by 2007, when an opinion poll carried out for the BBC World Service in twenty-seven countries found that 51 percent of respondents regarded the United States negatively, a figure surpassed only by their negative evaluations of Iran (54 percent) and Israel (56 percent). North Korea was regarded negatively by 48 percent of the respondents.[113] Since the Iraq War, the United States has undergone a shift in its profile from a status quo to a revisionist power.[114]

Washington's political isolation and the quagmire into which its forces sank in Iraq significantly reduced the Bush administration's leverage vis-à-vis its European and other allies. Lack of legitimacy for the invasion prevented the United States from effectively shifting a fair percentage of the cost on to others as it had in the Persian Gulf War of 1990–1. In that intervention, authorized by the Security Council, non-US financial contributions amounted to 88 percent of the $61 billion cost of the war. From March 2003 to 2006, the United States provided 85 percent of the $248 billion incremental costs, almost a complete reversal in funding.[115] Washington also lost the ability to restrain Iran and North Korea. Both countries used the opportunity to accelerate their efforts to acquire nuclear weapons. Iran withdrew from the non-proliferation (NPT) regime

---

[110] *Time Europe*, available at www.time.com/time/europe/gdml/peace2003.html.
[111] BBC News, March 18, 2003, available at http://news.bbc.co.uk/2/hi/americas/2862343. stm, showed that on the eve of the Iraq invasion only 34 percent of Europeans viewed the US positively, compared to 70 percent in 2002. In Spain, only 14 percent had a favorable image. In Eastern Europe, where the US is traditionally held in higher esteem, support dropped from 80 percent to 50 percent in Poland.
[112] The Pew Global Attitudes Project, "15-Nation Pew Global Attitudes Survey," release date June 13, 2006.
[113] *The Age* (Melbourne), March 6, 2007, p. 7.
[114] This last point is also made by Reus-Smit, "Unipolarity and Legitimacy."   [115] Ibid.

and expelled UN inspectors.[116] North Korea removed the seals from its processing plant and conducted a nuclear test, although it agreed in 2007 to freeze its nuclear program.[117] Ironically, the Bush administration's rhetoric and invasion of Iraq may have provided not only the opportunity to these countries to push ahead with their weapons programs but the perceived need to do so as well.[118]

In the first weeks of the Bush administration, high-ranking officials indicated to foreign officials and the media that they were deeply offended by the survival of Saddam's regime and were on the lookout for any pretext to invade Iraq.[119] They confided to friendly listeners that Saddam's removal would allow Washington to remake the map of the Middle East and dramatically increase its influence worldwide. They assumed Iraqis would welcome their American "liberators" with open arms and accept émigré puppet Ahmed Chalabi as their new ruler. A pro-American regime in the heart of the Middle East was expected to provide significant leverage over Saudi Arabia, Iran and the Palestinians. Administration officials also reasoned that a high-tech military campaign of "shock and awe" that paralyzed Iraqi forces at the outset with precision bombing and missile attack and overthrew Saddam with few American casualties would intimidate North Korea and Iran. "Iraq is not just about Iraq," a senior official confided, but about Iran, Libya and North Korea.[120] Victory was expected to encourage widespread bandwagoning, making countries around the world more intent on currying favor with the United States, while allowing Washington to put more pressure on countries like France that opposed its vision of world order.[121]

[116] Arms Control Association, "Questions Surround Iran's Nuclear Program," March 3, 2006, available at www.armscontrol.org/factsheets/Iran-IAEA-Issues.asp.
[117] Kerr, "North Korean Test Provokes Widespread Condemnation"; Cha and Kang, "The Korea Crisis"; Van Ness, "The North Korean Nuclear Crisis"; Howard W. French, "Korean Nuclear Talks Fail to Set Disarmament Timetable, but Yield Agreement on Goals," *New York Times*, July 19, 2007; Chose Sang-Hun, "U.N. Inspectors Confirm Shutdown of North Korean Reactor," *New York Times*, July 17, 2007.
[118] Daniel L. Byman and Kenneth Pollack, "What Next?," *Washington Post* August 20, 2006, p. BO1; Carpenter and Bandow, *The Korean Conundrum*, pp. 72–4; Selig S. Harrison, "North Korea: A Nuclear Threat," *Newsweek*, October 16, 2006, available at www.msnbc.msn.com/id/15175633/site/newsweek/.
[119] Hersh, *Chain of Command*, pp. 163–71; Mann, *Rise of the Vulcans*, pp. 294–310; Halper and Clarke, *America Alone*, pp. 28–35; Isikoff and Corn, *Hubris*, p. 16.
[120] David E. Sanger, "Viewing the War as a Lesson to the World," *New York Times*, April 6, 2003.
[121] Frum and Perle, *An End to Evil*, pp. 33, 212–13, 247–66.

The United States was king of the hill and basking in its "unipolar" glory.[122] Charles Krauthammer, a leading neocon who coined the term, nevertheless thought the US had failed to exploit its position by letting Saddam stay in power. Washington in his view should be "unashamedly laying down the rules of world order and being prepared to enforce them."[123] High-ranking administration officials were committed to using its military power to strengthen its hold on hegemony. Condoleezza Rice labeled China the most likely future challenger of the United States, and neocons favored a more confrontational policy toward Beijing. They had considered George Bush Senior's diplomatic response to Tiananmen Square weak and pushed for a more aggressive response to China's downing of an American EP-3 reconnaissance aircraft in April 2001.[124] As we have observed, standing is conceptually distinct from security, but is not unrelated to it in practice. With standing comes influence, which to some degree is fungible and can be used to enhance security or material well-being. Honor also entered into the picture, providing further evidence that standing, not security was the principal goal for some of the highest-ranking administration officials. Cheney felt disgraced by the American failure in Vietnam. He wanted a military victory that would erase that stain and also free the executive of the remaining shackles imposed on it in its aftermath.[125] Although the German defeat in World War I had been much more serious, and although the restrictions were imposed on the country, not merely its executive, the passions aroused were similar, if not as widespread.

Standing may have been an important personal consideration for President Bush. He has been described as a man of low self-esteem, and certainly had few, if any, serious accomplishments to his name. He made it clear to his closest confidants that he wanted to use the presidency to accomplish something great, something for which he would be remembered. Accounts of his presidency maintain that he found new purpose

---

[122] Krauthammer, "The Unipolar Moment"; Brooks and Wohlforth, "American Primacy in Perspective"; Wohlforth, "The Stability of a Unipolar World"; Reus-Smit, *American Power and World Order*, ch. 4 on the "idealism of preponderance."

[123] Krauthammer, "Unipolar Moment."

[124] Barbara Slavin, "Rice Called a Good Fit for Foreign Policy Post," *USA Today*, December 18, 2000; Testimony of Colin L. Powell before the U.S. Senate Committee on Foreign Relations, Washington, DC, March 8, 2000; Alfonsi, *Circle in the Sand*, pp. 381–3.

[125] Bob Woodward, "Vice President Praises Bush as Strong, Decisive Leader Who Has Helped Restore Office," *Washington Post*, January 20, 2005, p. AO7; Charlie Savage, "Dick Cheney's Mission to Expand – or 'Restore' – the Powers of the Presidency," *Boston Globe*, November 26, 2006; Jane Mayer, "The Hidden Power," *New Yorker*, March 12, 2006.

after the 9.11 attacks and reveled in his role as wartime leader following the invasion of Afghanistan.[126] George Bush freely admits that he idolized his father – "I love him, I love him more than anything" – and sought to imitate his accomplishments, including attendance at Choate and Yale, becoming president of the Delta Kappa Epsion fraternity, a member of the varsity baseball team, a combat pilot and president of the United States.[127] One does not need to be Sigmund Freud to surmise that all this playing copycat indicated a strong need to win his father's approval by equaling his accomplishments – and all the more so once he had become the "black sheep" of the family. By winning the "war against terrorism" and ridding the Middle East of Saddam Hussein he might convince himself and his parents that he was worthy of the presidency. We can speculate that the thought of bringing down the man who allegedly had tried to assassinate his father must have been particularly gratifying. At a September 2006 fundraiser in Texas, Bush described how Saddam tortured Iraqis, used gas against his Kurdish opponents and invaded Iran. And then came the clincher: "After all," he told his audience, "this is the guy that tried to kill my dad at one time."[128] Unnamed intelligence sources report that Cheney played upon Bush's concern to impress his parents by "cherry-picking" intelligence that could be used to make the case that Saddam had tried to assassinate his father. If true, anger and the desire for revenge, provided another incentive for Bush to consider an invasion of Iraq.[129] Bush's rage, like that of Achilles, drove the plot of this saga.

Like WMDs and links with Al-Qaeda, the assassination charge has no basis in fact. The story originated with the Kuwaiti government, who had strong motives of their own to extract a confession under torture from the alleged ringleader. The US ambassador at the time, Edward "Skip" Gnehm, denied having seen any evidence for the allegation, although the FBI at one point took the story seriously. Neither the Kuwaitis nor the FBI subsequently came up with any proof that such a plot ever existed.[130]

---

[126] Walsh, "Bush Addresses Silent Influences," *Washington Post*, October 25, 2000, for the quote; Especially, Renshon, *In his Father's Shadow*, pp. 137–58.

[127] Bush, *A Charge to Keep*, pp. 50–1, 167; Philipps, *American Dynasty*, pp. 43–5, 77; Renshon, *In his Father's Shadow*, pp. 31–4.

[128] Quoted in Isikoff and Corn, *Hubris*, p. 115.

[129] Seymour Hersh, "A Case Not Closed," *New Yorker*, November 1, 1993, revised version posted September 27, 2002, on the dubious nature of the alleged assassination attempt, at www.newyorker.com/archive/content/articles/020930fr_archive02?020930fr_archive02.

[130] Paul Quinn-Judge, "CIA Report Casts Doubt on Kuwait Assertion of Plot on Bush," *Boston Globe*, May 27, 1993; Seymour Hersh, "A Case Not Closed," *New Yorker*, November 1,

Republican House Majority Leader Dick Armey admitted that he "just cringed" when he read about the president's speech. "Wow," he told his wife, "I hope *that's* not what this is all about."[131]

The administration wanted war but could only wage it with the authorization of the Congress and this required public support. Public opinion looks to presidents for symbolic reassurance in the aftermath of catastrophes, and, not surprisingly, in the aftermath of 9.11 the president's approval rating shot up from 55 to 90 percent.[132] The administration sought to exploit this receptivity to guidance. It did a masterful job of transforming the terrorist attacks of 9.11 into a "war on terrorism" against tenebrous and threatening monsters. It won the support of 94 percent of the American people for the invasion of Afghanistan, and a much less impressive majority for the war in Iraq, by convincing them that Saddam possessed WMDs, or soon would, and had close ties with Al-Qaeda.[133] As a result, 77 of 100 senators and 296 of 435 House members voted to authorize the president to "use the armed forces of the United States as he determines to be necessary and appropriate in order to defend the national security of the United States against the continuing threat posed by Iraq."[134] The administration's success in winning over public opinion was helped by its persistent use of lies about WMD and Saddam's alleged links to Al-Qaeda and the reluctance of Democrats or the news media to challenge administration claims. The terrorist attacks had provoked anger across the political spectrum. Americans wanted revenge, and the administration cleverly pitched the invasions of both Afghanistan and Iraq as means of achieving it.[135]

1993; Isikoff and Corn, *Hubris*, p. 116, reporting on their interview with Ambassador Gnehm.

[131] Isikoff and Corn, *Hubris*, p. 116, reporting on their interview with Dick Armey.

[132] Edelman, *Constructing the Political Spectacle* and *The Politics of Misinformation*, on public needs and their exploitation by presidents. Woodward, *State of Denial*, p. 81, on the pubic opinion poll.

[133] Rich, *Greatest Story Ever Sold*, pp. 33–4, citing polls; Devetak, "The Gothic Scene of International Relations," for a depiction of the administration's rhetoric, deliberately gothic and intended to create a threatening atmosphere populated by monstrous and ghostly beings.

[134] Alison Mitchell and Carl Hulse, "Congress Authorizes Bush to Use Force Against Iraq, Creating a Broad Mandate," *New York Times*, January 13, 1991; for the resolution see History News Network, available at http://hnn.us/articles/1282.html.

[135] Woodward, *State of Denial*, p. 69, quoting Bush's comments on his impressions of the feelings of the New Yorkers he encountered on his first visit to the City after 9.11, on September 14, 2001.

The attacks of 9.11 wounded the United States physically and psychologically as Al-Qaeda killed a sizeable number of people, although many less than initial estimates. They destroyed a major landmark – the World Trade Center – an icon of American economic power – and damaged an even more hallowed landmark – the Pentagon – the center of American military might. The attacks were not conducted by another state, but by a rag-tag cabal of Middle Eastern terrorists, which made the offensive more intolerable still. That such an unworthy adversary could so successfully attack the United States aroused anger in the Aristotelian sense, and with it, strong desires for revenge. It also soon became apparent that terrorist attacks had succeeded because of refusal at the highest levels of government to take seriously the threat of terrorism and the remarkable incompetence on the part of the FBI.[136] The administration successfully exploited American anger, deflecting it away from itself and towards Saddam.

The Persian Gulf War of 1990–1 evoked memories of the Vietnam War and of the trauma arising from the American defeat. It provoked a display of yellow ribbons on cars, houses and trees, many of them with the logo: "Support our troops." Following the earlier lead of Ronald Reagan, rightwing revisionists encouraged the myth that America would have won the war if public opinion had supported the forces engaged in combat.[137] The Iraq War triggered a similar display of ribbons and other manifestations of patriotism, once again built around the home-grown *Dolchstoss* myth of "liberal" – by now a term of ill-repute – betrayal of victorious American forces. The stab-in-the-back thesis became prominent in the course of the Iraq occupation after it became evident that US forces were making no headway against the insurgents, could not provide security even within major urban centers or create an army, police force or government without loyalties to specific religious factions. In the 2006 mid-term elections, President Bush tried and failed to make the case for "staying the course," and Bush supporters, most of them in the neocon camp, publicized their

---

[136] Dan Eggen, "Pre 9/11 Missteps by FBI Detailed," *Washington Post*, June 10, 2005, p. A01.

[137] Moyar, *Triumph Forsaken*. Neo-Neocon, "Mind is a Difficult Thing to Change: Vietnam Interlude – after the Fall," April 28, 2005, available at http://neo-neocon.blogspot.com/2005/04/mind-is-difficult-thing-to-change.html; "Breaking the Big Stick: Removing the Threat of War to Achieve Peace," May 31, 2007, available at http://neoneocon.com/category/war/vietnam/; Robert Buzzanaco, "How I Learned to Stop Worrying and Love Vietnam and Iraq,"*Counterpunch*, April 16–17, 2005, available at www.counterpunch.org/buzzanco04162005.html. For serious analyses, Lembcke, *The Spitting Image*; Turner, *Echoes of Combat*; Hixon, *Historical Memory and Representations of the Vietnam War*.

revisionist take on Vietnam to mobilize support and intimidate opponents of the war.[138]

In post-World War I Germany, the stab-in-the-back myth, so effectively propagated by Nazis and other right-wing nationalists, responded to a deep-seated need of many Germans to deny their country's defeat because it was too threatening to their self-esteem. Defeat generated not only resentment and denial, but a strong desire for revenge to which Hitler pandered, and he gained tremendous support following his successful challenge of the limitations imposed by the Treaty of Versailles.[139] By focusing American opinion on security, and providing the opportunity to erase the stain of Vietnam through a successful war, George Bush reaped similar benefits. The combination of anger at the attacker and the still-lingering trauma of Vietnam provided the basis for popular support for the war that continued for some time after failure in Iraq should have been more widely evident. One reason for the delayed public disenchantment was the widely recognized reluctance of the media and elected Democratic officials to criticize the war. Clearly, the stab-in-the-back lie had served its purpose well. In the 2004 presidential election John Kerry and the Democrats made reasoned arguments about the national interest and were trumped by fear-mongering about national security.

One of the most striking aspects of the runup to war in Iraq was the extraordinary willingness of the Bush administration to embrace risk. Critiques of the administration's Iraq policy universally emphasize its failure to gather and use available intelligence for any kind of serious risk assessment, to employ a level of forces that would have reduced military risks, or devise in advance an occupation policy designed to achieve its political goals.[140] In chapter 7 I offered a reformulation of prospect theory to account for the diverse motives of actors. Actors responding to their appetites will generally behave as prospect theory predicts: they will be more willing to accept risks to avert perceived loss than to make perceived gains. When moved by fear – when security is their primary concern – actors will be find it more difficult to distinguish conceptually between loss and gain because security, like honor, is relational. They are accordingly more risk-accepting. When the spirit motivated actors to seek honor or standing, they become even more risk-prone. Honor and standing, especially in international affairs, historically have required actors to seek out

---

[138] "US 'Will Stay the Course' in Iraq, says Bush," US Department of Defense, American Forces Press Service, July 10, 2003.
[139] See chapter 8 for discussion.
[140] Ricks, *Fiasco*, pp. 42–3, 66–84, on military dissatisfaction.

and embrace risks, so the appearance of high risk can actually make the action in question more desirable. If, as I suggest, top policymakers of the Bush administration were motivated primarily by standing, their demonstrable propensity for risk-taking becomes understandable. Colin Powell, James Baker, Lawrence Eagleburger, Brent Scowcroft and Dick Armey were risk-averse because none of them framed the problem in terms of standing. They were moved by security concerns and perceived no threat to American interests that required an immediate military response.[141] In August 2002, Powell told Bush that an American invasion of Iraq could destabilize the entire region, put friendly regimes in Saudi Arabia, Jordan and Egypt in jeopardy, derail other important US foreign policy initiatives, including the war on terrorism, and do all this at enormous cost. Republican moderates also expected the economic costs to be staggering, potentially driving up the price of oil to unheard-of prices.[142]

The spirit also provides insight into the unexpected degree of resistance Iraqis offered to the American occupation. The spirit craves autonomy, and in many societies there are few things more dishonorable than visible subordination. Classical realists from Thucydides to Morgenthau understand this phenomenon and recognize that power must be masked to be effective.[143] Subordinate actors must be allowed – even encouraged – to believe that they are expressing their free will, not being coerced, are being treated as ends in themselves, not as means, and are respected as ontological equals, even in situations characterized by marked power imbalance.

The spirit is a universal attribute of human beings, but its relative importance varies from culture to culture. In so-called shame cultures, honor takes precedence over appetite even at the risk, or near certainty, of death. Viewed in this light, it is hardly surprising that the American occupation of Iraq provoked serious resistance, just as the Soviet invasion of Afghanistan had during the Cold War. The Bush administration expected its forces to be hailed as liberators and had no plans for a rapid

---

[141] Transcript of interview with Brent Scowcroft, *Face the Nation*, August 4, 2002; Brent Scowcroft, "Don't Attack Saddam," *Wall Street Journal*, August 15, 2002, p. A12; Todd Purdum and Patrick E. Tyler, "Top Republicans Break with Bush on Iraq Strategy," *New York Times*, August 16, 2002, p. A1; James A. Baker II, "The Right Way to Change a Regime," *New York Times*, August 25, 2002, section 4, p. 9; transcript of Lawrence Eagleburger, *Crossfire*, August 19, 2002; interview with Lawrence Eagleburger, *Fox News Sunday*, Washington, DC, August 18, 2002; Walter Gibbs, "Scowcroft Urges Wide Role for the U.N. in Postwar Iraq," *New York Times*, April 9, 2003; Eric Schmitt, "Iraq is Defiant as G.O.P. Leaders Oppose Attack," *New York Times*, August 9, 2002, p. A6.

[142] Woodward, *Bush at War*, pp. 332–4.   [143] Lebow, "Power and Ethics," for a discussion.

transfer of power to an independent Iraqi or international authority. They assumed tight control over the reins of civilian authority and installed a corrupt American puppet exile with no local support. American forces increasingly came to be seen as an army of occupation. Violent resistance triggered equally violent reprisals and set in motion an escalatory spiral which further cast the Americans in the role of occupiers. Insensitive to Iraqi needs for self-esteem, American authorities belatedly attempted to satisfy Iraqi appetites by restoring electricity, providing gasoline and diesel fuel, rebuilding schools and hospitals and doing their best to provide security. These programs – which the Bush administration repeatedly cited as evidence of its good will and commitment – did nothing to placate the spirit, and moreover were run in a manner that further highlighted Iraqi subordination. The same was true of dilatory American efforts to create an independent Iraqi governing authority, along with actions that made it apparent that Washington would continue to have the last word on all important matters. Interviews with Iraqis from all walks of life indicated fury at their perceived subordination. One respondent angrily admitted that Saddam may have killed thousands of Iraqi civilians, and the Americans only hundreds. The American occupation was still intolerable, as he put it, because "Saddam was one of ours."[144]

The failure of Anglo-American intervention led to a shift in goals within the Bush and Blair administrations, from winning the war to preventing a withdrawal of their military forces. Bush made frequent appeals to Americans to "stay the course" in Iraq on the grounds that it was not only essential for Iraqi democracy but for the honor of the United States.[145] The new goal of both leaders became avoiding being judged by history as the president or prime minister responsible for defeat in Iraq. Once again considerations of standing trumped those of security and material gain.

The invasion of Iraq had disastrous consequences for American influence in the Middle East, if not throughout the world.[146] Public opinion polls indicate that America's decline in standing began with the Afghanistan intervention and accelerated when it became apparent that Washington would invade Iraq. Negative evaluations of the United States increased again with the failure of the occupation. Had the Anglo-Americans not encountered an insurgency, or had quickly defeated or

---

[144] Interviews conducted and quote provided by Prof. Shawn Rosenberg.
[145] Ewen MacAskill, "Unrest in the Ranks as Bush Slogs on," and Commentary and Analysis, "Bush and Iraq: Defiance and Delusion," *Guardian Weekly*, January 15, 2007.
[146] Cox, "Meanings of Victory," for an argument that the administration's response to 9.11 initially strengthened US influence.

defused that insurgency, and withdrawn from Iraq within six months leaving behind a stable, pro-Western government, US prestige would not have suffered such a precipitous decline. This counterfactual undoubtedly involves more than a minimal rewrite of history because any invasion of Iraq was almost certain to heighten religious and ethnic tensions, making it extremely difficult, perhaps impossible, to cobble together a functioning coalition government. To succeed, such an effort would have required considerable political sophistication on the ground, and an occupation managed in a way to win the support rather than alienate wide segments of Iraqi opinion. It is difficult to imagine the Bush administration having met this goal given its proclivity for control, secrecy, scorn for compromise and contempt for diplomats and other professionals with local knowledge. Political success would have also required United Nations backing, if not a truly international coalition of military forces. This too was out of the question in the absence of incontrovertible evidence that Saddam possessed WMD or was close to developing them. Most demanding of all, it required an administration that was willing to lead a coalition of diverse states, with all the diplomacy and compromise this involves, rather than one intent on dictating policy or acting unilaterally.

The Bush administration has frequently been described as something of an anomaly, and it is difficult to find another administration that pursued such far-reaching goals that entailed such risk and with such a lack of preparation. The closest parallel may be Harry Truman's decision in June 1950 to cross the thirty-eighth parallel in Korea to seek unification of that country in the face of Chinese threats of intervention. Truman knew that moving north involved considerable risk, which he did his best to deny, and with tragic consequences for himself, American forces and Korea. The difference is that Truman believed himself to be facing the prospect of certain political loss at home if he failed to unify the Peninsula.[147] George Bush by comparison, was riding high in the polls in the aftermath of the Afghan invasion, and was under no domestic pressure to invade Iraq. The most important similarity between the two situations may be the extent to which the president were successfully manipulated by advisors. General Douglas MacArthur offered a wildly optimistic scenario to Truman and subsequently withheld critical information from him. Cheney and Rumsfeld did the same thing to Bush.[148]

The Bush administration's Iraq adventure, and its foreign policy more generally, is reminiscent of a parvenu power sensitive to challenges to its

[147] Lebow, *Between Peace and War*, pp. 148–228.   [148] Ibid., pp. 153–69 on Korea.

honor and anxious to win impressive victories to convince others of its standing. The United States meets some of the conditions of a parvenu power. It gained independence in 1775 but did not become a great power until its defeat of Spain at the end of the nineteenth century, a war motivated at least in part by the desire to achieve great power status.[149] In the interim it developed a variant of the parvenu discourse emphasizing its uniqueness and superiority to the corrupt cultures and political units of Europe. It combined Puritan ideas of "the city on the hill" and the image of the United States as the modern-day descendant of Athens.[150]

Under presidents McKinley and Roosevelt, the United States sought recognition as a great power through the acquisition of colonies, the development of a powerful navy – sent around the world by Roosevelt from 1907 to 1909 to impress others with American strength – participation or leadership at international conferences, and a say in all matters considered important by other great powers.[151] Theodore Roosevelt and many Republicans would have entered the European war before 1917, with or without any provocation by Germany, to assert America's role in the world.[152] After World War I, the Senate rejected the Treaty of Versailles and declined to participate in the League of Nations, but the United States was hardly isolationist with respect to the rest of the world. It took a leading role in restructuring German reparations with the Dawes (1924) and Young Plans (1930). It hosted the Washington Naval Conference (1921–2), which established ratios for capital ships among the major naval powers.[153] It employed bribes, threats and force in the Caribbean and Central America to maintain or install governments that would do the bidding of American corporations and investors.[154] Public opinion and Congress constrained President Franklin Roosevelt in the 1930s, but the executive gained a relatively free hand in foreign affairs after the Japanese attack on Pearl Harbor in December 1941. This pattern continued after World War II; Congress did not make a serious effort to check presidential authority until public opinion turned against the war in Indochina in the late 1960s.

---

[149] McCartney, *Power and Progress*, p. 10.
[150] The literature on American self-images is vast. A useful start, with particular emphasis on foreign policy, is Mead, *Special Providence*.
[151] Collin, *Theodore Roosevelt's Caribbean*, pp. 127–340, and *Theodore Roosevelt, Diplomacy and Expansion*; Burton, *Theodore Roosevelt*.
[152] Burton, *Theodore Roosevelt*, pp. 191–5; Gould, *The Presidency of Theodore Roosevelt*, pp. 261–74; Collin, *Theodore Roosevelt*, p. 193.
[153] Goldman, *Sunken Treaties*; Goldstein and Maurer, *The Washington Conference*; Kaufman, *Arms Control during the Prenuclear Era*.
[154] LaFeber, *Inevitable Revolutions*; Westad, *The Global Civil War*, pp. 143–52.

Cheney and Rumsfeld sought to use the war in Iraq as a vehicle to free the executive from the vestiges of legislation imposed by the Congress at the end of the Indochina war.[155]

Unlike most great powers, the restraints on the United States were more internal than external; Congress, not other powers, kept American presidents from playing a more active role in European affairs in the 1920s and 1930s, and forced a withdrawal from Indochina in the 1970s. American leaders and people were never spurned or humiliated by the other powers, but American presidents and their advisors did at times feel humiliated by the internal restraints imposed upon them, and not infrequently sought to commit the country to activist policies through membership in international institutions that involved various long-term obligations (e.g. IMF, NATO), *faits accomplis* in the form of executive actions (e.g. the 1940 destroyer deal, intervention in the Korean War, sending Marines to Lebanon in 1958), and congressional resolutions secured on the basis of false or misleading information (the Gulf of Tonkin and Iraq War resolutions).

Postwar American leaders and members of the national security community, including professors and think-tank than intellectuals, were deeply concerned, if not paranoid, about maintaining credibility. Parvenu powers are prone to interpret the behavior of other powers as insults that must be avenged. American leaders, and the national security community more generally during the Cold War, displayed a consistent tendency to interpret the behavior of others as challenges to American interests or resolve that required sharp responses. Concern for maintaining credibility was a primary cause of intervention in Korea and Vietnam, of a range of expensive strategic programs and even of Eisenhower's decision to reject the Rosenbergs' plea to have their sentence reduced from execution to life imprisonment.[156]

The US fixation on resolve has often been attributed to the so-called lessons of the 1930s: the assumption that failure to oppose Japan, Italy and Hitler at the outset encouraged their leaders to make more farreaching demands that ultimately led to a costly war. The practitioners and principal victims of appeasement in the 1930s were France and Britain, not the United States, and their leaders never manifested the same degree of

---

[155] Jane Mayer, "The Hidden Power," *New Yorker*, 24 July 2008; PBS *Frontline*, "The Dark Side," 19 June 2007, available at www.pbs.org/wgbh/pages/frontline/darkside/view/.

[156] Dwight David Eisenhower to Clyde Raymond Miller, June 10, 1953, and to John Sheldon Eisenhower, June 16, 1953, papers of Dwight David Eisenhower, XIV, available at www.eisenhowermemorial.org/presidential-papers/first-term/index/..%5Cdocuments%5C240.cfm.

concern for credibility as their American counterparts did in the postwar era. We must look elsewhere to explain this remarkable and often self-defeating behavior, and perhaps the answer lies in the experience of the 1920s, when a relatively new great power was prevented from continuing the role of *primus inter pares* that it had assumed at Versailles. Subsequent presidents had to settle for a secondary role, especially in Europe, then still the center of world affairs. When the United States asserted its leadership again, twenty years later during another world war, its leaders were all the more intent on maintaining it in the face of domestic and foreign challenges. Ironically, concern for credibility promoted ill-considered and open-ended commitments such as Vietnam and Iraq that led to the kinds of public opposition and congressional constraints that subsequent American presidents considered detrimental to their credibility. Rather than prompt a reassessment of national security strategy, it strengthened the commitment of some presidents and their advisors to break free of these constraints and assert leadership in the world, ushering in a new cycle of overextension, failure and new constraints. In a document prepared for defense secretary Cheney in 1992, intended to reorient American foreign policy after the Cold War, Paul Wolfowitz, Lewis Libby and Zalmay Khalilzad argued that the United States should use its unrivalled power to convince "potential competitors that they need not aspire to a greater role or pursue a more aggressive posture to protect their legitimate interests . . . [and must] discourage [potential competitors] from challenging [its leadership] or seeking to overturn the established political and economic order." The United States, moreover, should be prepared to act unilaterally toward this end "when collective action cannot be orchestrated."[157] Bush administration neocons in particular assumed that the United States not only had the power but the responsibility to spread American values, "doing something," as secretary of state Rice put it, "that benefits all humanity."[158]

Transformation of the international system

In Homer's world there was little or no differentiation among personal, city and international relations. By the time of classical Greece, *oikos* and polis were distinct, although there was no separate word or set of concepts

---

[157] Steven R. Weisman, "Pre-Emption Evolves from an Idea to Official Action," *New York Times*, March 22, 2004.
[158] Rice, "Promoting the National Interest."

to distinguish international from other forms of relations. In the Roman Republic, from an early date, legal distinctions differentiated Romans from other Latins and both of them from other Italians. However, it was not until the nineteenth century that the international realm became conceptually distinct, with profound implications for the practice and study of international relations. It is a distinguishing characteristic of the modern world.

Another key feature of the modern world is civil society. For a long time, the concept of *societas civilis* referred to the condition of living within a legal order that possessed sufficient force to guarantee its subjects security and good government.[159] Montesquieu was the first to make the connection between the spirit of liberty and personal independence on the one hand and the emergence of civil society (*l'état civile*) on the other. Rather than undermining order, he thought it had the potential to create a new form of public mores (*mœurs*) that could endow social relations with more consistency.[160] Adam Ferguson stressed the importance of civil society as a means of opposing illegitimate state authority.[161] Hegel redefined civil society (*die bürgerliche Gesellschaft*) to refer to an equality-based system of social relations among associations of people that was independent of the state and the family, which he thought to have first emerged in Europe in the seventeenth century. His civil society is characterized by free labor, a commodity market and a system of contract law enforcement.[162] In our time, the concept of civil society has been expanded to include a general strengthening of the rule of law and the development of voluntary associations not connected with commercial relations.[163]

Civil society encourages citizens to find satisfaction in the commercial and private sphere and to indulge their appetites as they see fit. It heralds a turning away from the state, the decline of man as a *zoon politikon* and an upgrading of the appetite in response to the perceived social benefits of individual greed. For all these reasons, civil society was anathema to many conservative supporters of the *ancien régime*, and regarded by radicals as at best a necessary evil. Marx considered civil society another means by

---

[159] It is used in this sense by Vattel, *Le droit des gens*; Kant, "Idea for a Universal History with a Cosmopolitan Purpose," and "Perpetual Peace."

[160] Montesquieu, *Spirit of the Laws*, I.3.6 and 19.27.

[161] Ferguson, *Essay on the History of Civil Society*, pp. 7–29.

[162] Hegel, *Philosophy of Right*, 157, 188; Jones, "Hegel and the Economics of Civil Society"; Cohen and Arato, *Civil Society and Politics Theory*, pp. 91–102.

[163] Cohen and Arato, *Civil Society and Political Theory*; Keane, *Civil Society and the State*; Seligman, *The Idea of Civil Society*; Bartelson, "Making Sense of Global Civil Society"; Koselleck, *Critique and Crisis*.

which the bourgeoisie could tighten its hold over society.[164] Montesquieu and Tocqueville sought to adapt the spirit to modern society in the hope that it could act as an effective check on central authority, and inspire politicians and civil servants to put aside their private interests in pursuit of projects that benefited the community as a whole.[165] Civil society not only legitimized the appetite as a drive, it facilitated its partial blending with the spirit to the extent that wealth became not only a marker of standing but a means of attaining it.

Civil society provided new domains and opportunities for achieving honor and standing. Some of these routes led to national, even international fame (e.g. sports, science, the creative and performing arts), while others led to renown in specialized or geographically restricted communities (e.g. law, mathematics, spelunking, community service). This diversity gave rise to multiple hierarchies in which individuals of varying talents and interests could compete for honor and standing, making it at least theoretically possible for everyone to achieve self-esteem. A critical development in this regard has been the increasing openness of many of these arenas to people of all class, religious and racial backgrounds. In Europe prior to the French Revolution, only aristocrats were allowed to compete for standing and honor. Recognition, in the form of admission into this elite, was barred to those with talent but the wrong religious affiliations or genealogical antecedents. Such prejudice has not altogether disappeared in Western societies, but even the most traditional elite hierarchies (e.g. military, diplomatic service and formerly aristocratic sports like tennis and golf) began to open up, offering opportunities for members of groups that have historically been at the bottom of the social ladder to rise to the top of these intensely competitive hierarchies. Henry Kissinger, Madeleine Albright, Colin Powell, Condoleezza Rice and Tiger Woods are cases in point.

The concept of the international and the emergence of civil society and democratic governments heightened the contrast between domestic and interstate relations. The former were rule-based, or at least expected to be, while the latter was considered anarchical and war-prone. To the extent the international system had any order, it was associated with that imposed by the great powers acting in concert to establish a rudimentary

---

[164] Marx, "On the Jewish Question."
[165] Tocqueville, *Democracy in America*, I.2.10, p. 383; II.4.7. Krause, *Liberalism without Honor*, Lebow and Lebow, *Running Red Lights and Ruling the World*, ch. 2.

form of the hierarchy I have associated with spirit-based worlds.[166] The different patterns of authority that characterized domestic and international relations encouraged the latter's conceptualization as a distinct level of analysis subject to rules of its own and provided the justification for its study as a separate field.

For realists, the most striking feature of the international system is its relative lack of order. From a constructivist perspective, its most interesting feature is the kind of order that exists: a single hierarchy in which only a relatively small number of actors can compete for honor and standing. The 1648 Peace of Westphalia facilitated the emergence of the state as unit actor in international affairs, something that became a reality in the nineteenth century.[167] By that time the legal concept of sovereignty had made states ontological equals, a status reflected today in the "one state, one vote" rule in the General Assembly of the United Nations and many other international bodies. In the nineteenth century, this development had the practical effect of limiting actors to a relatively small number of European political units. The number of recognized states gradually increased, and the United Nations currently has 192 members, most of them non-European. International organizations, many of them international non-governmental organizations (INGOs), also have legal standing. Important security decisions are nevertheless made in the Security Council, where each of the permanent members has a veto, or by the great powers acting in concert or with their allies. The major powers also have disproportionate influence over international economic policies, and tend to exercise it through "clubs" with select membership like the G-7, the G-8 or the Trilateral Commission. Great powerdom is an even more restrictive category. One the eve of the First World War, there were nine: Britain, France, Germany, Italy, Austria-Hungary, Russia, the Ottoman Empire, Japan and the United States. Between the wars, the number dropped to seven, and after World War II was superseded by a new category of "superpowers," of which there were two. Some realists claim that after the Cold War and the collapse of the Soviet Union, we

---

[166] Kratochwil, *Rules, Norms, and Decisions*; Franck, *The Power of Legitimacy*; Hurd, "Legitimacy and Authority in International Politics"; Bukovansky, *Legitimacy and Power Politics*; Coicaud, *Legitimacy and Politics*, all attribute some degree of hierarchical order to the international system.

[167] Osiander, "Sovereignty, International Relations, and the Westphalian Myth," on the nineteenth-century narratives that ahistorically traced this development back to Westphalia.

have entered a "unipolar world" with only one superpower, the United States.[168]

The criteria for standing among political units has been strikingly uniform across the millennia. It is achieved by power, measured in size, population, military strength, wealth and their symbolic manifestations.[169] Standing is mostly gained by victory in war, although it can be claimed secondarily through various forms of conspicuous consumption. Palaces, temples, shrines, mausoleums, sports arenas and elaborate public buildings all qualify. Egypt, Greece and Rome set the standard for the West and were emulated by modern European states who built many of their most impressive public buildings in the classical style, raised statues of their greatest political and military leaders clothed in togas, and imported obelisks from Egypt and Ethiopia – or erected their own (e.g. Nelson's Column, the Washington Monument) in central squares. While they did not parade captives through triumphal arches, they built such arches (e.g. the Arc de Triomphe, the Brandenburg Gate) and impressive museums – often, like the British Museum, with classical facades – in which to display art and artifacts, much of it booty from conquests. The obelisk was not an arbitrary choice; it was a symbol of masculinity and power for the Egyptians and Romans, and has remained so for their modern descendants. Victory in war and standing in international affairs continue to be advertised as expressions of sexual prowess and domination. The fifth-century Greek Eurymedon vase depicts a Greek preparing to rape a Persian prisoner of war.[170] After being shown pictures of the results of the US bombing of Haiphong Harbor in 1965, Lyndon Johnson exclaimed: "I just didn't screw Ho Chi Minh. I cut his pecker off."[171] President Bush is reported to have told Ariel Sharon that if the United States captured Osama bin Laden "I will screw him in the ass."[172]

In the modern age, the first powers to claim standing on some basis other than military power were the American and French republics.

---

[168] Krauthammer, "The Unipolar Moment," and "The Unipolar Moment Revisited"; Wohlforth, "The Stability of a Unipolar World"; Huntington, "The Lonely Superpower"; Mastanduno, "Preserving the Unipolar Moment."

[169] For attempts at measurement, Sprout and Sprout, *Foundations of International Politics*; Morgenthau, *Politics among Nations*, pp. 131, 180–1; Waltz, *Theory of International Politics*, pp. 131, 153, 180–1.

[170] Smith, "Eurymedon and the Evolution of Political Personifications in the Early Classical Period," esp. plate 8.

[171] Quoted in Topmiller, 1996 – A Missed Opportunity for Peace in Vietnam.

[172] Matthew Yglesias, "Strange Decorum," available at www.matthewyglesias.com/archives/2007/02/strange_decorum/.

French spokesmen especially insisted that their form of government set them apart from and made them superior to the other powers, a claim which resonated widely in Europe.[173] Similar claims were made in the twentieth century by the Soviet Union and People's Republic of China on the basis of their communist regimes. Revolutionary France was initially treated as a pariah by the other powers, as was the Soviet Union, and to a lesser extent, the People's Republic.[174] These governments had strong incentives to develop alternative criteria of standing and to appeal for recognition and support over the heads of governments to fellow republicans, communists, workers or oppressed peoples. France also claimed recognition on cultural grounds. Napoleon is supposed to have declared that every great scientist and artist was French no matter where they were born because Paris was the world's center of human achievement. Napoleon's career illustrates another phenomenon: the rapidity with which many revolutionary regimes – North Korea being an important exception – gradually transform themselves in the face of international constraints and opportunities and end up seeking recognition and standing on the basis of traditional criteria. Napoleon proclaimed himself emperor – the highest social and political rank in pre-revolutionary Europe – and married off his family to European royalty. The Soviet Union's accommodation was not quite so rapid or thorough, but by Khrushchev's time Moscow sought recognition from the United States as a coequal superpower and based its claim on its military and economic power. The Soviet Union also poured funds into science, arts, sports and chess with an eye to validating its system of government and increasing its standing internationally.[175] All of the communist states sought to excel in the oldest of all international competitions, the Olympic Games. The People's Republic of China also underwent a gradual transformation. Within fifty years of the communist victory in the civil war, its leaders were asserting primacy in the region in more or less the same way imperial Chinese dynasties had in the past.[176]

---

[173] Bukovansky, *Legitimacy and Power Politics*, pp. 194–202.

[174] Ibid.; Ulam, *Expansion and Coexistence*, pp. 12–31; Hinton, "China as an Asian Power"; Levine, "Perception and Ideology in Chinese Foreign Policy."

[175] Allison and Monnington, "Sport Prestige and International Relations"; Soltis, *Soviet Chess*.

[176] Hinton, "China as an Asian Power"; Kirby, "Traditions of Centrality, Authority, and Management in Modern China's Foreign Relations"; Shumbaugh, "Return to the Middle Kingdom?"; Zhang and Tang, "China's Regional Strategy"; Lampton, "China's Rise in Asia Need Not Be at America's Expense."

For much of recorded history, external honor has been associated with physical bravery and athletic prowess. However, these markers of standing have rarely been static, unproblematic or unique. In fifth-century Greece, external honor was broadened to include participation in politics and excellence in debate. In certain periods of Chinese history, it included intellectual distinction: honors and promotion in the civil service were achieved in large part through competitive examinations. In contemporary Britain, the titles "Sir" or "Lady" still command respect, and in the course of the last century knighthoods and peerages were extended to business tycoons, scholars, athletes and artists of all kinds, including, in 1996, one of the Beatles. Tracking changes in what societies – domestic, regional or international – value, and how they recognize those who achieve it, tells us a lot about the distribution of influence in these societies and the character of their politics.

Recognition as a great power or superpower depends primarily on military and economic might. For Vattel, Ranke and realists, great powers became great powers because of their power.[177] The concept of the "great powers" came into use in the eighteenth century but was only institutionalized by the Congress of Vienna.[178] Great powership is a status conferred by other states, and the criteria for this status have not only changed in the course of the last two centuries, but not every state that appears to meet the criteria of the moment achieves this status.[179] In her study of the American and French revolutionary regimes, Mlada Bukovansky shows that for this to happen state power must be considered legitimate by existing great powers, and "justified in principle because it rests not just on force but on acquiescence."[180] Failure to meet this criterion resulted in the non-recognition of the Soviet Union for some years after the Bolshevik Revolution and successful efforts by the United States and many of its allies from 1949 to 1971 to deny the People's Republic of China a seat

---

[177] Vattel defined a great power as a state that can stand up to any combination of others. For Ranke, "The Great Powers," great powers were states that had the military and economic power to maintain a sphere of influence in which other powers recognized their *droit de regard*.

[178] Kratochwil, *Rules, Norms, and Decisions*; Neumann, "Russian as a Great Power."

[179] Hobson and Sharman, "The Enduring Place of Hierarchy in World Politics"; Simpson, *Great Powers and Outlaw States*; Reus-Smit, *The Moral Purpose of the State*; Suzuki, "Seeking 'Legitimate' Great Power Status in Post-Cold War International Society."

[180] Bukovansky, *Legitimacy and Power Politics*, p. 70; Reus-Smit, *The Moral Purpose of the State*, p. 137; Clark, *Legitimacy in International Society*, p. 100.

in the United Nations.[181] As Shogo Suzuki observes, great power status, like the concert of Europe, is a social and socially legitimated hierarchy within international society.[182]

States sometimes retain great power status after their power has declined. According to Morgenthau, "brilliant diplomacy" can make up for raw power, and France retained its great power status after the Napoleonic Wars due to the diplomacy of Talleyrand.[183] Less powerful states have also been recognized as great powers as it serves the interest of other great powers. In 1945, France and China were made permanent members of the Security Council. At the time, France was weak and impoverished, and China weaker and poorer still and in the throes of a civil war. The China seat went to the Kuomintang although it controlled only parts of the country. Subsequent efforts to expand the number of permanent members of the Security Council have been resisted by states who feel they will lose prestige if their rivals are admitted or that the "club" will lose some of its value if its size increases.

Erik Ringmar describes international society as a ring of concentric circles with the great powers inhabiting the innermost one.[184] To become a great power, an aspiring state must identify and acquire the "status markers" associated with great power identity, and persuade existing great powers that it meets the normative requirements of great power status.[185] It must be willing and able to uphold the rules and core values of the society.[186] Great powers are in a privileged position, but their ability to exercise influence benefits from, and may even depend on, acceptance of their "right to rule" by others.[187] As Weber noted, acquiring prestige is essential for becoming a great power, just as becoming a great power

---

[181] According to Neumann, "Russia as a Great Power," this phenomenon pre- and post-dates the Soviet Union. Russia has often met the conditions for great power status but its European contemporaries have always doubted whether it qualified on normative grounds.

[182] Suzuki, "Seeking 'Legitimate' Great Power Status in Post-Cold War International Society."

[183] Morgenthau, *Politics among Nations*, 1st edn, p. 107; Kissinger, *Diplomacy*, p. 81; Clark, *Legitimacy in International Society*, pp. 99–101; Simpson, *Great Powers and Outlaw States*, p. 107.

[184] Ringmar, *Identity, Interest, and Action*.

[185] Russell, "Identity Diplomacy." Suzuki, "Seeking 'Legitimate' Great Power Status in Post-Cold War International Society," for elaboration.

[186] Wight, *Systems of States*; Bull, *Anarchical Society*, p. 171; Kratochwil, *Rules, Norms, and Decisions*, p. 52.

[187] Coicaud, *Legitimacy and Politics*, p. 10; Simpson, *Great Powers and Outlaw States*, p. 5.

confers prestige.[188] For our purposes, prestige is equivalent to status or standing.

The lowest rung of the prestige hierarchy is occupied by the "pariah" or "rogue" state. These are relatively recent concepts that made their appearance during the Reagan administration, and were applied to states like Libya and Cuba that the administration chose to ostracize because of their leadership and policies. The Clinton administration introduced the less offensive term "states of concern." George W. Bush brought "rogue states" back into use and made them a more central focus of US foreign policy. Iraq, Iran, North Korea and Cuba headed the administration's list of "rogue states" and were described as the "axis of evil." The term "pariah" or "rogue" state was also applied by the media and conservative scholars to Syria, Sudan, Afghanistan under the Taliban, and Libya before its about-face on weapons of mass destruction.[189] Critics of American policy responded in kind by labeling the Bush administration a rogue state by virtue of its use of force without legal international sanction.[190] Even more than great powers, the category of rogue state illustrates the highly contested and fundamentally political nature of any hierarchy in international relations.

Military power does not always confer prestige. The Ottoman Empire was denied recognition for centuries by the Western powers because of its Muslim faith, and non-Caucasian states were excluded on racial grounds.[191] Japan was discriminated against on racial grounds, and was not accepted as a great power until its defeat of Russia in 1904–5.[192] The prestige of the Soviet Union underwent a precipitous decline in the decades before its demise in 1992. This was due to the authoritarian character of its regime, the invasions of Hungary, Czechoslovakia and Afghanistan, and vast expenditure on its military at the expense of its

[188] See Weber, *From Max Weber*, p. 161, where he speaks of *Machtprestige* in combination as constituting the basis of great powerhood.
[189] John R. Bolton, "Remarks to the Conference of the Institute for Foreign Policy Analysis and the Fletcher School's International Security Studies Program," Washington, DC, December 2, 2003; Nincic, *Renegade Regimes*.
[190] Blum, *Rogue State*; Chomsky, "Rogue States," a noted critic of US policy, thinks the term unwarranted: see www.zmag.org/chomsky/articles/z9804-rogue.html.
[191] Naff, "The Ottoman Empire and the European States System"; Vincent, "Racial Equality."
[192] Bull, *Anarchical Society*, pp. 13–14; Watson, "New States in the Americas"; Suganami, "Japan's Entry into International Society"; Gong, "China's Entry into International Society," and *The Standard of "Civilization" in International Society*, pp. 13–14; Keene, *Beyond the Anarchical Society*, on the development of two patterns or order in world politics: one among European states and their offshoots, and the other between them and non-European political units.

civilian economy. In the 1980s, the Soviet Union retained its great power status almost entirely because of its military power. More recently, the prestige of the United States has been seriously eroded by its unilateral behavior, rejection of numerous international agreements and norms and the invasion of Iraq. European diplomacy up to the French Revolution, and arguably afterwards, was preoccupied with the prestige hierarchy, and was driven by efforts to maintain or elevate the standing of one's state. Chris Reus-Smit finds that the primary role of ambassadors in Renaissance Italian city states was to engage in "oratorical diplomacy" and cultivate an image of honor and glory for their city.[193] The Soviet Union under Khrushchev and Brezhnev sought to acquire and demonstrate its power to gain prestige, and was willing to make substantive concessions to the United States in exchange for recognition as a coequal superpower.[194] In a comparative study of the recent diplomacy of Russia and the Baltic states, Wynne Elizabeth Russell finds that Baltic representatives sought to portray their countries as worthy candidates for admission to the European club but Russia as both undeserving and a threat to European interests. The Russians did just the reverse. Both sides invoked characteristics of their states – democracy by the Baltics, and *derzhavnost'* (great power quality) by Russia to argue that their admission would raise the status of the "club," while letting the other in would lower it.[195] As these examples indicate, prestige can be an end in itself, a means to an end, or something appealed to in order to advance state interests.

Although military power does not necessarily confer prestige, rich states like Japan and Germany, who, by virtue of their past, have not sought to become dominant military powers, did not have the same degree of standing as they had earlier in the century. Unlike in domestic politics in countries with robust civil societies, there have been no equally good alternative means for states to achieve standing. Other criteria have been proposed from time to time by countries likely to benefit from a more pluralist approach, but they have not been accepted by existing great powers. A more serious challenge is now underway – a phenomenon I address below – but for the time being great power status is still based on the combination of economic power and military might. Standing in international relations more closely resembles that in traditional warrior

---

[193] Reus-Smit, *The Moral Purpose of the State*, pp. 65–7.
[194] This case is addressed in more detail in chapter 7.
[195] Russell, "Identity Diplomacy." See also Kuus, "Toward Co-operative Security?," and Lehti, "Challenging the 'Old' Europe."

societies than it does in modern democracies. It is achieved primarily through military prowess, and takes the form of a single hierarchy. This makes the culture of international relations something of an atavism, and radically differentiates it – in theory and practice – from standing and order in domestic political systems.

As I noted, all attempts by revolutionary powers to promulgate alternative criteria of standing have failed. Realists would attribute this outcome to their lack of power, but this is only part of the story. French revolutionary ideas were widely embraced by European intellectuals, and the country's standing rose accordingly. It was undercut by the reign of terror, Napoleon's autocratic rule and imperialism abroad. Soviet claims to be the harbinger of a new political–economic order were undermined by the purges, the Stalin–Hitler Pact and the postwar imposition of unpopular communist regimes in Eastern Europe. This loss of prestige occurred while the Soviet Union was still a rising power in terms of its economic and military capabilities. The People's Republic of China is another interesting case. It initially sought standing as a revolutionary opponent of imperialism and leader of national liberation movements. In recent decades, Chinese leaders have sought standing by more traditional means, and the country's standing in the region and world has risen in proportion to its economic and military power. At the same time, its communist regime lost standing because of Tiananmen Square and its corrupt and authoritarian character. It may lose standing in the future because of the environmental damage it is causing. The United States, arguably a quasi-revolutionary power for part of its history, claimed standing on the grounds that it represented the most democratic and progressive political and economic order. Its standing reached its high water mark at the end of World War II, and declined during the Cold War due to domestic and foreign policies that contradicted its proclaimed principles. These include capital punishment, military intervention in Indochina and support of right-wing dictatorships around the world.

In recent years, the most serious challenge to traditional conceptions of standing has come from religious fundamentalists. For many Christians in the United States and Muslims in the Middle East, South and Southeast Asia, the standing of a state depends on the degree to which its leaders follow practices, at home and abroad, they consider to reflect divine will. Iran and Saudi Arabia have both claimed standing on this basis, and like the French and Soviet revolutionary regimes before them, have won widespread support among sympathizers outside their respective countries. Less revolutionary but perhaps ultimately more successful challenges to traditional conceptions of standing are presently being made by such countries, or groups of countries, as Canada, Scandinavia and the European Union. Their claims for standing are based in the first instance on their economic wealth and democratic political systems, which have allowed them to provide a high standard of living and quality of life for their citizens, and secondarily on foreign policies (e.g. peace-keeping, development aid and programs, support for international institutions) intended to serve the international community as a whole. Both the Islamic and postindustrial claims for standing are really claims for status based on honor. Iranian and Saudi leaders claim that their domestic and foreign policies are rule-based and reflect divine law as revealed in the Koran. Canada, Scandinavia, the European Union and Japan assert that their most important foreign policy initiatives are coordinated in multilateral fora and reflect and respond to widely accepted secular goals, rules and norms. Both sets of claimants further maintain that their aid to third parties is in the service of their respective communities, which is another traditional basis for gaining honor.

Throughout the twentieth century, standing was largely divorced from honor. The United States achieved something approaching *hēgemonia* toward the end of World War I, but quickly lost it at Versailles where it came to be perceived as just another great power. It regained this status in the aftermath of World War II but squandered it through its support of right-wing, repressive regimes, the overthrow of democratically elected governments and unilateral resorts to force in Vietnam and Iraq. Neocons and their supporters are convinced that standing is still the principal means of gaining and exercising influence in international relations. Canada, Scandinavia, the European Union and Japan are hopeful that international society has become thick enough that honor can once again become a meaningful concept, that they can gain by acting as they are, and that with it will come increased influence.

Kenneth Waltz insists that "For a country to choose not to become a great power is a structural anomaly."[196] Almost a decade ago, he thought it likely that Japan would acquire nuclear weapons. It has not done so and continues to eschew most symbols of military status and power.[197] Sweden, Brazil, Argentina, Canada and the European Union have either terminated or never started nuclear programs. The European Union, which undeniably seeks to expand its influence on the world stage, has

[196] Waltz, "Structural Realism after the Cold War."
[197] Mearsheimer, "Back to the Future."

not encouraged members states to invest heavily in their armed forces. Germany, Japan, India and Brazil are all seeking permanent seats on the Security Council, and none of them are doing so on the basis of their military clout. They advance diverse arguments, including the need for regional and cultural diversity, commitments to peace and contributions to the general welfare of humankind. Their claims have not fallen on deaf ears. In January 2006, US influence in the world was rated lower than that of China.[198] A survey across twenty-three countries revealed a strong preference for Europe to become more influential than the United States in the future.[199] If states can gain prestige without becoming major military powers, and lose it by spending too much on their military instrument, or using it in inappropriate ways, then we need to disaggregate the concepts of power and prestige and examine them independently.

Regional political systems, and by extension the international system, must be regarded as sites of contestation where a variety of actors, by no means all of them states, claim standing on the basis of diverse criteria. States invest considerable resources in publicizing and justifying their claims and in making efforts to impress others. The growing diversity in claims for recognition, and the possible decline in the traditional military–economic basis of standing, points to a growing tension between the informal criteria used by many governments and peoples to award standing and the more formal recognition conferred by international institutions like the Security Council and the G-8. It will be interesting to see if this tension becomes more pronounced and the subject of an international discussion that leads to changes in the membership of existing institutions, internal changes in those institutions or the creation of new ones. One sign that a debate is already underway is a proposal by a panel commissioned by former UN secretary-general Kofi Annan to expand the Security Council to twenty-four members to make it more reflective of today's world. The panel also recognized that the credibility of the United Nations was threatened by allowing some of the worst violators of human rights (e.g. Cuba, Libya, Sudan) to serve on the Human Rights Commission.[200] The new Human Rights Council, its successor, disappointed supporters of

[198] Poll conducted in thirty-three countries in January 2006 by GlobeScan and the Program on International Policy Attitudes for the BBC World Service. World Public Opinion.org, June 14, 2006.
[199] World Public Opinion.org, "23 Nation Poll: Who Will Lead the World?," June 14, 2006.
[200] "Expansion of Security Council Proposed," *New York Times*, December 1, 2004, p. 1A.

human rights when it was stonewalled by some of the worst human rights offenders much to the chagrin of secretary-general Ban Ki-moon.[201]

Constructivist scholars have a tendency to assume the existence, or the possibility of the existence, of a single international society. They are accordingly interested in the global diffusion of norms.[202] International relations is far from homogeneous as different regions and countries display varying degrees of commitment to diverse values and norms. The international system is likely to continue this way for some time, and such diversity makes possible claims to status on differing bases, and with it the emergence of multiple, competitive hierarchies. Such diversity impedes the robustness of international society, but has the potential to strengthen regional orders. To the extent that regional actors share common values that differentiate them from other actors, they have strong incentives to build a community around those values to strengthen them collectively vis-à-vis other actors. In the 1950s, Karl Deutsch described how such a process could occur and suggested that it was underway in what he and his co-authors called the North Atlantic community.[203]

For realists, regional or international societies, and the sense of community and mutual support they enable, are no substitute for military power.[204] Realists assume that foreign policy does, or should, respond to system imperatives. As the international system is anarchical, and thus a self-help system, successful states are those that make security their first priority, and attempt to achieve it through economic self-sufficiency, military capability and alliances with like-minded actors. For realists, these means are not only rational but independent of culture; they are equally applicable to ancient and modern international relations among Western and non-Western political units.[205]

In practice, foreign policy reflects domestic values and practices, and does so for multiple, even reinforcing reasons. As numerous studies indicate, policymakers are cognitively predisposed to bring the set of expectations and practices to foreign policy that have served them well in domestic

---

[201] Warren Hogue, "Dismay Over New U.N. Human Rights Council," *New York Times*, March 9, 2007; Associated Press, "UN Urges Cooperation with Rights Panel," March 12, 2007, available at www.nytimes.com/aponline/world/AP-UN-Human-Rights-Council.html.

[202] For example, Clark, *Legitimacy in International Society*; Frost, "Tragedy, Ethics and International Relations."

[203] Deutsch *et al.*, *Political Community in the North Atlantic Area*.

[204] Mearsheimer, *The Tragedy of Great Power Politics*, for a particularly monochromatic presentation of this position.

[205] Morgenthau, *Politics among Nations*, pp. 3, 8.

society.[206] Ontological security, a concept explored in the introduction and elaborated in chapter 3, provides additional domestic incentives – especially in democratic societies – to pursue foreign policies that are consistent with the core values of society, or, with appropriate spin, can be made to appear so. In even minimally robust regional societies, there are systemic-level incentives and pressures to conduct foreign policies in accord with shared values and practices. With legitimacy comes influence, which is the positive side of the equation.[207] On the negative side, pressures to conform to accepted values and practices can be formal, arising from institutions and threats of punishment, or informal and associated with the fear of ostracism. Durkheim and Goffman emphasize the latter, and Paul Schroeder, as we observed in chapter 6, found this form of social control to be more effective in the nineteenth century than the balance of power. My cases from Greek to modern times offer additional confirmation of this point.

A powerful illustration of this phenomenon is provided by the largely successful socialization of the military organizations of southern Europe. Traditionally, officers in Portugal, Spain and Greece were anti-democratic and anti-socialist and relied on power and privileges that were the result of military coups or civil wars triggered by military coups. Beginning in the late 1950s officers from these countries began cross-training with other NATO armies and attending NATO staff and defense colleges. They established friendships and close working relationships with officers from the more democratic countries of northern Europe and North America, and gradually assimilated their values and professionalism. They began to play different roles in their political systems, becoming increasingly disengaged from domestic politics. In Spain, the defining moment came when the army intervened to crush an attempted coup against the post-Franco republic in February 1981 in which right-wing officers were implicated.[208] For social controls of this kind to work, three conditions must be met: those with an interest in maintaining the norms in question must be able to monitor the behavior of other actors and be willing to ostracize

---

[206] Goldgeier, *Leadership Style and Soviet Foreign Policy*, for persuasive examples of how this worked in Soviet foreign policy.

[207] On this point, see Kratochwil, *Rules, Norms, and Decisions*; Franck, *The Power of Legitimacy*; Hurd, "Legitimacy and Authority in International Politics"; Bukovansky, *Legitimacy and Power Politics*; Coicaud, *Legitimacy and Politics*; Reus-Smit, "Unipolarity and Legitimacy."

[208] Martínez Inglés, *El golpe que nunca existió*.

those who do not conform, and these actors must desire acceptance by the community.

Perhaps the strongest incentive that states have to adhere to widely shared norms is that policies in accord with them are more likely to succeed, and at less cost than policies at odds with accepted values and practices. It is easier to elicit support for policies that reflect shared norms because it is possible to persuade other actors that they are in the common interest. Policies contrary to accepted values and practices must rely on coercion or bribes, or a combination of the two, and are correspondingly more costly in resources. Cooperation archived on this basis last only so long as the dominant state retains the power to punish and reward.[209]

The Greek concept of *hēgemonia* nicely captures the distinction between persuasion and coercion. As employed by fifth- and fourth-century Greeks, *hēgemonia* distinguished legitimate international authority from *archē*, a form of rule based purely on the exercise of power. Greeks associated *hēgemonia* with *timē*, the gift of honor, which meant "esteem" in the abstract, but also the "office" to which one was accordingly entitled.[210] Sparta and Athens earned *timē* and the honorific status of "hegemons" by virtue of their contributions to Greece during the Persian Wars. *Timē* was also conferred on Athens in recognition of its literary, artistic, intellectual, political and commercial accomplishments that had made it, in Pericles words, the "school of Hellas."[211] Something similar developed in the Far East where China's claim to primacy was traditionally based not only on its power but its cultural supremacy and the economic benefits it provided to tributary states.[212] In both cultures, dominant and lesser powers alike saw advantages in legitimizing authority and establishing a hierarchy among actors. Like traditional domestic hierarchies, it allowed the hegemons to transform power into influence in efficient ways. Because their authority and leadership were acknowledged, it was easier to persuade others to follow their lead on a range of political, economic

---

[209] Lebow, "Power and Ethics"; Brooks and Wohlforth, "International Relations Theory and the Case against Unilateralism," and *The Challenge of American Primacy*, p. 517; Kane, *The Politics of Moral Capital*, p. 28; Reus-Smit, "International Crises of Legitimacy"; Hurd, "Breaking and Making Norms," for diverse elaborations of this argument.

[210] Perlman, "Hegemony and *Archē* in Greece"; Lebow, *Tragic Vision of Politics*, pp. 122, 126, 276–92, 297–302, 312–16 for a discussion.

[211] Thucydides, 2.4.

[212] Rossabi, "Traditional Chinese Foreign Policy and Intersocietal Cooperation" and *China among the Equals*; Kirby, "Traditions of Centrality, Authority, and Management in Modern China's Foreign Relations"; Hinton, "China as an Asian Power"; Kang, *China Reshapes Asia*; Shumbaugh, "Return to the Middle Kingdom?"

and cultural issues. From the perspective of the lesser powers, hegemony constrained dominant powers by enmeshing them in a dense network of mutual obligations and expectations; it limited their freedom of action and increased the cost of acting at odds with their obligations and others' expectations.

For the Greeks, *hēgemonia* is exercised primarily through a form of persuasion (*peithō*) that is characterized by frankness and accomplishes its goal by convincing others to act in support of common interests and identities. Greeks distinguished *peithō* from persuasion brought about by deceit (*dolos*), false logic, coercion and other forms of chicanery, which along with the use of force, they associated with *archē*. *Peithō* has consequences that go beyond narrow persuasion. Because it accepts the ontological equality of all the parties to a dialogue, regardless of their relative power or standing in the society, it can build friendships and mutual respect even when attempts at persuasion do not succeed. The dialogue *peithō* entails helps actors to define who they are, and this includes the actor attempting to persuade, not just those it seeks to influence. *Peithō* has the potential to foster cooperation that transcends discrete issues – that is, to create an enduring propensity to cooperate – and to create or strengthen collective identities through common acts of performance. By harmonizing interests and building friendships, *peithō* not only reduces conflict within a community, it reconciles those at the base of the hierarchy to its existence.

The Greek approach to "great powers" and how they gain status and exercise influence is a special case of the general principles I associate in chapter 2 with traditional spirit-based hierarchies. Such hierarchies contain rule packages which assign the most responsibility for maintaining order, assisting others and exercising self-restraint to actors with the highest status. They are based on a fundamental tradeoff. In return for prestige and all the privileges that come with it, high-ranking actors provide security and assume some responsibility for the well-being of lower-status actors. The system functions as long as powerful actors accept this arrangement and limit their own ambitions, which is another important objective of this kind of order. Much of the debate about the nature and sustainability of international order in the literature revolves around these two problems.[213] Historically, actors have found it difficult to coordinate their behavior through common institutions – not, as

---

[213] Dunne, "Society and Hierarchy in International Relations," for example, identifies two threats to international order: the need, identified by the English School, for powerful

liberals contend, because of the lack of institutions, but more fundamentally because of the absence of common values and understandings that would permit such institutions to form and function.[214] This problem still exists given the diversity of values among important actors and regions. The second problem – actors who consider themselves too powerful to accept conventional constraints on their behavior – is a perennial one in international relations and the United States is only the most recent example.

Contrary to the assumptions of realism, there are strong incentives for powerful actors to conform to the rules of the system – to the extent that regional or international society is thick enough for them to develop. It allows actors to translate their power into influence in the most efficient and effective manner. In return, they must limit the goals they seek to those others accept as legitimate and in the interest of the community as a whole. There are also strong unit-level incentives for actors to pursue foreign policies in accord with commonly accepted values.[215] As a general rule, individuals, groups, organizations and political units attempt to create, sustain and affirm identities in their interactions with other actors.[216] To the extent that identities help determine interests – and my case studies demonstrate how critical they are in this regard – they indirectly influence, if not directly shape, foreign policy behavior. The character of regional and international systems is not a function of so-called structural features such as anarchy or polarity, but of the values and norms (or their relative absence) that influence behavior at the system and unit levels. Systems at both levels are open-ended and contingent in their character. Unit identities are fluid and contingent and evolve in the course of interactions with other actors. They are also influenced by behavior in accord with, or in defiance of, norms and practices at the system level.

When enough powerful actors behave in a novel but similar way, they have the potential to transform the character of their system. If they are powerful and respected actors, they create strong incentives for others to follow their lead. Changes in the character of the system change the

---

actors to coordinate their actions and security through common institutions, and the need for the most powerful actors to accept the limits imposed by this order.

[214] On this point, see Lebow, "Reason, Emotion and Cooperation."

[215] In addition to the literature on ontological security referred to in chapter 3, see Reus-Smith, *The Moral Purpose of the State*, p. 31, for a persuasive argument about values and foreign policies.

[216] Taylor, *Sources of the Self,* p. 47; Giddens, *The Constitution of Society*. Claude, "Collective Legitimation as Political Function of the United Nations," for an application to international relations.

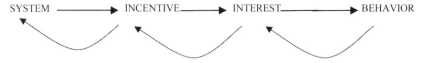

Fig. 9.1 *System transformation*

incentives for actors, which in turn encourages shifts in interests and behavior (see figure 9.1). Behavior in turn affects how states define their interests and ultimately their identities. The connection between interests and identities, I noted earlier, arises from the propensity of actors to bring their understandings of themselves in line with their behavior.

The chain of causation flows upwards from actors to the system, and downwards from the system to actors. The larger the system and the more diverse its character, the weaker these links will be and the more difficult the character will be to describe. Regional systems have a greater potential for robustness. They can form and sustain themselves in a weak international society, as the North Atlantic community has, and possess the potential to influence the behavior and character of other regions and the international system as a whole. Here too, influence is a two-way street. The more anarchical an international system becomes, the more threatening it is to the survival of even robust regional orders.

The contemporary international system is at best a weak society, as it is composed of members with diverse values and identities, who interact with one another in a variety of different ways. This makes it impossible to offer a meaningful characterization of the system, which is why liberal and realist theories capture only some of the dynamics at work. It is nevertheless important to acknowledge that a regime has emerged with substantive and procedural rules governing the legitimate use of force. Christ Reus-Smit describes this regime as based on four principles, all of them enshrined in the Charter of the United Nations: (1) recognized sovereign states are legal equals; (2) states possess a variety of rights, among them self-determination and non-intervention except in the most unusual circumstances; (3) to uphold these rights, the international use of force is confined to self-defense and collective peace enforcement; (4) only the Security Council of the United Nations can legitimize the use of force.[217]

---

[217] Reus-Smit, "Unipolarity and Legitimacy."

Some regional societies are more robust. Political, economic and cultural relations among the developed, industrial powers, especially the democratic ones, are very different in character than among authoritarian regimes with weak, corrupt and largely state-controlled economies and with large armies that often play important independent roles in domestic and foreign politics. Western Europe, North America and much of the Pacific increasingly resemble a Kantian world in their interactions with one another – although not with everyone else – while the Middle East, parts of Africa and the Indian subcontinent remain largely Hobbesian.

Contestation over standing in the international system is an indication of its diversity. Different claims to standing reflect different value systems, and in the absence of a value consensus, even among the most powerful actors, there is no effective way of adjudicating among them. Diversity is good for a system to the extent that it allows and legitimizes multiple hierarchies, making international society more like its domestic counterparts. Predictably, the United States, far and away the dominant military power, looks askance at this prospect because its national security elite sees only negative implications for its standing and influence. Since the emergence of the modern international system, great powers have always sought to maintain control over standing, the means by which it is determined and who is allowed to compete for it. The current situation is different in the sense that there is only one superpower, the United States, whose military capabilities dwarf those of any other power. Since the end of the Cold War, most countries have until quite recently cut back on military spending, while the United States has consistently increased its own. In 2003, the United States spent $417 billion on defense, 47 percent of the world total.[218] In 2008, it spent 41 percent of its national budget on the military and the cost of past wars, and accounted for almost 50 percent of world defense spending. This was twice the total of Japan, Russia, the United Kingdom, Germany and China combined. Not surprisingly, it is the only state with a global military reach.[219] Democratic and Republican administrations alike have bet that extraordinary levels of military expenditure will sustain, if not increase, the standing and influence that traditionally come with military dominance. It is intended to make the United

---

[218] SIPRI, "The Major Spenders in 2003," available at www.sipri.se.
[219] Global Issues, "World Military Spending," February 25, 2007, available at www.globalissues.org/Geopolitics/ArmsTrade/Spending.asp#USMilitarySpending; Christopher Hellman, "Highlights of the Fiscal Year 2008 Pentagon Spending Request," February 5, 2007, available at www.armscontrolcenter.org.

States, in the words of former secretary of state Madeleine Albright, "the indispensable nation," the only power capable of enforcing order.[220]

It is not difficult to imagine a world in which multiple hierarchies based on different conceptions of standing become increasingly a reality. The response to the invasion of Iraq by some of America's closest allies and trading partners indicates the extent to which considerable informal movement in this direction has already taken place. As we have seen, public opinion polls reveal that respect for the United States has plummeted by reason of its unilateral foreign policies and military intervention in Afghanistan and Iraq. This decline is independent of perceptions of American power, which remain uniformly high. This contrast indicates the extent to which criteria other than military and economic power have become important for standing. The interesting question, and one very much amenable to empirical investigation, is the extent to which this decline has been the result of a shift in values or a judgment that the United States has not acted in a manner consistent with values on which its claim to standing is based, or both. Regardless of the causes, declining respect for the United States, documented in every region of the world, helps to explain why the most powerful state in history finds it increasingly difficult to translate its power into influence. It has lost any *hēgemonia* it may have possessed and is increasingly judged an *archē*. In this circumstance, its military power is perceived as more of a threat than a benefit.

Multiple domestic hierarchies arise and flourish in civil society not only because states provide law and order but because actors seeking recognition and standing voluntarily accept limits on their powers. The more robust regional orders become, and the more peaceful the international environment becomes, the more multiple hierarchies can be expected to emerge at both regional and international levels. States will feel more confident about seeking standing in diverse ways and devoting resources toward this end that might otherwise be reserved for security. World public opinion has responded positively to these changes and by the ways these countries have sought standing. The BBC World Service poll conducted in early 2007, to which I referred earlier when documenting the low standing of the United States, indicates a significant increase in the standing of countries associated with alternate visions of the international system. When asked what countries exerted a positive influence in

---

[220] Quoted in Alison Mitchell, "Clinton Urges NATO Expansion in 1999," *New York Times*, October 23, 1996, p. A20.

the world, Canada and Japan topped the list at 54 percent, followed by France (50), Britain (45), China (42) and India (37).[221]

It is not inconceivable that the concept of honor could become relevant again to relations among states, supplementing or supplanting standing. Canada and Germany have already redirected their resources, and they are not alone. Their military budgets were slashed dramatically in the aftermath of the Cold War. At the same time, Germany dramatically increased the resources earmarked for development, directing most, but by no means all of them to the former East Germany. In February 2006, Donald Rumsfeld bitterly complained that Germany was spending only 1.45 percent of its GDP on defense, less that 10 percent of what the United States spends.[222] Canada increased its foreign aid and restructured its armed forces to make them a more effective tool for rapid intervention in civil emergencies at home and overseas.[223] New Zealand did something similar while the Cold War was still raging.[224] Leaders in both countries had little difficulty in selling these policies to public opinion as responses to real needs and national values. In Canada, international peacekeeping, foreign aid and the role of honest broker have been central to the national identify since the 1950s.[225]

Positive responses at home and abroad to foreign policies of this kind encourage leaders to pursue them. This can set up a positive reinforcement cycle in which praise and respect from third parties builds national esteem, plays well politically and strengthens the link between such policies and national identity. Such a processes has been underway for some time in Germany and Canada and to a lesser extent in Japan. In Japan, the end of the Cold War has served as a catalyst for a debate about the national identity, and the ways it is advanced or hindered by a pacifist–international versus a more nationalist–military orientation of the country's foreign

[221] *The Age* (Melbourne), March 6, 2007, p. 7.

[222] *Atlantic Review*, February 2, 2006, "Defense Budgets: US Spends too Much and Europe Spends too Little?," available at http://atlanticreview.org/archives/266-Defense-budget-US-spends-too-much-and-Europe-spends-too-little.html. The German figures refer to FY 2003. Under Chancellor Angela Merkel, defense spending increased to 23.9 billion euros in 2007.

[223] Minister's Monitoring Committee, *Final*, p. 9; Oliver, "How Much Was Never Enough?"

[224] Phil Goff, "New Zealand in the International Environment," speech to the "Leadership in Complex Environments" conference at Massey University, November 25, 2005, available at www.beehive.govt.nz/ViewDocument.aspx?DocumentID = 24456; Gentiles, "New Zealand Defence Policy"; O'Brien, "Influences on New Zealand Defence Policy." See also *The Government's Defence Policy Framework* (2000), available at www.nzdf.mil.nz/downloads/pdf/public-docs/defencepolicyframeworkjune2000.pdf.

[225] Chandler, *What is Canada?*

policy.[226] To the extent that the more international orientation remains dominant in Japan, China plays a responsible role in Asia, India and Pakistan avoid another military conflict, the Middle East remains troubled but its problems remain largely confined to its own region, the European Union prospers and successfully incorporates the countries of Eastern Europe, and Russia strengthens its economic and political links with both the EU and China, fear is likely to decline as a foreign policy motive, and appetite and spirit are likely to increase accordingly. States will have strong incentives to seek standing on the basis of criteria associated with these motives and to spend less on the maintenance of powerful military forces. Alternative conceptions of standing will develop and coexist, while claims for standing on the basis of military power will become less persuasive. As standing confers influence, states will have additional incentives to shift their foreign policies.

In such a world states would view even more negatively the use of force in the absence of unqualified international support, or at the very least authorization from the United Nations Security Council. From the vantage point of, say, the year 2030 we might look back on the Iraq War as one of the defining moments of the international relations of the twenty-first century because of the way it delegitimized the unilateral use of force and accelerated the emergence of alternative measures of standing. If so, the United States would be well advised to rethink its approach to international relations. Continued emphasis on military spending and the use of threats or actual force will become even less efficacious in attaining their goals and more corrosive of American standing internationally.

The world does not need to move down the path I have described. In different circumstances, it could become increasingly fear-driven, making security a more important, if not primary, concern for a larger number of actors. Imagine some kind of military confrontation on the Korean peninsula or in the Taiwan Straits, an Indo-Pakistani war, greater tensions in the Middle East involving Israel, Palestinians and their Arab neighbors, an implosion of Iraq that draws in Iranian and Turkish forces, Iranian development of nuclear weapons, military action against Iran by either Israel or the United States, an escalating conflict between Georgia and Russia and Russia and the Baltic states, bio- or nuclear terrorism by non-state actors or the use of nuclear weapons in any of these conflicts. Any of

---

[226] On Japan's debate about its identity as reflected in its foreign policy, Luck, "Tokyo's Quixotic Quest for Acceptance"; Rozman, "Japan's Quest for Great Power Identity"; Pyle, *The Japanese Question*; Hughes, "Japan's Re-emergence as a 'Normal' Military Power."

these developments, particularly if they reinforce one another in synergistic ways, would radically alter our understanding of the international
environment. In such a world, most states would direct more resources
to security, and the American military might be evaluated more positively by many of the actors who now regard it as a threat to peace and
international order – assuming that Washington is not perceived to be an
instigator of any of these conflicts, and is a status quo, not a revisionist
power. In this pessimistic scenario, not only would American standing
increase, but military power as a basis of standing would be reaffirmed.

As we all know, social expectations can be made self-fulfilling.[227] By
behaving as if there is really a "war against terror" and that Muslims hate
America, the Bush administration helped to transform its rhetoric into
an ever greater reality. Its invasion of Iraq arguably accelerated nuclear
proliferation by Iran and North Korea, which it was supposed to deter.
In classical Greece we observed how the seemingly robust regional norms
that helped to constitute Hellenic society were eroded during the runup
to the Peloponnesian War and were almost destroyed in the course of it.
The First World War and the crises preceding it offer another example
of this dynamic. In both cases, competition for standing, closely related
to needs for self-esteem, helped to transform the societies in question
into fear-based worlds. These transitions were accompanied by rhetoric
that portrayed the world as a never-ending struggle for power in which
any policies that advanced power and wealth by almost any means were
justified. Justice was equated with helping one's friends and hurting one's
enemies. Realist approaches to foreign affairs helped to bring about and
justify such worlds. The world is once again at a crossroads, and the
behavior of the most powerful actors in the international system has the
potential to reaffirm traditional modes of behavior or transform the character of the international system. That behavior, as always, is never simply
a response to the so-called "realities" of international life, but to understandings mediated by the conceptions intellectuals and policymakers
bring to bear. As Hans Morgenthau so well understood, the true role of
international theory is not to anchor policies in timeless verities but to
provide leaders with the conceptions they need to grasp the potential
and the feasibility of bringing about a positive change in the nature of
international politics.[228]

---

[227] Lebow, *White Britain and Black Ireland*, for an analysis of the dynamics of how this occurs
and its application to Anglo-Irish relations.
[228] Morgenthau, *Decline of Democratic Politics*, pp. 75–6.

Constructivism maintains that agents and structures are mutually constitutive. Individuals and states create societies that reflect their identities and interests, and these societies in turn influence, if not shape, the interests and identities of actors. Actors and societies continue to evolve through an interactive process. The first, and perhaps principal task constructivists confront is to understand the dynamics that drive this process so its outcomes can be monitored. Paradoxically, the stronger and more frequent the interactions between actors and their societies, the denser the networks linking them together, making it more difficult to discover those interactions most responsible for change. Their consequences are also difficult, if not impossible to predict, because they are almost certainly non-linear. Seemingly large changes can be dampened down over time, while small ones can be amplified. This section of the chapter, and this book more generally, have sought to identify some of the dynamics and the pathways by which changes in interests and identities interact among individual and social units. I will return to this question in the conclusion.

10

General findings and conclusions

Troia (nefas!) commune sepulcrum Asiae Europaeque
Troia virum et virtutum omnium acerba cinis . . .
Troy – the horror! – common grave of Asia and Europe,
Troy, cruel tomb of all heroes and heroism . . .

Catullus[1]

This book develops a framework for the study of politics and derives from it a theory of international relations. I elaborate only part of this theory in detail – that having to do with the spirit – because it is the motive more or less ignored by political science. I posit three fundamental motives that reflect universal human needs – appetite, spirit and reason – and a fourth – fear – that grows in importance in proportion to the failure of reason to constrain appetite or spirit. Each motive has an associated "logic" that prompts specific approaches to cooperation, conflict and risk-taking. Appetite, spirit and reason have the potential to generate orders, each associated with a different form of hierarchy and principle of justice, or a combination of principles in the case of reason. Fear can also produce order, but as Aristotle, Hobbes and Weber recognize, it is likely to be short-lived if it is not associated with some principle of justice that brings about a high voluntary degree of compliance.[2]

My theory is dynamic because it accepts change as the norm, defined as movement away from rather than towards any postulated equilibrium. So-called structures, including the orders and hierarchies I describe, are ideal types, never encountered in practice. They are also "snapshots" of an ever changing social reality. As change is the norm, robustness has nothing to do with an order's proclivity to return to a previous state. Rather it is a function in the first instance of the degree to which elites conform to the "rule packages" associated with their respective status or office, and thus act in accord with the principle of justice on which

---

[1] Catullus, 68th Poem, lines 89–90.   [2] See my discussion of these authors in chapter 2.

their status or office is based. Robustness is also affected by the degree of correspondence between hierarchies and the principles of justice on which they are based. Hierarchies and their associated practices evolve, as does the degree of support for different principles of justice, making them important catalysts of change in their own right.

My theory is dialectical in the same sense as Marxism. The success of appetite-, spirit- and even fear-based orders creates the conditions for their transformation by sharpening their inner tensions and making them more visible to actors. Unlike Marxism, my theory is not deterministic because it recognizes the fundamental importance of agency. Leadership, elite behavior and chance determine whether orders achieve their potential; it is not preordained as is the progressive evolution of feudalism, capitalism and socialism in Marxism. Agents, external pressures and chance also determine how long orders endure. My theory is open-ended in a more fundamental sense: it is embedded in a theory of history that predicts shifts between appetite- and spirit-based societies and the evolution in the ways these motives find expression. The same is true of the hierarchies on which these orders are based. I define progress in terms of growing complexity, but it is neither linear nor normative; there are numerous setbacks in the form of stagnant or collapsing orders, and some of the most reprehensible political orders displayed great complexity. Evolution does not lead to some culminating order, and with it an end to history. Human societies never stop evolving and much of their development is spurred by agents who push for change on the basis of reflection on their lives and the lessons of the past. Self-reflection shapes human goals and behavior, and is a catalyst for shifts in the hierarchy of motives and how they are expressed and the relative appeal of different and often competing conceptions of justice.

My theory is interactionist. Actors are not born with a hierarchy of motives but are socialized to them. This process is far from perfect, and behavior always displays considerable variation. In systems or societies where there is no consensus about values and norms actors have greater leeway and all the more so when competing discourses are available. Some deliberately choose to become deviants and violate the dominant norms. Social interaction occurs within and across levels of social aggregation. The former is by far the most important, as interactions among actors help to shape, sustain or change their hierarchy of motives, identities and interests. Changes in the identities and interests of actors can change the character of the society in which they interact. Modern societies are composed of large numbers of individuals, so change is unlikely to have an amplifying effect until it becomes quite widespread, and especially among elites. At the regional and international levels, where there are fewer actors, systems will be more sensitive to unit-level change. When powerful actors violate accepted norms, it can have a more disruptive, even transformative, effect. Changes at the system level create new incentives and constraints for actors, which in turn can accelerate the process of unit-level change.

My theory is rooted in the Greeks but draws heavily on Durkheim. I contend, and my cases offer support for the proposition, that compliance to norms is most effectively achieved through socialization and informal mechanisms of social control of the kind described by Durkheim.[3] Durkheim is connected to the Greeks through Montesquieu, who was a close reader of both Plato and Aristotle. Like Aristotle, Durkheim makes community and the human needs it fulfills the starting point of his analysis. He understands that the order communities need to function derives from the legitimacy of their *nomos*. Only when voluntary compliance is high can informal mechanisms of social control hope to reduce deviance. I largely ignore Durkheim's analysis of human needs and community and emphasize instead his mechanisms of social control.[4] I focus more on conflict than cooperation, not because I believe it is the default condition of international relations, but because realists claim conflict and war as their home turf. I want to demonstrate that these phenomena cannot be understood without taking the spirit into account and how in all but the most conflictual international environments, norms and compliance sustain at least a thin society that makes international relations far from the condition of anarchy assumed by most realists. In a follow-on volume that expands upon my conception of political order, Aristotle's and Durkheim's conceptions of human needs and community will figure prominently.

There is an important normative aspect to my theory. By normative I do not mean prescriptive, but rather concern for the kinds of social arrangements that promote human fulfillment. Greater complexity can give rise to orders with more open hierarchies and diverse routes for satisfying appetite and spirit. This outcome is far from inevitable as complexity can lead to new kinds of tyranny, some of them ostensibly democratic in form, as Tocqueville noted. Nor do societies with porous hierarchies

---

[3] Durkheim, *The Division of Labor in Society*, pp. 400–1.
[4] Comments by Bertrand Badie at my seminar presentation, Institut d'Études Politiques de Paris, April 3, 2007.

and diverse routes to honor and standing necessarily make for happier people. Enlightenment philosophers and their intellectual descendants naively believed that reason could sweep away superstition and oppression and replace it with just social orders that would enable people to find fulfillment. Modernity did not live up to this promise, and some thinkers, in the tradition of the anti-Enlightenment, hold reason responsible for the worst horrors of the twentieth century.[5] Beginning with Rousseau, various thinkers, among them Durkheim, identify alienation and anomie as quintessential modern ailments that can make people in commercial societies more miserable than their ancestors.[6] My theory suggests that social arrangements are only part of the solution to human happiness and fulfillment. They have the potential to create the conditions in which these ends become possible but their realization depends on agents. As Plato and Aristotle recognize, they must engage in a life-long process of self-education in which reason first constrains and then educates appetite and spirit alike. Aristotle and Tocqueville contend that they must also enter into relationships and engage in civic activities, both of which stretch the definition of self and bring satisfaction through social commitments and group achievements.

In this chapter I recapitulate my understanding of human motives and their implication for the behavior of individuals and states and the systems to which their interactions give rise. I offer a succinct restatement of my ideal-type description of honor-based societies, which I have used as a template for identifying spirit-based values and behavior in historical worlds. I review my empirical findings to assess the extent to which they offer evidence in support of the links I hypothesize between motives and behavior. My cases also suggest propositions that go beyond individual cases. They concern the rise of the state, prospect theory, the role of parvenu powers, power transition and the abuse of power. These findings prompt some concluding observations about the psychology of identity, the relationship between identity and order and that among power, influence and justice.

Motives

The spirit refers to the universal human drive for self-esteem. By excelling at activities valued by society we win the approbation of those who

---

[5] For example, Strauss, *Natural Right and History*; Bauman, *Modernity and Ambivalence*.
[6] Rousseau, *Discourse on the Origin and Foundations of Inequality*; Durkheim, *Suicide* and *Division of Labor in Society*.

matter and we feel good about ourselves. Institutions and states have neither psyche nor emotions. However, the people who comprise and run them do. They often project their psychological needs on to their political units, and feel better about themselves when those units win victories or perform well. In classical Greece the polis was the center of political life and a citizen's status was usually a reflection of that of his polis. Transference and standing by association are just as evident in the age of nationalism where the state has become the relevant unit.

The drive for esteem, reflected in the striving for honor or standing, is distinct from appetite and often at odds with it. We routinely refuse food, drink, gifts and sex in circumstances where they would be compromising. The active pursuit of honor and standing by individuals and states is often costly; vast sums have been spent on colonies, national airlines and space exploration, often with no expectation of net material gain. Foolhardy feats in battle, accepting war under unfavorable circumstances or building battle fleets that needlessly provoke a conflict with another major power indicate that honor and standing are not infrequently pursued at significant cost to security.

Following Plato and Aristotle, whose respective understandings of human motives I elaborate in chapter 3, I maintain that the spirit is only one of three fundamental human drives, the others being appetite and reason. We are familiar with the concept of appetite, which dominates contemporary thinking about the world and our paradigms of international relations. Liberalism, Marxism and Wendt's version of constructivism are rooted in appetite. They view appetite positively and imagine peaceful, productive worlds in which material well-being is a dominant value. They differ about how such worlds are to be achieved, and about the distribution of wealth within them. None of the principal theories within these paradigms admit that they are describing ideal-type worlds, although some recent formulations of Marxism come close to accepting the socialism envisaged by Marx as something akin to a Platonic form towards which we must strive but are unlikely ever to achieve.[7] Liberals, by contrast, offer their theories as descriptions of societies that already exist or are coming into being. Proponents of globalization predict the worldwide triumph of liberal, democratic, trading states. When this happens they expect the distinction between the "is" and the "ought" to disappear. In my judgment, we must keep this distinction clearly in mind

---

[7] Jessop, "Bringing the State Back In (Yet Again)," and *The Capitalist State*, pp. 258–9; Harvey, *The New Imperialism*.

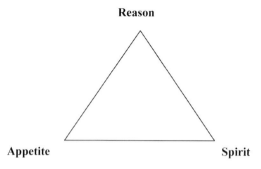

Fig. 10.1 *Motives*

and recognize that liberalism, like Marxism, describes different versions of an ideal-type appetite-based world.

We can represent human motives and their consequences for behavior with two triangles. The first triangle (figure 10.1) has reason at its apex and appetite and spirit at its base. It allows us to represent order; the closer to the reason apex any society resides, the more ordered it is. To the degree that order is based on some widely accepted principle of justice, it will also be more stable.

When reason loses control over appetite or spirit, *nomos* is no longer enacted habitually and is increasingly violated, raising the prospect of a rapid phase transition into a fear-based world. The vertices of triangle 2 (see figure 10.2) are accordingly represented by appetite, spirit and fear. It is an inverse triangle, a shape that allows me to represent a fear-based world on the bottom, in keeping with our long-standing Western tradition that movement towards order and justice is upwards and toward disorder and injustice is downwards.

Most real worlds are found within both triangles. Their actors are motivated by appetite, spirit and reason, and are located somewhere inside the first triangle. As reason never fully constrains and educates the appetite and spirit, many worlds also contain a component of fear. Historically, fear has always been present in the international system. Real worlds are mixed worlds because they are lumpy; different actors reveal different mixes of motives because systemic conditioning and incentives are never fully determining. They cannot be represented in either triangle by a point, but rather by a shaded area, darker where more actors are found, and lighter at the peripheries. By identifying roughly where societies reside within triangle 2 we can infer important things about their politics, including the

Fig. 10.2 *Fear*

basis and degree of cooperation, the nature of conflict and the frequency of violence or war, and actors' propensity for risk-taking. With a large number of cases we could determine the distribution of societies across time and cultures to see if certain mixtures of motives were more common and stable than other configurations.

I theorize two kinds of movement within my triangles. The first is up and down: that is, away from and towards fear-based worlds. When reason the drive loses control of either appetite or spirit, actors no longer understand why self-restraint is in their fundamental interest and behave in ways that threaten the ability of others to satisfy their appetites or spirits, and, in extreme circumstances, their survival. Tensions escalate as actors driven by fear seek to lock in their advantages through preemption or any other action that will confer an advantage. Domestic societies are generally least likely to descend toward fear-based worlds, although the phenomenon is hardly unknown. Regional societies are less robust, and more difficult to keep from breaking up and becoming fear-dominated. Historically, there was no such thing as international society, and relations among political units not part of the same regional society were interest- or fear-based. International society is a very recent phenomenon, having developed in the late nineteenth century at the earliest, and even today is extraordinarily lumpy and populated by actors and regions whose fundamental values are at odds with other actors and regions.[8]

The second kind of movement is horizontal, and consists of *longue durée* oscillation between appetite- and spirit-based worlds. Hunter-gatherer and early agricultural societies were appetite-based, as meeting basic needs, especially food, tended to be difficult. Once a division of labor forms, many of these societies gradually evolve into spirit-based worlds.

---

[8] Watson, *Evolution of International Society*, for the recent history and expansion of international society.

A warrior class often emerges and justifies its privileges on the basis of the security it provides for the society as a whole. With additional wealth, new classes arise – including merchants and administrators – who may challenge the primacy of the warrior elite, and if successful, initiate a shift back toward appetite as the dominant motive. If and when wealth becomes widespread, and with it access to the material goods that provide markers of standing, it becomes correspondingly more difficult to sustain a hierarchy based on affluence. This circumstance provides an incentive for movement back toward a spirit-based world, although one far removed from a warrior society. Postindustrial society, I contend, may be in its early stages of such a shift.

Reason, affect and order

One source of movement in my triangles is the change in the degree to which reason constrains and educates appetite and spirit. As the Greeks were the first to understand, reason exists on multiple levels. Instrumental reason, to use Weber's term, is its simplest expression, and describes the kinds of strategic calculations that enable us to pursue, and often satisfy, our desires in the external world. David Hume was right in calling it the "slave of the passions" because instrumental reason has no ability to alter or shape them; at best it can restrain them when action in inappropriate circumstances would likely lead to failure or punishment. A second, higher form of reason, is called *phronēsis* by Aristotle and is generally translated into English as practical reason. It is the product of reflection on the consequences of our behavior and that of others, especially positive role models. For Aristotle, it is concerned with particulars, but can help make for a better life by influencing how we attempt to achieve important goals.[9] Adam Smith describes a similar kind of reflection for which the market is a catalyst. It can teach self-interested people prudence, discipline and a set of qualities Smith calls "propriety," which leads us to defer short-term gratification for longer-term, more substantial rewards.[10] For Plato and Aristotle, reason is also a drive in its own right that seeks to understand what makes for the happy life and to educate the appetite and spirit to

---

[9] Aristotle, *Nichomachean Ethics*, 1139a29–30, 1139a29–1142a. Thucydides, 3.82.4 refers to something similar in describing the stasis at Corcyra. People were no longer able to practice moderation or act with "practical intelligence" (*to pros hapan xuneton*).

[10] Smith, *Theory of Moral Sentiments*, I.i.5, VI.i.

work with it toward that end.[11] It has the potential to lead us to wisdom. Plato created ideal-type reason-informed worlds in his *Republic* and *Laws*. In our own time, John Rawls and Jürgen Habermas have theorized about such worlds, based on different principles of justice. Reason-informed worlds will always remain an ideal, but any degree of order, whether in appetite- or spirit-based societies, must contain a significant component of reason.

Instrumental reason is a double-edged sword. It makes it possible for individuals to satisfy their appetites and spirit. It is the foundation of order because it makes human actions more regular and predictable. Instrumental reason allows people to make connections between ends and means to maximize their chances of getting what they want. It leads them to recognize the advantages of pursuing their goals in socially sanctioned ways. The majority of people stop on red and go on green, whether the signals emanate from traffic lights or prospective business or sex partners. Societies can accordingly shape their behavior by virtue of the motives they emphasize, the channels they deem appropriate for their attainment and the rules they associate with these channels. Instrumental reason can also be disruptive. Actors intent on achieving their goals recognize that there are shortcuts in the form of free-riding and cheating. Both kinds of behavior have the potential to undermine the *nomos* that sustains order and predictability. Free-riding and cheating arouse the concerns, if not the fears, of other actors, encouraging them to behave in similar ways, if only to protect themselves and their interests. When enough actors violate *nomos*, those who continue to play by the rules are at a serious disadvantage and have strong incentives to follow suit. We witnessed such downward spirals in Greece, the late Roman Republic, the Roman Empire and modern Europe.

The second level of reason – let us stay with Aristotle's characterization of it as *phronēsis* – leads actors to reformulate their behavior on the basis of reflection. It goes beyond simple feedback that lets actors calibrate their behavior to make it more accurate or effective. It involves learning about one's environment and how it works. It can enhance order and predictability when actors come to appreciate that their ability to satisfy their appetites or spirit is enhanced by, or even depends on, a robust society, and it is thus in their interest to act in ways to make that a reality.

---

[11] Deutsch, *Nerves of Government*, also offers a three-step approach to learning. The first two levels involve "steering," based on feedback. They allows people or organizations to calibrate behavior more effectively or to change strategies they use to reach the target. A third feedback loop allows them to refine or alter their goals.

Second-level reason provides incentives for the kinds of community-sustaining activities and individual self-restraint that Tocqueville, drawing on the Greeks, calls self-interest well understood.

Phronēsis for Aristotle and propriety for Smith also lead actors to formulate more refined and elaborate goals. These goals are even more dependent on order and predictability and give actors additional incentives to exercise self-restraint. *Phronēsis* can also prompt recognition that multiple and open hierarchies are ultimately in the common interest. In appetite-based worlds, it led to the counter-intuitive understanding that the world's wealth was not finite and unchanging and that mercantilism, based on this premise, was counter-productive for even powerful actors. *Phronēsis* and propriety are the foundations of successful spirit- and appetite-based worlds that set in motion the dialectical processes described in chapters 4 and 9 that bring about their transformation.

We are emotional beings, not computers. Reason always functions in tandem with affect and can have quite divergent consequences depending on how they interact. Reason combined with positive affect in the form of affection builds empathy. It encourages us to see others as our ontological equals and to recognize the self-actualizing benefits of close relationships. For Plato, *eros* can be educated by reason and directed toward the good and the beautiful and even the kind wisdom concerned with the ordering of states and families.[12] From Socrates to Gadamer, philosophers have maintained that dialogue has the potential to make us recognize the parochial and limited nature of our understandings of justice. Affection and reason together make us seek cooperation, not only as a means of achieving specific ends, but of becoming ourselves. They bring many of us – individuals and social collectivities – to the recognition that self-restraint – that is, self-imposed limitations on our appetites and spirit – is essential to sustain the kinds of environments in which meaningful cooperation becomes possible. Reason almost always interacts with affect. Instrumental reason divorced from emotional commitments only reinforces actors' conceptions of themselves as autonomous and egoistic. It leads them to act in selfish, if sometimes efficient, ways, and to frame relationships with others as purely strategic means of achieving goals. In these circumstances, reason can intensify conflict and prevent the emergence of, or undermine, the kinds of communities that enable actors to advance their interests and satisfy their spirit more effectively. Modern social science, which

---

[12] Plato, *Symposium*, 209a–b, who distinguishes *eros* from *epithumia*, unreasoning or animal desires, that at best can be brought under control; Hall, *Trouble with Passion*, p. 65.

welcomes, utilizes and propagates such an understanding of human beings, stands in sharp contrast to traditional philosophy, not only in its assumptions about human beings, but in the kinds of behavior it encourages and endorses.

Social science as a whole has given short shrift to the role of emotions. It is undeniably central to psychology, but for some decades that field attempted to subsume emotions to cognition, and it is only in recent years that emotions have become an important subject of study in their own right. Research in neuroscience indicates that emotions are involved in decision-making, generally in a positive way, and from the earliest stage of deciding what information deserves our attention.[13] In political science, emotions have always been recognized as important, but our discipline has stressed their negative influence on behavior.[14] The time is long overdue for both disciplines to acknowledge and study the positive contribution of emotions, harnessed to reason, order and cooperation. Reason and affect together have the potential to encourage the enlightened and restrained behavior necessary to preserve *nomos*, or reform it to more closely approximate widely accepted principles of justice.

Theory and cases

The core of my theory concerns the different logics governing cooperation, conflict and risk-taking I associate with reason-, spirit-, appetite- and fear-based worlds. These are described in chapter 2 and summarized below.

In *reason-informed worlds* cooperation is the norm because actors understand that it is a precondition for human happiness and fulfillment. Conflict exists but is relatively easy to resolve because actors share fundamentally similar goals and the same conception of justice. Propensity for risk-taking depends on the nature of the society and its principle of justice.

In *spirit-based worlds*, cooperation is also routine. It is based on appeals to friendship, common descent and mutual obligation more than it is on mutual interest. Actors of high status are expected to assist those dependent on them, while actors of lower status are obliged to serve their protectors or patrons. Cooperation in honor societies is most difficult among

---

[13] Important exceptions include the work of Clore, "Cognitive Phenomenology," and Clore *et al.*, "Affective Feelings as Feedback"; Damasio, *Descartes' Error*; Gray, *The Psychology of Fear and Stress*. For a good review of the literature, see McDermott, "The Feeling of Rationality."

[14] An important exception is Marcus *et al.*, *Affective Intelligence and Political Judgment*.

equals because no high-status actor wants to accept the leadership of another and thereby acknowledge that they have greater standing. This makes cooperation difficult even in situations where there are compelling mutual security concerns. Conflict is also routine, and warfare in traditional honor worlds tends to be frequent. Wars between political units in honor societies often resemble duels because they are rule-governed. The ends of warfare and the means by which it is waged also tend to be limited. These limitations generally do not apply to warfare against outsiders or non-elite members of one's own society. Honor-based societies are risk-accepting with respect to both gain and loss. In warrior societies, honor cannot be attained without risk, so leaders and followers alike welcome the opportunity to risk limbs and lives to gain or defend it. Risk-taking will be extended to the defense of material possessions and territory to the degree they have become symbols of honor. Actors will also defend their autonomy at almost any cost because it is so closely linked to honor, unless they can find some justification for disaggregating it from honor that is convincing to themselves and their peers.

In *appetite-based worlds* cooperation is also routine, indeed the norm, and based on common interests. However, it endures only as long as actors share these interests. Relations among actors resemble the kind of shifting coalitions *Federalist* no. 10 expects in the Congress.[15] Conflict is as common as cooperation because actors also have opposing interests. To the extent that reason is present, these conflicts will be non-violent and rule-governed because all actors recognize their overriding interest in maintaining peaceful relations and the institutions, procedures and general level of trust that enable them to best advance their material interests. The outcome of disputes depends on the relative power of actors, the structure and rules of the institutions in which their conflicts are adjudicated, and their skill in framing arguments, bargaining with opponents and building coalitions. Actors are risk-averse when it comes to making gains, and more risk-accepting when they frame the issue as preventing loss.

Fear-based worlds are highly conflictual, and neither the ends nor the means of conflict are constrained by norms. Actors make security their first concern and attempt to become strong enough to deter or defeat any possible combination of likely adversaries. Arms races, reciprocal escalation, alliances and forward deployments intensify everyone's insecurity, as the security dilemma predicts. Fear of a common adversary creates strong incentives for cooperation, but cooperation will last only as long

---

[15] *Federalist Papers*, no. 10 by James Madison.

as the perceived threat. Under some conditions, fear encourages band-wagoning, that is cooperation with the threatening actor, not with those allying against it. Risk-taking is prevalent because security is such an important goal, and loss of security is understood to have catastrophic consequences.

My descriptions of these several ideal-type worlds are drawn from Plato, Aristotle, Augustine and Rawls (reason), Homer and Thucydides (spirit), Smith, Kant and liberalism (appetite) and Thucydides, Hobbes and realism (fear). As Weber recognized, real societies never correspond to ideal types, but ideal types can be used to analyze societies that reveal some of their characteristics and dynamics. I expected to find evidence of all four motives in most, if not all, of my cases, and thus mixed worlds of different kinds. I theorized that multiple motives would reveal themselves as mixtures, not solutions; they would not blend but rather give rise to behavior associated with each of the motives present. Such behavior would present anomalies to existing theories of international relations because they are all rooted in fear- or appetite-based worlds. My emphasis on the spirit should allow me to explain behavior that theories in other paradigms could not, and my theory could do a better job of accounting for behavior more generally because it would not attempt to assimilate it to one motive, or simply ignore it, as other theories do, but explain it with reference to multiple motives.

I have set up two empirical tests for my theory. The first is to demon-strate the utility of the spirit in understanding the foreign policies and character of a wide range of political units and regional and international systems. The second is to show that mixed motives not only give rise to mixed forms of behavior, but behavior that reflect the hierarchy of motives among the actors that constitute the society or system in which they inter-act. This second test is more telling for the theory and more difficult to conduct for several reasons. In modern societies appetite and spirit have become intertwined so actors often seek wealth as a means of gaining sta-tus, making it more difficult to fathom their underlying motives. Actors and systems are no longer isolated the way they were in premodern times, making the international system in which they now act lumpy in the sense of displaying different, and even contradictory, forms of behavior.

My case studies, which comprise the core of chapters 2 through 9, span 2,500 years of Western history. They include one non-Western country: nineteenth- and twentieth-century Japan. My choice of cases reflects my knowledge of history and languages, but I do not doubt that my findings could be replicated in cases drawn from the international history of other parts of Asia, the Middle East, Africa and Latin America. These cases constitute "easy" and "hard" tests for my theory. Fifth-century Greece and the early and middle Roman Republics are relatively "easy" cases because they are recognized by contemporaries and present-day scholars as societies in which honor was among the most highly valued attributes of individuals and cities alike. The "hard" cases are nineteenth- and twentieth-century Europe, societies in which appetite became increasingly dominant and in which honor and standing diverged. In these centuries international relations is also the hardest domain in which to look for manifestations of the spirit, as international society was usually thinner than its domestic counterparts and for so many decades fear is generally considered to have been the paramount motive.

I have accordingly adopted somewhat different strategies for the premodern and modern cases. In chapters 4 through 6 I analyze key episodes in the international relations of ancient, medieval and post-Westphalian Europe. I attempt to ascertain the extent to which they exhibit some or all of the first eleven generic characteristics of spirit-based warrior societies I describe at the end of chapter 3. These characteristics are internal to the society itself. The remaining two characteristics of these societies pertain to cooperation, conflict and risk-taking. They are predictions of the patterns of behavior that we should find in such worlds, and should be manifest to the extent the society in question qualifies as such a world. As all the societies I analyze are mixed worlds, only some of the behavior I attribute to honor worlds will be evident, and accordingly I also look for behavior I associate with appetite and fear.

My remaining cases, which address events that took place between 1870 and 2003, occurred in worlds in which individual actors display a wider variation of motives. My goal is to explain European expansion, World Wars I and II, the course and ending of the Cold War and the Anglo-American invasion of Iraq. I do so by showing the difficulty that security (fear) and interest-based (appetite) explanations have in accounting for these events, and how explanations based on the spirit that connect foreign policy to the search for honor or standing offer more persuasive accounts. I thus attempt to show that the spirit is not only relevant to "hard cases," but that they cannot be understood without taking it into account.

The ancient world

My first case, classical Greece, is undeniably a world in which honor was a primary motive for the aristocratic elite and for many other citizens in democratic Athens. My analysis in chapter 4 indicates that it incorporates to some degree all of the defining characteristics of an honor world. As my theory predicts, it reveals the patterns of cooperation and conflict I associate with such worlds. As appetite and fear were also present, the correspondence is not perfect. There is ample evidence of behavior associated with these other motives: the Athenians invoke fear, honor and interest to explain the acquisition of their empire and their subsequent commitment to retain it. None of the principal actors are fully consistent in their behavior, but the seeking and defending of honor is a priority for many of them. Key individuals and states chose to defend their honor in circumstances where it involved great risk and sacrifice.

This pattern is replicated in Macedonia, Alexander modeled himself on Achilles, led his troops into battle and was wounded while charging the Persian king. It is also typical of the early and middle Roman Republics if Livy and later Roman sources are to be believed. Honor declines as a motive in the late Republic and is secondary to appetite and fear in the Roman Empire. As I expect, Roman politics and foreign policy in these periods only occasionally reflect the kinds of behavior I attribute to honor societies. They nevertheless remain most pronounced in the army, the most traditional Roman institution, where officers sought glory at great risk, not only to themselves, but to their cohorts or legions. However, bravery and the honor it conferred were increasingly sought as a means of obtaining higher rank and the wealth it had the potential to bring in its wake.

One of the more striking features of the ancient world is the extent to which honor and its behavioral implications were recognized, discussed and problematized by poets, historians and philosophers. Homer's *Iliad* was at the core of the Greek educational curriculum. Praise of the spirit and depreciation of appetite is a constant theme in the ancient world, and is even evident in Christian writers such as Augustine. In part this reflects a deeply entrenched cultural preference common to societies that began as warrior societies. It also served as a legitimizing discourse for aristocracies, and almost all of the writers in question came from such backgrounds. Even those able to rise above class prejudices, and a case can be made that Plato did, remain committed to the pursuit of the good life, contemplation and civic engagement, and thus consider appetite as dangerous and destructive.

In Greek and Roman, as in modern times, anti-appetite diatribes became vocal in direct proportion to perceived elite indulgence. This was evident in late fifth- and fourth-century Greece, and in last century of the middle Roman Republic. Aristocrats were the intended target of these critiques, but they also had the effect of making it more difficult to admit wealthy non-aristocrats into the inner circle in which it was possible to compete for standing and honor. The spirit-based discourse accordingly exacerbated class tensions. Because the wealthy non-aristocratic elites of Athens and Rome grew up and were educated in societies in which the spirit was dominant, they did not develop an alternative discourse of their own. They tended to assimilate its values, measure themselves in terms of them and craved entry into the aristocracy.

As honor and standing diverge, the ends and means of warfare undergo a transformation. In late fifth-century Greece, we see more wars in which the objective was no longer a symbolic victory to establish precedence but the decisive defeat of adversaries. The rules of warfare were increasingly honored in the breach. There was greater reliance on ambushes, sieges, peltasts, non-Greek allies, slaves and mercenaries. This in turn eroded the traditional meaning and purpose of battle. It further undermined the honor culture by making fear an increasingly paramount motive given the likely consequences of defeat. The late Roman Republic underwent a similar transformation, but with respect to internal competition. The struggle for power became so acute that high office was increasingly achieved through violence instead of election. Assassinations and riots encouraged ambitious generals to make their own bids for power, leading to Caesar's march on Rome and the end of the Republic. Caesar's assassination triggered off a struggle for power that pitted Roman generals and their armies against each other. Fear and interest became mutually supporting because failure to gain power usually meant one's demise.[16]

When honor and standing diverge, hypocrisy becomes pronounced. Individuals and their political units are intent on achieving standing, now increasingly equated with authority over others achieved by any means, but feel the need to justify their behavior on traditional grounds. They speak the language of the honor culture. At a certain point, hypocrisy becomes transparent and self-defeating, and in the interim the culture may have become more accepting of motives other than honor. The Melian Dialogue is a watershed in this regard, as the Athenians dispense with any pretense (*prophasis*), and justify their invasion of Melos on purely utilitarian grounds.[17] Cleon is said to have bought votes by throwing

[16] There are exceptions to this rule, as the success of Tiberius indicates. He absented himself from Rome and public office to avoid giving the appearance of threatening the succession to power of Agrippa's sons, Gius and Lucius. Only when they died of natural causes did he reemerge and eventually succeed Octavian.
[17] Lebow, *Tragic Vision of Politics*, pp. 124–6, 148 for an analysis.

feasts, and Alcibiades appealed to the assembly for an invasion of Sicily on the grounds that it would make citizens rich.[18] In Rome, generals coerced the Senate into granting them triumphs, deserved or not. The practice became sufficiently widespread that Augustus sought to establish his bona fides by refusing triumphs voted him by the Senate.[19]

The survival and stability of real honor societies depend on their ability to moderate and control the four tensions Homer associates with them. In Greece and Rome these tensions were synergistic. Failure to restrain competition and keep it within the limits established by governing norms facilitated a shift in goals from honor to standing and brought about the transition to a fear-based world in fifth-century Greece and the late Roman Republic. Failure to open elites to newcomers, expand the circle in which the attainment of honor was possible and the means by which it could be won, not only intensified class conflict, it ultimately marginalized the aristocracy and with it, the importance of honor in the society. This phenomenon was most apparent in the late Roman Republic. Admission of new members to the elite can invigorate the society and facilitate expansion and wealth, as it did in the Roman Empire. Success of this kind threatens to transform honor-based societies into societies dominated by appetite. The evidence from my cases offers support for the proposition that honor-based societies are inherently fragile and subject to decay and transformation by two diametrically opposed dialectical processes.

Medieval Europe

The Merovingian and Carolingian dynasties are of theoretical interest because they ruled over a warrior society in which honor was absent and in which appetite was the dominant drive. They were warrior-based appetite societies. Standing was important as a means of achieving wealth, and in the absence of honor, the struggle for standing was unconstrained by norms. The political order was highly unstable and this is the underlying reason why the Frankish Empire and other political units of the era were relatively short-lived. Charlemagne is an interesting figure because of his understanding of the limitations and dangers of rule based almost entirely on his ability to maintain the loyalty of an increasingly large body of retainers through gifts of land and booty gained from raids and conquest. As he could not expand his empire indefinitely, he was anxious

---

[18] Thucydides, 3.37.2.   [19] Eder, "Augustus and the Power of Tradition."

to find some other way of consolidating his rule and making that of his descendants more secure. In an effort to build legitimacy he drew on German and Roman traditions and attempted to reintroduce the concept of honor.

While innovative, Charlemagne's strategy can hardly be considered successful. He gained respect but not legitimacy, and had to put down at least one attempted palace coup. Appetite remained the governing motive, and despite Charlemagne's efforts to encourage piety, his nobles and most church officials remained largely hypocritical in their approach to Christianity and the Church. The Merovingian and Frankish Empires raise the broader question of the extent to which it is possible to have a warrior society without a meaningful concept of honor. The practices Charlemagne found so threatening were the inheritance of a German warrior society cut loose from tribal affiliations and traditions of loyalty and charity that presumably would have made chieftaincy and order easier to maintain. Difficulty also arose from the fact that the Merovingian and Carolingian elite, which had imposed itself on local, once Roman populations, controlled more and richer territory than Germanic tribes had in their traditional settings. Exposed to wealth at a new order of magnitude, their appetites became increasingly unconstrained. The Church was corrupt, and Roman traditions were sufficiently foreign to Charlemagne's immediate retinue that they failed to serve as an effective source of restraint.

I next analyze Anglo-French relations from the Norman invasion through the Hundred Years War, which I treat as two separate but related cases. The Norman invasion of England occurred during the early stages of state formation, at a time when competition for standing among leaders was acute and relatively unconstrained by the norms usually associated with honor societies. The Hundred Years War, the name given to a series of wars between England and France that began in 1337 and ended in 1453, represents another violent epoch of European history, but one in which honor had nevertheless become an important motive for rulers and aristocratic warriors. Chivalry had developed in the interim and some of its values influenced the conduct of warfare.

Like Frankish Gaul, Normandy was a warrior society in which the competition for standing was fierce and more or less unconstrained. England was a more developed society with institutions, traditions and something approaching national sentiment, which, as Edward the Confessor discovered, could only be ignored at considerable political risk. Like Charlemagne, William sought to mobilize local sentiment and legitimate his claims through the support of respected third parties. These were astute political moves having nothing to do with honor, which was not yet a meaningful political concept in either Normandy or England. The spirit was nevertheless omnipresent. It drove leaders to seek standing through office and wealth, and frustration by competitors provoked anger and violence. Tostig, Harald Hardraada and William all made assaults against England to enforce their claims to the throne.

One of the biggest differences between these two eras of European history is the causes of war. Charlemagne's campaigns were motivated as much by security as by the desire to enhance his standing through territorial expansion. The Frankish kingdom was vulnerable to Saxon and Muslim marauders. After the conquest of Lombardia, Avar incursions became a serious problem, as did Viking raids along the Channel coast. The Anglo-Norman conflict had little to do with security and everything to do with the relative standing of Harold and William. The same was true of the Hundred Years War, triggered by the conflicting claims of Edward II and Philip VI to the throne of France and the province of Guyenne.

Chivalry developed in the twelfth and thirteenth centuries and reached its peak in the fourteenth and fifteenth centuries during the Hundred Years War. It was rooted in legends about Arthur and Charlemagne, the *chansons de geste* and romantic poems, all suitably reworked to emphasize prowess (*prouesse*), a concept that encompasses courage, competitive assertiveness, loyalty, self-restraint, discipline and service. Chivalry was modeled on Roman *virtu* and its texts rely heavily on Sallust, Livy and other Roman writers. Its heroes are reminiscent of Achilles and are sometimes described with metaphors and similes reminiscent of Homer. Chivalry was a response to a disorderly, violent and appetite-driven world by intellectuals and religious leaders who hoped to create an honor culture and class of knights that would exercise nobility and self-restraint, police society and protect women, orphans and the poor. Instead, it generated an artificial world of jousts and tournaments in which knights competed – at considerable risk – for honor and access to high-born women. These competitions were encouraged by kings and other leaders as a means of winning the loyalty of fighters who in turn enhanced their status.

On the macro level, the Hundred Years War was waged by both sides to achieve political goals, and strategies were chosen or developed to attain those ends regardless of their consequences for non-combatants or the social hierarchy. At the micro level, both armies were brutal and rapacious, but chivalrous practices were also apparent. Discipline was weak, and knights behaved the way their namesakes, the *milites*, did in the early

Roman Republic. Engagements not infrequently threatened to dissolve into a series of Homeric-style one-on-one combats, with the killing of adversaries or taking of prisoners regarded by participants as more important than routing the adversary. In some key encounters chivalry dictated the tactics of armies, even when they were suicidal, as at Crécy in 1346.

As my theory suggests, the mix of motives (appetite, spirit and fear) that characterized this period was reflected in the mixed strategies and tactics of warfare. Some of this behavior (e.g. French tactics at Crécy, the ransoming of high-ranking prisoners, the rapine and pillage that accompanied English *chevauchées* through France) clearly worked against the goal of victory and would otherwise be anomalous. Chivalry on the whole softened war, making fighting less barbaric for the "officer class" of knights. There was a sharp decline in the torture and slaughter of prisoners, and a growing awareness that clerics and civilians should not be treated the same way as combatants.[20] Chivalry created a precedent, ultimately based on Homer, that helped to shape interstate European warfare down to the First World War. The spirit thus served as a source of war and a catalyst for the development of international law and rules governing the conduct of war, especially of sieges and the treatment and exchange of prisoners.[21]

Westphalia to the French Revolution

Europe between 1648 and 1789 offers an informative contrast to the era of the Hundred Years War. Domestic and international society were more robust, especially in Western Europe, making honor a feasible ordering principle. By the sixteenth century, honor had come to be regarded as a more personal attribute, closely associated with physical appearance, military prowess and reputation, qualities that were considered the natural inheritance of the nobility. Honor was thought to elude those who sought it too actively, but to attach itself to those who achieved or displayed it with a cultivated nonchalance.[22] Honor, standing and wealth were now conceptually distinct categories, although not fully differentiated in practice.

With the possible exception of Britain, the distinction between private and state interest had not yet developed. Louis XIV spoke of *la gloire*,

---

[20] Gillingham, "1066 and the Introduction to Chivalry in England"; Contamine, *War and Competition between States*, "Introduction."
[21] Vale, *War and Chivalry*, p. 8.
[22] Huguet, *Dictionnaire de la langue française*, pp. 497–8; Nye, *Masculinity and Male Codes of Honor in Modern France*, p. 16.

which meant his prestige (*considération*) and standing relative to other leaders. His idea of the state as a personal patrimony was widely shared by other rulers and prevailed up to and even beyond the French Revolution in some countries. Louis's vast expenditure on armies and war was a choice, not a necessity, as it was for rulers of the seventeenth and eighteenth centuries. Standing among rulers was determined in the first instance by their success in war. For this reason, so-called enlightened despots tended to be more aggressive than other rulers. Louis XIV and Swedish, Prussian and Austrian rulers also faced pressures from below to make war, as it was a preferred route to reputation, office and wealth for young noblemen. Monarchs had family and dynastic interests, which were not infrequently at odds with state interests, especially when they concerned the pursuit or defense of thrones. Thrones conferred standing and were a major source of conflict, although somewhat less so than in early modern Europe. Marriages, like alliances, were considered a form of statecraft, and intended to enhance a ruler's claims to a throne or a territory while undercutting those of rivals. Two of the major wars of the eighteenth century were triggered by competing claims to the thrones of Spain and Austria.

For most of the seventeenth century Louis XIV's France was at the top of the European status hierarchy. Voltaire compared its level of civilization to classical Greece and Augustan Rome, and French became the language of diplomacy and culture.[23] Palaces, balls, other forms of lavish display, as well as support for science and the arts became secondary arenas of competition and means of claiming standing. Other leaders emulated Louis's pursuit of *gloire*, on the battlefield and in drawing rooms. Palaces sprang up all over Europe, and while not copies of Versailles, their builders sought to emulate its grandeur and to become the focus of equally elaborate court rituals. Kings like Peter I of Russia and Frederick II of Prussia also built up their armies for conquest.

Seventeenth- and eighteenth-century France, and indeed most of Western Europe, represents a variant on the traditional honor society because appetite was positively valued. I see this difference as a reflection of modernity, and its conflation of appetite and spirit. Actors at all levels increasingly sought material possessions, not so much for their inherent use or enjoyment but for the status conferred by their ownership and display.

Between Westphalia and the French Revolution, warfare largely assumed the character I associate with honor societies. Wars were less

---

[23] Voltaire, *The Age of Louis XIV*, pp. 1–5.

frequent, although often on a far grander scale than in the past. Data sets indicate that early modern Europe was proportionately the most warlike era in terms of the number of years in which there was war, with one new war on average every three years. In the sixteenth and seventeenth centuries the great powers were at war 95 percent of the time. The frequency of war drops to 71 percent in the eighteenth century and to 29 percent in a modified nineteenth century (1815–1914).[24] The ends and means of war were limited in comparison to the recent past. Rulers on the whole no longer attempted to assassinate or poison their adversaries, treated ambassadors and other representatives with civility, and addressed each other in the most respectful terms, even when their countries were at war. International law underwent a correspondingly rapid development and was part of the broader effort to regulate and civilize the practice of war.

The most fundamental reason for the limits on warfare was the restricted goals for which wars were fought. For the most part, they were struggles over precedence, and only occasionally involved the destruction of other major political units or recognized buffer states. Relative standing could sometimes be decided by one victory, as in early fifth-century Greece, or by campaigns of maneuver that secured a province or recognition of a ruler's right to that province. The quest for *gloire* nevertheless contributed to the brutality of war, and was responsible, as it was in Roman times, for consistently higher casualty rates among officers. The French in particular sought to achieve fame through their audacity, and their preferred method of warfare was the bayonet charge. This was increasingly suicidal in an age where artillery and musket fire could destroy formations at a distance, and a further indication of the overriding importance of *gloire*.

In the religious wars of the sixteenth and the first half of the seventeenth century, spirit and appetite were important motives, but fear increasingly became the dominant one given the destructiveness of the conflict. The Thirty Years War (1618–48), the last and most destructive of these conflicts, ended in the Peace of Westphalia. It created the conditions for the restoration and enhancement of a transnational European society, which allowed and encouraged European rulers and their states to compete for honor and standing. The Thirty Years War was a catalyst for learning – just as the thirty years war of the first half of the twentieth century would be. Reason to some degree regained its authority over spirit and appetite,

---

[24] Wright, *A Study of War*, pp. 121, 237, 242, 248, 638; Levy, *War in the Modern Great Power System*, pp. 139–41. Hamilton, "The European Wars: 1815–1914," for an overview.

and conscious efforts, not always successful, were made to limit warfare and make it rule-based.

Between Westphalia and the French Revolution, there were numerous wars, at least one of them on a global scale, but violence was limited. With some notable exceptions, civilian populations fared considerably better in war zones, and rules gradually developed to govern their treatment. Another indicator of the restraining effects of reason is that these wars ended by diplomacy short of decisive victories by any of the protagonists. The major exception was the Great Northern War (1699–1721), which ended in the total defeat of Sweden, but only because Charles XII refused to accept a compromise outcome, foolishly invaded Russia and led his army into an exposed position deep in what is now Ukraine, where it was crushed at Poltava. Charles could not restrain his warlike spirit and drive to dominate.

Imperialism and World War I

From the eighteenth century on, Europe is increasingly a mixed society in that appetite and spirit are both important for the elite and growing middle classes. Among almost all the great powers the nobility remained dominant, especially in foreign and military affairs, where it helped to transform honor and standing from class into national goals. The European bourgeoisie did not behave as Marx expected; significant segments of them placed social over class interests and assimilated aristocratic values and practices, especially when it came to foreign policy. This novel and largely unexpected alignment, as Weber observed, allowed the aristocracy to maintain its privileges, and in some countries its political power, in the face of the twin political and economic challenges of working-class democracy and finance capital allied to export-oriented industry.[25] Imperialism was an expression of the partial "feudalization" of the European middle classes that encouraged them to buttress their esteem through the competitive achievements of their respective nations. As in more traditional honor societies, they became angry when their nation was checked or challenged and were willing to go to war in its defense.

My argument bears a superficial resemblance to that of Joseph Schumpeter, who attributes war to the power of the aristocracy and its premodern values. He dismisses the aristocratic preference for war as irrational and "atavistic" in contrast to the rational, interest-driven, peace-oriented

[25] Weber, *Economy and Society*, II, pp. 920–1.

preferences of the commercial classes.[26] I show that there was considerable diversity among European aristocrats in how they accommodated
to modernity, and also among the middle classes in their response to the
aristocracy and its values. The most aggressive policies were pursued by
countries where (1) there was a sizeable middle class; (2) a significant portion of the middle class had become semi-feudalized; (3) and aristocrats
with premodern values dominated government. These conditions were
most pronounced in Germany and Austria, less evident in France and
Russia (for different reasons), and least apparent of all in Great Britain.

My account for World War I is an extension of my analysis of imperialism and once again foregrounds the spirit. It builds on a familiar narrative:
competition becomes more intense when reason loses control of the spirit,
and actors increasingly violate the unwritten rules that are intended to
govern and restrain their competition. Actors are sorely tempted to take
short-cuts to improve their position. If the rules are consistently violated,
society loses its cohesion and honor becomes meaningless. In the course
of such a transition, honor and standing diverge, and actors generally opt
for the latter over the former. This dynamic captures the progression of
European international relations in the late nineteenth and early twentieth century. It helps to explain why Germans considered Britain, the
country that threatened them the least, their most serious adversary, a
phenomenon that constitutes a serious anomaly for any realist account.
A preference for standing over honor also explains German willingness
to invade Belgium in spite of its treaty obligation, dating back to 1839,
to uphold that country's neutrality. German chancellor Bethmann Hollweg publicly acknowledged that the invasion was an "injustice," which he
nevertheless justified on the grounds of necessity. It was only a "necessity" because of Field Marshal Moltke's military plan which called for
using almost all of Germany's available forces to invade and defeat France
before the more slowly mobilizing Russians could advance too far into
East Prussia. Moltke doubted that his plan would work; exercises revealed
that he did not have enough forces to encircle the French army. They also
showed that a defensive strategy would lead to a sure victory on both
the western and eastern fronts. Moltke nevertheless remained committed
to his war plan because he rejected a defensive strategy out of hand as a
violation of his values and code of honor.

While standing and honor diverged at the state level, honor was
very much alive at the personal level. In key decisions, ranging from

---

[26] Schumpeter, *Imperialism*.

commitments to offensive strategies, Austrian desire to seek revenge against Serbia, and German willingness to back Austria, German and Austrian military and political leaders put their personal and class honor above the national interest. At least some of these officials – including the Austrian emperor, foreign minister and chief-of-staff – recognized that their war with Serbia in 1914 was almost certain to trigger a continental war they could not win. The policies of Germany and Austria in 1914, and in the decade leading up to war, cannot effectively be explained in terms of either interest or security, and can readily be accounted for by reference to the spirit.

World War II and the Cold War

Given the seeming dominance of appetite and fear, the twentieth century should be the hardest era in which to demonstrate the importance of the spirit, and World War II the most difficult conflict in which to make this case. I attempt to show that neither appetite nor fear arising from security concerns are capable of explaining the decisions of Germany, Italy and Japan to go to war. Explanations based on spirit not only offer more compelling accounts of these decisions for Italy and Japan but help explain why leaders such as Hitler and Mussolini came to power.

I begin my analysis with post-World War I Germany and the consequences of defeat for the German people. There was deep resentment toward the allies and positive hatred of the Treaty of Versailles. Revealingly, its most offensive feature for many Germans was not the loss of territory, reparations or restrictions on the military that it imposed, but the articles that required Germany to accept responsibility for the war and hand over the Kaiser, and possibly other officials, for trial as war criminals. The Weimar Republic, compelled to sign the treaty by the allies, never achieved legitimacy. Right-wing opponents of democracy, Hitler among them, gained popular support by promising to restore Germany's position in Europe, and with it the esteem of the German people. Hitler's own motives for going to war were pathological because they went far beyond restoration of *status quo ante bellum* to the conquest of Europe, if not the world.[27] Many of his foreign policy and defense initiatives – among them withdrawal from the League of Nations, the rearmament of Germany, *Anschluss* with Austria and dismemberment of

[27] Weinberg, *The Foreign Policy of Hitler's Germany*, I, p. 358; Rich, *Hitler's War Aims*, I, pp. 3–10; Bullock, *Hitler*, pp. 10–11, 622; Fest, *Hitler*, pp. 213–18.

Czechoslovakia – were welcomed enthusiastically by most Germans and Austrians. His wars against Poland, Western Europe, Yugoslavia, Greece and the Soviet Union were less popular, but what support they did have derived in large part from the same motives.[28] The importance of honor to the officer corps secured Hitler the quiescence, if not the active support, of the German army, and its willingness to keep fighting long after officers of every rank realized the hopelessness, if not the evil character, of their cause.

The spirit was an equally important motive for Italy and Japan. Neither country was attempting to live down the consequences of defeat and partial territorial dismemberment, but their aggressive, expansionist policies can be described in large part as efforts to gain standing in the international system. Both countries achieved great power status only belatedly. Italy emerged as a nation state in the latter half of the nineteenth century and was a great power in name only. It was the last European country to obtain a colonial empire, suffered a grievous defeat in Ethiopia in 1896 and arguably put in the worst military performance of any major combatant in World War I. Although on the winning side, Italy satisfied only some of its far-ranging territorial ambitions, and right-wing anti-republican forces convinced many Italians that Britain and France had robbed them of their due. Their success in transforming Italy into a revisionist power was not merely the result of the right's tactical skill, but of the predisposition of middle-class Italians to see themselves and their country as weak, lacking respect and vulnerable to the machinations of other powers.

Territorial aspirations, disillusionment with a stagnant parliamentary system and a severe economic crisis made it possible for Mussolini to achieve power by a combination of legal and extra-legal means and gradually impose a dictatorship. His foreign policy, increasingly at odds with Italy's strategic and economic interests, was intended to consolidate and strengthen his regime by creating a modern-day Roman *imperium* that would enhance the esteem of Italians. Germany posed the principal threat to Italy, but Mussolini chose to ally with it against Britain and France because the latter two countries were considered the barriers to colonial expansion in the Mediterranean. Mussolini entered World War II erroneously believing that a German victory was all but inevitable and that Italy could only satisfy its territorial ambitions by being on the winning side. While his decision for war was idiosyncratic and based on bad judgment, the invasion of France was widely supported by the Italian elite.

---

[28] Kershaw, *The "Hitler Myth,"* pp. 151–68.

The Japanese had even more compelling reasons for hostility to the status quo powers, as they had been the object of European economic exploitation and racism and only grudgingly accepted as a great power. In an earlier stage of their history, they had struggled to assert their equality with China, from whom, via Korea, they had received much of their culture. Japanese colonialism in China and Korea was in large part motivated by the desire for recognition and standing, from Asian as well as European audiences. These motives also lay behind Japan's aggression against China in the 1930s, although it also reflected a desire for economic autarchy and the struggle for power between the army and the civilian leadership. Japanese military aggression had much to do with problems of modernity; threatened aristocrats clung to premodern values and the middle class also failed to develop the kind of world view Marx associated with the bourgeoisie. Japanese inability to bring the war in China to a successful conclusion prompted its leadership to begin a wider war against the European colonial powers and the United States. The attack on Pearl Harbor made no strategic sense given the military commitment Japan already had in China and the far greater military potential of the United States. Both the Japanese calculations about the American response, and their willingness to take extraordinary risks with their own security, must be understood in terms of the spirit-driven values of a traditional warrior class.

In my analysis of Germany, Italy and Japan, I offer four explanations for World War II: the survival of prefeudal values; late recognition of these three countries as great powers; leaders' needs to pursue aggressive foreign policies to sustain themselves in power; and pathological leaders driven to commit acts of aggression at home and abroad for personal rather than political reasons. These explanations are related and synergistic in their consequences, and collectively highlight the importance of the spirit as a motive for key actors in all three countries.

The origins of World War II show important differences and similarities with World War I. Among the initiators of that conflict, honor was less important for key actors in Germany and Italy. Neither Hitler nor Mussolini was concerned with honor, and nor could their behavior in any way be considered honorable. Both took a decided pride in duplicitous stratagems and violence to gain the upper hand against adversaries. Honor was a powerful motive for the middle classes and intellectuals in both countries, and both dictators successfully played upon their people's deep resentment of the outcome of World War I and the postwar settlement. Mussolini reached the highpoint of his popularity after the conquest of Abyssinia, and Hitler his after peacefully overturning the most offensive clauses of the Treaty of Versailles.

When society is robust, honor and standing are closely linked, and actors are correspondingly more restrained in their goals and the means they use to achieve them. This was evident in the eighteenth century when European society was the most robust it had ever been. When society is thinner, honor and standing more readily diverge, actors are less restrained and escalations in goals and means are likely to occur. Conflictual behavior of this kind further undermines society, as it did before and during both world wars. Warfare is not always destructive of *nomos*; in some circumstances, it can sustain the values of society. Where honor is paramount warfare can strengthen communal bonds, even those between adversaries, as it did in Homer's fictional account of the Trojan War and arguably in classical Greece during different periods of its history. Warfare is most likely to weaken or destroy society when reason loses control of the spirit or appetite and actors no longer feel constrained by the limitations governing warfare in their societies. Fear quickly becomes the dominant motive, and provides further incentives for violating *nomos*. Late fifth-century Greece, the late Roman Republic and Europe during the first half of the twentieth century show striking parallels in this respect.

Both world wars had unrelievedly negative consequences, not only because of the goals and strategies of the actors, but because of the ways in which they interacted. In the aftermath of the Napoleonic Wars, Carl von Clausewitz observed that force tends toward the extreme because if one side holds back the other will gain an advantage. Violence sets in motion a process of reciprocal escalation (*Wechselwirkung*). The use of poison gas and the course of submarine and anti-submarine warfare in World War I, and the bombing of cities in World War II, exemplify this phenomenon. Clausewitz also recognizes limiting factors to escalation. Like Homer and Thucydides, he believed they derive from the social conditions of states and the nature of their relationships. They exist *prior* to war, and are not a function of the conflict itself.[29] Conventional accounts of military escalation or restraint generally rely on strategic or organizational logic. They ignore cultural determinants of political–military behavior, which I have tried to show, with cases from ancient times to the present, are more important. They establish – or fail to establish – the

---

[29] Clausewitz, *On War*, book 1, ch. 1, pp. 75–6.

necessary preconditions for cooperation in peacetime and self-restraint during wars.[30]

Hitler to Bush

My final cases are the Cold War and the Anglo-American invasion of Iraq. The Cold War arose from the power vacuum created in central Europe by the defeat of Nazi Germany. Converging on Germany from opposite directions, allied forces and the Red Army sought to avoid a confrontation but also to impose their political and economic preferences on the territories they occupied. In these circumstances, some degree of conflict between the two superpowers and their allies was highly likely, and all the more so because of the antagonistic nature of their social systems and mutual resentments arising from wartime and occupation policies. Appetite (markets for the West, reparations for the Soviets), spirit (competition for standing in Europe) and fear (concern for the consequences of the other side gaining control of Europe's industrial base and resources) were all implicated and probably reinforcing at the onset of the Cold War. It would be fruitless to attempt to untangle these motives or assess their relative weight. In the West, different concerns were paramount for different actors at different times. In the Soviet Union, Stalin's voice was dominant, and all we can do is speculate about his hierarchy of motives and the ways in which cunning and paranoia combined to shape his policies.[31]

The spirit unambiguously enters into the picture with the Soviet Union's explosion of its first atomic device in August 1949, the "loss" of China in 1949 and the launching of Sputnik in 1957. The American reaction to all three events indicates the extent to which the Cold War was framed as a contest for standing by both superpowers.

I demonstrated how, during the Cuban missile crisis, issues of standing and reputation were central to Khrushchev's decision to deploy missiles in Cuba, Kennedy's response, the initial unwillingness of either side to make concessions and the ultimate resolution of the crisis. The compromises that led to the resolution of this crisis paved the way for détente. From the late 1960s, the dynamics of the Cold War increasingly came to

---

[30] Lebow, "Reason, Emotion and Cooperation."

[31] Volkogonov, *Stalin*, pp. 3–13, 70–1, 225–36; Tucker, *Stalin in Power*, pp. 278–80, 317–19, 620, 625; Holloway, *Stalin and the Bomb*, pp. 153–60, 171, 283–8, 368–70.

resemble European imperial competition in the latter part of the nineteenth century.

The end of the Cold War on terms highly favorable to the West was celebrated in America as a "triumph." There was, and continues to be, enormous resistance to evidence that the Soviet Union's search for accommodation had little to do with American pressure and was largely a response to "new thinking" by the Soviet elite.[32] American intellectuals and the public more generally have been remarkably receptive to what can only be called the myth that Washington "won" the Cold War by spending the Soviets into submission through the Reagan arms buildup and "Star Wars." Such a reading of the Cold War portrays it as a potlatch, a form of conspicuous consumption intended to determine relative standing. It provides stunning evidence of the extent to which the American elite and much of public opinion framed the Cold War as a competition for standing.

My final case is the Anglo-American invasion of Iraq. The attacks of 9.11 wounded the United States physically and psychologically. They killed thousands of people, destroyed the World Trade Center, an icon of American economic power, and damaged the Pentagon, an even more hallowed landmark of American military might. The attacks were not conducted by another state, but by a rag-tag cabal of Middle Eastern terrorists, who, it soon became apparent, only succeeded because of refusal at the highest levels to take the threat of terrorism seriously and incompetence on the part of the CIA and the FBI. That such an unworthy adversary could so successfully attack the United States aroused anger in the Aristotelian sense and with it an acute desire for revenge. The Bush administration successfully exploited this anger and focused it against Saddam.

There was no significant public pressure to invade Iraq, and what support became manifest was largely manufactured by the administration. The United States was basking in its allegedly "unipolar moment" and high-ranking administration officials were committed to using its military power to strengthen its hold on hegemony. By demonstrating its ability to conduct a campaign of "shock and awe," they unreasonably expected to remake the political map of the Middle East, intimidate Iran, North Korea and China and make ally and adversary alike more compliant. Honor also entered into the picture: Vice-President Cheney felt

---

[32] Lebow and Stein, "Reagan and the Russians," and postscript to *We All Lost the Cold War*; Herrmann, "Learning from the End of the Cold War."

disgraced by the American failure in Vietnam. He wanted a military victory that would erase that stain and also free the executive of the remaining shackles imposed in its aftermath. Standing may have been an important personal consideration for President Bush. He has been described as a man of low self-esteem, and certainly had few, if any, serious accomplishments to his name. He made it clear to his closest confidants that he wanted to use the presidency to accomplish something great, something for which he would be remembered.

The state

My case studies generated a series of general observations and propositions about the spirit and politics. They are developed in detail in the concluding sections of chapters 6 through 9 so I only briefly recapitulate them here. Readers wanting more discussion and evidence should turn to the relevant sections of these chapters.

The first proposition concerns the important role the spirit played in the development of the modern state. Social scientists and historians rightly consider warfare to have been critical to its development. Wars drove leaders to centralize authority, extract the resources necessary to fight them and develop bureaucracies that could field and supply ever larger standing armies and navies. After 1648, the distinction between domestic and foreign violence and war became more distinct, which allows me to generalize about the causes of war and the different character of civil and international war in the seventeenth and eighteenth centuries. I find that the principal motive for war was standing. Monarchs gained and maintained standing, or *gloire*, through military victories and the territorial expansion it allowed. Appetite was a secondary consideration, as wars often cost far more than any economic benefits new territories might be expected to confer. Even when conquered territories generated wealth, it was most often sought – as in the case of Frederick's conquest of Silesia – to augment a ruler's military might so that he might win more victories and further increase his standing.

Additional evidence for my thesis is provided by the extraordinary sums European rulers during this period lavished on their courts, palaces, churches, theaters, other public buildings, processions and festivals. Louis XIV built not only Versailles, but Vaux-le-Vicomte, and he extensively renovated the Louvre. He employed a stellar array of writers and artists and was a patron of the sciences. The rays of the Sun King illuminated other courts and inspired emulation. Louis's grandson, Philip V of Spain, had his portrait painted by the same artist, Hyacinthe Rigaud, for whom Louis had sat, and had his palace redecorated and his court re-modeled in the style of Versailles. Max Emmanuel of Bavaria spent 75 percent of his state's income on his court, while Ernst August of Hanover and Friedrich Karl von Schöborn, prince-bishop of Würzburg both spent over 50 percent of state income on their courts. Charles II of England followed Louis's example in founding the Royal Observatory (1675) and the Chelsea Hospital (1681). In Vienna, display determined status, and a very high percentage of the Viennese economy was based on the supply of servants, goods, comestibles and buildings such as the Residenz and the lesser establishments in its orbit. In Hungary and Poland, the Esterházys, Radziwills and Czartoryskis built enormous palaces on their estates, spent small fortunes on servants, orchestras, dependent gentry and private armies, all in pursuit of standing. Peter the Great wanted his Peterhof in Saint Petersburg to be recognized as a new Versailles.[33]

There was considerable variation in relative expenditure on courts and armies within and across states. In a number of major powers, expenditure on display regularly exceeded that of armies. In France, high-profile expenditure on display continued regardless of military requirements. On average, almost 50 percent of the state budget in 1770 went to the court, while only 20 percent went to the army. However, at peak periods of war, military spending could rise as high as 75 percent. In 1768, Vienna spent 23 percent on the court and 48 percent on the army, but this percentage dropped sharply afterwards when the army reforms were completed. In Bavaria in 1770, the court received 42 percent, and the army 30 percent. In Russia, Peter the Great devoted 80 percent of his income to his war machine, but his priorities underwent a considerable shift in favor of display after the Great Northern War.[34] The two great outliers were Saxony and Prussia. Toward the end of Frederick the Great's reign, Prussia directed 80 percent of its revenues to war-making. The Saxon kings of Poland, Augustus I (1697–1733) and Augustus II (1733–63), went to the other extreme. They devoted almost all of their resources to display, transforming Dresden into one of the most culturally exciting and beautiful courts of Europe. Augustus II, known as "the Strong," was also famous for fathering 354 illegitimate children by the legion of mistresses he supported. Saxony's neglect of its military made it an inviting target

---

[33] Swann, "Politics and the State in Eighteenth Century Europe"; Blanning, *Pursuit of Glory*, pp. 113–14; Burke, *The Fabrication of Louis XIV*, pp. 169–78.
[34] Schulze, "The Prussian Military State"; Parker, *The Military Revolution*, pp. 62–5.

for Prussian conquest. Territorial conquest in the eighteenth century was hardly the norm, and did not deter other rulers from continuing to spend vast sums on display.

In both war and peace the spirit played a large, if not dominant, role. The quest for standing and honor cannot by itself explain the rise of the modern state, but its development cannot be understood without taking them into account.

Prospect theory

Prospect theory tells us that people are willing to take greater risks to prevent losses than they are to make gains. Loss and gain are determined with reference to a benchmark established by actors themselves and subjective by nature.[35] Prospect theory was developed and tested with respect to material gains and losses, so it is above all a theory about appetite. In chapter 7, I suggest a reformulation of prospect theory based on the evidence of my cases, ancient and modern. These cases indicate that willingness to run risks varies as a function of the motive. They not only determine how actors frame the meaning of gain and loss but the possibility of distinguishing between them, which is so essential to prospect theory.

Table 10.1. *Prospect theory*

	Gains	Loss avoidance
Appetite	Risk-averse	Risk-accepting
Fear	Risk-averse	More or less risk-accepting
Spirit	Risk-accepting	Very risk-accepting

When appetite is dominant – when actors are concerned with material gains and losses – prospect theory appears to capture the risk propensity of actors (see table 10.1). They are risk-averse when seeking gains and more risk-accepting when attempting to prevent loss. When actors are motivated by fear – as they often are when security is their paramount concern – they will be much more or much less risk-accepting depending on their situation. They may balance, preempt or bandwagon. Security is always relational, which links gains and losses in a way that is

[35] Kahneman and Tversky, "Prospect Theory," and *Choices, Values, and Frames.*

not generally true for appetite, where one actor's gain or loss of wealth does not necessarily lead to a corresponding loss or gain for another actor. When one actor's gain is understood to be another's loss, and vice versa, the distinction between loss and gain loses all relevance for risk-taking.

When actors are motivated by the spirit – when they are concerned with winning or preserving honor – they will be risk-accepting with respect to either loss or gain. Loss of honor is intolerable to such actors, and even certain death is unlikely to deter them from action intended to avoid it. They are generally willing to embrace risk when it comes to gain because accepting risk is often an essential precondition for gaining honor or standing. For the warriors of the *Iliad*, knights in the Middle Ages, and Prussian officers in the nineteenth and early twentieth centuries, honor was directly proportional to the risk that actors ran to achieve it. In honor societies, to behave well, especially in circumstances where survival is doubtful, earns respect in the eyes of others, which is why Leonidas and the Spartans at Thermopylae remain to this day the ultimate symbols of duty and honor.

Leonidas and his Spartans had no difficulty in determining the risk they faced. In many circumstances risk is difficult to calculate – for actors at the time and analysts in retrospect.[36] Despite all the evidence now available about the Cuban missile crisis, students of the crisis make very different assessments of the risks of escalation inherent in an American air strike against the Soviet missile sites in Cuba.[37] For prospect theory it is the understanding of actors that matters, and case studies indicate that policymakers rarely make careful risk assessments, let alone articulate and defend them to others. The risk estimates they share with others are more often than not rhetorical moves intended to influence them. Cases in point are Moltke's assurances of victory to Bethmann Hollweg, Conrad's to Berchtold and Franz Josef, and MacArthur's to President Truman. The Bush administration assured the Congress and the American public of the presence of WMDs in Iraq (high threat) and that Iraqi oil would pay the cost of the war (low cost). It would be interesting to know if there is significant variation in risk assessment across motives. We know that policymakers driven by fear make higher threat assessments and

---

[36] Vertzberger, "Rethinking and Reconceptualizing Risk in Foreign Policy Decision Making"; Lebow, *Nuclear Crisis Management*, pp. 104–53; Lebow and Stein, *We All Lost the Cold War*, chs. 6 and 11.

[37] Lebow and Stein, *We All Lost the Cold War*, pp. 291–309.

display less cognitive complexity.[38] What about actors moved by the spirit? My cases provide some evidence that they also engage in biased threat assessment: Conrad's initial hope that he could defeat Serbia before Russia advanced deep into Galicia and the Japanese belief that the United States would accept a limited defeat in the Pacific rather than fight a prolonged war are striking examples of self-serving estimates. Moltke, however, did not delude himself that his military plan would encircle and defeat France. We know that motivated bias is most pronounced when policymakers face clashing threats to which they cannot find a solution. They are likely to address the threat they can most vividly picture and deny, ignore, distort or explain away information that suggests that their policy will fail.[39] Actors motivated by the spirit are less threatened by risk, which they embrace, or by the prospect of loss, which matters less if honor is attained. They should accordingly have fewer psychological incentives to bolster and deny.

Parvenu powers

My cases suggest the proposition that powers seeking acceptance as great powers are likely be particularly aggressive, and may continue to act this way for some time afterwards. Aggressive behavior is all the more likely if their leaders or peoples have been previously ostracized or otherwise humiliated by the dominant powers of the system. In chapter 6 I offer Sweden in the seventeenth century and Russia and Prussia in the eighteenth as examples. In chapter 7 I extend my argument to imperial Germany and argue that its aggressiveness was in part for the same reason. The Kaiser and the military officers and civilian officials he gathered around him were particularly sensitive to real or imagined slights to their standing or honor. So too, as we have seen, was the German middle class, many of whom sought or buttressed their self-esteem through the accomplishments of their state.

Beginning in the nineteenth century, one of the defining characteristics of parvenu powers became the development and wide appeal of discourses that stress their unique spiritual and creative qualities – hence,

---

[38] Holsti, "Crisis Decision Making"; Cohen, "Threat Perception in International Crisis," on threat perception. Lawler and Thye, "Bringing Emotion into Social Exchange Theory," for a review of the literature on fear and cognitive complexity.

[39] Janis and Mann, *Decision Making*; Lebow, *Between Peace and War*, chs. 5–6; Jervis *et al.*, *Psychology and Deterrence*, for theory and cases.

their superiority – over the alleged rationalism, individualism and crass materialism of the West. This discourse arose in Prussia during the Napoleonic Wars and became the basis for the *Sonderweg* thesis that emphasized Germany's unique historical development and was critical and dismissive of commerce and constitutional government. Germany was portrayed as the land of intellectual and artistic creativity and communal solidarity, qualities associated with a mythical conception of the German people (*Volk*). By emphasizing the role of the state as both the instrument and expression of this mission – a theme developed by Kant and Fichte that received fuller expression in the philosophy of Hegel – power could be concentrated in ways that facilitated unification and the emergence of imperial Germany as the dominant military power on the continent. Subsequent authors in this tradition, among them Werner Sombart, praised "the ancient German hero's spirit," which would make the German *Volk* the "chosen people" of the twentieth century.[40]

Russia and Japan developed variants on this theme. Russian nationalism stressed moral over material forces and contrasted the holy mission of the Russian people to Western rationalism and materialism. Slavophile ideology was equally *völkisch*. It emphasized the communal life of the Rus in contrast to the individualism of the West (which now included Germany), and hailed the Russian Empire as the successor to Rome and Byzantium. In Japan, prominent intellectuals created a mythical premodern past of consensual and happy village life, and stressed the superiority of this way of life to the crass and conflictual values of the West (which included Germany and Russia). The anti-Western, anti-materialist and anti-individualist ideologies that became prominent in these several countries and their common emphasis on their special mission suggests that national self-images are more a function of the relationship between political units and the dominant powers of the system than they are an expression of particular national cultures. All variants of this ideology nevertheless stress their country's allegedly unique past and the determining effects of "national character."

In chapter 8 I applied the concept of the parvenu power to the Soviet Union, and in chapter 9 to the United States, which, I argue, qualifies as one at least in part. These identities and their associated discourses may help explain the particular intensity of the Cold War and Washington's continuing aggressiveness after its demise.

---

[40] Sombart, *Händler und Helden*, pp. 125, 143.

Power transition and power abuse

Power transition theories predict conflict between rising powers and hegemons because the former want to remake the system to serve their interests, while the latter want to preserve order and hierarchies beneficial to them.[41] My theory and cases suggest a less cramped and less mechanical model of state motives and behavior. States pursue power as a means to diverse ends, which include security, access to wealth and status. My cases demonstrate that status is one of the most important of these ends, and that there are multiple routes by which it can be achieved.

I noted in chapter 2 that many spirit-based worlds originate as warrior societies in which the possibility of attaining honor, and with it high office, are open only to an aristocratic elite. In chapter 9 I suggested that the European regional system from Westphalia to at least 1945 resembled such a society, and that the international system still does in important ways. Westphalia integrated Catholic and Protestant powers in the same society. Participation and recognition as a great power, or its equivalent before the concept achieved institutional status at the Congress of Vienna, were initially restricted to European states but subsequently expanded to include the Ottoman Empire, the United States, Japan and ultimately all recognized sovereign states.

Not every actor allowed to compete for honor and office necessarily does so. Many domestic societies have alternative career paths and statuses available to people who opt out of such competition for whatever reason. The Sioux are particularly interesting in this respect because they were among the most competitive of all warrior societies: like the Spartans, they encouraged contests, often violent ones, among young boys as part of their training and socialization. Not every young man had the disposition, courage or physical attributes to become a warrior. The alternative was to dress like women and become a *winkte*. Such men became objects of disdain for "having the heart of a woman" and had to erect their tipis at the edge of camp alongside orphans and other outcasts. *Winktes* were nevertheless thought to have magical qualities, and they could achieve a degree of respect by demonstrating their healing powers.[42] In modern international relations, the closest analog is the neutral state: a country that opts out of the competition for standing by renouncing war for any purpose beyond self-defense. International law came to recognize the special

---

[41] Organski, *World Politics*; Organski and Kugler, *The War Ledger*; Gilpin, *War and Change in World Politics*; Doran and Parsons, "War and the Cycle of Relative Power."

[42] Hassrick, *Sioux*, pp. 133–8.

status of neutrals, and some (e.g. Switzerland, Sweden) gained respect for performing important services for the other powers, prisoners of war or the international community more generally. Like *winktes*, they carved out alternate niches for themselves. They can also lose status, as Switzerland has in recent years, in response to revelations about its wartime collaboration with the Nazis and the postwar conspiracy of its banks to keep funds and other assets deposited by Jews who later died in the Holocaust. Evidence that honor and standing gained in alternative niches is critical to national self-esteem comes from the reactions of leaders and public opinion in Switzerland and Austria to external criticism and threatened loss of status by virtue of not having performed their expected roles properly. Criticism appears to have provoked the same kind of national resentments that slights or humiliation do in the case of great powers.[43]

Other actors struggle to gain entry into the circle where it becomes possible to compete for honor and standing. There are several strategies toward this end. The most obvious is to gain recognition by emulating the accomplishments of high-status actors. This strategy will be most attractive to actors who have the right resources and temperament and live in societies with relatively open elites. Among the Sioux, it was possible for a young man from a low-status family, even an orphan, to gain admission to councils of men and achieve high status by performing a set of ceremonies. These ceremonies entailed gift-giving, hosting feasts and adopting a younger and less wealthy individual. To acquire the horses and blankets to give away the young man had to display extraordinary bravery on the battlefield and accumulate sufficient coups to earn a share of booty taken on raids. He could gain more wealth and status by becoming a *blotahunka*, or expedition leader, and demonstrating his tactical and leadership skills.[44]

Classical Greece offers a nice parallel at the regional level. Sparta was the unquestioned hegemon prior to the two Persian invasions of Greece (499–479 BCE), a position it earned by dint of the courage and success of its hoplites against other Greek cities and the Persians. Athens emerged as another possible hegemon because of the courage and success of its naval and land forces against the Persians, especially at Marathon and Salamis, and the leadership it provided in subsequent efforts to liberate the rest of Hellas from the Persian yoke. Sparta was not pleased by the prospect

---

[43] Ludi, "What Is So Special about Switzerland?"; Uhl, "From Victim to Co-Responsibility Thesis."
[44] Hassrick, *Sioux*, pp. 83–90, 296–308.

of sharing its hegemony, and in the immediate aftermath of Salamis proposed that Athens should not rebuild the protective walls on the spurious grounds that it could provide a fortified location for the Persians in a third invasion. Themistocles instructed Athenians to work around the clock to rebuild the walls around the harbor at Piraeus while he went off to Sparta to negotiate. When informed by an envoy that the walls were high enough to offer protection, he told the Spartiates that Athens was now invulnerable and that any discussion should be conducted on the basis of equality. The Spartans "showed no open signs of displeasure" and accepted Athens as an equal on the basis of the courage it had displayed against the Persians, although, Thucydides tells us, many felt privately aggrieved.[45] As I noted in chapter 9, *hēgemonia* was a purely honorific office associated with honor (*timē*), conferred by others for services rendered to the community. It put the recipient in a leadership position, but could be withdrawn if power was abused. It was the functional equivalent of chief and *blotahunka* among the Sioux.

A variant of the emulation strategy is to compete at the local rather than the general level for honor or standing – to become, in the words of the old adage, a big fish in a small pond. This is a common strategy in domestic societies where people seek recognition and honor in their community, state, province or region. In international relations, this has been an attractive option for middle-level powers. In eighteenth-century Europe, Prussia and the kingdom of Piedmont pursued this strategy, the former with enough verve and success to become a great power. In the postwar world, India, Argentina, Brazil, Mexico, Egypt, Syria, Iraq, Iran, Vietnam, China and Nigeria have at one time or another sought to establish themselves as dominant regional powers. China has since become a great power, and influential members of the political and intellectual elites of India and Brazil harbor similar ambitions for their countries.[46] Mexico appears to have opted out of the Latin American competition, and, beginning with NAFTA, to define itself more as a North American power. This reorientation fits with one of the findings of social identity theory: actors not infrequently desert low-status groups for higher status ones.[47]

---

[45] Thucydides, 189–92.
[46] Narilkar, "Peculiar Chauvinism or Strategic Calculation?"; Narilkar and Hurrell, *Pathways to Power.*
[47] Elmers, "Individual Upward Mobility and the Perceived Legitimacy of Intergroup Relations"; Abrams and Hogg, "Social Identification, Social Categorization and Social Influence."

Deviance is another possible strategy. It can appeal to actors who lack the resources to compete for standing or confront elites that are closed to them for whatever reason. Deviant actors attempt to gain attention and recognition by violating the norms of the system, and may attract like-minded actors to their entourage. Gangs often function in this way, and not infrequently coalesce around a dominant figure.[48] In international relations, deviance is most often a strategy of resentful, low-status, middle-resource actors. Cases in point are North Korea, Libya, Sudan, Iran and Iraq under Saddam Hussein. President Bush has referred to most of these states as being part of "the axis of evil," an inflammatory and unhelpful term. There is nevertheless truth to the claim that such states have violated a host of long-standing norms concerning non-interference in the internal affairs of other states, the kidnapping of foreigners, involvement in criminal activities and terrorism, as well as more recent norms about treatment of their own populations. High-status deviance is another possibility, and I shall shortly return to George Bush's America in this connection.

A more sophisticated and more difficult strategy is to challenge existing hierarchies as opposed to merely rebelling against them. Actors can try to open up these hierarchies, change the rules governing how honor and office are conferred or even develop alternative hierarchies. All of these moves require considerable resources and benefit from coordination among multiple actors who are similarly inclined. History offers all kinds of evidence of success and failure on the part of individuals, classes and states. One episode that featured prominently in chapter 7 is Marx's prediction that the rising bourgeoisie would organize to carry out a revolution against the aristocracy to replace its hierarchy and values with a new, more egalitarian social order. In much of central Europe, the upper levels of the bourgeoisie sought entry into the nobility instead, while many less affluent members of the middle class accepted its authority and assimilated its practices as best they could. The aristocracy, threatened by the rise of commercial and professional classes, unexpectedly had its status confirmed by them.

In chapter 9 I noted that individual states, most notably the French Republic, and to a lesser extent the United States, opted, at least initially, for a revolutionary strategy. They spurned the old order to varying degrees and appealed over the heads of states to their publics for honor

---

[48] Whyte, *Street Corner Society*, pp. 1–14 on "Doc" and his boys; Cara Buckley, "A Fearsome Gang and its Wannabes," *New York Times*, August 19, 2007, "News of the Week in Review," p. 3.

and standing on ideological grounds. They met with some initial success, as did the Soviet Union in the twentieth century, but soon sought standing on more traditional grounds by means of military prowess. New challenges are underway by some of the key states of the European Union, Scandinavia, Canada, Japan, and regionally by Iran, and their implications are analyzed in chapter 9. The most interesting aspect of these campaigns to gain acceptance for alternative conceptions of standing is their attempt to reintroduce the concept of honor in international relations. Neither the major industrial powers noted above nor Iran are claiming status on the basis of military feats, or even their power, but on how they govern themselves and use their resources in accord with ethical or religious codes.

Parvenu powers, it is apparent, embrace the dual strategies of assimilation and deviance. They seek entry into the ranks of great powers, and generally attempt to do so by the same means existing great powers achieved their status. They often do so with a vengeance, as in the Hohenzollerns' single-minded focus on their army and the conquests it facilitated. Only belatedly did Frederick the Great come to realize that there was a law of diminishing returns: the more threatening conquest became to the existing order, the more other powers combined to prevent it. The Soviet Union under Khrushchev and his successors not only directed enormous resources to its armed forces – including a relatively useless but very expensive blue water navy – but to high culture, athletic teams and chess masters to buttress the country's claims to superpower status. Deviance enters the picture in the form of aggressive behavior and other rule violations that may be motivated by a desire for acceptance and status, but can easily be perceived as threats by high-status actors. Prominent events of the Cold War conform to this pattern. Much of what the United States perceived as deviant behavior by the Soviet Union under Khrushchev and Brezhnev (e.g. scuttling the 1960 Paris summit, the Cuban missile deployment, Third World intervention in the 1970s), I argued in chapter 9, was a response to rebuffs, slights and humiliations following earlier efforts at normalization of relations or détente. They angered Soviet leaders and strengthened the hand of factions within the leadership committed to confrontational policies.

My theory and cases suggest that most rising states seek status commensurate with their power and accomplishments. On the whole they appear at least as interested in the prestige conferred by this status, its related offices and privileges as they are in any material or security benefits. Contrary to the predictions of power transition theories, rising powers seeking status are more often than not accommodated, especially when they are seen to act in accord with the rules and values of the system. Athens was accepted by Sparta, Rome by Etruscan cities. Austria, England, Prussia, Russia, the United States and Japan were all recognized as other hegemons, great powers or their equivalents. Russia was recognized as a great power, but never fully accepted as one because many of its domestic practices were considered uncivilized. The Soviet Union was initially spurned, but ultimately recognized by the United States as a coequal superpower. The People's Republic of China received great power status in 1971 when it was given a permanent seat on the Security Council. Its acceptance into the international community – measured in terms of organizations it has been invited to join – went way up when the regime gave up its deviant identity – symbolized by its vocal support for anti-capitalist revolution throughout the developing world – and began to behave like a "normal" power. From the mid-1960s to the mid-1980s, China moved out of virtual non-membership in international organizations – the UN being the principal exception – to memberships equal to 80 percent of other states with its level of economic development.[49]

Existing hegemons and great powers conflict in their responses to rising powers. They resent having to share their status with others, especially those who claim equality or higher status. Spartiates felt this way about Athens just as Americans did about the Soviet Union and many still do about China.[50] Such powers are nevertheless pleased that others have chosen to emulate them and enjoy the recognition this entails. Within reason, the status of clubs – and that of their members – increases when others want to join, and more so when only a few are admitted. Thucydides' account of Sparta's response to Athenian reconstruction of its walls nicely captures this ambivalence. One of the interesting and relatively unexplored questions of international relations is how great powers resolve this tension. In what circumstances do they allow or resist conferring equal status on rising actors? When and how do they deprive declining powers of their status? Are they more reluctant, as I suspect they are, to take great power status away from declining powers than they are to confer it on rising ones?

Realists are right in thinking that rising powers tend to be aggressive, but they misunderstand the reasons why this is so and are wrong in asserting that they start or provoke hegemonic wars. Rising powers are often

[49] Johnston, "Is China a Status Quo Power?"
[50] Bernstein and Munro, "The Coming Conflict with America"; Brzezinski and Mearsheimer, "Clash of the Titans"; Shirk, *China*, p. 10.

parvenu powers: latecomers to the game intent on demonstrating their qualifications as great powers. As military prowess has been the principal qualification for great power standing, they have embraced war as a means to this end. As noted earlier, they have also invested heavily in palaces, public buildings, fleets, nuclear arsenals, science, sports, culture, hosting Olympic Games, foreign aid programs and anything else that is considered essential or helpful in buttressing their claims to great power status. For the most part, however, rising powers have not initiated military challenges to hegemons or dominant great powers. Pericles intended to humble Corinth, not Sparta, although he did not shirk from a military showdown when it became apparent that withdrawing the Megarian decree and ending the siege of Potidaea, as Sparta demanded, would enhance Sparta's prestige at Athens' expense.

In the sixteenth century, England challenged Spain in ways that made war all but inevitable, but only after Philip II sought to remove Elizabeth I from the throne and replace her with her Catholic cousin, Mary Stuart.[51] Sweden went to war with Austria, the most striking example in the seventeenth century of a rising power attacking a dominant one. In 1744 Prussia made war on Austria, which was a great power, but for purposes of a limited territorial grab. Prussia's war with Austria in 1866 offers a closer fit with the predictions of power transition theories. Russia achieved great power status by defeating Sweden, a declining great power, in the Great Northern War, but it did not initiate the conflict. It also warred on the Ottomans, another declining power. Japan defeated China, a peripheral power, and then Russia in 1904–5 in a war it tried hard to prevent through diplomacy and compromise.[52] The United States became a great power by defeating Spain, another peripheral power. The Soviet Union was considered a great power before World War II but became a superpower by defeating Nazi Germany in a war Stalin desperately sought to avoid. China fought the United States to a standstill in the Korean War, a conflict that neither side desired. With the exception of the Austro-Prussian and Franco-Prussian Wars, none of the wars initiated by rising powers were intended to restructure the international order or even to change significantly the ranking of the great powers.

So-called hegemonic wars are almost invariably started by hegemons or highly ranked great powers, and rarely if ever because they are threatened

---

[51] Parker, *The Grand Strategy of Phillip II*, pp. 147–78.

[52] Okamoto, *Japanese Oligarchy and the Russo-Japanese War*; Lenson, *Russian Push toward Japan*; White, *Diplomacy of the Russo-Japanese War*; Nish, *Anglo-Japanese Alliance*, and *Japanese Foreign Policy*, pp. 93–125.

by the growing military power of would-be challengers. Citing Thucydides, who attributes the Spartan decision for war to fear "of the further growth of Athenian power," realists offer the Peloponnesian War as the first recorded example of a hegemonic war caused by power transition.[53] Elsewhere I argue that Spartan fear of Athens had little to do with its military power. The Spartan "war party" had little appreciation of Athenian military power and expected a quick victory as a result of a single engagement between their hoplite armies. The "peace party" was more cautious because of their more realistic appreciation of Athenian military, especially naval, capabilities. What both factions really feared was Athenian wealth and cultural primary, and with it the growth of its empire, because this threatened their status as the leading city in Greece, something integral to Spartan identity.[54]

The wars I analyzed in the Middle Ages took place before any state system was established so are not relevant to the issue at hand. There were several so-called hegemonic wars in the years between 1648 and 1789, most of them involving France. As we have seen, Louis XIV and his successors did not go to war because they felt threatened by rising powers, nor were they challenged by rising powers. Louis XIV's Dutch War and wider conflicts with England, Austria and Piedmont were motivated by a bid for continental hegemony. As in the case of Athens under Pericles, they were an expression of hubris. Not content with its leading position in their respective systems, France, like Athens before it, sought to extend its domain to win more glory for its kings and the *noblesse d'epée* and overreached itself in the process. Napoleon's wars of conquest followed the same narrative.

The German decision for war in 1914 is somewhat more complex, but cannot convincingly be explained with reference to power transition theory. Germany was the leading continental power, and peace, as Bismarck and later major industrialists and bankers recognized, was likely to widen its economic, cultural and scientific lead. The German military felt threatened by Russian railway and military reforms, but only because of its commitment to conduct an offensive in France. Moltke pushed for war for reasons that had nothing to do with security, but with his honor and identity as a soldier. The Kaiser agreed to support Austria-Hungary's desire for revenge against Serbia for similar reasons. The Austrians were

---

[53] Thucydides, 1.23.5–6 for his general explanation of the war and 1.88 for his account of the Spartan assembly's decision for war.
[54] Lebow, *Tragic Vision of Politics*, ch. 3.

also more interested in their honor than their security. World War I is another case where standing among the powers – at least for Germany, Austria and Russia – was knowingly pursued at the expense of security.

World War II does not fit the power transition mold either. Japan and Italy were in no position to challenge the Western powers, and did so for reasons unrelated to security or economic needs. Mussolini thought he was bandwagoning. The foreign policy of Hitler's Germany, and the efforts to overturn the territorial and other limitations of the Treaty of Versailles, cannot be explained only with reference to *raison d'état*. As I have tried to demonstrate, the widely shared need of the German people to buttress their self-esteem, and how this need was played upon by the German right and Hitler, offers a more compelling explanation. By contrast, Germany's invasions of Poland, Western Europe and the Soviet Union, which had much less popular support, are best understood as another case of a dictator striving to make a mark for himself, driven in this instance by the megalomaniacal ambition of world conquest. The Cold War was undeniably a contest between a dominant power and rising power, but war was averted, contrary to the predictions of power transition theory. The conflict ended when the rising power became a declining power, but well before that the superpowers had reached various accords that significantly reduced the likelihood of war and stabilized their competition. There is no evidence to support realist claims that Gorbachev sought to settle the Cold War on the best terms he could in realization that the Soviet Union's position was declining. On the contrary, documents, memoirs and the oral testimony of Soviet officials indicate that Gorbachev and his advisors wanted to end the Cold War because they regarded it as dangerous and an impediment to their domestic reform program.[55]

My cases reveal several patterns of behavior that suggest propositions quite at odds with power transition theory. The first concerns rising powers. For the most part, they do their best to avoid wars with dominant great powers, preferring, like vultures circling dying prey, to attack powers who are weak and declining or involved in other serious military confrontations. Prussia's attack on Silesia in 1740, Russia's several wars against a declining Ottoman Empire, Japan's invasion of China in 1931 and European colonial outposts in Asia in 1941, and Italy's invasion of France in 1940 are cases in point. Sometimes rising powers miscalculate, as Frederick the Great did during the Seven Years War, when his aggressive moves triggered invasions of Prussia by Austria, France, Russia, Saxony

---

[55] See chapter 9.

and Sweden that nearly led to a crushing defeat and dismemberment. Occasionally great powers start wars with rising powers, but not because they fear their growing might. Rather, they *underestimate* their power and treat them with contempt, as Russia did Japan in 1904.

The second pattern involves wars among the great powers. Many, if not most of them, appear to be started by hegemons or dominant great powers (e.g. Athens, France under Louis XIV and Napoleon, Wilhelmine Germany and the United States in Iraq) who are not content with their status, spurn the limitations associated with their office, succumb to hubris and behave as deviants. They start or set in motion (i.e. the Corcyrean alliance and the "blank check" to Austria) wars based on unrealistic assessments of their own power that lead to their defeat. Their wars often start as attacks on smaller states, which bring into being a coalition of great powers against them. Louis XIV's wars against the United Provinces, Frederick the Great's attack on Saxony and Hitler's invasion of Poland are cases in point. Hegemons and dominant powers are at least as likely to fight smaller states (e.g. the United States vs.Vietnam, Afghanistan, Iraq; the USSR vs. Czechoslovakia, Afghanistan) as they are to fight one another.

The least likely kind of war is between a rising power and a dominant great power, the kind of war predicted by power transition theory. Japan's attack on the United States is an obvious exception, but it was motivated by fear and expectation of a sharp, unfavorable downturn in the balance of power in the near future. This might be called power transition in reverse. Another exception is China's attack on US forces in Korea in 1950. Like Japan in 1904, China sought to avoid this war through a combination of diplomacy and military preparations, but US leaders, who were also keen to avoid war, were insensitive to Chinese warnings and oblivious to their preparations. American forces advanced to the Yalu, exposing themselves to flank attack by a much threatened China.[56] The pattern of great power wars suggests that dominant great powers have few concerns about challengers, and are motivated primarily by standing in their conflicts with other great powers. This is why historically dominant powers have repeatedly provoked coalitions of other great powers against them.

Power transition theorists are right in thinking that upwards and downwards mobility are key processes in international relations, but they are mistaken in their view that appetite in the form of territorial or material advantages is the primary motive of rising powers and that fear in the form of territorial and material loss is the dominant concern of

---

[56] Lebow, *Between Peace and War*, ch. 5.

dominant powers or hegemons. The patterns I observe are more consistent with the assumption that the spirit, and the drive for status and standing to which it gives rise, is paramount for both, at least in their mutual relations. My propositions must be tested against a more comprehensive data set and I intend to publish such an analysis in due course.

Power, influence, justice

To this point in my argument I have examined human motives and their implications for politics and foreign policy. I now shift my focus to the means actors use to influence one another's behavior. I argue that there are important connections between motives and influence, because an actor's ability to assist or impede others – which is one important basis of influence – depends very much on what those actors want to gain or preserve. I further contend that attempts to translate power into influence through strategic bargaining that ignores the spirit and its need for autonomy risk failure.

Realism and liberalism share similar conceptions of power and influence. Theories within these paradigms assume that the best way to influence actors is by manipulating their cost calculus through the judicious use of bribes, threats, or some combination of the two.[57] Well-timed and credible promises of rewards or punishments are intended to make some behavior too attractive to forego or too costly to enact.

My theory and cases indicate that power is not so readily transformed into influence because it is heavily context-dependent. Strategic bargaining can usefully be compared to the children's game of rock, scissors and paper. Each of the two protagonists makes a fist behind its back and decides whether to be a rock, a pair of scissors or a piece of paper. At the count of three, they thrust open their fists and reveal one (rock), two (scissors) or three (paper) fingers. The rock triumphs over the scissors because it can smash them, but is trumped by paper, which wraps rock. The scissors in turn defeat the paper because they can cut it up. The game highlights the relational nature of power. In the Cuban missile crisis, to cite one example, the American rock (nuclear and local conventional superiority) triumphed over the Soviet scissors (military forces and missiles in Cuba) because Khrushchev was desperate to avoid a humiliating military defeat. Soviet scissors (military aid) cut North Vietnam (paper) because Hanoi was dependent on it, and thus agreed to enter into negotiations with the

---

[57] Schelling, *Arms and Influence*, for the classic statement of this strategy.

United States But American compellence failed because Hanoi, although always at a serious military disadvantage, did not fear war and its costs the way Americans did. North Vietnamese paper (willingness to suffer) wrapped the American rock. Power only translates into bargaining leverage when it enables an actor to inflict losses that the other side fears, or confer gains that it is keen to make.

Context is important in a second sense. In many situations, especially international conflicts and crises, it is difficult to fathom, let alone rank-order, other actors' preferences. This is why deterrence and compellence not infrequently provoke the behavior they are intended to prevent – an observation first made by Diodotus in the Mytilenean debate and since documented in numerous case studies of twentieth-century confrontations.[58]

Threat-based strategies arouse anger in the Aristotelian sense of the term (see chapter 2 for Aristotle and anger) as most actors bridle when they become the objects of intimidation. Anger brings with it a desire for revenge and encourages a reframing of the bargaining encounter to make the threat its central feature. Leaders may conclude that restraint or compliance on their part will be perceived as weakness and invite new demands, making a confrontational response more attractive, even if it is understood to be risky or costly. The origins of the Peloponnesian War, the First World War and the Cuban missile crisis can be attributed in part to this dynamic. In the case of the missile crisis, the provocation was Kennedy's deployment of Jupiter missiles in Turkey, intended to demonstrate American resolve. The deployment infuriated Khrushchev and made him look for some way of getting even. It also convinced him of the need to reply in kind because he worried that Kennedy would interpret inaction as weakness. Khrushchev's identity was very closely linked to the Soviet Union. His country's economic accomplishments, defeat of the Nazi invader and development of nuclear weapons, all leading to its superpower status, made him very proud. The forward deployment of nuclear-tipped missiles in Turkey over his repeated objections indicated to him that Kennedy did not respect the Soviet Union, let alone recognize it as another superpower. Khrushchev sent missiles to Cuba to deter an American invasion of that island, offset American strategic superiority and, he hoped, convince Kennedy to pursue a policy of détente. But, above all, he acted in defense of his and his nation's identity and toward

---

[58] Thucydides, 3.36–50; Lebow, *Between Peace and War*, ch. 4, "Beyond Parsimony," and "Thucydides and Deterrence"; Jervis *et al.*, *Psychology of Deterrence*.

that end sought to compel the president to recognize the Soviet Union as America's equal and treat it with appropriate respect. Khrushchev made this motive abundantly clear in his first private letter to Kennedy during the crisis, which the ExComm, convinced of his aggressive intentions and insensitive to his perspective on the Jupiter deployment, dismissed as emotional ramblings.[59]

Not only threats of punishment but promises of rewards that highlight the subordinate status of actors are likely to be perceived as humiliating and arouse anger. In these circumstances the spirit can rise to the fore and trump appetite and fear as motives. When this happens, the targets of threats and bribes undergo an important shift in their preferences, which is another reason why they may be opaque and misunderstood by outsiders. The American occupation of Iraq, and Iraqi resistance to it, arguably illustrate this process.

Individuals, armies and political units are committed to asserting and maintaining their identities, and the former is often a means to the latter. As a general rule, actors are reluctant to act out of character with their identities even when the behavior in question would bring significant material gains or avert serious material or physical losses. Any rule has exceptions, and actors do not always act consistently with their conceptions of themselves. Many Greek cities in the path of Xerxes' army chose to "Medize" – to go over to the Persian side in lieu of near certain destruction. During the Cold War, the United States and the Soviet Union alike supported regimes that behaved in sharp contrast to their professed values. Behavior at odds with identity generates dissonance which must be reduced by explaining it away or somehow making it consistent with the values actors associate with their self-images.[60] Alternatively, actors can reformulate their self-images, to make them consistent with their behavior. Thus neocons have urged Americans to acknowledge and embrace their identity as an empire.[61]

It has long been recognized that actors seeking to influence others are more likely to succeed if they can convince them that the behavior in question is consistent with their interests. As the implications of behavior for

[59] Lebow and Stein, *We All Lost the Cold War*, chs. 2 and 3.

[60] Festinger, *A Theory of Cognitive Dissonance*. Lebow, *White Britain and Black Ireland*, for an application of cognitive dissonance to the politics of colonialism.

[61] For thoughtful reviews of this debate, Ciută, "What Are We Debating?"; Bisley, "Neither Empire nor Republic"; Cox, "Empire, Imperialism and the Bush Doctrine"; Ikenberry, "Liberalism and Empire"; Mann, "First Failed Empire"; Nexon and Wright, "What's at Stake in the American Empire Debate?"

one's interests or identity are not always self-evident, and are sometimes quite ambiguous, influence puts a premium on framing, communication and persuasion. With good reason, Morgenthau describes influence as "a psychological relationship."[62] Actors frequently need, and even want, to be convinced that their behavior, interests and identities are all consistent.

Persuasion on the basis of interest is undeniably an important level of influence. So too are appeals to identity. I argued in chapter 2 that such appeals are most effective when target actors are sensitive to questions of honor or standing. Examples of successful persuasion that came up in our cases included the Ionians' plea to Athens to come to their assistance on the basis of common ancestry, the Kaiser's support of Austria to show himself *Nibelungentreue* and Sir Edward Grey's ability to convince key members of his cabinet and the British public that the nation's honor required coming to the aid of France and honoring the country's commitment to defend Belgium's neutrality. Conversely, appeals to interest that ignore actors' concern for honor, standing and autonomy are much less likely to succeed. In chapter 9 I attribute the failure of the American occupation of Iraq to this cause. American rule, exercised first through an American overlord, then through America's puppet Ahmed Chalabi, and finally through an Iraqi government with little legitimacy, offended many Iraqis by driving home the extent to which they and their country were subordinate to a foreign occupying power. Ironically, efforts to rebuild Iraqi infrastructure, in which American officials and contractors played the leading role, may have had the same effect.

Interest and identity, while distinct concepts, are often closely related. Persuasion that succeeds on the basis of interest has the potential to build common identities when it leads to sustained cooperation in projects of mutual benefit. Hoodwinking or coercing actors has the opposite effect, making them resentful and keen to find an opportunity to assert their autonomy. The distinction between these two kinds of persuasion is another Greek contribution to our understanding of politics. In *Philoctetes*, Sophocles distinguishes between persuasion based on duplicity, false logic, coercion and other forms of chicanery (*dolos*), and that achieved by honest dialogue (*peithō*) that builds or strengthens friendships and upholds mutually valued norms and practices.[63]

Sophocles, Thucydides and Plato all consider *peithō* a more effective strategy than *dolos* because it has the potential to foster cooperation that

---

[62] Morgenthau, *Politics among Nations*, 1st edn, p. 14.
[63] Knox, *The Heroic Temper*, ch. 5; White, *Heracles' Bow*, pp. 3–27; Lebow, "Power and Ethics."

transcends discrete issues, builds and strengthens community and encourages a convergence of interests that facilitate further cooperation. For much the same reason, *peithō* has a restricted domain; it cannot persuade actors to act contrary to their interests or identities. *Dolos* can sometimes compel actors to behave this way.[64] *Dolos* is almost always costlier in a material sense because it depends on threats and rewards. Greeks refer to political units whose influence is primarily capability-based, and whose influence is often exercised through *dolos*, as *archē*. They are driven to pursue aggressive foreign policies intended to augment their material capabilities. Like Athens, Louis XIV, Napoleon, the axis powers in World War II and the United States in Iraq, they may try to expand beyond the limits of their capabilities. *Peithō*, by contrast, encourages self-restraint because it can only be exercised in the common interest and for policies worked out with others through consultation, discussion and debate.[65]

Standing and honor – which should not be confused with soft power – have important implications for influence. When a political unit is respected and trusted and has used its power for the benefit of the community, its attempts to exercise leadership are more likely to be accepted by others. In these conditions, persuasion (*peithō*) allows an actor to translate its power into influence in the most efficient manner. When standing is freed from honor and based largely, or entirely, on material capabilities, it is more difficult to exercise and institutionalize. Bribes and threats, often accompanied by *dolos*, become its principal levers, and they can be costly in terms of resources.[66] Influence based on superior capabilities provokes resentment, and resistance if the circumstances permit, because it degrades the spirit. This is all the more likely to occur when no effort is made to give it any aura of legitimacy through consultation, institutionalization, rhetorical appeals or self-restraint.

Identity is closely connected to autonomy regardless of the motive that is dominant. If it is fear, actors worry that dependence will make them vulnerable. If it is appetite, they worry that their access to material rewards will be restricted. When the spirit is dominant, autonomy is an end in its own right, making dependence on others that much more unpalatable. Weber and Morgenthau warn that the exercise of power involves the subordination of one actor to another. As neither people nor states willingly

---

[64] Plato, *Gorgias*, and *Republic*, 509d–511d, 531d–534c.

[65] Lebow, "Power and Ethics," for an application of Sophocles' concepts to international relations, and *Tragic Vision of Politics*, chs. 7–8 for a discussion of *archē* and *hēgemonia*.

[66] Polybius, *Rise of the Roman Empire*, 6.9; Lebow, "Power, Persuasion and Justice," for an elaboration of this argument.

give up their autonomy, Morgenthau argues that power must be masked to be successful. The most effective way of doing this is by making it legitimate. To do this, an actor's claim to and its exercise of leadership must be based on shared conceptions of justice, so that others can be convinced that it is being used for the benefit of the community as a whole. When powerful states act this way they may achieve *hēgemonia* (see chapters 2 and 4) in the sense that it is understood by the Greeks.

Two important conclusions emerge from this discussion. The first pertains to the power of discourses. Politics is at least as much about efforts to shape language and ideas as it is to shape behavior. One of the most important forms of power, as Marx and Gramsci recognized, is the ability to shape or alter discourses.[67] Marx and Gramsci thought this was dependent on, and an expression of, control over the means of production. Like realists, Marxists emphasize the centrality of material capabilities. My cases suggest that this relationship is not nearly so straightforward. Those with the power regularly attempt to foster and maintain discourses commensurate with their interests. However, discourses can never be fully controlled, something that was apparent even before the information age proliferated mass channels of communication. The use of bribes, threats and coercion to sustain discourses sometimes hastens their transformation or demise. This was the experience of Athens in the fifth century BCE and of so-called enlightened despots in the seventeenth and eighteenth centuries. We may be witnessing another example in the heavy-handed, even crude exercise of American propaganda in the runup and aftermath of the invasion of Iraq. The "war on terror" and the justification for the invasions of Afghanistan and Iraq in the name of national security and local democracy sold well at home but struck much of the world as duplicitous. The Bush administration's behavior and rhetoric accelerated the sharp decline in respect and sympathy for the United States. This phenomenon is indicative of the extent to which discourses surrounding the legitimate uses of military force underwent significant evolution during the course of the twentieth century. Discourses, like influence itself, arise from a complex interplay of ideas and capabilities, and any theory of international relations or foreign policy must take both into account. My theory at least highlights the importance of this relationship and by

---

[67] Gramsci, *Selections from the Prison Notebooks*; Cox, "Gramsci, Hegemony and International Relations"; Gill and Law, "Global Hegemony and the Structural Power of Capital." For non-Marxist applications to IR, Kratochwil, *Rules, Norms and Decisions*; Murphy, "Understanding IR"; Crawford, *Argument and Change in World Politics*; Finnemore and Toope, "Alternatives to 'Legalization.'"

focusing our attention on motives offers some insight into the nature of influence and how it is exercised.

My second conclusion concerns the utility of power as a concept. Ira Katznelson notes that power and the state have been the defining concerns of political science.[68] They are at the core of the realist paradigm. Power is, however, difficult to define or operationalize. Neither Morgenthau nor Waltz produced a useable definition. They define power in terms of its multiple components (e.g. territory, population, wealth, military capability) without providing any relative weighting of them. In his drive for parsimony, Waltz ends up redefining power as all but equivalent to military and economic might.[69] Such a narrow construction might be abstractly appealing but it flies in the face of empirical realities. Morgenthau, to his credit, recognizes that there is no absolute measure of state power because it is always relative and situation-specific. He acknowledges that the strategies and tactics that leaders used to transform the potential attributes of power into influence are just as important as the attributes themselves.[70]

The fundamental problem – most pronounced in Waltz, but evident in other realists and many liberals as well – is the tendency to equate material capabilities with power, and power with influence. My cases indicate that material capabilities are only one component of power, and that power is only one basis of influence. The Anglo-American invasion of Iraq offers dramatic evidence that power does not necessarily produce influence, and that its use in inappropriate ways – at odds with prevailing norms and practices – can seriously erode a state's influence. For the United States, it has led to the seeming paradox that the most powerful state the world has ever witnessed is increasingly incapable of translating its power into influence. This is an anomaly for most realist and liberal understandings of power, but not for a theory like mine that disaggregates influence from power, and directs our attention to the social construction of both, and the ways in which they interact. My cases suggest that international relations theory would greatly benefit from focusing on influence rather than power. Such a shift, while not ignoring material capabilities, would ground the study of influence in the shared discourses that make influence possible. It would return to and build on Hobbes's understanding in

---

[68] Katznelson, "At the Court of Chaos," quoting Watkins, *State as a Concept of Political Science*, p. 83.

[69] Waltz, *Theory of International Politics*, p. 153. Lebow, "The Long Peace, the End of the Cold War, and the Failure of Realism," for a critique of Waltz's conception of power.

[70] Morgenthau, *Politics among Nations*, 1st edn, pp. 14, 105. Lebow, *Tragic Vision of Politics*, ch. 4, for a discussion of Morgenthau's views of power.

Behemoth that "the power of the mighty hath no foundation but in the opinion and belief of the people."[71]

Identity and order

Realism and liberalism ignore the spirit. As we have seen, the few realists and liberals who discuss prestige in international relations do not treat it as an end in itself but as a means of maximizing power. These paradigms also treat the identities of actors as irrelevant or unproblematic. Identities are assumed to have a prior existence or develop in the course of interactions with other actors, interactions that are shaped, if not largely determined, by the character of the system in which they occur. Constructivism problematizes identity. Its adherents insist that it has profound implications for behavior, even under conditions of so-called anarchy. My cases offer strong support for this proposition.

Anarchy – defined as the absence of a unit powerful enough to impose and enforce order – characterized almost every regional and international system I studied. With the exception of the Mediterranean basin during the Roman Empire, there were always multiple political units competing for dominance. Despite the existence of anarchy, there was a wide variation in the degree of order of the systems in question. Greece during the Peloponnesian War, the Mediterranean and Middle East during the Hellenistic age, Italy and Western Europe for much of the duration Roman Republic and medieval Europe were largely unordered. Warfare was frequent, often unlimited in ends and means, cooperation was difficult and usually short-lived, and relations between units were not rule-governed. In some of these systems, most notably the late Roman Republic, the Roman Empire and the Frankish Kingdoms, domestic politics was characterized by the same degree of mistrust, violence and disorder. Other regional and international systems possessed a moderate degree of order: fourth-century Greece, eighteenth-century Europe and East–West relations during the last decades of the Cold War are cases in point. Classical Greece down to the Peloponnesian War – although not the wider Mediterranean and Middle Eastern systems in which it functioned – arguably revealed a higher degree of order.

The order in these systems had little to do with their polarity. Although classical Greece has incorrectly been described as bipolar, it more closely resembled a multipolar system that included powerful states (e.g.

[71] Hobbes, *Behemoth*, p. 59; Flathman, *Thomas Hobbes*, pp. 121–5, for an elaboration.

Syracuse) in addition to Sparta and Athens, and non-Greek actors such as Persia.[72] In the first few centuries of the empire, Rome and Persia came close to being a bipolar system, although they were both vulnerable to incursions from nomadic peoples. The order of systems, domestic, regional and international, is a function of the extent to which reason constrains and educates appetite and spirit. That in turn is the result of reflection upon the consequences of one's own and others' behavior. Some actors come to understand the extent to which the attainment of their own goals – whether it be honor or material well-being – depends on the existence and functioning of the social order. In ordered systems, restraint and conformity to norms are largely self-imposed. High levels of compliance make possible law enforcement and the informal control of deviance through the kinds of social pressures described by Durkheim. In fifth-century Greece and eighteenth- and nineteenth-century Europe informal and collective pressures on actors often succeeded in shaming them into acting into accord with existing *nomos*. When voluntary compliance declines, as it did in late fifth-century Greece or late nineteenth-century Europe, it becomes increasingly difficult to control deviance. Widespread deviance, or deviance on the part of powerful actors, can undermine order and bring about a phase transition into a fear-dominated world.

For realists and liberals alike, order and peace are closely linked. For Waltz they appear to be synonymous.[73] My theory and cases indicate that they need to be conceptualized independently. Spirit-based worlds that are warrior societies can be highly ordered but still characterized by frequent warfare. Order does not prevent war, but regulates it and keep it within bounds, as we observed at times in ancient Greece, and to a lesser extent in Europe between Westphalia and the French Revolution. Spirit-based worlds need not be warrior societies. It is entirely possible to have a society in which honor is a dominant motive but achieved through other forms of excellence. In chapter 2 I suggested that the postindustrialist world may be moving in this direction. Such a society would almost certainly put a premium on peaceful relations among its constituent units and would be more likely to rely on its reward structures and Durkheimian methods of social control in lieu of threats and the balance of power.

I have identified several kinds of hierarchies, each associated with a different kind of order. Those orders in turn reflect the primacy of different motives. Hierarchies exist in all social systems, and take the form of

[72] Lebow, *Tragic Vision of Politics*, pp. 96–9.
[73] Waltz, *Theory of International Politics*, pp. 161–3, 199.

standing in systems such as the international one that lack robust orders.[74] My cases suggest a relationship between legitimacy and order. The former is a source of the latter, just as the latter helps to sustain the former. In regional and international systems the behavior of powerful states is absolutely critical to the maintenance of both hierarchy and order. Such actors are expected to use their authority and power toward this end: to cajole, and if necessary coerce, others into respecting the rules that determine the hierarchy and its associated norms. Most importantly, powerful actors are expected to lead by the example of their own behavior. The more they conform to the norms on which their status is based, the more successful they are likely to be in convincing others to do so.

In chapter 2 I noted that all descriptions of reality are snapshots that freeze it and give the appearance of stability to the so-called structures they portray. All features of social reality are in flux, some more than others, of course. Hierarchies are generally among the more slowly evolving features of the social landscape, but they are subject to all kinds of pressures from within and without and only endure by responding to them. Over time evolution can bring about fundamental changes as dramatic as those associated with revolutions – which, if we keep our evolutionary metaphor, can be described as punctuated equilibria. In mixed worlds we expect to find a mix of motives, varying degrees of support for competing conceptions of justice, and multiple, if not mixed, forms of hierarchy.

Contemporary international relations give evidence to this pattern. States reveal competing conceptions of justice, secular and religious, based on fairness, equality, proportionality and other principles interpreted in diverse ways. The international system is characterized by hierarchies that reflect, or incorporate, some of these conceptions of justice. The United Nations General Assembly is based on the principle of equality, with each state having one vote, while the Security Council is based on the principle of proportionality, with the most powerful states having permanent seats and veto power. Efforts to expand the membership of the Security Council by states seeking permanent seats appeal to variants of both principles. The unipolarity discourse sponsored by realist and neoconservative American foreign policy intellectuals, and embraced by the Bush administration, is offered as justification for a particular kind of hierarchy and is opposed by others who speak the language of multilateralism. The concept of the concert of powers is also present in the various "G" organizations that bring together the leading industrial powers of the world to discuss,

---

[74] Notably, Bull, *Anarchical Society*; Wendt, "Anarchy Is What States Make of It."

and when possible to coordinate, their policies. Analysis of the nature and relative importance of these various hierarchies, their relationship to underlying conceptions of justice, and the ways in which they are being challenged and evolving (or not), would tell us as least as much about international relations as tracking relative shifts in the power of actors.

Hierarchies are institutions in their own right – if we use the anthropological understanding of the term – and manifestations of institutions – if we employ the narrower sociological understanding. In the field of international relations there is a large literature within the liberal paradigm that emphasizes the potential of institutions to facilitate cooperation.[75] These approaches draw their arguments from economics and contend that institutions provide information and mechanisms that increase the benefits of cooperation. They have the potential to encourage, even compel, actors to make binding commitments, which makes defection more costly. Over time, the rewards of working through institutions can also reduce the benefits of defection.[76] My cases suggest that institutions are far from decisive, as extensive cooperation developed in eras when there were no institutions in the sociological sense of the term.[77] In more recent times, the presence of a dense network of such institutions has not prevented failures of cooperation. I have argued elsewhere that liberal institutionalists may mistake cause for effect.[78] Excluding institutions imposed and maintained by coercion, successful institutions build on *prior* decisions, or at least inclinations, by would-be participants to regulate and coordinate their behavior. In the absence of this commitment, these institutions are unlikely to provide the advantages attributed to them. Institutions presuppose common interests, even the existence of a community with many shared values and goals, and only then can they become the custodians of their norms and procedures.[79] Once functioning, institutions have the potential to construct more common interests and identities and strengthen the bonds of community. The real question is why and how a prior inclination to cooperate develops. Here, I believe, we must look to

[75] Eichengreen, *Golden Fetters*; Simmons, *Who Adjusts*.

[76] North, *Institutions, Institutional Change and Economic Performance*; Keohane, *International Institutions and State Power*; Stein, *Why Nations Cooperate*; Shanks et al., "Inertia and Change in the Constellation of International Governmental Organizations, 1981–1991"; Ikenberry, *After Victory*.

[77] Greif, *Institutions and the Path to the Modern Economy*, p. 30, following common practice in economics defines an institution as any system of social factors that generate regularity in behavior. I use institutions in their narrower organizational sense.

[78] Lebow, "Reason, Emotion and Cooperation."

[79] Kratochwil, *Rules, Norms, and Decisions*, p. 64.

the combined power of reason and affect and the learning and sense of community they can encourage.

The psychology of identity

In the introduction, I noted that constructivism must develop a psychology of interaction that links behavior and identity. My theory takes some preliminary steps in this direction. It frames the relationship between identity and behavior as a dynamic one because our understandings of ourselves evolve in response to feedback from our behavior and its consequences. Thinking people also learn about themselves from studying their environment and other actors. Their reflections are not only about behavior and its consequences, but, as Aristotle suggests, about the motives behind such behavior.

There is no consensus about the meaning of identity. However, most definitions start from the premise that it embodies some sense of who we are that connects us to and differentiates us from others.[80] Identity can be constructed around membership in a community and a set of roles it expects us to fulfill, as appears to have been the case in ancient Greece and Rome.[81] In the modern West identity has also involved membership in the nation, but this is just one of many possible affiliations, and not always the most important one. Western identity has also been theorized as something internal to the individual, based on experiences, relationships, feelings and goals that distinguish a person from others. Reflecting the Romantic conception of freedom, Hegel insists that identity requires us to invent something particular for ourselves.[82]

Social and individual formulations of identity are equally problematic. Identity defined as a set of socially determined roles ignores the degree to which people can alter their understandings of these roles or construct identities for themselves different from or in opposition to their societies. The modern Romantic conception errs in the opposite direction by exaggerating the degree of our uniqueness and

---

[80] McCall and Simmons, *Identities and Interactions*; Yack, *The Fetishism of Modernities*; Fitzgerald, *Metaphors of Identity*; Lapid, "Culture's Ship," on the difficulties of defining culture and identity and relating them to each other.

[81] Durkheim, *The Division of Labor in Society*, preface and pp. 219–22; Finley, *The World of Odysseus*, p. 134, for the concept of mechanical solidarity.

[82] Hegel, *Philosophy of Right*, preface, and *Phenomenology*, Bb, Cc; Berman, *The Politics of Individualism*; Norton, *The Beautiful Soul*.

independence from society.[83] The problem of identity is further complicated by empirical evidence indicating that people have not one but multiple identities that reflect the complex ways in which we think of ourselves
in relation to other people, groups of people, institutions and political
units.[84]

I pursue a more restrictive, and admittedly limited, approach to identity that focuses on human goals. Individuals and their societies place
different values on appetite, spirit and reason and channel their expression in different ways. These choices are a major determinant of identity.
I further assume that identity requires some sense of community to allow
individuals to differentiate themselves from others, but not necessarily by
creating hostile binaries of "us" and "others."[85] Hierarchies take different
forms and generate many possible identities.

There are other components of identity and other frames of reference
than motives that actors use to describe themselves. This is unproblematic
because my purpose is not to offer a comprehensive analysis of identity
but rather to isolate one major component of it that can be shown to
vary across actors, and to have important implications for their sense of
who they are, how they frame their interests and how they behave. To
recapitulate, I assume that culture generates identity in a double sense.
It emphasizes some motives and downgrades others and regulates the
ways in which approved ones should be developed and expressed. It does
the same for the spirit by defining the activities that gain esteem and the
routes and mechanisms by which it is achieved and celebrated. It creates
the hierarchies that make social differentiation possible. We are what we
eat, so to speak and what we aspire to be. So motives are an important
constituent of identity, and identity is important because it determines
our interests, and interests in turn inform behavior (see figure 10.3).

This scheme appears to suggests that identity, interests and behavior
are socially determined. However, actors are not prisoners of their socialization.[86] Feedback exists at every step of this chain. The behavior of
actors has the potential to reshape their interests, and changes in interests
affect identities. Changes in the identities of important actors, or large

---

[83] Lebow, *Tragic Vision of Politics*, for a more extensive discussion of these issues and the
relevant psychological literature.

[84] Durkheim, *The Division of Labor in Society*, pp. xl–xli, 172–4; Tajfel, *Human Groups and
Social Categories*; Tajfel and Turner, "The Social Identity Theory of Intergroup Behavior";
Brewer, "The Social Self"; Brewer and Miller, *Intergroup Relations*.

[85] Hobbes, *Leviathan*, I.13, on this point.

[86] Coleman, *The Foundations of Social Theory*, on the need to combine agency and structure
in the study of social behavior.

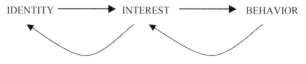

Fig. 10.3 *Identity*

numbers of them, can transform the character of the system in which they operate. Agency is as important as structure in this dynamic system. Agency is critical in another sense. Actors are influenced by their beliefs, not only by their behavior. Life experiences and the lessons they learn second-hand from education and reading give rise to beliefs about how the world works, who is a friend and who an enemy and the best ways to respond to both. National policymaking elites invariably contain people with varying outlooks on the world and associated policy preferences. Some of this variation can be explained with reference to the distribution of motives among actors. Fear, interest and honor give rise to different foreign policy orientations and specific preferences as we have observed in so many of my cases. Jacques Hymans uses a related scheme to show how conceptions of what a state stands for (solidarity) and how high it stands (status) vary within political elites. These conceptions combine to generate four national identity conceptions. Shifts in power among leaders with different conceptions do a better job than realism or bureaucratic and domestic politics in explaining the complex and shifting nuclear proliferation policies of France, Australia, Argentina and India. Leaders who fear their adversaries but feel superior to them are most likely to push for nuclear weapons.[87]

What kinds of feedback mechanisms are relevant here? In chapter 8 I noted that behavior is not always consistent with self-image and that actors commonly resort to cognitive sleights of hand to make it appear consistent and thereby reduce dissonance. Daryl Bem finds experimental evidence for the reverse process: reinterpretation of self-images to make them consistent with behavior. People appear to infer their attitudes from their behavior the same way an outside observer might. Self-perception theory is thus a special case of attribution theory.[88] Thucydides reveals a similar understanding in his discussion of how language is mobilized toward this end. His account of the Peloponnesian War implicitly

[87] Hymans, *Psychology of Nuclear Proliferation.*
[88] Bem, "Self-Perception" and "Self-Perception Theory"; Zanna and Cooper, "Dissonance and the Pill."

reveals – and his depiction of stasis in Corcyra does so explicitly – that changes in their behavior led people to reformulate their understandings of key concepts like justice, interest and reason. Their meanings were stretched to encompass, even justify, behavior at odds with their traditional meanings and accepted *nomos*. Changes in language allowed such behavior to become more widespread and accepted, which hastened the further transformation of the language. This process was consciously abetted by the rhetorical strategy of those in positions of authority. As their deeds became more at odds with traditional *nomos* they resorted to increasingly hypocritical arguments to make them appear consistent. They stretched language and logic and implicitly encouraged others to emulate them. At a certain point, when selfish behavior had become widespread and increasingly accepted, they gave up all pretence and adopted a blatant rhetoric of power and self-interest narrowly conceived.[89]

Anthropologist Erving Goffman describes another feedback process associated with what he calls the "interactive order." Drawing on Durkheim, he argues that society is held together by numerous everyday rituals. Personal relationships, including ephemeral encounters, only become a social reality through the rituals participants enact. The most banal gestures of politeness – among them greetings, handshakes, meaningless platitudes, goodbyes – fulfill the same functions that Durkheim attributes to religious ritual. Such micro-interactions, even though they allow deception and are susceptible to misunderstandings, structure social solidarity, and by extension the identity of participants. None of these interactions necessarily expresses the true feelings of participants and can be significantly at odds with them. Actors nevertheless realize the importance of enacting such rituals, and more generally of projecting an image of themselves and their behavior consistent with them.[90] A simple but revealing example are studies that indicate that a significantly higher percentage of people wash their hands before leaving public restrooms when other people are present and they can be observed.[91]

Actors who participate in rituals repeatedly – and all social encounters are embedded in rituals – cannot avoid reframing, at least in part, their conceptions of themselves to make them consistent with their behavior. Rituals reflect and instantiate a society's values, but they are malleable

---

[89] Thucydides, 3.53–68, 3.83.1–2, 5.89–99.

[90] Goffman, "The Nature of Difference and Demeanor," "Symbols of Class Status," *Presentation of Self in Everyday Life*, and *Stigma* and *Behavior in Public Places*.

[91] Monk-Turner *et al.*, "Predictors of Hand-Washing Behavior." The findings applied to women and minorities.

and change in response to the needs, values and preferences of actors. Changes in rituals have the potential to resocialize actors and ultimately to alter the discourses of the society. In Western countries, men used to doff their hats to "ladies" and open doors for them. This ritual affirmed and sustained the subordinate, if honored, role of women of a certain class. Both rituals gradually disappeared as women insisted on equality. Other rituals remain contested. At the time of writing marriage is high on the list in the United States, with many gays insisting on the right to participate in this ritual.

Bem's and Goffmann's actors are individual human beings and the mechanisms they describe are limited to individuals. But, as we have seen, the behavior of governments, and hierarchies more generally, is embedded in ritual. This also holds true for relations among political units. Diplomatic practice consists of elaborate and precise rituals that govern the interactions of state representatives and their leaders. They socialize all but the most recalcitrant actors to certain norms of behavior and help them to construct identities. Changes in interstate ritual should have the potential to alter the identities of states. Cases in point concern the procedures governing ships and fleets encountering one another on the high seas. In the seventeenth century the French asserted their primacy by insisting that his ambassadors take precedence over others and that other countries' naval vessels lower their flags or fire a salute in the presence of French ships. The British and Spanish refused, leading to violent exchanges, making the would-be ritual costly to ignore but impossible to enforce. In the nineteenth and twentieth centuries great powers were effective in asserting their primacy in diplomatic gatherings. The relative status of their country determined the precedence of diplomats and state representatives up to and including the Congress of Vienna, but this was replaced by the practice of establishing standing on the basis of years in service in a given posting. The change in this ritual was initially a convenient way of depoliticizing precedence but later became the harbinger of the emerging principle of equality among states.

The literature on ontological security, which derives in part from Goffmann's work, starts from the premise that actors of all kinds require consistent concepts of self that are generated and sustained through foreign policy routines. Some political scientists argue that these routines are embedded in biographical narratives of states that officials, media and intellectuals develop and invoke to explain and justify foreign policies. Policies at odds with these narratives and the values they encode bring shame on officials if public opinion judges their behavior at odds with their states' identity.[92] It seems equally likely that behavior consistently at odds with self-images will serve as the catalyst for changes in those self-images along the lines that Thucydides suggests. La Rochefoucauld and Tocqueville describe a roughly similar interaction between words and deeds in pre-revolutionary France.[93]

Identity and change

My theory addresses change at multiple levels. First, there is the process that I described in the previous section that connects the values of society to behavior through the identities and interests of actors. These links also work in reverse, allowing actors to influence and change the character of their society by altering their self-images and rituals of interaction. The analogy is to language.[94] We human beings need language to communicate and acquire it the way we do an identity. From early childhood we assimilate and practice the vocabulary, grammar and pronunciation of our mother tongue and the various social conventions associated with its use. As we mature, we introduce new words and expressions, devise new meanings to old words, let old words and meanings lapse, violate conventional grammar, and, most fundamentally, alter the social meanings associated with both the spoken and written language. Over time, the language evolves, and efforts to prevent it from doing so usually fail, as have the various measures of the French Academy and government to keep Anglicisms from creeping into the French lexicon.

Agents also have a powerful impact on the role of reason in their society. In chapter 2 I suggested that elites are particularly important in this regard because only they have the potential to create and instantiate discourses that emphasize and justify self-restraint. Spirit unconstrained by reason intensifies the competition for honor and gives rise to disruptive conflict within the elite. Unconstrained appetite undermines an elite's legitimacy and arouses resentment and envy on the part of other actors. It can bring about more pronounced imbalance in a society when other actors emulate elite self-indulgence and disregard the norms restraining the pursuit of wealth at others' expense. Loss of control to the spirit was a persistent threat to order in ancient Greece, the Roman

---

[92] Huysmans, "Security!"; McSweeny, *Security, Identity and Interests*; Mitzen, "Ontological Security in World Politics"; Manners, "European [Security] Union"; Steele, "Self-Identity and the IR State," p. 3; Berenskoetter, "Creating (In)Security from Within."

[93] Tocqueville, *Old Regime*, pp. 142–4; Furet, *Interpreting the French Revolution* p. 46.

[94] Wendt, "Anarchy Is What States Make of It," makes this analogy.

Republic, the Middle Ages and eighteenth-century Europe. In all these cases it was a major cause of civil and interstate wars. Loss of control to the appetite was not unknown in Greece, where it was initially associated with tyrants and oligarchies. In the modern world it is endemic to all kinds of regimes and their elites and has made rapacity a principal source of conflict at every level of order. This process is responsible for the first, most superficial, level of change: the oscillation of societies and the systems in which they interact along the continuum between reason- and fear-based worlds.

I describe two kinds of longer-term changes. The first consists of movement to and away from different ideal-type worlds and is determined largely by changes in the division of labor. Making allowance for considerable variation, human history begins with societies that are appetite-driven and subsequently transitions to worlds of the spirit, and much later back to appetite. The first iteration of appetite revolves around hunger, as hunter-gatherers and early agricultural settlements are consumed with the problem of subsistence. The spirit becomes more prominent in response to the division of labor and the accumulation of surplus. Surplus allows population growth, greater propinquity of settlements and greater competition for territory and other scarce resources. As external competition becomes more acute, or its material benefits more obvious, warriors increase their standing and authority in the society. Ideally, warrior-based honor societies maintain peace at home and deflect aggression abroad. The subsequent transformation back to an appetite world reflects further complexity in the division of labor. New classes emerge that initially seek entry into the existing elite, but if denied, may advance alternative claims to standing based on the benefits of appetite to society and the services they provide in that regard.

Transformations from appetite to spirit to interest-based worlds are progressive but not linear. They are not infrequently interrupted by breakdowns in order and the decay, even disappearance, of key political units, as well as regression into fear-based worlds. These breakdowns can and do occur at any stage of historical development. They may be repeated more than once in a unit or system before it transitions to the next stage of development. All of these transitions occur first in units but have the potential to transform the system when enough units have undergone a similar transition and pressures mount on other units to conform.

In *The Tragic Vision of Politics*, I argue that fifth-century Greece underwent a process of modernization that began to transform Athens from a spirit-based to an interest-based society.[95] This transformation was a fundamental cause of imbalance within Athens where reason lost control to both spirit and appetite, and between Sparta and Athens by virtue of Sparta's relative decline in standing. Both kinds of imbalance were fundamental causes of the Peloponnesian War. My cases in this book suggest that similar changes took place in early modern and modern Europe, where changes in emphasis and acceptability of motives – once again from spirit to appetite – helped to bring about civil breakdown and destructive wars. It is not coincidental that the Peloponnesian War and World Wars I and II occurred when those transitions were only partially completed. Transitions are danger periods because they can lead to reason's loss of control over the spirit without offsetting it by more effective control over the appetite.

A third and still deeper level of change involves changes in the ways appetite and spirit find expression. Wealth and education encourage more complex appetites and multiple routes by which honor and standing can be achieved. In the modern age, appetite and spirit became increasingly entwined as material possessions, from carriages to colonies, were sought after as markers of standing. To the extent that wealth, and the material possessions and leisure it permits, become increasingly widespread, they can no longer serve as effectively as markers of standing. In the postmodern world, appetite and spirit may become increasingly disaggregated, as I suggest in chapter 7. The search for meaning beyond affluence can only go in the direction of the spirit, to honor and recognition, and with it esteem, achieved on the basis of one's private achievements or public service. The present age may herald the tentative beginnings of such a transformation. In the wealthiest countries, a gradual shift is underway, most marked among the young, from "materialist" values (that stress economic and physical security) toward "post-materialist values" (that value self-expression and the quality of life).[96]

In Homer's world, bravery in battle and sporting prowess – both expression of *thumos* – were more highly regarded than anything else and were the principal claim for honor and standing. In the fifth century, skill in rhetoric and poetry supplemented athletic and military prowess as vehicles by which honor and standing could be attained. In the modern world, honor hierarchies have proliferated. Today, people can compete and excel in a wide range of activities, making it at least theoretically possible for

---

[95] Lebow, *Tragic Vision of Politics*, pp. 27–34, 152.
[96] Inglehart, *Culture Shift in Advanced Society*, and *Modernization and Postmodernization*.

everyone to exploit whatever talent they have to win the approbation of their peers and build their esteem. Most of these hierarchies have become increasingly open, breaking down, if not altogether doing away with, the traditional divide in honor societies between an elite allowed to compete for honor and standing and an underclass that cannot.

Viewed in this light, the international system is something of an atavism that still reflects many of the values of warrior societies. In contrast to societies in the developed world, there is still a single hierarchy of standing, and it is based on military power. In chapter 9 I noted that revolutionary powers (i.e. the United States, France, the Soviet Union, China and Iran) have challenged the legitimacy of this hierarchy and claimed standing on ideological grounds. These challenges failed, and most of the powers in question subsequently sought and achieved standing on traditional grounds. A more serious challenge is now underway, also described in chapter 9. It is spearheaded by a diverse group of countries, many of whom, such as Canada, Japan and the members of the European Union, claim standing on the basis of the multilateral nature of their foreign policies and how their wealth is used to benefit their citizens and those of less-developed countries. Their claims for status are based on honor, and rest on the hope that international society has become more like domestic societies in that multiple hierarchies are possible and thick enough to allow honor to replace standing as the basis of influence.

The transformation of the international system is by no means preordained, but it is a distinct possibility. In chapter 1 I offer a story line that leads us toward the proliferation of hierarchies at the regional and international levels and describes some of their likely consequences for interstate relations. Key to this transformation is the way in which discourses define what actors consider to be legitimate and illegitimate. Changes in the criteria for standing encourage shifts in foreign policy behavior, which in turn affect how states define their interests and ultimately their identities. As conflictual and violent as the current world is, and as remote an ideal a peaceful world appears, there is nevertheless a more realistic possibility than ever before of transforming the character of international relations to make it more closely resemble the more ordered and complex world of domestic societies. Troy – or Iraq – may ultimately become the tomb of heroes and heroism in the sense understood by Catullus, whom I quote at the outset of this chapter. It is important not to lose sight of this possibility, and for theory to show us how such a world could come about and renew our commitment to work toward its attainment.

BIBLIOGRAPHY

Abrams, Dominic and Michael Hogg, "Comments on the Motivational Status of Self-Esteem in Social Identity and Intergroup Discrimination," *European Journal of Social Psychology* 22 (1988), pp. 317–34.

"Social Identification, Social Categorization and Social Influence," *European Review of Social Psychology* 1 (1990), pp. 195–228.

eds., *Social Identity Theory: Constructive and Critical Advances* (New York: Springer, 1990).

Adams, Michael C., *The Great Adventure: Male Desire and the Coming of World War I* (Bloomington: University of Indiana Press, 1990).

Adamson, John, "The Kingdom of England and Great Britain: The Tudor and Stuart Courts 1509–1714," in John Adamson, ed., *The Princely Courts of Europe: Ritual, Politics and Culture under the Ancien Régime* (London: Weidenfeld and Nicolson, 1999), pp. 95–117.

Adcock, Frank E., *The Greek and Macedonian Art of War* (Berkeley: University of California Press, 1957).

Adkins, A. W. H., *Merit and Responsibility: A Study in Greek Values* (Oxford: Oxford University Press, 1960).

Adler, Emanuel, "Seizing the Middle Ground: Constructivism in World Politics," *European Journal of International Relations* 3 (1997), pp. 319–63.

Communitarian International Relations: The Epistemic Foundations of International Relations (London: Routledge, 2005).

Adler, Emanuel and Michael Barnett, eds., *Security Communities* (Cambridge: Cambridge University Press, 1998).

Aeschylus, *Aeschylus I: Oresteia*, ed. David Grene and Richmond Lattimore (Chicago: University of Chicago Press, 1953).

The Oresteia, trans. A. Shapiro and P. Burian (Oxford: Oxford University Press, 2003).

Afflerbach, Holger, *Falkenhayn. Politisches Denken und Handeln in Kaiserreich* (Munich: Oldenbourg, 1994).

Afflerbach, Holger and David Stevenson, *An Improbable War? The Outbreak of World War I and European Political Culture* (New York: Berghahn, 2007).

Agamben, Giorgio, *Homo Sacer: Sovereign Power and Bare Life*, trans. Daniel Heller-Roazen (Stanford, CA: Stanford University Press, 1998).

Agawa, Hiroyuki, *The Reluctant Admiral: Yamamoto and the Imperial Navy*, trans. John Bester (Tokyo: Kodansha, 1979).

Agnew, Jean-Christophe, *Worlds Apart: The Market and the Theater in Anglo-American Thought, 1550–1750* (Cambridge: Cambridge University Press, 1986).

Agnew, John A., "The Territorial Trap: The Geographical Assumptions of International Relations Theory," *Review of International Political Economy* 1 (Spring 1994), pp. 53–80.

"Spacelessness Versus Timeless Space in State-Centered Social Science," *Environment and Planning* 28 (1996), p. 11.

"Political Power and Geographical Scale," *Political Space: New Frontiers of Change and Governance in a Globalizing World*, in Ferguson and Jones, *Political Space*, pp. 115–29.

Agnew, John A. and Stuart Corbridge, *Mastering Space: Hegemony, Territory and International Political Economy* (New York: Routledge, 1995).

Aiko, Yuichi, "Rousseau and Saint-Pierre's Peace Project: A Critique of 'History of International Relations Theory,'" in Jahn, *Classical Theory in International Relations*, pp. 96–122.

Ainsworth, Peter F., *Jean Froissart and the Fabric of History* (Oxford: Oxford University Press, 1990).

Airlie, Stuart, "The Aristocracy," in McKitterick, *The New Cambridge Medieval History*, vol. II, pp. 431–50.

"Charlemagne and the Aristocracy: Captains and Kings," in Story, ed., *Charlemagne*, pp. 90–102.

Akbar, Ahmed S., *Jinnah, Pakistan and Islamic Identity: The Search for Saladin* (London: Routledge, 1997).

Islam under Siege: Living Dangerously in a Post-Honor World (Cambridge: Cambridge University Press, 2003).

Akin, David and Joel Robbins, eds., *Money and Modernity: State and Local Currencies in Melanesia* (Pittsburgh, PA: University of Pittsburgh Press, 1999).

Akira, Fujiwara, "The Role of the Japanese Army," in Borg and Okamoto, *Pearl Harbor as History*, pp. 189–96.

Albert, Matthias, David Jacobson and Yosef Lapid, eds., *Identities, Border, Orders: Rethinking International Relations* (Minneapolis: University of Minnesota Press, 2001).

Albertini, Luigi, *The Origins of the War of 1914*, trans. Isabella M. Massey, 3 vols. (Oxford: Oxford University Press, 1952–7).

Albin, Cecelia, *Justice and Fairness in International Negotiation* (Cambridge: Cambridge University Press, 2001).

Albrecht, Glenn, "Directionality Theory: Neo-Organicism and Dialectical Complexity," *Democracy and Nature* 6, no. 3 (November 2000), pp. 401–19.

Albright, Madeleine K., "United Nations," *Foreign Policy* 138 (September/October 2003), pp. 16–24.

Alekseev, Aleksandr A., "Karibskii krisis: kak eto bylo" [The Caribbean Crisis as it Really Was], *Ekho Planety*, no. 33 (November 1988), p. 29.

Alexander, Jeffrey, *Action and its Environments: Toward a New Synthesis* (New York: Columbia University Press, 1988).

Alexander, Jeffrey C. and Philip Smith, *The Cambridge Companion to Durkheim* (Cambridge: Cambridge University Press, 2005).

Alexander, Richard, *The Biology of Moral Systems* (New York: De Gruyter, 1987).

Alfonsi, Christian, *Circle in the Sand: Why We Went Back to Iraq* (New York: Doubleday, 2006).

Alford, C. Fred, *Levinas, the Frankfurt School and Psychoanalysis* (Middletown, CT: Wesleyan University Press, 2002).

Alford, John R. and John R. Hibbing, "The Origin of Politics: An Evolutionary Theory of Political Behavior," *Perspectives in Politics* 2 (December 2004), pp. 707–21.

Aliano, Richard A., *American Defense Policy from Eisenhower to Kennedy: The Politics of Changing Military Requirements, 1957–61* (Athens: Ohio University Press, 1975).

Alker, Hayward R., *Rediscoveries and Reformulations: Humanistic Methodologies for International Studies* (Cambridge: Cambridge University Press, 1996).

Al-Khalil, Samir, *The Monument: Art, Vulgarity, and Responsibility in Iraq* (Berkeley: University of California Press, 1991).

Allen, Colin, Marc Bekoff and George Lauder, eds., *Nature's Purposes* (Cambridge, MA: MIT Press, 1998).

Allen, Danielle, *The World of Prometheus: The Politics of Punishing in Democratic Athens* (Princeton, NJ: Princeton University Press, 2000).

Allen, William Sheridan, *The Nazi Seizure of Power: The Experience of a Single German Town, 1922–1945*, rev. edn (New York: Franklin Watts, 1984).

Allison, Graham T., *Essence of Decision: Explaining the Cuban Missile Crisis* (Boston: Little Brown, 1971).

Allison, June W., "Thucydides and *Polypragmosyne*," *American Journal of Ancient History* 4 (1979), pp. 10–22.

Allison, Lincoln, *The Global Politics of Sports* (London: Routledge, 2000).

Allison, Lincoln and Terry Monnington, "Sport Prestige and International Relations," in Allison, *The Global Politics of Sports*, pp. 5–25.

Allmand, C. T., *The Hundred Years War: England and France at War* (Cambridge: Cambridge University Press, 1988).

Allyn, Bruce J., James G. Blight and David A. Welch, eds., *Back to the Brink: Proceedings of the Moscow Conference on the Cuban Missile Crisis, January 27–28, 1989* (Lanham, MD: University Press of America, 1992).

Almond, Gabriel A., "The Return of the State," *American Political Science Review* 82 (September 1988), pp. 853–74.

A Discipline Divided (Newbury Park, CA: Sage, 1990).

Almond, Gabriel and Stephen J. Genco, "Clouds, Clocks, and the Study of Politics," *World Politics* 29, no. 4 (July 1977), pp. 496–522.

Almond, Gabriel and Sidney Verba, *The Civic Culture: Political Democracy in Five Nations* (Princeton, NJ: Princeton University Press, 1963).

Almond, Gabriel A., Taylor Cole and Roy C. Macridis, "A Suggested Research Strategy in Western European Government and Politics," *American Political Science Review* 49 (1955), pp. 1042–4.

Althusser, Louis, "Ideology and Ideological State Apparatuses (Notes Toward an Investigation)," in *Lenin and Philosophy and Other Essays*, trans. Ben Brewster (New York: Monthly Review Press, 1971), pp. 127–88.

For Marx, trans. Ben Brewster (London: Verso, 2005 [1965]).

Althusser, Louis and Étienne Balibar, *Reading Capital* (London: New Left Books, 1970).

Alvis, John, *Divine Purpose and Heroic Response in Homer and Virgil* (Lanham, MD: Rowman and Littlefield, 1995).

Ambrose, Stephen E., *Eisenhower*, 2 vols. (New York: Simon and Schuster, 1983–4).

Ames, Glenn J., *Colbert, Mercantilism, and the French Quest for Asian Trade* (Dekalb: Northern Illinois University Press, 1996).

Amin, Ash, ed., *Post-Fordism: A Reader* (Oxford: Basil Blackwell, 1994).

Anan, Noel, *Our Age: The Generation that Made Post-War Britain* (London: Fontana, 1990).

Anaya, James S., *Indigenous Peoples and International Law* (New York: Oxford University Press, 1996).

Andersen, Peter B., Niels O. Finneman and Peter V. Christiansen, eds., *Downward Causation* (Aarhus: Aarhus University Press, 2000).

Anderson, Benedict, *Imagined Communities*, 2nd edn (New York: Verso Press, 1991).

Anderson, James, "Questions of Democracy, Territoriality and Globalization," in James Anderson, ed., *Transnational Democracy: Political Spaces and Border Crossings* (London: Routledge, 2002), pp. 29–33.

Anderson, M. S., *Europe in the Eighteenth Century, 1713–1783* (New York: Holt, Rinehart and Winston, 1961).

"Eighteenth-Century Theories of the Balance of Power," in R. Hatton and M. S. Anderson, eds., *Studies in Diplomatic History* (London: Longman, 1970), pp. 183–98.

War and Society in Europe of the Old Regime, 1618–1789 (London: Fontana Books, 1988).

The War of the Austrian Succession, 1740–1748 (London: Longman, 1995).

Anderson, Margaret, *Practicing Democracy: Elections and Political Culture in Imperial Germany* (Princeton, NJ: Princeton University Press, 2000).

Anderson, Perry, *Lineages of the Absolutist State* (London: New Left Books, 1974).

Passages from Antiquity to Feudalism (London: New Left Books, 1974).

Andrew, C. M., P. Grupp and A. S. Kanya-Forstner, "The *groupe coloniale* in the French Chamber of Deputies, 1892–1932," *Historical Journal* 17 (1974), pp. 837–66.

"Le mouvement colonial française et ses principales personnalités, 1890–1914," *Revue Française d'Histoire d'Outre-Mer* 62 (1975), pp. 640–73.

"French Business and French Colonialists," *Historical Journal* 19 (1976), pp. 981–1000.

Andrew, Jean-Christophe, *Worlds Apart: The Market and the Theater in Anglo-American Thought, 1550–1750* (Cambridge: Cambridge University Press, 1986).

Annas, Julia, *The Morality of Happiness* (Oxford: Oxford University Press, 1993).

Apel, Karl-Otto, "Kant's 'Toward Perpetual Peace' as Historical Prognosis from the Point of View of Moral Duty," in James Bohmann and Matthias Lutz-Bachmann, eds., *Perpetual Peace: Essays on Kant's Cosmopolitan Ideal* (Cambridge, MA: MIT Press, 1997), pp. 79–112.

Appadurai, Arjun, *Modernity at Large* (Minneapolis: University of Minnesota Press, 1997).

Appian, *The Civil Wars*, ed. and trans. John Carter (New York: Penguin, 1996).

Apter, David, *Ideology and Discontent* (Glencoe, IL: Free Press, 1964).

Aquarone, Alberto, "Public Opinion in Italy before the Outbreak of World War II," in Roland Sarti, The *Ax Within. Italian Fascism in Action* (New York: New Viewpoints, 1974), pp. 209–22.

Arbatov, Georgi, *The System: An Insider's Life in Soviet Politics* (New York: Random House, 1992).

Archambault, Paul, "The Analogy of the Body in Renaissance Political Literature," *Bulletin d'Humanisme et Renaissance* 29 (1967), pp. 21–53.

Archibugi, Danielle and David Held, eds., *Cosmopolitan Democracy: An Agenda for a New World Order* (Cambridge: Polity, 1995).

"Introduction," to Archibugi and Held, *Democracy: An Agenda for a New World Order*, pp. 1–16.

Archibugi, Danielle, David Held and Martin Köhler, eds., *Re-Imagining Political Community: Studies in Cosmopolitan Democracy* (Stanford, CA: Stanford University Press, 1998).

Arend, Anthony Clark and Robert J. Beck, *International Law and the Use of Force* (New York: Routledge, 1994).

Arendt, Hannah, *The Human Condition* (Chicago: University of Chicago Press, 1958).

Eichmann in Jerusalem: A Report on the Banality of Evil (New York: Viking, 1964).

The Origins of Totalitarianism (New York: Harcourt, 1973).

Lectures on Kant's Political Philosophy (Chicago: University of Chicago Press, 1992).

Aristotle, *The Complete Works of Aristotle: The Revised Oxford Translation*, ed. Jonathan Barnes (Princeton, NJ: Princeton University Press, 1984).

Armitage, David, *The Ideological Origins of the British Empire* (Cambridge: Cambridge University Press, 2002).

Armstrong, John, "Nations Before Nationalism," in John Hutchinson and Anthony D. Smith, eds., *Nationalism* (New York: Oxford University Press, 1994), pp. 140–7.

Aron, Raymond, *Peace and War: A Theory of International Relations*, trans. Richard Howard and Annette Baker Fox (Garden City, NY: Doubleday, 1966 [1962]).

Arrian, *The Campaigns of Alexander*, trans. Aubrey de Sélincourt (New York: Barnes and Noble, 1971).

Arrighi, Giovanni, *The Long Twentieth Century: Money, Power, and the Origins of Our Times* (London: Verso 1994).

Artz, Lee, "War as Promotional 'Photo-Op': The *New York Times*'s Visual Coverage of the U.S. Invasion of Iraq," in Kamalipour and Snow, *War, Media, and Propaganda: A Global Perspective*, pp. 79–92.

Ashley, David, *History Without a Subject: The Postmodern Condition* (Boulder, CO: Westview, 1997).

Ashley, Richard K, "The Poverty of Neorealism," in Robert O. Keohane, *Neorealism and its Critics* (New York: Columbia University Press, 1986), pp. 255–300.

    "Reading Dissidence/Writing the Discipline: Crisis and the Question of Sovereignty in International Studies," *International Studies Quarterly*, 34, no. 3 (September 1990), pp. 367–416.

    "The Powers of Anarchy: Theory, Sovereignty, and the Domestication of Global Life," in James Der Derian, ed., *International Theory: Critical Investigations* (London: Macmillan, 1995), pp. 94–128.

Ashley, Richard K. and R. B. J. Walker, eds., "Speaking the Language of Exile: Dissidence in International Studies," *International Studies Quarterly*, 34, no. 3 (September 1990), pp. 259–68.

Aspaturian, Vernon, "Soviet Global Power and the Correlation of Forces," *Problems of Communism*, no. 20 (May/June 1980), pp. 1–8.

Attali, Jacques, "The Crash of Western Civilization: The Limits of the Market and Democracy," *Foreign Affairs* 107 (Summer 1997), pp. 54–64.

Auerbach, Erich, *Mimesis: The Representation of Reality in Modern Literature*, trans. Willar R. Trask (Princeton, NJ: Princeton University Press, 2003 [1946]).

Augelli, Enrico and Craig N. Murphy, *America's Quest for Supremacy and the Third World* (London: Pinter Publishers, 1998).

Augustine, *The City of God*, trans. Marcus Dods (New York: Modern Library, 1950).

    Confessions, trans. Henry Chadwick (Oxford: Oxford University Press, 1998).

Autrand, François, "France under Charles V and Charles VI," in Jones, *The New Cambridge Medieval History*, vol. VI, pp. 422–41.

Avineri, Shlomo, *Hegel's Theory of the Modern State* (Cambridge: Cambridge University Press, 1974).

Axelrod, Robert M., *The Evolution of Cooperation* (New York: Basic Books, 1984).

Axelrod, Robert M. and D. Dion, "The Further Evolution of Cooperation," *Science* 242 (1998), pp. 1385–90.

Axelrod, Robert M. and Robert O. Keohane, "Achieving Cooperation under Anarchy: Strategies and Institutions," *World Politics* 38, no. 1 (1985), pp. 226–54.

Aycoberry, Pierre, *The Nazi Question: An Essay on the Interpretations of National Socialism (1922–1975)*, trans, Robert Hurley (New York: Pantheon, 1981).

Ayers, Edward L., *Vengeance and Justice: Crime and Punishment in the 19th Century American South* (New York: Oxford University Press, 1984).

Ayton, Andrew and Philip Preston, eds., *The Battle of Crécy, 1346* (Woodbridge, Suffolk: Boydell Press, 2005).

Bacon, Francis, *The Advancement of Learning*, ed. William Wright (Oxford: Oxford University Press, 1920).

The Essayes or Counsels: Civill and Morall, ed. Michael Kiernan (Oxford: Oxford University Press, 1985).

Baddeley, A., "Is Memory all Talk?" *The Psychologist* 5 (1992), pp. 447–8.

Badian, Ernst, *Foreign Clientelae (264–70 B.C.)* (Oxford: Oxford University Press, 1958).

Roman Imperialism in the Late Republic (Ithaca, NY: Cornell University Press, 1968).

Badoglio, Pietro, *Italy in the Second World War: Memoirs and Documents* (Oxford: Oxford University Press, 1948).

Bae Ho Han and Soo Young Uh, *Korean Political Culture* (Seoul: Bupmon Publishing Co., 1987).

Baecque, Antoine de, *The Body Politic: Corporeal Metaphor in Revolutionary France, 1770–1800*, trans. Charlotte Mandell (Stanford, CA: Stanford University Press, 1977).

Baker, Keith Michael, ed., *The Old Regime and the French Revolution* (Chicago: University of Chicago Press, 1987).

"Enlightenment and the Institution of Society: Notes for a Conceptual History," in Kaviraj and Khilnani, eds., *Civil Society*, pp. 84–104.

Bakhtin, Mikhail, *Problems of Dostoevsky's Poetics* (Minneapolis: University of Minnesota Press, 1984).

Bakker, Egbert, *Poetry in Speech: Orality and Homeric Discourse* (Ithaca, NY: Cornell University Press, 1997).

Baldwin, John W., *The Government of Philip Augustus: Fundamentals of French Royal Power in the Middle Ages* (Berkeley: University of California Press, 1986).

Ball, Desmond, *Politics and Force Levels: The Strategic Missile Program of the Kennedy Administration* (Berkeley: University of California Press, 1980).

Ball, Terence, ed., *Idioms of Inquiry* (Albany: State University of New York Press, 1987).

Ball, Terence, James Farr and Russell L. Hanson, eds., *Political Innovation and Conceptual Change* (Cambridge: Cambridge University Press, 1989).

Balot, Ryan K., *Greed and Injustice in Classical Athens* (Princeton, NJ: Princeton University Press, 2001).

Balsdon, J. P., *Romans and Aliens* (Chapel Hill: University of North Carolina Press, 1979).

Bamba, Nobuya, *Japanese Diplomacy in a Dilemma: A New Light on Japan's Chikna Policy, 1924–49* (Vancouver: University of British Columbia Press, 1972).

Bank, David, *Breaking Windows: How Bill Gates Fumbled the Future of Microsoft* (New York: Free Press, 2001).

Baratelson, Jens, "Making Sense of Global Society," *European Journal of International Relations* 12, no. 3 (September 2006), pp. 371–96.

Barber, Benjamin R., *Strong Democracy: Participatory Politics for a New Age* (Berkeley: University of California Press, 1984).

    Jihad vs. McWorld (New York: Times Books, 1995).

Barber, Richard W., *The Knight and Chivalry* (Rochester, NY: Boydell, 1995).

Barbero, Alessandro, *Charlemagne: Father of a Continent*, trans. Allan Cameron (Berkeley: University of California Press, 2004).

Barclay, C. R., "Composing Protoselves Through Improvisation," in U. Neisser and R. Fivush, *The Remembering Self: Construction and Accuracy in the Self Narrative* (Cambridge: Cambridge University Press, 1994), pp. 55–7.

Barkawi, Tarak and Mark Laffey, "The Imperial Peace: Democracy, Force and Globalization," *European Journal of International Relations* 5, no. 4 (1999), pp. 403–34.

    eds., *Democracy, Liberalism, and War: Rethinking the Democratic Peace* (Boulder, CO: Lynne Rienner, 2001).

    "Retrieving the Imperial: Empire and International Relations," *Millennium* 31, no. 1 (2002), pp. 109–27.

Barker, Judith R. V., *The Tournament in England, 1100–1400* (Woodbridge, Suffolk: Boydell Press, 1986).

Barker, Rodney, *Political Legitimacy and the State* (Oxford: Oxford University Press, 1990).

Barkin, Samuel J., "Realist Constructivism and Realist-Constructivisms," *International Studies Review* 6, no. 2 (June 2004), pp. 348–52.

Barkow, Jerome H., Leda Cosmides and John Tooby, eds., *The Adapted Mind: Evolutionary Psychology and the Development of Culture* (New York: Oxford University Press, 1992).

Barlow, Ima C., *The Agadir Crisis* (Chapel Hill: University of North Carolina Press, 1940).

Barnaby, Frank, *The Gaia Peace Atlas: Survival into the Third Millennium* (New York: Doubleday, 1988).

Barnes, Jonathan, *The Presocratic Philosophers*. vol. I: *Thales to Zeno* (London: Routledge and Kegan Paul, 1979).

"Metaphysics," in Jonathan Barnes, ed., *The Cambridge Companion to Aristotle* (Cambridge: Cambridge University Press, 1995), pp. 66–108.

Barnett, Michael N., "Sovereignty, Nationalism, and Regional Order in the Arab States System," *International Organization*, 49, no. 3 (Summer 1995), pp. 479–510.

Barnhardt, Michael A., *Japan Prepares for Total War: The Search for Economic Security, 1919–1941* (Ithaca, NY: Cornell University Press, 1987).

Barnie, John, *War in Medieval English Society: Social Values in the Hundred Years War, 1337–99* (Ithaca, NY: Cornell University Press, 1974).

Barraclough, Geoffrey, *The Medieval Empire, Ideal and Reality* (London: G. Philip, 1950).

Barron, Caroline M., "The Reign of Richard II," in Jones, *The New Cambridge Medieval History*, vol. VI, pp. 297–333.

Barrow, Clyde, *Critical Theories of the State: Marxist, Neo-Marxist, Post-Marxist* (Madison: University of Wisconsin Press, 1993).

Barry, Michael, *An Affair of Honour* (Fermoy: Eglise Books, 1981).

Barshay, Andrew E., "'Double Cruelty': Marxism and the Presence of the Past in Japanese Capitalism," in Vlastos, *Mirror of Modernity*, pp. 243–51.

Bartelson, Jens, *A Genealogy of Sovereignty* (Cambridge: Cambridge University Press, 1995).

The Critique of the State (Cambridge: Cambridge University Press, 2001).

"Making Sense of Global Civil Society," *European Journal of International Relations* 12, no. 3 (2006), pp. 371–95.

Bartov, Omar, *The Eastern Front, 1941–45: German Troops and the Barbarization of Warfare* (New York: St. Martin's Press, 1985).

Hitler's Army: Soldiers, Nazis and the War in the Third Reich (New York: Oxford University Press, 1991).

"Basic Principles of Relations between the United States of America and the Union of Soviet Socialist Republics," *Department of State Bulletin*, June 26, 1972, pp. 898–9.

Bateman, Geoffrey and Philip Petit, *The Economy of Esteem: An Essay in Civil and Political Society* (Oxford: Oxford University Press, 2004).

Bauer, Yehuda, *Rethinking the Holocaust* (New Haven, CT: Yale University Press, 2000).

Bauman, Zygmunt, *Modernity and Ambivalence* (Cambridge: Polity, 1991).

"The Great War of Recognition," *Theory, Culture and Society* 18, nos. 2–3 (1997), pp. 137–50.

Baumeister, Roy F., "Violent Pride," *Scientific American*, 284, no. 4 (April 2001), pp. 96–101.

Baumeister, Roy F., L. Smart and J. Boden, "Relation of Threatened Egotism to Violence and Aggression: The Dark Side of Self-Esteem," *Psychological Review*, 103 (1996), pp. 5–33.

Baumeister, Roy F., Jennifer D. Campbell, Joachim I. Krueger and Kathleen D. Vohs, "Does High Self-Esteem Cause Better Performance, Interpersonal Success, Happiness, or Healthier Lifestyles?," *Psychological Science in the Public Interest* 4, no. 1 (May 2003), pp. 1–44.

"Exploding the Self-Esteem Myth," *Scientific American*, 292, no. 1 (January 2005), pp. 84–91.

Baumgold, Deborah, "Pacifying Politics: Resistance, Violence, and Accountability in Seventeenth Century Contract Theory," *Political Theory* 21, no. 1 (February 1993), pp. 6–27.

Baylis, John and Steve Smith, eds., *The Globalization of World Politics: An Introduction to International Relations* (Oxford: Oxford University Press, 1997).

Baynes, Kenneth, "Freedom and Recognition in Hegel and Habermas," *Philosophy and Social Criticism* 28, no. 1 (2002), pp. 1–17.

Beacham, Richard, "The Emperor as Impresario: Producing the Pageantry of Power," in Galinsky, *The Age of Augustus*, pp. 151–74.

Beard, Mary, *The Parthenon* (Cambridge, MA: Harvard University Press, 2003).

Beasley, William G., *The Meiji Restoration* (Stanford, CA: Stanford University Press, 1972).

Japanese Imperialism (Oxford: Oxford University Press, 1987).

Beccaria, Cesare, "On Crimes and Punishments," in Richard Bellamy, ed., *On Crimes and Punishments and Other Writings*, trans. Richard Davies and Virginia Cox (Cambridge: Cambridge University Press 1995 [1764]), pp. 1–114.

Bechtel, William, "Teleological Functional Analyses and the Hierarchical Organization of Nature," in Nicholas Rescher, ed., *Current Issues in Teleology* (Lanham, MD: University Press of America, 1986), pp. 26–47.

Becker, E., *The Birth and Death of Meaning* (New York: Free Press, 1962).

The Denial of Death (New York: Free Press, 1973).

Escape from Evil (New York: Free Press, 1975).

Becker, Marvin B., *Civility and Society in Western Europe, 1300–1600* (Bloomington: Indiana University Press, 1988).

Beeler, John, *Warfare in England, 1966–1189* (Ithaca, NY: Cornell University Press, 1966).

Beetham, David, *The Legitimation of Power* (Atlantic Highlands, NJ: Humanities Press, 1991).

Behnke, Andreas, "Grand Theory in the Age of its Impossibility: Contemplations on Alexander Wendt," in Guzzini and Leander, *Constructivism and International Relations*, pp. 48–56.

Beik, William, *Absolutism and Society in Seventeenth Century France* (Cambridge: Cambridge University Press, 1985).

Beisanz, M. H. B., R. Beisanz and K. Z. Beisanz, *The Ticos: Culture and Social Change in Costa Rica* (Boulder, CO: Lynne Rienner, 1999).

Bell, Daniel, *The End of Ideology* (Glencoe, IL: Free Press, 1960).

Bell, David A., *The Cult of Nation in France: Inventing Nationalism, 1680–1800* (Cambridge, MA: Harvard University Press, 2003).

Bell, Quentin, *On Human Finery* (London: Hogarth Press, 1976).

Bellah, Robert N., *Tokugawa Religion: The Values of Pre-Industrial Japan* (Glencoe, IL: Free Press, 1957).

"Durkheim and Ritual," in Alexander and Smith, *The Cambridge Companion to Durkheim*, pp. 183–210.

Beller, Steven, *Francis Joseph* (London: Longman, 1996).

Bem, Daryl J., "Self-Perception: An Alternative Interpretation of Cognitive Dissonance Phenomena," *Psychological Review*, 74 (1967), pp. 183–200.

"Self-Perception Theory," in L. Berkowitz, ed., *Advances in Experimental Social Psychology* (New York: Academic Press, 1972), vol. VI, pp. 1–62.

Bendix, Reinhard, *Nation-Building and Citizenship: Studies of our Changing Social Order* (New York: Wiley, 1964).

"Preconditions of Development: A Comparison of Japan and Germany," in R. P. Dore, ed., *Aspects of Social Change in Modern Japan* (Princeton, NJ: Princeton University Press, 1967), pp. 27–68.

Benedict, Ruth, *Patterns of Culture* (Boston: Houghton Mifflin, 1934).

The Chrysanthemum and the Sword: Patterns of Japanese Culture (Boston: Houghton Mifflin, 1946).

Benhabib, Seyla, *Claims of Culture: Equality and Diversity in the Global Era* (Princeton, NJ: Princeton University Press, 2002).

Benjamin, Roger and Raymond Duvall, "The Capitalist State in Context," in Roger Benjamin, *The Democratic State* (Lawrence: University of Kansas Press, 1985), pp. 19–57.

Benn, Charles, *China's Golden Age: Everyday Life in the Tang Dynasty* (New York: Oxford University Press, 2002).

Bennett, Andrew and Alexander George, *Case Studies and Theory Development* (Cambridge, MA: MIT Press, 2005).

Bentham, Jeremy, *An Introduction to the Principles of Morals and Legislation*, ed. J. H. Burns and H. L. A. Hart (Oxford: Oxford University Press, 1996).

Rights, Representation, and Reform: Nonsense Upon Stilts and Other Writings on the French Revolution, ed. Philip Schofield, Catherine Pease-Watkin and Cyprian Blamires (Oxford: Oxford University Press, 2002).

Berenskoetter, Felix, "Creating (In)Security from Within: Thoughts on the Ontological Purpose of Alliances," paper presented at the Deutsche Verein für Politische Wissenschaft, Arnoldsheim, May 2006.

"Friends, There are No Friends? An Intimate Reframing of the International," paper presented at the *Millennium* Annual Conference, London, October 21–22, 2006.

Berenstein, Richard J., *Beyond Objectivism and Relativism: Science, Hermeneutics and Praxis* (Philadelphia: University of Pennsylvania Press, 1983).

Berger, Gordon M., *Parties out of Power in Japan, 1931–1941* (Princeton, NJ: Princeton University Press, 1977).

Berger, Joseph and Morris Zelditch, eds., *Status, Power, and Legitimacy: Strategies and Theories* (New Brunswick, NJ: Transaction, 1998).

Berger, Peter, *The Capitalism Revolution: Fifty Propositions about Prosperity, Equality, and Liberty* (New York: Basic Books, 1986).

Berger, Peter and Thomas Luckman, *The Social Construction of Reality* (New York: Anchor, 1966).

Berger, Robert W., *A Royal Passion: Louis XIV as Patron of Architecture* (Cambridge: Cambridge University Press, 1994).

Berger, Suzanne and Ronald Dore, eds., *National Diversity and Global Capitalism* (Ithaca, NY: Cornell University Press, 1996).

Berger, Thomas, "Norms, Identity, and National Security in Germany and Japan," in Peter J. Katzenstein, ed., *The Culture of National Security: Norms and Identity in World Politics* (New York: Columbia University Press, 1996), pp. 317–56.

Berghahn, Volker R., *Der Tirpitz Plan, Genesis und Verfall einer innenpolitischen Krisenstrategie uner Wilhelm II* (Düsseldorf: Droste Verlag, 1971).

Germany and the Approach of War in 1914 (New York: St. Martin's Press, 1973).

Imperial Germany, 1871–1914 (Providence, RI: Berghahn, 1994).

"Structure and Agency in Wilhelmine Germany: The History of the German Empire – Past, Present, and Future," in Mombauer and Deist, *The Kaiser*, pp. 281–93.

Bergson, Henri, *Creative Evolution*, trans. Arthur Mitchell (New York: Modern Library, 1944).

The Creative Mind: An Introduction to Metaphysics, trans. Marabelle L. Anderson (New York: Citadel Press, 1946).

Berlin, Isaiah, *Four Essays on Liberty* (New York: Oxford University Press, 1969).

The Crooked Timber of Humanity: Chapters in the History of Ideas (New York: Vintage Books, 1992).

The Magus of the North: J. G. Hamann and the Origins of Modern Irrationalism (New York: Farrar, Straus and Giroux, 2001).

Berman, Harold, *Law and Revolution: The Formation of the Western Legal Tradition* (Cambridge, MA: Harvard University Press, 1983).

Berman, Marshall, *The Politics of Individualism: Radical Individualism and the Emergence of Modern Society* (London: Allen and Unwin, 1971).

Berman, Sheri E., "Modernization in Historical Perspective: The Case of Imperial Germany," *World Politics* 53 (April 2001), pp. 431–62.

Bernhardi, Friedrich von, *Deutschland und der nächste Krieg*, 2 vols. (Stuttgart: Cotta, 1912).

Bernstein, Richard and Ross H. Munro, "The Coming Conflict with America," *Foreign Affairs*, 76 (March/April 1997), pp. 18–31.

Bernstein, Steven, "The Challenged Legitimacy of International Organisations: A Conceptual Framework for Empirical Research," paper presented at the Berlin Conference on the Human Condition of Environmental Change, December 2005.

Berry, Christopher J., *The Idea of Luxury: A Conceptual and Historical Investigation* (Cambridge: Cambridge University Press, 1994).

Berstein, Richard J., *Beyond Objectivism and Relativism: Science, Hermeneutics, and Praxis* (Philadelphia: University of Pennsylvania Press, 1983).

Beschloss, Michael, *Mayday: Eisenhower, Khrushchev and the U-2 Affair* (New York: Harper and Row, 1986).

Bess, Michael, *Choices under Fire: Moral Dimension of World War II* (New York: Knopf, 2006).

Best, Geoffrey, *Humanity in Warfare* (New York: Columbia University Press, 1980).

War and Society in Revolutionary Europe, 1770–1870 (London: Fontana, 1982).

Betts, Richard K., *Nuclear Blackmail and Nuclear Balance* (Washington, DC: Brookings Institution, 1987).

"The New Threat of Mass Destruction," *Foreign Affairs*, 77, no. 1 (January/February 1998), pp. 26–41.

Bhaskar, Roy, *A Realist Theory of Science* (London: Verso, 1975).

The Possibility of Naturalism: A Philosophical Critique of the Contemporary Human Science (Brighton: Harvester Press, 1979).

Biddle, Stephen, "Victory Misunderstood: What the Gulf War Tells Us about the Future of Conflict," *International Security* 21, no. 2 (Fall 1996), pp. 139–79.

Military Power: Explaining Victory and Defeat in Modern Battle (Princeton, NJ: Princeton University Press, 2004).

Bieler, Andreas and Adam D. Morton, "The Gordian Knot of Agency-Structure in International Relations: A Neo-Gramscian Perspective," *European Journal of International Relations* 7 (2001), pp. 5–35.

Biersteker, Thomas J. and Cynthia Weber, "The Social Construction of State Sovereignty," in Biersteker and Weber, *State Sovereignty as a Social Construct*, pp. 1–21.

eds., *State Sovereignty as a Social Construct* (Cambridge: Cambridge University Press, 1996).

Binmore, Kenneth G., *Game Theory and the Social Contract: Just Playing* (Cambridge, MA: MIT Press, 1998).

Binski, Paul, *Westminster Abbey and the Plantagenets: Kingship and the Representation of Power, 1200–1400* (New Haven, CT: Yale University Press, 1995).

Bird, Graham, "The IMF and Developing Countries," *International Organization*, 50, no. 3 (Summer 1996), pp. 477–511.

Birnbaum, Karl E., *Peace Moves and U-Boat Warfare* (Stockholm: Almquist and Wiksell, 1958).

Bisley, Nick, "Neither Empire nor Republic: American Power and Regional Order in the Asia Pacific," *International Politics* 43, no. 2 (April 2006), pp. 197–218.

Black, Anthony, "Concepts of Civil Society in Pre-Modern Europe," in Kaviraj and Khilnani, *Civil Society*, pp. 33–38.

Black, Jeremy, *Eighteenth Century Europe, 1700–1798* (New York: St. Martin's Press, 1990).

    A Military Revolution? Military Change and European Society 1550–1800 (Basingstoke: Macmillan, 1991).

    European Warfare, 1660–1815 (New Haven, CT: Yale University Press, 1994).

    European International Relations: 1648–1815 (London: Palgrave, 2002).

Black, Max, ed., *The Social Theories of Talcott Parsons: A Critical Examination* (Englewood Cliffs, NJ: Prentice-Hall, 1951).

Blackbourn, David and Geoff Eley, *The Peculiarities of German History* (Oxford: Oxford University Press, 1984).

Blanning, T. C. W., *Joseph II and Enlightened Despotism* (New York: Harper and Row, 1970).

    "Introduction: The Beneficiaries and Casualties of Expansion," in T. C. W. Blanning, ed., *The Eighteenth Century: Europe, 1688–1815* (Oxford: Oxford University Press, 2000), pp. 1–10.

    The Culture of Power and the Power of Culture: Old Regime Europe, 1680–1789 (Oxford: Oxford University Press, 2002).

    The Pursuit of Glory: Europe 1648–1815 (London: Penguin, 2007).

Blattberg, Charles, *From Pluralist to Patriotic Politics: Putting Practices First* (Oxford: Oxford University Press, 2000).

Blau, Peter, "Critical Remarks on Weber's Theory of Authority," *American Political Science Review* 57, no. 2 (1963), pp. 305–16.

Bleicken, J., "Review of E. Badian, 'Foreign Clientelae,'" *Gnomon* 36 (1964), pp. 176–87.

Bloom, Allan, *The Closing of the American Mind* (New York: Simon and Schuster, 1987).

Bluche, François, *Louis XIV*, trans. Mark Greengrass (Oxford: Blackwell, 1990).

Blum, William, *Rogue State: A Guide to the World's Only Superpower* (Monroe, ME: Common Courage Press, 2000).

Blundell, Mary Whitlock, *Helping Friends and Harming Enemies: A Study in Sophocles and Greek Ethics* (Cambridge: Cambridge University Press, 1989).

Bobbio, Norberto, *Saggi sulla scienza politica in Italia* (Rome and Bari: Editori Laterza, 1996).

Bobrow, Davis B., "Complex Insecurity: Implications of Sobering Metaphor," *International Studies Quarterly* 40, no. 4 (1996), pp. 435–50.

    Prospects for International Relations: Conjectures about the Next Millennium, special edition of *International Studies Review* 1, no. 2 (Summer 1999), pp. 1–10.

Bock, Gisela, Quentin Skinner and Maurizio Viroli, *Machiavelli and Republicanism* (Cambridge: Cambridge University Press, 1990).

Bock, Kenneth, "Theories of Progress, Development, Evolution," in Tom Bottomore and Robert Nisbet, eds., *A History of Sociological Analysis* (New York: Basic Books, 1978), pp. 39–79.

Boemeke, Manfred F., Gerald D. Feldman and Elisabeth Glaser, eds., *Treaty of Versailles: A Reassessment after 75 Years* (New York: Cambridge University Press, 2006).

Boettcher, William A., *Presidential Risk Behavior in Foreign Policy: Prudence or Peril* (New York: Palgrave Macmillan, 2005).

Bohannon, J. N. and V. L. Symons, "Flashbulb Memories: Confidence, Consistency, and Quantity," in E. Winograd and U. Neisser, *Affect and Accuracy in Recall* (New York: Cambridge University Press, 1992), pp. 179–96.

Bohman, James and Matthias Lutz-Bachmann, eds., *Perpetual Peace: Essays on Kant's Cosmopolitan Ideal* (Cambridge, MA: MIT Press, 1997).

Bois, Guy, *La mutation de l'an mille* (Paris: Fayard, 1989).

Bonney, Richard, *The King's Debts* (Oxford: Oxford University Press, 1981).

Boog, Horst, Gerhard Krebs and Detlef Vogel, *Germany and the Second World War*, vol. VII: *The Strategic Air War in Europe and the War in West and East Asia, 1943–1944/5*, trans. Francisca Garvie *et al.* (New York: Oxford University Press, 2006).

Booth, Ken and Tim Dunne, eds., *Worlds in Collision: Terror and the Future of Global Order* (London: Palgrave, 2002).

Booth, William James, *Households: On the Moral Architecture of the Economy* (Ithaca, NY: Cornell University Press, 1993).

Borg, Dorothy and Shumpei Okamoto, eds., *Pearl Harbor as History* (New York: Columbia University Press, 1973).

Borton, Hugh, *Japan since 1931: Its Political and Social Development* (New York: Institute of Pacific Relations, 1940).

  Japan (Ithaca, NY: Cornell University Press, 1951).

Bosworth, R. J. B., *Italy, the Least of the Great Powers: Italian Foreign Policy before the First World War* (Cambridge: Cambridge University Press, 1979).

  Italy and the Approach of the First World War (New York: St. Martin's Press, 1983).

  The Italian Dictatorship: Problems and Perspectives in the Interpretation of Mussolini and Fascism (London: Arnold, 1998).

  Mussolini (London: Arnold, 2002).

Bottome, Edgar M., *The Missile Gap: A Study of the Formulation of Military and Political Policy* (Cranbury, NJ: Farleigh Dickenson University Press, 1971).

Boulding, Kenneth E., *Conflict and Defense: A General Theory* (New York: Harper and Row, 1962).

Boulton, D'Arcy Dacre Jonathan, *The Knights of the Crown: The Monarchical Orders of Knighthood in Later Medieval Europe, 1325–1520* (New York: St. Martin's Press, 1986).

Bourdieu, Pierre, "The Sentiment of Honor in Kabyle Society," in Peristiany, *Honor and Shame*, pp. 191–242.

    Outlines of a Theory of Practice, trans. Richard Nice (Cambridge: Cambridge University Press, 1977).

    Language and Symbolic Power, trans. Gino Raymond and Matthew Adamson (Cambridge, MA: Harvard University Press, 1991).

Bourdieu, Pierre, Jean-Claude Chamboredon and Jean-Claude Passeron, *The Craft of Sociology: Epistemological Preliminaries*, ed. Beate Krais, trans. Richard Nice (New York: De Gruyter, 1991).

Bourne, Kenneth, *The Foreign Policy of Victorian England, 1830–1902* (Oxford: Oxford University Press, 1970).

Bowen, H. V., Margaret Lincoln and Nigel Rigby, eds., *The Worlds of the East India Company* (Rochester, NY: Boydell Press, 2002).

Bowman, James, *Honor: A History* (New York: Encounter, 2006).

Boyarin, Jonathan, "Introduction," in Jonathan Boyarin, *Remapping Memory: The Politics of Timespace* (Minneapolis: University of Minnesota Press, 1994), pp. vii–xiv.

    "Space, Time, and the Politics of Memory," in Jonathan Boyarin, *Remapping Memory: The Politics of Timespace* (Minneapolis: University of Minnesota Press, 1994), pp. 1–38.

Boyd White, James, *Heracles' Bow: Essays on the Rhetoric and Poetics of the Law* (Madison: University of Wisconsin Press, 1985).

Boylan, Michael, "Monadic and Systemic Teleology," in Nicholas Rescher, *Current Issues in Teleology* (Lanham, MD: University Press of America, 1986), pp. 15–25.

Bozeman, Adda B., *Politics and Culture in International History* (Princeton, NJ: Princeton University Press, 1960).

Bracher, Karl Dietrich, *The German Dictatorship: The Origins, Structure, and Effects of National Socialism*, trans. Jean Steinberg (New York: Praeger, 1970).

    The German Dilemma: The Relationship of State and Democracy, trans. Richard Barry (New York: Praeger, 1975).

Bracken, Paul, *The Command and Control of Nuclear Forces* (New Haven, CT: Yale University Press, 1983).

Bramsted, Ernest K., *Aristocracy and the Middle Classes in Germany*, rev. edn (Chicago: University of Chicago Press, 1964 [1937]).

Braudel, Fernand, *On History*, trans. Sarah Matthews (Chicago: University of Chicago Press, 1980).

Brehm, J. W. and S. S. Brehm, *Psychological Reactance: A Theory of Freedom and Control* (New York: Academic Press, 1981).

Breiner, Peter, "'Unnatural Selection': Max Weber's Concept of *Auslese* and his Criticism of the Reduction of Political Conflict to Economics," *International Relations* 18 (September 2004), pp. 289–307.

Breitman, Richard, *The Architect of Genocide: Heinrich Himmler and the Final Solution* (New York: Knopf, 1991).

Bremer, Stuart A., *Simulated Worlds: A Computer Model of National Decision Making* (Princeton, NJ: Princeton University Press, 1987).

Brennan, Geoffrey and Philip Pettit, *The Economy of Esteem: An Essay on Civil and Political Society* (Oxford: Oxford University Press, 2004).

Brennan, T. Corey, "Power and Process under the Republican 'Constitution'," in Flower, *The Cambridge Companion to the Roman Republic*, pp. 31–65.

Breslauer, George, "Why Détente Failed: An Interpretation," in George, *Managing US–Soviet Rivalry*, pp. 319–40.

Brewer, Anthony, *Marxist Theories of Imperialism: A Critical Survey* (London: Routledge and Kegan Paul, 1980).

Brewer, Marilynn, "The Social Self: On Being the Same and Different at the Same Time," *Personality and Social Psychology Bulletin* 17, no. 5 (1991), pp. 475–82.

"The Psychology of Prejudice: In-Group Love or Out-Group Hate?," *Journal of Social Issues* 55, no. 3 (1999), pp. 429–44.

Brewer, Marilynn and N. Miller, *Intergroup Relations* (Pacific Grove, CA: Brooks-Cole, 2001).

Brewer, W. F., "What is Autobiographical Memory," in D. C. Rubin, *Autobiographical Memory* (Cambridge: Cambridge University Press, 1986), pp. 25–49.

Bridge, F. R., *Great Britain and Austria-Hungary, 1906–1914: A Diplomatic History* (London: Weidenfeld and Nicolson, 1972).

The Habsburg Monarchy among the Great Powers, 1815–1918 (New York: Berg, 1990).

Bridgman, Jon M., *The Revolt of the Hereros: Perspectives on Southern Africa* (Berkeley, University of California Press, 1981).

Brierly, J. L., *The Law of Nations*, 5th edn (New York: Oxford University Press, 1963).

Bright, Christopher, "Invasive Species: Pathogens of Globalization," *Foreign Policy*, no. 116 (Fall 1999), pp. 50–64.

Broadie, Alexander, *The Cambridge Companion to the Scottish Enlightenment* (Cambridge: Cambridge University Press, 2003).

Brodie, Bernard, *War and Politics* (New York: Macmillan, 1973).

Brooks, Stephen G., *The Globalization of Production and International Security* (New Haven, CT: Yale University Press, 2001).

Producing Security: Multinational Corporations, Globalization, and the Changing Calculus of Conflict (Princeton, NJ: Princeton University Press, 2005).

Brooks, Stephen G. and William Wohlforth, "American Primacy in Perspective," *Foreign Affairs* 81 (2002), pp. 20–33.

"From Old Thinking to New Thinking in Qualitative Research," *International Security* 26, no. 4 (Spring 2002), pp. 93–111.

"Hard Times for Soft Balancing," *International Security* 30 (Summer 2005), pp. 72–108.

"International Relations Theory and the Case Against Unilateralism," *Perspectives on Politics* 3, no. 3 (2005), pp. 509–24.

The Challenge of American Primacy (Princeton: Princeton University Press, 2007).

Broszat, Martin, *Hitler and the Collapse of Weimar Germany*, trans. V. R. Berghahn (New York: Berg, 1987).

Brown, Archie, *The Gorbachev Factor* (Oxford: Oxford University Press, 1996).

Brown, Chris, *International Relations Theory: New Normative Approaches* (New York: Columbia University Press, 1992).

"World Society and the English School. An International Society Perspective on World Society," *European Journal of International Relations* 7 (2001), pp. 423–42.

Sovereignty, Rights and Justice (Oxford: Polity, 2002).

"Reflections on the 'War on Terror,' Two Years On," *International Politics* 41 (2004), pp. 51–64.

Brown, Garrett Wallace, "State Sovereignty, Federation and Kantian Cosmopolitanism," *European Journal of International Relations* 11 (December 2005), pp. 495–522.

Brown, Giles, "Introduction to the Carolingian Renaissance," in Story, *Charlemagne*, pp. 1–51.

Brown, M. Kathryn and Travis W. Stanton, eds., *Ancient Indian Warfare* (Walnut Creek, CA: Rowman and Littlefield, 2003).

Brown, R. and J. Kulik, "Flashbulb Memories," *Cognition* 5 (1977), pp. 73–99.

Brown, Robert, *The Nature of Social Laws* (Cambridge: Cambridge University Press, 1984).

Brown, Roger Glenn, *Fashoda Reconsidered: The Impact of Domestic Politics on French Policy in Africa, 1893–98* (Baltimore, MD: Johns Hopkins University Press, 1970).

Brown, Rupert, "Social Identity Theory: Past Achievements, Current Problems and Future Challenges," *European Journal of Social Psychology* 30 (2000), pp. 745–78.

Brown, Rupert and Gabi Haeger, "Compared to What? Comparison Choice in an Inter-nation Context," *European Journal of Social Psychology*, 29 (1999), pp. 31–42.

Brubaker, Rogers and Frederick Cooper, "Beyond 'Identity'," *Theory and Society* 29 (2000), pp. 1–47.

Bruijn, Laap R., "States and their Navies from the Late Sixteenth to the End of the Eighteenth Centuries," in Contamine, *War and Competition Between States*, pp. 68–98.

Bruner, Jerome, "The 'Remembered' Self," in Ulrich Neisser and Robyn Fivush, *The Remembering Self: Construction and Accuracy in the Self Narrative* (Cambridge: Cambridge University Press, 1994), pp. 41–51.

Brunschwig, Henri, "Le parti coloniale français," *Revue Française d'Histoire d'Outre-Mer* 46 (1959), pp. 49–83.

French Colonialism, 1871–1914: Myths and Realities, trans. W. G. Brown (New York: Praeger, 1966).

Brunsson, Nils, *The Organization of Hypocrisy: Talk, Decisions, and Actions in Organizations,* trans. Nancy Adler (New York: Wiley, 1989).

Bryson, Anna, *From Courtesy to Civility: Changing Codes of Conduct in Early Modern England* (Oxford: Oxford University Press, 1998).

Brzezinski, Zbigniew, "The Competitive Relationship," in Charles Gati, ed., *Caging the Bear* (Indianapolis: Bobbs-Merrill, 1974), pp. 157–99.

Brzezinski, Zbigniew and John J. Mearsheimer, "Clash of the Titans," *Foreign Policy*, no. 146 (January/February 2005), pp. 1–3.

Buchheit, Lee C., *Secession: The Legitimacy of Self-Determination* (New Haven, CT: Yale University Press, 1978).

Buckle, Thomas, *History of Civilization in England* (London: John W. Parker, 1857).

Buckler, John, *The Theban Hegemony, 371–362 BC* (Cambridge, MA: Harvard University Press, 1980).

Buford, Norman, *Germany in the Eighteenth Century* (Cambridge: Cambridge University Press, 1965).

Builder, Carl H. and Brian Nichiporuk, *Information Technologies and the Future of Land Warfare* (Santa Monica, CA: Rand Corporation, 1995).

Bukovansky, Mlada, *Legitimacy and Power Politics: The American and French Revolutions in International Political Culture* (Princeton, NJ: Princeton University Press, 2002).

"The Hollowness of Anti-Corruption Discourse," *Review of International Political Economy* 13, no. 2 (May 2006), pp. 181–209.

"Liberal States, International Order, and Legitimacy: An Appeal for Persuasions over Prescription," *International Politics*, 44, no. 2 (March 2007), pp. 175–93.

Bull, Hedley, "The Grotian Conception of International Society," in Butterfield and Wight, *Diplomatic Investigations*, pp. 51–73.

"Recapturing the Just War for Political Theory," *World Politics* 31 (1979), pp. 588–99.

Bull, Hedley and Adam Watson, eds., *The Expansion of International Society* (Oxford: Oxford University Press, 1984).

Bullock, Alan, *Hitler: A Study in Tyranny,* rev. edn (New York: Harper, 1962).

Bulmer, Martin, "Concepts in the Analysis of Qualitative Data," *Sociological Review* 27, no. 4 (1979), pp. 651–77.

Bundy, McGeorge, *Danger and Survival: Choices About the Bomb in the First Fifty Years* (New York: Random House, 1988).

Bungay, Stephen, *The Most Dangerous Enemy: A History of the Battle of Britain* (London: Aurum, 2000).

Bunge, Mario, *Causality: The Place of the Causal Principle in Modern Science* (Cleveland, OH: Meridian Books, 1959).

Bunyeat, Myles F., "Aristotle on Learning to Be Good," in Amélie Oksenberg Rorty, *Essays on Aristotle's Ethics* (Berkeley: University of California Press, 1980), pp. 69–92.

Burbidge, John, "The Cunning of Reason," in Richard Hassing, *Final Causality in Nature and Human Affairs* (Washington, DC: Catholic University of America Press, 1997), pp. 151–62.

Burckhardt, Carl J., *Richelieu and his Age*, vol. III: *Power Politics and the Cardinal's Death* (London: Allen and Unwin, 1971).

Burke, Edmund, *A Philosophical Enquiry into the Origins of our Ideas of the Sublime and Beautiful*, 3rd edn, ed. Adam Phillips (New York: Oxford University Press, 1990).

  Reflections on the Revolution in France (Oxford: Oxford University Press, 1993 [1790]).

Burke, Peter, *The Fabrication of Louis XIV* (New Haven, CT: Yale University Press, 1992).

Burkitt, I., *Social Selves: Theories of the Social Formation of Personality* (London: Sage, 1991).

Burley (now Slaughter), Anne-Marie, "Law Among Liberal States: Liberal Internationalism and the Act of State Doctrine," *Columbia Law Review* 92, no. 8 (1992), pp. 1907–96.

Burns, J. H., *The Cambridge History of Medieval Political Thought, c. 350–1450* (Cambridge: Cambrige University Press, 1998).

Burrow, John W., *Evolution and Society* (Cambridge: Cambridge University Press, 1966).

  The Crisis of Reason: European Thought, 1848–1914 (New Haven, CT: Yale University Press, 2000).

Burton, David, *Theodore Roosevelt: Confident Imperialist* (Philadelphia: University of Pennsylvania Press, 1968).

Burton, John W., *World Society* (Cambridge: Cambridge University Press, 1972).

  Deviance, Terrorism and War: The Process of Solving Unsolved Social and Political Problems (New York: St. Martin's Press, 1979).

  Global Conflict (Brighton: Wheatsheaf Books, 1984).

Burton, Paul J., "*Clientela* or *Amicitia*?: Modeling Roman International Behaviour in the Middle Republic (264–146 B.C.)," *KLIO* 85, no. 2 (2003), pp. 333–69.

Bury, J. B., *The Idea of Progress: An Inquiry into its Origin and Growth* (London: Macmillan, 1920).

Bush, George W., *A Charge to Keep* (New York: Morrow, 1999).

Buss, Leo, *The Evolution of Individuality* (Princeton, NJ: Princeton University Press, 1987).

Butler, E. M., *The Tyranny of Greece over Germany* (Cambridge: Cambridge University Press, 1935).

Butler, Judith, *Excitable Speech: The Politics of the Performative* (New York: Routledge, 1997).

Butow, Robert J. C., *Japan's Decision to Surrender* (Stanford, CA: Stanford University Press, 1954).

John Doe Associates: Backdoor Diplomacy for Peace (Stanford, CA: Stanford University Press, 1974).

Butterfield, Herbert, *The Origins of Modern Science*, rev. edn (New York: Free Press, 1957).

The Whig Interpretation of History (Harmondsworth: Penguin, 1973).

Butterfield, Herbert and Martin Wight, *Diplomatic Investigations: Essays in the Theory of International Politics* (London: J. Allen and Unwin, 1966).

Buxton, R. G. A., *Persuasion in Greek Tragedy: A Study of Peitho* (Cambridge: Cambridge University Press, 1982).

Buzan, Barry, *From International to World Society? English School Theory and the Social Structure of Globalisation* (Cambridge: Cambridge University Press, 2004).

Buzan, Barry and Ole Waever, *Regions and Powers: The Structure of International Security* (Cambridge: Cambridge University Press, 2003).

Byass, Hugh, *Government by Assassination* (New York: Knopf, 1942).

Byerly, Henry, "Teleology and Evolutionary Theory: Mechanisms and Meanings," *Nature and System* 1 (1979), pp. 157–76.

Byock, Jesse, *Medieval Iceland: Society, Sagas, and Power* (Berkeley: University of California Press, 1988).

Viking Age Iceland (New York: Penguin Books, 2001).

Byung Nak Song, *Korean Economy*, 3rd edn (Seoul: Park Young Publishing, 1998).

Caesar, Julius, *The Conquest of Gaul*, trans. S. A. Handford (Harmondsworth: Penguin, 1951).

Cafagna, Luciano, *The Industrial Revolution in Italy, 1830–1914*, vol. IV, of *The Fontana Economic History of Europe* (London: Collins, 1971), ch. 6.

Caillois, Roger, *Man, Play, and Games* (New York: Schocken, 1961).

Cain, Peter and Tony Hopkins, *British Imperialism: 1688–2000*, rev. edn (London: Longman, 2001).

Cairncross, A. K., *Home and Foreign Investment, 1870–1913* (Cambridge: Cambridge University Press, 1953).

Calhoun, Craig, "The Problem of Identity in Collective Action," in J. Huber, *Macro-Micro Linkage in Sociology* (Beverly Hills, CA: Sage, 1991), pp. 51–75.

Callinicos, Alex, *New Mandarins of American Power: The Bush Administration's Plans for the World* (London: Polity, 2003).

Calvocoressi, Peter, Guy Wint and John Pritchard, *Total War: The Causes and Courses of the Second World War*, rev. edn (London: Penguin, 1989).

Campbell, D. T., "Common Fate, Similarity, and other Indices of the Status of Aggregates of Person as Social Entities," *Behavioural Science* 3 (1958), pp. 14–25.

Campbell, David, *Writing Security: United States Foreign Policy and the Politics of Identity* (Minneapolis: University of Minnesota Press, 1992).

Campbell, Donald, "'Downward Causation,' and Hierarchically Organized Biological Systems," in Francisco Ayala and Theodosius Dobzhansky, *Studies in the Philosophy of Biology* (Berkeley: University of California Press, 1974), pp. 179–86.

Canning, J. P., "Introduction: Politics, Institutions and Ideas," in Burns, *The Cambridge History of Medieval Political Thought*, pp. 341–67.

Caporaso, James, ed., *The Elusive State: International and Comparative Perspectives* (Newbury Park, CA: Sage, 1989).

Carlsnaes, Walter, "The Agent-Structure Problem in Foreign Policy Analysis," *International Studies Quarterly* 36, no. 3 (September 1992), pp. 254–70.

Carneiro, Robert, "Political Expansion as an Expression of the Principle of Competitive Exclusion," in Ronald Cohen and Elman Service, *Origins of the State* (Philadelphia, PA: Institute for the Study of Human Issues, 1978), pp. 205–23.

Carpenter, Ted Galen and Boug Bandow, *The Korean Conundrum: America's Troubled Relationship with North and South Korea* (London: Palgrave, 2004).

Carpi, Daniel, *Between Mussolini and Hitler: The Jews and the Italian Authorities in France and Tunisia* (Hanover, NH: University Press of New England, 1994).

Carr, Edward Hallett, *The Twenty Year's Crisis, 1919–1939: An Introduction to the Study of International Relations* (London: Macmillan, 1940).

Carroll, E. Malcom, *French Public Opinion and Foreign Affairs, 1970–1914* (New York: Century, 1931).

Carson, Thomas, "Perpetual Peace: What Kant Should Have Said," *Social Theory and Practice* 14, no. 2 (1988), pp. 173–214.

Carsten, F. L., *The Reichswehr and Politics, 1918 to 1933* (Oxford: Oxford University Press, 1966).

Cartledge, Paul, *The Greeks: A Portrait of Self and Others*, rev. edn (Oxford: Oxford University Press, 1997).

   Spartan Reflections (Berkeley: University of California Press, 2001).

   Alexander the Great: The Hunt for a New Past (London: Macmillan, 2004).

   The Spartans: The World of Warrior-Heroes in Ancient Greece (New York: Vintage, 2004).

Cartledge, Paul, Paul Miller and Sitta von Reden, eds., *Kosmos: Essays in Order, Conflict and Community in Classical Athens* (Cambridge: Cambridge University Press, 1998).

Castano, Emanuele, "In Case of Death, Cling to the Ingroup," *European Journal of Social Psychology*, 34 (2004), pp. 375–84.

"On the Advantages of Reifying the Ingroup," in V. Yzerbyt, C. M. Judd and O. Corneille, eds., *The Psychology of Group Perception: Perceived Variability, Entitativity, and Essentialism* (London: Psychology Press, 2004), pp. 381–400.

Castano, Emanuele and Mark Dechesne, "On Defeating Death: Group Reification and Social Identification as Immortality Strategies," *European Review of Social Psychology* 16 (2005), pp. 221–55.

Castano, E., M. P. Paladino, A. Coull and V. Yzerbyt, "Protecting the Ingroup: Motivated Allocation of Cognitive Resources in the Presence of Threatening Ingroup Members," *Group Processes and Intergroup Relations*, 4 (2001), pp. 327–39.

"Stereotype: Ingroup Identification and the Management of Deviant Ingroup Members," *British Journal of Social Psychology*, 41 (2002), pp. 365–85.

Castano, E., V. Yzerbyt and D. Bourguignon, "We Are One and I Like It: The Impact of Ingroup Entitativity on Ingroup Identification," *European Journal of Social Psychology*, 33 (2003), pp. 735–54.

Castano, Emanuele, V. Yzerbyt, D. Bourguignon and E. Seron, "Who May Come in? The Impact of Ingroup Identification on Ingroup-Outgroup Categorisation," *Journal of Experimental Social Psychology*, 38 (2002), pp. 315–22.

Castano, Emanuele, V. Yzerbyt and M. Paladino, "Fan Affiliation: The Effects of Mortality Salience on Fan Identification and Optimism," *European Journal of Social Psychology* 30 (2000), pp. 813–35.

"Transcending Oneself through Social Identification," in J. Greenberg, S. L. Koole and T. Pyszczynski, eds., *Handbook of Experimental Existential Psychology* (New York: Guilford Press, 2004), pp. 305–21.

Castano, Emanuele, V. Yzerbyt, M. P. Paladino and S. Sacchi, "I Belong, Therefore, I Exist: Ingroup Identification, Ingroup Entitativity, and Ingroup Bias," *Personality and Social Psychology Bulletin*, 28 (2002), pp. 135–43.

Castells, Manuel, *The Power of Identity* (Oxford: Blackwell, 1997).

Castoriadis, Cornelius, *Philosophy, Politics, Autonomy* (New York: Oxford University Press, 1991).

"The Greek *Polis* and the Creation of Democracy," in Castoriadis, *Philosophy, Politics, Autonomy*, pp. 81–123.

Catullus, *The Poems*, ed. Kenneth Quinn (New York: Macmillan, 1970).

Cecil, Lamar, *Albert Ballin: Business and Politics in Imperial Germany, 1888–1918* (Princeton, NJ: Princeton University Press, 1967).

"The Creation of Nobles in Prussia, 1871–1918," *American Historical Review* 75 (1970), pp. 757–95.

The German Diplomatic Service, 1871–1914 (Princeton, NJ: Princeton University Press, 1979).

Wilhelm II, 2 vols. (Chapel Hill: University of North Carolina Press, 1989–96).

"History as Family Chronicle: Kaiser Wilhelm II and the Dynastic Roots of the Anglo-German Antagonism," in Röhl and Sombart, *Kaiser Wilhelm II*, pp. 91–120.

Cederman, Lars-Erik, *Emergent Actors in World Politics: How States and Nations Develop and Dissolve* (Princeton, NJ: Princeton University Press, 1997).

   Constructing Europe's Identity: The External Dimension (London: Lynne Rienner, 2001).

   "Modeling the Democratic Peace as a Kantian Selection Process," *Journal of Conflict Resolution* 45, no. 4 (2001), pp. 470–502.

   "Modeling the Size of Wars: From Billiard Balls to Sandpiles," *American Political Science Review* 97 (2003), pp. 135–50.

Cerny, Philip C., "Globalization and Collective Action," *International Organization* 49, no. 4 (1995), pp. 595–626.

Chabod, Frederico, *A History of Italian Fascism*, trans. Muriel Grindrod (London: Weidenfeld and Nicolson, 1963).

   Italian Foreign Policy: The Statecraft of the Founders, trans. William McCluaig (Princeton, NJ: Princeton University Press, 1996).

Chaisson, Eric, *Cosmic Evolution: The Rise of Complexity in Nature* (Cambridge, MA: Harvard University Press, 2001).

Chalmers, David, *The Conscious Mind* (Oxford: Oxford University Press, 1996).

Chandler, David, *The Art of Warfare in the Age of Marlborough* (London: Batsford, 1976).

   "Building Global Society 'From Below'," *Millennium* 33, no. 2 (2004), pp. 313–40.

Chandler, Gareth, *What is Canada? A Wolf in Sheep's Clothing or the Leader in New Progress?* (Toronto: Trafford, 2000).

Chandler, Jerry and Gertrudis Van de Vijver, eds., "Closure: Emergent Organizations and their Dynamics," *Annals of the New York Academy of Sciences* 901 (2000), pp. 1–349.

Chang, Gordon H., *Friends and Enemies: The United States, China and the Soviet Union, 1948–1972* (Stanford, CA: Stanford University Press, 1990).

   Nuclear Showdown: North Korea Takes on the World (New York: Random House, 2006).

Chaniotis, Angelos, *War in the Hellenistic World* (Oxford: Blackwell, 2005).

Charny, Geoffroi de, *The Book of Chivalry of Geoffroi de Charny*, trans. Richard W. Kaeuper and Elspeth Kennedy (Philadelphia: University of Pennsylvania Press, 1996).

Chase-Dunn, Christopher, "World State Formation: Historical Processes and Emergent Necessity," *Political Geography Quarterly* 9, no. 2 (1990), pp. 108–30.

Chay, Jongsuk, ed., *Culture and International Relations* (New York: Praeger, 1990).

Checkel, Jeffrey T., *Ideas and International Political Change: Soviet/Russian Behavior and the End of the Cold War* (New Haven, CT: Yale University Press, 1997).

"Norms, Institutions and National Identity in Contemporary Europe," *International Organization* 51 (1997), pp. 31–63.

"Why Comply? Social Learning and European Identity Change," *International Organization* 55 (2001), pp. 553–88.

Chen, Jian, *Mao's China and the Cold War* (Chapel Hill: University of North Carolina Press, 2001).

Chernayev, Anatoly S., *My Six Years with Gorbachev*, trans. Robert English and Elizabeth Tucker (University Park, PA: Pennsylvania State University Press, 2000).

Chickering, Roger, *Imperial Germany and the Great War, 1914–1918* (Cambridge: Cambridge University Press, 1998).

Childers, Thomas, *The Nazi Voter: The Social Foundations of Fascism in Germany, 1919–1933* (Chapel Hill: University of North Carolina Press, 1983).

Childs, David, and Richard Popplewell, *The Stasi: The East German Intelligence and Security Service* (New York: New York University Press, 1996).

Chomsky, Noam and David Barsamian, *Imperial Ambitions: Conversations in the Post-9/11 World* (New York: Metropolitan Books, 2005).

Chopra, Jarat and Thomas G. Weiss, "Sovereignty Is No Longer Sacrosanct: Codifying Humanitarian Intervention," *Ethics and International Affairs* 6 (1992), pp. 473–93.

Christensen, Wayne, "A Complex Systems Theory of Teleology," *Biology and Philosophy* 11, no. 3 (1996), pp. 301–20.

Christian, David, *Maps of Time: An Introduction to Big History* (Berkeley: University of California Press, 2004).

"Progress: Directionality or Betterment?," *Historically Speaking*, 7, no. 4 (May/June 2006), pp. 22–5.

Christiansen, Thomas J. and Jack Snyder, "Chain Gangs and Passed Bucks: Predicting Alliance Patterns in Multipolarity," *International Organization* 44, no. 2 (1990), pp. 137–68.

Christie, Kenneth, ed., *Ethnic Conflict, Tribal Politics: A Global Perspective* (Richmond, VA: Curzon Press, 1999).

Churchill, Ward, *A Little Matter of Genocide: Holocaust and Denial in the Americas, 1492 to the Present* (San Francisco: City Lights, 1997).

Churchill, Winston, *The Second World War*, vol. III: *The Grand Alliance* (Boston: Houghton Mifflin, 1950).

Cialdini, R., R. Borden, A. Thorne, M. Walker, S. Freeman and L. Sloan, "Basking in Reflected Glory: Three (Football) Field Studies," *Journal of Personality and Social Psychology*, 34 (1976) pp. 366–75.

Ciano, Galeazzo, *Ciano's Diary, 1939–1943*, ed. Malcolm Muggeridge (London: Heinemann, 1947).

Cicero, *Tusculan Disputations*, trans. J. King (New York: Loeb Library, 1927).

Di Finibus, trans. H. Rackham (New York: Loeb Library, 1931).

Brutus, trans. G. L. Hendrickson (Cambridge, MA: Harvard University Press, 1939).

Pro Flacco, trans. C. MacDonald (New York: Loeb Library, 1977).

On Duties, ed. M. T. Griffin and E. M. Atkins (Cambridge: Cambridge University Press, 1991).

The Offices, trans. E. Atkins (Cambridge: Cambridge University Press, 1991).

Cienciala, Anna M., *Poland and the Western Powers, 1938–1939* (London: Routledge and Kegan Paul, 1968).

Cipolla, Carlo, *Before the Industrial Revolution*, 2nd edn (New York: Norton, 1980).

Cirincione, Joseph, Jessica T. Matthews and George Perkovich, *WMD in Iraq: Evidence and Implications* (Washington, DC: Carnegie Endowment for International Peace, 2004).

Ciută, Felix, "What Are We Debating? IR Theory between Empire and the 'Responsible' Hegemon," *International Politics* 43, no. 2 (April 2006), pp. 173–96.

Clark, Ian, *The Hierarchy of States: Reform and Resistance in the International Order* (Cambridge: Cambridge University Press, 1989).

Globalization and International Relations Theory (Oxford: Oxford University Press, 1999).

Legitimacy in International Society (New York: Oxford University Press, 2005).

"Setting the Revisionist Agenda for International Legitimacy," *International Politics*, 44, no. 2 (March 2007), pp. 325–35.

Clarke, Michael, "Manhood and Heroism," in Fowler, ed., *The Cambridge Companion to Homer*, pp. 74–90.

Clarke, Richard A., *Against All Enemies: Inside America's War on Terror* (New York: Free Press, 2004).

Claude, Inis L. Jr., "Collective Legitimation as Political Function of the United Nations," *International Organization* 20, no. 3 (1966), pp. 357–69.

Clausewitz, Carl von, *On War*, ed. and trans. Michael Howard and Peter Paret (Princeton, NJ: Princeton University Press, 1976).

Clendinnen, Inga, *Aztecs: An Interpretation* (Cambridge: Cambridge University Press, 1991).

Clifford Angell Bates, Jr., *Aristotle's 'Best Regime'* (Baton Rouge: Louisiana State University Press, 2003).

Clore, Gerald L., "Cognitive Phenomenology: Feelings and the Construction of Judgment," in Leonard Martin and Abraham Tesser, *The Construction of Social Judgments* (Hillsdale, NJ: Erlbaum, 1992), pp. 133–63.

Clore, Gerald L., Robert S. Wyer Jr., Bruce Dienes, Karen Gasper, Carol Gohm and Linda Isbell, "Affective Feelings as Feedback: Some Cognitive Consequences," in Leonard Martin and Gerald Clore, eds., *Theories of Mood and Cognition* (Mahwah, NJ: Erlbaum, 2002), pp. 27–62.

Clunas, Craig, *Superfluous Things: Material Culture and Social Status in Early Modern China* (Cambridge: Polity, 1991).

Cobban, Alfred, *The Social Interpretation of the French Revolution* (Cambridge, MA: Harvard University Press, 1964).

Coble, Parks M., *Facing Japan: Chinese Politics and Japanese Imperialism, 1931–1937* (Cambridge, MA: Harvard University Press, 1991).

Cochran, Molly, *Normative Theory in International Relations: A Pragmatic Approach* (Cambridge: Cambridge University Press, 1999).

Cohen, Albert, *Delinquent Boys: The Culture of the Gang* (London: Routledge and Kegan Paul, 1956).

Cohen, Benjamin, *The Geography of Money* (Ithaca, NY: Cornell University Press, 1998).

Cohen, Daniel, *The Wealth of the World and the Poverty of Nations*, trans. Jacqueline Lindenfeld (Cambridge, MA: MIT Press, 1998).

Cohen, David, "Sexuality, Violence and the Athenian Law of *Hubris*," *Greece and Rome* 38 (1991), pp. 171–88.

  Law, Violence and Community in Classical Athens (Cambridge: Cambridge University Press, 1995).

Cohen, G. A., *Karl Marx's Theory of History: A Defense* (Princeton, NJ: Princeton University Press, 1978).

  "Functional Explanation, Consequence Explanation, and Marxism," *Inquiry* 25, no. 1 (1982), pp. 27–56.

  "Self-Ownership, Communism, and Equality," *Proceedings of the Aristotelian Society*, supplementary vol. 16 (1990), pp. 25–44.

Cohen, Jean L., "Trust, Voluntary Association and Workable Democracy: The Contemporary American Discourse of Civil Society," in Mark E. Warren, *Democracy and Trust* (Cambridge: Cambridge University Press, 1999), pp. 208–48.

Cohen, Jean L. and Andrew Arato, *Civil Society and Political Theory* (Cambridge, MA: MIT Press, 1992).

Cohen, Jerome B., *Japan's Economy in War and Reconstruction* (Minneapolis: University of Minnesota Press, 1949).

Cohen, Mark N., "The Significance of Long-Term Changes in Human Diets and Food Economy," in Marvin Harris and Eric B. Ross, *Food and Evolution: Toward a Theory* (Philadelphia, PA: Temple University Press, 1987), pp. 261–84.

Cohen, Raymond, "Threat Perception in International Crisis," *Political Science Quarterly* 93, no. 1 (Spring 1978), pp. 93–107.

Cohen, William B., *Rulers of Empire: The French Colonial Service in Africa* (Stanford, CA: Hoover Institution Press, 1971).

Cohen, Youssef, Brian R. Brown and A. F. K. Organski, "The Paradoxical Nature of State Making: A Violent Creation of Order," *American Political Science Review* 75, no. 4 (December 1981), pp. 901–10.

Coicaud, Jean-Marc, *Legitimacy and Politics: A Contribution to the Study of Political Right and Political Responsibility* (Cambridge: Cambridge University Press, 2002).

Coker, Christopher, *Waging War Without Warriors: The Changing Culture of Military Conflict* (Boulder, CO: Lynne Reinner, 2002).

"The Unhappy Warrior," *Historically Speaking* 8, no. 4 (March/April 2006), pp. 34–9.

The Warrior Ethos: Military Culture and the War on Terror (London: Routledge, 2007).

Colarizi, Simona, *L'opinione degli italiani sotto il regime 1929–1943* (Laterza: Biblioteca Laterza Universale, 1991).

Cole, C. W., *Colbert and the Century of French Mercantilism*, 2 vols. (New York: Columbia University Press, 1939).

Coleman, James, "Problems of Quantitative Measurement in Sociology," in Coleman, ed., *Introduction to Mathematical Sociology* (New York: Free Press, 1964), pp. 1–6.

The Foundations of Social Theory (Cambridge, MA: Harvard University Press, 1990).

Collier, Andrew, *Critical Realism: An Introduction to Roy Bhaskar's Philosophy* (London: Verso, 1994).

Collin, Richard H., *Theodore Roosevelt: Culture, Diplomacy and Expansion* (Baton Rouge: Louisiana State University Press, 1985).

Theodore Roosevelt's Caribbean: The Panama Canal, the Monroe Doctrine, and the Latin American Context (Baton Rouge: Louisiana State University Press, 1990).

Collins, A. E., S. E. Gathercole, M. A. Conway and P. E. M. Morris, eds., *Theories of Memory* (Hillsdale, NJ: Erlbaum, 1993).

Collins, J. B., *Fiscal Limits of Absolutism: Direct Taxation in Early Seventeenth-Century France* (Berkeley: University of California Press, 1998).

Collins, Randall, *Weberian Sociological Theory*, (Cambridge: Cambridge University Press, 1986).

"Imperialism and Legitimacy: Weber's Theory of Politics," in Collins, *Weberian Sociological Theory*, pp. 145–66.

Collins, Roger, *Early Medieval Europe 300–1000* (New York: St. Martin's Press, 1991).

Collins, S., "Categories, Concepts or Predicaments? Remarks on Mauss' Use of Philosophical Terminology," in M. Carrithers, S. Collins and S. Lukes, *The Category of the Person: Anthropology, Philosophy, History* (Cambridge: Cambridge University Press, 1985), pp. 46–82.

Committee for the Compilation of Materials on Damage Caused by the Atomic Bombs in Hiroshima and Nagasaki, *Hiroshima and Nagasaki: The Physical, Medical, and Social Effects of the Atomic Bombings* (New York: Basic Books, 1981).

Comor, Edward A., "Governance and the Nation-State in a Knowledge-Based Political Economy," in Martin Hewson and Timothy J. Sinclair, *Approaches to Global Governance Theory* (Albany, NY: State University of New York Press, 1999), pp. 117–34.

"The Role of Communication in Global Civil Society: Forces, Processes, Prospects," *International Studies Quarterly* 45, no. 3 (September 2001), pp. 389–408.

Comte, Auguste, "Plan of the Scientific Work Necessary for the Reorganization of Society," in *Early Political Writings*, trans. and ed. H. S. Jones (Cambridge: Cambridge University Press, 1998), pp. 145–87.

Connolly, William E., *Identity/Difference: Democratic Negotiations of Political Paradox* (Ithaca, NY: Cornell University Press, 1991).

Connor, W. Robert, *The New Politicians of Fifth-Century Athens* (Princeton, NJ: Princeton University Press, 1971).

Thucydides (Princeton, NJ: Princeton University Press, 1984).

"Civil Society, Dionysiac Festival, and the Athenian Democracy," in Josiah Ober and Charles Hedrick, eds., *Dēmokratia: A Conversation on Democracies, Ancient and Modern* (Princeton, NJ: Princeton University Press, 1996), pp. 217–26.

Connor, Walker, "When Is a Nation?" in John Hutchinson and Anthony D. Smith, *Nationalism* (New York: Oxford, 1995), pp. 154–9.

Connor, Walter D., "Dissent in Eastern Europe: A New Coalition," *Problems of Communism* 29 (1980), pp. 21–37.

Conrad von Hötzendorf, Franz, *Aus meiner Dienstzeit*, 5 vols. (Vienna: Rikola, 1921–5).

Conrad von Hötzendorf, Virginia, *Mein Leben mit Conrad von Hötzendorf* (Leipzig: Grethlein, 1935).

Conroy, Hilary, *The Japanese Seizure of Korea* (Philadelphia: University of Pennsylvania Press, 1960).

Contamine, Philippe, ed., *Histoire militaire de la France*, vol. I: *Des origines à 1715* (Paris: Presses Universitaires de France, 1992).

War and Competition between States (Oxford: Oxford University Press, 2000).

"The Growth of State Control. Practices of War, 1300–1800: Ransom and Booty," in Contamine, *War and Competition Between States*," pp. 163–93.

Contreni, John J., "The Carolingian Renaissance: Education and Literary Culture," in McKitterick, *The New Cambridge Medieval History*, vol. II, pp. 709–57.

Cooley, Alexander, *Logics of Hierarchy: The Organization of Empires, States and Military Occupations* (Ithaca, NY: Cornell University Press, 2005).

Cooper, John M., "Aristotle on Friendship," in A. Rorty, *Essays on Aristotle's Ethics* (Berkeley: University of California Press, 1980), pp. 301–40.

Reason and Emotion: Essays on Ancient Moral Psychology and Ethical Theory (Princeton, NJ: Princeton University Press, 1999).

"Socrates and Plato in Plato's *Gorgias*," in Cooper, *Reason and Emotion: Essays on Ancient Moral Psychology and Ethical Theory* (Princeton, NJ: Princeton University Press, 1999), pp. 29–75.

Cooper, John Milton, Jr., "The Command of Gold Reverses: American Loans to Britain, 1915–1917," *Pacific Historical Review* 45 (1976), pp. 209–30.

"The United States," in Hamilton and Herwig, *The Origins of World War I*, pp. 415–42.

Cooper, Laurence D., *Rousseau, Nature and the Problem of the Good Life* (University Park: Pennsylvania State University Press, 1999).

Copeland, Dale, *The Origins of Major War* (Ithaca, NY: Cornell University Press, 2000).

Corfield, P. J., "Class by Name and Nature in Eighteenth-Century Britain," *History* 72 (1987), pp. 38–61.

Cornell, T. J., "Aeneas and the Twins: The Development of the Roman Foundation Legend," *Proceedings of the Cambridge Philological Society*, 21 (1983), pp. 1–32.

Cornford, F. M., *Thucydides Mythistoricus* (London: Arnold, 1907).

Cornil, Fernando, "Listening to the Subaltern: Postcolonial Studies and the Poetics of Neocolonial States," in Laura Chrisman and Benita Parry, eds., *Postcolonial Theory and Criticism* (Cambridge: D. S. Brewer, 2000), pp. 37–55.

Corradini, Enrico, "Report to the First Nationalist Congress," Florence, December 3, 1910, in Adrian Lyttelton, *Italian Fascisms: From Pareto to Gentile* (London: Jonathan Cape, 1973), pp. 135–64.

Cortell, Andrew P. and James W. Davis, Jr., "Understanding the Domestic Impact of International Norms: A Research Agenda," *International Studies Review* 2 (2000), pp. 65–90.

Coser, Lewis A., *The Functions of Social Conflict* (Glencoe, IL: Free Press, 1956).

Costello, John, *The Pacific War 1941–1945* (New York: Quill, 1982).

Coulbourn, Rushton, ed., *Feudalism in History* (Princeton, NJ: Princeton University Press, 1956).

Coverdale, John F., *Italian Intervention in the Spanish Civil War* (Princeton, NJ: Princeton University Press, 1975).

Covini, Maria N., "Political and Military Bonds in the Italian State System, Thirteenth to Sixteenth Centuries," in Contamine, *War and Competition between States*, pp. 9–36.

Cox, Robert W., "Social Forces, States and World Orders: Beyond International Relations Theory," in Robert O. Keohane, *Neorealism and its Critics* (New York: Columbia University, 1986), pp. 204–54.

"Gramsci, Hegemony and International Relations: An Essay in Method," in Stephen Gill, *Gramsci, Historical Materialism on International Relations* (Cambridge: Cambridge University Press, 1993), pp. 49–66.

"Meanings of Victory: American Power after the Towers," in Booth and Dunne, *Worlds in Collision*, pp. 152–61.

"Empire, Imperialism and the Bush Doctrine," *Review of International Studies* 30 (2004), pp. 585–608.

Cracraft, James, *The Revolution of Peter the Great* (Cambridge, MA: Harvard University Press, 2003).

Craig, Gordon A. and Felix Gilbert, eds., *The Diplomats 1919–1939*, vol. I: *The Twenties* (New York: Atheneum, 1965).

Crane, Gregory. *Thucydides and the Ancient Simplicity: The Limits of Political Realism* (Berkeley: University of California Press, 1998).

Crane, Jonathan, "The Epidemic Theory of Ghettos and Neighborhood Effects on Dropping Out and Teenage Childbearing," *American Journal of Sociology* 96 (1991), pp. 1226–59.

Craven, Wesley Frank and Frank Lea Cate, *The Army Air Forces in World War Two* (Washington, DC: Office of Air Force History, 1983), vol. V.

Crawcour, Sydney, "Industrialization and Technological Change, 1885–1920," in Peter Duus, *The Cambridge History of Japan*, vol. VI: *The Twentieth Century* (Cambridge: Cambridge University Press, 1988), pp. 1–54.

Crawford, Neta C., *Argument and Change in World Politics: Ethics, Decolonization, and Humanitarian Intervention* (Cambridge: Cambridge University Press, 2002).

Creveld, Martin Van, *The Rise and Decline of the State* (Cambridge: Cambridge University Press, 1999).

Croce, Benedetto, "Chi è fascista?" *Il Giornale di Napoli*, October 29, 1944, p. 3.

Croce, the King and the Allies: Extracts from a Diary, July 1943–June 1944, trans. Sylvia Sprigge (London: Allen and Unwin, 1950).

Crocker, J. and L. E. Park, "The Costly Pursuit of Self-Esteem," *Psychological Bulletin*, 130, no. 3 (2004), pp. 392–414.

Crook, J. A., A. Lintott and E. Rawson, eds., *Cambridge Ancient History*, 3rd edn, vol. IX: *The Last Age of the Roman Republic, 146–43 B.C.* (Cambridge: Cambridge University Press, 1994).

Cross, Charles, "Explanation and the Theory of Questions," *Erkenntnis* 34, no. 2 (1991), pp. 237–60.

Cross, R. C., "Logos and Form in Plato's Mind," *Mind* 63, no. 252 (1954), pp. 433–50.

Crouch, David, *William Marshall: Court, Career and Chivalry in the Angevin Empire, 1147–1219* (London: Longman, 1990).

The Birth of the Nobility: Constructing Aristocracy in England and France, 900–1300 (London: Longman, 2005).

Crowley, James B., *Japan's Quest for Autonomy: National Security and Foreign Policy, 1930–38* (Princeton, NJ: Princeton University Press, 1966).

"Intellectuals as Visionaries of the New Asian Order," in Morley, *Dilemmas of Growth in Prewar Japan*, pp. 319–74.

Culham, Phyllis, "Women in the Roman Republic," in Flower, *The Cambridge Companion to the Roman Republic*, pp. 139–59.

Cusack, Thomas R. and Richard J. Stoll, *Exploring Realpolitik: Probing International Relations Theory with Computer Simulation* (Boulder, CO: Lynne Rienner, 1990).

"Collective Security and State Survival in the Interstate System," *International Studies Quarterly* 38, no. 1 (1994), pp. 33–59.

Cutler, A. Claire, Virginia Haufler and Tony Porter, eds., *Private Authority and International Affairs* (Albany, NY: State University of New York Press, 1999).

"The Contours and Significance of Private Authority in International Affairs," in Cutler *et al., Private Authority and Intenational Affairs*, pp. 333–76.

Czempiel, Ernst-Otto and James N. Rosenau, eds., *Global Changes and Theoretical Challenges: Approaches to World Politics for the 1990s* (Lexington, MA: Lexington Books, 1992).

Daalder, Ivo H. and James M. Lindsay, *America Unbound: The Bush Revolution in Foreign Policy*, rev. edn (Hoboken, NJ: Wiley, 2005).

Dabashi, Hamid, *Authority in Islam: From the Rise of Muhammad to the Establishment of the Umayyads* (New Brunswick, NJ: Transaction Press, 1989).

Dahl, Robert A., "Power," in David L. Sills (ed.), *International Encyclopedia of the Social Sciences*, vol. XII (New York: Free Press, 1968), pp. 405–15.

Dahlstrom, Daniel, "Hegel's Appropriation of Kant's Account of Teleology in Nature," in Stephen Houlgate, ed., *Hegel and the Philosophy of Nature* (Albany: State University of New York Press, 1998), pp. 167–88.

Dahrendorf, Ralf, *Society and Democracy in Germany* (Garden City, NY: Doubleday, 1967).

Dallin, Alexander, *German Rule in Russia 1941–1945: A Study in Occupation Policies* (London: Macmillan, 1957).

Damasio, Anthony, *Descartes' Error: Emotion, Reason, and the Human Brain* (New York: Putnam, 1996).

Darby, Philip, "Pursuing the Political: A Postcolonial Rethinking of Relations International," *Millennium* 33, no. 1 (2004), pp. 1–34.

David, Stephen R., "Internal War: Causes and Cures," *World Politics* 49 (1997), pp. 552–76.

Davidson, Donald, "Actions, Reasons, and Causes," *Journal of Philosophy* 60, no. 23 (1963), pp. 685–700.

Inquiries into Truth and Interpretation (Oxford: Oxford University Press, 2001 [1984]).

Davidson, James N., *Courtesans and Fishcakes: The Consuming Passions of Classical Athens* (London: HarperCollins, 1997).

Davies, Norman, *God's Playground* (Oxford: Oxford University Press, 1981).

Davis, James A. and William Wohlforth, "German Unification," in Herrmann and Lebow, *Ending the Cold War*, pp. 131–60.

Davis, James W., *Terms of Inquiry: On the Theory and Practice of Political Science* (Baltimore, MD: Johns Hopkins University Press, 2005).

Davis, L. E. and R. A. Huttenback, *Mammon and the Pursuit of Empire* (Cambridge: Cambridge University Press, 1987).

Davis, R. H. C., *A History of Medieval Europe: From Constantine to Saint Louis*, 2nd edn (New York: Longman, 1988).

Dawe, R. D., "Some Reflections on *ate* and *hamartia*," *Harvard Studies in Classical Philology* 72 (1968), pp. 89–123.

Dawes, R., A. J. C. Van der Kraft and J. Orbell, "Cooperation for the Benefit of Us – Not Me, or My Conscience," in Jane Mansbridge, *Beyond Self-Interest* (Chicago: University of Chicago Press, 1990), pp. 97–110.

De Bruhl, Marshall, *Firestorm: Allied Air Power and the Destruction of Dresden* (New York: Random House, 2006).

De Felice, Renzo, *Mussolini*, 4 vols. (Turin: Einaudi, 1965–97).

Storia degli ebrei sotto il fascismo, 3rd. rev. edn (Turin: Einaudi, 1972).

The Interpretations of Fascism trans. Brenda Everett (Cambridge, MA: Harvard University Press, 1977).

Rosso e nero (Milan: Baldini e Castoldi, 1995).

De Jong, Irene. J. F., *Narrators and Focalizers* (Amsterdam: B. M. Grüner, 1987).

De Jong, Mayke, "Charlemagne's Church," in Story, ed., *Charlemagne*, pp. 103–35.

De Ste. Croix, G. E. M., *The Class Struggle in the Ancient World from the Archaic Age to the Arab Conquests* (Ithaca, NY: Cornell University Press, 1981).

De Vattel, Emmerich, "Preface to The Law of Nations," in Forsyth, *et al., The Theory of International Relations*, pp. 87–120.

Deak, Istvan, Jan T. Gross and Tony Judt, eds., *The Politics of Retribution in Europe: World War II and its Aftermath* (Princeton, NJ: Princeton University Press, 2000).

Dechesne, M., J. Greenberg, J. Arndt and J. Schimel, "Terror Management and Sports Fan Affiliation: The Effects of Mortality Salience on Fan Identification and Optimism," *European Journal of Social Psychology*, 30 (2000), pp. 813–35.

Dechesne, M., J. Janssen, J. and A. van Knippenberg, "Derogation and Distancing as Terror Management Strategies: The Moderating Role of Need for Structure and Permeability of Group Boundaries," *Journal of Personality and Social Psychology*, 79 (2000), pp. 923–32.

Dedijer, Vladimir, *The Road to Sarajevo* (New York: Simon and Schuster, 1966).

Deibert, Ronald J. "International Plug, 'n' Play? Citizen Activism, the Internet, and Global Public Policy," *International Studies Perspectives* 1, no 3 (December 2000), pp. 255–72.

Deist, Wilhelm, "Kaiser Wilhelm II in the Context of his Military and Naval Entourage," in Röhl and Sombart, *Kaiser Wilhelm II*, pp. 169–92.

Deleuze, Gilles and Felix Guattari, *A Thousand Plateaus: Capitalism and Schizophrenia*, vol. II (Minneapolis: University of Minnesota Press, 1987).

  What is Philosophy?, trans. Hugh Tomlinson and Graham Burcell (New York: Columbia University Press, 1994).

Demel, Walter, *Europäische Geschichte des 19. Jahrhunderts* (Stuttgart: Kohlhammer, 2000).

Deneen, Patrick J., *The Odyssey of Political Theory: The Politics of Departure and Return* (Lanham, MD: Rowman and Littlefield, 2000).

Denemark, Robert Allen, George Modelski, Barry K. Gills and Jonathan Friedman, eds., *World System History: The Science of Long-Term Change* (London: Routledge, 2000).

Derrida, Jacques, *Of Grammatology* (Baltimore, MD: Johns Hopkins University Press, 1974).

  Writing and Difference, trans. A. Bass (Chicago: University of Chicago Press, 1978).

  Positions (Chicago: University of Chicago Press, 1981).

  Otobiographies: l'enseignement de Nietzsche et la politique du nom propre (Paris: Éditions Galilée, 1984).

  "Force of Law: The 'Mystical Foundation of Authority,'" in D. Cornell, M. Rossenfeld and D. G. Carlson, eds., *Deconstruction and the Possibility of Justice* (New York: Routledge, 1992), pp. 3–67.

Descartes, René, *Regulae ad directionem ingenii, Rules for the Direction of Natural Intelligence: A Bilingual Edition of the Cartesian Treatise on Method*, ed. and trans. George Hefferman (Amsterdam: Rodopi, 1998).

Dessert, Daniel, *Argent, pouvoir et société au Grand Siècle* (Paris: Fayard, 1984).

  Fouquet (Paris: Fayard, 1987).

Dessert, Daniel and Jean-Louis Journet, "Le lobby Colbert: un royaume, ou une affaire du famille?," *Annales* 30, no. 6 (November/December 1975), pp. 1306–36.

Dessler, David, "What's at Stake in the Agent-Structure Debate?," *International Organization* 43, no. 3 (Summer 1989), pp. 441–73.

Deutsch, Karl W., *Nationalism and Social Communication* (Cambridge, MA: MIT Press, 1953).

  Nerves of Government: Models of Political Communication and Control (New York: Free Press, 1966).

Deutsch, Karl W. *et al.*, *Political Community and the North Atlantic Area* (Princeton, NJ: Princeton University Press, 1957).

Deutsch, Karl W., B. Fritsch, H. Jaguaribe and A. S. Markovits, eds., *Problems of World Modeling – Political and Social Implications* (Cambridge, MA: Ballinger, 1977).

Devetak, Richard, "The Gothic Scene of International Relations: Ghosts, Monsters, Terror and the Sublime after September 11," *Review of International Studies* 31 (2005), pp. 621–43.

DeVries, Willem, "The Dialectic of Teleology," *Philosophical Topics* 19, no. 2 (1991), pp. 51–70.

DeWald, Jonathan, *Aristocratic Experience and the Origins of Modern Culture: France, 1570–1715* (Berkeley: University of California Press, 1993).

Dewey, John, *Characters and Events: Popular Essays in Social and Political Philosophy*, vol. II (London: Allen and Unwin, 1929).

Dews, Peter, *Logics of Disintegration: Post-Structuralist Thought and Claims of Critical Theory* (London: Verso, 1987).

Diakonoff, Igor M., *The Paths of History* (Cambridge: Cambridge University Press, 1999).

Diamond, Jared, "The Diffusion of Language Groups in Africa," *Discover* 14 (1993), pp. 53–62.

Dicken, Peter, *Global Shift: Transforming the World Economy*, 3rd edn (New York: Guilford, 1998).

Dickey, Laurence W., *Hegel: Religion, Economics, and the Politics of the Spirit 1770– 1807* (Cambridge: Cambridge University Press, 1987).

Dickinson, Frederick, *World War I and Japan* (Cambridge, MA: Harvard University Press, 1997).

Dickinson, Goldsworthy Lowes, *The European Anarchy* (London: Allen and Unwin, 1916).

Dickson, P. G. M., *Finance and Government under Maria Theresa, 1740–1780*, 2 vols. (Oxford: Oxford University Press, 1987).

Dickson, P. G. M. and J. Stirling, "War Finance, 1689–1714," in S. Bromley, ed., *The New Cambridge Modern History* (Cambridge: Cambridge University Press, 1970), vol. IV, pp. 284–315.

Diels, Hermann and Walther Kranz, *Die Fragmente der Vorsokratiker*, 7th edn (Berlin: Weidmannsche, 1954).

Diephouse, D. J., "The Triumph of Hitler's Will," in Joseph Held, ed., *The Cult of Power. Dictators in the Twentieth Century* (New York: Columbia University Press, 1983), pp. 51–76.

Diesing, Paul, *How Does Social Science Work? Reflection on Practice* (Pittsburgh, PA: University of Pittsburgh Press, 1991).

Diggins, John P., *Max Weber: Politics and the Spirit of Tragedy* (New York: Basic Books, 1996).

Dingman, Roger, *Power in the Pacific* (Chicago: University of Chicago Press, 1976).

Dionysius of Halicarnassus, *On Thucydides*, trans. William K. Pritchett (Berkeley: University of California Press, 1975).

Dipper, Christof, "Orders and Classes: Eighteenth-Century Society under Pressure," in Blanning, *The Eighteenth Century*, pp. 52–90.

Dixon, Norman F., *On the Psychology of Military Incompetence* (New York: Basic Books, 1976).

Dockrill, M. L., "British Policy during the Agadir Crisis of 1911," in Hinsley, *British Foreign Policy under Sir Edward Grey*, pp. 271–87.

Dodds, E. R., *The Greeks and the Irrational* (Berkeley: University of California Press, 1951).

Dollimore, Jonathan and Alan Sinfield, *Political Shakespeare: Essays in Cultural Materialism*, 2nd edn (Ithaca, NY: Cornell University Press, 1994).

Dombrowski, Peter, *Policy Responses to the Globalization of American Banks* (Pittsburgh: University of Pittsburgh Press, 1978).

"Fragmenting Identities, Shifting Loyalties: The Influence of Individualisation on Global Transformations," *Global Society* 12, no. 3 (September 1998), pp. 363–88.

"Haute Finance and High Theory: Recent Scholarship on Global Financial Relations," *Mershon International Studies Review* 42 (May 1998), pp. 1–28.

Dombrowski, Peter and Richard W. Mansbach, "From Sovereign States to Sovereign Markets?" *International Politics* 36 (March 1999), pp. 1–23.

Dombrowski, Peter and Tom Rice, "Changing Identities and International Relations Theory: A Cautionary Note," *Nationalism and Ethnic Politics* 6, no. 4 (Winter 2000), pp. 83–105.

Donaldson, M., "What Is Hegemonic Masculinity?," *Theory and Society* 22 (1993), pp. 643–57.

Dondi, M., "The Fascist Mentality after Fascism," in R. J. B. Bosworth and P. Dogliani, *Italian Fascism: History, Memory and Representation* (London: Macmillan, 1999), pp. 141–56.

Donelan, Michael, ed., *The Reason of State* (London: Allen and Unwin, 1978).

Donlon, Walter, "Reciprocities in Homer," *Classical World* 75 (1981–2), pp. 137–85.

"Political Reciprocity in Dark Age Greece: Odysseus and his *hetairoi*," in Christopher Gill, Norman Postlethwaite and Richard Seaford, *Reciprocity in Ancient Greece* (Oxford: Oxford University Press, 1998), pp. 51–72.

Donnelly, Jack, "The Social Construction of International Human Rights," in Dunne and Wheeler, *Human Rights and Global Politics*, pp. 703–23.

Realism and International Relations (Cambridge: Cambridge University Press, 2000).

Doran, Charles and Wes Parsons, "War and the Cycle of Relative Power," *American Political Science Review* 74 (1980), pp. 947–65.

Dore, Ronald P., *British Factory: Japanese Factory* (London: Allen and Unwin, 1973). *Land Reform in Japan* (New York: Schocken Books, 1985).

Dore, Ronald P. and Tsutomu Ōuchi, "Rural Origins of Japanese Fascism," in Morley, *Dilemmas of Growth in Prewar Japan*, pp. 181–210.

Dorpalen, Andreas, *Hindenburg and the Weimar Republic* (Princeton, NJ: Princeton University Press, 1964).

Doty, Roxanne Lynn, "The Logic Of Difference in International Relations: U.S. Colonization of the Philippines," in Francis A. Beer and Robert Hariman, eds., *Post-Realism: The Rhetorical Turn in International Relations* (East Lansing: Michigan State University Press, 1996), pp. 331–46.

Doucet, Marc G., "The Democratic Paradox and Cosmopolitan Democracy," *Millennium* 24, no. 1 (2005), pp. 137–55.

Douglas, David C., *William the Conqueror* (Berkeley: University of California Press, 1964).

Douglas, Mary, *Natural Symbols: Explorations in Cosmology* (New York: Pantheon, 1970).

Dover, K. J., *Greek Popular Morality in the Time of Plato and Aristotle* (Berkeley: University of California Press, 1974).

    Greek Homosexuality, Updated with a New Postscript (Cambridge, MA: Harvard University Press, 1989).

Dowd, Maureen, *Bushworld: Enter at Your Own Risk* (New York: G. P. Putnam's Sons, 2004).

Dowden, Ken, "The Epic Tradition in Greece," in Fowler, ed., *The Cambridge Companion to Homer*, pp. 188–206.

Dower, John, *War without Mercy: Race and Power in the Pacific War* (New York: Pantheon, 1986).

    Embracing Defeat: Japan in the Wake of World War II (New York: Norton, 1999).

Downing, Brian M., "Constitutionalism, Warfare, and Political Change in Early Modern Europe," *Theory and Society* 17, no. 1 (January 1988), pp. 7–56.

    The Military Revolution and Political Change: Origins of Democracy and Autocracy in Early Modern Europe (Princeton, NJ: Princeton University Press, 1992).

Doyle, Michael W. "Kant, Liberal Legacies, and Foreign Affairs, Part 1," *Philosophy and Public Affairs* 12, no. 3 (1983), pp. 205–35.

    "Kant, Liberal Legacies, and Foreign Affairs, Part 2," *Philosophy and Public Affairs* 12, no. 4 (1983), pp. 323–53.

    Empires (Ithaca, NY: Cornell University Press, 1986).

    "Liberalism and World Politics," *American Political Science Review* 80 (1986), pp. 1151–69.

    Ways of War and Peace: Realism, Liberalism, and Socialism (New York: Norton, 1997).

Doyle, R. E., "The Objective Character of Atē in Aeschylean Tragedy," *Traditio* 28 (1972), pp. 1–28.

Doyle, William, *Old European Order, 1600–1800* (Oxford: Oxford University Press, 1978).

Drolet, Jean-François, "The Visible Hand of Neo-Conservative Capitalism," *Millennium* 35, no. 2 (2007), pp. 245–78.

Duara, Prasenjit, "Historicizing National Identity, or Who Imagines What and When," in Geoff Eley and Ronald Grigor Suny, *Becoming National: A Reader* (Oxford: Oxford University Press, 1996), pp. 151–77.

Duby, Georges, *La société aux XIe and XIIIe siècles dans la région mâconnaise* (Paris: Colin, 1953).

  Guerriers et paysans (Paris: Gallimard, 1973).

  "Lineage, Nobility and Chivalry in the Region of Mâcon During the Twelfth Century," in Robert Forster and Orest Ranum, eds., *Selections from the Annales Économies, Sociétés, Civilisations* Baltimore, MD: Johns Hopkins University Press, 1976), pp. 140–68.

Dudden, Alexis, *Japan's Colonization of Korea: Discourse and Power* (Honolulu: University of Hawaii Press, 2005).

Duffy, Christopher, *The Military Life of Frederick the Great* (New York: Atheneum, 1986).

  The Military Experience in the Age of Reason (London: Routledge and Kegan Paul, 1987).

Dukes, *Catherine the Great and the Russian Nobility* (Cambridge: Cambridge University Press, 1967).

Dumard, Adeline, *Les bourgeois de Paris au XIXe siècle* (Paris: Presses Universitaires de France, 1979).

Dumont, Louis, "The Modern Concept of the Individual: Notes on its Genesis and that of Concomitant Institutions," *Contributions to Indian Sociology* 6 (1965), pp. 13–61.

Dunabin, Jean, *France in the Making 843–1190* (Oxford: Oxford University Press, 1985).

Dunlop, Ian, *Louis XIV* (New York: St. Martins Press, 2000).

Dunn, John, "The Identity of the History of Ideas," in Peter Laslett, W. G. Runciman and Quentin Skinner, eds., *Philosophy, Politics and Society*, 4th series (Oxford: Blackwell, 1972), pp. 158–73.

  "Trust and Political Agency," in D. Gambetta, ed., *Trust* (Oxford: Blackwell, 1988), pp. 73–93.

  "The Contemporary Significance of John Locke's Conception of Civil Society," in Kaviraj and Khilnani, *Civil Society*, pp. 39–57.

Dunne, Tim, *Inventing International Society: A History of the English School* (New York: St. Martin's Press, 1998).

  "Society and Hierarchy in International Relations," *International Relations* 17, no. 3 (2003), pp. 303–20.

  "System, State and Society: How Does It All Hang Together," *Millennium* 24, no. 1 (2005), pp. 157–69.

  "'The Rules of the Game are Changing': Fundamental Human Rights in Crisis after 9/11," *International Politics* 44, no. 2 (March 2007), pp. 269–86.

Dunne, Tim and Nicholas J. Wheeler, eds., *Human Rights and Global Politics* (Cambridge: Cambridge University Press, 1999).

Durand, Yves, *Les fermiers généraux au XVIIIe siècle* (Paris: Presses Universitaires de France, 1971).

Durkheim, Émile, *Suicide: A Study in Sociology*, trans. George Spaulding and George Simpson (Glencoe, IL: Free Press, 1951).

The Division of Labor in Society, trans. W. D. Halls (New York: Macmillan, 1984).

Professional Ethics and Civic Morals (London: Routledge, 1992).

The Elementary Forms of the Religious Life, trans. Carol Cosman (Oxford: Oxford University Press, 2001).

Dutton, Paul Edward, *Charlemagne's Mustache and Other Cultural Clusters of a Dark Age* (New York: Palgrave Macmillan, 2004).

Duus, Peter, "Ōyama Ikuo and the Search for Democracy," in Morley, *Dilemmas of Growth in Prewar Japan*, pp. 423–60.

"Introduction," in Peter Duus, ed., *The Cambridge History of Japan*, vol. VI: *The Twentieth Century* (Cambridge: Cambridge University Press, 1988), pp. 1–54.

"Japan's Informal Empire in China, 1895–1937: An Overview," in Duus, Myers and Peattie, *Japanese Informal Empire in Asia*, pp. xi–xxix.

The Abacus and the Sword (Berkeley: University of California Press, 1995).

Duus, Peter, Raymon H. Myers and Mark R. Peattie, *Japanese Informal Empire in Asia* (Princeton, NJ: Princeton University Press, 1989).

Duvall, Raymond and Jutta Weldes, "The International Relations of Democracy, Liberalism and War: Directions for Future Research," in Tarak Barkawi and Mark Laffey, eds., *Democracy, Liberalism, and War* (Boulder, CO: Lynne Rienner, 2001), pp. 195–207.

Dwyer, Philip G., ed., *The Rise of Prussia, 1700–1830* (London: Longmans, 2000).

Eakin, Paul John, *How our Lives Become Stories: Making Selves* (Ithaca, NY: Cornell University Press, 1999).

Earl, Donald, *The Moral and Political Tradition of Rome* (Ithaca, NY: Cornell University Press, 1967).

Easterling, P. E. and B. M. W. Knox, eds., *The Cambridge History of Classical Literature*, vol. I, part 2: *Greek Drama* (Cambridge: Cambridge University Press, 1989).

Eckersley, Robyn, "Ambushed: The Kyoto Protocol, the Bush Administration's Climate Policy and the Erosion of Legitimacy," *International Politics*, 44, no. 2 (March 2007), pp. 306–24.

Eckholm, Erik, "A Trial Will Test China's Grip on the Internet," *New York Times*, November 16, 1998, A1.

Eckstein, Arthur M., "Hannibal at New Carthage: Polybius 3.15 and the Power of Irrationality," *Classical Philology* 84 (1989), pp. 1–15.

Moral Vision in the Histories of Polybius (Berkeley: University of California Press, 1995).

Mediterranean Anarchy, Interstate War and the Rise of Rome (Berkeley: University of California Press, 2006).

Eckstein, Harry, "Case Study and Theory in Political Science," in Fred Greenstein and Nelson Polsby, *Handbook of Political Science*, vol. VII: *Strategies of Inquiry* (Reading, MA: Addison-Wesley, 1975), pp. 79–135.

Edelman, G. M., *Bright Air, Brilliant Fire: On the Matter of the Mind* (New York: Basic Books, 1992).

Edelman, Murray, *Constructing the Political Spectacle* (Chicago: University of Chicago Press, 1988).

    The Politics of Misinformation (New York: Cambridge University Press, 2001).

Edelstein, Michael, *Overseas Investments in the Age of High Imperialism: The United Kingdom, 1850–1924* (New York: Columbia University Press, 1982).

Eder, Walter, "Augustus and the Power of Tradition," in Karl Galinsky, *The Age of Augustus*, pp. 13–33.

Edgeworth, F. Y., *Mathematical Psychics: An Essay on the Application of Mathematics to the Moral Sciences* (London: C. K. Paul, 1881).

Edkins, Jenny and Véronique Pin-Fat, "Through the Wire: Relations of Power and Relations of Violence," *Millennium* 24, no. 1 (2005), pp. 1–26.

Edwards, Anthony, *Achilles in the Odyssey: Ideologies of Heroism in the Homeric Epic* (Königstein: Hain, 1985).

Edwards, D., and J. Potter, "The Chancellor's Memory: Rhetoric and Truth in Discursive Remembering," *Applied Cognitive Psychology* 6 (1992), pp. 187–215.

Edwards, D., J. Potter and D. Middleton, "Toward a Discursive Psychology of Remembering," *The Psychologist* 5 (1992), pp. 441–6.

Edwards, M. W., *Homer, Poet of the Iliad* (Baltimore, MD: Johns Hopkins University Press, 1987).

Égret, Jean, *Louis XV et l'opposition parlementaire* (Paris: Armand Colin, 1970).

Ehrenberg, Victor, "*Polypragmosyne*: A Study in Greek Politics," *Journal of Hellenic Studies* 67 (1947), pp. 46–67.

    Sophocles and Pericles (Oxford: Blackwell, 1954).

Ehrenreich, Barbara, *Blood Rites: Origins and History of the Passions of War* (New York: Henry Holt & Co., 1997).

Eichengreen, Barry, *Golden Fetters: The Gold Standard and the Great Depression 1919–1939* (New York: Oxford University Press, 1992).

Einhard, *Life of Emperor Karl the Great*, trans. William Glaister (London: G. Bell, 1877).

    Vita Karoli Magni, ed. Evelyn Scherabon Firchow and Edwin H. Zeydel (Coral Gables, FL: University of Miami Press, 1972).

Eisenstadt, S. N., "Communication Patterns in Centralized Empires," in Lasswell *et al.*, *Propaganda and Communication in World History*, vol. I, pp. 536–51.

Ekstein, Michael G. and Zara Steiner, "The Sarajevo Crisis," in Hinsley, *British Foreign Policy Under Sir Edward Grey*, pp. 397–410.

Eksteins, Modris, *Rites of Spring: The Great War and the Birth of the Modern Age* (Boston: Houghton Mifflin, 1989).

Elazar, Dahlia S., *The Making of Fascism: Class, State, and Counter-Revolution, Italy 1919–1922* (Westport, CT: Praeger, 2001).

Eldredge, Niles, *Time Frames: The Rethinking of Darwinian Evolution and the Theory of Punctuated Equilibria* (New York: Simon and Schuster, 1985).

Eldredge, Niles and Stephen Jay Gould, "Punctuated Equilibria: An Alternative to Phyletic Gradualism," in T. J. Schopf, ed., *Models in Paleobiology* (San Francisco, CA: Freeman, Cooper, 1972), pp. 82–115.

Eley, Geoff, *Reshaping the German Right: Radical Nationalism and Political Change after Bismarck* (New Haven, CT: Yale University Press, 1980).

"The British Model and the German Road: Rethinking the Course of German History before 1914," in David Blackbourn and Geoff Eley, *The Peculiarities of German History: Bourgeois Society and Politics in Nineteenth-Century Germany* (Oxford: Oxford University Press, 1984), pp. 1–158.

"German History and the Contradictions of Modernity: The Bourgeoisie, the State and the Mastery of Reform," in Geoff Eley, ed., *Society, Culture, and the State in Germany, 1870–1930* (Ann Arbor: University of Michigan Press, 1996), pp. 67–104.

Eley, Geoff and Ronald Grigor Suny, eds., *Becoming National: A Reader* (Oxford: Oxford University Press, 1996).

Elias, Norbert, *The Civilizing Process* (Oxford: Oxford University Press, 1978 [1939]).

The History of Manners: The Civilizing Process I (Oxford: Basil Blackwell, 1978).

State Formation and Civilization: The Civilizing Process II (Oxford: Basil Blackwell, 1982).

The Court Society, trans. Edmund Jephcott (Oxford: Oxford University Press, 1983).

The Society of Individuals, ed. Michael Schröter, trans. Edmund Jephcott (Oxford: Basil Blackwell, 1991).

The Germans, trans. Eric Dunning and Stephen Mennell (Cambridge: Polity, 1996).

Elkins, David L., *Beyond Sovereignty: Territory and Political Economy in the Twenty-first Century* (Toronto: University of Toronto Press, 1995).

Elkins, David and Richard Simeon, "A Cause in Search of its Effect, or What Does Political Culture Explain?," *Comparative Politics* 11, no. 2 (January 1979), pp. 127–45.

Ellemers, Naomi, "Individual Upward Mobility and the Perceived Legitimacy of Intergroup Relations," in John Jost and Brenda Major, eds., *The Psychology of Legitimacy: Emerging Perspectives on Ideology, Justice, and Intergroup Relations* (New York: Cambridge University Press, 2001), pp. 205–22.

Elster, Jon, *The Cement of Society* (Cambridge: Cambridge University Press, 1989).

Nuts and Bolts for the Social Sciences (Cambridge: Cambridge University Press, 1989).

"Norms of Revenge," *Ethics* 100 (1990), pp. 862–85.

"Strategic Uses of Argument," in Kenneth Arrow, Robert H. Mnookin, Lee Ross, Amos Tversky and Robert Wilson, *Barriers to Conflict Resolution* (New York: W. W. Norton, 1995), pp. 236–57.

Elvin, Mark, *The Pattern of the Chinese Past: A Social and Economic Interpretation* (Stanford, CA: Stanford University Press, 1973).

Elwitt, Sanford, *The Making of the Third Republic: Class and Politics in France, 1868–1884* (Baton Rouge: Louisiana State University Press, 1975).

The Third Republic Defended: Bourgeois Reform in France, 1880–1914 (Baton Rouge: Louisiana State University Press, 1986).

Emerson, Rupert, *From Empire to Nation: The Rise to Self-Assertion of Asian and African Peoples* (Boston: Beacon Press, 1960).

Emmeche, Claus, Simo Koppe and Frederik Stjernfelt, "Levels, Emergence, and Three Versions of Downward Causation," in Peter Bogh Andersen, Claus Emmeche, Niels Ole Finneman and Peder Voetmann Christiansen, eds., *Downward Causation* (Aarhus: Aarhus University Press, 2000), pp. 13–34.

Enç, Berent and Fred Adams, "Functions and Goal-Directedness," in Colin Allen, Marc Bekoff and George Lauder, *Nature's Purposes* (Cambridge, MA: MIT Press, 1998), pp. 371–94.

English, Robert D., *Russia and the Idea of the West: Gorbachev, Intellectuals, and the End of the Cold War* (New York: Columbia University Press, 2000).

"Power, Ideas, and New Evidence on the Cold War's End: A Reply to Brooks and Wohlforth," *International Security* 26, no. 4 (2002), pp. 93–111.

Entman, Robert M., *Projections of Power: Framing News, Public Opinion and U.S. Foreign Policy* (Chicago: University of Chicago Press, 2004).

Epkenhans, Michael, *Die Wilhelminische Flottenrüstung 1908–1914. Weltmacht-streben, industrieller Fortschritt, soziale Integration* (Munich: Oldenbourg, 1991).

"Willhelm II and 'His' Navy, 1888–1918," in Mombauer and Deist, *The Kaiser*, pp. 12–36.

Epstein, Joshua M. and Robert Axtell, *Growing Artificial Societies: Social Science from the Bottom Up* (Washington, DC: Brookings Institution Press, 1996).

Erdmann, Karl Dietrich, "War Guilt 1914 Reconsidered: A Balance of New Research," in H. W. Koch, ed., *The Origins of the First World War*, 2nd edn (Oxford: Oxford University Press, 1984), pp. 343–70.

Erickson, John, *The Road to Stalingrad: Stalin's War with Germany* (London: Weidenfeld and Nicolson, 1975).

The Road to Berlin: Stalin's War with Germany (London: Weidenfeld and Nicolson, 1983).

Erikson, Erik, *Childhood and Society* (New York: Norton, 1950).

"The Development of Ritualization," in Donald R. Cutler, ed., *The Religious Situation* (Boston: Beacon, 1968), pp. 711–33.

Erikson, Kai, *Wayward Puritans: A Study in the Sociology of Deviance* (New York: Wiley, 1966).

Erlich, Alexander, *The Soviet Industrialization Debate 1924–1928* (Cambridge, MA: Harvard University Press, 1967).

Erskine, Toni, "'Citizen of Nowhere' or the 'Point where Circles Intersect'? Impartialist and Embedded Cosmopolitanisms," *Review of International Studies* 28 (2002), pp. 457–78.

Erspamer, Francesco, *La biblioteca di don Ferrante. Duello e onore nella cultura del Cinquecento* (Rome: Bulzoni, 1982).

Ertman, Thomas, *Birth of the Leviathan: Building States and Regimes in Medieval and Early Modern Europe* (Cambridge: Cambridge University Press, 1997).

Etzioni, Amitai, "The Epigenesis of Political Communities at the International Level," *American Journal of Sociology* 68, no. 4 (1963), pp. 407–21.

"The Evils of Self-Determination," *Foreign Policy*, no. 89 (Winter 1992–3), pp. 21–35.

"The Global Importance of Illiberal Moderates," *Cambridge Review of International Affairs* 19, no. 3 (September 2006), pp. 369–85.

Euben, J. Peter, *The Tragedy of Political Theory: The Road Not Taken* (Princeton, NJ: Princeton University Press, 1990).

"Democracy Ancient and Modern," *PS: Political Science and Politics* 26 (1993), pp. 478–80.

"Democracy and Political Theory: A Reading of Gorgias," in John R. Wallach, J. Peter Euben and Josiah Ober, *Athenian Political Thought and the Reconstitution of American Democracy* (Ithaca, NY: Cornell University Press, 1994), pp. 198–226.

"Reading Democracy: 'Socratic' Dialogues and the Political Education of Democratic Citizens," in J. Ober and C. Hedrick, *Dēmokratia: A Conversation on Democracies, Ancient and Modern* (Princeton, NJ: Princeton University Press, 1996), pp. 327–59.

Platonic Noise (Princeton, NJ: Princeton University Press, 2003).

Euben, J. Peter, John R. Wallach and Josiah Ober, *Athenian Political Thought and the Reconstruction of American Democracy* (Ithaca, NY: Cornell University Press, 1994).

Euripides, *Euripides*, ed. Richard Lattimore, 2 vols. (Chicago: University of Chicago Press, 1959).

Evangelista, Matthew, *Unarmed Forces: The Transnational Movement to End the Cold War* (Ithaca, NY: Cornell University Press, 1999).

"Turning Points in Arms Control," in Richard K. Herrmann and Richard Ned Lebow, *Ending the Cold War* (New York: Palgrave, 2004), pp. 83–106.

Evans, Gareth, *Cooperating for Peace: The Global Agenda for the 1990s and Beyond* (St. Leonards, Australia: Allen and Unwin, 1993).

Evans, Michael, "Of Arms and the Man: A Response to Christopher Coker's 'The Unhappy Warrior,'" *Historically Speaking* 8, no. 4 (March/April 2006), pp. 40–2.

Evans, Richard J., *Rethinking German History: Nineteenth Century Germany and the Origins of the Third Reich* (London: Unwin Hyman, 1987).

  "The Habsburg Monarchy and the Coming of War," in Evans and Pogge von Strandmann, *The Coming of the First World War*, pp. 33–56.

Evans, Richard J. and Hartmut Pogge von Strandmann, eds., *The Coming of the First World War* (Oxford: Oxford University Press, 1988).

Everson, Stephen, "Psychology," in Jonathan Barnes, ed., *The Cambridge Companion to Aristotle* (Cambridge: Cambridge University Press, 1995), pp. 168–94.

Eyck, Erich, *A History of the Weimar Republic*, trans. Harlan Hanson and Robert Waite, 2 vols. (Cambridge, MA: Harvard University Press, 1962–3).

Faber, Richard, *The Vision and the Need: Late Victorian Imperialist Aims* (London: Faber and Faber, 1966).

Fabian, Johannes, "Ethnographic Objectivity Revisited: From Rigor to Vigor," in Allan Megill, *Rethinking Objectivity* (Durham, NC: Duke University Press, 1994), pp. 81–108.

  Out of Our Minds: Reason and Madness in the Exploration of Central Africa (Berkeley: University of California Press, 2000).

Fairbank, John, *The Chinese World Order* (Cambridge, MA: Harvard University Press, 1968).

Fallows, James, "Blind into Baghdad," *Atlantic Monthly* (January/February 2004), pp. 52–74.

Falter, Jürgen, "The National Socialist Mobilisation of New Voters," in Thomas Childers, ed., *The Formation of the Nazi Constituency, 1919–33* (London: Croom Helm, 1986), pp. 202–31.

Falk, A., Fehr, E. and Fischbacher, U., "On the Nature of Fair Behavior," Institute for Empirical Research in Economics, University of Zurich, Working Paper no. 17 (August 1999).

Fantham, Elaine, "Literature in the Roman Republic," in Flower, *The Cambridge Companion to the Roman Republic*, pp. 271–94.

Farnham, Barbara, ed., *Avoiding Losses/Taking Risks: Prospect Theory and International Conflict* (Ann Arbor: University of Michigan Press, 1995).

Farr, James, "Understanding Conceptual Change Politically," in Terence Ball, S. T. Hanson and James Farr, eds., *Political Innovation and Conceptual Change* (Cambridge: Cambridge University Press, 1989), pp. 24–49.

Farrell, Joseph, "Roman Homer," in Fowler, *The Cambridge Companion to Homer*, pp. 254–71.

Fasolt, Constantin, *Limits of History* (Chicago: University of Chicago Press, 2004).

Favier, Jean, *Charlemagne* (Paris: Fayard, 1999).

Favro, Diane, "Making Rome a World City," in Galinsky, *The Age of Augustus*, pp. 234–63.

Fearon, James D., "Causes and Counterfactuals in Social Science: Exploring an Analogy Between Cellular Automata and Historical Processes," in Tetlock and Belkin, *Counterfactual Thought Experiments in World Politics*, pp. 39–67.

Featherstone, Mike, Scott Lash and Roland Robertson, eds., *Global Modernities* (London: Sage, 1995).

Feinstein, Lee and Anne-Marie Slaughter, "A Duty to Prevent," *Foreign Affairs* 83, no. 1 (2004), pp. 136–51.

Feis, Herbert, *Europe: The World's Banker, 1870–1914* (New Haven, CT: Yale University Press, 1930).

Feldner, Fritz, ed., *Schicksaljahre Osterreichs 1908–1919. Das politische Tagebuch Josef Redlich*, vol. I: *1908–1914* (Graz: Böhlaus, 1953–4).

Fellner, Fritz, "Die Mission Hoyos," in Wilhelm Alff, ed., *Deutschlands Sonderung von Europe, 1862–1945* (Frankfurt am Main: Lang, 1984), pp. 283–316.

Felson, Nancy and Laura M. Slatkin, "Gender and Homeric Epic," in Fowler, ed., *The Cambridge Companion to Homer*, pp. 91–116.

Fénelon, François de Salignac de La Mothe, "Sentiments on the Balance of Europe," in *Two Essays on the Balance of Europe* (London: n.p., 1720).

Fenoaltea, Stefano, "Italy," in Patrick O'Brien, ed., *Railways and the Economic Development of Western Europe, 1830–1914* (London: Macmillan, 1983), pp. 49–70.

Ferguson, Adam, *An Essay on the History of Civil Society*, 2nd edn (Edinburgh: A. Kincaid and J. Bell, 1768).

Principles of Moral and Political Science: Being Chiefly a Retrospect of Lectures Delivered in the College of Edinburgh, 2 vols. (London: A. Strahan and T. Cadell, 1792).

Ferguson, Arthur B., *The Indian Summer of English Chivalry: Studies in the Decline and Transformation of Chivalric Idealism* (Durham, NC: Duke University Press, 1960).

Ferguson, Niall, *The Pity of War* (London: Penguin, 1998).

Empire: How Britain Made the Modern World (London: Penguin, 2003).

Ferguson, R. Brian, "(Mis)understanding Resource Scarcity and Cultural Difference," *Anthropology Newsletter* (November 1995), pp. 136–54.

Ferguson, Yale H. and R. J. Barry Jones, eds., *Political Space: New Frontiers of Change and Governance in a Globalizing World* (Albany: State University of New York Press, 2002).

Ferguson, Yale H. and Rey Koslowski, "Culture, International Relations Theory, and Cold War History," in Odd Arne Westad, *Reviewing the Cold War: Approaches, Interpretations, Theory* (London: Frank Cass, 2000), pp. 149–79.

Ferguson, Yale H. and Richard W. Mansbach, *The Elusive Quest: Theory and International Politics* (Columbia: University of South Carolina Press, 1988).

"The Past as Prelude to the Future? Identities and Loyalties in Global Politics," in Yosef Lapid and Friedrich Kratochwil, eds., *The Return of Culture and Identity in IR Theory* (Boulder, CO: Lynne Rienner, 1996), pp. 21–44.

Polities: Authority, Identities, and Change (Columbia: University of South Carolina Press, 1996).

"Global Politics at the Turn of the Millennium: Changing Bases of 'Us' and 'Them,'" in Davis B. Bobrow, *Prospects for International Relations: Conjectures about the Next Millennium,* special edition *of International Studies Review* 1, no. 2 (Summer 1999), pp. 77–107.

"History's Revenge and Future Shock: The Remapping of Global Politics," in Martin Hewson and Timothy J. Sinclair, *Approaches to Global Governance Theory* (Albany: State University of New York Press, 1999), pp. 197–238.

"Stories of Global Politics: Continuity and Change, Anarchy and Order: Polities and Markets," paper delivered to the 4th Pan-European Conference on International Relations," Canterbury, UK, 2001.

"Remapping Political Space: Issues and Nonissues in Analyzing Global Politics in the Twenty-First Century," in Ferguson and Jones, *Political Space*, pp. 87–111.

"Reconstructing Theory in Global Politics: Beyond the Postmodern Challenge," in Darryl S. L. Jarvis, ed., *International Relations and the 'Third Debate': Postmodernism and its Critics* (Westport, CT: Greenwood, 2006), pp. 147–64.

Fernández-Armesto, Felipe, *Truth: A History and a Guide to the Perplexed* (London: Bantam, 1997).

Fest, Joachim, *Hitler*, trans. Richard and Clara Winslow (New York: Harcourt, Brace, Jovanovich, 1974).

Festinger, Leon, *A Theory of Cognitive Dissonance* (Stanford, CA: Stanford University Press, 1957).

Feuchtwanger, E. J., *Disraeli, Democracy and the Tory Party* (Oxford: Oxford University Press, 1968).

"Introduction," in Feuchtwanger, ed., *Upheaval and Continuity: A Century of German History* (Pittsburgh, PA: University of Pittsburgh Press, 1974), pp. 1–23.

Feyerabend, Paul, *Against Method* (London: New Left Books, 1975).

Fieldhouse, D. K., "'Imperialism': An Historiographical Revision," *Economic History Review* 14 (1961), pp. 187–209.

Economics and Empire, 1830–1914 (London: Weidenfeld and Nicolson, 1976).

The Colonial Empires: A Comparative Survey from the Eighteenth Century, 2nd edn (London: Macmillan, 1982).

Fierke, Karen M., "Whereof We Can Speak, Thereof We Must Not Be Silent: Trauma, Political Solipsism and War," *Review of International Studies* 30 (2004), pp. 471–92.

Finley, John H., "Euripides and Thucydides," *Harvard Studies in Classical Philology* 49 (1938), pp. 23–68.

Finley, Moses I., *The World of Odysseus* (New York: Viking, 1978).

Democracy Ancient and Modern, rev. edn (New Brunswick, NJ: Rutgers University Press, 1985).

Politics in the Ancient World (Cambridge: Cambridge University Press, 1991).

The Ancient Economy, 2nd rev. edn (Berkeley and Los Angeles: University of California Press, 1999).

Finley, Moses I. and H. W. Pleket, *The Olympic Games: The First Thousand Years* (London: Chatto and Windus, 1976).

Finnemore, Martha, *The Purpose of Intervention: Changing Beliefs about the Use of Force* (Ithaca, NY: Cornell University Press, 2003).

Finnemore, Martha and Kathryn Sikkink, "International Norm Dynamics and Political Change," *International Organization* 52, no. 4 (Autumn 1998), pp. 887–917.

Finnemore, Martha and Stephen Toope, "Alternatives to 'Legalization': Richer Views of Law and Politics," *International Organization* 55, no. 3 (2001), pp. 743–58.

Fischer, David Hackett, *Albion's Seed: Four British Folkways in America* (New York: Oxford University Press, 1989).

Fischer, Fritz, *Germany's Aims in the First World War* (New York: Norton, 1967).

War of Illusions: German Policies from 1911 to 1914, trans. Marian Jackson (New York: Norton, 1975 [1969]).

Fischer, Louis, *Russia's Road from Peace to War: Soviet Foreign Relations, 1917–1941* (New York: Harper and Row, 1969).

Fischer, Markus, *Well-Ordered License: On the Utility of Machiavelli's Thought* (Boulder, CO: Lexington Books, 2000).

Fitzgerald, T. K., *Metaphors of Identity* (Albany, NY: State University of New York Press, 1993).

Fivush, Robyn, "The Function of Event Memory," in U. Neisser and E. Winograd, *Remembering Reconsidered: Ecological and Traditional Approaches to the Study of Memory* (Cambridge: Cambridge University Press, 1988), pp. 277–83.

Flannery, Kent V., *The Early Mesoamerican Village* (New York: Academic Press, 1976).

Flathman, Richard, *Thomas Hobbes: Skepticism, Individuality, and Chastened Politics* (Newbury Park, CA: Sage, 1993).

Fletcher, Miles, *The Search for a New Order: Intellectuals and Fascism in Prewar Japan* (Chapel Hill: University of North Carolina Press, 1982).

Fletcher, Roger, "Recent Developments in German Historiography," *German Studies Review* 7 (October 1984), pp. 451–80.

Flockhart, Trine, "'Complex Socialization': A Framework for the Study of State Socialization," *European Journal of International Relations*, 12, no. 1 (2006), pp. 98–118.

Flower, Harriet I., ed., *The Cambridge Companion to the Roman Republic* (Cambridge: Cambridge University Press, 2003).

Flyvbjerg, Bent, *Making Social Science Matter: Why Social Inquiry Fails and How it Can Succeed Again* (Cambridge: Cambridge University Press, 2001).

Fogel, Joshua A., *Politics and Sinology* (Cambridge, MA: Harvard University Press, 1984).

    The Cultural Dimension of Sino-Japanese Diplomacy: Essays on the Nineteenth and Twentieth Centuries (New York: M. E. Sharpe, 1997).

    The Nanjing Massacre in History and Historiography (Berkeley: University of California Press, 2000).

Fogu, Claudio, "*Italiani brava gente*: The Legacy of Fascist Historical Culture," in Lebow, Kansteiner and Fogu, *The Politics of Memory in Postwar Europe*, pp. 147–76.

Foley, Helen P., *Female Acts in Greek Tragedy* (Princeton, NJ: Princeton University Press, 2001).

Foley, John Miles, *Homer's Traditional Art* (University Park: Pennsylvania State University Press, 1999).

    "Epic as Genre," in Fowler, *The Cambridge Companion to Homer*, pp. 177–87.

Fontane, Theodor, *Wanderungen durch die Mark Brandenburg*, 8 vols. (Berlin: Aufbau-Verlag, 1997–2004).

Force, Pierre, *Self-Interest before Adam Smith: A Genealogy of Economic Science* (Cambridge: Cambridge University Press, 2003).

Forster, Robert, *The Nobility of Toulouse in the Eighteenth Century* (Baltimore, MD: Johns Hopkins University Press, 1960).

    "The Survival of the Nobility during the French Revolution," in Johnson, *French Society and the Revolution*, pp. 132–47.

Forsyth, M. G., H. M. A. Keens-Soper and P. Savigear, *The Theory of International Relations* (New York: Atherton Press, 1970).

Fossier, Robert, *Enfance de l'Europe*, 2nd edn, 2 vols. (Paris: Presses Universitaires de France, 1989).

    The Cambridge Illustrated History of the Middle Ages, vol. I: *350–950* (Cambridge: Cambridge University Press, 1997).

Foucault, Michel, *The Archeology of Knowledge* (London: Tavistock, 1972).

    Language, Counter-Memory, Practice, ed. D. F. Bouchard (Ithaca, NY: Cornell University Press, 1977).

    The History of Sexuality, trans. Robert Hurley (New York: Random House, 1980).

    Power/Knowledge: Selected Interviews and Other Writings, 1973–77, ed. Colin Gordon (Brighton: Harvester Press, 1980).

    The Order of Things, An Archeology of the Human Sciences (New York: Vintage, 1994 [1971]).

Fouracre, Paul, "Frankish Gaul to 814," in McKitterick, *The New Cambridge Medieval History*, vol. II, pp. 85–109.

Fowler, Kenneth, *The Hundred Years War* (London: Macmillan, 1971).

Fowler, Robert, ed., *The Cambridge Companion to Homer* (Cambridge: Cambridge University Press, 2004).

"The Homeric Question," in Fowler, *The Cambridge Companion to Homer*, pp. 220–34.

Fox, Christopher, Roy Porter and Robert Wokler, eds., *Inventing Human Science: Eighteenth Century Domains* (Berkeley: University of California Press, 1995).

Fox, John, *Germany and the Far Eastern Crisis, 1931–38: A Study in Diplomacy and Ideology* (Oxford: Oxford University Press, 1982).

Franceschet, Antonio, "'One Powerful and Enlightened Nation': Kant and the Quest for a Global Rule of Law," in Jahn, *Classical Theories of International Relations*, pp. 74–95.

Franck, Thomas M., *The Power of Legitimacy among Nations* (New York: Oxford University Press, 1990).

The Power of Legitimacy (Oxford: Oxford University Press, 1991).

Fairness in International Law and Institutions (Oxford: Oxford University Press, 1995).

"Tribe, Nation, World: Self-Identification in the Evolving International System," *Ethics and International Affairs* 11 (1997), pp. 151–69.

Frank, Robert H., *Choosing the Right Pond: Human Behavior and the Quest for Status* (New York: Oxford University Press, 1985).

Franklin, John Hope, *The Militant South, 1800–1861* (Cambridge, MA: Harvard University Press, 1956).

Frantzen, Allen J., *Bloody Good: Chivalry, Sacrifice, and the Great War* (Chicago: University of Chicago Press, 2004).

Franzinelli, Mimmo, *Squadristi: protagonisti e technice della violenza facista, 1919–1922* (Milan: Mondadori, 2003).

Fraser, Nancy, "Rethinking Recognition," *New Left Review* 3 (May/June 2000), pp. 107–20.

Fravel, M. Taylor, "Regime Insecurity and International Cooperation: Explaining China's Compromises in Territorial Disputes," *International Security*, 30, no. 2 (Fall 2005), pp. 46–83.

Frederick, Howard, "Social and Industrial Policy for Public Networks," in L. M. Harasim, *Global Networks: Computers and International Communication* (Cambridge, MA: MIT Press, 1993), pp. 283–95.

Frederico, Giovanni, *The Economic Development of Italy since 1870* (Brookfield, VT: Elgar, 1994).

Freedman, Lawrence, *U.S. Intelligence and the Soviet Threat* (Princeton, NJ: Princeton University Press, 1986).

The Revolution in Strategic Affairs, Adelphi Paper 318 (New York: Oxford University Press, 1998).

"The Changing Forms of Military Conflict," *Survival* 40, no. 4 (Winter 1998–9), pp. 39–56.

Freeman, Mark A., "Liking Self and Social Structure: A Psychological Perspective on Sri Lanka," *Journal of Cross-Cultural Psychology*, 12, no. 1 (1981), pp. 291–308.

Frege, Gottlob, "On Concept and Object," in McGuinness, *Gottlob Frege*, pp. 182–94.

"On Sense and Meaning," in McGuinness, *Gottlob Frege*, pp. 157–77.

Frei, Norbert, "People's Community and War: Hitler's Popular Support," in Hans Mommsen, *The Third Reich between Vision and Reality: New Perspectives on German History, 1918–1945* (Oxford: Berg, 2001), pp. 59–78.

French, David, "Had We Known How Bad Things Were in Germany: We Might Have Got Stiffer Terms': Great Britain and the German Armistice," in Boemeke, Feldman and Glaser, *Treaty of Versailles*, pp. 69–86.

Freud, Sigmund, *Beyond the Pleasure Principle*, ed. and trans. James Strachey (New York: Norton, 1989).

Frevert, Ute, "Honor, Gender, and Power: The Politics of Satisfaction in Pre-War Europe," in Afflerbach and Stevenson, *An Improbable War?*, pp. 233–55.

Men of Honor: A Social and Cultural History of the Duel (Cambridge: Blackwell, 1995).

Fried, Johannes, "The Frankish Kingdoms, 817–911: The East and Middle Kingdoms," in McKitterick, *The New Cambridge Medieval History*, vol. II, pp. 142–68.

Fried, Morton, *The Evolution of Political Society: An Essay in Political Anthropology* (New York: Random House, 1967).

Frieden, Jeffrey, "International Investment and Colonial Control," *International Organization* 48 (1994), pp. 558–93.

Frieden, Jeffrey and David A. Lake, *International Political Economy: Perspectives on Global Power and Wealth* (New York: St. Martin's Press, 1987).

Friedlander, Henry and Sybil Miltons, eds., *The Holocaust: Ideology, Bureaucracy and Genocide* (Millwood, NJ: Kraus, 1980).

Friedman, Gil and Harvey Starr, *Agency, Structure, and International Politics* (London: Routledge, 1977).

Friedman, Milton and Rose Friedman, *Free to Choose* (New York: Avon Books, 1979).

Friedman, Thomas L., *The Lexus and the Olive Tree* (New York: Farrar, Straus and Giroux, 1999).

Longitudes and Attitudes: Exploring the World after September 11 (New York: Farrar, Straus and Giroux, 2002).

Friedrich, Carl J. and Zbigniew Brzezinski, *Totalitarian Dictatorship and Autocracy*, 2nd edn (Cambridge, MA: Harvard University Press, 1965).

Friedrichs, Jörg, "The Meaning of New Medievalism," *European Journal of International Relations* 7, no. 4 (2001), pp. 475–502.

Frissen, Paul, "The Virtual State: Postmodernisation, Informatisation and Public Administration," in Brian D. Loader, *The Governance of Cyberspace: Politics, Technology, and Global Restructuring* (London: Routledge, 1997), pp. 111–25.

Fritzsche, Peter, *A Nation of Fliers: German Aviation and the Popular Imagination* (Cambridge, MA: Harvard University Press, 1992).

Froissart, *Chronicles*, trans. Geoffrey Brereton (Baltimore, MD: Johns Hopkins University Press, 1968).

Fromm, Eric, *Escape From Freedom* (New York: Rinehart, 1941).

Frost, Alan, *The Global Reach of Empire: Britain's Maritime Expansion in the Indian and Pacific Oceans, 1764–1815* (Carlton, Vic.: Miegunyah Press, 2003).

Frost, Mervyn, *Ethics in International Relations: A Constitutive Theory* (Cambridge: Cambridge University Press, 1996).

"Tragedy, Ethics and International Relations," *International Relations* 17, no. 4 (2003), pp. 477–95.

Frost, Robert I., *State and Society in Northeastern Europe, 1558–1721* (Cambridge: Cambridge University Press, 1993).

Frum, David and Richard Perle, *An End to Evil: How to Win the War on Terror* (New York: Random House, 2003).

Frye, Timothy, *Brokers and Bureaucrats: Building Market Institutions in Russia* (Ann Arbor: University of Michigan Press, 2000).

Fujitani, Takashi, *Splendid Monarchy: Power and Pageantry in Modern Japan* (Berkeley: University of California Press, 1996).

Fukuyama, Francis, "The End of History?" *National Interest* (Summer 1989), pp. 3–18.

The End of History and the Last Man (New York: Free Press, 1992).

Fuller, J. F. C., *Armament and History: A Study of the Influence of Armament on History from the Dawn of Classical Warfare to the Second World War* (New York: Scribner's, 1945).

Fuller, Lon, *Anatomy of the Law* (New York: F. A. Praeger, 1968).

Furedi, Frank, *The New Ideology of Imperialism: Renewing the Moral Imperative* (Boulder, CO: Pluto Press, 1994).

Furet, François, *Interpreting the French Revolution* (Cambridge: Cambridge University Press, 1981 [1978]).

Gadamer, Hans-Georg, *Philosophical Hermeneutics*, trans. David E. Linge (Berkeley: University of California Press, 1976).

Dialogue and Dialectic: Eight Hermeneutical Studies on Plato, trans. P. Christopher Smith (New Haven, CT: Yale University Press, 1980).

"Plato and the Poets," in *Dialogue and Dialectic*, pp. 39–72.

"Text and Interpretation," in Diane Michelfelder and Richard Palmer, eds., *Dialogue and Deconstruction* (Albany: State University of New York Press, 1989), pp. 24–55.

Truth and Method, 2nd edn, trans. Joel Weinsheimer and Donald G. Marshall (New York: Crossroad, 1989).

"Reflections on My Philosophical Journey," in Lewis Edwin Hahn, ed., *The Philosophy of Hans-George Gadamer* (Chicago, IL: Open Court, 1997), pp. 3–63.

Gaddis, John Lewis, "Toward the Post-Cold World," *Foreign Affairs* 70 (1991), pp. 102–22.

Gaertner, L. and J. Schopler, J., "Perceived Ingroup Entitativity and Intergroup Bias: An Interconnection of Self and Others," *European Journal of Social Psychology* 28 (1998), pp. 963–80.

Gagliardo, John G., *Germany under the Old Regime, 1600–1790* (London: Longman, 1991).

Galagher, John and Ronald Robinson, "The Imperialism of Free Trade," *Economic History Review*, 2nd series, 6 (1953), pp. 1–15.

Galbraith, John Kenneth, *The Affluent Society* (Boston: Houghton Mifflin, 1984).

Galbraith, Peter W., *The End of Iraq: How American Incompetence Created a War Without End* (New York: Simon and Schuster, 2006).

Galeotti, Anna Elisabetta, *Toleration as Recognition* (Cambridge: Cambridge University Press, 2002).

Galinsky, Karl, ed., *The Age of Augustus* (Cambridge: Cambridge University Press, 2005).

Galston, William A., *Liberal Purposes: Goods, Virtues, and the Diversity of the Liberal State* (Cambridge: Cambridge University Press, 1991).

   Liberal Pluralism: The Implications of Value Pluralism for Political Theory and Practice (Cambridge: Cambridge University Press, 2002).

Gammon, W., "The Social Psychology of Collective Action," in A. D. Morris and C. McClure Mueller, *Frontiers in Social Movement Theory* (New Haven, CT: Yale University Press, 1992), pp. 122–41.

Ganguly, Šumit, "Explaining the Kashmir Insurgency: Political Mobilization and Institutional Decay," *International Security* 21, no. 2 (1997), pp. 76–107.

Ganshof, François Louis, "Charlemagne et les institutions de la monarchie franque," in Helmut Beumann, ed., *Karl der Grosse: Lebenswerk und Nachleben*, vol. I: *Persönlichkeit und Geschichte* (Düsseldorf: L. Schwann, 1965), pp. 364–88.

   Qu'est-ce que la féodalité? 5th edn (Paris: Tallandier, 1982).

Ganz, David, "Book Production in the Carolingian Empire and the Spread of Caroline Miniscule," in McKitterick, *The New Cambridge Medieval History*, vol. II, pp. 786–808.

Garcia, Luis Ribot, "Types of Armies: Early Modern Spain," in Contamine, *War and Competition between States*, pp. 37–68.

Garfinkel, Alan, *Forms of Explanation: Rethinking the Questions in Social Theory* (New Haven, CT: Yale University Press, 1981).

Garnett, George and John Hudson, *Law and Government in Medieval England and Normandy: Essays in Honour of Sir James Holt* (Cambridge: Cambridge University Press, 1994).

Garthoff, Raymond L., *Détente and Confrontation: American-Soviet Relations from Nixon to Reagan* (Washington, D.C.: Brookings Institution, 1985).

Reflections on the Missile Crisis, rev. edn (Washington: Brookings Institution, 1989).

The Great Transition: American Soviet Relations and the End of the Cold War (Washington, DC: Brookings Institution, 1994).

Gasser, Adolph, "Der deutsche Hegemonialkrieg von 1914," in Imanuel Geiss and Alexander Wendt, eds., *Deutschland in der Weltpolitik des 19 und 20. Jahrhunderts* (Düsseldorf: Bertelsmann, 1973), p. 310.

Preussischer Militärgeist und Kriegsentfesselung 1914. Drei Studien zum Ausbruch des Ersten Weltkrieges (Basel: Helbing und Lichtenhahn, 1985).

Gaukroger, Stephen, *Descartes: An Intellectual Biography* (Oxford: Oxford University Press, 1995).

Gauthier, David, "Morality and Advantage," *Philosophical Review* 76 (1961), pp. 460–75.

Gay, Peter, *The Enlightenment: An Interpretation,* vol. II: *The Science of Freedom* (New York: Norton, 1969).

Schnitzler's Century: The Making of Middle Class Culture, 1815–1914 (New York: Norton, 2002).

Geary, Dick, "The Industrial Elite and the Nazis in the Weimar Republic," in Stachura, *The Nazi Machtergreifung*, pp. 85–100.

Geddes, Barbara, "How the Cases you Choose Affect the Answers you Get: Selection Bias in Comparative Politics," *Political Analysis* 2, no. 1 (1990), pp. 131–50.

Geertz, Clifford, *The Interpretation of Numbers* (New York: Basic Books, 1973).

Negara: The Theater State in Nineteenth Century Bali (Princeton, NJ: Princeton University Press, 1980).

Local Knowledge (New York: Basic Books, 1983).

Gehrke, Hans-Joachim, *Stasis. Unterversuchungen zu den inneren Kriegen in den griechischen Staaten des 5. und 4. Jahrhunderts v. Chr.* (Munich: Beck, 1985).

Geiss, Imanuel, "The Outbreak of the First World War and German War Aims," *Journal of Contemporary History* 1 (July 1966), pp. 75–91.

July 1914: The Outbreak of the First World War. Selected Documents, trans. Henry Hughes (New York: Scribner's 1968).

German Foreign Policy, 1971–1914 (London: Kegan Paul, 1976).

Gellner, Ernest, *Plough, Sword and Book: The Structure of Human History* (London: Collins Harvill, 1988).

Encounters with Nationalism (Oxford: Blackwell, 1994).

"Nationalism and Modernization," in John Hutchinson and Anthony D. Smith, *Nationalism* (New York: Oxford, 1994), pp. 55–63.

Genovese, Eugene D., *The World the Slaveholders Made: Two Essays in Interpretation* (New York: Pantheon, 1969).

Gentile, Emilio, *Fascist Ideology, 1918–25* (New York: Enigma Books, 2005).

Gentiles, D., "New Zealand Defence Policy: Has it Been Transformed?," *New Zealand International Review* (July/August 2005), pp. 7–11.

George, Alexander L., *Towards a Soviet–American Crisis Prevention Regime: History and Prospects* (Los Angeles: UCLA, ACIS Working Paper 28, 1980).

Managing U.S.–Soviet Rivalry: Problems of Crisis Prevention (Boulder, CO: Westview, 1983).

Bridging the Gap: Theory and Practice in American Foreign Policy (Washington, D.C.: U.S. Institute of Peace Press, 1993).

George, Alexander L. and Richard Smoke, *Deterrence in American Foreign Policy: Theory and Practice* (New York: Columbia University Press, 1974).

George, Alexander L., Philip J. Farley and Alexander Dallin, *U.S.–Soviet Security Cooperation: Achievements, Failures, Lessons* (New York: Oxford University Press, 1988).

Geras, Norman, "The Controversy about Marx and Justice," in Alex Callinicos, *Marxist Theory* (Oxford: Oxford University Press, 1989), pp. 211–67.

Gergen, Kenneth J., "Mind, Text, and Society: Self-Memory in Social Context," in Ulrich Neisser and Robyn Fivush, *The Remembering Self: Construction and Accuracy in the Self Narrative* (Cambridge: Cambridge University Press, 1994), pp. 78–104.

An Invitation to Social Construction (London: Sage, 1999).

Germain, Randall and Michael Kenny, "Engaging Gramsci: International Relations Theory and the Neo-Gramscians," *Review of International Studies* 24 (1998), pp. 3–21.

Gerschenkron, Alexander, *Bread and Democracy in Germany* (Berkeley: University of California Press, 1943).

Economic Backwardness in Historical Perspective: A Book of Essays (Cambridge, MA: Harvard University Press, 1962).

"Agrarian Policies and Industrialization: Russia 1861–1917," in H. J Habakkuk and M. Postan, eds., *Cambridge Economic History of Europe* (Cambridge: Cambridge University Press, 1965), vol. VI, part 2, pp. 706–800.

Geyer, Dietrich, *Russian Imperialism: The Interaction of Domestic and Foreign Policy, 1860–1914*, trans. Bruce Little (New Haven, CT: Yale University Press, 1987).

Gibbon, Edward, *The Decline and Fall of the Roman Empire*, vol. II (New York: Modern Library, 1938).

Giddens, Anthony, *The Class Structure of Advanced Societies* (New York: Harper, 1975).

Central Problems in Social Theory (Berkeley: University of California Press, 1979).

The Constitution of Society: Outline of the Theory of Structuration (Cambridge: Polity, 1984).

The Consequences of Modernity (Stanford, CA: Stanford University Press, 1990).

"Jürgen Habermas," in Quentin Skinner, *The Return of Grand Theory in the Human Sciences* (Cambridge: Cambridge University Press, 1991), pp. 121–40.

Modernity and Self-Identity: Self and Society in the Late Modern Age (Cambridge: Polity, 1992).

The Third Way: The Renewal of Social Democracy (Cambridge: Polity, 1998).

Gierke, Otto, *Natural Law and the Theory of Society, 1500 to 1800*, trans. Ernest Barker (Boston: Beacon Press, 1957).

Gilbert, Margaret, *On Social Facts* (Princeton, NJ: Princeton University Press, 1989).

Gilbert, Martin, *The First World War: A Complete History* (New York: Holt, 1994).

Gill, Stephen and David Law, "Global Hegemony and the Structural Power of Capital," in Stephen Gill, ed., *Gramsci, Historical Materialism and International Relations* (Cambridge: Cambridge University Press, 1993), pp. 93–126.

"1066 and the Introduction of Chivalry into England," in Garnett and Hudson, *Law and Government in Medieval England and Normandy*, pp. 31–55.

Gillingham, John "War and Chivalry in the *History of William the Marshal*," in Matthew Strickland, ed., *Anglo-Norman Warfare: Studies in Late Anglo-Saxon and Anglo-Norman Military Organization and Warfare* (Woodbridge, Suffolk: Boydell, 1992), pp. 92–116.

Gills, Barry K. ed., *Globalization and the Politics of Resistance* (London: Palgrave, 2001).

Gilpin, Robert, *War and Change in World Politics* (Princeton, NJ: Princeton University Press, 1981).

The Political Economy of International Relations (Princeton, NJ: Princeton University Press, 1987).

Gintis, Herbert, "Beyond *Homo Economicus*: Evidence from Experimental Economics," *Ecological Economics* 35 (2000), pp. 311–22.

Gladwell, Malcolm, *The Tipping Point: How Little Things Can Make a Big Difference* (Boston: Back Bay Books, 2000).

Glahn, Gerhard von, *Law among Nations*, 7th edn (Boston: Allyn and Bacon, 1996).

Glantz, David M., *The Siege of Leningrad, 1941–44: 900 Days of Terror* (London: Collins, 2004).

Colossus Reborn: The Red Army at War, 1941–1943 (Lawrence: University of Kansas Press, 2005).

Glaser, David, ed., *Handbook of Criminology* (Chicago: Rand McNally, 1974).

Gleason, Abbot, *European and Muscovite: Ivan Kireevsky and the Origins of Slavophilism* (Cambridge, MA: Harvard University Press, 1972).

Totalitarianism: The Inner History of the Cold War (New York: Oxford University Press, 1985).

Gleditsch, Kristian S. and J. David Singer, "Distance and International War, 1816–1965," in M. R. Khan, *Proceedings of the International Peace Research Association, Fifth General Conference* (Oslo: International Peace Research Association, 1975), pp. 481–506.

Gluck, Carol, *Japan's Modern Myths: Ideology in the Late Meiji Period* (Princeton, NJ: Princeton University Press, 1985).

Goddard, Stacie E. and Daniel H. Nexon, "Paradigm Lost: Reassessing Theory of International Politics," *European Journal of International Relations* 11, no. 1 (March 2005), pp. 9–62.

Godefroy, Frédéric, ed., *Dictionnaire de l'ancienne langue française et de tous ses dialectes du IX au XV siècle*, vol. IV (Paris: F. Vieweg, 1881–1902).

Goebel, Stefan, *The Great War and Medieval Memory: War. Remembrance and Medievalism in Britain and Germany, 1914–1940* (Cambridge: Cambridge University Press, 2007).

Goertz, Gary and Jack Levy, eds., *Causal Explanations, Necessary Conditions, and Case Studies: World War I and the End of the Cold War* (New York: Palgrave, 2005).

Goethe, Johann Wolfgang, *Wilhelm Meisters Wanderjahre, oder, Die Entsagenden* ["Wilhelm Meister's Apprenticeship"] (Stuttgart: P. Reclam, 1982).

Goetz, Hans-Werner, "Social and Military Institutions," in McKitterick, *The New Cambridge Medieval History*, vol. II, pp. 451–80.

Goffman, Erving, "Symbols of Class Status," *British Journal of Sociology* 2, no. 4 (1951), pp. 294–304.

"On the Nature of Difference and Demeanor," *American Anthropologist* 58 (1956), pp. 473–502.

Presentation of Self in Everyday Life (New York: Doubleday, 1959).

Behavior in Public Places: Notes on the Social Organization of Gatherings (New York: Free Press, 1962).

Stigma: Notes on the Management of Spoiled Identity (New York: Simon and Schuster, 1963).

Interaction Ritual (Garden City, NY: Doubleday, 1967).

Goheen, Robert F., *The Imagery of Sophocles's Antigone* (Princeton, NJ: Princeton University Press, 1941).

Goldberg, Eric J., *Struggle for Empire: Kingship and Conflict under Louis the German, 817–876* (Ithaca, NY: Cornell University Press, 2006).

Goldenberg, J. L., S. K. McCoy, T. Pyszczynksi, J. Greenberg, and S. Solomon, "The Body as a Source of Self-Esteem: The Effects of Mortality Salience on Identification with One's Body, Interest in Sex, and Appearance Monitoring," *Journal of Personality and Social Psychology*, 79 (2000), pp. 118–30.

Goldgeier, James M., *Leadership Style and Soviet Foreign Policy: Stalin, Khrushchev, Brezhnev, Gorbachev* (Baltimore, MD: Johns Hopkins University Press, 1994).

Goldhill, Simon, *Reading Greek Tragedy* (Cambridge: Cambridge University Press, 1986).

Goldman, Emily O., *Sunken Treaties: Naval Arms Control between the Wars* (State College: Pennsylvania State University Press, 1994).

Goldstein, Erik, "Great Britain: The Home Front," in Boemeke, Feldman and Glaser, *Treaty of Versailles*, pp. 147–66.

Goldstein, Erik and John Maurer, eds., *The Washington Conference, 1921–22: Naval Rivalry, East Asian Stability and the Road to Pearl Harbor* (London: Frank Cass, 1994).

Goldsworthy, Adrian Keith, *The Roman Army at War 100 BC–AD 200* (Oxford: Oxford University Press, 1996).

"'Instinctive Genius:' The Depiction of Caesar the General," in Kathryn K. Welch and Anton Powell, eds., *Julius Caesar as Artful Reporter: The War Commentaries as Political Instruments* (London: Duckworth, 1998), pp. 193–219.

Gong, Gerritt W., "China's Entry Into International Society," in Bull and Watson, *The Expansion of International Society*, pp. 171–84.

The Standard of "Civilization" in International Society (Oxford: Oxford University Press, 1984).

Gooch, George, *Frederick the Great: The Ruler, the Writer, the Man* (New York: Knopf, 1947).

Goodwin, A., ed., *The New Cambridge Modern History*, vol. VIII: *The American and French Revolutions, 1763–1793* (Cambridge: Cambridge University Press, 1965).

Goody, Jack, *The Theft of History* (Cambridge: Cambridge University Press, 2006).

Gorbachev, Mikhail, *Memoirs* (New York: Doubleday, 1995).

Gordon, Andrew, *Labor and Imperial Democracy in Prewar Japan* (Berkeley: University of California Press, 1991).

Gordon, Michael R., "Domestic Conflict and the Origins of the First World War: The British and German Cases," *Journal of Modern History*, 46 (June 1974), pp. 191–226.

Gordon, Michael R. and Bernard E. Trainor, *Cobra II: The Inside Story of the Invasion and Occupation of Iraq* (New York: Pantheon, 2006).

Gotthelf, Allan, "Aristotle's Conception of Final Causality," in Allan Gotthelf and James G. Lennox, eds., *Philosophical Issues in Aristotle's Biology* (Cambridge: Cambridge University Press, 1987), pp. 204–42.

Gottlieb, Gidon, *Nation Against State: A New Approach to Ethnic Conflicts and the Decline of Sovereignty* (New York: Council on Foreign Relations Press, 1993).

Götz, Aly, *Final Solution: Nazi Propaganda Policy and the Murder of the European Jews* (London: Arnold, 1999).

Gould, Lewis L., *The Presidency of Theodore Roosevelt* (Lawrence: University of Kansas Press, 1991).

Gould, Stephen Jay, *Hen's Teeth and Horse's Tows* (New York: Norton, 1983).

Wonderful Life: The Burgess Shale and the Nature of History (New York: Norton, 1989).

Dinosaur in a Haystack: Reflections in Natural History (New York: Crown, 1996).

Full House: The Spread of Excellence from Plato to Darwin (New York: Harmony Books, 1996).

Gourevitch, Peter, "The Second Image Reversed: The International Sources of Domestic Politics," *International Organization* 32, no. 4 (Autumn 1978), pp. 881–911.

Gower, John, *Vox Clamantis*, in *The Cambridge History of English and American Literature*, 18 vols., vol. II: *The End of the Middle Ages* (Cambridge: Cambridge University Press, 1907–21), pp. 907–21.

Graebner, Norman A., "Hoover, Roosevelt, and the Chinese," in Borg and Okamoto, *Pearl Harbor as History*, pp. 25–52.

Graham, A. J., *Colony and Mother City in Ancient Greece* (Manchester: Manchester University Press, 1964).

Graham, Keith, *Practical Reasoning in a Social World: How We Act Together* (Cambridge: Cambridge University Press, 2002).

Gramsci, Antonio, *Selections from the Prison Notebooks of Antonio Gramsci*, ed. and trans. Quentin Hoare and G. Nowell Smith (London: Lawrence and Wishart, 1971).

   Quaderni del carcere, ed. V. Geratana, 4 vols. (Turin: Einaudi, 1975).

   Scritti di economia politica (Rome: Bollati Boringhieri, 1994).

Granatstein, J. L., *Canada's Army: Waging War and Keeping the Peace* (Toronto: University of Toronto Press, 2002).

Granovetter, Mark, "Threshold Models of Collective Behavior," *American Journal of Sociology*, 83 (1978), pp. 1420–43.

Grant, Ruth, *Hypocrisy and Integrity: Machiavelli, Rousseau and the Ethics of Politics* (Chicago: University of Chicago Press, 1997).

Gravdal, Kathryn, "Chretien de Troyes, Gratian, and the Medieval Romance of Sexual Violence," *Signs*, 17, no. 3 (Spring, 1992), pp. 558–85.

Gray, Colin, "RMAs and the Dimensions of Strategy," *Joint Forces Quarterly* (Autumn/Winter 1997–8), pp. 50–4.

Gray, Jeffrey, *The Psychology of Fear and Stress*, 2nd edn (Cambridge: Cambridge University Press, 1987).

Green, David P. and Ian Shapiro, *Pathologies of Rational Choice Theory: A Critique of Applications in Political Science* (New Haven, CT: Yale University Press, 1994).

Green, Peter, *Alexander to Actium: The Historical Evolution of the Hellenistic Age* (Berkeley: University of California Press, 1993).

   The Greco-Persian Wars, rev. edn (Berkeley: University of California Press, 1996).

Greenberg, J., J. Arndt, J. Schimel, T. Pyszczynski and S. Solomon, "Clarifying the Function of Mortality Salience-Induced Worldview Defense: Renewed Suppression or Reduced Accessibility of Death-Related Thoughts?," *Journal of Experimental Social Psychology*, 37 (2001), pp. 70–6.

Greenberg, J., S. L. Koole and T. Pyszczynski, eds., *Handbook of Experimental Existential Psychology* (New York: Guilford Press, 2004).

Greenberg, J., J. Porteus, L. Simon, T., Pyszczynski and S. Solomon, "Evidence of a Terror Management Function of Cultural Icons: The Effects of Mortality Salience on the Inappropriate Use of Cherished Cultural Symbols," *Personality and Social Psychology Bulletin*, 21 (1995), pp. 1221–8.

Greenberg, J., T. Pyszczynski and S. Solomon, "The Causes and Consequences of a Need for Self-Esteem: A Terror Management Theory," in F. Baumeister, ed., *Public Self and Private Self* (New York: Springer-Verlag, 1986), pp. 189–212.

Greenberg, J., Pyszczynski, S., Solomon, A. Rosenblatt, M. Veeder, S, Kirkland *et al.*, "Evidence for Terror Management II: The Effects of Mortality Salience on Reactions to Those who Threaten or Bolster the Cultural Worldview," *Journal of Personality and Social Psychology*, 58 (1990), pp. 308–18.

Greenberg, J., T. Pyszczynski, S. Solomon, L. Simon and M. Breus, "Role of Consciousness and Accessibility of Death-Related Thoughts in Mortality Salience Effects," *Journal of Personality and Social Psychology*, 67 (1994), pp. 627–37.

Greenberg, J., L. Simon, T. Pyszczynski, S. Solomon and D. Chatel, "Terror Management and Tolerance: Does Mortality Salience Always Intensify Negative Reactions to Others Who Threaten One's Worldview?," *Journal of Personality and Social Psychology* 63 (1992), pp. 212–20.

Greenberg, J., S. Solomon and T. Pyszczynski, "Terror Management Theory of Self-Esteem and Social Behaviour: Empirical Assessments and Conceptual Refinements," in M. P. Zanna, ed., *Advances in Experimental Social Psychology*, vol. XXIX (New York: Academic Press, 1997), pp. 61–139.

Greenberg, Kenneth S., *Honor and Slavery* (Princeton, NJ: Princeton University Press, 1996).

Greenblatt, Stephen L., "Learning to Curse: Aspects of Linguistic Colonialism in the Sixteenth Century," in Fred Chiappelli, ed., *First Images of America: The Impact of the New World on the Old* (Berkeley: University of California Press, 1976), vol. II, pp. 561–80.

"Invisible Bullets: Renaissance Authority and its Subversion, *Henry IV* and *Henry V*," in J. Dollimore and A. Sinfield, *Political Shakespeare: Essays in Cultural Materialism* (Manchester: Manchester University Press, 1996), pp. 18–48.

Greenfeld, Liah, *Nationalism: Five Roads to Modernity* (Cambridge, MA: Harvard University Press, 1992).

The Spirit of Capitalism: Nationalism and Economic Growth (Cambridge, MA: Harvard University Press, 2001).

Greenstein, Fred and Nelson W. Polsby, *Handbook of Political Science: Strategies of Inquiry*, vol. VII (Reading, MA: Addison-Wesley, 1975).

Greif, Avner, *Institutions and the Path to the Modern Economy: Lessons from Medieval Trade* (Cambridge: Cambridge University Press, 2006).

Grey, Edward, *Twenty-Five Years, 1892–1916* (New York: Stokes, 1925).

Griswold, Charles L., *Adam Smith and the Virtues of Enlightenment* (Cambridge: Cambridge University Press, 1999).

Groh, Dieter, "'Je eher, desto besser!' Innenpolitische Faktoren für die Präventivkreigsberietschaft des Deutschen Reiches 1913/14," *Politische Vierteljahrsschrift* 13 (1972), pp. 501–21.

Gross, Leo, "The Peace of Westphalia, 1648–1948," in Robert S. Wood, *The Process of Organization* (New York: Random House, 1971), pp. 35–56.

Grotius, Hugo, *De jure belli ac pacis libri tres*, trans. F. W. Kelsey (Oxford: Oxford University Press, 1925).

    Prolegomena to the Law of War and Peace (New York: Bobbs-Merrill, 1957).

Gruber, Lloyd, *Ruling the World: Power Politics and the Rise of Supranational Institutions* (Princeton, NJ: Princeton University Press, 2000).

Gruder, Vivian R., *The Royal Provincial Intendants: A Governing Elite in Eighteenth Century France* (Ithaca, NY: Cornell University Press, 1968).

Gruen, Erich S., *The Hellenistic World and the Coming of Rome* (Berkeley: University of California Press, 1984).

    Culture and National Identity in Republican Rome (Berkeley: University of California Press, 1992).

    "Rome and the Greek World," in Flower, *The Cambridge Companion to the Roman Republic*, pp. 242–70.

    "Augustus and the Making of the Principate," in Galinsky, *The Age of Augustus*, pp. 33–54.

Grundmann, Herbert, "Rotten and Brabanzonen: Söldnerheere im 12. Jahrdundert," *Deutsches Archiv für die Geschichte des Mittelalters*, 5 (1941–42), pp. 418–92.

Guehenno, Jean-Marie, *The End of the Nation-State*, trans. Victor Pesce Elliot (Minneapolis: University of Minnesota Press, 1995).

Gulick, Edward Vose, *Europe's Classical Balance of Power* (New York: Norton, 1955).

Gunn, J. A. W., *Politics and the Public Interest in the Seventeenth Century* (London: Routledge, 1969).

Gunnell, John G., *Philosophy, Science and Political Inquiry* (Morristown, NJ: General Learning Press, 1975).

    Between Philosophy and Politics (Amherst: University of Massachusetts Press, 1982).

    The Orders of Discourse: Philosophy, Social Science and Politic Lanham, MD: Rowman and Littlefield, 1988).

    "Handbooks and History: Is It Still the American Science of Politics?" *International Political Science Review* 23, no. 4 (2002), pp. 339–54.

Guoqi, Xu, *China and the Great War: China's Pursuit of a New National Identity and Internationalization* (Cambridge: Cambridge University Press, 2005).

Gurowitz, Amy, "Mobilizing International Norms: Domestic Actors, Immigrants and the Japanese State," *World Politics* 51 (1999), pp. 413–45.

Gurr, Ted Robert, *Minorities at Risk* (Washington, DC: US Institute of Peace, 1993).

Guttmann, Allen, *The Olympics: A History of the Modern Games* (Urbana: University of Illinois Press, 1992).

Guyer, Paul, "Nature, Morality, and the Possibility of Peace," in Guyer, *Kant on Freedom, Law, and Happiness* (Cambridge: Cambridge University Press, 2000), pp. 408–34.

Guzzini, Stefano, "Structural Power: The Limits of Neorealist Power Analysis," *International Organization* 47, no. 3 (1993), pp. 443–78.

    Realism in International Relations and International Political Economy: The Continuing Story of a Death Foretold (London: Routledge, 1998).

    "The Enduring Dilemmas of Realism in International Relations," *European Journal of International Relations* 10 (2004), pp. 533–68.

    "The Concept of Power: A Constructivist Analysis," *Millennium*, 33, no. 3 (2005), pp. 495–522.

Guzzini, Stefano and Anna Leander, *Constructivism and International Relations: Alexander Wendt and his Critics* (London: Routledge, 2006).

Haas, Michael, "A Plea for Bridge Building in International Relations," in Klaus Knorr and James N. Rosenau, *Contending Approaches to International Politics* (Princeton, NJ: Princeton University Press, 1969), pp. 158–76.

Habermas, Jürgen, *Knowledge and Human Interests*, trans. Jeremy Shapiro (Boston: Beacon Press, 1971).

    Theory and Practice, trans John Viertel (Boston: Beacon Press, 1973).

    Legitimation Crisis (Boston, MA: Beacon Press, 1975).

    The Theory of Communicative Action, trans. T. McCarthy, 2 vols. (Boston: Beacon Press, 1984–7).

    Moral Consciousness and Communicative Action, trans. Christian Lenhardt and Shierry Weber Nicholsen (Cambridge, MA: MIT Press, 1990).

    On the Logic of the Social Sciences (Cambridge, MA: MIT Press, 1994).

    "Kant's Idea of Perpetual Peace, with the Benefit of Two Hundred Years' Hindsight," in James Bohman and Matthias Lutz-Bachmann, *Perpetual Peace: Essays on Kant's Cosmopolitan Ideal* (Cambridge, MA: MIT Press, 1997), pp. 113–55.

Habib, Douglas F., "Chastity, Masculinity, and Military Efficiency: The United States Army in Germany, 1918–1923," *International History Review*, 28, no. 4 (December 2006), pp. 709–57.

Hacking, Ian, *The Social Construction of What?* (Cambridge, MA: Harvard University Press, 1999).

Haeussler, Helmut, *General William Groener and the German Army* (Madison: State Historical Society of Wisconsin, 1962).

Hafner, Katie and Matthew Lyons, *Where Wizards Stay Up Late: The Origins of the Internet* (New York: Simon and Schuster, 1996).

Hagan, J., "Domestic Political Systems and War Proneness," *Mershon International Studies Review* 38, no. 2 (1994), pp. 183–207.

Haimson, Leopold, ed., *The Mensheviks: From the Revolution of 1917 to the Second World War* (Chicago: University of Chicago Press, 1974).

Halbwachs, Maurice, *The Collective Memory*, trans. F. J. Ditter Jr. and V. Y. Ditter (New York: Harper and Row, 1980).

Haley, Usha C. V., Linda Low and Mun-Heng Toh, "Singapore Incorporated: Reinterpreting Singapore's Business Environments through a Corporate Metaphor," *Management Decision* 34, no. 9 (1996), pp. 17–28.

Hall, Cheryl, *The Trouble with Passion: Political Theory Beyond the Reign of Reason* (New York: Routledge, 2005).

Hall, Edith, *Inventing the Barbarian: Greek Self-Definition through Tragedy* (Oxford: Oxford University Press, 1989).

Hall, John A., *Powers and Liberties: The Causes and Consequences of the Rise of the West* (New York: Blackwell, 1985).

    States in History (Oxford: Basil Blackwell, 1986).

Hall, John Whitney, ed., *The Cambridge History of Japan*, vol. IV: *Early Modern Japan* (Cambridge: Cambridge University Press, 1991).

Hall, Rodney Bruce, *National Collective Identity: Social Constructs and International Systems* (New York: Columbia University Press, 1999).

Halliday, Fred, *Rethinking International Relations* (Vancouver: University of British Columbia Press, 1994).

    "The Future of International Relations: Fears and Hopes," in Steve Smith, Ken Booth and Marysia Zalewski, *International Theory: Positivism and Beyond* (Cambridge: Cambridge University Press, 1999), pp. 318–27.

Halloran, M. and E. Kashima, "Social Identity and Worldview Validation: The Effects of Ingroup Identity Primes and Mortality Salience on Value Endorsement," *Personality and Social Psychology Bulletin* 30 (2004), pp. 915–25.

Halper, Stefan and Jonathan Clarke, *America Alone: The Neo-Conservatives and the Global Order* (New York: Cambridge University Press, 2004).

Hamerow, Theodore S., *Restoration, Revolution, Reaction. Economics and Politics in Germany, 1815–1871* (Princeton, NJ: Princeton University Press, 1966).

Hamilton, Alexander, James Madison and John Jay, *The Federalist Papers*, ed. Roy P. Fairfield (Baltimore, MD: Johns Hopkins University Press, 1981).

Hamilton, D. and S. Sherman, "Perceiving Persons and Groups," *Psychological Review*, 103 (1996), pp. 336–55.

Hamilton, Richard F., *Who Voted for Hitler* (Princeton, NJ: Princeton University Press, 1982).

    The Social Misconstruction of Reality: Validity and Verification in the Scholarly Community (New Haven, CT: Yale University Press, 1996).

    Marxism, Revisionism, and Leninism: Explication, Assessment and Commentary (Westport, CT: Praeger, 2000).

    "The European Wars, 1815–1914," in Hamilton and Herwig, *The Origins of World War I*, pp. 45–91.

"On the Origins of the Catastrophe," in Hamilton and Herwig, *The Origins of World War I*, pp. 469–506.

Hamilton, Richard F. and Holger H. Herwig, *The Origins of World War I* (Cambridge: Cambridge University Press, 2003).

Hammer, Dean, *The Iliad as Politics: The Performance of Political Thought* (Norman: University of Oklahoma Press, 2002).

Hammer, Paul E. J., "Patronage at Court, Faction and the Earl of Essex," in John Guy, ed., *The Reign of Elizabeth I: Court and Culture in the Last Decade* (Cambridge: Cambridge University Press, 1995), pp. 65–86.

Hanawalt, Barbara, *"Of God and Ill Repute" – Gender and Social Control in Medieval England* (New York: Oxford University Press, 1998).

Handbuch über den koeniglich-preussischen Hof und Staat für das Jahr 1907 (Berlin: Prussia Staatsministerium, 1907).

Hankinson, R. J., "Philosophy of Science," in Jonathan Barnes, ed., *The Cambridge Companion to Aristotle* (Cambridge: Cambridge University Press, 1995), pp. 109–39.

Hansen, Lene and Ole Waever, eds., *European Integration and National Identity: The Challenge of the Nordic States* (London: Routledge, 2002).

Hanson, Russell L., *Political Innovation and Conceptual Change* (Cambridge: Cambridge University Press, 1989).

Hanson, Victor, *The Western Way of War: Infantry Battle in Classical Greece* (New York: Random House, 1989).

Hoplites: The Classical Greek Battle Experience (London: Routledge, 1991).

"Hoplites into Democrats: The Changing Ideology of Athenian Infantry," in Josiah Ober and Charles Hedrick, *Dēmokratia: A Conversation on Democracies, Ancient and Modern* (Princeton, NJ: Princeton University Press, 1996), pp. 289–312.

Hardt, Michael and Antonio Negri, *Empire* (Cambridge, MA: Harvard University Press, 1999).

Harkabi, Yehoshafat, *The Bar Kokhba Syndrome: Risk and Realism in International Politics*, trans. Max D. Ticktin (Chappaqua, NY: Rossel Books, 1983).

Harmat, Ulrike, "Divorce and Remarriage in Austria Hungary: The Second Marriage of Franz Conrad von Hötzendorf," *Austrian History Yearbook*, 32 (2002), pp. 69–103.

Harmon-Jones, E., J. Greenberg, S. Solomon and L. Simon, "The Effects of Mortality Salience on Intergroup Bias Between Minimal Groups," *European Journal of Social Psychology*, 25 (1996), pp. 781–85.

Harmon-Jones, E., L. Simon, J. Greenberg, T. Pyszczynski, S. Solomon and H. McGregor, "Terror Management Theory and Self-Esteem: Evidence that Increased Self-Esteem Reduces Mortality Salience Effects," *Journal of Personality and Social Psychology*, 72 (1997), pp. 24–36.

Harootunian, H. D., *Toward Restoration: The Growth of Political Consciousness in Tokugawa Japan* (Berkeley: University of California Press, 1970).

 Things Seen and Unseen: Discourse and Ideology in Tokugawa Japan (Chicago: University of Chicago Press, 1988).

Harouel, Jean-Louis, Jean Barbey, Eric Bournazel and Jacqueline Thibaut-Payen, *Histoire des institutions de l'époque franque à la Révolution*, 3rd edn (Paris: Presses Universitaires de France, 1990).

Harré, Rom, *The Principles of Scientific Thinking* (London: Macmillan, 1970).

 "Trust and its Surrogates: Psychological Foundations of Political Process," in Mark E. Warren, *Democracy and Trust* (Cambridge: Cambridge University Press, 1999), pp. 249–72.

Harré, Rom and Peter Secord, *The Explanation of Social Behavior* (Oxford: Basil Blackwell, 1973).

Harris, Bob, *Politics and the Nation: Britain in the Mid-Eighteenth Century* (Oxford: Oxford University Press, 2002).

Harris, J. Paul, "Great Britain," in Hamilton and Herwig, *The Origins of World War I*, pp. 266–99.

Harris, Marvin, "Foodways: Historical Overview and Theoretical Prolegomenon," in Marvin Harris and Eric B. Ross, *Food and Evolution: Toward a Theory of Human Food Habits* (Philadelphia, PA: Temple University Press, 1986), pp. 57–92.

Harris, Marvin and Eric B. Ross, *Death, Sex, and Fertility: Population Regulation in Preindustrial and Developing Societies* (New York: Columbia University Press, 1967).

Harris, Nigel, *The End of the Third World* (Harmondsworth: Penguin, 1986).

Harris, Robert and Jeremy Paxman, *A Higher Form of Killing* (New York: Hill and Wang, 1982).

Harris, William V., *War and Imperialism in Ancient Rome, 327–70 B.C.* (Oxford: Oxford University Press, 1979).

Harrison, Ewan, "Waltz, Kant and Systemic Approaches to IR," *Review of International Studies* 28, no. 1 (2002), pp. 143–62.

Harrison, Thomas, ed., *Greeks and Barbarians* (Edinburgh: Edinburgh University Press, 2002).

Hart, H. L. A., *The Concept of Law* (Oxford and New York: Oxford University Press, 1994 [1961]).

Harvey, David, *The Condition of Postmodernity* (Oxford: Blackwell, 1990).

 The New Imperialism (Oxford: Oxford University Press, 2003).

Harwit, Martin, *An Exhibit Denied: Lobbying the History of Enola Gay* (New York: Springer-Verlag, 1996).

Hasan, Fekri, "Imperialist Appropriations of Egyptian Obelisks," in David Jeffreys, ed., *Views of Ancient Egypt since Napoleon Bonaparte: Imperialism, Colonialism, and Modern Appropriations* (London: UCL Press, 2003), pp. 19–68.

Hasek, Jaroslav, *The Good Soldier Schweik*, trans. Paul Selver (New York: Unger, 1962).

Haslam, Jonathan, *No Virtue like Necessity: Realist Thought in International Relations since Machiavelli* (New Haven, CT: Yale University Press, 2002).

Hassig, Ross, *War and Society in Ancient Mesoamerica* (Berkeley: University of California Press, 1992).

    Aztec Warfare: Imperial Expansion and Political Control (Norman: University of Oklahoma Press, 1998).

Hassrick, Royal B., *The Sioux* (Norman: University of Oklahoma Press, 1964).

Hastings, Max, *Bomber Command* (New York: Dial Press, 1979).

Hatton, R. M., *Charles XII* (London: Weidenfeld and Nicolson, 1968).

Havens, Thomas R. H., *Farm and Nation in Modern Japan: Agrarian Nationalism, 1870–1940* (Princeton, NJ: Princeton University Press, 1974).

Hayek, Friedrich A., *The Road to Serfdom* (Chicago: University of Chicago Press, 1944).

    The Constitution of Liberty (Chicago, IL.: University of Chicago Press, 1960).

    Law, Legislation and Liberty, 3 vols. (Chicago: University of Chicago Press, 1973–9).

Hayes, Peter, "Hobbes' Bourgeois Moderation," *Polity* 31, no. 1 (Autumn, 1998), pp. 53–74.

Haykal, Muhammad, *The Sphinx and the Commissar: The Rise and Fall of Soviet Influence in the Middle East* (New York: Harper and Row, 1978).

Hayles, N. Katherine, "Chaos and Order," in *Complex Dynamics in Literature and Science* (Chicago: University of Chicago Press, 1991), pp. 91–114.

Haym, Ronald, *Britain's Imperial Century, 1815–1914* (London: Palgrave Macmillan, 2002).

Headrick, Annabeth, "Butterfly War at Teotihuacan," in Brown and Stanton, *Ancient Indian Warfare*, p. 162.

Heater, Derek, *National Self-Determination: Woodrow Wilson and his Legacy* (New York: St. Martin's Press, 1994).

Heath, Joseph, *Communicative Action and Rational Choice* (Cambridge, MA: MIT Press, 2000).

Heath, Malcolm, *The Poetics of Greek Tragedy* (Stanford, CA: Stanford University Press, 1987).

Hedrick, Charles W., "The Zero Degree of Society: Aristotle and the Athenian Citizen," in J. Peter Euben, John R. Wallach and Josiah Ober, *Athenian Political Thought and the Reconstruction of American Democracy* (Ithaca, NY: Cornell University Press, 1994). pp. 289–318.

Hegel, W. F. G., *Hegel's Philosophy of Right*, trans. T. M. Knox (Oxford: Oxford University Press, 1969).

    Lectures on the Philosophy of World History, trans. H. B. Nisbet (Cambridge: Cambridge University Press, 1975).

Phenomenology of Spirit, trans. A. V. Miller (Oxford: Clarendon Press, 1977).

Elements of the Philosophy of Right, ed. Allen H. Wood, trans. H. B. Nisbet (Cambridge: Cambridge University Press, 1991).

"The German Constitution," in Laurence Dickey and H. B. Nisbet, eds., *Political Writings*, trans. H. B. Nisbet (Cambridge: Cambridge University Press, 1999), pp. 6–101.

Heichelheim, Fritz M. and Cedric A. Yeo, *A History of the Roman People* (Englewood Cliffs, NJ: Prentice-Hall, 1962).

Heider, Fritz, *The Psychology of Interpersonal Relations* (New York: Wiley, 1958).

Heilbroner, Robert, *21st Century Capitalism* (New York: Norton, 1993).

Heine, S., M. Harihara and Y. Niiya, "Terror Management in Japan," *Asian Journal of Social Psychology*, 5 (2002), pp. 187–96.

Heinemann, Ulrich, *Die verdränge Niederlage: Politische Öffentlichkeit und Kriegsschuldfrage in der Weimarer Republik* (Göttingen: Vandenhoeck und Ruprecht, 1983).

Heinrich, Joseph, R. Boyd, S. Bowles *et al.*, "In Search of Homo Economicus: Behavioral Experiments in 15 Small-Scale Societies," *American Economic Review* 91 (May 2001), pp. 73–8.

Heinrichs, Waldo H., *Threshold of War: Franklin D. Roosevelt and American Entry into World War II* (New York: Oxford University Press, 1988).

Held, David, *Models of Democracy* (Stanford, CA: Stanford University Press, 1987).

Political Theory and the Modern State: Essays on State, Power, and Democracy (Stanford, CA: Stanford University Press, 1989).

Political Theory Today (Stanford, CA: Stanford University Press, 1991).

Democracy and the Global Order: From the Modern State to Cosmopolitan Governance (Cambridge: Polity, 1995).

"Cosmopolitan Democracy and the Global Order: A New Agenda" in J. Bohman and M. Lutz-Bachmann, eds., *Perpetual Peace: Essays on Kant's Cosmopolitan Ideal* (Cambridge, MA: MIT Press, 1997).

Held, David, Anthony McGrew, David Goldblatt, and Jonathan Perraton, *Global Transformations: Politics, Economics and Culture* (Cambridge: Polity, 1999).

Global Covenant: The Social Democratic Alternative to the Washington Consensus (Cambridge: Polity, 2004).

Helleiner, Eric, *States and the Reemergence of Global Finance: From Bretton Woods to the 1990s* (Ithaca, NY: Cornell University Press, 1994).

"Historicizing Territorial Currencies: Monetary Space and the Nation-State in North America," *Political Geography* 18 (1999), pp. 309–39.

Heller, Mark, "The Use and Abuse of Hobbes: The State of Nature in International Relations," *Polity* 13, no. 1 (1982), pp. 21–32.

Helman, Gerald B. and Steven R. Ratner, "Saving Failed States," *Foreign Policy*, No. 89 (Winter 1992–3), pp. 3–20.

Henderson, Gregory, *Korea: The Politics of the Vortex* (Cambridge, MA: Harvard University Press, 1968).

Henderson, Gregory and Richard Ned Lebow, "Conclusions," in Henderson, Lebow, and John G. Stoessinger, eds., *Divided Nations in a Divided World* (New York: David McKay Company, 1974), pp. 433–54.

Henry, Clement M. and Robert Springborg, *Globalization and the Politics of Development in the Middle East* (New York: Cambridge University Press, 2001).

Henshall, Nicholas, *The Myth of Absolutism: Change and Continuity in Early Modern European Monarchy* (New York: Longman, 1991).

Herbst, Jeffrey, "Responding to State Failure in Africa," *International Security*, 21, no. 3 (Winter 1996–7), pp. 120–44.

Herf, Jeffrey, *Reactionary Modernism: Technology, Culture, and Politics in Weimar and the Third Reich* (Cambridge: Cambridge University Press, 1984).

Divided Memory: The Nazi Past and the Two Germanies (Cambridge, MA: Harvard University Press, 1997).

Herman, Robert., "Identity, Norms, and International Security: The Soviet Foreign Policy Revolution and the End of the Cold War," in Peter J. Katzenstein, *The Culture of National Security: Norms and Identity in World Politics* (New York: Columbia University Press, 1996), pp. 271–316.

Herod, Andrew, Gearóid Ó Tuathail and Susan M. Roberts, eds., *An Unruly World? Globalization, Governance, and Geography* (London: Routledge, 1998).

Herodotus, *The Histories*, trans. Robin Waterfield (New York: Oxford University Press, 1998).

Herr, Michael, *Dispatches* (New York: Avon Books, 1978).

Herrera, Geoffrey, "Technology and International Systems," *Millennium* 32, no. 3 (2003), pp. 559–94.

Herrin, Judith, *The Formation of Christendom* (Oxford: Blackwell, 1987).

Herring, Eric, *Danger and Opportunity: Explaining International Crisis Outcomes* (Manchester: Manchester University Press, 1995).

Herrmann, David G., *The Arming of Europe and the Making of the First World War* (Princeton, NJ: Princeton University Press, 1996).

Herrmann, Richard K., *Perceptions and Behavior in Soviet Foreign Policy* (Pittsburgh, PA: University of Pittsburgh Press, 1985).

"Learning from the End of the Cold War," in Herrmann and Lebow, *Ending the Cold War*, pp. 219–38.

Herrmann, Richard K. and Marilynn Brewer, "Identities and Institutions: Becoming European in the EU," in Richard Herrmann, Thomas Risse and Marilynn Brewer, eds., *Transnational Identities: Becoming European in the EU* (Lanham, MD: Rowman and Littlefield, 2004), pp. 1–22.

Herrmann, Richard K. and Richard Ned Lebow, eds., *Ending the Cold War: Interpretations, Causation, and the Study of International Relations* (New York: Palgrave Macmillan, 2004).

"What Was the Cold War? When and Why Did it End?" in Herrmann and Lebow, *Ending the Cold War*, pp. 1–30.

Hersh, Seymour M., "Who Lied to Whom?," *New Yorker*, March 2003.
    Chain of Command: The Road from 9/11 to Abu Ghraib (New York: Harper, 2004).

Herwig, Holger H., *Das Elitekorps des Kaisers. Die Marineoffiziere in Wilhelminischen Deutschland* (Hamburg: Christians, 1977).
    Germany's Vision of Empire in Venezuela, 1871–1914 (Princeton, NJ: Princeton University Press, 1986).
    "Clio Deceived: Patriotic Self-Censorship in Germany After the Great War," *International Security* 12 (Fall 1987), pp. 5–44.
    "Luxury" Fleet: The Imperial German Navy, 1888–1918 (London: Ashfield Press, 1987).
    "Introduction," in Holger Herwig, *The Outbreak of World War I: Causes and Responsibilities* , 5th edn (Toronto: D. C. Heath, 1991), pp. 1–22.
    The First World War: Germany and Austria-Hungary, 1914–1918 (London: Arnold, 1998).
    "Germany," in Hamilton and Herwig, *The Origins of World War I*, pp. 150–87.
    "Why Did it Happen?" in Hamilton and Herwig, *The Origins of World War I*, pp. 443–68.
    "Hitler Wins in the East but Hitler Still Loses World War II," in Tetlock, Lebow and Parker, *Unmaking the West*, pp. 323–62.

Herz, John H., "Idealist Internationalism and the Security Dilemma," *World Politics* 12, no. 2 (1950), pp. 157–80.
    Political Realism and Political Idealism (Chicago: University of Chicago Press, 1951).
    "The Rise and Demise of the Territorial State," *World Politics* 9, no. 4 (1957), pp. 473–93.
    International Politics in the Atomic Age (New York: Columbia University Press, 1959).
    "The Territorial State Revisited – Reflections on the Future of the Nation-State," *Polity* 1, no. 1 (1968), pp. 11–34.
    The Nation-State and the Crisis of World Politics: Essays on International Politics in the Twentieth Century (New York: David McKay, 1976).
    "The Security Dilemma in International Relations: Background and Present Problems," *International Relations* 17 (2003), pp. 411–16.

Herzstein, Robert E., *The War that Hitler Won: Goebbels and the Nazi Media Campaign* (New York: Paragon House, 1987).

Hesiod, "Works and Days," in *Hesiod*, trans. Richard Lattimore (Ann Arbor: University of Michigan Press, 1978), pp. 15–118.

Hesk, Jens, *Deception and Democracy in Classical Athens* (Cambridge: Cambridge University Press, 2001).

Hewitt, H. J., *The Organization of War Under Edward III, 1338–62* (Manchester: Manchester University Press, 1966).

Hewson, Martin, "Did Global Governance Create Informational Governance?" in Hewson and Sinclair, *Approaches to Global Governance Theory*, pp. 97–115.

Hewson, Martin and Timothy J. Sinclair, eds. *Approaches to Global Governance Theory* (Albany: State University of New York Press, 1999).

Hibbard, Caroline, "The Theatre of Dynasty," in R. Malcolm Smuts, ed., *The Stuart Court and Europe. Essays in Politics and Political Culture* (Cambridge: Cambridge University Press, 1996), pp. 155–76.

Hilferding, Rudolf, *Das Finanzkapital, eine Stude über die jüngste Entwicklung des Kapitalismus* (Vienna: Verlag der Wiener Volksbuchlandlung, 1927 [1910]).

Hilgruber, Andreas, "Riezlers Theorie des kalkulieren Risikos und Bethmann Hollwegs politische Konzeption in der Julikrise 1914," *Historische Zeitschrift* 202 (April 1966), pp. 333–51.

Deutsche Grossmacht- und Weltpolitik im 19. und 20. Jahrhundert (Düsseldorf: Droste, 1977).

"Die 'Endlösung' und das deutsche Ostimperium als Kernstück des rassenideologischen Programms des Nationalsozialismus," in Hillgruber, *Deutsche Grossmacht- und Weltpolitik im 19. und 20. Jahrhundert* (Düsseldorf: Droste, 1977), pp. 252–75.

Hinsley, F. H., *Power and the Pursuit of Peace* (Cambridge: Cambridge University Press, 1963).

ed., *British Foreign Policy under Sir Edward Grey* (Cambridge: Cambridge University Press, 1977).

Sovereignty, 2nd edn (Cambridge: Cambridge University Press, 1986).

Hinton, Harold C., "China as an Asian Power," in Robinson and Shumbaugh, *Chinese Foreign Policy*, pp. 348–72.

Hintze, Otto, "Imperialismus und Weltpolitik," *Staat und Verfassung: Gesammelte Aufsätze zur allgemeinen Verfassungsgeschichte*, ed. Fritz Hartung (Göttingen: Vandenhock und Ruprecht, 1962), pp. 457–69.

The Historical Essays of Otto Hintze, ed. Felix Gilbert (New York: Oxford University Press, 1975).

Hironaka, Ann, *Neverending Wars: The International Community, Weak States, and the Perpetuation of Civil War* (Cambridge, MA: Harvard University Press, 2005).

Hirsch, Fred, *Social Limits of Growth* (London: Routledge and Kegan Paul, 1977).

Hirschman, Albert O., "The Search for Paradigms as a Hindrance to Understanding," *World Politics* 22, no. 3 (April 1970), pp. 329–43.

The Passions and the Interests: Political Arguments for Capitalism before its Triumph (Princeton, NJ: Princeton University Press, 1977).

"Rival Interpretations of Market Society: Civilizing, Destructive or Feeble?," *Journal of Economic Literature* 29 (December 1982), pp. 1463–84.

"The Concept of Interest: From Euphemism to Tautology," in Albert O. Hirschman, *Rival Views of Market Society and Other Recent Essays* (New York: Viking Penguin, 1986), pp. 48–82.

The Rhetoric of Reaction: Perversity, Futility, and Jeopardy (Cambridge, MA: Harvard University Press, 1991).

Hitchens, Christopher, *Thomas Jefferson: Author of America* (New York: Harper-Collins, 2005).

Hitti, Philip K., *The Arabs: A Short History* (Chicago: Henry Regnery Company, 1956).

Hixon, Walter L., *Historical Memory and Representations of the Vietnam War* (New York: Garland, 2000).

Hobbes, Thomas, *A Dialogue Between a Philosopher and a Student of the Common Laws of England*, ed. Joseph Cropsey (Chicago: University of Chicago Press, 1971).

Behemoth or The Long Parliament, ed. Ferdinand Tönnies (Chicago: University of Chicago Press, 1990).

De Cive, in Bernard Gert, ed., *Man and Citizen* (Indianapolis: Hackett, 1991 [1651]).

Leviathan, ed. Richard Tuck (Cambridge: Cambridge University Press, 1996).

Hobbs, Heidi, ed., *Pondering Postinternationalism* (Albany, NY: SUNY Press, 2000).

Hobsbawm, Eric J., *The Age of Revolution, 1789–1848* (London: Weidenfeld and Nicolson, 1962).

"Rules of Violence," in Hobsbawm, *Revolutionary: Contemporary Essays* (New York: Pantheon, 1973), pp. 209–15.

Nations and Nationalism since 1780 (New York: Cambridge University Press, 1990).

Hobson, John A. *Imperialism: A Study* (London: Allen and Unwin, 1938).

Hobson, John M. and J. C. Sharman, "The Enduring Place of Hierarchy in World Politics: Tracing the Social Logics of Hierarchy and Political Change," *European Journal of International Relations* 11, no. 1 (March 2005), pp. 9–62.

Hochman, Jiri, *The Soviet Union and the Failure of Collective Security, 1934–1938* (Ithaca, NY: Cornell University Press, 1984).

Hodges, Richard, *Dark Age Economics* (London: Duckworth, 1982).

Hodges, Richard and David Whitehouse, *Mohammed, Charlemagne and the Origins of Europe: Archeology and the Pirenne Thesis* (Ithaca, NY: Cornell University Press, 1983).

Hodgson, David, "Constraint, Empowerment, and Guidance: A Conjectural Classification of Laws of Nature," *Philosophy* 76, no. 3 (2001), pp. 341–70.

Hodgson, Geoffrey, "Reconstitutive Downward Causation," in Edward Fullbrook, ed., *Intersubjectivity in Economics* (London: Routledge, 2002), pp. 159–80.

Hoffmann, Stanley, "International Relations: The Long Road to Theory," *World Politics* 11, no. 3 (1959), pp. 346–77.

The State of War: Essays on the Theory and Practice of International Relations (New York: Praeger, 1965).

"Delusions of World Order," *New York Review of Books*, April 9, 1992, p. 37.

"The Crisis of Liberal Internationalism." *Foreign Policy* 98 (Spring 1995), pp. 159–77.

"The Clash of Globalizations," *Foreign Affairs* 81, no. 4 (July/August 2002), pp. 104–15.

Holbach, Paul Henri Theirry, baron de, *Système de la nature, ou les lois du monde physique et du monde moral*, 2 vols. (Geneva: Slatkine Reprints, 1973).

Holborn, Hajo, "Origins and Political Character of Nazi Ideology," *Political Science Quarterly*, 79 (1964), pp. 542–54.

Holland, D. and N. Quinn, eds., *Cultural Models in Language and Thought* (Cambridge: Cambridge University Press, 1987).

Hollis, Martin, *The Philosophy of Social Science* (Cambridge: Cambridge University Press, 1994).

Hollis, Martin and Steve Smith, *Explaining and Understanding International Relations* (Oxford: Clarendon Press, 1990).

Holloway, David, *Stalin and the Bomb: The Soviet Union and Atomic Energy, 1939–1956* (New Haven, CT: Yale University Press, 1994).

Holloway, Steven Kendall, *Canadian Foreign Policy: Defining the National Interest* (Toronto: Broadview Press, 2000).

Holmes, Richard, *Acts of War: The Behaviour of Men in Battle* (London: Weidenfeld and Nicolson, 1985).

Holquist, Michael and Katerina Clark, *Mikhail Bakhtin* (Cambridge, MA: Harvard University Press, 1984).

Holsti, Kalevi J., "Retreat from Utopia: International Relations Theory, 1945–1970," *Canadian Journal of Political Science* 4 (1971), pp. 165–77.

The Dividing Discipline: Hegemony and Diversity in International Theory (Boston: Allen and Unwin, 1985).

Peace and War: Armed Conflicts and International Order, 1648–1989 (Cambridge: Cambridge University Press, 1991).

The State, War, and the State of War (Cambridge: Cambridge University Press, 1996).

"The Problem of Change in International Relations," in Ferguson and Jones, *Political Space*, pp. 23–43.

Holsti, Ole, "Crisis Decision Making," in Philip A. Tetlock, L. Husbands, Robert Jervis *et al.*, eds., *Behavior, Society, and Nuclear War* (New York: Oxford University Press, 1989), vol. I, pp. 8–84.

Homans, George, *Social Behavior: Its Elementary Forms* (New York: Harcourt, 1961).

Homer, *The Iliad of Homer*, trans. Richard Lattimore (Chicago: University of Chicago Press, 1951).

The Iliad, trans. David Fagles (New York: Viking, 1990).

Homer-Dixon, Thomas, *Environment, Scarcity, and Violence* (Princeton, NJ: Princeton University Press, 1999).

Hondros, John L, *Occupation and Resistance: The Greek Agony, 1941–44* (New York: Pella, 1983).

Honig, Bonnie, "Declarations of Independence: Arendt and Derrida on the Problem of Founding a Republic," *American Political Science Review* 85 (March 1991), pp. 97–113.

  Political Theory and the Displacement of Politics (Ithaca, NY: Cornell University Press, 1993).

  Democracy and the Foreigner (Princeton, NJ: Princeton University Press, 2001).

Honneth, Axel, *The Struggle for Recognition* (Cambridge, MA: MIT Press, 1996).

Honneth, Axel and Nancy Fraser, *Recognition or Redistribution? A Political-Philosophical Exchange* (New York: Verso Press, 2003).

Honneth, Axel, Thomas McCarthy, Claus Offe *et al.*, eds., *Cultural-Political Interventions in the Unfinished Project of the Enlightenment*, trans. Barbara Fultner (Cambridge, MA: MIT Press, 1992).

Hont, Istvan, *Jealousy of Trade: International Competition and the Nation-State in Historical Perspective* (Cambridge, MA: Harvard University Press, 2005).

Hont, Istvan and Michael Ignatieff, eds., *Wealth and Virtue: The Shaping of Political Economy in the Scottish Enlightenment* (Cambridge: Cambridge University Press, 1983).

Hooker, T. J., "χαρις and αρειη in Thucydides," *Hermes* 102, no. 1 (1974), pp. 164–9.

Hoover, Kenneth B., *Economics as Ideology: Keynes, Laski, Hayek, and the Creation of Contemporary Politics* (Lanham, MD: Rowman and Littlefield, 2003).

Hopf, Ted, *Peripheral Visions: Deterrence Theory and American Foreign Policy in the Third World, 1965–1990* (Ann Arbor: University of Michigan Press, 1994).

  "Constructivism All the Way Down," *International Politics* 37 (2000), pp. 369–78.

  Social Construction of International Politics: Identities and Foreign Policies, Moscow, 1955 and 1999 (Ithaca, NY: Cornell University Press, 2002).

Hopkins, Raymond F., "The International Role of 'Domestic' Bureaucracy," *International Organization* 30, no. 3 (Summer 1976), pp. 405–32.

Horace, *Epistles, Book II; and, Epistle to the Pisones (Ars poetica)*, ed. Niall Rudd (Cambridge: Cambridge University Press, 1989).

Horn, Daniel, *The German Naval Mutinies of World War I* (New Brunswick, NJ: Rutgers University Press, 1969).

Horowitz, Donald L., *Ethnic Groups in Conflict* (Berkeley: University of California Press, 1985).

  The Deadly Ethnic Riot (Berkeley: University of California Press, 1995).

Hosoya, Chihiro, "Twenty-Five Years after Pearl Harbor: A New Look at Japan's Decision for War," in Grant K. Goodman, ed., *Imperial Japan and Asia* (New York: Columbia University Press, 1967), pp. 52–64.

"Retrogression in Japan's Foreign Policy Decision-Making Process," in Morley, *Dilemmas of Growth in Prewar Japan*, pp. 81–105.

"The Tripartite Pact, 1939–1940," in Morley, *Deterrent Diplomacy*, 191–258.

Housley, Norman, "*Pro deo et patria mori*: Sanctified Patriotism in Europe, 1400–1600," in Contamine, *War and Competition between States*, pp. 221–8.

Howarth, David, *1066: The Year of the Conquest* (New York: Viking Press, 1978).

Howe, Christopher, *The Origins of Modern Japanese Trade Supremacy: Development and Technology in Asia from 1540 to the Pacific War* (London: Hurst, 1966).

Howes, Dustin, "When States Choose to Die," *International Studies Quarterly* 47, no. 4 (2003), pp. 669–92.

Huddie, Leonie, "From Social to Political Identity: A Critical Examination of Social Identity Theory," *Political Psychology*, 22, no. 1 (2001), pp. 127–56.

Huggins, Mark, *The Victorians and Sport* (London: Hambledon, 2004).

Hughes, Christopher W., "Japan's Re-emergence as a 'Normal' Military Power," Adelphi Paper 368–9 (London: International Institute of Strategic Studies, 2004).

Hughes, Lindsey, *Peter the Great* (New Haven, CT: Yale University Press, 2002).

Huguet, Edmond, *Dictionnaire de la langue française* (Paris: Didier, 1980).

Huizinga, Johan, *The Waning of the Middle Ages, a Study of the Forms of Life, Thought and Art in France and the Netherlands in the XIVth and XVth Centuries* (London: E. Arnold, 1927).

Homo Ludens: A Study of the Play-Element in Culture (New York: Roy Publishers, 1950).

Hull, Isabel V., *The Entourage of Kaiser Wilhelm II, 1888–1918* (New York: Cambridge University Press, 1982).

"Military Culture: Wilhelm II, and the End of the Monarchy in the First World War," in Mombauer and Deist, *The Kaiser*, pp. 235–58.

Absolute Destruction: Military Culture and the Practices of War in Imperial Germany (Ithaca, NY: Cornell University Press, 2005).

Hulswit, Menno, "Teleology: A Peircean Critique of Ernst Mayr's Theory," *Transactions of the Charles S. Peirce Society* 32, no. 2 (1996), pp. 182–214.

Hume, David, *The Philosophical Works*, vol. II, ed. T. H. Green and T. H. Gorse (Aalen: Scientia, 1964 [1874–5]).

"Of Civil Liberty," in *Essays: Moral, Political and Literary*, ed. Eugene F. Miller (Indianapolis, IN: Liberty Classics, 1985), pp. 87–96.

Political Essays, ed. Knud Haakonssen (Cambridge: Cambridge University Press, 1994).

An Inquiry Concerning the Principles of Morals, ed. T. L. Beauchamp (New York: Oxford University Press, 1998).

A Treatise of Human Nature, ed. David Fate Norton and Mary Norton (Oxford: Oxford University Press, 2000).

Humphreys, Paul, *The Chances of Explanation: Causal Explanation in the Social, Medical, and Physical Sciences* (Princeton, NJ: Princeton University Press, 1989).

Hundert, E. G., *The Enlightenment's Fable: Bernard Mandeville and the Discovery of Society* (Cambridge: Cambridge University Press, 1994).

Hunter, Horst, *Politics as Friendship: The Origins of Classical Notions of Politics in the Theory and Practice of Friendship* (Waterloo, Ont.: Wilfrid Laurier University Press, 1978).

Hunter, Richard, "Homer and Greek Literature," in Fowler, *The Cambridge Companion to Homer*, pp. 235–53.

Huntington, Samuel P., *The Soldier and the State: The Theory and Politics of Civil–Military Relations* (New York: Vintage Books, 1957).

   Political Order in Changing Societies (New Haven, CT: Yale University Press, 1968).

   American Politics: The Promise of Disharmony (Cambridge, MA: Harvard University Press, 1981).

   "The Clash of Civilizations?" *Foreign Affairs*, 72, no. 3 (Summer 1993), pp. 22–49.

   "If Not Civilizations, What? – Paradigms of the Post-Cold War World," *Foreign Affairs*, 72, no. 5 (November/December 1993), pp. 186–94.

   The Clash of Civilizations and the Remaking of World Order (New York: Simon and Schuster, 1996).

   "The West Unique, Not Universal," *Foreign Affairs*, 75, no. 6 (November/December 1996), pp. 28–46.

   "The Erosion of American National Interests," *Foreign Affairs*, 76, no. 5 (September/October 1997), pp. 28–49.

   "The Lonely Superpower," *Foreign Affairs* 78 (1999), pp. 35–49.

Huntley, Wade, "Kant's Third Image: Systemic Sources of the Liberal Peace," *International Studies Quarterly* 40, no. 1 (1996), pp. 45–76.

Hurd, Ian, "Legitimacy and Authority in International Politics," *International Organization* 53 (Spring 1999), pp. 379–408.

   "Breaking and Making Norms: American Revisionism and Crises of Legitimacy," *International Politics*, 44, no. 2 (March 2007), pp. 194–213.

Hurlock, Elizabeth, "Sumptuary Law," in M. Roach and J. Eicher, eds., *Dress, Adornment and the Social Order* (New York: Wiley, 1965), pp. 295–301.

Hurrell, Andrew, "Kant and the Kantian Paradigm in International Relations," *Review of International Studies* 16, no. 3 (1990), pp. 183–205.

Hussey, Edward, "Heraclitus," in Long, *The Cambridge Companion to Early Greek Philosophy*, pp. 88–112.

Hutchinson, D. S., "Ethics," in Jonathan Barnes, ed., *The Cambridge Companion to Aristotle* (Cambridge: Cambridge University Press, 1995), pp. 195–232.

Hutchinson, John and Anthony D. Smith, eds., *Nationalism* (New York: Oxford, 1994).

Huth, Paul and Bruce Russett, "Deterrence Failure and Crisis Escalation," *International Studies Quarterly* 32 (1988), pp. 29–46.

"What Makes Deterrence Work? Cases from 1900 to 1980," *World Politics* 41 (1989), pp. 143–69.

Hutto, Daniel, "A Cause for Concern: Reasons, Causes and Explanations," *Philosophy and Phenomenological Research* 59, no. 2 (1999), pp. 381–401.

Huxley, Thomas, *Social Diseases and Worse Remedies* (London: Macmillan, 1891).

Huysmans, Jeff, "Security! What Do You Mean? From Concept to Thick Signifier," *European Journal of International Relations*, 4 (1998), pp. 226–55.

Hyde, K., *Society and Politics in Medieval Italy: The Evolution of the Civil Life, 1000–1350* (London: Macmillan, 1973).

Hyman, I. E., Jr., "Multiple Approaches to Remembering," *The Psychologist* 5 (1992), pp. 450–1.

Hymans, Jacques C., *The Psychology of Nuclear Proliferation: Identity, Emotions, and Foreign Policy* (Cambridge: Cambridge University Press, 2006).

Ienaga, Saburō, *The Pacific War: World War II and the Japanese, 1931–35* (New York: Pantheon, 1978).

Ignatieff, Michael, "Citizenship and Moral Narcissism," *Political Science Quarterly* 60 (1993), pp. 63–74.

The Warrior's Home: Ethnic War and the Modern Conscience (New York: Henry Holt, 1997).

"The Way We Live Now: The Year of Living Dangerously," *New York Times Magazine*, March 14, 2004.

Ike, Nobutaka, ed. and trans., *Japan's Decision for War: Records of the 1941 Policy Conferences* (Stanford, CA: Stanford University Press, 1967).

Ikegami, Eiko, *The Taming of the Samurai: Honorific Individualism and the Making of Modern Japan* (Cambridge, MA: Harvard University Press, 1995).

Ikenberry, G. John, *After Victory: Institutions, Strategic Restraint and the Rebuilding of Order after Major Wars* (Princeton: Princeton University Press, 2001).

America Unrivaled: The Future of the Balance of Power (Ithaca, NY: Cornell University Press, 2002).

"American Unipolarity: The Sources of Persistence and Decline," in Ikenberry, *America Unrivaled*, pp. 284–310.

"What States Can Do Now," in T. V. Paul, G. John Ikenberry and John Hall, *The Nation-State in Question* (Princeton, NJ: Princeton University Press, 2003), pp. 350–71.

"Liberalism and Empire: Logics of Order in the American Unipolar Age Doctrine," *Review of International Studies* 30 (2004), pp. 609–30.

Ikenberry, G. John and Michael Mastanduno, eds., *International Relations Theory and the Asia-Pacific* (New York: Columbia University Press, 2003).

Immerwar, Henry R., *Form and Thought in Herodotus* (Atlanta: Scholars Press, 1966).

Inayatulla, Naem, and David L. Blaney, "Knowing Encounters: Beyond Parochialism in International Relations Theory," in Lapid and Kratochwil, *The Return of Culture and Identity in IR Theory*, pp. 65–84.

    International Relations and the Problem of Difference (New York: Routledge, 2004).

    "The Savage Smith and the Temporal Walls of Capitalism," in Jahn, *Classical Theory in International Relations*, pp. 123–54.

Inglehart, Ronald, *Culture Shift in Advanced Society* (Princeton, NJ: Princeton University Press, 1990).

    Modernization and Postmodernization: Culture, Economic, and Political Change in 43 Societies (Princeton, NJ: Princeton University Press, 1997).

    "Trust, Well-Being and Democracy," in Mark Warren, *Democracy and Trust* (Cambridge: Cambridge University Press, 1999), pp. 88–120.

Ingram, Edward, "Pairing off Empires: The United States as Great Britain in the Middle East," in Tore T. Petersen, *Controlling the Uncontrollable? The Great Powers in the Middle East* (Trondheim: Tapir Books, 2006), pp. 1–32.

Innes, Harold and Rosamond McKitterick, "The Writing of History," in McKitterick, *Carolingian Culture*, pp. 193–220.

Innes, Matthew, "Charlemagne's Government," in Story, ed., *Charlemagne*, pp. 71–89.

Inwood, Stephen, *A History of London* (New York: Carroll and Graf, 1998).

Iriye, Akira, *After Imperialism: The Search for a New Order in the Far East, 1921–1931* (Cambridge, MA: Harvard University Press, 1965).

    "The Failure of Military Expansionism," in Morley, *Dilemmas of Growth in Prewar Japan*, pp. 107–38.

    Pacific Estrangement (Cambridge, MA: Harvard University Press, 1972).

    Power and Culture: The Japanese–American War, 1941–1945 (Cambridge, MA: Harvard University Press, 1981).

    The Origins of the Second World War in Asia and the Pacific (London: Longman, 1987).

    "Japan's Drive to Great Power Status," in Jansen, *The Emergence of Meiji Japan*, pp. 268–330.

    Japan and the Wider World: From the Eighteenth Century to the Present (New York: Longman, 1997).

Iriye, Akira and Warren Cohen, eds., *American, Chinese, and Japanese Perspectives on Wartime Asia* (Wilmington: University of Delaware Press, 1984).

Irwin, Terence H., "The Metaphysical and Psychological Basis of Aristotle's Ethics," in Amélie Rorty, *Essays on Aristotle's Ethics* (Berkeley: University of California Press, 1981), pp. 35–64.

    Plato's Ethics (Oxford: Oxford University Press, 1995).

Isaacson, Walter, *Kissinger: A Biography* (New York: Simon and Schuster, 1992).

Isaak, Robert A., *Managing World Economic Change*, 2nd edn (Englewood Cliffs, NJ: Prentice-Hall, 1995).

Isikoff, Michael and David Corn, *Hubris: The Inside Story of Spin, Scandal, and the Selling of the Iraq War* (New York: Crown, 2006).

Isocrates, *Isocrates*, trans. David Mirhady and Yun Lee Too, 2 vols. (Austin: University of Texas Press, 2000).

Israelian, Victor, *Inside the Kremlin during the Yom Kippur War* (College Park, PA: Pennsylvania State University Press, 1995).

Jackman, Robert W. and Ross A. Miller, *Before Norms: Institutions and Civic Culture* (Ann Arbor: University of Michigan Press, 2004).

Jackson, Frank and Philip Pettit, "Structural Explanation in Social Theory," in David Charles and Kathleen Lennon, *Reduction, Explanation, and Realism* (Oxford: Oxford University Press, 1993), pp. 97–131.

Jackson, Frank and Carol Rosenberg, "Why Africa's Weak States Persist: The Juridical and the Empirical in Statehood," *World Politics* 35 (1982), pp. 1–24.

Jackson, Patrick T. and Daniel H. Nexon, "Relations before States," *European Journal of International Relations* 5, no. 3 (1999), pp. 291–332.

"Constructivist Realism or Realist-Constructivism?," *International Studies Review* 6 (June 2004), pp. 337–41.

Jackson, Robert H., "Quasi-States, Dual Regimes, and Neoclassical Theory: International Jurisprudence and the Third World," *International Organization* 41, no. 4 (Autumn 1987), pp. 519–49.

Quasi-states: Sovereignty, International Relations and the Third World (Cambridge: Cambridge University Press, 1990).

Jackson, Robert H. and Mark W. Zacher, *The Territorial Covenant: International Society and the Stabilization of Boundaries*, Working Paper No. 15 (Vancouver, Canada: Institute of International Relations, University of British Columbia, 1997).

Jacobs, Jane, *The Death and Life of Great American Cities* (New York: Vintage, 1961).

Jacobs, Jonathan, "Teleological Form and Explanation," in Nicholas Rescher, *Current Issues in Teleology* (Lanham, MD: University Press of America, 1986), pp. 49–55.

Jaeger, C. Stephen, *The Origins of Courtliness: Civilizing Trends and the Formation of Courtly Ideals, 939–1210* (Philadelphia: University of Pennsylvania Press, 1985).

Jahn, Beate, *Classical Theory in International Relations* (Cambridge: Cambridge University Press, 2006).

"Classical Smoke, Classical Mirror: Kant and Mill in Liberal International Relations Theory," in Jahn, *Classical Theory in International Relations*, pp. 178–206.

James, Alan, *Sovereign Statehood: The Basis of International Society* (London: Allen and Unwin, 1986).

James, William, *The Meaning of Truth* (Cambridge, MA: Harvard University Press, 1975).

Janis, Irving L., *Victims of Groupthink: A Psychological Study of Foreign-Policy Decisions and Fiascoes* (Boston: Houghton Mifflin, 1972).

Janis, Irving L. and Leon Mann, *Decision Making: A Psychological Analysis of Conflict, Choice, and Commitment* (New York: Free Press, 1977).

Janowitz, Morris, *The Professional Soldier: A Social and Political Portrait* (New York: Free Press, 1960).

    Social Control of the Welfare State (New York: Elsevier, 1976).

Jansen, Marius B., *The Japanese and Sun Yat-sen* (Cambridge, MA: Harvard University Press, 1954).

    Japan in Transition from Tokugawa to Meiji (Princeton, NJ: Princeton University Press, 1986).

    The Emergence of Meiji Japan (Cambridge: Cambridge University Press, 1995).

    Japan and its World, rev. edn (Princeton: Princeton University Press, 1995).

Jarausch, Konrad, "The Illusion of Limited War: Chancellor Bethmann Hollweg's Calculated Risk, July 1914," *Central European History*, 2 (March 1969), pp. 48–76.

    The Enigmatic Chancellor: Bethmann Hollweg and the Hubris of Imperial Germany (New Haven, CT: Yale University Press, 1973).

Jarvis, D. S. L., *International Relations and the Challenge of Postmodernism* (Columbia: University of South Carolina Press, 2000).

Javitch, Daniel, "*The Philosopher of the Court*: A French Satire Misunderstood," *Comparative Literature* 23 (1971), pp. 97–124.

Jay, Martin, *Dialectical Imagination: History of the Frankfurt School and the Institute of Social Research, 1923–1950* (Boston: Little, Brown, 1973).

Jelavich, Barbara, *Russia's Balkan Entanglements, 1806–1914* (Cambridge: Cambridge University Press, 1991).

Jendrysik, Mark Stephen, *Explaining the English Revolution: Hobbes and his Contemporaries* (Lanham, MD: Rowman and Littlefield, 2002).

Jenkyns, Richard, *Victorians and Ancient Greece* (Cambridge, MA: Harvard University Press, 1980).

Jervis, Robert, *Perception and Misperception in International Relations* (Princeton, NJ: Princeton University Press, 1976).

    "Cooperation under the Security Dilemma," *World Politics* 40, no. 1 (1978), pp. 167–214.

    "War and Misperception," *Journal of Interdisciplinary History* 18, no. 4 (Spring 1988), pp. 675–700.

    The Meaning of the Nuclear Revolution (Ithaca, NY: Cornell University Press, 1989).

    System Effects: Complexity in Political and Social Life (Princeton, NJ: Princeton University Press, 1997).

"The Implications of Prospect Theory for Human Nature and Values," *Political Psychology* 25 (2004), pp. 163–76.

"Why the Bush Doctrine Cannot Be Sustained," *Political Science Quarterly* 120 (Fall 2005), pp. 351–78.

Jervis, Robert, Richard Ned Lebow and Janice Gross Stein, *Psychology and Deterrence* (Baltimore, MD: Johns Hopkins University Press, 1985).

Jessop, Bob, *The Capitalist State: Marxist Theory and Methods* (New York: New York University Press, 1982).

"Bringing the State Back In (Yet Again): Reviews, Revisions, Rejections, and Redirections," *International Review of Sociology* 11, no. 2 (2001), pp. 149–73.

Joffe, Joseph, "Defying History and Theory: The United States as the 'Last Remaining Superpower'," in Ikenberry, *America Unrivaled*, pp. 155–80.

Johnson, Cathryn, Timothy J. Dowd and Cecelia L. Ridgeway, "Legitimacy as a Social Process," *Annual Reviews of Sociology* 35 (August 2006), pp. 53–78.

Johnson, Chalmers, *MITI and the Japanese Miracle, 1925–1975* (Stanford, CA: Stanford University Press, 1982).

Blowback: The Costs and Consequences of American Empire (New York: Holt, 2000).

Johnson, Douglas, ed., *French Society and the Revolution* (Cambridge: Cambridge University Press, 1976).

Johnson, Hubert C., *Frederick the Great and his Officials* (New Haven, CT: Yale University Press, 1975).

Johnston, Alastair Ian, "Treating International Institutions as Social Environments," *International Studies Quarterly*, 45, no. 4 (2001), pp. 487–515.

"Is China a Status Quo Power?," *International Security*, 27, no. 4 (2003), pp. 5–56.

Joll, James, *1914: The Unspoken Assumptions* (London: Weidenfeld and Nicolson, 1968).

Jones, Gareth Stedman, "Hegel and the Economics of Civil Society," in Kaviraj and Khilnani, *Civil Society*, pp. 105–30.

Jones, Michael, "The Last Capetians and Early Valois Kings, 1314–1364," in Jones, *The New Cambridge Medieval History*, vol. VI, pp. 388–421.

ed., *The New Cambridge Medieval History*, vol. VI: *c.1300–c.1415* (Cambridge: Cambridge University Press, 2000).

Jones, R. E., "Why St. Petersburg?" in Lindsey Hughes, ed., *Peter the Great and the West: New Perspectives* (London: Palgrave, 2000), pp. 189–205.

Jones, R. J. Barry, *Globalisation and Interdependence in the International Political Economy* (London: Pinter, 1995).

Jönsson, Christer, Sven Tägil and Gunnar Törnquist, *Organizing European Space* (London: Sage, 2000).

Jonsson, Stefan, *Robert Musil and the History of Modern Thought* (Durham, NC: Duke University Press, 2000).

Jordan, William, *Louis IX and the Challenge of the Crusade* (Princeton, NJ: Princeton University Press, 1979).

Josephson, Peter, *The Great Art of Government: Locke's Use of Consent* (Lawrence: University Press of Kansas, 2002).

Josephus, Flavius, *The Jewish War*, rev. edn, ed. Betty Radice and E. Mary Smallwood, trans. G. A. Williamson (New York: Penguin, 1984).

Jouanna, Arlette, "Recherches sur la notion d'honneur," *Revue d'histoire moderne et contemporaine* 15 (1968), pp. 579–623.

Joyner, Christopher, *Governing the Frozen Commons* (Oxford: Oxford University Press, 2004).

Juarrero, Alicia, *Dynamics in Action: Intentional Behavior as a Complex System* (Cambridge, MA: MIT Press, 1999).

Juvenal, *Satire*, in *Juvenal and Perseus*, trans. G. G. Ramsay (New York: G. P. Putnam's Sons, 1924), pp. 124–248.

Kaeuper, Richard, "Charny's Career," in De Charny, *Book of Chivalry*, pp. 3–17.

  "Geoffroi de Charny and His Book," in De Charny, *Book of Chivalry*, pp. 3–66.

  War, Justice and Public Order: England and France in the Later Middle Ages (Oxford: Oxford University Press, 1988).

  Chivalry and Violence in Medieval Europe (Oxford: Oxford University Press, 1999).

  ed., *Violence in Medieval Society* (Woodbridge, Sussex: Boydell Press, 2000).

  "Chivalry and the 'Civilizing Process'," in Kaeuper, *Violence in Medieval Society*, pp. 21–38.

Kagan, Donald, *The Outbreak of the Peloponnesian War* (Ithaca, NY: Cornell University Press, 1969).

Kagan, Robert, "The Benevolent Empire," *Foreign Policy* 111 (Summer 1998), pp. 24–35.

  "Power and Weakness," *Policy Review* (June/July 2002), pp. 11–18.

  Paradise and Power: American and Europe in the New World Order (London: Atlantic Books, 2003).

Kahler, Miles, "Evolution, Choice, and International Change," in David Lake and Robert Powell, *Strategic Choice and International Relations* (Princeton, NJ: Princeton University Press, 1999), pp. 165–96.

Kahler, Miles and David A. Lake, *Governance in a Global Economy: Political Authority in Transition* (Princeton, NJ: Princeton University Press, 2003).

Kahn, E. J., *The China Hands: America's Foreign Service Officers and What Befell Them* (New York: Viking, 1972).

Kahn, Herman, *Thinking About the Unthinkable* (New York: Horizon Press, 1962).

Kahn, Victoria, *Machiavellian Rhetoric: From the Counter-Reformation to Milton* (Princeton, NJ: Princeton University Press, 1994).

Kahneman, Daniel and Amos Tversky, "Prospect Theory: An Analysis of Decision Making under Risk," *Econometrica* 47, no. 2 (March 1979), pp. 263–92.

eds., *Choices, Values, and Frames* (New York: Cambridge University Press, 2000).

Kaiser, David E., "Germany and the Origins of the First World War," *Journal of Modern History* 55 (September 1983), pp. 442–74.

Kaldor, Mary, *New and Old Wars: Organized Violence in a Global Era* (Stanford, CA: Stanford University Press, 1999).

Kam, Cindy D. and Donald R. Kinder, "Terror and Ethnocentrism: Foundations of American Support for the War on Terrorism," *Journal of Politics* 69, no. 2 (2007), pp. 320–38.

Kamalipour, Yahya and Nancy Snow, *War, Media, and Propaganda: A Global Perspective* (Boulder, CO: Rowman and Littlefield, 2004).

Kandel, Eric R., *In Search of Memory: The Emergence of a New Science of Mind* (New York: Norton, 2006).

Kane, John, *The Politics of Moral Capital* (Cambridge: Cambridge University Press, 2001).

Kang, David C., "Getting Asia Wrong: The Need for New Analytic Frameworks," *International Security* 27 (Spring 2003), pp. 57–85.

China Reshapes Asia (New York: Columbia University Press, forthcoming)

Kann, Robert A., *Kaiser Franz Josef und der Ausbruch des ersten Weltkrieges* (Vienna: Böhlau in Komm, 1971).

Kant, Immanuel, *The Groundwork of the Metaphysics of Morals*, trans. H. J. Paton (London: Hutchinson, 1949).

Kant's Critique of Practical Reason and Other Writings in Moral Philosophy, trans. Lewis White Beck (Chicago: University of Chicago Press, 1949).

Kant: Political Writings, ed. Hans Reiss, trans. H. B. Nisbet (Cambridge: Cambridge University Press, 1991).

"Conjectures on the Beginning of Human History," in *Kant: Political Writings*, pp. 221–34.

"Idea for a Universal History with a Cosmopolitan Purpose," in *Kant: Political Writings*, pp. 41–53.

"Perpetual Peace: A Philosophical Sketch," in *Kant: Political Writings*, pp. 93–130.

Ideas Toward a Universal History, in Henry Allison and Peter Heath, trans. Gary Hatfield, *Immanuel Kant: Theoretical Writings after 1781* (Cambridge: Cambridge University Press, 1992), pp. 105–8.

Prolegomena to any Future Metaphysics that Will Be Able to Come Forward as Science, ed. and trans. Gary Hatfield (Cambridge: Cambridge University Press, 2004).

Kantorowicz, Ernst. H., *The King's Two Bodies: A Study in Medieval Political Thought* (Princeton, NJ: Princeton University Press, 1957).

Kaplan, Morton, *System and Process in International Relations* (New York: Wiley, 1957).

Kaplan, Robert D., "The Coming Anarchy," *Atlantic Monthly* (February 1994), pp. 44–67.

 The Ends of the Earth: A Journey to the Frontiers of Anarchy (New York: Random House, 1996).

 The Coming Anarchy: Shattering the Dreams of the Post Cold War World (New York: Random House, 2000).

 Warrior Politics: Why Leadership Demands a Pagan Ethos (New York: Random House, 2002).

Kaplowitz, Noel, "Psychopolitical Dimensions of International Relations: The Reciprocal Effects of Conflict Strategies," *International Studies Quarterly* 23 (1984), pp. 373–406.

Karl, David J., "Proliferation, Pessimism and Emerging Nuclear Powers," *International Security* 21, no. 3 (1996), pp. 87–119.

Karnow, Stanley, *Vietnam: A History*, rev. edn (New York: Viking, 1991).

Kasfir, Nelson, "Domestic Anarchy, Security Dilemmas, and Violent Predation: Causes of Failure," in Robert I. Rotberg, *When States Fail: Causes and Consequences* (Princeton, NJ: Princeton University Press, 2004), pp. 53–76.

Katsumi, Usui, "The Role of the Foreign Ministry," in Borg and Okamoto, *Pearl Harbor as History*, pp. 127–48.

Katz, Mark N., "Nationalism and the Legacy of Empire," *Current History* (October 1994), pp. 322–36.

Katzenstein, Peter J., *The Culture of National Security. Norms and Identity in World Politics* (New York: Columbia University Press, 1996).

 "Introduction: Alternative Perspectives on National Security," in Katzenstein, *The Culture of National Security*, pp. 1–34.

Katznelson, Ira, *Desolation and Enlightenment: Political Knowledge after Total War, Totalitarianism, and the Holocaust* (New York: Columbia University Press, 2003).

 "At the Court of Chaos," *Perspectives in Politics*, 5, no. 1 (March 2007), pp. 3–16.

Kauffman, Stuart J., *At Home in the Universe* (Oxford: Oxford University Press, 1995).

 "The Fragmentation and Consolidation of International Systems," *International Organization* 51, no. 2 (1997), pp. 173–208.

Kauffman, Stuart J., Richard Little and William Wohlforth, eds., *The Fate of International Systems: Balancing and Balancing Failure, 850 BCE–1900* (forthcoming).

Kaufman, Robert Gordon, *Arms Control during the Prenuclear Era: The United States and Naval Limitation between the Two World Wars* (New York: Columbia University Press, 1990).

"To Balance or Bandwagon? Alignment Decisions in 1930s Europe," *Security Studies* 1, no. 3 (1992), pp. 417–47.

Kaufmann, Chaim, "Possible and Impossible Solutions to Ethnic Civil Wars," *International Security* 20 (1996), pp. 136–75.

Kaviraj, Sudipta and Sunil Khilnani, eds., *Civil Society: History and Possibilities* (Cambridge: Cambridge University Press, 2001).

Kazmi, Zaheer A., "Discipline and Power: Interpreting Global Islam: A Review Essay," *Review of International Studies* 30 (2004), pp. 245–54.

Keane, John, ed., *Civil Society and the State: New European Perspectives* (London: Verso, 1988).

"Despotism and Democracy: The Origins and Development of the Distinction between Civil Society and the State 1750–1850," in Keane, *Civil Society and the State,* pp. 91–116.

Global Civil Society? (Cambridge: Cambridge University Press, 2003).

Keating, Tom, *Canada and World Order: The Multilateralist Tradition in Canadian Foreign Policy,* 2nd edn (Dom Mills, Ont.: Oxford University Press, 2002), pp. 162–85.

Keegan, John, *The Face of Battle* (New York: Viking, 1976).

A History of Warfare (New York: Alfred A. Knopf, 1993).

Keeley, Lawrence, H., *War before Civilization* (New York: Oxford University Press, 1966).

Keen, Maurice, *Chivalry* (New Haven, CT: Yale University Press, 1984).

"Chivalry and the Aristocracy," in Jones, *The New Cambridge Medieval History,* vol. VI, pp. 209–21.

Keene, Edward, *Beyond the Anarchical Society* (Cambridge: Cambridge University Press, 2002).

"Images of Grotius," in Jahn, *Classical Theory in International Relations,* pp. 233–52.

Keens-Soper, H. M. A. and P. Savigear, eds., *The Theory of International Relations: Selected Texts from Gentili to Treitschke* (New York: Atherton Press, 1970).

Kehoe, Alice Beck, *Humans: An Introduction to Four-Field Anthropology* (London: Routledge, 1998).

Kehr, Eckart, *Der Primat der Innenpolitik* (Berlin: Walter de Gruyter, 1965).

"*Soziale und finanzielle Grundlagen der Tirpitzschen Flottenpropaganda,*" in Wehler, *Moderne deutsche Sozialgeschichte,* pp. 287–308.

Economic Interest, Militarism, and Foreign Policy: Essays on German History, trans. Grete Heinz (Berkeley: University of California Press, 1970).

Battleship Building and Party Politics in Germany, trans. Pauline R. and Eugene N. Anderson (Chicago: University of Chicago Press, 1973).

Kellert, Stephen H., *In the Wake of Chaos* (Chicago: University of Chicago Press, 1993).

Kelley, Terence Marshall, *The Collected Writings of Rousseau*, trans. Judith R. Bush (Hanover, NH: University Press of New England, 1992), vol. III.

Kelman, Herbert, "Patterns of Personal Involvement in the National System: A Social Psychological Analysis of Political Legitimacy," in James N. Rosenau, ed., *International Politics and Foreign Policy: A Reader in Research and Theory* (Glencoe, IL: Free Press, 1969), pp. 277–88.

"The Interdependence of Israeli and Palestinian Identities: The Role of the Other in Existential Conflicts," *Journal of Social Issues* 55, no. 3 (1999), pp. 581–600.

Kennedy, Elspeth, "The Quest for Identity and the Importance of Lineage in Thirteenth-Century France Prose Romance," in Christopher Harper-Bill and Ruth Harvery, eds., *The Ideals and Practice of Medieval Knighthood II* (Cambridge: Cambridge University Press, 1988), pp. 70–86.

ed., *Lancelot do Lac. The Non-Cyclic Old French Prose Romance*, 2 vols. (Oxford: Oxford University Press, 1980).

Kennedy, Paul M., *The Rise of Anglo-German Antagonism, 1860–1914* (London: Allen and Unwin, 1980).

"The Kaiser and German *Weltpolitik*: Reflections on Wilhelm II's Place in the Making of Germany Foreign Policy," in Röhl and Sombart, *Kaiser Wilhelm II*, pp. 143–68.

The Rise and Fall of the Great Powers: Economic Change and Military Conflict from 1500 to 2000 (New York: Random House, 1987).

Kennedy, Robert F., *Thirteen Days: A Memoir of the Cuban Missile Crisis* (New York: Norton, 1969).

Kennedy, W. P., *Industrial Structure, Capital Markets, and the Origins of British Economic Decline* (Cambridge: Cambridge University Press, 1987).

Keohane, Nannerl, *Philosophy and the State in France: The Renaissance and Enlightenment* (Princeton, NJ: Princeton University Press, 1980).

Keohane, Robert O., "The Theory of Hegemonic Stability and Changes in International Economic Regimes, 1967–1977," in Ole R. Holsti, Randolph M. Sieverson and Alexander L. George, eds., *Change in the International System* (Boulder, CO: Westview, 1980), pp. 131–62.

International Institutions and State Power: Essays in International Relations Theory (Boulder, CO: Westview Press, 1989).

After Hegemony: Cooperation and Discord in the World Political Economy (Princeton, NJ: Princeton University Press, 1984).

Neorealism and its Critics (New York: Columbia University, 1986).

Ideas and Foreign Policy: Beliefs, Institutions, and Political Change (Ithaca, NY: Cornell University Press, 1993).

Keohane, Robert O. and Lisa Martin, "The Promise of Institutionalist Theory," *International Security* 20, no. 1 (Summer 1995), pp. 39–52.

Kermode, Frank, *The Sense of an Ending: Studies in the Theory of Fiction with a New Epilogue* (New York: Oxford University Press, 2000).

Kerr, Paul, "North Korean Test Provokes Widespread Condemnation," *Arms Control Today* 36, no. 9 (November 2006), pp. 23–32.

Kershaw, Ian, "Ideology, Propaganda, and the Rise of the Nazi Party," in Stachura, *The Nazi Machtergreifung*, pp. 162–81.

    Popular Opinion and Political Dissent in the Third Reich: Bavaria 1933–1945 (Oxford: Oxford University Press, 1983).

    The "Hitler Myth": Image and Reality in the Third Reich (Oxford: Oxford University Press, 1987).

Kettering, Sharon, *French Society, 1589–1715* (London: Longmans, 2001).

Keuls, Eva C., *The Reign of the Phallus: Sexual Politics in Ancient Athens* (New York: Harper and Row, 1985).

Keynes, John Maynard, *The End of Laissez-Faire* (London: Hogarth Press, 1927).

    "Economic Possibilities for Our Grandchildren," in *Essays in Persuasion: The Collected Writings of John Maynard Keynes*, ed. Elizabeth Johnson and Donald Moggridge (Cambridge: Cambridge University Press, 1930), vol. IX, p. 329.

Khilnani, Sunil, "The Development of Civil Society," in Kaviraj and Khilnani, *Civil Society*, pp. 11–32.

Khoury, Philip and Joseph Kostiner, eds., *Tribes and State Formation in the Middle East* (Berkeley: University of California Press, 1990).

Khrushchev, Nikita, *Khrushchev Remembers*, trans. Strobe Talbott (Boston: Little, Brown, 1970).

    Khrushchev Remembers: The Last Testament, trans. Strobe Talbot (Boston: Little, Brown, 1975).

    Khrushchev Remembers: The Glasnost Tapes, ed. and trans. Jerrold L. Schechter (Boston: Little, Brown, 1990).

Khrushchev, Sergei, *Khrushchev on Khrushchev: An Inside Account of the Man and his Era*, trans. and ed. William Taubman (Boston: Little, Brown, 1990).

Kiernan, V. G., *The Duel in European History* (Oxford: Oxford University Press, 1988).

Kiesling, Eugenia C., "France," in Hamilton and Herwig, *The Origins of World War I*, pp. 227–65.

Kilbourne, Benjamin, "Fields of Shame: Anthropologists Abroad," *Ethos* 20 no. 2 (1992), pp. 230–53.

Kilgour, Raymond L., *The Decline of Chivalry as Shown in the French Literature of the Late Middle Ages* (Cambridge, MA: Harvard University Press, 1937).

Kim Dae Jung, "Is Culture Destiny? The Myth of Asia's Anti-Democratic Values," *Foreign Affairs* 73, no. 6 (November/December 1994), pp. 189–94.

Kim Eun Mee, *Big Business, Strong State: Collusion and Conflict in South Korean Development, 1960–1990* (Albany, NY: State University of New York Press, 1997).

Kim Key-Hiuk, *The Last Phase of the East Asian World Order: Korea, Japan, and the Chinese Empire, 1860–1882* (Berkeley: University of California Press, 1980).

Kimio, Itō, "The Invention of *Wa* and the Transformation of the Image of Prince Shōtoku in Modern Japan," in Vlastos, *Mirror of Modernity*, pp. 37–47.

Kimmel, Michael S., *Absolutism and its Discontents: State and Society in Seventeenth Century France and England* (New Brunswick, NJ: Transaction Books, 1998).

Kindleberger, Charles P., *The World in Depression, 1929–1939* (London: Allen Lane, 1973).

King, Gary, Robert O. Keohane and Sidney Verba, *Designing Social Inquiry: Scientific Inference in Quantitative Research* (Princeton, NJ: Princeton University Press, 1994).

Kirby, William C., "Traditions of Centrality, Authority, and Management in Modern China's Foreign Relations," in Robinson and Shumbaugh, *Chinese Foreign Policy*, pp. 13–29.

Kirk, G. S., *Homer and the Oral Tradition* (Cambridge: Cambridge University Press, 1976).

Kissinger, Henry, *A World Restored: Metternich, Castlereagh and the Problems of Peace, 1812–22* (Boston: Houghton Mifflin, 1957).

   Years of Upheaval (Boston: Little, Brown, 1972).

   "Detente with the Soviet Union: The Reality of Competition and the Imperative of Cooperation," *Department of State Bulletin*, October 14, 1974, pp. 505–19.

   White House Years (Boston: Little, Brown, 1979).

   Diplomacy (New York: Simon and Schuster, 1994).

Kitchen, Martin, *The German Officer Corps, 1890–1914* (Oxford: Oxford University Press, 1968).

Kleingeld, Pauline, "Kant, History, and the Idea of Moral Development," *History of Philosophy Quarterly* 16, no. 1 (1999), pp. 59–80.

Klotz, Audie, *Norms in International Regimes: The Struggle against Apartheid* (Ithaca, NY: Cornell University Press, 1995).

Knight, Frank H., *The Ethics of Competition and Other Essays* (London: Allen and Unwin, 1936).

Knorr, Klaus and James N. Rosenau, eds., *Contending Approaches to International Politics* (Princeton, NJ: Princeton University Press, 1969).

   "Tradition and Science in the Study of International Politics," in Knorr and Rosenau, *Contending Approaches to International Politics*, pp. 3–19.

Knorr, Klaus and Frank N. Trager, eds., *Economic Issues and National Security* (Lawrence: Regents Press of Kansas, 1977).

Knorr, Klaus and Sidney Verba, eds., *The International System: Theoretical Essays* (Princeton, NJ: Princeton University Press, 1961).

Knox, Bernard, *Oedipus at Thebes* (New York: Norton, 1970).

   The Heroic Temper: Studies in Sophoclean Tragedy (New York: Cambridge University Press, 1982).

   "Everybody but Shakespeare," *New Republic*, August 8, 1983, reprinted in Knox, *Essays: Ancient and Modern*, pp. 243–49.

Essays: Ancient and Modern (Baltimore, MD: Johns Hopkins University Press, 1989).

Knox, MacGregor, *Mussolini Unleashed, 1939–1941: Politics and Strategy in Fascist Italy's Last War* (Cambridge: Cambridge University Press, 1982).

Common Destiny: Dictatorships, Foreign Policy and War in Fascist Italy and Nazi Germany (Cambridge: Cambridge University Press, 1995).

"Fascism: Ideology, Foreign Policy, and War," in Adrian Lyttelton, ed., *Liberal and Fascist Italy, 1900–1945* (Oxford: Oxford University Press, 2002), pp. 105–38.

Knox, Paul L. and Peter J. Taylor, *World Cities in a World-System* (Cambridge: Cambridge University Press, 1995).

Kobrin, Stephen J., "Back to the Future: Neomedievalism and the Postmodern Digital World Economy," *Journal of International Affairs* 51, no. 2 (Spring 1998), pp. 361–86.

Koch, H. W. ed., *The Origins of the First World War*, 2nd edn (Oxford: Oxford University Press, 1984).

Kocka, Jürgen, "German History before Hitler: The Debate about the German *Sonderweg*," *Journal of Contemporary History*, 23, no. 1 (1988), pp. 3–16.

Koehler, John O., *STASI: The Untold Story of the East German Secret Police* (Boulder, CO: Westview, 1999).

Kohn, Richard H., "History at Risk: The Case of the Enola Gay," in Edward T. Linenthal and Tom Engelhardt, *History Wars: The Enola Gay and Other Battles for the American Past* (New York: Henry Holt, 1996), pp 140–71.

Kolodziej, Edward, "The Limits of Deterrence Theory," *Journal of Social Issues* 43, no. 4 (1987), pp. 130–1.

Komter, A. E., *The Gift: An Interdisciplinary Perspective* (Amsterdam: Amsterdam University Press, 1996).

Konstan, David, "*Philia* in Euripides' *Electra*," *Philologos* 129 (1985), pp. 176–85.

Friendship in the Classical World (Cambridge: Cambridge University Press, 1997).

Pity Transformed (London: Duckworth, 2004).

The Emotions of the Ancient Greeks: Studies in Aristotle and Classical Literature (Toronto: University of Toronto Press, 2006).

Konstan, David and N. Kreith Rutter, *Envy, Spite and Jealousy: The Rivalrous Emotions in Ancient Greece* (Edinburgh: Edinburgh University Press, 2003).

Korbel, Josef, *Poland between East and West: Soviet and German Diplomacy toward Poland, 1919–1933* (Princeton, NJ: Princeton University Press, 1963).

Korfmann, Manfred, "Die Arbeiten in Troia/Wilusa 2003," *Studia Troica* 14 (2004), pp. 1–34.

Koselleck, Reinhart, "Einleitung," in Otto Brunner, Werner Conor and Reinhard Koselleck, eds., *Geschichtliche Grundbegriffe, Historisches Lexicon zur Politisch-Sozialen Sprache in Deutschland* (Stuttgart: Klett-Cotta, 1972–7), vol I, pp. 1–24.

"*Begriffsgeschichte* and Social History," in Reinhart Koselleck, *Futures Past: On the Semantics of Historical Time* (Cambridge, MA: MIT Press, 1985), pp. 73–91.

Critique and Crisis: Enlightenment and the Pathogenesis of Modern Society (Oxford: Berg, 1988).

The Practice of Conceptual History: Timing History, Spacing Concepts, trans. Todd Damuel Pesner (Stanford, CA: Stanford University Press, 2002).

Koselleck, Reinhart and Hans-Georg Gadamer, *Hermaneutik and Historik* (Heidelberg: Carl Winter, 1987).

Koskenniemi, Martti, *The Gentle Civilizer of Nations: The Rise and Fall of International Law, 1870–1960* (Cambridge: Cambridge University Press, 2001).

Koslowski, Reynold and Friedrich V. Kratochwil, "Understanding Change in International Politics: The Soviet Empire's Demise and the International System," *International Organization* 48, no. 2 (Spring 1994), pp. 215–47.

Krailsheimer, A. J., *Studies in Self-Interest from Descartes to La Bruyère* (Oxford: Oxford University Press, 1962).

Kraines, D. and V., "Evolution of Learning Among Pavlov Strategies in a Competitive Environment with Noise," *Journal of Conflict Resolution* 39 (1995), pp. 439–66.

Krasner, Stephen D., *Defending the National Interest: Raw Materials Investments and U.S. Foreign Policy* (Princeton, NJ: Princeton University Press, 1978).

"Global Communications and National Power," *World Politics* 43, no. 3 (1991), pp. 336–66.

"Westphalia and All That," in Judith Goldstein and Robert O. Keohane, *Ideas and Foreign Policy: Beliefs, Institutions, and Political Change* (Ithaca, NY: Cornell University Press, 1993), pp. 235–64.

Sovereignty: Organized Hypocrisy (Princeton, NJ: Princeton University Press, 1999).

Kratochwil, Friedrich V., *Rules, Norms, and Decisions: On the Conditions of Practical and Legal Reasoning in International Relations and Domestic Affairs* (Cambridge: Cambridge University Press, 1989).

"Citizenship: On the Border of Order," in *The Return of Culture and Identity in IR Theory* (Boulder, CO: Lynne Rienner, 1996), pp. 181–97.

"Constructing a New Orthodoxy? Wendt's 'Social Theory of International Politics' and the Constructivist Challenge," *Millennium* 29, no. 1 (2000), pp. 73–101.

Kratochwil, Friedrich V. and John Gerard Ruggie, "International Organization: A State of the Art on the Art of the State," *International Organization* 40, no. 3 (Autumn 1986), pp. 753–75.

Krause, Andreas, *Scapa Flow. Die Selbstversenkung der wilhelminischen Flotte* (Berlin: Ullstein, 1999).

Krause, Sharon R., *Liberalism without Honor* (Cambridge, MA: Harvard University Press, 2002).

Krausnick, Helmut, *Die Truppe des Weltanschauungskrieges: die Einsatzgruppen der Sicherheitspolizei und des SD, 1938–1942* (Stuttgart: Deutsche Verlags-Anstalt, 1981).

Kraut, Richard, *Aristotle on the Human Good* (Princeton, NJ: Princeton University Press, 1999).

Aristotle: Political Philosophy (New York: Oxford University Press, 2002).

Krauthammer, Charles, "The Unipolar Moment," *Foreign Affairs* 70 (1990/1), pp. 23–33.

"The Unipolar Moment Revisited," *National Interest* 70 (Winter 2002), pp. 5–18.

Krentz, Peter, "Casualties in Hoplite Battles," *Greek, Roman and Byzantine Studies* 26 (1985), pp. 13–20.

Krieger, Leonard, *The German Idea of Freedom: History of a German Tradition* (Boston: Beacon Press, 1957).

Kristjánsson, Kristján, "Justice and Desert-Based Emotions," *Philosophical Explorations* 8, no. 1 (March 2005), pp. 53–68.

Kristol, Irving, *Two Cheers for Capitalism* (New York: Basic Books, 1978).

Kristol, William and Robert Kagan, "Towards a Neo-Reaganite Foreign Policy," *Foreign Affairs* 75, no. 4 (1996), pp. 18–32.

Kroener, Bernard R., "The Modern State and Military Society in the Eighteenth Century," in Contamine, *War and Competition between States*, pp. 195–220.

Kronenbitter, Günther, *Krieg im Frieden: die Führung der k.u.k. Armee und die Grossmachtpolitik Österreich-Ungarns 1906–1914* (Munich: Oldenbourg, 2003).

Krug, Wilhelm Traugott, *Geschichtliche Darstellung des Liberalismus alter und neuer Zeit. Ein historiker Versuch* (Leipzig: F. A. Brockhaus, 1823).

Krüger, Peter, *Deutschland und die Reparationen 1918–19: die Genesis des Reparationsproblems in Deutschland zwischen Waffenstillstand und Versailler Friedensschluss* (Stuttgart: Deutsche Verlags-Anstalt, 1973).

Krüger, Peter and Paul W. Schroeder, eds., in cooperation with Katja Wüstenbeker, "*The Transformation of European Politics, 1763–1848:*" *Episode or Model in History?* (Münster: Lit Verlag, 2002).

Kruglanski, A., *Lay Epistemics and Human Knowledge: Cognitive and Motivational Bases* (New York: Plenum Press, 1989).

"Motivated Social Cognition: Principles of the Interface," in E. Higgins and A. Kruglanski, eds., *Social Psychology: Handbook of Basic Principles* (New York: Guilford Press, 1996), pp. 493–520.

Krumeich, Gerd, "Die Dolchstoss-Legende," in Étienne François and Hagen Schulze, eds., *Deutsche Erinnerungsorte* (Munich: Beck, 2000), pp. 585–99.

Kubálková, Vendulka, Nicholas Onuf and Paul Kowert, *International Relations in a Constructed World* (Armonk, NY: M. E. Sharpe, 1998).

Kuhn, Thomas S., *The Structure of Scientific Revolutions* (Chicago: University of Chicago Press, 1962).

"Reflections on my Critics," in Imre Lakatos and Alan Musgrave, *Criticism and the Growth of Knowledge* (Cambridge: Cambridge University Press, 1970), pp. 231–78.

Kumar, Krishan, *From Post-Industrial to Post-Modern Society: New Theories of the Contemporary World* (Oxford: Blackwell, 1995).

Kundera, Milan, *Immortality* (London: Faber and Faber, 1991).

Kupchan, Charles A., *The Vulnerability of Empire* (Ithaca, NY: Cornell University Press, 1994).

"After Pax Americana: Benign Power, Regional Integration, and the Sources of Stable Multipolarity," *International Security* 23 (1998), pp. 40–79.

Kurke, Leslie, *The Traffic in Praise: Pindar and the Poetics of Social Economy* (Ithaca, NY: Cornell University Press, 1991).

Kuus, Merje, "Toward Co-operative Security? International Integration and the Construction of Identity in Estonia," *Millennium* 31, no. 2 (2001), pp. 297–317.

Kydd, Andrew, "Sheep in Sheep's Clothing: Why Security Seekers Do Not Fight One Another," *Security Studies* 7, no. 1 (Autumn 1997), pp. 141–54.

La Rochefoucauld, François de, *The Maxims*, trans. Louis Kronenberger (New York: Stackpole, 1936).

Lacey, Norris J., ed., *The Old French Arthurian Vulgate and Post-Vulgate in Translation* (New York: Routledge, 1995). Vol. I: *The History of the Holy Grail*, trans. Carol J. Chase; *The Story of Merlin*, trans. Rupert T. Pickens. Vol. II: *Lancelot*, part 1, trans. Samuel N. Rosenberg; part 2, trans. Carleton W. Carroll; part 3, trans. Samuel N. Rosenberg. Vol. III: *Lancelot*, part 4, trans. Roberta L. Krueger; part 5, trans. William W. Kibler; part 6, trans. Carleton W. Carroll. Vol. IV: *The Quest for the Holy Grail*, trans. E. Jane Burns; *The Death of Arthur*, trans. Norris J. Lacey; *The Post-Vulgate*, part I; *The Merlin Continuation*, intro. and trans. Martha Asher. Vol. V: *The Post-Vulgate*, parts I–III; *The Merlin Continuation* (end); *The Quest for the Holy Grail, The Death of Arthur*, trans. Martha Asher; chapter summaries for the Vulgate and Post-Vulgate cycles, by Norris J. Lacey; index of proper names by Samuel N. Rosenberg with Daniel Golembeski.

Lancelot-Grail Reader: Selections from the Medieval French Arthurian Cycle (New York: Garland, 2000).

Lacey, Walter K., *The Family in Classical Greece* (Ithaca, NY: Cornell University Press, 1984 [1968]).

Ladurie, Emmanuel Le Roy, *Saint-Simon and the Court of Louis XIV*, in collaboration with Jean Fitou, trans. Arthur Goldhammer (Chicago: University of Chicago Press, 2001).

LaFeber, Walter, *Inevitable Revolutions: The United States in Latin America* (New York: Norton, 1984).

The Clash: A History of U.S.–Japan Relations (New York: Norton, 1997).

Lafond, Jean, *La Rochefoucauld, Augustinisme et littérature*, 3rd edn (Paris: Klinck-sieck, 1986).

LaHaye, Tim and Jerry Jenkins, *Left Behind*, 12 vols. (Carol Stream, IL: Tyndale House, 1996–2005).

Laing, R. D., *The Divided Self: An Existential Study in Sanity and Madness* (New York: Penguin, 1990 [1969]).

Lakatos, Imre and Alan Musgrave, eds., *Criticism and the Growth of Knowledge* (Cambridge: Cambridge University Press, 1970).

Lakoff, George and Mark Johnson, *Philosophy in the Flesh. The Embodied Mind and its Challenge to Western Thought* (New York: Basic Books, 1999).

Laks, André and Malcolm Schofield, eds., *Justice and Generosity: Studies in Hellenistic Social and Political Philosophy* (Cambridge: Cambridge University Press, 1995).

Lampton, Daniel M., "China's Rise in Asia Need Not Be at America's Expense," in Shumbaugh, *Power Shift*, pp. 306–28.

Lane, Robert, *The Market Experience* (Cambridge: Cambridge University Press, 1991).

Langer, William L., *European Alliances and Alignments, 1871–1890*, 2nd edn (New York: Knopf, 1966).

Lapid, Yosef, "Culture's Ship: Returns and Departures in International Relations Theory," in Lapid and Kratochwil, *The Return of Culture and Identity in IR Theory*, pp. 3–20.

"Introduction. Identities, Border, Orders: Nudging International Relations Theory in a New Direction," in Albert, Jacobson and Lapid, *Identities, Border, Orders*, pp. 1–20.

Lapid, Yosef and Friedrich Kratochwil, eds., *The Return of Culture and Identity in IR Theory* (Boulder, CO: Lynne Rienner, 1996).

Lapidus, Gail W., "Contested Sovereignty: The Tragedy of Chechnya," *International Security* 23, no. 1 (1998), pp. 5–49.

Lapin, Hayim and Dale B. Martin, eds., *Jews, Antiquity, and the Nineteenth-Century Imagination* (College Park: University Press of Maryland, 2003).

Laplace, Pierre-Simon, *Théorie analytique des probabilités*, in *Oeuvres complètes de Laplace*, 3rd edn (Paris: Gauthier-Villars, 1820).

Large, Stephen S., *Emperor Hirohito and Shōwa Japan: A Political Biography* (London: Kegan Paul, 1992).

Lasch, Christopher, "The Revolt of the Elites: Have They Canceled their Allegiance to America?" *Harpers* (November 1994).

Laski, Harold, *Political Authority in the Modern State* (New Haven, CT: Yale University Press, 1919).

A Grammar of Politics (New Haven, CT: Yale University Press, 1925).

Lassman, Peter and Ronald Speirs, ed., *Weber: Political Writings* (Cambridge: Cambridge University Press, 1994).

"Introduction," in *Weber: Political Writings*, pp. vii–xxv.

Lasswell, Harold D., *World Politics and Personal Insecurity* (New York: McGraw-Hill, 1935).

Politics: Who Gets What, When, How (Cleveland, OH: Meridian Books, 1952).

Lasswell, Harold D., Daniel Lerner and Hans Speier, eds., *Propaganda and Communication in World History* (Honolulu: East-West Center, 1979).

Latacz, Joachim, *Troy and Homer: Towards a Solution of an Old Mystery*, trans. Kevin Windle and Rosh Ireland (Oxford: Oxford University Press, 2004).

Lateiner, Donald, "The *Iliad*: An Unpredictable Classic," in Fowler, *The Cambridge Companion to Homer*, pp. 11–30.

Laudan, Larry, *Beyond Positivism and Relativism: Theory, Method, and Evidence* (Boulder, CO: Westview Press, 1996).

Laue, Theodore H. von, *Leopold von Ranke: The Formative Years* (Princeton, NJ: Princeton University Press, 1950).

"Soviet Diplomacy: G. V. Chicherin, People's Commissar for Foreign Affairs, 1918–1930," in Gordon A. Craig and Felix Gilbert, *The Diplomats 1919–1939*, vol. I: *The Twenties* (New York: Atheneum, 1965), pp. 234–81.

Lavisse, Ernest, *Louis XIV: La Fronde, Le roi, Colbert (1644–85)* (Paris: Hachette, 1905).

Lawler, Edward J, and Shane R. Thye, "Bringing Emotion into Social Exchange Theory," *Annual Review of Sociology* 25 (1999), pp. 217–44.

Lawrence, Andrew, "Imperial Peace or Imperial Method: Skeptical Inquiries into Ambiguous Evidence for the 'Democratic Peace'," in Lebow and Lichbach, *Theory and Evidence in Comparative Politics and International Relations*, pp. 199–228.

Layne, Christopher, "The Unipolar Illusion: Why New Great Powers Will Arise," *International Security* 17 (1993), pp. 5–51.

"Kant or Cant: The Myth of Democratic Peace," *International Security* 19 (1994), pp. 5–49.

Le Baker, Geoffrey, *Chronicle*, in Richard Barber, ed., *The Life and Campaigns of the Black Prince: From Contemporary Letters, Diaries and Chronicles* (Woodbridge, Suffolk: Boydell Press, 1986).

Le Goff, Jacques, *St. Louis* (Paris: Gallimard, 1996).

Le Patourel, John, "The Origins of the War," in Fowler, *The Hundred Years War*, pp. 28–50.

Leach, William, *Country of Exiles* (New York: Pantheon Books, 1999).

Leaman, Bertha, "The Influence of Domestic Policy upon Foreign Affairs in France, 1898–1905," *Journal of Modern History* 14 (December 1942), pp. 449–79.

Lear, Jonathan, *Aristotle: The Desire to Understand* (Cambridge: Cambridge University Press, 1988).

Lebovics, Herman, *The Alliance of Iron and Wheat in the Third Republic, 1860–1914* (Baton Rouge: Louisiana State University Press, 1988).

Lebow, David Bohmer and Richard Ned Lebow, *Running Red Lights and Ruling the World* (New York: Oxford University Press, forthcoming).

Lebow, Katherine, *Socialism in One City: Nowa Huta and the Transformation of Poland, 1949–1980* (Princeton, NJ: Princeton University Press, forthcoming).

Lebow, Richard Ned, "Divided Ireland," in Henderson, Lebow and Stoessinger, *Divided Nations in a Divided World*, pp. 197–266.

    White Britain and Black Ireland: Colonial Stereotypes and Social Policy (Philadelphia, PA: Institute for the Study of Human Issues, 1976).

    Between Peace and War: The Nature of International Crisis (Baltimore, MD: Johns Hopkins University Press, 1981).

    "Misconceptions in American Strategic Assessment," *Political Science Quarterly* 97 (Summer 1982), pp. 187–206.

    "Superpower Management of Security Alliances: The Soviet Union and the Warsaw Pact," in Arlene Idol Broadhurst, ed., *The Future of European Alliance Systems* (Boulder, CO: Westview, 1982), pp. 185–236.

    "Miscalculation in the South Atlantic: British and Argentine Intelligence Failures in the Falkland Crisis," *Journal of Strategic Studies* 6 (March 1983), pp. 1–29.

    "Windows of Opportunity: Do States Jump Through Them?" *International Security* 9 (1984), pp. 147–86.

    "Conclusions," in Robert Jervis, Richard Ned Lebow and Janice Gross Stein, *Psychology and Deterrence* (Baltimore, MD: Johns Hopkins University Press, 1985), pp. 203–32.

    "The Soviet Offensive in Europe: The Schlieffen Plan Revisited?" *International Security* 9, vol. 4 (Spring 1985), pp. 44–78.

    Nuclear Crisis Management: A Dangerous Illusion (Ithaca, NY: Cornell University Press, 1987).

    "Malign Analysts or Evil Empire? A Critique of Western Studies of Soviet Strategy," *International Journal* 44 (Winter 1988–9), pp. 1–40.

    "The Long Peace, the End of the Cold War, and the Failure of Realism," *International Organization* 48 (1994), pp. 249–77.

    "Thomas Schelling and Strategic Bargaining," *International Journal* 51, no. 3 (1996), pp. 555–76.

    "Beyond Parsimony: Rethinking Theories of Coercive Bargaining," *European Journal of International Relations* 4, no. 1 (1998), pp. 31–66.

    "Contingency, Catalysts and International System Change," *Political Science Quarterly* 115, no. 4 (Winter 2000), pp. 591–616.

    "A Data Set Named Desire: A Reply to William P. Thompson," *International Studies Quarterly*, 47 (June 2003), pp. 475–58.

    The Tragic Vision of Politics: Ethics, Interests and Orders (Cambridge: Cambridge University Press, 2003).

"Constructive Realism," *International Studies Review* 6, no. 2 (June 2004), pp. 346–8.

"What Was the Cold War? When and Why Did it End?," in Herrmann and Lebow, *Ending the Cold War*, pp. 1–30.

"Power, Persuasion and Justice," *Millennium* 33, no. 3 (2005), pp. 551–82.

"Reason, Emotion and Cooperation," *International Politics*, 42, no. 3 (2005), pp. 283–313.

"Tragedy, Politics and Political Science," *International Relations* 19, no. 3 (Spring 2005), pp. 329–36.

"The Memory of Politics" in Lebow, Kansteiner and Fogu, *The Politics of Memory in Postwar Europe*, pp. 1–39.

"Thucydides and Deterrence," *Security Studies* 16, no. 2 (2007), pp. 1–26.

Lebow, Richard Ned, Wulf Kansteiner and Claudio Fogu, eds., *The Politics of Memory in Postwar Europe* (Durham, NC: Duke University Press, 2006).

Lebow, Richard Ned and Mark Lichbach, eds., *Theory and Evidence in Comparative Politics and International Relations* (New York: Palgrave, 2007).

Lebow, Richard Ned and Thomas Risse-Kappen, *International Relations Theory and the End of the Cold War* (New York: Columbia University Press, 1995).

Lebow, Richard Ned and Janice Gross Stein, "Rational Deterrence Theory: I Think Therefore I Deter," *World Politics* 41 (January 1989), pp. 208–24.

"Deterrence: The Elusive Dependent Variable," *World Politics* 42 (April 1990), pp. 336–69.

"Afghanistan, Carter and Foreign Policy Change: The Limits of Cognitive Models," in Dan Caldwell and Timothy J. McKeown, eds., *Diplomacy, Force, and Leadership: Essays in Honor of Alexander L. George* (Boulder, CO: Westview, 1993), pp. 95–128.

"Reagan and the Russians," *Atlantic Monthly* 273 (February 1994), pp. 35–7.

We All Lost the Cold War (Princeton, NJ: Princeton University, 1994).

"The End of the Cold War as a Non-Linear Confluence," in Herrmann and Lebow, *Ending the Cold War*, pp. 189–218.

Lefebvre, Georges, *Napoleon from 18 Brumaire to Tilsit, 1799–1807*, trans. Henry E. Stockhold (New York: Columbia University Press, 1969).

Legro, Jeffrey, *Cooperation under Fire: Anglo-American Restraint during World War II* (Ithaca, NY: Cornell University Press, 1995).

Lehti, Marko, "Challenging the 'Old' Europe: Estonia and Latvia in a 'New' Europe," paper presented at the 5th Pan-European International Relations Conference, The Hague, September 2004.

Lembcke, Jerry, *The Spitting Image: Myth, Memory, and the Legacy of Vietnam* (New York: New York University Press, 1998).

Lemke, Douglas, "Continuity of History: Power Transition Theory and the End of the Cold War," *Journal of Peace Research* 34 (1996), pp. 203–36.

Regions of War and Peace (New York: Cambridge University Press, 2002).

Lendon, J. E., *Soldiers and Ghosts: A History of Battle in Classical Antiquity* (New Haven, CT: Yale University Press, 2005).

Lenin, V. I., *State and Revolution* (Moscow: Progress Publishers, 1917).

Imperialism: The Highest Stage of Capitalism (New York: International Publishers, 1941 [1916]).

Lenski, Noel Emmanuel, *Failure of Empire: Valens and the Roman State in the Fourth Century AD* (London: University College Press, 2003).

Lenson, George, *The Russian Push toward Japan* (Princeton, NJ: Princeton University Press, 1959).

Lentin, Anthony, *Lloyd George, Woodrow Wilson, and the Guilt of Germany: An Essay in the Pre-History of Appeasement* (Leicester: Leicester University Press, 1984).

"A Comment," in Boemeke, Feldman and Glaser, *Treaty of Versailles*, pp. 221–43.

Lerman, Katherine A., "The Kaiser's Elite? Wilhelm II and the Berlin Administration, 1890–1914," in Mombauer and Deist, *The Kaiser*, pp. 63–90.

Lerner, Barbara, "Self-Esteem and Excellence: The Choice and the Paradox," *American Educator* (Winter 1985), pp. 10–16.

Lesaffer, Randall, "Peace Treaties from Lodi to Westphalia," in Lesaffer, *Peace Treaties and International Law in European History* (Cambridge: Cambridge University Press, 2004), pp. 9–44.

Levesque, J., *The Enigma of 1989: The USSR and the Liberation of Eastern Europe*, trans. K. Martin (Berkeley: University of California Press, 1997).

Levi, Ariel and Philip E. Tetlock, "A Cognitive Analysis of Japan's 1941 Decision for War," *Journal of Conflict Resolution*, 24, no. 2 (June 1980), pp. 195–211.

Levi, Margaret, "A Model, a Method, and a Map: Rational Choice in Comparative and Historical Analysis," in Mark I. Lichbach and Alan S. Zuckerman, *Comparative Politics: Rationality, Culture, and Structure* (Cambridge: Cambridge University Press, 1997), pp. 19–41.

Levine, Steven I., "Perception and Ideology in Chinese Foreign Policy," in Robinson and Shumbaugh, *Chinese Foreign Policy*, pp. 40–6.

Levite, Ariel E., "Never Say Never Again: Nuclear Restraint Revisited," *International Security* 27 (2002–3), pp. 59–88.

Levitt, Michael and Dennis Ross, *Hamas: Politics, Charity, and Terrorism in Service of Jihad* (New Haven, CT: Yale University Press, 2006).

Levy, Jack S., "Historical Trends in Great Power War, 1495–1975," *International Studies Quarterly* 26, no. 2 (June 1982), pp. 278–300.

War in the Modern Great Power System, 1495–1975 (Lexington, MA: Lexington Books, 1983).

"Learning and Foreign Policy: Sweeping a Conceptual Minefield," *International Organization* 48, no. 2 (Spring 1994), pp. 279–312.

"Loss Aversion, Framing, and Bargaining: The Implications of Prospect The-
    ory for International Conflict," *International Political Science Review / Revue
    internationale de science politique* 17, no. 2, (1996), pp. 179–95.
"Theory, Evidence, and Politics in the Evolution of International Relations
    Research Programs," in Lebow and Lichbach, *Theory and Evidence in Com-
    parative Politics and International Relations*, pp. 177–98.
Levy, Jack S. and William R. Thompson, "Hegemonic Threats and Great-Power
    Balancing in Europe, 1495–1999," *Security Studies* 14, no. 1 (January–March
    2005), pp. 1–30.
Levy, Marion J. Jr., "'Does It Matter If He's Naked?' Bawled the Child," in Klaus
    Knorr and James N. Rosenau, *Contending Approaches to International Rela-
    tions* (Princeton, NJ: Princeton University Press, 1969), pp. 87–109.
Lewis, David K., *Convention: A Philosophical Study* (Cambridge, MA: Harvard Uni-
    versity Press, 1969).
Lewis, Sinclair, *Babbitt* (New York: Harcourt, Brace, 1922).
Libicki, Martin, "Rethinking War: The Mouse's New Roar," *Foreign Policy*, no. 117
    (Winter 1999–2000), pp. 30–43.
Lieven, D., *Russia and the Origins of the First World War* (New York: St. Martin's
    Press, 1983).
Lilla, Mark, *G. B. Vico: The Making of an Anti-Modern* (Cambridge, MA: Harvard
    University Press, 1993).
Lind, Michael, "In Defense of Liberal Nationalism," *Foreign Affairs* 73, no. 3
    (May/June 1994), pp. 87–99.
Lindow, John, *Comitatus, Individuals and Honor: Studies in North Germanic Insti-
    tutional Vocabulary* (Berkeley: University of California Press, 1975).
Lindgren, Jan, "Men, Money and Means," in Contamine, *War and Competition
    Between States*, pp. 129–62.
Linklater, Andrew, *Men and Citizens in the Theory of International Relations*
    (London: Macmillan, 1982).
    "The Question of the Next Stage in International Relations Theory: A Critical-
        Theoretical Point of View," *Millennium: Journal of International Studies* 21,
        no. 1 (1992), pp. 77–98.
    The Transformation of Political Community (Columbia: University of South Car-
        olina Press, 1998).
    "The Problem of Harm in World Politics," *International Affairs* 78, no. 2 (2002),
        pp. 319–38.
    "Norbert Elias: the 'Civilizing Process' and the Sociology of International Rela-
        tions," *International Politics* 41 (2004), pp. 3–35.
Linklater, Andrew and Hidemi Suganami, *The English School of International
    Relations: A Contemporary Assessment* (Cambridge: Cambridge University
    Press, 2006).

Lintott, Andrew, *Violence, Civil Strife and Revolution in the Classical City* (Baltimore, MD: Johns Hopkins University Press, 1982).

Little, Lester K., *Religious Poverty and the Profit Economy in Medieval Europe* (Ithaca, NY: Cornell University Press: 1978).

Little, Richard, "The Growing Relevance of Pluralism?" in Steve Smith, Ken Booth, and Marysia Zalewski, *International Theory: Positivism and Beyond* (Cambridge: Cambridge University Press, 1996), pp. 66–86.

"Historiography and International Relations," *Review of International Studies* 25, no. 2 (1999), pp. 291–9.

"Reconfiguring International Political Space: The Significance of World History," in *Political Space: New Frontiers of Change and Governance in a Globalizing World* (Albany: State University of New York Press, 2002), pp. 45–60.

Livy, *The Early History of Rome*, books I–V of *The History of Rome from its Foundations*, trans. Aubrey de Sélincourt (London: Penguin, 1960).

Llosa, Mario Vargas, "The Culture of Liberty," *Foreign Policy*, no. 112 (January/February 2001), pp. 66–71.

Lloyd, G. E. R., *The Ambitions of Curiosity: Understanding the World in Ancient Greece and China* (Cambridge: Cambridge University Press, 2002).

Llull, Ramon, *Book of the Order of Chivalry*, trans. Edward Caxton, ed. Alfred T. P. Byles (Oxford: Oxford University Press, 1926).

Ramon Lull's Book of Knighthood and Chivalry, trans. William Caxton (Highland Village, TX: Chivalry Bookshelf, 2001).

Locke, John, *Two Treatises of Government* (New York: Cambridge University Press, 1988).

Lockwood, William W., *The Economic Development of Japan: Growth and Structural Change, 1868–1938* (Princeton, NJ: Princeton University Press, 1954).

Loen, Johann Michael von, *Der Adel* (Ulm: Scriptor Verlag Königstein, 1982 [1752]).

Loew, C. J., *The Reluctant Imperialists: British Foreign Policy, 1878–1902* (London: Routledge and Kegan Paul, 1967).

Loew, John, *The Great Powers, Imperialism, and the German Problem, 1865–1935* (London: Routledge, 1994).

Lone, Stewart, *Japan's First Modern War: Army and Society in the Conflict with China, 1894–95* (London: St. Martin's Press, 1994).

Long, A. A., ed., *The Cambridge Companion to Early Greek Philosophy* (Cambridge: Cambridge University Press, 1999).

Longmore, Norman, *The Bombers: The RAF Offensive against Germany 1939–1945* (London: Hutchinson, 1983).

Lopez, Robert, *The Commercial Revolution of the Middle Ages, 950–1350* (Cambridge: Cambridge University Press, 1976).

Loraux, Nicole, "Mourir devant Troie, tomber pour Athènes: De la gloire du héros à l'idée de la cité," in G. Gnoli and Jean-Pierre Vernant, eds., *La mort, les morts dans les anciennes sociétés* (Cambridge: Cambridge University Press, 1982), pp. 16–62.

The Experiences of Tiresias, trans. Paula Wissing (Princeton, NJ.: Princeton University Press, 1995).

Lord, Albert Bates, *The Singer of Tales* (Cambridge, MA: Harvard University Press, 2000).

Lord, Carnes and David K. O'Connor, eds., *Essays on the Foundations of Aristotelian Political Science* (Berkeley: University of California Press, 1991).

Lott, Trent, *Herding Cats: A Life in Politics* (New York: Regan Books, 2005).

Lough, John, ed., *Locke's Travels in France, 1675–1679 as Related in his Journals, Correspondence, and Other Papers* (Cambridge: Cambridge University Press, 1953).

Louis XIV, *Mémoires de Louis XIV pour l'instruction du dauphin*, ed. Charles Dreyss, 2 vols. (Paris, 1860).

Memoirs for the Instruction of the Dauphin, trans. Paul Sonnino (New York: Free Press, 1970).

Louis, William Roger, *Imperialism: The Robinson and Gallagher Controversy* (New York: Viewpoints, 1976).

Lovejoy, Arthur O. and George Boas, *Primitivism and Related Ideas in Antiquity* (Baltimore, MD: Johns Hopkins University Press, 1935).

Low, Polly, *Interstate Relations in Classical Greece* (Cambridge: Cambridge University Press, 2007).

Lowe, C. J. and F. Marzari, *Italian Foreign Policy, 1870–1940* (London: Routledge and Kegan Paul, 1975).

Luard, Evan, *War in International Society: A Study in International Sociology* (New Haven, CT: Yale University Press, 1987).

Lucas, Colin, "Nobles, Bourgeois and the Origins of the French Revolution," in Johnson, *French Society and the Revolution*, pp. 88–131.

Luck, Edward C., "Tokyo's Quixotic Quest for Acceptance," *Far Eastern Economic Review*, May 2005, pp. 5–10.

Ludi, Regula, "What is So Special about Switzerland? Wartime Memory as a National Ideology in the Cold War Era," in Lebow, Kansteiner and Fogu, *Politics of Memory in Postwar Europe*, pp. 210–48.

Luhmann, Niklas, *A Sociological Theory of Law*, trans. Elizabeth King and Martin Albrow (Boston: Routledge and Kegan Paul, 1972).

Two Works by Niklas Luhmann (New York: Wiley, 1979).

"Trust: A Mechanism for the Reduction of Social Complexity," in Luhmann, *Two Works by Niklas Luhmann*, pp. 4–103.

Essays in Self Reference (New York: Columbia University Press, 1990).

"The 'State' of the Political System," in Luhmann, *Essays on Self-Reference*, pp. 65–148.

Social Systems, trans. John Bednarz, Jr. with Dirk Baecker (Stanford, CA: Stanford University Press, 1995).

Lukács, Georg, *History and Class Consciousness: Studies in Marxist Dialectics*, trans. Rodney Livingstone (Cambridge, MA: MIT Press, 1971).

The Destruction of Reason (London: Merlin Press, 1980 [1962]).

Lukes, Steven, *Emile Durkheim: His Life and Work. A Historical and Critical Study* (Stanford, CA: Stanford University Press, 1973).

"Power and the Battle for Hearts and Minds," *Millennium* 33, no. 3 (2005), pp. 477–94.

Power: A Radical View, 2nd edn (London: Palgrave, 2005).

Lustick, Ian, "Multiple Historical Records and the Problem of Selection Bias," *American Political Science Review* 90, no. 3 (1996), pp. 505–18.

Lustig, Nora, Barry P. Bosworth, and Robert Z. Lawrence, eds., *North American Free Trade Agreement: Assessing the Impact* (Washington, DC: Brookings Institution, 1992).

Luvaas, Jay, *The Military Legacy of the Civil War: The European Inheritance* (Chicago: University of Chicago Press, 1959).

Luxemburg, Rosa, *The Accumulation of Capital*, trans. Agnes Schwarzchild (New Haven, CT: Yale University Press, 1951 [1913]).

Lynn, John A., *Giant of the Grand Sie: The French Army, 1610–1715* (Cambridge: Cambridge University Press, 1997).

Battle: A History of Combat and Culture (Boulder, CO: Westview, 2003).

Lyotard, Jean-François, *The Postmodern Condition: A Report on Knowledge*, trans. Geoff Bennington and Brian Massumi (Minneapolis: University of Minnesota Press, 1984).

Lyttelton, Adrian, *The Seizure of Power: Fascism in Italy, 1919–1929* (Princeton, NJ: Princeton University Press, 1988).

Ma, J. T., "Fighting Poleis in the Ancient World," in Van Wees, *War and Violence in Ancient Greece*, pp. 337–76.

Machamer, Peter, "Teleology and Selective Processes," in Robert Colody, *Logic, Laws, and Life* (Pittsburgh, PA: University of Pittsburgh Press, 1977), pp. 129–42.

Machiavelli, Niccolò, *The Prince and The Discourses*, Modern Library College Editions (New York: Random House, 1950).

Discourses on Livy, trans. Harvey Mansfield and Nathan Tarcov (Chicago: University of Chicago Press, 1996).

Machinist, Peter, "Final Response: On the Study of the Ancients, Language, Writing and the State," in Seth Sanders, ed., *Margins of Writing, Origins of Cultures* (Chicago: Oriental Institute, 2006), pp. 291–300.

"Kingship and Divinity in Imperial Assyria," in Gary Beckman and Theodore J. Lewis, *Text, Artifact, and Image: Revealing Ancient Israelite Religion* (Providence, RI: Brown Judaic Studies, 2006), pp. 152–88.

McAleer, Kevin, *Dueling: The Call of Honor in Fin-de-Siècle Germany* (Princeton, NJ: Princeton University Press, 1994).

McCall, G., and Simmons, J., *Identities and Interactions* (New York: Free Press, 1978).

McCanles, Michael, *The Discourse of Il Principe* (Malibu, CA: Undena, 1983).

McCartney, Paul T., *Power and Progress: American National Identity, the War of 1898, and the Rise of American Imperialism* (Baton Rouge: Louisiana State University Press, 2006).

McClellan, David S., *Dean Acheson: The State Department Years* (New York: Dodd, Mead, 1976).

McCrae, Robert, *Leibniz: Perception, Apperception, and Thought* (Toronto: University of Toronto Press, 1976).

"The Theory of Knowledge," in Nicholas Jolley, ed., *The Cambridge Companion to Leibniz* (Cambridge: Cambridge University Press, 1995), pp. 176–98.

McCulloch, David, *The Path Between the Seas: The Creation of the Panama Canal, 1870–1914* (New York: Simon and Schuster, 1977).

McDermott, Rose, *Risk-Taking in International Politics: Prospect Theory to American Foreign Policy* (Ann Arbor: University of Michigan, 1998).

"The Feeling of Rationality: The Meaning of Neuroscientific Advances for Political Science," *Perspectives in Politics* 2 (December 2004), pp. 691–706.

ed., special issue of *Political Psychology* on Prospect Theory, 25 (April 2004), pp. 147–312.

McDonald, David McLaren, *United Government and Foreign Policy in Russia, 1900–1914* (Cambridge, MA: Harvard University Press, 1992).

McGuinness, Brian, ed., *Gottlob Frege: Collected Papers on Mathematics, Logic and Philosophy* (Oxford: Basil Blackwell, 1984).

MacIntyre, Alasdair, *After Virtue*, 2nd edn (Notre Dame, IN: Notre Dame University Press, 1984).

McKendrick, Neil, *The Birth of A Consumer Society: The Commercialization of Eighteenth Century England* (London: Hutchinson, 1983).

McKenzie, Robert and Allan Silver, *Angels in Marble: Working Class Conservatives in Urban England* (Chicago: University of Chicago Press, 1968).

McKeown, Timothy, "The Limitations of 'Structural' Theories of Commercial Policy," *International Organization* 40 (1986), pp. 43–64.

McKitterick, Rosamond, *The Frankish Kingdoms under the Carolingians, 715–987* (London: Longman, 1983).

The Carolingians and the Written Word (Cambridge: Cambridge University Press, 1989).

ed., *Carolingian Culture: Emulation and Innovation* (Cambridge: Cambridge University Press, 1994).

ed., *The New Cambridge Medieval History,* vol. II: *c.700–c.900* (Cambridge: Cambridge University Press, 1995).

"Eighth-Century Foundations," in McKitterick, *The New Cambridge Medieval History*, vol. II, pp. 681–94.

"The Carolingian Renaissance of Culture and Learning," in Story, ed., *Charlemagne*, pp. 151–66.

Mack Smith, Denis, *Italy: A Modern History*, rev. edn (Ann Arbor: University of Michigan Press, 1969).

"Benedetto Croce: History and Politics," *Journal of Contemporary History* 8, no. 1 (January 1973), pp. 167–88.

Mussolini's Roman Empire (London: Longman, 1976).

Mussolini (New York: Knopf, 1982).

Mackay, Christopher S., *Ancient Rome: A Military and Political History* (Cambridge: Cambridge University Press, 2004).

Mackie, Hilary, *Graceful Errors: Pindar and the Performance of Praise* (Ann Arbor: University of Michigan Press, 2003).

McLaughlin, Peter, *What Functions Explain* (Cambridge: Cambridge University Press, 2001).

McLean, Roderick R., *Royalty and Diplomacy in Europe, 1890–1914* (Cambridge: Cambridge University Press, 2001).

MacMillan, John, *On Liberal Peace: Democracy, War and the International Order* (New York: Tauris, 1998).

"Immanuel Kant and the Democratic Peace," in Jahn, *Classical Theory in International Relations*, pp. 52–73.

MacMillan, Margaret, *Paris 1919: Six Months that Changed the World* (New York: Random House, 2001).

McNeill, William H., *The Pursuit of Power: Technology, Armed Force, and Society since A.D. 1000* (Chicago: University of Chicago Press, 1982).

Mythistory and Other Essays (Chicago: University of Chicago Press, 1986).

"Territorial States Buried Too Soon," *Mershon International Studies Review* 41, Supplement 2 (November 1997), pp. 273–4.

Macpherson, C. B., *The Political Theory of Possessive Individualism: Hobbes to Locke* (Oxford: Oxford University Press, 1962).

McSweeny, Bill, *Security, Identity and Interests: A Sociology of International Relations* (Cambridge: Cambridge University Press, 1999).

"Introduction" to Thomas Hobbes, *Leviathan* (London: Penguin, 1968), pp. 9–63.

Macy, Michael and Robert Willer, "From Factors to Actors: Computational Sociology and Agent-Based Modeling," *Annual Review of Sociology* 28 (2002), pp. 143–66.

Maffesoli, Michel, *The Time of the Tribes: The Decline of Individualism in Mass Society* (London: Sage, 1996).

Magendie, Maurice, *La politesse mondiane et les théories de l'honnêteté en France au XXIIe siècle, de 1600 à 1660* (Paris: F. Alcan, 1925).

Mahoney, James, "Path Dependence in Historical Sociology," *Theory and Society* 29, no. 4 (August 2000), pp. 507–48.

Mallaby, Sebastian, "The Reluctant Imperialist: Terrorism, Failed States, and the Case for American Empire," *Foreign Affairs* 81 (March/April 2002), pp. 2–7.

Malmesbury, James Edward Harris, *Memoirs of an Ex-Minister: An Autobiography* (London: Longmans, Green, 1884).

Mancini, G. Federico, "The Italians in Europe," *Foreign Affairs* 79, no. 2 (March/April 2000), 122–34.

Mandeville, Bernard, *The Fable of the Bees, or, Private Vices, Publick Benefits*, ed. F. B. Kaye (Indianapolis, IN: Liberty Fund, 1988).

Mann, James, *Rise of the Vulcans: The History of Bush's War Cabinet* (New York: Penguin, 2004).

Mann, Michael, "The Autonomous Power of the State: Its Origins, Mechanisms and Results," in John A. Hall, *States in History* (Oxford: Basil Blackwell, 1986), pp. 109–36.

 The Sources of Social Power, vol. I: *A History of Power from the Beginning to A. D. 1760* (Cambridge: Cambridge University Press, 1986).

 States, War and Capitalism: Studies in Political Sociology (Oxford: Basil Blackwell, 1988).

 "Nation-States in Europe and Other Continents: Diversifying, Developing, Not Dying," *Daedalus* 122 (1993), pp. 115–40.

 The Sources of Social Power, vol. II: *The Rise of Classes and Nation-States, 1760– 1914* (Cambridge: Cambridge University Press, 1993).

 "Neither Nation-State Nor Globalism," *Environment and Planning* 28, no. 11 (1996), pp. 1960–4.

 "The First Failed Empire of the 21st Century Doctrine," *Review of International Studies* 30 (2004), pp. 631–53.

Mann, Thomas, *Reflections of a Nonpolitical Man*, trans. Walter D. Morris (New York: Ungar, 1987).

Manners, Ian, "European [Security] Union: From Existential Threat to Ontological Security," International Institute of Security Working Paper, 2002.

Mannheim, Karl, *Man and Society in an Age of Reconstruction: Studies in Modern Social Structure* (London: Routledge and Kegan Paul, 1940).

Manning, C. A. W., *The Nature of International Society* (London: London School of Economics, 1962).

Mansbach, Richard W. and Franke Wilmer, "War and the Westphalian State of Mind," in Albert, Jacobson, and Lapid, *Identities, Borders, Orders*, pp. 51–71.

Mansbridge, Jane J., "The Rise and Fall of Self-Interest in the Explanation of Polit-ical Life," in Jane J. Mansbridge, *Beyond Self-Interest* (Chicago: University of Chicago Press, 1990).

"Complicating Oppositional Consciousness," in Jane J. Mansbridge and Aldon D. Morris, eds., *Oppositional Consciousness: The Subjective Roots of Social Protest* (Chicago: University of Chicago Press, 2001), pp. 1–31.

Mansfield, Edward D. and Jack Snyder, "Democratization and the Danger of War," *International Security* 20 (1995), pp. 5–38.

Electing to Fight: Why Emerging Democracies Go to War (Cambridge, MA: MIT Press, 2005).

Maoz, Zeev, *Paths to Conflict: International Dispute Initiation, 1816–1976* (Boulder, CO: Westview, 1982).

Maoz, Zeev and Nasrin Abdolali, "Regime Types and International Conflict, 1816–1976," *Journal of Conflict Resolution* 33, no. 1 (1989), pp. 3–35.

Marcellinus, Ammianus, *The Later Roman Empire: A.D. 354–378*, ed. Andrew Wallace-Hadrill, trans. Walter Hamilton (New York: Penguin, 1986).

March, James G. and Johan P. Olsen, "The Logic of Appropriateness," ARENA Working Paper Series (Oslo: Centre for European Studies, University of Oslo, 2004).

Marchand, Suzanne L., *Down from Olympus. Archaeology and Philhellenism in Ger-many, 1750–1970* (Princeton, NJ: Princeton University Press, 1996).

Marcus, George E., *The Sentimental Citizen: Emotion in Democratic Politics* (Uni-versity Park: Pennsylvania State University Press, 2002).

Marcus, George, W. R. Neuman and M. Mackuen, *Affective Intelligence and Political Judgment* (Chicago: University of Chicago Press, 2000).

Margolis, Joseph and Jacques Catudal, *The Quarrel Between Invariance and Flux: A Guide for Philosophers and Other Players* (University Park: State University of Pennsylvania Press, 2001).

Marion, Russ, *The Edge of Organization: Chaos and Complexity Theories of Formal Social Systems* (Thousand Oaks, CA: Sage, 1999).

Markell, Patchen, *Bound by Recognition* (Princeton, NJ: Princeton University Press, 2003).

Markey, Daniel, "Prestige and the Origins of War: Returning to Realism's Roots," *Security Studies* 8 (Summer 1999), pp. 126–73.

Marks, J., "The Ongoing *Neikos*: Thersites, Odysseus and Achilleus," *American Journal of Philology* 126 (2005), pp. 1–31.

Marrus, Michael R., *The Holocaust in History* (Hanover, NH: University Press of New England, 1987).

The Nuremberg War Crimes Trial, 1945–46: A Documentary History (Boston: Bedford Books, 1997).

Marseille, J., *Empire colonial et capitalisme français. Histoire d'un divorce* (Paris: A. Michel, 1984).

Marshall, Byron K., *Capitalism and Nationalism in Prewar Japan: The Ideology of the Business Elite, 1868–1941* (Stanford, CA: Stanford University Press, 1967).

Marshall, Jonathan, *To Have and Have Not* (Berkeley: University of California Press, 1995).

Marshall, P. J., *The Making and Unmaking of Empires: Britain, India, and America c. 1750–1783* (Oxford: Oxford University Press, 2005).

Marshall, T. H., *Class, Citizenship, and Social Development* (New York: Doubleday, 1949).

   Citizenship and Social Class (Cambridge: Cambridge University Press, 1950).

Martínez Inglés, Amadeo, *El golpe que nunca existió* (Madrid: Foca, 2001).

Maruyama, Masao, *Thought and Behavior in Modern Japanese Politics* (New York: Oxford University Press, 1966).

Marx, Anthony W., *Faith in Nation: Exclusionary Origins of Nationalism* (Oxford: Oxford University Press, 2003).

Marx, Karl, *Early Writings*, trans. and ed. T. B. Bottomore (New York: McGraw-Hill, 1963).

   Capital, 3 vols. (Moscow: Progress Publishers, 1966).

   Writings of the Young Marx on Philosophy and Society, ed. Lloyd Easton and Kurt Guddat (Garden City, NY: Doubleday, 1967).

   A Contribution to the Critique of Political Economy (Moscow: Progress Publishers, 1970 [1859])

   Critique of Hegel's Philosophy of Right (Cambridge: Cambridge University Press, 1970).

   "The Bourgeoisie and the Counter-Revolution," *Neue Rheinische Zeitung*, December 14, 1848, in Karl Marx, *The Revolutions of 1848* (Harmondsworth: Penguin, 1973), pp. 192–4.

   Grundrisse: Foundations of the Critique of Political Economy, trans. Martin Nicolaus (New York: Random House, 1973).

Marx, Karl and Friedrich Engels, *Selected Works in One Volume* (London: Lawrence and Wishart, 1968).

   "On the Jewish Question," in Marx and Engels, *Collected Works*, vol. III (New York: International Publishers, 1972), pp. 146–74.

   "The Communist Manifesto," in Marx and Engels, *Collected Works*, vol. VI (New York: International Publishers, 1975), pp. 477–519.

   The German Ideology (New York: Prometheus, 1998).

Marx, Leo and Bruce Mazlish, eds., *Progress: Fact or Illusion?* (Ann Arbor: University of Michigan Press, 1996).

Masaki, Hisashi, "The Financial Characteristics of the Zaibutsu in Japan: The Old Zaibatsu and their Closed Finance," in Keiichiro Nakagawa, ed., *Marketing and Finance in the Course of Industrialization*, part I, ch. 2 (Tokyo: Tokyo University Press, 1978), pp. 33–54.

Maslow, Abraham H., *Motivation and Personality* (New York: Harper and Row, 1954).

Toward a Psychology of Being (Princeton, NJ: Van Nostrand, 1962).

Massie, Robert K., *Peter the Great: His Life and World* (New York: Knopf, 1980).

Mastanduno, Michael, "Preserving the Unipolar Moment: Realist Theories and U.S. Grand Strategy after the Cold War," *International Security* 21 (1997), pp. 44–98.

Masters, Roger D., *The Nature of Politics* (New Haven, CT: Yale University Press, 1989).

Mastny, Vojtech, "Stalin and the Prospects of a Separate Peace in World War II," *American Historical Review*, 77, no. 5 (December 1972), pp. 1365–88.

Mathews, Jessica T., "Power Shift," *Foreign Affairs* 76, no. 1 (January/ February 1997), pp. 50–66.

Matthews, George, *The Royal General Farms in Eighteenth Century France* (New York: Columbia University Press, 1958).

Matthews, Robert, *Human Rights and Canadian Foreign Policy* (Montreal: McGill-Queen's University Press, 1989).

Matthias, P and P. O'Brien, "Taxation in Britain and France, 1715–1810: Comparison of the Social and Economic Incidence of the Taxes Collected for the Central Government," *Journal of European Economic History* 5 (1976), pp. 601–50.

Maurer, John H., *The Outbreak of the First World War: Strategic Planning, Crisis Decision Making, and Deterrence Failure* (Westport, CT: Praeger, 1995).

Mauss, Marcel, *The Gift: The Form and Reason for Exchange in Archaic Societies.* trans. W. D. Halls (New York: Norton, 1990 [1925]).

Maxon, Yale, *Control of Japanese Foreign Policy: A Study of Civil–Military Rivalry, 1930–1945* (Berkeley: University of California Press, 1957).

Mayall, James, *Nationalism and International Society* (Cambridge: Cambridge University Press, 1990).

"Tragedy, Progress and the International Order: A Response to Frost," *International Relations* 14, no. 4 (2003), pp 497–503.

Mayer, Arno, "Domestic Causes of the First World War," in Leonard Krieger and Fritz Stern, eds., *The Responsibility of Power* (Garden City, NY: Doubleday, 1967), pp. 308–24.

"Internal Causes and Purposes of War in Europe," *Journal of Modern History* 41 (1969), pp. 291–303.

Mayr, Ernst, "Teleological and Teleonomic: A New Analysis," in Henry Plotkin, *Learning, Development, and Culture* (New York: Wiley, 1982), pp. 17–38.

Mazlish, Bruce, "Progress in History," *Historically Speaking*, 7, no. 4 (May/June 2006), pp. 18–21.

Mead, George Herbert, *Mind, Self, and Society* (Chicago: University of Chicago Press, 1934).

Mead, Walter Russell, *Special Providence: American Foreign Policy and How It Changed the World* (New York: Knopf, 2001).

Mearsheimer, John, "Back to the Future: Instability in Europe after the Cold War," *International Security* 15 (1990), pp. 5–56.

    "The Case for Ukrainian Nuclear Deterrent," *Foreign Affairs* 72, no. 3 (Summer 1993), pp. 50–66.

    "The False Promise of International Institutions," *International Security* 19 (1994–5), pp. 5–49.

    The Tragedy of Great Power Politics (New York: Norton, 2001).

Mecca, Andrew M., Neil J. Smelser and John Vasconcellos, eds., *The Social Importance of Self-Esteem* (Berkeley: University of California Press, 1989).

Medick, Hans, "Plebian Culture in the Transition to Capitalism," in Raphael Samuel and Gareth Stedman-Jones, eds., *Culture, Ideology, and Politics* (Cambridge: Cambridge University Press, 1982), pp. 84–112.

Meek, Ronald L., *Social Science and the Ignoble Savage* (Cambridge: Cambridge University Press, 1976).

Meierhenrich, Jens, "Forming States after Failure," in Robert I. Rotberg, *When States Fail* (Princeton, NJ: Princeton University Press, 2004), pp. 153–69.

Meiggs, Russell, *The Athenian Empire* (Oxford: Oxford University Press, 1972).

Meinecke, Friedrich, *Weltbürgertum und Nationalstaat* (Berlin: Oldenbourg, 1911), trans. as *Cosmopolitanism and the National State* (Princeton: Princeton University Press, 1970).

    Die Idea der Staatsräson in der neuerer Geschichte (Munich: Oldenbourg, 1924).

Melucci, A., *Nomads of the Present* (London: Hutchinson, 1989).

Menon, Rajan and Graham E. Fuller, "Russia's Ruinous Chechen War," *Foreign Affairs* 79, no. 2 (March/April 2000), pp. 32–44.

Mercer, Jonathan, "Anarchy and Identity," *International Organization* 49, no. 2 (1995), pp. 229–52.

Merelman, Richard, "Learning and Legitimacy," *American Political Science Review* 60 (1960), pp. 548–61.

Merkl, Peter H., *Political Violence under the Swastika. 581 Early Nazis* (Princeton, NJ: Princeton University Press, 1975).

Mermin, Jonathan, *Debating War and Peace: Media Coverage of U.S. Intervention in the Post-Vietnam Era* (Princeton, NJ: Princeton University Press, 1999).

Merridale, Catherine, *Ivan's War: The Red Army 1939–1945* (London: Faber and Faber, 2005).

Merton, Robert K., "The Self-Fulfilling Prophecy," *Antioch Review* 8 (1948), pp. 193–210.

    Social Theory and Social Structure (Glencoe, IL: Free Press, 1957).

Merwin, M. S., *La chanson de Roland* (New York: Vintage Books, 1970).

Mesquita, Bueno de, *The War Trap* (New Haven, CT: Yale University Press, 1991).

Mettam, Roger, *Power and Faction in Louis XIV's France* (Oxford: Blackwell, 1988).

Metz, Stephen, "A Wake for Clausewitz: Toward a Philosophy of 21st-Century Warfare," *Parameters* (1994–5), pp. 126–32.

"Racing Toward the Future: The Revolution in Military Affairs," *Current History* (April 1997), pp. 184–5.

"Which Army After Next? The Strategic Implications of Alternative Futures," *Parameters* 27, no. 3 (Autumn 1997), pp. 16–21.

Armed Conflict in the 21st Century: The Information Revolution and Post-Modern Warfare (Carlisle, PA: Strategic Studies Institute, 2000).

Meyer, Jean, *La noblesse bretonne* (Paris: Flammarion, 1972).

"States, Roads, War, and the Organization of Space," in Contamine, *War and Competition between States*," pp. 99–127.

Meyering, Theo, "Physicalism and Downward Causation in Psychology and the Special Sciences," *Inquiry* 43, no. 2 (2000), pp. 181–202.

Michaelis, Meir, *Mussolini and the Jews: German-Italian Relations and the Jewish Question in Italy, 1922–1945* (Oxford: Oxford University Press, 1978).

Michels, Roberto, *Political Parties* (New York: Collier, 1962).

Migdal, Joel S., ed., *Boundaries and Belonging: States and Societies in the Struggle to Shape Identities and Local Practices* (Cambridge: Cambridge University Press, 2004).

Milgram, Stanley, *Obedience to Authority* (New York: Harper and Row, 1974).

Milich, Klaus J., "Fundamentalism Hot and Cold: George W. Bush and the 'Return of the Sacred'," *Cultural Critique* 62 (Winter 2006), pp. 1–35.

Mill, John Stuart, "A Few Words on Non-Intervention," in Mill, *Dissertations and Discussions: Political, Philosophical, and Historical* (Boston: W. V. Spencer, 1964–7), vol. III, pp. 153–78.

"M. de Tocqueville on Democracy in America," in Mill, *Dissertations and Discourses*, vol. II, pp. 79–161.

"Considerations on Representative Government," in Mill, *Three Essays* (Oxford: Oxford University Press, 1975), pp. 145–426.

Miller, David and Michael Walzer, *Pluralism, Justice, and Equality* (Oxford: Oxford University Press, 1995).

Miller, Stephen G., *Ancient Greek Athletics* (New Haven, CT: Yale University Press, 2004).

Millett, Paul, "The Rhetoric of Reciprocity in Classical Athens," in Christopher Gill, Norman Postlethwaite and Richard Seaford, *Reciprocity in Ancient Greece*, pp. 227–54.

Lending and Borrowing in Ancient Athens (New York: Cambridge University Press, 1991).

Miliband, Ralph, *The State in Capitalist Society* (London: Weidenfeld and Nicolson, 1969).

Mills, C. Wright, *The Sociological Imagination* (New York: Oxford University Press, 1959).

Milosz, Czeslaw, *The Captive Mind* (New York: Vintage, 1990 [1951]).

Milward, Alan S., *The European Rescue of the Nation-State* (Berkeley: University of California Press, 1992).

Minister's Monitoring Committee on Change in the Department of National Defence and the Canadian Forces, *Final Report – 1999* (Ottawa: Ministry of Defence, 1999).

Mintz, Sidney, *Sweetness and Power: The Place of Sugar in Modern History* (New York: Penguin, 1985).

Mishal, Shaul and Avraham Sela, *The Political Hamas: Vision, Violence and Coexistence* (New York: Columbia University Press, 1983).

Mitchell, Timothy, "The Limits of the State: Beyond Statist Approaches and their Critics," *American Political Science Review* 85 (March 1991), pp. 77–96.

Mitrany, David, *A Working Peace System* (London: Royal Institute of International Affairs, 1943).

Mitzen, Jennifer, "Ontological Security in World Politics: State Identity and the Security Dilemma," *European Journal of International Relations* 12, no. 3 (2006), pp. 341–70.

Moatti, Claude, *Le raison de Rome* (Paris: Seuil, 1997).

Modelski, George, "Agraria and Industria: Two Models of the International System," in Klaus Knorr and Sidney Verba, *The International System: Theoretical Essays* (Princeton, NJ: Princeton University Press, 1961), pp. 118–43.

"Is World Politics Evolutionary Learning?" *International Organization* 44, no. 1 (1990), pp. 1–24.

Modelski, George and Kazimerz Poznanski, "Evolutionary Paradigms in the Social Sciences," *International Studies Quarterly* 40, no. 3 (1996), pp. 315–19.

Moe, Terry M., "On the Scientific Status of Rational Models," *American Journal of Political Science* 23, no. 1 (1979), pp. 215–43.

Moisy, Claude, "Myths of the Global Information Village," *Foreign Affairs*, no. 107 (Summer 1997), pp. 78–87.

Molasky, M., *The American Occupation of Japan and Okinawa: Literature and Memory* (London: Routledge, 1999).

Moltke, Helmuth von, *Erinnerungen, Briefe, Dokuments, 1877–1916* (Stuttgart: Der Kommende Tag, 1922).

Mombauer, Annika, *Helmuth von Moltke and the Origins of the First World War* (Cambridge: Cambridge University Press, 2001).

The Origins of the First World War: Controversies and Consensus (New York: Longman, 2002).

Mombauer, Annika and Wilhelm Deist, eds., *The Kaiser: New Research on Wilhelm II's Role in Imperial Germany* (Cambridge: Cambridge University Press, 2003).

Mommsen, Hans, *The Rise and Fall of Weimar Democracy*, trans. Elborg Forster and Larry Jones (Chapel Hill: University of North Carolina Press, 1996).

Mommsen, Wolfgang J., *Das Zeitalter des Imperialismus* (Frankfurt: Fischer Bucherei, 1969).

"Domestic Factors in German Foreign Policy Before 1914," *Central European History* 6 (March 1973), pp, 24–43.

Theories of Imperialism, trans. P. S. Falla (Chicago: University of Chicago Press, 1977).

"The Topos of Inevitable War in Germany in the Decade before 1914," in Volker R. Berghahn and Martin Kitchen, eds., *Germany in the Age of Total War* (London: Croom Helm, 1981), pp. 23–45.

Max Weber and German Politics, 1890–1920, trans. Michael S. Steinberg (Chicago: University of Chicago Press, 1984).

Grossmachtstellung und Weltpolitik 1870–1914. Die Aussenpolitik des Deutschen Reiches (Frankfurt: Propyleaen, 1993).

Imperial Germany, 1867–1918: Politics, Culture and Society in an Authoritarian State, trans. Richard Deveson (London: Arnold, 1995).

"Max Weber and the Peace Treaty of Versailles," in Boemeke, Feldman and Glaser, *Treaty of Versailles*, pp. 535–46.

Mommsen, Wolfgang and Jürgen Osterhammel, eds., *Imperialism and After: Continuities and Discontinuities* (London: Allen and Unwin, 1986).

Monk-Turner, Elizabeth, Donald Edwards, Steve Poorman *et al.*, "Predictors of Hand-Washing Behavior," *Social Behavior and Personality* 30, no. 8 (December 2002), pp. 751–6.

Monoson, S. Sara, *Plato's Democratic Entanglements: Athenian Politics and the Practice of Philosophy* (Princeton, NJ: Princeton University Press, 2000).

Montaigne, Michel Eyquem de, *Essays*, trans. Donald Frame (Stanford, CA: Stanford University Press, 1965).

Montesquieu, Charles-Louis de Secondat, *The Greatness of the Romans and their Decline*, trans. David Bindon (Ithaca, NY: Cornell University Press, 1968).

The Spirit of the Laws, trans. Anne M. Cohler, Baisa Carolyn Miller and Harold Samuel Stone (Cambridge: Cambridge University Press, 1989).

Montgelas, Max and Walter Schücking, eds., *Die deutschen Dokumente zum Kriegsausbruch 1914*, 3 vols. (Berlin: Deutsche Verlagsgesellschaft für Politik und Geschichte, 1922).

Moon, Bruce E., *The Political Economy of Basic Human Needs* (Ithaca, NY: Cornell University Press, 1991).

Moore, Barrington, Jr., *Political Power and Social Theory* (Cambridge, MA: Harvard University Press, 1958).

Injustice (White Plains, NY: M. E. Sharpe, 1968).

Social Origins of Dictatorship and Democracy: Lord and Peasant in the Making of the Modern World (Boston: Beacon Press, 1966).

Morazé, Charles, *Les bourgeois conquérants: XIXeme siècle* (Paris: Colin, 1957).

Morgan, Roger, "A European 'Society of States' – But Only States of Mind," *International Affairs*, 766, no. 3 (July 2000), pp. 559–74.

Morganstern, Oskar, "Thirteen Critical Points in Contemporary Economic Theory," *Journal of Economic Literature* 10, no. 4 (1972), pp. 1164–5.

Morgenthau, Hans J., "Théorie des sanctions internationales," *Revue de droit international et de législation comparé*," 3rd series 16 (1935), pp. 474–503; 809–36.

Scientific Man vs. Power Politics (Chicago: University of Chicago Press, 1946).

Politics Among Nations: The Struggle for Power and Peace (New York: Alfred Knopf, 1948; 3rd edn 1962; 4th edn 1967; 6th rev. edn, ed. Kenneth W. Thompson, 1985).

The Decline of Democratic Politics (Chicago: University of Chicago Press, 1958).

Dilemmas of Politics (Chicago: University of Chicago Press, 1958).

Politics in the Twentieth Century, vol. I: *The Decline of Democratic Politics* (Chicago: University of Chicago Press, 1962).

"The Purpose of Political Science," in James C. Charlesworth, ed., *A Design for Political Science: Scope, Objectives and Methods* (Philadelphia: American Academy of Political and Social Science, 1966), pp. 63–79.

"Fragment of an Intellectual Autobiography: 1904–1932," in Kenneth W. Thompson and Robert J. Myers, *A Tribute to Hans Morgenthau* (Washington, DC: New Republic Book Co., 1977), pp. 1–17.

In Defense of the National Interest: A Critical Examination of American Foreign Policy (Lanham, MD: University Press of America, 1982).

Political Theory and International Affairs: Hans J. Morgenthau on Aristotle's "The Politics," ed. Anthony F. Lang Jr. (Westport, CT: Praeger, 2004).

Morineau, Michel, "Budget de l'État et gestion des finances royales en France au dix-huitième siècle," *Revue Historique* 264, no. 536 (October–December 1980), pp. 289–336.

Morley, James William, *The Japanese Thrust into Siberia* (New York: Columbia University Press, 1957).

ed., *Dilemmas of Growth in Prewar Japan* (Princeton, NJ: Princeton University Press, 1971).

"Introduction: Choice and Consequence," in Morley, *Dilemmas of Growth in Prewar Japan*, pp. 3–32.

ed., *Deterrent Diplomacy: Japan, Germany, and the USSR, 1935–1940* (New York: Columbia University Press, 1976).

The Fateful Choice: Japan's Advance into Southeast Asia 1939–1941 (New York: Columbia University Press, 1980).

ed., *The China Quagmire: Japan's Expansion on the Asian Continent 1933–1941* (New York: Columbia University Press, 1983).

ed., *Japan Erupts: The London Naval Conference and the Manchurian Incident, 1828–1932* (New York: Columbia University Press, 1984).

The Final Confrontation: Japan's Negotiations with the United States, 1941 (New York: Columbia University Press 1994).

Morris, Justin and Nicholas J. Wheeler, "The Security Council's Crisis of Legitimacy and the Use of Force," *International Politics* 44, no. 2 (March 2007), pp. 232–49.

Morris, Martin, *Rethinking the Communicative Turn: Adorno, Habermas and the Problem of Communicative Freedom* (Albany: State University of New York Press, 2001).

Morris, Simon Conway, *The Crucible of Creation* (Oxford: Oxford University Press, 1998).

Morton, Frederic, *Thunder at Twilight: Vienna 1913/14* (New York: Scribner's, 1989).

Mosca, Gaetano, *The Ruling Class*, trans. Hannah Kahn (New York: McGraw-Hill 1939).

Moss, Scott and Paul Davidson, *Multi-Agent-Based Simulation* (Berlin: Springer-Verlag, 2001), pp. 49–67.

Mosse, George, *The Crisis of German Ideology: Intellectual Origins of the Third Reich* (New York: Grosset and Dunlap, 1964).

The Nationalization of the Masses: Political Symbolism and Mass Movements in Germany from the Napoleonic Wars through the Third Reich (New York: Columbia University Press, 1975).

Mote, Frederick W., *Intellectual Foundations of China*, 2nd edn (New York: McGraw-Hill, 1989).

Moya, Alex, "Rethinking the Nation-State from the Frontier," *Millennium* 32 (2003), pp. 267–94.

Moyar, Mark, *Triumph Forsaken: The Vietnam War, 1954–1963* (New York: Cambridge University Press, 2006).

Moynihan, Daniel Patrick, *Pandaemonium: Ethnicity in International Politics* (New York: Oxford University Press, 1993).

Mruk, Christopher J., *Self-Esteem Research, Theory, and Practice: Toward a Positive Psychology of Self-Esteem*, 3rd edn (New York: Springer, 2006).

Muellner, Leonard Charles, *The Anger of Achilles: Mēnis in Greek Epic* (Ithaca, NY: Cornell University Press, 1966).

Muir, Edward, *Mad Blood Stirring: Vendetta and Faction in Fruili during the Renaissance* (Baltimore, MD: Johns Hopkins University Press, 1993).

Muller, Jerry Z., *The Mind and the Market: Capitalism in Modern European Thought* (New York: Knopf, 2002).

Munemitsu, Mutsu, *Kenkenroku: A Diplomatic Record of the Sino-Japanese War, 1894–95*, trans. Gordon Berger (Princeton, NJ: Princeton University Press, 1982).

Murdoch, Iris, *The Sovereignty of the Good* (London: Routledge and Kegan Paul, 1970).

Murphy, Alexander B., "The Sovereign State System as Political-Territorial Ideal: Historical and Contemporary Considerations," in Thomas J. Biersteker and Cynthia Weber, *State Sovereignty as Social Construct* (Cambridge: Cambridge University Press, 1996), pp. 81–120.

Murphy, Craig N., "Understanding IR: Understanding Gramsci," *Review of International Studies* 24, no 3 (1998), pp. 417–25.

   "Global Governance: Poorly Done and Poorly Understood," *International Affairs*, 76, no. 4 (October 2000), pp. 789–803.

Murphy, Craig N. and Roger Tooze, *The New International Political Economy* (Boulder, CO: Lynne Rienner, 1991).

Murray, Shoon Kathleen and Christopher Spinosa, "The Post-9/11 Shift in Public Opinion: How Long Will It Last?" in Eugene R. Wittkopf and James M. McCormick, *The Domestic Sources of American Foreign Policy*, 4th edn (Lanham, MD: Rowman and Littlefield, 2004), pp. 97–115.

Murray, Williamson, "Thinking About Revolutions in Military Affairs," *Joint Forces Quarterly* (Summer 1997), pp. 69–76.

Murray, Williamson and Allan R. Millett, *A War To Be Won: Fighting the Second World War* (Cambridge, MA: Harvard University Press, 2000).

Musil, Robert, *The Man Without Qualities*, trans. Sophie Wilkins (London: Picador, 1995).

Muthu, Sankar, *Enlightenment Against Empire* (Princeton, NJ: Princeton University Press, 2003).

Mutz, Diana C., *Hearing the Other Side: Deliberative versus Participatory Democracy* (Cambridge: Cambridge University Press, 2006).

Myers, Ramon and Mark Peattie, eds., *The Japanese Colonial Empire* (Princeton, NJ: Princeton University Press, 1984).

Naff, Thomas, "The Ottoman Empire and the European States System," in Bull and Watson, *Expansion of International Society*, pp. 143–70.

Nagei, Yonosuke and Akira Iriye, *The Origins of the Cold War in Asia* (Tokyo: University of Tokyo Press, 1977).

Nagy, Gregory, *The Best of the Acheans: Concepts of the Hero in Archaic Greek Poetry* (Baltimore, MD: Johns Hopkins University Press, 1999).

Naimark, Norman, *Russians in Germany: A History of the Soviet Zone* (Cambridge, MA: Harvard University Press, 1995).

Najita, Tetsuo, "Nakano Seigō and the Spirit of the Meiji Restoration in Twentieth Century Japan," in Morley, *Dilemmas of Growth in Prewar Japan*, pp. 375–422.

Nandy, Ashis, *The Intimate Enemy: Loss and Recovery of Self under Colonialism* (Delhi: Oxford University Press, 1983).

Nardin, Terry, *Laws, Morality, and the Relations of States* (Princeton, NJ: Princeton University Press, 1983).

   The Ethics of War and Peace: Religious and Secular Perspectives (Princeton, NJ: Princeton University Press, 1998).

Narilkar, Amrita, "Peculiar Chauvinism or Strategic Calculation? Explaining the Negotiating Strategy of a Rising India," *International Affairs* 82, no. 1 (2006), pp. 59–76.

Narilkar, Amrita and Andrew Hurrell, *Pathways to Power: Brazil and India in International Regimes*, forthcoming.

National Commission on Terrorist Attacks, *The 9/11 Commission Report: Final Report of the National Commission on Terrorist Attacks upon the United States* (New York: Norton, 2004).

Nees, Lawrence, *A Tainted Mantle: Hercules and the Classical Tradition at the Carolingian Court* (Philadelphia: University of Pennsylvania Press, 1991).

Nehamas, Alexander, *Nietzsche: Life as Literature* (Cambridge, MA: Harvard University Press, 1987).

Neiberg, Michael S., *Fighting the Great War: A Global History* (Cambridge, MA: Harvard University Press, 2005).

Neisser, Ulric, "John Dean's Memory: A Case Study," *Cognition* 9 (1981), pp. 1–22.

"The Psychology of Memory and the Socio-Linguistics of Remembering," *The Psychologist* 5 (1992), pp. 451–2.

ed., *The Perceived Self: Ecological and Interpersonal Sources of Self-Knowledge* (Cambridge: Cambridge University Press, 1993).

Neisser, Ulric and Fivush, R., *The Remembering Self: Construction and Accuracy in the Self Narrative* (Cambridge: Cambridge University Press, 1994).

"Self-Narratives: True and False," in Neisser and Fivush, *The Remembering Self*, pp. 1–18.

Nelson, Janet L., "The Frankish Kingdoms, 814–898: The West," in McKitterick, *The New Cambridge Medieval History*, vol. II, pp. 110–41.

"Kingship and Royal Government," in McKitterick, *The New Cambridge Medieval History*, vol. II, pp. 383–430.

"Kingship and Empire," in Burns, *The Cambridge History of Medieval Political Thought*, pp. 211–51.

"Kingship and Empire in the Carolingian World," in Story, *Charlemagne*, pp. 52–87.

Nelson, M. Frederick, *Korea and the Old Orders in East Asia* (Baton Rouge: Louisiana State University Press, 1945).

Neumann, Franz, *Behemoth: The Structure and Practice of National Socialism* (London: Gollancz, 1944).

Neumann, Iver B., *Uses of the Other: "The East" in European Identity Formation* (Minneapolis: University of Minnesota Press, 1999).

"Russia as a Great Power, 1815–2007," *Journal of Inernational Relations and Development* 11 (2008), pp. 128–51.

Neumann, Iver B. and Jennifer Welsh, "The Other in European Self-Definition: An Addendum to the Literature on International Society," *Review of International Studies* 17, no. 4 (1991), pp. 327–48.

Neuschel, Kristen B., *Word of Honor: Interpreting Noble Culture in Sixteenth Century France* (Ithaca, NY: Cornell University Press, 1989).

Neustadt, Richard, *Presidential Power: The Politics of Leadership* (New York: Wiley, 1960).

Newbolt, Henry, *The Book of the Happy Warrior* (London: Longmans and Green, 1917).

Newbury, C. W., "The Development of French Policy in the Lower and Upper Niger, 1880–1898," *Journal of Modern History* 31 (January 1959), pp. 16–26.

Newton, Stella Mary, *Fashion in the Age of the Black Prince: A Study of the Years 1340–1365* (Woodbrdge, Suffolk: Boydell, 1980).

Nexon, Daniel H. and Thomas Wright, "What's at Stake in the American Empire Debate?," *American Political Science Review* 101, no. 2 (May 2007), pp. 253–72.

Neyrey, Jerome H., *Honor and Shame in the Gospel of Matthew* (Louisville, KY: Westminster John Knox Press, 1998).

Ng, Wendy, *Japanese-American Internment in World War II: A History and Study Guide* (Westport, CT: Greenwood, 2002).

Nicasie, M. J., *Twilight of Empire: The Roman Army from the Reign of Diocletian until the Battle of Adrianople* (Amsterdam: J. C. Gieben, 1998).

Nicolson, Harold, *The Meaning of Prestige* (Cambridge: Cambridge University Press, 1937).

    The Congress of Vienna: A Study in Allied Unity, 1812–1822 (London: Methuen, 1961).

Nichols, J. Alden, *Germany after Bismarck: The Caprivi Era* (Cambridge, MA: Harvard University Press, 1958).

Nicholson, Nigel James, *Aristocracy and Athletics in Archaic and Classical Greece* (Cambridge: Cambridge University Press, 2005).

Nicholson, Peter, *The Political Philosophy of the British Idealists* (Oxford: Oxford University Press, 1990).

Nietzsche, Friedrich, *On the Genealogy of Morals*, trans. and ed. Walter Kaufmann (New York: Vintage, 1967).

    Human, All Too Human, trans. R. J. Hollingdale (Cambridge: Cambridge University Press, 1986).

    Thus Spake Zarathustra (New York: Dover, 1999 [1924]).

    The Gay Science, ed. Bernard Williams, trans. Josefine Nauckhoff and Adrian del Caro (Cambridge: Cambridge University Press, 2001).

Nincic, Miroslav, *Renegade Regimes: Confronting Deviant Behavior in World Politics* (New York: Columbia University Press, 1989).

Ninkovich, Frank, *Modernity and Power: A History of the Domino Theory in the Twentieth Century* (Chicago: University of Chicago Press, 1994).

Nippel, Wilfried, "The Construction of the 'Other,'" in Harrison, *Greeks and Barbarians*, pp. 278–310.

Nipperdey, Thomas, "Nationalidee und Nationaldenkmal in 19. Jahrhundert," *Historische Zeitschrift* 106 (1968), pp. 529–85.

Nachdenken über die deutsche Geschichte (Munich: Beck, 1986).

Nisbet, Richard E., *The Geography of Thought: How Asians and Westerners Think Differently . . . and Why* (New York: Free Press, 2003).

Nisbet, Robert, *Twilight of Authority* (New York: Oxford University Press, 1975).

Nish, Ian, *The Alliance in Decline: A Study in Anglo-Japanese Relations, 1908–23* (London: Athlone, 1972).

The Anglo-Japanese Alliance: The Diplomacy of Two Island Empires, 1894–1907, 2nd edn (London: Athlone, 1985).

Japan's Struggle with Internationalism (London: Athlone, 1992).

Japanese Foreign Policy in the Interwar Period (Westport, CT: Praeger, 2002).

Noakes, Jeremy, *Nazi Party in Lower Saxony* (Oxford: Oxford University Press, 1971).

Noble, Thomas F. X., "The Papacy in the Eighth and Ninth Centuries," in McKitterick, *The New Cambridge Medieval History*, vol. II, pp. 563–86.

Nordlinger, Eric, *On the Autonomy of the Democratic State* (Cambridge, MA: Harvard University Press, 1981).

North, Douglas C., *Structure and Change in Economic History* (New York: Norton, 1981).

Institutions, Institutional Change and Economic Performance (Cambridge: Cambridge University Press, 1990).

North, Douglas C. and Robert Paul Thomas, *Rise of the Western World: A New Economic History* (Cambridge: Cambridge University Press, 1973).

North, Dudley, *Discourses on Trade* (London, 1690).

Norton, Robert E., *The Beautiful Soul: Aesthetic Morality in the Eighteenth Century* (Ithaca, NY: Cornell University Press, 1995).

Nossal, Kim, *The Politics of Canadian Foreign Policy* (Toronto: Prentice-Hall, 1996).

Nove, Alec, "Was Stalin Really Necessary?" *Problems of Communism* 25, no. 4 (1976), pp. 49–62.

An Economic History of the Soviet Union (Harmondsworth: Penguin, 1982).

Nowak, M. A. and K. Sigmund, "A Strategy of Win-Shift, Lose-Stay that Outperforms Tit-for-Tat in the Prisoner's Dilemma Game," *Nature* 364 (1993), pp. 56–8.

Nowak, M.A., K. M. Page and K. Sigmund, "Fairness and Reason in the Ultimate Game," *Science* 289, September 8, 2000, pp. 1773–5.

Nozick, Robert, *Anarchy, State, and Utopia* (New York: Basic Books, 1974).

Nunn, Sam and Adam N. Stulberg, "The Many Faces of Modern Russia," *Foreign Affairs*, 79, no. 2 (March/April 2000), pp. 45–62.

Nussbaum, Martha, *The Fragility of Goodness: Luck and Ethics in Greek Tragedy and Philosophy* (New York: Cambridge University Press, 1986).

"Aristotelian Social Democracy," in R. Bruce Douglas, Gerald M. Mara and Henry S. Richardson, *Liberalism and the Good* (New York: Routledge, 1990).

Upheavals of Thought: The Intelligence of Emotion (Cambridge: Cambridge University Press, 2001).

Nye, Joseph S. Jr., *Bound to Lead: The Changing Nature of American Power* (New York: Basic Books, 1990).

Masculinity and Male Codes of Honor in Modern France (Oxford: Oxford University Press, 1993).

"The Decline of America's Soft Power," *Foreign Affairs* 83 (2004), pp. 16–21.

O'Brien, P. K., "Imperialism and the Rise and Decline of the British Economy, 1688–1989," *New Left Review* 238 (1998), pp. 48–80.

O'Neill, Barry, *Honor, Symbols, and War* (Ann Arbor: University of Michigan Press, 1999).

Oakley, S. P., *A Commentary on Livy, Books 1–5* (Oxford: Oxford University Press, 1997).

"The Early Republic," in Flower, *The Cambridge Companion to the Roman Republic*, pp. 15–30.

Ober, Josiah, *Mass and Elite in Democratic Athens: Rhetoric, Ideology, and the Power of the People* (Princeton, NJ: Princeton University Press, 1989).

"Aristotle's Political Sociology: Class, Status, and Order in the *Politics*," in Carnes Lord and David K. O'Conner, *Essays on the Foundations of Aristotelian Political Science* (Berkeley: University of California Press, 1991), pp. 112–35.

"How to Criticize Democracy in Late Fifth- and Fourth-Century Athens," in J. Peter Euben, John Wallach and Josiah Ober, *Athenian Political Thought and the Reconstruction of American Democracy* (Ithaca, NY: Cornell University Press, 1994), pp. 149–71.

Ober, Josiah and Charles Hedrick, eds., *Dēmokratia: A Conversation on Democracies, Ancient and Modern* (Princeton, NJ: Princeton University Press, 1996).

Offer, Avner, "Going to War in 1914: A Matter of Honour?," *Politics and Society*, 23 (1995), pp. 213–41.

"Costs and Benefits, Prosperity and Security, 1870–1914," in Andrew Porter and Aline Low, eds., *The Oxford History of the British Empire*, vol. III: *The Nineteenth Century* (Oxford: Oxford University Press, 1999), pp. 690–711.

Ogata, Sadako, *Defiance in Manchuria* (Berkeley: University of California Press, 1964).

Ogden, C. K. and I. A. Richards, *The Meaning of Meaning: A Study of the Influence of Language upon Thought and of the Science of Symbolism*, 4th rev. edn, with supplementary essays by B. Malinowski and F. G. Crookshank (New York: Harcourt Brace, 1936).

Ogden, Daniel, "Homosexuality and Warfare in Ancient Greece," in Alan B. Lloyd, ed., *Battle in Antiquity* (London: Duckworth, 1996), pp. 107–68.

Ōhata, Tokushirō, "The Anti-Comintern Pact, 1935–1939," in Morley, *Deterrent Diplomacy*, pp. 9–112.

Oka, Yoshitake, *Konoe Fumimaro: A Political Biography*, trans. Shumpei Okamoto and Patricia Murray (Tokyo: University of Tokyo Press, 1983).

Okamoto, Shumpei, *The Japanese Oligarchy and the Russo-Japanese War* (New York: Columbia University Press, 1970).

Okey, Robin, *The Hapsburg Monarchy* (New York: St. Martin's Press, 2001).

Oldmeadow, Julian and Susan T. Fiske, "System-Justifying Ideologies Moderate Status = Competence Stereotypes: Roles for Belief in a Just World and Social Dominance Orientation," *European Journal of Social Psychology* 37 (2007), pp. 1135–48.

Olender, Maurice, *The Languages of Paradise. Race, Religion, and Philology in the Nineteenth Century*, trans. Arthur Goldhammer (Cambridge, MA: Harvard University Press, 1992).

Oliver, Dean F., "How Much Was Never Enough? Canadian Defence and 11 September," in Norman Hillmer and Maureen Appel Molot, eds., *Canada Among Nations 2002: A Fading Power* (Dom Mills, Ont.: Oxford University Press, 2002), pp. 122–40.

Olson, M., *The Logic of Collective Action* (Cambridge, MA: Harvard University Press, 1965).

Olwig, Kenneth, *Landscape, Nature, and the Body Politic: From Britain's Renaissance to America's New World* (Madison: University of Wisconsin Press, 2002).

Ong, Graham Gerard, "Building and IR Theory with 'Japanese Characteristics': Nishida Kitarō and 'Emptiness,'" *Millennium* 33, no. 1 (2004), pp. 3–58.

Onuf, Nicholas G., *World of our Making* (Columbia: University of South Carolina Press, 1989).

"Levels," *European Journal of International Relations* 1, no. 1 (March 1995), pp. 35–8.

"Constructivism: A User's Manual," in Kubálková, Onuf and Kowert, *International Relations in a Constructed World*, pp. 58–78.

The Republican Legacy in International Thought (New York: Cambridge University Press, 1998).

"Writing Large: Habit, Skill, and Grandiose Theory," in Heidi Hobbs, *Pondering Postinternationalism* (Albany, NY: SUNY Press, 2000), pp. 99–113.

"The Politics of Constructivism," in K. M. and K. E. Jörgensen, *Constructing International Relations: The Next Generation* (London: M. E. Sharpe, 2001), pp. 236–54.

"Late Modern Civil Society," in Randall Germain and Michael Kenny, eds., *The Idea of Global Civil Society: Politics and Ethics in a Globalizing Era* (New York: Routledge, 2005), pp. 236–52.

Onuf, Nicholas G. and Paul Kowert, *International Relations in a Constructed World* (Armonk, NY: M. E. Sharpe, 1998).

Onuf, Nicholas G. and Peter Onuf, *Nations, Markets, and War: Modern History and the American Civil War* (Charlottesville: University of Virginia Press, 2006).

Opotow, Susan, "Moral Exclusion and Injustice," *Journal of Social Issues* 46, no. 1 (1990), pp. 1–20.

Oren, Ido, *Our Enemies and US: America's Rivalries and the Making of Political Science* (Ithaca, NY: Cornell University Press, 2003).

Organski, A. F. K., *World Politics*, 2nd edn (New York: Knopf, 1967).

Organski, A. F. K. and Jacek Kugler, *The War Ledger* (Chicago: University of Chicago Press, 1980).

Orgel, Stephen, *The Illusion of Power: Political Theater in the English Renaissance* (Berkeley: University of California Press, 1975).

 The Authentic Shakespeare and Other Problems of the Early Modern Stage (New York: Routledge, 2002).

Orla-Bukowska, Annamaria, "New Threads on an Old Loom: National Memory and Social Identity in Postwar and Post-Communist Poland," in Lebow, Kansteiner and Fogu, *The Politics of Memory in Postwar Europe*, pp. 177–209.

Ormrod, David, *The Rise of Commercial Empires: England and the Netherlands in the Age of Mercantilism, 1650–1770* (New York: Cambridge University Press, 2003).

Ormrod, W. Mark, "England: Edward II and Edward III," in Jones, *The New Cambridge Medieval History*, vol. VI, pp. 273–96.

Orren, Karen and Stephen Skowronek, "In Search of Political Development," in David F. Ericson and Louisa Bertch Green, *The Liberal Tradition in American Politics: Reassessing the Legacy of American Liberalism* (New York: Routledge, 1999), pp. 29–42.

Ortner, Sherry, "Resistance and the Problem of Ethnographic Refusal," *Comparative Studies in Society and History* 37, no. 1 (1995), pp. 173–93.

Orwin, Clifford, *The Humanity of Thucydides* (Princeton, NJ: Princeton University Press, 1994).

Osborne, Robin, "Homer's Society," in Fowler, *The Cambridge Companion to Homer*, pp. 206–19.

Osiander, Andreas, "Sovereignty, International Relations, and the Westphalian Myth," *International Organization* 55, no. 2 (Spring 2001), pp. 251–87.

Österreichs-Ungarns Aussenpolitik von der bosnischen Krise 1908 bis zum Kriegsausbruch 1914: Diplomatische Aktenstücke des Österreich-ungarischen Ministeriums des Äussen, ed. Ludwig von Bittner and Hans Uebersberger (Vienna: Österrichischer Bundesverlag, 1930).

Osterud, Oyvind, "The Narrow Gate: Entry to the Club of Sovereign States," *Review of International Studies*, 23, no. 2 (1997), pp. 167–84.

Ougaard, Morten and Richard Higgott, eds., *Towards a Global Polity* (London: Routledge, 2002).

Ovid, *The Metamorphoses*, trans. Allen Mandelbaum (New York: Harcourt Brace, 1993).

Amores, trans. Grant Showerman (Cambridge, MA: Harvard University Press, 1997).

Owen, John, "How Liberalism Produces the Democratic Peace," *International Security* 19 (1994), pp. 87–125.

Owens, Patricia, *Between War and Politics: International Relations and the Thought of Hannah Arendt* (Oxford: Oxford University Press, 2007).

Oz-Salzberger, Fania, "Civil Society in the Scottish Enlightenment," in Kaviraj and Khilnani, *Civil Society*, pp. 58–83.

Padrone, A., "Le reazioni dell'opinione pubblica italiana all'intervento nella seconda guerra mondiale," *Revista di storia della storiographica moderna* 6 (1985), pp. 57–90.

Pagden, Anthony, *The Fall of Natural Man: The American Indian and the Origins of Comparative Ethnology* (Cambridge: Cambridge University Press, 1982).

   ed., *The Languages of Political Theory in Early Modern Europe* (Cambridge: Cambridge University Press, 1987).

   Lords of All the World: Ideologies of Empire in Spain, Britain and France c. 1500–1800 (New Haven, CT: Yale University Press, 1995).

Pagels, Heinz, *The Cosmic Code: Quantum Physics as the Language of Nature* (London: Penguin Books, 1982).

Painter, S., *French Chivalry. Chivalric Ideas and Practices in Medieval France* (Baltimore, MD: Johns Hopkins University Press, 1940).

Palmer, R. R., "Frederick the Great, Guibert, Bulow: From Dynastic to National War," in Paret, *Makers of Modern Strategy*, pp. 91–119.

Pape, Helmut, "Final Causality in Peirce's Semiotics and his Classification of the Sciences," *Transactions of the Charles S. Peirce Society* 29, no. 4 (1993), pp. 581–607.

Pape, Robert A., "Soft Balancing: How States Pursue Security in a Unipolar World," annual meeting of the American Political Science Association, Chicago, September 2–5, 2004.

Paret, Peter, *Clausewitz and the State* (Oxford: Oxford University Press, 1976).

   ed., *Makers of Modern Strategy* (Princeton, NJ: Princeton University Press, 1986).

Pareto, Vilfredo, *The Rise and Fall of Elites: An Application of Theoretical Sociology* (New Brunswick, NJ: Transaction, 1991).

Parker, Geoffrey, *The Grand Strategy of Phillip II* (New Haven, CT: Yale University Press, 1998).

   The Military Revolution: Military Innovation and the Rise of the West 1500–1800, 3rd edn (Cambridge, MA: Cambridge University Press, 2000).

Parkin, Frank, *Class, Inequality and the Political Order* (New York: Praeger, 1971).

Parry, Clive, "The Function of Law in the International Community," in Max Sorensen, *Manual of Public International Law* (New York: St. Martin's Press, 1968), pp. 175–245.

Parry, J. and M. Bloch, *Money and the Morality of Exchange* (Cambridge: Cambridge University Press, 1989).

Parry, J. H., *The Establishment of the European Hegemony: 1415–1715*, 3rd rev. edn (New York: Harper Torchbooks, 1966).

Parry, Milman, *The Making of Homeric Verse* Oxford: (Oxford University Press, 1971).

Parson, Edward A., *Protecting the Ozone Layer* (Oxford: Oxford University Press, 2003).

Parsons, Craig, *How to Map Arguments in Political Science* (New York: Oxford University Press, forthcoming).

Parsons, Talcott, *The Structure of Social Action* (New York: McGraw-Hill, 1937).

    Essays in Sociological Theory (Glencoe, IL: Free Press, 1949).

    The Social System (Glencoe, IL: Free Press, 1951).

    Toward A General Theory of Action (Cambridge, MA: Harvard University Press, 1951).

    Economy and Society (Glencoe, IL: Free Press, 1957).

Pascal, Blaise, *Pensées*, trans. A. J. Krailsheimer (London: Penguin, 1966).

Patomäki, Heikki, "How to Tell Better Stories about World Politics," *European Journal of International Relations* 2, no. 1 (1996), pp. 105–34.

    "Problems of Democratizing Global Governance," *European Journal of International Relations* 9 (2003), pp. 347–76.

Patterson, Cynthia, "Other Sorts: Slaves, Foreigners, and Women in Periclean Athens," in Samons, *The Cambridge Companion to the Age of Pericles*, pp. 153–78.

Paul, T. V., "The Enduring Axioms of Balance of Power Theory and their Contemporary Relevance," in T. V. Paul, James J. Wirtz and Michel Fortmann, *Balance of Power: Theory and Practice in the 21st Century* (Stanford, CA: Stanford University Press, 2004), pp. 1–18.

Paul, T. V., G. John Ikenberry and John A. Hall, eds., *The Nation-State in Question* (Princeton, NJ: Princeton University Press, 2003).

Paxton, Robert, *Anatomy of Fascism* (New York: Knopf, 2004).

Peitsch, Helmut, Charles Burdett and Claire Gorrara, eds., *European Memories of the Second World War* (New York: Berghahn, 1999).

Pelcynski, Z. A., "The Hegelian Conception of the State," in Pelcynski, ed., *Hegel's Political Philosophy: Problems and Perspectives* (Cambridge: Cambridge University Press, 1975), pp. 1–29.

Peled, Alon, "The New Sciences, Self-Organization and Democracy," *Democratization* 7, no. 2 (2000), pp. 19–35.

Peltonen, Markku, *The Duel in Early Modern England: Civility, Politeness and Honour* (Cambridge: Cambridge University Press, 2003).

Pelz, Stephen E., *Race to Pearl Harbor* (Cambridge, MA: Harvard University Press, 1974).

Pennebaker, J. W., Paez, D. and Rimé, B., *Collective Memory of Political Events: Social Psychological Perspectives* (Mahwah, NJ: Lawrence Erlbaum, 1997).

Peperzak, Adriaan, "Hegel Contra Hegel in his Philosophy of Right: The Contradictions of International Politics," *Journal of the History of Philosophy* 32, no. 2 (1994), pp. 241–63.

Pepys, Samuel, *The Diary of Samuel Pepys*, 3 vols. (London: J. M. Dent, 1906).

Peristiany, J. G., ed., *Honour and Shame, the Values of Mediterranean Society* (Chicago: University of Chicago Press, 1966).

Perkel, Christine, "The Golden Age and its Contradictions in the Poetry of Virgil," *Virgilius* 48 (2002), pp. 3–39.

Perkins, Merle J., *The Moral and Political Philosophy of the Abbé de Saint Pierre* (Geneva: Droz, 1959).

Perlman, Shalom, "Panhellenism, the Polis and Imperialism," *Historia*, 25 (1976), pp. 1–30.

"Hegemony and *Archē* in Greece: Fourth Century Views," in Richard Ned Lebow and Barry S. Strauss, *Hegemonic Rivalry: From Thucydides to the Nuclear Age* (Boulder, CO: Westview, 1991), pp. 269–88.

Péronnet, Michel C., *Les évêques de l'ancienne France*, 2 vols. (Lille: Université de Lille, 1997).

Perré, Jean, *Les mutations de la guerre moderne: des origines à 1792* (Paris: Payot, 1948).

Persell, Stuart M., *The French Colonial Lobby, 1839–1938* (Stanford, CA: Hoover Institution Press, 1983).

Peters, Ralph, "Our Soldiers, their Cities," *Parameters*, 26, no. 1 (Spring 1996), p. 43.

Peterson, Eric, "Surrendering to Markets," *Washington Quarterly* 18 (1995), pp. 103–15.

Petrarch, Francesco, *Letters of Old Age. Rerum Senilium Libri I–XVIII*, trans. Aldo S. Bernardo, Saul Levin and Reta A. Bernardo (Baltimore, MD: Johns Hopkins University Press, 1992).

Petrovna, Margarita H., "The End of the Cold War: A Battle or Bridging Ground Between Rationalist and Ideational Approaches in International Relations?" *European Journal of International Relations* 9 (2003), pp. 115–63.

Pfaff, William, "A New Colonialism?" *Foreign Affairs*, 74, no. 1 (January/February 1995), pp. 2–6.

The Bullet's Song: Romantic Violence and Utopia (New York: Simon and Schuster, 2004).

Pflanze, Otto, *Bismarck and the Development of Germany*, 3 vols. (Princeton, NJ: Princeton University Press, 1963–90).

Phillips, David L., *Losing Iraq: Inside the Postwar Reconstruction Fiasco* (Boulder, CO: Westview, 2005).

Phillips, Kevin, *American Dynasty: Aristocracy, Fortune, and the Politics of Deceit in the House of Bush* (New York: Viking, 2004).

Phillips, Seymour, "Simon de Montfort (1250), the Earl of Manchester (1644), and Other Stories: Violence and Politics in Thirteenth-and Early Fourteenth-Century England," in Kaeuper, *Violence in Medieval Society*, pp. 79–90.

Piaget, Jean, *The Moral Development of the Child* (London: Free Press, 1965).

Pierson, Paul, "Increasing Returns, Path Dependence, and the Study of Politics," *American Political Science Review* 94, no. 2 (2000), pp. 251–67.

"Big, Slow-Moving, and . . . Invisible: Macro-Social Processes in the Study of Comparative Politics," in James Mahoney and Dietrich Rueschemeyer, *Comparative Historical Analysis in the Social Sciences* (Cambridge: Cambridge University Press, 2003), ch. 5.

Pindar, *The Compete Odes*, ed. Stephen Instone, trans. Anthony Verity (Oxford: Oxford University Press, 1997).

Pinkard, Terry P., *Hegel: A Biography* (Cambridge: Cambridge University Press, 2000).

German Philosophy, 1760–1860: The Legacy of Idealism (Cambridge: Cambridge University Press, 2002).

Pinker, Steven, *The Language Instinct* (New York: Morrow, 1994).

The Blank Slate: Modern Denial of Man's Nature (New York: Viking, 2002).

Pipes, Richard, "Historical Evolution of the Russian Intelligentsia," in Pipes, *The Russian Intelligentsia*, pp. 47–74.

The Russian Intelligentsia (New York: Columbia University Press, 1961).

"Why the Soviet Union Thinks It Could Fight and Win a Nuclear War," *Commentary*, no. 64 (July 1981), pp. 29–31.

Pippin, Robert, "What Is the Question for which Hegel's Theory of Recognition Is the Answer?" *European Journal of Philosophy* 8, no. 2 (2000), pp. 155–72.

Pirenne, Henri, *Mohammed and Charlemagne* (New York: Norton, 1939).

Piscatori, James, *Islam in a World of Nation-States* (New York: Cambridge University Press, 1986).

Pitkin, Hannah Fenichel, *Fortune is a Woman: Gender and Politics in the Thought of Niccolo Machiavelli* (Berkeley: University of California Press, 1984).

Pitt-Rivers, J., "Honor and Social Status," in Peristiany, *Honour and Shame*, pp. 21–77.

Plato, *The Collected Dialogues*, ed. Edith Hamilton and Huntington Cairns (Princeton, NJ: Princeton University Press, 1961).

Republic, ed. and trans. I. A. Richards (Cambridge: Cambridge University Press, 1996).

Platt, D. C. M., *Britain's Investment Overseas on the Eve of the First World War* (New York: St. Martin's Press, 1986).

Plautus, *Amphitruo*, ed. David Christenson (Cambridge: Cambridge University Press, 2000).

Plessner, Helmuth, *Die Verspätete Nation* (Stuttgart: Kohlhammer, 1959).

Plutarch, *The Lives of Noble Greeks and Romans*, trans. John Dryden (New York: Modern Library, 1932).

The Age of Alexander: Nine Lives by Plutarch, trans. Ian Scott-Kilvert (Harmondsworth: Penguin, 1973).

"Alexander," in *The Age of Alexander*, pp. 252–334.

"Demosthenes," in *The Age of Alexander*, pp. 188–217.

Pocock, J. G. A., *The Machiavellian Moment: Florentine Political Thought and the Atlantic Republic Tradition* (Princeton, NJ: Princeton University Press, 1975).

Virtue, Commerce and History (Cambridge: Cambridge University Press, 1985).

Podhoretz, Norman, "The Present Danger," *Commentary*, no. 69 (April 1980), pp. 27–40.

Pogge von Strandmann, Hartmut, "Germany and the Coming of War," in Evans and Pogge von Strandmann, *The Coming of the First World War*, pp. 87–124.

Poggi, Gianfranco, *The Development of the Modern State: A Sociological Introduction* (Stanford, CA: Stanford University Press, 1978).

Polanyi, Karl, *The Great Transformation* (Boston: Farrar and Rinehart, 1944).

"The Economy as an Instituted Process," in Karl Polanyi, Conrad M. Arensberg and Harry W. Pearson, *Trade and Market in the Early Empires: Economic History and Theory* (New York: Free Press, 1957), pp. 243–4.

The Livelihood of Man, ed. Henry W. Pearson (New York: Academic Press, 1977).

Polanyi, Karl, Conrad M. Arensberg, and Harry W. Pearson, eds., *Trade and Market in the Early Empires: Economic History and Theory* (New York: Free Press, 1957).

Polkinghorne, D., *Narrative Knowing and the Human Sciences* (Albany: State University of New York Press, 1988).

"Narrative and Self-Concept," *Journal of Narrative and Life History* 1 (1991), pp. 135–53.

Pollexfen, John, *A Discourse on Trade, Coyne, and Paper Credit* (London, 1697).

Polonsky, Anthony, *Politics in Independent Poland, 1921–1939* (Oxford: Oxford University Press, 1972).

Poly, Jean-Pierre and Eric Bournazel, *La mutation féodale: Xe–XIIe siècle*, 3rd edn (Paris: Presses Universitaires de France, 2004).

Polybius, "The Histories," in William Ebenstein, *Great Political Thinkers*, 4th edn (New York: Holt, Rinehart and Winston, 1969), pp. 112–23.

The Rise of the Roman Empire, trans. Ian Scott-Kilvery (London: Penguin, 1979).

Pomeranz, Kenneth, *The Great Divergence: China, Europe, and the Making of the Modern World Economy* (Princeton, NJ: Princeton University Press, 2000).

Portelli, Alessandro, "Uchronic Dreams: Working-Class Memory and Possible Worlds," in *The Death of Luigi Trastulli and Other Stories: Form and*

Meaning in Oral History (Albany: State University of New York Press, 1991), pp. 99–116.

Porter, Andrew, *European Imperialism, 1860–1914* (London: Macmillan, 1994).

Porter, Andrew and Alaine Low, eds., *The Oxford History of the British Empire*, vol. III: *The Nineteenth Century* (Oxford: Oxford University Press, 1999).

Porter, Bruce D., *War and the Rise of the State: The Military Foundations of Modern Politics* (New York: Free Press, 1994).

Porter, James I., "Homer: The History of an Idea," in Fowler, *The Cambridge Companion to Homer*, pp. 324–43.

Porter, Roy, *English Society in the Eighteenth Century* (Harmondsworth: Penguin, 1990).

Reassessing Foucault: Power, Medicine and the Body (London: Routledge, 1994).

Postlethwaite, Norman, "Akhilleus and Agamemnon: Generalized Reciprocity," in Christopher Gill, Norman Postlethwaite and Richard Seaford, eds., *Reciprocity in Ancient Greece* (New York: Oxford University Press, 1998), pp. 93–104.

Potter, David, "The Roman Army and Navy," in Flower, *The Cambridge Companion to the Roman Republic*, pp. 66–88.

Poulantzas, Nicos, *Classes in Contemporary Capitalism* (London: New Left Books, 1975).

State, Power, Socialism (London: New Left Books, 1978).

Pounds, N. J. G., *An Historical Geography of Europe, 450 BC–AD 1330* (Cambridge: Cambridge University Press, 1973).

Poundstone, William. *The Recursive Universe: Cosmic Complexity and the Limits of Scientific Knowledge* (Oxford: Oxford University Press, 1985).

Powaski, Ronald E., *Return to Armageddon: The United States and the Nuclear Arms Race, 1981–1999* (New York: Oxford University Press, 2000).

Powell, Colin, "US Forces: The Challenges Ahead," *Foreign Affairs* 71 (Winter 1992), pp. 32–45.

Powell, Robert, "Anarchy in International Relations Theory: The Neorealist-Neoliberal Debate," *International Organization*, 48, no. 2 (Spring 1994), pp. 313–44.

Prados, John, *The Soviet Estimate: U.S. Intelligence Analysis and Russian Military Strength* (New York: Dial Press, 1982).

Prestwich, J. O., "War and Finance in the Anglo-Norman State," *Transactions of the Royal Historical Society*, 5th series 4 (1954), pp. 19–54.

Price, Richard M., *The Chemical Weapons Taboo* (Ithaca, NY: Cornell University Press, 1997).

Pritchett, W. Kendrick, *The Greek State at War*, 4 vols. (Berkeley: University of California Press, 1971–85).

Procacci, Guiliano, *The History of the Italian People* (London: Penguin, 1968).

Pufendorf, Samuel, *De jure naturae et gentium libri octo*, trans. C. H. Oldfather and W. A. Oldfather (Oxford: Oxford University Press, 1934).

On the Duty of Man and Citizen according to Natural Law, trans. Michael Silverthorn (Cambridge: Cambridge University Press, 1991).

Puhle, Hans-Jürgen, *Von der Agrarkrise zum Präfaschismus* (Wiesbaden: Steiner, 1972).

Purdham, Todd S., *A Time of our Choosing: America's War in Iraq* (New York: Henry Holt, 2003).

Purifoy, Lewis M., *Harry Truman's China Policy: McCarthyism and the Diplomacy of Hysteria, 1947–1951* (New York: New Viewpoints, 1976).

Putnam, Hilary, *Meaning and the Moral Sciences* (London: Routledge and Kegan Paul, 1978).

Putnam, Michael C., "Troy in Latin Literature," *New England Classical Journal* 34, no. 3 (August 2007), pp. 195–206.

Putnam, Robert D., "Diplomacy and Domestic Politics: The Logic of Two-level Games," *International Organization*, 42, no. 3 (Summer 1988), pp. 427–60.

   Bowling Alone: The Collapse and Revival of American Community (New York: Simon and Schuster, 2000).

Pyle, Kenneth B., *The New Generation in Meiji Japan: Problems of Cultural Identity, 1885–95* (Stanford, CA: Stanford University Press, 1969).

   The Japanese Question: Power and Purpose in a New Era (Washington DC: AEI Press, 1996).

The Quest for the Holy Grail, trans. Pauline Matarasso (Harmondsworth: Penguin, 1969).

Quint, David, *Epic and Empire: The Politics and Generic Form from Virgil to Milton* (Princeton, NJ: Princeton University Press, 1993).

   "Duelling and Civility in Sixteenth Century Italy," *I Tatti Studies* 7 (1997), pp. 231–78.

Raaflaub, Kurt A., "Expansion und Machtbildung in frühren Polis-Systemen," in Walter Eder, *Staat und Staatlichkeit in der frühren römischen Republik* (Stuttgart: Steiner, 1990), pp. 511–45.

   "Equalities and Inequalities in Athenian Democracy," in Ober and Hedrick, *Dēmokratia*, pp. 139–74.

Radnitzky, Gerard and Gunnar Andersson, eds., *Progress and Rationality in Science* (Dordrecht: D. Reidel, 1978).

Rae, Heather, *Social Identities and the Homogenisation of Peoples* (Cambridge: Cambridge University Press, 2002).

Ragin, Charles, *The Comparative Method: Moving Beyond Qualitative and Quantitative Strategies* (Berkeley, CA: University of California Press, 1987).

Ragionieri, Ernesto, *Storia d'Italia,* vol. IV: *Dall'unità a oggi* (Turin: Einaudi, 1976).

Rahe, Paul, *Republics Ancient and Modern*, vol. I: *The Ancien Régime in Classical Greece* (Chapel Hill: University of North Carolina Press, 1994).

Randall, Jonathan, *Osama: The Making of a Terrorist* (New York: Knopf, 2004).

Randall, William S., *Thomas Jefferson* (New York: Henry Holt, 1993).

Randsborg, Klavs, *The First Millennium A.D. in Europe and the Mediterranean* (Cambridge: Cambridge University Press, 1991).

Ranke, Leopold von, "The Great Powers," in Theodor H. von Laue, *Ranke, the Formative Years* (Princeton, NJ: Princeton University Press, 1950 [1833]), pp. 181–218.

Rao, Rahul, "The Empire Writes Back (to Michael Ignatieff)," *Millennium* 33, no. 1 (2004), pp. 145–66.

Rappaport, Joanne, *The Politics of Memory* (New York: Cambridge University Press, 1990).

Rasler, Karen and William R. Thompson, "Malign Autocracies and Major Power Warfare: Evil, Tragedy and International Relations Theory," *Security Studies* 10 (2001), pp. 46–79.

Rattray, R. S., *Ashanti* (Oxford: Oxford University Press, 1923).

Rawls, John, *The Law of Peoples* (Cambridge, MA: Harvard University Press, 1999).
    "Some Reasons for the Maximum Criterion," in Rawls, *Collected Papers*, ed. Samuel Freeman (Cambridge, MA: Harvard University Press, 1999), pp. 225–31.
    A Theory of Justice, rev. edn (Cambridge, MA: Harvard University Press, 1999).
    Justice as Fairness, ed. Erin Kelly (Cambridge, MA: Harvard University Press, 2001).

Raz, Joseph, *The Authority of Law* (Oxford: Oxford University Press, 1979).
    The Morality of Freedom (Oxford: Oxford University Press, 1986).

Reden, Sitta von, *Exchange in Ancient Greece* (London: Duckworth, 1995).

Reed, J. D., *Virgil's Gaze: Nation and Poetry in the Aeneid* (Princeton, NJ: Princeton University Press, 2007).

Reeve, C. D. C., *Philosopher-Kings: The Argument of Plato's Republic* (Princeton, NJ: Princeton University Press, 1988).

Regele, Oskar, *Feldmarschall Conrad. Auftrag und Erfüllung 1906–1918* (Vienna: Herold, 1955).

Reich, Robert B., *The Work of Nations: Preparing Ourselves for 21st-Century Capitalism* (New York: Alfred A. Knopf, 1991).

Reinicke, Wolfgang H., *Global Public Policy: Governing without Government?* (Washington, DC: Brookings Institution, 1998).
    "The Other World Wide Web: Global Public Policy Networks," *Foreign Policy*, no. 117 (Winter 1999–2000), pp. 44–57.

Reischauer, Edwin O., "What Went Wrong?," in Morley, *Dilemmas of Growth in Prewar Japan*, pp. 489–510.

Reischauer, Robert K., *Japan: Government and Politics* (New York: Nelson, 1939).

Rengger, Nicholas, "Tragedy or Scepticism? Defending the Anti-Pelagian Mind in World Politics," *International Politics* 42, no. 3 (2005), pp. 321–8.

Renner, Karl, *Marxismus, Krieg und Internationale* (Stuttgart: Dietz, 1918).

Renshon, Stanley A., *In His Father's Shadow: The Transformation of George W. Bush* (New York: Palgrave Macmillan, 2004).

Rescher, Nicholas, *Process Metaphysics: An Introduction to Process Philosophy* (Albany: State University of New York Press, 1977).

    Leibniz's Metaphysics of Nature: A Group of Essays (Dordrecht: Reidel, 1981).

    Process Metaphysics: An Introduction to Process Philosophy (Albany: State University of New York Press, 1996).

    Process Philosophy: A Survey of Basic Issues (Pittsburgh, NJ: University of Pittsburgh Press, 2000).

Resnick, Evan, "Review of Schweller, *Unanswered Threats*," *Perspective on Politics* 5, no. 2 (June 2007), pp. 417–18.

Reus-Smit, Christian, *The Moral Purpose of the State: Culture, Social Identity, and Institutional Rationality in International Relations* (Princeton, NJ: Princeton University Press, 1999).

    "Politics and International Legal Obligation," *European Journal of International Relations* 9 (2003), pp. 591–626.

    American Power and World Order (Cambridge: Polity, 2004).

    "Liberal Hierarchy and the License to Use Force," *Review of International Studies* 31 (2005), pp. 71–92.

    "International Crises of Legitimacy," *International Politics* 44, no. 2 (March 2007), pp. 157–74.

    "Unipolarity and Legitimacy," forthcoming.

Reuter, Timothy, "Plunder and Tribute in the Carolingian Empire," *Transactions of the Royal Historical Society*, 5th series 35 (1985), pp. 75–94.

Reynolds, Susan, *Kingdoms and Communities in Western Europe 900–1300* (Oxford: Oxford University Press, 1984).

Rhodes, P. J., "Democracy and Empire," in Samons, *The Cambridge Companion to the Age of Pericles*, pp. 24–45.

Rhodes, Richard, *The Making of the Atomic Bomb* (New York: Simon and Schuster, 1986).

Rhodes, Robin Francis, *Architecture and Meaning on the Athenian Acropolis* (Cambridge: Cambridge University Press, 1995).

Riasanovsky, Nicholas V., *Russia and the West in the Teaching of the Slavophiles* (Gloucester, MA: Peter Smith, 1965).

Ricci, David, *The Tragedy of Political Science: Politics, Scholarship, and Democracy* (New Haven, CT: Yale University Press, 1984).

Rice, Condoleezza, "Promoting the National Interest," *Foreign Affairs* 79, no. 1 (January/February 2000), pp. 45–62.

Rich, David Alan, "Russia," in Hamilton and Herwig, *The Origins of World War I*, pp. 188–226.

Rich, Frank, *The Greatest Story Ever Sold: The Decline and Fall of Truth from 9/11 to Katrina* (New York: Penguin, 2006).

Rich, Norman, *Hitler's War Aims*, 2 vols. (New York: Norton, 1973–4).

   Why the Crimean War? A Cautionary Tale (Hanover, NH: University Press of New England, 1985).

Richter, Melvin, "Conceptual History (*Begriffsgeschichte*) and Political Theory," *Political Theory* 14, no. 4 (1986), pp. 604–37.

   The History of Political and Social Concepts: A Critical Introduction (Oxford: Oxford University Press, 1995).

Richthofen, Manfred von, *Der rote Kampfflieger* (Berlin: Ullstein, 1917).

Ricks, Thomas E., *Fiasco: The American Military Adventure in Iraq* (New York: Penguin, 2006).

Ricoeur, Paul, *Freud and Philosophy: An Essay in Interpretation* (New Haven, CT: Yale University Press, 1970).

   "The Model of the Text: Meaningful Action Considered as a Text," in Fred Dallmayer and T. McCarthy, eds., *Understanding and Social Inquiry* (Notre Dame, IN: Notre Dame University Press, 1977 [1971]), pp. 146–67.

   "The Political Paradox," in William Connolly, ed., *Legitimacy and the State* (New York: New York University Press, 1984), pp. 253–54.

   Time and Narrative, vol. III (Chicago: University of Chicago Press, 1988).

Riekhoff, Harald von, *German-Polish Relations, 1918–1933* (Baltimore, MD: Johns Hopkins University Press, 1971).

Riesman, David, Ruel Denney and Nathan Glazer, *The Lonely Crowd: A Study of the Changing American Character* (New Haven, CT: Yale University Press, 1950).

Rigaudière, Albert, "The Theory and Practice of Government in Western Europe," in Jones, *The New Cambridge Medieval History*, vol. VI, pp. 17–41.

Rimell, Raymond L., *Zeppelin! A Battle for Air Supremacy in World War I* (London: Conway Maritime Press, 1984).

Ringer, Fritz, *The Decline of the German Mandarins. The German Academic Community, 1890–1933* (Cambridge, MA: Harvard University Press, 1969).

Ringmar, Erik, *Identity, Interest and Action: A Cultural Explanation of Sweden's Intervention in the Thirty Years War* (Cambridge: Cambridge University Press, 1996).

   "On the Ontological Status of the State," *European Journal of International Relations* 2, no. 4 (1996), pp. 439–66.

   "The Recognition Game: Soviet Russia against the West," *Cooperation and Conflict* 37, no. 2 (2002), pp. 115–36.

Ripsman, Norrin M. and T. V. Paul, "Under Pressure? Globalisation and the National Security State," *Millennium* 33, no. 2 (2004), pp. 355–80.

Risse, Thomas, "'Let's Argue!' Communicative Action in World Politics," *International Organization* 54 (2000), pp. 1–40.

Risse, Thomas, S. C. Ropp and K. Sikkink, eds., *The Power of Human Rights: International Norms and Domestic Change* (Cambridge: Cambridge University Press, 1999).

Rist, John M., *Real Ethics: Rethinking the Foundations of Morality* (Cambridge: Cambridge University Press, 2002).

Ritter, Gerhard, *The Schlieffen Plan*, trans. Andrew and Eva Wilson (New York: Praeger, 1958).

"Eine neue Kriegsschuldthese?," *Historische Zeitschrift* 194 (June 1962), pp. 657–68.

The Sword and Scepter: The Problem of Militarism in Germany, trans. Heinz Norden, 4 vols. (Coral Gables: University of Miami Press, 1969–73).

Frederick the Great: A Historical Profile, ed. and trans. Peter Paret (Berkeley: University of California Press, 1975).

Robb, Kevin, *Literacy and Paideia in Ancient Greece* (New York: Oxford University Press, 1994).

Roberts, Michael, *The Military Revolution, 1560–1660* (Belfast: Queen's University Press, 1956).

The Age of Liberty, Sweden, 1719–1772 (Cambridge: Cambridge University Press, 1986).

Roberts, Walter A., *Tito, Mihailovic, and the Allies, 1941–45* (New Brunswick, NJ: Rutgers University Press, 1973).

Robertson, Roland, "Globalization: Time-Space and Homogeneity-Heterogeneity," in Mike Featherstone, Scott Lash and Roland Robertson, *Global Modernities* (London: Sage, 1995), pp. 25–44.

Robin, Corey, *Fear: The History of a Political Idea* (New York: Oxford University Press, 2004).

Robinson, J. A., "Sampling Autobiography," *Cognitive Psychology* 8 (1976), pp. 588–95.

Robinson, Ronald and John Gallagher, "The Imperialism of Free Trade," *Economic History Review* 6 (1953), pp. 1–15.

Robinson, Ronald and John Gallagher with Alice Denny, *Africa and the Victorians: The Climax of Imperialism in the Dark Continent* (New York: St. Martin's Press, 1961).

Robinson, Thomas W. and David Shumbaugh, eds., *Chinese Foreign Policy: Theory and Practice* (Oxford: Oxford University Press, 1994).

Robinson, William I., "Beyond Nation-State Paradigms: Globalization, Sociology, and the Challenge of Transnational Studies," *Sociological Forum* 13, no. 4 (1998), pp. 1–16.

Rodrik, Dani, *Has Globalization Gone Too Far?* (Washington, DC: International Institute for Economics, 1997).

Rogers, Clifford J., *War Cruel and Sharp: English Strategy under Edward III, 1327–1360* (Rochester, NY: Boydell Press, 2000).

Rogowski, Ronald, *Commerce and Coalitions: How Trade Affects Domestic Political Alignments* (Princeton, NJ: Princeton University Press, 1989).

Röhl, John G., *Germany Without Bismarck* (Berkeley: University of California Press, 1967).

    1914: Delusion or Design? The Testimony of Two German Diplomats (London: Elek, 1973).

    Young Wilhelm (Cambridge: Cambridge University Press, 1988).

    The Kaiser and his Court: Wilhelm II and the Government of Germany (Cambridge: Cambridge University Press, 1994).

    "Germany," in Keith Wilson, *Decisions for War, 1914* (New York: St. Martin's Press, 1995), pp. 27–54.

    Wilhelm II: The Kaiser's Personal Monarchy, 1888–1900 (Cambridge: Cambridge University Press, 2004).

Röhl, John G. and Nicolaus Sombart, eds., *Kaiser Wilhelm II: New Interpretations: The Corfu Papers* (Cambridge: Cambridge University Press, 1982).

Rohwer, Jürgen and Eberhard Jäckel, eds., *Der Mord an dem Juden im Zweiten Weltkrieg: Entschlussbildung und Verwicklung* (Stuttgart: Deutsche Verlags-Anstalt, 1985).

Röling, B. V. A., *The Tokyo Trial and Beyond: Reflections of a Peacemonger*, ed. Antonio Cassese (Cambridge: Polity, 1993).

Romano, Sergio, "La cultura della politica esterna italiana," in R. J. B. Bosworth and Sergio Romano, *La politica esterna italiana, 1860–1985* (Bologna: Il Mulino, 1991), pp. 17–34.

Rood, Tim, "Thucydides' Persian Wars," in Christina Shuttleworth Kraus, ed., *The Limits of Historiography: Genre Narrative in Ancient Historical Texts* (Leiden: Brill, 1999), pp. 141–68.

Rorty, Amélie Oksenberg, ed., *Essays on Aristotle's Ethics* (Berkeley, CA: University of California Press, 1980).

Rorty, Richard, *Philosophy and the Mirror of Nature* (Princeton, NJ: Princeton University Press, 1979).

    Contingency, Irony and Solidarity (Cambridge: Cambridge University Press, 1989).

Rose, Gideon, "Neoclassical Realism and Theories of Foreign Policy," *World Politics* 51 (1998), pp. 144–72.

Rosecrance, Richard N., *Action and Reaction in World Politics: International Systems in Perspective* (Boston: Little, Brown, 1963).

    The Rise of the Trading State: Commerce and Conquest in the Modern World (New York: Basic Books, 1986).

    "The Rise of the Virtual State," *Foreign Affairs* 75, no. 4 (July/August 1996), pp. 45–61.

    The Rise of the Virtual State: Wealth and Power in the Coming Century (New York: Basic Books, 1999).

Rosell, Steven A., *Renewing Governance: Governing by Learning in the Information Age* (New York: Oxford University Press, 1999).

Rosemberg, Justin, "Why There Is No International Historical Sociology?," *European Journal of International Relations* 12, no. 3 (September 2006), pp. 307–40.

Rosen, Stanley, *The Ancients and the Moderns: Rethinking Modernity* (South Bend, IN: St. Augustine's Press, 2002).

Rosen, Stephen Peter, *War and Human Nature* (Princeton, NJ: Princeton University Press, 2005).

Rosenau, James N., "Pre-theories and Theories of Foreign Policy," in R. Barry Farrell, *Approaches to Comparative and International Politics* (Evanston, IL: Northwestern University Press, 1966), pp. 27–93.

"Introduction," in James N. Rosenau, *The Domestic Sources of Foreign Policy* (New York: Free Press, 1967), pp. 1–10.

ed., *Linkage Politics: Essays on the Convergence of National and International Systems* (New York: Free Press, 1969).

"Toward the Study of National-International Linkages," in James N. Rosenau, *Linkage Politics* (New York: Free Press, 1969), pp. 44–63.

The Scientific Study of Foreign Policy (New York: Free Press, 1971).

"Global Changes and Theoretical Challenges: Toward a Postinternational Politics for the 1990s," in Ernst-Otto Czempiel and Rosenau, *Global Changes and Theoretical Challenges: Approaches to World Politics for the 1990s* (Lexington, MA: Lexington Books, 1989), pp. 1–20.

Turbulence in World Politics: A Theory of Change and Continuity (Princeton, NJ: Princeton University Press, 1990).

Rosenau, James N. and Mary Durfee, *Thinking Theory Thoroughly: Coherent Approaches to an Incoherent World* (Boulder, CO: Westview Press, 1995).

Rosenberg, Alexander, "Hume and the Philosophy of Social Science," in David Fate Norton, ed., *The Cambridge Companion to Hume* (Cambridge: Cambridge University Press, 1993), pp. 241–324.

Rosenberg, Arthur, *Imperial Germany: The Birth of the German Republic, 1871–1918*, trans. Ian Morrow (Boston: Beacon Press, 1964 [1928]).

Rosenberg, Hans, *Bureaucracy, Aristocracy, and Autocracy: The Prussian Experience, 1660–1815* (Cambridge, MA: Harvard University Press, 1958).

"Die Pseudodemokratisierung der Rittergutsbesitzerklasse," in Rosenberg, *Machteliten und Wirtschaftskonjunkturen: Studien zur neueren deutschen Sozial- und Wirtschaftsgeschichte* (Göttingen: Vandenhoeck und Ruprecht, 1978), pp. 124–46.

Rosenberg, Matthias von, *Friedrich Carl von Savigny (1779–1861) im Urteil seiner Zeit* (Frankfurt am Main: Verlag Lang, 2000).

Rosenberg, Morris, "The Self-Concept: Social Product and Social Force," in Morris Rosenberg and Ralph H. Turner, *Social Psychology: Sociological Perspectives* (New York: Basic Books, 1981), pp. 593–624.

Rosenberg, Shawn W., *The Not So Common Sense: Differences in How People Judge Social and Political Life* (New Haven, CT: Yale University Press, 2002).

Rosenblatt, A., J. Greenberg, S. Solomon, T. Pyszczynski and D. Lyon, "Evidence for Terror Management Theory I: The Effects of Mortality Salience on Reactions to those who Violate or Uphold Cultural Values," *Journal of Personality and Social Psychology*, 57 (1989), pp. 681–90.

Rosenmeyer, Thomas G., *The Art of Aeschylus* (Chicago: University of Chicago Press, 1982).

Roshchin, Evgeny, "The Concept of Friendship: From Princes to States," *European Journal of International Relations* 12, no. 4 (December 2006), pp. 599–624.

Ross, Eric B., "An Overview of Trends in Dietary Variation from Hunter-Gatherer to Modern Capitalist Societies," in Marvin Harris and Eric B. Ross, *Food and Evolution: Toward a Theory* (Philadelphia, PA: Temple University Press, 1987), pp. 7–56.

Rossabi, Morris, ed., *China Among the Equals: The Middle Kingdom and its Neighbors, 10th–14th Centuries* (Berkeley: University of California Press, 1983).

"Traditional Chinese Foreign Policy and Intersocietal Cooperation," paper presented at the Conference on Patterns of Cooperation in the Foreign Relations of Modern China, Wintergreen, VA, August 1987.

Rotberg, Robert I., ed., *When States Fail: Causes and Consequences* (Princeton, NJ: Princeton University Press, 2004).

Rotberg, Robert I. and Theodore K. Rabb, eds., *The Origin and Prevention of Major Wars* (Cambridge: Cambridge University Press, 1989).

Roth, Joseph, *The Radetzky March*, trans Joachim Neugroschel (London: Penguin, 1995).

Roth, Michael S., *Knowing and History: Appropriations of Hegel in Twentieth-Century France* (Ithaca, NY: Cornell University Press, 1988), pp. 189–224.

Rothenberg, Gunther E., *The Army of Francis Joseph* (West Lafayette, IN: Purdue University Press, 1976).

"Moltke, Schlieffen and the Doctrine of Envelopment," in Peter Paret, ed., *Makers of Modern Strategy: From Machiavelli to the Nuclear Age* (Princeton, NJ: Princeton University Press, 1985), pp. 296–325.

Rothkopf, David, "In Praise of Cultural Imperialism?" *Foreign Policy*, no. 107 (Summer 1997), pp. 38–77.

Rothkrug, Lionel, *Opposition to Louis XIV: The Political and Social Origins of the French Enlightenment* (Princeton, NJ: Princeton University Press, 1983).

Rothschild, Emma, *Economic Sentiments: Adam Smith, Condorcet and the Enlightenment* (Cambridge, MA: Harvard University Press, 2001).

Rotter, Julian B., "Generalized Expectancies for Internal vs. External Control of Reinforcement," *Psychological Monographs: General and Applied* 80 (1966), pp. 591–609.

Rouche, Michel, "Break-Up and Metamorphosis of the West: Fifth to Seventh Centuries," in Fossier, *The Cambridge Illustrated History of the Middle Ages*, vol. I, pp. 52–103.

"The Carolingian 'Renewal,'" in Fossier, *The Cambridge Illustrated History of the Middle Ages*, vol. I, pp. 416–73.

Rousseau, Jean-Jacques, *Oeuvres complètes* (Paris: J. P. Mayer, 1959–)

Du contrat social (Paris: Éditions Garnier Frères, 1962).

Discourse on the Origin and Foundations of Inequality (Second Discourse), in Roger D. Masters, trans. Roger D. Masters and Judith R. Masters, *The First and Second Discourses* (New York: St. Martin's Press, 1964), pp. 77–229.

"Abstract of the Abbé de Saint-Pierre's Project for Perpetual Peace," in M. G. Forsyth, H. M. A. Keens-Soper and P. Savigear, *The Theory of International Relations* (New York: Atherton Press, 1970), pp. 127–80.

Essais sur l'origine des langues, ed. Charles Porset (Bordeaux: Ducros, 1970).

Émile, trans. Allen Bloom (New York: Basic Books, 1979).

Rêveries (Paris: Larousse, 1993).

Rowe, Christopher, "Aristotelian Constitutions," in Christopher Rowe and Malcolm Schofield, eds., *The Cambridge History of Greek and Roman Political Thought* (Cambridge: Cambridge University Press, 2000), pp. 366–89.

Rowe, David M., "The Tragedy of Liberalism: How Globalization Caused the First World War," *Security Studies* 14 (July–September 2005), pp. 407–47.

Rowe, Michael, ed., *Collaboration and Resistance in Napoleonic Europe: State Formation in an Age of Upheaval, c. 1800–1815* (New York: Palgrave Macmillan, 2003).

Rowlands, Guy, *The Dynastic State and the Army under Louis XIV: Royal Service and Private Interest, 1661–1701* (Cambridge: Cambridge University Press, 2002).

Rozman, Gilbert, "Japan's Quest for Great Power Identity," *Orbis*, Winter 2002, pp. 73–91.

Rubin, D. C., ed., *Autobiographical Memory* (Cambridge: Cambridge University Press, 1986).

Rubin, M. and M. Hewstone, "Social Identity Theory's Self-Esteem Hypothesis: A Review and Some Suggestions for Clarification," *Personality and Social Psychology Review*, 2, no. 40 (1998), pp. 40–62.

Rudner, Richard, *Philosophy of Social Science* (Englewood Cliffs, NJ: Prentice-Hall, 1966).

Ruggie, John Gerard, "International Regimes, Transaction and Change: Embedded Liberalism and the Postwar Economic Regimes," *International Organization* 36 (1982), pp. 379–415.

"Continuity and Transformation in the World Polity: Toward a Neorealist Synthesis," *World Politics* 35, no. 2 (January 1983), pp. 261–85.

"Territoriality and Beyond: Problematizing Modernity in International Relations," *International Organization* 47 (Winter 1993), pp. 139–74.

Winning the Peace: America and World Order in the New Era (New York: Columbia University Press, 1996).

Constructing the World Polity (London: Routledge, 1998).

"What Makes the World Hang Together? Neo-utilitarianism and the Social Constructivist Challenge," *International Organization* 52, no. 4 (Autumn 1998), pp. 855–85.

Rummel, R. J., "Democracy, Power, Genocide, and Mass Murder," *Journal of Conflict Resolution* 39, no. 1 (1995), pp. 3–26.

Rupert, James, "Dateline Tashkent: Post-Soviet Central Asia," *Foreign Policy*, no. 87 (Summer 1992), pp. 175–95.

Rupert, Mark, *Producing Hegemony* (Cambridge: Cambridge University Press, 1993).

Russell, Bertrand, *Problems of Philosophy* (Oxford: Oxford University Press, 1959).

Russell, Wynee Elizabeth, "Identity Diplomacy: A Study in Diplomatic Representation and the Ordering of International Society," PhD dissertation, Department of International Relations, Australian National University, January 2003.

Russett, Bruce, *Community and Contention: Britain and America in the Twentieth Century* (Cambridge, MA: MIT Press, 1963).

Grasping the Democratic Peace: Principles for a Post-Cold War World (Princeton, NJ: Princeton University Press, 1993).

Russett, Bruce and John R. Oneal, *Triangulating Peace: Democracy, Interdependence, and International Organization* (New York: Norton, 2001).

Ryan, Alan, "John Rawls," in Quentin Skinner, *The Return of Grand Theory in the Human Sciences* (Cambridge: Cambridge University Press, 1985), pp. 101–20.

Ryberg, Inez Scott, "Virgil's Golden Age," *Transactions and Proceedings of the American Philological Association* 39 (1958), pp. 112–31.

Sabine, George, "The State," in *Encyclopedia of the Social Sciences* (New York: Macmillan, 1934).

Sacchi, E. and Emanuele Castano, "Entitative is Beautiful: The Importance of Perceiving the Ingroup as a Real Entity," paper presented to the 13th general meeting of the European Association of Experimental Social Psychology, San Sebastian, Spain, June 2002.

Sachs, Jeffrey, "Global Capitalism: Making it Work," *The Economist* (September 12, 1998), pp. 23–25.

Sadao, Asada, "The Japanese Navy and the United States," in Borg and Okamoto, *Pearl Harbor as History*, pp. 225–60.

Sagan, Scott D., "Why Do States Build Nuclear Weapons," *International Security* 21 (Winter 1996/7), pp. 54–86.

Sagan, Scott D. and Kenneth N. Waltz, *The Spread of Nuclear Weapons: A Debate* (New York: Norton, 1995).

Saggs, H. W. F., *The Might That Was Assyria* (London: Sidgwick and Jackson, 1984).

Sahlins, Marshall, *Stone Age Economics* (Chicago: Aldine-Atherton, 1972).

Saikal, Amin, "Reactions in the Muslim World to the Iraqi Conflict," in Ramesh Thakur and Waheguru Pal Singh Sidhu, *The Iraq Crisis and World Order: Structural, Institutional and Normative Challenges* (Tokyo: United Nations University Press, 2006), pp. 187–200.

Saintifaller, Leo, *Zur Geschichte der Ottonisch-Salischen Reichskirchensystems* (Vienna: Böhlaus Nachfolger, 1994).

Saint-Pierre, Abbé, *A Project for Settling an Everlasting Peace in Europe* (London: J. Watts, 1714).

Salisbury, Harrison E., *900 Days: The Siege of Leningrad* (New York: Harper and Row, 1969).

Salkever, Stephen, *Finding the Mean* (Princeton, NJ: Princeton University Press, 1991).

Sallust, *The Histories*, trans. Patrick McGushin, 2 vols. (Oxford: Oxford University Press, 1992–4).

  Bellum Catilinae, ed. J. T. Ramsey, 2nd edn (New York: Oxford University Press, 2007).

Salmon, Wesley, *Causality and Explanation* (New York: Oxford University Press, 1998).

Salter, Liora, "The Standards Regime for Communication and Information Technologies," in A. Claire Cutler, Virginia Haufler and Tony Porter, *Private Authority and International Affairs* (Albany: State University of New York Press, 1999), pp. 92–127.

Salthe, Stanley, *Development and Evolution* (Cambridge, MA: MIT Press, 1993).

Salthe, Stanley and Koichiro Matsuno, "Self-Organization in Hierarchical Systems," *Journal of Social and Evolutionary Systems* 18, no. 4 (1995), pp. 327–38.

Salvatorelli, Luigi and Giovanni Mira, *Storia d'Italia nel periodo fascista* (Milan: Einaudi, 1964).

Salvemini, Gaetano, *Prelude to World War II* (Garden City, NY: Doubleday, 1954 [1953]).

  The Origins of Fascism in Italy (New York: Harper and Row, 1973).

Samons, Loren J. III, ed., *The Cambridge Companion to the Age of Pericles* (Cambridge: Cambridge University Press, 2007).

Samuels, Richard J., *Rich Nation, Strong Army: National Security and the Technological Transformation of Japan* (Ithaca, NY: Cornell University Press, 1994).

  Machiavelli's Children: Leaders and their Legacies in Italy and Japan (Ithaca, NY: Cornell University Press, 2003).

  Securing Japan: Tokyo's Grand Strategy and the Future of East Asia (Ithaca, NY: Cornell University Press, 2007).

Samuelson, Robert J., "The Erosion of Confidence," *Newsweek* (June 17, 2002).

Sanderson, G. N., *England, Europe, and the Upper Nile* (Edinburgh: Edinburgh University Press, 1965).

Santarelli, Enzo, *Storia di movimento e de regime fascista*, 2 vols. (Rome: Editore Riunite, 1967).

Savigny, Friedrich Karl von, *System des heutigen Römischen Rechts*, vol. I (Berlin: Veit und Comp, 1840).

Sawyer, Keith, "Simulating Emergence and Downward Causation in Small Groups," in Robert Scalapino, *Democracy and the Party Movement in Prewar Japan: The Failure of the First Attempt* (Berkeley: University of California Press, 1953), pp. 551–85.

   "Emergence in Sociology: Contemporary Philosophy of Mind and Some Implications for Sociological Theory," *American Journal of Sociology* 107, no. 3 (2001), pp. 551–85.

Schalk, Ellery, "The Court as Civilizer," in Ronald Asch and Adolf Birk, eds., *Princes, Patronage and the Nobility: The Court at the Beginning of the Modern Age, c. 1450–1650* (Oxford: Oxford University Press, 1991), pp. 257–63.

Schama, Simon, *The Embarrassment of Riches. An Interpretation of Dutch Culture in the Golden Age* (New York: Knopf, 1987).

   Landscape and Memory (London: HarperCollins, 1996).

Schattschneider, E. E., *The Semisovereign People; A Realist's View of Democracy in America* (New York: Holt, Rinehart and Winston, 1960).

Schechter, Danny, "Selling the Iraq War: The Media Management Strategies We Never Saw," in Kamalipour and Snow, *War, Media, and Propaganda: A Global Perspective*, pp. 25–32.

Scheff, Thomas, "Shame in Social Theory," in Melvin R. Lansky and Andrew P. Morrison, eds., *The Widening Scope of Shame* (Hillsdale, NJ: Analytic Press, 1997) pp. 205–30.

Scheidel, Walter, and Sitta von Reden, *The Ancient Economy: Edinburgh Readings on the Ancient World* (New York: Routledge, 2002).

Scheiner, Irwin, "The Japanese Village: Imagined, Real, Contested," in Vlastos, *Mirror of Modernity*, pp. 67–78.

Schelling, Thomas, *The Strategy of Conflict* (Cambridge, MA: Harvard University Press, 1960).

   Arms and Influence (New Haven, CT: Yale University Press, 1966).

   "Dynamic Models of Segregation," *Journal of Mathematical Sociology* 1, no. 1 (1971), pp. 143–86.

   Micromotives and Macrobehavior (New York: Norton, 1978).

Schieder, Theodor, *Frederick the Great*, ed. and trans. Sabina Berkeley and H. M. Scott (London: Longman, 2000).

Schlesinger, Arthur Meier, Jr., *The Age of Jackson* (Boston: Little, Brown, 1945).

   A Thousand Days: John F. Kennedy in the White House (Boston: Houghton Mifflin, 1965).

   The Imperial Presidency (Boston: Houghton Mifflin, 1973).

   Robert Kennedy and his Times (Boston: Houghton Mifflin, 1978).

Schliefer, James T., *The Making of Tocqueville's "Democracy in America"* (Chapel Hill: University of North Carolina Press, 1980).

Schmidt, Brian C., *The Political Discourse of Anarchy: A Disciplinary History of International Relations* (Albany: State University of New York Press, 1998).

"Realism as Tragedy," *Review of International Studies* 30 (2004), pp. 427–41.

"Competing Realist Conceptions of Power," *Millennium* 33, no. 3 (2005), pp. 523–50.

Schmidt, Carl, *The Concept of the Political*, trans. Carol Schwab (New Brunswick, NJ: Rutgers University Press, 1976).

Schmidt, Dennis J., *On Germans and Other Greeks: Tragedy and Ethical Life* (Bloomington: Indiana University Press, 2001).

Schmidt, James, ed., *What Is Enlightenment? Eighteenth Century Answers and Twentieth Century Questions* (Berkeley: University of California Press, 1996).

Schmitt, Carl, *Political Theology: Four Chapters on the Concept of Sovereignty* (Cambridge: MIT Press, 1985).

Schneewind, J. B., *The Invention of Autonomy: A History of Modern Moral Philosophy* (New York: Cambridge University Press, 1998).

Schoenbaum, David, *Hitler's Social Revolution; Class and Status in Nazi Germany, 1933–1939* (Garden City, NY: Doubleday, 1966).

Schofield, Malcolm, "Political Friendship and the Ideology of Reciprocity," in Paul Cartledge, Paul Miller and Sitta von Reden, eds., *Kosmos: Essays in Order, Conflict and Community in Classical Athens* (Cambridge: Cambridge University Press, 1998), pp. 37–51.

The Stoic Idea of the City (Chicago: University of Chicago Press, 1999).

Schopenhauer, Arthur, "The Wisdom of Life," in *Essays from Parenga and Parlipomena*, trans. T. Bailey Saunders (London: Allen and Unwin, 1951), pp. 70–92.

Schorske, Carl E., *German Social Democracy, 1905–1917* (Cambridge, MA: Harvard University Press, 1955).

Schrift, Alan D., ed., *The Logic of the Gift: Toward an Ethic of Generosity* (New York: Routledge, 1997).

Schroeder, Paul W., "World War I as Galloping Gertie: A Reply to Joachim Remak," *Journal of Modern History* 44 (September 1972), pp. 319–45.

"The Transformation of Political Thinking, 1787–1848," in Robert Jervis, *Coping with Complexity in the International System* (Boulder, CO: Westview, 1993), pp. 47–70.

The Transformation of European Politics, 1763–1848 (Oxford: Oxford University Press, 1994).

"Necessary Conditions and World War I as an Unavoidable War," in Goertz and Levy, *Causal Explanations, Necessary Conditions, and Case Studies*, pp. 47–84.

"International Politics, Peace and War, 1815–1914," in T. C. W. Blanning, ed., *The Nineteenth Century* (Oxford: Oxford University Press, 2000), pp. 158–209.

Schulte, Theo, *The German Army and Nazi Policies in Occupied Russia* (Oxford: Berg, 1989).

Schulze, Hagen, "The Prussian Military State, 1763–1806," in Dwyer, *The Rise of Prussia*, pp. 201–19.

Schulzinger, Robert D., *A Time for War: The United States and Vietnam, 1941–1975* (New York: Oxford University Press, 1997).

Schuman, Frederick Lewis, *International Politics: An Introduction to the Western State* (New York: McGraw-Hill, 1958).

Schumpeter, Joseph A., *Imperialism and Social Classes*, trans. Heinz Norden (New York: Kelley, 1951).

Capitalism, Socialism, and Democracy (New York: Harper and Row, 1963).

The Theory of Economic Development (New Brunswick, NJ: Transaction, 1983).

Schwabe, Klaus, "Germany's Peace Aims and the Domestic and International Constraints," in Boemeke, Feldman and Glaser, *Treaty of Versailles*, pp. 37–68.

Schwartz, B. I., *The World of Thought in Ancient China* (Cambridge, MA: Harvard University Press, 1985).

Schwartz, Herman M., *States Versus Markets*, 2nd edn (New York: St. Martin's Press, 2000).

Schwartz, Joseph M., *The Permanence of the Political: A Democratic Critique of the Radical Impulse to Transcend Politics* (Princeton, NJ: Princeton University Press, 1995).

Schweller, Randall L. "Bandwagoning for Profit: Bringing the Revisionist State Back," *International Security* 19, no. 1 (1994), pp. 72–107.

Unanswered Threats: Political Constraints on the Balance of Power (Princeton, NJ: Princeton University Press, 2006).

Scobell, Andrew, *China's Use of Military Force: Beyond the Great Wall and the Long March* (New York: Cambridge University Press, 2003).

Scodel, Ruth, "The Story Teller and his Audience," in Fowler, *The Cambridge Companion to Homer*, pp. 45–58.

Scott, H. M., *Enlightened Absolutism: Reform and Reformers in Later Eighteenth-Century Europe* (Ann Arbor: University of Michigan Press, 1990).

"Prussia's Emergence as a European Great Power, 1740–1763," in Dwyer, *The Rise of Prussia*, 151–76.

The Birth of a Great Power System, 1740–1815 (London: Pearson Longman, 2006).

Scott, James C., *Domination and the Arts of Resistance: Hidden Transcripts* (New Haven, CT: Yale University Press, 1990).

Scott, Shirley V., "Is There Room for International Law in Realpolitik? Accounting for the US 'Attitude' towards International Law," *Review of International Studies* 30, no. 1 (2004), pp. 71–88.

Seabrooke, Leonard, "The Economic Taproot of U.S. Imperialism: The Bush *Rentier* Shift," *International Politics* 41 (2004), pp. 293–318.

Seaford, Richard, *Reciprocity and Ritual: Homer and Tragedy in the Developing City State* (Oxford: Oxford University Press, 1994).

Money and the Early Greek Mind (Cambridge: Cambridge University Press, 2004).

Searle, John, *Speech Acts: An Essay in the Philosophy of Language* (Cambridge: Cambridge University Press, 1969).

The Construction of Social Reality (New York: Free Press, 1995).

Sedikides, C. and A. P. Gregg, "Portraits of the Self," in M. A. Hogg and J. Cooper, eds., *Sage Handbook of Social Psychology* (London: Sage, 2003), pp. 110–38.

Sedley, David, "Parmenides and Melissus," in Long, *The Cambridge Companion to Early Greek Philosophy*, pp. 113–33.

Segal, Charles, *Oedipus Tyrannus: Tragic Heroism and the Limits of Knowledge*, 2nd edn (New York: Oxford University Press, 2001).

Sehon, Scott, "An Argument against the Causal Theory of Action Explanation," *Philosophy and Phenomenological Research* 60, no. 1 (2000), pp. 67–85.

Seigel, Jerrold, *The Idea of the Self: Thought and Experience in Western Europe since the Seventeenth Century* (Cambridge: Cambridge University Press, 2005).

Seiichi, Imai, "Cabinet, Emperor, and Senior Statesmen," in Borg and Okamoto, *Pearl Harbor as History*, pp. 53–82.

Seiler, Bernd, "'Dolchstoss' und 'Dolchstosslegende'," *Zeitschrift für Deutsche Sprache* 22 (1966), pp. 1–20.

Selden, Mark and Kuoko Selden, *The Atomic Bomb: Voices from Hiroshima and Nagasaki* (New York: M. E. Sharpe, 1989).

Seligman, Adam B., *The Idea of Civil Society* (Princeton, NJ: Princeton University Press, 1995).

Sellin, Thorsten, *The Death Penalty: Report for the Model Penal Code Project of the American Law Institute* (Philadelphia, PA: American Law Institute, 1959).

Semmel, Bernard, *Imperialism and Social Reform* (Cambridge, MA: Harvard University Press, 1960).

Sen, Amartya K., "Rational Fools: A Critique of the Behavioral Foundations of Economic Theory," in H. Harris, *Scientific Models and Men* (Oxford: Oxford University Press, 1978), pp. 317–44.

"Goals, Commitments and Identity," *Journal of Law, Economics, and Organization* 20 (1992), pp. 341–55.

Seton-Watson, Hugh, *The Russian Empire, 1801–1917* (Oxford: Oxford University Press, 1967).

Seward, Desmond, *The Hundred Years War: The English in France, 1337–1453* (New York: Penguin, 1978).

Shah, J., A. Kruglanski and E. Thompson, "Membership Has its (Epistemic) Rewards: Need for Closure Effects on In-Group Bias," *Journal of Personality and Social Psychology* 75 (1998), pp. 383–93.

Shanks, C., H. K. Jacobson, and J. H. Kaplan, "Inertia and Change in the Constellation of International Governmental Organizations, 1981–1991," *International Organization* 50 (1996), pp. 593–628.

Shannon, Vaughn P., "Wendt's Violation of the Constructivist Project: Agency and Why a World State Is *Not* Inevitable," *European Journal of International Relations* 11 (December 2005), pp. 581–606.

Shapcott, Richard, "IR as Practical Philosophy: Defining a 'Classical Approach'," *British Journal of Politics and International Relations* 6 (2004), pp. 271–91.

Shapiro, Andrew L., "The Internet," *Foreign Policy*, no. 115 (Summer 1999), pp. 14–27.

Shapiro, Gary and Alan Sica, eds., *Hermeneutics* (Amherst: University of Massachusetts Press, 1984).

Shapiro, Ian, *Moral Foundations of Politics* (New Haven, CT: Yale University Press, 2003).

   The State of Democratic Theory (Princeton, NJ: Princeton University Press, 2003).

Shaw, Martin, *Theory of the Global State: Globality as an Unfinished Revolution* (Cambridge: Cambridge University Press, 2000).

Shearer, David, "Outsourcing War," *Foreign Policy*, no. 112 (Fall 1998), pp. 68–80.

Sherif, Muzafer, "Subordinate Goals in the Reduction of Intergroup Conflict," *American Journal of Sociology* 63, no. 4 (1858), pp. 349–56.

Shewmaker, Kenneth E., *Americans and Chinese Communists, 1927–1945: A Persuading Encounter* (Ithaca, NY: Cornell University Press, 1971).

Shigeo, Misawa and Ninomiya Saburō, "The Role of the Diet and Political Parties," in Borg and Okamoto, *Pearl Harbor as History*, pp. 321–40.

Shilliam, Robert, "Hegemony and the Unfashionable Problematic of 'Primitive Accumulation," *Millennium* 33, no. 1 (2004), pp. 59–90.

   "The 'Other' in Classical Political Theory: Re-Contextualizing the Cosmopolitan/Communitarian Debate," in Jahn, *Classical Theory in International Relations*, 207–32.

Shilling, Chris and Philip A. Mellor, "Durkheim, Morality and Modernity: Collective Effervescence, *Homo Duplex* and the Sources of Moral Action," *British Journal of Sociology* 49, no. 2 (June 1998), pp. 193–209.

Shillony, Ben-Ami, *Politics and Culture in Wartime Japan* (Oxford: Oxford University Press, 1981).

Shils, Edmund, *Center and Periphery* (Chicago: University of Chicago Press, 1975).

Shively, Donald H., "Popular Culture," in Hall, *The Cambridge History of Japan*, vol. VI, pp. 706–70.

Shirk, Susan L., *China: Fragile Superpower* (New York: Oxford University Press, 2007).

Shklar, Judith, *Ordinary Vices* (Cambridge, MA: Harvard University Press, 1984).

   "Let us not be Hypocritical," in Shklar, *Ordinary Vices*, pp. 45–86.

"Liberalism of Fear," in Nancy Rosenblum, ed., *Liberalism and the Moral Life* (Cambridge, MA: Harvard University Press, 1989), pp. 21–38.

Short, T. L., "Teleology in Nature," *American Philosophical Quarterly* 20, no. 4 (1983), pp. 311–20.

"Darwin's Concept of Final Cause: Neither New nor Trivial," *Biology and Philosophy* 17, no. 3 (2002), pp. 323–40.

Shotter, John, "Social Accountability and the Social Construction of 'You,'" in John Shotter and Kenneth. J. Gergen, *Texts of Identity* (London: Sage, 1989), pp. 133–51.

Shöttler, Peter, "Historians and Discourse Analysis," *History Workshop* 27, no. 1 (1989), pp. 37–65.

Showalter, Dennis E., "German Grand Strategy: A Contradiction in Terms," *Militärgeschlichtliche Mitteilungen* 48, no. 2 (1980), pp. 65–102.

The Wars of Frederick the Great (London: Longman, 1996).

"The Eastern Front and German Military Planning, 1871–1914 – Some Observations," *East European Quarterly* 15 (1981), pp. 163–80.

Shumbaugh, David, ed., *Power Shift: China and Asia's New Dynamics* (Berkeley: University of California Press, 2005).

"Return to the Middle Kingdom? China and Asia in the Early Twenty-First Century," in Shumbaugh, *Power Shift*, pp. 23–47.

Shun, Inoue, "The Invention of the Martial Arts: Kanō Jigorō and Kōdōkan Judo," in Vlastos, *Mirror of Modernity*, pp. 163–72.

Shy, John and Thomas W. Collier, "Revolutionary War," in Peter Paret, ed., *Makers of Modern Strategy from Machiavelli to the Nuclear Age* (Princeton, NJ: Princeton University Press, 1986), pp. 815–62.

Sidney, Algernon, *Discourses Concerning Government* (London: London and Westminster, 1698).

Sigmund, K., *Games of Life: Explorations in Ecology, Evolution and Behavior* (Harmondsworth: Penguin, 1995).

Sigmund, K., E. Fehr and M. A. Nowak, "The Economics of Fair Play," *Scientific American* 286 (2002), pp. 82–7.

Silberman, Asher, *Between Past and Present: Archeology, Ideology, and Nationalism in the Modern Middle East* (New York: Henry Holt, 1989).

Silberman, Bernard S. and H. D. Harootunian, eds., *Japan in Crisis: Essays on Taishō Democracy* (Princeton, NJ: Princeton University Press, 1974).

Silk, M. S., ed., *Tragedy and the Tragic Greek Theatre and Beyond* (Oxford: Oxford University Press, 1998).

Simmel, Georg, *The Philosophy of Money*, 2nd edn, trans. Tom Bottomore and David Frisby (New York: Routledge, 2004).

Simmons, B. A., *Who Adjusts: Domestic Sources of Foreign Economic Policy during the Interwar Years* (Princeton, NJ.: Princeton University Press, 1994).

Simon, Robert L., *Fair Play: The Ethics of Sport*, 2nd edn (Boulder, CO: Westview, 2004).

Simpson, Gerry, *Great Powers and Outlaw States: Unequal Sovereigns in the International Legal Order* (Cambridge: Cambridge University Press, 2004).

Sims, Brendan, "The Connections between Foreign Policy and Domestic Politics in Eighteenth-Century Britain," *History Journal* 49, no. 2 (2006), pp. 605–24.

Sinclair, R. K., *Democracy and Participation in Athens* (Cambridge: Cambridge University Press, 1988).

Singer, J. David, "The Level-of-Analysis Problem in International Relations," *World Politics* 14, no. 1 (1961), pp. 77–92.

  "The Incompleat Theorist: Insight Without Evidence," in Knorr and Rosenau, *Contending Approaches to International Politics*, pp. 62–86.

  "Accounting for International War: The State of the Discipline," *Journal of Peace Research* 18, no. 1 (1981), pp. 1–18.

Singer, J. David and Melvin Small, *The Wages of War, 1816–1965: A Statistical Handbook* (New York: Wiley, 1972).

Skinner, Quentin, *Foundations of Modern Political Thought*, vol. I: *The Renaissance* (Cambridge: Cambridge University Press, 1978).

  Machiavelli (New York: Hill and Wang, 1981).

  ed., *The Return of Grand Theory in the Human Sciences* (Cambridge: Cambridge University Press, 1985).

  "Introduction: the Return of Grand Theory," in Skinner, *The Return of Grand Theory in the Human Sciences*, pp. 1–20.

  "Meaning and Understanding in the History of Ideas," in Tully, *Meaning and Context*, pp. 29–67.

  "A Reply to My Critics," in Tully, *Meaning and Context*, pp. 231–88.

  "Some Problems in the Analysis of Political Thought and Action," in Tully, *Meaning and Context*, pp. 97–118.

  "Language and Political Change," in Ball, Farr and Hanson, *Political Innovation and Conceptual Change*, pp 6–23.

  "Machiavelli's *Discoursi* and the Pre-humanist Origins of Republic Ideas," in Gisela Bock, Quentin Skinner and Maurizio Viroli, *Machiavelli and Republicanism* (Cambridge: Cambridge University Press, 1990), pp. 21–41.

  Reason and Rhetoric in the Philosophy of Hobbes (Cambridge: Cambridge University Press, 1996).

  Visions of Politics, vol. I: *Regarding Method* (Cambridge: Cambridge University Press, 2002).

  "The State of Princes to the Person of the State," in *Visions of Politics,* vol. II: *Renaissance Virtues* (Cambridge: Cambridge University Press, 2002), pp. 368–78.

Skocpol, Theda, *States and Social Revolutions: A Comparative Analysis of France, Russia, and China* (Cambridge: Cambridge University Press, 1979).

Skrowonek, Steven, *Building a New American State: The Expansion of National Administrative Capacities, 1877–1920* (Cambridge: Cambridge University Press, 1982).

Slomp, Gabriella, "Hobbes, Thucydides and the Three Greatest Things," *History of Political Thought*, 11 (Winter 1990), pp. 565–86.

Small, Melvin and J. David Singer, *Resort to Arms: International and Civil Wars, 1816–1980* (Beverly Hills, CA: Sage, 1982).

Smith, Adam, *An Inquiry into the Nature and Causes of the Wealth of Nations* (New York: Random House, 1937).

 Lectures on Jurisprudence, ed. R. L. Meek *et al.* (Oxford: Oxford University Press, 1978).

 The Theory of Moral Sentiments (Cambridge: Cambridge University Press, 2002 [1759]).

Smith, Amy, "Eurymedon and the Evolution of Political Personifications in the Early Classical Period," *Journal of Hellenic Studies*, 119 (1999), pp. 128–41.

Smith, Anthony D., *The Ethnic Origins of Nations* (New York: Basil Blackwell, 1986).

 National Identity (Reno: University of Nevada Press, 1991).

Smith, John Maynard and Eörs Szathmáry, *The Origins of Life: From the Birth of Life to the Origins of Language* (Oxford: Oxford University Press, 1999).

Smith, Paul, *Disraelian Conservatism and Social Reform* (London: Routledge and Kegan Paul, 1967).

Smith, Richard H., "Assimilative and Contrastive Emotional Reactions to Upward and Downward Social Comparison," *Journal of Experimental Social Psychology*, 41(2000), pp. 298–304.

Smith, Steve, "The Forty Years' Detour: The Resurgence of Normative Theory in International Relations," *Millennium* 21, no. 3 (1992), pp. 489–506.

 "Positivism and Beyond," in Smith, Booth and Zalewski, *International Theory: Positivism and Beyond*, pp. 11–44.

 "Wendt's World," *Review of International Studies* 26, no. 1 (2000), pp. 151–63.

Smith, Steve, Ken Booth, and Marysia Zalewski, eds., *International Theory: Positivism and Beyond* (Cambridge: Cambridge University Press, 1996).

Smith, Thomas W., "The New Law of War: Legitimizing Hi-Tech and Infrastructural Violence," *International Studies Quarterly*, 46, no. 3 (September 2002), pp. 355–74.

Smith, Tony, *The Pattern of Imperialism: The United States, Great Britain, and the Late-Industrializing World Since 1815* (Cambridge: Cambridge University Press, 1981).

Smuts, Malcolm R., "Art and the Material Culture of Majesty in Early Stuart England," in Smuts, ed., *The Stuart Court and Europe. Essays in Politics and Political Culture* (Cambridge: Cambridge University Press, 1996), pp. 86–112.

Snyder, Jack, "Civil Military Relations and the Cult of the Offensive, 1914 and 1984," *International Security* 9 (Summer 1984), pp. 108–46.

  The Ideology of the Offensive: Military Decision Making and the Disasters of 1914 (Ithaca, NY: Cornell University Press, 1984).

  "Perceptions of the Security Dilemma in 1914," in Jervis, Lebow and Stein, *Psychology and Deterrence*, pp. 153–79.

  From Voting to Violence: Democratization and Nationalist Conflict (New York: Norton, 2000).

Snyder, Jack and Karen Ballentine, "Nationalism and the Marketplace of Ideas," *International Security* 21, no. 2 (1997), pp. 5–40.

Solingen, Etel, *Regional Orders at Century's Dawn: Global and Domestic Influences on Grand Strategy* (Princeton, NJ: Princeton University Press, 1998).

Solomon, S., J. Greenberg, and T. Pyszczynski, "Terror Management Theory of Self Esteem," in C. R. Snyder and D. Forsyth, eds., *Handbook of Social and Clinical Psychology: The Health Perspective* (New York: Pergamon Press, 1991), pp. 21–40.

  "A Terror Management Theory of Social Behaviour: The Psychological Functions of Self-Esteem and Cultural Worldviews," in M. P. Zanna, ed., *Advances in Experimental Social Psychology*, vol. XXIV (New York: Academic Press, 1991), pp. 93–159.

  "The Cultural Animal: Twenty Years of Terror Management Theory and Research," in J. Greenberg, S. L. Koole and T. Pyszczynski, eds., *Handbook of Experimental Existential Psychology* (New York: Guilford, 2004), pp. 13–34.

Soltis, Andy, *Soviet Chess, 1917–1990* (Jefferson, NC: McFarland, 2000).

Sombart, Werner, *Händler und Helden: Patriotische Besinningen* (Munich: Duncker and Graefe, 1915).

  Der Moderne Kapitalismus, 2 vols. (Munich: Duncker and Humblot, 1916).

  Luxury and Capitalism, trans. W. R. Dittmar (Ann Arbor: University of Michigan Press, 1967).

Sondhaus, Lawrence, *Franz Conrad von Hötzendorf: Architect of the Apocalypse* (Boston: Humanities Press, 2000).

Sonnino, Paul, *Louis XIV and the Origins of the Dutch War* (Cambridge: Cambridge University Press, 1988).

Soper, Steven P., *Totalitarianism: A Conceptual Approach* (Lanham, MD: University Press of America, 1985).

Sophocles, *Antigone, Oedipus the King, Electra*, trans. H. D. F. Kitto (Oxford: Oxford University Press, 1962), pp. 1–46.

Sorabji, Richard, "Aristotle on the Role of Intellect in Virtue," in Rorty, *Essays on Aristotle's Ethics*, pp. 201–20.

Srensen, Georg, "An Analysis of Contemporary Statehood: Consequences for Conflict and Cooperation," *Review of International Studies*, 23 (1997), pp. 253–69.

Changes in Statehood: The Transformation of International Relations (London: Palgrave, 2001).

Sorensen, Max, ed., *Manual of Public International Law* (New York: St. Martin's Press, 1968).

Sorensen, Theodore C., *Kennedy* (New York: Harper and Row, 1965).

Sösemann, Bernd, "Hollow-Sounding Jubilees: Forms and Effects of Public Self-Display in Wilhelmine Germany," in Mombauer and Deist, *The Kaiser*, pp. 37–62.

Spalinger, Anthony J., *War in Ancient Egypt* (Oxford: Blackwell, 2005).

Spaulding, Robert M. Jr., "The Bureaucracy as a Political Force, 1920–45," in Morley, *Dilemmas of Growth in Prewar Japan*, pp. 33–80.

Spector, Ronald H., *The American War with Japan: Eagle against the Sun* (New York: Free Press, 1985).

Speer, James, "Hans Morgenthau and the World State," *World Politics* 20, no. 2 (1968), pp. 207–27.

Spence, D. P., *Narrative Truth and Historical Truth: Meaning and Interpretation in Psychoanalysis* (New York: Norton, 1982).

Spence, I. G., *The Cavalry of Classical Greece: A Social and Military History* (Oxford: Oxford University Press, 1993).

Spengler, Oswald, *The Decline of the West* (New York: Knopf, 1939).

Spindler, Arno, *La guerre sous-marine*, 3 vols. (Paris: Payot, 1933–5).

Spinner-Halev, Jeff and Elizabeth Theiss-Morse, "National Identity and Self-esteem," *Perspective on Politics* 1, no. 3 (September 2003), pp. 515–32.

Spiro, David, *The Hidden Hand of American Hegemony*. (Ithaca, NY: Cornell University Press, 1999).

Spirtas, Michael, "A House Divided: Tragedy and Evil in Realist Theory," *Security Studies* 5 (1996), pp. 385–423.

Sprout, Harold and Margaret Sprout, *Foundations of International Politics* (Princeton: Van Nostrand, 1962).

Spruyt, Hendrik, *The Sovereign State and its Competitors* (Princeton, NJ: Princeton University Press, 1994).

Spykman, Nicholas, "Geography and Foreign Policy 2," *American Political Science Review* 36 (April 1938), pp. 213–36.

Stachura, Peter D., ed., *The Nazi Machtergreifung* (London: Allen and Unwin, 1983).

"Introduction: Weimar, National Socialism and Historians," in Stachura, *The Nazi Machtergreifung*, pp. 1–14.

"The Nazis, the Bourgeoisie and the Workers during the *Kampfzeit*," in Stachura, *The Nazi Machtergreifung*, pp. 15–32.

Stalin, J. V., *Problems of Leninism* (Moscow: Foreign Languages Publishing House, 1953).

Stanlis, Peter J., *Edmund Burke: The Enlightenment and Revolution* (New Brunswick, NJ: Transaction Publishers, 1991).

Stannard, David E., *American Holocaust: Columbus and the Conquest of the New World* (New York: Oxford University Press, 1992).

Stauffer, Devin, "Reopening the Quarrel between the Ancients and the Moderns: Leo Strauss' Critique of Hobbes' 'New Political Science'," *American Political Science Review* 101, no. 2 (May 2007), pp. 223–33.

Stearns, Peter N., *Consumerism in World History: The Global Transformation of Desire* (London: Routledge, 2001).

Steffek, Jans, "The Legitimization of International Governance: A Discourse Approach," *European Journal of International Relations*, 9 (2003), pp. 249–75.

Steger, M. D., *Globalism: The New Market Ideology* (Lanham, MD: Rowman and Littlefield, 2002).

Stein, Arthur A., "Governments, Economic Interdependence, and International Cooperation," in Philip E. Tetlock, Jo L. Husbands, Robert Jervis, Paul C. Stern and Charles Tilly, *Behavior, Society and Nuclear War*, 3 vols. (New York: Oxford University Press, 1989), vol. III, pp. 242–324.

Why Nations Cooperate: Circumstance and Choice in International Relations (Ithaca, NY: Cornell University Press, 1990).

Stein, Janice Gross, "Calculation, Miscalculation, and Conventional Deterrence 1: The View from Cairo," in Jervis, Lebow and Stein, *Psychology and Deterrence*, pp. 34–59.

"Calculation, Miscalculation, and Conventional Deterrence 2: The View from Jerusalem," in Jervis, Lebow and Stein, *Psychology and Deterrence*, pp. 60–88.

"Proliferation, Non-Proliferation, and Anti-Proliferation: Egypt and Israel in the Middle East," in Steven Spiegel, Michael Yaffe and Elizabeth Matthews, eds., *The Dynamics of Middle East Nuclear Proliferation* (New York: Mellon Press, 2000), pp. 33–58.

Stein, Janice Gross *et al.*, "Five Scenarios of the Israeli-Palestinian Relationship in 2002: Works in Progress," *Security Studies* 7, no. 4 (1998), pp. 195–212.

Steinberg, Jonathan, "The Copenhagen Complex," *Journal of Contemporary History* 1 (1966), pp. 23–46.

"The German Background to Anglo-German Relations, 1905–1914," in Hinsley, *British Foreign Policy under Sir Edward Grey*, pp. 193–215.

All or Nothing: The Axis and the Holocaust 1941–43 (London: Routledge, 1990).

Steinberg, Richard H., "In the Shadow of Law or Power?: Consensus-Based Bargaining and Outcomes in the GATT/WTO," *International Organization* 56 (Spring 2002), pp. 339–74.

Steiner, George, *Antigones* (New York: Oxford University Press, 1984).

Steiner, Zara S., *Britain and the Origins of the First World War* (London: Macmillan, 1977).

Steinert, Marlis, *Hitler's War and the Germans*, ed. and trans. Thomas E. J. de Witt (Athens, OH: Ohio University Press, 1977).

Stenton, Frank, *Anglo-Saxon England*, 3rd edn (Oxford: Oxford University Press, 2001 [1943]).

Sterling-Folker, Jennifer, "Realist Environment, Liberal Process, and Domestic-Level Variables," *International Studies Quarterly* 41, no. 1 (1997), pp. 1–25.

Stern, Fritz, "Bethmann Hollweg and the War: The Limits of Responsibility," in Stern and Krieger, *The Responsibility of Power*, pp. 271–307.

   The Failure of Illiberalism: Essays on the Political Culture of Modern Germany (New York: Knopf, 1972).

   The Politics of Cultural Despair: A Study in the Rise of the Germanic Ideology (Berkeley: University of California Press, 1974).

   Gold and Iron; Bismarck, Bleichröder, and the Building of the German Empire (New York: Knopf, 1977).

Stern, Fritz and Leonard Krieger, eds., *The Responsibility of Power: Historical Essays in Honor of Hajo Holborn* (Garden City, NY: Doubleday, 1967).

Stern, Sheldon M., *Averting "The Final Failure": John F. Kennedy and the Secret Cuban Missile Crisis Meetings* (Stanford, CA: Stanford University Press, 2003).

Stevenson, David, *Armaments and the Coming of War in Europe, 1904–1914* (Oxford: Oxford University Press, 1996).

   "French War Aims and Peace Planning," in Boemeke, Feldman and Glaser, *Treaty of Versailles*, pp. 87–110.

Stewart, Ian, *Does God Play Dice? The New Mathematics of Chaos*, 2nd edn (Malden, MA: Blackwell, 2002).

Stigler, George and Gary Becker, "De Gustibus Non Est Disputant," *American Economic Review* 67, no. 2 (1977), pp. 76–90.

Stopes, Marie, *Married Love or Love in Marriage* (New York: Critic and Guide Co., 1918).

Storry, Richard, *Double Patriots: A Study of Japanese Nationalism* (Boston: Houghton Mifflin, 1957).

Story, Joanna, ed., *Charlemagne: Empire and Society* (Manchester: University of Manchester Press, 2005).

Stove, D. C., "Hume, Probability, and Induction," *Philosophical Review* 74 (1965), pp. 160–77.

Strachan, Hew, *The First World War*, 5 vols. (Oxford: Oxford University Press, 2001).

Strandmann, Hartmut Pogge von, "Germany and the Coming of War," in Evans and Strandmann, *The Coming of the First World War*, pp. 87–124.

Strang, David, "Anomaly and Commonplace in European Political Expansion: Realist and Institutionalist Accounts," *International Organization* 45 (1991), pp. 143–62.

Strauss, Barry, "On Aristotle's Critique of Athenian Democracy," in Lord and O'Connor, *Essays on the Foundations of Aristotelian Political Science*, pp. 212–33.

    "The Athenian Trireme, School of Democracy," in Ober and Hedrick, *Dēmokratia*, pp. 313–26.

    "The Melting Pot, the Mosaic and the Agora," in J. Peter Euben, John R. Wallach and Josiah Ober, *Athenian Political Thought and the Reconstruction of American American Democracy* (Ithaca, NY: Cornell University Press, 1994), pp. 252–64.

    The Battle of Salamis (New York: Simon and Schuster, 2004).

    The Trojan War (New York: Simon and Schuster, 2006).

Strauss, Jenny, *Hesiod's Cosmos* (Cambridge: Cambridge University Press, 2003).

Strauss, Leo, *The Political Philosophy of Hobbes, its Basis and its Genesis*, trans. Elsa M. Sinclair (Chicago: University of Chicago Press, 1952).

    Natural Right and History (Chicago: University of Chicago Press, 1953).

Strayer, Joseph R., *On the Medieval Origins of the Modern State* (Princeton, NJ: Princeton University Press, 1970).

    Medieval Statecraft and the Perspectives of History (Princeton, NJ: Princeton University Press, 1971).

Streit, Christian, *Keine Kameraden; deutsche Wehrmacht und die sojetische Kriesgefangenen, 1941–45* (Stuttgart: Deutsche Verlags-Anstalt, 1978).

Strickland, Matthew, "Against the Lord's Anointed: Aspects of Warfare and Baronial Rebellion in England and Normandy, 1075–1265," in Garnett and Hudson, *Law and Government in Medieval England and Normandy*, pp. 56–79.

Strong, Tracy B., *Friedrich Nietzsche and the Politics of Transfiguration*, expanded edn (Berkeley: University of California Press, 1988).

Stubbs, Richard and Geoffrey R. D. Underhill, *Political Economy and the Changing Global Order* (Toronto: M&S, 1994).

Stueck, William, *The Korean War: An International History* (Princeton, NJ: Princeton University Press, 1995).

Suganami, Hidemi, "Japan's Entry into International Society," in Bull and Watson, *Expansion of International Society*, pp. 117–26.

Sugden, Robert, "Thinking as a Team: Towards an Explanation for Nonselfish Behavior," *Social Philosophy and Policy* 10, no. 1 (1993), pp. 69–89.

Sullivan, Walter, *Restructuring Public Philosophy* (Berkeley: University of California Press, 1984).

Sumner, William Graham, *Folkways: A Study of the Sociological Importance of Usages, Manners, Customs, Mores, and Morals* (Boston: Ginn, 1940 [1907]).

Sumption, Jonathan, *The Hundred Years War*, 2 vols. (London: Faber and Faber, 1990–9).

Sun, Youli, *China and the Origins of the Pacific War, 1931–41* (New York: St. Martin's Press, 1993).

Suskind, Ron, *The One Percent Doctrine: Deep Inside America's Pursuit of its Enemies since 9/11* (New York: Simon and Schuster, 2006).

Suzuki, Shogo, "China's Quest for Great Power Status: The Social Mechanisms of Delinquent Gang Formation," University of Manchester, Centre of International Politics Working Paper Series no. 29, March 2007.

   "Seeking 'Legitimate' Great Power Status in Post-Cold War International Society: China's and Japan's Participation in UNPKO," *International Relations* 22, no. 1 (2008), pp. 45–63.

Swann, Julian, "Politics and the State in Eighteenth Century Europe," in Blanning, *The Eighteenth Century*, pp. 11–51.

Sweet, D. W., "Great Britain and Germany, 1905–1911," in Hinsley, *British Foreign Policy under Sir Edward Grey*, pp. 216–35.

Swenson, Rod, "Autocatakinetics, Evolution, and the Law of Maximum Entropy Production," in Lee Freese, *Advances in Human Ecology*, vol. VI (Greenwich, CT: JAI Press, 1997), pp. 1–47.

Sylvester, Christine, *Feminist Theory and International Relations in a Postmodern Era* (Cambridge: Cambridge University Press, 1994).

Syme, Ronald, *The Augustan Aristocracy* (Oxford: Oxford University Press, 1986).

Tacitus, *Germania*, trans, J. B. Rives (Oxford: Oxford University Press, 1999).

Tajfel, Henri, "Social Categorisation, Social Identity and Social Comparison," in Tajfel, *Differentiation Between Social Groups*, pp. 61–76.

   ed., *Differentiation Between Social Groups: Studies in the Psychology of Intergroup Relations* (London: Academic Press, 1978).

   Human Groups and Social Categories (Cambridge: Cambridge University Press, 1981).

Tajfel, Henri and John Turner, "The Social Identity Theory of Intergroup Behavior," in Stephen Worchel and William Austin, eds., *Psychology of Intergroup Relations* (Chicago: Nelson-Hall, 1986), pp. 7–24.

Tajfel, Henri, M. Billing, R. Bundy and C. Flament, "Social Categorization and Intergroup Behavior," *European Journal of Social Psychology* 1, no. 2 (1971), pp. 149–78.

Takashi, Itō, "The Role of Right-Wing Organizations in Japan," in Borg and Okamoto, *Pearl Harbor as History*, pp. 487–510.

Talbott, Strobe, "Globalization and Diplomacy: A Practitioner's Perspective," *Foreign Policy*, no. 108 (Fall 1997), pp. 69–83.

Tamir, Yael, *Liberal Nationalism* (Princeton, NJ: Princeton University Press, 1993).

"Who's Afraid of a Global State?," in Kjell Goldmann, Ulf Hannerz and Charles Westin, *Nationalism and Internationalism in the Post-Cold War Era* (London: Routledge, 2000), pp. 244–67.

Tandy, David W., *Warriors into Traders: The Power of the Market in Early Greece* (Berkeley: University of California Press, 1997).

Taplin, Oliver, *Homeric Soundings: The Shaping of the Iliad* (Oxford: Oxford University Press, 1992).

Tatu, Michel, *Power in the Kremlin: From Khrushchev to Kosygin* (New York: Viking, 1968).

Taubman, Ben-Ari O., V. Florian and M. Mikulincer, "The Impact of Mortality Salience on Reckless Driving – A Test of Terror Management Mechanisms," *Journal of Personality and Social Psychology* 76 (1999), pp. 35–45.

Taylor, A. J. P., *English History 1914–1945* (Oxford: Oxford University Press, 1965).
  The Struggle for the Mastery of Europe, 1848–1918 (Oxford: Oxford University Press, 1971).

Taylor, Charles, *Hegel* (Cambridge: Cambridge University Press, 1975).
  Hegel and Modern Society (Cambridge: Cambridge University Press, 1979).
  Philosophy and the Human Sciences: Philosophical Papers, vol. II (Cambridge: Cambridge University Press, 1985).
  "Interpretation and the Sciences of Man," in *Philosophy and the Human Sciences*, pp. 15–57.
  Sources of the Self: The Making of Modern Identity (Cambridge, MA: Harvard University Press, 1989).
  The Malaise of Modernity (Toronto: Anansi Press, 1991).
  "The Politics of Recognition," in Amy Gutmann, ed., *Multiculturalism: Examining the Politics of Recognition* (Princeton, NJ: Princeton University Press, 1994), pp. 25–74.
  "Politics," in Jonathan Barnes, ed., *The Cambridge Companion to Aristotle* (Cambridge: Cambridge University Press, 1995), pp. 233–58.
  "Living with Difference," in Anita Allen and Milton Regan, *Debating Democracy's Discontent* (Oxford: Oxford University Press, 1998), pp. 212–26.
  "The Atomists," in Long, *The Cambridge Companion to Early Greek Philosophy*, pp. 181–204.

Taylor, Charles and David A. Jodice, *World Handbook of Political and Social Indicators*, 3rd edn (New Haven, CT: Yale University Press, 1983).

Taylor, Donald M., "Multiple Group Membership and Self-Identity," *Journal of Cross-Cultural Psychology* 12, no. 1 (1981), pp. 61–79.

Taylor, Ian, "Taiwan's Foreign Policy and Africa: The Limitations of Dollar Diplomacy," *Journal of Contemporary China* 11, no. 30 (2002), pp. 125–40.

Taylor, Peter J., "The State as a Container: Territoriality in the Modern-World System," *Progress in Human Geography* 18, no. 2 (1994), pp. 151–62.

"Embedded Statism and the Social Sciences: Opening Up to New Spaces," *Environment and Planning* 28 (1996) pp. 1917–28.

Taylor, Telford, *The Anatomy of the Nuremberg Trials* (New York: Knopf, 1992).

Teitel, Rudi, "Transitional Justice: The Role of Law in Political Transformation," *Yale Law Journal* 106, no. 7 (May 1997), pp. 2009–80.

Tennenhouse, Leonard, "Strategies of State and Political Plays: *A Midsummer Night's Dream, Henry IV, Henry V, Henry VIII*," in Jonathan Dollimore and Alan Sinfield, *Political Shakespeare: Essays in Cultural Materialism* (Manchester: Manchester University Press, 1996), pp. 109–28.

Teschke, Benno, *The Myth of 1648: Class, Geopolitics, and the Making of Modern International Relations* (London: Verso, 2003).

"Debating 'The Myth of 1648': State Formation, the Interstate System and the Emergence of Capitalism in Europe," *International Politics* 45, no. 5 (November 2006), pp. 531–73.

Tesón, Fernando, *A Philosophy of International Law* (Boulder, CO: Westview, 1998).

Tesser, Abraham and James E. Collins, "Emotion in Social Reflection and Comparison Situations: Intuitive, Systematic, and Exploratory Approaches," *Journal of Personality and Social Psychology* 55 (1988), pp. 695–709.

Tetlock, Philip E. "Accountability and Complexity of Thought," *Journal of Personality and Social Psychology* 45 (July 1983), pp. 74–83.

Tetlock, Philip E. and Aaron Belkin, eds., *Counterfactual Thought Experiments in World Politics: Logical, Methodological, and Psychological Perspectives* (Princeton, NJ: Princeton University Press, 1996).

Tetlock, Philip A., Richard Ned Lebow and Geoffrey Parker, *Unmaking the West: Counterfactual and Contingency* (Ann Arbor: University of Michigan Press, 2006).

Thaler, Richard H., "Anomalies: The January Effect," *Journal of Economic Perspectives* 1 (1987), pp. 197–201.

Thaler, Richard H., *The Winner's Curse: Paradoxes and Anomalies of Economic Life* (New York: Free Press, 1992).

Thayer, Bradley A., *Darwin and International Relations: On the Evolutionary Origins of War and Ethnic Conflict* (Lexington: University Press of Kentucky, 2004).

The Stateman's Yearbook, 1914 (New York: Macmillan, 1914).

Thies, Jochen, *Architekt der Weltherrschaft: Die "Endziele" Hitlers* (Düsseldorf: Droste, 1976).

Thomas, Caroline, *In Search of Security: The Third World* (Boulder, CO: Lynne Rienner, 1987).

Thompson, J. Eric, *The Rise and Fall of Maya Civilization* (Norman: University of Oklahoma Press, 1964).

Thompson, Michael, *Rubbish Theory: The Creation and Destruction of Value* (Oxford: Oxford University Press, 1979).

Thompson, Norma, *The Ship of State: Statecraft and Politics from Ancient Greece to Democratic America* (New Haven, CT: Yale University Press, 2001).

Thompson, Wayne C., *In the Eye of the Storm: Kurt Riezler and the Crises of Modern Germany* (Iowa City: University of Iowa Press, 1980).

Thompson, William P., "A Streetcar Named Sarajevo: Catalysts, Multiple Causation Chains, and Rivalry Structures," *International Studies Quarterly*, 47 (September 2003), pp. 453–74.

Thompson, William R., "Democracy and Peace: Putting the Cart before the Horse?" *International Organization* 50 (1996), pp. 141–74.

   ed., *Evolutionary Interpretations of World Politics* (London: Routledge, 2001).

Thomson, Janice, *Mercenaries, Pirates, and Sovereigns* (Princeton, NJ: Princeton University Press, 1994).

Thomson, Janice and Stephen D. Krasner, "Global Transactions and the Consolidation of Sovereignty," in Czempiel and Rosenau, *Global Changes and Theoretical Challenges*, pp. 195–219.

Thucydides, *History of the Peloponnesian War*, trans. Rex Warner (New York: Viking-Penguin, 1972).

   The Landmark Thucydides: A Comprehensive Guide to the Peloponnesian War, ed. Robert B. Strassler (New York: Free Press, 1996).

Tibi, Bassam, "The Simultaneity of the Unsimultaneous: Old Tribes and Imposed Nation-States in the Modern Middle East," in Philip Khoury and Joseph Kostiner, *Tribes and State Formation in the Middle East* (Berkeley: University of California Press, 1990).

Tickner, J. Ann, "Identity in International Relations Theory: Feminist Perspectives," in Lapid and Kratochwil, *The Return of Culture and Identity in IR Theory*, pp. 147–62.

Tiedemann, Arthur E., "Big Business and Politics in Prewar Japan," in Morley, *Dilemmas of Growth in Prewar Japan*, pp. 267–318.

Tilly, Charles, *The Formation of National States in Western Europe* (Princeton, NJ: Princeton University Press, 1975).

   Big Structures, Large Processes and Huge Comparisons (New York: Russell Sage Foundation, 1984).

   "War-Making and State-Making as Organized Crime," in Peter B. Evans, Dietrich Rueschemeyer and Theda Skocpol, *Bringing the State Back In* (Cambridge: Cambridge University Press, 1985), pp. 169–91.

   "Entanglements of European Cities and States," in Charles Tilly and Wim P. Blockmans, eds., *Cities and the Rise of States in Europe, A.D. 1000 to 1800* (Boulder, CO: Westview, 1989), pp. 158–81.

   Coercion, Capital, and European States, AD 990–1990 (Oxford: Blackwell, 1990).

   "Citizenship, Identity and Social History," in Charles Tilly, *Citizenship, Identity, and Social History* (Cambridge: Press Syndicate of the University of Cambridge, 1996), pp. 1–18.

"International Communities, Secure or Otherwise," in Emanuel Adler and Michael Barnett, *Security Communities* (Cambridge: Cambridge University Press, 1998), pp. 397–412.

Tin-bor Hui, Victoria, *War and State Formation in Ancient China and Early Modern Europe* (New York: Cambridge University Press, 2005).

Tirpitz, Alfred von, *Erinnerungen* (Leipzig: K. F. Koehler, 1919).

Titmuss, Richard M., *Problems of Social Policy: 1907–1973* (London: HMSO, 1950).

Titus, David Anson, *Palace and Politics in Prewar Japan* (New York: Columbia University Press, 1974).

Toby, Ronald P., *State and Diplomacy in Early Modern Japan: Asia in the Development of the Tokugawa Bakufu* (Stanford, CA: Stanford University Press, 1991).

Tocqueville, Alexis de, *The Old Regime and the French Revolution*, trans. Stuart Gilbert (Garden City, NY: Doubleday Anchor, 1955).

Democracy in America, trans. and ed. Harvey C. Mansfield and Debra Winthrop (Chicago: University of Chicago Press, 2000).

Todorov, Tzvetan, *The Conquest of America: The Question of the Other* (New York: Harper and Row, 1984).

Toews, John, "Intellectual History after the Linguistic Turn: The Autonomy of Meaning and the Irreducibility of Experience," *American Historical Review* 92, no. 4 (1987), pp. 809–907.

Togliatti, Palmiro, *Lectures on Fascism* (New York: International Publishers, 1976).

Tollaksen, Jeff, "New Insights from Quantum Theory on Time, Consciousness, and Reality," in Stuart Hameroff, Alfred Kasczniak and Alwyn Scott, *Toward a Science of Consciousness* (Cambridge, MA: MIT Press, 1996), pp. 551–67.

Tolliday, Steven, ed., *The Economic Development of Modern Japan, 1868–1945*, vol. I: *From the Meiji Restoration to the Second World War* (Cheltenham: Elgar, 2001).

Tomes, Nancy, *The Gospel of Germs: Men, Women and the Microbe in American Life* (Cambridge, MA: Harvard University Press, 1998).

Tompkins, Daniel, "Fear, Honor and Profit: Ambiguity and Ideation in Thucydides," paper presented at the annual meeting of the American Political Science Association, Philadelphia, September 2006.

Tönnies, Ferdinand, *Gemeinschaft und Gesellschaft: Abhandlung des Communismus und des Socialismus als empirischer Kulturformen* (Leipzig: R. Reisland, 1887).

Topmiller, Robert, 'A Missed Opportunity for Peace in Vietnam – 1966," *Peace and Change* 27, no. 1 (2002), pp. 63–96.

Toulmin, Stephen, *Foresight and Understanding: An Inquiry into the Aims of Science* (Bloomington: Indiana University Press, 1961).

Cosmopolis: The Hidden Agenda of Modernity (New York: Free Press, 1990).

Travers, T. H. E., "Technology, Tactics, and Morale: Jean de Bloch, the Boer War, and British Military Theory, 1900–1914," *Journal of Modern History* 51 (June 1979), pp. 224–86.

Treasure, Geoffrey, *Louis XIV* (London: Longman, 2001).

    The Making of Modern Europe, 1648–1780 (London: Routledge, 2003).

Treitschke, Heinrich von, *Politik*, ed. M. Cornicelius (Leipzig: S. Hirzel, 1897–8).

Trevor-Roper, Hugh, ed., *Hitler's Secret Conversations, 1941–1944* (New York: Farrar, Straus and Young, 1953).

Tritle, Lawrence. "Warfare in Herodotus," in Carolyn Dewald and John Marincola, eds., *The Cambridge Companion to Herodotus* (Cambridge: Cambridge University Press, 2006), pp. 209–23.

Trotsky, Leon, *The Permanent Revolution* (New York: Merit, 1969).

Troyes, Chrétien de, *Arthurian Romances*, trans. William W. Kibler (London: Penguin, 1991).

Trumpener, Ulrich, "Junkers and Others: The Rise of Commoners in the Prussian Army, 1871–1914," *Canadian Journal of History* 14 (April 1979), pp. 29–47.

Tuathail, Gearóid O, Andrew Herod and Susan M. Roberts, "Negotiating Unruly Problematics," in Andrew Herod, Gearóid Ó Tuathail and Susan M. Roberts, *An Unruly World? Globalization, Governance, and Geography* (London: Routledge, 1998), pp. 1–24.

Tuchman, Barbara, *A Proud Tower: A Portrait of the World before the War 1890–1914* (New York: Ballentine Books, 1996).

Tuck, Richard, *Hobbes* (New York: Oxford University Press, 1989).

    Philosophy and Government, 1572–1651 (Cambridge: Cambridge University Press, 1993).

    "Hobbes' Moral Philosophy," in Tom Sorrell, ed., *The Cambridge Companion to Hobbes* (Cambridge: Cambridge University Press, 1996), pp. 175–207.

    The Rights of War and Peace: Political Thought and the International Order from Grotius to Kant (New York: Oxford University Press, 1999).

Tucker, Robert C., *Stalin as Revolutionary: A Study in the History of Personality, 1879–1929* (New York: Norton, 1973).

    Stalin in Power: The Revolution from Above, 1928–1941 (New York: Norton, 1990).

Tullio-Altan, Carlo, *La conscienza civile degli Italiani: valore e disvalore nella storia nazionale* (Udine: Paolo Gaspari, 1997).

Tully, James, ed., *Meaning and Context: Quentin Skinner and his Critics* (Princeton, NJ: Princeton University Press, 1988).

    An Approach to Political Philosophy: Locke in Context (Cambridge: Cambridge University Press, 1993).

Tunstall, Graydon A. Jr., *Planning for War against Russia and Serbia: Austro-Hungarian and German Military Strategies, 1871–1914* (New York: Columbia University Press, 1993).

"Bundesgenossen? Zur militärpolitischen Kooperation zwischen Berlin und Wien, 1912 bis 1914," in Walther L. Bernecker and Volker Dotterweich, eds., *Deutschland in den international Beziehungen des 19. und 20. Jahrhunderts* (Munich: Ernst Vögel, 1996), pp. 143–68.

"The Habsburg Command Conspiracy: The Austrian Falsification of Historiography on the Outbreak of World War I," *Austrian History Yearbook* 27 (1996), pp. 181–98.

"Austria-Hungary," in Hamilton and Herwig, *The Origins of World War I*, pp. 112–49.

Turner, Bryan S., *Status* (Minneapolis: University of Minnesota Press, 1988).

ed., *Citizenship and Social Theory* (London: Sage, 1993).

"Contemporary Problems in the Theory of Citizenship," in Turner, *Citizenship and Social Theory*, pp. 1–18.

Turner, Frank M., *The Greek Heritage in Victorian Britain* (New Haven, CT: Yale University Press, 1981).

Turner, Fred, *Echoes of Combat: The Vietnam War in American Memory* (New York: Anchor, 1996).

Turner, Henry Ashby Jr., *Geissel des Jahrhunderts: Hitler and seine Hinterlassenschaft* (Berlin: Siedler, 1989).

Turner, J. C., P. J. Oakes, S. A. Haslam and C. McGarty, "Self and Collective: Cognition in Social Context," *Personality and Social Psychological Bulletin*, 20 (1994), pp. 454–62.

Turner, J. C., P. J. Oakes, S. D. Reicher and M. S. Wetherell, *Rediscovering the Social Group: A Self-Categorization Theory* (Oxford: Blackwell, 1987).

Turner, John, R. Brown and Henri Tajfel, "Social Comparison and Group Interest in Intergroup Favoritism," *European Journal of Social Psychology* 9, no. 2 (1971), pp. 187–204.

Turner, Jonathan, *A Theory of Social Action* (Stanford, CA: Stanford University Press, 1988).

Turner, Stephen, *The Social Theory of Practices: Tradition, Tacit Knowledge, and Presuppositions* (Chicago: University of Chicago Press, 1994).

The Cambridge Companion to Weber (Cambridge: Cambridge University Press, 2000).

Tversky, Amos and Daniel Kahneman, "Loss Aversion in Riskless Choice: A Reference-Dependent Model," *Quarterly Journal of Economics* 104 (1991), pp. 1039–62.

Tyler, Tom R., "Psychological Perspectives on Legitimacy and Legitimation," *Annual Review of Psychology* 57 (January 2006), pp. 375–400.

Tylor, Edward B., *The Origins of Culture* (New York: Harper and Row, 1958 [1871]).

Uhl, Heidemarie, "From Victim to Co-Responsibility Thesis: Nazi Rule, World War II, and the Holocaust in Austrian Memory," in Lebow, Kansteiner and Fogu, *Politics of Memory in Postwar Europe*, pp. 40–72.

Ulam, Adam B., *Expansion and Coexistence: The History of Soviet Foreign Policy, 1917–1967* (New York: Praeger, 1968).

Ulanowicz, Robert, *Ecology: The Ascendant Perspective* (New York: Columbia University Press, 1997).

Ullmann-Margalit, Edna, "Invisible-Hand Explanations," *Synthèse* 39, no. 2 (1978), pp. 263–91.

Ungern-Sternberg, Jürgen von, "The Crisis of the Republic," in Flower, *The Cambridge Companion to the Roman Republic*, pp. 89–112.

United States Department of State, *The Washington Summit: General Secretary Brezhnev's Visit to the United States, June 18–25, 1973* (Washington, DC: Government Printing Office, 1973).

United States Senate, *Report on the U.S. Intelligence Community's Prewar Intelligence Assessments on Iraq* (Washington, DC: Government Printing Office, 2004).

Urbach, Karina, *European Aristocracies and the Radical Right, 1918–1939* (Oxford: Oxford University Press, 2007).

Vale, Juliet, "Violence and Tournament," in Kaeuper, *Violence in Medieval Society*, pp. 143–58.

Vale, M. G. A., *English Gascony, 1399–1453* (Oxford: Oxford University Press, 1970).
    War and Chivalry: Warfare and Aristocratic Culture in England, France and Burgundy at the End of the Middle Ages (London: Duckworth, 1981).
    The Princely Court: Medieval Courts and Culture in North-West Europe, 1270–1380 (Oxford: Oxford University Press, 2001).

Vallacher, Robin and Andrzej Nowak, "The Emergence of Dynamical Social Psychology," *Psychological Inquiry* 8, no. 2 (1997), pp. 73–99.

Van Creveld, Martin, *The Power of Power Politics: A Critique* (New Brunswick, NJ: Rutgers University Press, 1983).
    Technology and War: From 2000 B. C. to the Present (New York: Free Press, 1989).
    The Transformation of War (New York: Free Press, 1991).
    "The Fate of the State," *Parameters* (Spring 1996), pp. 4–17.
    The Rise and Decline of the State (Cambridge: Cambridge University Press, 1999).

Van Evera, Stephen, "The Cult of the Offensive and the Origins of the First World War," *International Security* 9, no. 1 (Summer 1984), pp. 58–107.
    Causes of War: Power and the Roots of Conflict (Ithaca, NY: Cornell University Press, 1999).

Van Ness, Peter, "The North Korean Nuclear Crisis: Four-Plus Two – an Idea Whose Time has Come," *Keynotes*, no. 4, Department of International Relations, Australia National University, November 2003.

Van Riper, Paul K. and F. G. Hoffman, "Pursuing the Real Revolution in Military Affairs: Exploiting Knowledge-Based Warfare," *National Security Studies Quarterly* 4 (Summer 1998), pp. 1–19.

Varela, Francisco, "Patterns of Life: Intertwining Identity and Cognition," *Brain and Cognition* 34, no. 1 (1997), pp. 72–87.

Varley, H. Paul, *Samurai* (New York: Delacorte Press, 1970).

Vasquez, John A., *The War Puzzle* (Cambridge: Cambridge University Press, 1993).
   The Power of Power Politics: From Classical Realism to Neotraditionalism (Cambridge: Cambridge University Press, 1998).

Vattel, Emmerich de, *Le droit des gens* (Washington, DC: Carnegie Institution, 1916).

Veblen, Thorstein, *The Theory of the Leisure Class: An Economic Study in the Evolution of Institutions* (New York: Modern Library, 1934 [1898]).
   Imperial Germany and the Industrial Revolution (New York: Viking, 1939).

Veitch, Colin, "'Play up! Play up! and Win the War!' Football, the Nation and the First World War 1914–15," *Journal of Contemporary History* 20 (1985), pp. 363–78.

Venette, Jean de, *The Chronicle of Jean de Venette*, trans. J. Birdsall, ed. R. A. Newhall (New York: Columbia University Press, 1953).

Venturi, Franco, *Roots of Revolution: A History of the Populist and Socialist Movements in Nineteenth Century Russia* (London: Weidenfeld and Nicolson, 1952).

Vernant, Jean Pierre, *Mythe et pensée chez les grecs, études de psychologie historique* (Paris: Maspero, 1966).
   "A 'Beautiful Death' and the Disfigured Corpse in Homeric Epic," in *Mortals and Immortals: Collected Essays*, ed. Froma I. Zeitlin (Princeton, NJ: Princeton University Press, 1991), pp. 50–74.

Vertzberger, Yaacov, Y. I., "Rethinking and Reconceptualizing Risk in Foreign Policy Decision Making: A Sociocognitive Approach," *Political Psychology* 16, no. 2 (1995), pp. 347–80.

Veyne, Paul, *Did the Greeks Believe in their Myths? An Essay in the Constitutive Imagination* (Chicago: University of Chicago Press, 1988).

Vico, Giambattista, *The New Science*, trans. T. G. Bergin and M. H. Fisch (Ithaca, NY: Cornell University Press, 1948).

Victor D. Cha and David C. Kang, "The Korea Crisis," *Foreign Policy*, 26 (May 2003), pp. 20–8.
   Nuclear North Korea: A Debate on Engagement Strategies (New York: Columbia University Press, 2003).

Vidal-Nacquet, Pierre, *The Black Hunter: Forms of Thought and Forms of Society in the Greek World*, trans. A. Szegedy-Maszak (Baltimore, MD: Johns Hopkins University Press, 1986).

Vincent, Andrew, "The Hegelian State and International Politics," *Review of International Politics* 9, no. 2 (1983), pp. 191–205.
   Theories of the State (Oxford: Blackwell, 1987).

Vincent, R. J., *Human Rights and International Relations* (Cambridge: Cambridge University Press, 1986).

"Racial Equality," in Bull and Watson, *Expansion of International Society*, pp. 239–54.

Viner, Jacob, "Power versus Plenty as Objectives of Foreign Policy in the Seventeenth and Eighteenth Centuries," *World Politics* 1, no. 1 (1948), pp. 1–29.

Virgil, *The Aeneid*, trans. David West (New York: Penguin, 1990).

Viroli, Maurizio, *From Politics to Reason of State: The Acquisition and Transformation of the Language of Politics 1250–1600* (Cambridge: Cambridge University Press, 1992).

Machiavelli (Oxford: Oxford University Press, 1998).

Vlastos, Gregory, *Socrates: Ironist and Moral Philosopher* (Cambridge: Cambridge University Press, 1991).

Vlastos, Stephen, "Opposition Movements in Early Meji, 1868–1885," in Jansen, *The Emergence of Meiji Japan*, pp. 203–67.

ed., *Mirror of Modernity: Invented Traditions of Modern Japan* (Berkeley: University of California Press, 1998).

"Tradition: Past/Present Culture and Modern Japanese History," in Vlastos, *Mirror of Modernity*, pp. 1–18.

"Agrarianism without Tradition: The Radical Critique of Prewar Japanese Modernity," in *Vlastos, Mirror of Modernity*, pp. 79–94.

Volkogonov, Dimitri, *Stalin: Triumph and Tragedy*, ed. and trans. Harold Shukman (London: Weidenfeld and Nicolson, 1991).

Voltaire [François-Marie Arouet] *Dictionnaire philosophique*, 3 vols. (Paris: Hachette, 1860).

"Envie," Questions sur l'encyclopédie (1771), in *Oeuvres complètes de Voltaire*, ed. Louis Moland (Paris: Garnier, 1878), vol. II, pp. 537–8.

The Age of Louis XIV, trans. Martyn P. Pollack (New York: E. P. Dutton, 1942).

Vygotsky, Lev S., *Mind in Society: The Development of Higher Psychological Processes*, ed. Michael Cole (Cambridge, MA: Harvard University Press, 1978).

Waever, Ole, "Securitization and Desecuritization," in Ronnie Lipschutz, *On Security* (New York: Columbia University Press, 1995), pp. 46–86.

"European Security Identities," *Journal of Common Market Studies*, 34, no. 1 (1996), pp. 103–32.

"The Sociology of a Not So International Discipline: American and European Developments in International Relations," *International Organization* 52, no. 4 (Autumn 1998), pp. 687–727.

Wakabayashi, Bob Tadashi, *Anti-Foreignism and Western Learning in Early-Modern Japan: The New Theses of 1825* (Cambridge, MA: Harvard University Press, 1986).

What Really Happened in Nanking: Refutation of a Common Myth (Tokyo: Shuppan, 2002).

Walbank, F. W., "Introduction," to Polybius, *The Rise of the Roman Empire*, pp. 9–39.

Waldron, Arthur, "After Deng the Deluge: China's Next Leap Forward," *Foreign Affairs* 74, no. 5 (September/October 1995), pp. 148–53.

Waldron, Jeremy, *God, Locke, and Equality: Christian Foundations in Locke's Political Thought* (Cambridge: Cambridge University Press, 2002).

Waley, Daniel, "The Army of the Florentine Republic from the Twelfth to the Fourteenth Century," in Nicolai Rubinstein, ed., *Florentine Studies: Politics and Society in Renaissance Florence* (London: Faber, 1968), pp. 70–108.

Walicki, Andrej, *The Slavophile Controversy: History of a Conservative Utopia in Nineteenth-Century Russian Thought*, trans. Hilda Andrews-Rusiecka (Oxford: Oxford University Press, 1975).

Walker, R. B. J., "The Concept of Culture in the Theory of International Relations," in Jongsuk Chay, *Culture and International Relations* (New York: Praeger, 1990), pp. 3–17.

Inside/Outside: International Relations as Political Theory (Cambridge: Cambridge University Press, 1993).

"Editorial Note: Re-engaging with the Political," *Alternatives* 25 (2001), pp. 1–2.

Wallace, James and Jim Erickson, *Hard Drive: Bill Gates and the Making of the Microsoft Empire* (New York: Wiley, 1992).

Wallace-Hadrill, Andrew, "*Mutatas Formas*: The Augustan Transformation of Roman Knowledge," in Galinsky, *The Age of Augustus*, pp. 55–84.

Wallach, John R., *The Platonic Political Art* (University Park: Pennsylvania State University Press, 2001).

Wallerstein, Immanuel, *The Modern World System*, 3 vols. (New York: Academic Press, 1974–89).

The Capitalist World Economy (Cambridge: Cambridge University Press, 1979).

The Politics of the World-Economy: The States, the Movements, and Civilization (Cambridge: Cambridge University Press, 1984).

"The Inter-State Structure of the Modern World-System," in Smith, Booth and Zalewski, *International Theory*, pp. 87–107.

Walt, Stephen M., "Alliance Formation and the Balance of World Power," *International Security* 9, no. 4 (1985), pp. 3–43.

The Origins of Alliances (Ithaca, NY: Cornell University Press, 1987).

"Testing Theories of Alliance Formation: The Case of Southwest Asia," *International Organization* 42, no. 2 (1998), pp. 275–316.

"Keeping the World 'Off Balance'," in Ikenberry, *America Unrivaled*, pp. 121–54.

Waltz, Kenneth N., *Man, the State and War* (New York: Columbia University Press, 1959).

Theory of International Politics (Reading, MA: Addison-Wesley, 1979).

"The Spread of Nuclear Weapons: More May Be Better," Adelphi Papers, no. 171 (London: International Institute for Strategic Studies, 1981).

"The Emerging Structure of International Politics," *International Security* 18 (1993), pp. 44–79.

"International Relations Is Not Foreign Policy," *Security Studies* 6 (1996), pp. 54–7.

"Structural Realism after the Cold War," *International Security* 25, no. 2 (2000), pp. 5–41.

Walzer, Michael, "On the Role of Symbolism in Political Thought," *Political Science Quarterly* 82, no. 2 (1967), pp. 191–204.

Spheres of Justice: A Defense of Pluralism and Equality (New York: Basic Books, 1983).

"The Reform of the International System," in Øyvind Østerud, ed., *Studies of War and Peace* (Oslo: Norwegian University Press, 1986), pp. 227–40.

"Citizenship," in Ball *et al.*, *Political Innovation and Conceptual Change*, pp. 211–219.

On Toleration (New Haven, CT: Yale University Press, 1997).

Wapner, Paul, "Politics Beyond the State: Environmental Activism and World Civic Politics," *World Politics* 47, no. 3 (April 1995), pp. 311–40.

Environmental Activism and World Civic Politics (Albany: State University of New York Press, 1996).

Warren, Mark E., ed., *Democracy and Trust* (Cambridge: Cambridge University Press, 1999).

"Democratic Theory and Trust," in Warren, *Democracy and Trust*, pp. 310–45.

Waswo, Ann, "The Origins of Tenant Unrest," in Silberman and Harootunian, *Japan in Crisis: Essays on Taishō Democracy*, pp. 374–97.

Waters, Sydney D., "*Achilles*" *at the River Plate* (Wellington, NZ: New Zealand Navy, Historical Publications Branch, 1948).

Watkins, Frederick M., *The State as a Concept of Political Science* (New York: Harper, 1934).

Watson, Adam, "New States in the Americas," in Bull and Watson, *The Expansion of International Society*, pp. 127–42.

"Hedley Bull, States, Systems and International Society," *Review of International Studies* 13, no. 2 (April 1987), pp. 147–53.

The Evolution of International Society (London: Routledge, 1992).

Weart, Spencer, *Never at War: Why Democracies Will Not Fight One Another* (New Haven, CT: Yale University Press, 1998).

Weber, Andreas and Francisco Varela, "Life after Kant: Natural Purposes and the Autopoietic Foundations of Biological Individuality," *Phenomenology and the Cognitive Sciences* 1, no. 2 (2002), pp. 97–125.

Weber, Bruce and David Depew, "Natural Selection and Self-Organization," *Biology and Philosophy* 11, no. 1 (1996), pp. 33–65.

Weber, Cynthia, *Simulating Sovereignty: Intervention, the State and Symbolic Exchange* (Cambridge: Cambridge University Press, 1995).

Weber, Max, "'Objectivity' in Social Science and Social Policy," in E. A. Shils and H. E. Finch, *Max Weber: The Methodology of the Social Sciences* (New York: Free Press, 1949), pp. 76–112.

On the Methodology of the Social Sciences, trans. and ed. Edward A. Shils and Henry A. Finch (Glencoe, IL: Free Press, 1949 [1904]), pp. 90–5.

The Sociology of Religion, trans. Talcott Parsons (Boston: Beacon Press, 1956).

From Max Weber: Essays in Sociology, trans. and ed. H. H. Gerth and C. Wright Mills (New York: Oxford University Press, 1958).

The Protestant Ethic and the Spirit of Capitalism, trans. Talcott Parsons (New York: Scribner's, 1958).

Economy and Society, 2 vols., ed. Guenther Roth and Claus Wittich (Berkeley: University of California Press, 1968).

The Profession and Vocation of Politics, in Lassman and Speirs, *Weber: Political Writings*, pp. 309–69.

"Suffrage and Democracy in Germany," [*Wahlrecht und Demokratie in Deutschland*, 1917], in Lassman and Speirs, *Weber: Political Writings*, pp. 80–129.

"Science as a Vocation," in Weber, *From Max Weber*, pp. 129–58.

Webster, Charles, *The Congress of Vienna* (London: Thames and Hudson, 1963).

Webster, Richard A., *Industrial Imperialism in Italy* (Berkeley: University of California Press, 1971).

Wedeen, Lisa, "Conceptualizing Culture: Possibilities for Political Science," *American Political Science Review* 96 (2002), pp. 713–28.

Wees, Hans Van, *Status Warriors: War, Violence and Society in Homer and History* (Amsterdam: J. C. Gieben, 1992).

"Politics and the Battlefield: Ideology in Greek Warfare," in Anton Powell, *The Greek World* (London: Routledge, 1995), pp. 153–78.

"Heroes, Knights and Nutters: Warrior Mentality in Homer," in Alan Lloyd, ed., *Battle in Antiquity* (London: Duckworth, 1996), pp. 1–86.

ed., *War and Violence in Ancient Greece* (London: Duckworth, 2000).

Greek Warfare: Myth and Realities (London: Duckworth, 2004).

Wehler, Hans-Ulrich, ed., *Moderne deutsche Sozialgeschichte. Neue wissenschaftliche Bibliotek: Geschichte*, vol. X (Cologne: Neue Wissenschaftliche Bibliotek, 1966).

Das deutsche Kaiserreich, 1871–1918 (Göttingen: Vandenhoeck und Ruprecht, 1977).

The German Empire, 1871–1918, trans. Kim Traynor (New York: Berg, 1985).

Weigley, Russell F., *The Age of Battles: The Quest for Decisive Warfare from Breitenfeld to Waterloo* (Bloomington: Indiana University Press, 1990).

Weinberg, Gerhard L., *The Foreign Policy of Hitler's Germany*, 2 vols. (Chicago: University of Chicago Press, 1970–80).

A World at Arms: A Global History of World War II (Cambridge: Cambridge University Press, 1994).

Germany, Hitler and World War II: Essays in Modern German and World History (Cambridge: Cambridge University Press, 1995).

Weinstein, Donald, "Fighting or Flying? Verbal Duelling in Mid-Sixteenth Century Italy," in Trevor Dean and K. J. P. Loew, eds., *Crime, Society and the Law in Renaissance Italy* (Cambridge: Cambridge University Press, 1994), pp. 204–20.

Weiss, Linda, *The Myth of the Powerless State* (Ithaca, NY: Cornell University Press, 1998).

Welch, David, *Propaganda and the German Cinema, 1933–1945* (Oxford: Oxford University Press, 1983).

Painful Choices: A Theory of Foreign Policy Change (Princeton, NJ: Princeton University Press, 2005).

Wendt, Alexander E., "The Agent-Structure Problem in International Relations Theory," *International Organization*, 17, no. 4 (1987), pp. 335–70.

"Anarchy Is What States Make of It: The Social Construction of Power Politics," *International Organization* 46, no. 2 (Spring 1992), pp. 391–425.

"Social Theory as Cartesian Science," in Guzzini and Leander, *Constructivism and International Relations*, pp. 181–219.

"Collective Identity Formation and the International State," *American Political Science Review* 88, no. 2 (June 1994), pp. 384–96.

"Constructing International Politics," *International Security* 20, no. 1 (Summer 1995), pp. 71–81.

"Identity and Structural Change in International Politics," in Lapid and Kratochwil, *The Return of Culture and Identity in IR Theory*, pp. 47–64.

"On Constitution and Causation in International Relations," *Review of International Studies* 24, no. 5 (1998), pp. 101–17.

Social Theory of International Politics (Cambridge: Cambridge University Press, 1999).

"Driving with the Rearview Mirror: On the Rational Science of Institutional Design," *International Organization* 55, no. 4 (2001), pp. 1019–49.

"Why a World State Is Inevitable," *European Journal of International Relations* 9 (2003), pp. 491–542.

"The State as Person in International Theory," *Review of International Studies* 30, no. 2 (2004), pp. 289–316.

"Agency, Teleology and the World State: A Reply to Shannon," *European Journal of International Relations*, 11 (December 2005), pp. 589–98.

Wengst, Udo, *Graf Brockdorff-Rantzau und die aussenpolitischen Anfänge der Weimarer Republik* (Berne: Lang, 1973).

Werner, Karl Ferdinand, *Histoire de France.* vol. I: *Les origines* (Paris: Fayard, 1984).

Wertsch, James, *Voices of the Mind* (Cambridge, MA: Harvard University Press, 1991).

Wesseling, H. L., *Divide and Rule: The Partition of Africa, 1880–1914*, trans. Arnold Pomerans (Westport, CT: Praeger, 1996).

Westad, Odd Arne, ed., *Reviewing the Cold War: Approaches, Interpretations, Theory* (London: Frank Cass, 2000).

The Global Cold War: Third World Interventions and the Making of Our Times (Cambridge: Cambridge University Press, 2003).

Westerfield, H. Bradford, *Foreign Policy and Party Politics: Pearl Harbor to Korea* (New Haven, CT: Yale University Press, 1955).

Westney, D. Eleanor, *Imitation and Innovation: The Transfer of Western Organizational Patterns to Meiji Japan* (Cambridge, MA: Harvard University Press, 1987).

Wheeler, Nicholas, *Saving Strangers: Humanitarian Intervention in International Society* (Oxford: Oxford University Press, 2000).

White, Donald W., "The Nature of World Power in American History: An Evaluation at the End of World War II," *Diplomatic History* 11, no. 3 (Summer 1987), pp. 181–202.

White, Hayden, *Tropics of Discourse: Essays in Cultural Criticism* (Baltimore, MD: Johns Hopkins University Press, 1978).

"Foucault Decoded: Notes from Underground," in White, *Tropics of Discourse*, pp. 230–60.

The Content of the Form. Narrative Discourse and Historical Representation (Baltimore, MD: Johns Hopkins University Press, 1987).

White, James Boyd, *When Words Lose their Meaning: Constitutions and Reconstitutions of Language, Character, and Community* (Chicago: University of Chicago Press, 1984).

Heracles' Bow: Essays on the Rhetoric and Poetics of the Law (Madison: University of Wisconsin Press, 1985).

White, John A., *The Diplomacy of the Russo-Japanese War* (Princeton, NJ: Princeton University Press, 1964).

White, R. D., "Rethinking Polgyny: Co-Wives, Codes and Cultural Systems," *Current Anthropology* 29 (1989), pp. 519–72.

White, R. T., "Recall of Autobiographical Events," *Applied Cognitive Psychology* 18 (1989), pp. 127–35.

White, William Foote, *Street Corner Society: The Social Structure of an Italian Slum* (Chicago: University of Chicago Press, 1955).

Whitehead, Alfred North, *The Concept of Nature* (Cambridge: Cambridge University Press, 1920).

Process and Reality (Cambridge: Cambridge University Press, 1929).

Whiting, Allen S., *China Crosses the Yalu: The Decision to Enter the Korean War* (Ann Arbor: University of Michigan Press, 1960).

Wickham, Chris, *Early Medieval Italy: Central Power and Local Society, 400–1000* (Totowa, NJ: Barnes and Noble, 1981).

Wiggershaus, Rolf, *The Frankfurt School: Its History, Theories and Politi-
    cal Significance*, trans. Michael Robertson (Cambridge, MA: MIT Press,
    1994).

Wight, Martin, "Why There Is No International Theory," in Butterfield and
    Wight, *Diplomatic Investigations: Essays in the Theory of International Politics*,
    pp. 17–35.

    Systems of States (Leicester: Leicester University Press, 1977).

    "The Three Traditions of International Theory," in G. Wight and B. Porter, eds.,
    International Theory: The Three Traditions (Leicester: Leicester University
    Press, 1991), pp. 7–14.

Wilhelm, H.-H., "Wie geheim war die 'Endlösung'?" in Wolfgang Benz, ed.,
    Miscellanea: Festschrift für Helmut Krausnick zum 75. Geburtstag (Stuttgart:
    Deutsche Verlags-Anstalt, 1980), pp. 131–8.

Wilkes, Kathleen V., "The Good Man and the Good for Man in Aristotle's Ethics,"
    in Rorty, *Essays on Aristotle's Ethics*, pp. 341–58.

Willetts, Peter, "The Role of 'Non-State Actors': Transnational Actors and Interna-
    tional Organizations in Global Politics," in John Baylis and Steve Smith, eds.,
    The Globalization of World Politics: An Introduction to International Relations
    (New York: Oxford University Press, 1997), pp. 287–310.

Williams, Bernard, *Shame and Necessity* (Berkeley and Los Angeles: University of
    California Press, 1993).

    Truth and Truthfulness: An Essay in Genealogy (Princeton, NJ: Princeton Univer-
    sity Press, 2002).

Williams, Howard, *Kant's Critique of Hobbes* (Cardiff: University of Wales Press,
    2003).

Williams, Melissa, "The Discipline of the Democratic Peace: Kant, Liberalism and
    the Social Constructivism of Security Communities," *European Journal of
    International Relations* 7 (2001), pp. 525–54.

Williams, Michael, "The Hobbesian Theory of International Relations," in Jahn,
    Classical Theory in International Relations, pp. 253–76.

Williams, Raymond, *Marxism and Literature* (Oxford: Oxford University Press,
    1978).

Williams, Robert, *Hegel's Ethics of Recognition* (Berkeley: University of California
    Press, 1997).

Williamson, Samuel R. Jr., "Influence, Power, and the Policy Process: The Case of
    Franz Ferdinand," *Historical Journal* 17 (June 1974), pp. 417–34.

    "Vienna and July 1914: The Origins of the Great War Once More," in Peter
    Paston and Samuel R. Williamson, Jr., eds., *Essays on World War I: Origins and
    Prisoners of War* (Brooklyn: Brooklyn College, Social Science Monographs,
    1983), pp. 19–34.

    "The Origins of World War I," *Journal of Interdisciplinary History* 18 (Spring
    1988), pp. 795–818.

Austria-Hungary and the Coming of the First World War (London: Macmillan, 1990).

Williamson, Samuel R. Jr. and Ernest R. May, "An Identity of Opinion: Historians and July 1914," *Journal of Modern History*, 79 no. 2 (June 2007), pp. 335–87.

Willis, Paul, *Learning to Labor: How Working Class Kids Get Working Class Jobs* (New York: Columbia University Press, 1977).

Wilmer, Franke, *The Indigenous Voice in World Politics: Since Time Immemorial* (Newbury Park, CA: Sage, 1993).

Wilson, Catherine, *Leibniz' Metaphysics: A Historical and Comparative Study* (Manchester: Manchester University Press, 1989).

Wilson, David Sloan, "Incorporating Group Selection into the Adaptationist Program: A Case Study Involving Human Decision Making," in Jeffrey A. Simpson and Douglas T. Kendrick, *Evolutionary Social Psychology* (Hillsdale, NJ: Erlbaum, 1997), pp. 345–86.

Wilson, Keith M., *The Policy of the Entente: Essays on the Determinants of British Foreign Policy, 1909–1914* (Cambridge: Cambridge University Press, 1985).

Wilson, Penelope, "Homer and the English Epic," in Fowler, ed., *The Cambridge Companion to Homer*, pp. 272–86.

Wilson, Robert, "Causal Depth, Theoretical Appropriateness, and Individualism in Psychology," *Philosophy of Science* 61, no. 1 (1994), pp. 55–75.

"Group-Level Cognition," *Philosophy of Science* 68 (2001), pp. 262–73.

Wilson, Trevor, *The Myriad Faces of War: Britain and the Great War, 1914–1918* (London: Polity, 1986).

Winch, Donald, *Riches and Poverty: An Intellectual History of Political Economy in Britain, 1750–1834* (Cambridge: Cambridge University Press, 1996).

Winkler, Heinrich August, *Der lange Weg nach Westen*, vol. II: *Deutsche Geschichte vom 'Dritten Reich' bis zur Wiedervereinigung* (Munich: Beck, 2000).

The Long Shadow of the Reich: Weighing up German History (London: German Historical Institute, 2002).

Winkler, John J., *The Constraints of Desire: The Anthropology of Sex and Gender in Ancient Greece* (New York: Routledge, 1990).

Winkler, J. and Froma Zeitlin, eds., *Nothing to Do with Dionysos? Athenian Drama in its Social Context* (Princeton, NJ: Princeton University Press, 1990).

Winnington-Ingram, R. P., *Sophocles: An Interpretation* (Cambridge: Cambridge University Press, 1980).

Winograd, E. and Ulrich Neisser, eds., *Affect and Accuracy in Recall* (New York: Cambridge University Press, 1992).

Wise, David and Thomas Ross, *The U-2 Affair* (New York: Random House, 1962).

Witt, Peter-Christian, *Finanzpolitik des deutschen Reiches von 1903 bis 1913* (Lübeck: Matthiesen, 1970).

Witt, Ulrich, "Self-Organization and Economics – What Is New?," *Structural Change and Economic Dynamics* 8, no. 4 (1997), pp. 489–507.

Wittgenstein, Ludwig, *Philosophical Investigations*, 2nd edn, ed. G. E. M. Anscombe (Oxford: Oxford University Press, 1958).

    Philosophical Grammar, ed. Rush Rhees, trans. Anthony Kenny (Berkeley: University of California Press, 1974).

Wittkopf, Eugene R. and James M. McCormick, eds., *The Domestic Sources of American Foreign Policy*, 4th edn (Lanham, MD: Rowman and Littlefield, 2004).

Wohl, Robert, *A Passion for Wings: Aviation and the Western Imagination 1908–1918* (New Haven, CT: Yale University Press, 1994).

Wohl, Victoria, *Love Among the Ruins: The Erotics of Democracy in Classical Athens* (Princeton, NJ: Princeton University Press, 2002).

Wohlforth, William C., *The Elusive Balance: Power and Perceptions during the Cold War* (Ithaca, NY: Cornell University Press, 1993).

    "The Stability of a Unipolar World," *International Security* 24 (1999), pp. 5–41.

    "U.S. Strategy in a Unipolar World," in Ikenberry, *America Unrivaled*, pp. 98–118.

Wohlforth, William, Richard Little, Stuart J. Kaufman *et al.*, "Testing Balance-of-Power Theory in World History," *European Journal of International Relations*, 12, no. 2 (June 2007), pp. 155–86.

Wolf, Klaus-Dieter, "The New Raison d'État as a Problem for Democracy in World Society," *European Journal of International Relations* 5, no. 3 (1999), pp. 333–63.

Wolfers, Arnold, *Discord and Collaboration: Essays on International Politics* (Baltimore, MD: Johns Hopkins University Press, 1962).

Wolin, Sheldon S., "Democracy: Electoral and Athenian," *PS: Political Science and Politics* 26 (1993), pp. 475–7.

    Politics and Vision: Continuity and Innovation in Western Political Thought (Princeton, NJ: Princeton University Press, 2004).

Wollheim, Richard, *On the Emotions* (New Haven, CT: Yale University Press, 1999).

Woloch, Isser, *Eighteenth-Century Europe: Tradition and Progress, 1714–1789* (New York: Norton, 1982).

Wood, Allen W., *Kant's Moral Religion* (Ithaca, NY: Cornell University Press, 1970).

    "Marx on Right and Justice," *Philosophy and Public Affair* 8, no. 3 (1979), pp. 267–95.

    Hegel's Ethical Thought (Cambridge: Cambridge University Press, 1990).

    "Kant's Practical Philosophy," in K. Ameriks, ed., *The Cambridge Companion to German Idealism* (Cambridge: Cambridge University Press, 2000), pp. 57–75.

Wood, John Cunningham, ed., *Adam Smith: Critical Assessments* (London: Croom-Helm, 1983).

Woodward, Bob, *Bush at War* (New York: Simon and Schuster, 2002).

Plan of Attack (New York: Simon and Schuster, 2004).

State of Denial: Bush at War, Part III (New York: Simon and Schuster, 2006).

Woolgar, Steve and Dorothy Pawluch, "Ontological Gerrymandering: The Anatomy of Social Problems Explanations," *Social Problems* 32, no. 3 (February 1985), pp. 214–27.

Wright, Georg von, *Explanation and Understanding* (Ithaca, NY: Cornell University Press, 1971).

Wright, Larry, *Teleological Explanations* (Berkeley: University of California Press, 1976).

Wright, Nicholas, *Knights and Peasants: The Hundred Years' War in the French Countryside* (Rochester, NY: Boydell Press, 1998).

Wright, Quincy, *A Study of War* (Chicago: University of Chicago Press, 1942).

Wright, Robert, *The Moral Animal: The New Science of Evolutionary Psychology* (New York: Pantheon, 1994).

Wrong, Dennis H., *Power: Its Forms, Bases and Uses* (New York: Harper and Row, 1979).

Wyatt-Brown, Bertram, *Southern Honor: Ethics and Behavior in the Old South* (New York: Oxford University Press, 1986).

The Shaping of Southern Culture: Honor, Grace and War, 1760s–1890s (Chapel Hill: University of North Carolina Press, 2001).

Xenophon, *Hellenica 11.3.11–IV.28*, ed. and trans. Peter Krentz (Warminster: Aris and Philips, 1990).

Memorabilia, trans. Amy L. Bonnette (Ithaca, NY: Cornell University Press, 1994).

Hiero the Tyrant and Other Treatises, trans. Robin Waterfield (New York: Penguin, 1997).

Xia, Yafeng, *Negotiating with the Enemy: U.S.-China Talks during the Cold War, 1949–1972* (Bloomington: Indiana University Press, 2006).

Yack, Bernard, *The Problems of a Political Animal* (Berkeley: University of California Press, 1993).

The Fetishism of Modernities: Epochal Self-Consciousness in Contemporary Social and Political Thought (Notre Dame, IN: University of Notre Dame Press, 1997).

Yamamura, Kozo, "The Founding of Mitsubishi: A Case Study," *Business History Review* 41, no. 2 (1967), pp. 141–60.

A Study of Samurai Income and Entrepreneurship: Quantitative Analysis of Economic and Social Aspects of the Samurai in Tokagawa and Meiji Japan (Cambridge, MA: Harvard University Press, 1974).

Yates, Frances A., *Theatre of the World* (Chicago: University of Chicago Press, 1969).

Yates, Robin, "The Song Empire: The World's First Superpower?," in Tetlock, Lebow and Parker, *Unmaking the West*, pp. 205–40.

Yergin, Daniel and J. Stanislaw, *The Commanding Heights* (New York: Simon and Schuster, 1998).

Yoneyama, L., *Historical Traces: Time, Space, and the Dialectics of Memory* (Berkeley: University of California Press, 1999).

Young, Charles, "Aristotle on Justice," *Southern Journal of Philosophy* 27 (1989), pp. 233–49.

Young, Graham, "Mao Zedong and the Class Struggle in Socialist Society," *Australian Journal of Chinese Affairs* 16 (July 1986), pp. 41–80.

Young, Louise, *Japan's Total Empire: Manchuria and the Culture of Wartime Imperialism* (Berkeley: University of California Press, 1997).

   "Colonizing Manchuria: The Making of an Imperial Myth," in Vlastos, *Mirror of Modernity*, pp. 95–109.

Young, Oran, "Anarchy and Social Choice: Reflections on the International Polity," *World Politics* 30, no. 2 (January 1978), pp. 241–63.

Yzerbyt, V. Y., C. M. Judd and O. Corneille, eds., *The Psychology of Group Perception: Perceived Variability, Entitativity, and Essentialism* (London: Psychology Press, 2004).

Zacher, Mark W., "The Territorial Integrity Norm: International Boundaries and the Use of Force," *International Organization* 55, no. 2 (Spring 2001), pp. 215–50.

Zacher, Mark W. and Richard A. Matthew, "Liberal International Theory: Common Threads, Divergent Strands," in Charles W. Kegley, ed., *Controversies in International Relations Theory: Realism and the Neoliberal Challenge* (New York: St. Martin Press, 1995), pp. 107–50.

Zamora, Margarita, *Reading Columbus* (Berkeley: University of California Press, 1993).

Zanker, Graham, "Beyond Reciprocity: The Akhilleus-Priam Scene in *Iliad* 24," in Christopher Gill, Norman Postlethwaite and Richard Seaford, *Reciprocity in Ancient Greece* (Oxford: Oxford University Press, 1998), pp. 93–104.

Zanna, M. P. and J. Cooper, "Dissonance and the Pill: An Attribution Approach to Studying the Arousal Properties of Dissonance," *Journal of Political and Social Psychology*, 29 (1974), pp. 703–9.

Zechlin, Egmont, "Deutschland zwischen Kabinettskrieg und Wirtschaftskrieg: Politik und Kriegführung in den ersten Monaten des Weltkrieges," *Historische Zeitschrift* 199 (1964), pp. 347–52.

   Krieg und Kriegsrisiko: Zur deutschen Politik im Ersten Weltkrieg (Düsseldorf: Droste, 1979).

Zehfuss, Maja, "Writing War, Against Good Conscience," *Millennium* 33, no. 1 (2004), pp. 91–122.

Zeitlin, Froma, "Thebes: Theater of Self and Society in Athenian Drama," in J. Peter Euben, *Greek Tragedy and Political Theory* (Berkeley and Los Angeles: University of California Press, 1986), pp. 101–41.

Zelditch, M., "Process of Legitimation: Recent Developments and New Directions," *Social Psychology Quarterly* 64, no. 1 (2001), pp. 4–17.

Zelditch, M. and H. A. Walker, "Normative Regulation of Power," in Shane R. Thye and Edward J. Lawler, eds., *Advances in Group Processes*, 20 (Greenwich, CT: JAI Press, 2000), pp. 155–78.

Zeller, Gaston, "French Diplomacy and Foreign Policy in the European Setting," in *The New Cambridge Modern History* (Cambridge: Cambridge University Press, 1970), vol. V, pp. 68–72.

Zeman, Z. A. B., "The Balkans and the Coming of War," in Evans and Strandmann, *The Coming of the First World War*, pp. 19–32.

Zeng, Ka, *Trade Threats, Trade Wars: Bargaining, Retaliation, and American Coercive Diplomacy* (Ann Arbor: University of Michigan Press, 2004).

Zhang, Shu Guang, *Deterrence and Strategic Culture: Chinese–American Confrontations, 1949–1958* (Ithaca, NY: Cornell University Press, 1993).

Zhang, Yungling and Tang Shiping, "China's Regional Strategy," in Shumbaugh, *Power Shift*, pp. 48–70.

Zhiumin, Chen, "Nationalism, Internationalism and Chinese Foreign Policy," *Journal of Contemporary China* 14, no. 42 (February 2005), pp. 35–53.

Ziegler, Karl-Heinz, "The Influence of Medieval Roman Law on Peace Treaties," in Randall Lesaffer, ed., *Peace Treaties and International Law in European History: From the Late Middle Ages to World War One* (Cambridge: Cambridge University Press, 2004), pp. 147–61.

Ziemke, Earl F., *Stalingrad to Berlin: The German Defeat in the East* (Washington, DC: Government Printing Office, 1968).

Moscow to Stalingrad: Decision in the East (Washington, DC: Government Printing Office, 1987).

Ziolkowski, Theodore, "Der Hunger nach dem Mythos: Zur seelischen Gastronomie der Deutschen in den Zwanziger Jahren," in Reinhold Grimm and Jost Hermand, eds., *Die sogenannten Zwanziger Jahre: First Wisconsin Workshop* (Bad Homburg: Gehlen, 1970), pp. 169–201.

Zuber, Terence, *Inventing the Schlieffen Plan: German War Planning, 1871–1914* (Oxford: Oxford University Press, 2002).

German War Planning, 1891–1914: Sources and Interpretations (Woodbridge, Sussex: Boydell, 2004).

Zubok, Vladislav, "Why Did the Cold War End in 1989? Explanations of 'The Turn,'" in Westad, *Reviewing the Cold War*, pp. 343–68.

Zuccotti, Susan, *The Italians and the Holocaust: Persecution, Rescue and Survival* (New York: Basic Books, 1987).

Zucker, Rose, *Democratic Distributive Justice* (Cambridge: Cambridge University Press, 2001).

Zuckert, Catherine H., *Understanding the Political Spirit: Philosophical Investigations from Socrates to Nietzsche* (New Haven, CT: Yale University Press, 1988).

Zukert, Michael P., *Launching Liberalism: On Lockean Political Philosophy* (Lawrence: University Press of Kansas, 2002).

Zunino, P. G., *L'ideologia del fascismo: miti, credenze, e valori della stabilizzazione* (Bologna: Il Mulino, 1985).

INDEX

ABC television, 463
Acheson, Dean, 445
Achilles (New Zealand ship), 143
Achilles, 19, 66, 70, 140, 141, 143–5,
    146–7, 148–9, 150–1, 152, 154,
    155–6, 172, 193, 195, 202, 203–4,
    212, 213, 215, 220, 223, 240, 248,
    341, 370, 386, 441, 471, 523
Acropolis, 175
Actium, battle of, 166, 388
Adrianople, Battle of, 210
Aeneas, 229–55
Aeschylus, 44, 100, 140, 173, 181,
    193–4, 218, 220
affect, 81, 113, 116, 129–31, 514–15,
    562
Afghanistan, 14, 440–1, 456, 457, 460,
    467, 471, 472, 475, 477, 488, 500,
    550, 556
Africa, 323
Agadir crisis, 364
Agamemnon, 66, 140, 143–5, 146,
    147–8, 149, 152, 155, 158, 248,
    341, 370, 441
Agamemnon, 174, 193, 195, 198, 213,
    215
agency, 35, 368–70, 504, 506–7, 563–6,
    567
Agincourt, Battle of, 249, 254, 259, 260,
    357
agon, 20, 143–5, 150, 153, 154, 194,
    195
Agreement on Prevention of Nuclear
    War (1973), 453
Ajax (New Zealand ship), 143
Ajax, 141, 150, 154, 168, 213, 386, 398
Aksakov, Konstantin S., 432

Albania, 395, 419
Albright, Madeleine, 482, 500
Alcibiades, 195–6, 216, 217, 521
Alcuin, 228, 229, 260
Alexander of Macedon, 124, 166, 191,
    201, 210, 212, 214, 218, 220, 239,
    519, 528
Alexander Severus, 209
Alexandria, 213
Algeria, 328
alienation, 508
Allende, Salvador, 455
alliances, 75, 516
al-Qaeda, 441, 461–2, 467, 471, 472–3
Althusser, Louis, 36
American Enterprise Institute, 466
amicitia, 214
amour de soi (love of self), 317
amour propre (self-esteem), 75, 318
anarchy, 90, 94, 182, 483, 493, 507, 529,
    558
ancien régime, 123, 306
anger, 62, 69, 146, 248, 279, 325, 379,
    441, 447, 473, 534, 552, 557
Anglo-Japanese alliance (1902), 360,
    404
Angola, 456
animus dominandi, 22
Annan, Kofi, 106, 492
anomie, 41, 508
Anschluss, 372, 529
Anti-Comintern Pact, 397
Antigone (Sophocles), 53–4, 158, 168
Antioch, 213
Antiphon, 44
anti-Semitism, 330, 381, 383, 386
anti-Westernism, 386

Aphrodite, 142
Apollo, 148, 240
appeasement, 479
appetite (*see also* motives), 14–15, 26,
    72–6, 125, 141–2, 162–3, 170, 199,
    209–10, 212, 216, 271–2, 301,
    366–8, 371, 444–5, 474, 476, 482,
    509–12, 535, 537
appetite-based worlds, 82–3, 106–7,
    516
Aquinas, Thomas, 315
Aquitaine, duchy of, 247–8
archē (control), 198, 214, 495, 500
archetypes, 314
Archidamus, 180, 185
Archilocus, 194
Arendt, Hannah, 18
aretē (excellence), 165, 166, 172, 187,
    198, 200
Argentina, 326, 491, 543, 564
Argos, 166, 176, 188
aristocracy, *see* nobility
Aristophanes, 194
Aristotle, 4–5, 14, 22, 29, 33, 41, 51, 60,
    78, 79–82, 83–4, 85–7, 88–9, 93,
    96–7, 98, 104, 116, 119, 120, 122,
    123, 127–8, 129–31, 165, 169, 193,
    219, 222, 233, 315, 317, 318, 332,
    362–3, 379, 441, 447, 448, 452,
    473, 505, 507, 508, 509, 512, 513,
    514, 517, 534, 552
Armey, Richard, 460, 470, 472, 475
arms races, 90, 516
Arnold, Matthew, 308
Artemisia, 192
Artemisium, 177
Arthur (king of Britain), 239, 240, 241,
    246, 253, 523
Asia, 323–4
Asquith, Herbert, 313
assimilation, 545
Assyria, 64
Athena, 151, 152
Athens, 5, 32, 36, 50, 64, 71, 73, 83, 84,
    85, 86–7, 100, 103, 157, 159–60,
    168, 173–4, 175, 177–8, 185, 190,
    195–6, 198, 201, 206, 212, 213,
    214, 220, 307, 311, 478, 495, 519,

529, 542–3, 546, 547, 548, 550,
    554, 558, 568–9
attribution theory, 564
Auerstädt, Battle of, 429
Augustine of Hippo, 76, 207, 255, 260,
    517, 519, 521, 529
Augustus (Gaius Octavius Thurinus),
    209, 217, 399
Augustus I (of Poland), 304
Augustus II (of Poland), 304, 536
Augustus III (of Poland), 536–7
Ausgleich, 369
Austerlitz, Battle of, 429
Australia, 414, 564
Austria (including Austria-Hungary),
    86, 264, 273, 274, 278, 285, 296,
    303, 304, 307, 312, 314, 325, 334,
    338, 339–41, 344–5, 348–52, 354,
    356, 359, 363, 366, 369, 372, 375,
    417–18, 429, 434, 519, 525, 528,
    529, 530, 536, 542, 546, 549, 554
Austro-Prussian War, 547
autonomy, 516, 556
avaritia, 207
Avars, 226, 227, 230, 231, 238, 523
Aztec Empire, 71, 124–5, 150

Babbitt (Sinclair Lewis), 319
Bacon, Francis, 1, 112
Badian, Ernst, 214
Badoglio, Pietro, 395
Baghdad Railway, 337
Baker, James, 460, 475
balance, 27, 47, 48, 50, 52–3, 84, 87–8,
    98, 113, 291, 567–8, 569
balance of power, 118, 119, 289, 559
Balbulus, Notker, 232
Balkans, 363
Ballin, Albert, 347
Baltic states, 423, 489, 502
Ban Ki-moon, 106, 493
bandwagoning, 517, 549
Bank of England, 280
bannum, 226
Bartelson, Jens, 40
Basic Principles Agreement (1972),
    453
Bauer, Gary, 460

Bavaria, 226, 264, 268, 282–3, 304, 536
Bay of Pigs invasion, 448, 450
Bayle, Pierre, 276
BBC, 468, 500
Beck, Józef, 432
Behemoth (Thomas Hobbes), 553
Belgium, 313, 338, 340, 353, 355, 356,
    359, 395, 421, 519, 520, 528, 554
Bem, Daryl, 566
Benedict, Ruth, 35
Bennett, William, 460
Bentham, Jeremy, 316
Beowulf, 255
Berchtold, Leopold von, 313, 349, 352,
    370, 538
Berghahn, Volker, 337, 363
Bergson, Henri, 57, 59
Berlin Wall, 458
Bernhardi, Friedrich von, 364
Bess, Michael, 425
Bethmann Hollweg, Theobald von,
    337, 340, 345, 348, 352, 353,
    354–5, 356, 363, 417, 519, 528, 538
Biden, Joseph, 463
Big Bang, 43
bin Laden, Osama, 441, 460, 467, 484
bio-technology, 28
bipolarity, *see* polarity
Bismarck, Otto von, 313, 324, 331,
    332–3, 334, 337, 356, 374, 388,
    430, 548
Black Death, 234, 248
Black Prince (Edward, Prince of
    Wales), 240, 249, 251–2, 259
Black, Jeremy, 283–4
Blair, Tony, 464, 476
blank check, 313, 365, 369, 370, 550
Blanning, Tim, 276
Bleichröder, Gerson, 331
blotahunka (expedition leader), 542–3
Boer War, 421
Bohemia, 264
Bonnie Prince Charlie (Charles Edward
    Stuart), 294
Book of the Order of Chivalry (Ramon
    Llull), 239
Borodino, Battle of, 281
Bosnia-Herzegovina, 340

Bosnian Annexation crisis, 434, 454
Bossuet, Jacques-Bénigne, 274
Bosworth, Clifford Edmund, 396
Bourbon dynasty, 420
Bourdieu, Pierre, 302
bourgeoisie, 293–5, 309, 324, 331,
    342–3, 396, 401, 527, 531–2, 539,
    544
Boxer Rebellion, 421
Bracher, Karl Dietrich, 382–3
Brazil, 491–2, 543
Brezhnev, Leonid, 453, 454–6, 489, 545
Briseis, 143–4, 148, 370
British East India Company, 280
Bronze Age, 222
Brooks, Stephen, 120–1, 122
Bukovansky, Mlada, 486
Bulgaria, 452
Bull, Hedley, 3, 58, 434
Bülow, Bernhard von, 313, 324, 337,
    353, 356, 363
bureaucracy, 409, 411, 564
Burgfrieden, 380
Burgundy, 264
Burma, 414
Bush, George H. W., 470, 471, 488
Bush, George W., 438, 442, 459–64,
    470–2, 473–5, 477, 520, 535, 537,
    544, 545
Bush administration (George W.), 440,
    503, 534, 538, 560
bushidō, 404–5, 415–16
Byng, John, 294
Byzantium, 225, 231, 540

Caesar, Julius, 207, 208, 209, 216–17,
    520
Calchas, 147
Camelot, 239
Camillus (*see also* Virgil), 165
Camp David, 448
Campbell, D. T., 134
Canada, 280, 491, 501, 545, 547, 570
Caprivi, Leo von, 334–5
Carloman, 225
Carlowitz peace conference, 279
Carthage, 73, 206, 207, 210
Castano, Emanuele, 134–5

caste solidarity, 251
Castro, Fidel, 448, 452
Catherine II (of Russia), 265, 296, 297
Catholicism, 375, 396
Cato the Elder, 208, 209
Catullus, 505, 570
cavalry, 357
CBS, 463
Central Intelligence Agency, 462–3, 534
Chaeronea, Battle of, 166, 201
Chalabi, Ahmed, 469, 476, 554, 559
Chamberlain, Joseph, 327
change and transformation, 96–111, 480, 505, 506, 567–70
Chanson de Roland, 232, 241, 243
chansons de geste, 227–8, 238, 241, 255, 256, 261, 523
chaos and complexity, 48
Chapman, George, 305, 308
Charlemagne, 222–34, 239, 241, 243, 253, 256, 258, 260–1, 300, 521–2, 523
Charles II (of England), 303, 536
Charles III (of Spain), 265
Charles IV (Holy Roman Emperor), 247
Charles V (Holy Roman Emperor), 249, 251, 281
Charles XII (of Sweden), 282, 284–5, 288–90, 527
Charny, Geoffroi de, 240, 243, 244, 256
Cheney, Richard, 459–60, 462–3, 465, 467, 470, 471, 477, 479, 480, 520, 535
chevauchée, 249–50, 524
Chiang Kai-shek, 412, 444
China, 18, 41, 64–5, 101, 109, 124, 157, 295, 373–4, 397, 398–9, 404, 407, 408–9, 412–14, 416, 417–19, 439, 444, 454, 470, 477, 485, 486–7, 490, 492, 495, 499, 501, 531, 534, 543, 546, 547, 549, 550, 570
Chirac, Jacques, 464
chivalry, 30, 222–4, 235, 239, 241, 255–7, 415, 522, 523–4
Chomsky, Noam, 465

Christianity, 219, 229, 243–4, 255, 306, 331, 385, 400, 431, 432, 490, 522
Chryseis, 147
Chryses, 147, 156
Chungking, 413
Churchill, Winston, 280
Ciano, Galeazzo, 394–5
Cicero, 209
Cimon, 195
Cincinnatus, Lucius Quinctius, 66
citizenship, 206
city state (polis), 43
civil society, 41, 481, 489
Clash of Civilizations (Samuel Huntington), 118, 120
class, 41, 87, 520, 521, 531
Clausewitz, Carl von, 10, 41, 42, 356, 420, 428, 532
Clemenceau, Georges, 379
Cleon, 83–6, 186, 217, 521
Clinton administration, 440, 488
Clytemnestra, 140, 174
cognition, 515, 539
cognitive psychology, 35
Coker, Christopher, 374
Colbert, Charles, 320, 321
Colbert, Jean-Baptiste, 265–6, 273, 277, 284, 286, 303
Cold War, 32, 37, 439–59, 475, 483, 490, 501–2, 533–4, 540, 545, 549, 553
comitatus, 233
Communist Party of Germany (KPD), 382
compellence, 552
competition, 27, 172, 218–21, 272, 419, 521, 528, 568
compliance, 4–5, 8–9, 13, 507, 559
concepts, 39, 118, 119
conflict, approaches to, 6, 59, 515
Confucianism, 399, 401, 416
Congress, US, 463, 472, 478, 516, 538
Congress of Vienna, 98–9, 420, 486, 541, 566
Conrad von Hötzendorf, Franz, 313, 348–52, 359, 370, 417, 509, 538
Conservative Party (Germany), 333

conspicuous consumption, 310–11, 319–20, 323, 337, 484

Constantine, 255

constructivism, 3, 16, 18, 34, 55, 58, 78, 119, 483, 503, 529, 562

contingency, 368–70

cooperation, approaches to, 4–6, 59, 72, 75, 91, 149, 428, 495, 507, 515, 561

Corcyra, 86, 90, 103, 178–9, 181–5, 188, 193, 565

Corinth, 103, 178–9, 188, 193, 213, 547

Corneille, Pierre, 315

Cornil, Fernando, 69

Corradini, Enrico, 390

Costa Rica, 109, 110

Crécy, Battle of, 249, 252–3, 254, 357

Creon, 158

Crete, 169

Crimean War, 24, 309, 433

Croatia, 419

Croce, Bendetto, 391

Crusades, 323

Cuba, 452, 455, 492

Cuban missile crisis, 32, 439, 444, 447–8, 534, 538, 545, 551, 552

culture, 118–19, 120, 122, 442

Curatii, 204

cyclicity, 28, 97

Cyclops, 147

Czartoryski, house of, 536

Czechoslovakia, 372, 377, 423, 432, 488, 530, 550

D'Annunzio, Gabriele, 388

Dante Alighieri, 315

Darius, 176, 203

Darwin, Charles, 129

David and Goliath, 150

Dawes Plan, 478

Decline of the West (Oswald Spengler), 387

Deiphobos, 154

Delbrück, Hans, 336, 379

Deleuze, Gilles, 39

Delian League, 175, 201–2, 213

Delphi, 174, 189, 194

Democracy in America (see also Tocqueville), 325

democracy, 461, 476

Democratic Party (US), 472, 474

Democratic Peace, 11, 224

Democritus of Abdera, 44, 56

Demosthenes, 196, 202

Denmark, 264, 377, 395

Derrida, Jacques, 36

Descartes, René, 302, 315

détente, 440, 449, 450, 453–4, 455–6, 533

deterrence, 100, 445, 552

Deutsch, Karl, 95, 493

Deutsche Bank, 337

deviance, 7, 543–4, 545, 550, 559

dialogue, 80–1

Diocletian, 209

Diodotus, 100, 131, 552

Diomedes, 141, 151, 154, 155

Dionysius of Halicarnassus, 187

Discourse on the Origin of Inequality (see also Rousseau), 318

discourse, 443–4, 556–7

disorder, see order

display, 310–11, 323, 484, 525, 535, 547

Disraeli, Benjamin, 324, 326–7, 334

dissonance, 553

divine right of kings, 265

division of labor (see also Durkheim), 101, 102, 104–5, 511, 568

Dobrynin, Anatoly F., 454

Doestoevsky, Fyodor, 432, 433

Dolchstoss (stab in the back), 386–7, 460, 473–4

dolos (deceit), 496, 555

Dresden, 536

Dreyfus Affair, 330

driving, 112–14, 135–6

dueling, 71, 149

Dulles, John Foster, 451

Dunn, John, 40

Durkheim, Émile, 7, 13, 18, 52, 101, 114, 119–20, 122, 181–2, 193, 310, 494, 507, 508, 559, 565

Dutch Republic (see also Holland, Netherlands), 263, 264, 265, 281, 298, 550

Dutch War (with England), 267
Dutch War (with France), 267, 279–80, 282
dynastic rivalry, 17

Eagleburger, Lawrence, 460, 475
education, 79–80, 569
Edward I (of England), 245
Edward II (of England), 247
Edward II (of France), 523
Edward III (of England), 244–6, 247–9, 251, 252–3
Edward the Confessor (king of England), 237, 238, 522
Egypt, 48, 175, 310, 327, 454, 455, 484, 543
Eichi, Shibusawa, 402
Einhard, 228, 232
Einstein, Albert, 1
Eisenhower, Dwight D., 448, 449–50, 451, 479
Eisenhower administration, 446
Electra, 168
Eley, Geoff, 337
Elias, Norbert, 276
Elis, 175
Elizabeth I (of England), 547
Elkins, David, 118, 119
Emden (ship), 422–3
emergent properties, 13, 117
Émile (*see also* Rousseau), 316
emotion, 113, 129–31
empathy, 514
empire, 102
England (*see also* Hundred Years War, Great Britain), 17–18, 30, 109, 223, 226, 235–8, 239, 242, 245, 247–57, 259–61, 264, 279, 286, 295, 298, 300, 343, 522–3, 546, 547
English School of international relations, 3, 23, 34
enlightened absolutism, 265–6
Enlightenment, 13, 14, 36, 37, 45, 47, 63, 96, 106, 123, 265–71, 306, 307, 315, 316, 342, 508
Ennius, 206
Enola Gay, 426
Entente Cordiale, 360
entiativity, 8, 134

epistēme (systematic knowledge), 41, 127
epistemological optimism, 36
epistemology, 28, 55
epithumia, 78, 79
equality, 105–7, 142, 197, 560, 566
equilibrium, 48, 55, 505
Erikson, Erik, 25, 26
Erklären, 34
Ernst August (of Hanover), 536
eros (love), 79, 514
Ertman, Thomas, 299–300
esteem, *see* self-esteem
Esterházy, house of, 536
Ethiopia, 388, 392, 393–6, 418, 456, 484, 530, 532
etic frameworks, 41
Etruscans, 206, 546
Euripides, 44, 64, 189, 194
European Union, 12, 220, 491–2, 502, 545, 570
Eurybiades, 177, 191
Eurymedon vase, 484
evolution, 38, 41, 55, 97, 98, 118, 506, 556–60
Executive Committee (ExComm) (*see also* Cuban missile crisis), 444, 553
Eyck, Erich, 381

fairness, 49, 560
Falkenhayn, Erich von, 345, 358
fame, 148
fascism, 388–90, 407
Fashoda crisis, 310, 329, 454
fear, 4–6, 27, 35, 88–93, 113, 118, 119, 158, 167, 199, 212, 215–16, 290, 474, 502, 503, 510–11, 537, 550
fear-based worlds, 32, 86, 162, 516–17, 559, 568
Federal Bureau of Investigation (FBI), 471, 473, 534
Federalist Papers, 75, 516
feedback, 507, 564–6, 567
Feith, Douglas, 459
Felice, Renzo de, 391, 395
Felton, William
feminism, 34, 35
Ferguson, Adam, 481
feudalism, 41

feudalization (of bourgoisie), 325, 344, 376, 527–8
Feyerabend, Paul, 35–6
Fichte, Johann Gottlieb, 307, 386, 430–7
Final Solution, 426
Finley, John, 195
Fischer, Fritz, 347–8, 381, 392
Flanders, 223, 235, 239, 245
Florence, 285
flux, 54–5
Foch, Ferdinand, 379
Fontane, Theodor, 330
food, 141–2
Forgách, János, 352
Foucault, Michel, 36
Fourteen Points, 377, 398
France, 24, 34, 75, 98, 99, 223, 224, 235–8, 242, 247–57, 262, 264, 265–9, 271, 272, 278, 279–84, 287–8, 289, 298–9, 301–2, 303–4, 310, 313, 321, 323, 325, 326, 327–30, 332, 338, 343, 346, 347, 352–3, 355–6, 358, 359, 373, 374, 377, 379, 392, 395, 419, 421, 430, 454, 461, 464, 469, 475, 479, 484–5, 487, 490–2, 501, 519–25, 526, 528, 530, 536, 539, 548, 549, 550, 554, 564, 566, 567, 570
Francke, Ernst, 336
Franco-Prussian War, 430, 547
Frankfurt School, 384
Frankish kingdoms, 30, 124, 223, 225–34, 238, 256, 258, 259–61, 521–2, 523–4, 558
Franz Ferdinand, Archduke, 339, 354, 369–70
Franz Josef, Emperor, 339, 351–2, 354, 369, 538
Franz, Günther, 264
Frederick I (of Prussia), 264, 270
Frederick II (of Prussia), 265, 268, 270, 271, 272, 276–7, 282, 288, 296, 301, 304, 519, 525, 535, 536, 537, 545, 549
Frege, Gottlob, 39
French Academy, 567
French language, 259, 260, 268, 276, 525

French Revolution, 12, 30, 123, 124, 266, 305–6, 307, 342, 419, 420, 437, 489, 525, 544
French Revolutionary and Napoleonic Wars, 267, 353, 356, 375, 419, 427, 428, 429, 532, 540
Freud, Sigmund, 45, 46, 132, 202, 316, 471
friendship, 81, 137, 184, 515
Froissart, Jean, 250
Fronde, 265

G-7, 483
G-8, 483, 492
Gadamer, Hans-Georg, 514
Galahad, 240
Galbraith, John Kenneth, 46
Galicia, 350
Galileo Galilei, 302
Gallagher, John, 324
games, 149
Gaugamela, Battle of, 203
Gaul, 207
Geertz, Clifford, 35, 302
Gelon, 176
genocide, 423
Georgia, 502
Gephardt, Richard, 463
German idealism, 332
German unification, 309, 457
Germany and the Next War (Friedrich von Bernhardi), 307
Germany, 17–18, 23, 32, 92, 97–8, 103, 224, 239, 242, 264, 295, 297, 300, 307–8, 311, 312, 313, 314, 324, 325, 329, 330, 338, 340–1, 342, 344–8, 352–62, 363, 365–6, 368–70, 372, 373, 374–86, 387, 388, 395, 407, 413, 417–19, 421–6, 429–31, 432, 434, 437, 439, 442, 443, 458, 464, 470, 474, 489, 492, 499, 501, 519–29, 530, 532, 533, 539–40, 548–9, 555
Germany, East (DDR), 457, 501
Gerschenkron, Alexander, 295
Gesta Karli Magni, 232
Gibbon, Edward, 263–4, 283
Giddens, Anthony, 25, 138
Giers, M. N., 366

gifts, 142, 147–8, 181
Gilpin, Robert, 22–3, 94
Gladstone, William, 327
Glaucus, 141, 151
globalization, 509
gloire (glory), 262, 266, 267, 282, 283,
    301, 315, 323, 524–5, 526, 535–6
Gnehm, Edward, 471
Godwine, earl of Essex, 237
Goebbels, Joseph, 384
Goethe, Johann Wolfgang von, 314,
    332
Goffman, Erving, 25, 494, 565, 566
Goltz, Colmar von der, 358
Gorbachev, Mikhail, 32, 440, 457–8,
    549
Goths, 210
Gournaym, Vincent de, 301
Gower, John, 240
Graf Spee, 143
Gramsci, Antonio, 556
grand theory, 1–2, 33, 58, 59, 112,
    120–1, 122
Granicus, Battle of, 203
Gratian, 211
Great Britain (*see also* England), 8, 73,
    224–57, 265–6, 274, 280–1, 294–5,
    307–8, 309–10, 313, 314, 323, 325,
    326–7, 329–30, 335, 338, 340, 343,
    345, 346–7, 359–61, 365, 373, 374,
    377, 379, 386, 392, 397, 404, 420,
    422, 430, 440, 454, 462, 464, 468,
    479, 499, 501, 524, 528, 529, 530,
    566
Great Depression, 92, 407
Great Northern War, 269, 280–1, 285,
    296, 304, 433, 527, 536, 547
great powers, 64, 65, 107, 262, 309,
    325–6, 429, 483–4, 486–9, 490,
    496, 499, 545, 548, 566
Great Red Spot of Jupiter, 56
Greater East Asian Co-Prosperity
    Sphere, 406, 411
Greece, 29, 52, 53–6, 75, 92, 161, 165,
    166, 222, 223, 254, 307, 372, 395,
    419, 429, 446, 484, 494, 518–20,
    521, 530, 531, 535, 558–9, 562,
    567–70

Greek language, 308
Greenfield, Liah, 40
Grey, Edward, 313, 388, 554
Gromyko, Andrei, 454
Grotius, Hugo, 9
groups, 7, 8, 16
Gruen, Eric, 214
Grundbegriffe (foundational concepts),
    44
Guantanamo, 468
Guattari, Felix, 39
Guernica, 424
Guesclin, Bertrand du, 252, 259
Guicciardini, Francesco, 392
Guinevere, 253
Gulf of Tonkin resolution, 479
Gulf War, 466, 468, 473
Gustav III (of Sweden), 265–9,
    296
Gutzkow, Karl, 334
Guyenne, 259–60, 261
Guzzini, Stefano, 111

Habermas, Jürgen, 36, 513
habit, 4–6
Habsburgs, 267, 288, 294
Haiti, 14
Halbach, Gustav Krupp von Bohlen
    und, 347, 354
hamartia (miscalculation), 98, 99
Hamas, 67
Hamerow, Theodore, 380–1
Hannibal, 208
Hardinge, Charles, 361, 388
Hardraada, Harald, 237, 238
Harold, king of England, 236,
    237
Harris, William, 207
Hartshorne, Paul, 57
Harvard University, 308
Hastings, Battle of, 237
Haugwitz, Christian Graf von,
    265
Hayashi, Tadasu, 408
Hayek, Friedrich, 117
Hector, 19, 66, 141, 147, 148–9, 150,
    151, 152, 153, 154, 195, 213
Hecuba, 147

Hegel, W. G. F., 8–9, 10, 12, 33, 36, 68–9, 73, 82, 87, 117, 219, 307–10, 430–5, 481, 562
hēgemōnia (hegemony), 33, 184, 186, 197, 198, 213, 491, 495–6, 500, 543, 556
hegemonic wars, 546–8
Heidegger, Martin, 18
Heider, Fritz, 133, 136
Heinsius, Anthonie, 265
Helen (of Troy), 139–41, 142, 144, 147, 152, 153, 155–6, 253
Hellenistic age, 166, 212, 218, 558
Helsinki Accords, 454
Henri I (of France), 235, 236
Henri V (of France), 249, 254, 259
Henshall, Nicholas, 266
Hephaestion, 203–4
Heracles, 171
Herald, Chandos, 251
hermeneutics, 6, 36–7, 38–42, 160
Hermes, 149
Herodotus, 44, 51, 100, 176, 187, 188, 189, 192, 194, 220, 314
Herr, Michael, 427
Herrero people, 421
Herrschaft (rule) (*see also* Max Weber), 2
Hesiod, 156
Hesse, Herman, 364, 380
hierarchy, 6, 26, 64–8, 74, 77, 84, 91–2, 105–7, 110, 117, 118–21, 146–8, 163, 164, 184, 197–8, 340–1, 343, 483, 496–7, 499, 500, 505–6, 507, 514, 544, 562, 563, 569–70
Hildebrand of Soana (Pope Gregory VII), 238
Hilferding, Rudolph, 326
Hindenburg, Paul von, 361, 382, 383, 386
Hippias of Elis, 44
Hippocratic physicians, 44
Hiroshima, 425, 426
Hirschman, Albert O., 321
Hitler, Adolf, 32, 203–5, 271, 372, 375, 383–6, 391–2, 393, 396–7, 418–19, 423, 429, 437, 442, 479, 520–1, 529–30, 531–2, 549, 550

Ho Chi Minh, 484
Hobbes, Thomas, 5, 12, 18, 24, 60, 66, 70, 222, 298, 315, 316, 505, 517, 557
Hobson, John, 326
Holstein, Friedrich von, 335
Holsti, K. J., 120, 122, 286–7
Holy Alliance, 325
Holy League, 285
Holy Roman Empire, 26, 234, 261, 267–74
Homer (*see also Iliad* and *Odyssey*), 5, 20, 44, 60, 70, 119, 120, 122, 123, 130, 156, 157, 167–8, 171, 176, 183, 190, 192, 194, 203, 204, 220, 222, 227–8, 240, 241, 242, 305, 308, 340, 416, 427, 428, 517, 523, 524, 532
homonoia (community), 76, 318
Hong Kong, 414
Honneth, Axel, 69
honor (*timē*), 4–6, 17, 18–19, 33, 61–6, 67, 68, 70–1, 105, 107, 121, 123, 127, 144, 146–7, 165, 167, 168, 170, 172, 175–80, 195, 197, 198, 200, 206, 213–19, 222, 223, 226, 232–3, 234, 259, 291–5, 309, 313, 340–1, 354, 362, 366, 372, 417–18, 419, 427, 428, 435, 474–5, 486, 491–2, 501, 509, 516, 518, 521, 523, 524, 532, 533, 534, 543, 545, 549, 554, 555, 559, 568, 569
honor-based worlds, 162–4
Horace, 204
Horatii, 204
Hoyos, Alexander, 354
hubris, 100, 440, 550
Huizinga, Johan, 20–1, 246, 250, 257
Hume, David, 15, 45, 315, 512
humiliation, 17, 376, 386, 437, 448, 545
Humphrey, Hubert, 426
Hundred Years War, 30, 223, 224, 235, 246–57, 259–61, 291, 300, 522, 523
Hungary, 303, 343, 369–70, 432, 488, 536
hunter-gatherer societies, 100, 104, 511–17

Leontius, 126
Leopold (grand duke of Tuscany), 265
Leopold I (of Austria), 264, 265–71
Leopold II, (Holy Roman Emperor), 276
Letterman, David, 463
Leucippas, 56
levels of analysis, 51–3, 98, 115–17, 158, 483
Lewis, Sinclair, 319
Libby, Lewis "Scooter", 460, 480
liberalism, 2–3, 15–16, 18, 34, 35, 51, 58, 59, 60, 76, 78, 94, 97, 159, 371, 497, 498, 509–10, 551, 557–8, 559, 561
Libya, 469, 492, 544
linguistic turn, 39
Livy (Titus Livius), 207, 209, 240, 519, 523, 528
Lloyd George, David, 378, 379
Llull, Ramon, 239, 242, 244
Locke, John, 36, 275
Lombardia, 523
Lombards, 225, 227, 231, 238
Louis IX (of France), 257
Louis XIV (of France), 98, 99, 109, 262, 264, 265–8, 272–3, 274–6, 277, 279–80, 282–3, 284, 285, 286, 287, 288–90, 292–3, 301–3, 307, 321, 323, 334, 337, 344, 524–5, 529, 535, 548, 550, 558
Louis XV (of France), 273
Louis the German, 234
Low Countries (*see also* Belgium, Dutch Republic, Netherlands), 307, 343
Luard, Evan, 287
Ludendorff, Erich, 361
Ludwig, Johann Christian, 274
Luhmann, Niklas, 48, 111
Luther, Martin, 332
luxuria, 207
Lycaon, 150–1
Lyotard, Jean-François, 35–8
Lysistrata, 194

MacArthur, Douglas, 477, 538
McCarthyism, 444–5

Macedonia, 83–5, 124, 161, 166, 201, 218, 220, 222, 519, 520, 528
McGovern, James, 463
Machiavelli, Niccolò, 60, 98, 158–9, 315, 391
Machtprestige (power-prestige), 20, 24
Mack Smith, Devis, 390–1
McKinley, William, 478
McNamara, Robert, 447
Malinovsky, Rodion, 452
Malplaquet, Battle of, 281
Manchuria, 397, 401–9
Mandeville, Bernard de, 320–1
Mann, Leon, 415
Mann, Thomas, 364, 380, 387
Mansbridge, Jane, 11
Mao Zedong, 86, 295, 450
Maori people, 124
Marathon, Battle of, 72, 171, 172, 173, 189, 199, 216, 218, 308, 542
Marchand, Jean-Baptiste, 329
Maria Theresa (of Austria), 276–7, 291–5
Mark Antony (Marcus Antonius), 209
markets, 74
Markey, Daniel, 24
Marlborough, Duke of (John Churchill), 281, 282
Marne, First Battle of, 357
marriage, 566
Marshall, William, 244, 246
Martel, Charles, 225
Marx, Karl, 33, 37, 74–7, 101, 141, 325, 331, 374, 481, 509, 527–8, 531, 544, 556
Marxism, 3, 15, 34, 35, 36, 41, 48, 58, 60, 94, 96, 97, 311, 418, 433, 506, 509–10, 556
Masa (restaurant), 109, 110
Maslow, Abraham, 132–3
Matscheko, Franz Baron von, 352
Matsuoka, Yōsuke, 371, 413, 416, 417–29
Matteotti, Giacomo, 390
Mauss, Marcel, 181
Max Emmanuel (of Bavaria), 276, 536
Max of Baden (Prince of Germany), 361, 377

Mazarin, Jules Cardinal, 262–6, 267, 271, 273
Mazinni, Giuseppe, 388
meden agan (middle way), 48, 186, 218
media, 463
Megara, 86, 547
Megarian Decree, 160
Meiji Restoration, 404, 435
Meinecke, Friedrich, 430
Melian Dialogue, 186–7, 197, 215, 217, 220–1, 520, 523
Menelaus, 139, 141, 142, 152, 213
mercantilism, 320, 321
Mermin, Jonathan, 463
Merton, Robert, 120
Meso-America, 101, 157
Mexico, 543
Midas, 46
Middle Ages, 124, 234
Middle East, 103, 157
middle-range theories, 120–1, 122
military cultures, 208–9
military plans, 350–1, 352, 355–7
milites, 242, 523
Mill, John Stuart, 11
Miller, Judith, 463
Mills, C. Wright, 35
Minseitō, 409
Mintz, Sidney, 109
miscalculation, 98–9
mixed worlds, 93–6, 224, 517, 560
Miyake, Setsurei, 435
mobility, 145–6
modernity, 14, 30–1, 63, 75, 108, 306–7, 311, 314–22, 374, 508
modernization, 437
Molière (Jean-Baptiste Poquelin), 34
Molotov–Ribbentrop Pact, 490
Moltke, Helmuth von, the Younger, 352–6, 366, 370, 417, 528, 538, 539, 548
Mommsen, Wolfgang, 335, 363–4, 378, 381
monarchy, 17
Mongols, 102
Montenegro, 348–9

Montesquieu, Charles de Secondat, baron de, 274, 321, 481, 482, 507
Montreal Protocol, 8–9
moral blindness, 140
morality, 315–16
Morazé, Charles, 327
Morgenthau, Hans J., 18, 22, 34, 41, 42, 70, 120–1, 122, 263, 475, 487, 503, 554, 555–6, 557
Morillon, Philippe, 427
Moroccan crises, 454
Mortimer, Roger, 247
motives (*see also* fear, honor, interest, psyche), 4–5, 45–7, 60–82, 160, 177–8, 199–201, 224, 257–8, 259, 291, 312, 314, 320, 339, 371–2, 379, 415, 416, 417–19, 443–4, 502, 505, 506–12, 517, 519–24, 528, 529, 533, 537–8, 550–1, 553, 555, 563, 564, 567–8, 569
Mount Olympus, 202
Mukden Incident, 408
Müller, Adam, 332
multipolarity, *see* polarity
Mund, 226
Munemitsu, Mutsu, 404
Mussolini, Benito, 32, 372, 373, 375, 388–97, 398, 405, 413, 418–19, 423, 437, 529, 530, 531–2, 549
Mustafava, Kara, 285
Mutz, Diana, 53
Myers, Richard, 460
Mytilenean Debate, 100, 131, 186, 552

Nagasaki, 425, 426
Nakano, Seigō, 435, 436
Nanjing, Rape of, 425–6
nano-technology, 28
Napoleon Bonaparte, 143, 203, 271, 290, 420, 429, 433, 548, 550, 558
Napoleon III, 328
Napoleonic Wars, *see* French Revolutionary and Napoleonic Wars
National Aeronautic and Space Administration (NASA), 446
National Air and Space Museum, 426
national interest, 158–9

Scheler, Max, 364
Schelling, Friedrich Wilhelm Joseph, 307
Schlegel, Friedrich, 332
Schleicher, Kurt von, 382
Schlieffen, Albert Graf von, 355, 357–8, 359
Schöborn, Friedrich Karl von, 536
Schmitt, Carl, 10, 11
Schroeder, Paul, 1–2, 281, 288, 309–10, 362, 494
Schumpeter, Joseph, 31, 75, 314, 339, 341–2, 527–8
Scipio Aemilianus, 204, 210
Scipio Africanus, 204–8
scope conditions, 111–12
Scotland, 248, 300, 344–5
Scowcroft, Brent, 460, 475
Sebastianus, 210
Second Athenian League, 201
security dilemma, 516
security, 91, 238, 267, 285–6, 367–8, 371, 374, 432, 435, 443–4, 445, 466–7, 475, 500, 503, 509, 516, 523, 529, 537, 549, 556
self-esteem, 5, 16, 17–18, 26, 32, 64, 120–1, 122, 125, 128–9, 131, 132–7, 143, 151, 162, 312, 314, 325, 337, 364, 366, 372, 374, 375, 392, 399, 417–18, 429–30, 445, 448, 476, 495, 501, 503, 508–9, 527, 528, 542, 549, 563
self-evaluation maintenance, 136–48
self-image, 564
self-interest, 316–22
self-interest well understood, 514
self-perception theory, 564
self-restraint, 82–3, 88, 514, 533
self-restraint, lack of (akrasia), 219
Senate, US, 478
Senegal, 328
separation of powers, 47–8
September 11, 2001 terrorist attacks (9.11), 11, 440–1, 459, 466, 471, 472, 534
September Program, 347–8, 377

Serbia, 340, 348, 349, 350–1, 354, 359, 366, 369, 370, 421, 424, 519, 529, 539, 548
Seven against Thebes (Aeschylus), 168
Seven Years War, 270, 287, 288, 294, 549
sex, 73, 169, 219, 484, 513
Shakespeare, William, 262, 314
shame, 63, 129
Sharon, Ariel, 484
Shelley, Percy, 308
Sherif, Muzafer, 11
Shidehara, Kijūrō, 405, 408
Shigetaka, Shiga, 404
Shilliam, Robert, 12
Shintoism, 400
Shiratori, Toshio, 436
Shogunate, 437
Shohō, Tokutomi, 404
Shōwa Research Association, 406
Siam, 399
Siberia, 405
Sicilian Debate, 215
Sicilian expedition, 185, 195–6
Sicily, 167–8, 217, 517, 521
Silesia, 270, 330, 535, 549
Simeon, Richard, 118, 119
Simmel, Georg, 18
Singapore, 414
Sino-Japanese War, 404, 405, 436
Sioux people, 68, 541, 542, 543
Skinner, Quentin, 36, 39–40
slavery, 73
Slavophilia, 432, 433, 540
Smith, Adam, 5, 30, 37, 46, 73, 74, 81, 101, 106–7, 108, 123, 295, 307, 316, 318–20, 321–2, 323, 337, 344, 512, 514, 517
Social Contract (see also Rousseau), 318
Social Darwinism, 312
social democracy, 334, 359, 363, 369
Social Democratic Party of Germany (USPD), 380
social identity theory (SIT), 133–5, 543
social imperialism, 324, 326–7, 334, 337
socialism (see also Marxism), 329

socialization, 507, 564

society, 184–7, 216, 222, 226, 231, 232–3, 258, 260–1, 288, 419, 427, 428, 504, 513, 532, 567–8

Society of St. George, 244

sociology, 16

Socrates (*see also* Plato), 44, 49–51, 62, 80, 83, 84, 125–6, 167–8, 199, 514

Solferino, Battle of, 351

Somalia, 14

Sombart, Werner, 342, 430

Sonderweg, 381, 540

Sophocles, 44, 53, 64, 130, 198, 220, 386, 554–5

South Africa, 8

South West Africa, 421

South Yemen, 456

Southeast Asia, 157

sovereignty, 10, 14, 483

Soviet Union, 92, 109, 225–6, 239, 258, 264, 268, 274, 278, 282, 285, 295, 298, 300, 323, 326, 338, 372, 374, 382, 419, 421, 423, 424, 434, 437, 439–59, 467, 478, 483, 485, 486, 488–9, 490–2, 494, 525, 530, 540, 544, 545, 546, 547, 549, 550, 551–3, 566, 570

Sparta, 25, 66, 71, 102, 103, 157, 159–60, 168, 169, 174, 175, 176, 177, 179–92, 193, 199, 201, 220–1, 495, 538, 541, 542–3, 546, 547, 548, 559, 569

Spengler, Oswald, 387

spirit (*see also* motives, psyche, *thumos*), 14–15, 19–21, 26, 32, 60–4, 72, 74, 105–6, 125, 159, 199, 216, 248, 264–71, 368, 374, 444, 461, 474–6, 482, 504, 505, 508–12, 515, 538, 554, 559

Spirit of the Laws (Montesquieu), 321

spirit-based worlds, 29, 82–3, 90

sports, 17–18, 85, 105, 170, 175, 184–5, 194, 202, 310–11, 322, 485

Sputnik, 444, 446, 533

Stalin, Josef V., 203, 295, 394, 434, 444, 533

standing, 5, 19–21, 33, 121, 123, 146–7, 175–80, 213–19, 223, 238, 267, 274–8, 291–5, 301, 309, 322, 323, 345, 365, 418, 419, 427–8, 448, 474–5, 476–7, 482, 484–93, 509, 520–1, 523, 525, 531–2, 543, 555, 560, 569–70

standing, markers of, 337, 344

stasis, 194, 565

state, rise of, 234–5, 248–9, 263, 298–304, 535–7

status, 105–6

Stein, Janice, 100

Stephen, Pope, 225

Stern, Fritz, 386

Steuart, James, 321

Sthenelaïdas, 180, 186

Stinnes, Hugo, 347

strategic bargaining, 553

Strategic Defense Initiative, 457, 534

stratification, 41, 245, 273, 291–5, 312

Strauss, Leo, 70

Stresemann, Gustav, 382

Sudan, 329, 544

Suetonius, 228

superpowers, 483

survival (state), 18, 70, 72, 162

Suzuki, Shogo, 487

Sweden, 25–6, 71, 262–3, 264, 274, 279, 280, 284–5, 288, 296, 297, 429, 433, 437, 491, 539, 547

Swiss Confederation, 263, 264

Switzerland, 542

Sylvan, David, 24

sympathetisches Nacherleben, 119, 120, 122

Syracuse, 86, 559

Syria, 441, 454, 455–6, 543

system-level theories, 1–2, 7–8, 116

Tacitus (Gaius Cornelius Tacitus), 226, 233, 397, 404, 444, 502

Tajfel, Henri, 8, 133

Takigawa, Seijirō, 436

Talleyrand-Périgord, Charles de, 439, 487

Tanaka, Giichi, 405

Tassilo, duke of Bavaria, 227

tautology, 118, 119, 120, 122

Taylor, Charles, 68–9

Telemachus, 141
telos, 37–8, 97, 315
Tenet, George, 462
Terror Management Theory, 135–49
Teucer, 154
The Civic Culture (Almond and Verba), 118, 119
The Quest for the Holy Grail, 240
Thebes, 86, 188, 201, 220
Themistocles, 100, 191, 195, 210, 543
Theoderic, 230
Theory of Moral Sentiments (Adam Smith), 318–20
Thermopylae, 172, 176–91, 212, 368
Thersites, 145, 146, 177, 198
Thespians, 172
Thetis, 149
Thirty Years War, 26, 37, 71, 263, 526
Thirty Years Peace, 193
Thököly, Imre, 285
Thucydides (*see also* Peloponnesian War), 3–5, 6, 12, 23, 24, 25, 41, 42, 43, 44, 51, 52–5, 64, 74, 77, 80, 83–4, 85–6, 87, 90–1, 92, 93, 96–7, 99, 100, 103, 104, 108, 116, 129, 131, 158, 159–60, 168, 172, 173–4, 177, 185–7, 193–4, 195, 197–8, 199, 215, 219, 220–1, 222, 314, 317, 428, 475, 517, 546, 547, 554–5, 564–5, 567
thumos, 569
Tiananmen Square, 470, 490
Tiberius Gracchus, 209
Tilly, Charles, 299
timē, 183–4, 495
Time magazine, 467–8
Tirpitz, Alfred von, 336, 360–1
Titus Manlius, 204
Tocqueville, Alexis de, 17, 123, 325–6, 482, 507, 508, 509, 514, 567
Tōjō, Hideki, 414, 416, 417–18, 437–8
Tokugawa shogunate, 399–400, 415, 436
Tönnies, Ferdinand, 18
Torah, 150
Tostig, 237

tournaments, 244, 251, 261, 523
trade, 326
tragedy, 53, 98, 99–100, 307, 314–15
tragic poets, 44
Tragic Vision of Politics (Lebow), 41, 54, 103, 568
Trajan, 210
transference, 120–1, 122
Treaty of Brest-Litovsk, 377, 421–3, 434, 458
Treaty of Nystad, 269, 280
Treaty of Shimonoseki, 404
Treaty of the Pyrenees, 263
Treaty of Tilsit, 420
Treaty of Utrecht, 276, 280
Treaty of Verdun, 260
Treaty of Versailles, 372, 376–80, 384, 386, 393, 418, 478, 480, 491, 529, 532, 549
Treitschke, Heinrich von, 10, 335
Trilateral Commission, 483
Triumph of the Will (film), 385–6
Trojan War, 139, 156, 198, 229, 253, 521, 532, 570
troubadours, 222
Troy (film), 19
Troy, 139–61, 203
Troyes, Chrétien de, 239, 242–3
Truman, Harry S., 451, 477, 538
Truman administration, 444, 446
Tunisia, 329
turbulence, 56
Turkey, 447, 450, 451, 502, 552
Turner, Henry, 381
typologies, 113
tyranny, 4–5, 98, 186, 199, 507
Tyrtaeus, 165

U-2 reconnaissance plane, 450, 451, 452
Ukichi, Taguchi, 404
unipolarity, 470, 484, 534
United Nations, 106, 463–4, 466–7, 477, 483, 487, 492, 498, 546, 560
United Nations, General Assembly, 483, 560
United Nations, Human Rights Commission, 492–3

United Nations, Security Council, 65–6, 461, 468, 474–5, 483, 492, 498, 502, 504
United Provinces *see* Dutch Republic
United States, 8–9, 11, 66, 75, 86, 97–8, 99, 108, 109, 111, 157, 159, 280, 307–8, 309, 310, 311, 323–4, 325–6, 347, 356, 374, 379, 408, 412, 413–15, 422, 426–7, 439–80, 484–5, 486, 489, 490, 491, 497, 499–500, 531, 540–6, 550, 551–2, 553, 554, 555, 556, 557, 570
University of Wales, 1
US–Soviet Trade Agreement, 456

Valens (Roman emperor), 210
Vattel, Emerich de, 9, 486
Veblen, Thorstein, 109, 307, 310–11, 318, 344
Venice, 285, 297
Verdun, Battle of, 361
Versailles, 274–6, 520, 525
Verstehen, 34
Vichy Regime, 327
Vico, Giambattista, 320
Victoria (queen of Great Britain), 327
Vienna, siege of, 431–2
Vienna summit, 450, 451
Vietnam (*see also* Indochina), 543, 550
Vietnam War, *see* Indochina War
Vikings, 67, 124, 163, 238, 523
Villas, Marshall Charles, 283
Virgil (Publius Vergilius Maro), 12, 220, 221
virtus (military valor), 204, 206, 218, 241, 259–60, 523
Visigoths, 211
Vita Karoli, 232
Voltaire (François-Marie Arouet), 268, 277, 343, 525

Waever, Ole, 12, 220
Wales, 248
Walpole, Robert, 265
Waltharius, 255
Waltz, Kenneth, 18–19, 24, 70, 91, 94, 111, 116, 491, 557, 558

Walzer, Michael, 302
Wanderungen durch die Mark Brandenburg (Fontane), 330
War of Austrian Succession, 270, 280, 283, 287, 557
war on terrorism, 472, 503
Warburg, Max, 347
warfare, 71–2, 86, 101, 110, 149–50, 151, 163–4, 166, 171–4, 188–92, 195, 196, 206–11, 231–3, 238, 258–9, 278–91, 299, 309, 375, 415, 416, 417–29, 516, 519–25, 532–3, 535, 558, 559
warfare, aerial, 421, 423, 424, 425, 427, 484, 532
warfare, naval, 421–2
warrior elites, 85, 90
warrior societies, 70, 72, 102, 105–6, 110, 123–4, 162, 416, 419, 516, 519–20, 521–2, 541, 554, 559
wars of German unification, 332
Warsaw Pact, 458
Washington, George, 66
Washington Naval Conference, 478
Waterloo, Battle of, 420, 429
Watson, Adam, 3
Way of the Subject, 437
Wayne, John, 427
wealth, 108–11, 141–2, 169, 172, 187, 215, 229, 233, 258, 311, 320, 321, 503, 512, 517, 522, 569
Wealth of Nations (Adam Smith), 98, 321
weapons of mass destruction (WMDs), 461–2, 463, 464, 466–7, 471, 472, 477
Weber, Max, 2–3, 19–20, 21, 22, 24, 32, 45, 93–4, 95, 98, 118, 119, 120, 122, 157, 225, 235, 302, 315, 325, 331, 333, 336, 342, 364, 396, 487, 505, 512, 527, 555
Weberian transformation, 298
Weekly Standard, 460, 466
Wees, Hans van, 187
Wehler, Hans-Ulrich, 337, 363, 381
Weiss, Paul, 57
Weltpolitik, 335, 337, 338, 359–61, 363

Wendt, Alexander, 24, 58, 97, 111, 116, 509
West Point (US Military Academy), 19
Westphalia, Treaties of, 12, 30, 541
Whitehead, Alfred North, 57
Wight, Martin, 12, 19, 434
Wilhelm II (of Germany), 312, 313, 339–40, 345, 352, 354, 357, 365–6, 369, 370, 372, 374, 377, 378, 383, 410, 429, 433, 529, 539, 548, 550, 554
William I (of England), 522
William of Orange, 280, 282
William, duke of Normandy (the Conqueror), 236–8, 259, 299
Wilson, Woodrow, 377, 398
winkte, 541–2
Witt, Johan de, 265, 271
Wittgenstein, Ludwig, 35–6, 39
Wolfowitz, Paul, 459–60, 480
Woods, Tiger, 482
Woolsey, James, 460
World Trade Center (*see also* September 11), 473
World War I, 24, 31, 32, 92, 104, 224, 311–14, 338–70, 373, 375, 385, 388, 398, 405, 416, 417–18, 419, 421–3, 427, 428, 429, 430–1, 470, 478, 483, 491, 503, 520, 524, 528, 530, 531, 532–3, 548–9, 552, 569

World War II, 31–2, 78, 98, 99–100, 104, 437, 438, 483–4, 491, 519–32, 533, 549, 569
worst case analysis, 92

xenia (guest friendship), 51, 139–40, 147, 183, 242
Xenophon, 165, 168, 169, 181
Xerxes, 187, 191, 192, 553

Yalu River, 550
Yamagata, Aritomo, 401, 403, 405, 407–8
Yamamoto, Isoroku, 401, 414
Young Plan, 478
Yugoslavia, 372, 388, 395, 427, 530

Zabern affair, 344
Zacharias, Pope, 225
zaibatsu, 402, 405, 411
Zamyatin, Leonid, 453
Zemlya i Volya (land and liberty), 433
Zentrumspartei (Germany), 335, 380
Zeus, 140, 149, 151, 175, 176
Zinni, Anthony, 473